PSYCHOLOGY
AN EXPLORATION

Important Dates in Psychology

Use this timeline to get a better understanding of key dates in the history of psychology.

1920 Francis Sumner becomes the first African American to receive a Ph.D. in psychology at Clark University.

1920 Watson and Rayner publish the "Little Albert" experiment.

1929 Hans Berger introduces EEG method for studying the human brain.

1906 Ivan Pavlov publishes his findings on classical conditioning.

360 Plato writes the *Theaetetus* examining theories of perception, knowledge, and truth.

350 Aristotle writes *De Anima* about the relationship of the soul to the body.

1848 Phineas Gage suffers brain damage and provides a famous case study of the effects of brain damage.

1859 Charles Darwin publishes the theory of natural selection, which influences the field of evolutionary psychology.

1884 James-Lange theory of emotion proposed.

1900 Freud publishes *The Interpretation of Dreams.*

1906 Ramon y Cajal discovers that the nervous system is composed of individual cells.

1908 Yerkes-Dodson law proposed to explain relationship between performance and arousal.

1921 The first neurotransmitter, acetylcholine, is discovered.

1921 The Rorschach Inkblot Test is developed.

1921 Allport proposes a trait theory of personality.

B.C.E.	400	C.E.	1650	1860	1900	1920

430 Hippocrates proposes that mental illnesses are caused by an imbalance of four major fluids in the human body.

1649 Descartes publishes *The Passion of the Soul,* outlining the pineal gland as the seat of the soul.

1860 Gustav Fechner is often credited with performing the first scientific experiments that would form thebasis for experimentation in psychology.

1861 Broca's Area and its role in speech production is discovered.

1874 Wernicke's Area and its role in language comprehension is discovered.

1890 William James publishes his book, *Principles of Psychology.*

1892 American Psychological Association (APA) founded and G. Stanley Hall elected first president.

1894 Margaret Floy Washburn is the first woman to receive a Ph.D. in psychology at Cornell University.

1879 Wilhelm Wundt establishes the first laboratory of psychology in Leipzig, Germany.

1904 Spearman proposes a general factor of intelligence.

1905 Mary Whiton Calkins becomes the first female president of the APA.

1905 Freud proposes his psychosexual theory of personality development.

1905 The first widely used IQ test, the Binet-Simon, was created.

1911 Thorndike proposes the Law of Effect.

1912 Gestalt psychology first developed by Max Wertheimer.

1912 The intelligence quotient is developed by William Stern.

1913 Carl Jung develops his theory of the collective conscious.

1915 Freud first proposes the concept of defense mechanisms.

1930 Tolman and Honzik demonstrate latent learning in rats.

1930 Jean Piaget proposes four stages of cognitive development.

1933 Sigmund Freud proposes the concept id, ego, and superego

1934 Lev Vygotsky proposes concept of zone of proximal development.

1935 Henry Mur creates the Them Apperception Tes

1935 Prefrontal lobotomy developed by Dr. Antonio Egas Mc

1950 Erik Erikson proposes his psychosocial stages of personality development.

1951 Soloman Asch's classic study on conformity conducted.

1952 The first edition of the *Diagnostic and Statistical Manual of Mental Disorders (DSM)* is published.

1952 Chlorpromazine first drug treatment introduced for the treatment of schizophrenia.

1938 B.F. Skinner introduces the concept of operant conditioning.

1938 Electroconvulsive shock first used on a human patient.

1939 Clark and Clark classic study on prejudice conducted.

1942 Carl Rogers develops client-centered therapy.

1942 The Minnesota Multiphasic Personality Inventory is created.

1961 Carl Rogers creates the concepts of ideal self, real self, conditional positive regard, and unconditional positive regard.

1961 Muzafer Sherif conducts the "Robber's Cave" study.

1967 Seligman demonstrates learned helplessness in dogs.

1967 Holmes and Rahe create the Social Readjustment Rating Scale.

1967 Beck proposes a cognitive theory for explaining depression.

1968 Roger Sperry demonstrates hemispheric specialization with split-brain patients.

1977 The stress-vulnerability model of schizophrenia proposed by Zubin and Spring.

1977 Thomas and Chess conduct studies of different types of infant temperament.

1978 Elizabeth Loftus puts into question the validity of eyewitness testimony with discovery of misinformation effect.

1979 Mary Ainsworth uses the Strange Situation experiment to study infant attachment styles.

1979 Thomas Bouchard begins the Minnesota study of twins reared apart to identify the influence of genetics and the environment on personality traits.

2000 Genetic researchers finish mapping human genome.

2002 Steven Pinker publishes *The Blank Slate* arguing the concept of *tabula rasa*.

2002 New Mexico is the first state to allow licensed psychologists to prescribe drug treatments for psychological disorders.

1994 Herrnstein and Murray publish *The Bell Curve*.

1995 Goleman proposes idea of emotional intelligence.

2004 Massachusetts first state in US to legalize same-sex marriage.

| 1940 | 1960 | 1970 | 1990 | 2010 |

1948 Alfred Kinsey begins survey research on sexual behavior.

1953 The American Psychological Association publishes the first edition of *Ethical Standards in Psychology*.

1962 Cognitive arousal theory of emotion proposed by Schachter and Singer.

1981 David Wechsler begins to devise IQ tests for specific age groups.

1996 McCrae and Costa propose the Big Five Personality dimensions.

1997 Elisabeth Kubler-Ross publishes *On Grief and Grieving*, exploring the process of grieving through expansion of her theory of the five stages of death from *On Death and Dying* (1969)

2004 Alexander Storch presents possibility of obtaining stem cells from adults to repair damaged neural tissue.

2005 FDA mandates black box warnings of increased suicide risk on antidepressants.

2008 Law passed requiring insurance companies to provide equal coverage for mental health services.

2009 US President Barack Obama lifts federal funding limits on scientific research involving human stem cells.

2013 DSM-V scheduled for publication.

1954 Abraham Maslow proposes a hierarchy of needs to describe human motivation.

1955 Albert Ellis proposes rational emotive behavioral therapy.

1956 Hans Selye proposes the General Adaptation Syndrome to describe responses to stress.

1959 Festinger and Carlsmith publish their study on cognitive dissonance.

1959 Harlow and Zimmerman demonstrate the importance of contact comfort with their study on infant monkeys.

1983 Gardner first proposes his theory of multiple intelligences.

1985 Robert Sternberg proposes the triarchic theory of intelligence.

1989 Albert Bandura proposes the concept of reciprocal determinism.

1963 Albert Bandura's "Bobo doll" study is conducted.

1963 Stanley Milgram conducts his classic study on obedience.

1963 Lawrence Kohlberg creates his theory of moral development.

1974 Friedman and Rosenman discover link between heart disease and Type-A personality.

1966 Masters and Johnson introduce four stages of sexual response cycle.

1974 The PET scan is first introduced as a brain imaging technique.

PSYCHOLOGY
AN EXPLORATION

Saundra K. Ciccarelli

Gulf Coast Community College

J. Noland White

Georgia College & State University

PEARSON

Boston Columbus Indianapolis New York San Francisco Upper Saddle River
Amsterdam Cape Town Dubai London Madrid Milan Munich Paris Montreal Toronto
Delhi Mexico City Sao Paulo Sydney Hong Kong Seoul Singapore Taipei Tokyo

Editorial Director: Craig Campanella
Editor in Chief: Jessica Mosher
Senior Editor: Amber Mackey
Director of Marketing: Brandy Dawson
Executive Marketing Manager: Jeanette Koskinas
Marketing Manager: Brigeth Rivera
Marketing Assistant: Jessica Warren
Senior Managing Editor: Maureen Richardson
Senior Project Manager/Liaison: Harriet Tellem
Operations Supervisor: Mary Fischer
Operations Specialist: Diane Peirano

Text and Cover Designer: Anne DeMarinis/DeMarinis Design LLC
Photographer, Student Images: Shayle Keating Photography
Cover Art: Circle Bokeh © Loskutnikov/Shutterstock.com, Fish © Monika Wisniewska/Shutterstock.com
Media Director: Brian Hyland
Media Editor, Editorial: Beth Stoner
Media Editor, Production: Pam Weldin
Full-Service Project Management: Rebecca Dunn/Preparé Inc.
Composition: Preparé Inc.
Printer/Binder: Courier Kendallville
Cover Printer: Lehigh–Phoenix Color

Credits and acknowledgments borrowed from other sources and reproduced, with permission, in this textbook appear on pages C–1–C–2.

We would like to thank all of the students who allowed us to use their photos in our book.

Library of Congress Cataloging-in-Publication Data

Ciccarelli, Saundra K.
    Psychology: an exploration / Saundra K. Ciccarelli, J. Noland White.—2nd ed.
        p. cm.
    Includes bibliographical references and index.
    ISBN 978-0-205-25641-9
    1. Psychology—Textbooks. I. White, J. Noland. II. Title.
    BF121.C522 2013
    150—dc23
                                                        2011046768

10 9 8 7 6 5 4 3 2 1

Student Edition ISBN 10: 0-205-25641-4
ISBN 13: 978-0-205-25641-9

Instructor's Review Copy: ISBN 10: 0-205-26054-3
ISBN 13: 978-0-205-26054-6

Á la Carte ISBN 10: 0-205-26052-7
ISBN 13: 978-0-205-26052-2

brief contents

Psychology in Action   Secrets to Surviving College: How to Improve Your Grades   PIA–2

1   The Science of Psychology   2

2   The Biological Perspective   40

3   Sensation and Perception   80

4   Learning   120

5   Memory   162

6   Consciousness and Cognition   196

7   Development Across the Life Span   228

8   Motivation and Emotion   270

9   Stress and Health   310

10   Social Psychology   344

11   Theories of Personality and Intelligence   384

12   Psychological Disorders   430

13   Psychological Therapies   464

Appendix A   Statistics in Psychology   A–1

Appendix B   Applied Psychology and Psychology Careers   B–1

contents

Preface xi
About the Authors 1

psychology in action

Secrets for Surviving College: How to Improve Your Grades PIA–2

Study Methods: Different Strokes for Different Folks PIA-4

Reading Textbooks: Textbooks Are Not Meatloaf PIA-6

How to Take Notes: Printing Out PowerPoint Slides is Not Taking Notes PIA-8

    Taking Notes While Reading the Text PIA-8

    Taking Notes During the Lecture PIA-8

Studying for Exams: Cramming Is Not an Option PIA-9

Writing Papers: Planning Makes Perfect PIA-12

applying psychology to everyday life
Strategies for Improving Your Memory PIA-14

Chapter Summary PIA-16   Test Yourself PIA-17

CONCEPT SUMMARY PIA-18

1 The Science of Psychology 2

What Is Psychology? 4

    The Field of Psychology 4

    Psychology's Goals 4

Psychology Then:
The History of Psychology 5

    In the Beginning: Wundt, Introspection, and the Laboratory 5

    Titchener and Structuralism in America 6

    William James and Functionalism 7

issues in psychology
Psychology's African American Roots 8

    Gestalt Psychology: The Whole Is Greater Than the Sum of Its Parts 9

    Sigmund Freud's Theory of Psychoanalysis 9

    Pavlov, Watson, and the Dawn of Behaviorism 10

Psychology Now: Modern Perspectives 12

    Psychodynamic Perspective 12

    Behavioral Perspective 12

    Humanistic Perspective 13

    Cognitive Perspective 13

    Sociocultural Perspective 13

    Biopsychological Perspective 14

    Evolutionary Perspective 15

Psychological Professionals and Areas of Specialization 16

    Areas of Specialization 16

Psychology: The Scientific Methodology 18

    Why Psychologists Use the Scientific Method 18

    Descriptive Methods 20

    Finding Relationships 23

issues in psychology
Stereotypes, Athletes, and College Test Performance 29

Ethics of Psychological Research 30

    The Guidelines for Doing Research with People 30

applying psychology to everyday life
Thinking Critically about Critical Thinking 32

Chapter Summary 34   Test Yourself 36

CONCEPT SUMMARY 38

2 The Biological Perspective 40

An Overview of the Nervous System 42

Neurons and Nerves: Building the Network 42

    Structure of the Neuron—The Nervous System's Building Block 43

    Generating the Message Within the Neuron—The Neural Impulse 44

    Sending the Message to Other Cells: The Synapse 47

    Neurotransmitters, Messengers of the Network 48

    Cleaning Up the Synapse: Reuptake and Enzymes 49

The Central Nervous System—The "Central Processing Unit" 51

    The Brain 51

    The Spinal Cord 51

psychology in the news
Fact or Fiction: Focus on the Brain, but Check Your Sources! 52

The Peripheral Nervous System—Nerves on the Edge 54

    The Somatic Nervous System 54

    The Autonomic Nervous System 55

Distant Connections: The Endocrine Glands 57

    The Pituitary, Master of the Hormonal Universe 58

    The Pineal Gland 58

    The Thyroid Gland 58

    Pancreas 58

    The Gonads 59

    The Adrenal Glands 59

Looking Inside the Living Brain 60
Lesioning Studies 60
Brain Stimulation 60
Mapping Structure 61
Mapping Function 62

From the Bottom Up: The Structures of the Brain 63
The Hindbrain 64
Structures under the Cortex 65
The Cortex 67
The Association Areas of the Cortex 70
The Cerebral Hemispheres: Are You in Your Right
Mind? 71

applying psychology to everyday life
Paying Attention to the Causes of Attention-Deficit/Hyperactivity
Disorder 73

Chapter Summary 74   Test Yourself 76

CONCEPT SUMMARY 78

3

Sensation and Perception 80

The ABCs of Sensation 82
What Is Sensation? 82
Sensory Thresholds 82
Habituation and Sensory Adaptation 83

The Science of Seeing 84
Perceptual Properties of Light: Catching the Waves 84
The Structure of the Eye 85
How the Eye Works 87
Perception of Color 88

The Hearing Sense: Can You Hear Me Now? 91
Perception of Sound: Good Vibrations 92
The Structure of the Ear: Follow the Vibes 93
Types of Hearing Impairments 95

**Chemical Senses: It Tastes Good and Smells
Even Better 96**
Gustation: How We Taste the World 96
The Sense of Scents: Olfaction 98

Somesthetic Senses: What the Body Knows 99
Perception of Touch, Pressure, and Temperature 99
Pain: Gate-Control Theory 100
The Kinesthetic Sense 101
The Vestibular Sense 101

The ABCs of Perception 102
The Constancies: Size, Shape, and Brightness 103
The Gestalt Principles 103
Depth Perception 105
Perceptual Illusions 108
Other Factors That Influence Perception 111

applying psychology to everyday life
Beyond "Smoke and Mirrors"—The Psychological Science and
Neuroscience of Magic 112

Chapter Summary 114   Test Yourself 115

CONCEPT SUMMARY 118

4

Learning 120

Definition of Learning 122

It Makes Your Mouth Water: Classical Conditioning 122
Pavlov and the Salivating Dogs 123
Elements of Classical Conditioning 123
Putting It All Together: Pavlov's Canine Classic, or Tick Tock,
Tick Tock 123
Conditioned Emotional Responses: Rats! 128
Watson and "Little Albert" 128
Other Conditioned Responses in Humans 128
Why Does Classical Conditioning Work? 129

What's in It for Me? Operant Conditioning 131
Frustrating Cats: Thorndike's Puzzle Box and the Law of
Effect 131
B. F. Skinner: The Behaviorist's Behaviorist 132
The Concept of Reinforcement 132
Positive and Negative Reinforcement 133
The Schedules of Reinforcement: Why the One-Armed Bandit Is
So Seductive 134
Variable Ratio Schedule of Reinforcement 137
The Role of Punishment in Operant Conditioning 138
Two Kinds of Punishment 139
Problems with Punishment 140

issues in psychology
The Link between Spanking and Aggression in Young Children 142
Stimulus Control: Slow Down, It's the Cops 142
Other Concepts in Operant Conditioning 143

classic studies in psychology
Biological Constraints on Operant Conditioning 144
Applying Operant Conditioning: Behavior Modification 145

Cognitive Learning Theory 147
Tolman's Maze-Running Rats: Latent Learning 148
Köhler's Smart Chimp: Insight Learning 148
Seligman's Depressed Dogs: Learned Helplessness 149

Observational Learning 151
Bandura and the Bobo Doll 151
The Four Elements of Observational Learning 152

applying psychology to everyday life
Can You Really Toilet Train Your Cat? 154

Chapter Summary 156   Test Yourself 158

CONCEPT SUMMARY 160

5

Memory 162

Three Processes of Memory 164
Putting It In: Encoding 164
Keeping It In: Storage 164
Getting It Out: Retrieval 164

Models of Memory 164

The Information-Processing Model: Three Stages of Memory 166
Sensory Memory: Why Do People Do Double Takes? 166
Short-Term and Working Memory 168
Long-Term Memory 170
Types of Long-Term Information 172

Getting It Out: Retrieval of Long-Term Memories 176
Retrieval Cues 176
Recall: Hmm...Let Me Think 177
Recognition: Hey, Don't I Know You from Somewhere? 178

classic studies in psychology
Elizabeth Loftus and Eyewitnesses 179
Automatic Encoding: Flashbulb Memories 180

The Reconstructive Nature of Long-Term Memory Retrieval: How Reliable Are Memories? 181
Constructive Processing of Memories 181
Memory Retrieval Problems 182
Reliability of Memory Retrieval 182

What Were We Talking About? Forgetting 184
Ebbinghaus and the Forgetting Curve 185
Encoding Failure 186
Memory Trace Decay Theory 186
Interference Theory 186

Neuroscience of Memory 188
Neural Activity and Structure in Memory Formation 188
The Hippocampus and Memory 188
When Memory Fails: Organic Amnesia 189

applying psychology to everyday life
Alzheimer's Disease 190

Chapter Summary 191   Test Yourself 193

CONCEPT SUMMARY 194

6

Consciousness and Cognition 196

What Is Consciousness? 198
Definition of Consciousness 198
Altered States of Consciousness 198

Altered States: Sleep 199
The Biology of Sleep 199
The Stages of Sleep 200
What Happens in REM Sleep? 203
Sleep Disorders 204

psychology in the news
Murder While Sleepwalking 204

How People Think 207
Mental Imagery 208
Concepts 209
Problem Solving and Decision Making 211
Problems with Problem Solving 215
Creativity 216

Language 218
The Levels of Language Analysis 218
The Relationship between Language and Thought 219

applying psychology to everyday life
Mental and Physical Exercises Combine for Better Cognitive Health 222

Chapter Summary 224   Test Yourself 225

CONCEPT SUMMARY 226

7

Development Across the Life Span 228

Issues in Studying Human Development 230
Research Designs 230
Nature Versus Nurture 230

The Basic Building Blocks of Development 231
Genetic and Chromosome Problems 232

Prenatal Development 234
Fertilization, the Zygote and Twinning 234

psychology in the news
Abby and Brittany Hensel, Together for Life 234
The Germinal Period 235

The Embryonic Period 236

The Fetal Period: Grow, Baby, Grow 236

Infancy and Childhood Development 238
Physical Development 238

Baby, Can You See Me? Baby, Can You Hear Me? Sensory Development 238
Cognitive Development 240
Autism Spectrum Disorder 245
Psychosocial Development 246

classic studies in psychology
Harlow and Contact Comfort 249

Gender Development 251
Gender Roles 252
Theories of Gender-Role Development 252

Adolescence 253
Physical Development 254
Cognitive Development 254
Psychosocial Development 256

Adulthood 258
Physical Development: Use It or Lose It 258
Cognitive Development 259
Psychosocial Development 260
Theories of Physical and Psychological Aging 262
Stages of Death and Dying 263

⁝ **applying psychology** to everyday life
⁝ Cross-Cultural Views on Death 264

Chapter Summary 265   Test Yourself 266

CONCEPT SUMMARY 268

8

Motivation and Emotion 270

Approaches to Understanding Motivation 272
Instinct Approaches 272
Drive-Reduction Approaches 273
Personality and nAch: Carol Dweck's Self-Theory of
  Motivation 275
Arousal Approaches 276
Incentive Approaches 278
Humanistic Approaches: Maslow's Hierarchy of Needs 279
Self-Determination Theory (SDT) 281

Psychoactive Drugs and Addiction 282
Physical Dependence 282
Psychological Dependence 283

Sexual Motivation 288
Sexual Orientation 290

⁝ **issues in psychology**
⁝ What Is the Evolutionary Purpose of Homosexuality? 293

Emotion 294
The Three Elements of Emotion 294

⁝ **classic studies in psychology**
⁝ The Angry/Happy Man 300

⁝ **applying psychology** to everyday life
⁝ When Motivation Is Not Enough 304

Chapter Summary 305   Test Yourself 306

CONCEPT SUMMARY 308

9

Stress and Health 310

Stress and Stressors 312
Definition of Stress 312
What Are Stressors? 312
Environmental Stressors: Life's Ups and Downs 313
Psychological Stressors: Stress and the Mind 315

Physiological Factors: Stress and Health 319
The General Adaptation Syndrome 319
Immune System and Stress 320

⁝ **issues in psychology**
⁝ Health Psychology and Stress 323
The Influence of Cognition and Personality on Stress 324
Personality Factors in Stress 325
Social Factors in Stress: People Who Need People 330

Stress, Hunger, and Eating 332
The Physiology of Hunger 333
Social Components of Hunger 333
Maladaptive Eating Problems 333

Stress and Sexual Dysfunction 334

Coping with Stress 336
Problem-Focused Coping 336
Emotion-Focused Coping 336
Meditation as a Coping Mechanism 337
How Culture Affects Coping 337
How Religion Affects Coping 338

⁝ **applying psychology** to everyday life
⁝ Exercising for Mental Health 339

Chapter Summary 339   Test Yourself 340

CONCEPT SUMMARY 342

10

Social Psychology 344

Social Influence: Conformity, Compliance, and Obedience 346
Conformity 346
Compliance 349
Obedience 350

**Social Cognition: Attitudes, Impression Formation, and
Attribution 353**
Attitudes 353
The ABC Model of Attitudes 354
Attitude Formation 355
Attitude Change: The Art of Persuasion 356
Cognitive Dissonance: When Attitudes and Behavior Clash 357

Impression Formation and Attribution 359
Social Categorization 359
Implicit Personality Theories 360
Attribution 360
Fundamental Attribution Error 361

Social Interaction: Prejudice, Love, and Aggression 363
Prejudice and Discrimination 363
Types of Prejudice and Discrimination 363

classic studies in psychology
Brown Eyes, Blue Eyes 364
How People Learn Prejudice 365
Overcoming Prejudice 366

Liking and Loving: Interpersonal Attraction 367
The Rules of Attraction 367
When Opposites Attract 368

psychology in the news
Facing Facebook—The Social Nature of Online Networking 369
Love Is a Triangle—Robert Sternberg's Triangular Theory of Love 369

Aggression and Prosocial Behavior 371
Aggression and Biology 371
The Power of Social Roles 372
Violence in the Media and Aggression 373
Prosocial Behavior 374
Why People Won't Help 375

applying psychology to everyday life
Anatomy of a Cult 377

Chapter Summary 378   Test Yourself 380

CONCEPT SUMMARY 382

The Third Force: Humanism and Personality 398
Carl Rogers and Self-Concept 399
Current Thoughts on the Humanistic View of Personality 400

Trait Theories: Who Are You? 401
Allport 401
Cattell and the 16PF 401
The Big Five: OCEAN, or the Five-Factor Model of Personality 401
Current Thoughts on the Trait Perspective 403

Assessment of Personality 404
Interviews 405
Problems with Interviews 405
Projective Tests 405
Behavioral Assessments 407
Personality Inventories 407

Intelligence 409
Definition 409
Theories of Intelligence 410
Measuring Intelligence 410
Individual Differences in Intelligence: Intellectual Disability and Giftedness 415

The Biology of Personality and Intelligence: Behavioral Genetics 419
Twin Studies 419

classic studies in psychology
Geert Hofstede's Four Dimensions of Cultural Personality 421

applying psychology to everyday life
The Biological Basis of the Big Five 423

Chapter Summary 424   Test Yourself 426

CONCEPT SUMMARY 428

11
Theories of Personality and Intelligence 384

Theories of Personality and Intelligence 386

The Man and the Couch: Sigmund Freud and the Psychodynamic Perspective 386
Freud's Cultural Background 386
The Unconscious Mind 387
The Divisions of the Personality 388
Superego: The Moral Watchdog 388
Stages of Personality Development 390
The Neo-Freudians 392
Current Thoughts on Freud and the Psychodynamic Perspective 394

The Behaviorist and Social Cognitive Views of Personality 396
Bandura's Reciprocal Determinism and Self-Efficacy 397
Rotter's Social Learning Theory: Expectancies 397
Current Thoughts on the Behaviorist and Social Cognitive Views 398

12
Psychological Disorders 430

What Is Abnormality? 432
A Very Brief History of Psychological Disorders 432
What Is Abnormal? 433
A Working Definition of Abnormality 434

issues in psychology
Abnormality Versus Insanity 435

Models of Abnormality 435
The Biological Model: Medical Causes for Psychological Disorders 436
The Psychological Models 436
Biopsychosocial Perspective: All of the Above 437

Diagnostic and Statistical Manual of Mental Disorders, Fourth Edition, Text Revision (DSM-IV-TR) 437
Categories in the DSM-IV-TR 437
How Common Are Psychological Disorders? 438
The Pros and Cons of Labels 439

Anxiety Disorders: What, Me Worry? 440
Phobic Disorders: When Fears Get Out of Hand 440
Panic Disorder 442
Obsessive-Compulsive Disorder 442
Acute Stress Disorder (ASD) and Posttraumatic Stress Disorder (PTSD) 443
Generalized Anxiety Disorder 444
Causes of Anxiety Disorders 444

Mood Disorders: The Effect of Affect 445
Major Depression 446
Bipolar Disorders 446
Causes of Mood Disorders 447

Eating Disorders 448
Anorexia Nervosa 448
Bulimia Nervosa 449

Schizophrenia: Altered Reality 451
Symptoms 451
Categories of Schizophrenia 452
Causes of Schizophrenia 453

Personality Disorders 455
Antisocial Personality Disorder 456
Borderline Personality Disorder 456
Causes of Personality Disorders 456

applying psychology to everyday life
Taking the Worry Out of Exams 458

Chapter Summary 459   Test Yourself 461

CONCEPT SUMMARY 462

13
Psychological Therapies 464

Two Kinds of Therapy 466
Psychotherapy 466
Biomedical Therapy 466

The Early Days: Ice-Water Baths and Electric Shocks 466
Early Treatment of the Mentally Ill 467
Pinel's Reforms 467

Psychotherapy Begins 467
Psychoanalysis 467
Dream Interpretation 468

Free Association 468
Evaluation of Psychoanalysis and Psychodynamic Approaches 468
Interpersonal Psychotherapy 469

Humanistic Therapy: To Err Is Human 470
Tell Me More: Rogers's Person-Centered Therapy 470
Gestalt Therapy 471
Evaluation of the Humanistic Therapies 472

Behavior Therapies: Learning One's Way to Better Behavior 473
Therapies Based on Classical Conditioning 473
Therapies Based on Operant Conditioning 474
Evaluation of Behavior Therapies 476

Cognitive Therapies: Thinking Is Believing 476
Beck's Cognitive Therapy 476
Ellis and Rational–Emotive Behavior Therapy (REBT) 477
Evaluation of Cognitive and Cognitive–Behavioral Therapies 478

Group Therapies: Not Just for the Shy 479
Types of Group Therapies 479
Advantages of Group Therapy 480
Disadvantages of Group Therapy 480

psychology in the news
Mental Health on Campus 481

Does Psychotherapy Really Work? 482
Studies of Effectiveness 482
Characteristics of Effective Therapy 483
Cultural, Ethnic, and Gender Concerns in Psychotherapy 484
Cybertherapy: Therapy in the Computer Age 485

Biomedical Therapies 486
Psychopharmacology 486
Electroconvulsive Therapy 489
Psychosurgery 490

applying psychology to everyday life
Virtual Realities 492

Chapter Summary 493   Test Yourself 494

CONCEPT SUMMARY 496

Appendix A: Statistics in Psychology A–1
Appendix B: Applied Psychology and Psychology Careers B–1
Answer Key AK–1
Glossary G–1
References R–1
Credits C–1
Name Index NI–1
Subject Index SI–1

why do you need this new edition?

If you're wondering why you should buy this new edition of *Psychology: An Exploration*, here are ten good reasons!

1 Engaging online resources to help you succeed! MyPsychLab provides you with online study resources to help make your study time even more effective. Improved with exciting resources, such as new video clips that reinforce and enrich the chapter content and an experiments application that allows you to participate first-hand in psychological experiments. MyPsychLab: Where you are always learning!

2 Get a better grade with the expanded and improved introductory chapter, Psychology in Action: Secrets for Surviving College and Improving Your Grades. It provides practical information on study methods as well as strategies for improving your memory.

3 A new "Study Tip" feature at the beginning of each chapter reminds you to refer back to Psychology in Action for helpful tips that will help you succeed in your course.

4 New and expanded coverage throughout. Every chapter of the second edition has been updated with current and relevant research citations; instructors will include this new information on your exams. Some highlights of the new and expanded coverage include:

5 Chapter 2, The Biological Perspective, is reorganized to improve its clarity. The section "Looking Inside the Living Brain" is expanded and reorganized to clearly present information on cutting-edge techniques psychologists use to study the brain.

6 Chapter 4, Learning, is reorganized to improve its clarity, and sections on learned helplessness and the effect of violent media on children are expanded.

7 Chapter 5, Memory, includes a new opening essay featuring a man known as "The Human Google" with the rare ability to recall almost any event from his past. The section "Models of Memory" has been reorganized, and new research is added on working memory and short-term memory.

8 Chapter 12, Psychological Disorders, is substantially restructured. Disorders previously covered in other chapters are now included here, such as eating disorders and PTSD.

9 Chapter 13, Psychological Therapies, includes an extended section on effective therapy, with new discussions of which therapies are the most effective for a variety of disorders.

10 New and compelling topics for many of the book's feature essays will enrich your understanding of how psychology impacts our lives today. New topics include: "Beyond 'Smoke and Mirrors'—The Psychological Science and Neuroscience of Magic," "The Link between Spanking and Aggression in Young Children," and "The Big Lie: Dr. Andrew Wakefield and the Vaccine Scandal."

the NEW MyPsychLab
Engage. Assess. Succeed.

The NEW MyPsychLab combines original online materials with powerful online assessment to engage students, assess their learning, and help them succeed. MyPsychLab helps ensure students are always learning and always improving.

new video

New Video New, exclusive 30-minute video episodes for every chapter take the viewer from the research laboratory to inside the brain to out on the street for real-world applications.

new experiments

A new experiments application allows students to experience psychology. Students do experiments online to reinforce what they are learning in class and reading about in the book.

new BioFlix animations

Bring difficult-to-teach biological concepts to life with dramatic "zoom" sequences and 3D movement.

eText

The Pearson eText lets students access their textbook anytime, anywhere, and in any way they want it, including listening to it online.

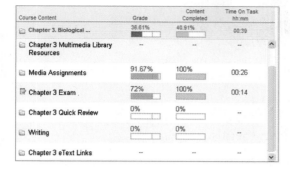

Course Content	Grade	Content Completed	Time On Task hh:mm
Chapter 3. Biological ...	36.61%	40.91%	00:39
Chapter 3 Multimedia Library Resources	--	--	--
Media Assignments	91.67%	100%	00:26
Chapter 3 Exam	72%	100%	00:14
Chapter 3 Quick Review	0%	0%	--
Writing	0%	0%	--
Chapter 3 eText Links	--	--	--

assessment

With powerful online assessment tied to every video, application, and chapter of the text, students can get immediate feedback. Instructors can see what their students know and what they don't know with just a few clicks. Instructors can then personalize MyPsychLab course materials to meet the needs of their students.

new APA assessments

A unique bank of assessment items allows instructors to assess student progress against the American Psychological Association's Learning Goals and Outcomes. These assessments have been keyed to the APA's latest progressive Learning Outcomes (basic, developing, advanced) published in 2008.

> Overall, students are much better prepared for class than students in classes where I don't have a tool like MyPsychLab.

> MyPsychLab allows us to take assessments and connect them to outcomes in accordance with APA guidelines.

> In nine years of experience MyPsychLab has been completely reliable and has never gone down.

Proven Results

Instructors and students have been using MyPsychLab for nearly ten years. To date, over 500,000 students have used MyPsychLab. During that time, three white papers on the efficacy of MyPsychLab were published. Both the white papers and user feedback show compelling results: MyPsychLab helps students succeed and improve their test scores. One of the key ways MyPsychLab improves student outcomes is by providing continuous assessment as part of the learning process. Over the years, both instructor and student feedback have guided numerous improvements that have made MyPsychLab even more flexible and effective.

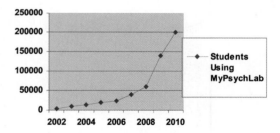

Faculty Advocate Program

Pearson is committed to helping instructors and students succeed with MyPsychLab. To that end, we offer a Psychology Faculty Advocate Program designed to provide peer-to-peer support to new users of MyPsychLab. Experienced Faculty Advocates help instructors understand how MyPsychLab can improve student performance. To learn more about the Faculty Advocate Program, please contact your local Pearson representative or one of the Faculty Advocates listed below:

Noland White at noland.white@gcsu.edu

Gabe Myland at gabe.mydland@dsu.edu

Teresa Stalvey at stalveyt@nfcc.edu

> MyPsychLab simplifies my life and allows me to be more informative, knowledgeable, creative, and entertaining. The entertainment factor increases the number of students that sign up for my class.

presentation resources for instructors
Powerful and Exclusive

Instructors consistently tell us that making their classroom lectures and online instruction exciting and dynamic is a top priority in order to engage students and bring psychology to life. We have been listening, and we have responded by creating state-of the-art presentation resources, putting the most powerful presentation resources at your fingertips.

NEW! MyPsychLab video series (17 episodes)

This brand-new video series offers instructors and students the most current and cutting-edge introductory psychology video content available anywhere. These exclusive videos take the viewer into today's research laboratories, inside the body and brain through breathtaking animations, and out into the street for real-world applications. Guided by the Design, Development, and Review team, a diverse group of introductory psychology instructors, this comprehensive new series features 17 half-hour episodes organized around the major topics of the introductory psychology course syllabus. For maximum flexibility, each 30-minute episode features several brief clips that bring psychology to life:

- *The Big Picture* introduces the topic of the episode and provides the hook to draw students fully into the topic.

- *The Basics* uses the power of video to present foundational topics, especially those that students find difficult to understand.

- *Special Topics* delves deeper into high-interest and cutting-edge topics, showing research in action.

- *Thinking Like a Psychologist* models critical thinking and explores research methods.

- *In the Real World* focuses on applications of psychological research.

- *What's in It for Me?* These clips show students the relevance of psychological research to their lives.

Available in MyPsychLab and also on DVD to adopters of Pearson psychology textbooks (ISBN 0205035817).

NEW! ClassPrep available in MyPsychLab

Finding, sorting, organizing, and presenting your instructor resources is faster and easier than ever before with MyClassPrep. This fully searchable database contains hundreds and hundreds of our best teacher resources, such as lecture launchers and discussion topics, in-class and out-of-class activities and assignments, handouts, as well as video clips, photos, illustrations, charts, graphs, and animations. Instructors can search or browse by topic, and it is easy to sort your results by type, such as photo, document, or animation. You can create personalized folders to organize and store what you like, or you can download resources. You can also upload your own content and present directly from MyClassPrep.

interactive PowerPoint slides

(ISBN 0205256791) These slides bring the powerful Ciccarelli/White design right into the classroom, drawing students into the lecture and providing wonderful interactive activities and rich visuals.

New with this edition, the Interactive PowerPoint Slides now offer embedded video clips, which allow instructors an easy and seamless way to show video content without leaving the slide presentation.

The slides are built around the text's learning objectives and offer multiple pathways or links between content areas.

Icons integrated throughout the slides indicate interactive exercises, simulations, and activities that can be accessed directly from the slides.

teaching and learning package
Integration and Feedback

It is increasingly true today that as valuable as a good textbook is, it is still only one element of a comprehensive learning package. The teaching and homework package that accompanies *Psychology: An Exploration,* second edition, is the most comprehensive and integrated on the market. We have made every effort to provide high-quality instructor resources that will save you preparation time and will enhance the time you spend in the classroom. Noland White has overseen the development of each component of the teaching and assessment package by working directly with the authors and reviewers to ensure consistency in quality and content.

The **Test Item File** (ISBN 0205256422) contains a primary test bank containing thousands of questions. Each chapter includes a two-page Total Assessment Guide that categorizes all test items by learning objective and question type (factual, conceptual, or applied) in an easy-to-reference grid.

The test item file has been thoroughly revised in response to feedback. It has also been analyzed line-by-line by a developmental editor and a copy editor in order to ensure clarity, accuracy, and delivery of the highest quality assessment tool.

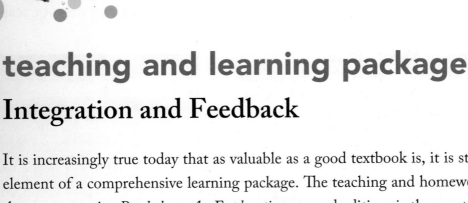

	TOTAL ASSESSMENT GUIDE	Chapter 5 Learning					
Learning Objective	Factual (Multiple Choice)	Conceptual (Multiple Choice)	Applied (Multiple Choice)	True/False Questions	Short Answer Questions	Essay Questions
5.1– What is learning?	1, 2	3, 4, 5		152		180
5.2– What is classical conditioning and who first studied it?	6, 7, 8, 9, 10, 11			153		
5.3– What are the important concepts in classical conditioning?	13, 14, 18, 19, 20		12, 15, 16, 17, 21, 22	154	167	181
5.4– What was Pavlov's classic experiment in conditioning?	23, 27, 28, 30, 31, 32, 33	24, 34	25, 26, 29	155, 156, 157	169, 173	179
5.5– What is a conditioned emotional response?	35, 42, 43, 44, 49, 50, 51, 53, 54	45, 47	36, 37, 38, 39, 40, 41, 46, 48, 52	158, 159	168, 172	177, 183
5.6– Why does classical conditioning work?		55, 56, 57, 58, 59	60		160	175
5.7– What is operant conditioning and	63, 64, 65	61, 62, 66		161		178

Answer Key

1. a Explanation: Alterations due to a genetic blueprint w examples of maturation.
(Page 166–167, Conceptual, LO 5.1)

2. b Explanation: The food acted as an unconditioned sti automatically evoked the conditioned response. Foo causes one to salivate. (Page 167, Applied, LO 5.3)

3. b Explanation: The UCS was a loud noise because it au evoked a fear response.
(Page 167, Applied, LO 5.5)

4. b Explanation: Thorndike was known for his work wit (Page 176, Factual, LO 5.7

Definitions of Learning

1. The process by which experience or practice results in a relatively permanent change in behavior or potential behavior is known as _____.
a. learning
b. intelligence formation
c. imprinting
d. cognition
Answer a   % correct 89   a= 89 b= 2 c= 5 d= 4   r = .40

2. Learning is a process by which experience results in _____.
a. acquisition of motivation
b. relatively permanent behavior change
c. amplification of sensory stimuli
d. delayed genetic behavioral contributions
Answer b   % correct 80   a= 10 b= 80 c= 10 d= 0   r = .23. Learning is a process by which

In addition to the high-quality test bank just described, a second bank of over 1,800 questions by Fred Whitford is available, which has been class-tested with item analysis available for each question.

An additional feature for the test bank, currently not found in any other introductory psychology texts, is the inclusion of rationales for the correct answer and the key distracter in the multiple-choice questions. The rationales help instructors reviewing the content to further evaluate the questions they are choosing for their tests and give instructors the option to use the rationales as an answer key for their students. Feedback from current customers indicates that this unique feature is very useful for ensuring quality and quick response to student queries.

The test bank comes with Pearson MyTest (ISBN 0205256805), a powerful assessment generation program that helps instructors easily create and print quizzes and exams. Questions and tests can be authored online, allowing instructors ultimate flexibility and the ability to efficiently manage assessments anytime, anywhere! Instructors can easily access existing questions and edit, create, and store using simple drag-and-drop and Word-like controls. Data on each question provides information on level of difficulty and page number. In addition, each question maps to the text's major section and learning objective. For more information go to **www.PearsonMyTest.com**.

- **Instructor's Resource Manual** (ISBN 0205259898) offers an exhaustive collection of resources in an easy-to-use format. For each chapter, you'll find activities, exercises, assignments, handouts, and demos for in-class use, as well as guidelines on integrating the many Pearson media resources into your classroom and syllabus. The electronic format features click-and-view hotlinks that allow instructors to quickly review or print any resource in a particular chapter. This resource saves prep work and helps you maximize your classroom time.

- **Create a Custom Text.** For enrollments of at least 25, you can create your own textbook by combining chapters from best-selling Pearson textbooks and/or reading selections in the sequence you want. To begin building your custom text, visit www.pearsoncustomlibrary.com. You may also work with a dedicated Pearson Custom editor to create your ideal text—publishing your own original content or mixing and matching Pearson content. *Contact your Pearson Publisher's Representative to get started.*

Accessing All Resources

For a list of all student resources available with Ciccarelli/White, *Psychology: An Exploration,* second edition, go to **www.mypearsonstore.com**, enter the text ISBN 0205256414, and check out the "Everything That Goes with It" section under the book cover.

For access to all instructor resources for Ciccarelli/White, *Psychology: An Exploration,* second edition, simply go to **http://pearsonhighered.com/irc** and follow the directions to register (or log in if you already have a Pearson user name and password). Once you have registered and your status as an instructor is verified, you will be e-mailed a login name and password. Use your login name and password to access the catalog. Click on the "online catalog" link, click on "psychology" followed by "introductory psychology" and then the Ciccarelli/White *Psychology: An Exploration,* second edition, text. Under the description of each supplement is a link that allows you to download and save the supplement to your desktop.

For technical support for any of your Pearson products, you and your students can contact **http://247.pearsoned.com**.

learner-centered approach
Curiosity and Dialogue

In recent years there has been an increased focus on a more learner-centered approach in higher education. A learner-centered approach encourages dialogue and recognizes the importance of actively engaging students. This textbook came about because we recognized the importance of motivating students to read. When we say "read," we mean really read the text, not just skim it looking for answers to some study guide questions or trying to cram it all in the night before the exam. We set out to write in a style that draws the reader into an ongoing dialogue about psychology. We also want to see students inspired to use the study materials integrated with the text. Our goal is to awaken students' curiosity and energize their desire to learn more; we are delighted with the feedback from students and instructors who have used our text and who tell us this approach is working.

chapter opening prologues
are designed to capture student interest immediately. Taken from a case study or recent event in the news, these openers engage students in the material from the very start of the chapter. The design truly captures the imagination of students and adds to the appeal of the chapter content.

Hey, now the afterimage of the flag has normal colors! Why does this happen?

● Hey, now the afterimage of the flag has normal colors! Why does this happen?
    The phenomenon of the color afterimage is explained by the second theory of color perception, called the **opponent-process theory** (De Valois & De Valois, 1993; Hurvich & Jameson, 1957), based on an idea first suggested by Edwald Hering in 1874 (Finger, 1994). In opponent-process theory, there are four primary colors: red, green, blue, and yellow. The colors are arranged in pairs, red with green and blue with yellow. If one member of a pair is strongly stimulated, the other member is inhibited and cannot be working—so there are no reddish-greens or bluish-yellows.

student voice questions
encourage students to stop, to clarify, and to think critically. Written by students for students, these questions create a dialogue between the text and the reader and encourage students to ask similar questions in the classroom or online. Cited by students and instructors alike as a truly unique and key feature, this feature highlights photographs of students who used the text in their introductory class and who provided questions, comments, and invaluable feedback on the book.

LINKS

Color-deficient vision involving one set of cones is inherited in a pattern known as *sex-linked inheritance*. The gene for color-deficient vision is *recessive*. To inherit a recessive trait, you normally need two of the genes, one from each parent. LINK to Chapter Seven: Development Across the Life Span, p. 154.

One thing that is often difficult for students to do is make connections from topics in one chapter to topics in other chapters. Throughout each chapter, when one topic has a relationship to another topic, a LINK symbol is shown that includes specific chapter and page numbers. The links refer to content covered within the same chapter or in earlier chapters as well as in subsequent chapters—giving students a real sense of the connections in all of the material.

MyPsychLab icons

indicate that students can find related video, podcasts, simulations, practice quizzes, and more in MyPsychLab to expand their learning. There are many more resources available in MyPsychLab than those highlighted in the book, but the icons draw attention to some of the most high-interest materials available at **www.mypsychlab.com**.

Watch on **MyPsychLab**

Listen on **MyPsychLab**

Explore on **MyPsychLab**

Simulate on **MyPsychLab**

Study and Review on **MyPsychLab**

Read on **MyPsychLab**

Survey on **MyPsychLab**

practice quiz   How much do you remember?

3.2   3.3

Pick the best answer.

1. Which of the following terms refers to the perceived effect of the amplitude of light waves?
   a. color
   b. brightness
   c. saturation
   d. hue

2. Which of the following represents the correct path of light through the eye?
   a. iris, cornea, lens, retina
   b. cornea, vitreous humor, iris, lens, aqueous humor, retina
   c. cornea, pupil, lens, vitreous humor, retina
   d. cornea, lens, pupil, iris, retina

3. If you wanted to locate a dimly lit star better at night, what should you do?
   a. Look directly at it because the cones will focus better at night.
   b. Look off to the side, using the cones in the periphery of the retina.
   c. Look directly at it because the rods can see sharply at night.
   d. Look off to the side, using the rods in the periphery of the retina.

4. Which theory of color vision best accounts for afterimages?
   a. trichromatic theory
   b. opponent-process theory
   c. both a and b
   d. neither a nor b

5. Which statement about color-deficient vision is TRUE?
   a. There are more men with color-deficient vision than women.
   b. All people with color-deficient vision see only in black and white.
   c. Some people with color-deficient vision see only in blue.
   d. Some people with color-deficient vision see only in blue and red.

ANSWERS ON PAGE AK-1.

practice quizzes

are included in each chapter at the end of every major section. Practice quizzes help students think critically and apply their understanding before moving on to the next section.

test yourself

Sample exams are found at the end of every chapter. Both the quizzes and the end-of-chapter tests are in multiple-choice format to replicate the experience most students have with graded assessments. Answers to all practice quizzes and end-of-chapter tests are in an **Answer Key** found in the back of the book.

TEST yourself

ANSWERS ON PAGE AK-1.

Study and Review on MyPsychLab   Ready for your test? More quizzes and a customized plan. www.MyPsychLab

Pick the best answer.

1. You find that you have to add 1 teaspoon of sugar to a cup of coffee that already has 5 teaspoons of sugar in it to notice the difference in sweetness. If you have a cup of coffee with 10 teaspoons of sugar in it, how many teaspoons would you have to add to notice the difference in sweetness at least half the time?
   a. 1
   b. 2
   c. 4
   d. 5

2. The process by which the brain stops attending to constant, unchanging information is called _____.
   a. adaptation.
   b. sensation.
   c. habituation.
   d. accommodation.

3. Which of the following terms refers to the psychological effect of the length of light waves?
   a. color
   b. brightness
   c. pitch
   d. amplitude

4. Which of the following is responsible for controlling how much light enters the eye?
   a. cornea
   b. lens
   c. retina
   d. iris

5. Which type of retinal cell forms the optic nerve?
   a. rods
   b. cones
   c. ganglion cells
   d. bipolar cells

6. Which type of retinal cell plays a role in color vision?
   a. rods
   b. cones
   c. ganglion cells
   d. bipolar cells

7. Which set of colors are the primary colors when mixing light?
   a. red, yellow, and blue
   b. red, blue, and green
   c. blue, green, and yellow
   d. red, green, and yellow

concept summaries

at the end of each chapter provide
students with a graphic summary
of content covered in the chapter.
By pulling the content together
in this highly visual manner,
students can better understand
the connections and grasp how
the chapter material fits together.

classic studies in psychology

Biological Constraints on Operant Conditioning

Raccoons are fairly intelligent animals and are sometimes used in learning
experiments. In a typical experiment, a behaviorist would use shaping and reinforcement to teach a raccoon a trick. The goal might be to get the raccoon to
pick up several coins and drop them into a metal container, for which the raccoon would
be rewarded with food. The behaviorist starts by reinforcing the raccoon for picking up a
single coin. Then the metal container is introduced, and the raccoon is now required to
drop the coin into the slot on the container in order to get reinforcement.

It is at this point that operant conditioning seems to fail. Instead of dropping the coin
in the slot, the raccoon puts the coin in and out of the slot and rubs it against the inside
of the container, then holds it firmly for a few seconds before finally letting it go. When
the requirement is upped to two coins, the raccoon spends several minutes rubbing them
against each other and dipping them into the container, without actually dropping them
in. In spite of the fact that this dipping and rubbing behavior is not reinforced, it gets
worse and worse until conditioning becomes impossible.

other features of each chapter

are special sections covering interesting topics
related to the chapter material, especially topics
of diversity and cultural interest. These sections
are not set off from the text in boxes, and the
authors refer to these features in the chapter
content, making it more likely that students
will read the enriching material. The test bank,
practice quizzes, and the tests at the end of
each chapter include questions on this material,
further encouraging students to read it. Each
section ends with **Questions for Further Study**
that encourage students to think critically about
the content they have just read.

psychology in the news

Facing Facebook—The Social Nature of Online Networking

There are some interesting research findings concerning the online networking phenomenon. For example, people using particular sites seem to have
certain things in common. The findings of one study suggest that the student's
choice of social network sites a college student is related to racial identity, ethnic identity,
and the education level of the student's parents (Hargittai, 2007). White students prefer
Facebook, and Hispanic students prefer MySpace; and while Asian and Asian American
students use Facebook more than MySpace, they use less popular sites like Xanga and
Friendster more than any other ethnic group does. The more education the parents
have, the more likely the student is to use Facebook and Xanga, and the less likely to
use MySpace.

In another study, researchers found that young people who already experience positive social relationships use the online sites to enhance those same relationships, contrary
to the stereotyped view that it would be the socially inept who would gravitate toward
the anonymous nature of online networking (Mikami et al., 2010). Those who are less well

applying psychology to everyday life

Beyond "Smoke and Mirrors"— The Psychological Science and Neuroscience of Magic

Many people enjoy watching magic acts in person or on television. Perhaps you
have been amazed by a Mindfreak® performed by Criss Angel or the performance and edgy antics of Penn & Teller. If you are one of those people, you
likely witnessed a performance that included many various illusions. And like many of us,
you probably wondered at some point in the performance, "How did they do that?!" Did
you think the tricks were due to some type of special device (such as a fake thumb tip for
hiding a scarf), or perhaps they were accomplished with "smoke and mirrors," or maybe
the magician distracted the audience with one movement while actually doing something
else to pull off the illusion? Magicians use many techniques to take advantage of, or
manipulate, our actual level of awareness of what is happening right in front of us or perhaps to manipulate our attention.

learning outcomes and assessment
Goals and Standards

In recent years many psychology departments have been focusing on core competencies and on how methods of assessment can better enhance students' learning. In response, the American Psychological Association (APA) established ten recommended goals for the undergraduate psychology major. Specific learning outcomes were established for each of the ten goals, and suggestions were made on how best to tie assessment practices to these goals. In 2008, the APA identified a progression of learning outcomes for the goals associated directly with the discipline of psychology moving from basic (retention and comprehension) to developing (application and analysis) to advanced (evaluation and creation). In writing this text, we have used the APA goals and assessment recommendations as guidelines for structuring content and integrating the teaching and homework materials. For details on the APA learning goals and assessment guidelines, please see **http://www.apa.org**.

Based on APA recommendations, each chapter is structured around detailed **Learning Objectives**. All of the instructor and student resources are also organized around these objectives, making the text and resources a fully integrated system of study. Instructors can choose which learning objectives are important in their course and when using the resources have the flexibility to pick the content they want their students to focus on.

learning objectives

3.1 How does sensation travel through the central nervous system, and why are some sensations ignored?

3.2 What is light, and how does it travel through the various parts of the eye?

3.3 How do the eyes see, and how do the eyes see different colors?

3.4 What is sound, and how does it travel through the various parts of the ear?

3.5 How do the senses of taste and smell work, and how are they alike?

3.6 What allows people to experience the sense of touch, pain, motion, and balance?

3.7 What are perception, perceptual constancies, and the Gestalt principles of perception?

3.8 What is depth perception, and what kind of cues are important for it to occur?

3.9 What are visual illusions and how can they and other factors influence and alter perception?

APA UNDERGRADUATE LEARNING GOALS AND OUTCOMES | **CICCARELLI/WHITE CONTENT**

Knowledge Base of Psychology

1

Demonstrate familiarity with the major concepts, theoretical perspectives, empirical findings, and historical trends in psychology.

1.1 Characterize the nature of psychology as a discipline.

1.2 Demonstrate knowledge and understanding representing appropriate breadth and depth in selected content areas of psychology: theory and research representing general domains, the history of psychology, relevant levels of analysis, overarching themes, and relevant ethical issues.

1.3 Use the concepts, language, and major theories of the discipline to account for psychological phenomena.

1.4 Explain major perspectives of psychology (e.g., behavioral, biological, cognitive, evolutionary, humanistic, psychodynamic, and sociocultural).

Ch 1: 1.1–1.5
Ch 2: 2.1–2.11, and Applying Psychology to Everyday Life: Paying Attention to the Causes of Attention-Deficit/Hyperactivity Disorder
Ch 3: 3.1–3.8
Ch 4: 4.1–4.11
Ch 5: 5.1–5.5, 5.7–5.11
Ch 6: 6.1–6.5
Ch 7: 7.1, 7.3–7.11
Ch 8: 8.1–8.9
Ch 9: 9.1–9.5
Ch 10: 10.1–10.4, 10.6, 10.11–10.12
Ch 11: 11.1–11.13
Ch 12: 12.1–12.9
Ch 13: 13.1–13.10
Appendix: Statistic A.1
Major concepts all reinforced with student study guide materials, online homework tools, and instructor's teaching and assessment package

Research Methods in Psychology

2

Understand and apply basic research methods in psychology, including research design, data analysis, and interpretation.

2.1 Describe the basic characteristics of the science of psychology.

2.2 Explain different research methods used by psychologists.
  a. Describe how various research designs address different types of questions and hypotheses.
  b. Articulate strengths and limitations of various research designs.
  c. Distinguish the nature of designs that permit causal inferences from those that do not.

2.3 Evaluate the appropriateness of conclusions derived from psychological research.
  a. Interpret basic statistical results.
  b. Distinguish between statistical significance and practical significance.
  c. Describe effect size and confidence intervals.
  d. Evaluate the validity of conclusions presented in research reports.

2.4 Design and conduct basic studies to address psychological questions using appropriate research methods.
  a. Locate and use relevant databases, research, and theory to plan, conduct, and interpret results of research studies.
  b. Formulate testable research hypotheses, based on operational definitions of variables.
  c. Select and apply appropriate methods to maximize internal and external validity and reduce the plausibility of alternative explanations.
  d. Collect, analyze, interpret, and report data using appropriate statistical strategies to address different types of research questions and hypotheses.
  e. Recognize that theoretical and sociocultural contexts as well as personal biases may shape research questions, design, data collection, analysis, and interpretation.

2.5 Follow the APA Code of Ethics in the treatment of human and nonhuman participants in the design, data collection, interpretation, and reporting of psychological research.

2.6 Generalize research conclusions appropriately based on the parameters of particular research methods.
  a. Exercise caution in predicting behavior based on limitations of single studies.
  b. Recognize the limitations of applying normative conclusions to individuals.
  c. Acknowledge that research results may have unanticipated societal consequences.
  d. Recognize that individual differences and sociocultural contexts may influence the applicability of research findings.

Ch 1: 1.6–1.12
Ch 2: 2.6
Ch 4: 4.12 and Classic Studies in Psychology: Biological Constraints of Operant Conditioning
Ch 5: Classic Studies in Psychology: Elizabeth Loftus and Eyewitnesses and Applying Psychology to Everyday Life: Current Research on Alzheimer's Disease
Ch 6: Psychology in the News: Murder While Sleepwalking
Ch 7: 7.1, 7.6, 7.11, and Classic Studies in Psychology: Harlow and Contact Comfort
Ch 8: Classic Studies in Psychology: The Angry/Happy Man
Ch 10: Classic Studies in Psychology: Brown Eyes, Blue Eyes
Ch 11: 11.8, 11.10, and Classic Studies in Psychology: Geert Hofstede's Four Dimensions of Cultural Personality and Applying Psychology to Everyday Life: The Biological Basis of the Big Five
Appendix A: Statistics A.1–A.6
Appendix B: Applied Psychology B.7 B.8
Methodology reinforced with student study guide materials, online homework tools, and instructor's teaching and assessment package

3 Critical Thinking Skills in Psychology

Respect and use critical and creative thinking, skeptical inquiry, and, when possible, the scientific approach to solve problems related to behavior and mental processes.

3.1 Use critical thinking effectively.

3.2 Engage in creative thinking.

3.3 Use reasoning to recognize, develop, defend, and criticize arguments and other persuasive appeals.

3.4 Approach problems effectively.

Ch 1: 1.13–1.14 and Applying Psychology to Everyday Life: Thinking Critically about Critical Thinking

Ch 3: Applying Psychology to Everyday Life: Beyond "Smoke and Mirrors"—The Psychological Science and Neuroscience of Magic

Ch 4: 4.13, Issues in Psychology: The Link between Spanking and Aggression in Young Children and Applying Psychology to Everyday Life: Can You Really Toilet Train Your Cat?

Ch 6: 6.6–6.7, 6.9–6.10

Ch 7: 7.2, 7.6, and Issues in Psychology: The Big Lie: Dr. Andrew Wakefield and the Vaccine Scandal

Ch 9: 9.5–9.6, 9.9–9.10

Ch 10: 10.5, 10.7, 10.9, 10.13, and Applying Psychology to Everyday Life: Anatomy of a Cult

Ch 11: 11.8, 11.12

Ch 12: 12.1 and Issues in Psychology: Abnormality versus Insanity

Ch 13: 13.5–13.7, 13.10, and Applying Psychology to Everyday Life: Virtual Realities

Critical thinking skills reinforced with student study guide materials, online homework tools, and instructor's teaching and assessment package

4 Application of Psychology

Understand and apply psychological principles to personal, social, and organizational issues.

4.1 Describe major applied areas of psychology (e.g., clinical, counseling, industrial/organizational, school, health).

4.2 Identify appropriate applications of psychology in solving problems.

4.3 Articulate how psychological principles can be used to explain social issues and inform public policy.

4.4 Apply psychological concepts, theories, and research findings as these relate to everyday life.

4.5 Recognize that ethically complex situations can develop in the application of psychological principles.

Introduction: Secrets for Surviving College: How to Improve Your Grades

Ch 1: 1.5, 1.13–1.14

Ch 2: Psychology in the News: Fact or Fiction—Focus on the Brain, but Check Your Sources! and Applying Psychology to Everyday Life: Paying Attention to the Causes of Attention Deficit/Hyperactivity Disorder

Ch 4: 4.13 and Applying Psychology to Everyday Life: Can You Really Toilet Train Your Cat?

Ch 5: 5.12

Ch 6: 6.10 and Applying Psychology to Everyday Life: Mental Exercises for Better Cognitive Health

Ch 7: 7.11–7.12, Issues in Psychology: The Facts and Myths about Immunizations, Applying Psychology to Everyday Life: Cross-Cultural Views on Death

Ch 8: 8.5, 8.7, and Applying Psychology to Everyday Life: A How-To of Happiness?

Ch 9: 9.2, 9.6–9.12, Applying Psychology to Everyday Life: Exercising for Mental Health, and Issues in Psychology: Health Psychology and Stress

Ch 10: 10.5, 10.7–10.9, 10.13, and Applying Psychology to Everyday Life: Anatomy of a Cult

Ch 11: 11.10–11.13

Ch 12: 12.1, 12.9, and Applying Psychology to Everyday Life: Taking the Worry Out of Exams

Ch 13: 13.1, 13.4–13.7, Psychology in the News: Mental Health on Campus, and Applying Psychology to Everyday Life: Virtual Realities

Appendix B: Applied Psychology

Applications reinforced with student study guide materials, online homework tools, and instructor's teaching and assessment package

APA UNDERGRADUATE LEARNING GOALS AND OUTCOMES   **CICCARELLI/WHITE CONTENT**

5 Values in Psychology

Value empirical evidence, tolerate ambiguity, act ethically, and reflect other values that are the underpinnings of psychology as a science.

5.1 Recognize the necessity for ethical behavior in all aspects of the science and practice of psychology.

5.2 Demonstrate reasonable skepticism and intellectual curiosity by asking questions about causes of behavior.

5.3 Seek and evaluate scientific evidence for psychological claims.

5.4 Tolerate ambiguity and realize that psychological explanations are often complex and tentative.

5.5 Recognize and respect human diversity and understand that psychological explanations may vary across populations and contexts.

5.6 Assess and justify their engagement with respect to civic, social, and global responsibilities.

5.7 Understand the limitations of their psychological knowledge and skills.

Ch 1: 1.13 1.14
Ch 4: 4.8, 4.10
Ch 6: 6.7, 6.9–6.10, and Psychology in the News: Murder While Sleepwalking
Ch 7: 7.2, 7.8, 7.12, and Issues in Psychology: The Big Lie: Dr. Andrew Wakefield and the Vaccine Scandal
Ch 9: 9.5–9.6, 9.11–9.12
Ch 10: 10.8–10.9, 10.12–10.13
Ch 11: 11.8–11.13, Classic Studies in Psychology: Geert Hofstede's Four Dimensions of Cultural Personality
Ch 12: 12.1, Issues in Psychology: Abnormality versus Insanity
Ch 13: 13.1, 13.7, 13.10
Values reinforced with content in student study guide and instructor's teaching and assessment package

6 Information and Technological Literacy

Demonstrate information competence and the ability to use computers and other technology for many purposes.

6.1 Demonstrate information competence at each stage in the following process: formulating a researchable topic, choosing relevant and evaluating relevant resources, and reading and accurately summarizing scientific literature that can be supported by database search strategies.

6.2 Use appropriate software to produce understandable reports of the psychological literature, methods, and statistical and qualitative analyses in APA or other appropriate style, including graphic representations of data.

6.3 Use information and technology ethically and responsibly.

6.4 Demonstrate basic computer skills, proper etiquette, and security safeguards.

Ch 1: 1.6–1.11
Ch 2: 2.6 and Psychology in the News: Fact or Fiction—Focus on the Brain, but Check Your Sources!
Ch 4: Classic Studies in Psychology: Biological Constraints on Operant Conditioning
Ch 5: Classic Studies in Psychology: Elizabeth Loftus and Eyewitnesses, and Current Research on Alzheimer's Disease
Ch 6: Psychology in the News: Murder While Sleepwalking
Ch 7: Classic Studies in Psychology: Harlow and Contact Comfort
Ch 8: Classic Studies in Psychology: The Angry/Happy Man
Ch 10: 10.2–10.5, 10.8–10.11, and Classic Studies in Psychology: Brown Eyes, Blue Eyes
Ch 11: Classic Studies in Psychology: Geert Hofstede's Four Dimensions of Cultural Personality
Appendix A: Statistics
Study Guide Chapter 1: Summary section on the scientific method and study hints.
Information and technological literacy reinforced with the Watch/Hear/Learn/Explore/Practice More icons integrated into the text, leading to Web-based expansions on topics and allowing instructors and students access to extra information, videos, podcasts, and simulations, as well as student study guide materials, online homework tools, and instructor's teaching and assessment package.

7 Communication Skills

Communicate effectively in a variety of formats.

7.1 Demonstrate effective writing skills in various formats (e.g., essays, correspondence, technical papers, note taking) and for various purposes (e.g., informing, defending, explaining, persuading, arguing, teaching).

7.2 Demonstrate effective oral communication skills in various formats (e.g., group discussion, debate, lecture) and for various purposes (e.g., informing. defending, explaining, persuading, arguing, teaching).

7.3 Exhibit quantitative literacy. Demonstrate effective interpersonal communication skills.

7.4 Exhibit the ability to collaborate effectively.

Ciccarelli Student Voice questions
Narrative of the text—like a dialogue between author and reader
Test bank essay questions
Instructor's Resource Manual—see student assignments, lecture launchers, and classroom activities sections
MyPsychLab online homework and assessment tools

8 Sociocultural and International Awareness

Recognize, understand, and respect the complexity of sociocultural and international diversity.

8.1 Interact effectively and sensitively with people from diverse backgrounds and cultural perspectives.

8.2 Examine the sociocultural and international contexts that influence individual differences.

8.3 Explain how individual differences influence beliefs, values, and interactions with others and vice versa.

8.4 Understand how privilege, power, and oppression may affect prejudice, discrimination, and inequity. Recognize prejudicial attitudes and discriminatory behaviors that might exist in themselves and others.

Ch 1: 1.13–1.14
Ch 6: 6.9
Ch 7: 7.2, 7.6, 7.8, 7.11–7.12, Applying Psychology to Everyday Life: Cross-Cultural Views on Death, and Psychology in the News: Abby and Brittany Hensel, Together for Life
Ch 8: 8.5–8.6
Ch 9: 9.2–9.3, 9.5–9.8, and 9.10–9.12
Ch 10: 10.1–10.3, 10.5–10.9, 10.11–10.13, and Classic Studies in Psychology: Brown Eyes, Blue Eyes
Ch 11: 11.10–11.13 and Classic Studies in Psychology: Geert Hofstede's Four Dimensions of Cultural Personality
Ch 12: 12.1 and Issues in Psychology: Abnormality versus Insanity
Ch 13: 13.1, 13.7
Diversity issues also covered in student study guide materials, online homework tools, and instructor's teaching and assessment package

9 Personal Development

Develop insight into their own and others' behavior and mental processes and apply effective strategies for self-management and self-improvement.

9.1 Reflect on their experiences and find meaning in them.

9.2 Apply psychological principles to promote personal development.

9.3 Enact self-management strategies that maximize healthy outcomes.

9.4 Display high standards of personal integrity with others.

Introduction: Secrets for Surviving College: How to Improve Your Grades
Ch 4: Applying Psychology to Everyday Life: Can You Really Toilet Train Your Cat?
Ch 5: Applying Psychology to Everyday Life: Current Research in Alzheimer's Disease
Ch 6: 6.10 and Applying Psychology to Everyday Life: Mental Exercises for Better Cognitive Health
Ch 7: Issues in Psychology: The Big Lie: Dr. Andrew Wakefield and the Vaccine Scandal
Ch 8: 8.5–8.7 and Applying Psychology to Everyday Life: A How-To of Happiness?
Ch 9: 9.2–9.3 9.5–9.12, and Applying Psychology to Everyday Life: Exercising for Mental Health
Ch 10: 10.5, 10.7–10.9, 10.12–10.13, and Applying Psychology to Everyday Life: Anatomy of a Cult
Ch 11: 11.8, 11.13
Ch 12: Applying Psychology to Everyday Life: Taking the Worry Out of Exams
Ch 13: Applying Psychology to Everyday Life: Virtual Realities and Psychology in the News: Mental Health on Campus
Appendix B: Applied Psychology
Each chapter-opening "Why Study" feature helps students understand the relevance and applicability of the chapter subject to their own lives.

10 Career Planning and Development

Pursue realistic ideas about how to implement their psychological knowledge, skills, and values in occupational pursuits in a variety of settings.

10.1 Apply knowledge of psychology (e.g., decision strategies, lifespan processes, psychological assessment, types of psychological careers) to formulating career choices.

10.2 Identify the types of academic experience and performance in psychology and the liberal arts that will facilitate entry into the workforce, post-baccalaureate education, or both.

10.3 Describe preferred career paths based on accurate self-assessment of abilities, achievement, motivation, and work habits.

10.4 Identify and develop skills and experiences relevant to achieving selected career goals.

10.5 Demonstrate an understanding of the importance of lifelong learning and personal flexibility to sustain personal and professional development as the nature of work evolves.

Introduction: Secrets for Surviving College: How to Improve Your Grades
Ch 1: 1.5
Appendix A: Statistic A.7
Appendix B: Applied Psychology B.1–B.6
Each chapter-opening "Why Study" feature helps students understand the relevance of psychological research. Career planning content is also found in student study guide materials, online homework tools, and instructor's teaching and assessment packages.

development story
Insight and Collaboration

The creation of this text and package is the result of the most extensive development investment in a text that this discipline has ever experienced. Over 1,000 instructors and students contributed to decisions regarding issues such as organization, content coverage, pedagogical innovation, and writing style through feedback from reviews and focus groups. A full-time development editor analyzed this feedback and worked with the authors, editing the prose line-by-line for clarity. Student reviewers who had used the book in their introductory psychology class provided valuable input by evaluating the writing style and in-text learning tools; you will see some of these student reviewers in the photos included with the Student Voice questions. The second edition continues to carry the benefit of this input and has been even further improved based on specific feedback from reviewers of the first edition, including expert reviewers for each major topic area who provided feedback on the currency and accuracy of the research. We are grateful to all who provided feedback on changes for the second edition text as well as changes to the design—which we hope you find as inviting as we do!

INSTRUCTORS

Alabama
Susan Anderson, University of South Alabama
Lisa D. Hager, Spring Hill College
Chan Roark, Troy University
Royce Simpson, Spring Hill College

Arizona
Olga Carranza, Pima Community College–Desert Vista
Lynda Mae, Arizona State University
Kam Majer, Glendale Community College
Gregory Privitera, Glendale Community College
Mike Todd, Paradise Valley Community College
Deborah Van Marche, Glendale Community College

Arkansas
Karen Yanowitz, Arkansas State University

California
Patricia Alexander, Long Beach City College
Ronald Barrett, Loyola Marymount University
John Billimek, University of California, Irvine
Jessica Cail, Long Beach City College
David Campbell, Humboldt State University
Linda Chaparro, Oxnard College
Kimberley Duff, Cerritos College
Vera Dunwoody, Chaffey College
Mark Eastman, Diablo Valley College
Michael Feiler, Merritt College

Maria Fitzpatrick, Chaffey College
Lenore Frigo, Shasta College
Gregg Gold, Humboldt State University
Mark Harmon, Reedley College–Clovis Center
Ann Hennessey, Los Angeles Pierce College
Melissa Holmes, San Joaquin Delta College
Karin Hu, City College of San Francisco
Senqi Hu, Humboldt State University
Lori Hubbard-Welsh, California State University–Chico
Steve Isonio, Golden West Community College
Inna Kanevsky, San Diego Mesa College
Lee Kooler, Modesto Junior College
Jennifer Lee, Cabrillo College
Randy Martinez, Cypress College
Terry Maul, San Bernardino Valley College
Lee Merchant, Modesto Junior College
Arthur Olguin, Santa Barbara City College
Fernando Ortiz, Santa Ana Community College
Jeff Pedroza, Santa Ana College
Michelle Pilati, Rio Hondo College
Scott Reed, California State University–Chico
Eileen Roth, Glendale Community College
Angela Sadowski, Chaffey College
Harry Saterfield, Foothill College
Cindy Selby, California State University–Chico
Alan Spivey, Shasta College
Mark Stewart, American River College
Kathleen Taylor, Sierra College

Joan Thomas-Spiegel, Los Angeles Harbor College
Inger Thompson, Glendale Community College
Herkie Williams, El Camino College–Compton Center
Dean Yoshizumi, Sierra College

Colorado
Layton Curl, Metropolitan State College
Karla Gingerich, Colorado State University
Jan Hickman, Westwood College
Misty Hull, Pikes Peak Community College
Diane Martichuski, University of Colorado at Boulder
Lisa Routh, Pikes Peak Community College
Frank Vattano, Colorado State University

Connecticut
Marlene Adelman, Norwalk Community College
Moises Salinas, Central Connecticut State University
Lawrence Venuk, Naugatuck Valley Community College

Florida
Melissa Acevedo, Valencia Community College–West
Kathleen Bey, Palm Beach Community College–Central
Gary Bothe, Pensacola Junior College
Kelvin Faison, Pasco Hernando Community College
Jodi Grace, St. Thomas University
Peter Gram, Pensacola Junior College
Joe Grisham, Indian River Community College
Marlene Grooms, Miami Dade College–Homestead Campus
Gregory Harris, Polk Community College
Sheryl Hartman, Miami Dade Community College
Debra Hollister, Valencia Community College
James Jakubow, Florida Atlantic University
Manuel Mares, Florida National College
Glenn J. Musgrove, Broward Community College–Central Campus
Jeanne O'Kon, Tallahassee Community College
Jennifer P. Peluso, Florida Atlantic University
Jeanine Plowman, Florida State University
Lawrence Siegel, Palm Beach Community College–South
Teresa Stalvey, North Florida Community College
Wayne Stein, Brevard Community College–Melbourne
Patricia Stephenson, Miami Dade Community College
Richard Townsend, Miami Dade Community College
Barbara Van Horn, Indian River Community College
Guillermo Wated, Barry University
Steven Zombory, Palm Beach Atlantic University

Georgia
Sheree Barron, Georgia College & State University
David Brackin, Young Harris College
Deb Briihl, Valdosta State University
Kristen Diliberto-Macaluso, Berry College
Dan Fawaz, Georgia Perimeter College
Deborah Garfin, Georgia State University
Adam Goodie, University of Georgia
Amy Hackney, Georgia Southern University
Michael Hoff, Dalton State College
John Lindsay, Georgia College & State University
Antoinette Miller, Clayton State University
Suzann Shepard, Middle Georgia College & John A. Logan College

Hawaii
Robert Dotson, Honolulu Community College

Idaho
Richard Cluff, Brigham Young University–Idaho
Tera Letzring, Idaho State University

Randy Simonson, College of Southern Idaho
Shannon Welch, University of Idaho

Illinois
Elizabeth Arnott-Hill, Chicago State University
Rachel Berry, Southeastern Illinois College
Paula J. Biedenharm, Aurora University
John Binning, Illinois State University
Martha Bonne, Joliet Junior College
Lorelei Carvajal, Triton College
David Das, Elgin Community College
Joseph Ferrari, DePaul University
Renae Franiuk, Aurora University
Pablo Gomez, DePaul University
Christine Grela, McHenry County College
Susan Harris-Mitchell, College of DuPage
Suzanne Hester, Oakton Community College
Charmaine Jake-Matthews, Prairie State College
Mary Johannesen-Schmidt, Oakton Community College
Lynnel Kiely, Harold Washington College
Shari Larson, College of Lake County
Karen Owens, College of Lake County
Deborah Podwika, Kankakee Community College
Eric Rogers, College of Lake County
Suzanne Valentine-French, College of Lake County
Ada Wainwright, College of DuPage
Joan Warmbold-Boggs, Oakton Community College

Indiana
Cathy Alsman, Ivy Tech Community College–Terre Haute
Dan Dickman, Ivy Tech Community College of Indiana
Patricia Kemerer, Ivy Tech Community College–Fort Wayne
Darrell Rudmann, Indiana East University
Don Shull, Ivy Tech–Evansville
Deb Stipp-Evans, Ivy Tech Community College–Gary
Colin William, Ivy Tech Community College–Lafayette
Martin Wolfger, Ivy Tech Community College of Indiana

Iowa
Tim Boffeli, Clarke College
William Dragon, Cornell College
James Rodgers, Hawkeye Community College
Lee Skeens, Southeastern Community College
Susan Troy, Northeast Iowa Community College

Kansas
Deborah Allen, Fort Scott Community College
Steve Hoekstra, Kansas Wesleyan University
Diane Kappen, Johnson County Community College
Rupert Klein, Kansas State University
John Sanders, Garden City Community College
Joe Slobko, Garden City Community College

Kentucky
Sabra Jacobs, Big Sandy Community and Technical College–Prestonburg
Sherry Rager, Hopkinsville Community College

Louisiana
Brett Heintz, Delgado Community College
Mike Majors, Delgado Community College–City Park
Jack Palmer, University of Louisiana–Monroe
Mary Boone Treuting, Louisiana State University–Alexandria

Maryland
Patrick Allen, College of Southern Maryland
Katherine Helfrich, Frederick Community College

Cynthia Koenig, St. Mary's College of Maryland
Misty Kolchakian, Anne Arundel Community College

Massachusetts
Marcelle Bartolo-Abela, Holyoke Community and Baypath Colleges
Shirley Cassarra, Bunker Hill Community College
Pamela Ludemann, Framingham State College
Lloyd Sheldon Johnson, Bunker Hill Community College
Chitra Ranganathan, Framingham State College

Michigan
Gregory Cutler, Bay de Noc Community College
Michael Drissman, Macomb Community College–South
Mary Eberly, Oakland University
Cassandra George-Sturges, Washtenaw Community College
Terri Heck, Macomb Community College–South
Patricia Lanzon, Henry Ford Community College
Paulina Multhaupt, Macomb Community College
Shawn Talbot, Kellogg Community College
Michael Vargo, Grand Rapids Community College

Minnesota
Dawn Albertson, Minnesota State University–Mankato
Ivonne Tjoe Fat, Rochester Community and Technical College

Mississippi
Collin Billingsley, Northeast Mississippi Community College
William Goggin, University of Southern Mississippi
Shaila Khan, Tougaloo Community College
Jeannette Murphey, Meridian Community College
Randy Vinzant, Jones County Junior College

Missouri
John Gambon, Ozarks Technical College
Julie Tietz, Cottey College
Matthew Westra, Metropolitan Community College–Longview

Nebraska
Patrick Dolan, Drew University
Jean Mandernach, University of Nebraska, Kearney
Keith Matthews, Northeast Community College
Linda Petroff, Central Community College
James Thomas, University of Nebraska–Omaha

New Hampshire
Mark Henn, University of New Hampshire

New Jersey
Fred Bonato, Saint Peter's College
Deborah Fish Ragin, Montclair State University
Joan Rafter, Hudson County Community College
John Ramirez, Middlesex County College
Darla Silverman, Sussex County Community College
Jonathon Springer, Kean University
Jordan Vosmik, Drew University
Anthony Zoccolillo, DeVry University

New Mexico
Katherine Demitrakis, Albuquerque Tech–Vocational Institute
Andrea Ericksen, San Juan College
Sarah Erickson, University of New Mexico
Jim Johnson, Central New Mexico Community College
Marisa McLeod, Santa Fe Community College
Brian Parry, Mesa State College
Ron Salazar, San Juan College

New York
Miles Groth, Wagner College
Melvyn King, SUNY–Cortland

Joe Lao, Teachers College, Columbia University
Michael Magee, Brooklyn College
George Meyer, Suffolk County Community College–Ammerman
Laurence Nolan, Wagner College
Billa Reiss, St. John's University

North Carolina
Beth Barton, Coastal Carolina Community College and University of North Carolina–Wilmington
Elizabeth Denny, University of North Carolina–Pembroke
Sarah Estow, Guilford College
Shirley Kuhn, Pitt Community College
Julie Lee, Cape Fear Community College
Michele Mathis, Cape Fear Community College
Micha Pitzen, Coastal Carolina Community College
John Schulte, Cape Fear Community College
Stephanie Williford, Coastal Carolina Community College

Ohio
Leslie Angel, Sinclair Community College
Nathan Arbuckle, Ohio State University
Bobby J. Beavers, Sinclair Community College
Ronald Craig, Cincinnati State College
Lorry Cology, Owens Community College
Chris Cunningham, Bowling Green State University
Diane Feibel, University of Cincinnati–Raymond Walters College
Carolyn Kaufman, Columbus State Community College
Elaine McLeskey, Belmont Technical College
Mark Rittman, Cuyahoga Community College
Keith Syrja, Owens Community College
John Ward, Miami University

Oklahoma
James Hunsicker, Southwestern Oklahoma State University
Mike Knight, University of Central Oklahoma
Jerrie Scott, Rose State College

Oregon
Barbara DeFilippo, Lane Community College

Pennsylvania
Joseph Hardy, Harrisburg Area Community College
Sharon Himmanen, Cedar Crest College
Daniel Klaus, Community College of Beaver County
Sonya Lott-Harrison, Community College of Philadelphia
Barbara Radigan, Community College of Allegheny County
Mark Rivardo, Saint Vincent College
Cathy Sigmund, Geneva College
Adrian Tomer, Shippensburg University
Peter Zubritzky, Community College of Beaver County

Rhode Island
Thomas Malloy, Rhode Island College
Michael Spiegler, Providence College

South Carolina
Dan Bellack, Trident Technical College
Eurnestine Brown, Winthrop University
Devin Byrd, University of South Carolina–Aiken
William House, University of South Carolina–Aiken
Laura May, University of South Carolina–Aiken
Barbara Oswald, Midlands Technical College and University of Cincinnati
Frank Provenzano, Greenville Technical College
Nancy Simpson, Trident Technical College

South Dakota
Gabe Mydland, Dakota State University

Tennessee

Erskine Ausbrooks, Dyersburg State Community College
Vivian Grooms, Jackson State Community College
Michelle Merwin, University of Tennessee–Martin
Aubrey Shoemaker, Walters State Community College

Texas

Dr. Joyce Bateman-Jones, Central Texas College
Robert Benefield, East Texas Baptist University
Diane Boudreaux-Kraft, Houston Community College–Southwest
Patrick Carroll, University of Texas–Austin
Monica Castator, Navarro College
Dr. Ili Castillo, Houston Community College–Northwest
Jane Cirillo, Houston Community College–Southeast
Wanda Clark, South Plains College
Perry Collins, Wayland Baptist University
Mary Cordell, Hill College–Hillsboro
Michael Devoley, Lonestar College–Montgomery
Wendy Domjan, University of Texas–Austin
Judith Easton, Austin Community College
Daniel Fox, Sam Houston State University
James Francis, San Jacinto College–South
Perry Fuchs, University of Texas, Arlington
Michael Garza, Brookhaven Community College
Robert C. Gates, Cisco Junior College
Jerry Green, Tarrant County College–Northwest
Brooke Hall, Lamar State College
Richard Harland, West Texas A&M University
Rose Hattoh, Austin Community College–South Austin
Jerwen Jou, University of Texas, Pan American
Helen Just, St. Edward's University
Judith Keith, Tarrant County Community College–Northeast
Shirin Khosropour, Austin Community College
Richard Kirk, Texas State Technical College
Irv Lichtman, Houston Community College–Northeast
Nancey Lobb, Alvin Community College
Don Lucas, Northwest Vista College
Lynn New, East Texas Baptist University
Annette Nolte, Tarrant County College–Northwest
Jane Ogden, East Texas Baptist University
Julie Penley, El Paso Community College
Jean Raniseski, Alvin Community College
Cynthia Reed, Tarrant County College–Northeast
Eric Reittinger, Texas A&M University
Karen Saenz, Houston Community College–Southeast
David Shepard, South Texas Community College
Sangeeta Singg, Angelo State University
Lynn Skaggs, Central Texas College
Peggy Skinner, South Plains College
Christopher L. Smith, Tyler Junior College
Jeanne Spaulding, Houston Community College–Northwest
Genevieve Stevens, Houston Community College–Central
Donna Thompson, Midland College
Cheryl Willard, Lee College
Tom Wood, Sam Houston State University
Melissa Wright, Victoria College
Andrea Zabel, Midland College
Clare Zaborowski, San Jacinto College–Central

Utah

Leigh Shaw, Weber State University
David Yells, Utah Valley State College

Virginia

Jeffrey Clark, Virginia Union University

Jeffrey Green, Virginia Commonwealth University
Alicia Grodsky, Northern Virginia Community College
Rosalyn King, Northern Virginia Community College–Loudoun
Cynthia Lofaso, Central Virginia Community College
Molly Lynch, NOVA–Manassas
Bethany Marcus, ECPI College of Technology
James O'Brien, Tidewater Community College
Theresa Tuttle, ECPI College of Technology

Washington

Pamela Costa, Tacoma Community College
Craig Cowden, Tacoma Community College
Brian Smith, Seattle Central Community College
Connie Veldink, Everett Community College

West Virginia

Chris LeGrow, Marshall University

Wisconsin

Andrew Berns, Milwaukee Area Technical College
Regan Gurung, University of Wisconsin–Green Bay
Kathleen Kavanaugh, Milwaukee Area Technical College
Bart Van Voorhis, University of Wisconsin–La Crosse
Carmen Wilson-Van Voorhis, University of Wisconsin–La Crosse

TEXT AND SUPPLEMENTS FOCUS GROUP PARTICIPANTS

Cathy Alsman, Ivy Tech Community College–Terre Haute
Kristin Anderson, Houston Community College–Southwest
Susan Anderson, University of South Alabama
Melissa Avecedo, Valencia Community College
Mike Barber, Lake City Community College
Dan Bellack, Trident Technical College
Andrew Berns, Milwaukee Area Technical College
Kathy Bey, Palm Beach Community College
Derek Borman, Mesa Community College
Saundra Boyd, Houston Community College
Pat Carroll, University of Texas–Austin
Jack Chuang, San Jacinto College–Central
Jane Cirillo, Houston Community College Southeast
Wanda Clark, South Plains College
Perry Collins, Wayland Baptist
Jacqueline Cuevas, Midwestern State
Barbara DeFilippo, Lane Community College
Vera Dunwoody, Chaffey College
Mark Eastman, Diablo Valley College
Ann Ewing, Mesa Community College
Dan Fawaz, Georgia Perimeter College
Brenda Fonseca, Mesa Community College
Perry Fuchs, University of Texas, Arlington
John Gambon, Ozarks Technical Community College
Dan Grangaard, Austin Community College
Jerry Green, Tarrant County College–Northwest
Amy Hackney, Georgia Southern University
Wayne Hall, San Jacinto College–Central
Sheryl Hartman, Miami Dade College
Dr. Nancy Woods Hernandez, Howard College
Karen Hoblit, Victoria College
Lisette Hodges, Lamar State College–Orange
Debra Hollister, Valencia Community College
Susan Hornstein, Southern Methodist University
Linda Jones, Blinn College
Shirin Khosropor, Austin Community College
Irv Lichtman, Houston Community College
Michael Magee, Brooklyn College
Jerry Marshall, Green River Community College

Randy Martinez, Cypress Community College
Michael McCoy, Cape Fear Community College
Marisa McLeod, Santa Fe Community College
Fred Miller, Portland Community College
Wendy Mills, San Jacinto College–North
Annette Nolte, Tarrant County College
Jane Ogden, East Texas Baptist University
Laura Overstreet, Tarrant County College
Jennifer Peluso, Florida Atlantic University
Skip Pollock, Mesa Community College
Cynthia Reed, Tarrant County College–Northeast
Darla Rocha, San Jacinto College
Lilian M. Romero, San Jacinto College–Central Campus
Gloria Scheff, Broward Community College

Nancy Simpson, Trident Technical College
Jason Spiegelman, Community College of Baltimore County
Genevieve Stevens, Houston Community College–Central
Larry Symon, Western Washington University
Joe Tinnin, Richland College
Richard Townsend, Miami Dade College
Charles Verschoor, Miami Dade Community College
Melissa B. Weston, El Centro College
Fred Whitford, Montana State University
Stephanie Williford, Coastal Carolina Community College
Madeline Wright, Houston Community College–Central
Andrea Zabel, Midland College
Clare Zaborowski, San Jacinto College–South

STUDENT REVIEWERS FOR *PSYCHOLOGY: AN EXPLORATION*

**Tompkins Cortland
Community College**
Regan Allen
Jamie Arce
Tenetrius Bell
Kurt Berry
Megan Beschler
Christine Brandon
Sarah Casselbury
Megan Daniels
Jaimie Edwards
Felix Ferreira
Christina Ferris
Elizabeth Foster
Bryan Grubb
Leeann Huntley
Chonee Kang
Joseph LaMontagne
Alyssa Mayo
Kimberly McDowell
Greg McEver
Lyndsey Miller
Joshua Moen
Bill Mooney
Justin Mott
Danielle O'Rarke
Amylynn Otis
Hang Thanh Pham
Joe Randall
Cristian Rojas

Nicolette Ruggiero
Monica Sacco
Robin Riemen Schneider
Amanda Shaw
Tanya Smith
Nicole Snell
Tinisha Taylor
Chelsea Titterington
Thomas Wilk
Kamar Williams
Kathie Wood
Alan Ytern

Jefferson Community College
Carissa Aznar-Beane
Stephen Babcock
Suzanne Bellinger
Alicia Bradberry
Luis Calvo
Nick D'Alessandro
Marya Diabo
Spencer Dingman
Thea Durant
Zach Ellis
Kaizamar Feliciano
Christina Flynn
Tamara Freeman
Caleb Gardner
Amanda Gaylord
Nichole Goodreault

Jayme Hale
Darlene Hubbard
Collin Keller
Justine Lamb
Jess MacCortney
Ashley Mattice
Ryan Mcintosh
Amy Morgan
Emma Ottinger
Fuji Panjadi
Diane Maitland Patterson
Megan Rector
Andrew Riordan
Spencer Roby
James Walter Scott III
Melanie Shambo
Bryant Staie
Christine Sullivan
Walter Thomas
Sandra Vinson
Steven Vivyan
Brandon Willams
Lyndsey Worthinton
Amanda Wright

University of South Carolina
Mudar Atra
Kanesha Batteaste
DaBrian Beckham
Jessica Britt

Maronica Brown
Justin Butler
Chad Canfall
Tracy Crump
Danielle DeVoss
Haley Gaston
Jasmine Grant
Ashley Grimsley
Shacola Jenkins
Curtis Kendrick
Amanda Lewis
Jeana Maher
Ciera Martinez
Adam Mast
Kenyatta Maxwell
Christy McDaniel
Kandace McDavid
Brittany McMickens
Madison Morgan
Ariel Rhodan
Loresa Starks
Jordan Wilson
James Wise
Instructor: Elizabeth Freeman

acknowledgments

I can hardly believe that this second edition of *Psychology: An Exploration* is here at last. With three editions of the original, larger text already floating around, it's hard to imagine that all of this began only ten years ago. I have to thank my dear friend Cindy Sullivan, who talked me into this text originally, as well as my editors, Jessica Mosher and Amber Mackey, who have supported me and Noland through this complex process. My husband, Joe Ciccarelli, and my young adult offspring Al and Liz deserve thanks for putting up with my working at odd hours of the day and night.

Yolanda de Rooy supported and advised me and put a tremendous amount of support behind this text—thank you so much. I have to thank Jessica Mosher, the editor who never quits and apparently sleeps very little and somehow manages to have a life squeezed into the spare moments between trips to visit schools. Special thanks to Jeanette Koskinas (Executive Marketing Manager), Brigeth Rivera (Marketing Manager), and Jessica Warren (Marketing Assistant) for a fantastic marketing campaign. Thank you again to Rochelle Diogenes for moral support and great guidance behind the scenes.

Anne DeMarinis is the designer extraordinaire who has once again created what I modestly think continues to be one of the most visually appealing textbooks to ever grace a student's desk. Harriet Tellem, a bastion of production know-how and good sense, kept us all on track (not an easy job!).

Thank you to my entire team of supplement authors who waited patiently for the final versions of this text so that they could finish revising all of their work.

And, of course, I can't forget Noland White, my co-author, surrogate son, and Grand High Nit-Picking Expert who helped in many ways to make this text soar to new heights. Could not do it without you, buddy! Last, but most certainly not least, to my dear friend and former developmental editor, Susanna Lesan, who made me believe in myself. Thank you from the bottom of my heart!

Sandy Ciccarelli
Gulf Coast Community College
Panama City, Florida
sciccarelli@gulfcoast.edu

I would like to personally thank:

My wife and best friend Leah, and our wonderful children, Sierra, Alexis, and Landon, thank you for your love, patience, and support. I would not be able to do any of this without you;

My lead author and collaborator Sandy Ciccarelli, for your assistance, advice, guidance, and continuing to be the best mentor that I could ever hope to work with!;

My students, for your inspiration and encouragement, along with those student and faculty users and reviewers of this text I have not met, for your very useful comments and suggestions;

My friends and colleagues in the Department of Psychological Science at Georgia College for your encouragement, frequent discussions, and feedback;

Jessica Mosher, for your enthusiasm, vision, support, and for being such a wonderful person;

Amber Mackey for your support, oversight, direction, and for being such a great editor and great person overall!;

Everyone who has worked so hard on updating and revising the supplements or providing other feedback, including Natalie Ceballos, Marcus Dickson, Kristie Morris, Holly Schofield, Jason Spiegelman, Fred Whitford, and Ted Whitley;

Harriet Tellem, Rebecca Dunn, Anne DeMarinis, Amber Mackey, Brigeth Rivera, Jeanette Koskinas, Stephen Frail, Paul DeLuca, Beth Stoner, Samantha Solana, Kerri Hart-Morris, and all of the other Pearson and associated staff, for your part in making all of this such a great experience.

Noland White
Georgia College
Milledgeville, Georgia
noland.white@gcsu.edu

about the authors

SAUNDRA K. CICCARELLI is a Professor of Psychology at Gulf Coast Community College in Panama City, Florida. She received her Ph.D. in Developmental Psychology from George Peabody College of Vanderbilt University, Nashville, Tennessee. She is a member of the American Psychological Association and the Association for Psychological Science. Originally interested in a career as a researcher in the development of language and intelligence in developmentally delayed children and adolescents, Dr. Ciccarelli had publications in the *Journal of Mental Deficiency* while still at Peabody. However, she discovered a love of teaching early on in her career. This led her to the position at Gulf Coast Community College, where she has been teaching Introductory Psychology and Human Development for over 30 years. Her students love her enthusiasm for the field of psychology and the many anecdotes and examples she uses to bring psychology to life for them. Before writing this text, Dr. Ciccarelli authored numerous ancillary materials for several introductory psychology and human development texts.

J. NOLAND WHITE is an Associate Professor of Psychology at Georgia College & State University (Georgia College), Georgia's Public Liberal Arts University, located in Milledgeville. He received both his B.S. and M.S. in Psychology from Georgia College and joined the faculty in 2001 after receiving his Ph.D. in Counseling Psychology from the University of Tennessee. As a licensed psychologist, Dr. White has worked as a consultant in a variety of settings, including adult mental health, developmental disabilities, and juvenile justice. Back on campus, he operates an active lab and with his students is currently investigating the psychophysiological characteristics and neuropsychological performance of adults with and without ADHD. Outside of the lab, Dr. White is engaged in collaborative research examining the effectiveness of incorporating technology in and out of the college classroom to facilitate student learning. He also serves as a mentor for other faculty wanting to expand their use of technology with their classes. In 2008, he was a recipient of the Georgia College Excellence in Teaching Award.

psychology in action
secrets for surviving college and improving your grades

why study how to study?

Pamela D's story on the facing page is not uncommon. Many students find that they need to study in different ways from the old "listen and write notes" that so many have used. This chapter will help you figure out your own study style as well as provide you with some helpful information to improve your reading, writing, and memory skills.

chapter outline

Study Methods: Different Strokes for Different Folks

Reading Textbooks: Textbooks Are Not Meatloaf

How to Take Notes: Printing Out PowerPoint Slides is Not Taking Notes

Studying for Exams: Cramming Is Not an Option

Writing Papers: Planning Makes Perfect

APPLYING PSYCHOLOGY TO EVERYDAY LIFE: Strategies for Improving Your Memory

Pamela D. was struggling in her introductory psychology class. She would read the assigned chapters in the text, but what she read just didn't seem to "stick," no matter how hard she tried or how many times she read it. The funny thing was that she understood nearly all of what the instructor was saying in class, but found it hard to take notes that made any kind of sense and to listen at the same time. Her test grades were mediocre C's, even though once the instructor went over the exam, she understood exactly what she had done wrong. Feeling depressed and overwhelmed, she finally went to the instructor to ask for advice.

Her instructor listened carefully to Pamela's tale of woe. She then told Pamela that her problem might be that she was not studying in the right way; different people, she said, sometimes learned in different ways. The instructor suggested that Pamela go to the college's counseling center and get tested for her learning style—something Pamela had never heard of or thought about before now. Sure enough, Pamela turned out to be the kind of learner who needed to listen more than write—she was an auditory learner. The instructor suggested a recorder for class, so that Pamela could listen to the lecture without worrying about taking notes until later. She also recommended that Pamela try a method for reading the text chapters that included reciting what she had just read aloud—something called the SQ3R method. As a result, Pamela's grades went from C's to A's, not just in her psychology class but in all of her classes. Now she knew how to tailor her study habits to fit her own style of learning, and it made all the difference in the world.

learning objectives

PIA.1 What are some different methods of studying?

PIA.2 How should you go about reading a textbook so that you get the most out of your reading efforts?

PIA.3 What are the best ways to take notes in class and while reading the text?

PIA.4 How should you approach studying for exams, and why do different kinds of test questions require different study approaches?

PIA.5 What are the key steps in writing papers for college?

PIA.6 How can you improve your memory for facts and concepts?

warning
Reading the following material may lead to higher grades and lower anxiety

I want to make better grades, But sometimes it seems that no matter how hard I study, the test questions turn out to be hard and confusing and I end up not doing very well. Is there some trick to getting good grades?

Teachers often use multiple methods to present a point, but trying to cover all learning methods in one lecture would not be practical.

I want to make better grades, But sometimes it seems that no matter how hard I study, the test questions turn out to be hard and confusing and I end up not doing very well. Is there some trick to getting good grades?

Many students would probably say that their grades are not what they want them to be. A big part of the problem is that despite many different educational experiences, students are rarely taught how to study. What worked for them in grade school and high school may not work in college, when the expectations from teachers are higher and the workload is far greater. There are five things students should know in order to do their absolute best in any college course:

- Their particular learning style.
- How to read a textbook and take notes so that they're understandable and memorable the first time.
- How to take useful notes during lectures.
- How to study efficiently for exams.
- How to write good term papers.

This Introduction presents various techniques and information for maximizing knowledge and skills in each of these five areas.

Study Methods: Different Strokes for Different Folks

PIA.1 What are some different methods of studying?

Most college students have probably heard something about the concept of a *learning style*, but what exactly is it? In general, a learning style is the particular way in which a person takes in, or absorbs, information (Dunn et al., 1989, 2001; Felder, 2010; Felder & Spurlin, 2005). Educators and others who use this concept believe that people absorb information in several ways: through the eyes, by reading text or looking at charts, diagrams, and maps; through the ears, by listening, talking things out, and discussing things with others; and through the sense of touch and the movement of the body, by touching things, writing things down, drawing pictures and diagrams, and learning by doing (Barsch, 1996; Felder & Brent, 2005).

For quite some time now, many educators and psychologists have believed that accommodating their teaching methods to each student's learning style is a key element of good instruction: you find out what the learning style is and then you adjust your method of teaching to that style. To adapt their teaching, educators began to supplement a straight lecture approach by adding visual elements such as slide presentations or videos, for example. This is not a bad thing, of course: The more varied the presentation, the more likely students are to pay attention. But trying to tailor one lecture to all of the various learning styles? Not so practical (Coffield et al., 2004; Willingham, 2005). Research strongly suggests that a strong and varied teaching style will yield better student success regardless of any differences in students' learning styles (Geake, 2008; Zhang, 2006).

In an article in *Psychological Science in the Public Interest,* a journal published by the Association for Psychological Science (Pashler et al., 2009), researchers did an extensive literature review of learning style studies and discovered several key points:

1. Students definitely have preferences about how information is presented to them.

2. Students do seem to have different capabilities when it comes to processing different kinds of information.

3. No real evidence exists to show that tailoring the presentation of information to different learning styles has any effect on a student's ability to learn the information (Pashler et al., 2009).

What? What was that last bit? There was *no real evidence* that tailoring the instructional method to the student's learning style makes any difference in the student's ability to learn that material. While some learning-styles theorists are critical of the researchers' conclusions (Braio et al., 1997; Drysdale et al., 2001; Dunn et al., 1986, 1995; Felder, 2010; Ford & Chen, 2001; Glenn, 2009), others go so far as to say that the implication that a student can have only one or two learning styles is a disservice to the student (Henry, 2007). Instead of trying to limit a student's study methods to just one or two modalities (which is simply not going to happen very often in the world outside academia), wouldn't it be better to help students learn several different styles of studying? Instead of focusing on the different learning styles, this *Psychology in Action* introduction will focus on different *study methods*—take the opportunity to try them out and find which methods work best for you. Table 1 lists some of the various methods that any student can use to improve both understanding of a subject and grades on tests.

No matter what the study method, students must read the textbook to be successful in the course. (While that may seem obvious to some, many students today seem to think that just taking notes on lectures or slide presentations will be enough. Others seem to think that they can just "soak it up" like vegetation soaks up sunshine. Not really a positive analogy, is it?) The next section deals with how to read textbooks for understanding rather than just to "get through" the material. ▣—|Read on MyPsychLab

Some students find it helpful to hear the content in addition to reading it. This is especially true when learning a new language. This woman is listening to an audio recording from her textbook as she follows along and looks at the figures and photos.

▣□—|Read the handbook *What Every Student Should Know about Study Skill*s in the library on **MyPsychLab**

---

table 1   Multiple Study Methods

VERBAL METHODS	VISUAL METHODS	AUDITORY METHODS	ACTION METHODS
Use flash cards to identify main points or key terms.	Make flash cards with pictures or diagrams to aid recall of key concepts.	Join or form a study group or find a study partner so that you can discuss concepts and ideas.	Sit near the front of the classroom and take notes by jotting down key terms and making pictures or charts to help you remember what you are hearing.
Write out or recite key information in whole sentences or phrases in your own words.	Make charts and diagrams and sum up information in tables.	While studying, speak out loud or into a digital recorder that you can play back later.	While studying, walk back and forth as you read out loud.
When looking at diagrams, write out a description.	Use different colors of highlighter for different sections of information in text or notes.	Make speeches.	Study with a friend.
Use "sticky" notes to remind yourself of key terms and information, and put them in the notebook or text or on a mirror that you use frequently.	Visualize charts, diagrams, and figures.	Record the lectures (with permission). Take notes on the lecture sparingly, using the recording to fill in parts that you might have missed.	While exercising, listen to recordings you have made of important information.
Practice spelling words or repeating facts to be remembered.	Trace letters and words to remember key facts.	Read notes or text material into a digital recorder or get study materials recorded and play back while exercising or doing chores.	Write out key concepts on a large board or poster.
Rewrite things from memory.	Redraw things from memory.	When learning something new, state or explain the information in your own words out loud or to a study partner.	Make flash cards, using different colors and diagrams, and lay them out on a large surface. Practice putting them in order.
		Use musical rhythms as memory aids, or put information to a rhyme or a tune.	Make a three-dimensional model.
			Spend extra time in the lab.
			Go to outside areas such as a museum or historical site to gain information.

Reading Textbooks: Textbooks Are Not Meatloaf

PIA.2 How should you go about reading a textbook so that you get the most out of your reading efforts?

Students make two common mistakes in regard to reading a textbook. The first mistake is simple: Many people don't bother to read the textbook *before* going to the lecture that will cover that material. Trying to get anything out of a lecture without reading the material first is like trying to find a new, unfamiliar place without using a map or any kind of directions. It's easy to get lost. This is especially true because of the assumption that most instructors make when planning their lectures: They take for granted that the students have already read the assignment. The instructors then use the lecture to go into detail on the information the students supposedly got from the reading. If the students haven't done the reading, the instructor's lecture isn't going to make a whole lot of sense.

The second mistake that most people make when reading textbook material is to try to read it the same way they would read a novel: They start at the first page and read continuously. With a novel, it's easy to do this because the plot is usually interesting and people want to know what happens next, so they keep reading. It isn't necessary to remember every little detail—all they need to remember are the main plot points. One could say that a novel is like meatloaf—some meaty parts with lots of filler. Meatloaf can be eaten quickly, without even chewing for very long.

With a textbook, the material may be interesting but not in the same way that a novel is interesting. A textbook is a big, thick steak—all meat, no filler. Just as a steak has to be chewed to be enjoyed and to be useful to the body, textbook material has to be "chewed" with the mind. You have to read slowly, paying attention to every morsel of meaning.

So how do you do that? Probably one of the best-known reading methods is called SQ3R, first used by F. P. Robinson in a 1946 book called *Effective Study* (1946,1970). The letters S-Q-R-R-R stand for:

SURVEY   Look at the chapter you've been assigned to read.

- Take a look at the outline at the beginning of the chapter or whatever opening questions, learning objectives, or other material the author has chosen to let you, the reader, know what the chapter is about.

- Flip through the chapter and read the headings of each section, and look at the tables, figures, graphs, and cartoons to get an idea about the kinds of things that you will be learning.

- Finally, quickly read through the chapter summary if there is one.

It might sound like it takes too much time to do this, but you should just be skimming at this point—a couple of minutes is all it should take. Why do this at all? Surveying the chapter, or "previewing" it, as some experts call it, helps you form a framework in your head around which you can organize the information in the chapter when you read it in detail. Organization is listed as one of the main ways to improve your memory for information. ⒧ⒾⓃⓀ to Chapter Five: Memory, p. 174. Think of it this way: As mentioned earlier, if you are going to drive to a new place, it's helpful to have a road map to give you an idea of what's up ahead. Surveying the chapter is giving yourself a "road map" for the material in the chapter.

QUESTION   After previewing the chapter, read the heading for the first section. Just the first section! Try to think of a question based on this heading that the section should answer as you read. For example, in Chapter One there's a section titled

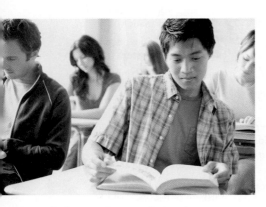

Before reading any chapter in a text, survey the chapter by reading the outline and the section headings

"Pavlov, Watson, and the Dawn of Behaviorism." You could ask yourself, "What did Pavlov and Watson do for psychology?" or "What is behaviorism?" Some textbooks even include questions at the start of many sections. In this text, a list of learning objectives for the key concepts in the chapter is presented in the form of questions that can be used with the SQ3R method. There are also student questions that can serve the same purpose. These questions, which are based on the author's years of hearing and answering similar questions from students in the classroom, will be in gray type in the margin, often with the picture of a typical student who is asking the question. Now when you read the section, you aren't *just* reading—you're reading to *find an answer*. That makes the material much easier to remember later on.

READ Now read the section, looking for the answer to your questions. As you read, take notes by making an outline of the main points and terms in the section. This is another area where some students make a big mistake. They assume that using a highlighter to mark words and phrases is as good as writing notes. One of the author's former students conducted research on the difference between highlighting and note-taking, and her preliminary findings were clear: Students who wrote their own notes during the reading of a text or while listening to a lecture scored significantly higher on their exam grades than students who merely used a highlighter on the text (Boyd & Peeler, 2004). Highlighting requires no real mental effort (no "chewing," in other words), but writing the words down yourself requires you to read the words in depth and understand them. When we study memory, you'll learn more about the value of processing information in depth. (LINK) to Chapter Five: Memory, p. 171.

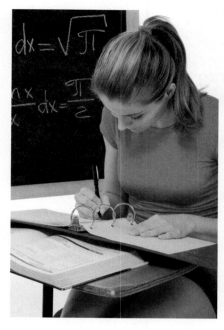

As you read, take notes. Write down key terms and try to summarize the key points of each paragraph and section in the chapter. These notes will be useful when you later review the chapter material.

RECITE It may sound silly, but reciting out loud what you can remember from the section you've just read is another good way to process the information more deeply and completely. How many times have you thought you understood something, only to find that when you tried to tell it to someone, you didn't understand it at all? Recitation forces you to put the information in your own words, just as writing it down in the form of notes does. Writing it down accesses your visual memory; saying it out loud gives you an auditory memory for the same information. If you have ever learned something well by teaching it to someone else, you already know the value of recitation. If you feel self-conscious about talking to yourself, talk into a digital recorder—it makes a great way to review.

Now repeat the Question, Read, and Recite instructions for each section, taking a few minutes' break after every two or three sections. Why take a break? There's a process that has to take place in your brain when you are trying to form a permanent memory for information, and that process takes a little bit of time. (LINK) to Chapter Five: Memory, p 188. When you take a break every 10 to 20 minutes, you are giving your brain time to do this process. Doing this avoids a common problem in reading texts in which when you find yourself reading the same sentence over and over again because your brain is too overloaded with trying to remember what you just read to continue reading.

RECALL/REVIEW Finally, you've finished reading the entire chapter. If you've used the guidelines listed previously, you'll only have to read the chapter in this depth once instead of having to read it over and over throughout the semester and just before exams. Once you've read the chapter, take a few minutes to try to remember as much of what you learned while reading it as you can. A good way to do this is to take any practice quizzes that might be available, either in your text or in a student workbook that goes with the text. Many publishers have Web sites for their textbooks that have practice quizzes available online. If there are no quizzes, read the chapter summary in

After reading a chapter section, take time to reflect on what the information means and how it might relate to real-world situations.

Here are two things that instructors love to see: attentive looks and note-taking during the lecture. And for the student who learns better just by listening, a small digital recorder (used with permission) can help for later review of the lecture. How should these students have prepared before coming to this class?

detail, making sure that you understand everything in it. If there's anything that's confusing, go back to that section in the chapter and read again until you understand it.

Some educators and researchers now add a fourth "R": "**Reflect**." To reflect means to try to think critically about what you have read by trying to tie the concepts into what you already know, thinking about how you can use the information in your own life, and deciding which of the topics you've covered interests you enough to look for more information on that topic (Richardson & Morgan, 1997). For example, if you have learned about the genetic basis for depression, you might understand why that disorder seems to run in your best friend's family. (LINK) to Chapter Twelve: Psychological Disorders, p. 448.

Reading textbooks in this way means that, when it comes time for the final exam, all you will have to do is carefully review your notes to be ready for it—you won't have to read the entire textbook all over again. What a time-saver! Recent research suggests that the most important steps in this method are the three R's: Read, Recite, and Review. In two experiments with college students, researchers found that when compared with other study methods such as rereading and note-taking study strategies, the 3R strategy produced superior recall of the material. (McDaniel et al., 2009).

How to Take Notes: Printing Out PowerPoint Slides Is Not Taking Notes

PIA.3 What are the best ways to take notes in class and while reading the text?

Remember the study showing that highlighting is not as effective as note-taking (Boyd & Peeler, 2004)? One of this researcher's earliest studies was a comparison of students who took notes by hand while listening to a lecture with PowerPoint slides and students who printed out the PowerPoint slides and merely used a highlighter to stress certain ideas on the printout. Students taking notes by hand scored an average of one letter grade higher on exams than did the students who used a highlighter on the printouts. PowerPoint slides are not meant to be notes at all; they are merely talking points that help the instructor follow a particular sequence in lecturing. Typically, the instructor will have more to say about each point on the slide, and that is the information students should be listening to and writing down. In Table 1, the suggestions to use highlighters of different colors are not meant to replace taking notes but instead to supplement the notes you do take.

Taking Notes While Reading the Text

How should you take notes? As stated earlier, you should try to take notes while reading the chapter by writing down the main points and the vocabulary terms *in your own words* as much as possible. This forces you to think about what you are reading. The more you think about it, the more likely it is that the concepts will become a part of your permanent memory. (LINK) to Chapter Five: Memory, p. 171.

Taking Notes During the Lecture

Taking notes while listening to the lecture is a slightly different procedure. First, you should have your notes from the reading in front of you, and it helps to leave plenty of space between lines to add notes from the lecture. As mentioned in the section on how to read a textbook, a major mistake made by many students is to come to the lecture without having read the material first. This is an EXTREMELY BAD IDEA. In case that didn't sink in the first time, let me repeat it: **Extremely Bad Idea.** If you come to the lecture totally unprepared, you will have no idea what is important enough to write down and what is just the instructor's asides and commentary. Reading the material first gives you a good idea of exactly what is important in the lecture and reduces the amount of notes you take.

If you are like Pamela in the opening story, ask your instructor if you can bring a digital recorder to class to record the lecture. You will then be able to listen during the class and use the recording to take notes from later on. Some students may prefer to jot down diagrams, charts, and other visual aids along with their written notes. When you have good notes taken while reading the text and from the lectures, you will also have ready-made study aids for preparing to take exams. The next section deals with the best ways to study for exams.

practice quiz   How much do you remember?

Pick the best answer:

1. Which of the following statements is NOT one of the conclusions drawn in the Pashler et al. 2009 study of learning styles?
   a. People have preferences about the way information is presented to them.
   b. People have different capabilities when processing different kinds of information.
   c. There is definite evidence that tailoring information presentation to different learning styles has a profound effect on student learning.
   d. All of the above are true of the Pashler study.

2. Which of the following statements is TRUE?
   a. You should approach reading a textbook in the same way that you would read a novel.
   b. Never take notes while reading—do it several days later.

   c. Read the text assignment *before* going to the lecture.
   d. Try not to look ahead in the chapter before starting your reading.

3. It is helpful to _____ when taking notes.
   a. Use your own words as much as possible.
   b. Write down every word on any PowerPoint slide.
   c. Use a highlighter and the text rather than write your own.
   d. Use the exact wording of the instructor or slides.

Brainstorming: What are some reasons that thinking about material to be learned in your own words would lead to stronger, longer lasting memories?

ANSWERS ON PAGE AK-1

Studying for Exams: Cramming Is Not an Option

PIA.4 **How should you approach studying for exams, and why do different kinds of test questions require different study approaches?**

There is a right way to study for a test, believe it or not. While many students would love to skip testing altogether, recent reseach provides support for what educators have long believed: in addition to measuring retention, test-taking helps people learn the material, and often better than other methods of studying (Karpicke & Blunt, 2011). Here are some good things to remember when preparing for an exam, whether it's a quiz, a unit test, a midterm, or a final (Carter et al., 2002; Hoffman & McGuire, 2010; Reynolds, 2002):

- **Timing is everything:** One of the worst things that students do is waiting until the last minute to study for the exam. Remember the analogy about "chewing" the steak? (Just as a steak has to be chewed to be enjoyed and to be useful to the body, textbook material has to be "chewed" with the mind.) The same concept applies to preparing for an exam: You have to give yourself enough time. If you've read your text material and taken good notes as discussed

Could this be you? The scattered materials, the frantic phone call to a friend or professor, the tense and worried facial expression are all hallmarks of that hallowed yet useless student tradition, cramming. Don't let this happen to you.

in the previous sections, you'll be able to save a lot of time in studying for the exam, but you still need to give yourself ample time to go over all of those notes. One helpful thing to do is to make a study schedule in which you plan out (at least a week before the exam) the hours of the day during which you intend to study and the topics you will cover in those hours. Always give yourself more time than you think you will need, just in case something comes up at the last minute to throw off your schedule: unexpected company, car trouble, or other unforeseen events that might require you to forgo studying for one night.

- **Find out as much as you can about the type of test and the material it will cover.** The type of test can affect the way in which you want to study the material. An objective test, for example, such as multiple choice or true/false, is usually fairly close to the text material, so you'll want to be very familiar with the wording of concepts and definitions in the text, although this is not a suggestion to memorize a lot of material. These kinds of tests can include one of three types of questions:

- **Factual:** Questions that ask you to remember a specific fact from the text material. For example, "Who built the first psychological laboratory?" requires that you recognize a person's name. (The answer is Wilhelm Wundt.)

- **Applied:** Questions that ask you to use, or apply, information presented in the text. For example, consider the following question from Chapter Four, Learning:

One-year-old Ben learned to say the word duck when his mother showed him a duck in their backyard. That evening he sees a cartoon with a rooster in it and says, "Duck!," pointing to the rooster. Ben is exhibiting _____.

  a. generalization.

  b. discrimination.

  c. spontaneous recovery.

  d. shaping.

This question requires you to take a concept (in this case, generalization) and apply it to a real-world example.

- **Conceptual:** Questions that demand that you think about the ideas or concepts presented in the text and demonstrate that you understand them by answering questions like the following: "Freud is to _____ as Watson is to _____." (The answers could vary, but a good set would be "the unconscious" and "observable behavior.")

Notice that although memorizing facts might help on the first type of question, it isn't going to help at all on the last two. Memorization doesn't always help on factual questions either, because the questions are sometimes worded quite differently from the text. It is far better to understand the information rather than be able to "spit it back" without understanding it. "Spitting it back" is memorization; understanding it is true learning. **LINK** to Chapter Five: Memory, p. 165. There are different levels of analysis for information you are trying to learn, and the higher the level of analysis, the more likely you are to remember (Anderson et al., 2001; Bloom, 1956). *Factual questions* are the lowest level of analysis: knowledge. *Applied questions* are a higher level and are often preferred by instructors for that reason—it's hard to successfully apply information if you don't really understand it. *Conceptual questions* are a kind of analysis, a level higher than either of the other two. Not only do you have to understand the concept, you have to understand it well enough to compare and contrast it with other concepts. They might be harder questions, but in the long run, you will get more "bang for your buck" as far as true learning with these kinds of questions is concerned.

Subjective tests, such as essay tests and short-answer exams, require that you not only be able to recall and understand the information from the course but also that you be able to organize it in your own words. To study for a subjective test means that you not only need to be familiar with the material but also that you need to be able to write it down. Make outlines of your notes. Rewrite both reading and lecture notes and make flash cards, charts, and drawings. Practice putting the flash cards in order. Talk out loud or study with someone else and discuss the possible questions that could be on an essay test. You may find that only a few of these methods work best for you, but the more ways in which you try to study, the better you will be able to retrieve the information when you need it. It may sound like a big investment of your time, but most students vastly underestimate how long it takes to study—and fail to recognize that many of these techniques are doable when first reading the textbook assignment and preparing for the classroom lecture. DON'T CRAM! You might also look at old tests (if the instructor has made them available) to see what kinds of questions are usually asked. If this is not possible, make sure that you pay close attention to the kinds of questions asked on the first exam so that you will know how to prepare for future tests. Write out your own test questions as if you were the instructor. Not only does this force you to think about the material the way it will appear on the test, but it also provides a great review tool. Other helpful advice:

- **Use SQ3R.** You can use the same method that you used to read the text material to go over your notes. Skim through your notes to get an overview of the material that will be on the test. Try to think of possible test questions that the instructor might include on an exam. Reread your notes, referring back to the text if necessary. Recite the main ideas and definitions of terms, either out loud, onto a tape, or to a friend or study group. Review by summarizing sections of material or by making an outline or flash cards that you can use in studying important concepts.

- **Use the concept maps provided.** When surveying the chapter, make sure you look over the concept maps provided at the end of the chapter. **Concept maps** are a visual organization of the key concepts, terms, and definitions that are found in each chapter and are an excellent way to "see" how various concepts are linked together (Carnot et al., 2001; Novak, 1995; Wu et al., 2004). They are also a great way to review the chapter once you have finished reading it, just to check for understanding—if the concept maps don't make sense, then you've missed something and need to go back over that section. You can also make your own concept maps as you take notes on the chapter. A guide to making concept maps, examples from your text, and a tool for creating them can be found on **mypsychlab**.

- **Take advantage of all the publisher's test materials.** Practice does help, and most textbooks come with a study guide or a Web site (such as **www.mypsychlab.com** for this text, see pp. x—x),. Those materials should have practice quizzes available—take them. The more types of quiz questions you try to answer, the more successful you will be at interpreting the questions on the actual exam. You'll also get a very good idea of the areas that you need to go back and review again. And remember, taking tests or quizzes is a great way to study according to research (Karpicke & Blunt, 2011)!

- **Make use of the resources.** If you find that you are having difficulty with certain concepts, go to the instructor well in advance of the exam for help.

concepts maps an organized visual representation of knowledge consisting of concepts and their relationships to other concepts.

Many students studying for exams ignore one of the most valuable resources to which they have access: the instructor. Most instructors are happy to answer questions or schedule time for students who are having difficulty understanding the material.

Holding your eyes open is not going to help you study when you are this tired. Sleep has been shown to improve memory and performance on tests, so get a good night's sleep before every exam.

(This is another good reason to manage your study time so that you aren't trying to do everything in a few hours the night before the exam.) There are help centers on most college and university campuses with people who can help you learn to study, organize your notes, or tutor you in the subject area.

- **Don't forget your physical needs.** Studies have shown that not getting enough sleep is very bad for memory and learning processes (Mander et al., 2011; Stickgold et al., 2001; Vecsey et al., 2009). Try to stop studying an hour or so before going to bed at a reasonable time to give your body time to relax and unwind. Get a full night's sleep if possible. Do not take sleep-inducing medications or drink alcohol, as these substances prevent normal stages of sleep, including the stage that seems to be the most useful for memory and learning (Davis et al., 2003). Do eat breakfast; hunger is harmful to memory and mental performance. A breakfast heavy on protein and light on carbohydrates is the best for concentration and recall (Benton & Parker, 1998; Dani et al., 2005; Pollitt & Matthews, 1998; Stubbs et al., 1996).

- **Use your test time wisely.** When taking the test, don't allow yourself to get stuck on one question that you can't seem to answer. If an answer isn't clear, skip that question and go on to others. After finishing all of the questions that you can answer easily, go back to the ones you have skipped and try to answer them again. This accomplishes several things: You get to experience success in answering the questions that you can answer, which makes you feel more confident and relaxed; other questions on the test might act as memory cues for just the information you need for one of those questions you skipped; and once you are more relaxed, you may find that the answers to those seemingly impossible questions are now clear because anxiety is no longer blocking them. This is a way of reducing stress by dealing directly with the problem, and Chapter Nine has more ways of dealing effectively with stress. Ⓛ Ⓘ Ⓝ Ⓚ to Chapter Nine: Stress and Health, pp. 336–338.

The next section gives some helpful information about another form of assessment: the term paper.

Writing Papers: Planning Makes Perfect

PIA.5 What are the key steps in writing papers for college?

Several steps are involved in writing a paper, whether it be a short paper or a long one. You should begin all of these steps well in advance of the due date for the paper (not the night before):

1. **Choose a topic.** The first step is to choose a topic for your paper. In some cases, the instructor may have a list of acceptable topics, which makes your job easier. If that is not the case, don't be afraid to go to your instructor during office hours and talk about some possible topics. Try to choose a topic that interests you, one that you would like to learn more about. The most common mistake students make is to pick a topic that is far too broad. For example, the topic "autism" could fill a book. A narrower topic might discuss a single form of autism in detail. Again, your instructor can help you narrow down your topic choices.

2. **Do the research.** Find as many sources as you can that have information about your topic. Don't limit yourself to encyclopedias or textbooks. Go to your school library and ask the librarian to point you in the direction of some good scientific journals that would have information about the topic. Be very careful about using the Internet to do research: Not everything on the Internet is

correct or written by true experts—avoid other students' papers and "ency-clopedia" Web sites that can be written and updated by darn near anyone.
✳ Explore on MyPsychLab

3. **Take notes.** While reading about your topic, use note cards to remember key points. On the back of the note card (a 3 × 5 card), write the reference that will go along with the reading. (You might also start a document on the computer and type your references into the document as you read, but that only works if you have your computer with you while reading.) References for psychology papers are usually going to be in APA (American Psychological Association) style, which can be found at **www.apastyle.org**. Write your notes about the reading on the front of the note card. Some people prefer two note cards, one for the notes and one for the reference, so that they can sort them separately. Remember, taking notes helps you avoid **plagiarism**—the copying of someone else's ideas or exact words (or a close imitation of the words) and presenting them as your own. Note-taking also helps you avoid using too many direct quotes—papers are supposed to be in *your* words, not someone else's, even if you give them credit.

4. **Decide on the thesis.** The thesis is the central message of your paper—the message you want to communicate to your audience—which may be your instructor, your classmates, or both, depending on the nature of the assign-ment. Some papers are persuasive, which means they are trying to convince the reader of a particular point of view, such as "Autism is not caused by immu-nizations." Some papers are informative, providing information about a topic to an audience that may have no prior knowledge, such as "Several forms of autism have been identified." 📖 Read on MyPsychLab

5. **Write an outline.** Using your notes from all your readings, create an outline of your paper—a kind of "road map" of how the paper will go. Start with an introduction (e.g., a brief definition and discussion of what autism is). Then decide what the body of the paper should be. If your paper is about a specific type of autism, for example, your outline would include sections about the different causes of that type. The last section of your outline should be some kind of conclusion. For example, you might have recommendations about how parents of a child with autism can best help that child to develop as fully as possible.

6. **Write a first draft.** Write your paper using the outline and your notes as guides. If using APA style, place citations with all of your statements and asser-tions. Failure to use citations (which point to the particular reference work from which your information came) is also a common mistake that many students make. It is very important that you avoid plagiarism, as discussed in tip 3. When you use a source, you are supposed to explain the information that you are using in your own words *and* cite the source, as in the following example:

In one study comparing both identical and fraternal twins, researchers found that stressful life events of the kind listed in the SRRS were excellent predictors of the onset of episodes of major depression (Kendler & Prescott, 1999).

The reference section would have the following citation: Kendler, K. S., & Prescott, C. A. (1999). A population-based twin study of lifetime major depression in men and women. *Archives of General Psychiatry, 56*(1): 39–44. (Author's note: the number in front of the parentheses is the volume of the journal, the one inside is the issue number, and the last numbers are the rel-evant pages of that article.)

Instructors are a good source of sugges-tions for paper topics—they know the kind of information they want to be reading and grading in the wee hours of the night.

✳ Explore the research process and find reliable sources in Research Navigator on **MyPsychLab**

plagiarism the copying of someone else's exact words (or a close imitation ofthe words) and presenting them as yourown.

📖 Read and handbook *What Every Student Should Know about Avoiding Plagiarismin* the library on **MyPsychLab**

In earlier times, people actually had to write or type their first, second, and sometimes third drafts on real paper. The advent of computers with word-processing programs that allow simple editing and revision have no doubt saved a lot of trees from the paper mill. This also means there is no good excuse for failing to write a first draft and for proofreading one's work.

7. **Let it sit.** Take a few days (if you have been good about starting the paper on time) to let the paper sit without reading it. Then go back over the paper and mark places that don't sound right and need more explanation, a citation, or any other changes. This is much easier to do after a few days away from the paper; the need to reword will be more obvious.

8. **Write the revised draft.** Some people do more than one draft, whereas others do only a first draft and a final. In either case, revise the draft carefully, making sure to check your citations—and your spelling!

practice quiz   How much do you remember?

Pick the best answer.

1. When studying for an exam, you should
   a. Wait until just before the scheduled exam, so that the information will be fresh in your mind.
   b. Study all night long before the exam—you can sleep after the test.
   c. Memorize as much of the information as possible.
   d. Tailor your studying to the type of test questions that will be on the exam, making sure that you are understanding the concepts in your own words.

2. When writing a paper, a "road map" of how the paper will go is provided by
   a. Your detailed notes on your readings.
   b. The first draft of the paper.
   c. An outline of the paper's major sections.
   d. Letting the paper "sit" for a while after writing the first draft.

Brainstorming: Given the research about protein and learning, can you think of a reason why attention problems might be on the rise in schoolchildren? What other reasons might there be for this increase?

ANSWERS ON PAGE AK-1

applying psychology to everyday life
. . . .
Strategies for Improving Your Memory

PIA.6 How can you improve your memory for facts and concepts?

 Everyone needs a little memory help now and then. Even memory experts use strategies to help them perform their unusual feats of remembering. These strategies may be unique to that individual, but there are many memory "tricks" that are quite simple and available for anyone to learn and use. A memory trick or strategy to help people remember is called a **mnemonic** from the Greek word for memory. Here are a few of the more popular mnemonics, some of which may sound familiar:

- **Linking.** Make a list in which items to be remembered are linked in some way. If trying to remember a list of the planets in the solar system, for example, a person could string the names of the planets together like this: *Mercury* was the messenger god, who carried lots of love notes to *Venus*, the beautiful goddess who sprang from the *Earth's* sea. She was married to *Mars*, her brother, which didn't please her father *Jupiter* or his father *Saturn*, and his uncle *Uranus* complained to the sea god, *Neptune*. That sounds like a lot, but once linked in this way, the names of the planets are easy to recall in proper order.

- **The peg word method.** In this method, it is necessary to first memorize a series of "peg" words, numbered words that can be used as keys for remembering items associated with them. A typical series of peg words is:

  - One is a bun
  - Two is a shoe
  - Three is a tree

mnemonic   a strategy or trick for aiding memory.

- Four is a door
- Five is a hive
- Six is bricks
- Seven is heaven
- Eight is a gate
- Nine is a line
- Ten is a hen

To use this method, each item to be remembered (e.g., on a grocery list) is associated with a peg word and made into an image. If the items to be remembered are cheese, milk, eggs, bread, and sugar, the series of images might be a bun with a big wedge of cheese in it, a shoe with milk pouring out of it, a tree with eggs hanging from it, a door made of a slice of bread, and a hive with little bags of sugar flying around it instead of bees. The images are bizarre, and that actually helps cement the memory. When retrieving the list, all the person has to do is recite, "One is a bun, cheese. Two is a shoe, milk . . ." and so on, and the images will pop up readily.

- **The method of loci (LOW-kee or LOW-sī).** This method, often credited to the ancient Romans and sometimes called the Roman Room Method, was actually invented by the Greeks. In both cultures, orators and speech makers used this method to keep track of the points they wanted to make in their speeches, which were often quite long and involved. There were no cue cards or tele-prompters, so they had to rely on memory alone. In this method, the person pictures a very familiar room or series of rooms in a house or other building. Each point of the speech is then made into an image and "placed" mentally in the room at certain locations. For example, if the first point was about military spending, the image might be a soldier standing in the doorway of the house throwing money out into the street. Each point would have its place, and all the person would need to do to retrieve the memories would be to take a "mental walk" around the house.

- **Verbal/rhythmic organization.** How do you spell relief? If when spelling a word with an ie or an ei in it, you resort to the old rhyme "I before E except after C, or when sounded as A as in neighbor or weigh," you have made use of a verbal/ rhythmic organization mnemonic. "Thirty days hath September, April, June, and November . . ." is another example of this technique. Setting information into a rhyme aids memory because it uses verbal cues, rhyming words, and the rhythm of the poem itself to aid retrieval. Sometimes this method is accomplished through making a sentence by using the first letters of each word to be remembered and making them into new words that form a sentence. The colors of the rainbow are ROY G. BIV (red, orange, yellow, green, blue, indigo, and violet). The notes on the musical staff are "Every Good Boy Does Fine." There are countless examples of this technique.

- **Put it to music (a version of the rhythmic method).** Some people have had success with making up little songs, using familiar tunes, to remember specific information. The best example of this? The alphabet song.

This *Psychology in Action* introduction has covered several different ways to help you get more out of your psychology class as well as all of your other college course work. If you follow the advice given in this section for reading, taking notes, studying, writing papers, and improving your memory, you will find that making good grades will be easier than ever before and that you will actually remember a great deal of what you've studied long after the last final exam is over.

1. The use of images appears to help form better memories. How might imagery be linked to the earliest kinds of memories we have?

2. What are some mnemonics that you or people you know have used? Which method do you think those personal mnemonics represent?

Other Resources

There are some excellent books and Web resources available for help in maximizing your studying. Three excellent books are the following:

Carter, C., Bishop, J., & Kravits, S. L. (2011). *Keys to effective learning: Study skills and habits for success*. Upper Saddle River, NJ: Prentice Hall.

Carter, C., Bishop, J., Kravits, S. L., and Block, J. (2009). *Keys to success: Building analytical, creative, and practical skills*. (6th ed.). Upper Saddle River, NJ: Prentice Hall.

Sellers, D., Dochen, C. W., & Hodges. R. W. (2011). *Academic transformation: The road to college success* (2nd ed.). Upper Saddle River, NJ: Prentice Hall.

Websites

The Virginia Polytechnic Institute and State University has a good online site at www.ucc.vt.edu/stdyhlp.html

Another good source created by Joe Landsberger is the Web site Study Guides and Strategies, available at www.studygs.net

A good resource for the background behind concept maps and how to use them is at http://cmap.ihmc.us/Publications/ResearchPapers/TheoryCmaps/TheoryUnderlying ConceptMaps.htm

psychology in action summary

PIA.1   What are some different methods of studying?

- In general, a learning style is the particular way in which a person takes in, or absorbs, information.

- Research strongly suggests that a strong and varied teaching style will yield better student success regardless of any differences in students' learning styles.

- Research by an APS group suggested that there was *no real evidence* that tailoring the instructional method to the student's learning style makes any difference in the student's ability to learn that material.

- Students can learn to use several different methods of studying to find what method works best for them.

PIA.2   How should you go about reading a textbook so that you get the most out of your reading efforts?

- Textbooks must be read in a different way from novels or popular books.

- The SQ3R method is an excellent way to approach reading a textbook: survey, question, read, recite, review.

PIA.3   What are the best ways to take notes in class and while reading the text?

- Notes should be in your own words and written or typed, not highlighted in the text or handouts.

- When taking notes from a lecture, you should be prepared by having the notes from your reading in front of you, and some people may benefit from recording the lecture and taking notes afterward.

PIA.4   How should you approach studying for exams, and why do different kinds of test questions require different study approaches?

- Don't wait until the last minute to study.

- Find out about the types of questions on the exam.

- Use concept maps, the SQ3R method, and the publisher's practice test materials.

- Get plenty of sleep and eat breakfast, preferably something with protein.

PIA.5   What are the key steps in writing papers for college?

- Key steps in writing a research paper are to choose a topic, read about the topic, take notes on your reading, decide upon the central message of your paper, write an outline and a first draft, and allow the paper to sit for a few days before going back and writing the final draft.

PIA.6   How can you improve your memory for facts and concepts?

- There are memory strategies called mnemonics, including methods that use imagery, rhymes, linking, and even music to improve memory.

TEST yourself

✓● Study and Review on MyPsychLab   Ready for your test? More quizzes and a customized plan. www.MyPsychLab

Pick the best answer.

1. Which of the following statements is one of the conclusions drawn in the Pashler et al. 2009 study of learning styles?
   a. People do not have preferences about the way information is presented to them.
   b. People have different capabilities when processing different kinds of information.
   c. There is little evidence that tailoring the presentation of information to different learning styles has a profound effect on student learning.
   d. There is no such thing as having a learning style.

2. Which of the following statements is FALSE?
   a. Textbooks can be read as easily as a novel if you are a good reader.
   b. Take notes while reading, putting the concepts into your own words.
   c. Read the text assignment *before* going to the lecture.
   d. Take a survey of the chapter's headings, figures, and outlines before reading in depth.

3. In the Boyd and Peeler (2004) study, highlighting:
   a. Produced better memory than relying on your own notes.
   b. Led to the same quality of memory as traditional note-taking.
   c. Was associated with GPAs a full letter grade below those of students who took notes by writing during the lecture.
   d. Produced results no different than taking notes during the lecture.

4. When studying for an exam, you should NOT
   a. Wait until just before the scheduled exam, so that the information will be fresh in your mind.
   b. Get a good night's sleep.
   c. Try to understand the information in your own words.
   d. Tailor your studying to the type of test questions that will be on the exam.

5. When writing a paper, the thesis is
   a. Your detailed notes on your readings.
   b. The central message of your paper.
   c. An outline of the paper's major sections.

psychology in action

secrets for surviving college and improving your grades

PIA.1   p. PIA-4

verbal methods
see and say

rewrite or recite key information in your own words

visual methods
use your eyes

use different colors of highlighter for different ideas in your notes

draw diagrams and summary tables of information from memory

Study Methods

action methods
use movement

auditory methods
use your hearing

study with a partner and discuss concepts and ideas; take turns explaining concepts to each other

talk out loud while studying or into an audio recorder

use exercise and movement while studying

walk around while reading out loud from your materials

write out and diagram key concepts on a poster or white board

create your own models or go on your own "field trips" to gather information

PIA.2   p. PIA-6

reading for learning
is not the same as reading for pleasure

break up your reading sessions
so you have time to process and understand the information

reading, reciting, and reviewing
is very effective

SQ3R

Reading Textbooks

PIA.3   p. PIA-8

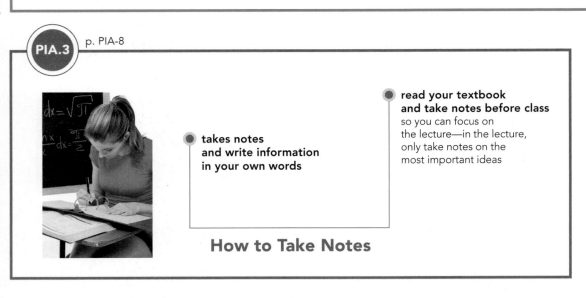

takes notes
and write information
in your own words

read your textbook
and take notes before class
so you can focus on the lecture—in the lecture, only take notes on the most important ideas

How to Take Notes

PIA.4 p. PIA-9

- **spacing out studying sessions**
  (distributed practice) is more effective than
  cramming (massed practice); start early!

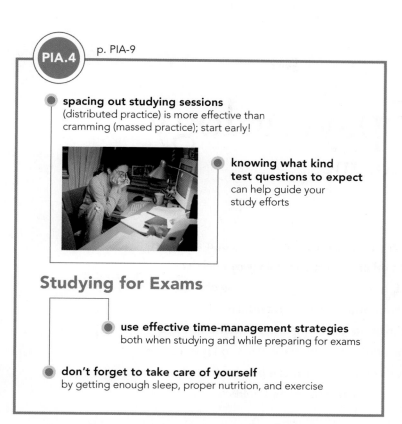

- **knowing what kind
  test questions to expect**
  can help guide your
  study efforts

Studying for Exams

- **use effective time-management strategies**
  both when studying and while preparing for exams

- **don't forget to take care of yourself**
  by getting enough sleep, proper nutrition, and exercise

PIA.5 p. PIA-12

- **quality papers require timely preparation,
  research, planning, and outlining**
  write an initial draft followed by a revised draft

- **don't forget to proofread**
  for spelling and grammar

Writing Papers

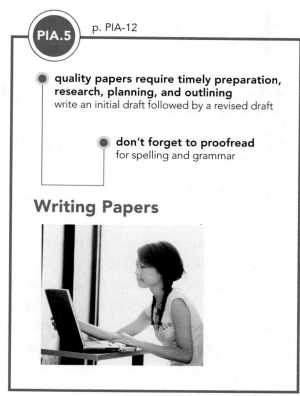

PIA.6 p. PIA-14

- **memory strategies (mnemonics)**
  can be helpful for some types
  of information
  - linking
  - peg-word method
  - method of loci
  - verbal or rhythmic organization —[put it to music

Strategies for Improving Your Memory

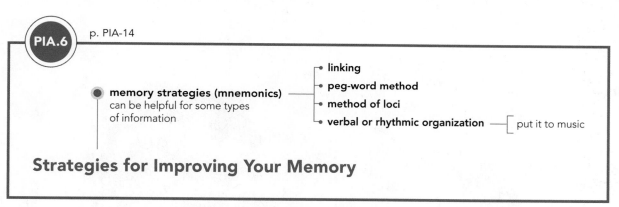

- **MyPsychLab**
  is an online resource
  that can help make your
  study time more effective

- **study tools**
  on MyPsychLab
  - **extra quizzing**
  - **concept mapping tool**
  - **videos**
  - **and more**

MyPsychLab®

- **icons**
  throughout this book direct you
  to additional content on MyPsychLab

- View
- Watch
- Listen
- Explore
- Simulate
- Study and Review
- Read
- Map the Concepts

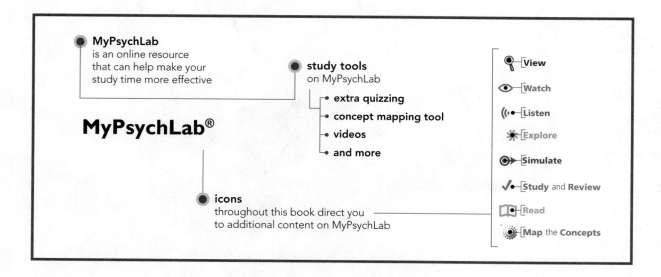

1

the science of psychology
what can psychology do for me?

why study psychology?

Psychology not only helps you understand why other people do the things they do, it also helps you better understand yourself and your reactions to other people. Psychology can help you understand how your brain and body are connected, how to improve your learning abilities and memory, and how to deal with the stresses of life, both ordinary and extraordinary. In studying psychology, an understanding of the methods psychologists use is important because research can be flawed, and knowing how research should be done can bring those flaws to light. Finally, psychology and its research methods promote critical thinking, which can be used to evaluate not just research but also claims of all kinds, including those of advertisers and politicians.

chapter outline

What Is Psychology?

Psychology Then:
The History of Psychology

ISSUES IN PSYCHOLOGY:
Psychology's African American
Roots

Psychology Now:
Modern Perspectives

Psychological Professionals
and Areas of Specialization

Psychology: The Scientific
Methodology

ISSUES IN PSYCHOLOGY:
Stereotypes, Athletes, and
College Test Performance

Ethics of Psychological Research

APPLYING PSYCHOLOGY
TO EVERYDAY LIFE:
Thinking Critically About
Critical Thinking

Have you ever wondered...

. . . why birds of a feather flock together, but opposites so often attract?

. . . how you can remember some things easily and at other times forget what you really need to remember?

. . . what dreams might mean and why we need to sleep at all?

. . . if ESP really exists?

. . . why some people become serial killers?

. . . how prejudice forms?

. . . what scores on an IQ test really mean?

. . . how the salesperson managed to talk you into buying more than you wanted to buy?

. . . how different men and women really are?

. . . why buying lottery tickets can be so addictive?

. . . why people tend to get sick right before final exam week?

. . . why identical twins aren't so identical when it comes to their personalities?

If you've ever been curious about any of these questions, this book is for you. Psychologists study all of these things and more. If you've puzzled about it, thought about doing it, or actually done it, chances are psychology has an explanation for it.

learning objectives

Study Help Note: For each section of every chapter in this text there are numbered learning objectives. These learning objectives represent the key concepts that students should be able to recognize, discuss, analyze, and use after reading the chapter. They appear at the beginning of each chapter, at the beginning of each relevant section in the chapter, and in the chapter summary.

These are your learning objectives for this chapter:

1.1 What defines psychology as a field of study, and what are psychology's four primary goals?

1.2 How did structuralism and functionalism differ, and who were the important people in those early fields?

1.3 What were the basic ideas and who were the important people behind the early approaches known as Gestalt, psychoanalysis, and behaviorism?

1.4 What are the basic ideas behind the seven modern perspectives, as well as the important contributions of Skinner, Maslow, and Rogers?

1.5 How does a psychologist differ from a psychiatrist, and what are the other types of professionals who work in the various areas of psychology?

1.6 Why is psychology considered a science, and what are the steps in using the scientific method?

1.7 How are naturalistic and laboratory settings used to describe behavior, and what are some of the advantages and disadvantages associated with these settings?

1.8 How are case studies and surveys used to describe behavior, and what are some drawbacks to each of these methods?

1.9 What is the correlational technique, and what does it tell researchers about relationships?

1.10 How are operational definitions, independent and dependent variables, experimental and control groups, and random assignment used in designing an experiment?

1.11 How do the placebo and experimenter effects cause problems in an experiment, and how can single-blind and double-blind studies control for these effects?

1.12 What are the basic elements of a real-world experiment?

1.13 What are some ethical concerns that can occur when conducting research with people and animals?

1.14 What are the basic principles of critical thinking, and how can critical thinking be useful in everyday life?

What Is Psychology?

The Field of Psychology

Some people believe psychology is just the study of people and what motivates their behavior. Psychologists do study people, but they study animals as well. To better understand what motivates behavior, psychologists study not only what people and animals do, but also what happens in their bodies and in their brains as they do it.

1.1 What defines psychology as a field of study, and what are psychology's four primary goals?

Psychology is the scientific study of behavior and mental processes. *Behavior* includes all of our outward or overt actions and reactions, such as talking, facial expressions, and movement. The term *mental processes* refers to all the internal, covert activity of our minds, such as thinking, feeling, and remembering. Why "scientific"? To study behavior and mental processes in both animals and humans, researchers have to observe them. Whenever a human being is observing anyone or anything, there's always a possibility the observer will see only what he or she expects to see. Psychologists don't want to let these possible biases* cause them to make faulty observations. They want to be as precise as possible and measure as carefully as they can, so they use the scientific method to study psychology.

Psychology's Goals

Every science has the common goal of learning how things work. The goals specifically aimed at uncovering the mysteries of human and animal behavior are description, explanation, prediction, and control.

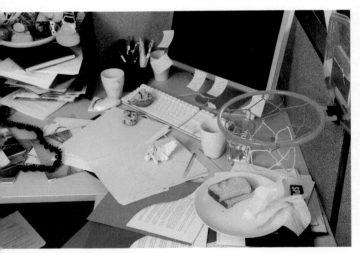

Is this an environment that you would want to work in? Some researchers have wondered if your answer might be influenced by your gender.

psychology the scientific study of behavior and mental processes.

DESCRIPTION: WHAT IS HAPPENING? The first step in understanding anything is to describe it. *Description* involves observing a behavior and noting everything about it: what is happening, where it happens, to whom it happens, and under what circumstances it seems to happen.

For example, a psychologist might wonder why so many computer scientists seem to be male. She makes further observations and notes that many "non-techies" stereotypically perceive the life and environment of a computer scientist as one in which someone lives and breathes at the computer, surrounds himself with computer games, junk food, and science-fiction gadgets—characteristics that add up to a very masculine ambiance.

That's what *seems* to be happening. The psychologist's observations are a starting place for the next goal: Why do females seem to avoid going into this environment?

EXPLANATION: WHY IS IT HAPPENING? Based on her observations, the psychologist might try to come up with a tentative explanation, such as "women feel they do not belong in such stereotypically masculine surroundings." In other words, she is trying to understand or find an *explanation* for the lower proportion of women in this field. Finding explanations for behavior is a very important step in the process of forming theories of behavior. A *theory* is a general explanation of a set of observations or facts. The goal of description provides the observations, and the goal of explanation helps to build the theory.

---

*Biases: personal judgments based on beliefs rather than facts.

The preceding example comes from a real experiment conducted by psychologist Sapna Cheryan and colleagues (Cheryan et al., 2009). Professor Cheryan (who teaches psychology at the University of Washington in Seattle), set up four experiments with more than 250 female and male student participants who were not studying computer science. In the first experiment, students came into a small classroom that had one of two sets of objects: either Star Trek® posters, video-game boxes, and Coke™ cans, or nature posters, art, a dictionary, and coffee mugs (among other things). Told to ignore the objects because they were sharing the room with another class, the students spent several minutes in the classroom. While still sitting in the classroom, they were asked to fill out a questionnaire asking about their attitude toward computer science. Although the attitudes of male students were not different between the two environments, women exposed to the stereotypically masculine setup were less interested in computer science than those who were exposed to the nonstereotypical environment. The three other similar experiments yielded the same results.

PREDICTION: WHEN WILL IT HAPPEN AGAIN?   Determining what will happen in the future is making a *prediction*. In the Cheryan et al. study, the prediction is clear: If we want more women to go into computer science, we must do something to change either the environment or the perception of the environment typically associated with this field. This is the purpose of the last of the four goals of psychology: changing or modifying behavior.

CONTROL: HOW CAN IT BE CHANGED?   The focus of *control*, or the modification of some behavior, is to change a behavior from an undesirable one (such as women avoiding a certain academic major) to a desirable one (such as more equality in career choices).

Professor Cheryan suggests that changing the image of computer science may help increase the number of women choosing to go into this field. Not all psychological investigations will try to meet all four of these goals. In some cases, the main focus might be on description and prediction, as it would be for a personality theorist who wants to know what people are like (description) and what they might do in certain situations (prediction). Some psychologists are interested in both description and explanation, as is the case with experimental psychologists who design research to find explanations for observed (described) behavior. Therapists may be more interested in controlling or influencing behavior and mental processes, although the other three goals would be important in achieving this objective.

Although these goals have not really changed over the years since psychology's beginnings, the methods of achieving them certainly have changed. In the next section, we'll take a look at the early pioneers in psychology. ☑•⌐**Survey** on **MyPsychLab**

☑•⌐**Survey** Participate in a survey: What do you know about psychology? on **MyPsychLab**

Psychology Then: The History of Psychology
In the Beginning: Wundt, Introspection, and the Laboratory

How long has psychology been around? ●

Psychology is a relatively new field in the realm of the sciences; it is only about 130 years old. It's not that no one thought about what makes people tick before then; on the contrary, many philosophers,* medical doctors, and physiologists** thought about little else. Famous philosophers such as Plato, Aristotle, and Descartes wrote about the relationship of the soul (or mind) and the body (Durrant, 1993; Everson, 1995;

How long has psychology been around?

---

*Philosophers: people who seek wisdom and knowledge through thinking and discussion.
**Physiologists: scientists who study the physical workings of the body and its systems.

German physiologist Wilhelm Wundt participates in an experiment in his laboratory as students look on.

✳ Explore with a time line of important dates in psychology on **MyPsychLab**

Structuralists would be interested in all of the memories and sensations this woman is experiencing as she smells the rose.

objective introspection the process of examining and measuring one's own thoughts and mental activities.

structuralism early perspective in psychology associated with Wilhelm Wundt and Edward Titchener, in which the focus of study is the structure or basic elements of the mind.

Jackson, 2001; Kenny, 1968, 1994). Philosophers tried to understand or explain the human mind and its connection to the physical body, whereas medical doctors and physiologists wondered about the physical connection between the body and the brain. For example, physician Hermann von Helmholtz (von Helmholtz, 1852, 1863) performed groundbreaking experiments in visual and auditory perception. ⓛⓘⓝⓚ to Chapter Three: Sensation and Perception, p. 88. ✳ Explore on **MyPsychLab**

1.2 How did structuralism and functionalism differ, and who were the important people in those early fields?

It really all started to come together in a laboratory in Leipzig, Germany, in 1879. It was here that Wilhelm Wundt (VILL-helm Voont, 1832–1920), a physiologist, attempted to apply scientific principles to the study of the human mind. In his laboratory, students from around the world were taught to study the structure of the human mind. Wundt believed that the mind was made up of thoughts, experiences, emotions, and other basic elements. In order to inspect these nonphysical elements, students had to learn to think objectively about their own thoughts—after all, they could hardly read someone else's mind. Wundt called this process **objective introspection**, the process of objectively examining and measuring one's own thoughts and mental activities (Rieber & Robinson, 2001). For example, Wundt might place an object, such as a rock, into a student's hand and have the student tell him everything that he was feeling as a result of having the rock in his hand—all the sensations stimulated by the rock. (Objectivity* was— and is—important because scientists need to remain unbiased. Observations need to be clear and precise, but unaffected by the individual observer's beliefs and values.)

Wundt's was the first attempt by anyone to bring objectivity and measurement to the concept of psychology. This attention to objectivity, together with the establishment of the first true experimental laboratory in psychology, is why Wundt is known as the "father of psychology."

Titchener and Structuralism in America

One of Wundt's students was Edward Titchener (1867–1927), an Englishman who eventually took Wundt's ideas to Cornell University in Ithaca, New York. Titchener expanded on Wundt's original ideas, calling his new viewpoint **structuralism** because the focus of study was the structure of the mind. He believed that every experience could be broken down into its individual emotions and sensations (Brennan, 2002). Although Titchener agreed with Wundt that consciousness, the state of being aware of external events, could be broken down into its basic elements, Titchener also believed that objective introspection could be used on thoughts as well as on physical sensations. For example, Titchener might have asked his students to introspect about things that are blue rather than actually giving them a blue object and asking for reactions to it. Such an exercise might have led to something like the following: "What is blue? There are blue things, like the sky or a bird's feathers. Blue is cool and restful, blue is calm," and so on.

In 1894, one of Titchener's students at Cornell University became famous for becoming the first woman to receive a Ph.D. in psychology (Goodman, 1980; Guthrie, 2004). Her name was Margaret F. Washburn, and she was Titchener's only graduate student for that year. In 1908 she published a book on animal behavior

---

*Objectivity: expressing or dealing with facts or conditions as they really are without allowing the influence of personal feelings, prejudices, or interpretations.

that was considered an important work in that era of psychology, *The Animal Mind* (Washburn, 1908).

Structuralism was a dominant force in the early days of psychology, but it eventually died out in the early 1900s, as the structuralists were busily fighting among themselves over just which key elements of experience were the most important. A competing view arose not long after Wundt's laboratory was established, shortly before structuralism came to America.

William James and Functionalism

Harvard University was the first school in America to offer classes in psychology in the late 1870s. These classes were taught by one of Harvard's most illustrious instructors, William James (1842–1910). James began teaching anatomy and physiology, but as his interest in psychology developed, he began teaching psychology almost exclusively (Brennan, 2002). His comprehensive textbook on the subject, *Principles of Psychology*, is so brilliantly written that copies are still in print (James, 1890, 2002).

Unlike Wundt and Titchener, James was more interested in the importance of consciousness to everyday life rather than just the analysis of it. He believed that the scientific study of consciousness itself was not yet possible. Conscious ideas are constantly flowing in an ever-changing stream, and once you start thinking about what you were just thinking about, what you were thinking about is no longer what you *were* thinking about, it's what you *are* thinking about, and . . . excuse me, I'm a little dizzy. I think you get the picture, anyway.

Instead, James focused on how the mind allows people to *function* in the real world—how people work, play, and adapt to their surroundings. He called this viewpoint **functionalism**. (James was heavily influenced by Charles Darwin's ideas about *natural selection*, in which physical traits that help an animal adapt to its environment and survive are passed on to its offspring, becoming part of the animal's traits.) If physical traits could aid in survival, why couldn't behavioral traits do the same? Animals and people whose behavior helped them to survive would pass those traits on to their offspring, perhaps by teaching or even by some mechanism of heredity.* (Remember that this was early in the days of trying to understand how heredity worked.) For example, a behavior such as avoiding the eyes of others in an elevator can be seen as a way of protecting one's personal space—a kind of territorial protection that may have its roots in the primitive need to protect one's home and source of food and water from intruders (Manusov & Patterson, 2006) or as a way of avoiding what might seem like a challenge to another person (Brown et al., 2005; Jehn et al., 1999).

One of James's early students was Mary Whiton Calkins, who completed every course and requirement for earning a Ph.D. but was denied that degree by Harvard University because she was a woman. Calkins eventually established a psychological laboratory at Wellesley College. Her work was some of the earliest research in the area of human memory and the psychology of the self. In 1905, she became the first female president of the American Psychological Association (Furumoto, 1979, 1991; Zedler, 1995). Unlike Washburn, Calkins never earned the elusive Ph.D. degree despite a successful career as a professor and researcher (Guthrie, 2004).

This is a good place to point out that women were not the only minority to make contributions in the early days of psychology. In 1920 Francis Cecil Sumner became the first African American to earn a Ph.D. in psychology at Clark University. He eventually became the chair of the psychology department at Howard University and

functionalism early perspective in psychology associated with William James, in which the focus of study is how the mind allows people to adapt, live, work, and play.

Mary Whiton Calkins, despite being denied a Ph.D. degree by Harvard because she was a woman, became the first female president of the American Psychological Association and had a successful career as a professor and researcher.
Source: Archives of the History of American Psychology–The University of Akron.

---

*Heredity: the transmission of traits and characteristics from parent to offspring through the actions of genes.

Is functionalism still an important point of view in psychology?

Francis Cecil Sumner, the first African American to receive a Ph.D. in psychology, went on to chair the psychology department at Howard University and is considered by many to be the father of African American psychology.

is assumed by many to be the father of African American psychology (Guthrie, 2004). Kenneth and Mamie Clark worked to show the negative effects of school segregation on African American children (Lal, 2002). Hispanic psychologist Jorge Sanchez conducted research in the area of intelligence testing, focusing on the cultural biases in such tests. While psychology recently has seen an increase in the contributions of all minorities, the percentages are still small when compared to the population at large. For a summary of the contributions of African Americans to the early days of psychology, see the following feature, *Issues in Psychology: Psychology's African American Roots.*

● Is functionalism still an important point of view in psychology?

In the new field of psychology, functionalism offered an alternative viewpoint to the structuralists. But like so many of psychology's early ideas, it is no longer a major perspective. Instead, one can find elements of functionalism in the modern fields of *educational psychology* (studying the application of psychological concepts to education) and *industrial/organizational psychology* (studying the application of psychological concepts to businesses, organizations, and industry), as well as other areas in psychology. Ⓛ Ⓘ Ⓝ Ⓚ to Appendix B: Applied Psychology and Psychology Careers, pp. B–2–B–12. Functionalism also played a part in the development of one of the more modern perspectives, evolutionary psychology, discussed later in this chapter.

issues in psychology
Psychology's African American Roots

Even the Rat Was White is an excellent and thought-provoking book. Written by the late Dr. Robert V. Guthrie in 1976 and recently republished (Guthrie, 2004), it is an enlightening summary of the history of African Americans in the field of psychology. The contributions of African American psychologists to early psychology have often been ignored in textbooks. Dr. Guthrie (who died from cancer in 2005 at the age of 75) includes in his text a detailed listing of the important African American psychologists and their contributions to the relatively new field of psychology. The following is a brief summary of just a few of the achievements of these often neglected scholars.

- Dr. Charles Henry Thompson (1896–1980) was the first African American to receive a doctorate in educational psychology (the University of Chicago, 1925). For 30 years he was the editor of the *Journal of Negro Education*.

- Dr. Albert Sidney Beckham (1897–1964) received his Ph.D. in psychology in 1930 from New York University. In the 1930s he was senior assistant psychologist at the National Committee for Mental Hygiene at the Illinois Institute for Juvenile Research; he also counseled many black youths in his role as the psychologist at DuSable High School in Chicago. He had many publications of his research in the areas of intelligence and social concerns of the African American youth of his time.

- Dr. Robert Prentiss Daniel (1902–1968) earned his Ph.D. in educational psychology from Columbia University in 1932. At one time the director of the Division of Educational Psychology and Philosophy at Virginia Union University, he became president of Shaw University in North Carolina and finally the president of Virginia State College.

- Dr. Inez Beverly Prosser (1897–1934) earned her Ph.D. in educational psychology from the University of Cincinnati in 1933 and was the first African American woman to earn this degree. Her promising teaching career met a tragic end when she died in an automobile accident only one year after earning her doctorate.

- Dr. Howard Hale Long (1888–1948) received his Ed.D. in educational psychology from Harvard University in 1933. After teaching psychology and doing research in educational psychology for many years, Dr. Long became dean of administration at Wilberforce State College in Ohio.

- Dr. Ruth Howard (1900–1997) is known as the first African American woman to earn the Ph.D. in psychology (not educational psychology) in 1934 from the University of Minnesota. She served with her husband, Dr. Albert Beckham, as codirector for the Center for Psychological Services and also maintained a private practice in clinical psychology.

These African American pioneers in the field of psychology represent only a fraction of all those who made important contributions to psychology's early days.

. . . .

Gestalt Psychology: The Whole Is Greater Than the Sum of Its Parts

Meanwhile, back in Germany, other psychologists were attacking the concepts of psychology in yet another way. Max Wertheimer (VERT-hi-mer), like James, objected to the structuralist point of view but for different reasons. Wertheimer felt that psychological events such as perceiving* and sensing** could not be broken down into any smaller elements and still be properly understood. As a melody is made up of individual notes that can only be understood if the notes are in the correct relationship to one another, so perception can only be understood as a whole, entire event. Hence, the familiar slogan, "The whole is greater than the sum of its parts." The Gestalt psychologists believed that people naturally seek out patterns ("wholes") in the sensory information available to them. See Figure 1.1 for an example of Gestalt perceptual patterns.

FIGURE 1.1 A Gestalt Perception
The eye tends to "fill in" the blanks here and see both of these figures as circles rather than as a series of dots or a broken line.

1.3 What were the basic ideas and who were the important people behind the early approaches known as Gestalt, psychoanalysis, and behaviorism?

Wertheimer and others devoted their efforts to studying sensation and perception in this new perspective called **Gestalt psychology**. *Gestalt* (Gesh-TALT) is a German word meaning "an organized whole" or "configuration," which fit well with the focus on studying whole patterns rather than small pieces of them. Today, Gestalt ideas are part of the study of *cognitive psychology*, a field focusing not only on perception but also on learning, memory, thought processes, and problem solving; the basic Gestalt principles of perception are still taught within this newer field (Ash, 1998; Kohler, 1992; Wertheimer, 1982). (L)(I)(N)(K) to Chapter Three: Sensation and Perception, pp. 103–105. The Gestalt approach has also been an influential concept in psychological therapy, becoming the basis for a major therapeutic technique called *Gestalt therapy*. (L)(I)(N)(K) to Chapter Thirteen: Psychological Therapies, pp. 470–472.

Sigmund Freud's Theory of Psychoanalysis

It should be clear by now that psychology didn't start in one place and at one particular time. People of several different viewpoints were trying to promote their own perspective on the study of the human mind and behavior in different places all over

Gestalt psychology early perspective in psychology focusing on perception and sensation, particularly the perception of patterns and whole figures.

---

*Perceiving: becoming aware of something through the senses.

**Sensing: seeing, hearing, feeling, tasting, or smelling something.

What about Freud? Everybody talks about him when they talk about psychology. Are his ideas still in use?

Psychoanalyst Sigmund Freud walks with his daughter Anna, also a psychoanalyst.

Physiologist Ivan Pavlov uses a dog to demonstrate the conditioned reflex to students at the Russian Military Medical Academy.

psychoanalysis the theory and therapy based on the work of Sigmund Freud.

the world. Up to now, this chapter has focused on the physiologists and philosophers who became interested in psychology, with a focus on understanding consciousness but little else. The medical profession took a whole different approach to psychology.

● **What about Freud? Everybody talks about him when they talk about psychology. Are his ideas still in use?**

Sigmund Freud had become a noted physician in Austria while the structuralists were arguing, the functionalists were specializing, and the Gestaltists were looking at the big picture. He was a medical doctor—a neurologist, someone who specializes in disorders of the nervous system—and he and his colleagues had long sought a way to understand the patients who were coming to them for help.

Freud's patients suffered from nervous disorders for which he and other doctors could find no physical cause. Therefore, it was thought, the cause must be in the mind, and that is where Freud began to explore. He proposed that there is an *unconscious* (unaware) mind into which we push, or *repress*, all of our threatening urges and desires. He believed that these repressed urges, in trying to surface, created the nervous disorders in his patients (Freud et al., 1990). Ⓛ Ⓘ Ⓝ Ⓚ to Chapter Eleven: Theories of Personality and Intelligence, pp. 386–392.

Freud stressed the importance of early childhood experiences, believing that personality was formed in the first six years of life; if there were significant problems, those problems must have begun in the early years.

Some of his well-known followers were Alfred Adler, Carl Jung, and his own daughter, Anna Freud. Anna Freud began what became known as the ego movement in psychology that produced one of the most famous psychologists in the study of personality development, Erik Erikson. Ⓛ Ⓘ Ⓝ Ⓚ to Chapter Seven: Development Across the Life Span, pp. 250–251.

Freud's ideas are still influential today, although in a somewhat modified form. He had a number of followers in addition to those already named. Many of them became famous by altering his theory to fit their own viewpoint, but his basic ideas are still discussed and debated today. Ⓛ Ⓘ Ⓝ Ⓚ to Chapter Eleven: Theories of Personality and Intelligence, pp. 392–394.

Although some might think that Sigmund Freud was the first person to deal with people suffering from various mental disorders, the truth is that mental illness has a fairly long (and not very pretty) history. For more on the history of mental illness, see the Ⓛ Ⓘ Ⓝ Ⓚ to Chapter Twelve: Psychological Disorders, p. 432.

Freudian **psychoanalysis**, the theory and therapy based on Freud's ideas, has been the basis of much modern *psychotherapy*—a process in which a trained psychological professional helps a person gain insights into and change his or her behavior. But another major and competing viewpoint has actually been more influential in the field of psychology as a whole.

Pavlov, Watson, and the Dawn of Behaviorism

Ivan Pavlov, like Freud, was not a psychologist. He was a Russian physiologist who, working with dogs, had shown that a reflex (an involuntary reaction) such as salivation, which is normally produced by actually having food in one's mouth, could be caused to occur in response to a totally new and formerly unrelated stimulus,* such as the sound of a ticking metronome. He would turn on the metronome, give the dogs food, and they would salivate. After several repetitions, the dogs would sali-

_____
*Stimulus: anything that causes an organism to have a reaction or response.

vate to the sound of the metronome *before* the food was presented—a learned (or "conditioned") reflexive response (Klein & Mowrer, 1989). This process was called *conditioning*. (L)(I)(N)(K) to Chapter Four: Learning, p. 123.

In the early 1900s, psychologist John B. Watson had tired of the arguing among the structuralists; he challenged the functionalist viewpoint, as well as psychoanalysis, with his own "science of behavior," or **behaviorism** (Watson, 1924). Watson wanted to bring psychology back to a focus on scientific inquiry, and he felt that the only way to do that was to ignore the whole "consciousness" issue and focus only on *observable behavior*—something that could be directly seen and measured. He had read of Pavlov's work and thought that conditioning could form the basis of his new perspective of behaviorism.

OF BABIES AND RATS Watson was certainly aware of Freud's work and his views on unconscious repression. Freud believed that all behavior stems from unconscious motivation, whereas Watson believed that all behavior is learned. Freud had stated that a *phobia*, an irrational fear, is really a symptom of an underlying, repressed conflict and cannot be "cured" without years of psychoanalysis to uncover and understand the repressed material.

Watson believed that phobias are learned through the process of conditioning and set out to prove it. He took a baby, known as "Little Albert," and taught him to fear a white rat by making a loud, scary noise every time the infant saw the rat, until finally just seeing the rat caused the infant to cry and become fearful (Watson & Rayner, 1920). Even though "Little Albert" was not afraid of the rat at the start, the experiment worked very well—in fact, "Little Albert" became afraid of other fuzzy things, including a rabbit, a dog, and a sealskin coat. ⊙⟶Watch on MyPsychLab

This sounds really bizarre—what does scaring a baby have to do with the science of psychology?

Watson wanted to prove that all behavior was a result of a stimulus–response relationship such as that described by Pavlov. Because Freud and his ideas about unconscious motivation were becoming a dominant force, Watson felt the need to show the world that a much simpler explanation could be found. Although scaring a baby sounds a little cruel, he felt that the advancement of the science of behavior was worth the baby's relatively brief discomfort.

One of Watson's students was Mary Cover Jones, who completed her master's degree in 1920 under Watson's supervision (Rutherford, 2000). She duplicated the "Little Albert" study with another child, "Little Peter," successfully conditioning Peter to be afraid of a white rabbit (Jones, 1924). She then began a process of *counterconditioning*, in which Peter was exposed to the white rabbit from a distance while eating a food that he really liked. The pleasure of the food outweighed the fear of the far-away rabbit. Day by day, the situation was repeated with the rabbit being brought closer each time, until Peter was no longer afraid of the rabbit. Jones went on to become one of the early pioneers of behavior therapy. She was also a key figure in the Oakland Growth Study, a study of 200 fifth- and sixth-grade children that followed their development from the beginning of puberty to the end of adolescence. It is her work that is often cited when textbook authors talk about the benefits and problems associated with early and late maturation in puberty. She and her husband, Harold Jones, published the first educational television course in child development in 1952 (Rutherford, 2000).

Behaviorism, like psychoanalysis, still represents a major perspective in psychology today. It has also influenced the development of other perspectives, such as *cognitive psychology*.

American psychologist John Watson is known as the father of behaviorism. Behaviorism focuses only on observable behavior.

This sounds really bizarre— what does scaring a baby have to do with the science of psychology?

⊙⟶Watch classic video footage of John Watson, Rosalie Rayner, and "Little Albert" on **MyPsychLab**

Mary Cover Jones, one of the early pioneers of behavior therapy, earned her master's degree under the supervision of John Watson. She had a long and distinguished career, including the publication in 1952 of the first educational television course in child development.

behaviorism the science of behavior that focuses on observable behavior only.

practice quiz   How much do you remember?

Study Help Note: These practice quizzes are spaced throughout each chapter to give you an opportunity to check your understanding of the material in each section and provide practice for exams.

Pick the best answer.

1. In the definition of psychology, *behavior* means _____.
   a. internal, covert processes.
   b. mental processes.
   c. outward or overt actions and reactions.
   d. only human behavior.

2. Dr. Edwards designs a special behavior program for children diagnosed with autism to learn to communicate with others. Dr. Edwards is most interested in the goal of _____.
   a. description.   c. prediction.
   b. explanation.   d. control.

3. Cheryan et al. (2009) tested for the reason why there are so few women in the computer science field. This study most clearly illustrates the goal of _____.
   a. description.   c. prediction.
   b. explanation.   d. control.

4. Which of the following early psychologists would have been most likely to agree with the statement, "The study of the mind should focus on how it allows us to adapt to our surroundings"?

   a. Wilhelm Wundt   c. John Watson
   b. William James   d. Sigmund Freud

5. Which early perspective would have been LEAST likely to agree with the structuralists?
   a. introspectionism   c. psychoanalysis
   b. functionalism   d. Gestalt

6. Who was the first woman president of the American Psychological Association?
   a. Mary Whiton Calkins   c. Margaret Washburn
   b. Mary Cover Jones   d. Eleanor Gibson

7. Who among the early African American psychologists eventually became president of two universities?
   a. Dr. Ruth Howard
   b. Dr. Robert Prentiss Daniel
   c. Dr. Inez Beverly Prosser
   d. Dr. Albert Sidney Beckham

Brainstorming: Would it be possible to do a study such as Watson and Rayner's "Little Albert" research today? Why or why not? What might justify such a study today?

ANSWERS ON PAGE AK–1

Psychology Now: Modern Perspectives

1.4 **What are the basic ideas behind the seven modern perspectives, as well as the important contributions of Skinner, Maslow, and Rogers?**

Even in the twenty-first century, there isn't one single perspective that is used to explain all human behavior and mental processes. There are actually seven modern perspectives, with two of those being holdovers from the early days of the field.

Psychodynamic Perspective

Many professionals still use Freud's theory in therapy situations. It is far less common today than it was a few decades ago, however, and even those who use his techniques modify them for contemporary use. In the more modern **psychodynamic perspective**, the focus may still include the unconscious mind and its influence over conscious behavior and on early childhood experiences, but there is less emphasis on sex and sexual motivations and more emphasis on the development of a sense of self, social, and interpersonal relationships, and the discovery of other motivations behind a person's behavior. (L)(I)(N)(K) to Chapter Eleven: Theories of Personality and Intelligence, pp. 392–394. Some modern psychodynamic practitioners have even begun to recommend that the link between neurobiology (the study of the brain and nervous system) and psychodynamic concepts should be more fully explored (Glucksman, 2006).

psychodynamic perspective   modern version of psychoanalysis that is more focused on the development of a sense of self and the discovery of other motivations behind a person's behavior than sexual motivations.

Behavioral Perspective

Like modern psychodynamic perspectives, behaviorism also remains very influential. When its primary supporter, John B. Watson, moved on to greener pastures in the world of advertising, B. F. Skinner became the new leader of the field.

Skinner not only continued research in classical conditioning, but he also developed a theory of how voluntary behavior is learned called *operant conditioning* (Skinner, 1938). In this theory, behavioral responses that are followed by pleasurable consequences are strengthened, or *reinforced*. For example, a child who cries and is rewarded by getting his mother's attention will cry again in the future. Skinner's work is discussed in much greater depth in Chapter Four. (L)(I)(N)(K) to Chapter Four: Learning, pp. 132–134. In addition to the psychodynamic and behavioral perspectives, five newer perspectives have developed within the last 50 years.

Humanistic Perspective

Often called the "third force" in psychology, humanism was really a reaction to both psychoanalytic theory and behaviorism. If you were a psychologist in the early to mid-1900s, you were either a psychoanalyst or a behaviorist—there weren't any other major viewpoints to rival those two.

In contrast to the psychoanalytic focus on sexual development and behaviorism's emphasis on external forces in guiding personality development, some professionals began to develop a perspective that would allow them to focus on people's ability to direct their own lives. Humanists held the view that people have *free will*, the freedom to choose their own destiny, and that they strive for *self-actualization*, the achievement of one's full potential. Two of the earliest and most famous founders of this view were Abraham Maslow (1908–1970) and Carl Rogers (1902–1987). Today, humanism exists as a form of psychotherapy aimed at self-understanding and self-improvement. (L)(I)(N)(K) to Chapter Thirteen: Psychological Therapies, pp. 470–472.

Cognitive Perspective

Cognitive psychology, which focuses on how people think, remember, store, and use information, became a major force in the field in the 1960s. It wasn't a new idea, as the Gestalt psychologists had themselves supported the study of mental processes of learning. The development of computers (which just happened to make ideal models of human thinking), the work of Piaget with children, Chomsky's analysis of Skinner's views of language, and discoveries in biological psychology all stimulated an interest in studying the processes of thought. The **cognitive perspective** with its focus on memory, intelligence, perception, thought processes, problem solving, language, and learning has become a major force in psychology. (L)(I)(N)(K) to Chapter Six: Consciousness and Cognition, pp. 207–223.

Within the cognitive perspective, the relatively new field of **cognitive neuroscience** includes the study of the physical workings of the brain and nervous system when engaged in memory, thinking, and other cognitive processes. Cognitive neuroscientists use tools for imaging the structure and activity of the living brain, such as magnetic resonance imaging (MRI), functional magnetic resonance imaging (fMRI), and positron emission tomography (PET). (L)(I)(N)(K) to Chapter Two: The Biological Perspective, pp. 61-63. The continually developing field of brain imaging is important in the study of cognitive processes.

Sociocultural Perspective

Another modern perspective in psychology is the **sociocultural perspective**, which actually combines two areas of study: *social psychology*, which is the study of groups, social roles, and rules of social actions and relationships; and *cultural psychology*, which is the study of cultural norms,* values, and expectations. These two areas are

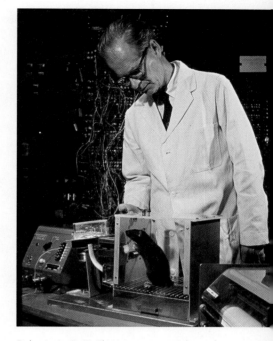

Behaviorist B. F. Skinner puts a rat through its paces. What challenges might arise from applying information gained from studies with animals to human behavior?

cognitive perspective modern perspective that focuses on memory, intelligence, perception, problem solving, and learning.

cognitive neuroscience study of the physical changes in the brain and nervous system during thinking.

sociocultural perspective perspective that focuses on the relationship between social behavior and culture.

---

*Norms: standards or expected behavior.

biopsychological perspective   perspective that attributes human and animal behavior to biological events occurring in the body, such as genetic influences, hormones, and the activity of the nervous system.

related in that both are about the effect that people have on one another, either individually or in a larger group such as a culture (Peplau & Taylor, 1997). LINK to Chapter Ten: Social Psychology, pp. 346–378. Russian psychologist Lev Vygotsky (1978) also used sociocultural concepts in forming his sociocultural theory of children's cognitive development. LINK to Chapter Seven: Development Across the Life Span, p. 244.

The sociocultural perspective is important because it reminds people that the way they and others behave (or even think) is influenced not only by whether they are alone, with friends, in a crowd, or part of a group but also by the social norms, fads, class differences, and ethnic identity concerns of the particular culture in which they live. *Cross-cultural research* also fits within this perspective. In cross-cultural research, the contrasts and comparisons of a behavior or issue are studied in at least two or more cultures. This type of research can help illustrate the different influences of environment (culture and training) when compared to the influence of heredity (genetics, or the influence of genes on behavior).

For example, in a classic study covered in Chapter Ten: Social Psychology (pp. 375–376), researchers Darley and Latané (1968) found that the presence of other people actually *lessened* the chances that a person in trouble would receive help. The phenomenon is called the "bystander effect," and it is believed to be the result of *diffusion of responsibility*, which is the tendency to feel that someone else is responsible for taking action when others are present. But would this effect appear in other cultures? Shorey (2001), in his discussion of the brutal beating death of a Somali prisoner in a Canadian military facility while bystanders looked on without acting, suggests that it just might. But is Canadian culture too similar to our own to lead us to this conclusion? Would another culture very different from Western culture show the same effect? This is exactly the kind of question that the sociocultural perspective asks and attempts to answer, using cross-cultural research.

Biopsychological Perspective

Biopsychology, or the study of the biological bases of behavior and mental processes, isn't really as new a perspective as one might think. Also known as physiological psychology, biological psychology, psychobiology, and behavioral neuroscience, biopsychology is part of the larger field of *neuroscience*: study of the physical structure, function, and development of the nervous system. Also, the previously discussed field of cognitive neuroscience often overlaps with biopsychology.

In the **biopsychological perspective**, human and animal behavior is seen as a direct result of events in the body. Hormones, heredity, brain chemicals, tumors, and diseases are some of the biological causes of behavior and mental events. LINK to Chapter Two: The Biological Perspective, pp. 42–74. Some of the topics researched by biopsychologists include sleep, emotions, aggression, sexual behavior, and learning and memory—as well as disorders. While disorders may have multiple causes (family issues, stress, or trauma, for example), research in biopsychology points clearly to biological factors as one of those causes.

For example, evidence continues to mount for a genetic cause for *schizophrenia*, a mental disorder involving delusions (false beliefs), hallucinations (false sensory impressions), and extremely distorted thinking (Brzustowicz et al., 2004; Maziade et al., 1997; Pogue-Geile & Yokley, 2010). LINK to Chapter Twelve: Psychological Disorders, pp. 453–455. Other research suggests that human sexual orientation may be related to the developing baby's exposure in the womb to testosterone (G. Brown et al., 2002) as well as the birth order of male children (Puts et al., 2006). The Puts, Jordan, and Breedlove (2006) study suggests that the more older brothers a male child

These scans show loss of gray matter in the brains of individuals with very early-onset, adolescent schizophrenia over a five-year period, highlighting one focus of the biological perspective.

has, the more likely he is to have a homosexual orientation. Still another example of research in this field is Escandon, Al-Hammadi, and Galvin's (2010) study finding a possible link between the tendency to lose one's train of thought in later adulthood—staring into space, unexplained excessive daytime sleepiness, and disorganized thinking, for example—and the development of Alzheimer's disease. **LINK** to Chapter Five: Memory, p. 190.

Evolutionary Perspective

The **evolutionary perspective** focuses on the biological bases for universal mental characteristics that all humans share. It seeks to explain general mental strategies and traits, such as why we lie, how attractiveness influences mate selection, why fear of snakes is so common, or why people universally like music and dancing. This approach may also overlap with biopsychology.

In this perspective, the mind is seen as a set of information-processing machines, designed by the same process of natural selection that Darwin (1859) first theorized, allowing human beings to solve the problems faced in the early days of human evolution—the problems of the early hunters and gatherers. For example, *evolutionary psychologists* (psychologists who study the evolutionary origins of human behavior) would view the human behavior of not eating substances that have a bitter taste (such as poisonous plants) as an adaptive* behavior that evolved as early humans came into contact with such bitter plants. Those who ate the bitter plants would die, while those who spit them out survived to pass on their "I-don't-like-this-taste" genes to their offspring, who would pass on the genes to *their* offspring, and so on, until after a long period of time there is an entire population of humans that naturally avoids bitter-tasting substances.

That explains why people don't like bitter stuff, like the white part of an orange peel, but that's really a physical thing. How would the evolutionary perspective help us understand something psychological like relationships?

Relationships between men and women are one of the many areas in which evolutionary psychologists conduct research. For example, in one study researchers surveyed young adults about their relationships with the opposite sex, asking the participants how likely they would be to forgive either a sexual infidelity or an emotional one (Shackelford et al., 2002). Evolutionary theory would predict that men would find it more difficult to forgive a woman who had sex with someone else than a woman who was only emotionally involved with someone because the man wants to be sure that the children the woman bears are his (Geary, 2000, 2012). Why put all that effort into providing for children who could be another man's offspring? Women, on the other hand, should find it harder to forgive an emotional infidelity, as they are always sure that their children are their own, but (in evolutionary terms, mind you) they need the emotional loyalty of the men to provide for those children (Buss et al., 1992; Daly et al., 1982; Edlund et al., 2006). The results of the study support the prediction: Men find it harder to forgive a partner's sexual straying and are more likely to break up with the woman than if the infidelity is purely emotional; for women, the opposite results were found. Other research concerning mating has found that women seem to use a man's kissing ability to determine his worthiness as a potential mate (Hughes et al., 2007; Walter, 2008).

---

*Adaptive: having the quality of adjusting to the circumstances or need; in the sense used here, a behavior that aids in survival.

evolutionary perspective perspective that focuses on the biological bases of universal mental characteristics that all humans share.

That explains why people don't like bitter stuff, like the white part of an orange peel, but that's really a physical thing. How would the evolutionary perspective help us understand something psychological like relationships?

Psychologists with an evolutionary perspective would be interested in how this couple selected each other as partners.

psychologist a professional with an academic degree and specialized training in one or more areas of psychology.

psychiatrist a medical doctor who has specialized in the diagnosis and treatment of psychological disorders.

psychiatric social worker a social worker with some training in therapy methods who focuses on the environmental conditions that can have an impact on mental disorders, such as poverty, overcrowding, stress, and drug abuse.

Read and learn more about psychological professionals on MyPsychLab

You said not all psychologists do counseling. But I thought that was all that psychologists do—what else is there?

Psychological Professionals and Areas of Specialization

Psychology is a large field, and the many professionals working within it have different training and different focuses, and may have different goals from the typical psychologist.

1.5 How does a psychiatrist differ from a psychologist, and what are the other types of professionals who work in the various areas of psychology?

A **psychologist** has no medical training but has a doctorate degree. Psychologists undergo intense academic training, learning about many different areas of psychology before choosing a specialization. Because the focus of their careers can vary so widely, psychologists work in many different vocational* settings. Figure 1.2a shows the types of settings in which psychologists work. Remember, not all psychologists are trained to do counseling! Psychologists in the counseling specialization must also be licensed to practice in their states. ☐▶ Read on MyPsychLab

In contrast, a **psychiatrist** has a medical (M.D. or D.O.) degree and is a medical doctor who has specialized in the diagnosis and treatment (including the prescription of medications) of psychological disorders. A **psychiatric social worker** is trained in the area of social work and usually possesses a master's degree in that discipline. These professionals focus more on the environmental conditions that can have an impact on mental disorders, such as poverty, overcrowding, stress, and drug abuse.

Areas of Specialization

You said not all psychologists do counseling. But I thought that was all that psychologists do—what else is there?

Although many psychologists do participate in delivering therapy to people who need help, there is a nearly equal number of psychologists who do other tasks:

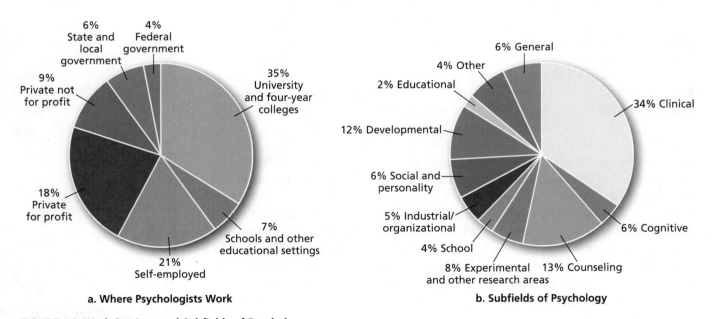

a. Where Psychologists Work

b. Subfields of Psychology

FIGURE 1.2 Work Settings and Subfields of Psychology
(a) There are many different work settings for psychologists. Although not obvious from the chart, many psychologists work in more than one setting. For example, a clinical psychologist may work in a hospital setting as well as teach at a university or college (Tsapogas et al., 2006).
(b) This pie chart shows the specialty areas of psychologists who recently received their doctorates (Hoffer et al., 2007).

*Vocational: having to do with a job or career.

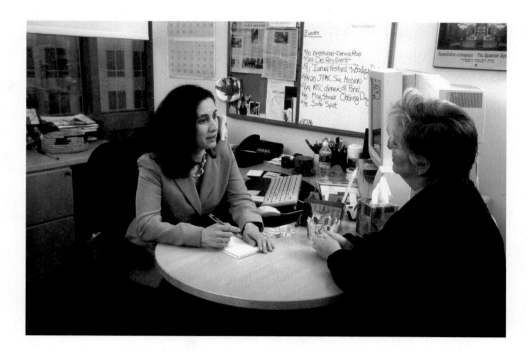

Psychiatric social workers help many kinds and ages of people. The woman on the right might be going through a divorce, dealing with the loss of a spouse, or even recovering from drug abuse.

researching, teaching, designing equipment and workplaces, and developing educational methods, for example. Also, not every psychologist is interested in the same area of human—or animal—behavior and most psychologists work in several different areas of interest, as shown in Figure 1.2b, Subfields of Psychology.

There are many other areas of specialization: Psychology can also be used in fields such as health, sports performance, legal issues, business concerns, and even in the design of equipment, tools, and furniture. For a more detailed look at some of these areas in which psychological principles can be applied and a listing of careers that can benefit from a degree in psychology, see **LINK** to Appendix B: Applied Psychology and Psychology Careers.

practice quiz   How much do you remember?

1.4   1.5

Pick the best answer.

1. Which of the following pairs represents the oldest of today's psychological perspectives?
   a. humanism and behaviorism
   b. behaviorism and psychodynamic
   c. psychodynamic and evolutionary psychology
   d. cognitive psychology and sociocultural psychology

2. Which perspective is known as the "third force" in psychology?
   a. psychoanalysis
   b. behaviorism
   c. cognitive psychology
   d. humanism

3. Wesley was behaving oddly and showing signs of memory problems and odd behavior. Doctors found that an earlier fall had created fluid pressure on his brain, causing the strange symptoms. Which of the following perspectives BEST explains Wesley's disordered behavior?
   a. psychodynamics
   b. cognitive psychology
   c. behaviorism
   d. biopsychology

4. Which perspective would a researcher be taking if she were studying the way children learn through reinforcement of their actions?
   a. psychoanalysis
   b. behaviorism
   c. cognitive psychology
   d. evolutionary perspective

5. Which of the following professionals in psychology focuses more on the environmental conditions that affect mental disorders?
   a. psychiatrist
   b. psychoanalyst
   c. psychiatric social worker
   d. psychologist

6. Dr. Roaden works in a school system, dealing directly with children who have emotional, academic, and behavioral problems. Dr. Roaden is most likely which type of psychologist?
   a. personality
   b. developmental
   c. school
   d. comparative

Brainstorming: Do you believe that violence is a part of human nature? Is violent behavior something that can someday be removed from human behavior or, at the very least, controlled? Think about this question from each of the perspectives discussed in this chapter.

ANSWERS ON PAGE AK–1

The scientific method can be used to determine if children who watch violence on television are more likely to be aggressive than those who do not.

Psychology: The Scientific Methodology

Why Psychologists Use the Scientific Method

Have you ever tried to guess what people do for a living based only on their appearance? People's guesses sometimes reveal the biases that they may have about certain physical appearances: Men with long hair are musicians, people wearing suits are executives, and so on.

1.6 Why is psychology considered a science, and what are the steps in using the scientific method?

In psychology, researchers want to see only what is really there, not what their biases might want them to see. The way to do that is by using the **scientific method**, a system for reducing bias and error in the measurement of data. The scientific method is a way to accomplish the goals of psychology as discussed earlier: description, explanation, prediction, and control.

The first step in any investigation is to have a question to investigate, right? So the first step in the scientific method is this:

1. **Perceiving the Question:** You notice something interesting happening in your surroundings for which you would like to have an explanation. An example might be that you've noticed that your children seem to get a little more aggressive with each other after watching a particularly violent children's cartoon program on Saturday morning. You wonder if the violence in the cartoon could be creating the aggressive behavior in your children. This step is derived from the goal of description: What is happening here?

   Once you have a question, you want an answer. The next logical step is to form a tentative* answer or explanation for the behavior you have seen. This tentative explanation is known as a **hypothesis**.

2. **Forming a Hypothesis:** Based on your initial observations about what's going on in your surroundings, you form an educated guess about the explanation for your observations, putting it into the form of a statement that can be tested in some way. Going back to the previous example, you might say, "Children who watch violent cartoons will become more aggressive." (Forming a hypothesis based on observations is related to the goals of *description* and *explanation*.)

   The next step is testing the hypothesis. People have a tendency to notice only things that agree with their view of the world, a kind of selective perception called *confirmation bias*. (L)(I)(N)(K) to Chapter Six: Consciousness and Cognition, p. 215. For example, if a person is convinced that all men with long hair smoke cigarettes, that person will tend to notice only those long-haired men who are smoking and ignore all the long-haired men who don't smoke. The scientific method is designed to overcome the tendency to look at only the information that confirms people's biases by forcing them to actively seek out information that might *contradict* their biases (or hypotheses). So when you test your hypothesis, you are trying to determine if the factor you suspect has an effect and that the results are not due to luck or chance. That's why psychologists keep doing research over and over—to get more evidence that hypotheses are "supported."

3. **Testing the Hypothesis:** The method you use to test your hypothesis will depend on exactly what kind of answer you think you might get. You might make more detailed observations or do a survey in which you ask questions of

scientific method system of gathering data so that bias and error in measurement are reduced.

hypothesis tentative explanation of a phenomenon based on observations.

---

*Tentative: something that is not fully worked out or completed as yet.

a large number of people, or you might design an experiment in which you would deliberately change one thing to see if it causes changes in the behavior you are observing. In the example, the best method would probably be an experiment in which you select a group of children, show half of them a cartoon with violence and half of them a cartoon with no violence, and then find some way of measuring aggressive behavior in the two groups.

What do you do with the results of your testing? Of course, testing the hypothesis is all about the goal of understanding behavior, which leads to the next step.

4. **Drawing Conclusions:** Once you know the results of your hypothesis testing, you will find that either your hypothesis was supported—which means that your little experiment worked, or your measurements supported your initial observations—or it wasn't supported, which means that you need to go back to square one and think of another possible explanation for what you have observed. (Could it be that Saturday mornings make children a little more aggressive? Or Saturday breakfasts?)

The results of any method of hypothesis testing won't be just the raw numbers or measurements. Any data that come from your testing procedure will be analyzed with some kind of statistical method that helps to organize and refine the data. ⓁⒾⓃⓀ to Appendix A: Statistics in Psychology. Drawing conclusions can be related to the goal of *prediction*: If your hypothesis is supported, you can make educated guesses about future, similar scenarios.

5. **Reporting Your Results:** You have come to some conclusion about your investigation's success or failure, and you want to let other researchers know what you have found.

Why tell anyone what happened if it failed? ●────

Just because one experiment or other study did not find support for the hypothesis does not necessarily mean that the hypothesis is incorrect. Your study might have been poorly designed, or there might have been factors not under your control that interfered with the study. But other researchers are asking the same kinds of questions that you might have asked. They need to know what has already been found out about the answers to those questions so that they can continue investigating and adding more knowledge about the answers to those questions. Even if your own investigation didn't go as planned, that tells other researchers what *not* to do in the future. So the final step in any scientific investigation is reporting the results.

At this point, you would want to write up exactly what you did, why you did it, how you did it, and what you found. If others can **replicate** your research (meaning, do exactly the same study over again and get the same results), it gives much more support to your findings. This allows others to predict behavior based on your findings and to use the results of those findings to modify or *control* behavior, the last goal in psychology.

This might be a good place to make a distinction between questions that can be scientifically or empirically studied and those that cannot. For example, "What is the meaning of life?" is not a question that can be studied using the scientific or empirical method. Empirical questions are those that can be tested through direct observation or experience. For example, "Has life ever existed on Mars?" is a question that scientists are trying to answer through measurements, experimentation, soil samples, and other methods. Eventually they will be able to say with some degree of confidence that life could have existed or could not have existed. That

Why tell anyone what happened if it failed?

replication in research repetition of a study or experiment to see if the same results will be obtained in an effort to demonstrate reliability of results.

is an empirical question because it can be supported or disproved by gathering real evidence. The meaning of life, however, is a question of belief for each person. One does not need proof to *believe*, but scientists need proof (in the form of objectively gathered evidence) to *know*.

In psychology, researchers try to find the answers to empirical questions. Questions that involve beliefs and values are best left to philosophy and religion.

Descriptive Methods

1.7 How are naturalistic and laboratory settings used to describe behavior, and what are some of the advantages and disadvantages associated with these settings?

There are a number of different ways to investigate the answers to research questions, and which one researchers use depends on the kind of question they want to answer. If they want to simply gather information about what has happened or what is happening, they would want a method that gives them a detailed description.

NATURALISTIC OBSERVATION   Sometimes all researchers need to know is what is happening to a group of animals or people. The best way to look at the behavior of animals or people is to watch them behave in their normal environment. That's why animal researchers go to where the animals live and watch them eat, play, mate, and sleep in their own natural surroundings. With people, researchers might want to observe them in their workplaces, homes, or on playgrounds. For example, if someone wanted to know how adolescents behave with members of the opposite sex in a social setting, that researcher might go to the mall on a weekend night.

What is the advantage of naturalistic observation? It allows researchers to get a realistic picture of how behavior occurs because they are actually watching that behavior. In a more artificial setting, like a laboratory, they might get behavior that is contrived or artificial rather than genuine. Of course, precautions must be taken. An observer should have a checklist of well-defined and specific behavior to record, perhaps using a special handheld computer to log each piece of data. In many cases, animals or people who know they are being watched will not behave normally anyway, in a process called the **observer effect**, so often the observer needs to remain hidden from view. When researching humans, this is often a difficult thing to do.

In the mall setting with the teenagers, a researcher might find that pretending to read a book is a good disguise, especially if one wears glasses to hide the movement of the eyes. Then the researchers would be able to look up at what goes on between the teens without them knowing that they were being watched. In other cases, researchers might use one-way mirrors, or they might actually become participants in a group, a technique called **participant observation**.

Are there disadvantages? Unfortunately, yes. One of the disadvantages of naturalistic observation is the possibility of **observer bias**. That happens when the person doing the observing has a particular opinion about what he or she is going to see or expects to see. If that is the case, sometimes that person sees only those actions that support that expectation and ignores actions that don't fit. One way to avoid observer bias is to use *blind observers*: people who do not know what the research question is and, therefore, have no preconceived notions about what they "should" see. It's also

This researcher is studying the behavior of a group of lemurs. Is this naturalistic observation? Why or why not?

observer effect   tendency of people or animals to behave differently from normal when they know they are being observed.

participant observation   a naturalistic observation in which the observer becomes a participant in the group being observed.

observer bias   tendency of observers to see what they expect to see.

a good idea to have more than one observer, so that the various observations can be compared.

Another disadvantage is that each naturalistic setting is unique and unlike any other. Observations that are made at one time in one setting may not hold true for another time, even if the setting is similar, because the conditions are not going to be exactly the same time after time—researchers don't have that kind of control over the natural world. For example, famed gorilla researcher Diane Fossey had to battle poachers who set traps for the animals in the area of her observations (Mowat, 1988). The presence and activities of the poachers affected the normal behavior of the gorillas she was trying to observe.

LABORATORY OBSERVATION Sometimes observing behavior in animals or people is simply not practical in a natural setting. For example, a researcher might want to observe the reactions of infants to a mirror image of themselves and record the reactions with a camera mounted behind the one-way mirror. That kind of equipment might be difficult to set up in a natural setting. In a laboratory observation, the researcher would bring the infant to the equipment, controlling the number of infants and their ages as well as everything else that goes on in the laboratory.

As mentioned previously, laboratory settings have the disadvantage of being an artificial situation that might result in artificial behavior—both animals and people often react differently in the laboratory than they would in the real world. The main advantage of this method is the degree of control that it gives to the observer.

Both naturalistic and laboratory observations can lead to the formation of hypotheses that can later be tested.

1.8 How are case studies and surveys used to describe behavior, and what are some drawbacks to each of these methods?

CASE STUDIES Another descriptive technique is called the **case study**, in which one individual is studied in great detail. In a case study, researchers try to learn everything they can about that individual. For example, Sigmund Freud based his entire theory of psychoanalysis on numerous case studies of his patients in which he gathered information about their childhoods and relationships with others from the very beginning of their lives to the present. (L I N K) to Chapter Eleven: Theories of Personality and Intelligence, pp. 386–389.

The advantage of the case study is the tremendous amount of detail it provides. It may also be the only way to get certain kinds of information. One famous case study is that of Phineas Gage, who had a large metal rod driven through his head and suffered a major personality change as a result (Damasio et al., 1994). Researchers couldn't study such a case with naturalistic observation, and of course an experiment is out of the question—you wouldn't get many volunteers for brain damage. Case studies are also good ways to study rare conditions such as multiple personality (now called *dissociative identity disorder*).

The disadvantage of the case study is that researchers can't really apply the results to other similar people. In other words, they can't assume that a person having the same kind of experiences as the person in their case study would turn out just like the subject of the case study. People are unique and have too many complicating factors in their lives to be that predictable. So what researchers find in one case won't necessarily apply or generalize to other cases. Another weakness of this method is that

The researcher in the foreground is watching the children through a one-way mirror to get a description of their behavior. Observations such as these are just one of many ways that psychologists have of investigating behavior. Why is it important for the researcher to be behind a one-way mirror?

After a gunpowder explosion, Phineas Gage ended up with a steel rod in his head. A model of Gage's head is shown next to his actual skull. Visible above the left side of his mouth is the entry point of the steel rod, and the exit point is at the top of the skull.

case study study of one individual in great detail.

case studies are a form of detailed observation and are vulnerable to bias on the part of the person conducting the case study, just as observer bias can occur in naturalistic or laboratory observation.

SURVEYS Sometimes psychologists want to know very personal things—such as what people do in their sexual relationships, for example. The only way to find out about very private (covert) behavior is to ask questions.

In the survey method, researchers will ask a series of questions about the topic they are studying. Surveys can be conducted in person in the form of interviews or on the telephone, the Internet, or with a questionnaire. The questions in interviews or on the telephone can vary, but usually the questions in a survey are all the same for everyone answering the survey. In this way, researchers can ask lots of questions and survey literally hundreds of people.

That is the big advantage of surveys, aside from their ability to elicit private information. Researchers can obtain a tremendous amount of data on a very large group of people. Of course, there are disadvantages. For one thing researchers have to be very careful about the group of people they survey. If they want to find out what college freshmen think about politics, for example, they can't really ask every single college freshman in the entire United States. But they can select a **representative sample** from that group. They can randomly* select a certain number of college freshmen from several different colleges across the United States, for example. Why randomly? Because the sample has to be *representative* of the **population**, which is the entire group in which the researcher is interested. If researchers selected only freshmen from Ivy League schools, for example, they would certainly get different opinions on politics than they might get from small community colleges. But if they take a lot of colleges and select their *participants* (people who are part of the study) randomly, they will be more certain of getting answers that a broad selection of college students would typically give.

That brings up the other major disadvantage of the survey technique: People don't always give researchers accurate answers. People tend to misremember things, distort the truth, and may lie outright—even if the survey is an anonymous** questionnaire. Remembering is not always a very accurate process, especially when people think that an honest answer might make them come off sounding undesirable or socially inappropriate. Other people deliberately give what they think is the more socially correct answer rather than their true opinion in order not to offend anyone; this process is called *courtesy bias*. Researchers must therefore take their survey results with a big grain of salt.[†]

Both the wording of survey questions and the order in which they appear on the survey can affect the outcome. It is difficult to word questions so that everyone who reads them will understand them in exactly the same way . For example, questions can be phrased in such a way that the desired answer becomes obvious (often resulting in courtesy bias–type answers), or a question that appears at the end of a survey might be answered quite differently than if it had appeared at the beginning.

"Next question: I believe that life is a constant striving for balance, requiring frequent trade-offs between morality and necessity, within a cyclic pattern of joy and sadness, forging a trail of bittersweet memories until one slips, inevitably, into the jaws of death. Agree or disagree?"

representative sample randomly selected sample of subjects from a larger population of subjects.

population the entire group of people or animals in which the researcher is interested.

---

*Randomly: in this sense, selected so that each member of the group has an equal chance of being chosen.

**Anonymous: not named or identified.

†Big grain of salt: a phrase meaning to be skeptical; to doubt the truth or accuracy of something.

practice quiz   How much do you remember?

1.6 **1.7** **1.8**

Pick the best answer.

1. In the scientific method, the first step is _____.
   a. reporting your results.
   b. perceiving a question.
   c. drawing conclusions.
   d. testing the hypothesis.

2. In a naturalistic observation, the phenomenon in which the behavior of the subjects being observed changes because they are being watched is called _____.
   a. observer bias.
   b. participant observation.
   c. observer effect.
   d. representative sampling.

3. The use of _____ helps to control for the effect of observer bias.
   a. blind observers
   b. a single trained observer
   c. randomly selected observers
   d. none of the above

4. The main disadvantage of a case study is that it is not _____.
   a. easily done due to the large number of subjects.
   b. detailed enough for most research questions.
   c. generalizable to other similar conditions.
   d. biased.

5. Which of the following is the BEST example of a representative sample?
   a. You ask your fellow students to be participants in a study of adult memory.
   b. You ask people from your church to participate in a study of family values.
   c. You choose people shopping in an expensive store in the mall to respond to your survey.
   d. You choose people randomly from the telephone book to respond to your survey.

Brainstorming: Let's assume that you want to find out if telepathy really exists. Would any of the descriptive methods for studying behavior be a good method to use in examining this question? Why or why not?

ANSWERS ON PAGE AK–1

Finding Relationships

The methods discussed so far only provide descriptions of behavior. Actually, only two methods give researchers more than just a description of what has happened: correlations and experiments. Correlation is a statistical technique, a particular way of organizing numerical information so that it is easier to look for patterns in the information. This method will be discussed here rather than in the statistics appendix found at the back of this text because correlation, like the experiment, is about finding relationships. In fact, the data from the descriptive methods just discussed are often analyzed using the correlational technique.

1.9 What is the correlational technique, and what does it tell researchers about relationships?

CORRELATIONS   A **correlation** is a measure of the relationship between two or more variables. A *variable* is anything that can change or vary—scores on a test, temperature in a room, gender, and so on. For example, researchers might be curious to know whether or not cigarette smoking is connected to life expectancy—the number of years a person can be expected to live. Obviously, the scientists can't hang around people who smoke and wait to see when those people die. The only way (short of performing a really unethical and lengthy experiment) to find out if smoking behavior and life expectancy are related to each other is to use the medical records of people who have already died. (For privacy's sake, personal information such as names and social security numbers would be removed, with only facts such as age, gender, and weight available to researchers.) Researchers would look for two facts from each record: the number of cigarettes the person smoked per day and the age of the person at death.

Now the researcher has two sets of numbers for each person in the study that go into a mathematical formula, ⓛⓘⓝⓚ to Appendix A: Statistics in Psychology, pp. A-10–A-12, to produce a number called the **correlation coefficient**. The correlation coefficient represents two things: the direction of the relationship and its strength.

correlation   a measure of the relationship between two variables.

correlation coefficient   a number derived from the formula for measuring a correlation and indicating the strength and direction of a correlation.

Direction? How can a mathematical relationship have a direction?

● Direction? How can a mathematical relationship have a direction?

Whenever researchers talk about two variables being related to each other, what they really mean is that knowing the value of one variable allows them to predict the value of the other variable. For example, if researchers find that smoking and life expectancy are indeed related, they should be able to predict how long someone might live if they know how many cigarettes a person smokes in a day. But which way does that prediction work? If a person smokes a lot of cigarettes, does that mean that he or she will live a longer life or a shorter one? Does life expectancy go up or down as smoking increases? That's what is meant by the *direction* of the relationship.

In terms of the correlation coefficient (represented by the small letter *r*), the number researchers get from the formula will either be a positive number or a negative number. If positive, the two variables increase in the same direction—as one goes up, the other goes up; as one decreases, the other also decreases. If negative, the two variables have an inverse* relationship. As one increases, the other decreases. If researchers find that the more cigarettes a person smoked, the younger that person was when he or she died, that would mean that the correlation between the two variables is negative. (As smoking goes up, life expectancy goes down—an inverse relationship.)

The strength of the relationship between the variables will be determined by the actual number itself. That number will always range between +1.00 and −1.00. The reason that it cannot be greater than +1.00 or less than −1.00 has to do with the formula and an imaginary line on a graph around which the data points gather, a graph called a scatterplot (see Figure 1.3). If the relationship is a strong one, the number will be closer to +1.00 or to −1.00. A correlation of +.89, for example, would be a very strong, positive correlation. That might represent the relationship between scores on the SAT and an IQ test, for example. A correlation of −.89 would be equally strong but negative. That would be more like the correlation researchers would probably find between smoking cigarettes and the age at which a person dies.

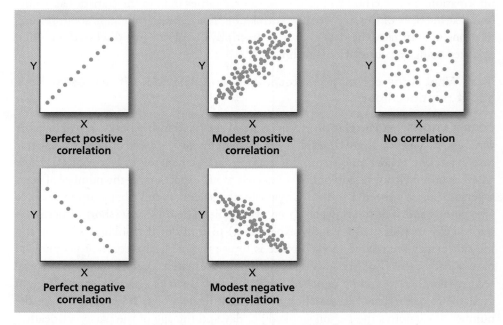

FIGURE 1.3 These scatterplots show direction and strength of correlation.
It should be noted that perfect correlations, whether positive or negative, rarely occur in the real world.

*Inverse: opposite in order.

Notice that the closer the number is to zero, the weaker the relationship becomes. Researchers would probably find that the correlation coefficient for the relationship between people's weight and the number of freckles they have is pretty close to zero, for example.

Go back to the cigarette example—if we found that the correlation between cigarette smoking and life expectancy was high, does that mean that smoking causes your life expectancy to be shortened?

Go back to the cigarette example—if we found that the correlation between cigarette smoking and life expectancy was high, does that mean that smoking causes your life expectancy to be shortened?

Not exactly. The biggest error that people make concerning correlation is to assume that it means one variable is the cause of the other. Remember that *correlation does not prove causation*. Although adverse health effects from cigarette smoking account for approximately 438,000 deaths each year in the United States alone, correlation by itself cannot be used to prove causation (Centers for Disease Control and Prevention, 2009b). Just because two variables are related to each other, researchers cannot assume that one of them causes the other one to occur. Both variables could be related to some other variable that is the cause of both. For example, cigarette smoking and life expectancy might be linked only because people who smoke may be less likely to take care of their health by eating right and exercising, whereas people who don't smoke may tend to eat healthier foods and exercise more than smokers do.

To sum up, a correlation will tell researchers whether there is a relationship between the variables, how strong the relationship is, and in what direction the relationship goes. If researchers know the value of one variable, they can predict the value of the other. If they know someone's IQ score, for example, they can predict what score that person should get on the SAT—not the exact score, just a reasonable estimate. Also, even though correlation does not prove causation, it can provide a starting point for examining causal relationships with another type of study, the experiment.

THE EXPERIMENT The only research method that will allow researchers to determine the cause of a behavior is the **experiment**. In an experiment, researchers deliberately manipulate (change in some purposeful way) the variable they think is causing some behavior while holding all the other variables that might interfere with the experiment's results constant and unchanging. That way, if they get changes in behavior (an effect, in other words), they know that those changes must be due to the manipulated variable. Remember the discussion of the steps in the scientific method? It focused on how to study the effects of watching violent cartoons on children's aggressive behavior. The most logical way to study that particular relationship is by an experiment.

First, researchers might start by selecting the children they want to use in the experiment. The best method to do that would be to make a random selection of a sample of children from a certain population as determined by the researchers—just as a sample would be selected for a survey. Ideally, researchers would decide on the age of child they wanted to study—say, children who are 3 to 4 years old. Then researchers would go to various day care centers and randomly select a certain number of children of that age. Of course, that wouldn't include the children who don't go to a day care center. Another way to get a sample in this age range might be to ask several pediatricians to send out letters to parents of children of that age and then randomly select the sample from those children whose parents responded positively.

experiment a deliberate manipulation of a variable to see if corresponding changes in behavior result, allowing the determination of cause-and-effect relationships.

The act of hitting each other with toy swords could be part of an operational definition of aggressive behavior.

operational definition definition of a variable of interest that allows it to be directly measured.

independent variable variable in an experiment that is manipulated by the experimenter.

dependent variable variable in an experiment that represents the measurable response or behavior of the subjects in the experiment.

Simulate to distinguish independent and dependent variables on **MyPsychLab**

If researchers do all of this and find that the children's behavior is aggressive, can they say that the aggressive behavior was caused by the violence in the cartoon?

1.10 How are operational definitions, independent and dependent variables, experimental and control groups, and random assignment used in designing an experiment?

The Variables Another important step is to decide on the variable the researchers want to manipulate (which would be the one they think causes changes in behavior) and the variable they want to measure to see if there are any changes (this would be the effect on behavior of the manipulation). Often the decision on the variables in the experiment comes before selection of the participants or subjects.

In the example of aggression and children's cartoons, the variable that researchers think causes changes in aggressive behavior is the violence in the cartoons. Researchers would want to manipulate that variable in some way, and in order to do that they have to define the term *violent cartoon*. They would have to find or create a cartoon that contains violence. Then they would show that cartoon to the participants and try to measure their aggressive behavior afterward. In measuring the aggressive behavior, the researchers would have to define exactly what they mean by "aggressive behavior" so that it can be measured. This definition is called an **operational definition** because it specifically names the operations (steps or procedures) that the experimenter must use to control or measure the variables in the experiment. An operational definition of aggressive behavior might be a checklist of very specific actions such as hitting and pushing that an observer can mark off as the children do the items on the list. If the observers were just told to look for "aggressive behavior," the researchers would probably get half a dozen or more different interpretations of what aggressive behavior is.

The name for the variable that is manipulated in any experiment is the **independent variable** because it is *independent* of anything the participants do. The participants in the study do not get to choose or vary the independent variable, and their behavior does not affect this variable at all. In the preceding example, the independent variable would be the presence or absence of violence in the cartoons.

The participants' response to the manipulation of the independent variable *is* a dependent relationship, so the response of the participants that is measured is known as the **dependent variable**. Their behavior, if the hypothesis is correct, should *depend* on whether or not they were exposed to the independent variable, and in the example, the dependent variable would be the measure of aggressive behavior in the children. The dependent variable is always the thing (response of subjects or result of some action) that is measured to see just how the independent variable may have affected it.

Simulate on **MyPsychLab**

The Groups

If researchers do all of this and find that the children's behavior is aggressive, can they say that the aggressive behavior was caused by the violence in the cartoon?

No, what has been described so far is not enough. The researchers may find that the children who watch the violent cartoon are aggressive, but how would they know if their aggressive behavior was caused by the cartoon or was just the natural aggressive level of those particular children or the result of the particular time of day they were observed? Those sorts of *confounding variables* (variables that interfere with each other and their possible effects on some other variable of interest) are the kind researchers have to control for in some way. For example, if most children in this experiment just happened to be from a fairly aggressive family background, any effects the violent cartoon in the experiment might have had on the children's behavior could be confused (confounded) with the possible effects of the family background. The researchers wouldn't know if the children were being aggressive because they watched the cartoon or because they liked to play aggressively anyway.

The best way to control for confounding variables is to have two groups of participants: those who watch the violent cartoon, and those who watch a nonviolent cartoon for the same length of time. Then the researchers would measure the aggressive behavior in both groups. If the aggressive behavior is significantly greater in the group that watched the violent cartoon (statistically speaking), then researchers can say that in this experiment, violent cartoon watching caused greater aggressive behavior.

The group that is exposed to the independent variable (the violent cartoon in the example) is called the **experimental group**, because it is the group that receives the experimental manipulation. The other group that gets either no treatment or some kind of treatment that should have no effect (like the group that watches the nonviolent cartoon in the example) is called the **control group** because it is used to *control* for the possibility that other factors might be causing the effect that is being examined. If researchers were to find that the group that watched the violent cartoon and the group that watched the noviolent cartoon were equally aggressive, they would have to assume that the violent content did not influence their behavior at all.

The Importance of Randomization   As mentioned previously, random selection is the best way to choose the participants for any study. Participants must then be assigned to either the experimental group or the control group. Not surprisingly, **random assignment** of participants to one or the other condition is the best way to ensure control over other interfering, or *extraneous*, variables. Random assignment means that each participant has an equal chance of being assigned to each condition. If researchers simply looked at the children and put all of the children from one day care center or one pediatrician's recommendations into the experimental group and the same for the control group, they would run the risk of biasing their research. Some day care centers may have more naturally aggressive children, for example, or some pediatricians may have a particular client base in which the children are very passive. So researchers want to take the entire participant group and assign each person randomly to one or the other of the groups in the study. Sometimes this process is as simple as picking names out of a hat.

1.11 How do the placebo and experimenter effects cause problems in an experiment, and how can single-blind and double-blind studies control for these effects?

Experimental Hazards: The Placebo Effect and the Experimenter Effect   A few other problems might arise in any experiment, even with the use of control groups and random assignment. These problems are especially likely when studying people instead of animals, because people are often influenced by their own thoughts or biases about what's going on in an experiment. Let's say there is a new drug that is supposed to improve memory in people who are in the very early stages of *Alzheimer's disease* (a form of mental deterioration that occurs in some people as they grow old). (LINK) to Chapter Five: Memory, pp. 190–191. Researchers wanting to test the drug to see if it really is effective in helping to improve memory would get a sample of people who are in the early stages of the disease, divide them into two groups, give one group the drug, and then test for improvement. They would probably have to do a test of memory both before and after the administration of the drug to be able to measure improvement.

Let me see if I've got this straight. The group that gets the drug would be the experimental group, and the one that doesn't is the control group, right?

Right, and getting or not getting the drug is the independent variable, whereas the measure of memory improvement is the dependent variable. But there's still a problem with doing it this way. What if the researchers do find that the drug group had greater memory improvement than the group that received nothing? Can they

experimental group   subjects in an experiment who are subjected to the independent variable.

control group   subjects in an experiment who are not subjected to the independent variable and who may receive a placebo treatment.

random assignment   process of assigning subjects to the experimental or control group randomly, so that each subject has an equal chance of being in either group.

Let me see if I've got this straight. The group that gets the drug would be the experimental group, and the one that doesn't is the control group, right?

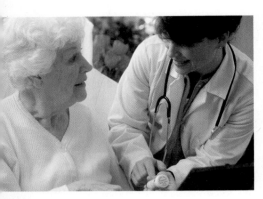

This elderly woman has Alzheimer's disease, which causes a severe loss of recent memory. If she were given a drug to improve her memory, the researcher could not be certain that any improvement shown was caused by the drug rather than by the elderly woman's belief that the drug would work. The expectations of any person in an experimental study can affect the outcome of the study, a phenomenon known as the placebo effect.

placebo effect　the phenomenon in which the expectations of the participants in a study can influence their behavior.

experimenter effect　tendency of the experimenter's expectations for a study to unintentionally influence the results of the study.

single-blind study　study in which the subjects do not know if they are in the experimental or the control group.

double-blind study　study in which neither the experimenter nor the subjects know if the subjects are in the experimental or control group.

really say that the drug itself caused the improvement? Or is it possible that the participants who received the drug *knew* that they were supposed to improve in memory and, therefore, made a major effort to do so? The improvement may have had more to do with participants' *belief* in the drug than the drug itself, a phenomenon* known as the **placebo effect**: The expectations and biases of the participants in a study can influence their behavior. In medical research, the control group is often given a harmless substitute for the real drug, such as a sugar pill or an injection of salt water, and this substitute (which has no medical effect) is called the *placebo*. If there is a placebo effect, the control group will show changes in the dependent variable even though the participants in that group received only a placebo.

Another way that expectations about the outcome of the experiment can influence the results, even when the participants are animals rather than people, is called the **experimenter effect**. It has to do with the expectations of the experimenter, not the participants. As discussed earlier in the section about naturalistic observations, sometimes observers are biased—they see what they expect to see. Observer bias can also happen in an experiment. When the researcher is measuring the dependent variable, it's possible that he or she could give the participants clues about how they are supposed to respond—with body language, tone of voice, or even eye contact. Although not deliberate, it does happen. It could go something like this in the example: You, the Alzheimer's patient, are in the experimenter's office to take your second memory test after trying the drug. The experimenter seems to pay a lot of attention to you and to every answer that you give in the test, so you get the feeling that you are supposed to have improved a lot. So you try harder, and any improvement you show may be caused only by your own increased effort, not by the drug. That's the experimenter effect: The behavior of the experimenter caused the participant to change his or her response pattern.

SINGLE-BLIND AND DOUBLE-BLIND STUDIES　Fortunately, there are ways to control for these effects. The classic way to control for the placebo effect is to give the control group an actual placebo—some kind of treatment that doesn't affect behavior at all. In the drug experiment, the placebo would have to be some kind of pill or solution that looks like and is administered just like the actual drug. The participants in both the experimental and the control groups would not know whether they got the real drug or the placebo. That way, if their expectations have any effect at all on the outcome of the experiment, the experimenter will be able to tell by looking at the results for the control group and comparing them to the results of the experimental group. Even if the control group improves a little, the drug group should improve significantly more if the drug is working. This is called a **single-blind study** because the participants are "blind" to the treatment they receive.

For a long time, that was the only type of experiment researchers did in psychology. But researchers Robert Rosenthal and Lenore Jacobson reported in their 1968 book, *Pygmalion in the Classroom*, that when teachers were told that some students had a high potential for success and others a low potential, the students showed significant gains or decreases in their performance on standardized tests depending on which "potential" they were supposed to have (Rosenthal & Jacobson, 1968). Actually, the students had been selected randomly and randomly assigned to one of the two groups, "high" or "low." Their performances on the tests were affected by the attitudes of the teachers concerning their potential. This study and similar studies after it highlighted the need to have the experimenter as well as the participants in research be "blind." So in a **double-blind study** neither the participants nor the person or persons measuring the dependent variable know who got what. That's why everything in a double-blind

*Phenomenon: an observable fact or event.

experiment gets coded in some way, so that only after all the measurements have been taken can anyone determine who was in the experimental group and who was in the control group.

For a good example of a typical experiment, read the following section about stereotypes, athletes, and test grades.

issues in **psychology**

Stereotypes, Athletes, and College Test Performance

1.12 What are the basic elements of a real-world experiment?

It seems that many people have a negative stereotype of college athletes—that they are graded and promoted on the basis of their ability on the athletic field and not on the basis of classroom performance. Evidence does exist that athletes turn in a poorer performance on academic tests in college than nonathletes (National Collegiate Athletic Association, 2002; Purdy et al., 1982; Upthegrove et al., 1999). If you are an athlete, can that negative stereotype actually have a negative impact on your test performance? Wesleyan University researchers Matthew Jameson, Robert Diehl, and Henry Danso have some evidence that such stereotypes can have just that kind of negative impact (Jameson et al., 2007).

In their experiment, 72 male college athletes from the sports teams of the university were given an intellectual test. Half of the athletes answered a brief questionnaire before taking the test, whereas the other half received the same questionnaire after taking the test. The questionnaire asked three questions, with the third question being, "Rate your likelihood of being accepted to the university without the aid of athletic recruiting." This item was designed to bring the negative stereotype of athletes ("dumb jocks") to the forefront of students' minds, creating a "high threat" for that stereotype. This difference in threat level between the two groups before taking the intellectual test represents the *independent variable* in this experiment.

Could knowing that other people might think your success in school is due to your athletic ability and not to your intelligence make you perform poorly on an academic test?

The results? Those students who answered the "high-threat" question *before* the intellectual test (the *experimental* group) scored significantly lower on that test (the measurement of the *dependent* variable) than those who answered the question *after* the test (the *control* group). The researchers also found a correlation between the students' exposure to the "high-threat" stereotype condition and accuracy on the intellectual test: The more students believed that they got into college primarily because of their ability in sports (based on their rating of that third question), the worse they performed on the subsequent test. Jameson and colleagues concluded that obvious negative stereotypes in higher education may be an important cause underlying the tendency of college athletes to underperform in academics.

QUESTIONS FOR FURTHER DISCUSSION

1. In this experiment, what might be some extraneous variables affecting the students' test performance?

2. What might educators do to try to prevent the effect of the "dumb jock" negative stereotype on college athletes?

Ethics of Psychological Research

The study that Dr. Watson did with "Little Albert" and the white rat seems pretty cruel when you think about it. Do researchers today do that kind of study?

Actually, as psychology began to grow and more research with people was being done, psychologists began to realize that some protections had to be put in place. No one wanted to be thought of as a "mad scientist," and if studies were permitted that could actually harm people, the field of psychology might die out pretty quickly. LINK to Chapter Four: Learning, p. 128; Chapter Ten: Social Psychology, pp. 350–353. Scientists in other areas of research were also realizing that ethical treatment of the participants in studies had to be ensured in some way. Ethical treatment, of course, means that people who volunteer for a study will be able to expect that no physical or psychological harm should come to them.

1.13 **What are some ethical concerns that can occur when conducting research with people and animals?**

Universities and colleges (where most psychological research is carried out) usually have *institutional review boards*, groups of psychologists or other professionals who look over each proposed research study and judge it according to its safety and consideration for the participants in the study. These review boards look at all aspects of the proposed research, from the written materials that explain the research to the potential subjects to the equipment that may be used in the study itself.

The Guidelines for Doing Research with People

Quite a few ethical concerns arise when dealing with human subjects in an experiment or other type of study. Here is a list of the most common ethical guidelines:

1. **Rights and well-being of participants must be weighed against the study's value to science.** In other words, people come first, research second.

2. **Participants must be allowed to make an informed decision about participation.** This means that researchers have to explain the study to the people they want to include before they do anything to them or with them—even children—and it has to be in terms that the participants can understand. If researchers are using infants or children, their parents have to be informed and give their consent. This is known as *informed consent*. Even in single- or

"He says he wants a lawyer."

double-blind studies, it is necessary to tell the participants that they may be members of either the experimental or the control group—they just won't find out which group they were actually in until after the experiment is concluded.

3. **Deception must be justified.** In some cases, it is necessary to deceive the participants because the study wouldn't work any other way. However, the participants have to be told after the study exactly why the deception was important. This is called *debriefing*.

4. **Participants may withdraw from the study at any time.** The participants must be allowed to drop out for any reason. For example, sometimes people get bored with the study, decide they don't have the time, or don't like what they have to do. Children participating in studies often decide to stop "playing" (play is a common part of studies of children). Researchers have to let them go, even if it means having to get more participants.

5. **Participants must be protected from risks or told explicitly of risks.** For example, if researchers are using any kind of electrical equipment, care must be taken to ensure that no participant will experience a physical shock from faulty electrical equipment.

6. **Investigators must debrief participants, telling the true nature of the study and expectations of results.** This is important in all types of studies but particularly in those involving a deception.

7. **Data must remain confidential.** Freud recognized the importance of confidentiality, referring to his patients in his books and articles with false names. Likewise, psychologists and other researchers today tend to report only group results rather than results for a single individual, so that no one could possibly be recognized.

8. **If for any reason a study results in undesirable consequences for the participant, the researcher is responsible for detecting and removing, or correcting, these consequences.** Sometimes people react in unexpected ways to the manipulations in an experiment, despite the researcher's best efforts to prevent any negative impact on participants. If this happens, the researcher must find some way of helping the participant overcome that impact (American Psychological Association, 2002).

Psychologists also study animals to find out about behavior, often drawing comparisons between what the animals do and what people might do under similar conditions.

But why not just study people in the first place? ●

Some research questions are extremely important but difficult or impossible to answer by using human participants. Animals live shorter lives, so looking at long-term effects becomes much easier. Animals are also easier to control—the scientist can control diet, living arrangements, and even genetic relatedness. The white laboratory rat has become a recognized species different from ordinary rats, bred with its own kind for many decades until each white rat is essentially a little genetic "twin" of all the others. Animals also engage in much simpler behavior than humans do, making it easier to see the effects of manipulations. But the biggest reason that researchers use animals in some research is that animals can be used in ways that researchers could never use people. For example, it took a long time for scientists to prove that the tars and other harmful substances in tobacco cause cancer because they had to do correlational studies with people and experiments only with animals. There's the catch—researchers can do many things to animals that they can't do to people. That might seem cruel at first, but when you think that without animal research there would be

But why not just study people in the first place?

no vaccines for deadly diseases, no insulin treatments for diabetics, no transplants, and so on, then the value of the research and its benefits to humankind far outweigh the hazards to which the research animals are exposed.

There are also ethical considerations when dealing with animals in research, just as there are with humans. With animals, though, the focus is on avoiding exposing them to any *unnecessary* pain or suffering. So if surgery is part of the study, it is done under anesthesia. If the research animal must die in order for the effects of some drug or other treatment to be examined in necropsy (autopsy performed on an animal), the death must be accomplished humanely. Animals are used in only about 7 percent of all psychological studies (Committee on Animal Research and Ethics, 2004).

practice quiz   How much do you remember?

1.9 1.10 1.11

Pick the best answer.

1. It's common knowledge that the more you study, the higher your grade will be. What kind of correlation is this relationship?
   a. positive
   b. negative
   c. zero
   d. causal

2. Which of the following would indicate the strongest relationship between two variables?
   a. +1.04
   b. −0.89
   c. +0.75
   d. +0.54

3. In an experiment to test the effects of alcohol on memory, the experimenter gives vodka mixed in orange juice to one group of subjects and orange juice with no vodka to the other group. She then measures the memory skills of both groups by means of a memory test. In this study, the independent variable would be _____.
   a. scores on the memory test.
   b. the presence or absence of vodka in the orange juice.
   c. intelligence.
   d. a placebo.

4. In that same experiment, the control group is the one that gets _____.
   a. only one drink of orange juice with vodka.
   b. a fake test of memory.
   c. only something to eat.
   d. the orange juice without vodka.

5. In a _____ study, neither the experimenter nor the participants know who is in the control group and who is in the experimental group.
   a. placebo
   b. single-blind
   c. double-blind
   d. triple-blind

6. In the "dumb jock" stereotype threat experiment, what was the dependent variable?
   a. the degree of stereotype threat
   b. the testing room
   c. the scores on the intellectual test
   d. the intelligence level of the athletes

7. Which of the following is NOT one of the common ethical rules?
   a. Participants have to give informed consent.
   b. Deception cannot be used in any studies with human beings.
   c. The rights and well-being of the participants must come first.
   d. Data must remain confidential.

8. We use animals in research because _____.
   a. animals have simple behavior that makes it easy to see changes.
   b. animals don't live as long as humans and are easier to control.
   c. we can do things to animals that we can't do to people.
   d. all of the above are true.

ANSWERS ON PAGE AK–1

applying psychology to everyday life
Thinking Critically about Critical Thinking

What good is all this focus on science and research going to do for me? I live in the real world, not a laboratory.

What good is all this focus on science and research going to do for me? I live in the real world, not a laboratory.

The real world is full of opportunities for scientific thinking. Think about all the commercials on television for miracle weight loss, hair restoration, or herbal remedies for arthritis, depression, and a whole host of physical and mental problems. Wouldn't it be nice to know how many of these claims people should believe? Wouldn't you like to know how to evaluate statements like these and possibly save yourself some time, effort, and money? That's exactly the kind of "real-world" problem critical thinking can help sort out.

The Criteria for Critical Thinking

1.14 What are the basic principles of critical thinking, and how can critical thinking be useful in everyday life?

critical thinking making reasoned judgments about claims.

According to Beyer (1995), **critical thinking** means making reasoned judgments. The word *reasoned* means that people's judgments should be logical and well thought out. Critical thinking also includes the ability to ask and seek answers for critical questions at the right time (Browne & Keeley, 2009). (A relevant example of a critical question might be, "Is someone paying you to do this research, and is this a conflict of interest?" or "Do you have any good evidence for your assertions, or are you just giving your opinion?")

While the word *critical* is often viewed as meaning "negative," that is not the use of this term here. Instead, it's more related to the word *criteria,** as in thinking that meets certain high criteria or standards (Nosich, 2008). People should remember four basic criteria for critical thinking when they are faced with statements about the world around them (Browne & Keeley, 2009; Gill, 1991; Shore, 1990):

1. **There are very few "truths" that do not need to be subjected to testing.** Although people may accept religious beliefs and personal values on faith, everything else in life needs to have supporting evidence. Questions that can be investigated empirically should be examined using established scientific methods. One shouldn't accept anything at face value but should always ask, "How do you know that? What is the evidence? Can you be more specific in your terms?" (These are more examples of those important questions to ask when thinking critically.) For example, many people still believe that astrology, the study of the supposed influence of the stars and planets on the birth of an infant, can be used to make predictions about that infant's personality and life events as he or she grows. But scientific investigations have shown us, time after time, that astrology is without any basis in truth or scientific fact (Ben-Shakhar et al., 1986; Bunge, 1984; Dean et al., 1992; Dean & Kelly, 2000; Hines, 2003; Kelly, 1980; Wiseman, 2007).

2. **All evidence is not equal in quality.** One of the most important, often overlooked steps in critical thinking is evaluating how evidence is gathered before deciding that it provides good support for some idea. For example, there are poorly done experiments, incorrect assumptions based on correlations rather than experiments, studies that cannot be replicated, and studies in which there is either no control group or no attempt made to control for placebo effects or experimenter effects. There are also studies that have been deliberately manipulated to produce the findings that the researcher (or whoever is paying the researcher) would prefer—sad but oh, so true, some people are more motivated by money than by the search for the truth. As a critical thinker you should be aware that the wilder the claim, the better the evidence should be: for example, I have not yet seen any evidence that convinces me of alien visitations or abductions!

3. **Just because someone is considered to be an authority or to have a lot of expertise does not make everything that person claims automatically true.** One should always ask to see the evidence rather than just take some expert's word for anything. How good is the evidence? Are there other alternative explanations? Is the alternative explanation simpler? If there are two explanations for some phenomenon and both account for the phenomenon equally well, the *simplest* explanation is *more often* the best one—a rule of thumb known as *the law of parsimony*.) For example, let's look at crop circles, those geometric patterns of flattened crop stalks that have at times been discovered in farmers' fields.

Many people believe that crop circles are created by alien visitors, despite clear evidence that crop circles are hoaxes created by ordinary people.

---

*Criteria: standards on which a judgment or decision may be based.

Two possible explanations for crop circles exist: either they are made by aliens in space ships—as is the claim by many alleged experts—or they are made by human beings as a hoax. Which explanation is simpler? Obviously, the hoax rationalization is the simplest, and it turned out to be correct for the crop circles that appeared in England in the late 1970s and 1980s. David Bower and Doug Chorley, two British men, confessed to creating the crop circles as a prank, thought up in a barroom and meant to make fun of people who believe in alien visitations (Nickell, 1995; M. Ridley, 2002; Schnabel, 1994).

4. **Critical thinking requires an open mind.** Although it is good to be a little skeptical, people should not close their minds to things that are truly possible. At the same time, it's good for people to have open minds but not so open that they are gullible* and apt to believe anything. Critical thinking requires a delicate balance between skepticism and willingness to consider possibilities—even possibilities that contradict previous judgments or beliefs. For example, scientists have yet to find any convincing evidence that there was once life on Mars. That doesn't mean that scientists totally dismiss the idea, just that there is no convincing evidence *yet*. I don't believe that there are Martians on Mars, but if I were shown convincing evidence, I would have to be willing to change my thinking—as difficult as that might be.

QUESTIONS **FOR FURTHER DISCUSSION**
1. How might critical thinking be applied to the issue of global climate change?
2. Why do you think some people (even very smart people) sometimes avoid thinking critically about issues such as politics, the existence of ESP, or the supernatural?

* *

_____

*Gullible: easily fooled or cheated.

chapter summary ((•⟍Listen on **MyPsychLab**   Listen to an audio file of your chapter www.MyPsychLab

What Is Psychology?

1.1 What defines psychology as a field of study, and what are psychology's four primary goals?
- Psychology is the scientific study of behavior and mental processes.
- The four goals of psychology are description, explanation, prediction, and control.

Psychology Then: The History of Psychology

1.2 How did structuralism and functionalism differ, and who were the important people in those early fields?
- In 1879 psychology began as a science of its own in Germany with the establishment of Wundt's psychology laboratory. He developed the technique of objective introspection.
- Titchener, a student of Wundt, brought psychology in the form of structuralism to America. Structuralism died out in the early twentieth century. Margaret F. Washburn, Titchener's student, was the first woman to receive a Ph.D. in psychology in 1894 and published *The Animal Mind*.
- William James proposed a countering point of view called functionalism, which stressed the way the mind allows us to adapt.

- Many of psychology's early pioneers were minorities such as the African Americans who, despite prejudice and racism, made important contributions to the study of human and animal behavior.
- Functionalism influenced the modern fields of educational psychology, evolutionary psychology, and industrial/organizational psychology.

issues in psychology: Psychology's African American Roots

1.3 What were the basic ideas and who were the important people behind the early approaches known as Gestalt, psychoanalysis, and behaviorism?
- Wertheimer and others studied sensation and perception, calling the new perspective Gestalt (an organized whole) psychology.
- Freud proposed that the unconscious mind controls much of our conscious behavior in his theory of psychoanalysis.
- Watson proposed a science of behavior called behaviorism, which focused only on the study of observable stimuli and responses.
- Watson and Rayner demonstrated that a phobia could be learned by conditioning a baby to be afraid of a white rat.
- Mary Cover Jones, one of Watson's more famous students in behaviorism and child development, later demonstrated that a learned phobia could be counterconditioned.

Psychology Now: Modern Perspectives

1.4 What are the basic ideas behind the seven modern perspectives, as well as the important contributions of Skinner, Maslow, and Rogers?

- Modern Freudians such as Anna Freud, Jung, and Adler changed the emphasis in Freud's original theory into a kind of neo-Freudianism.
- Skinner's operant conditioning of voluntary behavior became a major force in the twentieth century. He introduced the concept of reinforcement to behaviorism.
- Humanism, which focuses on free will and the human potential for growth, was developed by Maslow and Rogers, among others, as a reaction to the deterministic nature of behaviorism and psychoanalysis.
- Cognitive psychology is the study of learning, memory, language, and problem solving, and includes the field of cognitive neuroscience.
- Biopsychology emerged as the study of the biological bases of behavior, such as hormones, heredity, chemicals in the nervous system, structural defects in the brain, and the effects of phsyical diseases.
- The principles of evolution and the knowledge we currently have about evolution are used in this perspective to look at the way the mind works and why it works as it does. Behavior is seen as having an adaptive or survival value.

Psychological Professionals and Areas of Specialization

1.5 How does a psychiatrist differ from a psychologist, and what are the other types of professionals who work in the various areas of psychology?

- Psychologists have academic degrees and can do counseling, teaching, and research and may specialize in any one of a large number of areas within psychology.
- There are many different areas of specialization in psychology, including clinical, counseling, developmental, social, and personality as areas of work or study.
- Psychiatrists are medical doctors who provide diagnosis and therapy for persons with mental disorders.
- Psychiatric social workers are social workers with special training in the influences of the environment on mental illness.

Psychology: The Scientific Methodology

1.6 Why is psychology considered a science, and what are the steps in using the scientific method?

- The scientific method is a way to determine facts and control the possibilities of error and bias when observing behavior. The five steps are perceiving the question, forming a hypothesis, testing the hypothesis, drawing conclusions, and reporting the results.

1.7 How are naturalistic and laboratory settings used to describe behavior, and what are some of the advantages and disadvantages associated with these settings?

- Naturalistic observations involve watching animals or people in their natural environments but have the disadvantage of lack of control.
- Laboratory observations involve watching animals or people in an artificial but controlled situation, such as a laboratory.

1.8 How are case studies and surveys used to describe behavior, and what are some drawbacks to each of these methods?

- Case studies are detailed investigations of one subject, whereas surveys involve asking standardized questions of large groups of people that represent a sample of the population of interest.

- Information gained from case studies cannot be applied to other cases. People responding to surveys may not always tell the truth or remember information correctly.

1.9 What is the correlational technique, and what does it tell researchers about relationships?

- Correlation is a statistical technique that allows researchers to discover and predict relationships between variables of interest.
- Positive correlations exist when increases in one variable are matched by increases in the other variable, whereas negative correlations exist when increases in one variable are matched by decreases in the other variable.
- Correlations cannot be used to prove cause-and-effect relationships.

1.10 How are operational definitions, independent and dependent variables, experimental and control groups, and random assignment used in designing an experiment?

- Experiments are tightly controlled manipulations of variables that allow researchers to determine cause-and-effect relationships.
- The independent variable in an experiment is the variable that is deliberately manipulated by the experimenter to see if related changes occur in the behavior or responses of the participants and is given to the experimental group.
- The dependent variable in an experiment is the measured behavior or responses of the participants.
- The control group receives either a placebo treatment or nothing.
- Random assignment of participants to experimental groups helps to control for individual differences both within and between the groups that might otherwise interfere with the experiment's outcome.

1.11 How do the placebo and experimenter effects cause problems in an experiment, and how can single-blind and double-blind studies control for these effects?

- Experiments in which the subjects do not know if they are in the experimental or control groups are single-blind studies, whereas experiments in which neither the experimenters nor the subjects know this information are called double-blind studies.

issues in psychology: Stereotypes, Athletes, and College Test Performance

1.12 What are the basic elements of a real-world experiment?

- An experiment studying the effect of negative stereotypes on test performance of athletes (Jameson et al., 2007) found that athletes exposed to negative stereotypes prior to taking a test turned in a poorer performance than athletes whose exposure came after the test.

Ethics of Psychological Research

1.13 What are some ethical concerns that can occur when conducting research with people and animals?

- Ethical guidelines for doing research with human beings include the protection of rights and well-being of participants, informed consent, justification when deception is used, the right of participants to withdraw at any time, protection of participants from physical or psychological harm, confidentiality, and debriefing of participants at the end of the study. Researchers are also responsible for correcting any undesirable consequences that may result from the study.
- Animals in psychological research make useful models because they are easier to control than humans, they have simpler behavior, and they can be used in ways that are not permissible with humans.

applying psychology to everyday life: Thinking Critically About Critical Thinking

1.14 What are the basic principles of critical thinking, and how can critical thinking be useful in everyday life?

- Critical thinking is the ability to make reasoned judgments. The four basic criteria of critical thinking are that there are few concepts that do not need to be tested, evidence can vary in quality, claims by experts and authorities do not automatically make something true, and keeping an open mind is important.

TEST yourself

ANSWERS ON PAGE AK–1

✓●–[Study and Review on MyPsychLab   Ready for your test? More quizzes and a customized plan. www.MyPsychLab

Study Help Note: These longer quizzes appear at the end of every chapter and cover all the major learning objectives that you should know after reading the chapter. These quizzes also provide practice for exams. The answers to each Test Yourself section can be found in the Answer Key at the back of the book.

Pick the best answer.

1. In the definition of psychology, the term mental processes means _____.
   a. internal, covert processes.
   b. outward behavior.
   c. overt actions and reactions.
   d. only animal behavior.

2. A psychologist is interested in finding out why identical twins have different personalities. This psychologist is most interested in the goal of _____.
   a. description.   c. prediction.
   b. explanation.   d. control.

3. Psychologists who give potential employees tests that determine what kind of job those employees might be best suited for are interested in the goal of _____.
   a. description.   c. prediction.
   b. explanation.   d. control.

4. Which early theorist developed his perspective on psychology by basing it on Darwin's "survival of the fittest" doctrine?
   a. Wilhelm Wundt   c. John Watson
   b. William James   d. Sigmund Freud

5. "The whole is greater than the sum of the parts" is a statement associated with the perspective of _____.
   a. introspectionism.   c. psychoanalysis.
   b. functionalism.   d. Gestalt psychology.

6. _____ was (were) the focus of Watson's behaviorism.
   a. Conscious experiences   c. The unconscious mind
   b. Gestalt perceptions   d. Observable experiences

7. Who is most associated with the technique of introspection?
   a. Wundt   c. Watson
   b. James   d. Wertheimer

8. Who was denied a Ph.D. despite completing all the requirements for earning the degree?
   a. Mary Whiton Calkins   c. Margaret Washburn
   b. Mary Cover Jones   d. Eleanor Gibson

9. Which perspective focuses on free will and self-actualization?
   a. psychoanalysis   c. cognitive psychology
   b. behaviorism   d. humanism

10. Jenna suffers from a nervous tic of washing her hands repeatedly and being unable to resist washing them again and again. Which perspective would explain Jenna's hand-washing behavior as a result of repressed conflicts?
    a. psychodynamic perspective
    b. cognitive psychology
    c. behaviorism
    d. biopsychology

11. Which perspective looks at perception, learning, and memory?
    a. psychoanalysis   c. cognitive psychology
    b. behaviorism   d. evolutionary perspective

12. Which perspective emphasizes the biological bases for shared, universal mental characteristics?
    a. psychoanalysis   c. cognitive psychology
    b. behaviorism   d. evolutionary perspective

13. Which of the following professionals in psychology has the broadest area of interests and functions?
    a. psychiatrist   c. psychiatric social worker
    b. psychoanalyst   d. psychologist

14. A person who has suffered a major stroke and is now experiencing severe personality problems because of the damage would best be advised to see a _____.
    a. psychiatrist.   c. psychiatric social worker.
    b. psychoanalyst.   d. psychologist.

15. In the scientific method, forming an educated guess is called _____.
    a. reporting your results.   c. drawing conclusions.
    b. perceiving a question.   d. forming a hypothesis.

16. The main advantage of laboratory observation is _____.
    a. the degree of control it allows the observer.
    b. the degree of participation it allows the observer.
    c. the observer effect.
    d. the opportunity for representative sampling.

17. Harlan wanted to write realistically about street gangs, so he pretended to be a teenager and joined a real gang. This is most similar to the method of _____.
    a. laboratory observation.   c. the case study.
    b. the observer effect.   d. participant observation.

18. The main advantage of a case study is _____.
    a. the ease of generalizing the results to others.
    b. being able to determine cause and effect.
    c. the amount of detail it provides about an individual.
    d. the large number of people that can be studied at one time.

19. The entire group that a researcher is interested in is called a _____.
    a. sample.
    b. population.
    c. subject pool.
    d. survey.

20. Professor Jones surveyed her six classes and found that students who slept less than five hours the night before the exam received lower exam scores than those students who slept seven hours or more. What kind of correlation is this relationship between hours of sleep and scores?
    a. positive
    b. negative
    c. zero
    d. causal

21. Drinking orange juice is negatively correlated with the risk of cancer. Based on this information, which of the following statements is TRUE?
    a. The more orange juice you drink, the higher your risk of cancer.
    b. The more orange juice you drink, the lower your risk of cancer.
    c. The less orange juice you drink, the lower your risk of cancer.
    d. Drinking orange juice causes people to be cancer free.

22. A researcher designs an experiment to test the effects of playing video games on memory. What would be the dependent variable?
    a. scores on a memory test
    b. playing video games
    c. number of hours spent playing video games
    d. the type of video game played

23. In that same experiment, the experimental group would _____.
    a. not play the video games.
    b. take the memory test while the control group would not.
    c. not take the memory test while the control group would.
    d. play the video games.

24. In the stereotypes and athletes study, what was the independent variable?
    a. the test scores
    b. the room in which the test was given
    c. the control group
    d. the difference in threat level

25. In a _____ study, only the experimenter knows who is in the control group and who is in the experimental group.
    a. placebo
    b. single-blind
    c. double-blind
    d. triple-blind

26. Double-blind studies control for _____.
    a. the placebo effect.
    b. the experimenter effect.
    c. the placebo effect and the experimenter effect.
    d. extrinsic motivation.

27. Dr. Silverberg designed a study in which she tests infants for memory ability. Before she can begin her study, she must obtain _____.
    a. permission from the infants.
    b. permission from the parents.
    c. informed consent from the parents.
    d. confidential information from the parents.

28. Several years ago two scientists announced that they had achieved "cold fusion" in the laboratory, but further studies failed to replicate their findings and later other scientists found that the original two scientists had used sloppy methods. This highlights which of the following critical thinking principles?
    a. Few "truths" do not need to be tested.
    b. All evidence is not equal in quality.
    c. Authority or expertise does not make the claims of the authority or expert true.
    d. Critical thinking requires an open mind.

29. A famous newscaster advertises a new magnetic mattress for controlling pain. If Nathaniel decides to order the mattress because he believes that such a well-known personality should know if it works or not, he has made an error in which of the following?
    a. Few "truths" do not need to be tested.
    b. All evidence is not equal in quality.
    c. Authority or expertise does not make the claims of the authority or expert true.
    d. Critical thinking requires an open mind.

30. Critical thinking means making judgments based on _____.
    a. emotional issues.
    b. keeping a closed mind.
    c. reason and logical evaluation.
    d. authority and expertise.

1 the science of psychology

1.1 p. 4

Psychology
(is the scientific study of behavior and mental processes)

- has methods for studying phenomena
- has four primary goals
  - describe
  - explain
  - predict
  - control

1.2 **1.3** p. 5

Psychology Then: The History of Psychology
(has roots in several disciplines, including philosophy, medicine, and physiology, and has developed through several perspectives)

- A relatively new science that formally began in 1879 when Wilhelm Wundt ("father of psychology") established the first psychological laboratory in Leipzig, Germany

  - - - was a student of Wundt's - - -

  - **Structuralism**
    founded by Edward Titchener

  - **Functionalism**
    founded by William James

  - **Gestalt psychology**
    founded by Max Wertheimer

  - **Psychoanalysis**
    ideas put forth by Sigmund Freud

  - **Behaviorism**
    associated with work of John B. Watson, who was greatly influenced by Ivan Pavlov's work in conditioning/learning

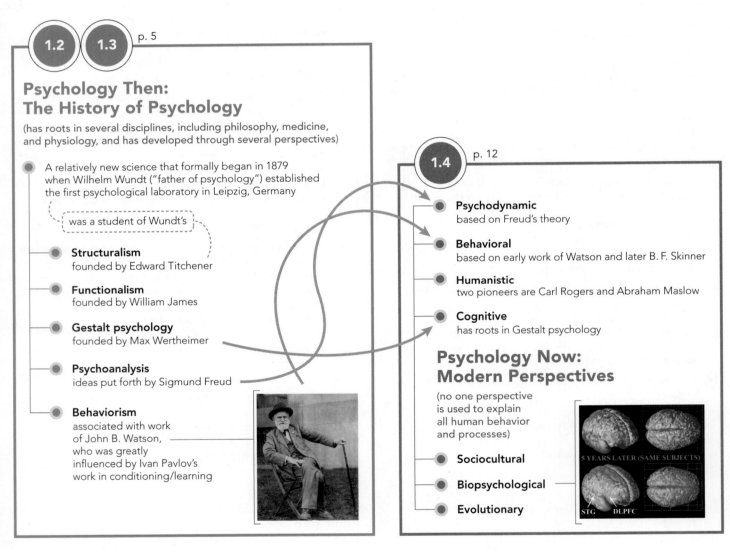

1.4 p. 12

- **Psychodynamic**
  based on Freud's theory

- **Behavioral**
  based on early work of Watson and later B. F. Skinner

- **Humanistic**
  two pioneers are Carl Rogers and Abraham Maslow

- **Cognitive**
  has roots in Gestalt psychology

Psychology Now: Modern Perspectives
(no one perspective is used to explain all human behavior and processes)

- **Sociocultural**
- **Biopsychological**
- **Evolutionary**

5 YEARS LATER (SAME SUBJECTS)

STG   DLPFC

1.5 p. 16

Types of Psychological Professionals
(people working in the field of psychology have a variety of training experiences and different focuses)

- **psychologist**
- **psychiatrist**
- **psychiatric social worker**
  - **LPC, MFT,** etc. (see Appendix B)

1.6 1.7 1.8   p. 18

scientific method
- perceiving the question
- forming a hypothesis
- testing the hypothesis
- drawing conclusions
- reporting your results

descriptive data collection methods
- naturalistic observation
- laboratory observation
- case studies
- surveys

Psychology: The Scientific Methodology
(psychology uses the scientific method to try to determine facts and reduce uncertainty)

1.9 1.10 1.11   p. 23

correlation
- is a measure of relationship between two or more variables
- produces a value called the *correlation coefficient*
- does not prove causation

experiments
the only research method that will allow researchers to determine the cause of a behavior by deliberately manipulating some variable and measuring changes in the variable of interest

- **operational definition** specifically names the steps or procedures used to control or measure the variable in the experiment
- have **groups**— experimental and control
- possible **hazards**— placebo effect and experimenter effects

Finding Relationships
(different ways to find out more than just descriptions of behavior)

1.13   p. 30

guidelines for research with humans
- rights and well-being of participants must be weighed against the study's value to science
- participants must be allowed to make an informed decision about participating (informed consent)
- deception must be justified
- participants may withdraw from the study at any time
- participants must be protected from risks or told explicitly of risks
- investigator must debrief participants, telling the true nature of the study and expectations of results
- data must remain confidential

Ethics of Psychological Research
(psychological scientists have a primary goal of protecting the health and welfare of their animal or human participants)

research with animals — primary focus is on avoiding any unnecessary pain or suffering

1.14   p. 32

scientific thinking can be applied to many real-world situations

Critical Thinking

four basic criteria for making reasoned judgments
- there are very few "truths" in the world that do not need to be subjected to testing
- all evidence is not equal in quality
- just because someone is considered to be an authority or to have a lot of expertise does not make everything that person claims automatically true
- critical thinking requires an open mind

2

the biological perspective

why study the nervous system and the glands?

How could we possibly understand any of our behavior, thoughts, or actions without knowing something about the incredible organs that allow us to act, think, and react? If we can understand how the brain, the nerves, and the glands interact to control feelings, thoughts, and behavior, we can begin to truly understand the complex organism called a human being.

chapter outline

An Overview of the Nervous System

Neurons and Nerves:
Building the Network

The Central Nervous System—
The "Central Processing Unit"

PSYCHOLOGY IN THE NEWS:
Fact or Fiction: Focus on the Brain,
but Check Your Sources!

The Peripheral Nervous System—
Nerves on the Edge

Distant Connections:
The Endocrine Glands

Looking Inside the Living Brain

From the Bottom Up:
The Structures of the Brain

APPLYING PSYCHOLOGY
TO EVERYDAY LIFE:
Paying Attention to the Causes
of Attention-Deficit/Hyperactivity
Disorder

Assisting the Brain

Team Hoyt is composed of Rick Hoyt and his father Dick Hoyt. Together, they have competed in over 1,000 races including six Ironman® competitions. The Ironman® competition consists of a 2.4-mile swim, a 112-mile bike ride, and a 26.2-mile run. Impressive as that is, what makes their accomplishments even more spectacular is that they approach each race a bit differently than any other competitors. For the swimming stage of a triathlon, Dick pulls Rick in a boat that is attached to a bungee cord, then he peddles Rick on a special two-seater bicycle for the biking segment. The third leg of the race is completed with Dick pushing Rick across the finish line in a customized running chair.

Rick was born with spastic quadriplegia and cerebral palsy as the result of oxygen deprivation to his brain during birth. Dick and Judy Hoyt discovered that although Rick could not walk or talk, he had a bright mind behind those bright eyes, and they worked hard to teach him the alphabet and basic words. In 1972, with a specially designed computer, Rick was able to communicate with his parents and others by tapping his head against a head piece attached to his wheelchair when specific letters of the alphabet were highlighted on a computer screen. Using this device, he eventually entered and graduated from high school and later from Boston University with a degree in Special Education.

Current research to help individuals with brain injuries or neurological conditions has moved far beyond the then-amazing but relatively simple computer that assisted Rick. Some of the most promising areas are in brain–computer interfaces (BCI) that use the brain's electrical activity to communicate with others. New developments in "hybrid" brain–computer interfaces use different sources of brain information, or even an external device (Pfurtscheller et al., 2010). It is possible that in the future, brain activity will enable individuals to control such assistive devices as prosthetic limbs or wheelchairs.

In this chapter, you will learn about the nervous system (which includes the brain) and some of the techniques used in brain research—research that may one day improve the quality of life for individuals like Rick and those with similar challenges.

learning objectives

2.1 What are the nervous system, neurons, and nerves, and how do they relate to one another?

2.2 How do neurons use neurotransmitters to communicate with each other and with the body?

2.3 How do the brain and spinal cord interact?

2.4 How do the somatic and autonomic nervous systems allow people and animals to interact with their surroundings and control the body's automatic functions?

2.5 How do the hormones released by glands interact with the nervous system and affect behavior?

2.6 How do psychologists study the brain and how it works?

2.7 What are the different structures of the bottom part of the brain, and what do they do?

2.8 What are the structures of the brain that control emotion, learning, memory, and motivation?

2.9 What parts of the cortex control the different senses and the movement of the body?

2.10 What parts of the cortex are responsible for higher forms of thought, such as language?

2.11 How does the left side of the brain differ from the right side?

study tip 2.1

As you are reading this chapter, refer to pages PIA-14–PIA-15 in *Psychology in Action* for some helpful memory strategies to use when learning the terminology in this chapter.

👁─Watch Episode 3: *Biological Psychology* in the MyPsychLab video series

An Overview of the Nervous System

2.1 What are the nervous system, neurons, and nerves, and how do they relate to one another?

This chapter will discuss a very complex system of cells, organs, and chemicals that work together to produce behavior, thoughts, and actions. The first part of this complex arrangement is the **nervous system**, a network of cells that carries information to and from all parts of the body. Before beginning the discussion on the cells that make up the nervous system, take a look at Figure 2.1. This figure shows the organization of the various parts of the nervous system and will help you understand how all the different parts work together in controlling the way people and animals think, act, and feel.

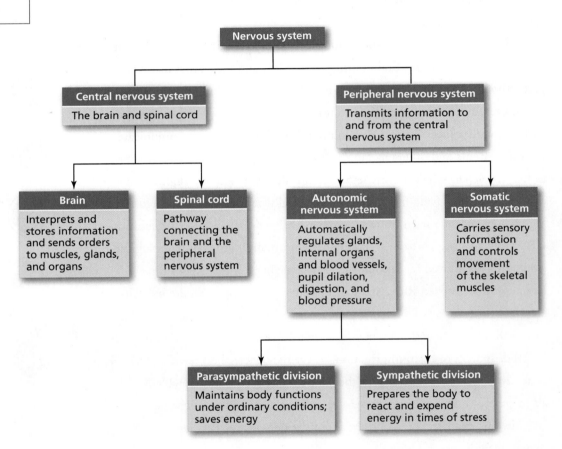

FIGURE 2.1 An Overview of the Nervous System

nervous system an extensive network of specialized cells that carries information to and from all parts of the body.

neuroscience a branch of the life sciences that deals with the structure and function of neurons, nerves, and nervous tissue.

biological psychology or **behavioral neuroscience** branch of neuroscience that focuses on the biological bases of psychological processes, behavior, and learning.

📖─Read and learn more about Cajal's influence and discoveries on **MyPsychLab**

Neurons and Nerves: Building the Network

The field of **neuroscience** is a branch of the life sciences that deals with the structure and functioning of the brain and the neurons, nerves, and nervous tissue that form the nervous system. It was Santiago Ramón y Cajal, a doctor studying slides of brain tissue, who in 1887 first theorized that the nervous system was made up of individual cells (Cajal, translation, 1995). In this discipline, the focus is on neural function in the central and peripheral nervous systems at the molecular, cellular, circuit, and behavioral levels. **Biological psychology**, or **behavioral neuroscience**, is the branch of neuroscience that focuses on the biological bases of psychological processes, behavior, and learning. 📖─Read on **MyPsychLab**

Structure of the Neuron—The Nervous System's Building Block

Although the entire body is composed of cells, each type of cell has a special purpose and function and, therefore, a special structure. Skin cells are flat, but muscle cells are long and stretchy. Most cells do have three things in common: a nucleus, a cell body, and a cell membrane holding it all together. The **neuron** is the specialized cell in the nervous system that receives and sends messages within that system. Neurons are one of the messengers of the body, and that means that they have a very special structure.

The parts of the neuron that receive messages from other cells are called the **dendrites**. The name *dendrite* means "branch," and this structure does indeed look like the branches of a tree. The dendrites are attached to the cell body, or **soma**, which is the part of the cell that contains the nucleus and keeps the entire cell alive and functioning. The **axon** (from the Greek for "axis") is a fiber attached to the soma, and its job is to carry messages out to other cells. (See Figure 2.2.)

Neurons make up only 10 percent of the cells in the brain. The other 90 percent of the brain is composed of **glial cells** that serve as a sort of structure on which the neurons develop and work and that hold the neurons in place. For example, during early brain development, radial glial cells (extending from inner to outer areas like the spokes of a wheel) help guide migrating neurons to form the outer layers of the brain. There are several different types of glial cells that perform various functions, such as getting nutrients to the neurons, cleaning up the remains of neurons that have died, communicating with neurons and other glial cells, and providing insulation for neurons. Recent research has found that some types of glial cells affect both the functioning and structure of neurons and specific types also have properties similar to

neuron the basic cell that makes up the nervous system and that receives and sends messages within that system.

dendrites branchlike structures that receive messages from other neurons.

soma the cell body of the neuron responsible for maintaining the life of the cell.

axon tubelike structure that carries the neural message to other cells.

glial cells cells that provide support for the neurons to grow on and around, deliver nutrients to neurons, produce myelin to coat axons, clean up waste products and dead neurons, influence information processing, and, during prenatal development, influence the generation of new neurons.

FIGURE 2.2 The Structure of the Neuron The electronmicrograph on the left shows myelinated axons.

myelin fatty substances produced by certain glial cells that coat the axons of neurons to insulate, protect, and speed up the neural impulse.

nerves bundles of axons coated in myelin that travel together through the body.

diffusion process of molecules moving from areas of high concentration to areas of low concentration.

stem cells, which allow them to develop into new neurons, both during prenatal development and in adulthood (Bullock et al., 2005; Kriegstein & Alvarez-Buylla, 2009).

Two special types of glial cells, called *oligodendrocytes* and *Schwann cells*, generate a layer of fatty substances called **myelin**. Oligodendrocytes produce myelin in the brain and spinal cord (the central nervous system); Schwann cells produce myelin in the neurons of the body. Myelin wraps around the shaft of the axons, forming a protective sheath. It's really the axons that do the bulk of the traveling through the body, with the somas clumped together near the spinal cord. So the axons of those various neurons can travel together throughout the body and never really touch each other directly. It's very similar to the concept of a telephone cable. Within the cable are lots of copper wires coated in plastic; the plastic serves the same insulating purpose for the wires as the myelin sheath does for the axons. Bundled all together, they form a cable that is much stronger and less vulnerable to breakage than any wire alone would be. It works the same way in the nervous system. Bundles of myelin-coated axons travel together in "cables" called **nerves**.

The myelin sheath is a very important part of the neuron. It not only insulates the neuron, but it also offers a little protection from damage and speeds up the neural message traveling down the axon. As shown in Figure 2.2, sections of myelin bump up next to each other on the axon, similar to the way sausages are linked together. The places where the myelin seems to bump are actually small spaces on the axon called nodes, which are not covered in myelin. When the electrical impulse that is the neural message travels down an axon coated with myelin, it "jumps" between the myelin sheath sections to the places where the axon is accessible at the nodes. That makes the message go much faster down the coated axon than it would down an uncoated axon of a neuron in the brain. In the disease called *multiple sclerosis* (MS), the myelin sheath is destroyed (possibly by the individual's own immune system), which leads to diminished or complete loss of neural functioning in those damaged cells. Early symptoms of MS may include fatigue, changes in vision, balance problems, and numbness, tingling, or muscle weakness in the arms or legs.

Exactly how does this "electrical message" work inside the cell?

● Exactly how does this "electrical message" work inside the cell?

Generating the Message Within the Neuron—The Neural Impulse

A neuron that's at rest—not currently firing a neural impulse or message—is actually electrically charged. The inside of the cell is really a semiliquid (jelly-like) solution in which there are charged particles, or *ions*. A semiliquid solution also surrounds the outside of the cell and contains ions, too. Although both positive and negative ions are located inside and outside of the cell, the relative charge of ions inside the cell is mostly negative, and the relative charge of ions outside the cell is mostly positive (due to both **diffusion** and electrostatic pressure). The cell membrane itself is *semipermeable*. This means some substances that are outside the cell can enter through tiny openings, or *channels*, in the membrane, while other substances in the cell can go outside. Many of these channels are gated—they open or close based on the electrical potential of the membrane (more about that in a minute). Inside the cell is a concentration of both smaller positively charged potassium ions and larger negatively charged protein ions. The negatively charged protein ions, however, are so big that they can't get out, which leaves the inside of the cell primarily negative when at rest. Outside the cell are lots of positively charged sodium ions and negatively charged chloride ions, but they are unable to enter the cell membrane when the cell is at rest because the ion channels that would allow them in are closed. But because the outside sodium ions are positive and the inside ions are negative, and because opposite electrical charges attract each other, the sodium ions will cluster around the membrane. This difference in charges creates an electrical potential.

Think of the ions inside the cell as a baseball game inside a stadium (the cell walls). The sodium ions outside the cell are all the fans in the area, and they want to get inside to see the game. When the cell is resting (the electrical potential is in a state called the **resting potential**, because the cell is at rest), the fans are stuck outside. The sodium ions cannot enter when the cell is at rest, because even though the cell membrane has all these channels, the *particular channels* for the big sodium ions aren't open yet. But when the cell receives a strong enough stimulation from another cell (meaning that the dendrites are activated), the cell membrane opens up those *particular* channels, one after the other, all down its surface, allowing the sodium ions (the "fans") to rush into the cell. That causes the inside of the cell to become mostly positive and the outside of the cell to become mostly negative, because many of the positive sodium ions are now inside the cell—at the point where the first ion channel opened. This electrical charge reversal will start at the part of the axon closest to the soma (the first ion channel) and then proceed down the axon in a kind of chain reaction. (Picture a long hallway with many doors in which the first door opens, then the second, and so on all the way down the hall.) This electrical charge reversal is known as the **action potential** because the electrical potential is now in action rather than at rest. Each action potential sequence takes about one-thousandth of a second, so the neural message travels very fast—from 2 miles per hour in the slowest, shortest neurons to 270 miles per hour in other neurons. (See Figure 2.3.) ✳ Explore on MyPsychLab

Now the action potential is traveling down the axon. When it gets to the end of the axon, something else happens—the message will get transmitted to another cell (that step will be discussed momentarily). Meanwhile, what is happening to the parts of the cell that the action potential has already left behind? How does the cell get the "fans" back outside? Remember, the action potential means that the cell is now positive inside and negative outside at the point where the channel opened. Several things happen to return the cell to its resting state. First, the sodium ion channels close immediately after the action potential has passed, allowing no more "fans" (sodium ions) to enter. The cell membrane also literally pumps the positive sodium ions back outside the cell, kicking the "fans" out until the next action potential opens the ion channels again. This pumping process is a little slow, so another type of ion gets into the act. Small, positively charged potassium ions inside the neuron move rapidly out of the cell after the action potential passes, helping to more quickly restore the inside of the cell to a negative charge. Now the cell becomes negative inside and positive outside, and the neuron is capable of "firing off" another message. Once the sodium pumps finish pumping out the sodium ions, the neuron can be said to have returned to its full resting potential, poised and ready to do it all again.

To sum all that up, when the cell is stimulated, the first ion channel opens and the electrical charge *at that ion channel* is reversed. Then the next ion channel opens and *that* charge is reversed, but in the meantime the *first* ion channel has been closed and the charge is returning to what it was when it was at rest. The action potential is the *sequence* of ion channels opening all down the length of the cell.

So if the stimulus that originally causes the neuron to fire is very strong, will the neuron fire more strongly than it would if the stimulus were weak?

Neurons actually have a threshold for firing, and all it takes is a stimulus that is just strong enough to get past that threshold to make the neuron fire. Here's a simple version of how this works: Each neuron is receiving many signals from other neurons. Some of these signals are meant to cause the neuron to fire, whereas others are meant to prevent the neuron from firing. The neuron constantly adds together the effects of the "fire" messages and subtracts the "don't fire" messages, and if the "fire" messages are great enough, the threshold is crossed and the neuron fires. When a neuron does fire, it fires in an **all-or-none** fashion. Neurons are either firing at full strength or not

resting potential the state of the neuron when not firing a neural impulse.

action potential the release of the neural impulse consisting of a reversal of the electrical charge within the axon.

all-or-none referring to the fact that a neuron either fires completely or does not fire at all.

✳ Explore neurons and neurotransmitters on **MyPsychLab**

So if the stimulus that originally causes the neuron to fire is very strong, will the neuron fire more strongly than it would if the stimulus were weak?

FIGURE 2.3 The Neural Impulse Action Potential
In the graph, voltage readings are shown at a given place on the neuron over a period of 20 or 30 milliseconds (thousandths of a second). At first the cell is resting; it then reaches threshold and an action potential is triggered. After a brief hyperpolarization period, the cell returns to its resting potential.

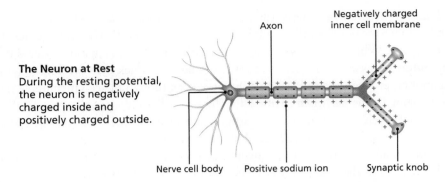

The Neuron at Rest
During the resting potential, the neuron is negatively charged inside and positively charged outside.

The Neural Impulse
The action potential occurs when positive sodium ions enter into the cell, causing a reversal of the electrical charge from negative to positive.

The Neural Impulse Continues
As the action potential moves down the axon toward the axon terminals, the cell areas behind the action potential return to their resting state of a negative charge as the positive sodium ions are pumped to the outside of the cell, and the positive potassium ions rapidly leave.

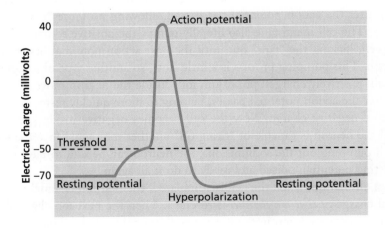

firing at all—there's no such thing as "partial" firing of a neuron. It is like turning on a light switch—it's either on or it's off.

So what's the difference between strong stimulation and weak stimulation? A strong message will cause the neuron to fire repeatedly (as if someone flicked the light switch on and off as quickly as possible), and it will also cause more neurons to fire (as if there were a lot of lights going on and off instead of just one).

● Now that we know how the message travels within the axon of the cell, what is that "something else" that happens when the action potential reaches the end of the axon?

Now that we know how the message travels within the axon of the cell, what is that "something else" that happens when the action potential reaches the end of the axon?

Sending the Message to Other Cells: The Synapse

2.2 How do neurons use neurotransmitters to communicate with each other and with the body?

Look once again at Figure 2.2 on page 43. The end of the axon fans out into several shorter fibers that have swellings or little knobs on the ends called **synaptic knobs** or **axon terminals** (may also be called *terminal buttons*). Figure 2.4 shows this knob enlarged to giant scale. Notice that the synaptic knob is not empty. It has a number of little saclike structures in it called **synaptic vesicles**. The word *vesicle* is Latin and means a "little blister" or "fluid-filled sac."

   Inside the synaptic vesicles are chemicals suspended in fluid, which are molecules of substances called **neurotransmitters**. The name is simple enough—they are inside a neuron and they are going to transmit a message. Next to the synaptic knob is the dendrite of another neuron (see Figure 2.4). Between them is a fluid-filled space called the **synapse** or the **synaptic gap**. Instead of an electrical charge, the vesicles at the end of the axon (also called the presynaptic membrane) contain the molecules of neurotransmitters, and the surface of the dendrite next to the axon (the postsynaptic membrane) contains ion channels that have **receptor sites**, proteins that allow only particular molecules of a certain shape to fit into it, just as only a particular key will fit into a keyhole.

   How do the neurotransmitters get across the gap? Recall the action potential making its way down the axon after the neuron has been stimulated. When that action potential, or electrical charge, reaches the synaptic vesicles, the synaptic vesicles release their neurotransmitters into the synaptic gap. The molecules then float across

This electromicrograph shows a motor neuron making contact with muscle fibers.

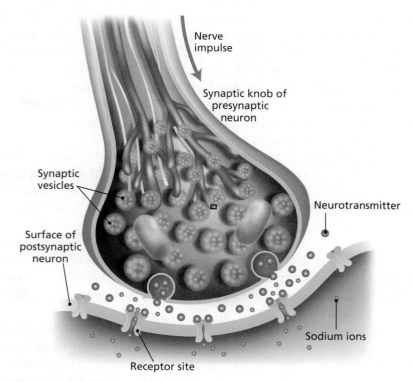

FIGURE 2.4 The Synapse
The nerve impulse reaches the synaptic knobs, triggering the release of neurotransmitters from the synaptic vesicles. The neurotransmitter molecules cross the synaptic gap to fit into the receptor sites that fit the shape of the molecules, opening the ion channel and allowing sodium ions to rush in.

synaptic knob   rounded areas on the end of the axon terminals.

axon terminals   branches at the end of the axon.

synaptic vesicles   saclike structures found inside the synaptic knob containing chemicals.

neurotransmitter   chemical found in the synaptic vesicles that, when released, has an effect on the next cell.

synapse (synaptic gap)   microscopic fluid-filled space between the synaptic knob of one cell and the dendrites or surface of the next cell.

receptor sites   three-dimensional proteins on the surface of the dendrites or certain cells of the muscles and glands, which are shaped to fit only certain neurotransmitters.

excitatory synapse synapse at which a neurotransmitter causes the receiving cell to fire.

inhibitory synapse synapse at which a neurotransmitter causes the receiving cell to stop firing.

antagonists chemical substances that block or reduce a cell's response to the action of other chemicals or neurotransmitters.

agonists chemical substances that mimic or enhance the effects of a neurotransmitter on the receptor sites of the next cell, increasing or decreasing the activity of that cell.

the synapse and many of them fit themselves into the receptor sites, opening the ion channels and allowing sodium to rush in, activating the next cell. It is this very activation that stimulates, or releases, the action potential in that cell. It is important to understand that the "next cell" may be a neuron, but it may also be a cell on a muscle or a gland. Muscles and glands have special cells with receptor sites on them, just like on the dendrite of a neuron.

So far, we've been talking about the synapse as if neurotransmitters always cause the next cell to fire its action potential (or, in the case of a muscle or gland, to contract or start secreting its chemicals). But the neurons must have a way to be turned *off* as well as on. Otherwise, when a person burns a finger, the pain signals from those neurons would not stop until the burn was completely healed. Muscles are told to contract or relax, and glands are told to secrete or stop secreting their chemicals. The neurotransmitters found at various synapses around the nervous system can either turn cells on (called an *excitatory* effect) or turn cells off (called an *inhibitory* effect), depending on exactly what synapse is being affected. Although some people refer to neurotransmitters that turn cells on as *excitatory* neurotransmitters and the ones that turn cells off as *inhibitory* neurotransmitters, it's really more correct to refer to **excitatory synapses** and **inhibitory synapses**. In other words, it's not the neurotransmitter itself that is excitatory or inhibitory, but rather it is the effect of that neurotransmitter that is either excitatory or inhibitory at the receptor sites of a particular synapse.

Neurotransmitters, Messengers of the Network

At least 100 neurotransmitters have been identified (Snyder, 2002), and possibly many more exist. The first neurotransmitter to be identified was named *acetylcholine*. It is found at the synapses between neurons and muscle cells. Acetylcholine serves to stimulate the skeletal muscles to contract but actually slows contractions in the heart muscle. If acetylcholine receptor sites on the muscle cells are blocked in some way, then the acetylcholine can't get to the site and the muscle will be incapable of contracting—paralyzed, in other words. This is exactly what happens when *curare*, a drug used by South American Indians on their blow darts, gets into the nervous system. Curare's molecules are just similar enough to fit into the receptor site without actually stimulating the cell, making curare an **antagonist** (a chemical substance that blocks or reduces the effects of a neurotransmitter) for acetylcholine.

What would happen if the neurons released too much acetylcholine? The bite of a black widow spider does just that. Its venom stimulates the release of excessive amounts of acetylcholine and causes convulsions and possible death. Black widow spider venom is an **agonist** (a chemical substance that mimics or enhances the effects of a neurotransmitter) for acetylcholine.

Acetylcholine also plays a key role in memory, arousal, and attention. For example, acetylcholine is also found in the hippocampus, an area of the brain that is responsible for forming new memories. Low levels of acetylcholine have been associated with Alzheimer's disease, the most common type of dementia. (L I N K) to Chapter Five: Memory, p. 190.

Since the discovery of acetylcholine, many other neurotransmitters have been identified. These substances have a variety of roles ranging from general excitatory and inhibitory effects to influencing eating, sleeping, movement, and consciousness. Others influence cognition, memory, and mood. Refer to Table 2.1 for an overview of various neurotransmitters and their functions.

The venom of the black widow spider causes a flood of acetylcholine to be released into the body's muscle system, causing convulsions.

table 2.1 Neurotransmitters and Their Functions

NEUROTRANSMITTERS	FUNCTIONS
Acetylcholine	Excitatory or inhibitory; involved in memory and controls muscle contractions.
Serotonin	Excitatory or inhibitory; involved in mood, sleep, and appetite.
GABA (gamma-aminobutyric acid)	Major inhibitory neurotransmitter; involved in sleep and inhibits movement.
Glutamate	Major excitatory neurotransmitter; involved in learning, memory formation, and nervous system development.
Norepinephrine	Mainly excitatory; involved in arousal and mood.
Dopamine	Excitatory or inhibitory; involved in control of movement and sensations of pleasure.
Endorphins	Inhibitory neural regulators; involved in pain relief.

Some neurotransmitters directly control the release of other neurotransmitters. These special neurotransmitters are called *neural regulators* or *neural peptides* (Agnati et al., 1992), and *endorphins*—pain-controlling chemicals in the body—are transmitters that you may have heard about. When a person is hurt, a neurotransmitter that signals pain is released. When the brain gets this message, it triggers the release of endorphins. The endorphins bind to receptors that open the ion channels on the axon. This causes the cell to be unable to fire its pain signal, and the pain sensations eventually lessen. For example, you might bump your elbow and experience a lot of pain right at first, but the pain will quickly subside to a much lower level. Sports players may injure themselves during an event and yet not feel the pain until after the event when the endorphin levels go down.

The name *endorphin* comes from the term *endogenous morphine*. (*Endogenous* means "native to the area"—in this case, native to the body.) Scientists studying the nervous system found receptor sites that fit morphine molecules perfectly and decided that there must be a natural substance in the body that has the same effect as morphine. Endorphins are the reason that heroin and the other drugs derived from opium are so addictive—when people take morphine or heroin, their bodies neglect to produce endorphins. When the drug wears off, they are left with no protection against pain at all, and *everything* hurts. This pain is why most people want more heroin, creating an addictive cycle of abuse. **LINK** to Chapter Eight: Motivation and Emotion, pp. 285–286.

If the neurotransmitters are out there in the synaptic gap and in the receptor sites, what happens to them when they aren't needed anymore?

reuptake process by which neurotransmitters are taken back into the synaptic vesicles.

> If the neurotransmitters are out there in the synaptic gap and in the receptor sites, what happens to them when they aren't needed anymore?

Cleaning Up the Synapse: Reuptake and Enzymes

The neurotransmitters have to get out of the receptor sites before the next stimulation can occur. Some just drift away through the process of diffusion, but most will end up back in the synaptic vesicles in a process called **reuptake**. (Think of a little suction tube, sucking the chemicals back into the vesicles.) In this way the synapse is cleared for the next release of neurotransmitters. Some drugs, like cocaine, affect the nervous system by blocking the reuptake process. See Figure 2.5 for a visual representation of how dopamine is affected by cocaine.

There is one neurotransmitter that is not taken back into the vesicles, however. Because acetylcholine is responsible for muscle activity, and

FIGURE 2.5 Reuptake of Dopamine
Dopamine is removed from the synapse by reuptake sites. Cocaine acts by blocking dopamine reuptake sites, allowing dopamine to remain active in the synapse longer.

muscle activity needs to happen rapidly and continue happening, it's not possible to wait around for the "sucking up" process to occur. Instead, an enzyme* specifically designed to break apart acetylcholine clears the synaptic gap very quickly (a process called **enzymatic degradation**). There are enzymes that break down other neurotransmitters as well.

● I think I understand the synapse and neurotransmitters now, but how do I relate that to the real world?

Knowing how and why drugs affect us can help us understand why a doctor might prescribe a particular drug or why certain drugs are dangerous and should be avoided. Because the chemical molecules of various drugs, if similar enough in shape to the neurotransmitters, can fit into the receptor sites on the receiving neurons just like the neurotransmitters do, drugs can act as agonists or antagonists. Drugs acting as agonists, for example, can mimic or enhance the effects of neurotransmitters on the receptor sites of the next cell. This can result in an increase or decrease in the activity of the receiving cell, depending on what the effect of the original neurotransmitter (excitatory or inhibitory) was going to be. So if the original neurotransmitter was excitatory, the effect of the agonist will be to increase that excitation. If it was inhibitory, the effect of the agonist will be to increase that inhibition. Another deciding factor is the nervous system location of the neurons that use a specific neurotransmitter.

For example, some antianxiety medications, such as diazepam (Valium®), are classified as benzodiazepines (Ⓛ Ⓘ Ⓝ Ⓚ to Chapter Thirteen: Psychological Therapies, p. 488) and are agonists for GABA, the primary inhibitory neurotransmitter in the brain. Areas of the brain that play a role in controlling anxiety, agitation, and fear include the amygdala, orbitofrontal cortex, and the insula (Julien et al., 2008; Naqvi et al., 2006). By increasing the inhibitory (calming) action of GABA, the benzodiazepines directly calm these specific brain areas (Julien et al., 2008; Preston et al., 2008).

Other drugs act as antagonists, blocking or reducing a cell's response to the action of other chemicals or neurotransmitters. Although an antagonist might sound like it has only an inhibitory effect, it is important to remember that if the neurotransmitter that the antagonist affects is inhibitory itself, the result will actually be an *increase* in the activity of the cell that would normally have been inhibited; the antagonist *blocks* the inhibitory effect.

Lastly, some drugs yield their agonistic or antagonistic effects by impacting the amount of neurotransmitter in the synapse. They do so by interfering with the regular reuptake or enzymatic degradation process. Remember that the neurotransmitter serotonin helps regulate and adjust people's moods, but in some people the normal process of adjustment is not working properly. In one theory of depression, serotonin is either not produced or not released in great enough amounts, so it can't fully activate the receptors on the next neuron, leaving the person in a state of depression. Some of the drugs used to treat depression are called SSRIs (selective serotonin reuptake inhibitors). SSRIs block the reuptake of serotonin, leaving more serotonin available in the synapse to bind with the receptor sites. Eventually, this elevates mood and lifts the depression.

This section covered the neuron and how neurons communicate. The next section looks at the bigger picture—the nervous system itself.

---

study tip 2.2

For this part of the section, if you focus your attention on the general ideas about agonistic and antagonistic effects, the brain areas will soon make more sense to you. You may also want to revisit this information after reading the sections on brain anatomy.

I think I understand the synapse and neurotransmitters now, but how do I relate that to the real world?

---

enzymatic degradation   process by which structure of neurotransmitter is altered so it can no longer act on a receptor.

central nervous system (CNS)   part of the nervous system consisting of the brain and spinal cord.

spinal cord   a long bundle of neurons that carries messages between the body and the brain and is responsible for very fast, lifesaving reflexes.

---

*Enzyme: a complex protein that is manufactured by cells.

practice quiz   How much do you remember?

Pick the best answer.

1. Which part of the neuron receives messages from other cells?
   a. axon
   b. dendrite
   c. soma
   d. myelin

2. Which one of the following is NOT a function of the myelin sheath?
   a. insulates the axon
   b. speeds up the neural message
   c. protects the nerve fiber from damage
   d. aids in reuptake

3. When a neuron's action potential occurs, _____ ions are rushing into the axon through openings on the membrane.
   a. sodium
   b. potassium
   c. chloride
   d. oxygen

4. When the action potential reaches the end of the axon terminals, it causes the release of _____.
   a. an electrical spark that sets off the next neuron.
   b. positively charged ions that excite the next cell.
   c. negatively charged ions that inhibit the next cell.
   d. neurotransmitters that excite or inhibit the next cell.

5. Receiving neurons have special _____ that fit the shape of certain molecules.
   a. synaptic vesicles
   b. gaps
   c. receptor sites
   d. branches

6. Which of the following is associated with sleep, mood, and appetite?
   a. acetylcholine
   b. GABA
   c. serotonin
   d. endorphin

ANSWERS ON PAGE AK–1.

The Central Nervous System— The "Central Processing Unit"

The **central nervous system (CNS)** is composed of the brain and the spinal cord. Both the brain and the spinal cord are composed of neurons and glial cells that control the life-sustaining functions of the body as well as all thought, emotion, and behavior.

2.3 How do the brain and spinal cord interact?

The Brain

The brain is the core of the nervous system, the part that makes sense of the information received from the senses, makes decisions, and sends commands out to the muscles and the rest of the body. Later parts of this chapter will cover the brain in more detail. Without the spinal cord, however, the brain would be useless.

The Spinal Cord

The **spinal cord** is a long bundle of neurons that serves two vital functions for the nervous system. Look at the cross-sectional view of the spinal cord in Figure 2.6. Notice that it seems to be divided into two areas, one around the outside and one inside the cord. If it were a real spinal cord, the outer section would appear to be white and the inner section would seem gray. That's because the outer section is composed mainly of myelinated axons and nerves, which appear white, whereas the inner section is mainly composed of cell bodies

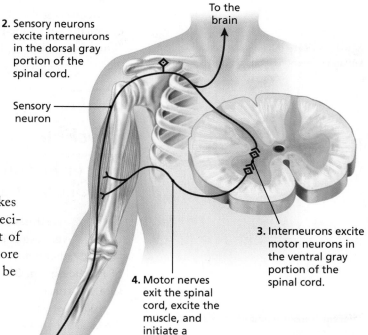

2. Sensory neurons excite interneurons in the dorsal gray portion of the spinal cord.

Sensory neuron

To the brain

3. Interneurons excite motor neurons in the ventral gray portion of the spinal cord.

4. Motor nerves exit the spinal cord, excite the muscle, and initiate a movement.

1. Flame stimulates pain receptors (sensory neurons).

FIGURE 2.6 The Spinal Cord Reflex
The pain from the burning heat of the candle flame stimulates the afferent nerve fibers, which carry the message up to the interneurons in the middle of the spinal cord. The interneurons then send a message out by means of the efferent nerve fibers, causing the hand to jerk away from the flame.

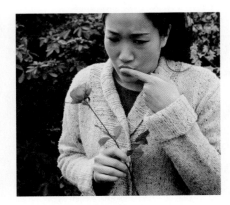

The look on this young woman's face clearly indicates that she has experienced pain in her finger. Pain is a warning signal that something is wrong—in this case that touching the thorns on the stem of the rose was a bad idea. What might be some of the problems encountered by a person who could feel no pain at all?

⊙▶ **Simulate** the nerve impulse in afferent and efferent neurons on **MyPsychLab**

of neurons, which appear gray. The purpose of the outer section is to carry messages from the body up to the brain and from the brain down to the body. It is simply a message "pipeline."

THE REFLEX ARC: THREE TYPES OF NEURONS   The inside section, which is made up of cell bodies separated by glial cells, is actually a primitive sort of "brain." This part of the spinal cord is responsible for certain reflexes—very fast, lifesaving reflexes. To understand how the spinal cord reflexes work, it is important to know there are three basic types of neurons: **afferent (sensory) neurons** that carry messages from the senses to the spinal cord, **efferent (motor) neurons** that carry messages from the spinal cord to the muscles and glands, and **interneurons** that connect the afferent neurons to the motor neurons (and make up the inside of the spinal cord and the brain itself). (See Figure 2.6.) Touch a flame or a hot stove with your finger, for example, and an afferent neuron will send the pain message up to the spinal column where it enters into the central area of the spinal cord. The interneuron in that central area will then receive the message and send out a response along an efferent neuron, causing your finger to pull back. This all happens very quickly. If the pain message had to go all the way up to the brain before a response could be made, the response time would be greatly increased and more damage would be done to your finger. So having this kind of **reflex arc** controlled by the spinal cord alone allows for very fast response times. (A good way to avoid mixing up the terms *afferent* and *efferent* is to remember "afferent neurons <u>a</u>ccess the spinal cord, <u>e</u>fferent neurons <u>e</u>xit.") The pain message does eventually get to the brain, where other motor responses may be triggered, like saying "Ouch!" and putting the finger in your mouth. ⊙▶ **Simulate** on **MyPsychLab**

afferent (sensory) neuron a neuron that carries information from the senses to the central nervous system.

efferent (motor) neuron a neuron that carries messages from the central nervous system to the muscles of the body.

interneuron a neuron found in the center of the spinal cord that receives information from the afferent neurons and sends commands to the muscles through the efferent neurons. Interneurons also make up the bulk of the neurons in the brain.

reflex arc the connection of the afferent neurons to the interneurons to the efferent neurons, resulting in a reflex action.

psychology in the news

Fact or Fiction: Focus on the Brain, but Check Your Sources!

🔊 As stressed in Chapter One, critical thinking is a valuable skill and one that is very useful in the study of psychology. One of the basic points highlighted was that not all evidence is equal in quality. Ⓛ Ⓘ Ⓝ Ⓚ to Chapter One: The Science of Psychology, p. 32. Have you ever heard a claim about the brain that you were not sure was true?

Whether you get your news from blogs or from Web sites, listen to podcasts, or watch the local or national news on your television, computer, or smartphone, you have probably read/heard/seen a segment that addresses some aspect of the human brain. Some recent, and not-so-recent brain-related news items have included the following:

"Older brains can't make new cells"

"Listening to classical music makes you smarter—also known as *The Mozart Effect*"

"Autism is caused by childhood vaccinations"

"People only use 10 percent of their brain"

Items adapted from *Neuromyth Busters: Eight Myths about the Brain*, Society for Neuroscience. Available at *www.sfn.org/skins/main/pdf/neuromyth_busters/neuromyth_busters.pdf*

Do any of the above "headlines" look familiar? Given the inherent interest in many of these topics and the number of people who reportedly "know" these facts, they have often been considered the truth. But in fact, all of the above items have been found to be false or have not been supported by conclusive, scientific evidence. So how do you go about evaluating brain-related news the next time it flashes across the headlines or shows up on your news feed?

Some of the best sources are the original research studies, assuming the researchers collected data in an unbiased manner and followed established research methods. Ⓛ Ⓘ Ⓝ Ⓚ *to Chapter One: The Science of Psychology, pp. 18-29.* Findings that are published in peer-reviewed journals (where research is reviewed by other experts in that area) are especially helpful, as are edited books with contributions by experts in the associated field. The challenge for students early in their psychological studies is that it is not so easy to fully understand the methods, statistics, or terminology used in the studies.

For students, aside from your textbooks and professors, other good resources are the educational materials provided by professional organizations. For psychology in general, the American Psychological Association (APA) and the Association for Psychological Science (APS) are two great sources of information. In addition to various peer-reviewed journals and other educational publications, they both have informative Web sites.

For information more specifically related to the brain and neuroscience, one of the best sources of research and educational material is the Society for Neuroscience (SfN). The four misconceptions mentioned earlier are based on eight myths about the brain that are covered in one of their educational publications *Neuromyth Busters: Eight Myths about the Brain* and is available from their Web site, *www.sfn.org/skins/main/pdf/neuromyth_busters/neuromyth_busters.pdf*

So the next time you see a news item about the brain, check your sources and remain mindful that some sources are certainly more helpful than others.

Useful Web sites:

American Psychological Association (APA)—*www.apa.org*

Association for Psychological Science (APS)—*www.psychologicalscience.org*

Society for Neuroscience (SfN)—*www.sfn.org/home.aspx*

QUESTIONS FOR FURTHER DISCUSSION

1. How might your personal experience with a brain-related disorder (e.g., grandparent with Alzheimer's disease) affect your ability to critically evaluate a claim related to the disorder (e.g., "Cure for Alzheimer's Found!")?
2. As a student in psychological science, how would you explain the need for replicability in research to a family member who is not as familiar with the scientific method?

If the spinal cord is such an important link between the body and the brain, what happens if it is damaged?

Damage to the central nervous system was once thought to be permanent. Neurons in the brain and spinal cord were not seen as capable of repairing themselves. When people recovered from a stroke, for example, it was assumed that healthy brain cells took over the function of the damaged ones. Scientists have known for a while now that some forms of central nervous system damage can be repaired by the body's systems, and in recent years great strides have been made in repairing spinal cord damage. The brain actually exhibits a great deal of **neuroplasticity**, the ability to constantly change both the structure and function of many cells in the brain in response to experience and even trauma (Neville & Bavelier, 2000; Rossini et al., 2007; Sanders et al., 2008). Scientists have been able to *implant* nerve fibers from outside the spinal cord onto a damaged area and then "coax" the damaged spinal nerves to grow through these "tunnels" of implanted fibers (Cheng et al., 1996). The first human trials have

> If the spinal cord is such an important link between the body and the brain, what happens if it is damaged?

neuroplasticity the ability within the brain to constantly change both the structure and function of many cells in response to experience or trauma.

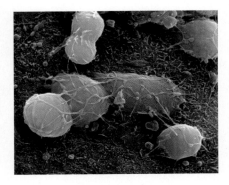

This electronmicrograph shows a stem cell in the process of becoming a neuron.

already begun (Blits & Bunge, 2006; Bunge & Pearse, 2003). It is also now known that the brain can change itself quite a bit by adapting neurons to serve new functions when old neurons die or are damaged. Dendrites grow and new synapses are formed in at least some areas of the brain, as people learn new things throughout life (Abraham & Williams, 2003).

Researchers are constantly looking for new ways to repair the brain. One avenue of research has involved scientists investigating the possibility of transplanting **stem cells** to repair damaged or diseased brain tissue. Stem cells can become other cells, such as blood cells, nerve cells, and brain cells (National Institutes of Health, 2007), and may offer promise for addressing diseases such as Parkinson's and Alzheimer's, or the repair of damaged spinal cords or brain tissue. If stem cells can be implanted into areas that have been damaged, the newly developed neurons may assume the roles that the original (now damaged) neurons can no longer perform.

The Peripheral Nervous System—Nerves on the Edge

Okay, that takes care of the central nervous system, except for the detail on the brain. How does the central nervous system communicate with the rest of the body?

The term *peripheral* refers to things that are not in the center or that are on the edges of the center. The **peripheral nervous system** or **PNS** (see Figure 2.7 and also Figure 2.1, p. 42) is made up of all the nerves and neurons that are not contained in the brain and spinal cord. It is this system that allows the brain and spinal cord to communicate with the sensory systems of the eyes, ears, skin, and mouth and enables the brain and spinal cord to control the muscles and glands of the body. The PNS can be divided into two major systems, the **somatic nervous system** and the **autonomic nervous system (ANS)**.

2.4 How do the somatic and autonomic nervous systems allow people and animals to interact with their surroundings and control the body's automatic functions?

The Somatic Nervous System

One of the parts of a neuron is the soma, or cell body (the word *soma* means "body"). The somatic nervous system is made up of the **sensory pathway**, which is all the nerves carrying messages from the senses to the central nervous system (those nerves containing afferent neurons), and the **motor pathway**, which is all of the nerves carrying messages from the central nervous system to the voluntary, or skeletal,*

FIGURE 2.7 The Peripheral Nervous System

stem cells special cells found in all the tissues of the body that are capable of manufacturing other cell types when those cells need to be replaced due to damage or wear and tear.

peripheral nervous system (PNS) all nerves and neurons that are not contained in the brain and spinal cord but that run through the body itself.

somatic nervous system division of the PNS consisting of nerves that carry information from the senses to the CNS and from the CNS to the voluntary muscles of the body.

autonomic nervous system (ANS) division of the PNS consisting of nerves that control all of the involuntary muscles, organs, and glands.

sensory pathway nerves coming from the sensory organs to the CNS consisting of afferent neurons.

motor pathway nerves coming from the CNS to the voluntary muscles, consisting of efferent neurons.

*Skeletal: having to do with the bones of the body, or skeleton.

muscles of the body—muscles that allow people to move their bodies (those nerves composed of efferent neurons). When people are walking, raising their hands in class, smelling a flower, or directing their gaze toward the person they are talking to or to look at a pretty picture, they are using the somatic nervous system. (As seen in the discussion of spinal cord reflexes, although these muscles are called the voluntary muscles, they can move involuntarily when a reflex response occurs. They are called "voluntary" because they *can* be moved at will but are not limited to only that kind of movement.)

Involuntary* muscles, such as the heart, stomach, and intestines, together with glands such as the adrenal glands and the pancreas are all controlled by clumps of neurons located on or near the spinal column. (The words *on* or *near* are used quite deliberately here. The neurons *inside* the spinal column are part of the central nervous system, not the peripheral nervous system.) These large groups of neurons near the spinal column make up the *autonomic nervous system*.

The Autonomic Nervous System

The word *autonomic* suggests that the functions of this system are more or less automatic, which is basically correct. Whereas the somatic division of the peripheral nervous system controls the senses and voluntary muscles, the autonomic division controls everything else in the body—organs, glands, and involuntary muscles. The autonomic nervous system is divided into two systems, the **sympathetic division** and the **parasympathetic division**. (See Figure 2.8.) (For a visual representation of how all the various sections of the nervous system are organized, look back at Figure 2.1 on page 42.)

THE SYMPATHETIC DIVISION The sympathetic division is also called the *fight-or-flight system* because it allows people and animals to deal with all kinds of stressful events. Ⓛ Ⓘ Ⓝ Ⓚ to Chapter Nine: Stress and Health, p. 319. Emotions during these

*Involuntary: not under deliberate control.

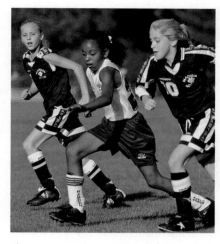

These young soccer players are using their senses and voluntary muscles controlled by the somatic division of the peripheral nervous system. What part of the autonomic nervous system are these girls also using at this time?

sympathetic division (fight-or-flight system) part of the ANS that is responsible for reacting to stressful events and bodily arousal.

parasympathetic division part of the ANS that restores the body to normal functioning after arousal and is responsible for the day-to-day functioning of the organs and glands.

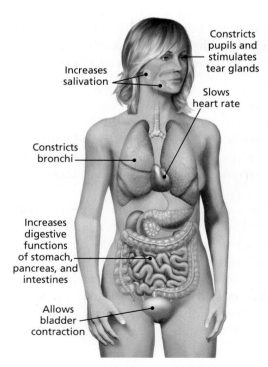

Increases salivation

Constricts pupils and stimulates tear glands

Slows heart rate

Constricts bronchi

Increases digestive functions of stomach, pancreas, and intestines

Allows bladder contraction

Parasympathetic Division

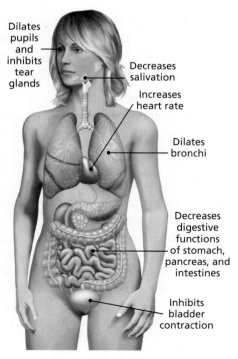

Dilates pupils and inhibits tear glands

Decreases salivation

Increases heart rate

Dilates bronchi

Decreases digestive functions of stomach, pancreas, and intestines

Inhibits bladder contraction

Sympathetic Division

FIGURE 2.8 **Functions of the Parasympathetic and Sympathetic Divisions of the Nervous System**

Snowboarder Shaun White of the U.S.A. 2010 Olympics Team won the gold medal in the halfpipe competition in Vancouver. What part of the autonomic nervous system is likely to be working as Shaun flies through the air, as in this picture?

events might be anger (hence, the term *fight*) or fear (that's the *flight* part, obviously) or even extreme joy or excitement. Yes, even joy can be stressful. The sympathetic division's job is to get the body ready to deal with the stress.

What are the specific ways in which this division readies the body to react? (See Figure 2.8.) The pupils seem to get bigger, perhaps to let in more light and, therefore, more information. The heart starts pumping faster and harder, drawing blood away from nonessential organs such as the skin (so at first the person may turn pale) and sometimes even the brain itself (so the person might actually faint). Blood needs lots of oxygen before it goes to the muscles, so the lungs work overtime, too (so the person may begin to breathe faster). One set of glands in particular receives special instructions. The adrenal glands will be stimulated to release certain stress-related chemicals (members of a class of chemicals released by glands called *hormones*) into the bloodstream. These stress hormones will travel to all parts of the body, but they will only affect certain target organs. Just as a neurotransmitter fits into a receptor site on a cell, the molecules of the stress hormones fit into receptor sites at the various target organs—notably, the heart, muscles, and lungs. This further stimulates these organs to work harder. (There are other hormones for other functions that have nothing to do with stress. For more about hormones and glands, see the section that follows, Distant Connections: The Endocrine Glands.) But not every organ or system will be stimulated by the activation of the sympathetic division. Digestion of food and excretion* of waste are not necessary functions when dealing with stressful situations, so these systems tend to be "shut down" or inhibited. Saliva, which is part of digestion, dries right up (ever try whistling when you're scared?). Food that was in the stomach sits there like a lump. Usually, the urge to go to the bathroom will be suppressed, but if the person is really scared the bladder or bowels may actually empty (this is why people who die under extreme stress, such as hanging or electrocution, will release their urine and waste). The sympathetic division is also going to demand that the body burn a tremendous amount of fuel, or blood sugar.

Now, all this bodily arousal is going on during a stressful situation. If the stress ends, the activity of the sympathetic division will be replaced by the activation of the parasympathetic division. If the stress goes on too long or is too intense, the person might actually collapse (as a deer might do when being chased by another animal). This collapse occurs because the parasympathetic division overresponds in its inhibition of the sympathetic activity. The heart slows, blood vessels open up, blood pressure in the brain drops, and fainting can result.

THE PARASYMPATHETIC DIVISION If the sympathetic division can be called the fight-or-flight system, the parasympathetic division might be called the "eat-drink-and-rest" system. The neurons of this division are located at the top and bottom of the spinal column on either side of the sympathetic division neurons (*para* means "beyond" or "next to" and in this sense refers to the neurons located on either side of the sympathetic division neurons).

In looking at Figure 2.8, it might seem as if the parasympathetic division does pretty much the opposite of the sympathetic division, but it's a little more complex than that. The parasympathetic division's job is to restore the body to normal functioning after a stressful situation ends. It slows the heart and breathing, constricts the pupils, and reactivates digestion and excretion. Signals to the adrenal glands stop because the parasympathetic division isn't connected to the adrenal glands. In a sense, the parasympathetic division allows the body to put back all the energy it burned—which is why people are often very hungry *after* the stress is all over.

---

*Excretion: in this sense, the act of eliminating waste products from the body.

The parasympathetic division does more than just react to the activity of the sympathetic division. It is the parasympathetic division that is responsible for most of the ordinary, day-to-day bodily functioning, such as regular heartbeat and normal breathing and digestion. People spend the greater part of their 24-hour day eating, sleeping, digesting, and excreting. So it is the parasympathetic division that is normally active. At any given moment, then, one or the other of these divisions, sympathetic or parasympathetic, will determine whether people are aroused or relaxed.

endocrine glands glands that secrete chemicals called hormones directly into the bloodstream.

Distant Connections: The Endocrine Glands

How do the glands fit into all of this? Aren't there more glands than just the adrenal glands? How do they affect our behavior?

Earlier we addressed the subject of neurons and the neurotransmitters and how they release into the synapse to communicate with postsynaptic neurons. This type of chemical communication is fairly specific, primarily affecting neurons in the immediate vicinity of the originating neuron, and also very fast (almost immediate). Other structures also use chemical communication but do so at a different rate and act in a more far-reaching manner. For example, glands are organs in the body that secrete chemicals. Some glands, such as salivary glands and sweat glands, secrete their chemicals directly onto the body's tissues through tiny tubes, or ducts. This kind of gland affects the functioning of the body but doesn't really affect behavior. Other glands, called **endocrine glands**, have no ducts and secrete their chemicals directly into the bloodstream. (See Figure 2.9.) The chemicals secreted by this type of gland are called

How do the glands fit into all of this? Aren't there more glands than just the adrenal glands? How do they affect our behavior?

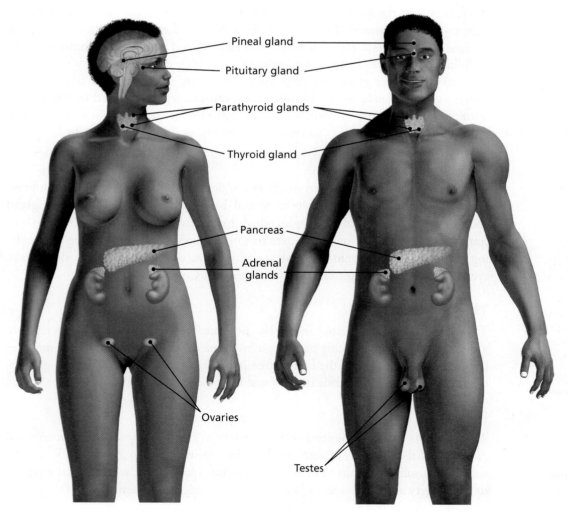

FIGURE 2.9 The Endocrine Glands

The endocrine glands secrete hormones directly into the bloodstream, which carries them to organs in the body, such as the heart, pancreas, and sex organs.

hormones. As mentioned earlier in the chapter when talking about the sympathetic division of the autonomic nervous system, these hormones flow into the bloodstream, which carries them to their target organs. The molecules of these hormones then fit into receptor sites on those organs to fulfill their function, affecting behavior as they do so. As compared to synaptic communication, endocrine communication is generally slower due to the time it takes hormones to travel to target organs; the behaviors and responses they affect may not occur until hours, weeks, or years later.

2.5 How do the hormones released by glands interact with the nervous system and affect behavior?

The hormones affect behavior and emotions by stimulating muscles, organs, or other glands of the body. Some theories of emotion state that the surge in certain hormones actually triggers the emotional reaction (Izard, 1988; Zajonc, 1980, 1984). (LINK) to Chapter Eight: Motivation and Emotion, p. 294. Some of the hormones produced by endocrine glands also influence the activity of the brain, producing excitatory or inhibitory effects (Mai et al., 1987).

The Pituitary, Master of the Hormonal Universe

The **pituitary gland** is located in the brain itself, just below the hypothalamus. The hypothalamus (see p. 66) controls the glandular system by influencing the pituitary. That is because the pituitary gland is the *master gland*, the one that controls or influences all of the other endocrine glands. One part of the pituitary controls things associated with pregnancy, such as production of milk for nursing infants and the onset of labor, as well as the levels of salt and water in the body. Another part of the pituitary secretes several hormones that influence the activity of the other glands. Most notable of these hormones is a *growth hormone* that controls and regulates the increase in size as children grow from infancy to adulthood.

As the master gland, the pituitary forms a very important part of a feedback system, one that includes the hypothalamus and the organs targeted by the various hormones. The balance of hormones in the entire endocrine system is maintained by feedback from each of these "players" to the others. ✳ Explore on MyPsychLab

The Pineal Gland

The **pineal gland** is also located in the brain, near the back, directly above the brain stem. It plays an important role in several biological rhythms. The pineal gland secretes a hormone called melatonin, which helps track day length (and seasons). In some animals, this hormone influences seasonal behaviors such as breeding and molting. In humans, melatonin levels are more influential in regulating the sleep–wake cycle. (LINK) to Chapter Six: Consciousness and Cognition, p. 199.

The Thyroid Gland

The **thyroid gland** is located inside the neck and secretes hormones that regulate growth and metabolism. One of these, a hormone called thyroxin, regulates metabolism (controlling how fast the body burns its available energy). As related to growth, the thyroid plays a crucial role in body and brain development.

Pancreas

The **pancreas** controls the level of blood sugar in the body by secreting *insulin* and *glucagons*. If the pancreas secretes too little insulin, it results in *diabetes*. If it secretes too much insulin, it results in *hypoglycemia*, or low blood sugar, which causes a person to feel hungry all the time and often become overweight as a result.

✳ Explore the endocrine glands on MyPsychLab

hormones chemicals released into the bloodstream by endocrine glands.

pituitary gland gland located in the brain that secretes human growth hormone and influences all other hormone-secreting glands (also known as the master gland).

pineal gland endocrine gland located near the base of the cerebrum; secretes melatonin.

thyroid gland endocrine gland found in the neck; regulates metabolism.

pancreas endocrine gland; controls the levels of sugar in the blood.

The Gonads

The **gonads** are the sex glands, including the **ovaries** in the female and the **testes** in the male. They secrete hormones that regulate sexual behavior and reproduction. They do not control all sexual behavior, though. In a very real sense, the brain itself is the master of the sexual system—human sexual behavior is not only controlled by instincts and the actions of the glands as in the animal world but also by psychological factors such as attractiveness.

The Adrenal Glands

Everyone has two **adrenal glands**, one on top of each kidney. The origin of the name is simple enough; *renal* comes from a Latin word meaning "kidney" and *ad* is Latin for "to," so *adrenal* means "to or on the kidney." Each adrenal gland is actually divided into two sections, the *adrenal medulla* and the *adrenal cortex*. It is the adrenal medulla that releases ephinephrine and norepinephrine when people are under stress and that aids in sympathetic arousal.

    The adrenal cortex produces over 30 different hormones called *corticoids* (also called steroids) that regulate salt intake and help initiate* and control stress reactions; it also provides a source of sex hormones in addition to those provided by the gonads. One of the most important of these adrenal hormones is *cortisol*, released when the body experiences stress, both physical stress (such as illness, surgery, or extreme heat or cold) and psychological stress (such as an emotional upset). L I N K to Chapter Nine: Stress and Health, p. 311. Cortisol is important in the release of glucose into the bloodstream during stress, providing energy for the brain itself, and in the release of fatty acids from the fat cells that provide the muscles with energy.

*Initiate: begin or start.

When the pancreas does not secrete enough insulin, the result is diabetes. Many diabetic people must give themselves insulin shots to supply enough of the hormone.

gonads   sex glands; secrete hormones that regulate sexual development and behavior as well as reproduction.

ovaries   the female gonads.

testes   the male gonads.

adrenal glands   endocrine glands located on top of each kidney that secrete over 30 different hormones to deal with stress, regulate salt intake, and provide a secondary source of sex hormones affecting the sexual changes that occur during adolescence.

practice quiz   How much do you remember?

2.3 **2.4** **2.5**

Pick the best answer.

1. If you burn your finger, your immediate reaction will probably involve all BUT which of the following?
  a. the brain
  b. the spinal cord
  c. afferent neurons
  d. efferent neurons

2. If you are typing on the computer keyboard, the motions of your fingers on the keys are probably being controlled by _____.
  a. the autonomic nervous system.
  b. sensory pathway neurons.
  c. motor pathway neurons.
  d. autonomic neurons.

3. The neurons of the motor pathway control _____.
  a. stress reactions.
  b. organs and glands.
  c. involuntary muscles.
  d. voluntary muscles.

4. What type of cell can become other types of cells in the body?
  a. blood cells
  b. stem cells
  c. neurons
  d. basal cells

5. Which of the following is NOT a function of the sympathetic division?
  a. increasing digestive activity to supply fuel for the body
  b. dilating the pupils of the eyes
  c. increasing the heart rate
  d. increasing the activity of the lungs

6. Which of the following would be active if you are sleeping?
  a. sympathetic division
  b. parasympathetic division
  c. somatic division
  d. motor division

7. Andrew never really grew to be very tall. The doctor told his parents that Andrew's _____ gland did not secrete enough growth hormone, causing his small stature.
  a. pituitary
  b. adrenal
  c. thyroid
  d. pancreas

8. If the pancreas secretes too little insulin, it causes _____.
  a. diabetes.
  b. hypoglycemia.
  c. hypothyroidism.
  d. virilism.

deep lesioning insertion of a thin, insulated wire into the brain through which an electrical current is sent that destroys the brain cells at the tip of the wire.

Looking Inside the Living Brain

2.6 How do psychologists study the brain and how it works?

Scientists can't be sure what brain tissue really looks like when it's inside the skull of a living person—nor can they be certain that it looks identical to that of a brain sitting on a dissecting table. How can scientists find out what the various parts of the brain do?

Lesioning Studies

One way to get some idea of the functions that various areas of the brain control is to study animals or people with damage in those areas. In animals, that may mean researchers will deliberately damage a part of the brain, after which, they test the animal to see what has happened to its abilities. In such an experiment, once the test animal is anesthetized and given medication for pain, a thin wire, which is insulated everywhere but at its tip, is surgically inserted into the brain. An electrical current strong enough to kill off the target neurons is sent through the tip of the wire. This procedure is called **deep lesioning**. (When cells are destroyed on the surface of the brain or just below it, the process is sometimes called *shallow lesioning.*)

It should be obvious that researchers cannot destroy areas of brains in living human beings. One method they can use is to study and test people who already have brain damage. However, this is not an ideal way to study the brain. No two case studies of humans are likely to present damage in exactly the same area of the brain, nor would the cases involve exactly the same amount of damage.

Brain Stimulation

In contrast to lesioning, a less harmful way to study the brain is to temporarily disrupt or enhance the normal functioning of specific brain areas through electrical stimulation, and then study the resulting changes in behavior or cognition. The procedure of stimulating a specific area of the brain is much the same as in lesioning, but the much milder current in this research does no damage to the neurons. It does cause the neurons to react as if they had received a message. This is called *electrical stimulation of the brain*, or *ESB*. It has become an important technique in psychology, as its use in animals (and in humans under very special circumstances such as testing before surgery to address seizure disorders) has informed us in many areas of investigation, including new directions for therapy.

INVASIVE TECHNIQUES: STIMULATING FROM THE INSIDE A specific type of ESB called *deep brain stimulation (DBS)* has been shown to be very helpful in some disorders in humans. In this procedure, neurosurgeons place electrodes in specific deep-brain areas and then route the electrode wires to a pacemaker-like device called an impulse generator that is surgically implanted under the collarbone. The impulse generator then sends impulses to the implanted electrodes, stimulating the specific brain areas of interest. Deep brain stimulation has been widely used as a treatment for Parkinson's disease and may play an important role in the treatment of seizure disorder, chronic pain, and possibly some psychiatric disorders (Fisher et al., 2010; Rabins et al., 2009; Weaver et al., 2009) among other areas. Techniques such as DBS are typically used only after all other less intrusive treatments have been shown to be ineffective or whose side effects have been deemed undesirable.

NONINVASIVE TECHNIQUE: STIMULATING FROM THE OUTSIDE There are also noninvasive techniques for stimulating the brain that contribute to research and our knowledge of the brain in a variety of areas. In *repetitive transcranial magnetic stimulation* (rTMS), magnetic pulses are applied to the cortex using special copper wire coils that

A researcher at the National Institute of Mental Health in Bethesda, Maryland, uses an electromagnet as part of an experimental treatment for depression. This treatment, called Repetitive Transcranial Magnetic Stimulation (rTMS), excites neurons in the brain, triggering activity.

are positioned over the head. The resulting magnetic fields stimulate neurons in the targeted area of the cortex. Another procedure, called *transcranial direct current stimulation* (tDCS), uses scalp electrodes to pass very low amplitude direct currents to the brain to change the excitability of cortical neurons directly below the electrodes. Both rTMS and tDCS are being evaluated as research tools in studies of cognition such as memory retrieval and decision making (Boggio et al., 2010; Boggio, Fregni et al., 2009) and as possible treatment options for a variety of psychological disorders including posttraumatic stress disorder (PTSD) and depression, and physical disorders due to suffering a stroke (Boggio, Rocha et al., 2009; Nitsche, Boggio, Fregni, & Pascual-Leone, 2009; Williams, Pascual-Leone, & Fregni, 2010).

Note: tDCS is NOT the same as electroconvulsive therapy, which uses much higher levels of current through the entire brain, resulting in a grand mal seizure and changes in the brain chemistry associated with depression. ⒧ⒾⓃⓀ to Chapter Thirteen: Psychological Therapies, p. 489.

All of these methods of stimulation yield important information about the brain and behavior, but they do not allow us to see what is going on inside the brain. Instead, various neuroimaging techniques can do this, either by directly imaging the brain's structure (the different parts) or its function (how the parts work). These methods also vary in their degree of spatial resolution (ability to see fine detail) and temporal resolution (ability to time lock a recorded event.)

Mapping Structure

COMPUTED TOMOGRAPHY (CT) Scientists have several ways to look inside the human brain without causing harm to the person. One way is to take a series of X-rays of the brain, aided by a computer. This is accomplished during a CT scan (**computed tomography** involves mapping "slices" of the brain by computer). CT scans can show stroke damage, tumors, injuries, and abnormal brain structure. (See Figures 2.10a and 2.10b.) CT scans are also useful for imaging possible skull fractures and are the imaging method of choice when there is metal in the body (e.g., a bullet or surgical clips).

MAGNETIC RESONANCE IMAGING (MRI) As useful as a CT scan can be for imaging the skull, it doesn't show very small details within the brain. The relatively newer technique of **magnetic resonance imaging**, or **MRI**, provides much more detail (see Figures 2.10c and 2.10d), even allowing doctors to see the effects of very small strokes. The person getting an MRI scan is placed inside a machine that generates a powerful magnetic field to align hydrogen atoms in the brain tissues (these normally spin in a random fashion); then radio pulses are used to make the atoms spin at a

computed tomography (CT) brain-imaging method using computer-controlled X-rays of the brain.

magnetic resonance imaging (MRI) brain-imaging method using radio waves and magnetic fields of the body to produce detailed images of the brain.

a.

b.

c.

d.

FIGURE 2.10 Mapping Brain Structure
Figure 2.10a: CT scan from a 5-year-old girl with a head injury and skull fracture, depicting the brain and swelling associated with the injury; Figure 2.10b: same CT scan highlighting the skull fracture (indicated by the red arrow). Contrast the brain detail of Figure 2.10a with the MRI scan in Figure 2.10c (different, adult individual). Note that the scans are in the horizontal plane, separating the brain into upper and lower portions. Figure 2.10d uses the same MRI data to provide an estimate of what the left external surface of the brain looks like. Figure 2.10a, b, and c images created with OsiriX software; Figure 2.10d cortical reconstruction was performed with the Freesurfer image analysis suite. CT and MRI data courtesy of N. White.

electroencephalograph machine designed to record the electroencephalogram.

electroencephalogram (EEG) a recording of the electrical activity of large groups of cortical neurons just below the skull, most often using scalp electrodes.

particular frequency and direction. The time it takes for the atoms to return to their normal spin allows a computer to create a three-dimensional image of the brain and display "slices" of that image on a screen.

Using MRI as a basis, researchers have developed several techniques that allow us to study other aspects of the brain. *MRI spectroscopy* allows researchers to estimate the concentration of specific chemicals and neurotransmitters in the brain. Another fascinating technique is called *DTI,* or *diffusion tensor imaging.* The brain has two distinct color regions, *gray matter,* the outer areas consisting largely of neurons with unmyelinated axons, and *white matter,* the fiber tracts consisting of myelinated axons (the myelin is responsible for the lighter color). DTI uses MRI technology to provide a way to measure connectivity in the brain by imaging these white matter tracts. DTI has been used to investigate many disorders and conditions, including multiple sclerosis, dementia, and schizophrenia (Assaf & Pasternak, 2008; Bremmer, 2005; Ulmer, Parsons, Moseley, & Gabrieli, 2006; Voineskos et al., 2010).

Mapping Function

FIGURE 2.11 Mapping Brain Function Various methods for mapping brain function. An EEG record is shown in Figure 2.11a, a PET scan image in Figure 2.11b, and an image from an fMRI study in Figure 2.11c.

THE ELECTROENCEPHALOGRAM (EEG) As important as imaging brain structure is, it is sometimes important to know how different brain areas function. A fairly harmless way to study the activity of the living brain is to record the electrical activity of the cortex just below the skull using a device called an **electroencephalograph**. The first **electroencephalogram (EEG)** recording in humans was accomplished in 1924 by Hans Berger (Niedermeyer, 2005). Recording the EEG involves using small metal-disk or sponge-like electrodes placed directly on the scalp, and a special solution to help conduct the electrical signals from the cortex just below. These electrodes are connected to an amplifier and then to a computer to view the information. The resulting electrical output forms waves that indicate many things, such as stages of sleep, seizures, and even the presence of tumors. The EEG can also be used to help determine which areas of the brain are active during various mental tasks that involve memory and attention.

EEG activity can be classified according to appearance and frequency. Very fast, irregular waves called *beta waves* indicate waking activity. Slightly more regular and slower waves called *alpha waves* are a sign of relaxation (seen in the bottom two lines in Figure 2.11a), *theta waves* are associated

a.

b.

c.

with drowsiness and sleep, and much slower, larger waves called *delta waves* indicate deep sleep. (These waveforms are covered in more detail in Chapter Six.) Ⓛⓘⓝⓚ to Chapter Six: Consciousness and Cognition, p. 201.

Another common EEG-based technique focuses on *event-related potentials*, or *ERPs*. In ERP studies, multiple presentations of a stimulus are measured during an EEG and then averaged to remove variations in the ongoing brain activity that is normally recorded during the EEG. The result is a measurement of the response of the brain related to the stimulus event itself, or an event-related potential. ERPs allow the study of different stages of cognitive processing. For example, one recent study has investigated differences in brain processing associated with the recognition of facial expression of emotion in individuals with and without schizophrenia (Lee, Kim, Kim, & Bae, 2010); in another study, ERPs are being studied as a possible method of lie detection (Rosenfeld et al., 2008). This modality is also being used as part of brain–computer interfaces (BCI) to assist people like Rick from the chapter opener better communicate and interact with others and the world around them. 📖┤Read on MyPsychLab

POSITRON EMISSION TOMOGRAPHY (PET) The functional neuroimaging methods discussed so far rely on the electrical activity of the brain. Other techniques make use of other indicators of brain activity, including energy consumption or changes in blood oxygen levels (if areas of the brain are active, they are likely using fuel and oxygen). In **positron emission tomography (PET)**, the person is injected with a radioactive glucose (a kind of sugar). The computer detects the activity of the brain cells by looking at which cells are using up the radioactive glucose and projecting the image of that activity onto a monitor. The computer uses colors to indicate different levels of brain activity, with lighter colors often indicating greater activity. (See Figure 2.11b.) With this method, researchers can actually have the person perform different tasks while the computer shows what his or her brain is doing during the task. A related technique is **single photon emission computed tomography (SPECT)**, which measures brain blood flow and uses more easily obtainable radioactive tracers than those used for PET (Bremmer, 2005).

FUNCTIONAL MRI (FMRI) Although traditional MRI scans only show structure, there is a technique called **functional MRI (fMRI)** in which the computer tracks changes in the oxygen levels of the blood (see Figure 2.11c). By superimposing this picture of where the oxygen goes in the brain over the picture of the brain's structure, researchers can identify what areas of the brain are active. By combining such images taken over a period of time, a sort of "movie" of the brain's functioning can be made (Lin et al., 2007). Functional MRIs can give more detail, tend to be clearer than PET scans, and are an incredibly useful tool for research into the workings of the brain. For example, fMRI has been used to demonstrate that older adults with a genetic risk for Alzheimer's disease show greater activation in brain areas associated with semantic knowledge and word retrieval when compared to older adults without that genetic risk. This finding may one day help clinicians and researchers identify individuals at risk for Alzheimer's much earlier in the disease process (Wierenga et al., 2010).

Okay, now I understand a little more about how we look inside the brain. What exactly IS inside the brain?

From the Bottom Up: The Structures of the Brain

Now it's time to look at the various structures of the brain, starting from the bottom and working up to the top. (A word of caution: This text won't be discussing every single part of the brain; only the parts interesting to psychologists as explorers of

positron emission tomography (PET) brain-imaging method in which a radioactive sugar is injected into a person and a computer compiles a color-coded image of the activity of the brain.

single photon emission computed tomography (SPECT) neuroimaging method that is similar to PET but uses a different radioactive tracer and can be used to examine brain blood flow.

functional magnetic resonance imaging (fMRI) MRI-based brain-imaging method that allows for functional examination of brain areas through changes in brain oxygenation.

📖┤Read and learn more about EEG and related techniques on **MyPsychLab**

Okay, now I understand a little more about how we look inside the brain. What exactly IS inside the brain?

medulla the first large swelling at the top of the spinal cord, forming the lowest part of the brain, which is responsible for life-sustaining functions such as breathing, swallowing, and heart rate.

pons the larger swelling above the medulla that connects the top of the brain to the bottom and that plays a part in sleep, dreaming, left–right body coordination, and arousal.

reticular formation (RF) an area of neurons running through the middle of the medulla and the pons and slightly beyond that is responsible for general attention, alertness, and arousal.

human behavior will be covered. Many parts of the brain also overlap in their functions, but a full understanding of the brain is not truly possible within one chapter of an introductory psychology text.)

2.7 What are the different structures of the bottom part of the brain, and what do they do?

The Hindbrain

MEDULLA The **medulla** is located at the top of the spinal column. In Figure 2.12, it is the first "swelling" at the top of the spinal cord, just at the very bottom of the brain. This is the part of the brain that a person would least want to have damaged, as it controls life-sustaining functions such as heartbeat, breathing, and swallowing. It is in the medulla that the sensory nerves coming from the left and right sides of the body cross over, so that sensory information from the left side of the body goes to the right side of the brain and vice versa.

PONS The **pons** is the larger "swelling" just above the medulla. This term means "bridge," and the pons is indeed the bridge between the lower parts of the brain and the upper sections. As in the medulla, there is a crossover of nerves, but in this case it is the motor nerves carrying messages from the brain to the body. This allows the pons to coordinate the movements of the left and right sides of the body. (It will be useful to remember these nerve crossovers when reading about the functions of the left and right sides of the brain in a later part of this chapter.) The pons also influences sleep, dreaming, and arousal.

THE RETICULAR FORMATION The **reticular formation (RF)** is an area of neurons running through the middle of the medulla and the pons and slightly beyond. These neurons are responsible for people's ability to selectively attend to certain kinds of

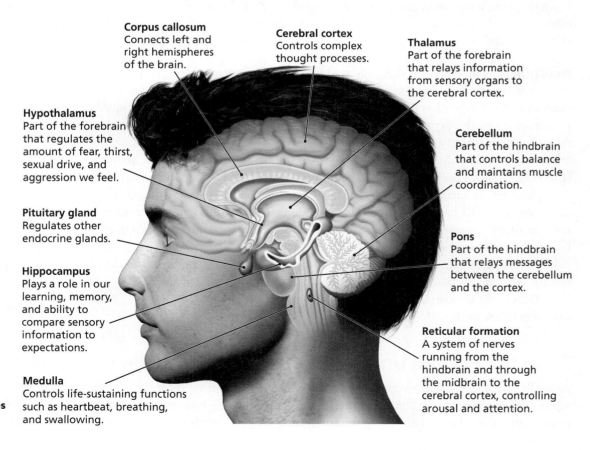

FIGURE 2.12 Major Structures of the Human Brain

Corpus callosum
Connects left and right hemispheres of the brain.

Cerebral cortex
Controls complex thought processes.

Thalamus
Part of the forebrain that relays information from sensory organs to the cerebral cortex.

Hypothalamus
Part of the forebrain that regulates the amount of fear, thirst, sexual drive, and aggression we feel.

Cerebellum
Part of the hindbrain that controls balance and maintains muscle coordination.

Pituitary gland
Regulates other endocrine glands.

Pons
Part of the hindbrain that relays messages between the cerebellum and the cortex.

Hippocampus
Plays a role in our learning, memory, and ability to compare sensory information to expectations.

Reticular formation
A system of nerves running from the hindbrain and through the midbrain to the cerebral cortex, controlling arousal and attention.

Medulla
Controls life-sustaining functions such as heartbeat, breathing, and swallowing.

information in their surroundings. Basically, the RF allows people to ignore constant, unchanging information (such as the noise of an air conditioner) and become alert to changes in information (for example, if the air conditioner stopped, most people would notice immediately).

The reticular formation is also the part of the brain that helps keep people alert and aroused. One part of the RF is called the *reticular activating system (RAS)*, and it stimulates the upper part of the brain, keeping people awake and alert. When a person is driving along and someone suddenly pulls out in front of the vehicle, it is the RAS that brings the driver to full attention. It is also the system that lets a mother hear her baby cry in the night, even though she might sleep through other noises.

Studies have shown that when the RF of rats is electrically stimulated while they are sleeping, they immediately awaken. If the RF is destroyed (by deep lesioning, for example), they fall into a sleeplike coma from which they never awaken (Moruzzi & Magoun, 1949; Steriade & McCarley, 1990). The RF is also implicated in comas in humans (Plum & Posner, 1985).

CEREBELLUM   At the base of the skull, behind the pons and below the main part of the brain, is a structure that looks like a small brain. (See Figure 2.12 on page 64.) The **cerebellum** (meaning "little brain") is the part of the lower brain that controls all involuntary, rapid, fine motor movement. People can sit upright because the cerebellum controls all the little muscles needed to keep them from falling out of their chair. It also coordinates voluntary movements that have to happen in rapid succession, such as walking, diving, skating, gymnastics, dancing, typing, playing a musical instrument, and even the movements of speech. Learned reflexes, skills, and habits are also stored here, which allows them to become more or less automatic. Because of the cerebellum, people don't have to consciously think about their posture, muscle tone, and balance.

So if your cerebellum is damaged, you might be very uncoordinated? ●

Yes. In fact, in a disease called *spinocerebellar degeneration* the first symptoms are tremors, an unsteady walk, slurred speech, dizziness, and muscle weakness. The person suffering from this disease will eventually be unable to walk, stand, or even get a spoon to his or her own mouth (Schöls et al., 1998). These symptoms are similar to what one might see in a person who is suffering from alcohol intoxication.

2.8 What are the structures of the brain that control emotion, learning, memory, and motivation?

Structures under the Cortex

The cortex, which is discussed in detail later in this chapter, is the outer wrinkled covering of the brain. A number of important structures are located just under the cortex and above the brain stem. Each of these subcortical structures (the prefix *sub-* means "under" or "below") plays a part in our behavior. (See Figure 2.13.)

LIMBIC SYSTEM   The **limbic system** (the word *limbic* means "marginal," and these structures are found in the inner margin of the upper brain) includes the thalamus, hypothalamus, hippocampus, amygdala, and the cingulate cortex. In general, the limbic system is involved in emotions, motivation, and learning. ◉▶ Simulate on **MyPsychLab**

Thalamus   Have you ever had to go to the emergency room of a hospital? You may find yourself getting past the receptionist, but most of the time you will have to wait to see a triage nurse before you ever get to see the doctor—if you ever get to see the doctor. (The word *triage* refers to a process for sorting injured people into groups based on their need for or likely benefit from immediate medical treatment.) Triage nurses will ask people questions about their complaints. They may be able to partially treat minor complaints before the person sees a doctor. Then they will send the person

cerebellum   part of the lower brain located behind the pons that controls and coordinates involuntary, rapid, fine motor movement.

limbic system   a group of several brain structures located primarily under the cortex and involved in learning, emotion, memory, and motivation.

◉▶ Simulate the limbic system on **MyPsychLab**

So if your cerebellum is damaged, you might be very uncoordinated?

This pitcher must count on his cerebellum to help him balance and coordinate the many fine motor commands that allow him to pitch the baseball accurately and swiftly. What other kinds of professions depend heavily on the activity of the cerebellum?

FIGURE 2.13 The Limbic System

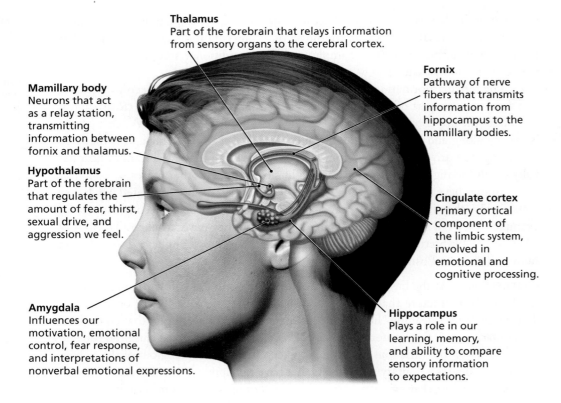

Thalamus
Part of the forebrain that relays information from sensory organs to the cerebral cortex.

Mamillary body
Neurons that act as a relay station, transmitting information between fornix and thalamus.

Hypothalamus
Part of the forebrain that regulates the amount of fear, thirst, sexual drive, and aggression we feel.

Fornix
Pathway of nerve fibers that transmits information from hippocampus to the mamillary bodies.

Cingulate cortex
Primary cortical component of the limbic system, involved in emotional and cognitive processing.

Amygdala
Influences our motivation, emotional control, fear response, and interpretations of nonverbal emotional expressions.

Hippocampus
Plays a role in our learning, memory, and ability to compare sensory information to expectations.

thalamus part of the limbic system located in the center of the brain, this structure relays sensory information from the lower part of the brain to the proper areas of the cortex and processes some sensory information before sending it to its proper area.

olfactory bulbs two projections just under the front of the brain that receive information from the receptors in the nose located just below.

hypothalamus small structure in the brain located below the thalamus and directly above the pituitary gland, responsible for motivational behavior such as sleep, hunger, thirst, and sex.

hippocampus curved structure located within each temporal lobe, responsible for the formation of long-term memories and the storage of memory for location of objects.

to a treatment room with the equipment that might be needed for the ailment, and eventually the person will see a doctor.

The **thalamus** ("inner chamber") is similar to a triage nurse. This somewhat round structure in the center of the brain acts as a relay station for incoming sensory information. Like a nurse, the thalamus might perform some processing of that sensory information before sending it on to the part of the cortex that deals with that kind of sensation—hearing, sight, touch, or taste. Damage to the thalamus might result in the loss or partial loss of any or all of those sensations. **LINK** to Chapter Three: Sensation and Perception, p. 108.

The sense of smell is unique in that signals from the neurons in the sinus cavity go directly into special parts of the brain called **olfactory bulbs**, just under the front part of the brain. Smell is the only sense that cannot be affected by damage to the thalamus.

Hypothalamus A very small but extremely powerful part of the brain is located just below and in front of the thalamus (see Figure 2.13). The **hypothalamus** ("below the inner chamber") regulates body temperature, thirst, hunger, sleeping and waking, sexual activity, and emotions. It sits right above the *pituitary gland*, which is called the "master gland" because it controls the functions of all the other endocrine glands that will be discussed later in this chapter. The hypothalamus controls the pituitary, so the ultimate regulation of hormones lies with the hypothalamus.

Hippocampus The **hippocampus** is the Greek word for "seahorse," and it was so-named because the scientists who first dissected the brain thought it looked like a seahorse. Research has shown that the hippocampus is instrumental in forming long-term (permanent) declarative memories that are then stored elsewhere in the brain (Bigler et al., 1996). As mentioned earlier, acetylcholine, the neurotransmitter involved in muscle control, is also involved in the memory function of the hippocampus. People who have Alzheimer's, for example, have much lower levels of acetylcholine in that structure than is normal, and the drugs given to these people boost the levels of acetylcholine. The hippocampus is located within the medial temporal lobes on each side of the brain (*medial* means "toward the middle"), and electrical stimulation of this area may produce memory-like or dreamlike experiences.

Amygdala   The **amygdala** ("almond") is an area of the brain located near the hippocampus. These two structures seem to be responsible for fear responses and memory of fear. Information from the senses goes to the amygdala before the upper part of the brain is even involved, so that people can respond to danger very quickly, sometimes before they are consciously aware of what is happening. In 1939 researchers found that monkeys with large amounts of their temporal lobes removed—including the amygdala—were completely unafraid of snakes and humans, both of which are normally fear-provoking stimuli (Klüver & Bucy, 1939). This effect came to be known as the *Klüver-Bucy syndrome*. Rats that have damaged amygdala structures will also show no fear when placed next to a cat (Maren & Fanselow, 1996). Case studies of humans with damage to the amygdala also show a link to decreased fear response (Adophs et al., 2005).

Cingulate Cortex   The cingulate cortex is the limbic structure that is actually found in the cortex. It is found right above the corpus callosum (see page 64) in the frontal and parietal lobes (see pages 69 and 70) and plays an important role in both emotional and cognitive processing. It has been shown to be active during a variety of cognitive tasks such as selective attention, written word recognition, and working memory (Cabeza & Nyberg, 2000) and has been implicated in a variety of psychological and mental disorders, including attention-deficit/hyperactivity disorder (Bush et al., 1999; Bush et al., 2008), schizophrenia, major depressive disorder, and bipolar disorder (Fornito et al., 2009; Maletic et al., 2007). The next section further explores the cortex and its functions.

This young woman's thirst is regulated by her hypothalamus.

amygdala   brain structure located near the hippocampus, responsible for fear responses and memory of fear.

cortex   outermost covering of the brain consisting of densely packed neurons, responsible for higher thought processes and interpretation of sensory input.

practice quiz   How much do you remember?

2.6   2.7   2.8

Pick the best answer.

1. Which of the following techniques uses a radioactive sugar to look at the functioning of the brain?
   a. EEG
   b. CT
   c. MRI
   d. PET

2. Which brain structure is most responsible for our balance, posture, and muscle tone?
   a. medulla
   b. cerebellum
   c. reticular formation
   d. pons

3. Which brain structure would most likely result in death if damaged?
   a. medulla
   b. cerebellum
   c. reticular formation
   d. pons

4. If you were to develop a rare condition in which signals from your eyes were sent to the area of the brain that processes sound, and signals from the ears were sent to the area of the brain that processes vision, which part of the brain would most likely be damaged?
   a. hippocampus
   b. hypothalamus
   c. thalamus
   d. amygdala

5. If you have problems storing away new memories, the damage is most likely in the _____ area of the brain.
   a. hippocampus
   b. hypothalamus
   c. cerebellum
   d. amygdala

ANSWERS ON PAGE AK–1.

The Cortex

As stated earlier, the **cortex** ("rind" or outer covering) is the outermost part of the brain, which is the part of the brain most people picture when they think of what the brain looks like. It is made up of tightly packed neurons and actually is only about one-tenth of an inch thick on average (Fischl et al., 2001; MacDonald et al., 2000; Zilles, 1990). The cortex is very recognizable surface anatomy because it is full of wrinkles.

Why is the cortex so wrinkled? ●

Why is the cortex so wrinkled?

From top to bottom, a rat brain, sheep brain, and human brain (not to scale!). Note the differences in the amount of corticalization, or wrinkling, of the cortex between these three brains. Greater amounts of corticalization are associated with increases in size and complexity. Images are courtesy of Dr. Walter Isaac.

cerebral hemispheres the two sections of the cortex on the left and right sides of the brain.

corpus callosum thick band of neurons that connects the right and left cerebral hemispheres.

occipital lobe section of the brain located at the rear and bottom of each cerebral hemisphere containing the visual centers of the brain.

The wrinkling of the cortex allows a much larger area of cortical cells to exist in the small space inside the skull. If the cortex were to be taken out, ironed flat, and measured, it would be about 2 to 3 square feet. (The owner of the cortex would also be dead, but that's fairly obvious, right?) As the brain develops before birth, it forms a smooth outer covering on all the other brain structures. This will be the cortex, which will get more and more wrinkled as the brain increases in size and complexity. This increase in wrinkling is called "corticalization."

2.9 What parts of the cortex control the different senses and the movement of the body?

THE LOBES AND THEIR SPECIALTIES The brain is divided into two sections called the **cerebral hemispheres**, which are connected by a thick, tough band of neural fibers (axons) called the **corpus callosum** (literally meaning "hard bodies," as calluses on the feet are hard). (See Figure 2.12 on page 64.) The corpus callosum allows the left and right hemispheres to communicate with each other. Each hemisphere can be roughly divided into four sections by looking at the deeper wrinkles, or fissures, in its surface (see Figure 2.14).

OCCIPITAL LOBES At the base of the cortex, toward the back of the brain is an area called the **occipital lobe** (the term *occipital* refers to the rear of the head). This area processes visual information from the eyes in the *primary visual cortex*. The *visual association cortex*, also in this lobe, is the part of the brain that helps identify and make sense of the visual information from the eyes. The famed neurologist Oliver Sacks once had a patient who had a tumor in his right occipital lobe area. He could still see objects perfectly well and even describe them in physical terms, but he could not identify

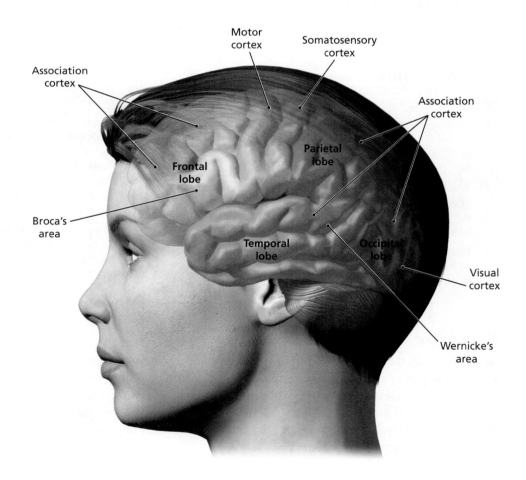

FIGURE 2.14 The Lobes of the Brain: Occipital, Parietal, Temporal, and Frontal

them by sight alone. For example, Sacks once gave him a rose to look at. The man turned it around and around and began to describe it as a "red inflorescence" of some type with a green tubular projection. Only when he held it under his nose (stimulating the sense of smell) did he recognize it as a rose (Sacks, 1990). Each area of the cortex has these association areas that help people make sense of sensory information.

PARIETAL LOBES   The **parietal lobes** (*parietal* means "wall") are at the top and back of the brain, just under the parietal bone in the skull. This area contains the **somatosensory cortex**, an area of neurons (see Figure 2.15) running down the front of the parietal lobes on either side of the brain. This area processes information from the skin and internal body receptors for touch, temperature, and body position. The somatosensory cortex is laid out in a rather interesting way—the cells at the top of the brain receive information from the bottom of the body, and as one moves down the area, the signals come from higher and higher in the body. It's almost as if a little upside-down person were laid out along this area of cells. (See Figure 2.15.)

TEMPORAL LOBES   The beginning of the **temporal lobes** (*temporal* means "of or near the temples") are found just behind the temples of the head. These lobes contain the *primary auditory cortex* and the *auditory association area*. Also found in the left temporal lobe is an area that in most people is particularly involved with language. The sense of taste also seems to be processed in the temporal lobe, deep inside a fold of the cortex (Fresquet et al., 2004).

FRONTAL LOBES   These lobes are at the front of the brain, hence, the name **frontal lobes**. (It doesn't often get this easy in psychology; feel free to take a moment to

parietal lobes   sections of the brain located at the top and back of each cerebral hemisphere containing the centers for touch, taste, and temperature sensations.

somatosensory cortex   area of neurons running down the front of the parietal lobes responsible for processing information from the skin and internal body receptors for touch, temperature, body position, and possibly taste.

temporal lobes   areas of the brain located along the side, starting just behind the temples, containing the neurons responsible for the sense of hearing and meaningful speech.

frontal lobes   areas of the brain located in the front and top, responsible for higher mental processes and decision making as well as the production of fluent speech.

This boxer must rely on his parietal lobes to sense where his body is in relation to the floor of the ring and the other boxer, his occipital lobes to see his target, and his frontal lobes to guide his hand and arm into the punch.

Motor Cortex   Somatosensory Cortex

FIGURE 2.15 The Motor and Somatosensory Cortex
The motor cortex in the frontal lobe controls the voluntary muscles of the body. Cells at the top of the motor cortex control muscles at the bottom of the body, whereas cells at the bottom of the motor cortex control muscles at the top of the body. Body parts are drawn larger or smaller according to the number of cortical cells devoted to that body part. For example, the hand has many small muscles and requires a larger area of cortical cells to control it. The somatosensory cortex, located in the parietal lobe just behind the motor cortex, is organized in much the same manner and receives information about the sense of touch and body position.

As this boy imitates the motions his father goes through while shaving, certain areas of his brain are more active than others, areas that control the motions of shaving. But even if the boy were only *watching* his father, those same neural areas would be active—the neurons in the boy's brain would *mirror* the actions of the father he is observing.

appreciate it.) Here are found all the higher mental functions of the brain—planning, personality, memory storage, complex decision making, and (again in the left hemisphere in most people) areas devoted to language. The frontal lobe also helps in controlling emotions by means of its connection to the limbic system. The most forward part of the frontal lobes is called the prefrontal cortex. The middle area toward the center (medial prefrontal cortex) and bottom surface above the eyes (orbitofrontal prefrontal cortex—right above the orbits of the eye) have strong connections to the limbic system. Phineas Gage, who was mentioned in Chapter One (p. 21), suffered damage to his frontal lobe. Following his accident, he lacked emotional control because of the damage to this lobe's connection with the limbic system structures, particularly the amygdala. People with damage to the frontal lobe may also experience problems performing mental tasks, getting stuck on one step or one wrong answer and repeating it over and over again (Goel & Grafman, 1995).

The frontal lobes also contain the **motor cortex**, a band of neurons located at the back of each lobe. (See Figure 2.14.) These cells control the movements of the body's voluntary muscles by sending commands out to the somatic division of the peripheral nervous system. The motor cortex is laid out just like the somatosensory cortex, which is right next door in the parietal lobes. This area of the brain has been the focus of a great deal of recent research, specifically as related to the role of a special type of neuron. These neurons are called **mirror neurons**, which fire when an animal performs an action—but they also fire when an animal observes that same action being performed by another. Previous brain-imaging studies in humans suggested that we, too, have mirror neurons in this area of the brain (Buccino et al., 2001; Buccino et al., 2004; Iacoboni et al., 1999). However, recent single-cell and multicell recordings in humans have demonstrated that neurons with mirroring functions are found not only in motor regions but also in parts of the brain involved in vision and memory. This suggests that such neurons provide much more information than previously thought about our own actions as compared to the actions of others (Mukamel et al., 2010). These new findings may have particular relevance for better understanding or treating specific clinical conditions that are believed to involve a faulty mirror system in the brain such as autism (Oberman & Ramachandran, 2007; Rizzolatti et al., 2009). ⓛⓘⓝⓚ to Chapter Seven, Development Across the Life Span, p. 245.

● You've mentioned association cortex a few times. Do the other lobes of the brain contain association cortex as well?

You've mentioned association cortex a few times. Do the other lobes of the brain contain association cortex as well?

The Association Areas of the Cortex

2.10 What parts of the cortex are responsible for higher forms of thought, such as language?

Association areas are made up of neurons in the cortex that are devoted to making connections between the sensory information coming into the brain and stored memories, images, and knowledge. In other words, association areas help people make sense of the incoming sensory input. Although the association areas in the occipital and temporal lobes have already been mentioned, much of the brain's association cortex is in the frontal lobes. Some special association areas are worth talking about in more detail.

BROCA'S AREA In the left frontal lobe of most people is an area of the brain devoted to the production of speech. (In a small portion of the population, this area is in the right frontal lobe.) More specifically, this area allows a person to speak smoothly and fluently. It is called *Broca's area* after nineteenth-century neurologist Paul Broca, who first studied people with damage to this area (Leonard, 1997). Damage to Broca's area causes a person to be unable to get words out in a smooth, connected fashion.

motor cortex rear section of the frontal lobe, responsible for sending motor commands to the muscles of the somatic nervous system.

mirror neurons neurons that fire when an animal or person performs an action and also when an animal or person observes that same action being performed by another.

association areas areas within each lobe of the cortex responsible for the coordination and interpretation of information, as well as higher mental processing.

People with this condition may know exactly what they want to say and understand what they hear others say, but they cannot control the actual production of their own words. Speech is halting and words are often mispronounced, such as saying "cot" instead of "clock" or "non" instead of "nine." Some words may be left out entirely, such as "the" or "for." This is called **Broca's aphasia**. *Aphasia* refers to an inability to use or understand either written or spoken language (Goodglass et al., 2001). (Stuttering is a somewhat different problem in getting words *started*, rather than mispronouncing them or leaving them out, but may also be related to Broca's area.)

WERNICKE'S AREA   In the left temporal lobe (again, in most people) is an area called *Wernicke's area*, named after the physiologist and Broca's contemporary, Carl Wernicke, who first studied problems arising from damage in this location. This area of the brain appears to be involved in understanding the meaning of words (Goodglass et al., 2001). A person with **Wernicke's aphasia** would be able to speak fluently and pronounce words correctly, but the words would be the wrong ones entirely. For example, Elsie suffered a stroke to the temporal lobe, damaging this area of the brain. In the emergency room the nurse tried to take her blood pressure, and when the cuff inflated, Elsie said, "Oh, that's so Saturday hard." Now, what does "Saturday hard" mean? Neither the nurse nor Elsie's daughter could figure that one out, but Elsie *thought* she was making sense. She also had trouble understanding what the people around her were saying to her. In another instance, Ernest suffered a stroke at the age of 80 and also showed signs of Wernicke's aphasia. For example, he asked his wife to get him some milk out of the air conditioner. Right idea, wrong word.

UNILATERAL SPATIAL NEGLECT   A condition that can sometimes occur following a stroke is **unilateral spatial neglect**, in which a person with damage to the right parietal and occipital lobes of the cortex will ignore everything in the left visual field. Unilateral refers to one side of the body, and this type of brain damage most often only affects attention to objects in the left visual field. Damage to areas of the frontal and temporal lobes may also play a part along with the parietal damage. Spatial neglect can affect the left hemisphere, but this condition occurs less frequently and in a much milder form than right-hemisphere neglect (Corbetta et al., 2005; Heilman et al., 1993; Springer & Deutsch, 1998).

Dr. V. S. Ramachandran reported an interesting case of unilateral spatial neglect in his book, *Phantoms in the Brain* (Ramachandran & Blakeslee, 1998). A woman who was typically neat and conscientious about her appearance was discovered by her son on a visit to look messy and totally odd. Her hair was uncombed on the left side. Her green shawl was hanging neatly over her right shoulder but hanging onto the floor on the left. Her lipstick was neatly applied to the right side of her lips, and *only to the right side—the left side of her face was completely bare of makeup!* Yet her eyeliner, mascara, and rouge were all neatly applied to the right side of her face. This woman had suffered a stroke that left her with unilateral spatial neglect.

The Cerebral Hemispheres: Are You in Your Right Mind?

I've heard that some people are right-brained and some are left-brained. Are the two sides of the brain really that different?

Most people tend to think of the two cerebral hemispheres as identical twins. Both sides have the same four lobes and are arranged in much the same way. But language seems to be confined to the left hemisphere in about 90 percent of the population (Toga & Thompson, 2003). What other special tasks do the two halves of the **cerebrum** (the upper part of the brain consisting of the two hemispheres and the structures connecting them) engage in, and how do researchers know about such functions? ⊙▶ Simulate on **MyPsychLab**

Broca's aphasia   condition resulting from damage to Broca's area, causing the affected person to be unable to speak fluently, to mispronounce words, and to speak haltingly.

Wernicke's aphasia   condition resulting from damage to Wernicke's area, causing the affected person to be unable to understand or produce meaningful language.

unilateral spatial neglect   condition produced most often by damage to the parietal lobe association areas of the right hemisphere resulting in an inability to recognize objects or body parts in the left visual field.

cerebrum   the upper part of the brain consisting of the two hemispheres and the structures that connect them.

As this woman brushes the right side of her hair, is she really "seeing" the left side? If she has spatial neglect, the answer is "no." While her eyes work just fine, her damaged right hemisphere refuses to notice the left side of her visual field.

⊙▶ Simulate the cerebrum on **MyPsychLab**

I've heard that some people are right-brained and some are left-brained. Are the two sides of the brain really that different?

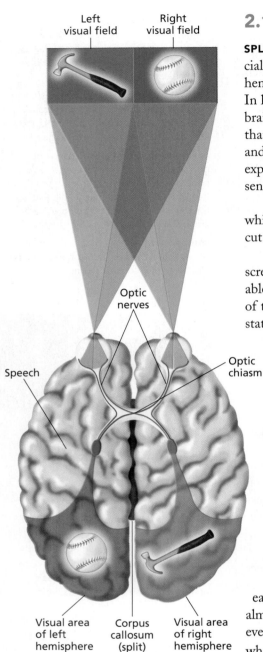

FIGURE 2.16 The Split-Brain Experiment
Roger Sperry created this experiment to demonstrate the specialization of the left and right hemispheres of the brain.

So there really are left-brained and right-brained people?

*Explore an experiment on hemispheric specialization on **MyPsychLab***

2.11 How does the left side of the brain differ from the right side?

SPLIT-BRAIN RESEARCH Roger Sperry was a pioneer in the field of hemisphere specialization. He won a Nobel Prize for his work in demonstrating that the left and right hemispheres of the brain specialize in different activities and functions (Sperry, 1968). In looking for a way to cure epilepsy (severe muscle spasms or seizures resulting from brain damage), Sperry cut through the corpus callosum, the thick band of neural fibers that joins the two hemispheres. In early research with animals, this technique worked and seemed to have no side effects. The first people to have this procedure done also experienced relief from their severe epileptic symptoms, but testing found that (in a sense) they now had two brains in one body.

The special testing involves sending messages to only one side of the brain, which is now possible because the connecting tissue, the corpus callosum, has been cut. Figure 2.16 shows what happens with a typical split-brain patient.

In a split-brain patient, if a picture of a ball is flashed to the right side of the screen, the image of the ball will be sent to the left occipital lobe. The person will be able to say that he or she sees a ball. If a picture of a hammer is flashed to the left side of the screen, the person will not be able to verbally identify the object or be able to state with any certainty that something was seen. But if the left hand (controlled by the right hemisphere) is used, the person can point to the hammer he or she "didn't see." The right occipital lobe clearly saw the hammer, but the person could not verbalize that fact (Sperry, 1968). By conducting studies such as these, researchers have found that the left hemisphere specializes in language, speech, handwriting, calculation (math), sense of time and rhythm (which is mathematical in nature), and basically any kind of thought requiring analysis. The right hemisphere appears to specialize in more global (widespread) processing involving perception, visualization, spatial perception, recognition of patterns, faces, emotions, melodies, and expression of emotions. It also comprehends simple language but does not produce speech.

Springer and Deutsch (1998) found that, in general, the left hemisphere processes information in a sequence and is good at breaking things down into smaller parts or performing analysis. The right hemisphere, by contrast, processes information all at once and simultaneously; in this sense it is a more global or holistic* style of processing. Remember the discussion in Chapter One of the early days of psychology, the structuralists, and the Gestalt psychologists? One could almost say that the left hemisphere of the brain is a structuralist who wants to break everything down into its smallest parts, and the right side of the brain is a Gestaltist, who wants to study only the whole. (See Table 2.2.) *Explore on **MyPsychLab***

So there really are left-brained and right-brained people?

Actually, unless one is a split-brain patient, the two sides of the brain are always working together as an integrated whole. For example, the right side might recognize someone's face, while the left side struggles to recall the person's name. People aren't really left- or right-brained; they are "whole-brained." Michael Gazzaniga was one of Roger Sperry's students, collaborator, and is a long-time researcher in the area of brain asymmetry and cognitive neuroscience. Gazzaniga's continuing work in brain lateralization has led to insights of the integrated mind, and he continues to work in related areas including human consciousness, perception, and neuroethics (Gazzaniga, 2006, 2009).

The separate functions of the left and right sides of the brain are often confused with handedness, or the tendency to use one hand for most fine motor skills. While most right-handed people also have their left hemisphere in control of their other fine

---

*Holistic: relating to or concerned with complete systems or wholes.

table 2.2 Specialization of the Two Hemispheres

LEFT HEMISPHERE	RIGHT HEMISPHERE
Controls the right hand	Controls the left hand
Spoken language	Nonverbal
Written language	Visual-spatial perception
Mathematical calculations	Music and artistic processing
Logical thought processes	Emotional thought and recognition
Analysis of detail	Processing of the whole
Reading	Pattern recognition
	Facial recognition

motor skills, such as speech, a few right-handers actually have their language functions in the right hemisphere, in spite of the dominance of the left hemisphere for controlling the right hand. Among left-handed people, there are also many who, although right-brain dominant, still have their language functions on the left side of the brain. Why? How much time do you have? There are far too many theories of why we use one hand rather than the other to cover in this text. Read on MyPsychLab

Read and learn more about right and left handedness on MyPsychLab

practice quiz   How much do you remember?

2.9 2.10 2.11

Pick the best answer.

1. In which of the following lobes of the cortex would you find the primary auditory area?
   a. frontal
   b. temporal
   c. occipital
   d. parietal

2. The higher mental functions, such as thinking and problem solving, are found in the _____ lobes.
   a. frontal
   b. parietal
   c. temporal
   d. corpus

3. In an old *Twilight Zone* episode, a man wakes up one morning to find that people around him are using words that make no sense to him, and they also don't seem to understand him. His wife tells him that their son forgot his dinosaur today, and when he looks puzzled, she holds up the son's lunchbox and repeats, "You know, his dinosaur." This man's predicament is most like which of the following disorders?
   a. Wernicke's aphasia
   b. Broca's aphasia
   c. apraxia
   d. spatial neglect

4. Dr. Ramachandran's unilateral spatial neglect patient suffered a stroke that most likely caused damage to her _____.
   a. thalamus.
   b. left temporal lobe.
   c. right parietal lobe.
   d. corpus callosum.

5. If you are a split-brain patient, which of the following would be true?
   a. Objects in your left visual field would be easily named.
   b. Objects in your left visual field are invisible.
   c. Objects in your right visual field would be easily named.
   d. Objects in your right visual field are invisible.

Brainstorming: If a person with unilateral spatial neglect only eats the food on the right side of the plate, what could caregivers do to help that person get enough to eat? What other odd things might a person with unilateral spatial neglect do that a person with normal functioning would not? What other things might a person with unilateral spatial neglect fail to do?

ANSWERS ON PAGE AK–1.

applying psychology to everyday life

Paying Attention to the Causes of Attention-Deficit/Hyperactivity Disorder

Attention-Deficit/Hyperactivity Disorder (ADHD) is a developmental disorder involving behavioral and cognitive aspects of inattention, impulsivity, and hyperactivity. Previously referred to as Attention Deficit Disorder (ADD), this disorder currently is listed as having three diagnostic categories in the *Diagnostic and Statistical*

Manual of Mental Disorders (DSM-IV-TR). These categories are ADHD predominantly hyper-active type, ADHD predominantly inattentive type, and ADHD combined type (American Psychiatric Association, 2000). Although ADHD is most commonly diagnosed in children, the disorder tends to persist into adolescence and adulthood. Inattention and impulsivity are often reported in adults, whereas symptoms of hyperactivity tend to decline with age. The ADHD-related problems in adults can range from strained relations with family, friends, or a significant other to problems with substance abuse, traffic accidents, or job stability (Barkley, Murphy, & Fischer, 2008).

The brain areas involved in the behavioral and cognitive characteristics of ADHD are typically divided into those responsible for regulating attention and cognitive control and those responsible for alertness and motivation (Nigg, 2010). The cortical and subcortical brain areas involved, and found to be smaller in neuroimaging studies of ADHD, are the prefrontal cortex (primarily on the right side), basal ganglia (subcortical structures involved in response control), cerebellum, and corpus callosum (Nigg, 2006).

Since ADHD involves a variety of behaviors and cognitive aspects, research has often looked for specific markers that may lead to the actual causes of the disorder. These markers may be biological, cognitive, or behavioral measures (Nigg, 2010). To assess individual mark-ers, researchers may combine neuroimaging and electrophysiological studies of individuals with ADHD while at rest or while they perform specific cognitive tasks (like various tests of attention). Some studies use EEG or ERPs (Clarke et al., 2007; Loo et al., 2009; van der Stelt et al., 2010) whereas others use MRI, fMRI, or PET (Bush et al., 2008; Volkow et al., 2007).

As Nigg points out, much of the research over the past 10 years has focused on the cognitive markers for ADHD, such as attention problems, that may or may not be com-bined with neuroimaging. More recent research suggests that some aspects of attention are actually normal in individuals with ADHD. The aspect of attention with which individu-als with ADHD do have problems is vigilance (being able to "watch out" for something important). Another cognitive area that appears to be impaired is being able to effectively control one's own cognitive processes such as staying on task, maintaining effort, or engaging in self-control (Nigg, 2010).

These recent findings have prompted researchers to reexamine the causes of ADHD and have highlighted the likelihood of more than one cause and more than one brain route to ADHD. Current research is looking at a variety of areas including environmental factors such as low-level lead exposure, genetic influences, the role of heredity and familial fac-tors, and personality factors (Nigg, 2010). Granted, some of these areas of investigation are not completely new and have been examined before, but the possibility of multiple causes and interactions between these causes has not been studied as closely as it is at present in ADHD research.

QUESTIONS FOR FURTHER DISCUSSION

1. How might a psychology professional help parents or teachers understand the neuro-imaging techniques and brain areas associated with ADHD?
2. If a college student has ADHD, what aspects of his or her school or personal life might be impacted by problems with vigilance or cognitive control?

chapter summary ((•─[Listen on **MyPsychLab**   Listen to an audio file of your chapter **www.MyPsychLab**

An Overview of the Nervous System

2.1 What are the nervous system, neurons, and nerves, and how do they relate to one another?

• The nervous system is a complex network of cells that carries informa-tion to and from all parts of the body.

Neurons and Nerves: Building the Network

2.2 How do neurons use neurotransmitters to communicate with each other and with the body?

• The brain is made up of two types of cells, neurons and glial cells.

- Neurons have dendrites, which receive input, a soma or cell body, and axons, which carry the neural message to other cells.

- Glial cells separate, support, and insulate the neurons from each other and make up 90 percent of the brain.

- Myelin insulates and protects the axons of neurons that travel in the body. These axons bundle together in "cables" called nerves. Myelin also speeds up the neural message.

- Neurons in the peripheral nervous system are also coated with neurilemma, which allows the nerves to repair themselves.

- A neuron contains charged particles called ions. When at rest, the neuron is negatively charged on the inside and positively charged on the outside. When stimulated, this reverses the charge by allowing positive sodium ions to enter the cell. This is the action potential.

- Neurons fire in an all-or-nothing manner. It is the speed and number of neurons firing that tell researchers the strength of the stimulus.

- Synaptic vesicles in the end of the axon terminal release neurotransmitter chemicals into the synapse, or gap, between one cell and the next. The neurotransmitter molecules fit into receptor sites on the next cell, stimulating or inhibiting that cell's firing. Neurotransmitters may be either excitatory or inhibitory.

- The first known neurotransmitter was acetylcholine. It stimulates muscles and helps in memory formation. Curare is a poison that blocks its effect.

- GABA is the major inhibitory neurotransmitter; high amounts of GABA are released when drinking alcohol.

- Serotonin is associated with sleep, mood, and appetite.

- Dopamine is associated with Parkinson's disease and schizophrenia.

- Endorphins are neural regulators that control our pain response.

- Most neurotransmitters are taken back into the synaptic vesicles in a process called reuptake.

- Acetylcholine is cleared out of the synapse by enzymes that break up the molecules.

The Central Nervous System— The "Central Processing Unit"

2.3 How do the brain and spinal cord interact?

- The central nervous system consists of the brain and the spinal cord.

- The spinal cord serves two functions. The outer part of the cord transmits messages to and from the brain, whereas the inner part controls lifesaving reflexes such as the pain response.

- Spinal cord reflexes involve afferent neurons, interneurons, and efferent neurons, forming a simple reflex arc.

- Great strides are being made in spinal cord repair and the growth of new neurons in the central nervous system.

Psychology in the News Fact or Fiction: Focus on the Brain, but Check Your Sources!

- Information about the brain and brain research comes from a variety of sources, but sources such as peer-reviewed journals and publications from professional associations offer the most reliable information.

The Peripheral Nervous System—Nerves on the Edge

- The peripheral nervous system is all the neurons and nerves that are not part of the brain and spinal cord and that extend throughout the body.

- There are two systems within the peripheral nervous system, the somatic nervous system and the autonomic nervous system.

2.4 How do the somatic and autonomic nervous systems allow people and animals to interact with their surroundings and control the body's automatic functions?

- The somatic nervous system contains the sensory pathway, or neurons carrying messages to the central nervous system, and the motor pathway, or neurons carrying messages from the central nervous system to the voluntary muscles.

- The autonomic nervous system consists of the parasympathetic division and the sympathetic division. The sympathetic division is our fight-or-flight system, reacting to stress, whereas the parasympathetic division restores and maintains normal day-to-day functioning of the organs.

Distant Connections: The Endocrine Glands

2.5 How do the hormones released by glands interact with the nervous system and affect behavior?

- Endocrine glands secrete chemicals called hormones directly into the bloodstream, influencing the activity of the muscles and organs.

- The pituitary gland is found in the brain just below the hypothalamus. It has two parts, the anterior and the posterior. It controls the levels of salt and water in the system and, in women, the onset of labor and lactation, as well as secreting growth hormone and influencing the activity of the other glands.

- The pineal gland is also located in the brain. It secretes melatonin, a hormone that regulates the sleep–wake cycle in response to changes in light.

- The thyroid gland is located inside the neck. It controls metabolism (the burning of energy) by secreting thyroxin.

- The pancreas controls the level of sugar in the blood by secreting insulin and glucagons. Too much insulin produces hypoglycemia, whereas too little causes diabetes.

- The gonads are the ovaries in women and testes in men. They secrete hormones to regulate sexual growth, activity, and reproduction.

- The adrenal glands, one on top of each kidney, control the stress reaction through the adrenal medulla's secretion of epinephrine and norepinephrine. The adrenal cortex secretes over 30 different corticoids (hormones) controlling salt intake, stress, and sexual development.

Looking Inside the Living Brain

2.6 How do psychologists study the brain and how it works?

- We can study the brain by using deep lesioning to destroy certain areas of the brain in laboratory animals or by electrically stimulating those areas (ESB).

- We can use case studies of human brain damage to learn about the brain's functions but cannot easily generalize from one case to another.

- rTMS and tDCS are noninvasive methods for stimulating the brain.

- Different neuroimaging methods allows scientists to investigate the structure or the function of the living brain.

- The electroencephalograph allows researchers to look at the electroencephalogram (EEG), or electrical activity of the surface of the brain, through the use of electrodes placed on the scalp that are then amplified and viewed using a computer. ERPs allow researchers to look at the timing and progression of cognitive processes.

- CT scans are computer-aided X-rays of the brain and show the skull and brain structure.

- MRI scans use a magnetic field, radio pulses, and a computer to give researchers an even more detailed look at the structure of the brain.

- fMRI allows researchers to look at the activity of the brain over a time period.
- PET scans use a radioactive sugar injected into the bloodstream to track the activity of brain cells, which is enhanced and color-coded by a computer. SPECT allows for the imaging of brain blood flow.

From the Bottom Up: The Structures of the Brain

2.7 What are the different structures of the bottom part of the brain and what do they do?

- The medulla is at the very bottom of the brain and top of the spinal column. It controls life-sustaining functions such as breathing and swallowing. The nerves from each side of the body also cross over in this structure to opposite sides.
- The pons is above the medulla and acts as a bridge between the lower part of the brain and the upper part. It influences sleep, dreaming, arousal, and coordination of movement on the left and right sides of the body.
- The reticular formation runs through the medulla and the pons and controls our general level of attention and arousal.
- The cerebellum is found at the base and back of the brain and coordinates fine, rapid motor movement, learned reflexes, posture, and muscle tone.

2.8 What are the structures of the brain that control emotion, learning, memory, and motivation?

- The thalamus is the switching station that sends sensory information to the proper areas of the cortex.
- The hypothalamus controls hunger, thirst, sleep, sexual behavior, sleeping and waking, and emotions. It also controls the pituitary gland.
- The limbic system consists of the thalamus, hypothalamus, hippocampus, amygdala, and the cingulate cortex.
- The hippocampus is the part of the brain responsible for the formation of long-term declarative memories and remembering locations of objects.
- The amygdala controls our fear responses and memory of fearful stimuli.

2.9 What parts of the cortex control the different senses and the movement of the body?

- The cortex is the outer covering of the cerebrum and consists of a tightly packed layer of neurons about one-tenth of an inch in thickness. Its wrinkles, or corticalization, allow for greater cortical area and are associated with greater brain complexity.
- The brain is divided into two cerebral hemispheres connected by a thick band of neural fibers called the corpus callosum.

- The occipital lobes at the back and base of each hemisphere process vision and contain the primary visual cortex.
- The parietal lobes at the top and back of the brain contain the somatosensory area, which processes our sense of touch, temperature, and body position. Taste is also processed in this lobe.
- The temporal lobes contain the primary auditory area and are also involved in understanding language.
- The frontal lobes contain the motor cortex, which controls the voluntary muscles, and are also where all the higher mental functions occur, such as planning, language, and complex decision making.

2.10 What parts of the cortex are responsible for higher forms of thought, such as language?

- Association areas of the cortex are found in all the lobes but particularly in the frontal lobes. These areas help people make sense of the information they receive from the lower areas of the brain.
- An area called Broca's area in the left frontal lobe is responsible for producing fluent, understandable speech. If damaged, the person has Broca's aphasia in which words will be halting and pronounced incorrectly.
- An area called Wernicke's area in the left temporal lobe is responsible for the understanding of language. If damaged, the person has Wernicke's aphasia in which speech is fluent but nonsensical. The wrong words are used.
- Unilateral spatial neglect comes from damage to the parietal lobe association areas on one side of the cortex, usually the right side. A person with this condition will ignore information from the opposite side of the body or the opposite visual field.

2.11 How does the left side of the brain differ from the right side?

- Studies with split-brain patients, in which the corpus callosum has been severed to correct epilepsy, reveal that the left side of the brain seems to control language, writing, logical thought, analysis, and mathematical abilities. The left side also processes information sequentially.
- The right side of the brain processes information globally and controls emotional expression, spatial perception, recognition of faces, patterns, melodies, and emotions. Information presented only to the left hemisphere can be verbalized, but information sent only to the right cannot.

applying psychology to everyday life: Paying Attention to the Causes of Attention-Deficit/Hyperactivity Disorder

- ADHD may be caused by the interaction of a variety of factors and often persists into adulthood.

TEST yourself

ANSWERS ON PAGE AK–1

✓ Study and Review on MyPsychLab   Ready for your test? More quizzes and a customized plan. www.MyPsychLab

Pick the best answer.

1. In the structure of the neuron, the _____ sends information to other cells.
   a. axon
   b. dendrite
   c. soma
   d. myelin

2. Which type of cell makes up 10 percent of the brain?
   a. glial cells
   b. neurons
   c. stem cells
   d. afferent cells

3. Damaged nerve fibers in the peripheral nervous system can repair themselves because they are coated with _____, which forms a protective tunnel around the nerve fibers.
   a. glial
   b. soma
   c. myelin
   d. neurilemma

4. When a neuron is in the resting potential state, where are the sodium ions?
   a. inside the cell
   b. outside the cell
   c. inside the soma
   d. in the synapse

5. How does one neuron communicate with another neuron?
   a. An electrical spark jumps over the gap between cells.
   b. Charged particles leap from one cell to the next.
   c. Chemicals in the end of one neuron float across the gap to fit into holes on the next neuron.
   d. The end of one neuron extends to touch the other neuron.

6. Which neurotransmitter is associated with the control of the pain response?
   a. acetylcholine
   b. GABA
   c. serotonin
   d. endorphin

7. Which of the following is the correct path of a reflex arc?
   a. efferent neuron to interneuron to afferent neuron
   b. efferent neuron to afferent neuron to interneuron
   c. afferent neuron to interneuron to efferent neuron
   d. afferent neuron to efferent neuron to the brain

8. Voluntary muscles are controlled by the _____ nervous system.
   a. somatic
   b. autonomic
   c. sympathetic
   d. parasympathetic

9. Your heart races. You begin to breathe faster. Your pupils enlarge and your appetite is gone. Your _____ division has just been activated.
   a. sympathetic
   b. parasympathetic
   c. autonomic
   d. somatic

10. The _____ division controls ordinary, day-to-day bodily functions.
    a. sympathetic
    b. parasympathetic
    c. central
    d. somatic

11. Anya is beautifully proportioned, but at 18 years of age she is still no taller than the average 10-year-old. Anya most likely had a problem in her _____ gland(s) while she was growing up.
    a. pituitary
    b. adrenal
    c. thyroid
    d. pineal

12. The function of hormones in the bloodstream is most similar to which of the following?
    a. the function of sodium ions in the action potential
    b. the function of myelin surrounding the axons
    c. the function of glial cells in the brain
    d. the function of neurotransmitters in the synapse

13. Sleep is influenced by levels of _____, secreted by the _____ gland(s).
    a. growth hormone; pituitary
    b. insulin; pancreas
    c. thyroxin; thyroid
    d. melatonin; pineal

14. Which of the following techniques for imaging the brain would not be advisable for a person with a metal spike in his or her head?
    a. EEG
    b. CT
    c. MRI
    d. PET

15. Which technique of studying the brain involves recording the electrical activity of large groups of cortical neurons?
    a. EEG
    b. deep lesioning
    c. ESB
    d. MRI

16. Which technique of studying the brain actually damages neurons?
    a. EEG
    b. deep lesioning
    c. ESB
    d. MRI

17. Maria suffered a stroke that damaged a part of her brain. She fell into a sleeplike coma and could not be awakened. If we know that the area of damage is somewhere in the brain stem, which structure is most likely damaged?
    a. medulla
    b. pons
    c. reticular formation
    d. cerebellum

18. Alexis is learning several new routines in her gymnastics class. After enough practice, her _____ will play an important role in helping her to perform the routines correctly and smoothly.
    a. medulla
    b. pons
    c. reticular formation
    d. cerebellum

19. Which sensory information does NOT have to be first sent to the thalamus before going to the cortex?
    a. auditory (hearing)
    b. olfactory (smell)
    c. gustatory (taste)
    d. visual (vision)

20. Which part of the brain is the primary link to the glandular system?
    a. hippocampus
    b. thalamus
    c. hypothalamus
    d. amygdala

21. Jeff is undergoing brain surgery to remove a tumor. The surgeon applies electrical simulation to various areas around the tumor, causing Jeff to report tingling sensations in various areas of his skin. The tumor is most likely in which lobe of Jeff's brain?
    a. frontal
    b. temporal
    c. occipital
    d. parietal

22. George has a small stroke that results in a partial paralysis of his left side. The damaged area is most likely in his _____ lobe.
    a. right frontal
    b. left frontal
    c. right parietal
    d. left temporal

23. Linda is recovering from damage to her brain. Her main symptom is a speech problem; instead of saying, "I am going to P.T. (physical therapy) at nine o'clock" she says, "I go...P.T....non o'cot." Linda's problem is _____.
    a. spatial neglect.
    b. visual agnosia.
    c. Broca's aphasia.
    d. Wernicke's aphasia.

24. In the split-brain operation, the _____ is severed, which is the primary communication pathway between the two hemispheres.
    a. cingulate cortex
    b. corpus callosum
    c. caudate
    d. cerebellum

25. Recognizing the face of someone you run into at the mall is a function of the _____ hemisphere; being able to retrieve that person's name from memory is a function of the _____ hemisphere.
    a. left; right
    b. right; left
    c. right; right
    d. left; left

2 the biological perspective

p. 42

2.1 **2.2**

Neurons and Nerves

(the brain is comprised of glial cells and neurons)

- have an electrical charge at rest—the resting potential (see Fig. 2.3, p. 46)
- are affected by neurotransmitters (see Table 2.1, p. 49)
- are separated by a gap called the synapse (see Fig. 2.4)

● **neurons**
specialized cells in nervous system — have specialized components →

● **glial cells**
provide physical and metabolic support to neurons

Axon terminal
(synaptic knobs)

Nucleus

Myelin sheath

Soma

Axon

Axon

Dendrites

Brain (CNS)

Spinal cord (CNS)

Nerves (PNS)

p. 51

2.3

The Central Nervous System

(comprised of the brain and spinal cord)

● **brain**
true core of nervous system: takes information from senses, processes it, makes decisions, sends commands to rest of body

● **spinal cord**
long bundle of neurons that carries information to and away from the brain; helps control pain response

p. 54

2.4

The Peripheral Nervous System

(comprised of the nerves and neurons not contained in the brain and spinal cord)

● **somatic nervous system**
controls voluntary muscles of the body

● **autonomic nervous system**
controls automatic functions of the body

2.5 p. 57

Distant Connections: The Endocrine Glands

- **glands**
  organs in the body
  that secrete chemicals

- **endocrine glands**
  secrete chemicals called
  hormones into bloodstream
  - pituitary gland
  - pineal gland
  - thyroid gland
  - pancreas
  - gonads
  - adrenal glands

2.6 p. 60

Looking Inside the Living Brain

(methods for studying the structures and/or activity of the living brain)

- **mapping structure**
  - computed tomography (CT)
  - magnetic resonance imaging (MRI)

- **mapping function**
  - electroencephalogram (EEG)
  - positron emission tomography (PET)
  - fMRI

2.7 **2.8** p. 63   **2.9** **2.10** **2.11** p. 67

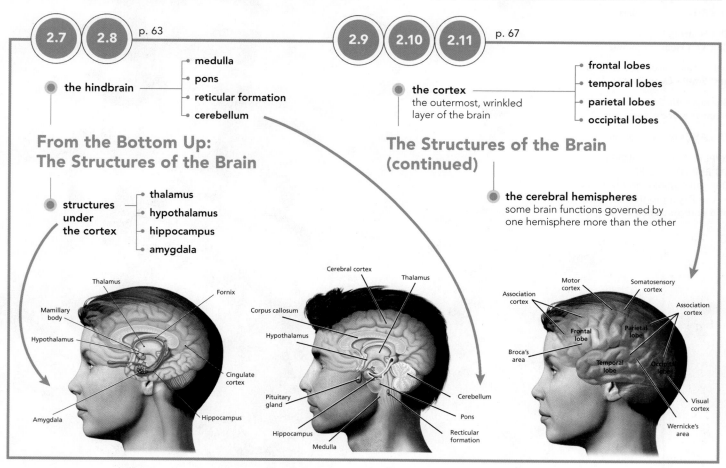

- **the hindbrain**
  - medulla
  - pons
  - reticular formation
  - cerebellum

From the Bottom Up: The Structures of the Brain

- **structures under the cortex**
  - thalamus
  - hypothalamus
  - hippocampus
  - amygdala

- **the cortex**
  the outermost, wrinkled
  layer of the brain
  - frontal lobes
  - temporal lobes
  - parietal lobes
  - occipital lobes

The Structures of the Brain (continued)

- **the cerebral hemispheres**
  some brain functions governed by
  one hemisphere more than the other

Thalamus
Fornix
Mamillary body
Hypothalamus
Amygdala
Cingulate cortex
Hippocampus

Cerebral cortex
Thalamus
Corpus callosum
Hypothalamus
Pituitary gland
Hippocampus
Medulla
Cerebellum
Pons
Recticular formation

Motor cortex
Somatosensory cortex
Association cortex
Association cortex
Frontal lobe
Parietal lobe
Broca's area
Temporal lobe
Occipital lobe
Visual cortex
Wernicke's area

3

sensation and perception

why study sensation and perception?

Without sensations to tell us what is outside our own mental world, we would live entirely in our own minds, separate from one another and unable to find food or any other basics that sustain life. Sensations are the mind's window to the world that exists around us. Without perception, we would be unable to understand what all those sensations mean—perception is the process of interpreting the sensations we experience so that we can act upon them.

chapter outline

The ABCs of Sensation

The Science of Seeing

The Hearing Sense:
Can You Hear Me Now?

Chemical Senses: It Tastes Good
and Smells Even Better

Somesthetic Senses:
What the Body Knows

The ABCs of Perception

APPLYING PSYCHOLOGY
TO EVERYDAY LIFE:
Beyond "Smoke and Mirrors"
—The Psychological Science
and Neuroscience of Magic

Seeing Sounds and Hearing Colors: Synesthesia

"There was a piece of music by a group called Uman. The first note was grey and it was like a band of grey with a slight curve to it, and it was a gradient—light grey going to dark grey—it had gold specks on it. The background was black but it was being broken up by other colours, moving shapes of fuchsia and there was a small sound like a click, almost like a drumbeat, something being struck, and as it was struck, a black shape appeared, and the shapes appeared from left to right, going horizontally across the bottom of this—like a movie screen that I was watching. And the shapes were so exquisite, so simple, so pure and so beautiful, I wanted somehow to be able to capture them, but they were moving too quickly and I couldn't remember them all."—Carol Steen (1996), New York artist and synesthete, quoted from ABC Radio National Transcripts, Health Report with Robin Hughes

Ms. Steen is a most unusual artist because she is able to perceive a world where sounds have colors and shapes, an ability she often turns into unusual and beautiful sculptures. A *synesthete* is a person with **synesthesia**, which literally means "joined sensation." People with this condition are rare—about 1 in 25,000. In the synesthete, the signals that come from the sensory organs, such as the eyes or the ears, go to places in the brain where they weren't originally meant to be, causing those signals to be interpreted as more than one sensation. A fusion of sound and sight is most common, but touch, taste, and even smell can enter into the mix (Cytowic, 1989).

Although research on the physical causes of synesthesia is ongoing, some studies suggest that areas of the left side of the brain deep inside the temporal lobe and nearby in the parietal lobe may be responsible (Ramachandran & Hubbard, 2003; Rouw & Scholte, 2007). (LINK) to Chapter Two: The Biological Perspective, pp. 69–70.

learning objectives

3.1 How does sensation travel through the central nervous system, and why are some sensations ignored?

3.2 What is light, and how does it travel through the various parts of the eye?

3.3 How do the eyes see, and how do the eyes see different colors?

3.4 What is sound, and how does it travel through the various parts of the ear?

3.5 How do the senses of taste and smell work, and how are they alike?

3.6 What allows people to experience the sense of touch, pain, motion, and balance?

3.7 What are perception, perceptual constancies, and the Gestalt principles of perception?

3.8 What is depth perception, and what kinds of cues are important for it to occur?

3.9 What are visual illusions, and how can they and other factors influence and alter perception?

synesthesia disorder in which the signals from the various sensory organs are processed in the wrong cortical areas, resulting in the sense information being interpreted as more than one sensation.

How do we get information from the outside world into our brains?

In some parts of the United States, "coffee regular" refers to coffee with two creams and two sugars. How much more sugar would you need to add to taste a difference?

sensation the process that occurs when special receptors in the sense organs are activated, allowing various forms of outside stimuli to become neural signals in the brain.

transduction the process of converting outside stimuli, such as light, into neural activity.

just noticeable difference (jnd or the **difference threshold)** the smallest difference between two stimuli that is detectable 50 percent of the time.

absolute threshold the lowest level of stimulation that a person can consciously detect 50 percent of the time the stimulation is present.

The ABCs of Sensation

How do we get information from the outside world into our brains?

Information about the world has to have a way to get into the brain, where it can be used to determine actions and responses. The way into the brain is through the sensory organs and the process of sensation.

What Is Sensation?

3.1 How does sensation travel through the central nervous system, and why are some sensations ignored?

Sensation occurs when special receptors in the sense organs—the eyes, ears, nose, skin, and taste buds—are activated, allowing various forms of outside stimuli to become neural signals in the brain. (This process of converting outside stimuli, such as light, into neural activity is called **transduction**.) Let's take a closer look at these special receptors.

SENSORY RECEPTORS The *sensory receptors* are specialized forms of neurons, the cells that make up the nervous system. Instead of receiving neurotransmitters from other cells, these receptor cells are stimulated by different kinds of energy—for example, the receptors in the eyes are stimulated by light, whereas the receptors in the ears are activated by vibrations. Touch receptors are stimulated by pressure or temperature, and the receptors for taste and smell are triggered by chemical substances.

Sensory Thresholds

Ernst Weber (1795–1878) did studies trying to determine the smallest difference between two weights that could be detected. His research led to the formulation known as Weber's law of **just noticeable differences** (**jnd**, or the **difference threshold**). A jnd is the smallest difference between two stimuli that is detectable 50 percent of the time, and Weber's law simply means that whatever the difference between stimuli might be, it is always a *constant*. If to notice a difference the amount of sugar a person would need to add to a cup of coffee that is already sweetened with 5 teaspoons is 1 teaspoon, then the percentage of change needed to detect a just noticeable difference is one-fifth, or 20 percent. So if the coffee has 10 teaspoons of sugar in it, the person would have to add another 20 percent, or 2 teaspoons, to be able to taste the difference half of the time. Most people would not typically drink a cup of coffee with 10 teaspoons of sugar in it, let alone 12 teaspoons, but you get the point.

Gustav Fechner (1801–1887) expanded on Weber's work by studying something he called the **absolute threshold** (Fechner, 1860). An absolute threshold is the lowest level of stimulation that a person can consciously detect 50 percent of the time the stimulation is present. (Remember, the jnd is detecting a difference *between two* stimuli.) For example, assuming a very quiet room and normal hearing, how far away can someone sit and you might still hear the tick of their analog watch on half of the trials? For some examples of absolute thresholds for various senses, see Table 3.1.

table 3.1	Examples of Absolute Thresholds
SENSE	**THRESHOLD**
Sight	A candle flame at 30 miles on a clear, dark night
Hearing	The tick of a watch 20 feet away in a quiet room
Smell	One drop of perfume diffused throughout a three-room apartment
Taste	1 teaspoon of sugar in 2 gallons of water
Touch	A bee's wing falling on the cheek from 1 centimeter above

I've heard about people being influenced by stuff in movies and on television, things that are just below the level of conscious awareness. Is that true?

Stimuli that are below the level of conscious awareness are called *subliminal stimuli*. (The word *limin* means "threshold," so *sublimin* means "below the threshold.") These stimuli are just strong enough to activate the sensory receptors but not strong enough for people to be consciously aware of them. Many people believe that these stimuli act upon the unconscious mind, influencing behavior in a process called *subliminal perception*.

At one time, many people believed that a market researcher named James Vicary had demonstrated the power of subliminal perception in advertising. It was five years before Vicary finally admitted that he had never conducted a real study (Merikle, 2000; Pratkanis, 1992). Furthermore, many researchers have gathered scientific evidence that subliminal perception does not work in advertising (Bargh et al., 1996; Broyles, 2006; Moore, 1988; Pratkanis & Greenwald, 1988; Trappey, 1996; Vokey & Read, 1985).

This is not to say that subliminal perception does not exist—there is a growing body of evidence that we process some stimuli without conscious awareness, especially stimuli that are fearful or threatening (LeDoux & Phelps, 2008; Öhman, 2008). In this effort, researchers have used *event-related potentials* (ERPs) and functional magnetic resonance imaging (fMRI) to verify the existence of subliminal perception and associated learning in the laboratory (Babiloni et al., 2010; Bernat et al., 2001; Fazel-Rezai & Peters, 2005; Sabatini et al., 2009). However, as in about every other case where subliminal perception has reportedly occurred, these studies use stimuli that are *supraliminal*—"above the threshold"—and detectable by our sensory systems. However, they are below the level of conscious perception, and participants are not aware or conscious that they have been exposed to the stimuli due to masking or manipulation of attention. Furthermore, the stimuli typically influence automatic reactions (such as an increase in facial tension) rather than direct voluntary behaviors (such as going to buy something suggested by advertising).

The real world is full of complex motives that are not as easily influenced as one might think (Pratkanis, 1992). Even the so-called hidden pictures that some artists airbrush into the art in advertisements aren't truly subliminal—if someone points one out, it can be seen easily enough.

Habituation and Sensory Adaptation

In Chapter Two it was stated that the lower centers of the brain filter sensory stimulation and "ignore" or prevent conscious attention to stimuli that do not change. The brain is only interested in changes in information. That's why people don't really "hear" the noise of the air conditioner unless it suddenly cuts off or the noise made in some classrooms unless it gets very quiet. Although they actually are *hearing* it, they aren't paying attention to it. This is called **habituation**, and it is the way the brain deals with unchanging information from the environment. All of our senses are subject to habituation (LINK) to Chapter Two: The Biological Perspective, p. 65.

Sometimes I can smell the odor of the garbage can in the kitchen when I first come home, but after a while the smell seems to go away—is this also habituation?

Although different from habituation, **sensory adaptation** is another process by which constant, unchanging information from the sensory receptors is effectively ignored. In habituation, the sensory receptors are still responding to stimulation but the lower centers of the brain are not sending the signals from those receptors to the cortex. The process of sensory adaptation differs because the receptor cells *themselves* become less responsive to an unchanging stimulus—garbage odors included—and the receptors no longer send signals to the brain.

I've heard about people being influenced by stuff in movies and on television, things that are just below the level of conscious awareness. Is that true?

This young woman does not feel the piercings on her ear and nose because sensory adaptation allows her to ignore a constant, unchanging stimulation from the metal rings. What else is she wearing that would cause sensory adaptation?

Sometimes I can smell the odor of the garbage can in the kitchen when I first come home, but after a while the smell seems to go away—is this also habituation?

habituation tendency of the brain to stop attending to constant, unchanging information.

sensory adaptation tendency of sensory receptor cells to become less responsive to a stimulus that is unchanging.

For example, when you eat, the food that you put in your mouth tastes strong at first, but as you keep eating the same thing, the taste does fade somewhat, doesn't it? As with habituation, all of our senses are subject to sensory adaptation.

You might think, then, that if you stare at something long enough, it would also disappear, but the eyes are a little different. Even though the sensory receptors in the back of the eyes adapt to and become less responsive to a constant visual stimulus, under ordinary circumstances the eyes are never entirely still. There's a constant movement of the eyes, tiny little vibrations called "microsaccades" or "saccadic movements" that people don't consciously notice. These movements keep the eyes from adapting to what they see. (That's a good thing, because otherwise many students would no doubt go blind from staring off into space.)

---

practice quiz   How much do you remember?   **(3.1)**

Pick the best answer.

1. The smallest difference between two stimuli that can be detected 50 percent of the time it is present is called _____.
   a. absolute threshold.
   b. just noticeable difference.
   c. sensation.
   d. sensory adaptation.

2. When receptor cells for the senses are activated, the process called _____ has begun.
   a. perception
   b. sublimination
   c. adaptation
   d. sensation

3. You have a piece of candy that you are holding in your mouth. After a while, the candy doesn't taste as strong as it did when you first tasted it. What has happened?
   a. sensory adaptation
   b. subliminal perception
   c. habituation
   d. perceptual defense

4. While driving down the road looking for the new restaurant you want to try out, not hearing the clicking of the turn signal you forgot to turn off until one of your friends points it out is likely due to _____.
   a. accommodation.
   b. adaptation.
   c. sublimation.
   d. habituation.

ANSWERS ON PAGE AK-1.

The Science of Seeing

> I've heard that light is waves, but I've also heard that light is made of particles—which is it?

● I've heard that light is waves, but I've also heard that light is made of particles—which is it?

Light is a complicated phenomenon. Although scientists have long argued over the nature of light, they finally have agreed that light has the properties of both waves and particles. The following section gives a brief history of how scientists have tried to "shed light" on the mystery of light.

Perceptual Properties of Light: Catching the Waves

3.2 **What is light, and how does it travel through the various parts of the eye?**

It was Albert Einstein who first proposed that light is actually tiny "packets" of waves. These "wave packets" are called *photons* and have specific wavelengths associated with them (Lehnert, 2007; van der Merwe & Garuccio, 1994).

When people experience the physical properties of light, they are not really aware of its dual, wave-like and particle-like, nature. With regard to its psychological properties, there are three aspects to our perception of light: *brightness, color,* and *saturation.*

Brightness is determined by the amplitude of the wave—how high or how low the wave actually is. The higher the wave, the brighter the light appears to be. Low waves are dimmer. *Color*, or hue, is largely determined by the length of the wave. Long wavelengths (measured in nanometers) are found at the red end of the *visible spectrum* (the portion of the whole spectrum of light that is visible to the human eye; see Figure 3.1), whereas shorter wavelengths are found at the blue end. (Note that when combining different colors, light behaves differently than pigments or paint. We will look at this distinction when we examine perception of color.)

Saturation refers to the purity of the color people perceive: A highly saturated red, for example, would contain only red wavelengths, whereas a less saturated red might contain a mixture of wavelengths. For example, when a child is using the red paint from a set of poster paints, the paint on the paper will look like a pure red, but if the child mixes in some white paint, the paint will look pink. The hue is still red, but it will be less of a saturated red because of the presence of white wavelengths. Mixing in black or gray would also lessen the saturation.

FIGURE 3.1 The Visible Spectrum
The wavelengths that people can see are only a small part of the whole electromagnetic spectrum.

White light

Prism

Visible light
400–700 nm

Gamma rays	X-rays	Ultra-violet rays		Infrared rays	Radar	Radio waves FM TV AM	AC circuits

10^{-5} 10^{-3} 10^{-1} 10^{1} 10^{3} 10^{5} 10^{7} 10^{9} 10^{11} 10^{13} 10^{15} 10^{17}

Wavelength in nanometers (nm; billionths of a meter)

The Structure of the Eye

The best way to talk about how the eye processes light is to talk about what happens to an image being viewed as the photons of light from that image travel through the eye. Refer to Figure 3.2 to follow the path of the image. ✳ Explore on **MyPsychLab**

✳ Explore the visual system in the Virtual Brain on **MyPsychLab**

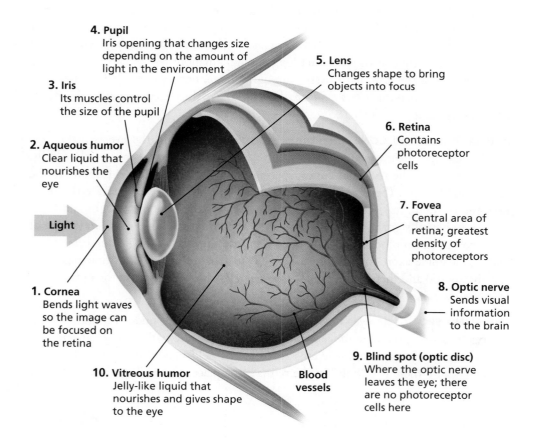

4. Pupil
Iris opening that changes size depending on the amount of light in the environment

3. Iris
Its muscles control the size of the pupil

2. Aqueous humor
Clear liquid that nourishes the eye

Light

1. Cornea
Bends light waves so the image can be focused on the retina

10. Vitreous humor
Jelly-like liquid that nourishes and gives shape to the eye

Blood vessels

5. Lens
Changes shape to bring objects into focus

6. Retina
Contains photoreceptor cells

7. Fovea
Central area of retina; greatest density of photoreceptors

8. Optic nerve
Sends visual information to the brain

9. Blind spot (optic disc)
Where the optic nerve leaves the eye; there are no photoreceptor cells here

FIGURE 3.2 Structure of the Eye
Light enters the eye through the cornea and pupil. The iris controls the size of the pupil. From the pupil, light passes through the lens to the retina, where it is transformed into nerve impulses. The nerve impulses travel to the brain along the optic nerve.

This photo illustrates an optical illusion caused by the refraction of light. The straw is not really broken although it appears that way.

FROM FRONT TO BACK: THE PARTS OF THE EYE Light enters the eye directly from a source (such as the sun) or indirectly by reflecting off of an object. To see clearly, a single point of light from a source or reflected from an object must travel through the structures of the eye and end up on the retina as a single point. Light bends as it passes through substances of different densities, through a process known as refraction. For example, have you ever looked at a drinking straw in a glass of water through the side of the glass? It appears that the straw bends, or is broken, at the surface of the water. That optical illusion is due to the refraction of light. The structures of the eye play a vital role in both collecting and focusing of light so that we can see clearly.

The surface of the eye is covered in a clear membrane called the *cornea*. The cornea not only protects the eye but also is the structure that focuses most of the light coming into the eye. The cornea has a fixed curvature, like a camera that has no option to adjust the focus. However, this curvature can be changed somewhat through vision-improving techniques that change the shape of the cornea. For example, oph-thalmologists can use both *photoreactive keratectomy (PRK)* and *laser-assisted in situ keratomileusis (LASIK)* procedures to remove small portions of the cornea, changing its curvature, and thus the focus in the eye.

The next visual layer is a clear, watery fluid called the *aqueous humor*. This fluid is continually replenished and supplies nourishment to the eye. The light from the visual image then enters the interior of the eye through a hole, called the *pupil*, in a round muscle called the *iris* (the colored part of the eye). The iris can change the size of the pupil, letting more or less light into the eye. That also helps focus the image; people try to do the same thing by squinting.

Behind the iris, suspended by muscles, is another clear structure called the *lens*. The flexible lens finishes the focusing process begun by the cornea. In a process called **visual accommodation**, the lens changes its shape from thick to thin, enabling it to focus on objects that are close or far away. The variation in thickness allows the lens to project a sharp image on the retina. People lose this ability as the lens hardens through aging (a disorder called *presbyopia*). Although people try to compensate* for their inability to focus on things that are close to them, eventually they usually need bifocals because their arms just aren't long enough anymore.

Once past the lens, light passes through a large, open space filled with a clear, jelly-like fluid called the *vitreous humor*. This fluid, like the aqueous humor, also nour-ishes the eye and gives it shape.

RETINA, RODS, AND CONES The final stop for light within the eye is the *retina*, a light-sensitive area at the back of the eye containing three layers: ganglion cells, bipolar cells, and the **rods** and **cones**, special cells (*photoreceptors*) that respond to the various light waves. (See Figures 3.3a and b.) The rods and the cones are the business end of the retina—the part that actually receives the photons of light and turns them into neural signals to the brain, sending them first to the *bipolar cells* (a type of interneuron; called bipolar or "two-ended" because they have a single dendrite at one end and a single axon on the other; Ⓛ Ⓘ Ⓝ Ⓚ to Chapter Two: The Biological Per-spective, p. 43) and then to the retinal *ganglion cells* whose axons form the optic nerve. (See Figure 3.3a.)

THE BLIND SPOT The eyes don't adapt to constant stimuli under normal circum-stances because of saccadic movements. But if people stare with one eye at one spot long enough, objects that slowly cross their visual field may at one point disappear briefly because there is a "hole" in the retina—the place where all the axons of those

visual accommodation the change in the thickness of the lens as the eye focuses on objects that are far away or close.

rods visual sensory receptors found at the back of the retina, responsible for non-color sensitivity to low levels of light.

cones visual sensory receptors found at the back of the retina, responsible for color vision and sharpness of vision.

---

*Compensate: to correct for an error or defect.

FIGURE 3.3 **The Parts of the Retina**
(a) Light passes through ganglion and bipolar cells until it reaches and stimulates the rods and cones. Nerve impulses from the rods and cones travel along a nerve pathway to the brain. (b) On the right of the figure is a photomicrograph of the long, thin rods and the shorter, thicker cones; the rods outnumber the cones by a ratio of about 20 to 1. (c) The blind spot demonstration. Hold the book in front of you. Close your right eye and stare at the picture of the dog with your left eye. Slowly bring the book closer to your face. The picture of the cat will disappear at some point because the light from the picture of the cat is falling on your blind spot.

ganglion cells leave the retina to become the optic nerve. There are no rods or cones here, so this is referred to as the **blind spot**. You can demonstrate the blind spot for yourself by following the directions in Figure 3.3c.

How the Eye Works

3.3 How do the eyes see, and how do the eyes see different colors?

THROUGH THE EYES TO THE BRAIN   You may want to first look at Figure 3.4 for a moment before reading this section. Light entering the eyes can be separated into the left and right visual fields. Light from the right visual field falls on the left side of each eye's retina; light from the left visual field falls on the right side of each retina. Light travels in a straight line through the cornea and lens, resulting in the image projected on the retina actually being upside down and reversed from left to right as compared to the visual fields. Thank goodness our brains can compensate for this!

The areas of the retina can be divided into halves, with the halves toward the temples of the head referred to as the temporal retinas and the halves toward the center, or nose, called the nasal retinas. Look at Figure 3.4 again. Notice that the information from the left visual field (falling on the right side of each retina) goes directly to the right visual cortex, while the information from the right visual field (falling on the left side of each retina) goes directly to the left visual cortex. This is because the axons from the temporal halves of each retina project to the visual cortex on the same side of the brain while the axons from the nasal halves cross over to the visual cortex on the opposite side of the brain. The optic chiasm is the point of crossover.

blind spot   area in the retina where the axons of the three layers of retinal cells exit the eye to form the optic nerve, insensitive to light.

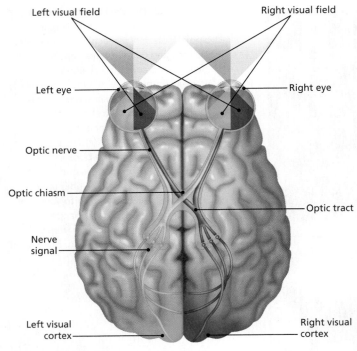

FIGURE 3.4 Crossing of the Optic Nerve
Light falling on the left side of each eye's retina (from the right visual field, shown in yellow) will stimulate a neural message that will travel along the optic nerve to the visual cortex in the occipital lobe of the left hemisphere. Notice that the message from the temporal half of the left retina goes directly to the left occipital lobe, while the message from the nasal half of the right retina crosses over to the left hemisphere (the optic chiasm is the point of crossover). The optic nerve tissue from both eyes joins together to form the left optic tract before going on to the left occipital lobe. For the left visual field (shown in blue), the messages from both right sides of the retinas will travel along the right optic tract to the right visual cortex in the same manner.

> Earlier you said the cones are used in color vision. There are so many colors in the world—are there cones that detect each color? Or do all cones detect all colors?

dark adaptation the recovery of the eye's sensitivity to visual stimuli in darkness after exposure to bright lights.

light adaptation the recovery of the eye's sensitivity to visual stimuli in light after exposure to darkness.

trichromatic theory theory of color vision that proposes three types of cones: red, blue, and green.

Let's go back now to the photoreceptors in the retina, the rods and cones responsible for different aspects of vision. The rods (about 120 million of them in each eye) are found all over the retina except in the very center, which contains only cones. Rods are sensitive to changes in brightness but not to changes in wavelength, so they see only in black and white and shades of gray. They can be very sensitive because many rods are connected to a single bipolar cell, so that if even only one rod is stimulated by a photon of light, the brain perceives the whole area of those rods as stimulated (because the brain is receiving the message from the single bipolar cell). But because the brain doesn't know exactly what part of the area (which rod) is actually sending the message, the visual acuity (sharpness) is quite low. That's why things seen in low levels of light, such as twilight or a dimly lit room, are fuzzy and grayish. Because rods are located on the periphery of the retina, they are also responsible for peripheral vision.

Because rods work well in low levels of light, they are also the cells that allow the eyes to adapt to low light. **Dark adaptation** occurs as the eye recovers its ability to see when going from a brightly lit state to a dark state. (The light-sensitive pigments that allow us to see are able to regenerate or "recharge" in the dark.) The brighter the light was, the longer it takes the rods to adapt to the new lower levels of light (Bartlett, 1965).

When going from a darkened room to one that is brightly lit, the opposite process occurs. The cones have to adapt to the increased level of light, and they accomplish this **light adaptation** much more quickly than the rods adapt to darkness—it takes a few seconds at most (Hood, 1998). There are 6 million cones in each eye; of these, 50,000 have a private line to the optic nerve (one bipolar cell for each cone). This means that the cones are the receptors for visual acuity. Cones are located all over the retina but are more concentrated at its very center where there are no rods (the area called the *fovea*). Cones also need a lot more light to function than the rods do, so cones work best in bright light, which is also when people see things most clearly. Cones are also sensitive to different wavelengths of light, so they are responsible for color vision.

Perception of Color

> Earlier you said the cones are used in color vision. There are so many colors in the world—are there cones that detect each color? Or do all cones detect all colors?

Although experts in the visual system have been studying color and its nature for many years, at this point in time there is an ongoing theoretical discussion about the role the cones play in the sensation of color.

THEORIES OF COLOR VISION Two theories about how people see colors were originally proposed in the 1800s. The first is called the **trichromatic** ("three colors") **theory.** First proposed by Thomas Young in 1802 and later modified by Hermann von Helmholtz in 1852, this theory proposed three types of cones: red cones, blue cones, and green cones, one for each of the three primary colors of light.

Most people probably think that the primary colors are red, yellow, and blue, but these are the primary colors when talking about *painting*—not when talking about *light*. Paints *reflect* light, and the way reflected light mixes is different from the way direct light mixes. For example, if an artist were to blend red, yellow, and blue paints together, the result would be a mess—a black mess. The mixing of paint (reflected light) is subtractive, removing more light as you mix in more colors. As all of the colors are mixed, the more light waves are absorbed and we see black. But if the artist were to blend a red, green, and blue light together by focusing lights of those three colors on one common spot, the result would be white, not black. The mixing of direct light is additive, resulting in lighter colors, more light, and when mixing red, blue, and green, we see white, the reflection of the entire visual spectrum.

In the trichromatic theory, different shades of colors correspond to different amounts of light received by each of these three types of cones. These cones then fire their message to the brain's vision centers. It is the combination of cones and the rate at which they are firing that determines the color that will be seen. For example, if the red and green cones are firing in response to a stimulus at fast enough rates, the color the person sees is yellow. If the red and blue cones are firing fast enough, the result is magenta. If the blue and green cones are firing fast enough, a kind of cyan color (blue-green) appears.

Brown and Wald (1964) identified three types of cones in the retina, each sensitive to a range of wavelengths, measured in nanometers (nm), and a peak sensitivity that roughly corresponds to three different colors (although hues/colors can vary depending on brightness and saturation). The peak wavelength of light the cones seem to be most sensitive to turns out to be just a little different from Young and von Helmholtz's original three corresponding colors: Short-wavelength cones detect what we see as blue-violet (about 420 nm), medium-wavelength cones detect what we see as green (about 530 nm), and long-wavelength cones detect what we see as green-yellow (about 560 nm). Interestingly, none of the cones identified by Brown and Wald has a peak sensitivity to light where most of us see red (around 630 nm). Keep in mind though that each cone responds to light across a range of wavelengths, not just its wavelength of peak sensitivity. Depending on the intensity of the light, both the medium- and long-wavelength cones respond to light that appears red.

THE AFTERIMAGE The trichromatic theory would, at first glance, seem to be more than adequate to explain how people perceive color. But there's an interesting phenomenon that this theory cannot explain. If a person stares at a picture of the American flag for a little while—say, a minute—and then looks away to a blank white wall or sheet of paper, that person will see an afterimage of the flag. **Afterimages** occur when a visual sensation persists for a brief time even after the original stimulus is removed. The person would also notice rather quickly that the colors of the flag in the afterimage are all wrong—green for red, black for white, and yellow for blue. If you follow the directions for Figure 3.5, in which the flag is yellow, green, and black, you should see a flag with the usual red, white, and blue.

While this deer may see quite well when using its rods at night, the bright headlights of a car will activate the cones. The cones will adapt rather quickly, but it takes time for the deer's pupil to contract, leaving the deer blinded by the light until then.

In trichromatic theory, the three types of cones combine to form different colors much as these three colored lights combine.

afterimages images that occur when a visual sensation persists for a brief time even after the original stimulus is removed.

FIGURE 3.5 Color Afterimage
Stare at the white dot in the center of this oddly colored flag for about 30 seconds. Now look at a white piece of paper or a white wall. Notice that the colors are now the normal, expected colors of the American flag. They are also the primary colors that are opposites of the colors in the picture and provide evidence for the opponent-process theory of color vision.

opponent-process theory   theory of color vision that proposes visual neurons (or groups of neurons) are stimulated by light of one color and inhibited by light of another color.

So which theory accounts for color blindness? I've heard that there are two kinds of color blindness: when you can't tell red from green and when you can't tell blue from yellow.

Why are most of the people with color-deficient vision men?

● Hey, now the afterimage of the flag has normal colors! Why does this happen?

The phenomenon of the color afterimage is explained by the second theory of color perception, called the **opponent-process theory** (De Valois & De Valois, 1993; Hurvich & Jameson, 1957), based on an idea first suggested by Edwald Hering in 1874 (Finger, 1994). In opponent-process theory, there are four primary colors: red, green, blue, and yellow. The colors are arranged in pairs, red with green and blue with yellow. If one member of a pair is strongly stimulated, the other member is inhibited and cannot be working—so there are no reddish-greens or bluish-yellows.

So how can this kind of pairing cause a color afterimage? From the level of the bipolar and ganglion cells in the retina, all the way through the thalamus, and on to the visual cortical areas in the brain, some neurons (or groups of neurons) are stimulated by light from one part of the visual spectrum and inhibited by light from a different part of the spectrum. For example, let's say we have a red-green ganglion cell in the retina whose baseline activity is rather weak when we expose it to white light. However, the cell's activity is increased by red light, so we experience the color red. If we stimulate the cell with red light for a long enough period of time, the cell becomes fatigued. If we then swap out the red light with white light, the now-tired cell responds even less than the original baseline. Now we experience the color green because green is associated with a decrease in the responsiveness of this cell.

So which theory is the right one? Both theories play a part in color vision. Trichromatic theory can explain what is happening with the raw stimuli, the actual detection of various wavelengths of light. Opponent-process theory can explain afterimages and other aspects of visual perception that occur after the initial detection of light from our environment. In addition to the retinal bipolar and ganglion cells, opponent-process cells are contained inside the thalamus in an area called the lateral geniculate nucleus (LGN). The LGN is part of the pathway that visual information takes to the occipital lobe. It is when the cones in the retina send signals through the retinal bipolar and ganglion cells that we see the red versus green pairings and blue versus yellow pairings. Together with the retinal cells, the cells in the LGN appear to be the ones responsible for opponent-processing of color vision and the afterimage effect.

● So which theory accounts for color blindness? I've heard that there are two kinds of color blindness: when you can't tell red from green and when you can't tell blue from yellow.

COLOR BLINDNESS   From the mention of red-green and yellow-blue color blindness, one might think that the opponent-process theory explains this problem. But in reality "color blindness" is caused by defective cones in the retina of the eye and as a more general term, *color-deficient vision* is more accurate, as most people with "color blindness" have two type of cones working and can see many colors.

There are really three kinds of color-deficient vision. In a very rare type, *monochrome color blindness*, people either have no cones or have cones that are not working at all. Essentially, if they have cones, they only have one type and, therefore, everything looks the same to the brain—shades of gray. The other types of color-deficient vision, or *dichromatic vision*, are caused by the same kind of problem—having one cone that does not work properly. *Protanopia* (red-green color deficiency) is due to the lack of functioning red cones, and *deuteranopia* (another type of red-green color deficiency) results from the lack of functioning green cones. In both of these types, the individual confuses reds and greens, seeing the world primarily in blues, yellows, and shades of gray. A lack of functioning blue cones is much less common and is called *tritanopia* (blue-yellow color deficiency). These individuals see the world primarily in reds, greens, and shades of gray. To get an idea of what a test for color-deficient vision is like, look at Figure 3.6.

● Why are most of the people with color-deficient vision men?

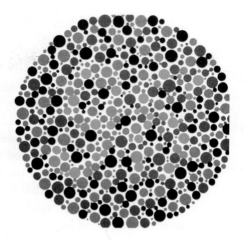

FIGURE 3.6 Ishihara Color Test Example
Two facsimiles of the Ishihara Color Test. In the circle on the left, the number 5 should be easier to see for those with normal color vision, and on the right, the number 96. In both circles, individuals with color-deficient vision will have difficulty identifying the numbers or may see nothing but a circle of dots.

Color-deficient vision involving one set of cones is inherited in a pattern known as *sex-linked inheritance*. The gene for color-deficient vision is *recessive*. To inherit a recessive trait, you normally need two of the genes, one from each parent. (L I N K) to Chapter Seven: Development Across the Life Span, p. 232. But the gene for color-deficient vision is attached to a particular chromosome (a package of genes) that helps to determine the sex of a person. Men have one X chromosome and one smaller Y chromosome (named for their shapes), whereas women have two X chromosomes. The smaller Y has fewer genes than the larger X, and one of the genes missing is the one that would suppress the gene for color-deficient vision. For a woman to have color-deficient vision, she must inherit two recessive genes, one from each parent, but a man only needs to inherit *one* recessive gene—the one passed on to him on his mother's X chromosome. His odds are greater; therefore, more males than females have color-deficient vision. Read on MyPsychLab

Read and learn more about color blindness on **MyPsychLab**

practice quiz How much do you remember?

3.2 3.3

Pick the best answer.

1. Which of the following terms refers to the perceived effect of the amplitude of light waves?
   a. color
   b. brightness
   c. saturation
   d. hue

2. Which of the following represents the correct path of light through the eye?
   a. iris, cornea, lens, retina
   b. cornea, vitreous humor, iris, lens, aqueous humor, retina
   c. cornea, pupil, lens, vitreous humor, retina
   d. cornea, lens, pupil, iris, retina

3. If you wanted to locate a dimly lit star better at night, what should you do?
   a. Look directly at it because the cones will focus better at night.
   b. Look off to the side, using the cones in the periphery of the retina.
   c. Look directly at it because the rods can see sharply at night.
   d. Look off to the side, using the rods in the periphery of the retina.

4. Which theory of color vision best accounts for afterimages?
   a. trichromatic theory
   b. opponent-process theory
   c. both a and b
   d. neither a nor b

5. Which statement about color-deficient vision is TRUE?
   a. There are more men with color-deficient vision than women.
   b. All people with color-deficient vision see only in black and white.
   c. Some people with color-deficient vision see only in blue.
   d. Some people with color-deficient vision see only in blue and red.

ANSWERS ON PAGE AK-1.

The Hearing Sense: Can You Hear Me Now?

If light works like waves, then do sound waves have similar properties? ●

The properties of sound are indeed similar to those of light, as both senses rely on waves. But the similarity ends there, as the physical properties of sound are different from those of light.

If light works like waves, then do sound waves have similar properties?

"And only you can hear this whistle?"

Perception of Sound: Good Vibrations

3.4 What is sound, and how does it travel through the various parts of the ear?

Sound waves do not come in little packets the way light comes in photons. Sound waves are simply the vibrations of the molecules of air that surround us. Sound waves do have the same properties of light waves though—wavelength, amplitude, and *purity*. Wavelengths are interpreted by the brain as the frequency or *pitch* (high, medium, or low). Amplitude is interpreted as *volume*, how soft or loud a sound is. (See Figure 3.7.) Finally, what would correspond to saturation or purity in light is called *timbre* in sound, a richness in the tone of the sound. And just as people rarely see pure colors in the world around us, they also seldom hear pure sounds. The everyday noises that surround people do not allow them to hear many pure tones.

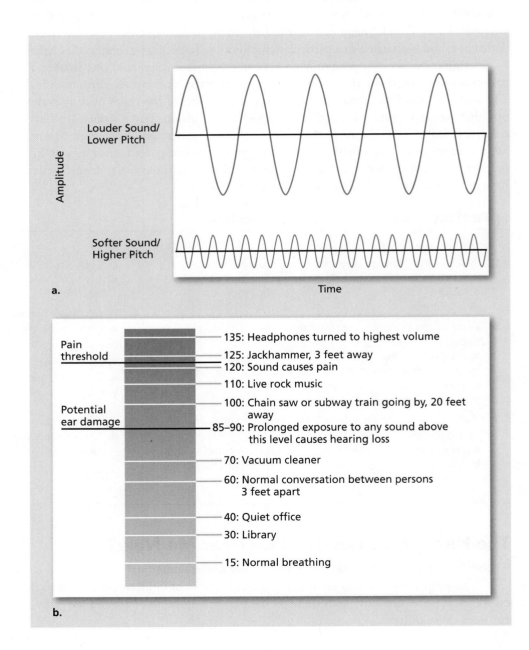

FIGURE 3.7 Sound Waves and Decibels

(a) Two sound waves. The higher the wave, the louder the sound; the lower the wave, the softer the sound. If the waves are close together in time (high frequency), the pitch will be perceived as a high pitch. Waves that are farther apart (low frequency) will be perceived as having a lower pitch. (b) Decibels of various stimuli. A *decibel* is a unit of measure for loudness. Psychologists study the effects that noise has on stress, learning, performance, aggression, and psychological and physical well-being.

Just as a person's vision is limited by the visible spectrum of light, a person is also limited in the range of frequencies he or she can hear. Frequency is measured in cycles (waves) per second, or **hertz (Hz)**. Human limits are between 20 and 20,000 Hz, with the most sensitivity from about 2000 to 4000 Hz, which is very important for conversational speech. (In comparison, dogs can hear between 50 and 60,000 Hz, and dolphins can hear up to 200,000 Hz.) Because music comprises a greater range (approximately 20 to 5000 Hz), to hear the higher and lower frequencies of a piece of music on a CD, for example, a person would need to increase the amplitude or volume—which explains why some people like to "crank it up." However, be careful not to crank it up too loudly (as can be the case with ear "buds" that do not block out ambient sound) as it requires relatively more volume/higher amplitudes to hear lower-frequency sounds as compared to higher frequencies. You can therefore cause damage that will lead to hearing loss in the range associated with normal speech. In other words, cranking it up now can possibly lead to hearing problems in the future.

The Structure of the Ear: Follow the Vibes

The ear is a series of structures, each of which plays a part in the sense of hearing, as shown in Figure 3.8.

THE OUTER EAR The **pinna** is the visible, external part of the ear that serves as a kind of concentrator, funneling* the sound waves from the outside into the structure of the ear. The pinna is also the entrance to the **auditory canal** (or ear canal), the short tunnel that runs down to the *tympanic membrane*, or eardrum. When sound waves hit the eardrum, they cause three tiny bones in the middle ear to vibrate.

✹ Explore on MyPsychLab

hertz (Hz) cycles or waves per second, a measurement of frequency.

pinna the visible part of the ear.

auditory canal short tunnel that runs from the pinna to the eardrum.

✹ Explore perception and hearing in the Virtual Brain on **MyPsychLab**

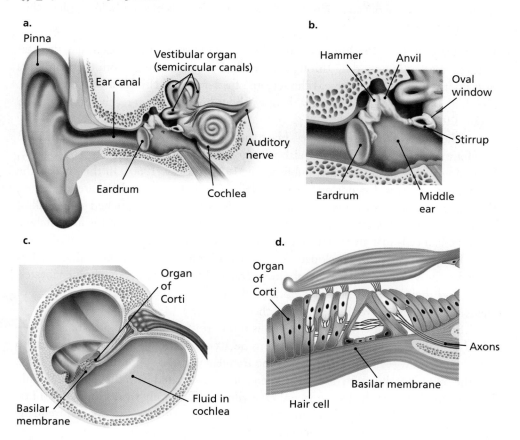

FIGURE 3.8 The Structure of the Ear
(a) This drawing shows the entire ear, beginning with the outer ear (pinna, ear canal, and eardrum). The vestibular organ includes the semicircular canals and the otolith organs (inside the round structures just above the cochlea). (b) The middle ear. Sound waves entering through the ear canal cause the eardrum to vibrate, which causes each of the three bones of the middle ear to vibrate, amplifying the sound. The stirrup rests on the oval window, which transmits its vibration to the fluid in the inner ear. (c) The inner ear. Large spaces are filled with fluid (shown in purple) that vibrates as the oval window vibrates. A thin membrane suspended in this fluid is called the basilar membrane, which contains the organ of Corti, the structure composed of the hairlike cells that send signals to the auditory cortex of the brain by way of the auditory nerve. (d) A close-up view of the basilar membrane (in dark pink) with the hair cells of the organ of Corti (in lighter pink). Notice the axons (small green lines) leaving the hair cells to form the auditory nerve.

*Funneling: moving to a focal point.

cochlea   snail-shaped structure of the inner ear that is filled with fluid.

auditory nerve   bundle of axons from the hair cells in the inner ear.

pitch   psychological experience of sound that corresponds to the frequency of the sound waves; higher frequencies are perceived as higher pitches.

place theory   theory of pitch that states that different pitches are experienced by the stimulation of hair cells in different locations on the organ of Corti.

frequency theory   theory of pitch that states that pitch is related to the speed of vibrations in the basilar membrane.

> I think I have it straight—but all of that just explains how soft and loud sounds get to the brain from the outside. How do we hear different kinds of sounds, like high pitches and low pitches?

THE MIDDLE EAR: HAMMER, ANVIL, AND STIRRUP   The three tiny bones in the middle ear are known as the hammer (*malleus*), anvil (*incus*), and stirrup (*stapes*), each name stemming from the shape of the respective bone. The vibration of these three bones amplifies the vibrations from the eardrum. The stirrup, the last bone in the chain, causes a membrane covering the opening of the inner ear to vibrate.

THE INNER EAR   This membrane is called the *oval window*, and its vibrations set off another chain reaction within the inner ear.

Cochlea   The inner ear is a snail-shaped structure called the **cochlea**, which is filled with fluid. When the oval window vibrates, it causes the fluid in the cochlea to vibrate. This fluid surrounds a membrane running through the middle of the cochlea called the *basilar membrane*.

Basilar Membrane and the Organ of Corti   The *basilar membrane* is the resting place of the *organ of Corti*, which contains the receptor cells for the sense of hearing. When the basilar membrane vibrates, it vibrates the organ of Corti, causing it to brush against a membrane above it. On the organ of Corti are special cells called *hair cells*, which are the receptors for sound. When these auditory receptors or hair cells are bent up against the other membrane, it causes them to send a neural message through the **auditory nerve** (which contains the axons of all the receptor neurons) and into the brain, where the auditory cortex will interpret the sounds (the transformation of the vibrations of sound into neural messages is transduction). The louder the sound in the outside world, the stronger the vibrations that stimulate more of those hair cells—which the brain interprets as loudness.

● I think I have it straight—but all of that just explains how soft and loud sounds get to the brain from the outside. How do we hear different kinds of sounds, like high pitches and low pitches?

PERCEIVING PITCH   **Pitch** refers to how high or low a sound is. For example, the bass tones in the music pounding through the wall of your apartment from the neighbors next door is a low pitch, whereas the scream of a 2-year-old child is a very high pitch. *Very* high. There are three primary theories about how the brain receives information about pitch.

The oldest of the three theories, **place theory**, is based on an idea proposed in 1863 by Hermann von Helmholtz and elaborated on and modified by Georg von Békésy, beginning with experiments first published in 1928 (Békésy, 1960). In this theory, the pitch a person hears depends on where the hair cells that are stimulated are located on the organ of Corti. For example, if the person is hearing a high-pitched sound, all of the hair cells near the oval window will be stimulated, but if the sound is low pitched, all of the hair cells that are stimulated will be located farther away on the organ of Corti.

Frequency theory, developed by Ernest Rutherford in 1886, states that pitch is related to how fast the basilar membrane vibrates. The faster this membrane vibrates, the higher the pitch; the slower it vibrates, the lower the pitch. (In this theory, all of the auditory neurons would be firing at the same time.)

So which of these first two theories is right? It turns out that both are correct—up to a point. For place-theory research to be accurate, the basilar membrane has to vibrate unevenly—which it does when the frequency of the sound is *above* 1000 Hz. For the frequency theory to be correct, the neurons associated with the hair cells would have to fire as fast as the basilar membrane vibrates. This only works up to 1000 Hz, because neurons don't appear to fire at exactly the same time and rate when frequencies are faster than 1,000 times per second.

The frequency theory works for low pitches, and place theory works for moderate to high pitches. Is there another explanation? Yes, and it is a third theory, developed by Ernest Wever and Charles Bray, called the **volley principle** (Wever, 1949; Wever & Bray, 1930), which appears to account for pitches from about 400 Hz up to about 4000. In this explanation, groups of auditory neurons take turns firing in a process called *volleying*. If a person hears a tone of about 3000 Hz, it means that three groups of neurons have taken turns sending the message to the brain—the first group for the first 1000 Hz, the second group for the next 1000 Hz, and so on.

volley principle theory of pitch that states that frequencies from about 400 Hz to 4000 Hz cause the hair cells (auditory neurons) to fire in a volley pattern, or take turns in firing.

Types of Hearing Impairments

Hearing impairment is the term used to refer to difficulties in hearing. A person can be partially hearing impaired or totally hearing impaired, and the treatment for hearing loss will vary according to the reason for the impairment.

CONDUCTION HEARING IMPAIRMENT *Conduction hearing impairment* means that sound vibrations cannot be passed from the eardrum to the cochlea. The cause might be a damaged eardrum or damage to the bones of the middle ear (usually from an infection). In this kind of impairment, hearing aids may be of some use in restoring hearing.

NERVE HEARING IMPAIRMENT In *nerve hearing impairment*, the problem lies either in the inner ear or in the auditory pathways and cortical areas of the brain. Normal aging causes loss of hair cells in the cochlea, and exposure to loud noises can damage hair cells. *Tinnitus* is a fancy word for an extremely annoying ringing in one's ears, and it can also be caused by infections or loud noises—including loud music in headphones, so you might want to turn down that music player!

Because the damage is to the nerves or the brain, nerve hearing impairment cannot be helped with ordinary hearing aids, which are basically sound amplifiers. A technique for restoring some hearing to those with nerve hearing impairment makes use of an electronic device called a *cochlear implant*. This device sends signals from a microphone worn behind the ear to a sound processor worn on the belt or in a pocket, which then translates those signals into electrical stimuli that are sent to a series of electrodes implanted directly into the cochlea, allowing transduction to take place and stimulating the auditory nerve. (See Figure 3.9.) The brain then processes the electrode information as sound.

FIGURE 3.9 Cochlear Implant

(a) In a cochlear implant, a microphone implanted just behind the ear picks up sound from the surrounding environment. A speech processor, attached to the implant and worn outside the body, selects and arranges the sound picked up by the microphone. The implant itself is a transmitter and receiver, converting the signals from the speech processor into electrical impulses that are collected by the electrode array in the cochlea and then sent to the brain. (b) This child is able to hear with the help of a cochlear implant. Hearing spoken language during the early years of a child's life helps in the development of the child's own speech.

practice quiz   How much do you remember?

Pick the best answer.

1. Which of the following properties of sound would be the most similar to the color or hue of light?
   a. pitch
   b. loudness
   c. purity
   d. timbre

2. The eardrum is also called the _____.
   a. pinna.
   b. oval window.
   c. tympanic membrane.
   d. cochlea.

3. The _____ theory best explains how we hear sounds above 4000 Hz.
   a. place
   b. frequency
   c. volley
   d. adaptive

4. If the bones of the middle ear begin to deteriorate, you will develop _____ hearing impairment.
   a. nerve
   b. stimulation
   c. brain pathway
   d. conduction

ANSWERS ON PAGE AK-1.

Chemical Senses: It Tastes Good and Smells Even Better

3.5 How do the senses of taste and smell work, and how are they alike?

The sense of taste (taste in food, not taste in clothing or friends) and the sense of smell are very closely related. Have you ever noticed that when your nose is all stopped up, your sense of taste is affected, too? That's because the sense of taste is really a combination of taste and smell. Without the input from the nose, there are actually only four, and possibly five, kinds of taste sensors in the mouth.

Gustation: How We Taste the World

TASTE BUDS   *Taste buds* is the common name for the taste receptor cells, special kinds of neurons found in the mouth that are responsible for the sense of taste, or **gustation**. Most taste buds are located on the tongue, but there are a few on the roof of the mouth, the cheeks, and under the tongue as well. How sensitive people are to various tastes depends on how many taste buds they have; some people have only around 500, whereas others have 20 times that number. The latter are called "supertasters" and need far less seasoning in their food than those with fewer taste buds (Bartoshuk, 1993).

So taste buds are those little bumps I can see when I look closely at my tongue?

● So taste buds are those little bumps I can see when I look closely at my tongue?

No, those "bumps" are called *papillae*, and the taste buds line the walls of these papillae. (See Figure 3.10.)

Each taste bud has about 20 receptors that are very similar to the receptor sites on receiving neurons at the synapse. Ⓛ Ⓘ Ⓝ Ⓚ to Chapter Two: The Biological Perspective, p. 47. In fact, the receptors on taste buds work exactly like receptor sites on neurons—they receive molecules of various substances that fit into the receptor like a key into a lock. Taste is often called a chemical sense because it works with the molecules of foods people eat in the same way the neural receptors work with neurotransmitters. When the molecules (dissolved in saliva) fit into the receptors, a signal is fired to the brain, which then interprets the taste sensation.

What happens to the taste buds when I burn my tongue? Do they repair themselves? I know when I have burned my tongue, I can't taste much for a while, but the taste comes back.

● What happens to the taste buds when I burn my tongue? Do they repair themselves? I know when I have burned my tongue, I can't taste much for a while, but the taste comes back.

In general, the taste receptors get such a workout that they have to be replaced every 10 to 14 days (McLaughlin & Margolskee, 1994). And when the tongue is burned, the damaged cells no longer work. As time goes on, those cells get replaced and the taste sense comes back.

gustation   the sensation of a taste.

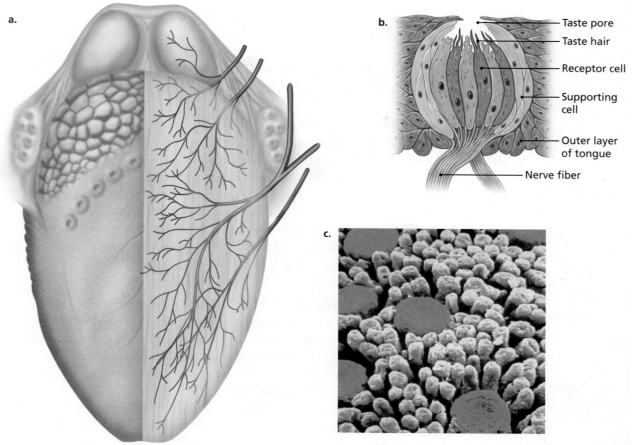

a.

b.
- Taste pore
- Taste hair
- Receptor cell
- Supporting cell
- Outer layer of tongue
- Nerve fiber

c.

FIGURE 3.10 The Tongue and Taste Buds—A Crosscut View of the Tongue (a) The right side of this drawing shows the nerves in the tongue's deep tissue. (b) The taste bud is located inside the papillae and is composed of small cells that send signals to the brain when stimulated by molecules of food. (c) Microphotograph of the surface of the tongue, showing two different sizes of papillae. The taste buds are located under the surface of the larger red papillae, whereas the smaller and more numerous papillae form a touch-sensitive rough surface that helps in chewing and moving food around the mouth.

THE FIVE BASIC TASTES In 1916 a German psychologist named Hans Henning proposed that there are four primary tastes: sweet, sour, salty, and bitter. Lindemann (1996) supported the idea that there is a fifth kind of taste receptor that detects a pleasant "brothy" taste associated with foods like chicken soup, tuna, kelp, cheese, and soy products, among others. Lindemann proposed that this fifth taste be called *umami*, a Japanese word first coined in 1908 by Dr. Kikunae Ikeda of Tokyo Imperial University to describe the taste. Dr. Ikeda had succeeded in isolating the substance in kelp that generated the sensation of umami—glutamate (Beyreuther et al., 2007). **LINK** to Chapter Two: The Biological Perspective, p. 49. Glutamate exists not only in the foods listed earlier, but is also present in human breast milk; also, it is the reason that the seasoning MSG—monosodium *glutamate*—adds a pleasant flavor to foods.

The five taste sensations work together, along with the sense of smell and the texture, temperature, and "heat" of foods, to produce thousands of taste sensations. Although researchers used to believe that certain tastes were located on certain places on the tongue, it is now known that all of the taste sensations are processed all over the tongue (Bartoshuk, 1993).

Just as individuals and groups can have varying food preferences, they can also vary on level of perceived sweetness. For example, obese individuals have been found to experience less sweetness than individuals who are not obese; foods that are both sweet and high in fat tend to be especially attractive to individuals who are obese (Bartoshuk et al., 2006). Such differences (as well as genetic variations like the supertasters) complicate direct comparison of food preferences. One possible solution is to have individuals rate taste in terms of an unrelated "standard" sensory experience of known intensity, such as the brightness of a light or the loudness of a sound or preference in terms of all pleasurable experiences, and not just taste (Bartoshuk, Fast, & Snyder, 2005; Snyder & Bartoshuk, 2009).

olfaction (olfactory sense) the sensation of smell.

Turning our attention back to how things taste for us as individuals, have you ever noticed that when you have a cold, food tastes very bland? Everything becomes bland or muted because you can taste only sweet, salty, bitter, sour, and umami—and because your nose is stuffed up with a cold, you don't get all the enhanced variations of those tastes that come from the sense of smell.

The Sense of Scents: Olfaction

Like the sense of taste, the sense of smell is a chemical sense. The ability to smell odors is called **olfaction**, or the **olfactory sense**.

The outer part of the nose serves the same purpose for odors that the pinna and ear canal serve for sounds: Both are merely ways to collect the sensory information and get it to the part of the body that will translate it into neural signals.

The part of the olfactory system that transduces odors—turns odors into signals the brain can understand—is located at the top of the nasal passages. This area of olfactory receptor cells is only about an inch square in each cavity, yet contains about 10 million olfactory receptors. (See Figure 3.11.)

OLFACTORY RECEPTOR CELLS The *olfactory receptor cells* each have about a half dozen to a dozen little "hairs," called *cilia*, that project into the cavity. Like taste buds, there are receptor sites on these hair cells that send signals to the brain when stimulated by the molecules of substances that are in the air moving past them.

 Wait a minute—you mean that when I can smell something like a skunk, there are little particles of skunk odor IN my nose?

● Wait a minute—you mean that when I can smell something like a skunk, there are little particles of skunk odor IN my nose?

Yes. When a person is sniffing something, the sniffing serves to move molecules of whatever the person is trying to smell into the nose and into the nasal cavities. That's okay when it's the smell of baking bread, apple pie, flowers, and the like, but when it's skunk, rotten eggs, dead animals—well, try not to think about it too much.

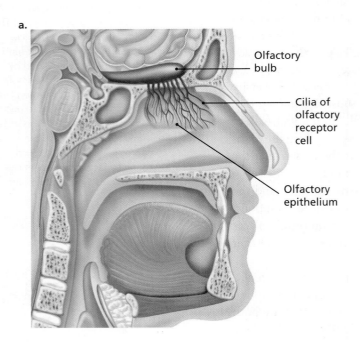

a.

Olfactory bulb

Cilia of olfactory receptor cell

Olfactory epithelium

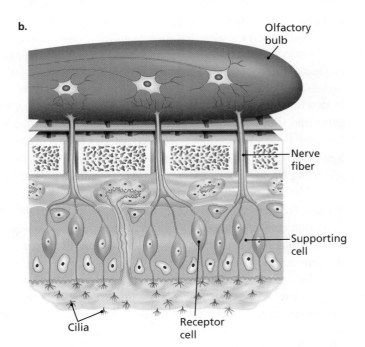

b.

Olfactory bulb

Nerve fiber

Supporting cell

Cilia

Receptor cell

FIGURE 3.11 The Olfactory Receptors

(a) A cross section of the nose and mouth. This drawing shows the nerve fibers inside the nasal cavity that carry information about smell directly to the olfactory bulb just under the frontal lobe of the brain (shown in green). (b) A diagram of the cells in the nose that process smell. The olfactory bulb is on top. Notice the cilia, tiny hairlike cells that project into the nasal cavity. These are the receptors for the sense of smell.

Olfactory receptors are like taste buds in another way, too. Olfactory receptors also have to be replaced as they naturally die off, about every 5 to 8 weeks. Unlike the taste buds, there are far more than five types of olfactory receptors—in fact, there are at least 1,000 of them.

You might remember from Chapter Two that signals from the olfactory receptors in the nasal cavity do not follow the same path as the signals from all the other senses. Vision, hearing, taste, and touch all pass through the thalamus and then on to the area of the cortex that processes that particular sensory information. But the sense of smell has its own special place in the brain—the olfactory bulbs, which are actually part of the brain.

THE OLFACTORY BULBS The **olfactory bulbs** are located right on top of the sinus cavity on each side of the brain directly beneath the frontal lobes. (Refer back to Figure 3.11.) The olfactory receptors send their neural signals directly up to these bulbs, bypassing the thalamus, the relay center for all other sensory information. The olfactory information is then sent from the olfactory bulbs to higher cortical areas, including the primary olfactory cortex (the *piriform cortex*), the orbitofrontal cortex, and the amygdala (remember from Chapter Two that the orbitofrontal cortex and amygdala play important roles in emotion). ⓛⓘⓝⓚ to Chapter Two: The Biological Perspective, p. 50.

Somesthetic Senses: What the Body Knows

So far, this chapter has covered vision, hearing, taste, and smell. That leaves touch. What is thought of as the sense of touch is really several sensations, originating in several different places in—and on—the body. It's really more accurate to refer to these as the body senses, or **somesthetic senses**. The first part of that word, *soma*, means "body," as mentioned in Chapter Two. The second part, *esthetic*, means "feeling," hence, the name. There are three somesthetic sense systems, the **skin senses** (having to do with touch, pressure, temperature, and pain), the **kinesthetic sense** (having to do with the location of body parts in relation to each other), and the **vestibular senses** (having to do with movement and body position).

Perception of Touch, Pressure, and Temperature

3.6 What allows people to experience the sense of touch, pain, motion, and balance?

Here's a good trivia question: What organ of the body is about 20 square feet in size? The answer is the skin. Skin is an organ. Its purposes include more than simply keeping bodily fluids in and germs out; skin also receives and transmits information from the outside world to the central nervous system (specifically, to the somatosensory cortex). ⓛⓘⓝⓚ to Chapter Two: The Biological Perspective, p. 69. Information about light touch, deeper pressure, hot, cold, and even pain is collected by special receptors in the skin's layers.

TYPES OF SENSORY RECEPTORS IN THE SKIN There are about half a dozen different receptors in the layers of the skin. (See Figure 3.12.) Some of them will respond to only one kind of sensation. For example, the *Pacinian corpuscles* are just beneath the skin and respond to changes in pressure. There are nerve endings that wrap around the ends of the hair follicles, a fact people may be well aware of when they tweeze their eyebrows, or when someone pulls their hair. These nerve endings are sensitive to both pain and touch. There are *free nerve endings* just beneath the uppermost layer of the skin that respond to changes in temperature and to pressure—and to pain.

How exactly does pain work? Why is it that sometimes I feel pain deep inside? Are there pain receptors there, too?

olfactory bulbs areas of the brain located just above the sinus cavity and just below the frontal lobes that receive information from the olfactory receptor cells.

somesthetic senses the body senses consisting of the skin senses, the kinesthetic sense, and the vestibular senses.

skin senses the sensations of touch, pressure, temperature, and pain.

kinesthetic sense sense of the location of body parts in relation to the ground and each other.

vestibular senses the sensations of movement, balance, and body position.

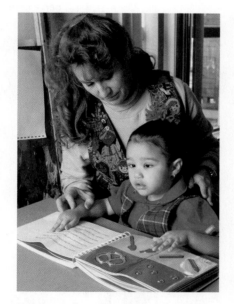

Her sense of touch is allowing this blind girl to "read" a Braille book with her fingers. The fingertips are extremely sensitive to fine differences in texture, allowing her to distinguish between small dots representing the different letters of the alphabet.

How exactly does pain work? Why is it that sometimes I feel pain deep inside? Are there pain receptors there, too?

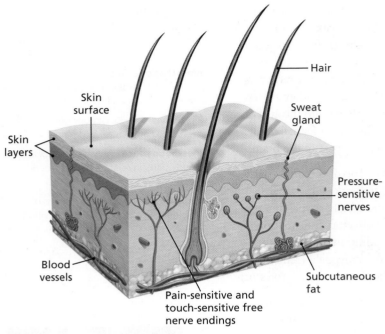

FIGURE 3.12 Cross Section of the Skin and Its Receptors

The skin is composed of several types of cells that process pain, pressure, and temperature. Some of these cells are wrapped around the ends of the hairs on the skin and are sensitive to touch on the hair itself, whereas others are located near the surface, and still others just under the top layer of tissue.

Congenital insensitivity to pain with anhidrosis (CIPA) is a rare genetic disorder that makes 5-year-old Ashlyn unable to feel pain. She must be examined carefully for scrapes and cuts after recess at school because she cannot feel when she hurts herself, putting her at risk for infection. What are some of the problems that Ashlyn and her parents may face as she grows older?

Yes, there are pain nerve fibers in the internal organs as well as receptors for pressure. How else would people have a stomachache or intestinal* pain—or get that full feeling of pressure when they've eaten too much or their bladder is full?

There are actually different types of pain. There are receptors that detect pain (and pressure) in the organs, a type of pain called *visceral pain*. Pain sensations in the skin, muscles, tendons, and joints are carried on large nerve fibers and are called *somatic pain*. Somatic pain is the body's warning system that something is being, or is about to be, damaged and tends to be sharp and fast. Another type of somatic pain is carried on small nerve fibers and is slower and more of a general ache. This somatic pain acts as a kind of reminder system, keeping people from further injury by reminding them that the body has already been damaged. For example, if you hit your thumb with a hammer, the immediate pain sensation is of the first kind—sharp, fast, and bright. But later the bruised tissue simply aches, letting you know to take it easy on that thumb.

People may not like pain, but its function as a warning system is vitally important. There are people who are born without the ability to feel pain, rare conditions called *congenital analgesia* and *congenital insensitivity to pain with anhidrosis (CIPA)*. Children with these disorders cannot feel pain when they cut or scrape themselves, leading to an increased risk of infection when the cut goes untreated (Mogil, 1999). They fear nothing—which can be a horrifying trial for the parents and teachers of such a child. These disorders affect the neural pathways that carry pain, heat, and cold sensations. (Those with CIPA have an additional disruption in the body's heat–cold sensing perspiration system [anhidrosis], so that the person is unable to cool off the body by sweating.)

A condition called *phantom limb pain* occurs when a person who has had an arm or leg removed sometimes "feels" pain in the missing limb (Nikolajsen & Jensen, 2001; Woodhouse, 2005). As many as 50 to 80 percent of people who have had amputations experience various sensations: burning, shooting pains, or pins-and-needles sensations where the amputated limb used to be. Once believed to be a psychological problem, some now believe that it is caused by the traumatic injury to the nerves during amputation (Ephraim et al., 2005).

Pain: Gate-Control Theory

The best current explanation for how the sensation of pain works is called *gate-control theory*, first proposed by Melzack and Wall (1965) and later refined and expanded (Melzack & Wall, 1996). In this theory, the pain signals must pass through a "gate" located in the spinal cord. The activity of the gate can be closed by nonpain signals coming into the spinal cord from the body and by signals coming from the brain. The gate is not a physical structure but instead represents the relative balance in neural activity of cells in the spinal cord that receive information from the body and then send information to the brain.

*Intestinal: having to do with the tubes in the body that digest food and process waste material.

Stimulation of the pain receptor cells releases a chemical called *substance P* (for "pain," naturally). Substance P released into the spinal cord activates other neurons that send their messages through spinal gates (opened by the pain signal). From the spinal cord, the message goes to the brain, activating cells in the thalamus, somatosensory cortex, areas of the frontal lobes, and the limbic system. The brain then interprets the pain information and sends signals that either open the spinal gates further, causing a greater experience of pain, or close them, dampening the pain. Of course, this decision by the brain is influenced by the psychological aspects of the pain-causing stimulus. Anxiety, fear, and helplessness intensify pain, whereas laughter, distraction, and a sense of control can diminish it. (This is why people might bruise themselves and not know it if they were concentrating on something else.) Pain can also be affected by competing signals from other skin senses, which is why rubbing a sore spot can reduce the feeling of pain.

Those same psychological aspects can also influence the release of the *endorphins*, the body's natural version of morphine. Ⓛ Ⓘ Ⓝ Ⓚ to Chapter Two: The Biological Perspective, p. 49. Endorphins can inhibit the transmission of pain signals in the brain, and in the spinal cord they can inhibit the release of substance P.

I've always heard that women are able to stand more pain than men. Is that true?

On the contrary, research has shown that women apparently feel pain more intensely than do men, and they also report pain more often than men do (Chesterton et al., 2003; Faucett et al., 1994; Norrbrink Budh et al., 2003). Men have been shown to cope better with many kinds of pain, possibly because men are often found to have a stronger belief than women that they can (or should) control their pain by their own efforts (Jackson et al., 2002).

The Kinesthetic Sense

Special receptors located in the muscles, tendons, and joints are part of the body's sense of movement and position in space—the movement and location of the arms, legs, and so forth in relation to one another. This sense is called *kinesthesia*, from the Greek words *kinein* ("to move") and *aesthesis* ("sensation"). When you close your eyes and raise your hand above your head, you know where your hand is because these special receptors, called proprioceptors, tell you about joint movement or the muscles stretching or contracting.

If you have ever gotten sick from traveling in a moving vehicle, you might be tempted to blame these proprioceptors. Actually, it's not the proprioceptors in the body that make people get sick. The culprits are special structures in the ear that tell us about the position of the body in relation to the ground and movement of the head that make up the *vestibular sense*—the sense of balance.

The Vestibular Sense

The name of this particular sense comes from a Latin word that means "entrance" or "chamber." The structures for this sense are located in the innermost chamber of the ear. There are two kinds of vestibular organs, the otolith organs and the semicircular canals.

The *otolith organs* are tiny sacs found just above the cochlea. These sacs contain a gelatin-like fluid within which tiny crystals are suspended (much like pieces of fruit in a bowl of Jell-O®). The head moves and the crystals cause the fluid to vibrate, setting off some tiny hairlike receptors on the inner surface of the sac, telling the person that he or she is moving forward, backward, sideways, or up and down. (It's pretty much the way the cochlea works but with movement being the stimulus instead of sound vibrations.)

The *semicircular canals* are three somewhat circular tubes that are also filled with fluid that will stimulate hairlike receptors when rotated. Having three tubes allows one

This tightrope-walking violinist is performing an amazing feat of coordination and muscular control. He must not only use his vestibular organs to help maintain his balance, but also his kinesthetic sense to be aware of exactly where each foot is in relation to the rope.

sensory conflict theory an explanation of motion sickness in which the information from the eyes conflicts with the information from the vestibular senses, resulting in dizziness, nausea, and other physical discomfort.

to be located in each of the three planes of motion. Remember learning in geometry class about the x-, y-, and z-axes? Those are the three planes through which the body can rotate, and when it does, it sets off the receptors in these canals. When you spin around and then stop, the fluid in the horizontal canal is still rotating and will make you feel dizzy because your body is telling you that you are still moving, but your eyes are telling you that you have stopped.

MOTION SICKNESS This disagreement between what the eyes say and what the body says is pretty much what causes *motion sickness*, the tendency to get nauseated when in a moving vehicle, especially one with an irregular movement. Normally, the vestibular sense coordinates with the other senses. But for some people, the information from the eyes may conflict a little too much with the vestibular organs, and dizziness, nausea, and disorientation are the result. This explanation of motion sickness is known as **sensory conflict theory** (Oman, 1990; Reason & Brand, 1975). The dizziness is the most likely cause of the nausea. Many poisons make a person dizzy, and the most evolutionarily adaptive thing to do is to expel the poison. Even without any poison in a case of motion sickness, the nausea occurs anyway (Treisman, 1977).

One way some people overcome motion sickness is to focus on a distant point or object. This provides visual information to the person about how he or she is moving, bringing the sensory input into agreement with the visual input. This is also how ballerinas and ice skaters manage not to get sick when turning rapidly and repeatedly—they focus their eyes at least once on some fixed object every so many turns.

practice quiz How much do you remember?

(3.5) (3.6)

Pick the best answer.

1. The receptors on our taste buds work most like _____.
   a. receptors in the ears.
   b. receptors in the eyes.
   c. receptor sites on neurons.
   d. receptors in the skin.

2. Which of the following statements about olfactory receptors is FALSE?
   a. Olfactory receptors are replaced every few years.
   b. There are at least 1,000 types of olfactory receptors.
   c. Signals from the receptors go directly to the olfactory bulbs in the brain.
   d. Olfactory receptors have hairlike projections called cilia.

3. After some time has passed, you can no longer smell the odor of wet paint that you noticed when you first entered your classroom. Which is the most likely reason for this?
   a. The smell has gone away.
   b. You've adapted to the smell, even though it's still there.
   c. Your nose fell asleep.
   d. You fell asleep.

4. Pain sensations in the skin, muscles, tendons, and joints that are carried on large nerve fibers are called _____.
   a. visceral pain.
   b. somatic pain.
   c. referred pain.
   d. indigenous pain.

5. In gate-control theory, substance P _____.
   a. opens the spinal gates for pain.
   b. closes the spinal gates for pain.
   c. is unrelated to pain.
   d. is similar in function to endorphins.

6. A bowl of gelatin with fruit in it will wiggle more than if it contained no fruit. This is most similar to the way the _____ work.
   a. semicircular canals
   b. proprioceptors
   c. otolith organs
   d. both a and b

ANSWERS ON PAGE AK-1.

The ABCs of Perception

3.7 What are perception, perceptual constancies, and the Gestalt principles of perception?

perception the method by which the sensations experienced at any given moment are interpreted and organized in some meaningful fashion.

Perception is the method by which the brain takes all the sensations people experience at any given moment and allows them to be interpreted in some meaningful fashion. Perception has some individuality to it. For example, two people might be looking at a cloud and while one thinks it's shaped like a horse, the other thinks it's more like a cow. They both *see* the same cloud, but they *perceive* that cloud differently. As individual as perception might be, some similarities exist in how people perceive the world around them, as the following section will discuss.

The Constancies: Size, Shape, and Brightness

One form of perceptual constancy* is **size constancy**, the tendency to interpret an object as always being the same size, regardless of its distance from the viewer (or the size of the image it casts on the retina). So if an object that is normally perceived to be about 6 feet tall appears very small on the retina, it will be interpreted as being very far away.

Another perceptual constancy is the tendency to interpret the shape of an object as constant, even when it changes on the retina. This **shape constancy** is why a person still perceives a coin as a circle even if it is held at an angle that makes it appear to be an oval on the retina. Dinner plates on a table are also seen as round, even though from the angle of viewing they are oval. (See Figure 3.13.)

A third form of perceptual constancy is **brightness constancy**, the tendency to perceive the apparent brightness of an object as the same even when the light conditions change. If a person is wearing black pants and a white shirt, for example, in broad daylight the shirt will appear to be much brighter than the pants. But if the sun is covered by thick clouds, even though the pants and shirt have less light to reflect than previously, the shirt will still appear to be just as much brighter than the pants as before—because the different amount of light reflected from each piece of clothing is still the same difference as before (Zeki, 2001).

The Gestalt Principles

Remember the discussion of the Gestalt theorists in Chapter One? Their original focus on human perception can still be seen in certain basic principles today, including the basic principles of the Gestalt tendency to group objects and perceive whole shapes.

FIGURE–GROUND RELATIONSHIPS   Take a look at the drawing of the cube in Figure 3.14. Which face of the cube is in the front? Look again—do the planes and corners of the cube seem to shift as you look at it?

This is called the "Necker cube." It has been around officially since 1832, when Louis Albert Necker, a Swiss scientist who was studying the structure of crystals, first drew it in his published papers. The problem with this cube is that there are conflicting sets of depth cues, so the viewer is never really sure which plane or edge is in the back and which is in the front—the visual presentation of the cube seems to keep reversing its planes and edges.

A similar illusion can be seen in Figure 3.15. In this picture, the viewer can switch perception back and forth from two faces looking at each other to the outline of a goblet in the middle. Which is the figure in front and which is the background?

Figure–ground relationships refer to the tendency to perceive objects or figures as existing on a background. People seem to have a preference for picking out figures from backgrounds even as early as birth. The illusions in Figures 3.14 and 3.15 are **reversible figures**, in which the figure and the ground seem to switch back and forth.

---

*Constancy: something that remains the same, the property of remaining stable and unchanging.

FIGURE 3.13 Shape Constancy
Three examples of shape constancy are shown here. The opening door is actually many different shapes, yet we still see it as basically a rectangular door. We do the same thing with a triangle and a circle—and, although when we look at them from different angles they cast differently shaped images on our retina, we experience them as a triangle and a circle because of shape constancy.

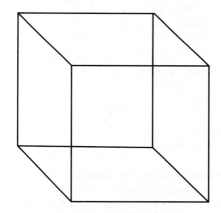

FIGURE 3.14 The Necker Cube
This is an example of a reversible figure. It can also be described as an ambiguous figure, since it is not clear which pattern should predominate.

size constancy   the tendency to interpret an object as always being the same actual size, regardless of its distance.

shape constancy   the tendency to interpret the shape of an object as being constant, even when its shape changes on the retina.

brightness constancy   the tendency to perceive the apparent brightness of an object as the same even when the light conditions change.

figure–ground   the tendency to perceive objects, or figures, as existing on a background.

reversible figures   visual illusions in which the figure and ground can be reversed.

FIGURE 3.15 Figure–Ground Illusion
What do you see when you look at this picture? Is it a wine goblet? Or two faces looking at each other? This is an example in which the figure and the ground seem to "switch" each time you look at the picture.

proximity the tendency to perceive objects that are close to each other as part of the same grouping.

similarity the tendency to perceive things that look similar to each other as being part of the same group.

closure the tendency to complete figures that are incomplete.

continuity the tendency to perceive things as simply as possible with a continuous pattern rather than with a complex, broken-up pattern.

FIGURE 3.16 Gestalt Principles of Grouping
The Gestalt principles of grouping are shown here. These are the human tendency to organize isolated stimuli into groups on the basis of five characteristics: proximity, similarity, closure, continuity, and common region.

Proximity: The dots on the left can be seen as horizontal or vertical rows—neither organization dominates. But just by changing the proximity of certain dots, as in the other two examples, we experience the dots as vertical columns (middle) or horizontal rows (right).

Similarity: The similarity of color here makes you perceive these dots as forming black squares and color squares rather than two rows of black and colored dots.

Closure: Even though the lines are broken, we still see these figures as a circle and a square—an example of how we tend to "close" or "fill in" missing parts from what we know of the whole.

Continuity: Because of continuity, we are much more likely to see the figure on the left as being made up of two lines, A to B and C to D, than we are to see it as a figure made up of lines A to D and C to B or A to C and B to D.

Common Region: Similarity would suggest that people see two groups, stars and circles. But the colored backgrounds define a visible common region, and the tendency is to perceive three different groups.

PROXIMITY Another very simple rule of perception is the tendency to perceive objects that are close to one another as part of the same grouping, a principle called **proximity**, or "nearness." (See Figure 3.16.)

SIMILARITY **Similarity** refers to the tendency to perceive things that look similar as being part of the same group. When members of a sports team wear uniforms that are all the same color, it allows people viewing the game to perceive them as one group even when they are scattered around the field or court.

CLOSURE **Closure** is the tendency to complete figures that are incomplete. A talented artist can give the impression of an entire face with just a few cleverly placed strokes of the pen or brush—the viewers fill in the details.

CONTINUITY The principle of **continuity** is easier to see than it is to explain in words. It refers to the tendency to perceive things as simply as possible with a continuous pattern rather than with a complex, broken-up pattern. Look at Figure 3.16 for an example of continuity. Isn't it much easier to see the figure on the left as two wavy lines crossing each other than as the little sections in the diagrams to the right?

CONTIGUITY **Contiguity** isn't shown in Figure 3.16 because it involves not just nearness in space but nearness in time also. Basically, contiguity is the tendency to perceive two things that happen close together in time as being related. Usually the first event that occurs is seen as causing the second event. Ventriloquists* make vocalizations without appearing to move their own mouths but move their dummy's mouth instead. The tendency to believe that the dummy is doing the talking is due largely to contiguity.

There is one other principle of perceptual grouping that was not one of the original principles. It was added to the list (and can be seen at the bottom of Figure 3.16) by Stephen Palmer (Palmer, 1992). In *common region*, the tendency is to perceive objects that are in a common area or region as being in a group. In Figure 3.16, people could perceive the stars as one group and the circles as another on the basis of similarity. But the colored backgrounds so visibly define common regions that people instead perceive three groups—one of which has both stars and circles in it. ✳ Explore on MyPsychLab

Depth Perception

3.8 What is depth perception, and what kinds of cues are important for it to occur?

The capability to see the world in three dimensions is called **depth perception**. It's a handy ability because without it you would have a hard time judging how far away objects are. How early in life do humans develop depth perception? It seems to develop very early in infancy, if it is not actually present at birth. People who have had sight restored have almost no ability to perceive depth if they were blind from birth. Depth perception, like the constancies, seems to be present in infants at a very young age.

Various cues exist for perceiving depth in the world. Some require the use of only one eye (**monocular cues**), and some are a result of the slightly different visual patterns that exist when the visual fields** of both eyes are used (**binocular cues**).

MONOCULAR CUES Monocular cues are often referred to as **pictorial depth cues** because artists can use these cues to give the illusion of depth to paintings and drawings. Examples of these cues are discussed next and can be seen in Figure 3.17.

1. **Linear perspective:** When looking down a long interstate highway, the two sides of the highway appear to merge together in the distance. This tendency for lines that are actually parallel to *seem* to converge† is called **linear perspective**. It works in pictures because people assume that in the picture, as in real life, the converging lines indicate that the "ends" of the lines are a great distance away from where the people are as they view them.

2. **Relative size:** The principle of size constancy is at work in **relative size**, when objects that people expect to be of a certain size appear to be small and are, therefore, assumed to be much farther away. Movie makers use this principle to make their small models seem gigantic but off in the distance.

3. **Overlap:** If one object seems to be blocking another object, people assume that the blocked object is behind the first one and, therefore, farther away. This cue is also known as **interposition**.

---

*Ventriloquist: an entertainer who, through the use of misdirection and skill, makes other objects, such as a dummy, appear to talk.
**Visual field: the entire area of space visible at a given instant without moving the eyes.
†Converge: come together.

a.

c.

b.

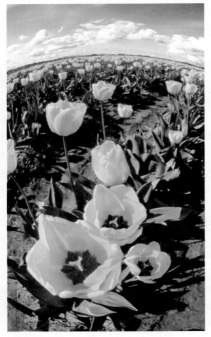

d.

FIGURE 3.17 Examples of Pictorial Depth Cues
(a) Both the lines of the trees and the sides of the road appear to come together or converge in the distance. This is an example of *linear perspective*. (b) Notice how the larger pebbles in the foreground seem to give way to smaller and smaller pebbles near the middle of the picture. *Texture gradient* causes the viewer to assume that as the texture of the pebbles gets finer, the pebbles are getting farther away. (c) In *aerial* or *atmospheric perspective*, the farther away something is the hazier it appears because of fine particles in the air between the viewer and the object. Notice that the road and farmhouse in the foreground are in sharp focus while the mountain ranges are hazy and indistinct. (d) The depth cue of *relative size* appears in this photograph. Notice that the flowers in the distance appear much smaller than those in the foreground. Relative size causes smaller objects to be perceived as farther away from the viewer.

aerial (atmospheric) perspective the haziness that surrounds objects that are farther away from the viewer, causing the distance to be perceived as greater.

texture gradient the tendency for textured surfaces to appear to become smaller and finer as distance from the viewer increases.

motion parallax the perception of motion of objects in which close objects appear to move more quickly than objects that are farther away.

accommodation as a monocular cue, the brain's use of information about the changing thickness of the lens of the eye in response to looking at objects that are close or far away.

4. **Aerial (atmospheric) perspective:** The farther away an object is, the hazier the object will appear to be due to tiny particles of dust, dirt, and other pollutants in the air, a perceptual cue called **aerial (atmospheric) perspective**. This is why distant mountains often look fuzzy, and buildings far in the distance are blurrier than those that are close.

5. **Texture gradient:** If there are any large expanses of pebbles, rocks, or patterned roads (such as a cobblestone street) nearby, go take a look at them one day. The pebbles or bricks that are close to you are very distinctly textured, but as you look farther off into the distance, their texture becomes smaller and finer. **Texture gradient** is another trick artists use to give the illusion of depth in a painting.

6. **Motion parallax:** The next time you're in a car, notice how the objects outside the car window seem to zip by very fast when they are close to the car, and objects in the distance, such as mountains, seem to move more slowly. This discrepancy in motion of near and far objects is called **motion parallax**.

7. **Accommodation:** A monocular cue that is not one of the pictorial cues, **accommodation** makes use of something that happens inside the eye. The

lens of the human eye is flexible and held in place by a series of muscles. The discussion of the eye earlier in this chapter mentioned the process of visual accommodation as the tendency of the lens to change its shape, or thickness, in response to objects near or far away. The brain can use this information about accommodation as a cue for distance. Accommodation is also called a "muscular cue."

convergence the rotation of the two eyes in their sockets to focus on a single object, resulting in greater convergence for closer objects and lesser convergence if objects are distant.

binocular disparity the difference in images between the two eyes, which is greater for objects that are close and smaller for distant objects.

BINOCULAR CUES As the name suggests, these cues require the use of two eyes.

1. **Convergence:** Another muscular cue, **convergence**, refers to the rotation of the two eyes in their sockets to focus on a single object. If the object is close, the convergence is pretty great (almost as great as crossing the eyes). If the object is far, the convergence is much less. Hold your finger up in front of your nose, and then move it away and back again. That feeling you get in the muscles of your eyes is convergence. (See Figure 3.18, left.)

2. **Binocular disparity:** **Binocular disparity** is a scientific way of saying that because the eyes are a few inches apart, they don't see exactly the same image. The brain interprets the images on the retina to determine distance from the eyes. If the two images are very different, the object must be pretty close. If they are almost identical, the object is far enough away to make the retinal disparity very small. You can demonstrate this cue for yourself by holding an object in front of your nose. Close one eye, note where the object is, and then open that eye and close the other. There should be quite a difference in views. But if you do the same thing with an object that is across the room, the image doesn't seem to "jump" or move nearly as much, if at all. (See Figure 3.18, right.)

In spite of all the cues for perception that exist, even the most sophisticated perceiver can still fail to perceive the world as it actually is, as the next section demonstrates.

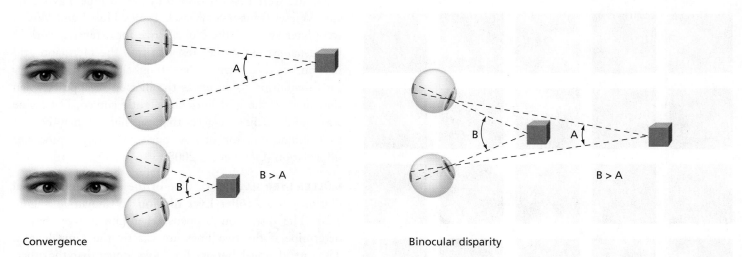

Convergence

Binocular disparity

FIGURE 3.18 Binocular Cues to Depth Perception
(left) Convergence is a depth cue that involves the muscles of the eyes. When objects are far away, the eye muscles are more relaxed; when objects are close, the eye muscles move together, or converge. (right) Binocular disparity. Because your eyes are separated by several centimeters, each eye sees a slightly different image of the object in front of you. In A, the object is far enough away that the difference is small. In B, while the object is closer, there is a greater difference between what each eye sees. The brain interprets this difference as the distance of the object.

You've mentioned the word *illusion* several times. Exactly what are illusions, and why is it so easy to be fooled by them?

Perceptual Illusions

● You've mentioned the word *illusion* several times. Exactly what are illusions, and why is it so easy to be fooled by them?

An *illusion* is a perception that does not correspond to reality: People *think* they see something when the reality is quite different. Another way of thinking of illusions is as visual stimuli that "fool" the eye. (Illusions are not hallucinations: an illusion is a distorted perception of something that is really there, but a hallucination originates in the brain, not in reality.)

3.9 What are visual illusions, and how can they and other factors influence and alter perception?

Research involving illusions can be very useful for both psychologists and neuroscientists. These studies often provide valuable information about how the sensory receptors and sense organs work and how humans interpret sensory input.

Sometimes illusions are based on early sensory processes, subsequent processing, or higher-level assumptions made by the brain's visual system (Eagleman, 2001; Macknik et al., 2008).

We've already discussed one visual illusion, color afterimages, which are due to opponent-processes in the retina or lateral geniculate nucleus (LGN) of the thalamus after light information has been detected by the rods and cones. Another postdetection, but still rather early, process has been offered for yet another illusion.

THE HERMANN GRID Look at the matrix of squares in Figure 3.19. Notice anything interesting as you look at different parts of the figure, particularly at the intersections of the white lines? You probably see gray blobs or diamonds that fade away or disappear completely when you try to look directly at them. This is the Hermann grid.

One explanation for this illusion is attributed to the responses of neurons in the primary visual cortex that respond best to bars of light of a specific orientation (Schiller & Carvey, 2005). Such neurons are called "simple cells" and were first discovered by David Hubel and Torsten Wiesel (Hubel & Wiesel, 1959). Hubel and Wiesel were later awarded the Nobel Prize for extensive work in the visual system. Other research into the Hermann grid illusion has documented that straight edges are necessary for this illusion to occur, as the illusion disappears when the edges of the grid lines are slightly curved, like a sine wave, and further suggests that the illusion may be due to a unique function of how our visual system processes information (Geier et al., 2008).

MÜLLER-LYER ILLUSION One of the most famous visual illusions, the **Müller-Lyer illusion**, is shown in Figure 3.20. The distortion happens when the viewer tries to determine if the two lines are exactly the same length. They are identical, but one line looks longer than the other. (It's always the line with the angles on the end facing outward.) Why is this illusion so powerful? The explanation is that most people live in a world with lots of buildings. Buildings have corners. When a person is outside a building, the corner of the building is close to that person, while the walls seem to be moving away (like the line with the

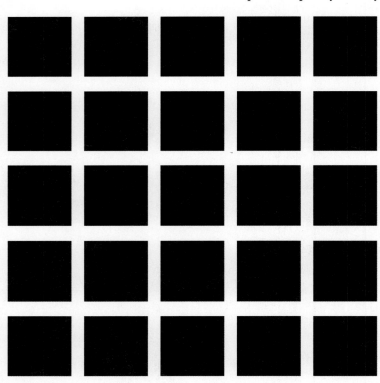

FIGURE 3.19 The Hermann Grid
Look at this matrix of squares. Do you notice anything interesting at the white intersections? What happens if you focus your vision directly on one of the intersections?

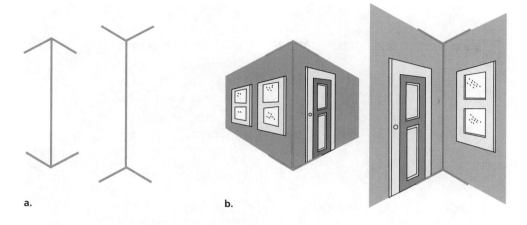

a.   b.

FIGURE 3.20 The Müller-Lyer Illusion
(a) Which line is longer? In industrialized Western countries, people generally see the lines in part (a) in situations similar to those in part (b). According to one theory, people have become accustomed to seeing right angles in their environment and assume that the short, slanted lines are forming a right angle to the vertical line. They make that assumption because they are accustomed to seeing corners, such as the ones depicted in the house interiors shown on the right in part (b). Consequently, in part (a), they tend to perceive the line on the right as slightly longer than the line on the left.

Müller-Lyer illusion   illusion of line length that is distorted by inward-turning or outward-turning corners on the ends of the lines, causing lines of equal length to appear to be different.

angles facing inward). When the person is inside a building, the corner of the room seems to move away from the viewer while the walls are coming closer (like the line with the angles facing outward). In their minds, people "pull" the inward-facing angles toward them like the outside corners of a building, and they make the outward-facing angles "stretch" away from them like the inside corners of the room (Enns & Coren, 1995; Gregory, 1990).

Segall and colleagues (Segall et al., 1966) found that people in Western cultures, having carpentered buildings with lots of straight lines and corners (Segall and colleagues refer to this as a "carpentered world"), are far more susceptible to this illusion than people from non-Western cultures (having round huts with few corners—an "uncarpentered world"). Gregory (1990) found that Zulus, for example, rarely see this illusion. They live in round huts arranged in circles, use curved tools and toys, and experience few straight lines and corners in their world.

THE MOON ILLUSION   Another common illusion is the *moon illusion*, in which the moon on the horizon* appears to be much larger than the moon in the sky (Plug & Ross, 1994). One explanation for this is that the moon high in the sky is all alone, with no cues for depth surrounding it. But on the horizon, the moon appears behind trees and houses, cues for depth that make the horizon seem very far away. The moon is seen as being behind these objects and, therefore, farther away from the viewer. Because people know that objects that are farther away from them and yet still appear large are very large indeed, they "magnify" the moon in their minds—a misapplication of the principle of size constancy. This explanation of the moon illusion is called the *apparent distance hypothesis*. This explanation goes back to the second century A.D., first written about by the Greek-Egyptian astronomer Ptolemy and later further developed by an eleventh-century Arab astronomer, Al-Hazan (Ross & Ross, 1976).

ILLUSIONS OF MOTION   Sometimes people perceive an object as moving when it is actually still. One example of this phenomenon takes place as part of a famous experiment in conformity called the *autokinetic effect*. In this effect, a small, stationary light in a darkened room will appear to move or drift because there are no surrounding cues to indicate that the light is *not* moving. Another is the *stroboscopic motion* seen in motion pictures, in which a rapid series of still pictures will seem to be in motion. Many a student has discovered that drawing little figures on the edges of a notebook and then flipping the pages quickly will also produce this same illusion of movement.

The moon illusion. When this moon is high in the night sky, it will still be the same size to the eye as it is now. Nevertheless, it is perceived to be much larger when on the horizon. In the sky, there are no objects for comparison, but on the horizon, objects such as this tree are seen as being in front of a very large moon.

---

*Horizon: the place where the earth apparently meets the sky.

FIGURE 3.21 "Rotating Snakes"
Notice anything as you move your eyes over this image? The image is not moving; seeing the "snakes" rotate is due at least in part to movements of your eyes.
Created by and courtesy of Dr. Akiyoshi Kitaoka, Ritsumeikan University.

FIGURE 3.22 "Reinterpretation of Enigma"
As in Figure 3.21, the motion you see in this static image is because of movements of your eyes, this time due more to tiny movements called *microsaccades*.
Created by and courtesy of Jorge Otero-Millan, Martinez-Conde Laboratory, Barrow Neurological Institute.

Another movement illusion related to stroboscopic motion is the *phi phenomenon*, in which lights turned on in sequence appear to move. For example, if a light is turned on in a darkened room and then turned off, and then another light a short distance away is flashed on and off, it will appear to be one light moving across that distance. This principle is used to suggest motion in many theater marquee signs—flashing arrows indicating direction that have a series of lights going on and off in a sequence, and even in strings of decorative lighting, such as the "chasing" lights seen on houses at holiday times.

What about seeing motion in static images? There are several examples, both classic and modern, of illusory movement or apparent motion being perceived in a static image. The debate about the causes for such illusions, whether they begin in the eyes or the brain, has been going on for at least 200 years (Troncoso et al., 2008).

Look at Figure 3.21. What do you see?

The "Rotating Snakes" illusion is one of many motion-illusion images designed by Dr. Akiyoshi Kitaoka. A variety of explanations have been offered for this type of motion illusion, ranging from factors that depend on the image's luminance and/or the color arrangement, or possibly slight differences in the time it takes the brain to process this information. When fMRI and equipment used to track eye movements was used to investigate participants' perception of the illusion, researchers found that there was an increase in brain activity in a visual area sensitive to motion. However, this activity was greatest when accompanied by guided eye movements, suggesting eye movements play a significant role in the perception of the illusion (Kuriki et al., 2008).

Eye movements have also been found to be a primary cause for the illusory motion seen in images based on a 1981 painting by Isia Levant, *Enigma*. Look at the center of Figure 3.22: notice anything within the green rings? Many people will see the rings start to "sparkle" or the rings rotating. Why does this occur? By using special eye-tracking equipment that allowed them to record even the smallest of eye movements, researchers found that tiny eye movements called *microsaccades*, discussed earlier in the chapter, are directly linked to the perception of motion in *Enigma* and are at least one possible cause of the illusion (Troncoso et al., 2008).

These two studies highlight some of the advances researchers have made in examining questions related to visual perception. For more information about the study of visual illusions as used in magic, and the study of such illusions from a neuroscientific perspective, see the Applying Psychology section at the end of the chapter.

Other Factors That Influence Perception

Human perception of the world is obviously influenced by things such as culture and misinterpretations of cues. Following are other factors that cause people to alter their perceptions.

PERCEPTUAL SETS AND EXPECTANCIES People often misunderstand what is said to them because they were expecting to hear something else. People's tendency to perceive things a certain way because their previous experiences or expectations influence them is called **perceptual set** or **perceptual expectancy**. Although expectancies can be useful in interpreting certain stimuli, they can also lead people down the wrong path. For example, look at Figure 3.23. The drawing in the middle is a little hard to identify. People who look at these five drawings and start with the drawing on the far left (which is clearly a man's face) tend to see the middle drawing as a man's face. But people who begin looking from the far right (where the drawing is a kneeling woman with one arm over her chest and one touching her knee) see the middle picture as a woman. What you see depends on what you expect to see. ⊙➤ Simulate on MyPsychLab

The way in which people *interpret* what they perceive can also influence their perception. For example, people can try to understand what they perceive by fusing information they already have (as is the case of perceptual expectancy). But if there is no existing information that relates to the new information, they can look at each feature of what they perceive and try to put it all together into one whole.

Anyone who has ever worked on a jigsaw puzzle knows that it's a lot easier to put it together if there is a picture of the finished puzzle to refer to as a guide. It also helps to have worked the puzzle before—people who have done the puzzle already know what it's going to look like when it's finished. In the field of perception, this is known as **top-down processing**—the use of preexisting knowledge to organize individual features into a unified whole. This is also a form of perceptual expectancy.

If the puzzle is one the person has never worked before or if that person has lost the top of the box with the picture on it, he or she would have to start with a small section, put it together, and keep building up the sections until the recognizable picture appears. This analysis of smaller features and building up to a complete perception is called **bottom-up processing** (Cave & Kim, 1999). In this case, there is no expectancy to help organize the perception, making bottom-up processing more difficult in some respects. Fortunately, the two types of processing are often used together in perceiving the surrounding world.

perceptual set (perceptual expectancy) the tendency to perceive things a certain way because previous experiences or expectations influence those perceptions.

top-down processing the use of preexisting knowledge to organize individual features into a unified whole.

bottom-up processing the analysis of the smaller features to build up to a complete perception.

The Ames Room illusion. Because people expect rooms to be square, the tendency in the Ames Room Illusion is to perceive the boy on the right as very large, and the man on the left as very small. In reality, the room is constructed so that the left "corner" is very far away compared to the "right" corner.

⊙➤ Simulate the concept of perceptual expectancy with an activity on ambiguous figures on **MyPsychLab**

FIGURE 3.23 Perceptual Set
Look at the drawing in the middle. What do you see? Now look at the drawings on each end. Would you have interpreted the middle drawing differently if you had looked at the drawing of the man's face or the sitting woman first?

FIGURE 3.24 The Devil's Trident
At first glance, this seems to be an ordinary three-pronged figure. But a closer look reveals that the three prongs cannot be real as drawn. Follow the lines of the top prong to see what goes wrong.

✳ Explore top-down processing on MyPsychLab

Would people of different cultures perceive objects differently because of different expectancies? Some research suggests that this is true. For example, take a look at Figure 3.24. This figure is often called the "devil's trident." Europeans and North Americans insist on making this figure three dimensional, so they have trouble looking at it—the figure is impossible if it is perceived in three dimensions. But people in less technologically oriented cultures have little difficulty with seeing or even reproducing this figure, because they see it as a two-dimensional drawing, quite literally a collection of lines and circles rather than a solid object (Deregowski, 1969). By contrast, if you give Europeans and North Americans the task of reproducing a drawing of an upside-down face, their drawings tend to be more accurate because the upside-down face has become a "collection of lines and circles." That is, they draw what they actually see in terms of light and shadow rather than what they "think" is there three dimensionally.
✳ Explore on MyPsychLab

practice quiz How much do you remember?

3.7 3.8 3.9

Pick the best answer.

1. The tendency to perceive a quarter as being round even when it is viewed at an angle is called _____.
   a. size constancy.
   b. shape constancy.
   c. brightness constancy.
   d. color constancy.

2. A reversible figure, such as the Necker cube, makes use of which principle of perception?
   a. shape constancy
   b. expectancy
   c. figure–ground relationships
   d. depth perception

3. Which of the following is NOT a monocular cue for depth?
   a. convergence
   b. linear perspective
   c. overlap
   d. texture gradient

4. An illusion _____.
   a. is the same thing as a hallucination.
   b. exists only in the brain cells of the viewer.
   c. is a distorted perception of an actual stimulus.
   d. corresponds directly to reality.

5. Ned found a decaying carcass lying on the beach one day. Looking at the size of the body (which had decomposed quite a bit), Ned decided that it was the body of a sea monster, something like the Loch Ness monster in Scotland. If we know that Ned loves to read about weird, mythical animals, we might expect that he has made an error of perception due to _____.
   a. perceptual set.
   b. perceptual defense.
   c. bottom-up processing.
   d. cognitive convergence.

6. The first time Joe had to put together a child's bicycle, it took a long time. But several bicycles later, he's a whiz at constructing them. His improved speed and skill can be attributed to _____.
   a. bottom-up processing.
   b. top-down processing.
   c. perceptual expectancy.
   d. perceptual set.

ANSWERS ON PAGE AK-1.

applying psychology to everyday life
Beyond "Smoke and Mirrors"—The Psychological Science and Neuroscience of Magic

Many people enjoy watching magic acts in person or on television. Perhaps you have been amazed by a Mindfreak® performed by Criss Angel or the performance and edgy antics of Penn & Teller. If you are one of those people, you likely witnessed a performance that included many various illusions. And like many of us, you probably wondered at some point in the performance, "How did they do that?!" Did you think the tricks were due to some type of special device (such as a fake thumb tip for hiding a scarf), or perhaps they were accomplished with "smoke and mirrors," or maybe the magician distracted the audience with one movement while actually doing something else to pull off the illusion? Magicians use many techniques to take advantage of, or manipulate, our actual level of awareness of what is happening right in front of us or perhaps to manipulate our attention.

Though magic is not a new topic of interest in psychology, there has been renewed interest in recent years, especially in the neuroscientific study of magic. This view suggests that researchers can work alongside magicians in order to gain a better understanding of various cognitive and perceptual processes by not only examining the sensory or physical mechanics behind magic tricks, or even the psychological explanations, but to look further by examining what is happening in the brain (Macknik & Martinez-Conde, 2009).

Penn & Teller have performed together for over 30 years and have joined neuroscientists in the effort to gain insights into the brain mechanisms behind magical illusions.

Dr. Stephen L. Macknik and Dr. Susanna Martinez-Conde of the Barrow Neurological Institute are two neuroscientists who have teamed up with professional magicians to study their techniques and tricks in the effort to better understand the brain mechanisms underlying the illusions and how researchers can use that information in the laboratory. They have identified several types of illusions that can be used alone or in combination with others to serve as a basis for various magic tricks; two of these are visual illusions and cognitive illusions (Macknik et al., 2008).

As discussed earlier in the chapter, visual illusions occur when our individual perception does not match a physical stimulus. These illusions are caused by organizational or processing biases in the brain. Furthermore, our brain activity from the perception does not directly match the brain activity associated with the physical stimulus (Macknik et al., 2008). One example Dr. Macknik and Dr. Martinez-Conde point out is similar to a trick you may have performed yourself in grade school. Did you ever take a pencil or pen, grasp it in the middle, and then shake or wiggle it up and down? If you did it correctly, the pen or pencil would appear to bend or be made of rubber. Magicians use this illusion when they "bend" solid objects, such as spoons. So what is the brain explanation? We have special neurons in the visual cortex that are sensitive to both motion and edges called *end-stopped neurons*. These neurons respond differently if an object is bouncing or moving up and down quickly, causing us to perceive a solid spoon or pencil as if it is bending.

Another effect or trick that is based on the functioning of our visual system is when a magician makes an object disappear, such as a ball vanishing into the air or perhaps the outfit of an assistant changing suddenly. By showing the audience the target object, such as the ball or outfit, and then removing it very quickly from the visual field, the *persistence of vision* effect will make it appear that the object is still there. This is due to a response in vision neurons called the after-discharge, which will create an afterimage that lasts for up to 100 milliseconds after a stimulus is removed (Macknik et al., 2008). Again, you may have performed a similar trick if you have ever taken a lit sparkler or flashlight and twirled it around quickly to make a trail of light in the dark. Read on MyPsychLab

Read and learn more about the science of magic on **MyPsychLab**

QUESTIONS FOR FURTHER DISCUSSION

1. The examples highlighted in this discussion are based on visual illusions; can you think of a magic trick or performance that may have been based on an illusion in a different sensory modality?

2. Of the neuroimaging methods covered in Chapter Two, which methods might be best for examining the brain activity of someone who is watching a magic performance? Why?

chapter summary

The ABCs of Sensation

3.1 How does sensation travel through the central nervous system, and why are some sensations ignored?

- Sensation is the activation of receptors located in the eyes, ears, skin, nasal cavities, and tongue.
- Sensory receptors are specialized forms of neurons that are activated by different stimuli such as light and sound.
- A just noticeable difference is the point at which a stimulus is detectable half the time it is present.
- Weber's law of just noticeable differences states that the just noticeable difference between two stimuli is always a constant.
- Absolute thresholds are the smallest amount of energy needed for conscious detection of a stimulus at least half the time it is present.
- Subliminal stimuli are stimuli presented just below the level of conscious awareness and subliminal perception has been demonstrated in the laboratory. It has not been shown to be effective in advertising.
- Habituation occurs when the brain ignores a constant stimulus.
- Sensory adaptation occurs when the sensory receptors stop responding to a constant stimulus.

The Science of Seeing

3.2 What is light, and how does it travel through the various parts of the eye?

- Brightness corresponds to the amplitude of light waves, whereas color corresponds to the length of the light waves.
- Saturation is the psychological interpretation of wavelengths that are all the same (highly saturated) or varying (less saturated).
- Light enters the eye and is focused through the cornea, passes through the aqueous humor, and then through the hole in the iris muscle called the pupil.
- The lens also focuses the light on the retina, where it passes through ganglion and bipolar cells to stimulate the rods and cones.

3.3 How do the eyes see, and how do the eyes see different colors?

- Rods detect changes in brightness but do not see color and function best in low levels of light. They do not respond to different colors and are found everywhere in the retina except the center, or fovea.
- Cones are sensitive to colors and work best in bright light. They are responsible for the sharpness of visual information and are found in the fovea.
- Trichromatic theory of color perception assumes three types of cones: red, green, and blue. All colors would be perceived as combinations of these three.
- Opponent-process theory of color perception assumes four primary colors of red, green, blue, and yellow. Colors are arranged in pairs, and when one member of a pair is activated, the other is not.
- Color blindness is a total lack of color perception, whereas color-deficient vision refers to color perception that is limited primarily to yellows and blues or reds and greens only.

The Hearing Sense: Can You Hear Me Now?

3.4 What is sound, and how does it travel through the various parts of the ear?

- Sound has three aspects: pitch (frequency), loudness, and timbre (purity).
- Sound enters the ear through the visible outer structure, or pinna, and travels to the eardrum and then to the small bones of the middle ear.
- The bone called the stirrup rests on the oval window, causing the cochlea and basilar membrane to vibrate with sound.
- The organ of Corti on the basilar membrane contains the auditory receptors, which send signals to the brain about sound qualities as they vibrate.
- Place theory states that the location of the hair cells on the organ of Corti correspond to different pitches of sound. This can explain pitch above 1000 Hz.
- Frequency theory states that the speed with which the basilar membrane vibrates corresponds to different pitches of sound. This can explain pitch below 1000 Hz.
- The volley principle states that neurons take turns firing for sounds above 400 Hz and below 4000 Hz.
- Conduction hearing impairment is caused by damage to the outer or middle ear structures, whereas nerve hearing impairment is caused by damage to the inner ear or auditory pathways in the brain.

Chemical Senses: It Tastes Good and Smells Even Better

3.5 How do the senses of taste and smell work, and how are they alike?

- Gustation is the sense of taste. Taste buds in the tongue receive molecules of substances, which fit into receptor sites.
- The five basic types of taste are sweet, sour, salty, bitter, and umami (brothy).
- Olfaction is the sense of smell. The olfactory receptors in the upper part of the nasal passages receive molecules of substances and create neural signals that then go to the olfactory bulbs under the frontal lobes.

Somesthetic Senses: What the Body Knows

- The somesthetic senses include the skin senses and the vestibular senses.

3.6 What allows people to experience the sense of touch, pain, motion, and balance?

- Pacinian corpuscles respond to pressure, certain nerve endings around hair follicles respond to pain and pressure, and free nerve endings respond to pain, pressure, and temperature.
- The gate-control theory of pain states that when receptors sensitive to pain are stimulated, a neurotransmitter called substance P is released into the spinal cord, activating other pain receptors by opening "gates" in the spinal column and sending the message to the brain.
- The kinesthetic senses allow the brain to know the position and movement of the body through the activity of special receptors responsive to movement of the joints and limbs.
- The vestibular sense also contributes to the body's sense of spatial orientation and movement through the activity of the otolith organs (up-and-down movement) and the semicircular canals (movement through arcs).
- Motion sickness is explained by sensory conflict theory, in which information from the eyes conflicts with information from the vestibular sense, causing nausea.

The ABCs of Perception

3.7 What are perception, perceptual constancies, and the Gestalt principles of perception?

• Perception is the interpretation and organization of sensations.

• Size constancy is the tendency to perceive objects as always being the same size, no matter how close or far away they are.

• Shape constancy is the tendency to perceive objects as remaining the same shape even when the shape of the object changes on the retina of the eye.

• Brightness constancy is the tendency to perceive objects as a certain level of brightness, even when the light changes.

• The Gestalt psychologists developed several principles of perception that involve interpreting patterns in visual stimuli. The principles are figure–ground relationships, closure, similarity, continuity, contiguity, and common region.

3.8 What is depth perception, and what kinds of cues are important for it to occur?

• Depth perception is the ability to see in three dimensions.

• Monocular cues for depth perception include linear perspective, relative size, overlap, aerial (atmospheric) perspective, texture gradient, motion parallax, and accommodation.

• Binocular cues for depth perception include convergence and binocular overlap.

3.9 What are visual illusions, and how can they and other factors influence and alter perception?

• Illusions are perceptions that do not correspond to reality or are distortions of visual stimuli.

• Perceptual set or expectancy refers to the tendency to perceive objects and situations in a particular way because of prior experiences.

• Top-down processing involves the use of preexisting knowledge to organize individual features into a unified whole.

• Bottom-up processing involves the analysis of smaller features, building up to a complete perception.

applying psychology to everyday life: Beyond "Smoke and Mirrors" —The Psychological Science and Neuroscience of Magic

• Magicians take advantage of some well-known properties of our visual system to accomplish a variety of magic tricks.

• By collaborating with magicians, psychologists and neuroscientists can learn more about magic and the brain processes responsible for our perception of magic tricks.

TEST yourself

ANSWERS ON PAGE AK-1.

✓• Study and Review on MyPsychLab   Ready for your test? More quizzes and a customized plan. www.MyPsychLab

Pick the best answer.

1. You find that you have to add 1 teaspoon of sugar to a cup of coffee that already has 5 teaspoons of sugar in it to notice the difference in sweetness. If you have a cup of coffee with 10 teaspoons of sugar in it, how many teaspoons would you have to add to notice the difference in sweetness at least half the time?
   a. 1
   b. 2
   c. 4
   d. 5

2. The process by which the brain stops attending to constant, unchanging information is called _____.
   a. adaptation.
   b. sensation.
   c. habituation.
   d. accommodation.

3. Which of the following terms refers to the psychological effect of the length of light waves?
   a. color
   b. brightness
   c. pitch
   d. amplitude

4. Which of the following is responsible for controlling how much light enters the eye?
   a. cornea
   c. retina
   b. lens
   d. iris

5. Which type of retinal cell forms the optic nerve?
   a. rods
   b. cones
   c. ganglion cells
   d. bipolar cells

6. Which type of retinal cell plays a role in color vision?
   a. rods
   b. cones
   c. ganglion cells
   d. bipolar cells

7. Which set of colors are the primary colors when mixing light?
   a. red, yellow, and blue
   b. red, blue, and green
   c. blue, green, and yellow
   d. red, green, and yellow

8. Which of the following properties of sound would be the most similar to the brightness of light?
   a. pitch
   b. loudness
   c. purity
   d. timbre

9. The thin membrane stretched over the opening to the inner ear is the _____.
   a. pinna.
   b. oval window.
   c. tympanic membrane.
   d. cochlea.

10. The _____ theory appears to account for how we hear sounds between 400 and 4000 Hz.
    a. wave
    b. frequency
    c. volley
    d. adaptive

11. If a severe ear infection damages the bones of the middle ear, you may develop _____ hearing impairment.
    a. nerve
    b. stimulation
    c. brain pathway
    d. conduction

12. The sense of taste is closely related to the sense of _____.
    a. sight.
    b. hearing.
    c. smell.
    d. touch.

13. The "bumps" on the tongue that are visible to the eye are the _____.
    a. taste buds.
    b. papillae.
    c. taste receptors.
    d. olfactory receptors.

14. The olfactory receptor cells are located in the _____.
    a. tops of the nasal passages.
    b. auditory passages.
    c. roof of the mouth.
    d. lining of the outer nose.

15. Which of the following statements about olfactory receptors is TRUE?
    a. Olfactory receptors are replaced every 5 to 8 weeks.
    b. There are fewer than 50 types of olfactory receptors.
    c. Signals from the receptors go through the brain stem and then to the cortex.
    d. Olfactory receptors respond to pressure.

16. In the spinal cord, _____ inhibit(s) the release of substance P.
    a. hormones
    b. serotonin
    c. norepinephrine
    d. endorphins

17. We know when we are moving up and down in an elevator because of the movement of tiny crystals in the _____.
    a. outer ear.
    b. inner ear.
    c. otolith organs.
    d. middle ear.

18. Ellis turns around and around in a circle. When he stops, he feels like his head is still spinning. What is responsible for this sensation?
    a. semicircular canals
    b. proprioceptors
    c. otolith organs
    d. otolith crystals

19. An old comedy routine on television had a character who would line up the heads of people who were very far away from him between his fingers. Then he would pinch his fingers together and say gleefully, "I'm crushing your head, I'm crushing your head." The comedian was playing around with which perceptual constancy?
    a. size constancy
    b. shape constancy
    c. brightness constancy
    d. color constancy

20. Which Gestalt principle is at work when a ventriloquist moves the dummy's mouth while doing the talking, making it seem like the dummy is talking?
    a. closure
    b. similarity
    c. contiguity
    d. continuity

21. Which of the following is occurring when looking down a set of railroad tracks, they appear to merge together in the distance?
    a. convergence
    b. linear perspective
    c. overlap
    d. texture gradient

22. The Müller-Lyer illusion exists in cultures in which there are _____.
    a. more men than women.
    b. more women than men.
    c. lots of trees.
    d. buildings with lots of corners.

23. Allison opened her new jigsaw puzzle but soon realized that the puzzle pieces inside had nothing to do with the picture on the box. With no picture to go by, she realized she would have to use _____.
   a. bottom-up processing.
   b. top-down processing.
   c. perceptual expectancy.
   d. perceptual set.

24. Juan just attended a terrific magic show. In one of the tricks, the magician made a ball disappear that had just been in plain sight. Which aspect of our visual system likely allowed the magician to accomplish this illusion?
   a. lateral inhibition
   b. microsaccades of the eyes
   c. persistence of vision
   d. achromatopsia

3 sensation and perception

3.1 p. 82

The ABCs of Sensation — ● **sensation**
process by which information from
the outside world enters the brain

- related to the activation of receptors
  in the various sense organs
- related to changes in physical stimuli

3.2 3.3 p. 84

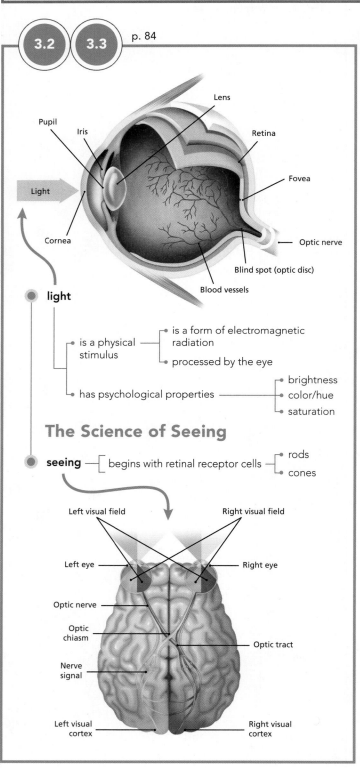

Lens
Pupil
Iris
Retina
Light
Fovea
Cornea
Optic nerve
Blind spot (optic disc)
Blood vessels

● **light**

- is a physical
  stimulus
  - is a form of electromagnetic
    radiation
  - processed by the eye

- has psychological properties
  - brightness
  - color/hue
  - saturation

The Science of Seeing

● **seeing** — begins with retinal receptor cells
  - rods
  - cones

Left visual field
Right visual field
Left eye
Right eye
Optic nerve
Optic
chiasm
Optic tract
Nerve
signal
Left visual
cortex
Right visual
cortex

3.4 p. 91

● **sound**

- is a physical
  stimulus
  - composed of
    sound waves
  - processed by the ear
  - processing can
    be impaired

- has psychological properties
  - **frequency** or **pitch**
  - **volume**
  - **timbre**

The Hearing Sense

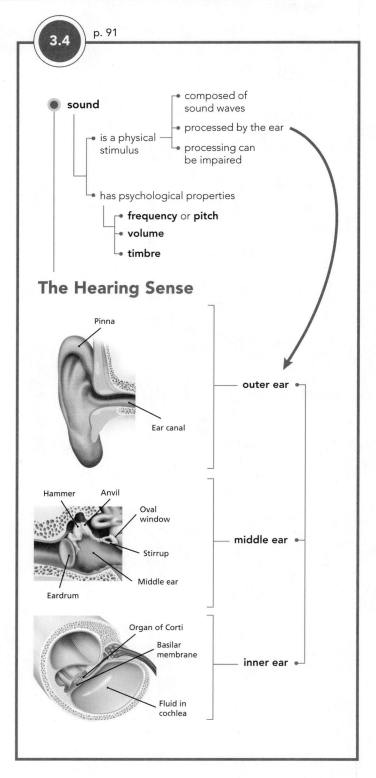

Pinna
Ear canal

Hammer
Anvil
Oval
window
Stirrup
Middle ear
Eardrum

Organ of Corti
Basilar
membrane
Fluid in
cochlea

outer ear

middle ear

inner ear

3.5 p. 96

- **smell/olfaction**
  - called a chemical sense because substance molecules are suspended in the air, carried to the nasal cavity, and fit into receptor sites
  - nose serves as a collection device
  - unique in that signals do not first travel to the thalamus before going to the brain

Olfactory bulb

Cilia of olfactory receptor cell

Olfactory epithelium

Chemical Senses

Taste pore

Taste hair

Receptor cell

Supporting cell

Outer layer of tongue

Nerve fiber

- **taste/gustation**
  - made possible largely through the role of taste buds (taste receptor cells)
  - five basic tastes (receptor types)
  - called a chemical sense because food molecules dissolve in saliva, which then fits into receptor sites

3.6 p. 99

Somesthetic Senses

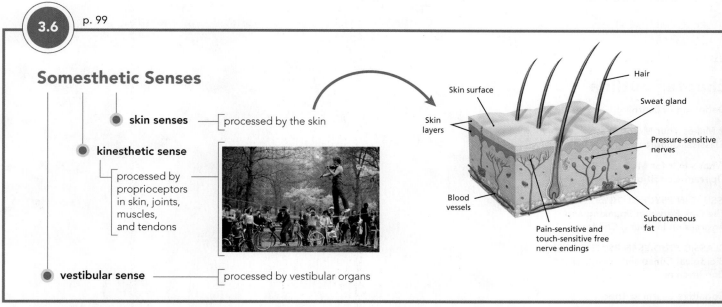

- **skin senses** — processed by the skin
- **kinesthetic sense**
  - processed by proprioceptors in skin, joints, muscles, and tendons
- **vestibular sense** — processed by vestibular organs

Skin surface

Skin layers

Blood vessels

Pain-sensitive and touch-sensitive free nerve endings

Hair

Sweat gland

Pressure-sensitive nerves

Subcutaneous fat

3.7 **3.8** **3.9** p. 102

The ABCs of Perception

- **perception**
  - method by which the sensations experienced at any given moment are interpreted and organized in some meaningful fashion
  - may have unique features depending on sensory modality
  - may not always be based on an accurate interpretation of the stimulus

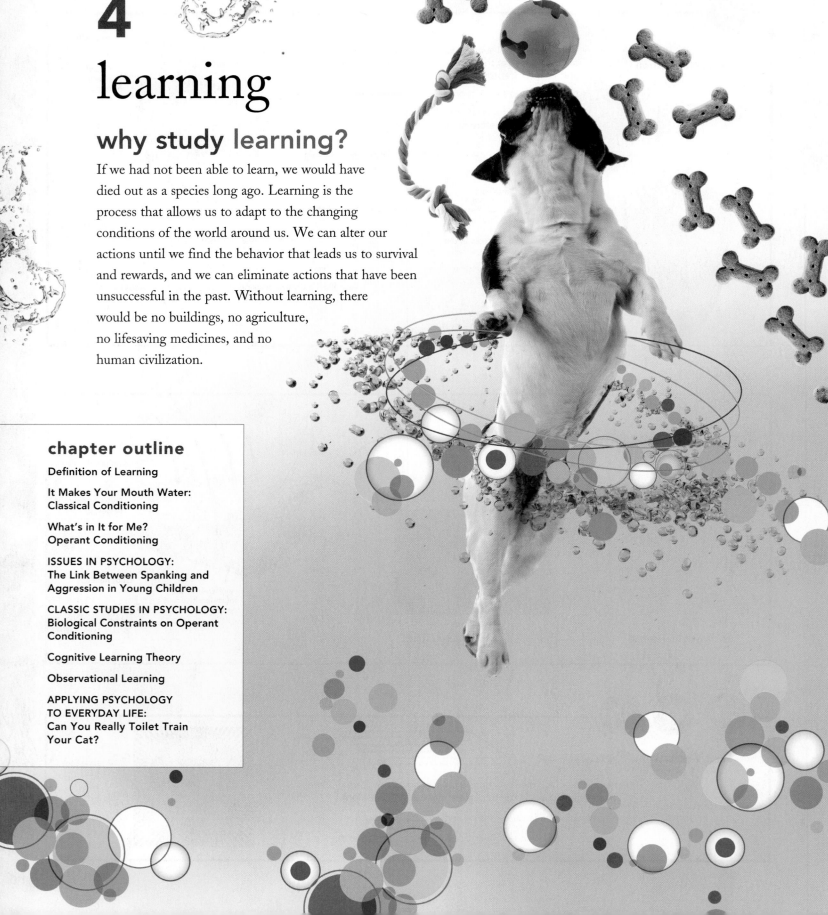

4
learning

why study learning?

If we had not been able to learn, we would have died out as a species long ago. Learning is the process that allows us to adapt to the changing conditions of the world around us. We can alter our actions until we find the behavior that leads us to survival and rewards, and we can eliminate actions that have been unsuccessful in the past. Without learning, there would be no buildings, no agriculture, no lifesaving medicines, and no human civilization.

chapter outline

Definition of Learning

It Makes Your Mouth Water:
Classical Conditioning

What's in It for Me?
Operant Conditioning

ISSUES IN PSYCHOLOGY:
The Link Between Spanking and
Aggression in Young Children

CLASSIC STUDIES IN PSYCHOLOGY:
Biological Constraints on Operant
Conditioning

Cognitive Learning Theory

Observational Learning

APPLYING PSYCHOLOGY
TO EVERYDAY LIFE:
Can You Really Toilet Train
Your Cat?

Why Clowns Can Be Scary

Angelica was only 5 years old when her parents took her to the circus. While she enjoyed seeing the animals and acrobats, she was not sure about the clowns. One clown, attempting to amuse the little girl, suddenly jumped in front of her and laughed loudly while making what was supposed to be a funny face. The sudden movement and noise, together with the unfamiliar clown makeup, scared Angelica badly.

Small wonder, then, that Angelica began to show fear in the presence of any clown, including the clown pictures on the walls of what used to be her favorite fast-food restaurant! Angelica's fear of clowns was a result of a special type of learning called *classical conditioning*. In this type of learning, objects or situations (such as a scary clown at the circus) can become associated or linked with other kinds of situations (such as the restaurant clown). Once the association is made, similar objects or situations can cause the same response (e.g., fear) that the earlier situation caused.

learning objectives

4.1 What does the term *learning* really mean?

4.2 How was classical conditioning first studied, and what are the important elements and characteristics of classical conditioning?

4.3 What is a conditioned emotional response, and how do cognitive psychologists explain classical conditioning?

4.4 How does operant conditioning occur, and what were the contributions of Thorndike and Skinner?

4.5 What are the important concepts in operant conditioning?

4.6 What are the schedules of reinforcement?

4.7 How does punishment differ from reinforcement?

4.8 What are some of the problems with using punishment?

4.9 How do operant stimuli control behavior, and what are some other concepts that can enhance or limit operant conditioning?

4.10 What is behavior modification, and how can behavioral techniques be used to modify involuntary biological responses?

4.11 How do latent learning, learned helplessness, and insight relate to cognitive learning theory?

4.12 What occurs in observational learning, including findings from Bandura's classic Bobo doll study and the four elements of observational learning?

4.13 What is a real-world example of the use of conditioning?

study tip

As you are reading this chapter, take a look back at page PIA-11 in *Psychology in Action* for some useful information about how practice and the use of small successes can influence learning and performance.

👁 Watch Episode 7: *Learning* in the MyPsychLab video series

What does "relatively permanent" mean? And how does experience change what we do?

the neighborhood. Jerry Van Amerongen

An instantaneous learning experience.
© Reprinted with special permission of King Features Syndicate.

Definition of Learning

4.1 What does the term *learning* really mean?

The term *learning* is one of those concepts whose meaning is crystal clear until one has to put it into actual words. "Learning is when you learn something." "Learning is learning how to do something." A more useful definition is as follows: *Learning* is any relatively permanent change in behavior brought about by experience or practice.

● What does "relatively permanent" mean? And how does experience change what we do?

The "relatively permanent" part of the definition refers to the fact that when people learn anything, some part of their brain is physically changed to record what they've learned. This is actually a process of memory, for without the ability to remember what happens, people cannot learn anything. Although there is no conclusive proof as yet, research suggests strongly that once people learn something, it is always present somewhere in memory (Barsalou, 1992; Smolen et al., 2008). They may be unable to "get" to it, but it's there. (L I N K) to Chapter Five: Memory, p. 171.

As for the inclusion of experience or practice, think about the last time you did something that caused you a lot of pain. Did you do it again? You didn't want to experience that pain again, so you changed your behavior to avoid the painful consequence.* This is how children learn not to touch hot stoves. Remember Angelica in the chapter opener? Her reaction to clowns, such as the one in the fast-food restaurant, changed to fear after her experience with the circus clown. In contrast, if a person does something resulting in a very pleasurable experience, that person is more likely to do that same thing again. This is another change in behavior and is explained by the law of effect (see page 131).

Not all change is accomplished through learning. Changes like an increase in height or the size of the brain are another kind of change controlled by a genetic blueprint. This kind of change is called *maturation* and is due to biology, not experience. For example, children learn to walk *when* they do because their nervous systems, muscle strength, and sense of balance have reached the point where walking is possible for them—all factors controlled by maturation, not by how much practice those children have had in trying to walk. No amount of experience or practice will help that child walk before maturation makes it possible—in spite of what some eager parents might wish.

It Makes Your Mouth Water: Classical Conditioning

4.2 How was classical conditioning first studied, and what are the important elements and characteristics of classical conditioning?

In the early 1900s, research scientists were unhappy with psychology's focus on mental activity. (L I N K) to Chapter One: The Science of Psychology, pp. 10–11. Many were looking for a way to bring some kind of objectivity and scientific research to the field. It was a Russian *physiologist* (a person who studies the workings of the body) named Ivan Pavlov (1849–1936) who pioneered the empirical study of the basic principles of a particular kind of learning (Pavlov, 1906, 1926).

Studying the digestive system in his dogs, Pavlov had built a device that would accurately measure the amount of saliva produced by the dogs when they were fed a measured amount of food. Normally, when food is placed in the mouth of any animal, the salivary glands automatically start releasing saliva to help with chewing and digestion.

---

*Consequence: an end result of some action.

This is a normal *reflex* (involuntary* response) in both animals and humans. The food causes the particular reaction of salivation. A *stimulus* can be defined as any object, event, or experience that causes a *response*, the reaction of an organism. In the case of Pavlov's dogs, the food is the stimulus and salivation is the response. ◉⎯[Watch on **MyPsychLab**

◉⎯[Watch video classic footage of Pavlov on **MyPsychLab**

Pavlov and the Salivating Dogs

Pavlov soon discovered that his dogs began salivating when they weren't supposed to be salivating. Some dogs would start salivating when they saw the lab assistant bringing their food, others when they heard the clatter of the food bowl from the kitchen, and still others when it was the time of day they were usually fed. Pavlov spent the rest of his career studying what eventually he termed **classical conditioning**, learning to make a reflex response to a stimulus other than the original, natural stimulus that normally produces it.

Elements of Classical Conditioning

Pavlov eventually identified several key elements that must be present and experienced in a particular way for conditioning to take place.

UNCONDITIONED STIMULUS The original, naturally occurring stimulus mentioned in the preceding paragraph is called the **unconditioned stimulus (UCS)**. The term *unconditioned* means "unlearned" or "naturally occurring." This is the stimulus that ordinarily leads to the involuntary reflex response. In the case of Pavlov's dogs, the food is the unconditioned stimulus.

UNCONDITIONED RESPONSE The reflex response to the unconditioned stimulus is called the **unconditioned response (UCR)** for much the same reason. It is unlearned and occurs because of genetic "wiring" in the nervous system. For example, in Pavlov's experiment, the salivation to that food is the UCR (unconditioned response).

CONDITIONED STIMULUS Pavlov determined that almost any kind of stimulus could become associated with the unconditioned stimulus (UCS) if it is paired with the UCS often enough. In his original study, for example, the sight of the food dish itself became a stimulus for salivation *before* the food was given to the dogs. Every time they got food (to which they naturally salivated), they saw the dish. At this point, the dish was called a **neutral stimulus (NS)** because it had no effect on salivation. After being paired with the food so many times, the dish came to produce the same salivation response, although a somewhat weaker one, as did the food itself. When a previously neutral stimulus, through repeated pairing with the unconditioned stimulus, begins to cause the same kind of reflexive response, learning has occurred. The neutral stimulus can now be called a **conditioned stimulus (CS)**. (*Unconditioned* means "unlearned," and *conditioned* means "learned.")

CONDITIONED RESPONSE The response that is given to the CS (conditioned stimulus) is not usually quite as strong as the original unconditioned response (UCR), but it is essentially the same response. However, because it comes as a response to the conditioned stimulus (CS), it is called the **conditioned response (CR)**.

Putting It All Together: Pavlov's Canine Classic, or Tick Tock, Tick Tock

Pavlov did a classic experiment in which he paired the ticking sound of a metronome (a simple device that produces a rhythmic ticking sound) with the presentation of food

Dr. Ivan Pavlov and students working in his laboratory. Pavlov, a Russian physiologist, was the first to study and write about the basic principles of classical conditioning.

classical conditioning learning to make an involuntary (reflex) response to a stimulus other than the original, natural stimulus that normally produces the reflex.

unconditioned stimulus (UCS) a naturally occurring stimulus that leads to an involuntary (reflex) response.

unconditioned response (UCR) an involuntary (reflex) response to a naturally occurring or unconditioned stimulus.

neutral stimulus (NS) stimulus that has no effect on the desired response.

conditioned stimulus (CS) stimulus that becomes able to produce a learned reflex response by being paired with the original unconditioned stimulus.

conditioned response (CR) learned reflex response to a conditioned stimulus.

---

*Involuntary: not under personal control or choice.

FIGURE 4.1 Classical Conditioning
Before conditioning takes place, the sound of the metronome does not cause salivation and is a neutral stimulus, or NS. During conditioning, the sound of the metronome occurs just before the presentation of the food, the UCS. The food causes salivation, the UCR. When conditioning has occurred after several pairings of the metronome with the food, the metronome will begin to elicit a salivation response from the dog without any food. This is learning, and the sound of the metronome is now a CS and the salivation to the bell is the CR.

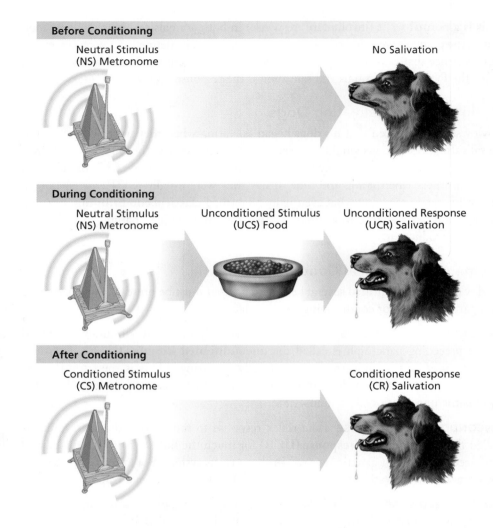

Before Conditioning

Neutral Stimulus (NS) Metronome → No Salivation

During Conditioning

Neutral Stimulus (NS) Metronome → Unconditioned Stimulus (UCS) Food → Unconditioned Response (UCR) Salivation

After Conditioning

Conditioned Stimulus (CS) Metronome → Conditioned Response (CR) Salivation

Could this be you? The anxiety that many people feel while in the dentist's office is a conditioned response, with the dentist's chair and the smells of the office acting as conditioned stimuli.

to see if the dogs would eventually salivate at the sound of the metronome (Pavlov, 1927). Since the metronome's ticking did not normally produce salivation, it was the neutral stimulus (NS) before any conditioning took place. The repeated pairing of the NS and the UCS (unconditioned stimulus) is usually called *acquisition*, because the organism is in the process of acquiring learning. Figure 4.1 is a chart of how each element of the conditioning relationship worked in Pavlov's experiment.

Notice that the responses, CR (conditioned response) and UCR (unconditioned response), are the same—salivation. They simply differ in what they are the response *to*. An *unconditioned* stimulus (UCS) is always followed by an *unconditioned* response (UCR), and a *conditioned* stimulus (CS) is always followed by a *conditioned* response (CR).

Is this rocket science? No, not really. Classical conditioning is actually one of the simplest forms of learning. It's so simple that it happens to people all the time without them even being aware of it. Does your mouth water when you merely *see* an advertisement for your favorite food on television? Does your stomach get upset every time you hear the high-pitched whine of the dentist's drill? These are both examples of classical conditioning.

After all the dog stories, the salivation to the TV ad probably needs no explanation, but what about the dentist's drill? Over the course of many visits, the body comes to associate that sound (CS) with the anxiety or fear (UCR) the person has felt while receiving a painful dental treatment (UCS), and so the sound produces a feeling of anxiety (CR) whether that person is in the chair or just in the outer waiting area.

Although classical conditioning happens quite easily, there are a few basic principles that Pavlov and other researchers discovered (although we will see that there are a few exceptions to some of these principles):

1. The CS must come *before* the UCS. If Pavlov started the metronome just after he gave the dogs the food, they did not become conditioned (Rescorla, 1988).

2. The CS and UCS must come very close together in time—ideally, no more than 5 seconds apart. When Pavlov tried to stretch the time between the potential CS and the UCS to several minutes, no association or link between the two was made. Too much could happen in the longer interval of time to interfere with conditioning (Pavlov, 1926; Wasserman & Miller, 1997). Recent studies have found that the interstimulus interval (ISI, or the time between the CS and UCS) can vary depending on the nature of the conditioning task and even the organism being conditioned. In these studies, shorter ISIs (less than 500 milliseconds) have been found to be ideal for conditioning (Polewan et al., 2006).

3. The neutral stimulus must be paired with the UCS several times, often many times, before conditioning can take place (Pavlov, 1926).

4. The CS is usually some stimulus that is distinctive* or stands out from other competing stimuli. The ticking was a sound that was not normally present in the laboratory and, therefore, distinct (Pavlov, 1926; Rescorla, 1988).

STIMULUS GENERALIZATION AND DISCRIMINATION   Pavlov did find that similar sounds would produce the same conditioned response from his dogs. He and other researchers found that the strength of the response to the similar sounds was not as strong as to the original one, but the more similar the other sound was to the original sound (be it a metronome or any other kind of sound), the more similar the strength of the response was as well (Siegel, 1969). (See Figure 4.2.) The tendency to respond to a stimulus that is only similar to the original conditioned stimulus is called **stimulus generalization**. For example, a person who reacts with anxiety to the sound of a dentist's drill might react with some slight anxiety to a similar-sounding machine, such as an electric coffee grinder. Of course, Pavlov did not give the dogs any food after the similar ticking sound. It didn't take long for the dogs to stop responding (generalizing) to the "fake" ticking sounds altogether. Because only the real CS was followed with food, they learned to tell the difference, or *discriminate*, between the "fake" ticking and the CS ticking, a process called **stimulus discrimination**. Stimulus discrimination occurs when an organism learns to respond to different stimuli in different ways. For example, although the sound of the coffee grinder might produce a little anxiety in the dental-drill-hating person, after a few uses that sound will no longer produce anxiety because it isn't associated with dental pain. **Simulate** on **MyPsychLab**

EXTINCTION AND SPONTANEOUS RECOVERY   What would have happened if Pavlov had stopped giving the dogs food after the real CS? Pavlov did just that, and the dogs gradually stopped salivating to the sound of the ticking. When the metronome's ticking (CS or conditioned stimulus) was repeatedly presented in the absence of the UCS (unconditioned stimulus or food, in this case), the salivation (CR or conditioned response) "died out" in a process called **extinction**.

Why does the removal of an unconditioned stimulus lead to extinction of the conditioned response? One theory is that the presentation of the CS alone leads to new learning. During extinction, the CS–UCS association that was learned is weakened,

---

*Distinctive: separate, having a different quality from something else.

stimulus generalization   the tendency to respond to a stimulus that is only similar to the original conditioned stimulus with the conditioned response.

stimulus discrimination   the tendency to stop making a generalized response to a stimulus that is similar to the original conditioned stimulus because the similar stimulus is never paired with the unconditioned stimulus.

extinction   the disappearance or weakening of a learned response following the removal or absence of the unconditioned stimulus (in classical conditioning) or the removal of a reinforcer (in operant conditioning).

Simulate stimulus generalization and stimulus discrimination on **MyPsychLab**

FIGURE 4.2 Strength of the Generalized Response
An example of stimulus generalization. The UCS was an electric shock and the UCR was the galvanic skin response (GSR), a measure associated with anxiety. The subjects had been conditioned originally to a CS tone (0) of a given frequency. When tested with the original tone, and with tones 1, 2, and 3 of differing frequencies, a clear generalization effect appeared. The closer the frequency of the test tone to the frequency of tone 0, the greater was the magnitude of the galvanic skin response to the tone (Hovland, 1937).

spontaneous recovery the reappearance of a learned response after extinction has occurred.

higher-order conditioning occurs when a strong conditioned stimulus is paired with a neutral stimulus, causing the neutral stimulus to become a second conditioned stimulus.

as the CS no longer predicts the UCS. In the case of Pavlov's dogs, through extinction they learned to not salivate to the metronome's ticking, as it no longer predicted that food was on its way.

Look back at Figure 4.1. Once conditioning is acquired, the conditioned stimulus (CS) and conditioned response (CR) will always come *before* the original unconditioned stimulus (UCS). The UCS, which comes after the CS and CR link, now serves as a strengthener, or reinforcer, of the CS–CR association. Remove that reinforcer, and the CR it strengthens will weaken and disappear—at least for a while.

The term *extinction* is a little unfortunate in that it seems to mean that the original conditioned response is totally gone, dead, never coming back, just like the dinosaurs. Remember that the definition of learning is any relatively *permanent* change in behavior. The fact is that once people learn something, it's almost impossible to "unlearn" it. People can learn new things that replace it or lose their way to it in memory, but it's still there. In the case of classical conditioning, this is easily demonstrated.

After extinguishing the conditioned salivation response in his dogs, Pavlov waited a few weeks, putting conditioned stimulus (e.g., the metronome) away. There were no more training sessions, and the dogs were not exposed to the metronome's ticking in that time at all. But when Pavlov took the metronome back out and set it ticking, the dogs all began to salivate, although it was a fairly weak response and didn't last very long. This brief recovery of the conditioned response proves that the CR is "still in there" somewhere (remember, learning is *relatively permanent*). It is just suppressed or inhibited by the lack of an association with the unconditioned stimulus of food (which is no longer reinforcing or strengthening the CR). As time passes, this inhibition weakens, especially if the original conditioned stimulus has not been present for a while. In **spontaneous recovery** the conditioned response can briefly reappear when the original CS returns, although the response is usually weak and short-lived. See Figure 4.3 for a graph showing both extinction and spontaneous recovery. People experience classical conditioning in many ways. People who are allergic to cats sometimes sneeze when they see a *picture* of a cat.

HIGHER-ORDER CONDITIONING Another concept in classical conditioning is **higher-order conditioning** (see Figure 4.4). This occurs when a strong conditioned stimulus is paired with a neutral stimulus. The strong CS can actually play the part of a UCS, and the previously neutral stimulus becomes a *second* conditioned stimulus.

✳ Explore higher-order conditioning on **MyPsychLab**

✳ Explore on **MyPsychLab**

For example, let's assume that Pavlov has conditioned his dogs to salivate at the sound of the metronome. What would happen if just before Pavlov turned on

FIGURE 4.3 Extinction and Spontaneous Recovery
This graph shows the acquisition, extinction, spontaneous recovery, and reacquisition of a conditioned salivary response. Typically, the measure of conditioning is the number of drops of saliva elicited by the CS on each trial. Note that on the day following extinction, the first presentation of the CS elicits quite a large response.

Stage 1

Metronome (CS₁)   UCR (salivation)   Conditioning   Metronome (CS₁)   CR (salivation)
US (food)

Stage 2

Metronome (CS₁)   CR (salivation)   High-Order Conditioning   CS₂   CR (salivation)

FIGURE 4.4 Higher-Order Conditioning
In Stage 1, a strong salivation response is conditioned to occur to the sound of the metronome (CS₁). In Stage 2, finger snapping (CS₂) is repeatedly paired with the ticking of the metronome (CS₁) until the dog begins to salivate to the finger snapping alone. This is called higher-order conditioning because one CS is used to create another, "higher" CS.

the metronome, he snapped his fingers? The sequence would now be "snap-ticking-salivation," or "NS-CS-CR" ("neutral stimulus/conditioned stimulus/conditioned response"). If this happens enough times, the finger snap will eventually also produce a salivation response. The finger snap becomes associated with the ticking through the same process that the ticking became associated with the food originally and is now another conditioned stimulus. Of course, the food (UCS) would have to be presented every now and then to maintain the original conditioned response to the metronome's ticking. Without the UCS, the higher-order conditioning would be difficult to maintain and would gradually fade away.

practice quiz   How much do you remember?

4.1 **4.2**

Pick the best answer.

1. Which of the following statements about learning is NOT TRUE?
   a. Learning is another word for maturation.
   b. Learning is relatively permanent.
   c. Learning involves changes in behavior.
   d. Learning involves experiences.

2. Ed noticed that whenever he used his electric can opener, his cat would come into the kitchen and act hungry—drooling and mewing pitiably. He reasoned that because he used the can opener to open the cat's food, the sound of the can opener had become a(n) _____.
   a. unconditioned stimulus.
   b. conditioned stimulus.
   c. unconditioned response.
   d. conditioned response.

3. Which of the following statements about conditioning is FALSE, according to Pavlov?
   a. The CS and UCS must come close together in time.

   b. The CS must come immediately after the UCS.
   c. The neutral stimulus and UCS must be paired several times before conditioning takes place.
   d. The CS is usually a rather distinctive stimulus.

4. The prologue is about Angelica's fear of clowns as a child. The fact that she was not only afraid of the circus clown but also other types of clowns is an example of _____.
   a. extinction.
   c. stimulus discrimination.
   b. spontaneous recovery.
   d. stimulus generalization.

5. A conditioned response that briefly reappears after it has been extinguished is called _____.
   a. spontaneous recovery.
   c. extinction.
   b. higher-order conditioning.
   d. stimulus generalization.

6. The use of a strong CS to create a second CS is called _____.
   a. spontaneous recovery.
   c. extinction.
   b. higher-order conditioning.
   d. stimulus generalization.

conditioned emotional response (CER) emotional response that has become classically conditioned to occur to learned stimuli, such as a fear of dogs or the emotional reaction that occurs when seeing an attractive person.

vicarious conditioning classical conditioning of a reflex response or emotion by watching the reaction of another person.

FIGURE 4.5 Conditioning of "Little Albert"
After "Little Albert" had been conditioned to fear a white rat, he also demonstrated fear to a rabbit, a dog, and a sealskin coat (although it remains uncertain if stimulus generalization actually occurred, as this fear was to a single rabbit, a single dog, etc.). Can you think of any emotional reactions you experience that might be classically conditioned emotional responses?

👁‍🗨 **Watch** classic footage of Little Albert on **MyPsychLab**

Conditioned Emotional Responses: Rats!

Later scientists took Pavlov's concepts and expanded them to explain not only animal behavior but also human behavior. One of the earliest of these studies showed that even an emotional response could be conditioned.

4.3 **What is a conditioned emotional response, and how do cognitive psychologists explain classical conditioning?**

Watson and "Little Albert"

In the first chapter of this text, John B. Watson's classic experiment with "Little Albert" and the white rat was discussed. This study was a demonstration of the classical conditioning of a phobia—an irrational fear response (Watson & Rayner, 1920).

Watson paired the presentation of the white rat to the baby with a loud, scary noise. Although the baby was not initially afraid of the rat, he was naturally afraid of the loud noise and started to cry. Soon, every time the baby saw the rat, he started to cry. In conditioning terms, the loud noise was the UCS, the fear of the noise the UCR, the white rat became the CS, and the fear of the rat (the phobia) was the CR. (See Figure 4.5.) (It should be pointed out that Watson didn't really "torture" the baby—Albert's fright was temporary. Of course, no ethics committee today would approve an experiment in which an infant experiences such psychological distress.) 👁‍🗨 **Watch** on **MyPsychLab**

The learning of phobias is a very good example of a certain type of classical conditioning, the **conditioned emotional response (CER)**. Conditioned emotional responses are some of the easiest forms of classical conditioning to accomplish and our lives are full of them. It's easy to think of fears people might have that are conditioned or learned: a child's fear of the dentist's chair, a puppy's fear of a rolled-up newspaper, or the fear of dogs that is often shown by a person who has been attacked by a dog in the past. But other emotions can be conditioned, too.

The next time you watch television, watch the commercials closely. Advertisers often use certain objects or certain types of people in their ads to generate a specific emotional response in viewers, hoping that the emotional response will become associated with their product. Sexy models, cute little babies, and adorable puppies are some of the examples of stimuli the advertising world uses to tug at our heartstrings, so to speak.

It is even possible to become classically conditioned by simply watching someone else respond to a stimulus in a process called **vicarious conditioning** (Bandura & Rosenthal, 1966; Hygge & Öhman, 1976; Jones & Menzies, 1995). Many years ago, children received vaccination shots in school. The nurse lined the children up, and one by one they had to go forward to get a needle in the arm. When some children received their shots, they cried quite a bit. By the time the nurse got near the end of the line of children, they were all crying—many of them before she ever touched needle to skin. They had learned their fear response from watching the reactions of the other children.

Other Conditioned Responses in Humans

Are there any foods that you just can't eat anymore because of a bad experience with them? Believe it or not, your reaction to that food is a kind of classical conditioning.

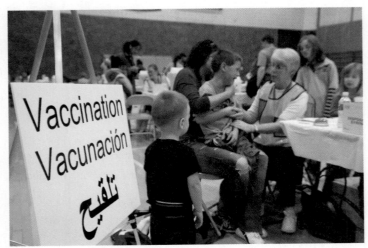

What kind of conditioning could be happening to the children who are waiting to get their vaccination?

Many experiments have shown that laboratory rats will develop a **conditioned taste aversion** for any liquid or food they swallow up to 6 hours before becoming nauseated. Researchers (Garcia et al., 1989; Garcia & Koelling, 1966) found that rats that were given a sweetened liquid and then injected with a drug or exposed to radiation* that caused nausea would not touch the liquid again. In a similar manner, alcoholics who are given a drug to make them violently nauseated when they drink alcohol may learn to avoid drinking any alcoholic beverage. The chemotherapy drugs that cancer patients receive also can create severe nausea, which causes those people to develop a taste aversion for any food they have eaten before going in for the chemotherapy treatment (Berteretche et al., 2004).

But I thought that it took several pairings of these stimuli to bring about conditioning. How can classical conditioning happen so fast?

BIOLOGICAL PREPAREDNESS Conditioned taste aversions, along with phobic reactions, are an example of **biological preparedness**. Most mammals find their food by smell and taste and will learn to avoid any food that smells or tastes like something they ate just before becoming ill. It's a survival mechanism, because if they kept on eating a "bad" food, they might die. The mammalian** body seems to be prepared to associate smell and taste with getting sick (Garcia & Koelling, 1966; Seligman, 1970). Although most conditioning requires repeated pairings of CS with UCS, when the response is nausea, one pairing—even after a period of time has passed—seems to be all that is necessary. Taste aversion conditioning is so effective that renowned psychologist Dr. John Garcia and colleagues have even used it as a tool to stop coyotes from killing ranchers' sheep and also to stop the ranchers from wiping out the coyote population entirely (Gustavson et al., 1976). Garcia and his fellow researchers laced sheep meat with lithium chloride and left it for the coyotes to find. The coyotes ate the drugged meat, got extremely sick, and avoided eating sheep for quite some time afterward. The coyotes got to live and the ranchers got to keep their sheep.

It's interesting to note that birds, which find their food by sight, will avoid any object or insect that simply *looks* like the one that made them sick. There is a certain species of moth with coloring that mimics the monarch butterfly. The butterfly is poisonous to birds, but the moth isn't. The moths' mimicry causes birds to avoid eating them, even though they are quite edible. Whereas mammals are biologically prepared to associate taste with illness, birds are biologically prepared to associate visual characteristics with illness (Shapiro et al., 1980).

As for phobias, fear is a reflex emotional response that has ties to survival—we need to remember what the fear-inducing stimuli are so that we can safely avoid them in future. It shouldn't take more than one snake bite to learn to avoid snakes! Nausea and fear are both examples of reflexes that help organisms survive to reproduce and pass on their genetic material, so the innate tendency to make quick and strong associations between stimuli and these reflexes has evolutionary importance.

Why Does Classical Conditioning Work?

There are two ways to explain how one stimulus comes to "stand in" for another. One is the original explanation given by Pavlov, whereas the other is based on a cognitive explanation. Pavlov believed that the conditioned stimulus, through its association close in time with the unconditioned stimulus, came to activate the same place in the

conditioned taste aversion development of a nausea or aversive response to a particular taste because that taste was followed by a nausea reaction, occurring after only one association.

biological preparedness referring to the tendency of animals to learn certain associations, such as taste and nausea, with only one or a few pairings due to the survival value of the learning.

> But I thought that it took several pairings of these stimuli to bring about conditioning. How can classical conditioning happen so fast?

Conditioned taste aversions in nature. This moth is not poisonous to birds, but the monarch butterfly whose coloring the moth imitates is quite poisonous. Birds find their food by vision and will not eat anything that resembles the monarch.

---

*Radiation: beams of energy.
**Mammalian: having to do with mammals (animals with fur or hair that feed their young with milk from milk glands).

stimulus substitution original theory in which Pavlov stated that classical conditioning occurred because the conditioned stimulus became a substitute for the unconditioned stimulus by being paired closely together.

cognitive perspective modern theory in which classical conditioning is seen to occur because the conditioned stimulus provides information or an expectancy about the coming of the unconditioned stimulus.

animal's brain that was originally activated by the unconditioned stimulus. He called this process **stimulus substitution**. But if a mere association in time is all that is needed, why would conditioning *fail to happen* when the CS is presented immediately *after* the UCS?

Robert Rescorla (1988) found that the CS has to provide some kind of information about the coming of the UCS in order to achieve conditioning. In other words, the CS must predict that the UCS is coming. In one study, Rescorla exposed one group of rats to a tone, and just after the tone's onset and while the tone was still audible, an electric shock was administered for some of the tone presentations. Soon the rats became agitated* and reacted in fear by shivering and squealing at the onset of the tone, a kind of conditioned emotional response. With a second group of rats, Rescorla again sounded a tone but administered the electric shock only *after* the tone *stopped*, not while the tone was being heard. That group of rats responded with fear to the *stopping* of the tone (Rescorla, 1968; Rescorla & Wagner, 1972).

The tone for the second group of rats provided a different kind of information than the tone in the first instance. For the first group, the tone meant the shock was coming, whereas for the second group, the tone meant there was no shock while the tone was on. It was the particular *expectancy* created by pairing the tone or its absence with the shock that determined the particular response of the rats. Because this explanation involves the mental activity of consciously expecting something to occur, it is an example of an explanation for classical conditioning called the **cognitive perspective**.

---

*Agitated: excited, upset.

practice quiz How much do you remember?

4.3

Pick the best answer.

1. In Watson's experiment with "Little Albert," the unconditioned stimulus was _____.
   a. the white rat.
   b. the loud noise.
   c. the fear of the rat.
   d. the fear of the noise.

2. Often people with certain types of cancer must take chemotherapy treatments. The drugs used in these treatments are powerful and usually cause strong nausea reactions. If Cindy had scrambled eggs for breakfast and then took a chemotherapy treatment later that same morning, what might we predict based on conditioned taste aversion research?
   a. Cindy will probably develop a strong liking for scrambled eggs.
   b. Cindy will probably be able to eat scrambled eggs with no nausea at all.
   c. Cindy will probably get nauseated the next time she tries to eat scrambled eggs.
   d. None of the above is likely.

3. Your pet parakeet eats some cooked spaghetti noodles. Later the poor bird gets very ill. What would the research on biological preparedness predict?

   a. The parakeet will probably not eat shell macaroni because it smells similar to spaghetti.
   b. The parakeet will probably not eat shell macaroni because it tastes similar to spaghetti.
   c. The parakeet will probably not eat linguini noodles because they are long and thin and look similar to spaghetti.
   d. The parakeet will eat spaghetti again.

4. The fact that the CS must come immediately *before* the UCS, and not after, is a problem for the _____ theory of why classical conditioning works.
   a. stimulus substitution
   b. cognitive perspective
   c. cognitive substitution
   d. stimulus perspective

5. Rescorla found that the CS must _____ the UCS for conditioning to take place.
   a. replace
   b. come after
   c. come at the same time as
   d. predict

So far, all learning seems to involve reflex behavior, but I know that I am more than just reflexes. People do things on purpose, so is that kind of behavior also learned?

What's in It for Me? Operant Conditioning

4.4 How does operant conditioning occur, and what were the contributions of Thorndike and Skinner?

All organisms are capable of two kinds of behavior: involuntary (reflexive) and voluntary. If Inez blinks her eyes because a gnat flies close to them, that's a reflex and totally involuntary. But if she then swats at the gnat to frighten it, that's a voluntary choice. She *had* to blink, but she *chose* to swat.

Classical conditioning is the kind of learning that occurs with reflexive, involuntary behavior. The kind of learning that applies to voluntary behavior is called **operant conditioning**, which is both different from and similar to classical conditioning.

Frustrating Cats: Thorndike's Puzzle Box and the Law of Effect

Edward L. Thorndike (1874–1949) was one of the first researchers to explore and attempt to outline the laws of learning voluntary responses, although the field was not yet called operant conditioning. Thorndike placed a hungry cat inside a "puzzle box" from which the only escape was to press a lever located on the floor of the box. Thorndike placed a dish of food *outside* the box, so that the hungry cat would be highly motivated to get out. Thorndike observed that the cat would move around the box, pushing and rubbing up against the walls in an effort to escape. Eventually, the cat would accidentally push the lever, opening the door. Upon escaping, the cat was fed from a dish placed just outside the box. The lever is the stimulus, the pushing of the lever is the response, and the consequence is both escape (good) and food (even better).

The cat did not learn to push the lever and escape right away. After a number of trials (and many errors) in a box like this one, the cat took less and less time to push the lever that would open the door (see Figure 4.6). It's important not to assume that the cat had "figured out" the connection between the lever and freedom—Thorndike kept moving the lever to a different position, and the cat had to learn the whole process over again. The cat would simply continue to rub and push in the same general area that led to food and freedom the last time, each time getting out and fed a little more quickly.

Based on this research, Thorndike developed the **law of effect**: If an action is followed by a pleasurable consequence, it will tend to be repeated. If an action is followed by an unpleasant consequence, it will tend not to be repeated (Thorndike, 1911). This is the basic principle behind learning voluntary behavior. In the case of the cat in the box, pushing the lever was followed by a pleasurable consequence (getting out and getting fed), so pushing the lever became a repeated response.

So did Thorndike call this operant conditioning?

No, but Thorndike's important and groundbreaking work began the study of what would eventually become *operant conditioning*.

So far, all learning seems to involve reflex behavior, but I know that I am more than just reflexes. People do things on purpose, so is that kind of behavior also learned?

operant conditioning the learning of voluntary behavior through the effects of pleasant and unpleasant consequences to responses.

law of effect law stating that if an action is followed by a pleasurable consequence, it will tend to be repeated, and if followed by an unpleasant consequence, it will tend not to be repeated.

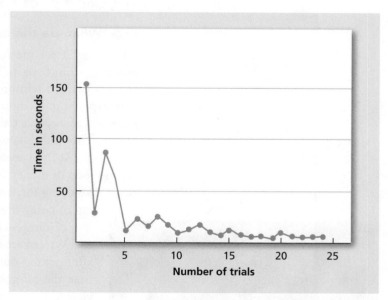

FIGURE 4.6 Graph of the Time to Learn in Thorndike's Experiment
This is one of the earliest "learning curves" in the history of the experimental study of conditioning. The time required by one of Thorndike's cats to escape from the puzzle box gradually decreased with trials but with obvious reversals.

So did Thorndike call this operant conditioning?

operant any behavior that is voluntary.

reinforcement any event or stimulus that, when following a response, increases the probability that the response will occur again.

Simulate stimulus generalization and stimulus discrimination on **MyPsychLab**

B. F. Skinner: The Behaviorist's Behaviorist

B. F. Skinner (1904–1990) was the behaviorist who assumed leadership of the field after John Watson. He was even more determined than Watson that psychologists should study only measurable, observable behavior. In addition to his knowledge of Pavlovian classical conditioning, Skinner found in the work of Thorndike a way to explain all behavior as the product of learning. He even gave the learning of voluntary behavior a special name: *operant conditioning* (Skinner, 1938). Voluntary behavior is what people and animals do to *operate* in the world. When people perform a voluntary action, it is to get something they want or avoid something they don't want, right? So voluntary behavior, for Skinner, is **operant** behavior, and the learning of such behavior is operant conditioning.

The heart of operant conditioning is the effect of consequences on behavior. Thinking back to the section on classical conditioning, learning a reflex really depends on what comes *before* the response—the unconditioned stimulus and what will become the conditioned stimulus. These two stimuli are the *antecedent* stimuli (antecedent means something that comes before another thing). But in operant conditioning, learning depends on what happens *after* the response—the consequence. In a way, operant conditioning could be summed up as this: "If I do this, what's in it for me?" **Simulate** on **MyPsychLab**

The Concept of Reinforcement

4.5 What are the important concepts in operant conditioning?

"What's in it for me?" represents the concept of **reinforcement**, one of Skinner's major contributions to behaviorism. The word itself means "to strengthen," and Skinner defined reinforcement as anything that, when following a response, causes that response to be more likely to happen again. Typically, this means that reinforcement is a consequence that is in some way pleasurable to the organism, which relates back to Thorndike's law of effect. The "pleasurable consequence" is what's in it for the organism. (Keep in mind that a "pleasurable consequence" might be something like getting food or money when you need it, but it might also mean *avoiding* a tiresome chore, like doing the dishes or taking out the garbage. I'll do almost anything to get out of doing the dishes, myself!)

Going back to Thorndike's puzzle box research, what was "in it" for the cat? We can see that the escape from the box and the food that the cat received after getting out are both *reinforcement* of the lever-pushing response. Every time the cat got out of the box, it got reinforced for doing so. In Skinner's view, this reinforcement is the reason that the cat learned anything at all. In operant conditioning, reinforcement is the key to learning.

Skinner had his own version of a puzzle box called a "Skinner box" or "operant conditioning chamber" (see Figure 4.7). His early research often involved placing a rat into one of these chambers and training it to push down on a bar to get food.

FIGURE 4.7 A Typical Skinner Box
This rat is learning to press the bar in the wall of the cage in order to get food (delivered a few pellets at a time in the food trough on lower left). In some cases, the light on the top left might be turned on to indicate that pressing the bar will lead to food or to warn of an impending shock delivered by the grate on the floor of the cage.

PRIMARY AND SECONDARY REINFORCERS The events or items that can be used to reinforce behavior are not all alike. Let's say that a friend of yours asks you to help her move some books from the trunk of her car to her apartment on the second floor. She offers you a choice of $25 or a candy bar. Unless you've suffered recent brain damage, you'll most likely choose the money, right? With $25, you could buy more than one candy bar. (At today's prices, you might even be able to afford three.)

Now pretend that your friend offers the same deal to a 3-year-old child who lives downstairs for carrying up some of the paperback books: $25 or a candy bar. Which reward will the child more likely choose? Most children at that age have no real idea of the value of money, so the child will probably choose the candy bar. The money and the candy bar represent two basic kinds of **reinforcers**, items or events that when following a response will strengthen it. The reinforcing properties of money must be learned, but candy gives immediate reward in the form of taste and satisfying hunger.

A reinforcer such as a candy bar that satisfies a basic need like hunger is called a **primary reinforcer**. Examples would be any kind of food (hunger drive), liquid (thirst drive), or touch (pleasure drive). Infants, toddlers, preschool-age children, and animals can be easily reinforced by using primary reinforcers. (It's not a good idea, however, to start thinking of reinforcers as rewards—freedom from pain is also a basic need, so pain itself can be a primary reinforcer when it is *removed*. Removal of a painful stimulus fills a basic need just as eating food when hungry fills the hunger need.)

A **secondary reinforcer** such as money, however, gets its reinforcing properties from being associated with primary reinforcers in the past. A child who is given money to spend soon realizes that the ugly green paper can be traded for candy and treats—primary reinforcers—and so money becomes reinforcing in and of itself. If a person praises a puppy while petting him (touch, a primary reinforcer), the praise alone will eventually make the puppy squirm with delight.

That sounds very familiar. Isn't this related to classical conditioning? ●——————

Secondary reinforcers do indeed get their reinforcing power from the process of classical conditioning. After all, the pleasure people feel when they eat, drink, or get a back rub is an automatic response, and any automatic response can be classically conditioned to occur to a new stimulus. In the case of money, the candy is a UCS for pleasure (the UCR), and the money is present just before the candy is obtained. The money becomes a CS for pleasure, and people certainly do feel pleasure when they have a lot of that green stuff, don't they?

In the case of the puppy, the petting is the UCS, the pleasure at being touched and petted is the UCR. The praise, or more specifically the tone of voice, becomes the CS for pleasure. Although classical and operant conditioning often "work together," as in the creation of secondary reinforcers, they are two different processes. Table 4.1 presents a brief look at how the two types of conditioning differ from each other.

Positive and Negative Reinforcement

Reinforcers can also differ in the way they are used. Most people have no trouble at all understanding that following a response with some kind of pleasurable consequence (like a reward) will lead to an increase in the likelihood of that response being repeated. This is called **positive reinforcement**, the reinforcement of a response by the *addition* or experience of a pleasurable consequence, such as a reward or a pat on

reinforcers any events or objects that, when following a response, increase the likelihood of that response occurring again.

primary reinforcer any reinforcer that is naturally reinforcing by meeting a basic biological need, such as hunger, thirst, or touch.

secondary reinforcer any reinforcer that becomes reinforcing after being paired with a primary reinforcer, such as praise, tokens, or gold stars.

positive reinforcement the reinforcement of a response by the addition or experience of a pleasurable stimulus.

That sounds very familiar. Isn't this related to classical conditioning?

---

table 4.1 Comparing Two Kinds of Conditioning

OPERANT CONDITIONING	CLASSICAL CONDITIONING
End result is an increase in the rate of an already occurring response.	End result is the creation of a new response to a stimulus that did not normally produce that response.
Responses are voluntary.	Responses are involuntary and reflexive.
Consequences are important in forming an association.	Antecedent stimuli are important in forming an association.
Reinforcement should be immediate.	CS must occur immediately before the UCS.
An expectancy develops for reinforcement to follow a correct response.	An expectancy develops for UCS to follow CS.

negative reinforcement the reinforcement of a response by the removal, escape from, or avoidance of an unpleasant stimulus.

the back. But many people have trouble understanding that the opposite is also true: Following a response with *the removal or escape* from something *unpleasant* will also increase the likelihood of that response being repeated—a process called **negative reinforcement**. Remember the idea that pain can be a reinforcer if it is removed? If a person's behavior gets pain to stop, the person is much more likely to do that same thing again—which is part of the reason people can get addicted to painkilling medication. (We'll discuss the concepts of positive and negative reinforcement in more detail later on.)

We've discussed what reinforcement is and how it affects the behavior that follows the reinforcement. In the next section we'll discuss the different ways in which reinforcement can be administered as well as the difference between reinforcement and punishment. We'll also look at the role of the stimuli that come *before* the behavior that is to be reinforced and a few other operant conditioning concepts.

practice quiz How much do you remember?

4.4 **4.5**

Pick the best answer.

1. In Thorndike's puzzle-box experiments, the cats were rewarded by _____.
   a. getting out of the box.
   b. getting food.
   c. being petted and praised.
   d. both a and b.

2. _____ is an example of a primary reinforcer, whereas _____ is an example of a secondary reinforcer.
   a. A candy bar; a gold star
   b. A gold star; money
   c. Food; a drink
   d. A gold star; candy

3. Carmen hates to clean up after dinner. One night she volunteers to bathe the baby before cleaning up. When she finishes with the baby and returns to the kitchen, her husband has cleaned everything up for her. Which of the following statements is most *likely* TRUE?
   a. Carmen will start cleaning up the kitchen before she bathes the baby.
   b. Carmen's husband has positively reinforced her for bathing the baby.
   c. Carmen's husband has negatively reinforced her for bathing the baby.
   d. Carmen will never bathe the baby again.

4. Bennie is afraid of snakes. He won't even look at pictures of them but turns the page or closes the book instead. When he sees a picture of a snake, his anxiety goes up, but when he avoids looking at the picture, his anxiety goes down. It is *most* correct to say that Bennie's avoidance behavior is being _____.
   a. punished because he feels anxious after doing so.
   b. punished because he will never get better.
   c. positively reinforced because he is rewarded by his anxiety going down.
   d. negatively reinforced because he is rewarded by his anxiety going down.

Brainstorming: What type of reinforcement worked best for you when you were in grade school? Positive or negative? Did this change in high school?

ANSWERS ON PAGE AK–1

The Schedules of Reinforcement: Why the One-Armed Bandit Is So Seductive

The timing of reinforcement can make a tremendous difference in the speed at which learning occurs and the strength of the learned response. Skinner (1956) found that reinforcing each and every response was not necessarily the best schedule of reinforcement for long-lasting learning.

4.6 What are the schedules of reinforcement?

THE PARTIAL REINFORCEMENT EFFECT Alicia's mother gives her a quarter every night she remembers to put her dirty clothes in the clothes hamper. Bianca's mother gives her a dollar at the end of the week, but only if Bianca has put her clothes in the hamper every night. Alicia learns more quickly than does Bianca because responses that are reinforced each time they occur are more easily and quickly learned. After a time, the mothers stop giving the girls the money. Which child will stop putting her clothes in the hamper more quickly?

The answer might be surprising. It will more likely be Alicia, who has expected to get a reinforcer (the quarter) after *every single response*. As soon as the reinforcers stop, the behavior extinguishes. Bianca has expected to get a reinforcer only after *seven correct responses*. When the reinforcers stop, Bianca might continue to put the clothes in the hamper for several more days or even another whole week, hoping that the reinforcer will eventually come anyway. Bianca may have learned more slowly than Alicia, but once she learned the connection between putting her clothes in the hamper and getting that dollar, she was less likely to stop doing it—even when her mother failed to give the dollar as expected.

Bianca's behavior illustrates the **partial reinforcement effect** (Skinner, 1956): A response that is reinforced after some, but not all, correct responses will be more resistant to extinction than a response that receives **continuous reinforcement** (a reinforcer for each and every correct response). Although it may be easier to teach a new behavior using continuous reinforcement, partially reinforced behavior is not only more difficult to suppress but also more like real life. Imagine being paid for every hamburger you make or every report you turn in. In the real world, people tend to receive partial reinforcement rather than continuous reinforcement for their work.

Partial reinforcement can be accomplished according to different patterns or schedules. For example, it might be a certain interval of time that's important, such as an office safe that can only be opened at a certain time of day. It wouldn't matter how many times one tried to open the safe if the effort didn't come at the right *time*. On the other hand, it may be the number of responses that is important, as it would be if one had to sell a certain number of raffle tickets in order to get a prize. When the timing of the response is more important, it is called an *interval schedule*. When it is the number of responses that is important, the schedule is called a *ratio schedule* because a certain number of responses is required for each reinforcer (e.g., 50 raffle tickets for each prize). The other way in which schedules of reinforcement can differ is in whether the number of responses or interval of time is *fixed* (the same in each case) or *variable* (a different number or interval is required in each case). So it is possible to have a fixed interval schedule, a variable interval schedule, a fixed ratio schedule, and a variable ratio schedule (Skinner, 1961), as shown in Figure 4.8.

FIXED INTERVAL SCHEDULE OF REINFORCEMENT The kind of reinforcement schedule most people are more familiar with is called a **fixed interval schedule of reinforcement**, in which a reinforcer is received after a certain, fixed interval of time has passed. If Professor Conner were teaching a rat to press a lever to get food pellets, she might require it to push the lever for 2 minutes to get a pellet. It wouldn't matter how many times the rat pushed the bar press, it would only get the pellet after 2 minutes had passed. If people receive a paycheck once every two weeks (provided that they show up to work in those two weeks), they are being reinforced on this kind of schedule.

As shown in the graph in the upper left corner of Figure 4.8, this schedule of reinforcement does not produce a fast rate of responding (notice that the line doesn't go "up" as fast as in the graph on the right). Since it only matters that at least *one* response is made *during* the specific interval of time, speed is not that important. Eventually, the rat will start pushing the lever only as the interval of time nears its end, causing the *scalloping* effect you see in the graph. The response rate goes up just before the reinforcer and then drops off immediately after, until it is almost time

"Remember, every time he gives you a pellet, reinforce that behavior by pulling the lever." ©The New Yorker Collection 2005 Joe Dator from cartoonbank.com. All Rights Reserved.

partial reinforcement effect the tendency for a response that is reinforced after some, but not all, correct responses to be very resistant to extinction.

continuous reinforcement the reinforcement of each and every correct response.

fixed interval schedule of reinforcement schedule of reinforcement in which the interval of time that must pass before reinforcement becomes possible is always the same.

FIGURE 4.8 Schedules of Reinforcement

These four graphs show the typical pattern of responding for both fixed and variable interval and ratio schedules of reinforcement. The responses are cumulative, which means new responses are added to those that come before, and all graphs begin after the learned pattern is well established. Slash marks mean that a reinforcement has been given. In both the fixed interval and fixed ratio graphs, there is a pause after each reinforcement as the learner briefly "rests." The "scalloped" shape of the fixed interval curve is a typical indicator of this pause, as is the stair-step shape of the fixed ratio curve. In the variable interval and ratio schedules, no such pause occurs, because the reinforcements are unpredictable. Notice that both fixed and variable interval schedules are slower (less steep) than the two ratio schedules because of the need to respond as quickly as possible in the ratio schedules.

| Fixed interval | Fixed ratio |
| Variable interval | Variable ratio |

So if a scheduled test is a fixed interval, then would a pop quiz be a variable interval schedule?

When people go fishing, they never know how long they may have to dangle the bait in the water before snagging a fish. This is an example of a variable interval schedule of reinforcement and explains why some people, such as this father and son, are reluctant to pack up and go home.

for the next food pellet. This is similar to the way in which factory workers speed up production just before payday and slow down just after payday (Critchfield et al., 2003).

Paychecks aren't the only kind of fixed schedule that people experience. When do you study the hardest? Isn't it right before a test? If you know when the test is to be given, that's like having a fixed interval of time that is predictable, and you can save your greatest studying efforts until closer to the exam. (Some students save *all* of their studying for the night before the exam, which is not exactly the best strategy.) Another example of a fixed interval schedule would be the way that most people floss and brush their teeth most rigorously* the few days before their next dental exam. In this case, they are probably hoping for negative reinforcement. The cleaner they get their teeth before the appointment, the less time they might have to spend in that chair.

● So if a scheduled test is a fixed interval, then would a pop quiz be a variable interval schedule?

VARIABLE INTERVAL SCHEDULE OF REINFORCEMENT Pop quizzes are unpredictable. Students don't know exactly what day they might be given a pop quiz, so the best strategy is to study a little every night just in case there is a quiz the next day. Pop quizzes are good examples of a **variable interval schedule of reinforcement**. The interval of time after which the organism must respond in order to receive a reinforcer changes from one time to the next. In a more basic example, a rat might receive a food pellet when it pushes a lever, every 5 minutes on average. Sometimes the interval might be 2 minutes, sometimes 10, but the rat must push the lever at least once *during* that interval to get the pellet. Because the rat can't predict how long the interval is going to be, it pushes the bar more or less continuously, producing the smooth graph in the lower left corner of Figure 4.8. Once again, speed is not important, so the rate of responding is slow but steady.

Another example of a variable interval schedule might be the kind of fishing in which people put the pole in the water and wait—and wait, and wait, until a fish takes the bait—if they are lucky. They only have to put the pole in once, but they might refrain from taking it out for fear that just when they do, the biggest fish in the world would swim by. Dialing a busy phone number is also this kind of schedule, as people don't know *when* the call will go through, so they keep dialing and dialing.

---

*Rigorously: strictly, consistently.

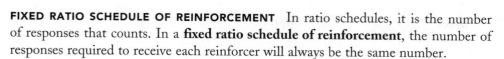

FIXED RATIO SCHEDULE OF REINFORCEMENT In ratio schedules, it is the number of responses that counts. In a **fixed ratio schedule of reinforcement**, the number of responses required to receive each reinforcer will always be the same number.

Notice two things about the graph in the upper right corner of Figure 4.8. The rate of responding is very fast, especially when compared to the fixed interval schedule on the left, and there are little "breaks" in the response pattern immediately after a reinforcer is given. The rapid response rate occurs because the rat wants to get to the next reinforcer just as fast as possible, and the number of lever pushes counts. The pauses or breaks come right after a reinforcer, because the rat knows "about how many" lever pushes will be needed to get to the next reinforcer because it's always the same. Fixed schedules—both ratio and interval—are predictable, which allows rest breaks.

In human terms, anyone who does piecework, in which a certain number of items have to be completed before payment is given, is reinforced on a fixed ratio schedule. Some sandwich shops give out punch cards that get punched one time for each sandwich purchased. When the card has 10 punches, for example, the person might get a free sandwich.

Variable Ratio Schedule of Reinforcement

In Figure 4.8 the graph on the lower right is also very fast, but it's so much smoother, like the variable interval graph on the left. Why are they similar?

A **variable ratio schedule of reinforcement** is one in which the number of responses changes from one trial to the next. In the rat example, the rat might be expected to push the bar an average of 20 times to get reinforcement. That means that sometimes the rat would push the lever only 10 times before a reinforcer comes, but at other times it might take 30 lever pushes or more.

The graph at the lower right of Figure 4.8 shows a curve that is just as rapid a response rate as the fixed ratio schedule because the *number* of responses still matters. But the graph is much smoother because the rat is taking no rest breaks. It can't afford to do so because it *doesn't know* how many times it may have to push that lever to get the next food pellet. It pushes as fast as it can and eats while pushing. It is the *unpredictability* of the variable schedule that makes the responses more or less continuous—just as in a variable interval schedule. ⊙▸ Simulate on **MyPsychLab**

In human terms, people who shove money into the one-armed bandit, or slot machine, are being reinforced on a variable ratio schedule of reinforcement (they hope). They put their coins in (response), but they don't know how many times they will have to do this before reinforcement (the jackpot) comes. People who do this tend to sit there until they either win or run out of money. They don't dare stop because the "next one" might hit that jackpot. Buying lottery tickets is much the same thing, as is any kind of gambling. People don't know how many tickets they will have to buy, and they're afraid that if they don't buy the next one, that will be the ticket that would have won, so they keep buying and buying.

Regardless of the schedule of reinforcement one uses, there are some things that can be done to make using reinforcement of a behavior as effective as possible. One thing also concerns timing: A reinforcer should be given as immediately as possible after the desired behavior. Delaying reinforcement tends not to work well, especially when dealing with animals and small children. (Older children and adults can think about future reinforcements, such as saving up one's money to buy a highly desired item, so delayed reinforcement can work with them.) Care should also be taken to reinforce *only* the desired behavior—for example, many parents make the mistake of giving a child who has not done some chore the promised treat anyway, which completely undermines the child's learning of that chore or task.

variable interval schedule of reinforcement schedule of reinforcement in which the interval of time that must pass before reinforcement becomes possible is different for each trial or event.

fixed ratio schedule of reinforcement schedule of reinforcement in which the number of responses required for reinforcement is always the same.

variable ratio schedule of reinforcement schedule of reinforcement in which the number of responses required for reinforcement is different for each trial or event.

In Figure 4.8 the graph on the lower right is also very fast, but it's so much smoother, like the variable interval graph on the left. Why are they similar?

⊙▸ **Simulate** the schedules of reinforcement on **MyPsychLab**

Slot machines provide reinforcement in the form of money on a variable ratio schedule, making the use of these machines very addictive for many people. People don't want to stop for fear the next pull of the lever will be that "magic" one that produces a jackpot.

So I think I get reinforcement now, but what about punishment? How does punishment fit into the big picture?

● So I think I get reinforcement now, but what about punishment? How does punishment fit into the big picture?

The Role of Punishment in Operant Conditioning

Let's go back to the discussion of positive and negative reinforcement. These strategies are important for *increasing* the likelihood that the targeted behavior will occur again. But what about behavior that we do not want to reoccur?

4.7 How does punishment differ from reinforcement?

People experience two kinds of things as consequences in the world: things they like (food, money, candy, sex, praise, and so on) and things they don't like (spankings, being yelled at, and experiencing any kind of pain, to name a few). In addition, people experience these two kinds of consequences in one of two ways: Either people experience them directly (such as getting money for working or getting yelled at for misbehaving) or they don't experience them, such as losing an allowance for misbehaving or avoiding a scolding by lying about misbehavior. These four consequences are named and described in Table 4.2.

First, take a look at the left column of Table 4.2, the one labeled "Reinforcement." Getting money for working is an example of *positive reinforcement*, the reinforcement of a response by the *addition* or experience of a *pleasurable* consequence, as mentioned earlier. That one everyone understands. But what about avoiding a penalty by turning one's income tax return in on time? That is an example of *negative reinforcement*, the reinforcement of a response by the *removal or escape* from an *unpleasant* consequence. Because the behavior (submitting the return before the deadline) results in *avoiding* an unpleasant stimulus (a penalty), the likelihood that the person will behave that way again (turn it in on time in the future) is *increased*—just as positive reinforcement will increase a behavior's likelihood. Examples are the best way to figure out the difference between these two types of reinforcement, so try to figure out which of the following examples would be positive reinforcement and which would be negative reinforcement:

1. Arnie's father nags him to wash his car. Arnie hates being nagged, so he washes the car so his father will stop nagging.

2. Trey learns that talking in a funny voice gets him lots of attention from his classmates, so now he talks that way often.

3. Allen is a server at a restaurant and always tries to smile and be pleasant because that seems to lead to bigger tips.

table 4.2   Four Ways to Modify Behavior

	REINFORCEMENT	PUNISHMENT
Positive (Adding)	Something valued or desirable	Something unpleasant
	Positive Reinforcement	*Punishment by Application*
	Example: getting a gold star for good behavior in school	Example: getting a spanking for disobeying
Negative (Removing/ Avoiding)	Something unpleasant	Something valued or desirable
	Negative Reinforcement	*Punishment by Removal*
	Example: avoiding a ticket by stopping at a red light	Example: losing a privilege such as going out with friends

4. An Li turns her report in to her teacher on the day it is due because papers get marked down a letter grade for every day they are late.

Here are the answers:

1. Arnie is being negatively reinforced for washing his car because the nagging (unpleasant stimulus) stops when he does so.

2. Trey is getting positive reinforcement in the form of his classmates' attention.

3. Allen's smiling and pleasantness are positively reinforced by the customers' tips.

4. An Li is avoiding an unpleasant stimulus (the marked-down grade) by turning in her paper on time, which is an example of negative reinforcement.

Two Kinds of Punishment

I'm confused—I thought taking something away was a kind of punishment? ●────
People get confused because "negative" sounds like it ought to be something bad, like a kind of punishment. **Punishment** is actually the opposite of reinforcement. It is any event or stimulus that, when following a response, causes that response to be less likely to happen again. Punishment *weakens* responses, whereas reinforcement (no matter whether it is positive or negative) *strengthens* responses. There are two ways in which punishment can happen, just as there are two ways in which reinforcement can happen.

Now take a look at the right column of Table 4.2, labeled "Punishment." **Punishment by application** occurs when something unpleasant (such as a spanking, scolding, or other unpleasant stimulus) is added to the situation or *applied*. This is the kind of punishment that most people think of when they hear the word *punishment*. This is also the kind of punishment that many child development specialists strongly recommend parents avoid using with their children because it can easily escalate into abuse (Dubowitz & Bennett, 2007; Saunders & Goddard, 1998; Straus, 2000; Straus & Stewart, 1999; Straus & Yodanis, 1994; Trocmé et al., 2001). A spanking might be *physically* harmless if it is only two or three swats with a hand, but if done in anger or with a belt or other instrument, it becomes abuse, both physical and emotional.

Punishment by removal, on the other hand, is the kind of punishment most often confused with negative reinforcement. In this type of punishment, behavior is punished by the removal of something pleasurable or desired after the behavior occurs. "Grounding" a teenager is removing the freedom to do what the teenager wants to do and is an example of this kind of punishment. Other examples would be placing a child in time-out (removing the attention of the others in the room), fining someone for disobeying the law (removing money), and punishing aggressive behavior by taking away television privileges. This type of punishment is far more acceptable to child development specialists because it involves no physical aggression and avoids many of the problems caused by more aggressive punishments.

The confusion over the difference between negative reinforcement and punishment by removal makes it worth examining the difference just a bit more. Negative reinforcement occurs when a response is followed by the *removal* of an *unpleasant* stimulus. If something unpleasant has just gone away as a consequence of that response, wouldn't that response tend to happen again and again? If the response increases, the consequence has to be a kind of *reinforcement*. The problem is that the name sounds like it should be some kind of punishment because of the word *negative*, and that's exactly the problem that many people experience when they are trying to understand negative reinforcement. They get negative reinforcement mixed up with punishment by removal, in which a *pleasant* thing is removed (like having your driver's license

punishment any event or object that, when following a response, makes that response less likely to happen again.

punishment by application the punishment of a response by the addition or experience of an unpleasant stimulus.

punishment by removal the punishment of a response by the removal of a pleasurable stimulus.

I'm confused—I thought taking something away was a kind of punishment?

This young man's father is applying punishment by removal as he takes the car keys away from his son.

table 4.3 Negative Reinforcement Versus Punishment by Removal

EXAMPLE OF NEGATIVE REINFORCEMENT	EXAMPLE OF PUNISHMENT BY REMOVAL
Stopping at a red light to avoid getting in an accident.	Losing the privilege of driving because you got into too many accidents.
Mailing an income tax return by April 15 to avoid paying a penalty.	Having to lose some of your money to pay the penalty for late tax filing.
Obeying a parent before the parent reaches the count of "three" to avoid getting a scolding.	Being "grounded" (losing your freedom) because of disobedience.

taken away because you caused a bad accident). Because something is removed (taken away) in both cases, people think that they will both have the effect of punishment, or weakening a response. The difference between them lies in *what* is taken away: In the case of negative reinforcement, it is an *unpleasant* thing; in the case of this particular form of punishment, it is a *pleasant* or desirable thing. For a head-to-head comparison of negative reinforcement and this particular type of punishment by removal, see Table 4.3.

Problems with Punishment

4.8 **What are some of the problems with using punishment?**

Although punishment can be effective in reducing or weakening a behavior, it has several drawbacks. The job of punishment is much harder than that of reinforcement. In using reinforcement, all one has to do is strengthen a response that is already there. But punishment is used to weaken a response, and getting rid of a response that is already well established is not that easy. (Ask any parent or pet owner.) Many times punishment only serves to temporarily suppress or inhibit a behavior until enough time has passed. For example, punishing a child's bad behavior doesn't always eliminate the behavior completely. As time goes on, the punishment is forgotten, and the "bad" behavior may occur again in a kind of spontaneous recovery of the old (and probably pleasurable for the child) behavior.

Look back at Table 4.2 under the "Punishment" column. Punishment by application can be quite severe, and severe punishment does do one thing well: It stops the behavior immediately (Bucher & Lovaas, 1967; Carr & Lovass, 1983). It may not stop it permanently, but it does stop it. In a situation in which a child might be doing something dangerous or self-injurious, this kind of punishment is sometimes more acceptable (Duker & Seys, 1996). For example, if a child starts to run into a busy street, the parent might scream at the child to stop and then administer several rather severe swats to the child's rear. If this is not usual behavior on the part of the parent, the child will most likely never run into the street again.

Other than situations of immediately stopping dangerous behavior, severe punishment has too many drawbacks to be really useful. It should also be discouraged because of its potential for leading to abuse (Dubowitz & Bennett, 2007; Gershoff, 2000; Trocmé et al., 2001):

• Severe punishment may cause the child (or animal) to avoid the punisher instead of the behavior being punished, so the child (or animal) learns the wrong response.

• Severe punishment may encourage lying to avoid the punishment (a kind of negative reinforcement)—again, not the response that is desired.

- Severe punishment creates fear and anxiety, emotional responses that do not promote learning (Baumrind, 1997; Gershoff, 2000, 2002). If the point is to teach something, this kind of consequence isn't going to help.

- Hitting provides a successful model for aggression (Gershoff, 2000; Milner, 1992).

That last point is worth a bit more discussion. In using an aggressive type of punishment, such as spanking, the adult is actually modeling (presenting a behavior to be imitated by the child). After all, the adult is using aggression to get what the adult wants from the child. Children sometimes become more likely to use aggression to get what they want when they receive this kind of punishment (Bryan & Freed, 1982; Larzelere, 1986), and the adult has lost an opportunity to model a more appropriate way to deal with parent–child disagreements. Since aggressive punishment does tend to stop the undesirable behavior, at least for a while, the parent who is punishing actually experiences a kind of negative reinforcement: "When I spank, the unpleasant behavior goes away." This may increase the tendency to use aggressive punishment over other forms of discipline and could even lead to child abuse (Dubowitz & Bennett, 2007). Finally, some children are so desperate for attention from their parents that they will actually misbehave on purpose. The punishment is a form of attention, and these children will take whatever attention they can get, even negative attention.

Punishment by removal is less objectionable to many parents and educators and is the only kind of punishment that is permitted in many public schools. But this kind of punishment also has its drawbacks—it teaches the child what *not* to do but not what the child should do. Both punishment by removal and punishment by application are usually only temporary in their effect on behavior. After some time has passed, the behavior will most likely return as the memory of the punishment gets weaker, allowing spontaneous recovery.

If punishment doesn't work very well, what can a parent do to keep a child from behaving badly?

If punishment doesn't work very well, what can a parent do to keep a child from behaving badly?

HOW TO MAKE PUNISHMENT MORE EFFECTIVE The way to make punishment more effective involves remembering a few simple rules:

1. **Punishment should immediately follow the behavior it is meant to punish.** If the punishment comes long after the behavior, it will not be associated with that behavior. (This is also true of reinforcement.)

2. **Punishment should be consistent.** This actually means two things. First, if the parent says that a certain punishment will follow a certain behavior, then the parent must make sure to follow through and do what he or she promised to do. Second, punishment for a particular behavior should stay at the same intensity or increase slightly but never decrease. For example, if a child is scolded for jumping on the bed the first time, the second time this behavior happens the child should also be punished by scolding or by a stronger penalty, such as removal of a favorite toy. But if the first misbehavior is punished by spanking and the second by only a scolding, the child learns to "gamble" with the possible punishment.

3. **Punishment of the wrong behavior should be paired, whenever possible, with reinforcement of the right behavior.** Instead of yelling at a 2-year-old for eating with her fingers, the parent should pull her hand gently out of her plate while saying something such as, "No, we do not eat with our fingers. We eat with our fork," and then placing the fork in the child's hand and praising her for using it. "See, you are doing such a good job with your fork. I'm so proud of you." Pairing punishment (the mild correction of pulling her

hand away while saying "No, we do not eat with our fingers") with reinforcement allows parents (and others) to use a much milder punishment and still be effective. It also teaches the desired behavior rather than just suppressing the undesired one.

The following section discusses some very recent research on the problems that can be generated by a particular form of punishment by application: spanking.

issues in psychology

The Link between Spanking and Aggression in Young Children

To spank or not to spank has been a controversial issue for many years now. Child development experts have typically advised parents to use other methods of disciplining their children, citing the possibility of encouraging child abuse as well as the role spanking plays in the modeling of aggression. Now the results of a new study suggest that there is a significantly increased risk of higher levels of aggression at age 5 when spanking is used at age 3 (C. Taylor et al., 2010).

While older studies have found similar results, the study by Dr. Catherine Taylor and her colleagues, Drs. Jennifer Manganello, Shawna Lee, and Janet Rice, differs from those earlier studies in that possible maternal risk factors such as neglect, the mother's use of drugs, and maternal psychological problems were measured and controlled.

In this study, 2,461 mothers participated in reporting their use of spanking at age 3 as well as their children's aggressive behavior at age 3 and then 2 years later at age 5. Factors such as child maltreatment by the mothers, psychological maltreatment, neglect, aggression from the mother's intimate partner, victimization, stress, depression, substance abuse, and the mother's consideration of abortion were also assessed. The Taylor study found that when mothers stated that they spanked their 3-year-olds more than twice in the previous month, those same children at 5 years of age were much more likely to be more aggressive (bullying, for example) when compared to children of mothers who spanked less than twice or not at all when their children were 3. This result held even when the individual differences between the natural aggression levels of the 3-year-olds and the other possible confounding factors were taken into account.

The conclusion seems to be that sparing the rod may spare the child (and those around the child) from an unpleasant personality trait. ▯●▯ Read on **MyPsychLab**

QUESTIONS FOR FURTHER DISCUSSION

1. How did your own parents discipline you, and do you think that it affected you in a positive or negative way?
2. Why would spanking at age 3 lead to higher aggression in that same child at age 5?

This dog has been trained to help its physically challenged owner. Operant conditioning principles can be used to train animals to do many useful tasks, including opening the refrigerator.

▯●▯ Read about the controversy surrounding spanking on **MyPsychlab**

Stimulus Control: Slow Down, It's the Cops

4.9 How do operant stimuli control behavior, and what are some other concepts that can enhance or limit operant conditioning?

You see a police car in your rearview mirror and automatically slow down, even if you weren't speeding. The traffic light turns red, so you stop. When you want to get into a store, you head for the door and push or pull on the handle. All of these things—slowing down, stopping, using the door handle—are learned. But how do you know what learned response to make, and when? The police car, the stoplight, and the door handle are all cues, stimuli that tell you what behavior will get you what you want.

DISCRIMINATIVE STIMULI   As stated earlier, a **discriminative stimulus** is any stimulus that provides an organism with a cue for making a certain response in order to obtain reinforcement. For example, a police car is a discriminative stimulus for slowing down, and a stop sign is a cue for stopping because both of these actions are usually followed by negative reinforcement—people don't get a ticket or don't get hit by another vehicle. A doorknob is a cue for where to grab the door in order to successfully open it. In fact, if a door has a knob, people always turn it, but if it has a handle, people usually pull it, right? The two kinds of opening devices each bring forth a different response from people, and their reward is opening the door.

Other Concepts in Operant Conditioning

Operant conditioning is more than just the reinforcement of simple responses. For example, have you ever tried to teach a pet to do a trick? Yes, it was really hard.

How do the circus trainers get their animals to do all those complicated tricks? ●

SHAPING   When you see an animal in a circus or in a show at a zoo perform tricks, you are seeing the result of applying the rules of conditioning—both classical and operant—to animals. But the more complex tricks are a process in operant conditioning called **shaping**, in which small steps toward some ultimate goal are reinforced until the goal itself is reached.

For example, if Jody wanted to train his dog to jump through a hoop, he would have to start with some behavior that the dog is already capable of doing on its own. Then he would gradually "mold" that starting behavior into the jump—something the dog is capable of doing but not likely to do on its own. Jody would have to start with the hoop on the ground in front of Rover's face and then call the dog through the hoop, using the treat as bait. After Rover steps through the hoop (as the shortest way to the treat), Jody should give Rover the treat (positive reinforcement). Then he could raise the hoop just a little, reward him for walking through it again, raise the hoop, reward him . . . until Rover is jumping through the hoop to get the treat. The goal is achieved by reinforcing each **successive approximation** (small steps one after the other that get closer and closer to the goal). This process is shaping (Skinner, 1974). Through pairing of a sound such as a whistle or clicker with the primary reinforcer of food, animal trainers can use the sound as a secondary reinforcer and avoid having an overfed learner.

EXTINCTION, GENERALIZATION, AND SPONTANEOUS RECOVERY IN OPERANT CONDITIONING   *Extinction* in classical conditioning involves the removal of the UCS, the unconditioned stimulus that eventually acts as a reinforcer of the CS–CR bond. It should come as no surprise, then, that extinction in operant conditioning involves the removal of the reinforcement. Have you ever seen a child throw a temper tantrum in the checkout line because the little one wanted some candy or toy? Many exasperated* parents will cave in and give the child the treat, positively reinforcing the tantrum. The parent is also being negatively reinforced for giving in, because the obnoxious** behavior stops. The only way to get the tantrum behavior to stop is to remove the reinforcement, which means no candy, no treat, and if possible, no attention from the parent. (Not only is this hard enough to do while enduring the tantrum, but also the tantrum behavior may actually get worse before it extinguishes!)

discriminative stimulus   any stimulus, such as a stop sign or a doorknob, that provides the organism with a cue for making a certain response in order to obtain reinforcement.

shaping   the reinforcement of simple steps in behavior that lead to a desired, more complex behavior.

successive approximations   small steps in behavior, one after the other, that lead to a particular goal behavior.

How do the circus trainers get their animals to do all those complicated tricks?

One way to deal with a child's temper tantrum is to ignore it. The lack of reinforcement for the tantrum behavior will eventually result in extinction.

---

*Exasperated: irritated or annoyed.
**Obnoxious: highly offensive or undesirable.

Just as in classical conditioning, operantly conditioned responses also can be generalized to stimuli that are only similar to the original stimulus. For example, what parent has not experienced that wonderful moment when Baby, who is just learning to label objects and people, refers to every man she sees as "Dada"? The name "Dada" is a response to the presence of her own father and is reinforced by his delight and attention to her. But in the beginning, she will generalize her "Dada" response to any man. As other men fail to reinforce her for this response, she'll learn to discriminate between them and her father and only call her father "Dada." In this way, the man who is actually her father becomes a discriminative stimulus just like the stoplight or the doorknob mentioned earlier.

Spontaneous recovery (the recurrence of a conditioned response after extinction) will also happen with operant responses. Remember the hoop-jumping dog? Anyone who has ever trained animals to do several different tricks will say that when first learning a new trick, most animals will try to get reinforcers by performing their *old* tricks. Rover might very well have tried to roll over, speak, and shake paws to get that treat before finally walking through the hoop.

While animals can learn many types of behavior through the use of operant conditioning, it seems that not every animal can be taught *anything*. For more on this topic, see the following section on biological constraints.

classic studies in psychology
Biological Constraints on Operant Conditioning

Raccoons are fairly intelligent animals and are sometimes used in learning experiments. In a typical experiment, a behaviorist would use shaping and reinforcement to teach a raccoon a trick. The goal might be to get the raccoon to pick up several coins and drop them into a metal container, for which the raccoon would be rewarded with food. The behaviorist starts by reinforcing the raccoon for picking up a single coin. Then the metal container is introduced, and the raccoon is now required to drop the coin into the slot on the container in order to get reinforcement.

It is at this point that operant conditioning seems to fail. Instead of dropping the coin in the slot, the raccoon puts the coin in and out of the slot and rubs it against the inside of the container, then holds it firmly for a few seconds before finally letting it go. When the requirement is upped to two coins, the raccoon spends several minutes rubbing them against each other and dipping them into the container, without actually dropping them in. In spite of the fact that this dipping and rubbing behavior is not reinforced, it gets worse and worse until conditioning becomes impossible.

Keller and Marian Breland, in their attempt to train a raccoon, found that this problem was not limited to the raccoon (Breland & Breland, 1961). They ran into a similar difficulty with a pig that was being trained to pick up a total of five large wooden coins and put them into a "piggy bank." Although at first successful, the pig became slower and slower at the task over a period of weeks, dropping the coin, rooting (pushing) it around with its nose, picking it up, dropping it again, and rooting some more. This behavior became so persistent that the pig actually did not get enough to eat for the day.

The Brelands concluded that the raccoon and the pig were reverting* to behavior that was instinctual for them. Instinctual behavior is genetically determined and not under the influence of learning. Apparently, even though the animals were at first able to learn the tricks, as the coins became more and more associated with food, the animals began to drift back into the instinctual patterns of behavior that they used with real food. Raccoons

Raccoons commonly dunk their food in and out of water before eating. This "washing" behavior is controlled by instinct and is difficult to change even using operant techniques.

---

*Reverting: to go back in action, thought, speech, and so on.

rub their food between their paws and dip it in and out of water. Pigs root and throw their food around before eating it. The Brelands called this tendency to revert to genetically controlled patterns **instinctive drift**.

In their 1961 paper describing these and other examples of instinctive drift, the Brelands (both trained by Skinner himself) determined that three assumptions in which most Skinnerian behaviorists believed were not actually true. The three false assumptions were as follows:

1. The animal comes to the laboratory a *tabula rasa*, or "blank slate," and can, therefore, be taught anything with the right conditioning.
2. Differences between species of animals are insignificant.
3. All responses are equally able to be conditioned to any stimulus.

As became quickly obvious in their studies with these animals, each animal comes into the world (and the laboratory) with certain genetically determined instinctive patterns of behavior already in place. These instincts differ from species to species, with the result that there are some responses that simply cannot be trained into an animal regardless of conditioning.

QUESTIONS FOR FURTHER DISCUSSION

1. What other kinds of limitations do animals have in learning?
2. What kinds of behavior might people do that would be resistant to conditioning?
3. How can these research findings about animal behavior be generalized to human behavior?

Applying Operant Conditioning: Behavior Modification

4.10 What is behavior modification, and how can behavioral techniques be used to modify involuntary biological responses?

Operant conditioning principles such as reinforcement and the process of shaping have been used for many years to change undesirable behavior and create desirable responses in animals and humans—particularly in schoolchildren. The term **behavior modification** refers to the application of operant conditioning (and sometimes classical conditioning) to bring about such changes. People might recall their grade school teacher offering gold stars or some other incentive* as a reward for reading a certain number of books or giving a reward like a wooden stick that could be traded in for a treat.

For example, if a teacher wants to use behavior modification to help a child learn to be more attentive during the teacher's lectures, the teacher may do the following:

1. Select a target behavior, such as making eye contact with the teacher.
2. Choose a reinforcer. This may be a gold star applied to the child's chart on the wall, for example.
3. Put the plan in action. Every time the child makes eye contact, the teacher gives the child a gold star. Inappropriate behavior (such as looking out of the window) is not reinforced with gold stars.
4. At the end of the day, the teacher gives the child a special treat or reward for having a certain number of gold stars. This special reward is decided on ahead of time and discussed with the child.

Both gold stars and wooden sticks can be considered *tokens*, secondary reinforcers that can be traded in for other kinds of reinforcers. The use of tokens to modify behavior is called a **token economy**. ⓁⒾⓃⓀ to Chapter Thirteen: Psychological

---

*Incentive: something that encourages a particular action.

---

instinctive drift tendency for an animal's behavior to revert to genetically controlled patterns.

behavior modification the use of operant conditioning techniques to bring about desired changes in behavior.

token economy type of behavior modification in which desired behavior is rewarded with tokens.

applied behavior analysis (ABA) modern term for a form of functional analysis and behavior modification that uses a variety of behavioral techniques to mold a desired behavior or response.

biofeedback use of feedback about biological conditions to bring involuntary responses, such as blood pressure and relaxation, under voluntary control.

neurofeedback form of biofeedback using brain-scanning devices to provide feedback about brain activity in an effort to modify behavior.

Therapies, p. 475. In the example, the child is collecting gold stars to "buy" the special treat at the end of the day. When one thinks about it, the system of money is very much a token economy. People are rewarded for working for money, which they then trade for food, shelter, and so on.

Another tool that behaviorists can use to modify behavior is the process of *time-out*. Time-out is a form of mild punishment by removal in which a misbehaving animal, child, or adult is placed in a special area away from the attention of others. Essentially, the organism is being "removed" from any possibility of positive reinforcement in the form of attention. When used with children, time-out should be limited to 1 minute for each year of age with a maximum time-out of 10 minutes (longer than that and the child can forget why the time-out occurred).

Applied behavior analysis (ABA) is the modern term for a form of behavior modification that uses both analysis of current behavior and behavioral techniques to mold a desired behavior or response. It can be said to have begun with the work of Lovaas (1964) and his associates, although the basic techniques are those first outlined by Skinner. Lovaas used small pieces of candy as reinforcers to teach social skills and language to children with *autism*. Autism is a disorder in which the person has great difficulty in communicating with others, often refusing to look at another person. LINK to Chapter Seven: Development Across the Life Span, p. 245. People who are autistic may also fail to learn to speak at all, and they normally do not like to be touched. (The character played by Dustin Hoffman in the movie *Rainman* was autistic.)

In ABA, skills are broken down to their simplest steps and then taught to the child through a system of reinforcement. Prompts (such as moving a child's face back to look at the teacher or the task) are given as needed when the child is learning a skill or refuses to cooperate. As the child begins to master a skill and receives reinforcement in the form of treats or praise, the prompts are gradually withdrawn until the child can do the skill independently. Applied behavior analysis is a growing field, with many colleges and universities offering excellent degrees at both the undergraduate and graduate levels. Typical uses for ABA are treating with children with disorders, training animals, and developing effective teaching methods for children and adults of all levels of mental abilities (Baer et al., 1968).

Other techniques for modifying behavior have been developed so that even behavior that is normally considered involuntary such as blood pressure and muscle tension can be brought under conscious control. For nearly 60 years, scientists have known how to use feedback of a person's biological information (such as heart rate) to create a state of relaxation (Margolin & Kubic, 1944). **Biofeedback** is the traditional term used to describe this kind of biological feedback of information, and through its use many problems can be relieved or controlled.

A relatively newer biofeedback technique called **neurofeedback** involves trying to change brain-wave activity. Traditionally, to record brain-wave activity, a person would have to be connected to a stand-alone *electroencephalograph*, a machine that amplifies and records the brain's electrical activity. In today's modern age, biofeedback and neurofeedback amplifers are often connected to a computer that records and analyzes the physiological activity of the brain. Neurofeedback applications can also be used with functional magnetic resonance imaging (fMRI). Neurofeedback can be integrated with video-game–like programs that individuals can use to learn how to produce brain waves or specific types of brain activity associated with specific cognitive or behavioral states (e.g., increased attention, staying focused, relaxed awareness). Individuals learn to make these changes through the principles of operant conditioning. ▶Read on MyPsychLab

▶Read and learn more about neurofeedback on MyPsychLab

practice quiz   How much do you remember?

Pick the best answer.

1. In a once-popular television series, Desmond lived in a bunker underground on a mysterious island. He had one task: When the alarm sounds, type in a series of numbers on the computer and push enter. Desmond was being reinforced for doing so by avoiding some terrible disaster that would occur if he did *not* type in the numbers at the right time—every 108 minutes. What kind of schedule of reinforcement was Desmond on?
   a. fixed interval
   b. fixed ratio
   c. variable interval
   d. variable ratio

2. Joe was trying to get tickets to a concert and called the ticket outlet only to find that the phone line was busy. He dialed again—busy—and then again and again, sometimes waiting a minute, sometimes a few minutes, not knowing how much time would go by before his call would go through. What schedule of reinforcement is evident here?
   a. fixed interval
   b. fixed ratio
   c. variable interval
   d. variable ratio

3. Jessica's mother was upset to find that Jessica had used her crayons to draw flowers on her bedroom wall. Her mother took the crayons away from her and made Jessica wash the drawings off the wall. Which of the following statements is TRUE?
   a. Having her crayons taken away was a form of punishment by removal.
   b. Being made to wash off the drawings was a form of punishment by application.
   c. Having her crayons taken away was a form of negative reinforcement.
   d. Both a and b are true.

4. Which of the following is NOT a problem with punishment?
   a. The effect of punishment is often temporary.
   b. Severe punishment creates fear and anxiety.
   c. Mild punishment can be paired with reinforcement of the correct behavior.
   d. Aggressive punishment can model aggressive behavior for the child.

5. Elizabeth's parents want her to put her clothes in the hamper. At first, they praise her for putting the clothes together in one pile. Then they praise her for getting the clothes on the same side of the room as the hamper. When she gets the clothes on top of the hamper, she gets praise. Finally, her parents praise her when she puts her clothes in the hamper. This is an example of _____.
   a. negative reinforcement.
   b. punishment.
   c. extinction.
   d. shaping.

6. Ella is teaching her parrot a new word. Every time the parrot says a sound that is close to the new word, she gives it a treat. But the parrot keeps repeating other words it has learned in the past, trying to get a treat that way. The parrot is exhibiting _____.
   a. generalization.
   b. extinction.
   c. spontaneous recovery.
   d. discrimination.

7. Applied behavior analysis _____.
   a. involves the process of shaping.
   b. is useful only for teaching autistic children.
   c. is different from behavior modification.
   d. cannot be used with animals.

Brainstorming: How did your parents discipline you when you were a child? What type of reinforcement or punishment did they use most often?

ANSWERS ON PAGE AK–1

Cognitive Learning Theory

4.11 How do latent learning, learned helplessness, and insight relate to cognitive learning theory?

In the early days of behaviorism, the original focus of Watson, Skinner, and many of their followers was on observable, measurable behavior. Anything that might be occurring inside a person or animal's head during learning was considered to be of no interest to the behaviorist because it could not be seen or directly measured. Other psychologists, however, were still interested in the mind's influence over behavior. Gestalt psychologists, for instance, were studying the way that the human mind tried to force a pattern on stimuli in the world around the person. LINK to Chapter One: The Science of Psychology, p. 9. This continued interest in the mind was followed, in the 1950s and 1960s, by the comparison of the human mind to the workings of those fascinating "thinking machines," computers. Soon after, interest in *cognition*, the mental events that take place inside a person's mind while behaving, began to dominate experimental psychology. Many behavioral psychologists could no longer ignore the thoughts, feelings, and expectations that clearly existed in the mind and that seemed to influence observable behavior and eventually began to develop a cognitive learning theory to supplement the more traditional theories of learning (Kendler, 1985). Three important figures often cited as key theorists in the early days of the development of cognitive learning theory were the Gestalt psychologists Edward Tolman and Wolfgang Köhler and modern psychologist Martin Seligman.

"Bathroom? Sure, it's just down that hall to the left, jog right, left, another left, straight past two more lefts, then right, and it's at the end of the third corridor on your right." ©The New Yorker Collection 2000 Pat Byrnes from cartoonbank.com. All Rights Reserved.

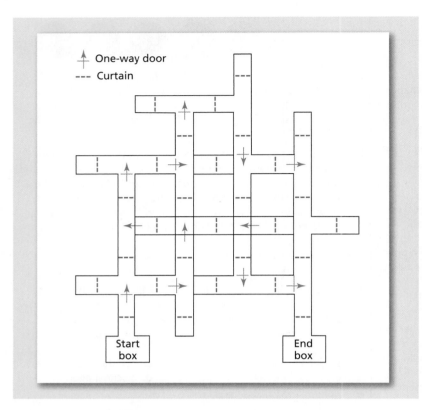

One-way door
--- Curtain

Start box

End box

FIGURE 4.9 A Typical Maze
This is an example of a maze like the one used in Tolman's experiments in latent learning. A rat is placed in the start box, and the trial is over when the rat gets to the end box.

Tolman's Maze-Running Rats: Latent Learning

One of Gestalt psychologist Edward Tolman's best-known experiments in learning involved teaching three groups of rats the same maze, one at a time (Tolman & Honzik, 1930). In the first group, each rat was placed in the maze and reinforced with food for making its way out the other side. The rat was then placed back in the maze, reinforced, and so on until the rat could successfully solve the maze with no errors—the typical maze-learning experiment (see Figure 4.9).

The second group of rats was treated exactly like the first, except that they never received any reinforcement upon exiting the maze. They were simply put back in again and again, until the tenth day of the experiment. On that day, the rats in the second group began to receive reinforcement for getting out of the maze. The third group of rats, serving as a control group, was also not reinforced and was not given reinforcement for the entire duration of the experiment.

A strict Skinnerian behaviorist would predict that only the first group of rats would learn the maze successfully because learning depends on reinforcing consequences. At first, this seemed to be the case. The first group of rats did indeed solve the maze after a certain number of trials, whereas the second and third groups seemed to wander aimlessly around the maze until accidentally finding their way out.

On the 10th day, however, something happened that would be difficult to explain using only Skinner's basic principles. The second group of rats, upon receiving the reinforcement for the first time, *should* have then taken as long as the first group to solve the maze. Instead, they began to solve the maze almost immediately (see Figure 4.10).

Tolman concluded that the rats in the second group, while wandering around in the first nine days of the experiment, had indeed learned where all the blind alleys, wrong turns, and correct paths were and stored this knowledge away as a kind of "mental map," or *cognitive map* of the physical layout of the maze. The rats in the second group had learned and stored that learning away mentally but had not *demonstrated* this learning because there was no reason to do so. The cognitive map had remained hidden, or latent, until the rats had a reason to demonstrate their knowledge by getting to the food. Tolman called this **latent learning**. The idea that learning could happen without reinforcement, and then later affect behavior, was not something traditional operant conditioning could explain. ✳ Explore on MyPsychLab

Köhler's Smart Chimp: Insight Learning

Another exploration of the cognitive elements of learning came about almost by accident. Wolfgang Köhler (1887–1967) was a Gestalt psychologist who became marooned* on an island in the Canaries (a series of islands off the coast of North Africa)

✳ Explore an experiment on learning in MyPsychLab

latent learning learning that remains hidden until its application becomes useful.

---

*Marooned: in this sense, being placed on an island from which escape is impossible.

when World War I broke out. Stuck at the primate research lab that had first drawn him to the island, he turned to studies of animal learning.

In one of his more famous studies (Köhler, 1925), he set up a problem for one of the chimpanzees. Sultan the chimp was faced with the problem of how to get to a banana that was placed just out of his reach outside his cage. Sultan solved this problem relatively easily, first trying to reach through the bars with his arm, using a stick that was lying in the cage to rake the banana into the cage. As chimpanzees are natural tool users, this behavior is not surprising and is still nothing more than simple trial-and-error learning.

But then the problem was made more difficult. The banana was placed just out of reach of Sultan's extended arm with the stick in his hand. At this point there were two sticks lying around in the cage, which could be fitted together to make a single pole that would be long enough to reach the banana. Sultan first tried one stick, then the other (simple trial and error). After about an hour of trying, Sultan seemed to have a sudden flash of inspiration. He pushed one stick out of the cage as far as it would go toward the banana and then pushed the other stick behind the first one. Of course, when he tried to draw the sticks back, only the one in his hand came. He jumped up and down and was very excited, and when Köhler gave him the second stick, he sat on the floor of the cage and looked at them carefully. He then fitted one stick into the other and retrieved his banana. Köhler called Sultan's rapid "perception of relationships" **insight** and determined that insight could not be gained through trial-and-error learning alone (Köhler, 1925). Although Thorndike and other early learning theorists believed that animals could not demonstrate insight, Köhler's work seems to demonstrate that insight requires a sudden "coming together" of all the elements of a problem in a kind of "aha" moment that is not predicted by traditional animal learning studies. ⓛⓘⓝⓚ to Chapter Six: Consciousness and Cognition, p. 221. More recent research has also found support for the concept of animal insight (Heinrich, 2000; Heyes, 1998; Zentall, 2000), but there is still controversy over how to interpret the results of those studies (Wynne, 1999).

Seligman's Depressed Dogs: Learned Helplessness

Martin Seligman is now famous for founding the field of *positive psychology*, a new way of looking at the entire concept of mental health and therapy. But in the mid- to late 1960s Seligman, a learning theorist, and his colleagues accidentally discovered an unexpected phenomenon while doing experiments on dogs using classical conditioning (Seligman, 1975). Their original intention was to study escape and avoidance learning. Seligman and colleagues presented a tone followed by a harmless but painful electric shock to one group of dogs (Overmier & Seligman,

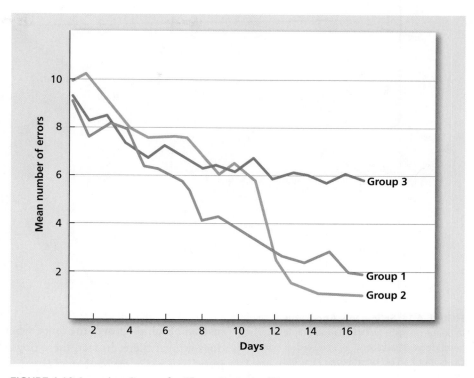

FIGURE 4.10 Learning Curves for Three Groups of Rats
In the results of the classic study of latent learning, Group 1 was rewarded on each day, while Group 2 was rewarded for the first time on Day 11. Group 3 was never rewarded. Note the immediate change in the behavior of Group 2 on Day 12 (Tolman & Honzik, 1930).

insight the sudden perception of relationships among various parts of a problem, allowing the solution to the problem to come quickly.

Another of Köhler's chimpanzees, Grande, has just solved the problem of how to get to the banana by stacking boxes. Does this meet the criteria for insight, or was it simple trial-and-error learning?

Speaker

Dog

Speaker

Hurdle

Shock grid floor

FIGURE 4.11 Seligman's Apparatus
In Seligman's studies of learned helplessness, dogs were placed in a two-sided box. Dogs that had no prior experience with being unable to escape a shock would quickly jump over the hurdle in the center of the box to land on the "safe" side. Dogs that had previously learned that escape was impossible would stay on the side of the box in which the shock occurred, not even trying to go over the hurdle.

I know some people who seem to act just like those dogs—they live in a horrible situation but won't leave. Is this the same thing?

1967; Seligman & Maier, 1967). (See Figure 4.11.) The dogs in this group were harnessed so that they could not escape the shock. The researchers assumed that the dogs would learn to fear the sound of the tone and later try to escape from the tone before being shocked.

These dogs, along with another group of dogs that had not been conditioned to fear the tone, were placed into a special box consisting of a low fence that divided the box into two compartments. The dogs, which were now unharnessed, could easily see over the fence and jump over if they wished—which is precisely what the dogs that had not been conditioned did as soon as the shock occurred. Imagine the researchers' surprise when, instead of jumping over the fence when the tone sounded, the previously conditioned dogs just sat there. In fact, these dogs showed distress but didn't try to jump over the fence *even when the shock itself began.*

Why would the conditioned dogs refuse to move when shocked? The dogs that had been harnessed while being conditioned had apparently learned in the original tone/ shock situation that there was nothing they could do to escape the shock. So when placed in a situation in which escape was possible, the dogs still did nothing because they had learned to be "helpless." They believed they could not escape, so they did not try.

More recently, Seligman's colleague and co-researcher in those early studies, Steven F. Maier, has revisited the phenomenon of learned helplessness from a neuroscientific approach, and this work has provided some new insights. Maier and others have focused on an area of the brain stem that releases serotonin and can play a role in activating the amygdala (which plays an important role in fear and anxiety) but also participates in decreasing activity in brain areas responsible for the "fight-or-flight" response. (L I N K) to Chapter Two: The Biological Perspective, p. 55. This combination of increased fear/anxiety with non-escape or freezing is the very behavior associated with learned helplessness. This part of the brain stem (the dorsal raphe nucleus) is a much older part of the brain and not able to determine what type of stressors are controllable. Their research suggests that a higher-level area, a part of the frontal lobe called the *ventromedial prefrontal cortex* (vmPFC), is able to help determine what is controllable. In turn, the vmPFC inhibits the brain stem area and calms the amygdala's response, allowing an animal to effectively respond to a stressor and exhibit control (Amat et al., 2005; Maier et al., 2006; Maier & Watkins, 2005). In other words, it is possible that the dogs in the early studies, rather than learning to be helpless were *not* learning how to relax and take control of the situation. Maier and colleagues suggest that both training and input from the vmPFC are necessary for animals to learn how to take control (Maier et al., 2006).

● I know some people who seem to act just like those dogs—they live in a horrible situation but won't leave. Is this the same thing?

Seligman extended this theory of **learned helplessness**, the tendency to fail to act to escape from a situation because of a history of repeated failures in the past, to explain *depression.* Depressed people seem to lack normal emotions and become somewhat apathetic, often staying in unpleasant work environments or bad marriages or relationships rather than trying to escape or better their situation. Seligman proposed that this depressive behavior is a form of learned helplessness. Depressed people may have learned in the past that they seem to have no control over what happens to them (Alloy & Clements, 1998). A sense of powerlessness and hopelessness is common to depressed people, and certainly this would seem to apply to Seligman's dogs as well.

Think about how this might apply to other situations. There are many students who feel that they are bad at math because they have had problems with it in the past. Is it possible that this belief could make them not try as hard or study as much as they should? Isn't this kind of thinking also an example of learned helplessness?

Cognitive learning is also an important part of a fairly well-known form of learning, often simplified as "monkey see, monkey do." Let's take a look at learning through watching the actions of others.

Observational Learning

4.12 What occurs in observational learning, including findings from Bandura's classic Bobo doll study and the four elements of observational learning?

Observational learning is the learning of new behavior through watching the actions of a model (someone else who is doing that behavior). Sometimes that behavior is desirable, and sometimes it is not, as the next section describes.

Bandura and the Bobo Doll

Bandura's classic study in observational learning involved having a preschool child in a room in which the experimenter and a model interacted with toys in the room in front of the child (Bandura et al., 1961). In one condition, the model interacted with the toys in a nonaggressive manner, completely ignoring the presence of a "Bobo" doll (a punch-bag doll in the shape of a clown). In another condition, the model became very aggressive with the doll, kicking it and yelling at it, throwing it in the air and hitting it with a hammer. 👁—Watch on **MyPsychLab**

When each child was left alone in the room and had the opportunity to play with the toys, a camera filming through a one-way mirror caught the children who were exposed to the aggressive model beating up on the Bobo doll in exact imitation of the model (See Figure 4.12). The children who saw the model ignore the doll did not act aggressively toward the toy. Obviously, the aggressive children had learned their aggressive actions from merely watching the model—with no reinforcement necessary. The fact that learning can take place without actual performance (a kind of latent learning) is called the **learning/performance distinction**.

learned helplessness the tendency to fail to act to escape from a situation because of a history of repeated failures in the past.

observational learning learning new behavior by watching a model perform that behavior.

learning/performance distinction referring to the observation that learning can take place without actual performance of the learned behavior.

👁—Watch footage from Bandura's Bobo doll experiment on **MyPsychLab**

FIGURE 4.12 Bandura's Bobo Doll Experiment
In Albert Bandura's famous Bobo doll experiment, the doll was used to demonstrate the impact of observing an adult model performing aggressive behavior on the later aggressive behavior of children. The children in these photos are imitating the adult model's behavior even though they believe they are alone and are not being watched.

Ah, but would that child have imitated the model if the model had been punished? Wouldn't the <u>consequences</u> of the model's behavior make a difference?

● Ah, but would that child have imitated the model if the model had been punished? Wouldn't the *consequences* of the model's behavior make a difference?

In later studies, Bandura showed a film of a model beating up the Bobo doll. In one condition, the children saw the model rewarded afterward. In another, the model was punished. When placed in the room with toys, the children in the first group beat up the doll, but the children in the second group did not. But when Bandura told the children in the second group that he would give them a reward if they could show him what the model in the film did, each child duplicated the model's actions. Both groups had learned from watching the model, but only the children watching the successful (rewarded) model imitated the aggression with no prompting (Bandura, 1965). Apparently, consequences do matter in motivating a child (or an adult) to imitate a particular model. The tendency for some movies and television programs to make "heroes" out of violent, aggressive "bad guys" is particularly disturbing in light of these findings. In fact, Bandura began this research to investigate possible links between children's exposure to violence on television and aggressive behavior toward others.

In a recent nationwide study of youth in the United States, it was found that young people ages 8 to 18 spend on average almost 7.5 hours per day involved in media consumption (television, computers, video games, music, cell phones, print, and movies), 7 days a week. Furthermore, given the prevalence of media multitasking (using more than one media device at a time), they are packing in approximately 10 hours and 45 minutes of media during those 7.5 hours! (Rideout et al., 2010). While not all media consumption is of violent media, it is quite easy to imagine that some of that media is of a violent nature.

Correlational research stretching over nearly two decades suggests that a link exists between viewing violent television and an increased level of aggression in children (Bushman & Huesmann, 2001; Engelhardt et al., in press; Huesmann & Eron, 1986; Sacks et al., 2011). ⓛⓘⓝⓚ to Chapter One: The Science of Psychology, pp. 23–25. While correlations do not prove that viewing violence on TV is the *cause* of increased violence, one cannot help but be curious as to the effects, especially given the continuing rise of media consumption in young people, coupled with the multiple ways young people interact with media. As such, there has been an ongoing debate as to the validity of the links between aggression and exposure to media violence (primarily focusing on television, movies, video games, and music). Although still a topic of debate for some (Ferguson, 2010), there appears to be a strong body of evidence that exposure to media violence does have immediate and long-term effects, increasing the likelihood of aggressive verbal and physical behavior and aggressive thoughts and emotions—and the effects appear to impact children, adolescents, and adults (Anderson et al., 2003). ✳[Explore on **MyPsychLab**

✳[Explore Bandura's study on observational learning on **MyPsychLab**

The Four Elements of Observational Learning

Bandura (1986) concluded, from these studies and others, that observational learning required the presence of four elements.

ATTENTION   To learn anything through observation, the learner must first pay *attention* to the model. For example, a person at a fancy dinner party who wants to know which utensil to use has to watch the person who seems to know what is correct. Certain characteristics of models can make attention more likely. For example, people pay more attention to those people they perceive as similar to them and to people whom they perceive as attractive.

MEMORY   The learner must also be able to retain the *memory* of what was done, such as remembering the steps in preparing a dish that was first seen on a cooking show.

IMITATION   The learner must be capable of reproducing, or *imitating*, the actions of the model. A 2-year-old might be able to watch someone tie shoelaces and might even remember most of the steps, but the 2-year-old's chubby little fingers will not have the dexterity* necessary for actually tying the laces. A person with extremely weak ankles might be able to watch and remember how some ballet move was accomplished but will not be able to reproduce it. The mirror neurons discussed in Chapter Two may be willing, but the flesh is weak. LINK to Chapter Two: The Biological Perspective, p. 70.

MOTIVATION   Finally, the learner must have the desire or *motivation* to perform the action. That person at the fancy dinner, for example, might not care which fork or which knife is the "proper" one to use. Also, if a person expects a reward because one has been given in the past, or has been promised a future reward (like the children in the second group of Bandura's study), or has witnessed a model getting a reward (like the children in the first group), that person will be much more likely to imitate the observed behavior. Successful models are powerful figures for imitation, but rarely would we be motivated to imitate someone who fails or is punished.

(An easy way to remember the four elements of modeling is to remember the letters AMIM, which stand for the first letters of each of the four elements. This is a good example of using a strategy to improve memory. LINK to Introduction, pp. PIA-14–PIA-16).

---

*Dexterity: skill and ease in using the hands.

practice quiz   How much do you remember?

4.11   4.12

Pick the best answer.

1. Cognition refers to _____.
   a. behavior that is observable and external.
   b. behavior that is directly measurable.
   c. the mental events that take place while a person is behaving.
   d. memories.

2. In Tolman's maze study, the fact that the group of rats receiving reinforcement only after the tenth day of the study solved the maze far more quickly than did the rats who had been reinforced from the first day can be interpreted to mean that these particular rats _____.
   a. were much smarter than the other rats.
   b. had already learned the maze in the first nine days.
   c. had the opportunity to cheat by watching the other rats.
   d. were very hungry and, therefore, learned much more quickly.

3. Seligman found many similarities between his "helpless" dogs and people suffering from _____.
   a. aggressive behavior syndrome.   c. schizophrenia.
   b. mental illness.   d. depression.

4. Köhler determined that Sultan's two-stick solution to the banana problem was an example of insight because it was _____.
   a. the result of trial-and-error learning.
   b. sudden and rapid.
   c. arrived at after a long time period.
   d. intelligent.

5. In Bandura's study with the Bobo doll, the children in the group that saw the model punished did not imitate the model at first. They would only imitate the model if given a reward for doing so. The fact that these children had obviously learned the behavior without actually performing it is an example of _____.
   a. latent learning.
   b. operant conditioning.
   c. classical conditioning.
   d. insight learning.

6. Miranda wanted to make a casserole she saw on a food show on TV. She bought the ingredients, put them together, baked it, and served it at dinner that night. To her horror, it tasted awful. She realized that she had left out a key ingredient and vowed next time to write everything down as she watched the show. Miranda's dinner disaster was an example of failing at which of Bandura's four elements of observational learning?
   a. attention
   b. memory
   c. imitation
   d. motivation

Brainstorming: Do you think that watching violence on television increases violence and aggression in viewers? Why or why not?

ANSWERS ON PAGE AK–1

applying psychology to everyday life

....

Can You Really Toilet Train Your Cat?

4.13 What is a real-world example of the use of conditioning?

(This article has been excerpted with permission of the author and cat-trainer extraordinaire, Karawynn Long. Karawynn Long is a published writer and Web designer who lives in Seattle with her family. Sadly, since this article was written, her cat, Misha has passed away. Ms. Long can be reached at her Web site **www.karawynn.net/mishacat/toilet.html**. The italicized words in brackets are the author's "editorial" comments.)

There have been more books and articles about toilet-training cats than you'd think. In the summer of 1989, when Misha was a small kitten with big ears and enough meow for five cats, I searched out and read a half-dozen of them. And then tried it myself, and discovered there were a couple of things they all failed to mention . . . here's what worked for me and Misha.

The central idea is that the transition from litter box to toilet should be accomplished in a series of stages. [*This is shaping.*] You make a small change and then give your cat time to adjust before you make another small change. If at any time Felix gives the whole thing up and goes on the rug instead, you're pushing him too far too fast; back up a stage or two and try again, more slowly.

Ready? First start by training yourself. . .

The very most important thing to remember is: Lid Up, Seat Down. Post a note on the back of the door or the lid of the toilet if you think you (or your housemates or guests) might forget. And if you are accustomed to closing the bathroom door when it's empty, you'll have to break that habit too. [*In operant conditioning, this is part of "preparing the training arena."*]

Begin by moving the cat's current litter box from wherever it is to one side of the toilet. Make sure he knows where it is and uses it. Rest (this means doing nothing for a period of between a day and a week, depending on how flappable your cat is). Next put something— a stack of newspapers, a phone book, a cardboard box—under the litter box to raise it, say, about an inch. (Magazines are too slick; you don't want the litter box sliding around and making your cat feel insecure. Tape the litter box down if you need to.) Rest. Get another box or phone book and raise it a little higher. Rest. Continue this process until the bottom of the litter box is level with the top of the toilet seat. (For Misha I raised it about two inches per day.) [*Notice that this is the step-by-step process typically used in shaping.*]

At the beginning of this process, your cat could just step into the litter box; later he began jumping up into it, until at some point he probably started jumping up onto the toilet seat first and stepping into the box from there. Lift the seat on your toilet and measure the inside diameter of the top of the bowl at its widest point. Venture forth and buy a metal mixing bowl of that diameter. Do not (I discovered this the hard way) substitute a plastic bowl. A plastic bowl will not support the cat's weight and will bend, dropping into the toilet bowl and spilling litter everywhere, not to mention startling the cat.

Now you move the litter box over so that it's sitting directly over the toilet seat. (If your cat has shown reluctance over previous changes, you might want to split this into two stages, moving it halfway onto the seat and then fully over.) Take away the stack of phone books or whatever you used. Rest. [*Again, notice that everything has to be done in small steps. This is the heart of the shaping process—requiring too large a step will stop the process.*]

Misha's first attempt without the box. He scored two out of a possible four.

Here's the cool part. Take away the litter box entirely. (Ta da!) Nestle the metal mixing bowl inside the toilet bowl and lower the seat. Fill the bowl with about two inches of litter (all of this is much easier if you have the tiny granules of litter that can be scooped out and flushed).

Naturally, any humans using the toilet at this point will want to remove the metal bowl prior to their own use and replace it afterward. The next week or two the whole process is likely to be something of an annoyance; if you begin to think it's not worth it, just remember that you will never have to clean a litter box again.

Watch your cat using the bathroom in the metal bowl. Count the number of feet he gets up on the toilet seat (as opposed to down in the bowl of litter). The higher the number, the luckier you are and the easier your job is going to be...

...because next you have to teach him proper squatting posture. Catch him beginning to use the toilet as much of the time as possible and show him where his feet are supposed to go. Just lift them right out of the bowl and place them on the seat (front legs in the middle, hind legs on the outside). If he starts out with three or, heaven forbid, all four feet in the bowl, just get the front two feet out first. Praise him all over the place every time he completes the activity in this position. [*The praise is the positive reinforcement and should be done with each successful step.*]

(Misha is very doglike in that he craves approval and praise. If your cat is indifferent to this sort of thing, you can also reward him with small food treats and wean him from them later when the toilet behavior has "set." Just keep the treats as small and infrequent as possible—half a Pounce™ or similar treat per occasion should be plenty.) [*If treats are too frequent, it will make it difficult to phase out the reinforcer after the behavior is well learned.*]

When he is regularly using the toilet with his front feet out (and some cats naturally start from this position), begin lifting a hind foot out and placing it on the seat outside the front paws. Your cat will probably find this awkward at first and try to replace the foot in the litter. Be persistent. Move that foot four times in a row if you have to, until it stays there. Praise and/or treat.

Repeat with the other hind foot, until your cat learns to balance in that squat. Once he's getting all four feet regularly on the seat, it's all easy from here.

Which is fortunate, because the last bit is also the most unpleasant. I suggest that you postpone this stage until you have at least a weekend, and preferably several days, when you (or another responsible party) will be at home most of the time. I skipped through this part in about two days; I only hope that your cat allows you to move along that fast.

Begin reducing the litter in the bowl. Go as fast as he'll feel comfortable with, because as the litter decreases, the odor increases. You'll want to be home at this point so that you can praise him and dump out the contents of the bowl immediately after he's finished, to minimize both the smell and the possibility that your cat, in a confused attempt to minimize the smell on his own, tries to cover it up with litter that no longer exists and ends up tracking unpleasantness into the rest of the house.

By the time you're down to a token teaspoonful of litter in the bottom of the bowl, your next-door neighbors will probably be aware of the precise instant your cat has used the toilet. This is as bad as it gets. The next time you rinse out the metal bowl, put a little bit of water in the bottom. Increase the water level each time, just as you decreased the litter level. Remember—if at any point Felix looks nervous enough about the change to give the whole thing up and take his business to the corner behind the door, back up a step or two and try the thing again more slowly. [*Shaping takes a lot of patience, depending on the behavior being shaped and the learning ability of the animal—or person.*]

Once the water in the mixing bowl is a couple of inches deep and your cat is comfortable with the whole thing, you get to perform the last bit of magic. Take the mixing bowl away, leaving the bare toilet. (Lid Up, Seat Down.)

Misha demonstrates proper squatting posture. Note the look of firm concentration.

Voila! Your cat is now toilet trained.

Some useful books on using operant conditioning to toilet train cats:

> Brotman, E. (2001). *How to Toilet Train Your Cat: The Education of Mango.* Sherman Oaks, CA: Bird Brain Press.
>
> DeCarlo, P. (2008). *Kick Litter: Nine-Step Program for Recovering Litter Addicts.* Coeur d'Alene, ID: CDA Press.
>
> Kunkel, P. & Mead K. P. (1991). *How to Toilet Train Your Cat: 21 Days to a Litter-Free Home.* New York: Workman Publishing Company.

QUESTIONS **FOR FURTHER DISCUSSION**

1. Why would this technique probably not work with a dog?
2. Are there any safety concerns with teaching a cat in this way?
3. Are there any other difficulties that might arise when doing this training?

chapter summary

((•⌐Listen on MyPsychLab   Listen to an audio file of your chapter **www.MyPsychLab**

Definition of Learning

4.1 What does the term *learning* really mean?

- Learning is any relatively permanent change in behavior brought about by experience or practice and is different from maturation that is genetically controlled.

It Makes Your Mouth Water: Classical Conditioning

4.2 How was classical conditioning first studied, and what are the important elements and characteristics of classical conditioning?

- Pavlov accidentally discovered the phenomenon in which one stimulus can, through pairing with another stimulus, come to produce a similar response. He called this classical conditioning.
- The unconditioned stimulus (UCS) is the stimulus that is naturally occurring and produces the reflex, or involuntary unconditioned response (UCR). Both are called "unconditioned" because they are not learned.
- The conditioned stimulus (CS) begins as a neutral stimulus but when paired with the unconditioned stimulus eventually begins to elicit the reflex on its own. The reflex response to the conditioned stimulus is called the conditioned response (CR), and both stimulus and response are learned.
- Pavlov paired a sound with the presentation of food to dogs and discovered several principles for classical conditioning: The neutral stimulus (NS) and UCS must be paired several times and the CS must precede the UCS by only a few seconds.
- Other important aspects of classical conditioning include stimulus generalization, stimulus discrimination, extinction, spontaneous recovery, and higher-order conditioning.

4.3 What is a conditioned emotional response, and how do cognitive psychologists explain classical conditioning?

- Watson was able to demonstrate that an emotional disorder called a phobia could be learned through classical conditioning by exposing a baby to a white rat and a loud noise, producing conditioned fear of the rat in the baby.

- Conditioned taste aversions occur when an organism becomes nauseated some time after eating a certain food, which then becomes aversive to the organism.
- Some kinds of conditioned responses are more easily learned than others because of biological preparedness.
- Pavlov believed that the NS became a substitute for the UCS through association in time.
- The cognitive perspective asserts that the CS has to provide some kind of information or expectancy about the coming of the UCS in order for conditioning to occur.

What's in It for Me? Operant Conditioning

4.4 How does operant conditioning occur, and what were the contributions of Thorndike and Skinner?

- Thorndike developed the law of effect: A response followed by a pleasurable consequence will be repeated, but a response followed by an unpleasant consequence will not be repeated.
- B. F. Skinner named the learning of voluntary responses operant conditioning because voluntary responses are what we use to operate in the world around us.

4.5 What are the important concepts in operant conditioning?

- Skinner developed the concept of reinforcement, the process of strengthening a response by following it with a pleasurable, rewarding consequence.
- A primary reinforcer is something such as food or water that satisfies a basic, natural drive, whereas a secondary reinforcer is something that becomes reinforcing only after being paired with a primary reinforcer.
- In positive reinforcement, a response is followed by the presentation of a pleasurable stimulus, whereas in negative reinforcement, a response is followed by the removal or avoidance of an unpleasant stimulus.
- Shaping is the reinforcement of successive approximations to some final goal, allowing behavior to be molded from simple behavior already present in the organism.

- Extinction, generalization and discrimination, and spontaneous recovery also occur in operant conditioning.

4.6 What are the schedules of reinforcement?

- Continuous reinforcement occurs when each and every correct response is followed by a reinforcer.
- Partial reinforcement, in which only some correct responses are followed by reinforcement, is much more resistant to extinction. This is called the partial reinforcement effect.
- In a fixed ratio schedule of reinforcement, a certain number of responses are required before reinforcement is given.
- In a variable ratio schedule of reinforcement, a varying number of responses are required to obtain reinforcement.
- In a fixed interval schedule of reinforcement, at least one correct response must be made within a set interval of time to obtain reinforcement.
- In a variable interval schedule of reinforcement, reinforcement follows the first correct response made after an interval of time that changes for each reinforcement opportunity.

4.7 How does punishment differ from reinforcement?

- Punishment is any event or stimulus that, when following a response, makes that response less likely to happen again.
- In punishment by application, a response is followed by the application or experiencing of an unpleasant stimulus, such as a spanking.
- In punishment by removal, a response is followed by the removal of some pleasurable stimulus, such as taking away a child's toy for misbehavior.

4.8 What are some of the problems with using punishment?

- A person who uses aggressive punishment, such as spanking, can act as a model for aggressive behavior. This will increase aggressive behavior in the one being punished, which is an undesirable response.
- Punishment of both kinds normally has only a temporary effect on behavior.
- Punishment can be made more effective by making it immediate and consistent and by pairing punishment of the undesirable behavior with reinforcement of the desirable one.

issues in psychology: The Link between Spanking and Aggression in Young Children

A recent study has found that children who were spanked at age 3 are more likely to be aggressive at age 5 than children who were not spanked.

4.9 How do operant stimuli control behavior, and what kind of behavior is resistant to operant conditioning?

- Discriminative stimuli are cues, such as a flashing light on a police car or a sign on a door that says "Open," that provide information about what response to make in order to obtain reinforcement.
- Shaping, extinction, generalization and discrimination, and spontaneous recovery are other concepts in operant conditioning.

classic studies in psychology: Biological Constraints on Operant Conditioning

- Instinctive behavior in animals is resistant to conditioning or modification. Although an animal may change its behavior at first through conditioning, the behavior will revert to the instinctual pattern in a process called instinctive drift.

4.10 What is behavior modification, and how can behavioral techniques be used to modify involuntary biological responses?

- Operant conditioning can be used in many settings on both animals and people to change, or modify, behavior. This use is termed *behavior modification* and includes the use of reinforcement and shaping to alter behavior.
- Token economies are a type of behavior modification in which secondary reinforcers, or tokens, are used.
- Applied behavior analysis (ABA) is the modern version of behavior modification and makes use of functional analysis and behavioral techniques to change human behavior.
- Neurofeedback is a type of biofeedback in which the person is typically connected to an electroencephalograph, a machine that records the brain's electrical activity.

Cognitive Learning Theory

4.11 How do latent learning, learned helplessness, and insight relate to cognitive learning theory?

- Cognitive learning theory states that learning requires cognition, or the influence of an organism's thought processes.
- Tolman found that rats that were allowed to wander in a maze but were not reinforced still showed evidence of having learned the maze once reinforcement became possible. He termed this hidden learning *latent learning*, a form of cognitive learning.
- Seligman found that dogs that had been placed in an inescapable situation failed to try to escape when it became possible to do so, remaining in the painful situation as if helpless to leave. Seligman called this phenomenon learned helplessness and found parallels between learned helplessness and depression.
- Köhler found evidence of insight, the sudden perception of the relationships among elements of a problem, in chimpanzees.

Observational Learning

4.12 What occurs in observational learning, including findings from Bandura's classic Bobo doll study and the four elements of observational learning?

- Observational learning is learning through watching others perform, or model, certain actions.
- Bandura's famous Bobo doll experiment demonstrated that young children will imitate the aggressive actions of a model even when there is no reinforcement for doing so.
- Bandura determined that four elements needed to be present for observational learning to occur: attention, memory, imitation, and motivation.

applying psychology to everyday life: Can You Really Toilet Train Your Cat?

4.13 What is a real-world example of the use of conditioning?

- Writer Karawynn Long used shaping, reinforcement, and classical conditioning to train her cat to use the toilet in her bathroom instead of a litter box.

TEST yourself

✓●─ **Study** and **Review** on **MyPsychLab**   Ready for your test? More quizzes and a customized plan. www.MyPsychLab

Pick the best answer.

1. Learning is _____.
   a. any temporary change in behavior.
   b. a change in behavior due to maturation.
   c. any relatively permanent change in behavior brought about by experience.
   d. any permanent change in behavior due to maturation.

2. In your college dorm, any time you take a shower, someone always flushes the toilet and causes the water in your shower to turn icy cold, making you cringe. After several episodes like this, you find that you tend to cringe whenever you hear a toilet flush, no matter where you are. In this example, what is the conditioned stimulus?
   a. the cold water
   b. the sound of the flushing
   c. the cringing reaction
   d. the sight of a toilet

3. A child has been classically conditioned to fear a white rat. If the child also shows fear when shown a white rabbit, this is called _____.
   a. stimulus generalization.
   b. stimulus discrimination.
   c. spontaneous recovery.
   d. extinction.

4. You move out of your dorm into an apartment shared with three other people. Unlike the shower in the dorm, this shower does not turn cold when the toilet is flushed, and you eventually stop cringing every time you hear the flushing sound. What has occurred?
   a. stimulus generalization
   b. stimulus discrimination
   c. spontaneous recovery
   d. extinction

5. When one conditioned stimulus is used to create another, this is called _____.
   a. spontaneous recovery.
   b. extinction.
   c. higher-order conditioning.
   d. shaping.

6. Tenia ate out with some friends and had fried oysters. The next morning she was nauseated and sick for much of the day. The next time she saw someone eating fried oysters, she felt queasy and quickly looked away. Her queasiness at the sight of the fried oysters was probably due to _____.
   a. higher-order conditioning.
   b. a conditioned taste aversion.
   c. stimulus substitution.
   d. stimulus generalization.

7. The fact that some kinds of stimuli (like a taste) are more easily and quickly connected to a response (like nausea) is explained by the concept of _____.
   a. biological preparedness.
   b. psychological preparedness.

   c. instinctive drift.
   d. stimulus substitution.

8. The key to the cognitive perspective of classical conditioning is that the presentation of the conditioned stimulus must _____.
   a. provide information about the coming of the unconditioned response.
   b. provide information about the coming of the unconditioned stimulus.
   c. provide information about the coming of the conditioned response.
   d. act as a substitute for the unconditioned stimulus.

9. In classical conditioning, the _____ are important in learning, but in operant conditioning, it is the _____ that determine whether learning will occur.
   a. antecedents; consequences
   b. consequences; antecedents
   c. rewards; punishments
   d. punishments; rewards

10. Who added the concept of reinforcement to learning theory?
    a. Watson
    b. Thorndike
    c. Skinner
    d. Pavlov

11. Which of the following is an example of a secondary reinforcer?
    a. a candy bar
    b. a glass of water
    c. petting a dog
    d. praising a child

12. Joaquin's parents have given his 2-year-old daughter, Marie, a very noisy jack-in-the-box toy for her birthday. Marie loves to turn the crank and make the puppet pop up, over and over and over. Desperate to have some peace and quiet, Joaquin gives Marie a popsicle, which distracts her and produces the quiet he was craving. But when the popsicle is finished, Marie goes back to the toy, cranking and cranking. Joaquin tries another popsicle. What kind of reinforcement process is taking place in this situation?
    a. Marie is being positively reinforced for playing with the toy by receiving the treat.
    b. Joaquin is being positively reinforced for giving her the treat by the quiet that follows.
    c. Joaquin is being negatively reinforced for giving her the treat by the absence of the noise.
    d. Both a and c are correct.

13. Sherry wants her dog to "heel" on command. At first she gives the dog a treat for coming to her when she speaks the command, "Heel!" Then she only rewards the dog when it stands at her side when she gives the command and, finally, she rewards the dog only when it is at her side and facing front. Sherry is using _____.
    a. higher-order conditioning.
    b. biological readiness.
    c. shaping.
    d. generalization.

14. One-year-old Ben learned to say the word *duck* when his mother showed him a duck in their backyard. That evening he sees a cartoon with a rooster in it and says "duck," pointing to the rooster. Ben is exhibiting _____.
    a. generalization.
    b. discrimination.
    c. spontaneous recovery.
    d. shaping.

15. For every 10 boxes of cookies that Lisa sells, her scout troop gets a dollar. Lisa is being reinforced on which type of schedule?
    a. fixed ratio
    b. fixed interval
    c. variable ratio
    d. variable interval

16. Dennis buys a lottery ticket every Saturday, using the same set of numbers. Although he has only won $25 on one occasion, he keeps buying the tickets. In fact, he's a little afraid that if he doesn't buy a ticket, that would be the one that would win really big. The fact that Dennis seems addicted to buying lottery tickets is a common characteristic of which schedule of reinforcement?
    a. fixed ratio
    b. fixed interval
    c. variable ratio
    d. variable interval

17. Sandy had learned that if her mother was smiling at her when she came into the kitchen, it meant that Sandy would probably be given a treat to eat if she asked nicely. But if her mother was frowning, she would not give Sandy anything and instead would shoo her away. Sandy's mother's facial expression was serving as a _____.
    a. conditioned stimulus.
    b. discriminative stimulus.
    c. positive reinforcer.
    d. negative reinforcer.

18. Liz failed her math test, so her parents told her that she could not play video games for a month. Her parents are using _____.
    a. positive reinforcement.
    b. negative reinforcement.
    c. punishment by removal.
    d. punishment by application.

19. To make punishment more effective, it should be _____.
    a. very intense.
    b. applied every other time the bad behavior occurs.
    c. an aggressive type, such as spanking.
    d. paired with reinforcement of the correct behavior.

20. In applied behavior analysis, _____.
    a. skills are broken down into their smallest steps and then reinforced.
    b. punishment by application is often used to control behavior.
    c. researchers develop new theories of learning rather than actually solving problems.
    d. the basic form of learning used is classical conditioning.

21. Jody has had repeated failures at asking guys out on dates. Finally, she gives up. One day at the office a really nice guy seems interested in her, but she refuses to even approach him. What concept might explain her reluctance?
    a. latent learning
    b. learned helplessness
    c. insight learning
    d. observational learning

22. Jared's father is ill and cannot prepare his famous chili recipe, which Jared has watched his father make many times. When his father tells Jared that he must cook the chili, he panics at first. But then Jared finds that he knows how to put the recipe together anyway. His ability to prepare the recipe is an example of _____.
    a. latent learning.
    b. learned helplessness.
    c. insight learning.
    d. discovery learning.

23. Archimedes was told by the king to find a way to prove that a gold crown was really gold. While in his bath, he noticed the water that his body displaced out of the tub and shouted, "Eureka!" which means "I have found it!" If the crown was really gold, it should displace the same amount of water as an equal amount of real gold. This is a famous example of _____.
    a. latent learning.
    b. learned helplessness.
    c. insight.
    d. observational learning.

24. Jared realized that he had learned how to prepare his father's famous chili recipe by watching his father in the kitchen for many years. This kind of learning is called _____.
    a. discovery learning.
    b. helplessness learning.
    c. insight learning.
    d. observational learning.

25. Barry would really like to learn to do ballroom dancing, but he has a severe limp in his left leg. Although he watches ballroom dancing on television and can remember all the moves and dips, he will be very unlikely to be able to learn to dance this way because he is missing a key element of observational learning. What is it?
    a. attention
    b. memory
    c. imitation
    d. motivation

4 learning

4.1 p. 122

Definition of Learning

(any relatively permanent change in behavior brought about by experience or practice)

- "relatively permanent" aspect of learning refers to learning being associated with physical changes in the brain

- although physical changes may be present we may not always be able to "get" to the information

4.2 p. 122

- **discovered by Ivan Pavlov** worked with salivating dogs — focused on observable, measurable behavior

- **several key elements must be present and experienced**
  - unconditioned stimulus (UCS)
  - unconditioned response (UCR)
  - conditioned stimulus (CS)
  - conditioned response (CR)

Classical Conditioning

(learning to make an involuntary response to a stimulus other than the original, natural stimulus that normally produces it)

Before Conditioning
Neutral Stimulus (NS) Metronome → No Salivation

During Conditioning
Neutral Stimulus (NS) Metronome → Unconditioned Stimulus (UCS) Food → Unconditioned Response (UCR) Salivation

After Conditioning
Conditioned Stimulus (CS) Metronome → Conditioned Response (CR) Salivation

- **basic principles for classical conditioning to occur**
  - CS must come before the UCS
  - CS and UCS must come very close together in time (< 5 sec)
  - CS must be paired with the UCS many times
  - CS must be distinct from other competing stimuli

- **key features**
  - stimulus generalization
  - stimulus discrimination
  - extinction
  - spontaneous recovery
  - higher-order conditioning

4.3 p. 128

- conditioned emotional responses
- conditioned taste aversion
- vicarious conditioning
- **other features**

Classical Conditioning (continued)

(learning to make an involuntary response to a stimulus other than the original, natural stimulus that normally produces it)

- **Why does it work?**
  - **Pavlov** - stimulus substitution
  - **cognitive perspective**

4.4 4.5 p. 131

- **Thorndike** was among the first to study learning of voluntary responses — developed law of effect

- **Skinner** led field of behaviorism after Watson — coined term *operant conditioning*

"Remember, every time he gives you a pellet, reinforce that behavior by pulling the lever."

Operant Conditioning

(learning to make voluntary responses through the effects of positive or negative consequences)

- **reinforcement** any event or stimulus, that when following a response increases the probability that the response will occur again
  - primary reinforcers
  - secondary reinforcers
  - positive reinforcement
  - negative reinforcement

4.6 **4.7** **4.8** **4.9** **4.10** p. 134

Operant Conditioning (continued)

(learning to make voluntary responses through the effects of positive or negative consequences)

punishment is any event or stimulus that, when following a response, decreases the probability that the response will occur again

● schedules of reinforcement
- timing of reinforcement
- continuous reinforcement
- partial reinforcement

● other features
- discriminative stimuli
- shaping
- extinction, generalization, spontaneous recovery
- instinctive drift

● behavior modification

table 4.2 **Four Ways to Modify Behavior**

	REINFORCEMENT	PUNISHMENT
Positive (Adding)	Something valued or desirable	Something unpleasant
	Positive Reinforcement	*Punishment by Application*
	Example: getting a gold star for good behavior in school	Example: getting a spanking for disobeying
Negative (Removing/Avoiding)	Something unpleasant	Something valued or desirable
	Negative Reinforcement	*Punishment by Removal*
	Example: avoiding a ticket by stopping at a red light	Example: losing a privilege such as going out with friends

4.11 p. 147

Cognitive Learning Theory

(focuses on role of cognition, or thought processes, on learning)

● **Tolman**
worked with rats in a maze

● **Köhler**
worked with chimpanzees; set up a problem situation

● **Seligman**
originally studied escape and avoidance learning in dogs

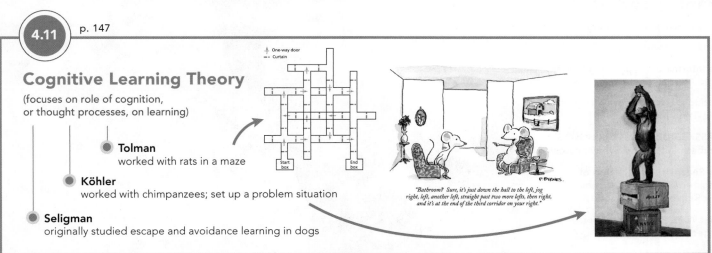

"Bathroom? Sure, it's just down the hall to the left, jog right, left, another left, straight past two more lefts, then right, and it's at the end of the third corridor on your right."

4.12 p. 151

Observational Learning

(the learning of a new behavior through the observation of a model; typically associated with classic work of Bandura and "Bobo doll" study)

● **children observing**
an adult model's aggressive or nonaggressive behaviors tended to later act in the same manner they saw modeled; no reinforcement was necessary

● **key elements for learner**
- pay attention to the model
- able to remember what was done
- capable of reproducing, or imitating, the actions of the model
- have the desire or motivation to perform the action

later research suggested that potential consequences can influence motivation to imitate a particular model

5

memory

why study memory?

Without memory, how would we be able to learn anything? The ability to learn is the key to our very survival, and we cannot learn unless we can remember what happened the last time a particular situation arose. Why study forgetting? If we can learn about the ways in which we forget information, we can apply that learning so that forgetting occurs less frequently.

chapter outline

Three Processes of Memory

Models of Memory

The Information-Processing Model: Three Memory Systems

Getting It Out: Retrieval of Long-Term Memories

CLASSIC STUDIES IN PSYCHOLOGY: Elizabeth Loftus and Eyewitnesses

The Reconstructive Nature of Long-Term Memory Retrieval: How Reliable Are Memories?

What Were We Talking About? Forgetting

Neuroscience of Memory

APPLYING PSYCHOLOGY TO EVERYDAY LIFE: Alzheimer's Disease

Unforgettable: Brad Williams, the "Human Google"

Most of us, at some point in our busy lives, have trouble remembering things. This is especially true of the events of the past—how much do you really remember about your own childhood? What if you could remember nearly every day of your life? This rare ability is possessed by individuals with a syndrome called *hyperthymesia* (hī-pər-thī-mē-sē-uh). A person with hyperthymesia not only has an astonishing and rare ability to recall specific events from his or her personal past (called *autobiographical memory*) but also spends an unusually large amount of time thinking about that personal past (Parker et al., 2006). To date, memory researchers are studying only a few people with hyperthymesia.

Brad Williams is one of those few. Known as the "Human Google," Brad can recall almost any news event or personal event he himself has experienced, particularly specific dates—and even the weather on those dates. Brad Williams is otherwise a pretty ordinary guy, likeable and possessed of a good sense of humor. A radio broadcaster in the city of La Crosse, Wisconsin, Brad is involved in the local theater group (he never forgets his lines) and is well known to his listening audience as the man with the amazing memory. Callers try to stump him by asking him trivia questions—as long as the questions are about anything but sports, a subject Brad does not follow (Edwards & Williams, 2010).

When the neuroscientists at The Center for the Neurobiology of Learning and Memory at the University of California at Irvine began to study Brad, his brother, Eric Williams, began filming a documentary about Brad and his extraordinary abilities. Titled *Unforgettable*, the 88-minute documentary chronicles Brad's childhood through his moments of fame as a guest on talk shows as he demonstrates his amazing ability. If you'd like to know more about Brad and hyperthymesia, you can reach Eric Williams at **www.unforgettabledoc.com**.

Ironically, CBS premiered a television drama during the fall of 2011 called "*Unforgettable*," about a police detective with hyperthymesia. Neither Brad nor Eric Williams was involved in the program.

learning objectives

5.1 What are the three processes of memory and the different models of how memory works?

5.2 How does sensory memory work?

5.3 What is short-term memory, and how does it differ from working memory?

5.4 How is long-term memory different from other types of memory?

5.5 What are the various types of long-term memory, and how is information stored in long-term memory organized?

5.6 What kinds of cues help people remember?

5.7 How do the retrieval processes of recall and recognition differ, and how reliable are our memories of events?

5.8 How are long-term memories formed, and how can this process lead to inaccuracies in memory?

5.9 What is false memory syndrome?

5.10 Why do we forget?

5.11 How and where are memories formed in the brain?

5.12 How does amnesia occur?

5.13 What are the facts about Alzheimer's disease?

Brad Williams, the man with the amazing memory described in the opening pages of this chapter, is seen here with famous neuroscientist Dr. Oliver Sacks.

memory an active system that receives information from the senses, puts that information into a usable form, organizes it as it stores it away, and then retrieves the information from storage.

encoding the set of mental operations that people perform on sensory information to convert that information into a form that is usable in the brain's storage systems.

storage holding onto information for some period of time.

retrieval getting information that is in storage into a form that can be used.

information-processing model model of memory that assumes the processing of information for memory storage is similar to the way a computer processes memory in a series of three stages.

Three Processes of Memory

5.1 **What are the three processes of memory and the different models of how memory works?**

Is memory a place or a process? The answer to that question is not simple. In reading through this chapter, it becomes clear that memory is a process but that it also has a "place" in the brain. Perhaps the best definition of **memory** is an active system that receives information from the senses, puts that information into a usable form, organizes it as it stores it away, and then retrieves the information from storage (Baddeley, 1996, 2003).

Although there are several different models of how memory works, all of them involve the same three processes: getting the information into the memory system, storing it there, and getting it back out.

Putting It In: Encoding

The first stage in the memory system is to get sensory information (sight, sound, etc.) into a form that the brain can use in a process called **encoding**. Encoding is the set of mental operations that people perform on sensory information to convert that information into a form that is usable in the brain's storage systems. For example, when people hear a sound, their ears turn the vibrations in the air into neural messages from the auditory nerve (*transduction*), which makes it possible for the brain to interpret that sound. ⓛⓘⓝⓚ to Chapter Three: Sensation and Perception, p. 82. Encoding is accomplished differently in each of the three memory storage systems. In one storage system, encoding may involve rehearsing information over and over to keep it in memory, whereas in another system encoding involves elaborating on the meaning of the information—but let's elaborate on that later.

Keeping It In: Storage

The next step in memory is to hold on to the information for some period of time in a process called **storage**. This period of time will vary depending on the storage system being used. For example, in one system people hold on to information just long enough to work with it, about 20 seconds or so. In another system, people hold on to information more or less permanently.

Getting It Out: Retrieval

The biggest problem many people have is **retrieval**, getting the information they know they have out of storage. Have you ever handed in an essay test and *then* remembered several other things you could have said? Retrieval problems are discussed in a major section of this chapter.

Models of Memory

Exactly how does memory work? When the storage process occurs, where does that information go and why? Memory experts have proposed several different ways of looking at memory. The model that many researchers feel is the most comprehensive* and has perhaps been the most influential over the last several decades is the **information-processing model**. This approach focuses on the way information is handled, or processed, through three different systems of memory. The processes of encoding, storage, and retrieval are seen as part of this model.

---

*Comprehensive: all inclusive, covering everything.

While it is common to refer to the three systems of the information-processing model as *stages* of memory, that term seems to imply a sequence of events. While many aspects of memory formation may follow a series of steps or stages, there are those who see memory as a simultaneous* process, with the creation and storage of memories taking place across a series of mental networks "stretched" across the brain (McClelland & Rumelhart, 1988; Plaut & McClelland, 2010; Rumelhart et al., 1986). This simultaneous processing allows people to retrieve many different aspects of a memory all at once, facilitating much faster reactions and decisions—something Brad Williams in our opening story seems to be very good at. This model of memory, derived from work in the development of artificial intelligence (AI), is called the **parallel distributed processing (PDP) model**. In the AI world, PDP is related to *connectionism* the use of artificial neural networks to explain the mental abilities of humans (Bechtel & Abrahamsen, 2002; Clark, 1991; Marcus, 2001; Schapiro & McClelland, 2009).

The information-processing model assumes that the length of time that a memory will be remembered depends on the stage of memory in which it is stored. Other researchers have proposed that a memory's duration depends on the depth (i.e., the effort made to understand the meaning) to which the information is processed or encoded (Cermak & Craik, 1979; Craik & Lockhart, 1972). If the word *BALL* is flashed on a screen, for example, and people are asked to report whether the word was in capital letters or lowercase, the word itself does not have to be processed very much at all—only its visual characteristics need enter into conscious attention. But if those people were to be asked to use that word in a sentence, they would have to think about what a ball is and how it can be used. They would have to process its meaning, which requires more mental effort than processing just its "looks." This model of memory is called the **levels-of-processing model**. Numerous experiments have shown that thinking about the meaning of something is a deeper level of processing and results in longer retention of the word (Cermak & Craik, 1979; Craik & Tulving, 1975; Paul et al., 2005; Watson et al., 1999).

Each of these models can be used to explain some, if not all, research findings about memory. Whether one of these models will one day become the preferred model of memory has yet to be determined. In science, newer theories may often be combined, sometimes with one another and sometimes with older theories. They may be reworked into a new theory with more power to explain existing data. So although in this textbook the information-processing model of memory (see Figure 5.1) may take

*Simultaneous: all at the same time.

parallel distributed processing (PDP) model a model of memory in which memory processes are proposed to take place at the same time over a large network of neural connections.

levels-of-processing model model of memory that assumes information that is more "deeply processed," or processed according to its meaning rather than just the sound or physical characteristics of the word or words, will be remembered more efficiently and for a longer period of time.

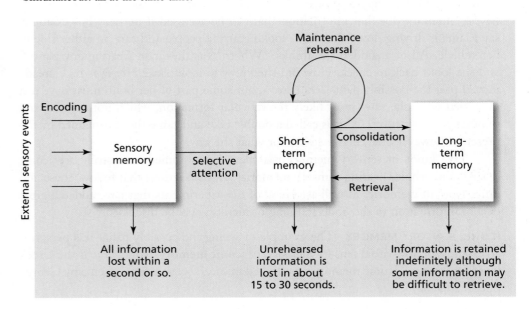

FIGURE 5.1 Three-Stage Process of Memory
Information enters through the sensory system, briefly registering in sensory memory. Selective attention moves the information into short-term memory, where it is held while attention (rehearsal) continues. If the information receives enough rehearsal, it will enter and be stored in long-term memory.

⊙➤ Simulate encoding, storage, and retrieval in memory on **MyPsychLab**

"center stage" for now, it is important to remember the concepts of the levels at which information is processed and the way in which those processes may take place while reading the rest of this chapter. ⊙➤ Simulate on **MyPsychLab**

practice quiz   How much do you remember?

5.1

Pick the best answer.

1. Eldon has just finished his essay test and handed it in. As he walks out of the classroom, he realizes that there were a few more things he should have included in the essay. Eldon's problem is in the memory process of _____.
   a. encoding.
   b. storage.
   c. retrieval.
   d. retention.

2. When Edie studies her psychology terms, she tries to tie in each concept to something she already knows. She thinks about the meaning of the concept rather than just saying the words over and over. Which model of memory would best explain Edie's approach to encoding memories?
   a. levels-of-processing model
   b. parallel distributed processing model
   c. information-processing model
   d. three-stage model

ANSWERS ON PAGE AK–1

The Information-Processing Model: Three Stages of Memory

Information-processing theory looks at how thought processes such as memory work and uses as its model for human thought the way that a computer functions (Massaro & Cowan, 1993). It was information-processing theorists who first proposed that there are three stages or types of memory systems (see Figure 5.1): sensory memory, short-term memory, and long-term memory (Atkinson & Shiffrin, 1968).

⊙➤ Simulate the information-processing model on **MyPsychLab**

⊙➤ Simulate on **MyPsychLab**

Sensory Memory: Why Do People Do Double Takes?

5.2 How does sensory memory work?

Sensory memory is the first stage of memory, the point at which information enters the nervous system through the sensory systems—eyes, ears, and so on. Information is encoded into sensory memory as neural messages in the nervous system. As long as those neural messages are traveling through the system, it can be said that people have a "memory" for that information that can be accessed if needed. For example, say Elaina is driving down the street, looking at the people and cars on either side of her vehicle. All of a sudden she thinks, "What? Was that man wearing any pants?" and she looks back to check. How did she know to look back? Her eyes had already moved past the possibly pants-less person, but some part of her brain must have just processed what she saw (most likely the reticular formation, which notices new and important information). This is called a double take and can only be explained by the presence, however brief, of a memory for what she saw.

Two kinds of sensory memory that have been studied extensively are iconic (visual) and echoic (hearing) sensory memories. In the sections that follow, these and other types of memories as well as several of the experiments that have added a great deal of information to the understanding of memory will be discussed.

ICONIC SENSORY MEMORY The example of seeing the possibly pants-less person is an example of how visual sensory memory, or **iconic memory**, works. *Icon* is the Greek word for "image." Iconic memory was studied in several classic experiments by George Sperling (1960).

sensory memory the very first stage of memory; the point at which information enters the nervous system through the sensory systems.

iconic memory visual sensory memory, lasting only a fraction of a second.

eidetic imagery the ability to access a visual memory for 30 seconds or more.

echoic memory the brief memory of something a person has just heard.

Capacity of Iconic Memory   Sperling had found in his early studies that if he presented a row of letters using a machine that allowed very fast presentation, his subjects could only remember about four or five of the letters, no matter how many had been presented.

Sperling became convinced that this method was an inaccurate measure of the capacity of iconic memory because the human tendency to read from top to bottom took long enough that the letters at the top of the grid may have faded from memory by the time the person had "read" the letters on the bottom. He developed a method called the *partial report method*, in which he showed a grid of letters similar to those in Figure 5.2, but immediately sounded a high, medium, or low tone just after the grid was briefly displayed. Subjects were told to report the top row of letters if they heard the high tone, the middle row for the medium tone, or the lowest row for the low tone. As they didn't hear the tone until after the grid went away, they couldn't look at just one row in advance (see Figure 5.2).

Using this method, Sperling found that subjects could accurately report any of the three rows. This meant that the entire grid was in iconic memory and available to the subjects. The capacity of iconic memory is everything that can be seen at one time.

Duration of Iconic Memory   Sperling also found that if he delayed the tone for a brief period of time, after about half a second, subjects could no longer recall any of the letters from the grid. The icon had completely faded out of sensory memory in that brief time.

In real life, information that has just entered iconic memory will be pushed out very quickly by new information, a process called *masking* (Cowan, 1988, 1995). Research suggests that after only a quarter of a second, old information is replaced by new information.

Some people may have what is properly called **eidetic imagery**, or the ability to access a visual memory over a long period of time. While similar to iconic memory, eidetic imagery is not quite the same thing (Gummerman et al., 1972; Haber, 1979). People with eidetic imagery ability might be able to look quickly at a page in a book, and then by focusing on a blank wall or piece of paper, "read" the words from the image that still lingers in their memory. There is controversy surrounding the existence of this ability, but it is generally believed to be more common in children and diminishes by adolescence or young adulthood (Haber, 1979; Leask et al., 1969; Stromeyer & Psotka, 1971).

If iconic memory lasts such a brief time, what use is it to us? ●

Function of Iconic Memory   Iconic memory actually serves a very important function in the visual system. Chapter Three discussed the way the eyes make tiny little movements called *saccades* that keep vision from adapting to a constant visual stimulus, so that what is stared at steadily doesn't slowly disappear. Iconic memory helps the visual system to view surroundings as continuous and stable in spite of these saccadic movements. It also allows enough time for the brain stem to decide if the information is important enough to be brought into consciousness—like the possibly pants-less person.

ECHOIC SENSORY MEMORY   The other type of sensory memory is **echoic memory**, or the brief memory of something a person has heard. A

Rows of Letters	Tone Signaling Which Row to Report
LHTY	High tone
EPNR	Medium tone
SBAX	Low tone

FIGURE 5.2 Iconic Memory Test
Sample grid of letters for Sperling's test of iconic memory. To determine if the entire grid existed in iconic memory, Sperling sounded a tone associated with each row after the grid's presentation. Participants were able to recall the letters in the row for which they heard the tone. The graph shows the decrease in the number of letters recalled as the delay in presenting the tone increased.

If iconic memory lasts such a brief time, what use is it to us?

Pablo Picasso was one of the most creative artists of his time. Here he is seen drawing an abstract of a woman in the air with a flashlight, using multiple exposures of the camera. What does his ability to "hold" the light image in his head long enough to complete the abstract tell us about his visual memory?

Once these piano strings have been attached to the tuning pins, the piano can be tuned. Tuning a piano requires the use of echoic sensory memory. What other occupations might find a good echoic memory to be an asset?

What happens if the lower brain centers send the information on to the higher centers?

Each person at this gathering is involved in a conversation with others, with dozens of such conversations going on at the same time all around. Yet if a person in another conversation says the name of one of the people in the crowd, that person in the crowd will be able to selectively attend to his or her name. This is known as the "cocktail party effect."

good example of echoic memory is the "What?" phenomenon. You might be reading or concentrating on the television, and your parent, roommate, or friend walks up and says something to you. You sit there for a second or two and then say "What? Oh— yes, I'm ready to eat now," or whatever comment is appropriate. You didn't really process the statement from the other person as he or she said it. You heard it, but your brain didn't interpret it immediately. Instead, it took several seconds for you to realize that (1) something was said, (2) it may have been important, and (3) you'd better try to remember what it was. If you realize all this within about 4 seconds, you will more than likely be able to "hear" an echo of the statement in your head, a kind of "instant replay." Echoic memory's capacity is limited to what can be heard at any one moment and is smaller than the capacity of iconic memory, although it lasts longer—about 2 to 4 seconds (Schweickert, 1993).

Echoic memory is very useful when a person wants to have meaningful conversations with others. It allows the person to remember what someone said just long enough to recognize the meaning of a phrase. As with iconic memory, it also allows people to hold on to incoming auditory information long enough for the lower brain centers to decide if the information is important enough to become conscious. It is echoic memory that allows a musician to tune a musical instrument, for example. The memory of the tuning fork's tone lingers in echoic memory long enough for the person doing the tuning to match that tone on the instrument.

● What happens if the lower brain centers send the information on to the higher centers?

Short-Term and Working Memory

5.3 What is short-term memory, and how does it differ from working memory?

Information typically moves from sensory memory to the next stage of memory, called **short-term memory (STM)**, through the process of **selective attention**, the ability to focus on only one stimulus from among all sensory input (Broadbent, 1958). When a person is thinking actively about some information, that information is said to be conscious (see Chapter Six). It can also be said to be in short-term memory, the memory system in which information is held for brief periods of time while being used.

Selective attention is responsible for the "cocktail party effect" that has been long established in studies of perception and attention (Bronkhorst, 2000; Cherry, 1953; Handel, 1989). If you've ever been at a party where there's a lot of noise and conversations going on in the background but you are able to notice when someone says your name, you have experienced this effect. The areas of the brain that are involved in selective attention were working even though you were not consciously aware of it, and when that important bit of information (your name) appeared, those areas brought the information to your conscious awareness (Hopfinger et al., 2000; Stuss et al., 2002).

Dr. Anne M. Treisman (Treisman, 2006; Triesman & Gelade, 1980) proposed that selective attention operates in a two-stage filtering process: In the first stage, incoming stimuli in sensory memory are filtered on the basis of simple physical characteristics. This is very similar to Broadbent's original idea, but instead of being sent to STM or not sent (lost), the stimuli are assigned different "signal strengths." Unattended sensory stimuli are lessened, or *attenuated*, when compared to attended stimuli, but are still available to the second-stage filter, which processes only the stimuli that meet a certain threshold of importance.

Something as subjectively important as one's own name may be able to be "plucked" out of the attenuated incoming stimuli. Even when deeply asleep, when the selective attention filter is not working at its peak level, it still functions: A mother awakens, hearing her infant's soft cries but sleeps through the nightly noises that come from the nearby train that passes by every night (LaBerge, 1980). The train sound may be louder but is not important (i.e., has been attenuated), whereas the baby's cry is most certainly important. The threshold of meaning for the baby's cry has been lowered, while that of the predictable, yet louder, train has been raised. Short-term memory tends to be encoded in auditory (sound) form. That simply means that people tend to "talk" inside their own heads. Although some images are certainly stored in STM in a kind of visual "sketchpad" (Baddeley, 1986), auditory storage accounts for much of short-term encoding. Even a dancer planning out moves in her head will not only visualize the moves but also be very likely to verbally describe the moves in her head as she plans. An artist planning a painting has visual information in STM but may also keep up an internal dialogue that is primarily auditory. Research in which participants were asked to recall numbers and letters showed that errors were nearly always made with numbers or letters that *sounded like* the target but not with those that *looked like* the target word or number (Acheson et al., 2010; Conrad & Hull, 1964).

Some memory theorists use the term *working memory* as another way of referring to short-term memory. This is not entirely correct: Short-term memory has traditionally been thought of as a thing or a place into which information is put. **Working memory** is more correctly thought of as an active system that processes the information present in short-term memory. Working memory is thought to consist of three interrelated systems: a central executive (a kind of "CEO" or "Big Boss") that controls and coordinates the other two systems, a visual "sketchpad" of sorts, and a kind of auditory "recorder" (Baddeley, 1986; Baddeley & Hitch, 1974; Baddeley & Larsen, 2007; Engle & Kane, 2004). The central executive acts as interpreter for both the visual and auditory information, and the visual and auditory information is itself contained in short-term memory. For example, when a person is reading a book, the sketchpad will contain images of the people and events of the particular passage being read, while the recorder "plays" the dialogue in the person's head. The central executive helps interpret the information from both systems and pulls it all together. In a sense, then, short-term memory can be seen as being a part of the working memory system (Acheson et al., 2010; Bayliss et al., 2005; Colom et al., 2006; Kail & Hall, 2001).

Another way to think about short-term memory is as if it were a kind of desk where you do your work. You might pull some files out of storage (permanent memory) or someone might hand you some files (sensory input). While the files are on your desk, you can see them, read them, and work with them (working memory). The "files" are now conscious material and will stay that way as long as they are on the desk. If they are not that important or only necessary for a little while, they get "thrown out" (forgotten as you fail to pay attention to them). If they are important, they might get stored away in the filing system (permanent memory), where they are not conscious until they are once again retrieved—brought out onto the desk.

CAPACITY: THE MAGICAL NUMBER SEVEN George Miller (1956) wanted to know how much information humans can hold in short-term memory at any one time. He reviewed several memory studies, including some using a memory test called the *digit-span test*, in which a series of numbers is read to subjects in the study who are then asked to recall the numbers in order. Each series gets longer and longer, until the subjects cannot recall any of the numbers in order (see Figure 5.3). ❋ Explore on **MyPsychLab**

Miller reported that the capacity of STM is about seven items or pieces of information, plus or minus two items, or from five to nine bits of information. Miller called

This woman must hold the phone number she is reading in short-term memory long enough to dial it on the phone next to her.

6 8 2 5

5 7 2 1 4

3 5 9 7 2 1

9 2 5 4 6 3 8

2 8 3 7 1 5 6 9

7 3 2 4 9 6 8 5 1

6 5 4 7 8 9 3 2 1 7

FIGURE 5.3 Digit-Span Test
Instructions for the digit-span test: Listen carefully as the instructor reads each string of numbers out loud. As soon as each string is ended (the instructor may say "go"), write down the numbers in the exact order in which they were given.

❋ Explore an experiment on the digit-span test on **MyPsychLab**

short-term memory (STM) the memory system in which information is held for brief periods of time while being used.

selective attention the ability to focus on only one stimulus from among all sensory input.

working memory an active system that processes the information in short-term memory.

this the "magical number seven, plus or minus two." So the "desk" isn't really very big and can hold only so many "files." Newer research suggests that younger adults can only hold three to five items at a time without using a memory strategy, and if the information consists of long, confusing, or unfamiliar words the capacity is further reduced (Cowan, 2001; Cowan et al., 2005; Palva et al., 2010).

Chunking   There is a way to "fool" STM into holding more information than is usual. (Think of it as "stacking" related files on the desk.) If the bits of information are combined into meaningful units, or chunks, more information can be held in STM. If someone were to recode the last sequence of numbers in Figure 5.3 as "654-789-3217," for example, instead of 10 bits of information, there would only be three "chunks" that read like a phone number. This process of recoding, or reorganizing, the information is called *chunking.*

WHY DO YOU THINK THEY CALL IT SHORT TERM?   How long is the "short" of short-term memory? Research has shown that short-term memory lasts from about 12 to 30 seconds without rehearsal (Atkinson & Shiffrin, 1968; Brown, 1958; Peterson & Peterson, 1959). After that, the memory seems to rapidly "decay" or disappear. The findings of a study with mice suggest that in order to form new memories, old memories must be "erased" by the formation of newly formed neurons (Kitamura et al., 2009). Some memories formed in the hippocampus will, without rehearsal, decay as new neurons (and newer memories) are added to the already existing neural circuits.

● What do you mean by rehearsal? How long can short-term memories last if rehearsal is a factor?

Most people learn that saying something they want to remember over and over again in their heads, such as repeating a phone number they need just long enough to dial it, can help them remember longer, a process called **maintenance rehearsal**. With maintenance rehearsal, a person is simply continuing to pay attention to the information to be held in memory, and since attention is how that information got into STM in the first place, it works quite well (Atkinson & Shiffrin, 1968; Rundus, 1971). With this type of rehearsal, information will stay in short-term memory until rehearsal stops. When rehearsal stops, the memory rapidly decays and is forgotten. If anything interferes with maintenance rehearsal (such as someone asking you the time of day while you are trying to count money), memories are also likely to be lost.

Interference in STM can also happen if the amount of information to be held in STM exceeds its capacity (about five to nine "bits" of information, remember). Information already in STM may be "pushed out" to make room for newer information. This is why it might be possible to remember the first few names of people you meet at a party, but as more names are added, they displace the older names. A better way to remember a person's name is to associate the name with something about the person's appearance, a process that helps move the name from STM into more permanent storage. This more permanent storage is long-term memory, which is the topic of the next section.

Long-Term Memory

5.4 How is long-term memory different from other types of memory?

Long-term memory (LTM) is the system into which all the information is placed to be kept more or less permanently. In terms of capacity, LTM is unlimited (Bahrick, 1984; Barnyard & Grayson, 1996). Think about it: Would there ever really come a time when you could not fit one more piece of information into your head? When you could learn nothing more? There is always room for more information (in spite of what some students may believe).

What do you mean by rehearsal? How long can short-term memories last if rehearsal is a factor?

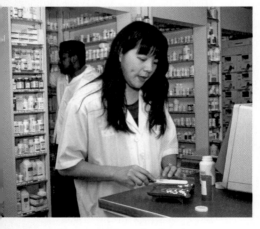

It is very important for this pharmacist to count out the number of pills in the prescription accurately. Short-term memory allows her to remember the last number she counted, but if she is interrupted, she will have to start all over again. Short-term memory is very susceptible to interference.

maintenance rehearsal   practice of saying information to be remembered over and over in one's head in order to maintain it in short-term memory.

long-term memory (LTM)   the system of memory into which all the information is placed to be kept more or less permanently.

As for duration,* the name *long term* says it all. There is a relatively permanent physical change in the brain itself when a long-term memory is formed. That means that many of the memories people have stored away for a long, long time—even since childhood—may still be there. That does not mean that people can always retrieve those memories. The memories may be *available* but not *accessible*. That is, they are still there, but for various reasons (discussed later under the topic of forgetting) people cannot get to them.

I once memorized a poem by repeating it over and over—that's maintenance rehearsal, right? Since I still remember most of the poem, it must be in long-term memory. Is maintenance rehearsal a good way to get information into long-term memory?

Information that is rehearsed long enough may actually find its way into long-term memory. After all, it's how most people learned their Social Security number and the letters of the alphabet (although people cheated a little on the latter by putting the alphabet to music, which makes it easier to retrieve). Most people tend to learn poems and the multiplication tables by maintenance rehearsal, otherwise known as rote learning. *Rote* is like "rotating" the information in one's head, saying it over and over again. But maintenance rehearsal is not the most efficient way of putting information into long-term storage, because to get the information back out, one has to remember it almost exactly as it went in. Try this: What is the fifteenth letter of the alphabet? Did you have to recite or sing through the alphabet song to get to that letter?

Although many long-term memories are encoded as images (think of the *Mona Lisa*), sounds, smells, and tastes (Cowan, 1988), in general LTM is encoded in meaningful form, a kind of mental storehouse of the meanings of words, concepts, and all the events that people want to keep in mind. Even the images, sounds, smells, and tastes involved in these events have some sort of meaning attached to them that gives them enough importance to be stored long term. If STM can be thought of as a working "surface" or desk, then LTM can be thought of as a huge series of filing cabinets behind the desk, in which files are stored in an organized fashion, according to meaning. Files have to be placed into the cabinets in a certain organized fashion to be useful. How else could anyone ever remember any kind of information quickly if the files were not in some order? The best way to encode information into LTM in an organized fashion is to make it meaningful through *elaborative rehearsal*.

ELABORATIVE REHEARSAL **Elaborative rehearsal** is a way of transferring information from STM into LTM by making that information meaningful in some way (Postman, 1975). The easiest way to do this is to connect new information with something that is already well known (Craik & Lockhart, 1972; Harris & Qualls, 2000; Postman, 1975). For example, the French word *maison* means "house." A person could try to memorize that (using maintenance rehearsal) by saying over and over, "*Maison* means house, *maison* means house." But it would be much easier and more efficient if that person simply thought, "*Maison* sounds like masons, and masons build houses." That makes the meaning of the word tie in with something the person already knows (masons, who lay stone or bricks to build houses) and helps in remembering the French term.

As discussed in the beginning of this chapter, Craik and Lockhart (1972) theorized that information that is more "deeply processed," or processed according to its meaning rather than just the sound or physical characteristics of the word or words, will be remembered more efficiently and for a longer period of time. As the levels-of-processing approach predicts, elaborative rehearsal is a deeper kind of processing than maintenance rehearsal and so leads to better long-term storage (Craik & Tulving, 1975).

I can remember a lot of stuff from my childhood. Some of it I learned in school and some of it is more personal, like the first day of school. Are these two different kinds of long-term memories?

---

*Duration: how long something lasts.

elaborative rehearsal a method of transferring information from STM into LTM by making that information meaningful in some way.

These students are rehearsing for a concert. They will use maintenance rehearsal (repeating the musical passages over and over) until they can play their parts perfectly. The movements of their fingers upon the strings of their instruments will be stored in long-term memory. How is this kind of long-term memory different from something like the memorized lines of one's part in a play?

I once memorized a poem by repeating it over and over—that's maintenance rehearsal, right? Since I still remember most of the poem, it must be in long-term memory. Is maintenance rehearsal a good way to get information into long-term memory?

I can remember a lot of stuff from my childhood. Some of it I learned in school and some of it is more personal, like the first day of school. Are these two different kinds of long-term memories?

Procedural knowledge, such as tying one's shoes, often must be learned by doing, as it is difficult to put into words. Once this child learns how to tie shoes, the knowledge will always be there to retrieve.

FIGURE 5.4 Tower of Hanoi
The Tower of Hanoi is a puzzle that is solved in a series of steps by moving one disk at a time. The goal is to move all of the disks from peg A to peg C; the rules are that a larger disk cannot be moved on top of a smaller one and a disk cannot be moved if there are other disks on top of it. Amnesia patients were able to learn the procedure for solving the puzzle but could not remember that they knew how to solve it.

procedural (nondeclarative) memory
type of long-term memory including memory for skills, procedures, habits, and conditioned responses. These memories are not conscious but are implied to exist because they affect conscious behavior.

anterograde amnesia   loss of memory from the point of injury or trauma forward, or the inability to form new long-term memories.

implicit memory   memory that is not easily brought into conscious awareness, such as procedural memory.

Types of Long-Term Information

5.5 What are the various types of long-term memory, and how is information stored in long-term memory organized?

Long-term memories include general facts and knowledge, personal facts, and even skills that can be performed. Memory for skills is called *procedural (nondeclarative) memory* because it usually involves a series of steps or procedures; memory for facts is called *declarative memory* because facts are things that are known and can be declared (stated outright). These two types of long-term memory are quite different, as the following sections will explain.

Procedural (Nondeclarative) LTM Memories for skills that people know how to do, like tying shoes and riding a bicycle, are a kind of LTM called **procedural (nondeclarative) memory**. Procedural memories also include emotional associations, habits, and simple conditioned reflexes that may or may not be in conscious awareness, which are often very strong memories. **LINK** to Chapter Four: Learning, p. 123. Referring back to Chapter Two, we will recall that the amygdala is the most probable location for emotional associations, such as fear, and the cerebellum in the hindbrain is responsible for storage of memories of conditioned responses, skills, and habits (Dębiec et al., 2010; Squire et al., 1993).

Evidence that separate areas of the brain control procedural memory comes from studies of people with damage to the hippocampus area of the brain. This damage causes them to have **anterograde amnesia**, in which new long-term declarative memories cannot be formed. (This disorder is fairly accurately represented by the character of Lenny in the 2000 motion picture *Memento*.) One of the more famous anterograde amnesia patients, H. M., is discussed in detail later in this chapter on page 188.

In one study (Cohen et al., 1985), patients with this disorder were taught how to solve a particular puzzle called the Tower of Hanoi (see Figure 5.4). Although the patients were able to learn the sequence of moves necessary to solve the puzzle, when brought back into the testing room at a later time they could not remember ever having seen the puzzle before—or, for that matter, the examiner. Each trial was like the first one ever for these patients, as they were unable to store the long-term memory of having been in the room or having met the examiner previously. Yet they were able to solve the puzzle even while claiming that they had never seen it before. Their procedural memories for how to solve the puzzle were evidently formed and stored in a part of the brain separate from the part controlling the memories they could no longer form.

The patients in this study had the kind of memory problems that people with Alzheimer's disease have. Yet even people with Alzheimer's disease do not forget how to walk, talk, fasten clothing, or even tie shoes (although they do lose motor ability because the brain eventually fails to send the proper signals). These are all procedural, nondeclarative memories. They may not be able to tell someone who asks that they know how to do these things, but they can still do them. Alzheimer's disease affects the hippocampus and the frontal cortex (involved in decision making and planning) and eventually affects other areas of the brain after it has progressed nearly to the end (Kanne et al., 1998). In fact, it would be rare to find someone who has lost procedural memory. Literally, these are the kind of memories people "never forget."

Procedural memory is similar to the concept of **implicit memory** because memories for these skills, habits, and learned reflexes are not easily retrieved into conscious awareness (i.e., nondeclarative). The fact that people have the knowledge of how to tie their shoes, for example, is *implied* by the fact that they can actually tie them. But have you ever tried to tell someone how to tie shoes without using your hands to show them? Such knowledge is in people's memories because they use this information, but they are often not consciously aware of this knowledge (Roediger, 1990). Although procedural memories are very often implicit, not all implicit memories are necessarily procedural. A memory from one's early childhood of being frightened by a dog, for example, may not be a conscious memory in later childhood but may still be the cause of that older child's fear of dogs. Conscious memories for events in childhood, on the other hand, are usually considered to be a different kind of long-term memory called declarative memory.

Declarative LTM Procedural memory is about the things that people can *do*, but **declarative memory** is about all the things that people can *know*—the facts and information that make up knowledge. People know things such as the names of the planets in the solar system, that adding two and two makes four, and that a noun is the name of a person, place, or thing—all facts that are readily available to anyone who wants to learn them. People can also know more personal facts—what they had for breakfast, their birthdates, and other facts that are not readily available to others. Therefore, there are two types of declarative long-term memories, *semantic* and *episodic* (Nyberg & Tulving, 1996).

General knowledge that anyone has the ability to know and that is often learned in school or by reading is called **semantic memory**. The word *semantic* refers to meaning, so this kind of knowledge is the awareness of the meanings of words, concepts, and terms as well as names of objects, math skills, and so on. This is also the type of knowledge that is used on game shows such as *Jeopardy* and *Cash Cab*. Semantic memories, like procedural memories, are relatively permanent. But it is possible to "lose the way to" this kind of memory, as discussed in the section on forgetting.

The other kind of factual memory is the personal knowledge that each person has of his or her daily life and personal history, a kind of autobiographical* memory. Memories of what has happened to people each day, certain birthdays, anniversaries that were particularly special, childhood events, and so on are called **episodic memory** because they represent episodes from their lives. Unlike procedural and semantic long-term memories, episodic memories tend to be updated and revised more or less constantly. You can probably remember what you had for breakfast today, but what you had for breakfast two years ago on this date is most likely a mystery. Episodic memories that are especially *meaningful*, such as the memory of the first day of school or your first date, are more likely to be kept in LTM (although they may not be as exact as people sometimes assume they are). The updating process is a kind of survival mechanism, because although semantic and procedural memories are useful and necessary on an ongoing basis, no one really needs to remember every little detail of every day. As becomes obvious later, the ability to forget some kinds of information is very necessary.

Episodic and semantic memories are forms of **explicit memory**, memories that are easily made conscious and brought from long-term storage into short-term memory. The knowledge of semantic memories such as word meanings, science concepts, and so on can be brought out of the "filing cabinet" and placed on the "desk" where that knowledge becomes *explicit*, or obvious. The same is often true of personal, episodic memories.

But sometimes I can't remember all the names of the planets or what I had for breakfast yesterday. Doesn't that make these memories implicit instead of explicit?

The difference between implicit memories, such as how to balance on a bicycle, and explicit memories, such as naming all the planets, is that it is impossible or extremely difficult to bring implicit memories into consciousness. Explicit memories can be forgotten but always have the potential to be made conscious. When someone reminds you of what you had for breakfast the day before, for example, you will remember that you had that knowledge all along—it was just temporarily "mislaid." For a look at the connections among all these types of LTM, see Figure 5.5.

declarative memory type of long-term memory containing information that is conscious and known.

semantic memory type of declarative memory containing general knowledge, such as knowledge of language and information learned in formal education.

episodic memory type of declarative memory containing personal information not readily available to others, such as daily activities and events.

explicit memory memory that is consciously known, such as declarative memory.

But sometimes I can't remember all the names of the planets or what I had for breakfast yesterday. Doesn't that make these memories implicit instead of explicit?

---

*Autobiographical: the story of a person's life as told by that person.

FIGURE 5.5 Types of Long-Term Memories

Long-term memory can be divided into declarative memories, which are factual and typically conscious (explicit) memories, and nondeclarative memories, which are skills, habits, and conditioned responses that are typically unconscious (implicit). Declarative memories are further divided into episodic memories (personal experiences) and semantic memories (general knowledge).

```
                    Long-term memory

        Declarative memory              Procedural memory
        (Explicit memory)               (Implicit memory)
                                        Motor skills, habits,
                                        classically conditioned reflexes

  Episodic memory      Semantic memory
  Events experienced   Facts, general
  by a person          knowledge
```

LONG-TERM MEMORY ORGANIZATION As stated before, LTM has to be fairly well organized for retrieval to be so quick. Can you remember the name of your first-grade teacher? If you can, how long did it take you to pull that name out of LTM and "put it on the desk" of STM? It probably took hardly any time at all. Think of it this way: If a person who puts documents in a filing cabinet just stuffs them in any drawer with no system of organization, when a particular document is needed it requires searching through every drawer. But if documents are filed away alphabetically, and perhaps even according to type of document (deeds in one drawer, power of attorney forms in another, etc.), it becomes very easy to retrieve a particular document.

Research suggests that long-term memory is organized in terms of related meanings and concepts (Collins & Loftus, 1975; Collins & Quillian, 1969). In their original study, Collins and Quillian (1969) had subjects respond "true" or "false" as quickly as possible to sentences such as "a canary is a bird" and "a canary is an animal." Looking at Figure 5.6, we clearly see that information exists in a network with nodes (focal points) of related information linked to each other in a hierarchy.* To verify the statement "a canary is a bird" requires moving to only one node, but "a canary is an animal" would require moving through two nodes and should take longer. This was exactly the result of the 1969 study, leading the researchers to develop the **semantic network model**, which assumes that information is stored in the brain in a connected fashion with concepts that are related to each other stored physically closer to each other than concepts that are not highly related (Collins & Quillian, 1969).

The parallel distributed processing model (Rumelhart et al., 1986) discussed earlier in this chapter can be used to explain how rapidly the different points on the networks can be accessed. Although the access of nodes within a particular category (for example, *birds*) may take place in a serial fashion, explaining the different response times in the Collins and Quillian (1969) study, access across the entire network may take place in a parallel fashion, allowing several different concepts to be targeted at the same time (for example, one might be able to think about *birds*, *cats*, and *trees* simultaneously).

Perhaps the best way to think of how information is organized in LTM is to think about the Internet. A person might go to one Web site and from that site link to many other related sites. Each related site has its own specific information but is also linked to many other related sites, and a person can have more than one site open at the same time. This may be very similar to the way in which the mind organizes the information stored in LTM.

semantic network model model of memory organization that assumes information is stored in the brain in a connected fashion, with concepts that are related stored physically closer to each other than concepts that are not highly related.

---

*Hierarchy: an ordered list or series.

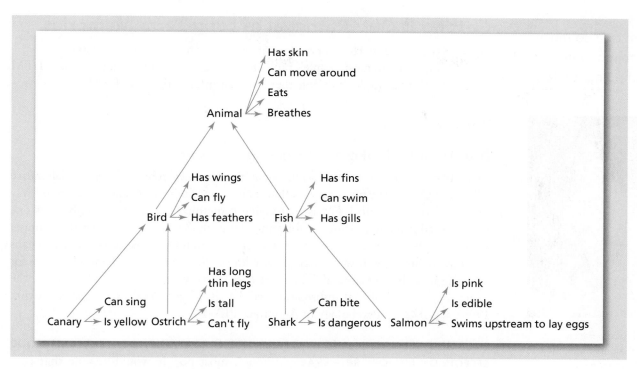

FIGURE 5.6 An Example of a Semantic Network
In the semantic network model of memory, concepts that are related in meaning are thought to be stored physically near each other in the brain. In this example, canary and ostrich are stored near the concept node for "bird," whereas shark and salmon are stored near "fish." But the fact that a canary is yellow is stored directly with that concept.

practice quiz   How much do you remember?

5.2   5.3   5.4   5.5

Pick the best answer.

1. Long ago (in the dark ages of television), when a television set was turned off, it took a while for the last image that was on the screen to fade away. This is most like _____.
   a. iconic memory.
   b. echoic memory.
   c. short-term memory.
   d. long-term memory.

2. Which type of memory is used to keep the flow of conversations going by allowing a person to remember what was just said?
   a. iconic memory
   b. echoic memory
   c. short-term memory
   d. long-term memory

3. Fethia learned her multiplication facts by repeating them over and over until she had them memorized. Fethia was using what kind of rehearsal?
   a. repetitive
   b. imagery
   c. elaborative
   d. maintenance

4. Of the following, which is most similar to the concept of long-term memory?
   a. a revolving door
   b. a filing cabinet
   c. a desktop
   d. a computer keyboard

5. Long-term memories are encoded in terms of _____.
   a. sounds.
   b. visual images.
   c. meanings of words and concepts.
   d. all of the above.

6. Which type of LTM is seldom, if ever, lost by people with Alzheimer's disease?
   a. procedural
   b. semantic
   c. episodic
   d. both b and c

7. In the game show *Who Wants to Be a Millionaire?* contestants are asked a series of questions of general information, although of increasing difficulty. The type of memory needed to access the answers to these kinds of questions is _____.
   a. procedural.
   b. semantic.
   c. episodic.
   d. working.

8. The Internet, with its series of links from one site to many others, is a good analogy for the organization of _____.
   a. short-term memory.
   b. episodic memory.
   c. long-term memory.
   d. procedural memory.

Brainstorming: In thinking about a typical day, how do you use each type of memory: procedural, episodic, and semantic?

My problem isn't so much getting information *into* my head as finding it later.

When this bride and groom dance together later on in their marriage, they will be able to recall this moment at their wedding and the happiness they felt at that time. State-dependent learning makes it easier for people to recall information stored while in a particular emotional state (such as the happiness of this couple) if the recall occurs in a similar emotional state.

Getting It Out: Retrieval of Long-Term Memories

● My problem isn't so much getting information *into* my head as finding it later.

Oddly enough, most people's problems with getting information stored in LTM back out again has to do with *how* they put that information *into* LTM.

Retrieval Cues

5.6 What kinds of cues help people remember?

Remember the previous discussion about maintenance rehearsal versus elaborative rehearsal? One of the main reasons that maintenance rehearsal is not a very good way to get information into LTM is that saying something over and over only gives one kind of **retrieval cue** (a stimulus for remembering), the sound of the word or phrase. When people try to remember a piece of information by thinking of what it means and how it fits in with what they already know, they are giving themselves cues for meaning in addition to sound. The more cues stored with a piece of information, the easier the retrieval of that information will be (Roediger, 2000; Roediger & Guynn, 1996). ⓁⒾⓃⓀ to Psychology in Action, p. PIA-14.

ENCODING SPECIFICITY AND STATE-DEPENDENT LEARNING: CONTEXT AND MOOD EFFECTS ON MEMORY RETRIEVAL Although most people would assume that cues for retrieval would have to be directly related to the concepts being studied, the fact is that almost anything in one's surroundings is capable of becoming a cue. Have you ever had to take a test in a different classroom than the one in which you learned the material being tested? Do you think that your performance on that test was hurt by being in a different physical context? Researchers have found strong evidence for the concept of **encoding specificity**, the tendency for memory of any kind of information to be improved if the physical surroundings available when the memory is first formed are also available when the memory is being retrieved (Reder et al., 1974; Tulving & Thomson, 1973; Vaidya et al., 2002). For example, encoding specificity would predict that the best place to take one's chemistry test is in the same room in which you learned the material. Also, it's very common to walk into a room and know that there was something you wanted, but in order to remember it, you have to go back to the room you started in to use your surroundings as a cue for remembering.

In one study, researchers had students who were learning to scuba dive in a pool also learn lists of words while they were either out of the pool or in the pool under the water (Godden & Baddeley, 1975). Subjects were then asked to remember the two lists in each of the two conditions. Words that were learned while out of the pool were remembered significantly better when the subjects were out of the pool, and words that were learned underwater were more easily retrieved if the subjects were underwater while trying to remember (see Figure 5.7).

Physical surroundings at the time of encoding a memory are not the only kinds of cues that can help in retrieval. In *state-dependent learning*, memories formed during a particular physiological or psychological state will be easier to remember while in a similar state. For example, when you are arguing with someone, it's much easier to remember all of the bad things that person has done than

retrieval cue a stimulus for remembering.

encoding specificity the tendency for memory of information to be improved if related information (such as surroundings or physiological state) available when the memory is first formed is also available when the memory is being retrieved.

Beetle Bailey by Mort Walker

to remember the good times. In one study (Eich & Metcalfe, 1989), researchers had subjects try to remember words that they had read while listening to music. Subjects read one list of words while listening to sad music (influencing their mood to be sad) and another list of words while listening to happy music. When it came time to recall the lists, the researchers again manipulated the mood of the subjects. The words that were read while subjects were in a happy mood were remembered better if the manipulated mood was also happy but far less well if the mood was sad. The reverse was also true.

5.7 How do the retrieval processes of recall and recognition differ, and how reliable are our memories of events?

Why do multiple-choice tests seem so much easier than essay tests?

There are two kinds of retrieval of memories, recall and recognition. It is the difference between these two retrieval methods that makes some kinds of exams seem harder than others. In **recall**, memories are retrieved with few or no external cues, such as filling in the blanks on an application form. **Recognition**, on the other hand, involves looking at or hearing information and matching it to what is already in memory. A word-search puzzle, in which the words are already written down in the grid and simply need to be circled, is an example of recognition. The following section takes a closer look at these two important processes.

Recall: Hmm...Let Me Think

When someone is asked a question such as "Where were you born?" the question acts as the cue for retrieval of the answer. This is an example of recall, as are essay question, short-answer, and fill-in-the-blank tests that are used to measure a person's memory for information (Borges et al., 1977; Gillund & Shiffrin, 1984; Raaijmakers & Shiffrin, 1992).

RETRIEVAL FAILURE: IT'S RIGHT ON THE TIP OF MY TONGUE Whenever people find themselves struggling for an answer, recall has failed (at least temporarily). Sometimes the answer seems so very close to the surface of conscious thought that it feels like it's "on the tip of the tongue." (If people could just get their tongues out there far enough, they could read it.) This is sometimes called the *tip of the tongue (TOT)* phenomenon (Brown & McNeill, 1966; Burke et al., 1991). Although people may be able to say how long the word is or name letters that start or even end the word, they cannot retrieve the sound or actual spelling of the word to allow it to be pulled into the auditory "recorder" of STM so that it can be fully retrieved. The best way to overcome this problem is to think about something else. Eventually the information just "pops out."

THE SERIAL POSITION EFFECT Another interesting feature of recall is that it is often subject to a kind of "prejudice" of memory retrieval, in which information at the beginning and the end of a list, such as a poem or song, tends to be remembered more easily and accurately. This is called the **serial position effect** (Murdock, 1962).

A good demonstration of this phenomenon involves instructing people to listen to and try to remember words that are read to them that are spaced about 4 or 5 seconds apart. People typically use maintenance rehearsal by repeating each word in their

FIGURE 5.7 Recall of Target Words in Two Contexts
The results of the Godden and Baddeley (1975) study indicated the retrieval of words learned while underwater was higher when the retrieval also took place underwater. Similarly, words learned while out of the water (on land) were retrieved at a higher rate out of the water.

Why do multiple-choice tests seem so much easier than essay tests?

recall type of memory retrieval in which the information to be retrieved must be "pulled" from memory with very few external cues.

recognition the ability to match a piece of information or a stimulus to a stored image or fact.

serial position effect tendency of information at the beginning and end of a body of information to be remembered more accurately than information in the middle of the body of information.

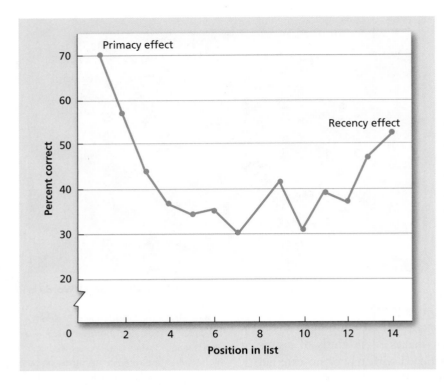

FIGURE 5.8 Serial Position Effect
In the serial position effect, information at the beginning of a list will be recalled at a higher rate than information in the middle of the list (primacy effect), because the beginning information receives more rehearsal and may enter LTM. Information at the end of a list is also retrieved at a higher rate (recency effect) because the end of the list is still in STM, with no information coming after it to interfere with retrieval.

These people are waiting to audition for a play. The person who auditioned first and the one who auditioned last have the greatest chance of being remembered when the time comes for the director to choose. The serial position effect will cause the impression made by the actors who come in the "middle" to be less memorable.

primacy effect tendency to remember information at the beginning of a body of information better than the information that follows.

recency effect tendency to remember information at the end of a body of information better than the information at the beginning of it.

heads. They are then asked to write as many of the words down as they can remember. If the frequency of recall for each word in the list is graphed, it will nearly always look like the graph in Figure 5.8.

Words at the very beginning of the list tend to be remembered better than those in the middle of the list. This effect is called the **primacy effect** and is due to the fact that the first few words, when the listener has nothing already in STM to interfere with their rehearsal, will receive far more rehearsal time than the words in the middle, which are constantly being replaced by the next word on the list (Craik, 1970; Murdock, 1962). In fact, the first words may actually move into LTM if they are rehearsed long enough, because rote memorization, although not the best way to remember something, can lead to long-term storage.

At the end of the graph there is another increase in recall. This is the **recency effect**; it is usually attributed to the fact that the last word or two was *just heard* and is still in short-term memory for easy retrieval, with no new words entering to "push" the most recent word or words out of memory (Bjork & Whitten, 1974; Murdock, 1962). The serial position effect works with many different kinds of information. Business schools, for example, often teach their students that they should try not to be "in the middle" for job interviews. Going first or last in the interview process is much more likely to make a person's interview more memorable.

Can knowledge of the serial position effect be of help to students trying to remember the information they need for their classes? Yes—students can take advantage of the recency effect by skimming back over their notes just before an exam. Knowing that the middle of a list of information is more likely to be forgotten means that students should pay more attention to the middle items, and breaking the study sessions up into smaller segments helps reduce the amount of "middle to muddle." (Students can also use *mnemonic strategies* to help offset this memory problem, as well as others. Ⓛⓘⓝⓚ to Psychology in Action, p. PIA-14.)

Recognition: Hey, Don't I Know You from Somewhere?

The other form of memory retrieval is *recognition*, the ability to match a piece of information or a stimulus to a stored image or fact (Borges et al., 1977; Gillund & Shiffrin, 1984; Raaijmakers & Shiffrin, 1992). Recognition is usually much easier than recall because the cue is the actual object, word, sound, and so on that one is simply trying to detect as familiar and known. Examples of tests that use recognition are multiple-choice, matching, and true–false tests. The answer is right there and simply has to be matched to the information already in memory.

Recognition tends to be very accurate for images, especially human faces. In one study, over 2,500 photographs were shown to participants at the rate of one every 10 seconds. Participants were then shown pairs of photographs in which one member of each pair was one of the previously seen photographs. Accuracy for identifying the previous photos was between 85 and 95 percent (Standing et al., 1970).

FALSE POSITIVES Recognition isn't foolproof, however. Sometimes there is just enough similarity between a stimulus that is not already in memory and one that is in memory so that a **false positive** occurs (Muter, 1978). A false positive occurs when a person thinks that he or she has recognized something or someone but in fact does not have that something or someone in memory.

False positives can become disastrous in certain situations. In one case, in a series of armed robberies in Delaware, word had leaked out that the suspect sought by police might be a priest. When police put Father Bernard Pagano in a lineup for witnesses to identify, he was the only one in the lineup wearing a priest's collar. Seven eyewitnesses identified him as the man who had robbed them. Fortunately for Father Pagano, the real robber confessed to the crimes halfway through Pagano's trial (Loftus, 1987). Eyewitness recognition can be especially prone to false positives, although most people seem to think that "seeing is believing." For more about the problems with eyewitnesses, see the following Classic Studies in Psychology feature.

"Hey, good buddy! How you doin'?" "Can't kick, big fella. What's shakin'?"

© The New Yorker Collection 1988 Lee Lorenz from cartoonbank.com. All Rights Reserved.

classic studies in psychology
....
Elizabeth Loftus and Eyewitnesses

Elizabeth Loftus is a Distinguished Professor of Social Ecology, a Professor of Law, and a Professor of Cognitive Science at the University of California in Irvine. One of the world's leading memory researchers, her focus has been on the accuracy of recall of memories—or rather, the inaccuracies of memory retrieval. She has been an expert witness at more than 200 trials, including that of Ted Bundy, the serial killer who was finally executed in Florida (Neimark, 1996).

Loftus and many others have demonstrated time and again that memory is not an unchanging, stable process but rather is a constantly changing one. People continually update and revise their memories of events without being aware that they are doing so, and they incorporate information gained after the actual event, whether correct or incorrect.

In one classic experiment, Loftus (1975) showed subjects a 3-minute video clip taken from the movie *Diary of a Student Revolution*. In this clip, eight demonstrators run into a classroom and eventually leave after interrupting the professor's lecture in a noisy confrontation. At the end of the video, two questionnaires were distributed containing one key question and 90 "filler" questions. The key question for half of the subjects was, "Was the leader of the four demonstrators who entered the classroom a male?" The other half was asked, "Was the leader of the twelve demonstrators who entered the classroom a male?" One week later, a new set of questions was given to all subjects in which the key question was, "How many demonstrators did you see entering the classroom?" Subjects who were previously asked the question incorrectly giving the number as "four" stated an average recall of 6.4 people, whereas those who read the question incorrectly giving the number as "twelve" recalled an average of 8.9 people. Loftus concluded that subjects were trying to compromise the memory of what they had actually seen—eight demonstrators—with later information. This study, along with the Father Pagano story and many others, clearly demonstrates the heart of Loftus's research: What people see and hear about an event after the fact can easily affect the accuracy of their memories of that event.

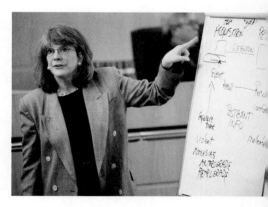

Dr. Elizabeth Loftus is an internationally known expert on the accuracy of eyewitness testimony. She is often called on to testify in court cases.

false positive error of recognition in which people think that they recognize some stimulus that is not actually in memory.

automatic encoding   tendency of certain kinds of information to enter long-term memory with little or no effortful encoding.

flashbulb memories   type of automatic encoding that occurs because an unexpected event has strong emotional associations for the person remembering it.

QUESTIONS FOR FURTHER DISCUSSION

1. How might police officers taking statements about a crime avoid getting inaccurate information from eyewitnesses?

2. How might Loftus's research apply to situations in which a therapist is trying to help a client recover memories that may have been repressed? What should the therapist avoid doing?

Automatic Encoding: Flashbulb Memories

Although some long-term memories need extensive maintenance rehearsal or effortful encoding in the form of elaborative rehearsal to enter from STM into LTM, many other kinds of long-term memories seem to enter permanent storage with little or no effort at all, in a kind of **automatic encoding** (Kvavilashvili et al., 2009; Mandler, 1967; Schneider et al., 1984). People unconsciously notice and seem able to remember a lot of things, such as the passage of time, knowledge of physical space, and frequency of events. For example, a person might make no effort to remember how many times cars have passed down the street but when asked can give an answer of "often," "more than usual," or "hardly any."

A special kind of automatic encoding takes place when an unexpected event or episode in a person's life has strong emotional associations, such as fear, horror, or joy. Memories of highly emotional events can often seem vivid and detailed, as if the person's mind took a "flash picture" of the moment in time. These kinds of memories are called **flashbulb memories** (Neisser, 1982; Neisser & Harsch, 1992; Winningham et al., 2000).

Many people share certain flashbulb memories. People of the "baby boomer" generation remember exactly where they were when the news came that President John F. Kennedy had been shot. Younger generations may remember the explosions of the space shuttles *Challenger* and *Columbia* and certainly remember the horrific events of September 11, 2001. But personal flashbulb memories also exist. These memories tend to be major emotional events, such as a first date, an embarrassing event, or a particularly memorable birthday party.

Why do flashbulb memories seem so vivid and exact? The answer lies in the emotions felt at the time of the event. Emotional reactions stimulate the release of hormones that have been shown to enhance the formation of long-term memories (Dolcos et al., 2005; McEwen, 2000; McGaugh, 2004; Sharot et al., 2004). While there is evidence for a high degree of accuracy in flashbulb memories of *major events*, the election of President Barack Obama in November 2008 or the death of pop legend Michael Jackson in June 2009, other research reveals that flashbulb memories are just as subject to decay and alterations over time as other kinds of memories (Neisser & Harsch, 1992). Apparently, no memories are completely accurate after the passage of time. The next section will discuss some of the reasons for faulty memories.

Fans of entertainer Michael Jackson may remember the moment they heard of his death on June 25, 2009. Events like this are so emotional for many people that the memories for the event are stored automatically, as if the mind had taken a "flash" picture of that moment in time. Such "flashbulb" memories seem to be very accurate but are actually no more accurate than any other memory.

practice quiz   How much do you remember?

Pick the best answer.

1. The best place to take your math exam to ensure good retrieval of math concepts is in _____.
   a. the math classroom.
   b. an auditorium to prevent cheating.
   c. the English classroom.
   d. the special testing room used for all exams.

2. Sarah can remember the names of the first two people she was introduced to at Ted's party, and she can remember the name of the last person she met, but the names of the dozen or so people in between are gone. This is an example of the _____.
   a. encoding specificity effect.
   b. serial position effect.
   c. tip-of-the-tongue effect.
   d. redintegrative effect.

3. This quiz question, as well as the other quiz questions, makes use of which form of retrieval of memories?
   a. rehearsal
   b. relearning
   c. recall
   d. recognition

4. Which of the following statements about Loftus's classic study is TRUE?
   a. All of the subjects were able to correctly recall the number of demonstrators.
   b. Subjects given a question stating that there were four demonstrators remembered only three demonstrators.
   c. Subjects given a question stating that there were twelve demonstrators remembered eight demonstrators.
   d. Subjects either increased or decreased the number of demonstrators in an attempt to compromise their memory with the later false information.

5. Which of the following statements about flashbulb memories is FALSE?
   a. They may be formed by the hormones released at emotional moments.
   b. They are vivid and detailed.
   c. They are unusually accurate.
   d. They can be personal or concern world events.

Brainstorming: Can you name all of the presidents of the United States? Which ones are harder to recall? Which ones are easier? What memory retrieval effect does this exemplify?

ANSWERS ON PAGE AK-1

The Reconstructive Nature of Long-Term Memory Retrieval: How Reliable Are Memories?

I think my memory is pretty good, but my brother and I often have arguments about things that happened when we were kids. Why don't we have the same exact memories? We were both there!

> I think my memory is pretty good, but my brother and I often have arguments about things that happened when we were kids. Why don't we have the same exact memories? We were both there!

People tend to assume that their memories are accurate when actually memories are revised, edited, and altered on an almost continuous basis. The reason for the changes that occur in memory has to do with the way in which memories are formed as well as how they are retrieved.

Constructive Processing of Memories

5.8 **How are long-term memories formed, and how can this process lead to inaccuracies in memories?**

Many people have the idea that when they recall a memory, they are recalling it as if it were an "instant replay." As new memories are created in LTM, old memories can get "lost," but they are more likely to be changed or altered in some way (Baddeley, 1988). In reality, memories (including those very vivid flashbulb memories) are never quite accurate, and the more time that passes, the more inaccuracies creep in. Psychologist John Kihlstrom, when talking about the early twentieth-century memory schema theorist Sir Frederic Bartlett's (1932) book on the constructive nature of memory, essentially says that "remembering is more like making up a story than it is like reading one printed in a book. For Bartlett, every memory is a blend of knowledge and inference. Remembering is problem-solving activity, where the problem is to give a

These men may engage in "Monday morning quarterbacking" as they apply hindsight to their memories of this game. Their memories of the game may be altered by information they get afterward from the television, newspapers, or their friends.

coherent* account of some past event, and the memory is the solution to that problem" (Kihlstrom, 2002, p. 3).

Loftus, along with other researchers (Hyman, 1993; Hyman & Loftus, 1998, 2002), has provided ample evidence for the **constructive processing** view of memory retrieval. In this view, memories are literally "built" from the pieces stored away at encoding. Each time a memory is retrieved, it may be altered or revised in some way to include new information, or details that were there at encoding may be left out of the new retrieval.

An example of how memories are reconstructed occurs when people, upon learning the details of a particular event, revise their memories to reflect their feeling that they "knew it all along." They will discard any incorrect information they actually had and replace it with more accurate information gained after the fact. This tendency of people to falsely believe that they would have accurately predicted an outcome without having been told about it in advance is called **hindsight bias** (Bahrick et al., 1996; Hoffrage et al., 2000). People who have ever done some "Monday morning quarterbacking" by saying that they knew all along who would win the game have fallen victim to hindsight bias.

Memory Retrieval Problems

Some people may say that they have "total recall." What they usually mean is that they feel that their memories are more accurate than those of other people. As should be obvious by now, true total recall is not a very likely ability for anyone to have. Here are some reasons why people have trouble recalling information accurately.

THE MISINFORMATION EFFECT Police investigators sometimes try to keep eyewitnesses to crimes or accidents from talking with each other. The reason is that if one person tells the other about something she has seen, the other person may later "remember" that same detail, even though he did not actually see it at the time. Such false memories are created by a person being exposed to information after the event. That misleading information can become part of the actual memory, affecting its accuracy (Loftus et al., 1978). This is called the **misinformation effect**. Elizabeth Loftus, in addition to her studies concerning eyewitness testimony, has also done several similar studies that demonstrate the misinformation effect. In one study, subjects viewed a slide presentation of a traffic accident. The actual slide presentation contained a stop sign, but in a written summary of the presentation, the sign was referred to as a yield sign. Subjects who were given this misleading information after viewing the slides were far less accurate in their memories for the kind of sign present than were subjects given no such information. One of the interesting points to be made by this study is that information that comes not only after the original event but also in an entirely different format (i.e., written instead of visual) can cause memories of the event to be incorrectly reconstructed.

Reliability of Memory Retrieval

5.9 What is false memory syndrome?

If memory is edited and changed when people are in a state of waking consciousness, alert and making an effort to retrieve information, how much more might memory be changed when people are in an altered state of conscious, such as hypnosis? *False*

constructive processing referring to the retrieval of memories in which those memories are altered, revised, or influenced by newer information.

hindsight bias the tendency to falsely believe, through revision of older memories to include newer information, that one could have correctly predicted the outcome of an event.

misinformation effect the tendency of misleading information presented after an event to alter the memories of the event itself.

---

*Coherent: understandable.

memory syndrome refers to the creation of inaccurate or false memories through the suggestion of others, often while the person is under hypnosis (Hochman, 1994).
⏵ Simulate on **MyPsychLab**

⏵ Simulate the creation of false memories on **MyPsychLab**

Research has shown that, although hypnosis may make it easier to recall some real memories, it also makes it easier to create false memories (Bowman, 1996). Hypnosis also has been found to increase the confidence people have in their memories regardless of whether those memories are real or false. False memories have been accidentally created by therapists' suggestions during hypnotic therapy sessions (especially those that involve age regression). Another study revealed that false memories are created in the brain in much the same way as real memories are formed and that people who look at real visual images and are also asked to imagine looking at visual images were often unable to later distinguish between the real and imagined images (Gonsalves et al., 2004). For more information on false memory syndrome, visit the Web site at **www.fmsfonline.org**.

Clearly, memories obtained through hypnosis should not be considered accurate without solid evidence from other sources.

But I've heard about people who under hypnosis remember being abused as children. Aren't those memories sometimes real?

But I've heard about people who under hypnosis remember being abused as children. Aren't those memories sometimes real?

The fact that some people recover false memories under certain conditions does not mean that child molestation* does not really happen; nor does it mean that a person who was molested might not push that unwanted memory away from conscious thought. Molestation is a sad fact, with one conservative estimate stating that nearly 20 percent of all females and 7 percent of all males have experienced molestation during childhood (Abel & Osborn, 1992). There are also many therapists and psychological professionals who are quite skilled at helping clients remember events of the past without suggesting possible false memories, and they find that clients do remember information and events that were true and able to be verified but were previously unavailable to the client (Dalenberg, 1996). False memory syndrome is not only harmful to the persons directly involved but also makes it much more difficult for genuine victims of molestation to be believed when they do recover their memories of the painful traumas of childhood.

So can we trust any of our memories at all? There is evidence to suggest that false memories cannot be created for just any kind of memory. The "memories" must at least be plausible, according to the research of cognitive psychologist and memory expert Kathy Pezdek, who with her colleagues has done several studies demonstrating the resistance of children to the creation of implausible false memories (Hyman et al., 1998; Pezdek et al., 1997; Pezdek & Hodge, 1999).

In the 1999 study, Pezdek and Hodge asked children to read five different summaries of childhood events. Two of these events were false, but only one of the two false events was plausible (e.g., getting lost). Although the children were told that all of the events happened to them as small children, the results indicated that the plausible false events were significantly more likely to be remembered as false memories than were the implausible false events (e.g., getting a rectal enema). A second experiment (Pezdek & Hodge, 1999) found similar results: Children were significantly less likely to form a false memory for an implausible false event than for a plausible false event.

The idea that only plausible events can become false memories runs contrary to the earlier work of Loftus and colleagues and to research concerning some very implausible false memories that have been successfully implanted, such as a memory for satanic rituals and alien abductions (Mack, 1994). Loftus and colleagues (Mazzoni

As this girl observes the activity below, she is storing some of the things she sees into memory while ignoring others. If she were to witness a crime, how would investigators know if her memories of the events were accurate or not? Would hypnotizing her to help her remember be effective? Why or why not?

*Molestation: unwanted or improper sexual activity.

et al., 2001) conducted several experiments in which they found that implausible events could be made more plausible by having the experimenters provide false feedback to the participants, who read articles telling of the implausible events as if they had actually happened to other people. The false feedback involved telling the participants that their responses to a questionnaire about fears were typical of people who had been through one of the false events (much as a well-meaning therapist might suggest to a client that certain anxieties and feelings are typical of someone who has been abused). These manipulations were so successful that participants not only developed false memories for the events but also even contradicted their own earlier statements in which they denied having these experiences in childhood. The researchers concluded that two steps must occur before people will be likely to interpret their thoughts and fantasies about false events as true memories:

1. The event must be made to seem as plausible as possible.

2. Individuals are given information that helps them believe that the event could have happened to them personally.

Other variables that are associated with a tendency to recall false events as real (Clancy et al., 2002) may be susceptibility to hypnosis, symptoms of depression, and the tendency to exhibit odd behavior and unusual beliefs (such as alien abduction, past-life regression, or the healing ability of crystals).

practice quiz   How much do you remember?

5.8   5.9

Pick the best answer.

1. The phenomenon of hindsight bias is an example of the _____ of long-term memory retrieval.
   a. instant replay view
   b. constructive processing view
   c. levels-of-processing view
   d. misinformation effect

2. In Loftus's 1978 study, subjects viewed a slide presentation of an accident. Later, some of the subjects were asked a question about a yield sign when the actual slides contained pictures of a stop sign. When these same subjects were later asked about what kind of sign was at the accident, they were very likely to be confused in this situation. This is an example of the _____.
   a. instant replay effect.
   b. constructive processing effect.
   c. levels-of-processing effect.
   d. misinformation effect.

3. Which of the following statements about memory retrieval while under hypnosis is TRUE?

   a. These memories are more accurate than other kinds of memories.
   b. People recalling memories under hypnosis are more confident in their memories, regardless of accuracy.
   c. Hypnosis makes it harder to recall memories in general.
   d. Age regression through hypnosis can increase the accuracy of recall of early childhood memories.

4. Pezdek and colleagues found that for a person to interpret thoughts and fantasies about false events as true memories _____.
   a. the event must seem as plausible as possible.
   b. the person must believe in repression.
   c. there is very little information provided about the event.
   d. they only need to hear about the event once.

Brainstorming: Think about the last time you argued with a family member about something that happened when you were younger. How might hindsight bias have played a part in your differing memories of the event?

ANSWERS ON PAGE AK–1

Why do we forget things? And why do we forget some things but not others?

What Were We Talking About? Forgetting

Why do we forget things? And why do we forget some things but not others?

5.10 Why do we forget?

Brad Williams, the Human Google of the opening story, seems to have a fairly normal life despite his unusual memory abilities. But the same has not been true of other people with not only the ability to remember nearly everything, but also the inability to *forget*. That is exactly the problem experienced in the case of A. R. Luria's (1968) famous *mnemonist*, Mr. S. (A mnemonist is a memory expert or someone with exceptional memory ability.) Mr. S. was a performing mnemonist, astonishing his audiences with lists of numbers that he memorized in minutes. But Mr. S. found that he *was unable to forget* the lists. He also could not easily separate important memories from trivial ones, and each time he looked at an object or read a word, images stimulated by that object or word would flood his mind. He eventually invented a way to "forget" things—by writing them on a piece of paper and then burning the paper (Luria, 1968).

The ability to forget seems necessary to one's sanity if the experience of Mr. S. is any indicator. But how fast do people forget things? Are there some things that are harder or easier to forget?

Ebbinghaus and the Forgetting Curve

Hermann Ebbinghaus (1913) was one of the first researchers to study forgetting. Because he did not want any verbal associations to aid him in remembering, he created several lists of "nonsense syllables," pronounceable but meaningless (such as GEX and WOL). He memorized a list, waited a specific amount of time, and then tried to retrieve the list, graphing his results each time. The result has become a familiar graph: the **curve of forgetting**. This graph clearly shows that forgetting happens quickly within the first hour after learning the lists and then tapers off gradually. (See Figure 5.9.) In other words, forgetting is greatest just after learning. This curve can be applied to other types of information as well. Although meaningful material is forgotten much more slowly and much less completely, the pattern obtained when testing for forgetting is similar (Conway et al., 1992).

DISTRIBUTED PRACTICE   In his early studies, Ebbinghaus (1885) found that it is also important not to try to "cram" information you want to remember into your brain. Research has found that spacing out one's study sessions, or **distributed practice**, will produce far better retrieval of information studied in this way than does *massed practice*, or the attempt to study a body of material all at once. For example, studying your psychology material for 3 hours may make you feel that you've done some really hard work, and you have. Unfortunately, you won't remember as much of what you studied as you would if you had shorter study times of 30 minutes to an hour followed by short breaks (Cepeda et al., 2006; Dempster & Farris, 1990; Donovan & Radosevich, 1999; Simon & Bjork, 2001). Ⓛ Ⓘ Ⓝ Ⓚ to Psychology in Action, p. PIA-11.

curve of forgetting   a graph showing a distinct pattern in which forgetting is very fast within the first hour after learning a list and then tapers off gradually.

distributed practice   spacing the study of material to be remembered by including breaks between study periods.

FIGURE 5.9 Curve of Forgetting
Ebbinghaus found that his recall of words from his memorized word lists was greatest immediately after learning the list but rapidly decreased within the first hour. After the first hour, forgetting leveled off.

encoding failure   failure to process information into memory.

memory trace   physical change in the brain that occurs when a memory is formed.

decay   loss of memory due to the passage of time, during which the memory trace is not used.

disuse   another name for decay, assuming that memories that are not used will eventually decay and disappear.

The fact that this woman can remember the things shown in the pictures even after many years makes it unlikely that the memory trace decay theory can explain all forgetting in long-term memory.

Encoding Failure

There are several reasons why people forget things. One of the simplest reasons is that some things never get encoded in the first place. Your friend, for example, may have said something to you as he walked out the door, and you may have heard him, but if you weren't paying attention to what he said, it would not get past sensory memory. This isn't forgetting so much as it is **encoding failure**, the failure to process information into memory. Researchers (Nickerson & Adams, 1979) developed a test of encoding failure using images of pennies. Looking at Figure 5.10, do you know which view of a penny is the correct one? People see pennies nearly every day, but how many people actually look at what's on the penny and try to remember it?

Memory Trace Decay Theory

One of the older theories of forgetting involves the concept of a **memory trace**. A memory trace is some physical change in the brain, perhaps in a neuron or in the activity between neurons, which occurs when a memory is formed (Brown, 1958; Peterson & Peterson, 1959). Over time, if these traces are not used, they may **decay**, fading into nothing. It would be similar to what happens when a number of people walk across a particular patch of grass, causing a path to appear in which the grass is trampled down and perhaps turning brown. But if people stop using the path, the grass grows back and the path disappears.

Forgetting in sensory memory and short-term memory seems easy to explain as decay: Information that is not brought to attention in sensory memory or continuously rehearsed in STM will fade away. But is decay a good explanation for forgetting from long-term memory? When referring to LTM, decay theory is usually called **disuse**, and the phrase "use it or lose it" takes on great meaning (Bjork & Bjork, 1992). Although the fading of information from LTM through disuse sounds logical, often people can recall memories they had assumed were long forgotten. There must be other factors involved in the forgetting of long-term memories.

Interference Theory

A possible explanation of LTM forgetting is that although most long-term memories may be stored more or less permanently in the brain, those memories may not always be accessible to attempted retrieval because other information

FIGURE 5.10 Which Penny Is Real?
Most people do not really look at the face of a penny. Which of these pennies represents an actual penny? The answer can be found on page 188.

interferes (Anderson & Neely, 1995). (And even memories that are accessible are subject to constructive processing, which can lead to inaccurate recall.) An analogy might be this: The can of paint that Phillip wants may very well be on some shelf in his storeroom, but there's so much other junk in its way that he can't see it and can't get to it. In the case of LTM, interference can come from two different "directions."

PROACTIVE INTERFERENCE Have you ever switched from driving a car with the gearshift on the wheel to one with the gearshift on the floor of the car? If the answer is yes, you probably found that you had some trouble when you first got into the new car. You may have grabbed at the wheel instead of reaching to the gearshift on the floor. The reason you reached for the gearshift in the "old" place is called **proactive interference**: the tendency for older or previously learned material to interfere with the learning (and subsequent retrieval) of new material (See Figure 5.11.)

Another example of proactive interference often occurs when someone gets a new cell phone. People in this situation often find themselves remembering their old cell phone number or some of its digits instead of the new cell phone number when they are trying to give the new number to friends.

RETROACTIVE INTERFERENCE When newer information interferes with the retrieval of older information, this is called **retroactive interference**. (See Figure 5.11.) What happens when you change back from the car with the gearshift on the floor to the older car with the gearshift on the wheel? You'll probably reach down to the floor at least once or twice because the newer skill retroactively interferes with remembering the old way of doing it.

How might interference work in each of the following cases?

1. Moving from the United States to England, where people drive on the left instead of the right side of the road.

2. Trying to program your old VCR after having the new one for a year.

3. Moving from one computer operating system to a different one, such as from Windows to Mac.

The different ways that forgetting occurs are summarized in Table 5.1.

proactive interference memory problem that occurs when older information prevents or interferes with the learning or retrieval of newer information.

retroactive interference memory retrieval problem that occurs when newer information prevents or interferes with the retrieval of older information.

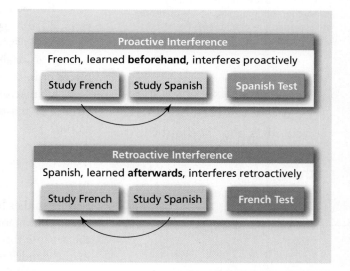

FIGURE 5.11 Proactive and Retroactive Interference
If a student were to study for a French exam and then a Spanish exam, interference could occur in two directions. When taking the Spanish exam, the French information studied first may proactively interfere with learning of the Spanish information. But when taking the French exam, the more recently studied Spanish information may retroactively interfere with the retrieval of the French information.

table 5.1 Reasons for Forgetting

REASON	DESCRIPTION
Encoding Failure	The information is not attended to and fails to be encoded.
Decay or Disuse	Information that is not accessed decays from the storage system over time.
Proactive Interference	Older information already in memory interferes with the learning of newer information.
Retroactive Interference	Newer information interferes with the retrieval of older information.

consolidation the changes that take place in the structure and functioning of neurons when a memory is formed.

[Read] and learn more about how researchers are mapping where memories are stored in the brain on **MyPsychLab**

All that explains is the "where" of memory. Did scientists ever find out the "what" or the exact physical change that happens in the brain when memories are stored?

The answer to **Figure 5.10** on page 186 is A.

Henry Gustav Molaison.

Neuroscience of Memory

5.11 How and where are memories formed in the brain?

Researchers have evidence that specific areas of the brain are physically altered during memory formation and that different areas may be involved for different types of memory. For example, procedural memories seem to be stored in the cerebellum (Boyd & Winstein, 2004; Daum & Schugens, 1996). Research involving PET scanning techniques strongly suggests that short-term memories are stored in the prefrontal cortex (the very front of the frontal lobe) and the temporal lobe (Goldman-Rakic, 1998; Rao et al., 1997). Memories of fear seem to be stored in the amygdala (Dębiec et al., 2010). [Read] on **MyPsychLab**

As for semantic and episodic long-term memories, evidence suggests that these memories are also stored in the frontal and temporal lobes but not in exactly the same places or in the same location as short-term memories (Weis et al., 2004).

● All that explains is the "where" of memory. Did scientists ever find out the "what" or the exact physical change that happens in the brain when memories are stored?

Neural Activity and Structure in Memory Formation

Several studies have offered evidence that memory formation involves not one physical change but many: changes in the number of receptor sites, changes in the sensitivity of the synapse through repeated stimulation (called *long-term potentiation*), and changes in the dendrites and in the proteins within the neurons (Alkon, 1989; Kandel & Schwartz, 1982; Shomrat et al., 2008; Squire & Kandel, 1999). All of these changes serve to increase the neural connections and make connections that already exist more sensitive to stimulation. These changes that take place as a memory is forming are called **consolidation**. Consolidation may take only a few minutes for some memories, such as learning a new friend's name, but may take years for others, such as learning a new language (Dudai, 2004).

The Hippocampus and Memory

In the discussion of the *hippocampus* (a part of the limbic system) in Chapter Two (p. 66), it was identified as the part of the brain that is responsible for the formation of new long-term declarative memories. A classic case study in psychology provides fairly clear evidence of the role of the hippocampus (Milner et al., 1968). H. M. was a 16-year-old suffering from severe epileptic seizures. H. M.'s hippocampi and adjacent medial temporal lobe structures were removed in an experimental operation that the surgeon hoped would stop his seizures. The hippocampus was not the source of his problem, but it was apparently the source of his ability to store any new information he encountered because without either hippocampus, he was completely unable to remember anything new. H. M., who can now be revealed as Henry Gustav Molaison, died in December 2008, at the age of 82. You can read more about H.M.'s contributions to science at Suzanne Corkin's Web site: **http://web.mit.edu/bnl/publications** (Carey, 2009).

When Memory Fails: Organic Amnesia

5.12 How does amnesia occur?

Problems in the functioning of the memory areas of the brain cause two forms of severe loss of memory disorders. These problems can result from concussions, brain injuries brought about by trauma, alcoholism (Korsakoff's syndrome), or disorders of the aging brain.

RETROGRADE AMNESIA If the hippocampus is that important to the formation of memories, what would happen if it got temporarily "disconnected"? People who are in accidents in which they received a head injury often are unable to recall the accident itself. Sometimes they cannot remember the last several hours or even days before the accident. This type of amnesia (literally, "without memory") is called **retrograde amnesia**, which is loss of memory from the point of injury backwards (Hodges, 1994). What apparently happens in this kind of memory loss is that the consolidation process, which was busy making the physical changes to allow new memories to be stored, gets disrupted and loses everything that was not already nearly "finished." It's similar to what happens when a computer's power goes out: Whatever you were working on that was not yet saved is gone.

One of the therapies for severe depression is *ECT*, or *electroconvulsive therapy*. LINK to Chapter Thirteen: Psychological Therapies, pp. 489–490. In one study with depressed patients who were being treated with ECT (Squire et al., 1975), patients were tested for their memory of certain television programs both before and after the treatment. Before treatment, recent programs were recalled in more detail and more often than older ones. But after treatment, these patients seemed to forget the *last three years of programs*, remembering only the older ones. Not only does this indicate that memories are lost when consolidation is interrupted (as it is by the seizure caused by the treatment) but also that consolidation may take not just days or months but sometimes years to be completed.

ANTEROGRADE AMNESIA Concussions can also cause a more temporary version of the kind of amnesia experienced by H. M. This kind of amnesia is called *anterograde amnesia*, or the loss of memories from the point of injury or illness forward (Squire & Slater, 1978). People with this kind of amnesia, like H. M., have difficulty remembering anything new. This is also the kind of amnesia most often seen in people with *senile dementia*, a mental disorder in which severe forgetfulness, mental confusion, and mood swings are the primary symptoms. (Dementia patients also may suffer from retrograde amnesia in addition to anterograde amnesia.) If retrograde amnesia is like losing a document in the computer because of a power loss, anterograde amnesia is like discovering that your hard drive has become defective—you can read data that are already on the hard drive, but you can't store any new information. As long as you are looking at the data in your open computer window (i.e., attending to the data), you can access the data, but as soon as you close that window (stop thinking about it), the information is lost, because it was never transferred to the hard drive (long-term memory). Read on **MyPsychLab**

This is the reason that elderly people with a dementia such as Alzheimer's will sometimes take several doses of medicine because they cannot remember having already taken a dose. It also makes for some very repetitive conversations, such as

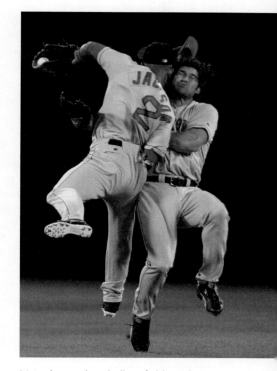

Major league baseball outfielder Johnny Damon (seen here colliding with player Damian Jackson) suffered a concussion after this injury. Concussions such as this can "wipe out" whatever was in the process of being consolidated into long-term memory. Which type of amnesia would you expect Johnny Damon to have, retrograde or anterograde?

Read and learn more about the fascinating topic of amnesia on **MyPsychLab**

retrograde amnesia loss of memory from the point of some injury or trauma backwards, or loss of memory for the past.

being told the same story or asked the same question numerous times in the space of a 20-minute conversation. For more about Alzheimer's disease, see Applying Psychology to Everyday Life at the bottom of this page.

practice quiz   How much do you remember?

5.10 5.11 5.12

Pick the best answer.

1. Salvatore was introduced to a number of new people on his first day at his new job. According to Ebbinghaus, when should Salvatore expect to have forgotten the greatest number of the names he has just learned?
   a. within the first hour after learning the names
   b. within the first day after learning the names
   c. near the end of the first week on the job
   d. near the middle of the first week on the job

2. When a person "forgets" what someone has just said because he wasn't paying attention to the speaker at all, it is an example of the _____ explanation of forgetting.
   a. interference
   b. memory trace
   c. encoding failure
   d. repression

3. Edna took sociology in the fall semester and is now taking psychology. Some of the concepts are similar, and Edna finds that she has trouble recalling some of the major sociology theorists. She keeps getting them confused with psychology theorists. Edna's problem is most likely due to _____.
   a. encoding failure.
   b. retroactive interference.
   c. proactive interference.
   d. none of the above.

4. Brian went from the United States, where he grew up, to England. The first week he was there, he had a terrible time remembering to drive on the left side of the road. His problem was most likely due to _____.
   a. encoding failure.
   b. retroactive interference.
   c. proactive interference.
   d. none of the above.

5. Katherine is trying to hold the names of the students she just met in her psychology class in short-term memory. According to studies, these short-term memories will be stored in what part of the brain?
   a. cerebellum
   b. hippocampus
   c. amygdala
   d. prefrontal lobes

6. Research suggests that memory formation is a function of _____.
   a. changes in the number of receptor sites.
   b. changes in the sensitivity of the synapse.
   c. changes in the dendrites and proteins within neurons.
   d. all of the above.

7. The role of the _____ in the formation of new long-term declarative memories was first made apparent in the case of H. M., a famous case study in amnesia.
   a. hippocampus
   b. amygdala
   c. frontal lobes
   d. cerebellum

8. T. J. was in a car accident and suffered a concussion. After he recovered, he found that he could not remember the accident itself or the events of the morning leading up to the accident. T. J. had which kind of amnesia?
   a. retrograde
   b. anterograde
   c. Alzheimer's disease
   d. infantile amnesia

Brainstorming: Why do you think that amnesia (no matter what type it is) seems to affect mainly episodic memories?

ANSWERS ON PAGE AK–1

applying psychology to everyday life
Alzheimer's Disease

5.13 What are the facts about Alzheimer's disease?

Nearly 5.3 million Americans have Alzheimer's disease (Alzheimer's Association, 2010). It is the most common type of dementia found in adults and the elderly, accounting for nearly 60 to 80 percent of all cases of dementia. It is estimated that 1 out of 8 people over the age of 65 has Alzheimer's disease. It has also become the third leading cause of death in late adulthood, with only heart disease and cancer responsible for more deaths (Alzheimer's Association, 2010; Antuono et al., 2001). In the past, the only way to diagnose Alzheimer's effectively was in an autopsy, but a recent study suggests that those who develop the disease may show signs of degeneration of the nervous system decades prior to the actual onset of the disease, leading to the hope that one day Alzheimer's may be diagnosed early enough to make full use of current treatments (Mortimer et al., 2008).

Symptoms usually begin with changes in memory, which may be rather mild at first but which become more severe over time, causing the person to become more and more forgetful about everyday tasks, such as remembering to turn off the stove. Eventually more dangerous forgetting occurs, such as taking extra doses of medication or leaving something cooking on the stove unattended. It is a costly disease to care for, and care-givers often face severe emotional and financial burdens in caring for a loved one who is slowly becoming a stranger.

What causes Alzheimer's disease is not completely understood. While it is normal for the brain to begin to form beta-amyloid protein deposits (plaques) and for strands of the protein tau to become twisted ("tangles"), people who suffer from Alzheimer's disease are found to have far more of these physical signs of an aging brain. One of the neurotransmitters involved in the formation of memories in the hippocampus is acetylcholine, and the neurons that produce this chemical break down in the early stages of the disease. While one early-onset form of Alzheimer's appears to be genetic and involves several different genetic variations, this seems to be the case for fewer than 5 percent of the total cases of the disease (Alzheimer's Association, 2010; Bertram & Tanzi, 2005). The sad truth is that there is not one cause, but many, and even those who do NOT have Alzheimer's disease are not safe from other forms of dementia, such as dementia caused by strokes, dehydration, medications, and so on.

Treatments can slow but not halt or reverse the course of the disease. Five drugs are currently approved for treatment, but as yet they only slow down the symptoms for an average of 6 to 12 months. Many experimental therapies are in human trials, but it will be a while before any are known to be successful and are put into practice. What is known is that the risk factors for Alzheimer's (and many other forms of dementia) are something that can be managed: high cholesterol, high blood pressure, smoking, obesity, Type II diabetes, a high-fat diet, and lack of exercise all contribute (Alzheimer's Association, 2010; Calon et al., 2008; Sweat, 2010). Keeping the brain mentally active is also a way to help prolong good cognitive health. One recent study's findings indicate that continued every-day learning stimulates brain-derived neurotrophic factors (BDNF), a key protein involved in the formation of memories (L. Y. Chen et al., 2010).

QUESTIONS FOR FURTHER DISCUSSION
1. People are now living much longer than their ancestors, and it is no longer unusual to hear of people who are well over 100 years of age. How might this extension of life expectancy be related to an increased rate of Alzheimer's disease?
2. What kinds of social programs or interventions could help people who are taking care of a relative with Alzheimer's?

chapter summary
((• Listen on MyPsychLab   Listen to an audio file of your chapter www.MyPsychLab

Three Processes of Memory

5.1 What are the three processes of memory and the different models of how memory works?

- Memory can be defined as an active system that receives information from the senses, organizes and alters it as it stores it away, and then retrieves the information from storage.
- The three processes are encoding, storage, and retrieval.

Models of Memory

- In the levels-of-processing model of memory, information that gets more deeply processed is more likely to be remembered.
- In the parallel distributed processing model of memory, information is simultaneously stored across an interconnected neural network that stretches across the brain.

The Information-Processing Model: Three Stages of Memory

5.2 How does sensory memory work?

- Iconic memory is the visual sensory memory in which an afterimage or icon will be held in neural form for about one-fourth to one-half second.
- Echoic memory is the auditory form of sensory memory and takes the form of an echo that lasts up to 4 seconds.

5.3 What is short-term memory, and how does it differ from working memory?

- Short-term memory is where information is held while it is conscious and being used. It holds about seven plus or minus two chunks of information and lasts about 30 seconds without rehearsal.
- Working memory is an active system responsible for processing the information in STM.
- STM is easily lost through decay or interference.

5.4 How is long-term memory different from other types of memory?

- Long-term memory is the system in which memories that are to be kept more or less permanently are stored and is unlimited in capacity and relatively permanent in duration.

- Information that is more deeply processed, or processed according to meaning, will be retained and retrieved more efficiently.

5.5 What are the various types of long-term memory, and how is information stored in long-term memory organized?

- Procedural memories are memories for skills, habits, and conditioned responses. Declarative memories are memories for general facts and personal experiences and include both semantic memories and episodic memories.

- Implicit memories are difficult to bring into conscious awareness, whereas explicit memories are those that a person is aware of possessing.

- LTM is organized in the form of semantic networks, or nodes of related information spreading out from a central piece of knowledge.

Getting It Out: Retrieval of Long-Term Memories

5.6 What kinds of cues help people remember?

- Retrieval cues are words, meanings, sounds, and other stimuli that are encoded at the same time as a new memory.

- Encoding specificity occurs when physical surroundings become encoded as retrieval cues for specific memories.

- State-dependent learning occurs when physiological or psychological states become encoded as retrieval cues for memories formed while in those states.

5.7 How do the retrieval processes of recall and recognition differ, and how reliable are our memories of events?

- Recall is a type of memory retrieval in which the information to be retrieved must be "pulled" out of memory with few or no cues, whereas recognition involves matching information with stored images or facts.

- The serial position effect, or primacy or recency effect, occurs when the first items and the last items in a list of information are recalled more efficiently than items in the middle of the list.

classic studies in psychology: Elizabeth Loftus and Eyewitnesses

- Loftus and others have found that people constantly update and revise their memories of events. Part of this revision may include adding information acquired later to a previous memory. That later information may also be in error, further contaminating the earlier memory.

- Automatic encoding of some kinds of information requires very little effort to place information into long-term memory.

- Memory for particularly emotional or traumatic events can lead to the formation of flashbulb memories, memories that seem as vivid and detailed as if the person were looking at a snapshot of the event but that are no more accurate than any other memories.

The Reconstructive Nature of Long-Term Memory Retrieval: How Reliable Are Memories?

5.8 How are long-term memories formed, and how can this process lead to inaccuracies in memory?

- Memories are reconstructed from the various bits and pieces of information that have been stored away in different places at the time of encoding in a process called constructive processing.

- Hindsight bias occurs when people falsely believe that they knew the outcome of some event because they have included knowledge of the event's true outcome into their memories of the event itself.

- The misinformation effect refers to the tendency of people who are asked misleading questions or given misleading information to incorporate that information into their memories for a particular event.

5.9 What is false memory syndrome?

- Rather than improving memory retrieval, hypnosis makes the creation of false memories more likely.

- False memory syndrome is the creation of false or inaccurate memories through suggestion, especially while hypnotized.

- Pezdek and colleagues assert that false memories are more likely to be formed for plausible false events than for implausible ones.

What Were We Talking About? Forgetting

5.10 Why do we forget?

- Ebbinghaus found that information is mostly lost within 1 hour after learning and then gradually fades away. This is known as the curve of forgetting.

- Some "forgetting" is actually a failure to encode information.

- Memory trace decay theory assumes the presence of a physical memory trace that decays with disuse over time.

- Forgetting in LTM is most likely due to proactive or retroactive interference.

Neuroscience of Memory

- Evidence suggests that procedural memories are stored in the cerebellum, whereas short-term memories are stored in the prefrontal and temporal lobes of the cortex.

- Semantic and episodic memories may be stored in the frontal and temporal lobes as well but in different locations than short-term memory, whereas memory for fear of objects is most likely stored in the amygdala.

5.11 How and where are memories formed in the brain?

- Consolidation consists of the physical changes in neurons that take place during the formation of a memory.

- The hippocampus appears to be responsible for the storage of new long-term declarative memories. If it is removed, the ability to store anything new is completely lost.

5.12 How does amnesia occur?

- In retrograde amnesia, memory for the past (prior to the injury) is lost, which can be a loss of only minutes or a loss of several years.

- ECT, or electroconvulsive therapy, can disrupt consolidation and cause retrograde amnesia.

- In anterograde amnesia, memory for anything new becomes impossible, although old memories may still be retrievable.

applying psychology to everyday life: Alzheimer's Disease

5.13 What are the facts about Alzheimer's disease?

- The primary memory difficulty in Alzheimer's is anterograde amnesia, although retrograde amnesia can also occur as the disease progresses.

- Alzheimer's disease has multiple causes, many of which are not yet identified.

- There are various drugs in use or in development for use in slowing or stopping the progression of Alzheimer's disease.

- Exercising the brain and tending to the health of the cardiovascular system can help put off or prevent various forms of dementia, including Alzheimer's disease.

Study and Review on MyPsychLab   Ready for your test? More quizzes and a customized plan. www.MyPsychLab

Pick the best answer.

1. Memory can best be described as _____.
   a. a series of storage bins or boxes.
   b. a process of storage.
   c. an active system that encodes, stores, and retrieves information.
   d. a series of passive data files.

2. In the _____ model of memory, memories are simultaneously created and stored across a mental network.
   a. levels-of-processing
   b. parallel distributed processing
   c. transfer-appropriate processing
   d. information-processing

3. Roberta looked up from her book, realizing that Joaquin had just said something to her. What was it? Oh, yes, he had just asked her if she wanted to go out to dinner. Roberta's ability to retrieve what Joaquin said is due to her _____.
   a. iconic sensory memory.
   b. echoic sensory memory.
   c. short-term memory.
   d. tactile sensory memory.

4. Although Sperling found evidence that iconic memory lasts about half a second, in reality information gets pushed out rather quickly by newer information. Evidence suggests that iconic memory really lasts about _____ of a second.
   a. three-quarters
   b. half
   c. one-quarter
   d. one-tenth

5. The duration of echoic memory is _____ than iconic memory, but its capacity is probably _____.
   a. shorter; larger.
   b. longer; smaller.
   c. longer; about the same.
   d. shorter; about the same.

6. When Greg tried to remember the name of his employer's wife, he had trouble getting the right name. At first he thought it might be Sandy or Candy but finally realized that it was Mandy. Greg's confusion is evidence that short-term memories are primarily encoded in _____ form.
   a. acoustic
   b. visual
   c. tactile
   d. optical

7. Although the capacity of short-term memory is limited, more items can be held in this kind of storage through the process of _____.
   a. chunking.
   b. decoding.
   c. rote rehearsal.
   d. data compression.

8. The best method for encoding long-term memories is probably to use _____.
   a. maintenance rehearsal.
   b. rote rehearsal.
   c. elaborative rehearsal.
   d. sleep learning.

9. The levels-of-processing concept of Craik and Lockhart would suggest that which of the following questions would lead to better memory of the word *frog*?
   a. Does it rhyme with *blog*?
   b. Is it in capital letters?
   c. Is it written in cursive?
   d. Would it be found in a pond?

10. Which type of long-term memory is revised and updated more or less constantly?
    a. procedural
    b. declarative
    c. semantic
    d. episodic

11. Knowledge that we gain from school is called _____ memory.
    a. procedural
    b. declarative
    c. semantic
    d. episodic

12. The semantic network model of memory would suggest that which of the following questions would take longest to answer?
    a. Is a collie a dog?
    b. Is a collie a mammal?
    c. Is a collie an animal?
    d. There would be no difference in answering times.

13. The research of Eich and Metcalfe would suggest that if you were really angry when you were learning Spanish, you should be _____ when taking the final exam for best retrieval.
    a. really calm
    b. unemotional
    c. angry
    d. depressed

14. Which of the following is NOT an example of a test using recall?
    a. short answer
    b. essay
    c. fill in the blanks
    d. true–false

15. The serial position effect predicts that the _____ of the list will be remembered best.
    a. beginning
    b. end
    c. middle
    d. beginning and the end

16. Melanie was having a difficult time describing the man who took her purse in the mall parking but was able to identify him from pictures the officer showed to her. Melanie's situation is a reminder that in comparing recognition to recall, recognition tends to be _____.
    a. easier.
    b. slower.
    c. more difficult.
    d. less accurate.

17. Is eyewitness testimony usually accurate?
    a. Yes, because seeing is believing.
    b. No, because eyewitnesses are not usually honest.
    c. Yes, because eyewitnesses are very confident.
    d. No, because there is a great possibility of a "false positive" identification.

18. The passage of time and frequency of events are examples of knowledge that is often subject to _____.
    a. encoding specificity.
    b. automatic encoding.
    c. flashbulb memories.
    d. eidetic imagery.

19. When retrieving a long-term memory, bits and pieces of information are gathered from various areas and put back together in a process called _____.
    a. consolidation.
    b. redintegration.
    c. constructive processing.
    d. automatic processing.

20. A problem with using decay or disuse theory to explain forgetting from long-term memory is that _____.
    a. older people can still remember things from their early years.
    b. there is no physical change in the brain when forming long-term memories.
    c. older memories get lost, whereas newer memories remain.
    d. older people cannot remember events in their childhood.

21. You started out by using WordPerfect and then moved to Microsoft Word. If you have trouble with Word, it is most likely due to _____.
    a. proactive interference.
    b. retroactive interference.
    c. anterograde interference.
    d. consolidation problems.

22. The earliest and main type of memory problem that people with dementia typically have is called _____.
    a. psychogenic amnesia.
    b. retrograde amnesia.
    c. retroactive amnesia.
    d. anterograde amnesia.

5 memory

5.1   p. 164

- an active system that receives, organizes, stores, and retrieves information

All information lost within a second or so.

Unrehearsed information is lost in about 15 to 30 seconds.

Information is retained indefinitely although some information may be difficult to retrieve.

Three Processes of Memory

- three basic steps
  - **encoding**
  - **storage**
  - **retrieval**

Models of Memory

- **information-processing model**
  - focuses on the way information is processed through different stages of memory

- **parallel distributed processing (PDP) model**
  - focuses on simultaneous processing of information across multiple neural networks

- **levels-of-processing model**
  - focuses on the depth of processing associated with specific information
  - deeper processing associated with longer retention

5.2   5.3   5.4   5.5   p. 166

The Information-Processing Model

(proposes three stages that vary both in duration and capacity; information must be processed effectively at earlier stages before long-term storage occurs)

- **sensory memory**
  capacity limited, duration <1 sec to 4 sec
  - **iconic** (visual)
  - **echoic** (auditory)

- **short-term and working memory**
  capacity limited (3–5 items), duration 12–30 secs without rehearsal
  - chunking and maintenance rehearsal can be used to increase capacity and duration, respectively

- **long-term memory**
  capacity seemingly unlimited, duration relatively permanent
  - associated with physical changes in the brain; hippocampus and cortex involved in consolidation of information from short-term to long-term memory
  - different types, based on information stored; different brain areas associated with each
  - organized in terms of related meanings and concepts
  - **semantic network model**
  - **parallel distributed processing model**

5.6 5.7 p. 176

getting it out ━━
- retrieval cues
- encoding specificity
- state-dependent learning

Retrieval of Long-Term Memories

recall vs. recognition ━━
- **recall:** few or no external cues required
- **recognition:** match incoming sensory information (e.g., see or hear) to what is already in memory

automatic encoding ━━ strong emotional associations can lead to vivid and detailed "flashbulb" memories

ED? TED? FRED? NED? TIM? JIM?

WILL? BILL? HARRY? LARRY? BARRY?

"Hey, good buddy! How you doin'?"   "Can't kick, big fella. What's shakin'?"

5.8 5.9 p. 181

constructive processing of memories ━━
- memories are rarely completely accurate and become less accurate over time
- Loftus and others have suggested that memory retrieval is a constructive process; memories are "built" at time of retrieval

The Reconstructive Nature of Long-Term Memory

memory retrieval problems ━━
- **misinformation effect**
- **reliability of memory retrieval**

5.10 p. 184

Forgetting

(originally studied by Ebbinghaus in 1913, research produced forgetting curve)

distributed practice produces far better retrieval than massed practice (cramming)

encoding failure nonattended information is not encoded into memory

memory trace decay over time, if not used, neuronal connections can weaken or decay

interference other information interferes with accurate retrieval

table 5.1 Reasons for Forgetting

REASON	DESCRIPTION
Encoding Failure	The information is not attended to and fails to be encoded.
Decay or Disuse	Information that is not accessed decays from the storage system over time.
Proactive Interference	Older information already in memory interferes with the learning of newer information.
Retroactive Interference	Newer information interferes with the retrieval of older information.

Proactive Interference

French, learned **beforehand**, interferes proactively

Study French | Study Spanish | Spanish Test

Retroactive Interference

Spanish, learned **afterwards**, interferes retroactively

Study French | Study Spanish | French Test

5.11 5.12 p. 188

different brain areas are associated with different types of memory ━━
- **procedural memories**
- **short-term memories**
- **semantic and episodic long-term memories**

amnesia
- **organic amnesia**
- **infantile amnesia**

several physical changes in brain are associated with memory formation (consolidation)
- changes at receptor (long-term potentiation)
- changes in dendrites

Neuroscience of Memory ━━ **hippocampus** plays a vital role in the formation of new declarative long-term memories

6

consciousness and cognition

why study consciousness, the nature of thought, and communication?

Consciousness, as humans experience it, is the key difference between humans and the lower animals. Waking thought, sleeping, and other forms of conscious awareness make up the better part of the human experience. Many theorists also see language as the major "dividing line" between humans and animals, but that line seems to be blurring—or is it? In a very real sense, to understand consciousness is to understand what it means to be who we are. We need to understand more about the thought processes that occur when we are asleep or awake. Why do we need to sleep at all? What is the difference between dreaming thought and waking thought? How do we organize our thoughts and use them to solve problems? How do we communicate those thoughts to others? How close do animals really come to true language?

chapter outline

What Is Consciousness?

Altered States: Sleep

PSYCHOLOGY IN THE NEWS:
Murder While Sleepwalking

How People Think

Language

APPLYING PSYCHOLOGY
TO EVERYDAY LIFE:
Mental and Physical Exercises
Combine for Better Cognitive Health

What Do You Mean, It's All Over?

While the doctor and nurses assured Latashia that she would not feel any discomfort or even remember anything about her colonoscopy, she wasn't so sure. As she lay on the gurney, the nurse came by and said, "I'm going to put the medication in your IV now." Latashia watched as the nurse inserted the hypodermic needle into the IV tubing and then walked away. She waited for some kind of "sleepy" feeling, but nothing seemed to be happening.

In what Latashia estimated to be about 5 minutes later, the nurse returned and asked if she wanted some juice to drink. Surprised that she was being offered something, Latashia said, "Can I have something to drink before the procedure?" The nurse just smiled and pointed to the clock on the wall. "Honey, the procedure was over nearly an hour ago." The drug Latashia received had completely erased her memories of the last 2 hours! How could a drug have such a powerful affect on her awareness? Read on!

learning objectives

6.1 What does it mean to be conscious, and are there different levels of consciousness?

6.2 Why do people need to sleep, and how does sleep work?

6.3 What are the different stages of sleep, including the stage of dreaming and its importance?

6.4 How do sleep disorders interfere with normal sleep?

6.5 How are mental images and concepts involved in the process of thinking?

6.6 What are the methods people use to solve problems and make decisions?

6.7 Why does problem solving sometimes fail, and what is meant by creative thinking?

6.8 How is language defined, and what are its different elements and structure?

6.9 Does language influence the way people think, and are animals capable of learning language?

6.10 What are some ways to improve thinking?

study tip

As you are reading this chapter, take a look back at page PIA-12 in *Psychology in Action* for some useful information about how sleep affects your ability to remember what you study.

👁 **Watch** Episode 6: *Consciousness* and Episode 10: *Cognition and Language* in the MyPsychLab video series

What exactly is meant by the term *consciousness*? I've heard it a lot, but I'm not sure that I know everything it means.

So where does that leave us in the search for a working definition of consciousness?

consciousness a person's awareness of everything that is going on around him or her at any given moment, which is used to organize behavior.

waking consciousness state in which thoughts, feelings, and sensations are clear and organized, and the person feels alert.

altered state of consciousness state in which there is a shift in the quality or pattern of mental activity as compared to waking consciousness.

What Is Consciousness?

6.1 What does it mean to be conscious, and are there different levels of consciousness?

● What exactly is meant by the term *consciousness*? I've heard it a lot, but I'm not sure that I know everything it means.

Consciousness is one of those terms that most people think they understand until someone asks them to define it. Various sorts of scientists, psychologists, neuroscientists, philosophers, and even computer scientists (who have been trying to develop an artificial intelligence for some time now), have tried to define consciousness, and so there are several definitions—one for nearly every field in which consciousness is studied. Although early psychologist William James spoke of a "stream of consciousness" in which ideas, sensations, and thoughts flow from one into another (James, 1890), philosopher Daniel Dennett asserts that there is no single stream of consciousness but rather multiple "channels," each of which is handling its own tasks (Dennett, 1991). All of these channels operate in parallel, in a kind of chaos of consciousness. People must somehow organize all this conscious experience, and their particular social groups and culture influence that organization.

Do animals experience consciousness in the same way as people? That is a question too complex to answer fully here, but many researchers into animal behavior, language, and cognition have some reason to propose that a kind of consciousness exists in at least some animals, although its organization would naturally not be the same as human consciousness (Block, 2005; Browne, 2004; Hurley & Nudds, 2006; Koch & Mormann, 2010). In their chapter on neurobiology and consciousness, Dr. Christof Koch and Dr. Florian Mormann (Koch & Mormann, 2010, p. 1225) state that "there is little reason to doubt that other mammals share conscious feelings . . . with humans." Later in this chapter a discussion of animal language touches on some of these issues.

Definition of Consciousness

● So where does that leave us in the search for a working definition of consciousness?

For our purposes, a more useful definition of consciousness might be the following: **Consciousness** is your awareness of everything that is going on around you and inside your own head at any given moment, which you use to organize your behavior (Farthing, 1992), including your thoughts, sensations, and feelings. In a cognitive neuroscience view, consciousness is generated by a set of action potentials in the communication among neurons just sufficient to produce a specific perception, memory, or experience in our awareness (Crick & Koch, 1990, 2003; Koch & Mormann, 2010). In other words, your eyes see a dog, the neurons along the optic pathway to the occipital lobe's visual cortex are activated, and the visual association cortex is activated to identify the external stimulus as a "dog." Bam!—consciousness! ⓁⒾⓃⓀ to Chapter Two: The Biological Perspective, p. 68.

Much of people's time awake is spent in a state called **waking consciousness** in which their thoughts, feelings, and sensations are clear and organized, and they feel alert. But there are many times in daily activities and in life when people experience states of consciousness that differ from this organized waking state. These variations are called "altered states of consciousness."

Altered States of Consciousness

An **altered state of consciousness** occurs when a shift takes place in the quality or pattern of your mental activity. Thoughts may become fuzzy and disorganized and you may feel less alert, or your thoughts may take bizarre turns, as they so often do in dreams. Sometimes being in an altered state may mean being in a state of *increased* alertness, as when you are under the influence of a stimulant. You may also divide your conscious awareness, as when you drive to work or school and then wonder how you got there—one level of conscious awareness was driving, while the other was thinking about the day ahead, perhaps. This altered state of divided consciousness can be a dangerous thing, as many people who try to drive and talk on a cell phone at the same time have discovered. Driving and carrying on a phone conversation are both processes that should demand focused attention, and it is simply not possible to do both at once in a safe and efficient manner. Studies have shown that driving while talking on a cell phone, even a hands-free phone, puts a person at the same degree of risk as driving under the influence of alcohol (Alm & Nilsson, 1995; Briem & Hedman, 1995; Strayer & Drews, 2007; Strayer & Johnston, 2001; Strayer et al., 2006). Texting while driving is more than risky—it can be murderous (Eastern Virginia Medical School, 2009).

There are many forms of altered states of consciousness, such as being under the influence of certain drugs, daydreaming, being hypnotized, or achieving a meditative state. (LINK) to Chapter Nine: Stress and Health, p. 337. But the most common altered state people experience is the one they spend about a third of their lives in on a nightly basis—sleep.

The driver of this car has several competing demands on his attention: working his cell phone, listening to the passenger read from a letter, and driving his car. If he manages to get himself and his passenger safely to their destination, it's possible that he won't even remember the trip—he may be driving in an altered state of consciousness.

Altered States: Sleep

Have you ever wondered why people have to sleep? They could get so much more work done if they didn't have to sleep, and they would have more time to play and do creative things.

The Biology of Sleep

6.2 Why do people need to sleep, and how does sleep work?

Sleep was once referred to as "the gentle tyrant" (Webb, 1992). People can try to stay awake, and sometimes they may go for a while without sleep, but eventually they *must* sleep. One reason for this fact is that sleep is one of the human body's *biological rhythms*, that is, natural cycles of activity that the body must go through. Some biological rhythms are monthly, like the cycle of a woman's menstruation, whereas others are far shorter—the beat of the heart is a biological rhythm. But many biological rhythms take place on a daily basis, like the rise and fall of blood pressure and body temperature or the production of certain body chemicals (Moore-Ede et al., 1982). The most obvious of these is the sleep–wake cycle (Baehr et al., 2000).

THE RHYTHMS OF LIFE: CIRCADIAN RHYTHMS The sleep–wake cycle is a **circadian rhythm**. The term actually comes from two Latin words, *circa* ("about") and *diem* ("day"). So a circadian rhythm is a cycle that takes "about a day" to complete.

For most people, this means that they will experience several hours of sleep at least once during every 24-hour period. The sleep–wake cycle is ultimately controlled by the brain, specifically by an area within the *hypothalamus*, the tiny section of the brain that influences the glandular system. (LINK) to Chapter Two: The Biological Perspective, p. 66.

Ever heard of melatonin? A lot of people were buying supplements of *melatonin* (a hormone normally secreted by the pineal gland) several years ago, hoping to sleep better and perhaps even slow the effects of aging (Folkard et al., 1993; Herxheimer & Petrie, 2001; Young, 1996). The release of melatonin is influenced by a structure deep within the

circadian rhythm a cycle of bodily rhythm that occurs over a 24-hour period.

rapid eye movement (REM)   stage of sleep in which the eyes move rapidly under the eyelids and the person is typically experiencing a dream.

non-REM (NREM) sleep   any of the stages of sleep that do not include REM.

alpha waves   brain waves that indicate a state of relaxation or light sleep.

theta waves   brain waves indicating the early stages of sleep.

delta waves   long, slow waves that indicate the deepest stage of sleep.

So are there different kinds of sleep? Do you go from being awake to being asleep and dreaming —is it instant?

hypothalamus in an area called the *suprachiasmatic* (SOO-prah-ki-AS-ma-tik) *nucleus*, the internal clock that tells people when to wake up and when to fall asleep (Quintero et al., 2003; Yamaguchi et al., 2003; Zisapel, 2001). The suprachiasmatic nucleus, or SCN, is sensitive to changes in light. As daylight fades, the SCN tells the pineal gland (located in the base of the brain) to secrete melatonin (Bondarenko, 2004; Delagrange & Guardiola-Lemaitre, 1997). As melatonin accumulates, a person will feel sleepy. As the light coming into the eyes increases (as it does in the morning), the SCN tells the pineal gland to stop secreting melatonin, allowing the body to awaken.

HOW MUCH SLEEP DO PEOPLE NEED?   How much sleep is enough sleep? The answer varies from person to person depending on age and possibly inherited sleep needs (Feroah et al., 2004), but most young adults need about 7 to 9 hours of sleep each 24-hour period in order to function well. (See Figure 6.1.) Some people are short sleepers, needing only 4 or 5 hours, whereas others are long sleepers and require more than 9 hours of sleep (McCann & Stewin, 1988). As we age, we seem to sleep less during each night until the average length of sleep approaches only 6 hours.

The Stages of Sleep

So are there different kinds of sleep? Do you go from being awake to being asleep and dreaming—is it instant?

There are actually two kinds of sleep: **REM (rapid eye movement) sleep** and **non-REM (NREM) sleep**. REM sleep is a relatively active type of sleep when most of a person's dreaming takes place, whereas non-REM sleep is a much deeper, more restful kind of sleep. In REM sleep, the voluntary muscles are inhibited, meaning that the person in REM sleep moves very little, whereas in non-REM sleep the person's body is free to move around (including kicking one's bed partner!). There are also several different stages of sleep that people go through each night in which REM sleep and non-REM sleep occur. A machine called an electroencephalograph allows scientists to record the brain-wave activity as a person passes through the various stages of sleep and to determine what type of sleep the person has entered (Aserinsky & Kleitman, 1953). See Figure 6.2 for a look at what happens in each stage of sleep.

A person who is wide awake and mentally active will show a brain-wave pattern on the electroencephalogram (EEG) called **beta waves**. Beta waves are very small and very fast. As the person relaxes and gets drowsy, slightly larger and slower **alpha waves** appear. The alpha waves are eventually replaced by even slower and larger **theta waves**. In the deepest stages of sleep, the largest and slowest waves appear, called **delta waves**.

FIGURE 6.1 Sleep Patterns of Infants and Adults

Infants need far more sleep than older children and adults. Both REM sleep and NREM sleep decrease dramatically in the first 10 years of life, with the greater decrease being in REM sleep. Nearly 50 percent of an infant's sleep is REM, compared to only about 20 percent for a normal, healthy adult (Roffwarg et al., 1966).

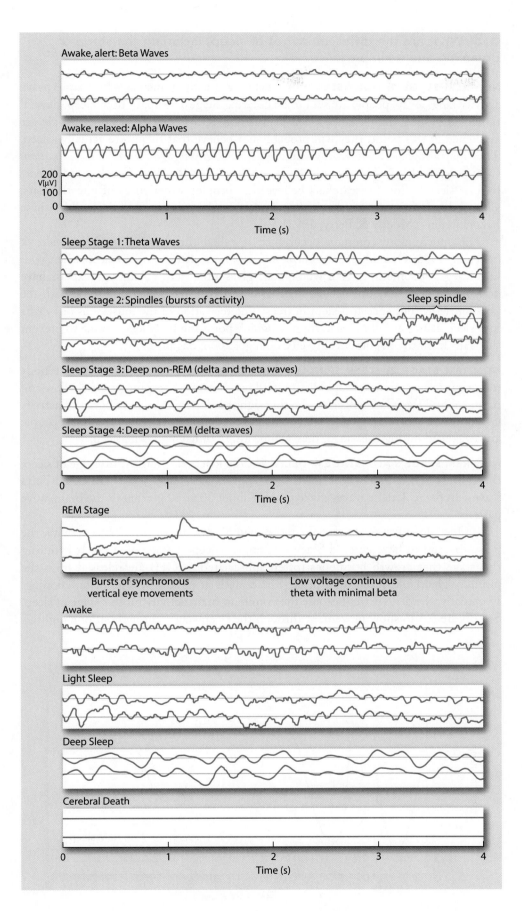

FIGURE 6.2 Brain Activity during Sleep
The EEG reflects brain activity during both waking and sleep. This activity varies according to level of alertness while awake (top two segments) and the stage of sleep (middle segments). Sleep Stages 3 and 4 are indicated by the presence of delta activity, which is much slower and accounts for the larger, slower waves on these graphs. [*Note*: The American Academy of Sleep Medicine (Iber et al., 2007) has recently published updated guidelines for the scoring of sleep activity, and one major change has been to combine NREM stages 3 and 4 into a single stage, now indicated by N3.] REM has activity that resembles alert wakefulness but has relatively no muscle activity except rapid eye movement. The bottom segments illustrate how EEG activity differs between wakefulness, light and deep sleep, and lastly what it looks like when brain activity has ceased in cerebral death. EEG data and images in this figure are courtesy of Dr. Leslie Sherlin.

6.3 What are the different stages of sleep, including the stage of dreaming and its importance?

NON-REM STAGE 1: LIGHT SLEEP As theta wave activity increases and alpha wave activity fades away, people are said to be entering Stage 1 sleep, or light sleep. Several rather interesting things can happen in this non-REM stage of sleep. If people are awakened at this point, they will probably not believe that they were actually asleep. They may also experience vivid visual events called *hypnogogic images* or *hallucinations* (Mavromatis, 1987; Mavromatis & Richardson, 1984). (The Greek word *hypnos* means "sleep.") Some researchers believe that peoples' experiences of ghostly visits, alien abductions, and near-death experiences may be most easily explained by these hallucinations (Moody & Perry, 1993).

A much more common occurrence is called the *hypnic jerk* (Mahowald & Schenck, 1996; Oswald, 1959). Have you ever been drifting off to sleep when your knees, legs, or sometimes your whole body gives a big "jerk"? Although experts have no solid proof of why this occurs, many believe that it has something to do with the possibility that our ancestors slept in trees: The relaxation of the muscles as one drifts into sleep causes a "falling" sensation, at which point the body jerks awake to prevent the "fall" from the hypothetical tree (Coolidge, 2006; Sagan, 1977).

NON-REM STAGE 2: SLEEP SPINDLES As people drift further into sleep, the body temperature continues to drop. Heart rate slows, breathing becomes more shallow and irregular, and the EEG will show the first signs of *sleep spindles*, brief bursts of activity lasting only a second or two. Theta waves still predominate in this stage, but if people are awakened during this stage, they will be aware of having been asleep.

NON-REM STAGE 3 AND STAGE 4: DELTA WAVES ROLL IN In the third stage of sleep, the slowest and largest waves make their appearance. These waves are called **delta waves**. In Stage 3, delta waves make up only about 20 to 50 percent of the brain-wave pattern.

Once delta waves account for more than 50 percent of total brain activity, the person is said to have entered Stage 4 sleep, the deepest stage of sleep. It is during this stage that growth hormones (often abbreviated as GH) are released from the pituitary gland and reach their peak. The body is at its lowest level of functioning. Eventually, the delta waves become the dominant brain activity for this stage of sleep. See Figure 6.3 to show movement through the sleep stages throughout one night.

FIGURE 6.3 A Typical Night's Sleep The graph shows the typical progression through the night of the different stages of sleep. The four non-REM stages are indicated on the *y*-axis; REM stages are represented by the green curves on the graph. The REM periods occur about every 90 minutes throughout the night (Dement, 1974).

Children spend more time in deep sleep so that their bodies will grow and are even harder to wake up during this stage than are adults. The fact that children do sleep so deeply may explain why certain sleep disorders are more common in childhood. Indeed, many sleep disorders are more common in boys than in girls because boys sleep more deeply than do girls due to high levels of the male hormone testosterone (Miyatake et al., 1980; Thiedke, 2001). ✳️Explore on MyPsychLab

✳️ Explore sleep and dreaming in the Virtual Brain on **MyPsychLab**

What Happens in REM Sleep?

After spending some time in Stage 4, the sleeping person will go back up through Stage 3, Stage 2, and then into a stage in which body temperature increases to near-waking levels, the eyes move rapidly under the eyelids, the heart beats much faster, and brain waves resemble beta waves—the kind of brain activity that usually signals wakefulness. The person is still asleep but in the stage known as rapid eye movement sleep (REM).

When a person in REM sleep is awakened, he or she almost always reports being in a dream state (Shafton, 1995). REM sleep is, therefore, associated with dreaming, and 90 percent of dreams actually take place in REM sleep. People do have dreams in the other non-REM (or NREM) stages, but REM dreams tend to be more vivid, more detailed, longer, and more bizarre than the dreams of NREM sleep. NREM dreams tend to be more like thoughts about daily occurrences and far shorter than REM dreams (Foulkes & Schmidt, 1983; Takeuchi et al., 2003). Fortunately, the body is unable to act upon these dreams under normal conditions because the voluntary muscles are paralyzed during REM sleep, a condition known as **REM paralysis**. Some people have a rare disorder in which the brain mechanisms that normally inhibit the voluntary muscles fail, allowing the person to thrash around and even get up and act out nightmares. This disorder is called **REM behavior disorder**, which is a fairly serious condition (Shafton, 1995). Usually seen in men over age 60, it can happen in younger men and in women. (For more about this disorder, see Psychology in the News: Murder While Sleepwalking, later in this section.)

THE NEED FOR REM SLEEP Why two kinds of sleep? REM sleep seems to serve a different purpose than does NREM, or deep sleep. After a very physically demanding day, people tend to spend more time in NREM deep sleep than is usual as the body recovers. But an emotionally stressful day leads to increased time in REM sleep (Horne & Staff, 1983). Perhaps the dreams people have in REM sleep are a way of dealing with the stresses and tensions of the day, whereas physical activity would demand more time for recovery of the body in NREM sleep. Also, if deprived of REM sleep (as would occur with the use of sleeping pills or other depressant drugs), a person will experience greatly increased amounts of REM sleep the next night, a phenomenon called **REM rebound** (Vogel, 1975, 1993).

An early study of REM sleep deprivation (Dement, 1960) seemed to suggest that people deprived of REM sleep would become paranoid, seemingly mentally ill from lack of this one stage of sleep. This is called the *REM myth* because later studies failed to reliably produce the same results (Dement et al., 1969).

REM sleep in early infancy differs from adult REM sleep in a couple of ways: Babies spend nearly 50 percent of their sleep in REM as compared to adults' 20 percent, the brain-wave patterns on EEG recordings are not exactly the same in infant REM when compared to adult REM recordings, and infants can and do move around quite a bit during REM sleep (Carskadon & Dement, 2005; Davis et al., 2004; Sheldon, 2002; Tucker et al., 2006). These differences can be explained: When infants are engaged in REM sleep, they are not dreaming but rather forming new connections between neurons (Carskadon & Dement, 2005; Davis et al., 2004; Sheldon, 2002).

While this infant is sleeping, her REM sleep (occurring about half of the time she is asleep) allows her brain to make new neural connections.

REM paralysis the inability of the voluntary muscles to move during REM sleep.

REM behavior disorder a rare disorder in which the mechanism that blocks the movement of the voluntary muscles fails, allowing the person to thrash around and even get up and act out nightmares.

REM rebound increased amounts of REM sleep after being deprived of REM sleep on earlier nights.

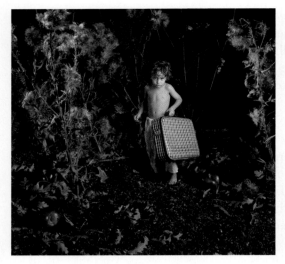

Nightmares are common in children and often involve being chased by a monster or similar frightening creature or being lost in a strange place like this young boy.

The infant brain is highly plastic, and much of brain growth and development takes place during REM sleep. (L I N K) to Chapter Two: The Biological Perspective, p. 53. As the infant's brain nears its adult size by age 5 or 6, the proportion of REM sleep has also decreased to a more adultlike ratio of REM to non-REM. For infants, to sleep is perchance to grow synapses.

Sleep Disorders

6.4 How do sleep disorders interfere with normal sleep?

NIGHTMARES **Nightmares** are bad dreams that take place during REM sleep, and some nightmares can be utterly terrifying. Children tend to have more nightmares than adults do because they spend more of their sleep in the REM state, as discussed earlier. As they age, they have fewer nightmares because they have less opportunity to have them. But some people still suffer from nightmares as adults.

STAGE FOUR SLEEP DISORDERS True **sleepwalking**, or **somnambulism**, occurs in about 20 percent of the population and is at least partially due to heredity (Abe et al., 1984; Kales et al., 1980). It is much more common in childhood and also occurs more frequently in boys than in girls. Although the old movies portray sleepwalkers as zombie-like and with arms outstretched, in reality a sleepwalker may do nothing more than sit up in bed. But other sleepwalking episodes may involve walking around the house, looking in the refrigerator or even eating, and getting into the car. Most sleepwalkers do not recall their nightly activities the next morning.

This lack of memory is typical of most sleepwalking episodes. The only real precaution that the families of people who sleepwalk should take is to clear their floors of obstacles and to put not-easy-to-reach locks on the doors. And although it is not dangerous to wake sleepwalkers, they may seem confused or disoriented, and strike out at others before awakening.

NIGHT TERRORS **Night terrors** are a rare disorder, although one that is more likely in children and also likely to disappear as the child grows older (Garland & Smith, 1991). A night terror is essentially a state of panic experienced while sound asleep. People may sit up, scream, run around the room, or flail at some unseen attacker. It is not uncommon for people to feel unable to breathe as well. Considering that people suffering a night terror episode are in a deep stage of sleep and breathing shallowly, one can understand why breathing would seem difficult when they are suddenly active. As with sleepwalking, most people do not remember what happened during a night terror episode, although a few people can remember vividly the images and terror they experienced.

psychology in the news
....
Murder While Sleepwalking

nightmares bad dreams occurring during REM sleep.

sleepwalking (somnambulism) occurring during deep sleep, an episode of moving around or walking around in one's sleep.

night terrors relatively rare disorder in which the person experiences extreme fear and screams or runs around during deep sleep without waking fully.

 A number of cases of "murder while *sleepwalking*" have been recorded in the past several decades. The term *sleepwalking* as used in these cases most likely refers to the very real condition called REM behavior disorder rather than ordinary sleepwalking. Use of this disorder as a defense in a murder trial has sometimes been successful. Here are short descriptions of two cases and their outcomes.

Case One: Scott Falater, 43 years old, was accused of murdering his wife in 1997. A neighbor, looking over a fence, witnessed Scott holding his wife's head underwater in the swimming pool. He called the police, who found a bloody pool and the body of Yamila Falater with 44 stab wounds.

Falater had performed a series of very deliberate and time-consuming actions in cleaning up after the murder. But Falater claimed to be sleepwalking during all of these actions. Although sleep experts for the defense stated that Falater's story was possible, the prosecution pointed to marital troubles as motive. Most damaging to his case was the witness who stated that three weeks before the murder, Falater had been discussing the case of a Canadian man's acquittal for murder based on a sleepwalking defense. The jury found Falater guilty of murder in the first degree, and he was given a life sentence (Martin, 2004; Tresniowski, 1999).

Case Two: In July of 2008 Brian Thomas of South Wales in Great Britain, a devoted husband and father of two children, killed his wife while dreaming of intruders breaking into their camper. Thomas had a history of sleepwalking and normally slept apart from his wife. Experts found that he suffered from night terrors, and he was acquitted of her murder by reason of temporary insanity (Morris, 2009).

QUESTIONS FOR FURTHER DISCUSSION

1. Should sleepwalking be a valid defense for a crime as serious as murder? What about other kinds of crimes?

2. What kind of evidence should be required to convince a jury that a crime was committed while sleepwalking?

This woman has insomnia. In insomnia, a person has trouble getting to sleep, staying asleep, or getting enough sleep. How will this woman feel when she gets up in the morning?

INSOMNIA Most people think that **insomnia** is the inability to sleep. Although that is the literal meaning of the term, in reality insomnia is the inability to get to sleep, stay asleep, or get a good quality of sleep (Kryger, Lavie, & Rosen, 1999). There are many causes of insomnia, both psychological and physiological. Some of the psychological causes are worrying, trying too hard to sleep, or having anxiety. Some of the physiological causes are too much caffeine, indigestion, or aches and pain.

People can take several steps to help them sleep. Obvious ones are taking no caffeinated drinks or foods that cause indigestion before bedtime, taking medication for pain, and dealing with anxieties in the daytime rather than facing them at night. That last bit of advice is easy to say but not always easy to do. Here are some other helpful hints (Kupfer & Reynolds, 1997; National Sleep Foundation, 2009):

1. Go to bed only when you are sleepy. Rather than trying too hard to go to sleep, after 20 minutes of lying there, get up and do something like reading or other light activity (avoid watching TV or being in front of a computer screen) until you feel sleepy, and then go back to bed.

2. Don't do anything in your bed but sleep. Your bed should be a cue for sleeping, not for studying or watching television. Using the bed as a cue for sleeping is a kind of learning called *classical conditioning*, or the pairing of cues and automatic responses. ⓁⒾ Ⓝ Ⓚ to Chapter Four: Learning, p. 123.

3. Don't try too hard to get to sleep, and especially do not look at the clock and calculate how much sleep you aren't getting. That just increases the tension and makes it harder to sleep.

4. Keep to a regular schedule. Go to bed at the same time and get up at the same time, even on days that you don't have to go to work or class.

5. Don't take sleeping pills or drink alcohol or other types of drugs that slow down the nervous system. These drugs force you into deep sleep and increase the probability of REM rebound, which will cause you to feel tired and sleepy the next day.

insomnia the inability to get to sleep, stay asleep, or get a good quality of sleep.

sleep apnea disorder in which the person stops breathing for nearly half a minute or more.

narcolepsy sleep disorder in which a person falls immediately into REM sleep during the day without warning.

If none of these steps seems to be working, there are sleep clinics and sleep experts who can help people with insomnia. The American Academy of Sleep Medicine has an excellent Web site at **www.aasmnet.org** that provides links to locate sleep clinics in many areas. One treatment that seems to have more success than any kind of sleep medication is the use of cognitive-behavior therapy, a type of therapy in which both rational thinking and controlled behavior are stressed (Bastien et al., 2004; Irwin et al., 2006; Morin et al., 2006). ⓁⒾⓃⓀ to Chapter Thirteen: Psychological Therapies, pp. 477–478.

SLEEP APNEA Snoring is fairly common, occurring when the breathing passages (nose and throat) get blocked. Most people snore only when they have a cold or some other occasional problem, but some people snore every night and quite loudly. It is this type of snoring that is often associated with a condition called **sleep apnea**, in which the person stops breathing for nearly half a minute or more. When breathing stops, there will be a sudden silence, followed shortly by a gasping sound as the person struggles to get air into the lungs. Many people do not wake up while this is happening, but they do not get a good, restful night's sleep because of the apnea.

Apnea is a serious problem. Not only does it disturb nightly sleep, making the person excessively sleepy in the daytime, but also it can cause heart problems (Flemons, 2002). If a person suspects the presence of apnea, a visit to a physician is the first step in identifying the disorder and deciding on a treatment. With mild apnea, treatment may be a device worn on the nose at night to open the nostrils and prevent blockage. Obesity is a primary cause of apnea, especially in men, so another solution might be to lose excess weight. There are also sprays that are supposed to shrink the tissues lining the throat (much as a nasal decongestant spray shrinks the tissues of the nasal passages). Some people sleep with a device that delivers a continuous stream of air under mild pressure, called a *continuous positive airway pressure (CPAP) device*. Others undergo a simple surgery in which the *uvula* (the little flap that hangs down at the back of the throat) and some of the soft tissues surrounding it are removed.

Some very young infants also experience a kind of apnea due to immaturity of the brain stem. These infants are typically placed on monitors that sound an alarm when breathing stops, allowing caregivers to help the infant begin breathing again. Although sleep apnea in infants is often associated with sudden infant death syndrome, or SIDS, it is not necessarily caused by it: Many infants who die of SIDS were never diagnosed with sleep apnea (Blackmon et al., 2003). 📖●─┤Read on **MyPsychLab**

📖●─┤Read and learn more about SIDS on **MyPsychLab**

NARCOLEPSY A disorder affecting one in every 2,000 persons, **narcolepsy** is a kind of "sleep seizure." In narcolepsy, the person may slip suddenly into REM sleep during the day (especially when the person experiences strong emotions). Another symptom is excessive daytime sleepiness that results in the person falling asleep throughout the day at inappropriate times and in inappropriate places (Overeem et al., 2001). These sleep attacks may occur many times and without warning, making the operation of a car or other machinery very dangerous for the *narcoleptic* (person who suffers from narcolepsy). The sudden REM attacks are especially dangerous because of the symptom of *cataplexy*, or a sudden loss of muscle tone. This REM paralysis may cause injuries if the person is standing when the attack occurs. The same hypnogogic images that may accompany Stage 1 sleep may also occur in the narcoleptic person. Table 6.1 has a more detailed list of known, treatable sleep disorders.

table 6.1 Sleep Disorders

NAME OF DISORDER	PRIMARY SYMPTOMS
Somnambulism	Sitting, walking, or performing complex behavior while asleep
Night terrors	Extreme fear, agitation, screaming while asleep
Restless leg syndrome	Uncomfortable sensations in legs causing movement and loss of sleep
Nocturnal leg cramps	Painful cramps in calf or foot muscles
Hypersomnia	Excessive daytime sleepiness
Circadian rhythm disorders	Disturbances of the sleep–wake cycle such as jet lag and shift work
Enuresis	Urinating while asleep in bed

practice quiz   How much do you remember?

6.1 6.2 6.3 6.4

Pick the best answer.

1. When our mental activity undergoes a change in quality or pattern, this is called a(n) _____.
   a. waking consciousness.
   b. altered state of consciousness.
   c. transient state of consciousness.
   d. hallucination.

2. The sleep–wake cycle is a(n) _____ rhythm, normally occurring every 24 hours.
   a. annual
   b. monthly
   c. circadian
   d. nocturnal

3. The suprachiasmatic nucleus instructs the _____ gland to release _____.
   a. pineal; melatonin.
   b. pineal; serotonin.
   c. pituitary; melatonin.
   d. pituitary; serotonin.

4. In which stage(s) of sleep is a person hardest to wake?
   a. Stage 1
   b. Stage 2
   c. Stages 3 and 4
   d. REM

5. Which of the following is NOT a characteristic of REM sleep?
   a. paralysis of voluntary muscles
   b. increased heart rate
   c. slower, deeper breathing
   d. increased body temperature

6. Acting out your nightmares is a rare condition called _____.
   a. sleep apnea.
   b. night terrors.
   c. narcolepsy.
   d. REM behavior disorder.

7. Which of the following is bad advice for someone suffering from insomnia?
   a. Do not watch TV or work on your computer in bed.
   b. Avoid coffee, tea, and other caffeine-containing products late in the day or in the evening.
   c. Do not study or work in bed.
   d. Lie in bed until you fall asleep, even if it takes several hours.

8. Nightmares occur in _____ sleep, whereas night terrors occur in _____ sleep.
   a. Stage 1; Stage 2
   b. REM; NREM
   c. Stage 4; Stage 1
   d. NREM; REM

Brainstorming: What are the possible consequences for teenagers and young adults who choose to consume large quantities of caffeine? Do you think they will have more sleep difficulties than people who do not use caffeine? How might their school or work performance be impacted by sleep problems or lack of sleep?

ANSWERS ON PAGE AK-1

How People Think

One very important characteristic of consciousness is the ability to think, but what does it mean to think? People are thinking all the time and talking about thinking as well: "What do you think?" "Let me think about that." "I don't think so." **Thinking**, or **cognition** (from a Latin word meaning "to know"), can be defined as mental activity that goes on in the brain when a person is processing information—organizing it, understanding it, and communicating it to others. Thinking includes memory, but it is much more. When people think, they are not only aware of the information in the brain but also are making decisions about it, comparing it to other information, and using it to solve problems.

thinking (cognition) mental activity that goes on in the brain when a person is organizing and attempting to understand information and communicating information to others.

mental images mental representations that stand for objects or events and have a picture-like quality.

Thinking also includes more than just a kind of verbal "stream of consciousness." When people think, they often have images as well as words in their minds.

6.5 How are mental images and concepts involved in the process of thinking?

Mental Imagery

As stated in Chapter Five, short-term memories are encoded in the form of sounds and also as visual images, forming a mental picture of the world. Thus, **mental images** (representations that stand in for objects or events and have a picturelike quality) are one of several tools used in the thought process.

Here's an interesting demonstration of the use of mental images. Get several people together and ask them to tell you *as fast as they can* how many windows are in the place where they live. Usually you'll find that the first people to shout out an answer have fewer windows in their houses than the ones who take longer to respond. You'll also notice that most of them say that to determine the number of windows, they pictured where they live and simply counted windows as they "walked through" the image they created in their mind.

> So more windows means more time to count them in your head? I guess mentally "walking" through a bigger house in your head would take longer than "walking" through a smaller one.

• So more windows means more time to count them in your head? I guess mentally "walking" through a bigger house in your head would take longer than "walking" through a smaller one.

That's what researchers think, too. They have found that it does take longer to view a mental image that is larger or covers more distance than a smaller, more compact one (Kosslyn et al., 2001; Ochsner & Kosslyn, 1994). In one study (Kosslyn et al., 1978), participants were asked to look at a map of an imaginary island (see Figure 6.4). On this map were several landmarks, such as a hut, a lake, and a grassy area. After viewing the map and memorizing it, participants were asked to imagine a specific place on the island, such as the hut, and then to "look" for another place, like the lake. When they mentally "reached" the second place, they pushed a button that recorded reaction time. The greater the physical distance on the map between the two locations, the longer it took participants to scan the image for the second location. The participants were apparently looking at their mental image and scanning it just as if it were a real, physical map.

Mental imagery is something people use every day. It helps them remember where they parked the car, find furniture that fits in their dorm room or apartment, and relax by creating daydreams. It allows people to find their way home and to get to other places by using their learned "mental maps" of how to get to familiar locations. (LINK) to Chapter Four: Learning, p. 148. As discussed in the introduction to this text, mental imagery is also a very useful tool for remembering other ideas and concepts, such as remembering your grocery list by linking the items on it to a series of standard images (Paivio, 1971, 1986; Thomas, 2001). (LINK) to Psychology in Action, p. PIA-6–PIA-8.

People are even able to mentally rotate, or turn, images (Shepherd & Metzler, 1971). Kosslyn (1983) asked participants questions such as the following: "Do frogs have lips and a stubby tail?" He found that most participants reported visualizing a frog, starting with the face ("no lips"), then mentally rotating the image so it was facing away from them, and then "zooming in" to look for the stubby tail ("yes, there it is"). A very important aspect of the research on mental rotation is that we tend to engage *mental* images in our mind much like we engage or interact with *physical* objects. When we rotate an object in our minds (or in other ways interact with or manipulate mental images), it is not instantaneous—it takes time, just as it would if we were rotating a physical object with our hands.

FIGURE 6.4 Kosslyn's Fictional Island
In Kosslyn's 1978 study, participants were asked to push a button when they had imagined themselves moving from one place on the island to another. As the graph below the picture shows, participants took longer times to complete the task when the locations on the image were farther apart (Kosslyn et al., 1978).

In the brain, creating a mental image is almost the opposite of seeing an actual image. With an actual image, the information goes from the eyes to the visual cortex of the occipital lobe and is processed, or interpreted, by other areas of the cortex that compare the new information to information already in memory. ⓁⒾⓃⓀ to Chapter Two: The Biological Perspective, p. 68. In creating a mental image, areas of the cortex associated with stored knowledge send information to the visual cortex, where the image is perceived in the "mind's eye" (Kosslyn et al., 1993; Sparing et al., 2002). PET scans show areas of the visual cortex being activated during the process of forming an image, providing evidence for the role of the visual cortex in mental imagery (Kosslyn et al., 1993, 1999, 2001).

Through the use of functional magnetic resonance imagery (fMRI), researchers have been able to see the overlap that occurs in brain areas activated during visual mental imagery tasks as compared to actual tasks involving visual perception (Ganis et al., 2004). During both types of tasks, activity was present in the frontal cortex (cognitive control), temporal lobes (memory), parietal lobes (attention and spatial memory), and occipital lobes (visual processing). However, the amount of activity in these areas differed between the two types of tasks. For example, activity in the visual cortex was stronger during perception than in imagery, suggesting that sensory input activates this area more strongly than memory input. And an important finding overall was that those areas activated during visual imagery were a subset of those activated during visual perception, with the greatest similarity in the frontal and parietal regions rather than the temporal and occipital regions. What does this mean? It indicates simply that there is commonality between the processes of visual imagery and visual perception but it *is not* a complete overlap, and, as the authors point out, the greater overlap *was not* in the temporal and occipital regions (memory and vision functions) that might be assumed to be the most likely areas of overlap given the visual nature of the tasks (Ganis et al., 2004).

Perception | Imagery | Perception - Imagery

Z score 7.7 3.7 -3.7 -3.7

In the fMRI images above, the areas of the brain activated during perception and imagery showed a great deal of overlap but were not identical. Adapted from Ganis, G., Thompson, W. L., & Kosslyn, S. M. (2004). Images courtesy of, and used with permission from, Dr. Giorgio Ganis and Elsevier.

Concepts

Images are not the only way we think, are they? ●

Mental images are only one form of mental representation. Another aspect of thought processes is the use of concepts. **Concepts** are ideas that represent a class or category of objects, events, or activities. People use concepts to think about objects or events without having to think about all the specific examples of the category. For example, a person can think about "fruit" without thinking about every kind of fruit there is in the world, which would take far more effort and time. This ability to think in terms of concepts allows us to communicate with each other: If I mention a bird to you, you know what I am referring to, even if we aren't actually thinking of the same *type* of bird.

Concepts not only contain the important features of the objects or events people want to think about, but also they allow the identification of new objects and events that may fit the concept. For example, dogs come in all shapes, sizes, colors, and lengths of fur. Yet most people have no trouble recognizing dogs as dogs, even though they may never before have seen that particular breed of dog. Friends of the author have a dog called a briard, which is a kind of sheepdog. Even though this dog is easily the size of a small pony, the author had no trouble recognizing it as a dog, albeit a huge and extremely shaggy one.

Concepts can represent many different levels of objects or events. Concepts can be of a very general form, such as "fruit," called a **superordinate concept**. The concept

Both of these animals are dogs. They both have fur, four legs, a tail—but the similarities end there. With so many variations in the animals we call "dogs," what is the prototype for "dog"?

Images are not the only way we think, are they?

concepts ideas that represent a class or category of objects, events, or activities.

superordinate concept the most general form of a type of concept, such as "animal" or "fruit."

basic-level type   an example of a type of concept around which other similar concepts are organized, such as "dog," "cat," or "pear."

subordinate concept   the most specific category of a concept, such as one's pet dog or a pear in one's hand.

formal concepts   concepts that are defined by specific rules or features.

natural concepts   concepts people form as a result of their experiences in the real world.

prototype   an example of a concept that closely matches the defining characteristics of a concept.

> But what about things that don't easily fit the rules or features? What if a thing has some, but not all, features of a concept?

A duck-billed platypus is classified as a mammal, yet shares features with birds, such as webbed feet and a bill, and also lays eggs. The platypus is an example of a "fuzzy" natural concept. Courtesy of Dave Watts, Nature Picture Library.

"apple" is more specific but can still be a **basic-level type**. "Pear," "orange," and "watermelon" would also be basic level. A "Granny Smith apple" would be a **subordinate concept**, or one that is the most specific example (Mandler, 2000, 2003; Rosch et al., 1976). As discussed in Chapter Five, concepts are thought to form a network of associations based on these levels. (See Figure 5.6, on page 175.)

Concepts can have very strict definitions. Those defined by specific rules or features are called **formal concepts** and are quite rigid. To be a square, for example, an object must be a two-dimensional figure with four equal sides and four angles adding up to 360 degrees. If an object has those features, it is not only a square, but also it cannot be anything BUT a square. Science and mathematics are full of formal concepts: Acid, limestone, asteroid, and wavelength are a few scientific formal concepts; in geometry, there are triangles, squares, rectangles, polygons, and lines. In psychology, there are double-blind experiments, sleep stages, and conditioned stimuli, to name a few. Each of these concepts must fit very specific features to be considered true examples.

● But what about things that don't easily fit the rules or features? What if a thing has some, but not all, features of a concept?

In everyday life, people are surrounded by objects, events, and activities that are not as clearly defined as the concepts of science and mathematics. What is a vehicle? Cars and trucks leap immediately to mind, but what about a bobsled? How about a raft? Those last two objects aren't quite as easy to classify as vehicles immediately, but they fit some of the rules for "vehicle." These are examples of **natural concepts**, concepts people form not as a result of the application of a strict set of rules, but rather as the result of their experiences with these concepts in the real world (Ahn, 1998; Barton & Komatsu, 1989; Gelman, 1988; Rosch, 1973). Whereas formal concepts are well defined, natural concepts are "fuzzy" (Hampton, 1998). Is a whale a fish or a mammal? Is a platypus a mammal or a bird? People may know that whales are technically mammals, but whales also share a lot of fish-defining characteristics. Mammals have fur; birds lay eggs and have beaks. The duck-billed platypus has and does all three (has fur, lays eggs, and has a beak), yet it is classified as a mammal, not a bird.

Natural concepts are important in helping people understand their surroundings in a less structured manner than the formal concepts that are taught in school, and they form the basis for interpreting those surroundings and the events that may occur in everyday life.

PROTOTYPES   When someone says "fruit," what's the first image that comes to mind? More than likely, it's a specific kind of fruit like an apple, a pear, or an orange. It's less likely that someone's first impulse will be to say "guava" or "papaya," or even "banana," unless that person comes from a tropical area. In the United States, apples are a good example of a **prototype**, a concept that closely matches the defining characteristics of the concept (Mervis & Rosch, 1981; Rosch, 1977). Fruit is sweet, grows on trees, has seeds, and is usually round—all very applelike qualities. Coconuts are sweet and they also grow on trees, but many people in the Northern Hemisphere have never actually seen a coconut tree. They have more likely seen countless apple trees. So someone who grew up in the northwestern United States where there are many apple trees would most likely think of apples as more prototypical than coconuts, whereas someone growing up in the tropics might see coconuts as a prototypical fruit (Aitchison, 1992). Research suggests that what a person knows about a particular type of object does affect the person's prototype for the category (Lynch et al., 2000; Shafto & Coley, 2003). For example, people who are not that knowledgeable about trees tend to pick a tree that is found where they live as the prototypical tree (such as an oak tree), whereas experts in tree identification tend to select trees that have more ideal characteristics

table 6.2 From Prototypes to Atypical Examples (Most Typical to Least Typical)

VEHICLES	FRUITS
Car	Orange
Bus	Apple
Train	Peach
Bicycle	Grape
Airplane	Strawberry
Boat	Grapefruit
Wheelchair	Watermelon
Sled	Date
Skates	Tomato
Elevator	Olive

Source: Adapted from Rosch & Mervis (1975), p. 576.

(tall, for example) rather than one specific type of tree. For nonexperts, familiarity is important in selecting a prototype, while for experts, central characteristics more representative of trees in general are the standard (Lynch et al., 2000).

Culture also matters in the formation of prototypes. Research on concept prototypes across various cultures found greater differences and variations in prototypes between cultures that were dissimilar, such as Taiwanese and American, than between cultures that are more similar, such as Hispanic Americans and non–Hispanic Americans living in Florida (Lin et al., 1990; Lin & Schwanenflugel, 1995; Schwanenflugel & Rey, 1986).

How do prototypes affect thinking? People tend to look at potential examples of a concept and compare them to the prototype to see how well they match—which is why it takes most people much longer to think about olives and tomatoes as fruit because they aren't sweet, one of the major characteristics of the prototype of fruit (Rosch & Mervis, 1975). Table 6.2 presents some prototypical American examples of the concepts "vehicle" and "fruit" as well as less typical examples.

No matter what type, concepts are one of the ways people deal with all the information that bombards* their senses every day and allows them to organize their perceptions of the world around them. This organization may take the form of *schemas*, mental generalizations about objects, places, events, and people (for example, one's schema for "library" would no doubt include books and bookshelves), or *scripts*, a kind of schema that involves a familiar sequence of activities (for example, "going to a movie" would include traveling there, getting the ticket, buying snacks, finding the right theater, etc.). Concepts not only help people think, but also they are an important tool in *problem solving*, a type of thinking that people engage in every day and in many different situations.

Problem Solving and Decision Making

Problem solving is certainly a big part of any college student's life. Is there any one "best" way to go about solving a problem?

Problem solving is certainly a big part of any college student's life. Is there any one "best" way to go about solving a problem?

---

*Bombards: attacks again and again.

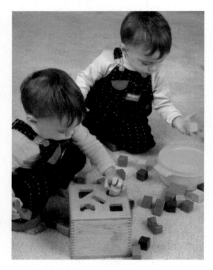

These children try one possible sequence of moves after another until finding just the right combination. This is an example of trial-and-error learning.

problem solving process of cognition that occurs when a goal must be reached by thinking and behaving in certain ways.

trial and error (mechanical solution) problem-solving method in which one possible solution after another is tried until a successful one is found.

algorithms very specific, step-by-step procedures for solving certain types of problems.

heuristic an educated guess based on prior experiences that helps narrow down the possible solutions for a problem. Also known as a "rule of thumb."

representative heuristic assumption that any object (or person) sharing characteristics with the members of a particular category is also a member of that category.

Think about it as you read on and solve the following: Put a coin in a bottle and then cork the opening. How can you get the coin out of the bottle without pulling out the cork or breaking the bottle? (For the solution, see page 214.)

As stated earlier, images and concepts are mental tools that can be used to solve problems. For the preceding problem, you are probably trying to create an image of the bottle with a coin in it. **Problem solving** occurs when a goal must be reached by thinking and behaving in certain ways. Problems range from figuring out how to cut a recipe in half to understanding complex mathematical proofs to deciding what to major in at college. There are several different ways in which people can think in order to solve problems.

6.6 What are the methods people use to solve problems and make decisions?

TRIAL AND ERROR (MECHANICAL SOLUTIONS) One method is to use **trial and error**, also known as a **mechanical solution**. Trial and error refers to trying one solution after another until finding one that works. For example, if Shelana has forgotten the PIN for her online banking Web site, she can try one combination after another until she finds the one that works, if she has only a few such PINs that she normally uses. Mechanical solutions can also involve solving by *rote*, or a learned set of rules. This is how word problems were solved in grade school, for example. One type of rote solution is to use an algorithm.

ALGORITHMS **Algorithms** are specific, step-by-step procedures for solving certain types of problems. Algorithms will always result in a correct solution, if there is a correct solution to be found, and you have enough time to find it. Mathematical formulas are algorithms. When librarians organize books on bookshelves, they also use an algorithm: Place books in alphabetical order within each category, for example. Many puzzles, like a Rubik's Cube®, have a set of steps that, if followed exactly, will always result in solving the puzzle. But algorithms aren't always practical to use. For example, if Shelana didn't have a clue about what those four numbers might be, she *might* be able to figure out her forgotten PIN by trying *all possible combinations* of four digits, 0 through 9. She would eventually find the right four-digit combination—but it might take years! Computers, however, can run searches like this one very quickly, so the systematic search algorithm is a useful part of some computer programs.

HEURISTICS Unfortunately, humans aren't as fast as computers and need some other way to narrow down the possible solutions to only a few. One way to do this is to use a heuristic. A **heuristic**, or "rule of thumb," is a simple rule that is intended to apply to many situations. Whereas an algorithm is very specific and will always lead to a solution, a heuristic is an educated guess based on prior experiences that helps narrow down the possible solutions for a problem. For example, if a student is typing a paper in a word-processing program and wants to know how to format the page, he or she could try to read an entire manual on the word-processing program. That would take a while. Instead, the student could type "format" into the help feature's search program or click on the word *Format* on the toolbar. Doing either action greatly reduces the amount of information the student will have to look at to get an answer. Using the help feature or clicking on the appropriate toolbar word will also work for similar problems.

Will using a rule of thumb always work, like algorithms do? Using a heuristic is faster than using an algorithm in many cases, but unlike algorithms, heuristics will *not* always lead to the correct solution. What you gain in speed is sometimes lost in accuracy. For example, a **representative heuristic** is used for categorizing objects and simply assumes that any object (or person) that shares characteristics with the members of a particular category is also a member of that category. This is a handy tool when it comes to classifying plants but doesn't work as well when applied to people. Are all people with dark skin from Africa? Does everyone with red hair also have a bad temper? Are all blue-eyed blondes from Sweden? See the point? The representative heuristic can be used—or misused—to create and sustain stereotypes (Kahneman & Tversky, 1973; Kahneman et al., 1982).

Another heuristic that can have undesired outcomes is the **availability heuristic**, which is based on our estimation of the frequency or likelihood of an event based on how easy it is to recall relevant information from memory or how easy it is for us to think of related examples (Tversky & Kahneman, 1973). Imagine, for example, that after you have already read this entire textbook (it could happen!) you are asked to estimate how many words in the book start with the letter *K* and how many have the letter *K* as the third letter in the word. Which place do you think is more frequent, the first letter or as the third letter? Next, what do you think the ratio of the more frequent placement is to the less frequent placement? What is easier to think of, words that begin with the letter *K* or words that have *K* as the third letter? Tversky and Kahneman (1973) asked this same question of 152 participants for five consonants (*K, N, L, R, V*) that appear more frequently in the third position as compared to the first in a typical text. Sixty-nine percent of the participants indicated that the first position was the more frequent placement and the median estimated ratio was 2:1, and for the letter *K*—there are typically twice as many words with *K* as the third letter as compared to the first. Can you think of an example where you may have used the availability heuristic and it did not work in your favor?

A useful heuristic that works much of the time is to *work backward from the goal*. For example, if you want to know the shortest way to get to the new coffee shop in town, you already know the goal, which is finding the coffee shop. There are probably several ways to get there from your house, and some are shorter than others. Assuming you have the address of the store, for many the best way to determine the shortest route is to look up the location of the store on an Internet map, a GPS, or a smart phone, and compare the different routes by the means of travel (walking versus driving). People actually used to do this with a physical map and compare the routes manually! Think about it, does technology help or hinder some aspects of problem solving? What are the benefits, if any, to using technology for solving some problems as compared to actively engaging in problem solving as a mental challenge?

What if my problem is writing a term paper? Starting at the end isn't going to help me much!

Sometimes it's better to break a goal down into *subgoals*, so that as each subgoal is achieved, the final solution is that much closer. Writing a term paper, for example, can seem overwhelming until it is broken down into steps: Choose a topic, research the topic, organize what has been gathered, write one section at a time, and so on. Other examples of heuristics include making diagrams to help organize the information concerning the problem or testing possible solutions to the problem one by one and eliminating those that do not work.

Another kind of heuristic is **means–end analysis,** in which a person determines the difference between the current situation and the goal and then tries to reduce that difference by various means (methods). For example, Katrina wanted a certain kind of invitation for her wedding, but buying it already made was very expensive and well over her budget. She ordered one sample of the invitation and examined it carefully. It had a pocket inside that held the response cards for people to send back to Katrina, a

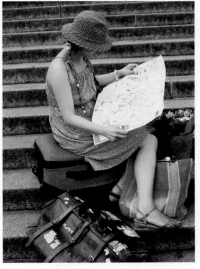

One rule of thumb, or heuristic, involves breaking down a goal into subgoals. This woman is consulting the map to see which of several possible paths she needs to take to get to her goal destination.

Smartphones and other portable devices provide tools for easy navigation. How might the use or overuse of these tools affect our ability to navigate when we do not have access to them?

What if my roblem is writing a term paper? Starting at the end isn't going to help me much!

availability heuristic   estimating the frequency or likelihood of an event based on how easy it is to recall relevant information from memory or how easy it is for us to think of related examples.

means–end analysis   heuristic in which the difference between the starting situation and the goal is determined and then steps are taken to reduce that difference.

decorative seashell tied onto the outside of the card with fancy ribbon, and a small box instead of an envelope. Her goal was to make 200 of these invitations by hand. Her subgoals were to find the paper, take the invitation carefully apart to see how to put one together, buy the little shells, find and buy the right size boxes for mailing, and assemble the invitations. What might have seemed an impossible task became doable once it was broken down into smaller subgoals.

INSIGHT

Sometimes I have to find answers to problems one step at a time, but in other cases the answer seems to just "pop" into my head all of a sudden. Why do some answers come so easily to mind?

When the solution to a problem seems to come suddenly to mind, it is called insight. Chapter Four (p. 149) contained a discussion of Köhler's (1925) work with Sultan the chimpanzee, which demonstrated that even some animals can solve problems by means of a sudden insight. In humans, insight often takes the form of an "aha!" moment—the solution seems to come in a flash. A person may realize that this problem is similar to another one that he or she already knows how to solve or may see that an object can be used for a different purpose than its original one, like using a dime as a screwdriver.

Remember the problem of the bottle discussed earlier in this chapter? The task was to get the coin out of the bottle without removing the cork or breaking the bottle. The answer is simple: *Push the cork into the bottle and shake out the coin. Aha!*

Insight is not really a magical process, although it can seem like magic. What usually happens is that the mind simply reorganizes a problem, sometimes while the person is thinking about something else (Durso et al., 1994).

Here's a problem that can be solved with insight: Marsha and Marjorie were born on the same day of the same month of the same year to the same mother and the same father, yet they are not twins. How is that possible? Think about it and then look for the answer on p. 215.

In summary, thinking is a complex process involving the use of mental imagery and various types of concepts to organize the events of daily life. Problem solving is a special type of thinking that involves the use of many tools, such as trial-and-error thinking, algorithms, and heuristics, to solve different types of problems.

> Sometimes I have to find answers to problems one step at a time, but in other cases the answer seems to just "pop" into my head all of a sudden. Why do some answers come so easily to mind?

practice quiz   How much do you remember?

(6.5) (6.6)

Pick the best answer.

1. Mental images _____.
   a. represent abstract ideas.
   b. have a picture-like quality.
   c. consist entirely of unconscious information.
   d. are always prototypes.

2. Knowing that the definition of psychology is the scientific study of behavior and mental processes is an example of a _____.
   a. prototypical concept.
   b. natural concept.
   c. formal concept.
   d. mental image.

3. A "rule of thumb" is another name for a _____.
   a. heuristic.
   b. algorithm.
   c. trial-and-error solution.
   d. means–end analysis.

4. What type of problem-solving strategy would be best to use when solving a problem in algebra class?
   a. heuristic
   b. algorithm
   c. trial-and-error solution
   d. means–end analysis

5. Miguel was struggling with the answer to one of the questions on his psychology midterm. Seeing that the answer was not going to come easily, he went on to answer some of the other easier questions. Then, suddenly, the answer to the problematic question just seemed to "pop" into his head. Miguel's experience is an example of _____.
   a. means–end analysis.
   b. a heuristic.
   c. an algorithm.
   d. insight.

ANSWERS ON PAGE AK-1

Problems with Problem Solving

6.7 Why does problem solving sometimes fail, and what is meant by creative thinking?

Using insight to solve a problem is not always foolproof. Sometimes a solution to a problem remains just "out of reach" because the elements of the problem are not arranged properly or because people get stuck in certain ways of thinking that act as barriers to solving problems. Such ways of thinking occur more or less automatically, influencing attempts to solve problems without any conscious awareness of that influence. Here's a classic example:

Two strings are hanging from a ceiling but are too far apart to allow a person to hold one and walk to the other. Nearby is a table with a pair of pliers on it. The goal is to tie the two pieces of string together. How? For the solution to this problem, see Figure 6.5 on page 167.

People can become aware of automatic tendencies to try to solve problems in ways that are not going to lead to solutions, and in becoming aware they can abandon the "old" ways for more appropriate problem-solving methods. Three of the most common barriers* to successful problem solving are functional fixedness, mental sets, and confirmation bias. ✳ Explore on MyPsychLab

FUNCTIONAL FIXEDNESS One problem-solving difficulty involves thinking about objects only in terms of their typical uses, which is a phenomenon called **functional fixedness** (literally, "fixed on the function"). Have you ever searched high and low for a screwdriver to fix something around the house? All the while there are several objects close at hand that could be used to tighten a screw: a butter knife, a key, or even a dime in your pocket. Because the tendency is to think of those objects in terms of cooking, unlocking, and spending, respectively, we sometimes ignore the less obvious possible uses. The string problem introduced before is an example of functional fixedness. The pair of pliers is often seen as useless until the person realizes it can be used as a weight. (See p. 217, Figure 6.5.)

MENTAL SETS Functional fixedness is actually a kind of **mental set**, which is defined as the tendency for people to persist in using problem-solving patterns that have worked for them in the past. Solutions that have worked in the past tend to be the ones people try first, and people are often hesitant or even unable to think of other possibilities. Look at the accompanying figure.

Can you draw four straight lines so that they pass through all nine dots *without lifting your pencil from the page and without touching any dot more than once?*

People are taught from the earliest grades to stay within the lines, right? That tried-and-true method will not help in solving the dot problem. The solution involves drawing the lines beyond the actual dots, as seen in Figure 6.6 on p. 218.

CONFIRMATION BIAS Another barrier to logical thinking, called **confirmation bias**, is the tendency to search for evidence that fits one's beliefs while ignoring any evidence to the contrary. This is similar to a mental set, except that what is "set" is a belief rather than a method of solving problems. Believers in ESP tend to remember the few studies that seem to support their beliefs and psychic predictions that worked out while at the same time "forgetting" the cases in which studies found no proof or psychics made predictions that failed to come true. They remember only that which confirms their bias toward a belief in the existence of ESP. Similarly, people who believe that they

---

*Barrier: something that blocks one's path; an obstacle preventing a solution.

Answer to insight problem on p. 214: *Marsha and Marjorie are two of a set of triplets. Gotcha!*

✳ Explore the two-string problem and confirmation bias on **MyPsychLab**

functional fixedness a block to problem solving that comes from thinking about objects in terms of only their typical functions.

mental set the tendency for people to persist in using problem-solving patterns that have worked for them in the past.

confirmation bias the tendency to search for evidence that fits one's beliefs while ignoring any evidence that does not fit those beliefs.

The driver of this train was texting from his cell phone immediately before this crash that killed 25 people and injured more than 130 others.

are good multitaskers and can safely drive a motor vehicle while talking or texting on their cell phones may tend to remember their own personal experiences, which may not include any vehicle accidents or "near-misses" (that they are aware of). While it might be tempting to think of one's self as a "supertasker," recent research suggests otherwise. When tested on driving simulators while having to perform successfully on two attention-demanding tasks, over 97 percent of individuals were unable to do so without significant impacts on their performance. During the dual-task condition, only 2.5 percent of individuals were able to perform without problems (Watson & Strayer, 2010). This specific example can be quite dangerous as it is estimated that at least 28 percent of all traffic crashes are caused by drivers using their cell phone and/or texting (National Safety Council, 2010). [Note that the availability heuristic and representative heuristic could also come into play here and, when misapplied, are often barriers to effective problem solving or the cause of errors in reasoning.]

Creativity

So far, we've only talked about logic and pretty straightforward thinking. How do people come up with totally new ideas no one has thought of before?

Not every problem can be answered by using information already at hand and the rules of logic in applying that information. Sometimes a problem requires coming up with entirely new ways of looking at the problem or unusual, inventive solutions. This kind of thinking is called **creativity**: solving problems by combining ideas or behavior in new ways (Csikszentmihalyi, 1996; pronounced chǐck-sĕnt-mē-HĪ-ē).

DIVERGENT AND CONVERGENT THINKING The logical method for problem solving that has been discussed so far is based on a type of thinking called **convergent thinking**. In convergent thinking, a problem is seen as having only one answer and all lines of thinking will eventually lead to (converge on) that single answer by using previous knowledge and logic (Ciardiello, 1998). For example, the question, "In what ways are a pencil and a pen alike?" can be answered by listing the features that the two items have in common: Both can be used to write, have similar shapes, and so on, in a simple comparison process. Convergent thinking works well for routine problem solving but may be of little use when a more creative solution is needed.

Divergent thinking is the reverse of convergent thinking. Here a person starts at one point and comes up with many different, or divergent, ideas or possibilities based on that point (Finke, 1995). For example, if someone were to ask the question, "What is a pencil used for?," the convergent answer would be "to write." But if the question is put this way: "How many different uses can you think of for a pencil?" the answers multiply: "writing, poking holes, a weight for the tail of a kite, a weapon." Divergent thinking has been attributed not only to creativity but also to intelligence (Guilford, 1967). Survey on **MyPsychLab**

What are the characteristics of a creative, divergent thinker? Theorists in the field of creative thinking have examined the habits of highly creative people and have found that the most productive periods of divergent thinking for those people tend to occur when they are doing some task or activity that is more or less automatic, such as walking or swimming (Csikszentmihalyi, 1996; Gardner, 1993a; Goleman, 1995). These automatic tasks take up some attention processes, leaving the remainder to devote to creative thinking. The fact that all of one's attention is not focused on the problem is actually a benefit: because divergent thinkers often make links and connections at a level of consciousness just below alert awareness, ideas can flow freely without being censored* by the higher mental processes (Goleman, 1995). In other

So far, we've only talked about logic and pretty straightforward thinking. How do people come up with totally new ideas that no one has thought of before?

Survey Participate in a survey: What is creativity? on **MyPsychLab**

creativity the process of solving problems by combining ideas or behavior in new ways.

convergent thinking type of thinking in which a problem is seen as having only one answer, and all lines of thinking will eventually lead to that single answer, using previous knowledge and logic.

divergent thinking type of thinking in which a person starts from one point and comes up with many different ideas or possibilities based on that point.

_____

*Censored: blocked from conscious awareness as unacceptable thoughts.

table 6.3 Stimulating Divergent Thinking

Brainstorming	Generate as many ideas as possible in a short period of time without judging each idea's merits until all ideas are recorded.
Keeping a Journal	Carry a journal to write down ideas as they occur or a recorder to capture those same ideas and thoughts.
Freewriting	Write down or record everything that comes to mind about a topic without revising or proofreading until all of the information is written or recorded in some way. Organize it later.
Mind or Concept Mapping	Start with a central idea and draw a "map" with lines from the center to other related ideas, forming a visual representation of the concepts and their connections.

FIGURE 6.5
The solution to the string problem is to use the pliers as a pendulum to swing the second string closer to you.

words, having part of one's attention devoted to walking, for example, allows the rest of the mind to "sneak up on" more creative solutions and ideas.

Creative, divergent thinking is often a neglected topic in the education of young people. Although some people are naturally more creative, it is possible to develop one's creative ability. The ability to be creative is important—coming up with topics for a research paper, for example, is difficult for many students. Cross-cultural research (Basadur et al., 2002; Colligan, 1983) has found that divergent thinking and problem-solving skills cannot be easily taught in the Japanese or Omaha Native American cultures, for example. In these cultures, creativity in many areas is not normally prized, and the preference is to hold to well-established, cultural traditions, such as traditional dances that have not varied for centuries. See Table 6.3 for some ways to become a more divergent thinker.

Many people believe that creative people are also a little different from other people. There are artists and musicians, for example, who actually encourage others to see them as eccentric. But the fact is that creative people are actually pretty normal. According to Csikszentmihalyi (1997), creative people usually are knowledgeable about many topics, are good at mental imagery and often have more vivid dreams and daydreams than others; they are also independent and unafraid to be different. They may be unconventional in their work but not in other areas of life.

Divergent thinking is the stepping stone to some very creative—and often unusual—ideas for uses for ordinary objects. This young man is creating some new sounds in a very "hands-on" way, by literally putting his hands on the record on the turntable to create the scratching sound so often found in rap and other forms of modern music.

practice quiz   How much do you remember?

6.7

Pick the best answer.

1. Al goes out one frosty morning to find that his car is covered with a layer of thick frost. He needs to get to work and looks for his ice scraper. Unable to find it, he thinks a moment, goes into the house, and returns with a hard plastic spatula from the kitchen. In using the spatula as a makeshift ice scraper, Al has overcome _____.
   a. functional fixedness.
   b. confirmation bias.
   c. creativity bias.
   d. confirmation fixedness.

2. Randall believes that aliens crashed in the western United States in the 1950s. When looking for information about this on the Internet, he ignores any sites that are skeptical of his belief and only visits and talks with his friends about the sites that support his belief. This is an example of _____.
   a. functional fixedness.
   b. confirmation bias.
   c. creativity bias.
   d. confirmation fixedness.

3. When a problem is seen as having only one answer, with all lines of thinking leading to that answer, this is known as _____ thinking.
   a. divergent
   b. creative
   c. convergent
   d. mental-set

4. Which of the following statements about creative people is TRUE?
   a. They are not very good at mental imagery.
   b. They are not afraid to be different.
   c. They value their dependence on others.
   d. They are often very conventional in their work.

ANSWERS ON PAGE AK-1

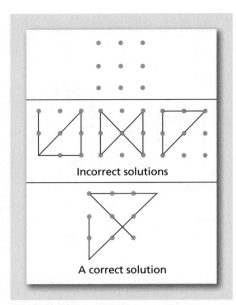

FIGURE 6.6 The Solution to the Dot Problem
When people try to solve this problem, a mental set causes them to think of the dots as representing a box, and they try to draw the line while staying in the box. The only way to connect all nine dots without lifting the pencil from the paper is to draw the line so that it extends out of the box of dots—literally "thinking outside the box."

language a system for combining symbols (such as words) so that an unlimited number of meaningful statements can be made for the purpose of communicating with others.

grammar the system of rules governing the structure and use of a language.

syntax the system of rules for combining words and phrases to form grammatically correct sentences.

morphemes the smallest units of meaning within a language.

semantics the rules for determining the meaning of words and sentences.

phonemes the basic units of sound in language.

Language

6.8 How is language defined, and what are its different elements and structure?

Language is a system for combining symbols (such as words) so that an infinite* number of meaningful statements can be made for the purpose of communicating with others. Language allows people not only to communicate with one another but also to represent their own internal mental activity. In other words, language is a very important part of consciousness and how people think.

The Levels of Language Analysis

The structures of languages all over the world share common characteristics. Languages involve word order, word meanings, the rules for making words into other words, the sounds that exist within a language, the rules for practical communication with others, and the meanings of sentences and phrases.

GRAMMAR **Grammar** is the system of rules governing the structure and use of a language. According to famed linguist Noam Chomsky (Chomsky, 2006; Chomsky et al., 2002), humans have an innate ability to understand and produce language through a device he calls the *language acquisition device,* or *LAD.* While humans may learn the *specific* language (English, Spanish, Mandarin, etc.) through the processes of imitation, reinforcement, and shaping, Ⓛ Ⓘ Ⓝ Ⓚ to Chapter Four: Learning, p. 132, the complexities of the grammar of a language are, according to Chomsky, to some degree "wired in" to the developing brain. The LAD "listens" to the language input of the infant's world and then begins to produce language sounds and eventually words and sentences in a pattern found across cultures. This pattern is discussed in greater detail in the next chapter. Ⓛ Ⓘ Ⓝ Ⓚ to Chapter Seven: Development Across the Life Span, pp. 244–245. Grammar includes rules for the order of words known as syntax, morphology (the study of the formation of words), phonemes (the basic sounds of language), and pragmatics (the practical social expectations and uses of language).

SYNTAX **Syntax** is a system of rules for combining words and phrases to form grammatically correct sentences. Syntax is quite important, as just a simple mix-up can cause sentences to be completely misunderstood. An example of the importance of syntax can be found in the lobby of a Moscow hotel across from a monastery: "You are welcome to visit the cemetery where famous composers, artists, and writers are buried daily except Thursday." So if people want to watch famous composers, artists, and writers being buried, they should not go to this monastery on Thursday.

MORPHEMES **Morphemes** are the smallest units of meaning within a language. For example, the word *playing* consists of two morphemes, *play* and *ing.* Morphemes themselves are governed by **semantics**, rules for determining the meaning of words and sentences. Sentences, for example, can have the same semantic meaning while having different syntax: "Johnny hit the ball" and "the ball was hit by Johnny."

PHONEMES **Phonemes** are the basic units of sound in a language. The *a* in the word *car* is a very different phoneme from the *a* in the word *day,* even though it is the same letter of the alphabet. The difference is in how we say the sound of the *a* in each word. Phonemes are more than just the different ways in which we pronounce single letters, too. *Th, sh,* and *au* are also phonemes. Phonemes for different languages are also different, and one of the biggest problems for people who are trying to learn

---

*Infinite: unlimited, without end.

another language is the inability to both hear and pronounce the phonemes of that other language. Although infants are born with the ability to recognize all phonemes (Werker & Lalonde, 1988), after about nine months, that ability has deteriorated and the infant recognizes only the phonemes of the language to which the infant is exposed (Boyson-Bardies et al., 1989).

PRAGMATICS   The **pragmatics** of language has to do with the practical aspects of communicating with others, or the social "niceties" of language. Simply put, pragmatics involves knowing things like how to take turns in a conversation, the use of gestures to emphasize a point or indicate a need for more information, and the different ways in which one speaks to different people (Yule, 1996). For example, adults speak to small children differently than they do to other adults by using simpler words. Both adults and children use higher pitched voices and many repeated phrases when talking to infants; such child-directed speech plays an important role in the development of language in children. Part of the pragmatics of language includes knowing just what rhythm and emphasis to use when communicating with others, called *intonation*. When speaking to infants, adults and children are changing the inflection when they use the higher pitch and stress certain words differently than others. Some languages, such as Japanese, are highly sensitive to intonation, meaning that changing the stress or pitch of certain words or syllables of a particular word can change its meaning entirely (Beckman & Pierrehumbert, 1986). For example, the Japanese name "Yoshiko" should be pronounced with the accent or stress on the first syllable: YO-she-koh. This pronunciation of the name means "woman-child." But if the stress is placed on the second syllable (yo-SHE-ko), the name can be interpreted as "woman who urinates."

Pragmatics involves the practical aspects of communicating. This young mother is talking and then pausing for the infant's response. In this way, the infant is learning about taking turns, an important aspect of language development. What kinds of games do adults play with infants that also aid the development of language?

The Relationship between Language and Thought

6.9 Does language influence the way people think, and are animals capable of learning language?

As with the controversy of nature versus nurture, researchers have long debated the relationship between language and thought. Does language actually influence thought, or does thinking influence language?

Two very influential developmental psychologists, Jean Piaget and Lev Vygotsky, often debated the relationship of language and thought (Duncan, 1995). Piaget (1926, 1962) theorized that concepts preceded and aided the development of language. For example, a child would have to have a concept or mental schema for "mother" before being able to learn the word "mama." In a sense, concepts become the "pegs" on which words are "hung." Piaget also believed that the tendency of young children to talk to themselves, even in the presence of another child, was very egocentric (from the child's point of view only, with no regard for the listener), and that as the child became more socially involved and less egocentric, these nonsocial speech patterns would become less frequent.

Vygotsky believed almost the opposite. He theorized that language actually helped develop concepts and that language could also help the child learn to control behavior—including social behavior (Vygotsky, 1962, 1978, 1987). For Vygotsky, the word helped form the concept: Once a child had learned the word "mama," the various elements of "mama-ness"— *warm, soft, food, safety,* and so on—could come together around that word. Vygotsky also believed that the "egocentric" speech of the preschool child was actually a way for the child to form thoughts and control actions. This "private speech" was a way for children to plan their behavior, develop self-control in the presence of other children, and organize actions so that their goals could be obtained. Vygotsky believed that private speech would actually *increase* as children became more

pragmatics aspects of language involving the practical ways of communicating with others, or the social "niceties" of language.

linguistic relativity hypothesis the theory that thought processes and concepts are controlled by language.

cognitive universalism theory that concepts are universal and influence the development of language.

socially active in the preschool years. The evidence seems to bear out Vygotsky's view: Children, especially bright children, do tend to use more private speech when learning how to socialize with other children or when working on a difficult task (Berk, 1992; Berk & Spuhl, 1995; Bivens & Berk, 1990).

LINGUISTIC RELATIVITY HYPOTHESIS The hypothesis that language shapes and influences thoughts was accepted by many theorists, with a few notable exceptions, such as Piaget. One of the best-known versions of this view is the Sapir-Whorf hypothesis (named for the two theorists who developed it, Edward Sapir and his student, Benjamin Lee Whorf). This hypothesis assumes that the thought processes and concepts within any culture are determined by the words of the culture (Sapir, 1921; Whorf, 1956). It has come to be known as the **linguistic relativity hypothesis**, meaning that thought processes and concepts are controlled by (relative to) language. That is, the words people use determine much of the way in which they think about the world around them.

Is there evidence for the linguistic relativity hypothesis? Neither Sapir nor Whorf provided any scientific studies that would support their proposition. There have been numerous studies by other researchers, however. For example, in one study researchers assumed that a language's names for colors would influence the ability of the people who grew up with that language to distinguish among and perceive colors. The study found that basic color terms did directly influence color recognition memory (Lucy & Shweder, 1979). But an earlier series of studies on the perception of colors (Rosch-Heider, 1972; Rosch-Heider & Olivier, 1972) had already found just the opposite effect: Members of the Dani tribe, who have only two names for colors, were no different in their ability to perceive all of the colors than were the English speakers in the study. More recent studies (Davies et al., 1998a, 1998b; Laws et al., 1995; Pinker & Bloom, 1990) support Rosch-Heider's findings and the idea of a **cognitive universalism** (concepts are universal and influence the development of language) rather than linguistic relativity.

Other research suggests that although the linguistic relativity hypothesis may not work for fine perceptual discriminations such as those in the Rosch-Heider studies, it may be an appropriate explanation for concepts of a higher level. In one study, researchers showed pictures of two animals to preschool children (Gelman & Markman, 1986). The pictures were of a flamingo and a bat. The children were told that the flamingo feeds its baby mashed-up food but the bat feeds its baby milk. Then they were shown a picture of a blackbird (which looked more like the bat than the flamingo). Half of the children were told that the blackbird was a bird, while the other children were not. When asked how the blackbird fed its baby, the children who had been given the bird label were more likely to say that it fed its baby mashed-up food than were the children who were not given the label. This finding indicated that the preschoolers were making inferences about feeding habits based on category membership rather than perceptual similarity—the word *bird* helped the children who were given that label to place the blackbird in its proper higher level category.

Research continues on the investigation of relationships between language and thought. Thus far, this research appears to support linguistic relativity and how language can shape our thoughts about space, time, colors, and objects (Boroditsky, 2001, 2009). However, researchers do not always agree. For some studies that offer support, there are others that reinterpret the data, fail to replicate, or offer critiques of the original studies, so findings are sometimes still in question (J. Y. Chen, 2007; January & Kako, 2007).

Psychologists cannot deny the influence of language on problem solving, cognition, and memory. Sometimes a problem can simply be worded differently so that the solution becomes obvious, and memory (**LINK** to Chapter Five: Memory, pp. 173–174) is certainly stored in terms of the semantics of language. Language can definitely influence the perception of others as well. "Computer geek" and "software engineer" might be used to describe the same person, for example, but one phrase is obviously less flattering and the image brought to mind is different for the two terms. In the end, trying to determine whether language influences thoughts or thoughts influence language may be like trying to determine which came first, the chicken or the egg.

ANIMAL STUDIES IN LANGUAGE

I've heard that chimpanzees can be taught to use sign language. Is this for real, or are the chimps just performing tricks like the animals in the circus or the zoo?

I've heard that chimpanzees can be taught to use sign language. Is this for real, or are the chimps just performing tricks like the animals in the circus or the zoo?

There are really two questions about animals and language: "Can animals communicate?" and "can animals use language?" The answer to the first question is a definite "yes." Animals communicate in many ways. They use sounds such as the rattle of a rattlesnake or the warning growl of an angry dog. There are also physical behaviors, such as the "dance" of honeybees that tells the other bees where a source of pollen is (Gould & Gould, 1994). But the answer to the second question is more complicated, because language is defined as the use of symbols, and symbols are things that stand for something else. Words are symbols, and gestures can be symbols. But the gestures used by animals are instinctual; that is, they are controlled by the animal's genetic makeup. The honeybee doing the "dance" is controlled completely by instinct, as is the growling dog. In human language, symbols are used quite deliberately and voluntarily, not by instinct, and abstract symbols have no meaning until people assign meaning to them. (Although Chomsky's innate language acquisition device might lead some to think that language for humans is instinctual, it should be noted that the infant's production of speech sounds becomes quite deliberate within a short period of time.)

Can animals be taught to use abstract symbols? Attempts have been made to teach animals (primates and dolphins) how to use sign language (as animals lack the vocal structure to form spoken words), but many of these attempts were simply not "good science." The most successful of these experiments (which is not without its critics as well) has been with Kanzi, a bonobo chimpanzee trained to press abstract symbols on a computer keyboard (Savage-Rumbaugh & Lewin, 1994). Kanzi actually was not the original subject of the study—his mother, Matata, was the chimp being trained. She did not learn many of the symbols, but Kanzi watched his mother use the keyboard and appeared to learn how to use the symbols through that observation. At last count, Kanzi could understand about 150 spoken English words. Trainers who speak to him are not in his view, so he is not responding to physical cues or symbols. He has managed to follow correctly complex instructions up to the level of a 2-year-old child (Savage-Rumbaugh et al., 1998). The most recent studies with Kanzi have him making sounds that seem to have consistent meaning across different situations (Tagliatatela et al., 2003). Nearly 100 videotaped hours of Kanzi engaged in day-to-day activities were analyzed for these sounds. The researchers were able to identify four sounds that seemed to represent banana, grapes, juice, and the word *yes*. (However, remember that four sounds do not come close to making an entire language.)

Other studies, with dolphins (Herman et al., 1993) and with parrots (Pepperberg, 1998, 2007), have also met with some success. Is it real language? The answer seems to be a qualified "yes." The qualification is that none of the animals that have achieved success so far can compare to the level of language development of a 3-year-old human child (Pinker, 1995). However, linguists still debate whether these animals are truly learning language if they are not also learning how to use syntax—combining words into grammatically correct sentences as well as being able to understand the differences between sentences such as "The girl kissed the boy" and "The boy kissed the girl." As yet, there is no conclusive evidence that any of the animals trained in language have been able to master syntax (Demers, 1988; Johnson, 1995; Pinker, 1995).

Read on MyPsychLab

Dr. Irene Pepperberg, a research scientist at MIT, is shown with her star pupil, Alex the gray parrot, who was the main subject of her research into animal language until his death in September 2007.

Read and learn more about animal studies and language on MyPsychLab

practice quiz   How much do you remember?

6.8 6.9

Pick the best answer.

1. The system of rules for combining words and phrases to make meaningful sentences is called _____.
   a. grammar.
   c. syntax.
   b. phonics.
   d. morphology.

2. Grammar includes all but which of the following aspects of language?
   a. tone
   c. order
   b. sounds
   d. meaning

3. The sounds of the letters *b, z, c,* and *d* are examples of _____.
   a. morphemes.
   c. semantics.
   b. phonemes.
   d. syntax.

4. The Dani have only two words for color, yet can distinguish between many different colors. This finding supports the language theory of _____.
   a. Sapir and Whorf.
   c. Pullum.
   b. Lucy and Shweder.
   d. Rosch.

5. The quality of language produced by animals cannot yet compare to the level achieved by a _____ human.
   a. 1-year-old
   b. 2-year-old
   c. 3-year-old
   d. 5-year-old

ANSWERS ON PAGE AK-1

applying psychology to everyday life

Mental and Physical Exercises Combine for Better Cognitive Health

6.10 What are some ways to improve thinking?

You may have heard the saying "use it or lose it," and you likely think of it in terms of maintaining physical fitness. But it is not limited to that; in many regards, the saying applies as well to our ability to maintain cognitive fitness. However, just as there is a difference between physical activity and physical exercise, there is a difference in mental *activity* and mental *exercise*.

Quite a few computerized brain-training programs and devices have hit the market in the last few years. In addition, a lot of attention in the media has focused on the benefits of specific computer-based brain exercises you can do to improve your cognitive fitness. While some are more scientifically grounded and offer the possibility of real benefits, many more appear to be riding the current wave of interest and may not be useful. For some individuals, practicing certain mental skills through cognitive exercises appears to help with those same skills when tested later. In general, however, research has not identified any benefits that transfer to untrained areas (A. M. Owen et al., 2010). Just as being physically active in general will not make you an Olympic athlete, to tune up your cognitive fitness you have to perform proper, focused cognitive exercises.

Wait a minute! You just said most skills don't transfer. That's correct, some do not, but just as in physical training, if you select the proper foundational exercises, you can benefit higher level cognitive functions. For example, impaired verbal working memory is one of the cognitive dysfunctions in schizophrenia. Deficits in early auditory processing are also present and have negative implications for both verbal learning and memory, and for understanding the semantics and emotional content of speech (M. Fisher et al., 2009). Imagine the difficulty you would have if you could not follow a conversation with another person because you could not remember what they just said or because you could not comprehend the meaning or the emotions they were expressing in their speech.

In a recent study, it was found that for a group of individuals with schizophrenia, computerized cognitive exercises that placed increasing demands on auditory perception (a foundational skill) were beneficial (M. Fisher et al., 2009). Those same individuals later demonstrated significant progress in verbal working memory and global cognition tasks (higher level skills). Although the cognitive exercise group originally received daily training for 10 weeks, when some participants were studied 6 months later, the researchers found that some of the gains were still evident and that gains overall were positively correlated with improved quality of life at the 6-month assessment point (Fisher et al., 2009). The authors acknowledged that some of the positive effects might have been due to the number of hours of training and the amount of repetition (the authors noted that each exercise was practiced for thousands of trials!). Furthermore, approximately 16 hours were devoted to tasks that had word stimuli or a learning/memory component, while over 30 hours were spent performing tasks that focused on auditory perception, which also engaged working memory.

The noting of the auditory perception tasks involving *working memory* (L I N K to Chapter Five, Memory, pp. 169–170) in the M. Fisher et al. (2009) study is very interesting, especially in light of recent research suggesting that challenging, adaptive training in working memory appears to improve *fluid intelligence* in young adults (Jaeggi et al., 2008). Fluid intelligence is the ability to adapt and deal with new problems or challenges the first time you encounter them, without having to depend on knowledge you already possess.

What else can you do more generally to benefit your cognitive health? Exercise! And this time, we are referring to physical exercise. Physical activity and specifically aerobic fitness have repeatedly been demonstrated to be associated with improved cognitive function across the life span. A physically active lifestyle and greater aerobic fitness have been implicated with better executive control and memory processes in preadolescent children (Chaddock et al., 2010; Hillman et al., 2009), better educational outcomes later in life and improved affect and visuospatial memory in young adults (Åberg et al., 2009; Stroth et al., 2009), increased hippocampal volume (associated with better memory) in elderly adults (Erickson et al., 2009), and as a useful intervention in a group of individuals at high risk of cognitive decline or impairment, especially for females in the group (Baker et al., 2010).

At least one possible benefit of regular aerobic activity is promoting or maintaining functional connectivity among key brain areas of the frontal, temporal, and parietal lobes (Voss et al., 2010). The increases in oxygen and blood flow to the brain play key roles. Other benefits include increased levels of mood-related neurotransmitters including serotonin, norepinephrine, and dopamine, along with neurogenesis in specific brain areas including the hippocampus (Ratey & Hagerman, 2008). In another study, three months of aerobic activity and increased fitness were associated with small increases in the size of the hippocampus and improved memory in individuals with schizophrenia. Interestingly, controls without schizophrenia in this research *also* showed increases in their hippocampi associated with increases in aerobic fitness (Pajonk et al., 2010).

So instead of "use it or lose it," perhaps a better saying to keep in mind is "what is good for the heart or body is also good for the mind." If you want to learn more, an interesting overview of research related to exercise and brain health can be found in the book, *Spark: The Revolutionary New Science of Exercise and the Brain*, by John Ratey and Eric Hagerman (2008).

QUESTIONS **FOR FURTHER DISCUSSION**

1. Aside from those exercises involving working memory, what other kinds of focused mental exercises might help to keep the brain fit?
2. Should doctors suggest aerobic exercise for their patients interested in maintaining or improving their cognitive functions? What about psychologists working with individuals who have mood or anxiety disorders, or clients with attention problems?
3. Based on this information, what might the implications be for schools that are reducing or eliminating their physical education requirements? What about college students who may experience a decrease in physical activity as compared to when they were in high school?

chapter summary

What Is Consciousness?

6.1 What does it mean to be conscious, and are there different levels of consciousness?
- Consciousness is a person's awareness of everything that is going on at any given moment. Most waking hours are spent in waking consciousness.
- Altered states of consciousness are shifts in the quality or pattern of mental activity.

Altered States: Sleep

6.2 Why do people need to sleep, and how does sleep work?
- The sleep–wake cycle is a circadian rhythm that occurs over a 24-hour period and is controlled by the activity of the hypothalamus and glandular system.
- The average amount of sleep needed by most young adults is about 7 to 9 hours within each 24-hour period.

6.3 What are the different stages of sleep, including the stage of dreaming and its importance?
- Stage One sleep is light sleep.
- Stage Two sleep is indicated by the presence of sleep spindles, bursts of activity on the EEG.
- Stage Three is highlighted by the first appearance of delta waves, the slowest and largest waves, whereas Stage Four is predominantly delta waves, and the body is at its lowest level of functioning.
- REM sleep occurs four or five times a night, replacing Stage 1 after a full cycle through Stages 1 through 4 and then back to Stage 1. It is accompanied by paralysis of the voluntary muscles but rapid movement of the eyes.

6.4 How do sleep disorders interfere with normal sleep?
- Sleepwalking and sleeptalking occur in Stage Four sleep.
- Night terrors are attacks of extreme fear that the victim has while sound asleep.
- REM behavior disorder is a rare condition in which REM paralysis fails and the person moves violently while dreaming, often acting out the elements of the dream.
- Nightmares are bad or unpleasant dreams that occur during REM sleep.

psychology in the news: Murder While Sleepwalking
- Sleepwalking has been used as a defense in several cases of murder. In some of these cases, the defendant has been acquitted because of the sleepwalking defense.
- Insomnia is an inability to get to sleep, stay asleep, or get enough sleep.
- Sleep apnea occurs when a person stops breathing for nearly half a minute or more, followed by gasping for breath.
- Narcolepsy is a genetic disorder in which the person suddenly and without warning collapses into REM sleep.

How People Think

- Thinking (cognition) is mental activity that occurs in the brain when information is being organized, stored, communicated, or processed.

6.5 How are mental images and concepts involved in the process of thinking?
- Mental images represent objects or events and have a picture-like quality.
- Concepts are ideas that represent a class or category of events, objects, or activities.
- Prototypes are examples of a concept that more closely match the defining characteristics of that concept.

6.6 What are the methods people use to solve problems and make decisions?
- Problem solving consists of thinking and behaving in certain ways to reach a goal.
- Mechanical solutions include trial-and-error learning and rote solutions.
- Algorithms are a type of rote solution in which one follows step-by-step procedures for solving certain types of problems.
- A heuristic or "rule of thumb" is a strategy that narrows down the possible solutions for a problem.
- Insight is the sudden perception of a solution to a problem.

6.7 Why does problem solving sometimes fail, and what is meant by creative thinking?
- Functional fixedness is the tendency to perceive objects as having only the use for which they were originally intended and, therefore, failing to see them as possible tools for solving other problems.
- Confirmation bias is the tendency to search for evidence that confirms one's beliefs, ignoring any evidence to the contrary.
- Divergent thinking involves coming up with as many different answers as possible. This is a kind of creativity (combining ideas or behavior in new ways).
- Creative people are usually good at mental imagery and have knowledge on a wide range of topics, are unafraid to be different, value their independence, and are often unconventional in their work but not in other areas.

Language

6.8 How is language defined, and what are its different elements and structure?
- Language is a system for combining symbols so that an infinite number of meaningful statements can be created and communicated to others.
- Grammar is the system of rules by which language is governed and includes the rules for using phonemes, morphemes, and syntax. Pragmatics refers to practical aspects of language.

6.9 Does language influence the way people think, and are animals capable of learning language?
- Sapir and Whorf originally proposed that language controls and helps the development of thought processes and concepts, an idea that is known as the linguistic relativity hypothesis.
- Other researchers have found evidence that concepts are universal and directly influence the development of language, called the cognitive universalism viewpoint.
- Studies with chimpanzees, parrots, and dolphins have been somewhat successful in demonstrating that animals can develop a basic kind of language, including some abstract ideas.
- Controversy exists over the lack of evidence that animals can learn syntax, which some feel means that animals are not truly learning and using language.

applying psychology to everyday life: Mental and Physical Exercises Combine for Better Cognitive Health

6.10 What are some ways to improve thinking?
- Both specific mental exercises (such as those involving working memory) and physical exercise promoting aerobic fitness are important for optimal cognitive functioning.

TEST yourself

✔●─ Study and Review on MyPsychLab   Ready for your test? More quizzes and a customized plan. www.MyPsychLab

Pick the best answer.

1. Most of our time awake is spent in a state called _____, in which our thoughts, feelings, and sensations are clear and organized, and we feel alert.
   a. altered state of consciousness
   b. waking consciousness
   c. unconsciousness
   d. working consciousness

2. Which of the following situations is NOT an altered state of consciousness?
   a. You are daydreaming.
   b. You have been drinking beer.
   c. You are concentrating on a math test.
   d. You are asleep.

3. Which of the following is NOT an example of a circadian rhythm?
   a. menstrual cycle
   b. sleep–wake cycle
   c. blood pressure changes
   d. body temperature changes

4. When light begins to fade at the end of the day, the suprachiasmatic nucleus in the _____ signals the pineal gland to release _____.
   a. hippocampus; melatonin.
   b. hippocampus; serotonin.
   c. hypothalamus; melatonin.
   d. hypothalamus; serotonin.

5. What is the first stage of sleep in which, if awakened, you will realize that you were asleep?
   a. Stage One
   b. Stage Two
   c. Stage Three
   d. Stage Four

6. In which stage(s) of sleep do night terrors occur?
   a. Stage One
   b. Stage Two
   c. Stage Three
   d. Stage Four

7. Sleepwalking _____.
   a. is partly hereditary.
   b. occurs more frequently in girls than in boys.
   c. occurs in about 50 percent of the population.
   d. lasts well into late adulthood in most people.

8. Night terrors _____.
   a. are the same thing as nightmares.
   b. are always vividly remembered afterward.
   c. are more common in children.
   d. take place in one of the lighter stages of sleep.

9. Which of the following statements about REM sleep is FALSE?
   a. The eyes move rapidly back and forth under the eyelids.
   b. Most people report that they were dreaming if awakened.
   c. The body is aroused and brain waves resemble waking beta waves.
   d. Lack of REM sleep produces psychological disorders.

10. If you are in REM sleep but are able to move around and act out your dreams, you may have a rare condition called _____.
    a. REM behavior disorder.
    b. somnambulism.
    c. nightmare disorder.
    d. narcolepsy.

11. If you suddenly and without warning slip into REM sleep during the day, often falling down as you do so, you may have the condition called _____.
    a. sleep apnea.
    b. insomnia.
    c. narcolepsy.
    d. epilepsy.

12. A sleep disorder that may require the use of a machine to force air gently into the nasal passages is called _____.
    a. sleep apnea.
    b. insomnia.
    c. narcolepsy.
    d. cataplexy.

13. Mental activity that goes on in the brain when a person is processing information is called _____.
    a. mentation.
    b. thinking.
    c. a concept.
    d. mental imagery.

14. Concepts that are formed as a result of everyday experience, which are not always well defined, are known as _____ concepts.
    a. formal
    b. natural
    c. prototypical
    d. mental

15. On a popular quiz show, contestants are asked to match the audience in naming certain items. One contestant, when asked to "name a type of vehicle," replied "elevator!" The audience groaned, because they knew that the contestant was pretty far off the mark. The contestant should have picked a vehicle that was closer to a _____ for vehicles to match the audience's response.
    a. formal concept
    b. natural concept
    c. fuzzy concept
    d. prototype

16. Algorithms are a type of _____.
    a. mechanical solution.
    b. heuristic.
    c. rule of thumb.
    d. means–end analysis.

17. The _____ heuristic can be used to create and maintain stereotypes.
    a. availability
    b. representative
    c. insight
    d. means–end analysis

18. When people persist in trying to solve a problem the same way they have always gone about solving problems, they have developed _____.
    a. a mental set.
    b. functional fixedness.
    c. confirmation bias.
    d. transformation bias.

19. Which of the following questions would be more likely to produce divergent thinking?
    a. "What is a coffee cup?"
    b. "How do you spell coffee cup?"
    c. "How many uses can you think of for a coffee cup?"
    d. "What does a coffee cup look like?"

20. The basic units of sound are called _____.
    a. morphemes.
    b. phonemes.
    c. semantics.
    d. syntax.

21. The linguistic relativity hypothesis states that _____.
    a. language shapes thoughts.
    b. thoughts shape language.
    c. language and thought develop independently.
    d. language and thought influence each other.

22. Research has supported the role of _____ in the maintenance of mental fitness and improved cognitive function.
    a. visual activity
    b. specific mental exercises such as those involving working memory
    c. higher levels of aerobic fitness
    d. b and c

6 consciousness and cognition

6.1   p. 198

- people's awareness of everything that is going on around them at any given moment (thoughts, sensations, and feelings) — much of the day is spent in waking consciousness where these are clear and organized

What Is Consciousness?

- altered states of consciousness occur when there is a shift in the quality or pattern of mental activity as compared to waking consciousness — alertness, thought content, and focus can vary greatly

6.2   6.3   6.4   p. 199

- people can live without sleep for a while, can't live without it altogether
  - **sleep deprivation:** can be a serious issue
  - **amount of sleep needed:** averages 7–9 hrs a night but varies by individual and age

Altered States: Sleep

(sleep is one of the body's daily [circadian] biological rhythms; sleep—wake cycle controlled by the brain including the hypothalamus and the neurotransmitter serotonin)

- consist of both REM (rapid eye movement) and non-REM stages
  - **non-REM Stage 1**
  - **non-REM Stage 2**
  - **non-REM Stages 3 and 4**
  - **REM sleep**

- sleep disorders
  - **insomnia**
  - **sleep apnea**
  - **narcolepsy**

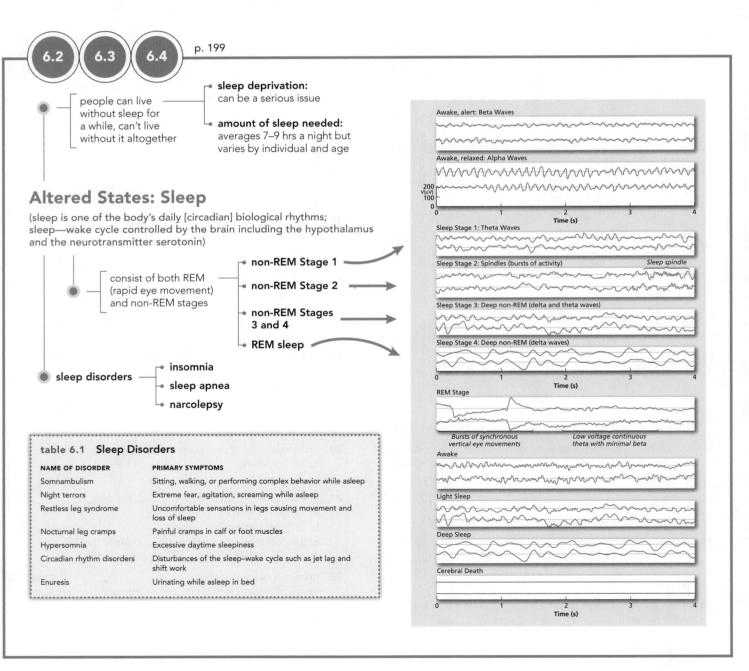

table 6.1   Sleep Disorders

NAME OF DISORDER	PRIMARY SYMPTOMS
Somnambulism	Sitting, walking, or performing complex behavior while asleep
Night terrors	Extreme fear, agitation, screaming while asleep
Restless leg syndrome	Uncomfortable sensations in legs causing movement and loss of sleep
Nocturnal leg cramps	Painful cramps in calf or foot muscles
Hypersomnia	Excessive daytime sleepiness
Circadian rhythm disorders	Disturbances of the sleep—wake cycle such as jet lag and shift work
Enuresis	Urinating while asleep in bed

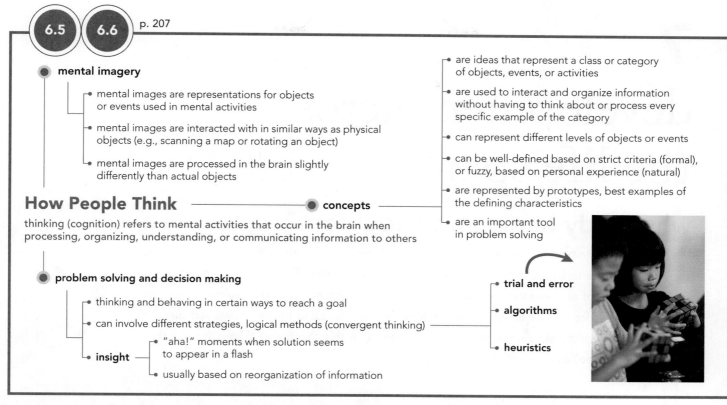

p. 207

6.5 **6.6**

- **mental imagery**
  - mental images are representations for objects or events used in mental activities
  - mental images are interacted with in similar ways as physical objects (e.g., scanning a map or rotating an object)
  - mental images are processed in the brain slightly differently than actual objects

How People Think

thinking (cognition) refers to mental activities that occur in the brain when processing, organizing, understanding, or communicating information to others

- **concepts**
  - are ideas that represent a class or category of objects, events, or activities
  - are used to interact and organize information without having to think about or process every specific example of the category
  - can represent different levels of objects or events
  - can be well-defined based on strict criteria (formal), or fuzzy, based on personal experience (natural)
  - are represented by prototypes, best examples of the defining characteristics
  - are an important tool in problem solving

- **problem solving and decision making**
  - thinking and behaving in certain ways to reach a goal
  - can involve different strategies, logical methods (convergent thinking)
    - trial and error
    - algorithms
    - heuristics
  - **insight**
    - "aha!" moments when solution seems to appear in a flash
    - usually based on reorganization of information

p. 215

6.7

- **problems with problem solving**
  - solutions to problems are not always apparent
  - problems can be caused by three common barriers

Problem Solving and Decision Making

table 6.3	**Stimulating Divergent Thinking**
Brainstorming	Generate as many ideas as possible in a short period of time without judging each idea's merits until all ideas are recorded.
Keeping a Journal	Carry a journal to write down ideas as they occur or a recorder to capture those same ideas and thoughts.
Freewriting	Write down or record everything that comes to mind about a topic without revising or proofreading until all of the information is written or recorded in some way. Organize it later.
Mind or Concept Mapping	Start with a central idea and draw a "map" with lines from the center to other related ideas, forming a visual representation of the concepts and their connections.

- **creativity**
  - consists of new ways of combining ideas or behavior
  - typically the result of divergent thinking

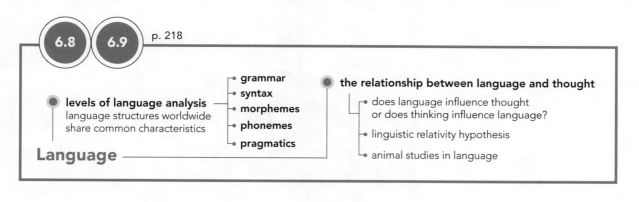

p. 218

6.8 **6.9**

- **levels of language analysis**
  language structures worldwide share common characteristics
  - **grammar**
  - **syntax**
  - **morphemes**
  - **phonemes**
  - **pragmatics**

- **the relationship between language and thought**
  - does language influence thought or does thinking influence language?
  - linguistic relativity hypothesis
  - animal studies in language

Language

7
development across the life span

why study human development?

Beginning to understand how we come to be the people we are is a critical step in understanding ourselves as we are today and who we may become as we grow older. From the moment of conception, each of us is headed down a pathway of change, influenced by our biology, environment, and social interactions, to a final destination that is the same for all of us. The twists and turns of the pathway are what make each of us unique individuals. In this chapter, we'll look at the influences that help determine our developmental pathway through life.

chapter outline

Issues in Studying Human Development

The Basic Building Blocks of Development

Prenatal Development

PSYCHOLOGY IN THE NEWS: Abby and Brittany Hensel, Together for Life

Infancy and Childhood Development

CLASSIC STUDIES IN PSYCHOLOGY: Harlow and Contact Comfort

Gender Development

Adolescence

Adulthood

APPLYING PSYCHOLOGY TO EVERYDAY LIFE: Cross-Cultural Views on Death

Not Your Average 16-Year-Old

At a time when many teenage girls are dating or shopping at the mall with friends, Jessica Watson was on a mission to become the youngest individual to sail nonstop and unassisted around the world. The 16-year-old left Sydney, Australia, on October 18, 2009. Seven months later, on May 15, 2010, she sailed back into Sydney, unofficially breaking the previous record, set by then 17-year-old Michael Perham (Marks, 2010; Munoz, 2010).

In January 2010, 16-year-old Abby Sunderland launched her own attempt to break the record. Setting sail from California, her attempt failed when her mast broke, forcing the teenager to send up two emergency beacons. She was rescued in early June of 2010 and flew back to her home in California two weeks later (Tran, 2010). Had she succeeded, Abby, like Jessica before her, would probably have been denied official recognition by the World Speed Sailing Record Council because the council wants to discourage what it considers dangerous and foolhardy attempts by those who are too young.

Adolescence is one among many stages of life, and while this chapter will cover several of the common features of human development in all of those stages, the stories of Jessica Watson and Abby Sunderland and their parents should be a reminder that each of us is an individual, with different motivations, goals, and desires. As you learn about the developing person in this chapter, keep in mind that the stages and ages discussed herein are generalities only. Like Jessica and Abby, each individual charts his or her own destiny.

learning objectives

7.1 What are some of the special research methods used to study development?

7.2 What is the relationship between heredity and environmental factors in determining development?

7.3 How do chromosomes and genes determine the inheritance of disorders, and what causes multiple births?

7.4 What happens during the germinal, embryonic, and fetal periods of pregnancy, and what are some hazards in prenatal development?

7.5 What kind of physical changes take place in infancy and childhood?

7.6 What are two ways of looking at cognitive development, and how does language develop?

7.7 How do infants and children develop personalities and form relationships with others, and what are Erikson's stages of psychosocial development for children?

7.8 What is gender, and how do gender roles develop?

7.9 What are the physical, cognitive, and personality changes that occur in adolescence, including concepts of morality and Erikson's search for identity?

7.10 What are the physical, cognitive, and personality changes that occur during adulthood and aging, including Erikson's last three psychosocial stages, and patterns of parenting?

7.11 How do psychologists explain why aging occurs, and what are the stages of death and dying?

7.12 What are some cross-cultural differences in views of death and dying?

human development the scientific study of the changes that occur in people as they age from conception until death.

longitudinal design research design in which one participant or group of participants is studied over a long period of time.

cross-sectional design research design in which several different age-groups of participants are studied at one particular point in time.

cross-sequential design research design in which participants are first studied by means of a cross-sectional design but are also followed and assessed for a period of no more than six years.

nature the influence of our inherited characteristics on our personality, physical growth, intellectual growth, and social interactions.

nurture the influence of the environment on personality, physical growth, intellectual growth, and social interactions.

Issues in Studying Human Development

What is development? In the context of life, **human development** is the scientific study of the changes that occur in people as they age, from conception until death. This chapter will touch on almost all of the topics covered in the other chapters of this text, such as personality, cognition, biological processes, and social interactions. But in this chapter, all of those topics will be studied in the context of changes that occur as a result of the process of human development.

Research Designs

7.1 What are some of the special research methods used to study development?

Research in development is affected by the problem of age. In any experiment, the participants who are exposed to the independent variable (the variable in an experiment that is deliberately manipulated by the experimenter) should be randomly assigned to the different experimental conditions. ⓛⓘⓝⓚ to Chapter One: The Science of Psychology, p. 27. The problem in developmental research is that the age of the people in the study should always be an independent variable, but people cannot be randomly assigned to different age-groups.

Special designs used in researching age-related changes are the **longitudinal design**, in which one group of people is followed and assessed at different times as the group ages; the **cross-sectional design**, in which several different age-groups are studied at one time; and the **cross-sequential design**, which is a combination of the longitudinal and cross-sectional designs (Baltes et al., 1988; Schaie & Willis, 2010).

The longitudinal design has the advantage of looking at real age-related changes as those changes occur in the same individuals. The disadvantages of this method are the lengthy amount of time, money, and effort involved in following participants over the years as well as the loss of participants when they move away, lose interest, or die. The cross-sectional design has the advantages of being quick, relatively inexpensive, and easier to accomplish than the longitudinal design. The main disadvantage is that one is no longer comparing changes in the same individuals as they age; instead, individuals of different ages are being compared to one another. Differences between age-groups are often a problem in developmental research. For example, in comparing the IQ scores of 30-year-olds to 80-year-olds to see how aging affects intelligence, questions arise concerning the differing experiences those two age-groups have had in educational opportunities that might affect IQ scores in addition to any effects of aging. Table 7.1 shows a comparison of a *longitudinal design,* a *cross-sectional design*, and a *cross-sequential design.*

In studying human development, developmental psychologists have outlined many theories of how these age-related changes occur. There are some areas of controversy, however, and one of these is the issue of nature versus nurture.

Nature Versus Nurture

7.2 What is the relationship between heredity and environmental factors in determining development?

Nature refers to heredity, the influence of inherited characteristics on personality, physical growth, intellectual growth, and social interactions. **Nurture** refers to the influence of the environment on all of those same things and includes parenting styles, physical surroundings, economic factors, and anything that can have an influence on development that does not come from within the person.

table 7.1   A Comparison of Three Developmental Research Designs

CROSS-SECTIONAL DESIGN

Different participants of various ages are compared at one point in time to determine age-related *differences*.	**Group One:** 20-year-old participants	Research done in 2012
	Group Two: 40-year-old participants	
	Group Three: 60-year-old participants	

LONGITUDINAL DESIGN

The **same** participants are studied at various ages to determine age-related *changes*.	**Study One:** 20-year-old participants	Research done in 1972
	Study Two: Same participants are 40 years old	Research done in 1992
	Study Three: Same participants are now 60 years old	Research done in 2012

CROSS-SEQUENTIAL DESIGN

Different participants of various ages are compared at several points in time, for a period of no more than six years, to determine both age-related *differences* and age-related *changes*.	**Study One:** Group One: 20-year-old participants Group Two: 40-year-old participants	Research done in 2012
	Study Two: Group One: participants will be 25 years old Group Two: participants will be 45 years old	Research to be done in 2017

So, is a person like Hitler born that way, or did something happen to make him the person he was?

How much of a person's personality and behavior is determined by nature, and how much is determined by nurture? This is a key question, and the answer is quite complicated. It is also quite important: Are people like Hitler, the infamous serial killer Ted Bundy, and Timothy McVeigh (the man responsible for the Oklahoma bombing of the Federal Building) the result of bad genes? Or was it bad parenting or life-altering experiences in childhood? Or are they the unique combination of both hereditary and environmental influences? After many years of scientific research, most developmental psychologists now agree that the last possibility is the most likely explanation for most of human development: All that people are and all that people become is the product of an interaction between nature and nurture (Insel & Wang, 2010; Ridley, 1999; Sternberg & Grigorenko, 2006). This does not mean that the controversy no longer exists; for example, intelligence is still a "hot topic" with regard to how much is inherited and how much is learned. There are researchers and theorists who assume a large genetic influence (Bouchard & Segal, 1985; Herrnstein & Murray, 1994; Jensen, 1969; Johnson et al., 2007; Kristensen & Bjerkedal, 2007) and those who believe that culture, economics, nutrition in early childhood, and educational opportunities have a greater impact (Gardner et al., 1996; Gould, 1996; Rose et al., 1984; Wahlsten, 1997).

Behavioral genetics is a relatively new field in the investigation of the origins of behavior in which researchers try to determine how much of behavior is the result of genetic inheritance and how much is due to a person's experiences. For more on behavioral genetics and links to other sites, go to **www.ornl.gov/sci/techresources/Human_Genome/elsi/behavior.shtml.**

So, is a person like Hitler born that way, or did something happen to make him the person he was?

The Basic Building Blocks of Development

Any study of the human life span must begin with looking at the complex material contained in the cells of the body that carries the instructions for life itself. After discussing the basic building blocks of life, we will discuss how the processes of conception and the development of the infant within the womb take place.

FIGURE 7.1 In this model of a DNA molecule, the two strands making up the sides of the "twisted ladder" are composed of sugars and phosphates. The "rungs" of the ladder that link the two strands are amines. Amines contain the genetic codes for building the proteins that make up organic life.

Read and learn more about DNA, genes, and chromosomes on **MyPsychLab**

Down syndrome is a form of developmental delay caused by an extra chromosome 21.

dominant referring to a gene that actively controls the expression of a trait.

recessive referring to a gene that influences the expression of a trait only when paired with an identical gene.

Genetic and Chromosome Problems

7.3 How do chromosomes and genes determine the inheritance of disorders, and what causes multiple births?

Genetics is the science of heredity. Understanding how genes transmit human characteristics and traits involves defining a few basic terms.

The basic building blocks of life are special *DNA molecules* that contain the instructions for all of an organism's traits (see Figure 7.1). These "instructions" known as *genes* are sections of the DNA molecules. Genes that are more active in influencing a trait are called **dominant**. A dominant gene will always be expressed in the observable trait. Some disorders, such as Huntington's disease and Marfan's syndrome, are carried by dominant genes. In these disorders, only one parent needs to have the gene for the disorder to be passed on to offspring. More often genetic disorders are carried by recessive genes. **Recessive** genes tend to recede, or fade, into the background when paired with a dominant gene. Diseases carried by recessive genes are only inherited when a child receives *two* recessive genes, one from each parent. Examples of disorders inherited in this manner are cystic fibrosis (a disease of the respiratory and digestive tracts), sickle-cell anemia (a blood disorder), Tay-Sachs disorder (a fatal neurological disorder), and phenylketonuria or PKU (a problem with digesting the amino acid phenylalanine, which can lead to brain damage). Figure 7.2 illustrates a typical pattern of inheritance for PKU. **Read** on **MyPsychLab**

Chromosomes are rod-shaped structures found in the nucleus of each cell and are nothing more than tightly wound strands of genes. Sometimes the chromosome itself is the problem. Although each egg and each sperm (the sex cells for females and males, respectively) are only supposed to have 23 chromosomes, in the creation of these cells a chromosome can end up in the wrong cell, leaving one cell with only 22 and the other with 24. If either of these cells survives to "mate," the missing or extra chromosome can cause mild to severe problems in development (American Academy of Pediatrics, 1995; Barnes & Carey, 2002; Centers for Disease Control, 2009; Gardner & Sutherland, 1996).

Examples of chromosome disorders include *Down syndrome*, a disorder in which there is an extra chromosome in what would normally be the twenty-first pair. Symptoms include almond-shaped, wide-set eyes and intellectual disability (Barnes & Carey, 2002; Hernandez & Fisher, 1996). Other chromosome disorders occur when there is an extra sex chromosome in the twenty-third pair, such as *Klinefelter's syndrome*, in which the twenty-third set of sex chromosomes is XXY, with the extra X producing a male with reduced masculine characteristics, enlarged breasts, obesity, and excessive height (Bock, 1993), and *Turner's syndrome*, in which the twenty-third pair is actually missing an X, so that the result is a lone X chromosome (Ranke & Saenger, 2001). These females tend to be very short, infertile, and sexually underdeveloped (American Academy of Pediatrics, 1995; Rovet, 1993).

Frank and Ernest

I HATE BEING A DNA MOLECULE. THERE'S SO MUCH TO REMEMBER!

©1986 Thaves. Reprinted with permission. Newspaper dist. by NEA, Inc.

Mother — Carries recessive PKU gene

Father — Does not carry recessive PKU gene

a.

Mother contributes either P or p

Father contributes either P or P

PP — Normal

PP — Normal

pP — Carrier

pP — Carrier

Result: No child will be afflicted with PKU, although 2 in 4 will carry the recessive gene

Mother — Carries recessive PKU gene

Father — Carries recessive PKU gene

b.

Mother contributes either P or p

Father contributes either P or p

PP — Normal

Pp — Carrier

pP — Carrier

pp — Afflicted with PKU

Result: 1 in 4 children will inherit two dominant genes and will not have PKU; 2 in 4 will inherit one recessive gene and not be afflicted with PKU but will carry the recessive gene; and 1 in 4 will have PKU

FIGURE 7.2 Dominant and Recessive Genes and PKU

This figure shows the variation of parents carrying zero, one, or two recessive genes and the result of this in their offspring.
(a) If only one parent carries the PKU gene, the children might be carriers but will not have PKU.
(b) Only if both parents are carriers of PKU will a child have the 1 in 4 possibility of having PKU.

practice quiz   How much do you remember?

Pick the best answer.

1. In a _____ design, several different age-groups of participants are studied at one time.
   a. longitudinal
   b. cross-sectional
   c. cross-sequential
   d. cross-longitudinal

2. In the analogy of the twisted ladder, the sequence of amines would be represented by the _____ of the ladder.
   a. sides
   b. length
   c. rungs
   d. wood

3. Brandon has blue eyes, even though both his mother and father have brown eyes. What do we know about Brandon's parents?
   a. At least one of his parents has a recessive blue-eye-color gene.
   b. Each of his parents must have one recessive blue-eye-color gene.
   c. Each of his parents must have one dominant blue-eye-color gene.
   d. Neither of his parents has a blue-eye-color gene.

4. Which of the following is a disorder caused by having an extra chromosome?
   a. Tay-Sachs
   b. PKU
   c. cystic fibrosis
   d. Down syndrome

ANSWERS ON PAGE AK-1.

ovum the female sex cell, or egg.

fertilization the union of the ovum and sperm.

zygote cell resulting from the uniting of the ovum and sperm.

monozygotic twins identical twins formed when one zygote splits into two separate masses of cells, each of which develops into a separate embryo.

dizygotic twins often called fraternal twins, occurring when two eggs each get fertilized by two different sperm, resulting in two zygotes in the uterus at the same time.

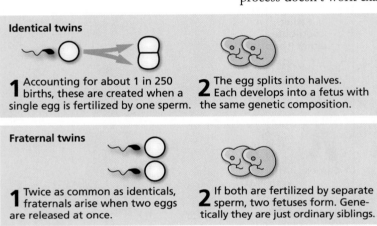

Identical twins

1 Accounting for about 1 in 250 births, these are created when a single egg is fertilized by one sperm.

2 The egg splits into halves. Each develops into a fetus with the same genetic composition.

Fraternal twins

1 Twice as common as identicals, fraternals arise when two eggs are released at once.

2 If both are fertilized by separate sperm, two fetuses form. Genetically they are just ordinary siblings.

FIGURE 7.3 Monozygotic and Dizygotic Twins
Because identical twins come from one fertilized egg (zygote), they are called monozygotic. Fraternal twins, who come from two different fertilized eggs, are called dizygotic.

Read and learn more about mitosis and meiosis on **MyPsychLab**

Prenatal Development

From conception to the actual birth of the baby is a period of approximately 9 months, during which a single cell becomes a complete infant. It is also during this time that many things can have a positive or negative influence on the developing infant.

Fertilization, the Zygote and Twinning

When an egg (also called an **ovum**) and a sperm unite in the process of **fertilization**, the resulting single cell will have a total of 46 chromosomes and is called a **zygote**. Normally, the zygote will begin to divide, first into two cells, then four, then eight, and so on, with each new cell also having 46 chromosomes because the DNA molecules produce duplicates of themselves before each division. (This division process is called *mitosis*.) Eventually, the mass of cells becomes a baby. When this division process doesn't work exactly this way, twins or multiples are sometimes the result.

There are actually two main types of twins. Twins who are commonly referred to as "identical" are **monozygotic twins**, meaning that the two babies come from one (mono) fertilized egg (zygote). Early in the division process, the mass of cells splits completely—no one knows exactly why—into two separate masses, each of which will develop into a separate infant. The infants will be the same sex and have identical features because they each possess the same set of 46 chromosomes. Nonidentical twins are more an accident of timing and are more common in women who are older and who are from certain ethnic groups (Allen & Parisi, 1990; Bonnelykke, 1990; Imaizumi, 1998). A woman's body may release more than one egg at a time or release an egg after she has already conceived once. If two eggs are fertilized, the woman may give birth to fraternal or **dizygotic twins** (two zygotes) or possibly triplets or some other multiple number of babies (Bryan & Hallett, 2001). This is also more likely to happen to women who are taking fertility drugs to help them get pregnant. (See Figure 7.3.)

Twins are important because they provide developmental psychologists with another way to look at the contribution of nature and nurture to human development. Researchers may seek out identical twins who have been separated at birth, looking at all the ways those twins are alike in spite of being raised in different environments. **LINK** to Chapter Eleven: Theories of Personality and Intelligence, pp. 419–421.

Read on **MyPsychLab**

Sometimes in the twinning process, the mass of cells does not completely split apart. When this occurs, the resulting *conjoined twins* will be joined at the point where the two cell masses remained "stuck." Sometimes this joining may involve only soft tissues. It may also involve the sharing of certain body parts, like the case of Abby and Brittany, which is discussed in the Psychology in the News section that follows.

psychology in the news
··
Abby and Brittany Hensel, Together for Life

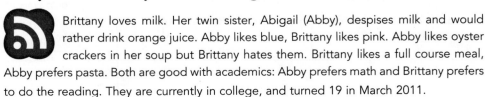

Brittany loves milk. Her twin sister, Abigail (Abby), despises milk and would rather drink orange juice. Abby likes blue, Brittany likes pink. Abby likes oyster crackers in her soup but Brittany hates them. Brittany likes a full course meal, Abby prefers pasta. Both are good with academics: Abby prefers math and Brittany prefers to do the reading. They are currently in college, and turned 19 in March 2011.

Abby and Brittany sound like many other siblings, each with separate likes and dislikes as well as different interests. But Abby and Brittany are not separate and can never truly be separate, for they have two separate heads yet share one lower body. No more than four sets of surviving conjoined twins in recorded history have this condition. In the case of Abby and Brittany Hensel, they each have their own heart, stomach and pair of lungs. Their spines are joined at the pelvis, and below the waist they have only one set of organs. Each controls one arm and one leg on one side of the body, yet they somehow manage to move as one (Miller & Doman, 1996).

The girls play sports, swim, and put on makeup just like any other girls their age. Yet every action they undertake has to be a miracle of coordination, and they do it without even seeming to think about it. If Brittany coughs, *Abby's* hand may reflexively go up to cover Brittany's mouth. When Brittany is sick, she can't take the medicine for it (her stomach is sensitive) but Abby can take it for her (her stomach isn't sensitive).

In 2002, the girls received surgery to correct a severe curve in each of their spines, the result of their unusual joining of spinal columns (Kaveny, 2001). They each gained about 2 inches in height and find that to be an advantage on the soccer field. Now 19 years old, they are healthy and seem to be both happy and well adjusted, surrounded by a loving mother, father, younger brother, and sister.

QUESTIONS FOR FURTHER DISCUSSION

1. What kinds of difficulties might Abby and Brittany have in adolescence?
2. How would being conjoined affect career decisions?
3. How can conjoined twins have different personalities?
4. If they decide to have a child (which is physically possible), who will claim the child, or will they both be the baby's mother?

Abby and Brittany Hensel are conjoined twins who share one body from the waist down but are two distinctly different individuals.

The Germinal Period

7.4 What happens during the germinal, embryonic, and fetal periods of pregnancy, and what are some hazards in prenatal development?

Once fertilization has taken place, the zygote begins dividing and moving down to the *uterus*, the muscular organ that will contain and protect the developing infant. This process takes about a week, followed by about a week during which the mass of cells, now forming a hollow ball, firmly attaches itself to the wall of the uterus. This two-week period is called the **germinal period** of pregnancy. The *placenta* also begins to form during this period. The placenta is a specialized organ that provides nourishment and filters away waste products from the developing baby. The *umbilical cord* also begins to develop at this time, connecting the organism to the placenta.

How does a mass of cells become a baby with eyes, nose, hands, feet, and so on? How do all those different things come from the same original single cell?

During the germinal period, the cells begin to differentiate, or develop into specialized cells, in preparation for becoming all the various kinds of cells that make up the human body—skin cells, heart cells, and so on. Perhaps the most important of these cells are the *stem cells*, which stay in a somewhat immature state until needed to produce more cells. Researchers are currently looking into ways to use stem cells found in the umbilical cord to grow new organs and tissues for transplant or to repair

> How does a mass of cells become a baby with eyes, nose, hands, feet, and so on? How do all those different things come from the same original single cell?

germinal period first two weeks after fertilization, during which the zygote moves down to the uterus and begins to implant in the lining.

The three periods of pregnancy are the germinal period, lasting about two weeks, the embryonic period, from about two to eight weeks, and fetal period, which lasts from eight weeks until the end of pregnancy.

neurological damage (Chen & Ende, 2000; Holden & Vogel, 2002; Lu & Ende, 1997; Moreno-Manzanoa et al., 2009). (LINK) to Chapter Two: The Biological Perspective, p. 48.

The Embryonic Period

Once firmly attached to the uterus, the developing organism is called an **embryo**. The **embryonic period** will last from two weeks after conception to eight weeks, and during this time the cells will continue to specialize and become the various organs and structures of a human infant. By the end of eight weeks after conception, the embryo is about 1 inch long and has primitive eyes, nose, lips, teeth, little arms and legs, and a beating heart. Although no organ is fully developed or completely functional at this time, nearly all are "there."

CRITICAL PERIODS As soon as the embryo begins to receive nourishment from the mother through the placenta, it becomes vulnerable to hazards such as diseases of the mother, drugs, and other toxins that can pass from the mother through the placenta to the developing infant. (Since the developing organism in the germinal stage is not yet connected to the mother's system, the organism is not usually vulnerable to outside influences in that stage.) It is during the embryonic period that we most clearly see **critical periods**, times during which some environmental influence can have an impact—often devastating—on the development of the infant. The structural development of the arms and legs, for example, is only affected during the time that they are developing (3½ to 8 weeks), whereas the heart's structure is most affected very early in this period (2½ to 6½ weeks). Other physical and structural problems can occur with the central nervous system (2 to 5 weeks), eyes (3½ to 8½ weeks), and the teeth and roof of the mouth (about 7 to 12 weeks).

PRENATAL HAZARDS: TERATOGENS Any substance such as a drug, chemical, virus, or other factor that can cause a birth defect is called a **teratogen**. Table 7.2 shows some common teratogens and their possible negative effects on the developing embryo.

The Fetal Period: Grow, Baby, Grow

The **fetal period** is the time from about eight weeks after conception until the birth of the child (now called a **fetus**) and is a period of tremendous growth. The fetus's length increases by about 20 times, and its weight increases from about 1 ounce at 2 months to a little over 7 pounds. The organs, while accomplishing most of their differentiation in the embryonic period, continue to develop and become functional. At this time, teratogens will more likely affect the physical functioning (physiology) of the organs rather than their structure. The functioning of the central nervous system, for example, is vulnerable throughout the fetal period, as are the eyes and the external sexual organs.

embryo name for the developing organism from two weeks to eight weeks after fertilization.

embryonic period the period from two to eight weeks after fertilization, during which the major organs and structures of the organism develop.

critical periods times during which certain environmental influences can have an impact on the development of the infant.

teratogen any factor that can cause a birth defect.

fetal period the time from about eight weeks after conception until the birth of the child.

fetus name for the developing organism from eight weeks after fertilization to the birth of the baby.

table 7.2 Common Teratogens

TERATOGENIC AGENT	EFFECT ON DEVELOPMENT
Measles, Mumps, and Rubella	Blindness, deafness, heart defects, brain damage
Marijuana	Irritability, nervousness, tremors; infant is easily disturbed, startled
Cocaine	Decreased height, low birth weight, respiratory problems, seizures, learning difficulties; infant is difficult to soothe
Alcohol	Fetal alcohol syndrome (intellectual disability, delayed growth, facial malformation), learning difficulties, smaller than normal heads
Nicotine	Miscarriage, low birth weight, stillbirth, short stature, intellectual disability, learning disabilities
Mercury	Intellectual disability, blindness
Vitamin A (high doses)	Facial, ear, central nervous system, and heart defects
Caffeine	Miscarriage, low birth weight
Toxoplasmosis	Brain swelling, spinal abnormalities, deafness, blindness, intellectual disability
High Water Temperatures	Increased chance of neural tube defects

Sources: March of Dimes Foundation (2009); Organization of Teratology Information Specialists (2011); Shepard, T. H. (2001)

Muscles begin to contract in the third month. In the fourth month, the mother will begin to feel this movement as a tiny "flutter" or "quickening" at first, and by the fifth month, the flutter will become a "kick." The last few months continue the development of fat and the growth of the body, until about the end of the thirty-eighth week. At that time, the fetus is pushed out of the mother's body in the process of labor and childbirth and becomes a baby. Babies born before 38 weeks are called *preterm* and may need life support to survive. This is especially true if the baby weighs less than about 5½ pounds at birth.

The most likely time for a *miscarriage*, or *spontaneous abortion*, is in the first three months, as the organs are forming and first becoming functional (Katz, 2007; Speroff et al., 1999). Some 15 to 20 percent of all pregnancies end in miscarriage, many so early that the mother may not have even known she was pregnant (Hill, 1998; Medical Economics Staff, 1994). When a miscarriage occurs, it is most likely caused by a genetic defect in the way the embryo or fetus is developing that will not allow the infant to survive. In other words, there isn't anything that the mother did wrong or that could have been done to prevent the miscarriage.

This pregnant woman is getting a sonogram. Sonograms allow doctors to see any physical deformities and make accurate measurements of gestational age without risk to the mother or the fetus.

practice quiz   How much do you remember?

7.4

Pick the best answer.

1. The fertilized egg cell is called a _____ .
    a. zygote.
    b. ovum.
    c. sperm.
    d. blastocyst.

2. Which of the following statements about Abby and Brittany Hensel is FALSE?
    a. They are able to coordinate their actions.
    b. They are remarkably healthy.
    c. They could have been successfully separated.
    d. They are one of only four sets of living dicephalic twins.

3. The first two weeks of pregnancy are called the _____ period.
    a. fetal
    b. embryonic
    c. placental
    d. germinal

4. Which of the following does NOT happen in the germinal period?
    a. dividing mass of cells travels to the uterus
    b. developing organs can be affected by toxins passing through the placenta
    c. mass of cells forms a hollow ball
    d. cells begin to differentiate

5. The period of pregnancy that contains the clearest examples of critical periods is the _____ period.
    a. germinal
    b. embryonic
    c. fetal
    d. gestational

6. Intellectual disability and blindness are possible outcomes of the effects of _____ on the developing baby.
    a. alcohol
    b. caffeine
    c. cocaine
    d. mercury

What can babies do? Aren't they pretty much unaware of what's going on around them at first?

Infancy and Childhood Development

● What can babies do? Aren't they pretty much unaware of what's going on around them at first?

Surprisingly, babies can do a lot more than researchers used to believe they could. A lot of the early research on infants just after birth was done on babies who were still very drowsy from the general anesthesia that used to be given to their mothers during the labor process. Drowsy babies don't tend to respond well, as one might imagine. In the next few sections, it becomes obvious that infants accomplish a great deal throughout infancy, even in the first few days of life on the outside.

Physical Development

7.5 What kind of physical changes take place in infancy and childhood?

Immediately after birth, several things start to happen. The respiratory system begins to function, filling the lungs with air and putting oxygen into the blood. The blood now circulates only within the infant's system because the umbilical cord has been cut. Body temperature is now regulated by the infant's own activity and body fat (which acts as insulation) rather than by the amniotic fluid. The digestive system probably takes the longest to adjust to life outside the womb. This is another reason for the excess body fat. It provides fuel until the infant is able to take in enough nourishment on its own. That is why most babies lose a little weight in the first week after birth.

REFLEXES Babies come into this world able to interact with it. Infants have a set of *innate* (existing from birth) involuntary* behavior patterns called *reflexes*. Until an infant is capable of learning more complex means of interaction, reflexes help the infant to survive. Figure 7.4 shows five infant reflexes. Pediatricians use these and other reflexes to determine whether or not an infant's nervous system is working properly.

Baby, Can You See Me? Baby, Can You Hear Me? Sensory Development

I've heard that babies can't see or hear very much at birth. Is that true?

● I've heard that babies can't see or hear very much at birth. Is that true?

Although most infant sensory abilities are fairly well developed at birth, some require a bit more time to reach "full power." The sense of touch is the most well developed, which makes perfect sense when one realizes how much skin-to-womb contact the baby has had in the last months of pregnancy. The sense of smell is also highly developed. Breast-fed babies can actually tell the difference between their own mother's milk scent and another woman's milk scent within a few days after birth.

Taste is also nearly fully developed. At birth, infants show a preference for sweets (and human breast milk is very sweet) and by four months have developed a preference for salty tastes (which may come from exposure to the salty taste of their mother's skin). Sour and bitter, two other taste sensations, produce spitting up and the making of horrible faces (Ganchrow et al., 1983).

Hearing is functional before birth but may take a little while to reach its full potential after birth. The fluids of the womb must clear out completely. From birth, newborns seem most responsive to high pitches, as in a woman's voice, and low pitches, as in a male's voice.

The least functional sense at birth is vision. As stated in Chapter Three, the eye is quite a complex organ. (LINK) to Chapter Three: Sensation and Perception, pp. 85–88. The rods, which see in black and white and have little visual acuity, are fairly well developed at birth, but the cones, which see color and provide sharpness of vision, will take

---

*Involuntary: in this sense, not under conscious, deliberate control.

a.   b.   c.

d.   e.

FIGURE 7.4 Five Infant Reflexes
Shown here are (a) grasping reflex,
(b) startle reflex (also known as the Moro
reflex), (c) rooting reflex (when you touch
a baby's cheek it will turn toward your
hand, open its mouth, and search for the
nipple), (d) stepping reflex, and (e) sucking
reflex. These infant reflexes can be used to
check on the health of an infant's nervous
system. If a reflex is absent or abnormal, it
may indicate brain damage or some other
neurological problem.

about another six months to fully develop. So the newborn has relatively poor color perception when compared to sharply contrasting lights and darks until about two months of age (Adams, 1987) and has fairly "fuzzy" vision, much as a nearsighted person would have. The lens of the newborn stays fixed until the muscles that hold it in place mature. Until then the newborn is unable to shift what little focus it has from close to far. Thus, newborns actually have a fixed distance for clear vision of about 7 to 10 inches, which is the distance from the baby's face to the mother's face while nursing (Slater, 2000).

Newborns also have visual preferences at birth, as discovered by researchers using measures of the time that infants spent looking at certain visual stimuli (Fantz, 1961). They found that infants prefer to look at complex patterns rather than simple ones, three dimensions rather than two, and that the most preferred visual stimulus was a human face. The fact that infants prefer human voices and human faces (DeCasper & Fifer, 1980; DeCasper & Spence, 1986; Fantz, 1964; Maurer & Young, 1983) makes it easier for them to form relationships with their caregivers and to develop language later on. ✳️Explore on MyPsychLab

✳️Explore infants' perceptual and cognitive milestones on **MyPsychLab**

FROM CRAWLING TO A BLUR OF MOTION: MOTOR DEVELOPMENT Infants manage a tremendous amount of development in motor skills from birth to about 2 years of age. Figure 7.5 shows some of the major physical milestones of infancy. When looking at the age ranges listed, remember that even these ranges are averages based on large samples of infants. An infant may reach these milestones earlier or later than the average and still be considered to be developing normally.

a.

b.

c.

d.

e.

f.

FIGURE 7.5 Six Motor Milestones
Shown here are (a) raising head and chest—2 to 4 months, (b) rolling over—2 to 5 months, (c) sitting up with support—4 to 6 months, (d) sitting up without support—6 to 7 months, (e) crawling—7 to 8 months, and (f) walking—8 to 18 months. The motor milestones develop as the infant gains greater voluntary control over the muscles in his or her body, typically from the top of the body downward. This pattern is seen in the early control of the neck muscles and the much later development of control of the legs and feet.

Cognitive Development

By the time the average infant has reached the age of 1 year, it has tripled its birth weight and added about another foot to its height. The brain triples its weight in the first two years, reaching about 75 percent of its adult weight. By age 5, the brain is at 90 percent of its adult weight. This increase makes possible a tremendous amount of major advances in **cognitive development**, including the development of thinking, problem solving, and memory.

7.6 What are two ways of looking at cognitive development, and how does language develop?

PIAGET'S THEORY: FOUR STAGES OF COGNITIVE DEVELOPMENT　One way of examining the development of cognition is found in the work of Jean Piaget. Piaget believed, based on observations of his own children and others, that children form mental concepts or **schemes** as they experience new situations and events. For example, if Sandy points to a picture of an apple and tells her child, "that's an apple," the child forms a scheme for "apple" that looks something like that picture. Piaget also believed that children first try to understand new things in terms of schemes they already possess in a process called *assimilation*. The child might see an orange and say "apple" because both objects are round. When corrected, the child might alter the scheme for apple to include "round" and "red." The process of altering or adjusting old schemes to fit new information and experiences is *accommodation* (Piaget, 1952, 1962, 1983).

cognitive development　the development of thinking, problem solving, and memory.

scheme　in this case, a mental concept formed through experiences with objects and events.

table 7.3 Piaget's Stages of Cognitive Development

STAGE		COGNITIVE DEVELOPMENT
Sensorimotor	Birth to 2 years old	Children explore the world using their senses and ability to move. They develop object permanence and the understanding that concepts and mental images represent objects, people, and events.
Preoperational	2 to 7 years old	Young children can mentally represent and refer to objects and events with words or pictures, and they can pretend. However, they can't conserve, logically reason, or simultaneously consider many characteristics of an object.
Concrete Operations	7 to 12 years old	Children at this stage are able to conserve, reverse their thinking, and classify objects in terms of their many characteristics. They can also think logically and understand analogies but only about concrete events.
Formal Operations	12 years old to adulthood	People at this stage can use abstract reasoning about hypothetical events or situations, think about logical possibilities, use abstract analogies, and systematically examine and test hypotheses. Not everyone can eventually reason in all these ways.

Piaget also proposed that there are four distinct stages of cognitive development that occur from infancy to adolescence, as shown in Table 7.3 (Piaget, 1952, 1962, 1983).

The Sensorimotor Stage The **sensorimotor stage** is the first of Piaget's stages. It concerns infants from birth to age 2. In this stage, infants use their senses and motor abilities to learn about the world around them. At first, infants only have the involuntary reflexes present at birth to interact with objects and people. As their sensory and motor development progresses, they begin to interact deliberately with objects by grasping, pushing, tasting, and so on. Infants move from simple repetitive actions, such as grabbing their toes, to complex patterns, such as trying to put a shape into a sorting box. ◉─Watch on **MyPsychLab**

◉─Watch classic footage on sensorimotor development with Jean Piaget on **MyPsychLab**

By the end of the sensorimotor stage, infants have fully developed a sense of **object permanence**, the knowledge that an object exists even when it is not in sight. For example, the game of "peek-a-boo" is important in teaching infants that Mommy's smiling face is always going to be behind her hands. This is a critical step in developing language (and eventually abstract thought), as words themselves are symbols of things that may not be present. Symbolic thought, which is the ability to represent objects in one's thoughts with symbols such as words, becomes possible by the end of this stage, with children at 2 years old capable of thinking in simple symbols and planning out actions.

Why is it so easy for children to believe in Santa Claus and the Tooth Fairy when they're little?

Why is it so easy for children to believe in Santa Claus and the Tooth Fairy when they're little?

The Preoperational Stage The **preoperational stage** (ages 2–7) is a time of developing language and concepts. Children, who can now move freely about in their world, no longer have to rely only on senses and motor skills but now can ask questions and explore their surroundings more fully. Pretending and make-believe play become possible because children at this stage can understand, through symbolic thinking, that a line of wooden blocks can "stand in" for a train. They are limited, however, in several ways. They are not yet capable of logical thought—they can use simple mental concepts but are not able to use those concepts in a more rational, logical sense. They believe that anything that moves is alive, a quality called *animism*. They tend to believe that what they see is literally true, so when children of this age see Santa Claus in a book, on television, or at the mall, Santa Claus becomes real to them. It doesn't occur to them to think about how Santa might get to every child's house in one night or why those toys are the same ones they saw in the store just last week. They may be able to count up to 10 or 20, but they won't see that in the bottom example in Figure 7.6

sensorimotor stage Piaget's first stage of cognitive development in which the infant uses its senses and motor abilities to interact with objects in the environment.

object permanence the knowledge that an object exists even when it is not in sight.

preoperational stage Piaget's second stage of cognitive development in which the preschool child learns to use language as a means of exploring the world.

Type of conservation	Initial presentation	Transformation	Question	Preoperational child's answer
Liquids	Two equal glasses of liquid	Pour one into a taller, narrower glass.	Which glass contains more?	The taller one.
Number	Two equal lines of pennies	Increase spacing of pennies in one line.	Which line has more pennies?	The longer one.

FIGURE 7.6 Conservation Experiment

A typical conservation task consists of pouring equal amounts of water into two glasses of the same size and shape. When the water from one of these glasses is poured into a taller, narrower glass, children who cannot yet conserve tend to focus (centrate) on the height of the water in the second glass, assuming that the second glass now has more water than the first one. In the second example, pennies are laid out in two equal lines. When the pennies in the top line are spaced out, the child who cannot yet conserve will centrate on the top line and assume that there are actually more pennies in that line.

both rows have the same number of coins, because they focus on the longer *appearance* of the top row of coins.

Another limitation is **egocentrism**, the inability to see the world through anyone else's eyes except one's own. For the preoperational child, everyone else must see what the child sees, and what is important to the child must be important to everyone else. For example, 2-year-old Vicki, after climbing out of her crib for the third time, was told by her mother, "I don't want to see you in that living room again tonight!" So Vicki's next appearance was made with her hands over her eyes—if she couldn't see her mother, her mother couldn't see *her*. Egocentrism is not the same as being egotistical or selfish—it would also be egocentric, but completely unselfish, if 4-year-old Kenny wants to give his grandmother an action figure for her birthday because that's what *he* would want.

Remember that children in this stage are also overwhelmed by appearances, as in the pennies example. A child who complains that his piece of pie is smaller than his brother's may be quite happy once his original piece is cut into two pieces—now he thinks he has "more" than his brother. He has focused only on the number of pieces, not the actual amount of the pie. Focusing only on one feature of some object rather than taking all features into consideration is called **centration**. In the pennies example in Figure 7.6, children of this stage will focus (or center) on the length of the top line of pennies only and ignore the number of pennies. Centration is one of the reasons that children in this stage often fail to understand that changing the way something looks does not change its substance. The ability to understand that altering the appearance of something does not change its amount (as in the pennies example), its volume, or its mass is called **conservation**.

Preoperational children fail at conservation not only because they centrate (focusing on just one feature, such as the number of pieces of pie) but also because

egocentrism the inability to see the world through anyone else's eyes.

centration in Piaget's theory, the tendency of a young child to focus only on one feature of an object while ignoring other relevant features.

conservation in Piaget's theory, the ability to understand that simply changing the appearance of an object does not change the object's nature.

they are unable to "mentally reverse" actions. This feature of preoperational thinking is called **irreversibility**. For example, if a preoperational child sees liquid poured from a short, wide glass into a tall, thin glass, the child will assume that the second glass holds more liquid. This failure to "conserve" (save) the volume of liquid as it takes on a different shape in the tall, thin glass is not only caused by the child's centration on the height of the liquid in the second glass but also by the inability of the child to imagine pouring the liquid back into the first glass and having it be the same amount again. Similar "reasoning" causes children of this age to assume that a ball of clay, when rolled out into a "rope" of clay, is now greater in mass.

Concrete Operations In the **concrete operations stage** (ages 7–12), children finally become capable of conservation and reversible thinking. Centration no longer occurs, as children become capable of considering all the relevant features of any given object. They begin to think more logically about beliefs such as Santa Claus, and they ask questions, eventually coming to their own more rational conclusions about the fantasies of early childhood. They are in school, learning all sorts of science and math, and are convinced that they know more than their parents at this point.

The major limitation of this stage is the inability to deal effectively with *abstract concepts*. Abstract concepts are those that do not have some physical, *concrete*, touchable reality. For example, "freedom" is an abstract concept. People can define it, they can get a good sense of what it means, but there is no "thing" that they can point to and say, "This is freedom." *Concrete concepts*, which are the kind of concepts understood by children of this age, are about objects, written rules, and real things. Children need to be able to see it, touch it, or at least see it in their heads to be able to understand it.

Formal Operations In the last of Piaget's stages, **formal operations** (age 12 to adulthood), abstract thinking becomes possible. Teenagers not only understand concepts that have no physical reality, but also they get deeply involved in hypothetical thinking, or thinking about possibilities and even impossibilities. "What if everyone just got along?" "If women were in charge of countries, would there be fewer wars?"

Piaget did not believe that everyone would necessarily reach formal operations. Studies show that only about half of all adults in the United States reach formal operations (Sutherland, 1992). Adults who do not achieve formal operations tend to use a more practical, down-to-earth kind of intelligence that suits their particular lifestyle. Successful college students, however, need formal operational thinking to succeed in their college careers, as most college classes require critical thinking, problem-solving abilities, and abstract thinking based on formal operational skills (Powers, 1984). Sadly, evidence suggests that only 35 percent of all college students reach formal operations (Huitt & Hummel, 2003).

Piaget saw children as active explorers of their surroundings, engaged in the discovery of the properties of objects and organisms within those surroundings. Educators have put Piaget's ideas into practice by allowing children to learn at their own pace, by "hands-on" experience with objects, and by teaching concepts to children that are at an appropriate cognitive level (Brooks & Brooks, 1993). But Piaget's theory has also been criticized on several points. Some researchers believe that the idea of distinct stages of cognitive development is not completely correct and that changes in thought are continuous and gradual rather than reached by jumping from one stage to another (Courage & Howe, 2002; Feldman, 2003; Schwitzgebel, 1999; Siegler, 1996). Others point out that preschoolers are not as egocentric as Piaget seemed to believe (Flavell, 1999) and that object permanence exists much earlier than Piaget thought (Aguiar & Baillargeon, 2003; Baillargeon, 1986).

These concrete operational children, seen in a science class, have begun to think logically and are able to solve many kinds of problems that were not possible for them to solve while in the preoperational stage.

irreversibility in Piaget's theory, the inability of the young child to mentally reverse an action.

concrete operations stage Piaget's third stage of cognitive development in which the school-age child becomes capable of logical thought processes but is not yet capable of abstract thinking.

formal operations stage Piaget's last stage of cognitive development, in which the adolescent becomes capable of abstract thinking.

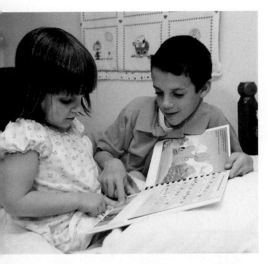

This boy is helping his younger sister learn to read a book. Vygotsky's view of cognitive development states that the help of skilled others aids in making cognitive advances such as this one.

VYGOTSKY'S THEORY: THE IMPORTANCE OF BEING THERE Russian psychologist Lev Vygotsky developed a theory of how children think that did not match the prevailing political ideas in Russia. After his death from tuberculosis in 1934, his ideas were suppressed by the government but kept alive by his students and later republished. Vygotsky's pioneering work in developmental psychology has had a profound influence on school education in Russia, and interest in his theories continues to grow throughout the world (Bodrova & Leong, 1996). Vygotsky wrote about children's cognitive development but differed from Piaget in his emphasis on the role of others in cognitive development (Vygotsky, 1934/1962, 1978, 1987). Whereas Piaget stressed the importance of the child's interaction with objects as a primary factor in cognitive development, Vygotsky stressed the importance of social interactions with other people, typically more highly skilled children and adults. Vygotsky believed that children develop cognitively when someone else helps them by asking leading questions and providing examples of concepts in a process called **scaffolding**. In scaffolding, the more highly skilled person gives the learner more help at the beginning of the learning process and then begins to withdraw help as the learner's skills improve (Rogoff, 1994).

Vygotsky also proposed that each developing child has a **zone of proximal development (ZPD)**, which is the difference between what a child can do alone versus what that child can do with the help of a teacher. For example, if little Jenny can do math problems up to the fourth-grade level on her own but with the help of a teacher can successfully work problems at a sixth-grade level, her ZPD is two years. Suzi might be the same age as Jenny (and might even score the same on a traditional IQ test), but if Suzi can only work math problems at a fifth-grade level with the help of the teacher, Suzi's ZPD is not as great as Jenny's. This might be a better way of thinking about intelligence: It isn't what you know (as measured by traditional tests), it's what you *can do*.

Other researchers have applied Vygotsky's social focus on learning to the development of a child's memory for personal (autobiographical) events, finding evidence that children learn the culturally determined structures and purposes of personal stories from the early conversations they have with their parents. This process begins with the parent telling the story to the very young child, followed by the child repeating elements of the story as the child's verbal abilities grow. The child reaches the final stage at around age 5 or 6 when the child creates the personal story entirely—an excellent example of scaffolding (Fivush & Nelson, 2004; Fivush et al., 1996; Nelson, 1993). Vygotsky's ideas have been put into practice in education through the use of cooperative learning, in which children work together in groups to achieve a common goal, and in reciprocal teaching, in which teachers lead students through the basic strategies of reading until the students themselves become capable of teaching the strategies to others.

STAGES OF LANGUAGE DEVELOPMENT The development of language is a very important milestone in the cognitive development of a child because language allows children to think in words rather than just images, to ask questions, to communicate their needs and wants to others, and to form concepts (L. Bloom, 1974; P. Bloom, 2000). Early views of language development were based on Skinnerian principles of reinforcement. However, Noam Chomsky argued strongly against this. He proposed a LAD (language acquisition device), an innate "program" that contained a schema for human language. The children matched the language they heard against this schema and, thus, language developed in a well-researched sequence (Chomsky, 1957, 1964, 1981, 1986).

scaffolding process in which a more skilled learner gives help to a less skilled learner, reducing the amount of help as the less skilled learner becomes more capable.

zone of proximal development (ZPD) Vygotsky's concept of the difference between what a child can do alone versus what that child can do with the help of a teacher.

Newer theories of language development are focusing on environmental influences on language such as *child-directed speech* (the way adults and older children talk to infants and very young children, with higher pitched, repetitious, sing-song speech patterns). Infants and toddlers attend more closely to this kind of speech, which creates a learning opportunity in the dialogue between caregiver and infant (Dominey & Dodane, 2004; Fernald, 1984, 1992; Küntay & Slobin, 2002). Other researchers are looking at the infant's use of gestures and signs (Behne et al., 2005; Lizskowski et al., 2006; Moll & Tomasello, 2007; Tomasello et al., 2007).

Infants also seem to understand far more than they can produce, a phenomenon known as the *receptive-productive lag* (Stevenson et al., 1988). They may be able to produce only one or two words, but they understand much longer sentences from their parents and others.

There are several stages of language development that all children experience, no matter what culture they live in or what language they will learn to speak (Brown, 1973):

1. **Cooing:** At around 2 months of age, babies begin to make vowel-like sounds.

2. **Babbling:** At about 6 months, infants add consonant sounds to the vowels to make a babbling sound, which at times can almost sound like real speech. Deaf children actually decrease their babbling after 6 months while increasing their use of primitive hand signs and gestures (Petitto & Marentette, 1991; Petitto et al., 2001).

3. **One-word speech:** Somewhere just before or around age 1, most children begin to say actual words. These words are typically nouns and may seem to represent an entire phrase of meaning. They are called *holophrases* (whole phrases in one word) for that reason. For example, a child might say "Milk!" and mean "I want some milk!" or "I drank my milk!"

4. **Telegraphic speech:** At around a year and a half, toddlers begin to string words together to form short, simple sentences using nouns, verbs, and adjectives. "Baby eat," "Mommy go," "Doggie go bye-bye" are examples of telegraphic speech. Only the words that carry the meaning of the sentence are used.

5. **Whole sentences:** As children move through the preschool years, they learn to use grammatical terms and increase the number of words in their sentences, until by age 6 or so they are nearly as fluent as an adult, although the number of words they know is still limited when compared to adult vocabulary.

Autism Spectrum Disorder

Before leaving the topic of cognitive development in infancy, let's briefly discuss a topic that has been making the news for a number of years: the causes underlying autism spectrum disorder. Autism spectrum disorder (ASD) is actually a whole range of disorders (with what may be an equally broad range of causes), which cause problems in thinking, feeling, language, and social skills in relating to others (Atladóttir et al., 2009; Johnson & Myers, 2007). Rumors and misinformation about the causes of autism have been circulating on the Internet for many years.

The major source of misinformation began in 1998, when British gastroenterologist Dr. Andrew Wakefield published the results of two studies that seemed to link the MMR (measles, mumps, and rubella) vaccine to autism and bowel disease in children (Wakefield et al., 1998). With a sample size of only 12 children, no control groups, and with neither study being blind—single or double—the studies were quickly denounced as inadequate and dangerous by autism specialists and others (Fitzpatrick, 2004; Judelsohn, 2007; Matthew & Dallery, 2007; Novella, 2007; Stratton et al., 2001a, 2001b). ⒧ⒾⓃⓀ to Chapter One: The Science of Psychology,

This infant has already learned some of the basics of language, including the use of gestures to indicate meaning and enhance communication.

One of the most important things parents can do for the continued health and safety of their infant is to have the baby immunized, following an approved schedule for each type of vaccine. Immunizations today are safe and effective and prevent dangerous and often deadly childhood diseases, such as rubella.

pp. 27–29. Nevertheless, Wakefield's publication was followed by measles epidemics due to parents refusing the MMR inoculation for their children. The myth of a link persists, in spite of numerous studies that have consistently failed to show any link between the MMR vaccine and autism (Burns, 2010; Gilberg & Coleman, 2000; Johnson & Myers, 2007; Madsen et al., 2002; Mars et al., 1998; Taylor et al., 1999; Thompson et al., 2007). In 2009, the final blow came to Wakefield's credibility when it was discovered that he had falsified his data. In 2004, the other authors listed on the study formally retracted the 1998 paper.

As a result of the British Medical Council's investigation into Wakefield's actions, Wakefield's medical license was revoked in May of 2010, after the council found him guilty of "serious professional misconduct."

practice quiz   How much do you remember?

7.5 **7.6**

Pick the best answer.

1. Which sense is least functional at birth?
   a. touch
   b. taste
   c. smell
   d. vision

2. What is the first voluntary movement that allows an infant to get from one place to another?
   a. sitting without support
   b. rolling over
   c. raising the head when placed face down
   d. standing

3. In which of Piaget's stages would a child be who has just developed object permanence?

   a. sensorimotor
   b. preoperational
   c. concrete operations
   d. formal operations

4. Vygotsky defines _____ as the difference between what a child can do alone and what that child can do with help.
   a. scaffolding
   b. habituation
   c. zone of proximal development
   d. metamemory

5. "Daddy go bye-bye" is an example of _____.
   a. telegraphic speech.
   b. babbling.
   c. a holophrase.
   d. cooing.

ANSWERS ON PAGE AK–1.

Psychosocial Development

7.7 How do infants and children develop personalities and form relationships with others, and what are Erikson's stages of psychosocial development for children?

The psychological and social development of infants and children involves the development of personality, relationships, and a sense of being male or female. Although these processes begin in infancy, they will continue in many respects well into adulthood.

Why are some children negative and whiny while others are sweet and good-natured?

● Why are some children negative and whiny while others are sweet and good-natured?

TEMPERAMENT   One of the first ways in which infants demonstrate that they have different personalities (long-lasting characteristics that make each person different from others) is in their **temperament**, the behavioral and emotional characteristics that are fairly well established at birth. Researchers (Chess & Thomas, 1986; Thomas & Chess, 1977) have been able to identify three basic temperament styles of infants:

1. **Easy:** "Easy" babies are regular in their schedules of waking, sleeping, and eating and are adaptable to change. Easy babies are happy babies and when distressed are easily soothed.

temperament the behavioral characteristics that are fairly well established at birth, such as easy, difficult, and slow to warm up.

2. **Difficult:** "Difficult" babies are almost the opposite of easy ones. Difficult babies tend to be irregular in their schedules and are very unhappy about change of any kind. They are loud, active, and tend to be crabby rather than happy.

3. **Slow to warm up:** This kind of temperament is associated with infants who are less grumpy, quieter, and more regular than difficult children but who are slow to adapt to change. If change is introduced gradually, these babies will "warm up" to new people and new situations.

Of course, not all babies will fall neatly into one of these three patterns—some children may be a mix of two or even all three patterns of behavior, as Chess and Thomas (1986) discovered. Even so, longitudinal research strongly suggests that these temperament styles last well into adulthood (Kagan, 1998; Kagan et al., 2007; Korn, 1984; Scarpa et al., 1995), although they are somewhat influenced by the environment in which the infant is raised. For example, a "difficult" infant who is raised by parents who are themselves very loud and active may not be perceived as difficult by the parents, whereas a child who is slow to warm up might be perceived as difficult if the parents themselves like lots of change and noise. The first infant is in a situation in which the "goodness of fit" of the infant's temperament to the parents' temperament is very close, but the parents of the second infant are a poor fit in temperament for that less active child (Chess & Thomas, 1986).

I'd sure hate to have a difficult child! How does a baby's temperament affect the way the parents deal with the baby?

Parents of babies with easy temperaments can make plans for shopping or dinner around the infant's schedule. Planning around the varying sleeping and eating behaviors of a difficult infant is much trickier (Bates, 1989; Sheeber & Johnson, 1992). As children grow, their temperament and how well it matches a parent's own temperament becomes an issue in discipline and in the formation of emotional bonds to the parents or other caregivers (Cameron et al., 1989; Goldsmith & Campos, 1982; Skolnick, 1986).

ATTACHMENT The emotional bond that forms between an infant and a primary caregiver is called **attachment**. Attachment is a very important development in the social and emotional life of the infant, usually forming within the first six months of the infant's life and showing up in a number of ways during the second six months, such as wariness of strangers and fear of being separated from the caregiver. Although attachment to the mother is usually the primary attachment, infants can attach to fathers and to other caregivers as well.

Mary Ainsworth (Ainsworth, 1985; Ainsworth et al., 1978) came up with a special experimental design to measure the attachment of an infant to the caregiver called the *Strange Situation* (exposing an infant to a series of leave-takings and returns of the mother and a stranger). Through this measurement technique, Ainsworth and another colleague identified four attachment styles:

1. **Secure:** Infants labeled as secure were willing to get down from their mother's lap when they first entered the room with their mothers. They explored happily, looking back at their mothers and returning to them every now and then (sort of like "touching base"). When the stranger came in, these infants were wary but calm as long as their mother was nearby. When the mother left, the infants got upset. When the mother returned, the infants approached her, were easily soothed, and were glad to have her back.

2. **Avoidant:** In contrast, avoidant babies, though somewhat willing to explore, did not "touch base." They did not look at the stranger or the mother and

attachment the emotional bond between an infant and the primary caregiver.

I'd sure hate to have a difficult child! How does a baby's temperament affect the way the parents deal with the baby?

This toddler shows reluctance to explore her environment, instead clinging to her father's leg. Such clinging behavior, if common, can be a sign of an ambivalent attachment.

reacted very little to her absence or her return, seeming to have no interest or concern.

3. **Ambivalent:** The word *ambivalent* means to have mixed feelings about something. Ambivalent babies in Ainsworth's study were clinging and unwilling to explore, very upset by the stranger regardless of the mother's presence, protested mightily when the mother left, and were hard to soothe. When the mother returned, these babies would demand to be picked up, but at the same time push the mother away or kick her in a mixed reaction to her return.

4. **Disorganized-disoriented:** In subsequent studies, other researchers (Main & Hesse, 1990; Main & Solomon, 1990) found that some babies seemed unable to decide just how they should react to the mother's return. These disorganized-disoriented infants would approach her but with their eyes turned away from her, as if afraid to make eye contact. In general, these infants seemed fearful and showed a dazed and depressed look on their faces.

It should come as no surprise that the mothers of each of the four types of infants also behaved differently from one another. Mothers of secure infants were loving, warm, sensitive to their infant's needs, and responsive to the infant's attempts at communication. Mothers of avoidant babies were unresponsive, insensitive, and coldly rejecting. Mothers of ambivalent babies tried to be responsive but were inconsistent and insensitive to the baby's actions, often talking to the infant about something totally unrelated to what the infant was doing at the time. Mothers of disorganized-disoriented babies were found to be abusive or neglectful in interactions with the infants.

Attachment is not necessarily the result of the behavior of the mother alone, however. The temperament of the infant may play an important part in determining the reactions of the mothers (Goldsmith & Campos, 1982; Skolnick, 1986). For example, an infant with a difficult temperament is hard to soothe. A mother with this kind of infant might come to avoid unnecessary contact with the infant, as did the mothers of the avoidant babies in Ainsworth's studies.

Critics of Ainsworth's Strange Situation research focus on the artificial nature of the design and wonder if infants and mothers would behave differently in the more familiar surroundings of home, even though Ainsworth's experimental observers also observed the infants and mothers in the home prior to the Strange Situation (Ainsworth, 1985). Other research has found results supporting Ainsworth's findings in home-based assessments of attachment (Blanchard & Main, 1979). Other studies have also found support for the concept of attachment styles and stability of attachment over the first six years of life (Lutkenhaus et al., 1985; Main & Cassidy, 1988; Owen et al., 1984; Wartner et al., 1994). Even adult relationships can be seen as influenced by the attachment style of the adult—those who are avoidant tend to have numerous shallow and brief relationships with different partners, whereas those who are ambivalent tend to have repeated breakups and makeups with the same person (Bartholomew, 1990; Hazan & Shaver, 1987).

As day care has become more widely acceptable and common, many parents have been concerned about the effect of day care on attachment. Psychologist Jay Belsky and colleagues (Belsky, 2005; Belsky & Johnson, 2005; Belsky et al., 2007) have studied the attachment of infants in day care and concluded that although higher quality of day care (low child-to-caregiver ratio, low turnover in caregivers, and caregivers well educated in child care techniques and theory) is important, especially for cognitive development, positive development including attachment was more clearly related to the quality of parenting the infants and toddlers received at home.

Although there are some cultural differences in attachment, such as the finding that mothers in the United States tend to wait for a child to express a need before trying to fulfill that need, whereas Japanese mothers prefer to anticipate the child's needs (Rothbaum et al., 2000), attachment does not seem to suffer in spite of the differences in sensitivity. Evidence that similar attachment styles are found in other cultures demonstrates the need to consider attachment as an important first step in forming relationships with others. It may set the stage for all relationships that follow (Hu & Meng, 1996; Juffer & Rosenboom, 1997; Keromoian & Leiderman, 1986). ☑●⎾Survey on **MyPsychLab**

Before leaving the topic of attachment, let's take a look at one of the first studies that examined the key factors necessary for attachment.

classic studies **in psychology**

Harlow and Contact Comfort

As psychologists began to study the development of attachment, they at first assumed that attachment to the mother occurred because the mother was associated with satisfaction of primary drives such as hunger and thirst. The mother is always present when the food (a primary reinforcer) is presented, so the mother becomes a secondary reinforcer capable of producing pleasurable feelings. ⓁⒾⓃⓀ to Chapter Four: Learning, p. 133.

Psychologist Harry Harlow felt that attachment had to be influenced by more than just the provision of food. He conducted a number of studies of attachment using infant Rhesus monkeys (Harlow, 1958). Noticing that the monkeys in his lab liked to cling to the soft cloth pad used to line their cages, Harlow designed a study to examine the importance of what he termed *contact comfort*, the seeming attachment of the monkeys to something soft to the touch.

He isolated eight baby Rhesus monkeys shortly after their birth, placing each in a cage with two surrogate (substitute) "mothers." The surrogates were actually a block of wood covered in soft padding and terry cloth and a wire form, both heated from within. For half of the monkeys, the wire "mother" held the bottle from which they fed, while for the other half the soft "mother" held the bottle. Harlow then recorded the time each monkey spent with each "mother." If time spent with the surrogate is taken as an indicator of attachment, then learning theory would predict that the monkeys would spend more time with whichever surrogate was being used to feed them. ●⎾Watch on **MyPsychLab**

The results? Regardless of which surrogate was feeding them, the monkeys all spent significantly more time with the soft, cloth-covered surrogate. In fact, all monkeys spent very little time with the wire surrogate, even if this was the one with the bottle. Harlow and his colleagues concluded that "contact comfort was an important basic affectional or love variable" (Harlow, 1958, p. 574).

Harlow's work represents one of the earliest investigations into the importance of touch in the attachment process and remains an important study in human development.

QUESTIONS **FOR FURTHER DISCUSSION**

1. Even though the cloth surrogate was warm and soft and seemed to provide contact comfort, do you think that the monkeys raised in this way would behave normally when placed into contact with other monkeys? How might they react?

2. What might be the implications of Harlow's work for human mothers who feed their infants with bottles rather than breast-feeding?

☑●⎾**Survey** Participate in a survey about a father's parental role on **MyPsychLab**

The wire surrogate "mother" provides the food for this infant Rhesus monkey. But the infant spends all its time with the soft, cloth-covered surrogate. According to Harlow, this demonstrates the importance of contact comfort in attachment.

●⎾**Watch** classic footage on nature and the development of affection with Harry Harlow on **MyPsychLab**

I've heard that you shouldn't pick a baby up every time it cries—that if you do, it might spoil the baby.

ERIKSON'S THEORY

I've heard that you shouldn't pick a baby up every time it cries—that if you do, it might spoil the baby.

Unfortunately, a lot of people have not only heard this advice but also acted on it by frequently ignoring an infant's crying, which turns out to be a very bad thing for babies. When a baby under 6 months of age cries, it is an instinctive reaction meant to get the caregiver to tend to the baby's needs—hunger, thirst, pain, and even loneliness. Research has shown that babies whose cries are tended to consistently (that is, the infant is fed when hungry, changed when wet, and so on) in the early months are more securely attached as late as age 1 than those infants whose caregivers frequently

table 7.4 Erikson's Psychosocial Stages of Development

STAGE	DEVELOPMENTAL CRISIS	SUCCESSFUL DEALING WITH CRISIS	UNSUCCESSFUL DEALING WITH CRISIS
1. **Infant** Birth to 1 year old	**Trust Versus Mistrust** Babies learn to trust or mistrust others based on whether or not their needs—such as food and comfort—are met.	If babies' needs are met, they learn to trust people and expect life to be pleasant.	If babies' needs are not met, they learn not to trust.
2. **Toddler** 1 to 3 years old	**Autonomy Versus Shame and Doubt** Toddlers realize that they can direct their own behavior.	If toddlers are successful in directing their own behavior, they learn to be independent.	If toddlers' attempts at being independent are blocked, they learn self-doubt and shame for being unsuccessful.
3. **Preschool Age** 3 to 5 years old	**Initiative Versus Guilt** Preschoolers are challenged to control their own behavior, such as controlling their exuberance when they are in a restaurant.	If preschoolers succeed in taking responsibility, they feel capable and develop initiative.	If preschoolers fail in taking responsibility, they feel irresponsible, anxious, and guilty.
4. **Elementary School Age** 5 to 12 years old	**Industry Versus Inferiority** School-aged children are faced with learning new social and academic skills. Social comparison is a primary source of information.	When children succeed at learning new skills, they develop a sense of industry, a feeling of competence and self-esteem arising from their work and effort.	If children fail to develop new abilities, they feel incompetent, inadequate, and inferior.
5. **Adolescence** 13 to early twenties	**Identity Versus Role Confusion** Adolescents are faced with deciding who or what they want to be in terms of occupation, beliefs, attitudes, and behavior patterns.	Adolescents who succeed in defining who they are and finding a role for themselves develop a strong sense of identity.	Adolescents who fail to define their identity become confused and withdraw or want to inconspicuously blend in with the crowd.
6. **Early Adulthood** Twenties and thirties	**Intimacy Versus Isolation** The task facing those in early adulthood is to be able to share who they are with another person in a close, committed relationship.	People who succeed in this task will have satisfying intimate relationships.	Adults who fail at this task will be isolated from other people and may suffer from loneliness.
7. **Middle Adulthood** Forties and fifties	**Generativity Versus Stagnation** The challenge is to be creative, productive, and nurturant of the next generation.	Adults who succeed in this challenge will be creative, productive, and nurturant, thereby benefiting themselves, their family, community, country, and future generations.	Adults who fail will be passive and self-centered, feel that they have done nothing for the next generation, and feel that the world is no better off for their being alive.
8. **Late Adulthood** Sixties and beyond	**Ego Integrity Versus Despair** The issue is whether a person will reach wisdom, spiritual tranquility, a sense of wholeness, and acceptance of his or her life.	Elderly people who succeed in addressing this issue will enjoy life and not fear death.	Elderly people who fail will feel that their life is empty and will fear death.

allow the infants to cry when there is a need for attention—hunger, pain, or wetness, for example (Brazelton, 1992; Heinicke et al., 2000). Erikson, a psychodynamic theorist who emphasized the importance of social relationships in the development of personality, would certainly disagree with letting a baby "cry it out," although allowing an infant who has been fed, changed, burped, and checked to cry on occasion will not damage attachment.

Erikson trained as a Freudian psychoanalyst but became convinced that social interactions were more important in development than Freud's emphasis on sexual development. Erikson believed that development occurred in a series of eight stages, with the first four of these stages occurring in infancy and childhood (Erikson, 1950; Erikson & Erikson, 1997). (Freud's stages of psychosexual development are covered in detail in a later chapter.) Ⓛ Ⓘ Ⓝ Ⓚ to Chapter Eleven: Theories of Personality and Intelligence, pp. 390–392. Each stage is an emotional *crisis*, or a turning point, in personality, and the crisis in each stage must be successfully met for normal, healthy psychological development.

Erikson focused on the relationship of the infant and the child to significant others in the immediate surroundings—parents and then later teachers and even peers. Table 7.4 summarizes the conflict in each of Erikson's eight stages and some of the implications for future development (Erikson, 1950; Erikson & Erikson, 1997). For now, look at the first four stages in particular.

practice quiz   How much do you remember?

⑺⑺
7.7

Pick the best answer.

1. According to Thomas and Chess, a child who is very irregular in sleeping and eating, resists change, and is negative and loud is labeled a(n) _____ child.
   a. easy
   b. difficult
   c. slow-to-warm-up
   d. negative

2. What kind of attachment, according to Ainsworth, is shown by a baby who explores the room, gets upset when the mother leaves but is easily soothed, and is happy to see the mother when she returns?
   a. secure   c. ambivalent
   b. avoidant   d. disorganized-disoriented

3. Mothers who were abusive and/or neglectful were associated with the _____ type of attachment.
   a. secure
   b. avoidant
   c. ambivalent
   d. disorganized-disoriented

4. In Erikson's _____ stage of psychosocial development, the child learns self-control and begins to feel more capable.
   a. trust versus mistrust
   b. autonomy versus shame and doubt
   c. initiative versus guilt
   d. industry versus inferiority

ANSWERS ON PAGE AK–1.

Gender Development

7.8 What is gender, and how do gender roles develop?

When do little kids learn the difference between girls and boys? ●

Most children begin to realize the difference between girls and boys at about age 2, and most can say which one they are at that age. But knowing one's *sex* (the physical characteristic of being male or female) is not the same as knowing the different behavior expected of a male or a female (**gender**). The behavior that goes along with being male or female is heavily influenced by cultural expectations as well as biology and is referred to as **gender identity**.

When do little kids learn the difference between girls and boys?

gender   the behavior associated with being male or female.

gender identity   the individual's sense of being male or female.

gender roles the culture's expectations for masculine or feminine behavior, including attitudes, actions, and personality traits associated with being male or female in that culture.

Read and learn more about one such case with the story of David Reimer's life MyPsychLab

Gender Roles

Gender roles are the culture's expectations for behavior of a person who is perceived as male or female, including attitudes, actions, and personality traits associated with a particular gender within that culture (Tobach, 2001; Unger, 1979). The process of developing a person's *gender identity* (a sense of being male or female) is influenced by both biological and environmental factors (in the form of parenting and other child-rearing behaviors), although which type of factor has greater influence is still controversial. Most researchers today would agree that biology has an important role in gender identity, at least in certain aspects of gender identity and behavior (Diamond & Sigmundson, 1997; Money, 1994; Reiner, 1999, 2000). In one study, 25 genetically male children who were born with ambiguous genitalia were surgically altered and raised as girls. Now older children and teenagers, they prefer male play activities. Fourteen of these children have openly declared themselves to be boys (Reiner, 2000). Read on MyPsychLab

Environment must also play its part. In most cultures, there are certain roles that males and females are expected to play (gender roles, in other words), and the pressure that can be brought to bear on a person who does not conform to these expectations can be tremendous. In most Western cultures, the pressure to be masculine is even greater for males than the pressure to be feminine is for girls. The term *tomboy* is not generally viewed as an insult, but there are no terms for a boy who acts in a feminine manner that are not insulting—*sissy*, for example, is not a nice term at all. And although studies of parents' influence on their children's gender typing show that both parents have an impact, they also show that the fathers are almost always more concerned about their sons showing male gender behavior than their daughters showing female gender behavior (Lytton & Romney, 1991). Cultures that are more individualistic and have fairly high standards of living are becoming more nontraditional, especially for women in those cultures, whereas the more traditional views seem to be held by collectivistic cultures that have less wealth, although even in the latter, women were more likely to be less traditional than men (Forbes et al., 2009; Gibbons et al., 1991). Other studies have found that the most nontraditional ideas about gender roles and gender behavior are found in countries such as the Netherlands, Germany, Italy, and England, whereas the most traditional ideas predominate in African and Asian countries such as Nigeria, Pakistan, and Japan (Best & Williams, 2001). The United States, often seen as very nontraditional by researchers, actually was somewhere in the middle in these studies, perhaps due to the large variation in subcultures that exists within this multicultural country. Environment, even in the form of culture, seems to play at least a partial and perhaps dominant role in gender behavior.

Theories of Gender-Role Development

How do children acquire the knowledge of their society or culture's gender-role expectations? How does that knowledge lead to the development of a gender identity? Although early psychodynamic theorists such as Freud, (L I N K) to Chapter Eleven: Theories of Personality and Intelligence, pp. 390–392, believed that children would learn their gender identities as a natural consequence of resolving the sexual conflicts of early childhood, many modern theorists focus on learning and cognitive processes for the development of gender identity and behavior.

SOCIAL LEARNING THEORY Social learning theory, which emphasizes learning through observation and imitation of models, attributes* gender-role development

---
*Attributes: explains as a cause.

to those processes. Children observe their same-sex parents behaving in certain ways and imitate that behavior. When the children imitate the appropriate gender behavior, they are reinforced with positive attention. Inappropriate gender behavior is either ignored or actively discouraged (Fagot & Hagan, 1991; Mischel, 1966).

GENDER SCHEMA THEORY A theory of gender-role development that combines social learning theory with cognitive development is called **gender schema theory** (Bem, 1987, 1993). In this theory based on the Piagetian concept of schemas, children develop a schema, or mental pattern, for being male or female in much the same way that they develop schemas for other concepts such as "dog," "bird," and "big." As their brains mature, they become capable of distinguishing among various concepts. For example, a "dog" might at first be anything with four legs and a tail, but as children encounter dogs and other kinds of animals and are given instruction, "dog" becomes more specific and the schema for "dog" becomes well defined.

In a similar manner, children develop a concept for "boy" and "girl." Once that schema is in place, children can identify themselves as "boy" or "girl" and will notice other members of that schema. They notice the behavior of other "boys" or "girls" and imitate that behavior. Rather than being simple imitation and reinforcement, as in social learning theory, children acquire their gender role behavior by organizing that behavior around the schema of "boy" or "girl." Evidence for this theory includes the finding that children can discriminate between male and female faces and voices before age 1 (Martin, 2000), a sign that the world is already being organized into those two concepts.

gender schema theory theory of gender identity acquisition in which a child develops a mental pattern, or schema, for being male or female and then organizes observed and learned behavior around that schema.

practice quiz   How much do you remember?

7.8

Pick the best answer.

1. The development of a person's sense of being male or female is called _____.
   a. gender role.
   b. gender identity.
   c. gender typing.
   d. gender stereotyping.

2. Which of the following is not a biological influence on gender?
   a. hormones secreted during fetal development
   b. the influence of hormones taken by the pregnant mother
   c. exposure to playmates of a particular gender
   d. sex chromosomes

3. In _____ cultures, gender roles are seen as more traditional, whereas in _____ cultures they may be more nontraditional, especially for women.
   a. individualistic; collectivistic
   b. collectivistic; individualistic
   c. European; Asian
   d. affluent; poor

4. Studies have shown that _____ are more concerned about appropriate gender behavior in their children, particularly their _____ children.
   a. fathers; male
   b. fathers; female
   c. mothers; male
   d. mothers; female

5. Alex sees his father hammering some nails into a loose board on their house. Later Alex takes his toy hammer and pretends to hammer in some imaginary nails. Of which theory of gender development would this be a good example?
   a. gender schema theory
   b. gender-role theory
   c. psychoanalytic theory
   d. social learning theory

ANSWERS ON PAGE AK-1.

Adolescence

Adolescence is the period of life from about age 13 to the early twenties, during which a young person is no longer physically a child but is not yet an independent, self-supporting adult. Although in the past, adolescence was always defined as the "teens," from ages 13 to 19, adolescence isn't necessarily determined by chronological age. It also concerns how a person deals with life issues such as work, family, and relationships. So although there is a clear age of onset, the end of adolescence may come earlier or later for different individuals.

adolescence the period of life from about age 13 to the early twenties, during which a young person is no longer physically a child but is not yet an independent, self-supporting adult.

Physical Development

Isn't adolescence just the physical changes that happen to your body?

PUBERTY

7.9 **What are the physical, cognitive, and personality changes that occur in adolescence, including concepts of morality and Erikson's search for identity?**

The clearest sign of the beginning of adolescence is the onset of **puberty**, the physical changes in both *primary sex characteristics* (growth of the actual sex organs such as the penis or the uterus) and *secondary sex characteristics* (changes in the body such as the development of breasts and body hair) that occur in the body as sexual development reaches its peak. Puberty occurs as the result of a complex series of glandular activities, stimulated by the "master gland" or the pituitary gland, when the proper genetically determined age is reached. Certain psychosocial and environmental factors such as stress, exercise, and nutrition may also have an impact on the timing of puberty (Ellis et al., 1999; Graber et al., 1995). The thyroid gland increases the rate of growth, and the adrenal glands and sex glands stimulate the growth of characteristics such as body hair, muscle tissue in males, and the menstrual cycle in girls, for example (Grumbach & Kaplan, 1990; Grumbach & Styne, 1998). Puberty often begins about two years after the beginning of the *growth spurt*, the rapid period of growth that takes place at around age 10 for girls and around age 12 for boys.

In addition to an increase in height, physical characteristics related to being male or female undergo rapid and dramatic change. In fact, the rate of growth and development in puberty approaches that of development in the womb. For females, breast tissue begins to enlarge, hips begin to widen, the uterus grows, and eventually the menstrual cycle begins. For boys, the penis and testicles increase in size, muscles become more defined, and the voice begins to deepen. For both sexes, oily secretions increase (causing pimples and even acne in many teens), hair grows on the pubic area and under the arms, and body odor becomes more noticeable. After about four years, the changes of puberty are relatively complete.

Cognitive Development

If I'm remembering correctly, teenagers should be in Piaget's formal operations stage. So why don't many teenagers think just like adults?

The cognitive development of adolescents is less visible than the physical development but still represents a major change in the way adolescents think about themselves, their peers and relationships, and the world around them.

PIAGET'S FORMAL OPERATIONS REVISITED Adolescents, especially those who receive a formal high school education, move into Piaget's final stage of formal operations, in which abstract thinking becomes possible. This cognitive advance

---

Isn't adolescence just the physical changes that happen to your body?

If I'm remembering correctly, teenagers should be in Piaget's formal operations stage. So why don't many teenagers think just like adults?

puberty the physical changes that occur in the body as sexual development reaches its peak.

is primarily due to the final development of the frontal lobes of the brain, the part of the brain that is responsible for organizing, understanding, and decision making (Giedd et al., 1999; Sowell et al., 1999). Teenagers begin to think about hypothetical situations, leading to a picture of what an "ideal" world would be like. Many become convinced that such a world is possible to achieve if only everyone else would just listen to the teenager. (It should be noted that although adolescents have reached the formal operations stage, not all adolescents—or adults—use their formal operational thought processes equally well. In a sense, they've graduated to "bigger and better" mental tools but don't necessarily know how to use those tools effectively. More formal educational processes or demanding life experiences help adolescents and adults become skilled "tool users.")

As discussed earlier, Piaget's concept of stages has been criticized as being too simplistic. The evidence now points to gradual, continuous cognitive development (Feldman, 2003; Siegler, 1996). Even so, Piaget's theory has had a tremendous impact in the education of children and in stimulating research about children's cognitive development (Satterly, 1987). Children in varying cultures usually come to understand the world in the way that Piaget described, although the age at which this understanding comes varies from one child to another.

Although headed into an adult style of thinking, adolescents are not yet completely free of egocentric thought. At this time in life, however, their egocentrism shows up in their preoccupation* with their own thoughts. They do a lot of introspection (turning inward) and may become convinced that their thoughts are as important to others as they are to themselves. Two ways in which this adolescent egocentrism emerges are the personal fable and the imaginary audience (Elkind, 1985; Lapsley et al., 1986; Vartanian, 2000).

In the **personal fable**, adolescents have spent so much time thinking about their own thoughts and feelings that they become convinced that they are special, one of a kind, and that no one else has ever had these thoughts and feelings before them. "You just don't understand me, I'm different from you" is a common feeling of teens. The personal fable is not without a dangerous side. Because they feel unique, teenagers may feel that they are somehow protected from the dangers of the world and so do not take the precautions that they should. This may result in an unwanted pregnancy, severe injury or death while racing in a car, drinking and driving, and drug use, to name a few possibilities. "It can't happen to me, I'm special" is a risky but common thought.

The **imaginary audience** shows up as extreme self-consciousness in adolescents. They become convinced that *everyone is looking at them* and that they are always the center of everyone else's world, just as they are the center of their own. This explains the intense self-consciousness that many adolescents experience concerning what others think about how the adolescent looks or behaves.

MORAL DEVELOPMENT Another important aspect in the cognitive advances that occur in adolescence concerns the teenager's understanding of "right" and "wrong." Harvard University professor Lawrence Kohlberg was a developmental psychologist who, influenced by Piaget and others, outlined a theory of the development of moral thinking through looking at how people of various ages responded to stories about people caught up in moral dilemmas (see Figure 7.7 for an example of a dilemma). Kohlberg (1973) proposed three levels of moral development, or the knowledge of

personal fable   type of thought common to adolescents in which young people believe themselves to be unique and protected from harm.

imaginary audience   type of thought common to adolescents in which young people believe that other people are just as concerned about the adolescent's thoughts and characteristics as they themselves are.

---

*Preoccupation: extreme or excessive concern with something.

> **Example of a Moral Dilemma**
>
> The ant worked long and hard over the summer to gather food for himself and his family. The grasshopper, who preferred to play and be lazy all summer, laughed at the ant for working so hard. The ant said, "you will be sorry this winter when you have no food." Sure enough, when winter came the very sorry grasshopper, cold and hungry, came to the ant and begged for food and shelter. Should the ant give food and shelter to the grasshopper?

FIGURE 7.7 Example of a Moral Dilemma

right and wrong behavior. These levels are summarized in Table 7.5, along with an example of each type of thinking. Although these stages are associated with certain age-groups, adolescents and adults can be found at all three levels. For example, a juvenile delinquent tends to be preconventional in moral thinking.

Kohlberg's theory has been criticized as being male oriented, especially since he used only males in his studies (Gilligan, 1982). Carol Gilligan (1982) proposed that men and women have different perspectives on morality: Men tend to judge as moral the actions that lead to a fair or just end, whereas women tend to judge as moral the actions that are nonviolent and hurt the fewest people. Researchers, however, have not found consistent support for gender differences in moral thinking (Walker, 1991). Another criticism is that Kohlberg's assessment of moral development involves asking people what they think should be done in hypothetical moral dilemmas. What people say they will do and what people actually do when faced with a real dilemma are often two different things. ▯▯┤Read on **MyPsychLab**

▯▯┤Read and learn more about Carol Gilligan's three stages of morality for women on **MyPsychLab**

Psychosocial Development

The development of personality and social relationships in adolescence primarily concerns the search for a consistent sense of self or personal identity.

---

table 7.5 Kohlberg's Three Levels of Morality

LEVEL OF MORALITY	HOW RULES ARE UNDERSTOOD	EXAMPLE
Preconventional morality (typically very young children)	The consequences determine morality; behavior that is rewarded is right; that which is punished is wrong.	A child who steals a toy from another child and does not get caught does not see that action as wrong.
Conventional* morality (older children, adolescents, and most adults)	Conformity to social norms is right; nonconformity is wrong.	A child criticizes his or her parent for speeding because speeding is against the posted laws.
Postconventional morality (about 20 percent of the adult population)	Moral principles determined by the person are used to determine right and wrong and may disagree with societal norms.	A reporter who wrote a controversial story goes to jail rather than reveal the source's identity.

*The term *conventional* refers to general standards or norms of behavior for a particular society, which will differ from one social group or culture to another.

ERIKSON'S IDENTITY VERSUS ROLE CONFUSION   The psychosocial crisis that must be faced by the adolescent, according to Erikson, is that of **identity versus role confusion** (see Table 7.6). In this stage, the teenager must choose from among many options for values in life and beliefs concerning things such as political issues, career options, and marriage (Feldman, 2003). From those options, a consistent sense of self must be found. Erikson believed that teens who have successfully resolved the conflicts of the earlier four stages are much better "equipped" to resist peer pressure to engage in unhealthy or illegal activities and find their own identity during the adolescent years. Those teens who are not as successful come into the adolescent years with a lack of trust in others, feelings of guilt and shame, low self-esteem, and dependency on others. Peer pressure is quite effective on teenagers who desperately want to "fit in" and have an identity of some sort and who feel that others will not want to be with them unless they conform to the expectations and demands of the peer group. They play the part of the model child for the parents, the good student for the teachers, and the "cool" juvenile delinquent to their friends and will be confused about which of the many roles they play are really their own identity.

PARENT/TEEN CONFLICT   Even for the majority of adolescents who end up successfully finding a consistent sense of self, there will be conflicts with parents. Many researchers believe that a certain amount of "rebellion" and conflict is a necessary step in breaking away from childhood dependence on the parents and becoming a self-sufficient* adult. Although many people think that these conflicts are intense and concern very serious behavior, the reality is that most parent/teen conflict is over trivial issues—hair, clothing, taste in music, and so on. On the really big moral issues, most parents and teens would be quite surprised to realize that they are in agreement. ◉─│Watch on MyPsychLab

Actresses Lindsay Lohan, Amanda Seyfried, Lacey Chabert, and Rachel McAdams on the set of Mark S. Waters's comedy movie *Mean Girls*. This movie portrays the ins and outs of peer pressure and the desire to fit in that many adolescents face.

identity versus role confusion   fifth stage of personality development in which the adolescent must find a consistent sense of self.

◉─│Watch footage on adolescent behavior including egocentrism, teen drinking, and teen pregnancy on **MyPsychLab**

---

practice quiz   How much do you remember?

7.9

Pick the best answer.

1. Which of the following statements about adolescence is FALSE?
   a. It begins with the onset of puberty.
   b. It is a time during which the young person is no longer a child but is not yet an adult.
   c. It ends when puberty is complete.
   d. It is a time of preoccupation with one's own thoughts.

2. Which term refers to the feeling of being unique and protected?
   a. formal operations   c. personal fable
   b. imaginary audience   d. puberty

3. According to Kohlberg, most adolescents are at the _____ level of morality.
   a. preconventional
   b. conventional
   c. postconventional
   d. preliminary

4. According to Erikson, the task of the adolescent is to _____.
   a. find a consistent sense of self.
   b. develop a sense of initiative.
   c. find intimacy with another.
   d. develop a sense of industry.

5. Which of the following issues typically creates a lot of conflict between most teens and their parents?
   a. serious issues of drug and alcohol use
   b. trivial issues of hair, clothing, and music choices
   c. issues of postconventional morality
   d. issues of achieving an identity

Brainstorming: Have you ever had a decision to make that challenged your moral thinking? In which of Kohlberg's three levels would you classify your decision?

ANSWERS ON PAGE AK–1.

---

*Self-sufficient: able to function without outside aid; capable of providing for one's own needs.

When exactly does adulthood begin?

Adulthood

Physical Development: Use It or Lose It

● When exactly does adulthood begin?

Adulthood can be thought of as the period of life from the early twenties until old age and death. Exactly when adulthood begins is not always easy to determine. In some cultures, adulthood is reached soon after puberty (Bledsoe & Cohen, 1993; Ocholla-Ayayo et al., 1993). Some people feel that it begins after graduation from high school, whereas others would say adulthood doesn't begin until after graduation from college. Others define it as the point when a person becomes totally self-sufficient with a job and a home separate from his or her parents. In that case, some people are not adults until their late thirties.

7.10 **What are the physical, cognitive, and personality changes that occur during adulthood and aging, including Erikson's last three psychosocial stages, and patterns of parenting?**

Adulthood can also be divided into at least three periods: young adulthood, middle age, and late adulthood. Physical changes in young adulthood are relatively minimal. The good news is that the twenties are a time of peak physical health, sharp senses, fewer insecurities, and mature cognitive abilities. The bad news is that even in the early twenties, the signs of aging are already beginning. Oil glands in the neck and around the eyes begin to malfunction, contributing to wrinkles in those areas near the end of the twenties and beginning of the thirties. The thirties may not bring noticeable changes, but vision and hearing are beginning to decline and by around age 40, bifocal lenses may become necessary as the lens of the eye hardens, becoming unable to change its shape to shift focus. Hearing loss may begin in the forties and fifties but often does not become noticeable until the sixties or seventies, when hearing aids may become necessary.

In the forties, while most adults are able to experience some security and stability without the worries and concerns of adolescence and young adulthood, physical aging continues: Skin begins to show more wrinkles, hair turns gray (or falls out), vision and hearing decline further, and physical strength may begin to decline (Frontera et al., 1991). In the fifties, these changes continue. Throughout middle age, weight may increase as the rate at which the body functions slows down but eating increases and less time is spent exercising. Height begins to decrease, with about half an inch of height lost for every 10 years past age 40, although people with the bone-loss disease osteoporosis may lose up to 8 inches or more (Cummings & Melton, 2002). Although sexual functioning usually does not decline in middle age, opportunities for sexual activity may be fewer than in the days of young adulthood (Hodson & Skeen, 1994; Williams, 1995). Children, mortgages, and career worries can put a damper on middle-age romance.

MENOPAUSE For women, the forties are a time of great physical changes. At this time in life a woman's reproductive organs begin functioning inconsistently, as levels of the female hormone estrogen decline in preparation for the end of reproduction. The uterus slowly begins to get smaller in size, menstrual cycles become irregular, and some women begin to experience "hot flashes," a sudden sensation of heat and sweating that may keep them up at night. Interestingly, in some cultures, particularly those in which the diet contains high amounts of soy products, hot flashes are almost nonexistent (Cassidy et al., 1994; Lock, 1994). These changes are called the *climacteric*, and the period of five to ten years over which these changes occur is called *perimenopause*. At an average age of 51, most women will cease ovulation altogether, ending their reproductive years. The cessation of ovulation and the menstrual cycle is called **menopause** (Mishell, 2001). Many women look forward to the freedom from

menopause the cessation of ovulation and menstrual cycles and the end of a woman's reproductive capability.

monthly menstruation and fear of unplanned pregnancies (Adler et al., 2000; Hvas, 2001; Leon et al., 2007).

Do men go through anything like menopause? ●

Men also go through a time of sexual changes, but it is much more gradual and less dramatic than menopause. In males, **andropause** (Carruthers, 2001) usually begins in the forties with a decline in several hormones, primarily testosterone (the major male hormone). Physical symptoms are also less dramatic but no less troubling: fatigue, irritability, possible problems in sexual functioning, and reduced sperm count. Males, however, rarely lose all reproductive ability.

EFFECTS OF AGING ON HEALTH It is in middle age that many health problems first occur, although their true cause may have begun in the young adulthood years. Young adults may smoke, drink heavily, stay up late, and get dark tans, and the wear and tear that this lifestyle causes on their bodies will not become obvious until their forties and fifties.

Some of the common health problems that may show up in middle age are high blood pressure, skin cancer, heart problems, arthritis, and obesity. High blood pressure can be caused by lifestyle factors such as obesity and stress but may also be related to hereditary factors (Rudd & Osterberg, 2002). Sleep problems, such as loud snoring and sleep apnea (in which breathing stops for 10 seconds or more), may also take their toll on physical health. There is some evidence that high blood pressure and apnea are linked, although the link may be as simple as the common cause of obesity (Nieto et al., 2000). The most common causes of death in middle age are heart disease, cancer, and stroke—in that order (McGinnis & Foege, 1993).

Cognitive Development

Intellectual abilities do not decline overall, although speed of processing (or reaction time) does slow down. Compared to a younger adult, a middle-aged person may take a little longer to solve a problem. However, a middle-aged person also has more life experience and knowledge to bring to bear on a problem, which counters the lack of speed. In one study (Salthouse, 1984), for example, older typists were found to outperform younger typists, even though they typed more slowly than the younger subjects. The older typists, because of years of practice, had developed a skill of looking farther ahead in the document they were typing, so that they could type more continuously without looking back at the document. This allowed them to complete their typing more quickly than the younger typists.

CHANGES IN MEMORY Changes in memory ability are probably the most noticeable changes in middle-aged cognition. People find themselves having a hard time remembering a particular word or someone's name. This difficulty in retrieval is probably not evidence of a cognitive decline but is more likely caused by the stresses a middle-aged person experiences and the sheer amount of information that a person of middle years must try to keep straight (Craik, 1994; Launer et al., 1995; Sands & Meredith, 1992). One study suggests that thinking about the positive events of the past activates areas of the brain connected to the brain areas that form newer memories, improving that new memory formation (Addis et al., 2010). Think positive!

HOW TO KEEP YOUR BRAIN YOUNG People who exercise their mental abilities have been found to be far less likely to develop memory problems and even senile dementias such as Alzheimer's in old age (Ball et al., 2002; Colcombe et al., 2003; Fiatarone, 1996). "Use it or lose it" is the phrase to remember. Working challenging crossword puzzles, for example, can be a major factor in maintaining a healthy level of cognitive functioning. Reading, having an active social life, going to plays, taking classes, and staying physically active can all have a positive impact on the continued well-being of the brain (Bosworth & Schaie, 1997; Cabeza et al., 2002; Singh-Manoux et al., 2003).

andropause gradual changes in the sexual hormones and reproductive system of middle-aged males.

Do men go through anything like menopause?

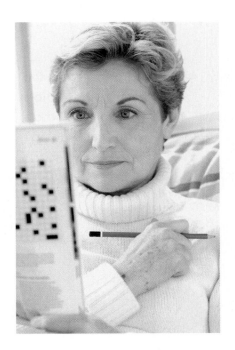

This middle-aged woman works on a crossword puzzle. Mental exercises such as this are one way to keep the brain healthy and fit. What might be some other ways to exercise one's brain?

intimacy an emotional and psychological closeness that is based on the ability to trust, share, and care, while still maintaining a sense of self.

generativity providing guidance to one's children or the next generation, or contributing to the well-being of the next generation through career or volunteer work.

authoritarian parenting style of parenting in which parent is rigid and overly strict, showing little warmth to the child.

Psychosocial Development

In adulthood, concerns involve career, relationships, family, and approaching old age. The late teens and early twenties may be college years for many, although other young people go to work directly from high school. Choosing and entering a career is a very serious task that many young adults have difficulty accomplishing. College students may change majors more than once during the first few years of college, and even after obtaining a bachelor's degree many may either get a job in an unrelated field or go on to a different type of career choice in graduate school. Those who are working may also change careers several times (perhaps as many as five to seven times) and may experience periods of unemployment while between jobs.

ERIKSON'S INTIMACY VERSUS ISOLATION: FORMING RELATIONSHIPS In young adulthood, Erikson saw the primary task to be finding a mate. True **intimacy** is an emotional and psychological closeness that is based on the ability to trust, share, and care (an ability developed during the earlier stages such as trust versus mistrust), while still maintaining one's sense of self. ⓁⒾⓃⓀ to Chapter Ten: Social Psychology, p. 370. Young adults who have difficulty trusting others and who are unsure of their own identities may find *isolation* instead of intimacy—loneliness, shallow relationships with others, and even a fear of real intimacy. For example, many marriages end in divorce within a few years, with one partner leaving the relationship—and even the responsibilities of parenting—to explore personal concerns and those unfinished issues of identity. Table 7.6 summarizes the last four stages in Erikson's theory.

ERIKSON'S GENERATIVITY VERSUS STAGNATION: PARENTING In middle adulthood, persons who have found intimacy can now focus outward on others (Table 7.6). Erikson saw this as parenting the next generation and helping them through their crises, a process he called **generativity**. Educators, supervisors, health care professionals, doctors, and community volunteers might be examples of positions that allow a person to be generative. Other ways of being generative include engaging in careers or some major life work that can become one's legacy to the generations to come. Those who are unable to focus outward and are still dealing with issues of intimacy or even identity are said to be *stagnated*. People who frequently hand the care of their children over to grandparents or other relatives so that they can go out and "have fun" may be unable to focus on anyone else's needs but their own.

● What kind of parent is the best parent—one who's really strict or one who's pretty easygoing?

What kind of parent is the best parent—one who's really strict or one who's pretty easygoing?

✴ Explore more with a simulation on Baumrind's parenting styles on **MyPsychLab**

PARENTING STYLES Parenting children is a very important part of most people's middle adulthood. Diana Baumrind (1967) outlined three basic styles of parenting, each of which may be related to certain personality traits in the child raised by that style of parenting. ✴ Explore on **MyPsychLab**

Authoritarian parenting tends to be overly concerned with rules. This type of parent is stern, rigid, demanding perfection, controlling, uncompromising,* and has a tendency to use physical punishment. The parent who does the punishment often shows little warmth or affection to the child—which may be from a desire to appear stern more than from an actual lack of love. Children raised in this way are often insecure, timid, withdrawn, and resentful. As teenagers, they will very often rebel against parental authority in very negative and self-destructive ways, such as delinquency (criminal acts committed by minor children), drug use, or premarital sex (Baumrind, 1991, 2005).

---

*Uncompromising: not making or accepting any viewpoint other than one's own, allowing no other viewpoints.

table 7.6 Erikson's Psychosocial Adolescent and Adult Stages

STAGE	DEVELOPMENTAL CRISIS	SUCCESSFUL DEALING WITH CRISIS	UNSUCCESSFUL DEALING WITH CRISIS
5. Adolescence 13 to early twenties	**Identity Versus Role Confusion** Adolescents are faced with deciding who or what they want to be in terms of occupation, beliefs, attitudes, and behavior patterns.	Adolescents who succeed in defining who they are and find a role for themselves develop a strong sense of identity.	Adolescents who fail to define their identity become confused and withdraw or want to inconspicuously blend in with the crowd.
6. Early Adulthood Twenties and thirties	**Intimacy Versus Isolation** The task facing those in early adulthood is to be able to share who they are with another person in a close, committed relationship.	People who succeed in this task will have satisfying intimate relationships.	Adults who fail at this task will be isolated from other people and may suffer from loneliness.
7. Middle Adulthood Forties and fifties	**Generativity Versus Stagnation** The challenge is to be creative, productive, and nurturant of the next generation.	Adults who succeed in this challenge will be creative, productive, and nurturant, thereby benefiting themselves, their family, community, country, and future generations.	Adults who fail will be passive and self-centered, feel that they have done nothing for the next generation, and feel that the world is no better off for their being alive.
8. Late Adulthood Sixties and beyond	**Ego Integrity Versus Despair** The issue is whether a person will reach wisdom, spiritual tranquility, a sense of wholeness, and acceptance of his or her life.	Elderly people who succeed in addressing this issue will enjoy life and not fear death.	Elderly people who fail will feel that their life is empty and will fear death.

Source: Erikson, 1950/1963.

Permissive parenting occurs when parents put very few demands on their children for behavior. **Permissive neglectful** parents simply aren't involved with their children, ignoring them and allowing them to do whatever they want until it interferes with what the parent wants. At that point, this relationship may become an abusive one. **Permissive indulgent** parents seem to be *too* involved with their children, allowing their "little angels" to behave in any way they wish, refusing to set limits on the child's behavior or to require any kind of obedience. Children from both kinds of permissive parenting tend to be selfish, immature, dependent, lacking in social skills, and unpopular with peers.

Authoritative parenting involves combining firm limits on behavior with love, warmth, affection, respect, and a willingness to listen to the child's point of view. Authoritative parents are more democratic, allowing the child to have some input into the formation of rules but still maintaining the role of final decision maker. Punishment tends to be nonphysical, such as restrictions, time-out, or loss of privileges. Authoritative parents set limits that are clear and understandable, and when a child crosses the limits, they allow an explanation and then agree on the right way to handle the situation.

ERIKSON'S EGO INTEGRITY VERSUS DESPAIR: DEALING WITH MORTALITY As people enter the stage known as late adulthood, life becomes more urgent as the realities of physical aging and the approaching end of life become harder and harder to ignore. (See Table 7.6.) Erikson (1980) believed that at this time people look back on the life they have lived in a process called a *life review*. In the life review people must deal with mistakes, regrets, and unfinished business. If people can look back and feel that their lives were relatively full and come to terms with regrets and losses, then a feeling of **integrity** or wholeness results. Integrity is the final completion of the identity, or ego. If people have many regrets and lots of unfinished business, they feel *despair*, a sense of deep regret over things that will never be accomplished because time has run out.

permissive parenting style of parenting in which parent makes few, if any, demands on a child's behavior.

permissive neglectful permissive parenting in which parents are uninvolved with a child or child's behavior.

permissive indulgent permissive parenting in which parents are so involved that children are allowed to behave without set limits.

authoritative parenting style of parenting in which parents combine warmth and affection with firm limits on a child's behavior.

integrity sense of wholeness that comes from having lived a full life and the ability to let go of regrets; the final completion of the ego.

practice quiz   How much do you remember?

Pick the best answer.

1. The period of five to ten years during which a woman's reproductive system begins to decline is called _____.
   a. climacteric.
   b. perimenopause.
   c. menopause.
   d. all of the above.

2. Which of the following has NOT been shown to help maintain a healthy level of cognitive functioning?
   a. working crossword puzzles
   b. reading
   c. going to plays
   d. sedentary lifestyle

3. Today's worker may change careers as many as _____ times.
   a. one to two
   b. three to five
   c. five to seven
   d. eight to nine

4. According to Erikson, achieving true intimacy is difficult if one's _____ is not already established.
   a. identity
   b. independence
   c. career
   d. marriage

5. According to Baumrind, _____ parenting may lead to an abusive relationship.
   a. authoritarian
   b. authoritative
   c. permissive neglectful
   d. permissive indulgent

6. In Erikson's last crisis, the life review is _____.
   a. a process of assigning blame.
   b. looking back on the life one has lived.
   c. an analysis of one's parents' lives.
   d. the writing of a biography.

7. A sense of completeness of one's ego, or identity, is called _____.
   a. life review.
   b. intelligence.
   c. integrity.
   d. generativity.

ANSWERS ON PAGE AK–1.

Theories of Physical and Psychological Aging

7.11 How do psychologists explain why aging occurs, and what are the stages of death and dying?

Why do people age? What makes us go through so many physical changes?

Why do people age? What makes us go through so many physical changes?

There are a number of theories of why people physically age. Some theories of physical aging point to biological changes in cellular structure, whereas others focus on the influence of external stresses on body tissues and functioning.

CELLULAR CLOCK THEORY One of the biologically based theories is the *cellular clock theory* (Hayflick, 1977). In this theory, cells are limited in the number of times they can reproduce to repair damage. Evidence for this theory is the existence of *telomeres*, structures on the ends of chromosomes that shorten each time a cell reproduces (Martin & Buckwalter, 2001). When telomeres are too short, cells cannot reproduce; damage accumulates, resulting in the effects of aging. (Sounds almost like what happens when the warranty is up on a car, doesn't it?)

FREE RADICAL THEORY One older theory points to outside influences such as stress, physical exertion, and bodily damage and is known as the *wear-and-tear theory of aging*. In this theory, the body's organs and cell tissues simply wear out with repeated use and abuse. The *free radical theory* is actually the latest version of the wear-and-tear theory in that it gives a biological explanation for the damage done to cells over time. *Free radicals* are oxygen molecules that have an unstable electron (negative particle). They bounce around the cell, stealing electrons from other molecules and increasing the damage to structures inside the cell. As people get older, more and more free radicals do more and more damage, producing the effects of aging (Hauck & Bartke, 2001; Knight, 1998).

I've heard that most older people just want to be left alone and have some peace and quiet. Is that true?

I've heard that most older people just want to be left alone and have some peace and quiet. Is that true?

activity theory theory of adjustment to aging that assumes older people are happier if they remain active in some way, such as volunteering or developing a hobby.

ACTIVITY THEORY **Activity theory** (Havighurst et al., 1968) proposes that an elderly person adjusts more positively to aging when remaining active in some way. Elderly people who volunteer at hospitals or schools, those who take up new hobbies or throw themselves full time into old ones, and those who maintain their friendships with others and continue to have social activities have been shown to be happier and live longer than those who withdraw themselves from activity.

Stages of Death and Dying

There are several ways of looking at the process of dying. One of the more well-known theories is that of Elisabeth Kübler-Ross (Kübler-Ross, 1997), who conducted extensive interviews with dying persons and their caregivers.

One way to age successfully and maintain psychological health is to remain active and involved in life. This woman is volunteering in a grade school classroom as a teacher's aide. This not only allows her to feel useful but also helps her to stay mentally alert and socially involved.

Elisabeth Kübler-Ross theorized that people go through five stages of reaction when faced with death (Backer et al., 1994; Kübler-Ross, 1997). These stages are *denial*, in which people refuse to believe that the diagnosis of death is real; *anger*, which is really anger at death itself and the feelings of helplessness to change things; *bargaining*, in which the dying person tries to make a deal with doctors or even with God; *depression*, which is sadness from losses already experienced (e.g., loss of a job or one's dignity) and those yet to come (e.g., not being able to see a child grow up); and finally *acceptance*, when the person has accepted the inevitable* and quietly awaits death.

Obviously, some people do not have time to go through all of these stages or even go through them in the listed order (Schneidman, 1983, 1994). Some theorists do not agree with the stage idea, seeing the process of dying as a series of ups and downs, with hope on the rise at times and then falling, to be replaced by a rise in despair or disbelief (Schneidman, 1983, 1994; Weisman, 1972). Still others question the idea of common reactions among dying people, stating that the particular disease or condition and its treatment, the person's personality before the terminal diagnosis, and other life history factors make the process of dying unique and unpredictable (Kastenbaum & Costa, 1977). The danger in holding too strictly to a stage theory is that people may feel there is a "right" way to face death and a "wrong" way when in fact each person's dying process is unique.

---

*Inevitable: something that cannot be avoided or escaped.

---

practice quiz   How much do you remember?

7.11

Pick the best answer.

1. According to research, if an older person wants to adjust more positively to aging, he or she should _____.
   a. quietly withdraw from social life.
   b. limit his or her range of activities.
   c. disengage from life.
   d. remain active in some way.

2. In which theory of aging do telomeres become the major means of aging cells?
   a. wear-and-tear theory
   b. cellular clock theory

   c. free radical theory
   d. hormonal imbalance theory

3. In the _____ stage of reaction to death and dying, a person may promise to do everything the doctor says if the doctor will say that the person can live a little longer.
   a. denial
   b. anger
   c. bargaining
   d. depression
   e. acceptance

applying psychology to everyday life

Cross-Cultural Views on Death

7.12 What are some cross-cultural differences in views of death and dying?

In the 1987 movie *The Princess Bride*, a character called Miracle Max (wonderfully played by comedian and actor Billy Crystal) says, "It just so happens that your friend here is only MOSTLY dead. There's a big difference between mostly dead and all dead. Mostly dead is slightly alive." As it turns out, that far-fetched idea of "mostly dead" is not unheard of in other cultures. While Westerners see a person as either dead or alive, in some cultures a person who, by Western standards is clearly alive, is mourned as already dead—as is the case in many Native American cultures. Let's take a look at two diverse cultures and their views on death and dying, remembering to contrast them with what you know of death and funeral rites common in your own culture.

The washed and wrapped body of a Hindu man is being carried to the crematorium by his family members.

- In a wealthy Hindu family in India, the dying person is surrounded by family members, even while in the hospital. In addition, many visitors will attend to the dying person, creating a nearly constant flow of visitors in and out of the room. Once the person has passed away, preparations for the funeral period—which can take nearly two weeks—are begun. The body is not sent to a funeral home, but rather is taken into the family home until the actual day of the funeral, where a cremation will take place. During the funeral preparation period, visitors and family stream in and out of the deceased's home and an abundance of food—all vegetarian at this time—are prepared and eaten. Until the day of the funeral, mattresses are placed on the floor, and all but the very old and infirm are expected to sleep there; the body of the deceased is also placed on the floor. The family members themselves will eventually wash the body in preparation for wrapping and the trip to the crematorium (Laungani, 1997). In Hinduism, it is believed that the dead person's soul will be reincarnated at either a higher level or a lower level of status, depending upon how the person lived his or her life.

- In the culture of the Northern Cheyenne Native American tribe, death is considered only the end of the physical body, while the self and one's Cheyenne nature will persist. The very old and the very young are said to be "close to the spirit," meaning that the infant has just come from the nonphysical world and the aged person is close to returning to it. The Cheyenne, like the Hindi, also believe in reincarnation, so many infants are seen to be the living embodiment of ancestors. Death itself is a long process, with various aspects of one's spirit leaving at different times. The first such "leaving" results in changes in the behavior and the mental activity of the dying person, but the person may still be able to walk and communicate. The second leads to loss of the senses, then consciousness, and finally, breathing. The very last essence to leave is the life principle, the first life given into an infant but the last to leave. This life principle stays in the skeleton until the bones begin to crumble into dust. Thus some Cheyenne believe that bones can become alive again (Strauss, 2004).

QUESTIONS FOR FURTHER DISCUSSION

1. How has your own experience with death, if any, affected you and your outlook on life? What were the cultural trappings of the days leading up to the death and/or the funeral arrangements?

2. How do the customs of the wealthy Hindu family differ from those of the Cheyenne, and how are they alike?

chapter summary

((•–[Listen on **MyPsychLab**   Listen to an audio file of your chapter **www.MyPsychLab**

Issues in Studying Human Development

7.1 What are some of the special research methods used to study development?

- Three special research methods used in developmental research are the longitudinal design, the cross-sectional design, and the cross-sequential design.

7.2 What is the relationship between heredity and environmental factors in determining development?

- Behavioral genetics is a field investigating the relative contributions to development of heredity (nature) and environment (nurture). Most developmental psychologists agree that development is a product of the interaction between nature and nurture.

The Basic Building Blocks of Development

7.3 How do chromosomes and genes determine the inheritance of disorders, and what causes multiple births?

- Dominant genes control the expression of a trait, whereas recessive gene traits are only expressed when paired with another recessive gene for the same trait. Almost all traits are the result of combinations of genes working together in a process called polygenic inheritance.

- Chromosome disorders include Down syndrome, Klinefelter's syndrome, and Turner's syndrome, whereas genetic disorders include PKU, cystic fibrosis, sickle-cell anemia, and Tay-Sachs disease.

Prenatal Development

- The fertilized egg cell is called a zygote and divides into many cells, eventually forming the baby.

- Monozygotic twins are formed when the zygote splits into two separate masses of cells, each of which will develop into a baby identical to the other. When the two masses do not fully separate, conjoined twins occur.

- Dizygotic twins are formed when the mother's body releases multiple eggs and at least two are fertilized or when another ovulation occurs even though the mother has already become pregnant.

psychology in the news: Abby and Brittany Hensel, Together for Life

- Conjoined twins Abby and Brittany Hensel are relatively healthy, well adjusted, and participate fully in many normal activities for young people of their age.

7.4 What happens during the germinal, embryonic, and fetal periods of pregnancy, and what are some hazards in prenatal development?

- The germinal period is the first two weeks of pregnancy in which the dividing mass of cells (blastocyst) moves down the fallopian tube into the uterus.

- The embryonic period begins at two weeks after conception and ends at eight weeks. The vital organs and structures of the baby form during this period, making it a critical one for teratogens to adversely affect the development of those organs and structures.

- The fetal period is from the beginning of the ninth week until the birth of the baby. During the fetal period, tremendous growth occurs, length and weight increase, and organs continue to become fully functional.

Infancy and Childhood Development

7.5 What kind of physical changes take place in infancy and childhood?

- Four critical areas of adjustment for the newborn are respiration, digestion, circulation, and temperature regulation.

- Infants are born with reflexes that help the infant survive until more complex learning is possible. These reflexes include sucking, rooting, Moro (startle), grasping, and stepping.

- The senses, except for vision, are fairly well developed at birth. Vision is blurry and lacking in full color perception until about 6 months of age. Gross and fine motor skills develop at a fast pace during infancy and early childhood.

7.6 What are two ways of looking at cognitive development, and how does language develop?

- Piaget's stages include the sensorimotor stage of sensory and physical interaction with the world, preoperational thought in which language becomes a tool of exploration, concrete operations in which logical thought becomes possible, and formal operations in which abstract concepts are understood and hypothetical thinking develops.

- Vygotsky believed that children learn best when being helped by a more highly skilled peer or adult in a process called scaffolding. The zone of proximal development is the difference between the mental age of tasks the child performs without help and those the child can perform with help.

- The stages of language development are cooing, babbling, one-word speech (holophrases), and telegraphic speech. Although some language is learned through imitation and reinforcement, infants may possess a language acquisition device that governs the learning of language during infancy and early childhood.

- Dr. Andrew Wakefield falsified data that led to parents refusing to have their children immunized against measles, mumps, and rubella, leading to epidemic outbreaks of these diseases.

7.7 How do infants and children develop personalities and form relationships with others, and what are Erikson's stages of psychosocial development for children?

- The three basic infant temperaments are easy (regular, adaptable, and happy), difficult (irregular, nonadaptable, and irritable), and slow to warm up (need to adjust gradually to change).

- The four types of attachment are secure, avoidant (unattached), ambivalent (insecurely attached), and disorganized-disoriented (insecurely attached and sometimes abused or neglected).

- In trust versus mistrust, the infant must gain a sense of predictability and trust in caregivers or risk developing a mistrustful nature; in autonomy versus shame and doubt, the toddler needs to become physically independent.

- In initiative versus guilt, the preschool child is developing emotional and psychological independence; in industry versus inferiority, school-age children are gaining competence and developing self-esteem.

classic studies in psychology: Harlow and Contact Comfort

- Harlow's classic research with infant Rhesus monkeys demonstrated the importance of contact comfort in the attachment process, contradicting the earlier view that attachment was merely a function of associating the mother with the delivery of food.

Gender Development

7.8 What is gender, and how do gender roles develop?

- Gender is the psychological aspects of being male or female.
- Gender roles are the culture's expectations for male and female behavior and personality.
- Gender identity is a person's sense of being male or female.
- There are both biological influences, in the form of hormones and chromosomes, and environmental influences, in the form of parenting, surroundings, and culture, on the formation of gender identity.
- Social learning theorists believe that gender identity is formed through reinforcement of appropriate gender behavior as well as imitation of gender models.
- Gender schema theorists believe that gender identity is a mental schema that develops gradually, influenced by the growth of the brain and organization of observed male or female behavior around the schema.

Adolescence

- Adolescence is the period of life from about age 13 to the early twenties during which physical development reaches completion.

7.9 What are the physical, cognitive, and personality changes that occur in adolescence, including concepts of morality and Erikson's search for identity?

- Puberty is a period of about four years during which the sexual organs and systems fully mature and during which secondary sex characteristics such as body hair, breasts, menstruation, deepening voices, and the growth spurt occur.
- Adolescents engage in two kinds of egocentric thinking called the imaginary audience and the personal fable.
- Kohlberg proposed three levels of moral development: preconventional morality, conventional morality, and postconventional morality.
- In Erikson's identity versus role confusion crisis the job of the adolescent is to achieve a consistent sense of self from among all the roles, values, and futures open to him or her.

Adulthood

7.10 What are the physical, cognitive, and personality changes that occur during adulthood and aging, including Erikson's last three psychosocial stages, and patterns of parenting?

- Adulthood begins in the early twenties and ends with death in old age. It can be divided into young adulthood, middle adulthood, and late adulthood.
- The twenties are the peak of physical health; in the thirties the signs of aging become more visible, and in the forties visual problems may occur, weight may increase, strength may decrease, and height begins to decrease.

- Women experience a physical decline in the reproductive system called the climacteric, ending at about age 50 with menopause, when a woman's estrogen levels are at zero and her reproductive capabilities are at an end. Men go through andropause, a less dramatic change in testosterone and other male hormones, beginning in the forties.
- Many health problems such as high blood pressure, skin cancers, and arthritis begin in middle age, with the most common causes of death in middle age being heart disease, cancer, and stroke.
- Reaction times slow down, but intelligence and memory remain relatively stable.
- Erikson's crisis of young adulthood is intimacy versus isolation, in which the young adult must establish an intimate relationship, usually with a mate.
- The crisis of middle adulthood is generativity versus stagnation, in which the task of the middle-aged adult is to help the next generation through its crises, either by parenting, mentoring, or a career that leaves some legacy to the next generation.
- Baumrind proposed three parenting styles: authoritarian (rigid and uncompromising), authoritative (consistent and strict but warm and flexible), and permissive (either indifferent and unconcerned with the daily activities of the child or indulgent and unwilling to set limits on the child).
- Erikson's final crisis is integrity versus despair, in which an older adult must come to terms with mortality.
- Research strongly indicates that remaining active and involved results in the most positive adjustment to aging.

7.11 How do psychologists explain why aging occurs, and what are the stages of death and dying?

- The cellular clock theory is based on the idea that cells only have so many times that they can reproduce; once that limit is reached, damaged cells begin to accumulate.
- The free radical theory states that oxygen molecules with an unstable electron move around the cell, damaging cell structures as they go.
- The five stages of reaction to death and dying are denial, anger, bargaining, depression, and acceptance.

applying psychology to everyday life
Cross-Cultural Views on Death

7.12 What are some cross-cultural differences in views of death and dying?

- In wealthy Hindu families, a dying person is surrounded by family and friends and then honored with a funeral process of nearly two weeks.
- In Northern Cheyenne culture, death is seen as part of the process of the life cycle, and takes place in three stages.

TEST yourself

ANSWERS ON PAGE AK-1

✓● Study and Review on MyPsychLab Ready for your test? More quizzes and a customized plan. www.MyPsychLab

Pick the best answer.

1. Differences between age-groups would cause the most serious problems for which developmental research method?
   a. longitudinal design
   b. cross-cultural design
   c. cross-sectional design
   d. cross-sequential design

2. If a person has one gene for cystic fibrosis but does not have the disease, cystic fibrosis must be a _____ disorder.
   a. dominant
   b. recessive
   c. sex-linked
   d. polygenic

3. In _____ syndrome, the twenty-third pair of chromosomes is missing an X, resulting in short, infertile females.
   a. PKU
   b. Down
   c. Klinefelter's
   d. Turner's

4. Which of the following represents dizygotic twins?
a. One egg is fertilized by two different sperm.
b. One egg splits and is then fertilized by two different sperm.
c. Two eggs get fertilized by two different sperm.
d. Two eggs are fertilized by the same sperm.

5. The spongelike organ that provides nourishment for the growing baby and filters away waste products is called the _____.
a. fallopian tube.
b. uterus.
c. umbilical cord.
d. placenta.

6. The critical period for pregnancy is the _____.
a. germinal period.
b. embryonic period.
c. fetal period.
d. last trimester.

7. Mary's baby was born with a smaller than normal head, some facial malformations, and is intellectually disabled. Mary most likely _____ during her early pregnancy.
a. ate fish with mercury in it
b. drank too much caffeine
c. drank alcohol
d. smoked marijuana

8. In the _____ reflex, the baby moves its head toward any light touch to its face.
a. sucking
b. startle
c. rooting
d. grasping

9. Which of the newborn's senses is the most fully developed at birth?
a. hearing **c.** smell **b.** vision **d.** touch

10. At what age can the typical infant sit without support?
a. 3 months **c.** 8 months **b.** 6 months **d.** 12 months

11. By age 5, the brain is at _____ percent of its adult weight.
a. 25 **c.** 90 **b.** 50 **d.** 100

12. In which of Piaget's stages does the child become capable of understanding conservation?
a. sensorimotor
b. preoperational
c. formal operations
d. concrete operations

13. According to Vygotsky, giving a child help in the form of asking leading questions and providing examples is called _____.
a. scaffolding.
b. the zone of proximal
c. private speech.
d. habituation development.

14. Infants seem to understand far more language than they can produce, a phenomenon known as _____.
a. productive–receptive lag.
b. receptive–productive lag.
c. accomodation.
d. child–directed speech.

15. Little Kashif held his empty cup up to his mother and said, "Milk!" His use of this word is labeled _____.
a. a holophrase.
b. telegraphic speech.
c. babbling.
d. cooing.

16. As an infant, Liz never liked change, but if you introduce new things gradually, she will eventually accept them without too much fuss. Liz is most likely _____.
a. easy.
b. difficult.
c. slow to warm up.
d. securely attached.

17. In the Strange Situation, _____ babies were clinging, unwilling to explore, very upset when Mommy left the room, and demanded to be held but pushed her away at the same time when she returned.
a. secure
b. avoidant
c. ambivalent
d. disorganized-disoriented

18. In Erikson's crisis of _____, children are developing a sense of competence and self-esteem.
a. trust versus mistrust
b. autonomy versus shame and doubt
c. initiative versus guilt
d. industry versus inferiority

19. The culture's expectations for male and female behaviors are called _____.
a. gender roles.
b. gender typing.
c. gender identity.
d. gender constancy.

20. What happened in the study of 25 genetic males born with ambiguous genitalia who were surgically altered to be females?
a. They all successfully identified themselves as female.
b. They became lesbians.
c. They preferred male games and toys, and most have openly declared themselves to be boys.
d. They became more traditionally feminine as they grew older.

21. In gender schema theory, gender identity _____.
a. first forms as a mental concept of "boy" or "girl."
b. is acquired through simple imitation of models.
c. occurs through observational learning.
d. is acquired through positive reinforcement of appropriate gender behavior.

22. Samantha refuses to go to school because her chin has a "huge" pimple on it and she is afraid that everyone will laugh at her and point. Samantha is a victim of _____.
a. the imaginary audience.
b. the personal fable.
c. abstract egocentrism.
d. formal operations.

23. Erikson's fifth stage of psychosocial development is _____.
a. identity versus role confusion.
b. intimacy versus isolation.
c. generativity versus stagnation.
d. integrity versus despair.

24. Vision and hearing begin to decline in the _____.
a. twenties. **b.** thirties. **c.** forties. **d.** fifties.

25. A decline in testosterone in the forties is called _____.
a. perimenopause.
b. menopause.
c. climacteric.
d. andropause.

26. The crisis of middle adulthood, according to Erikson, is _____.
a. identity versus role confusion.
b. generativity versus stagnation.
c. intimacy versus isolation.
d. integrity versus despair.

27. Rebellion in the teenage years is the most likely outcome of _____ parenting.
a. authoritarian
b. authoritative
c. permissive neglectful
d. permissive indulgent

28. Damage caused by unstable molecules is the main idea of the _____ theory of aging.
a. wear-and-tear
b. cellular clock
c. free radical
d. active

29. According to Kübler-Ross, when bargaining fails, _____ usually results.
a. denial
b. anger
c. depression
d. acceptance

30. Which culture discussed in the Applying Psychology section has a belief in reincarnation?
a. Hindu
b. Cheyenne
c. Navajo
d. Both Hindu and Cheyenne

7 development across the life span

7.1 **7.2** **7.3** p. 230

- **research designs**
  - longitudinal
  - cross-sectional
  - cross-sequential

- nature/genetics
- nurture/environment
- most developmental psychologists agree that the most likely explanation for most human development is based on the interaction between nature and nurture

Issues in Studying Human Development
(scientific study of changes that occur in people as they age)

- **basic building blocks of development**
  - **genetics** is the science of heredity
  - **DNA (deoxyribonucleic acid):** contains genetic codes and chromosomes
  - dominant and recessive genes
  - genetic and chromosome problems

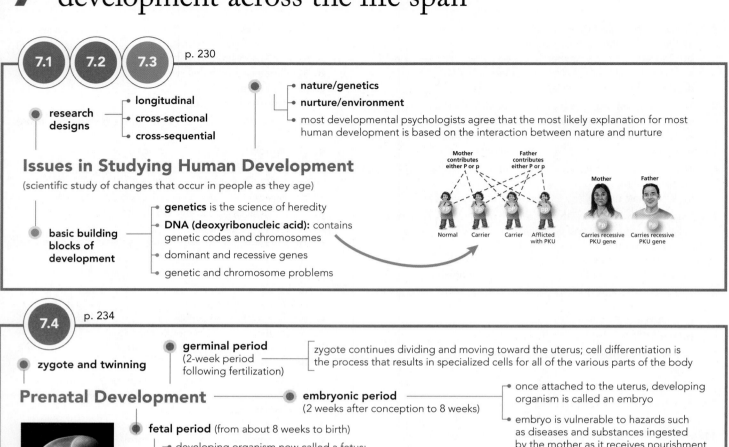

Mother contributes either P or p   Father contributes either P or p

Normal   Carrier   Carrier   Afflicted with PKU

Mother — Carries recessive PKU gene   Father — Carries recessive PKU gene

---

7.4 p. 234

- **zygote and twinning**

- **germinal period** (2-week period following fertilization) — zygote continues dividing and moving toward the uterus; cell differentiation is the process that results in specialized cells for all of the various parts of the body

Prenatal Development

- **embryonic period** (2 weeks after conception to 8 weeks)
  - once attached to the uterus, developing organism is called an embryo
  - embryo is vulnerable to hazards such as diseases and substances ingested by the mother as it receives nourishment through the placenta

- **fetal period** (from about 8 weeks to birth)
  - developing organism now called a fetus; time of tremendous growth and development
  - muscles begin to contract during the 3rd month, mother can start to feel "flutters" by 4th month, kicks felt by 5th month
  - full-term birth occurs around end of 38th week

table 7.3 Piaget's Stages of Cognitive Development		
STAGE		**COGNITIVE DEVELOPMENT**
Sensorimotor	Birth to 2 years old	Children explore the world using their senses and ability to move. They develop object permanence and the understanding that concepts and mental images represent objects, people, and events.
Preoperational	2 to 7 years old	Young children can mentally represent and refer to objects and events with words or pictures, and they can pretend. However, they can't conserve, logically reason, or simultaneously consider many characteristics of an object.
Concrete Operations	7 to 12 years old	Children at this stage are able to conserve, reverse their thinking, and classify objects in terms of their many characteristics. They can also think logically and understand analogies but only about concrete events.
Formal Operations	12 years old to adulthood	People at this stage can use abstract reasoning about hypothetical events or situations, think about logical possibilities, use abstract analogies, and systematically examine and test hypotheses. Not everyone can eventually reason in all these ways.

7.5 **7.6** p. 238

- **physical development**
  - immediately after birth, body systems start to function (i.e., respiratory, circulatory, temperature regulation, digestive)
  - babies are born with (innate) reflex behaviors (see Fig. 7.4)

- **sensory development**
  - touch, taste, and smell are well developed
  - hearing is functional but not fully developed
  - vision is least developed (rods are functional, cones take about six months to fully develop)

- **motor development**
  - normal motor development is related to many factors, such as nutrition, care, and health
  - birth to 2 years = period of rapid development (see Fig. 7.5)

- **cognitive development**
  - **Piaget's theory**
    - suggests children form mental concepts or schemes
    - proposes four distinct stages of cognitive development that span infancy to adolescence
  - **Vygotsky's theory**
    - stresses the importance of social interactions with others, typically more highly skilled children and adults
    - children's cognitive development occurs when someone helps them by asking leading questions and providing examples of concepts (scaffolding)
    - cognitive development occurs when others provide scaffolding and each child has a zone of proximal development
  - **stages of language development**
    - language allows children to think in words, ask questions, communicate needs and wants, and form concepts
    - various views of development
    - universal progressive stages

Infancy and Childhood Development

7.7 p. 246

psychosocial development — involves development of personality, relationships, and a sense of being male or female; process begins in infancy and continues into adulthood

Erikson's theory
- suggests development occurs in a series of eight stages (see Table 7.4)
- at each stage an emotional crisis must be successfully met for normal development to occur

important early concepts
- infants demonstrate personality through their temperament (e.g., easy, difficult, slow to warm up), which can also affect, and is affected by, parenting and the environment
- attachment (emotional bond between infant and a primary caregiver) is very important

Infancy and Childhood Development: Psychosocial Development

7.8 p. 251

gender — is defined as the psychological aspects of being masculine or feminine
- **gender roles:** cultural behavioral expectations for males or females
- **gender identity:** sense of being male or female (influenced by both biology and environment)
- **biological influences:** sexual characteristics of the genitals and hormonal differences
- **environmental and cultural influences:** parental influences and cultural expectations to adhere to gender roles

Gender Development

theories of gender role development
- **social learning theory:** gender roles learned through observation and imitation of models
- **gender schema theory** (Bem): Piaget-like schemas and concepts for male and female develop and influence gender roles

7.9 p. 253

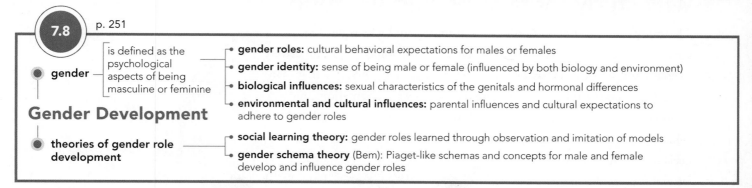

physical development
- increase in height and changes in both primary and secondary sex characteristics
- occurs as the result of glandular and hormonal activities
- tends to occur about 2 years after beginning of growth spurt

cognitive development
- final maturation of the frontal lobes allows cognitive advances (e.g., abstract thought/Piaget's formal operations)
- despite advances, still have egocentric thought that emerges in a variety of ways

Adolescence
(period of life from about age 13 to early 20s)

moral development
- understanding of what is "right" and "wrong"
- early theory was proposed by Kohlberg; suggested three levels of moral development
- some researchers (e.g., Gilligan) suggest that Kohlberg's ideas applied more to males; others suggest that assessment was based on hypothetical, rather than real-life, dilemmas

psychosocial development
- adolescence is largely marked by the search for a consistent sense of self or personal identity
- Erikson: the psychosocial crisis that must be resolved is identity vs. role confusion
- parent–teen conflict to be expected

7.10 p. 258

Adulthood
(period of life from early 20s until old age and death; age of onset can vary by culture)

physical development
- young adulthood
- middle age
- late adulthood

cognitive development
- cognitive skills often highest in 20s; processing and reaction time slow in middle age but are often compensated by greater life and situational knowledge
- memory issues begin in middle age, likely due to stress and information overload
- mental abilities aided by active cognitive engagement (challenging crossword puzzles, reading, etc.) and physical activity

psychosocial development
- typical life concerns involve career, relationships, family, and approaching old age
- Erikson's stage

7.11 p. 262

theories on aging
vary focus from biological changes to influence on external stressors
- cellular-clock theory
- wear-and-tear theory
- free-radical theory

activity theory — positive psychological adjustment associated with continued activity and involvement

stages of death and dying
(based on work of Kübler-Ross)
- denial
- anger
- bargaining
- depression
- acceptance

Adulthood: Aging

8

motivation and emotion

why study motivation and emotion?

The study of motivation not only helps us understand why some people are more driven to achieve than others but also why some people are driven to abuse drugs. Sexual behavior is another motivated activity, one that many struggle to understand—why are there different sexual orientations, for example? Emotions are a part of everything we do, affecting our relationships with others and our own health, as well as influencing important decisions. In this chapter, we will explore the motives behind our actions and the origins and influences of emotions.

chapter outline

Approaches to Understanding Motivation

Psychoactive Drugs and Addiction

Sexual Motivation

ISSUES IN PSYCHOLOGY:
What is the Evolutionary Purpose of Homosexuality?

Emotion

CLASSIC STUDIES IN PSYCHOLOGY:
The Angry/Happy Man

APPLYING PSYCHOLOGY TO EVERYDAY LIFE:
When Motivation is Not Enough

Making the Grade

Jennifer had worked hard in high school, making straight A's her junior and senior years, and nothing less than a B throughout. She was involved in a variety of school activities but her classes and grades always came first. Good grades were her ticket for possibly getting a scholarship for college. This was a goal she really wanted, but it would be impossible without a scholarship: Her family simply couldn't afford it.

Jennifer's hard work paid off, and she received an academic scholarship requiring her to maintain at least a 3.0 average on the university's 4-point grading scale. She needed B's or better. She was very thankful and did not think it would be too difficult.

Jennifer was excited about college and really enjoyed her courses and instructors. She also enjoyed the newfound freedoms of college life. With the seemingly more relaxed class schedule and abundance of social opportunities, she found several new extracurricular activities to pursue. She felt like she had plenty of time to do it all.

She got her first exam grade 4 weeks into the semester, a D. She was shocked; she had never received a D in high school. However, she admitted to herself she had not been prepared, relying on an intense cramming session the morning of the exam. She was disappointed but was sure it was only a fluke. Unfortunately, her behavior did not change, and she finished her first semester with a B, three C's, and a D; a 2.0 GPA. The next semester was a bit better but her overall GPA was only a 2.2, and she lost her scholarship.

With the help of her academic adviser, Jennifer was ultimately able to identify specific time-management and studying strategies for improving her grades. More importantly, she renewed her personal focus and motivation. By learning to balance her academic and social lives, she was better able to prioritize the time her courses required. Her renewed focus enabled her to raise her GPA, later regain and maintain her scholarship, and ultimately graduate.

learning objectives

8.1 How do psychologists define motivation, and what are the key elements of the early instinct and drive-reduction approaches to motivation?

8.2 What are the characteristics of the three types of needs?

8.3 What are the key elements of the arousal and incentive approaches to motivation?

8.4 How do Maslow's humanistic approach and self-determination theory explain motivation?

8.5 How does drug addiction occur?

8.6 What motivates sexual behavior and its variations?

8.7 What are the three elements of emotion?

8.8 How do the James-Lange and Cannon-Bard theories of emotion differ?

8.9 What are the key elements in cognitive arousal theory, the facial feedback hypothesis, and the cognitive-mediational theory of emotion?

"How much would you pay for all the secrets of the universe? Wait, don't answer yet. You also get this six-quart covered combination spaghetti pot and clam steamer. Now, how much would you pay?"
©The New Yorker Collection 1981 Michael Maslin from cartoonbank.com All Rights Reserved.

motivation   the process by which activities are started, directed, and continued so that physical or psychological needs or wants are met.

extrinsic motivation   type of motivation in which a person performs an action because it leads to an outcome that is separate from or external to the person.

intrinsic motivation   type of motivation in which a person performs an action because the act itself is rewarding or satisfying in some internal manner.

instincts   the biologically determined and innate patterns of behavior that exist in both people and animals.

instinct approach   approach to motivation that assumes people are governed by instincts similar to those of animals.

Approaches to Understanding Motivation

8.1 How do psychologists define motivation, and what are the key elements of the early instinct and drive-reduction approaches to motivation?

Motivation is the process by which activities are started, directed, and continued so that physical or psychological needs or wants are met (Petri, 1996). The word itself comes from the Latin word *movere*, which means "to move." Motivation is what "moves" people to do the things they do. For example, when a person is relaxing in front of the television and begins to feel hungry, the physical need for food might cause the person to get up, go into the kitchen, and search for something to eat. If the hunger is great enough, the person might even cook something. The physical need of hunger caused the action (getting up), directed it (going to the kitchen), and sustained the search (finding or preparing something to eat). Hunger is only one example, of course. Loneliness may lead to calling a friend or going to a place where there are people. The desire to get ahead in life motivates many people to go to college. Pain may cause a person to seek relief in drug use. Sexual arousal may motivate a person to look for a sexual partner. Just getting out of bed in the morning is motivated by the need to keep a roof over one's head and food on the table by going to work.

There are different types of motivation. Sometimes people are driven to do something because of an external reward (or the avoidance of an unpleasant consequence), as when someone goes to work at a job to make money and avoid losing possessions such as a house or a car. **LINK** to Chapter Four: Learning, p. 133. When the motivation is external (coming from outside the self), it is called **extrinsic motivation**. In extrinsic motivation, a person performs an action because it leads to an outcome that is separate from the person (Ryan & Deci, 2000). Other examples would be giving a child money for every "A" on a report card, offering a bonus to an employee for increased performance, or tipping a server in a restaurant for good service. The child, employee, and server are motivated to work for the external or extrinsic rewards. In contrast, **intrinsic motivation** is the type of motivation in which a person performs an action because the act itself is rewarding or satisfying in some internal manner. Psychologist Teresa Amabile (Amabile et al., 1976) found that children's creativity was affected by the kind of motivation for which they worked: Extrinsic motivation decreased the degree of creativity shown in the experimental group's artwork when compared to the creativity levels of the children in the intrinsically motivated control group.

Instinct Approaches

Early attempts to understand motivation focused on the biologically determined and innate patterns of behavior called **instincts** that exist in both people and animals. Just as animals are governed by their instincts to migrate, build a nest, mate, and protect their territory, early researchers proposed that human beings may also be governed by similar instincts (James, 1890; McDougall, 1908). According to **instinct approach** theorists, in humans the instinct to reproduce is responsible for sexual behavior, and the instinct for territorial protection may be related to aggressive behavior.

William McDougall (1908) proposed a total of 18 instincts for humans, including curiosity, flight (running away), pugnacity (aggressiveness), and acquisition (gathering possessions). As the years progressed, psychologists added more and more instincts to the list until there were thousands of proposed instincts. However, none of these early theorists did much more than give names to these instincts. Although there were plenty of descriptions, such as "submissive people possess the instinct of submission," there was no attempt to explain why these instincts exist in humans, if they exist at all (Petri, 1996).

Freud's psychoanalytic theory still includes the concept of instincts that reside in the id (which contains all the basic human needs and drives). (L I N K) to Chapter Eleven: Theories of Personality and Intelligence, p. 388. Even so, instinct approaches have faded away because, although they could describe human behavior, they could not explain it. But these approaches did force psychologists to realize that some human behavior is controlled by hereditary factors. This idea remains central in the study of human behavior today. For example, research on the genetics of both cognitive and behavioral traits suggests that hereditary factors can account for more than 50 percent of the variance in some aspects of human cognition, temperament, and personality; and much of this variance is due to the influence of multiple genes or hereditary factors, not just one (Kempf & Weinberger, 2009; Plomin et al., 1994; Plomin & Spinath, 2004).

Drive-Reduction Approaches

The next approach to gain support involved the concepts of needs and drives. A **need** is a requirement for some material (such as food or water) that is essential for survival of the organism. When an organism has a need, it leads to a psychological tension as well as a physical arousal that motivates the organism to act in order to fulfill the need and reduce the tension. This tension is called a **drive** (Hull, 1943).

Drive-reduction theory proposes just this connection between internal physiological states and outward behavior. In this theory, there are two kinds of drives. **Primary drives** involve the survival needs of the body such as hunger, thirst, and sexual intercourse, whereas **acquired (secondary) drives** are learned through experience or conditioning, such as the need for money or social approval, or the need of recent former smokers to have something to put in their mouths. If this sounds familiar, it should. The concepts of primary and secondary reinforcers from Chapter Four are related to these drives. Primary reinforcers satisfy primary drives, and secondary reinforcers satisfy acquired, or secondary, drives. (L I N K) to Chapter Four: Learning, p. 133.

This theory also includes the concept of **homeostasis**, or the tendency of the body to maintain a steady state. One could think of homeostasis as the body's version of a thermostat—thermostats keep the temperature of a house at a constant level, and homeostasis does the same for the body's functions. When there is a primary drive need, the body is in a state of imbalance. This stimulates behavior that brings the body back into balance, or homeostasis. For example, if Jarrod's body needs food, he feels hunger and the state of tension/arousal associated with that need. He will then seek to restore his homeostasis by eating something, which is the behavior stimulated to reduce the hunger drive (see Figure 8.1).

Although drive-reduction theory works well to explain the actions people take to reduce tension created by needs, it does not explain all human motivation. People don't always seek to reduce their inner arousal—sometimes they seek to increase it. Bungee-jumping, parachuting as a recreation, rock climbing, and watching horror movies are all activities that increase the inner state of tension and arousal, and many people love doing these activities. Why? The answer is complex: There are different types of needs, different effects of arousal, different incentives, and different levels of importance attached to many forms of behavior. The following theories explore some of these factors in motivation.

need a requirement of some material (such as food or water) that is essential for survival of the organism.

drive a psychological tension and physical arousal arising when there is a need that motivates the organism to act in order to fulfill the need and reduce the tension.

drive-reduction theory approach to motivation that assumes behavior arises from physiological needs that cause internal drives to push the organism to satisfy the need and reduce tension and arousal.

primary drives those drives that involve needs of the body such as hunger and thirst.

acquired (secondary) drives those drives that are learned through experience or conditioning, such as the need for money or social approval.

homeostasis the tendency of the body to maintain a steady state.

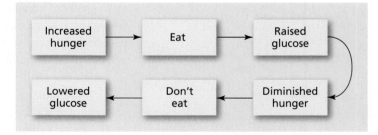

FIGURE 8.1 Homeostasis
In homeostasis, the body maintains balance in the body's physical states. For example, this diagram shows how increased hunger (a state of imbalance) prompts a person to eat. Eating increases the level of glucose (blood sugar), causing the feelings of hunger to decrease. After a period without eating, the glucose levels become low enough to stimulate the hunger drive once again, and the entire cycle is repeated.

(left) The human body needs water, especially when a person is working hard or under stress, as this man appears to be. Thirst is a survival need of the body, making it a primary drive, according to drive-reduction theory. What other kinds of needs might be primary drives?

(right) Some people are driven to do strenuous, challenging activities even when there is no physical need to do so. When a drive is acquired through learning, it is called an acquired or secondary drive. Fulfilling an acquired drive provides secondary reinforcement. What might this rock climber find reinforcing about scaling this steep cliff?

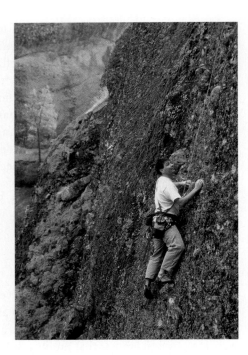

DIFFERENT STROKES FOR DIFFERENT FOLKS: NEEDS Obviously, motivation is about needs. Drive-reduction theory talks about needs, and other theories of motivation include the concept of needs. In many of these theories, most needs are the result of some inner physical drive (such as hunger or sex) that demands to be satisfied. Harvard University psychologist David C. McClelland (1961, 1987) proposed a theory of motivation that highlights the importance of three psychological needs not typically considered by the other theories: achievement, affiliation, and power.

8.2 What are the characteristics of the three types of needs?

NEED FOR ACHIEVEMENT: HOW TO SUCCEED BY EXCELLING AT EVERYTHING The **need for achievement** (abbreviated as **nAch** in McClelland's writings) involves a strong desire to succeed in attaining goals, not only realistic ones but also challenging ones. People who are high in nAch look for careers and hobbies that allow others to evaluate them because these high achievers also need to have feedback about their performance in addition to the achievement of reaching the goal. Although many of these people do become wealthy, famous, and publicly successful, others fulfill their need to achieve in ways that lead only to their own personal success, not material riches—they just want the challenge.

Achievement motivation appears to be strongly related to success in school, occupational success, and the quality and amount of what a person produces (Collins et al., 2004; Gillespie et al., 2002; Spangler, 1992). The chapter-opening story of Jennifer is a good example of the need for achievement. Jennifer's desire to improve her study habits and grades in order to keep her scholarship showed a strong desire to achieve a challenging goal.

need for achievement (nAch) a need that involves a strong desire to succeed in attaining goals, not only realistic ones but also challenging ones.

need for affiliation (nAff) the need for friendly social interactions and relationships with others.

NEED FOR AFFILIATION: POPULARITY RULES Another psychological need is for friendly social interactions and relationships with others. People high in this need, called the **need for affiliation (nAff)**, seek to be liked by others and to be held in high regard by those around them. This makes high-affiliation people good team players, whereas a person high in achievement just might run over a few team members on the way to the top. [●] Read on **MyPsychLab**

[●] Read and learn more about the need for affiliation on **MyPsychLab**

NEED FOR POWER: THE ONE WHO DIES WITH THE MOST TOYS WINS The final psychological need proposed by McClelland is the **need for power (nPow)**. Power is not about reaching a goal but about having control over other people. People high in this need would want to have influence over others and make an impact on them. They want their ideas to be the ones that are used, regardless of whether or not their ideas will lead to success. Status and prestige are important, so these people wear expensive clothes, live in expensive houses, drive fancy cars, and dine in the best restaurants. Whereas someone who is a high achiever may not need a lot of money to validate the achievement, someone who is high in the need for power typically sees the money (and cars, houses, jewelry, and other "toys") as the achievement. For the person high in the need for power, it's all about who has the most expensive "toys" in the end.

need for power (nPow) the need to have control or influence over others.

Personality and nAch: Carol Dweck's Self-Theory of Motivation

How do people get to be high achievers? ●

According to motivation and personality psychologist Carol Dweck (1999), the need for achievement is closely linked to personality factors, including a person's view of how *self* can affect the understanding of how much a person's actions can influence his or her success. (Dweck defines *self* as the beliefs one holds about one's abilities and relationships to others.) This concept is related to the much older notion of *locus of control*, in which people who assume that they have control over what happens in their lives are considered to be *internal* in locus of control, and those who feel that their lives are controlled by powerful others, luck, or fate are considered to be *external* in locus of control (A. P. MacDonald, 1970; Rotter, 1966).

Dweck has amassed a large body of empirical research, particularly in the field of education, to support the idea that people's "theories" about their own selves can affect their level of achievement motivation and their willingness to keep trying to achieve success in the face of failure (Dweck, 1986; Dweck & Elliott, 1983; Dweck & Leggett, 1988; Elliott & Dweck, 1988). According to this research, people can form one of two belief systems about intelligence, which in turn affects their motivation to achieve. Those who believe intelligence is fixed and unchangeable often demonstrate an external locus of control, leading them to give up easily or avoid situations in which they might fail—often ensuring their own failure in the process. They are prone to developing learned helplessness, the tendency to stop trying to achieve a goal because past failure has led them to believe that they cannot succeed. **LINK** to Chapter Four: Learning, pp. 150–151. Their goals involve trying to "look smart" and outperform others ("See, at least I did better than she did"). For example, a student faced with a big exam may avoid coming to class that day, even though that might mean getting an even lower score on a makeup exam.

This does not mean that students with this view of intelligence are always unsuccessful. In fact, Dweck's research (1999) suggests that students who have had a long history of successes may be most at risk for developing a learned helplessness after a big failure precisely because their previous successes have led them to believe in their own fixed intelligence. For example, a child who had never earned anything less than an A in school who then receives his first C might become depressed and refuse to do any more homework, ensuring future failure.

The other type of person believes that intelligence is changeable and can be shaped by experiences and effort in small increases, or increments. These people tend to show an internal locus of control, believing that their own actions and efforts will

How do people get to be high achievers?

Donald Trump stands triumphant at the opening of his Trump International Hotel and Tower in New York. Many people who are as wealthy as "The Donald" continue to buy new houses, businesses, clothing, and cars (among other things) even though they do not need them. Such actions are examples of the need for power. How might this need for power be expressed in a person's relationships with others, such as a spouse, employee, or friend?

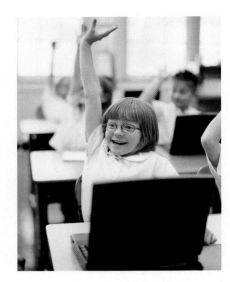

Many people are driven by a need to attain both realistic and challenging goals. This young girl seems eager to provide an answer to the teacher's question, and the teacher's positive feedback will help foster the girl's need for achievement.

improve their intelligence (Dweck & Molden, 2008). They work at developing new strategies and get involved in new tasks with the goal of increasing their "smarts." They are motivated to master tasks, and they don't allow failure to destroy their confidence in themselves or prevent them from trying again and again, using new strategies each time.

Based on this and other research, Dweck recommends that parents and teachers encourage children to value the learning process more than "looking smart" by always having the right answer (and only responding when sure of that answer, for example). Errors should not be viewed as failures but as a way to improve future performance on the road to mastering whatever the goal in question is. Essentially, this means praising efforts and the methods that children use to make those efforts, not just successes or ability. Instead of saying, "You're right, how smart you are," the parent or teacher should say something such as, "You are really thinking hard," or "That was a very clever way to think about this problem." In the past, teachers and parents have been told that praise is good and criticism is bad because it might damage a child's self-esteem. Dweck believes that constructive criticism, when linked with praise of effort and the use of strategies, will be a better influence on the child's self-esteem than endless praise that can become meaningless when given indiscriminately.

practice quiz   How much do you remember?

8.1   **8.2**

Pick the best answer.

1. The process by which activities are started, directed, and sustained to meet a person's wants is called _____.
   a. drive.
   b. incentive.
   c. motivation.
   d. instinct.

2. Liz picked out "her" desk on the first day of class. But in the second class period, someone else is sitting in "her" chosen seat. Liz's territorial attitude about that desk and her negative feelings toward the "interloper" sitting there might best be explained by which of the following?
   a. extrinsic approach
   b. intrinsic approach
   c. drive-reduction approach
   d. instinct approach

3. People high in the need for _____ want to be liked by others and are good team players.

   a. achievement
   b. affiliation
   c. power
   d. emotion

4. Ronnie believes that people are just born smart or not smart, and he thinks of himself as "not smart." As a result, Ronnie doesn't really try all that hard to succeed in school. Dweck would say that Ronnie's achievement motivation is being affected by his _____.
   a. external locus of control.
   b. internal locus of control.
   c. need for homeostasis.
   d. centralized locus of control.

Brainstorming: How might the three types of needs discussed in this section relate to the goals of many politicians? Would some needs be more important than others?

ANSWERS ON PAGE AK–1.

Arousal Approaches

8.3 What are the key elements of the arousal and incentive approaches to motivation?

Another explanation for human motivation involves the recognition of yet another type of need, the need for stimulation. A **stimulus motive** is one that appears to be unlearned but causes an increase in stimulation. Examples would be curiosity, playing, and exploration.

In **arousal theory**, people are said to have an optimal (best or ideal) level of tension. Task performances, for example, may suffer if the level of arousal is too high (such as severe test anxiety) or even if the level of arousal is too low (such as boredom). For many kinds of tasks, a moderate level of arousal seems to be best. This

stimulus motive a motive that appears to be unlearned but causes an increase in stimulation, such as curiosity.

arousal theory theory of motivation in which people are said to have an optimal (best or ideal) level of tension that they seek to maintain by increasing or decreasing stimulation.

relationship between task performance and arousal has been explained by the **Yerkes-Dodson law** (Teigen, 1994; Yerkes & Dodson, 1908), although Yerkes and Dodson formulated the law referring to stimulus intensity, not arousal level (Winton, 1987). However, this effect is modified by the difficulty level of the task: Easy tasks demand a somewhat "high-moderate" level for optimal performance, whereas difficult tasks require a "low-moderate" level. Figure 8.2 shows this relationship in graphic form.

Maintaining an optimal level of arousal, then, may involve reducing tension or creating it (Hebb, 1955). For example, husbands or wives who are underaroused may pick a fight with their spouse. Students who experience test anxiety (a high level of arousal) may seek out ways to reduce that anxiety in order to improve test performance. Students who are not anxious at all may not be motivated to study well, lowering their test performance. Many arousal theorists believe that the optimal level of arousal for most people under normal circumstances is somewhere in the middle, neither too high nor too low.

If people are supposed to be seeking a level of arousal somewhere around the middle, why do some people love to do things like bungee-jumping?

Even though the average person might require a moderate level of arousal to feel content, some people need less arousal and some need more. The person who needs more arousal is called a **sensation seeker** (Zuckerman, 1979, 1994). Sensation seekers seem to need more complex and varied sensory experiences than do other people. The need does not always have to involve danger. For example, students who travel to other countries to study tend to score higher on scales of sensation seeking than do students who stay at home (Schroth & McCormack, 2000). Sensation seeking may be related to temperament, as discussed in Chapter Seven. Table 8.1 has some sample items from a typical sensation-seeking scale.

In one study (Putnam & Stifter, 2002), researchers found evidence of sensation-seeking behavior in children as young as age 2. In this study, 90 children were studied at the ages of 6, 12, 24, and 25 months. In a test of the youngest participants, the babies were shown two sets of toys: (1) a block, a plate, and a cup; and (2) a flashing light, a toy beeper, and a wind-up dragon. The first set was considered a low-intensity stimulus, whereas the second set was labeled a high-intensity stimulus. The infants who reached out for the toys more quickly, particularly the high-intensity toys, were labeled "approach motivated."

The same children at age 2 were given an opportunity to explore a black box with a hole in one side. The children who were labeled "low approach motivated" at 6 and 12 months were unwilling to put their hands into the hole to see what might be in the box, whereas the "high-approach-motivated" children not only put their hands in but also in some cases tried to climb into the box.

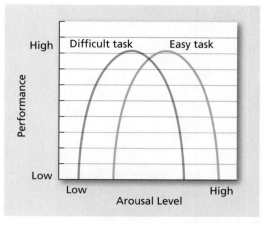

FIGURE 8.2 Arousal and Performance The optimal level of arousal for task performance depends on the difficulty of the task. We generally perform easy tasks well if we are at a high-moderate level of arousal (green) and accomplish difficult tasks well if we are at a low-moderate level (red).

If people are supposed to be seeking a level of arousal somewhere around the middle, why do some people love to do things like bungee-jumping?

---

table 8.1 **Sample Items from the Zuckerman-Kuhlman Personality Questionnaire**

SCALE ITEM	SENSATION SEEKING
I sometimes do "crazy" things just for fun.	High
I prefer friends who are excitingly unpredictable.	High
I am an impulsive person.	High
Before I begin a complicated job, I make careful plans.	Low
I usually think about what I am going to do before doing it.	Low

Source: Adapted from Zuckerman (2002).

Yerkes-Dodson law law stating performance is related to arousal; moderate levels of arousal lead to better performance than do levels of arousal that are too low or too high. This effect varies with the difficulty of the task: Easy tasks require a high-moderate level, whereas more difficult tasks require a low-moderate level.

sensation seeker someone who needs more arousal than the average person.

Does this look fun? If so, you may score relatively higher in sensation seeking.

This daring preschool boy has climbed high into this massive tree and looks as though he might try to climb higher still.

Last Thanksgiving, I had eaten about all I could. Then my aunt brought out a piece of her wonderful pumpkin pie and I couldn't resist—I ate it, even though I was not at all hungry. What makes us do things even when we don't have the drive or need to do them?

Is a sensation-seeking personality something people have when they are born? Although it is tempting to think of 6-month-old children as having little in the way of experiences that could shape their personalities, the fact is that the first six months of life are full of experiences that might affect children's choices in the future. For example, a very young infant might, while being carried, stick a hand into some place that ends up causing pain. This experience might affect that infant's willingness in the future to put his or her hand in something else through the simple learning process of operant conditioning. (L I N K) to Chapter Four: Learning, pp. 131–134. Determining the origins of sensation seeking clearly requires further research.

Incentive Approaches

Last Thanksgiving, I had eaten about all I could. Then my aunt brought out a piece of her wonderful pumpkin pie and I couldn't resist—I ate it, even though I was not at all hungry. What makes us do things even when we don't have the drive or need to do them?

It's true that sometimes there is no physical need present, yet people still eat, drink, or react as if they did have a need. Even though that piece of pie was not necessary to reduce a hunger drive, it was very rewarding, wasn't it? And on past occasions, that pie was also delicious and rewarding, so there is anticipation of that reward now. The pie, in all its glorious promise of flavor and sweetness, becomes an incentive to eat. **Incentives** are things that attract or lure people into action. In fact, the dictionary (Merriam-Webster, 2003) lists *incentive* as meaning the same thing as *motive*.

In **incentive approaches**, behavior is explained in terms of the external stimulus and its rewarding properties. These rewarding properties exist independently of any need or level of arousal and can cause people to act only upon the incentive. Thus, incentive theory is actually based, at least in part, on the principles of learning that were discussed in Chapter Four. (L I N K) to Chapter Four: Learning, pp. 131–134.

One of the earliest incentive approaches clearly demonstrates the relationship to learning, particularly the early cognitive learning theories found in the work of Edward Tolman (1932). **Expectancy-value theories** are a class of incentive theories based on the work of Tolman and others (Lewin, 1936; Rotter, 1954). In general, these theories assume that the actions of humans cannot be predicted or fully understood without understanding the beliefs, values, and importance that people attach to those beliefs and values at any given moment in time. Tolman's work with animals (the latent learning studies with rats discussed in Chapter Four, p. 000) demonstrated that organisms are capable of remembering what had happened in the past, anticipating future events, and adjusting their own actions according to those cognitive *expectancies* (a set of beliefs about what will happen in the future based on past experiences). Kurt Lewin (1936) applied these concepts to the estimated likelihood of future success or failure in his field theory of decision making. Julian Rotter's (1954) social learning theory included expectancy as one of the three factors that predict people's behavior—if Terry's past experiences with writing papers, for example, have led to an expectancy of failing to get a high grade, Terry is unlikely to take on the task of an extra term paper to earn bonus points.

By itself, the incentive approach does not explain the motivation behind all behavior. Many theorists today see motivation as a result of both the "push" of internal needs or drives and the "pull" of a rewarding external stimulus. For example, sometimes a person may actually be hungry (the push) but choose to satisfy that drive by selecting a candy bar instead of a celery stick. The candy bar has more appeal to most people, and it therefore has more "pull" than the celery. (Frankly, to most people, just about anything has more pull than celery.)

Humanistic Approaches: Maslow's Hierarchy of Needs

8.4 **How do Maslow's humanistic approach and self-determination theory explain motivation?**

A final approach to the study of motivation is based on the work of Abraham Maslow (1943, 1987). Maslow was one of the early humanistic psychologists who rejected the dominant theories of psychoanalysis and behaviorism in favor of a more positive view of human behavior ⓛⓘⓝⓚ to Chapter One: The Science of Psychology, p. 13. Maslow proposed that there are several levels of needs that a person must strive to meet before achieving the highest level of personality fulfillment. According to Maslow, **self-actualization** is the point that is seldom reached at which people have satisfied the lower needs and achieved their full human potential.

These needs include both deficiency needs and growth needs. Deficiency needs are needs of the body, such as the need for food or water, whereas growth needs are for desires such as having friends or feeling good about oneself. For a person to achieve self-actualization, which is the highest level of growth needs, the primary, basic needs must first be fulfilled. Figure 8.3 shows the typical way to represent Maslow's series of needs as a pyramid, with the most basic needs for survival at the bottom and the highest needs at the top. This type of ranking is called a hierarchy.*

The lowest level of the pyramid consists of physiological needs such as food, water, and rest. Once those needs are met, safety becomes important and involves feeling secure. Belongingness and love are the needs for friends and companions as well as to be accepted by others, and self-esteem is the need to feel that one has accomplished something good or earned the esteem of others. Although Maslow's original hierarchy included only one more level of self-actualization needs, Maslow later inserted two other needs just below this level (Maslow, 1971; Maslow & Lowery, 1998). Just above the esteem needs on the hierarchy come the cognitive needs, or the need to know and understand the world. This need is typical of an academic person who learns for the sake of gathering knowledge, and all people have a natural curiosity. Above the cognitive needs are the aesthetic needs, which include the need for order and beauty and are typical of artistic people.

incentives things that attract or lure people into action.

incentive approaches theories of motivation in which behavior is explained as a response to the external stimulus and its rewarding properties.

expectancy-value theories incentive theories that assume the actions of humans cannot be predicted or fully understood without understanding the beliefs, values, and the importance that a person attaches to those beliefs and values at any given moment in time.

self-actualization according to Maslow, the point that is seldom reached at which people have sufficiently satisfied the lower needs and achieved their full human potential.

FIGURE 8.3 Maslow's Hierarchy of Needs
Maslow proposed that human beings must fulfill the more basic needs, such as physical and security needs, before being able to fulfill the higher needs of self-actualization and transcendence.

Transcendence needs: to help others achieve self-actualization

Self-actualization needs: to find self-fulfillment and realize one's potential

Aesthetic needs: to appreciate symmetry, order, and beauty

Cognitive needs: to know, understand, and explore

Esteem needs: to achieve, be competent, gain approval and recognition

Belongingness and love needs: to be with others, be accepted, and belong

Safety needs: to feel secure and safe, out of danger

Physiological needs: to satisfy hunger, thirst, fatigue, etc.

---

*Hierarchy: a graded or ranked series.

In the movie *Castaway*, Tom Hanks's character is stranded on a deserted island. His first concern is to find something to eat and fresh water to drink—without those two things, he cannot survive. Even while he is building a crude shelter, he is still thinking about how to obtain food. Once he has those needs met, however, he gets lonely. He finds a volleyball, paints a handprint and then a crude face on it, and names it "Wilson." He talks to the volleyball as if it were a person, at first as a kind of way to talk out the things he needs to do and later as a way of staying relatively sane. The need for companionship is that strong.

Explore Maslow's Hierarchy of Needs on **MyPsychLab**

Does this theory apply universally?

peak experiences according to Maslow, times in a person's life during which self-actualization is temporarily achieved.

(It should be noted that all people also seem to like to express themselves artistically—even if it's only graffiti on a wall.) Once all these needs are met, it is possible to be concerned about self-actualization needs, or needs that help a person reach his or her full potential and capabilities as a human being. As you can see in Figure 8.3, Maslow also added a higher need called transcendence above the self-actualization needs (Maslow, 1971). Transcendence involves helping others to achieve their full potential. This aspect of Maslow's hierarchy is very similar to a stage in another theorist's work. Erik Erikson theorized a stage in personality development called generativity, in which people focus on helping the next generation through earlier crises of personality development. **LINK** to Chapter Seven: Development Across the Life Span, p. 260.

People move up the pyramid as they go through life, gaining wisdom and the knowledge of how to handle many different situations. But a shift in life's circumstances can result in a shift down to a lower need. For example, you might have a job you love and a loving family and life is good. If you lose the job, you might have to take a menial one to make ends meet. You dropped from the peak of the pyramid to the level of security, working your way back up the hierarchy. Moving up and down and then back up can occur frequently—even from one hour to the next. The times in a person's life in which self-actualization is achieved, at least temporarily, are called **peak experiences**. For Maslow, the process of growth and self-actualization is the striving to make peak experiences happen again and again. **Explore** on **MyPsychLab**

Maslow's theory has had a powerful influence on the field of management (Heil et al., 1998) and has spawned new ideas and concepts of what might be an appropriate revised hierarchy. **LINK** to Appendix B: Applied Psychology and Psychology Careers, pp. B-10–B-11. In spite of this influence, Maslow's theory is not without its critics. There are several problems with his theory, and the most serious is that there is little scientific support (Drenth et al., 1984). Like Sigmund Freud, Maslow developed his theory based on his own personal observations of people rather than any empirically gathered observations or research. Although many people report that while they were starving, they could think of nothing but food, there is anecdotal evidence in the lives of many people, some of them quite well known, that the lower needs do not have to be satisfied before moving on to a higher need (Drenth et al., 1984). For example, artists and scientists throughout history have been known to deny their own physical needs while producing great works (a self-actualization need).

● Does this theory apply universally?

Maslow's work was based on his studies of Americans. Cross-cultural research suggests that the order of needs on the hierarchy does not always hold true for other cultures, particularly those cultures with a stronger tendency than U.S. culture to avoid uncertainty, such as Greece and Japan. In those countries security needs are much stronger than self-actualization needs in determining motivation (Hofstede, 1980; Hofstede et al., 2002). This means that people in those cultures value job security more than they do job satisfaction (holding an interesting or challenging job). In countries such as Sweden and Norway that stress quality of life over what a person produces, social needs may be more important than self-actualization needs (Hofstede et al., 2002). **LINK** to Chapter Eleven: Theories of Personality and Intelligence, pp. 421–422.

Other theorists have developed and refined Maslow's hierarchy. Clayton Alderfer, for example, developed one of the more popular versions of this refinement. In his theory, the hierarchy has only three levels: *existence needs*, which include the physiological needs and basic safety needs that provide for the person's continued existence; *relatedness needs*, which include some safety issues as well as belongingness and self-esteem needs and are related to social relationships; and *growth needs*, which include some self-esteem issues and the self-actualization needs that help people develop their full potential as human beings (Alderfer, 1972). Alderfer believed that more than one need could be active at a time and that progression up and down the hierarchy is common as one type of need assumes greater importance at a particular time in a person's life than other needs.

Another modification to Maslow's original hierarchy incorporates dynamics between internal motives and environmental threats and opportunities (Kenrick et al., 2010). This revision has not been without critique and has spawned further contemplation. Some elements of Kenrick's theory have been challenged, including a questioning of its focus on evolutionary aspects instead of human cultural influences (Kesebir et al., 2010), and its removal of self-actualization from both the pinnacle of the pyramid and from the hierarchy altogether as a stand-alone motive (Peterson & Park, 2010). Just as there are many aspects to motivation, any revision or discussion of an appropriate hierarchy of needs will need to take into account a wide variety of opinions and viewpoints.

Self-Determination Theory (SDT)

Another theory of motivation that is similar to Maslow's hierarchy of needs is the **self-determination theory (SDT)** of Ryan and Deci (2000). In this theory, there are three inborn and universal needs that help people gain a complete sense of self and whole, healthy relationships with others. The three needs are *autonomy*, or the need to be in control of one's own behavior and goals (i.e., self-determination); *competence*, or the need to be able to master the challenging tasks of one's life; and *relatedness*, or the need to feel a sense of belonging, intimacy, and security in relationships with others. These needs are common in several theories of personality; the relatedness need is, of course, similar to Maslow's belongingness and love needs, and both autonomy and competence are important aspects of Erikson's theory of psychosocial personality development (Erikson, 1950, 1980). ⓛⓘⓝⓚ to Chapter Seven: Development Across the Life Span, pp. 250–251.

Ryan, Deci, and their colleagues (Deci et al., 1994; Ryan & Deci, 2000) believe that satisfying these needs can best be accomplished if the person has a supportive environment in which to develop goals and relationships with others. Such satisfaction will not only foster healthy psychological growth but also increase the individual's intrinsic motivation (actions are performed because the act is internally rewarding or satisfying). Evidence suggests that intrinsic motivation is increased or enhanced when a person not only feels competence (through experiencing positive feedback from others and succeeding at what are perceived to be challenging tasks) but also a sense of autonomy or the knowledge that his or her actions are self-determined rather than controlled by others (deCharms, 1968; Deci & Ryan, 1985).

Previous research has found a negative impact on intrinsic motivation when an external reward is given for the performance (Deci et al., 1999). A more recent paper, however, discusses the results of other studies that find negative effects only for tasks that are not interesting in and of themselves (Cameron et al., 2001). When the task itself is interesting to the person (as might be an assignment that an instructor or manager has explained in terms of its importance and future value), external rewards may increase intrinsic motivation, at least in the short term. Although this finding is intriguing, further research is needed to determine if the long-term effects of extrinsic rewards on intrinsic motivation are consistently negative, as the bulk of the research has shown up to now.

But don't we sometimes do things for both kinds of motives? ●——

There are usually elements of both intrinsic and extrinsic motives in many of the things people do. Most teachers, for example, work for money to pay bills (the extrinsic motive) but may also feel that they are helping young children to become better adults in the future, which makes the teachers feel good about themselves (the intrinsic motive).

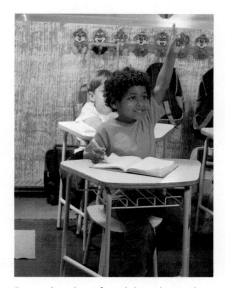

"That is the correct answer, Bill, but I'm afraid you don't win anything for it."
©The New Yorker Collection 1986 Lee Lorenz from *cartoonbank.com* All Rights Reserved.

Researchers have found that when tasks are interesting, external rewards may actually increase intrinsic motivation, at least for a short while. This boy seems actively engaged in the learning process in his classroom, suggesting that he finds the subject interesting. External rewards such as praise from the teacher or gold stars may actually enhance his intrinsic motivation to succeed in this class. How might this child's enthusiasm for learning affect the teacher's intrinsic motivation?

But don't we sometimes do things for both kinds of motives?

self-determination theory (SDT) theory of human motivation in which the social context of an action has an effect on the type of motivation existing for the action.

practice quiz how much do you remember?

8.3 8.4

Pick the best answer.

1. In the _____ approach, people are said to have an optimal level of tension.
   a. drive-reduction
   b. arousal
   c. incentive
   d. humanistic

2. Which of the following approaches to motivation has ties to the basic principles of learning and the concept of reinforcement?
   a. arousal
   b. humanistic
   c. incentive
   d. self-determination

3. The most basic needs in Maslow's hierarchy are _____ needs.
   a. esteem
   b. love
   c. safety
   d. physiological

4. Jamal gets a new toy for every good grade on his report card in first grade. Jamal is receiving _____.
   a. intrinsic motivation.
   b. extrinsic motivation.
   c. need motivation.
   d. intrinsic rewards.

Brainstorming: What motivates you while you are in this psychology course? In what ways are you intrinsically motivated? Extrinsically motivated?

ANSWERS ON PAGE AK–1.

> What motivates people to use mind-altering drugs, and what makes some people become addicted to certain drugs?

Simulate psychoactive drugs on **MyPsychLab**

Psychoactive Drugs and Addiction

● What motivates people to use mind-altering drugs, and what makes some people become addicted to certain drugs?

Many people use drugs that alter thinking, perception, memory, or some combination of those abilities called **psychoactive drugs**. Although many such drugs have practical purposes (sedation during surgery, control of pain, or controlling anxiety, for example), there are often dangers in using these drugs. One danger is their potential to create either a physical or psychological dependence, which can lead to a lifelong pattern of abuse as well as the risk of taking increasingly larger doses, leading to one of the clearest dangers of dependence: a drug overdose. Drug overdoses do not happen only with illegal drugs; even certain additives in so-called natural supplements can have a deadly effect. For example, in January 2003, Steve Bechler, a prospective pitcher for the Baltimore Orioles, died after taking three Ephedra pills on an empty stomach (Shekelle et al., 2003). Ephedra is a substance derived from a shrub found in desert areas and has been used in supplements that claim to promote weight loss.

Simulate on **MyPsychLab**

The motivation for using drugs varies and people may turn to drugs to alleviate psychological pain as well as physical pain. At some point, a line is crossed and addiction becomes a reality.

8.5 How does drug addiction occur?

Physical Dependence

Drugs that people can become physically dependent on cause the user's body to crave the drug (Abadinsky, 1989; Fleming & Barry, 1992; Pratt, 1991). After using the drug for some period of time, the body becomes unable to function normally without the drug, and the person is said to be dependent or addicted, a condition commonly called **physical dependence**.

DRUG TOLERANCE One sign of physical dependence is the development of a *drug tolerance* (Pratt, 1991). As the person continues to use the drug, larger and larger doses of the drug are needed to achieve the same initial effects of the drug.

WITHDRAWAL Another sign of a physical dependence is the user's experience of **withdrawal** when deprived of the drug. Depending on the drug, these symptoms can range from headaches, nausea, and irritability to severe pain, cramping, shaking, and dangerously elevated blood pressure. These physical sensations occur because

psychoactive drugs drugs that alter thinking, perception, and memory.

physical dependence condition occurring when a person's body becomes unable to function normally without a particular drug.

withdrawal physical symptoms that can include nausea, pain, tremors, crankiness, and high blood pressure, resulting from a lack of an addictive drug in the body systems.

the body is trying to adjust to the absence of the drug. Many users will take more of the drug to alleviate the symptoms of withdrawal, which makes the entire situation worse. This is actually an example of *negative reinforcement*, the tendency to continue a behavior that leads to the removal of or escape from unpleasant circumstances or sensations. Negative reinforcement is a very powerful motivating factor, and scores of drug-dependent users exist as living proof of that power. LINK to Chapter Four: Learning, pp. 133–134.

But not all drugs produce physical dependence, right? For example, some people say that you can't get physically dependent on marijuana. If that's true, why is it so hard for some people to quit smoking pot?

Psychological Dependence

Not all drugs cause physical dependence; some cause **psychological dependence**, or the belief that the drug is needed to continue a feeling of emotional or psychological well-being, which is a very powerful factor in continued drug use. People will continue to use the drug only because they *think* they need it. In this case, it is the rewarding properties of using the drug that cause a dependency to develop. This is an example of *positive reinforcement*, or the tendency of a behavior to strengthen when followed by pleasurable consequences. LINK to Chapter Four: Learning, pp. 133–134. Negative reinforcement is also at work here, as taking the drug will lower levels of anxiety.

Although not all drugs produce physical dependence, *any* drug can become a focus of psychological dependence. Indeed, because there is no withdrawal to go through and from which to recover, psychological dependencies can last forever. Some people who gave up smoking pot decades ago still say that the craving returns every now and then (Roffman et al., 1988).

The effect of a particular drug depends on the category to which it belongs and the particular neurotransmitter the drug affects. LINK to Chapter Two: The Biological Perspective, pp. 48–50. There are four major drug categories: **stimulants** (drugs that increase the functioning of the nervous system), **depressants** (drugs that decrease the functioning of the nervous system), **narcotics** (painkilling depressant drugs derived from the opium poppy), and **hallucinogenics** (drugs that alter perceptions and may cause hallucinations).

STIMULANTS Stimulants are a class of drugs that cause either the sympathetic division or the central nervous system (or both) to increase levels of functioning, at least temporarily. In simple terms, stimulants "speed up" the nervous system—the heart may beat faster or the brain may work faster, for example. Many of these drugs are called "uppers" for this reason.

Examples of stimulants include **amphetamines** that are synthesized (made) in laboratories rather than being found in nature. Among the amphetamines are drugs like Benzedrine, Methedrine, and Dexedrine.

People who take amphetamines often develop a physical dependency on the drug and quickly develop a tolerance. Drug tolerance ensures that the person taking these pills will find that it takes more and more pills to get the same stimulant effect. Doses can easily become toxic and deadly. Nausea, vomiting, high blood pressure, and strokes are possible, as is a condition called *amphetamine psychosis*. This condition causes addicts to become delusional (losing contact with what is real) and paranoid (Kratofil et al., 1996).

Unlike amphetamines, **cocaine** is a natural drug found in coca plant leaves. It produces feelings of euphoria (a feeling of great happiness), energy, power, and pleasure. It also deadens pain and suppresses the appetite. Cocaine is a highly dangerous drug, and some people have convulsions and may even die when using cocaine for the

One of the dangers of psychoactive drugs is that they may lead to physical or psychological dependence. Cocaine is a powerful and addictive stimulant and can be sniffed in through the nose or injected, as the man in this photograph is doing.

But not all drugs produce physical dependence, right? For example, some people say that you can't get physically dependent on marijuana. If that's true, why is it so hard for some people to quit smoking pot?

psychological dependence the feeling that a drug is needed to continue a feeling of emotional or psychological well-being.

stimulants drugs that increase the functioning of the nervous system.

depressants drugs that decrease the functioning of the nervous system.

narcotics a class of opium-related drugs that suppress the sensation of pain by binding to and stimulating the nervous system's natural receptor sites for endorphins.

hallucinogenics drugs including hallucinogens and marijuana that produce hallucinations or increased feelings of relaxation and intoxication.

amphetamines stimulants that are synthesized (made) in laboratories rather than being found in nature.

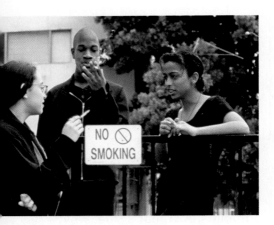

Hasn't nicotine just been the victim of a lot of bad press? After all, unlike cocaine and heroin, it's legal.

Nicotine is highly addictive, and many smokers will go to great lengths to be able to smoke—including smoking right next to the "no smoking" sign.

cocaine a natural drug derived from the leaves of the coca plant.

nicotine the active ingredient in tobacco.

caffeine a mild stimulant found in coffee, tea, and several other plant-based substances.

barbiturates depressant drugs that have a sedative effect.

benzodiazepines drugs that lower anxiety and reduce stress.

first time (Lacayo, 1995). Children born to mothers who use cocaine may have learning disabilities, hyperactivity, delayed language development, and tremors, among other symptoms (Blatt et al., 2000; Frank et al., 2001).

● Hasn't nicotine just been the victim of a lot of bad press? After all, unlike cocaine and heroin, it's legal.

Every year, nearly 430,000 people in the United States die from illnesses related to smoking cigarettes, which is more than the number of people whose deaths are caused by accidents in motor vehicles, alcohol, cocaine, heroin, and other drug abuse, AIDS, suicide, and homicide *combined* (Centers for Disease Control and Prevention [CDC], 2008). Remember, cocaine, heroin, morphine, and many other currently controlled substances or illegal drugs once used to be legal.

Nicotine is a relatively mild but nevertheless toxic stimulant, producing a slight "rush" or sense of arousal as it raises blood pressure and accelerates the heart, as well as providing a rush of sugar into the bloodstream by stimulating the release of adrenalin (Rezvani & Levin, 2001). As is the case with many stimulants, it also has a relaxing effect on most people and seems to reduce stress (Pormerleau & Pormerleau, 1994).

The physical withdrawal symptoms from nicotine abuse can be as bad as those resulting from alcohol, cocaine, or heroin abuse (Epping-Jordan et al., 1998). People don't think about nicotine as being as bad as cocaine or heroin because nicotine is legal and easily obtainable, but in terms of its addictive power, it is actually *more powerful* than heroin or alcohol (Henningfield et al., 1990).

There is one stimulant that almost everyone uses, with many using it every day. This is **caffeine**, the stimulant found in coffee, tea, most sodas, chocolate, and even many over-the-counter drugs. Caffeine is another natural substance, like cocaine and nicotine, and is found in coffee beans, tea leaves, cocoa nuts, and at least 60 other types of plants (Braun, 1996). It is a mild stimulant, helps maintain alertness, and can increase the effectiveness of some pain relievers such as aspirin. For that reason caffeine is often added to pain relievers and is the key ingredient in medications meant to keep people awake. But caffeine is also addictive for many people, and withdrawal can result in headaches, fever, sleeplessness, and other physical problems.

DEPRESSANTS Depressants slow the nervous system and are often used in medical procedures. Commonly known as the *major tranquilizers* (drugs that have a strong depressant effect) or sleeping pills, **barbiturates** are drugs that have a sedative (sleep-inducing) effect. The effects, depending on dosage levels, range from mild sedation or sleepiness to unconsciousness or coma. Overdoses can lead to death as breathing and heart action are stopped. Barbiturates are highly addictive and users can quickly develop a tolerance. Withdrawal can be as serious as convulsions, which are life threatening (Olin, 1993).

Another danger of barbiturate use is the combination of one of these drugs with alcohol, another kind of depressant drug. A person who takes a dose of barbiturates that is not deadly in and of itself may die from the interaction of that dose with alcohol. This is called a *drug interaction* and is a major contributor to many unfortunate deaths.

The *minor tranquilizers* (drugs having a relatively mild depressant effect) are called **benzodiazepines**. These drugs are used to lower anxiety and reduce stress. They are considered safer than barbiturates and are now the drugs of choice to treat sleep problems, nervousness, and anxiety. Some of the most common are Valium, Xanax, Halcion, Ativan, and Librium.

Rohypnol is a minor tranquilizer that has become notorious as the "date rape" drug. The unsuspecting victim drinks something with Rohypnol in it and will not be able to remember rape or other forms of assault (Armstrong, 1997; Gable 2004).

Alcohol The most commonly used and abused depressant is **alcohol**, the chemical resulting from fermentation or distillation of various kinds of vegetable matter. Anywhere from 10 to 20 million people in the United States suffer from alcoholism. Aside from the obvious health risks to the liver, brain, and heart, alcohol is associated with loss of work time, loss of a job, and loss of economic stability.

The dangers of abusing alcohol cannot be stressed enough. According to the National Center for Health Statistics (National Center for Health Statistics [NCHS], 2007), the number of alcohol-induced deaths (in which the body can no longer handle the alcohol) in 2003 was 20,687. Of these deaths, 12,360 were attributed to liver disease caused by alcoholism. The National Institute on Alcoholism and Alcohol Abuse (National Institute on Alcoholism and Alcohol Abuse [NIAAA], 2007) reports that from 2001 to 2002 the rate of psychiatric disorders, including alcohol and other drug abuse as well as depression and anxiety disorders, increased from 2.5 percent for a light drinker to 13.2 percent for a moderate drinker and 17.1 percent for a heavy drinker. Alcohol was involved in nearly 22.5 percent of the fatal traffic crashes for drivers under 21 and 24.8 percent of the fatal crashes for those over 21 (NIAAA, 2007).

If you are concerned about your own drinking or are worried about a friend or loved one, there is a free and very simple online assessment at this site on the Internet: **www.alcoholscreening.org.** 👁️⟩**Watch** on **MyPsychLab**

NARCOTICS *Narcotics* are a class of drugs that suppress the sensation of pain by binding to and stimulating the nervous system's natural receptor sites for endorphins, the neurotransmitters that naturally deaden pain sensations (Olin, 1993). Because they also slow down the action of the nervous system, drug interactions with alcohol and other depressants are possible—and deadly. All narcotics are a derivative of a particular plant-based substance—opium.

Opium, made from the opium poppy, has pain-relieving and euphoria-inducing properties that have been known for at least 2,000 years. Used in the 1800s as *laudanum*, it was still prescribed as *paregoric* for teething infants in the mid-1900s. In 1803 opium was developed for use as a medication by a German physician. The new form—morphine—was hailed as "God's own medicine" (Hodgson, 2001).

Morphine was thought to be a wonder drug, although its addictive qualities soon became a major concern to physicians and their patients. Morphine is still used today but in carefully controlled doses and for short periods of time.

Ironically, **heroin** was also first hailed as a wonder drug—a derivative of morphine that did not have many of the disagreeable side effects of morphine. It did not take long, however, for doctors and others to realize that heroin was even more powerfully addictive than morphine or opium. Although its use as a medicine ceased, many people still become addicted to it.

Why are morphine and heroin so addictive? ⬤

Think back to Chapter Two, which discussed the roles of endorphins in relieving pain. Opium and its derivatives, morphine and heroin, duplicate the action of endorphins so well that the nervous system slows or stops its production of the neurotransmitter. When the drug wears off, there is no protection against any kind of pain, causing the severe symptoms of withdrawal associated with these drugs. The addict who tries to quit using the drug feels such pain that the urge to use again becomes unbearable.

Methadone is also a derivative of opium but does not produce the euphoric "high" of morphine or heroin. It is used to control heroin dependency and can be taken only once a day to control the withdrawal symptoms that would otherwise follow when stopping heroin use (Kahan & Sutton, 1998). Two other drugs, buprenorphine and

alcohol the chemical resulting from fermentation or distillation of various kinds of vegetable matter.

opium substance derived from the opium poppy from which all narcotic drugs are derived.

morphine narcotic drug derived from opium, used to treat severe pain.

heroin narcotic drug derived from opium that is extremely addictive.

👁️⟩**Watch** videos on alcohol and the brain and alcoholism on **MyPsychLab**

Although many young adults see drinking as a rite of passage into adulthood, few may understand the dangers of "binge" drinking, or drinking four to five drinks within a limited amount of time. Inhibitions are lowered and poor decisions may be made, such as driving while intoxicated. Binge drinking, a popular activity on some college campuses, can also lead to alcoholism.

Why are morphine and heroin so addictive?

hallucinogens drugs that cause false sensory messages, altering the perception of reality.

LSD (lysergic acid diethylamide) powerful synthetic hallucinogen.

PCP synthesized drug now used as an animal tranquilizer that can cause stimulant, depressant, narcotic, or hallucinogenic effects.

MDMA (Ecstasy or X) designer drug that can have both stimulant and hallucinatory effects.

stimulatory hallucinogenics drugs that produce a mixture of psychomotor stimulant and hallucinogenic effects.

mescaline natural hallucinogen derived from the peyote cactus buttons.

psilocybin natural hallucinogen found in certain mushrooms.

Many of these young people enjoying themselves at a rave may be using MDMA, or Ecstasy. The dehydrating effect of the drug, together with the intense dancing and physical activity at raves like this one, can have a deadly effect on the user.

[◄●├Read and learn more about other dangerous synthetic drugs on **MyPsychLab**

naltrexone, are also used to treat opiate addictions (Kakko et al., 2003; Ward et al., 1999). Eventually, as the addicted person is weaned from these drugs, the natural endorphin system starts to normalize. This means that one does not have to take these other drugs forever.

HALLUCINOGENS The last major category of drugs is the **hallucinogenics**, a category including both hallucinogens and marijuana. Hallucinogenics actually cause the brain to alter its interpretation of sensations (Olin, 1993) and can produce sensory distortions very similar to the disorder *synesthesia*, Ⓛ Ⓘ Ⓝ Ⓚ to Chapter Three: Sensation and Perception, p. 81, in which sensations cross over each other—colors have sound, sounds have smells, and so on. False sensory perceptions, called *hallucinations*, are often experienced, especially with the more powerful hallucinogens. Although not usually associated with physical addiction, hallucinogenics can become psychologically addictive.

LSD, or **lysergic acid diethylamide**, is a hallucinogen synthesized from a grain fungus called *ergot*. Ergot fungus commonly grows on rye grain but can be found on other grains as well. First manufactured in 1938, LSD is one of the most potent, or powerful, hallucinogens (Johnston et al., 2007; Lee & Shlain, 1986). It takes only a very tiny drop of LSD to achieve a "high."

People who take LSD usually do so to get that high feeling. But the fact is that LSD takes people out of the real world and dumps them into a world of the brain's creation. "Bad trips" are quite common, and there is no way to control what kind of "trip" the brain is going to decide to take.

Another synthesized hallucinogen was found to be so dangerous that it became useful only in veterinary medicine as a tranquilizer. The drug is **PCP** (which stands for *p*henyl *c*yclohexyl *p*iperidine, a name that is often contracted as *phencyclidine*) and can have many different effects. Depending on the dosage, it can be a hallucinogen, stimulant, depressant, or analgesic (painkilling) drug. PCP can lead to acts of violence against others or suicide (Brecher et al., 1988; Cami et al., 2000; Johnston et al., 2007).

MDMA is technically an amphetamine but is capable of producing hallucinations as well. In fact, both MDMA (a "designer drug" known on the streets as **Ecstasy** or simply **X**) and PCP are now classified as **stimulatory hallucinogenics**—drugs that produce a mixture of psychomotor stimulant and hallucinogenic effects (National Institute on Drug Abuse, 2006; Shuglin, 1986). Although many users of MDMA believe that it is relatively harmless, in actuality it can be deadly. MDMA is a common drug at "raves" or all-night dance parties. Among other things, this drug dehydrates the body and raises body temperature, so it is very important that someone taking this drug drink enough water. But excessive drinking of water can also lead to coma and death: Excess fluid can disrupt the salt content of body tissue, making it impossible for all body parts to function properly. Adding to the risk is the possibility that Ecstasy users are also consuming alcohol; that interaction increases the dehydration and rise in body temperature (Leccese et al., 2000). [◄●├Read on **MyPsychLab**

A number of substances found in nature can produce hallucinogenic effects. Naturally produced drugs can still be dangerous especially when performing tasks that require a clear head and focused attention.

Mescaline comes from the buttons found on the peyote cactus and has long been a part of many Native American religious and spiritual rituals. Its hallucinogenic effects can last longer than those of LSD (Aghajanian & Marek, 1999; Johnston et al., 2007; Lyvers, 2003). **Psilocybin** (sigh-luh-SIGH-bun) is another naturally occurring hallucinogen, contained in a certain kind of mushroom, often referred to as "magic mushrooms." Like mescaline, it has also been used in similar rituals by several native cultures (Aghajanian & Marek, 1999; Griffiths et al., 2006).

Is using mescaline or psilocybin addictive? •───────

Is using mescaline or psilocybin addictive?

Neither mescaline nor psilocybin has been shown to create physical dependency, but as with any psychoactive drug, psychological dependency is possible (Lyvers, 2003). Eating psilocybin has been linked, however, to a psychiatric disorder called hallucinogen-persisting perception disorder (HPPD), as has marijuana (Espiard et al., 2005).

MARIJUANA One of the best known and most commonly abused of the hallucinogenic drugs (Hall & Degenhardt, 2009), **marijuana** (also called *pot* or *weed*) comes from the leaves and flowers of the hemp plant called *cannabis sativa*. (*Hashish* is the concentrated substance made by scraping the resin from these leaves, and both marijuana and hashish contain *cannabinoids*.) The most psychoactive cannabinoid, and the active ingredient in marijuana, is *tetrahydrocannabinol* (THC). Marijuana is best known for its ability to produce a sense of well-being, mild intoxication, and mild sensory distortions or hallucinations (Olin, 1993; Tart, 1970).

The effects of marijuana are mild relative to the other hallucinogens. Most people do report a feeling of mild euphoria and relaxation, along with an altered sense of time and mild visual distortions. Higher doses can lead to hallucinations, delusions, and the all-too-common paranoia. While most studies of marijuana's effects have concluded that marijuana does not produce physical dependency or physical withdrawal symptoms, newer studies suggest that long-term marijuana use can produce signs of withdrawal such as irritability, memory difficulties, sleep difficulties, and increased aggression (Block & Ghoneim, 1993; Budney et al., 2001; Kouri et al., 1999; Pope et al., 2001). A recent study of the long-term effects of marijuana use has also correlated smoking marijuana with an increased risk of psychotic behavior, with a greater risk for heavier users (Moore et al., 2007).

Marijuana smokers also get considerably more exposure to *carcinogens* (cancer-causing substances), carbon dioxide, and tar than do the smokers of ordinary cigarettes. This is partly caused by the higher content of these substances in marijuana and partly by the pot smoker's tendency to inhale more deeply and hold the smoke longer than tobacco smokers do (Wu et al., 1988).

Table 8.2 summarizes the various types of drugs, their common names, and their effects on human behavior.

marijuana mild hallucinogen (also known as *pot* or *weed*) derived from the leaves and flowers of a particular type of hemp plant.

table 8.2 How Drugs Affect Consciousness

DRUG CLASSIFICATION	COMMON NAME	MAIN EFFECT	ADVERSE EFFECTS
Depressants			
Alcohol	Beer, wine, spirits	Relaxation	Alcoholism, health problems, depression, increased risk of accidents, death
Barbiturates (tranquilizers)	Nembutal, Seconal		Addiction, brain damage, death
Stimulants			
Amphetamines	Methamphetamine, speed, Ritalin, Dexedrine	Stimulation, excitement	Risk of addiction, stroke, fatal heart problems, psychosis
Cocaine	Cocaine, crack		Risk of addiction, stroke, fatal heart problems, psychosis
Nicotine	Tobacco		Addiction, cancer
Caffeine	Coffee, tea		Caffeinism, high blood pressure
Narcotics			
Opiates	Morphine, heroin	Euphoria	Addiction, death
Hallucinogens	Marijuana, hashish, LSD, Ecstasy	Distorted consciousness, altered perception	Possibly permanent memory problems, bad "trips," suicide, overdose, and death

practice quiz　How much do you remember?

Pick the best answer.

1. What are two signs of physical dependency?
   a. drug tolerance and psychological cravings
   b. psychological cravings and withdrawal
   c. drug tolerance and withdrawal
   d. psychological cravings and nausea

2. Larger and larger doses of amphetamines can lead to a severe mental disturbance and paranoia called _____.
   a. amphetamine neurosis.
   b. amphetamine psychosis.
   c. amphetaminism.
   d. amphetamine toxicity.

3. The "date rape" drug, Rohypnol, is one of the _____.
   a. major tranquilizers.
   b. barbiturates.
   c. minor tranquilizers.
   d. opiates.

4. Of the following, which comes from the peyote cactus?
   a. mescaline
   b. psilocybin
   c. marijuana
   d. ergot

ANSWERS ON PAGE AK–1.

Sexual Motivation

8.6　What motivates sexual behavior and its variations?

The study of sexual behavior is not the study of the sex act but rather when, with whom, and under what circumstances sexual acts take place. Although other attempts were made to study human sexual behavior before the mid-twentieth-century studies of Alfred Kinsey (Kinsey et al., 1948; Kinsey et al., 1953), his original work remains an important source of information concerning the different ways in which people engage in the sex act. A well-received movie based on Kinsey's life and work was released in the United States in 2004. Remarkably, even more than half a century later and well into the sexual revolution, Kinsey's work is still so controversial that many movie theaters in the United States refused to show the film.

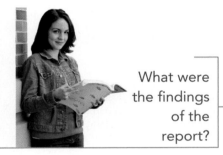

What were the findings of the report?

● What were the findings of the report?

THE KINSEY STUDY　In 1948, zoologist Alfred Kinsey published a controversial report on the results of a massive survey of sexual behavior he had collected over 10 years (Kinsey et al., 1948). His findings concerning the frequency of behavior such as masturbation, anal sex, and premarital sex rocked many people, who were apparently not ready to believe that so many people had tried alternative sexual behaviors. Kinsey believed that sexual orientation was not an either/or situation in which one is either completely heterosexual or completely homosexual but instead that sexual orientation is on a continuum* with some people falling at either extreme and some falling closer to the middle. The idea that there were many people who fit into that middle range of sexual orientation was shocking and, for many, unbelievable.

Kinsey used highly trained interviewers who conducted face-to-face interviews with the participants, who were all male in the original study. A later survey was published in 1953 that dealt exclusively with females (Kinsey et al., 1953). The participants were volunteers supposedly from both rural and urban areas and from different socioeconomic, religious, and educational backgrounds. In reality, a large portion of

---

*Continuum: a sequence of values, elements, or behavior that varies by small degrees.

Alfred Kinsey conducted many of his interviews face-to-face, as seen here. How might having to answer questions about one's sexual behavior be affected by Kinsey's presence?

the participants were well-educated, urban, young Protestants. Table 8.3 lists some of the more interesting findings of the Kinsey study.

Although Kinsey's data are still quoted in many discussions of sexual behavior, his original surveys were far from perfect. As stated earlier, the participants were almost exclusively white, middle class, and college educated. Older people, those who lived in rural regions, and less educated people were not well represented. Some critics claimed that Kinsey gave far more attention to sexual behavior that was considered unusual or abnormal than he did to "normal" sexual behavior (Geddes, 1954). Also, Kinsey's surveys were no less susceptible to the exaggerations, falsifications, and errors of any method using self-report techniques. Finally, a face-to-face interview might cause some people being interviewed to be inhibited about admitting to certain kinds of sexual behavior, or others might exaggerate wildly, increasing the likelihood of inaccurate data.

---

table 8.3   Key Findings from Kinsey's Sexual Behavior Surveys

Males reporting anal sex with spouse: 11 percent.

Nearly 46 percent of males had bisexual experiences.

Between 6 and 14 percent of females had bisexual experiences.

Whereas nearly 21 percent of the males had experienced intercourse at age 16, only 6 percent of females had done so.

Males reporting premarital sex: 67 to 98 percent (varied by economic level).

Females reporting premarital sex: 50 percent.

Nearly 50 percent of all married males had some extramarital experiences, whereas 26 percent of married females had extramarital experiences.

About 10 percent of males were predominantly homosexual.

Between 2 and 6 percent of females were predominantly homosexual.

Males who reported masturbating: 92 percent.

Females who reported masturbating: 62 percent.

Source: Gebhard and Johnson (1979/1998).

---

table 8.4   Findings from the Janus Report

Full sexual relations by age 14: men—19 percent, women—7.5 percent.

Overall, nearly 80 percent of men and 70 percent of women said they had masturbated, with about a quarter to a third saying that it was rarely.

At least one homosexual experience: 22 percent of men, 17 percent of women.

Males reporting premarital sex: 67 percent.

Females reporting premarital sex: 46 percent.

About 40 percent of men and about 26 percent of women reported having had at least one extramarital affair.

About 9 percent of males were predominantly homosexual.

About 5 percent of females were predominantly homosexual.

Source: Janus and Janus (1993).

---

sexual deviance behavior that is unacceptable according to societal norms and expectations.

sexual orientation a person's sexual attraction and affection for members of either the opposite or the same sex.

THE JANUS REPORT In 1993, Dr. Samuel S. Janus and Dr. Cynthia L. Janus published the results of the first large-scale study of human sexual behavior since those of Kinsey and colleagues (1948) and Masters and Johnson (1966). This national survey, begun in 1983, sampled 3,000 people from all 48 mainland states. Professors in the fields of sociology, psychology, psychiatry, history, biology, and political science received special training in the survey method and supervised experienced graduate student researchers who also collected survey data. Data were collected through interviews and mass questionnaires. Survey respondents ranged in age from 18 to over 65 and represented all levels of marital status, educational backgrounds, and geographical regions in the United States.

One finding of this massive survey was that nearly 80 percent of men and 70 percent of women had masturbated (although about a fourth to a third stated that this occurred rarely). Other responses indicated that 19 percent of men and nearly 8 percent of women had been involved in full sexual intercourse by age 14. Premarital sex was more commonly reported in men than in women (67 percent for males, 46 percent for females), and men were nearly twice as likely as women to report having had at least one extramarital affair. Whereas more than a fifth of the male respondents and only slightly fewer female respondents reported having at least one homosexual experience, only 9 percent of males and 5 percent of females identified themselves as predominantly homosexual.

Table 8.4 summarizes some of the findings from this massive survey. In addition to the topics in the table, *The Janus Report on Sexual Behavior* also looked at **sexual deviance** (sexual behavior that is unacceptable according to social norms), single people's sexual behavior, marriage, divorce, the decision to have children, and the effect of religion, political orientation, education, wealth, and geographical region on sexual behavior. 📖 Read on **MyPsychLab**

A more recent survey highlights the fact that age is not necessarily a barrier to being sexually active. The survey of over 3,000 people aged 57 to 85 found that many people are sexually active well into their eighties (Lindau et al., 2007). The most common barriers to sexual activity are health problems or lack of a partner rather than lack of desire.

📖 Read and learn more about sexual behavior on **MyPsychLab**

Sexual Orientation

What makes some people attracted to the same sex?

The term **sexual orientation** refers to a person's sexual attraction and affection for members of either the opposite or the same sex. One of the more important questions that researchers are trying to answer is whether sexual orientation is the product of learning and experience or whether it is biological in origin.

HETEROSEXUAL The most common sexual orientation is **heterosexual**, in which people are sexually attracted to members of the opposite physical sex, as in a man being attracted to a woman or vice versa. (The Greek word *hetero* means "other," so *heterosexual* means "other sexual" or attraction for the other sex.) Heterosexuality is a socially acceptable form of sexual behavior in all cultures.

HOMOSEXUAL It is difficult to get an accurate percentage for **homosexual** orientation, or sexual attraction to members of one's own sex. (The Greek word *homo* means "same.") The problem concerns the discrimination, prejudice, and mistreatment that homosexual people face in most cultures, making it more likely that a homosexual person will lie about his or her sexual orientation to avoid such negative treatment. The most recent surveys estimate that about 9 percent of men and 5 percent of women are homosexuals, meaning that their sexual orientations are exclusively or predominantly homosexual (Janus & Janus, 1993). However, the same surveys indicate that 22 percent of men and 17 percent of women have had at least one homosexual experience (see Table 8.4). Apparently, it is not unusual for people to experiment with alternative sexual behavior while deciding their true sexual identity.

If people have had homosexual as well as heterosexual experiences, does that make them bisexuals?

BISEXUAL A person who is **bisexual** may be either male or female and is attracted to both sexes. Although, as stated in the survey results, a portion of the population has had experiences with both sexes, this does not make these people bisexual, except in the most literal sense, and only for that period of experimentation. In other words, people can have bisexual experiences but are not bisexuals unless this becomes their preferred, stable, sexual identity.

Bisexual people do not necessarily have relationships with both men and women at the same time and may vary in the degree of attraction to one sex or the other over time. Many bisexuals may not act on their desires but instead have a long-term monogamous relationship with only one partner.

DEVELOPMENT OF SEXUAL ORIENTATION Although heterosexuality may be socially acceptable across cultures, in various cultures homosexuality and bisexuality are not considered acceptable and so people of those orientations have faced prejudice, discrimination, harassment, and much worse. Although attitudes in these cultures are becoming more positive (Loftus, 2001; Tucker & Potocky-Tripodi, 2006), full acceptance of alternatives to heterosexuality is still a long way off.

Is sexual orientation a product of the environment, biology, or both?

This is a very controversial issue for both heterosexuals and homosexuals (Diamond, 1995). If homosexuality is a product of upbringing and environmental experiences, it can be assumed to be a behavior that can be changed, placing a burden of choice to be "normal" or "abnormal" squarely on the shoulders of homosexual people. If it is biological, either through genetic influences or hormonal influences during pregnancy, then it can be seen as a behavior that is no more a choice than whether the infant is born a male or a female. The implications of homosexuality

heterosexual person attracted to the opposite sex.

homosexual person attracted to the same sex.

bisexual person attracted to both men and women.

If people have had homosexual as well as heterosexual experiences, does that make them bisexuals?

Is sexual orientation a product of environment, biology, or both?

Homosexuality is a sexual orientation that has faced discrimination and prejudice in many cultures. Shelly Bailes and Ellen Pontac, partners for 34 years, highlight the fact that their "coupleness" and a sense of commitment are not limited to heterosexual pairs alone.

as biological lead to some volatile* issues: If it is not a choice or a learned behavior pattern, then society will no longer be able to expect or demand that homosexuals change their sexual behavior or orientation. Homosexuality then becomes an issue of diversity rather than one of socially unacceptable behavior. A survey of gay and bisexual college students (Elliott & Brantley, 1997) revealed that while a few of these young adults knew of their orientation as early as grade school, most were aware by high school or shortly after.

In the past several decades, a large body of research in the areas of biological differences in the brains of heterosexual and homosexual males, genetic influences on sexual orientation, and even prenatal influences on sexual orientation has been amassed. One of the earliest studies, for example, found that severe stress experienced by pregnant women during the second trimester of pregnancy (the time during which the sexual differences in genitalia are formed) results in a significantly higher chance of any male children becoming homosexual in orientation (Ellis et al., 1988). Another study found that homosexual men and heterosexual women respond similarly (and quite differently than heterosexual men) to a testosterone-based pheromone (glandular chemical) that is secreted in perspiration (Savic et al., 2005).

Birth order has also been the subject of research in this area, with studies suggesting that the more older brothers a man has, the more likely the younger man is to be homosexual in orientation (Blanchard, 2001; McConaghy et al., 2006). The hypothesis is that with each male birth, the mother of these males develops a kind of "antibody" effect against the Y chromosome and these antibodies pass through the placenta and affect the sexual orientation of the later born males.

Finally, a recent study used neuroimaging techniques on heterosexual men and women and homosexual men and women. It found that the *heterosexual* men and *homosexual* women (both attracted to women, remember) seemed neurologically similar; while *homosexual* men and *heterosexual* women (both attracted to males) were neurologically similar (Savic & Lindström, 2008).

The evidence for genetic influences on sexual orientation is increasingly convincing. In studies of male and female homosexuals who have identical twins, fraternal twins, or adopted siblings, researchers found that 52 percent of the identical twin siblings were also gay, compared to 22 percent of the fraternal twins and only 11 percent of the adopted brothers and sisters (Bailey & Pillard, 1991). In a similar study with lesbian women only, 48 percent of identical twins were also gay compared to 16 percent of the fraternal twins and 6 percent of the adopted siblings (Bailey et al., 1993). Other research along similar lines has supported these findings (Bailey et al., 2000; Dawood et al., 2000). However, these findings, too, should be interpreted with caution. Twin studies are difficult to conduct without the influence of environment on behavior. Even twins who are raised apart tend to be reared in similar environments, so that the influence of learning and experience on sexual orientation cannot be entirely ruled out.

Some research suggests that homosexuality may be transmitted by genes carried on the X chromosome, which is passed from mother to son but not from father to son. In 33 out of 40 homosexual brothers, Hamer and colleagues (Hamer et al., 1993) found an area on the X chromosome (in a location called Xq28) that contains several hundred genes that the homosexual brothers had in common in every case, even though other genes on that chromosome were different. This was taken as evidence that the brothers had both inherited a set of genes, donated on

*Volatile: explosive.

the mother's X chromosome, which might be responsible for their sexual orientation. These findings have since been supported in other research (Hu et al., 1994; Turner, 1995).

One of the most common behavioral findings about male homosexuals is that they are consistently feminine as children, according to developmental psychologist J. Michael Bailey (Bailey & Zucker, 1995). Bailey has determined that about three-fourths of feminine boys (defined as boys who are uninterested in sports or rough play, have a desire to be girls, or have a reputation as a "sissy") are homosexual as adults, a far greater rate than in the general population of males. Bailey and colleague Ken Zucker interpret these findings as further support for the biological foundations of sexual orientation. Of course, those differences in childhood behavior could also have been the result of attention and other forms of reinforcement from the social environment. It is simply very difficult to separate environmental from biological influences on any aspect of behavior.

One thing is certain: The issue of what causes sexual orientation will continue to generate research and controversy for a long time to come.

Some scientists have wondered why homosexuality still exists, because from an evolutionary point of view—if it is genetic—the genes for homosexuality should have been removed from the gene pool long ago. The following special section takes a look at this issue.

issues in psychology
....
What Is the Evolutionary Purpose of Homosexuality?

Homosexuals do not often reproduce, so why hasn't the trait gone away? One recent theory has to do with something called the "kin selection hypothesis." Even though a homosexual member of a family may not reproduce himself or herself, by nurturing other family members such as nieces and nephews, they would be helping to continue many of their own genes through those kin (Iemmola & Camperio Ciani, 2008; Rahman & Hull, 2005). In Samoa, researchers Paul Vasey and Doug VanderLaan (Vasey & VanderLaan, 2010) studied the *fa'afafine*, men who prefer men as sexual partners and are accepted within that culture as neither man nor woman, much as the winkte in Lakota culture. Seeking to determine whether the kin selection hypothesis was a valid hypothesis in this society, the researchers gave fa'afafine, women, and heterosexual men in this culture a survey to measure their willingness to help nieces and nephews in various ways, as well as their willingness to do these same things for unrelated children. The survey results strongly support the kin selection hypothesis, with the fa'afafine far more likely than the women or heterosexual men to help their own kin rather than children in general.

QUESTIONS FOR FURTHER DISCUSSION

1. Samoan culture is not like Western culture. Would the kin selection hypothesis work in the United States to explain homosexuality's continued existence?

2. How do Western homosexual men and women transmit or protect their own genetic material?

....

practice quiz How much do you remember?

8.6

Pick the best answer.

1. In Kinsey's original data, more _____ than _____ reported having bisexual experiences.
   a. homosexuals; heterosexuals
   b. heterosexuals; homosexuals
   c. women; men
   d. men; women

2. Which group was NOT one of the groups poorly represented in the Kinsey study?
   a. older people
   b. white, middle class
   c. people with little education
   d. people living in rural areas

3. Compared to the Kinsey data, the data from the Janus Report revealed the age of the first sexual experience for about 20 percent of the men and 8 percent of the women to be _____.

   a. 14.   b. 16.   c. 17.   d. 12.

4. The Savic et al. 2005 study found that homosexual men responded to a pheromone in the same way as
   a. heterosexual men
   b. transsexual men
   c. heterosexual women
   d. homosexual women

5. Which of the following is NOT one of the possible causes of homosexuality, according to research?
   a. birth order
   b. abuse
   c. severe stress in the mother's second trimester of pregnancy
   d. genetics

ANSWERS ON PAGE AK–2

The first section of this chapter has looked at the various motives—achievement, power, and sex, to name a few—that drive human behavior. But people do more than just behave—feelings accompany every human action. The last section of this chapter explores the world of human emotions and how those emotions are connected to both thinking and actions.

What part does the way we feel about things play in our daily activities—what exactly causes feelings?

Emotion

What part does the way we feel about things play in all of our daily activities—what exactly causes feelings?

Human beings are full of feelings, or emotions, and although emotions may be internal processes, there are outward physical signs of what people are feeling.

The Three Elements of Emotion

8.7 What are the three elements of emotion?

The Latin word meaning "to move" is the source of both words used in this chapter over and over again—*motive* and *emotion*. **Emotion** can be defined as the "feeling" aspect of consciousness, characterized by three elements: a certain physical arousal, a certain behavior that reveals the feeling to the outside world, and an inner awareness of feelings.

THE PHYSIOLOGY OF EMOTION Physically, when a person experiences an emotion, an arousal is created by the sympathetic nervous system. **LINK** to Chapter Two: The Biological Perspective, pp. 55–56. The heart rate increases, breathing becomes more rapid, the pupils dilate, and the mouth may become dry. Think about the last time you were angry and then about the last time you were frightened. Weren't the physical symptoms pretty similar? Although facial expressions do differ among various emotional responses (Ekman, 1980; Ekman & Friesen, 1978; Ekman et al., 1969), emotions are difficult to distinguish from one another on the basis of outward bodily reactions alone. For example, it is quite easy to mistake a person who is actually afraid or angry as being aroused if the person's face is not clearly visible, which can lead to much miscommunication and misunderstanding. However, in the laboratory using devices to measure the heart rate, blood pressure, and skin temperature, researchers

emotion the "feeling" aspect of consciousness, characterized by a certain physical arousal, a certain behavior that reveals the emotion to the outside world, and an inner awareness of feelings.

have found that different emotions may be associated with different physiological reactions: Fear is associated with a decrease in skin temperature, whereas anger is associated with an increase in skin temperature and a greater increase in blood pressure (Larsen et al., 2008; Levenson, 1992; Levenson et al., 1992).

Which parts of the brain are involved in various aspects of emotion? As discussed in Chapter Two, the *amygdala*, a small area located within the limbic system on each side of the brain, is associated with fear in both humans and animals (Davis & Whalen, 2001; Fanselow & Gale, 2003) and is also involved in the facial expressions of human emotions (Morris et al., 1998). When the amygdala is damaged in rats, they cannot be classically conditioned to fear new objects—they apparently cannot remember to be afraid (Davidson et al., 2000; Fanselow & Gale, 2003). In humans, damage to the amygdala has been associated with similar effects (LaBar et al., 1995) and with impairment of the ability to determine emotions from looking at the facial expressions of others (Adolphs & Tranel, 2003).

Research now suggests that emotional stimuli travel to the amygdala by both a fast, crude "low road" (subcortical) and a slower but more involved cortical "high road" (LeDoux, 1996, 2007; LeDoux & Phelps, 2008). The direct route allows for quick responses to stimuli that are possibly dangerous, sometimes before we actually know what the stimuli are. However, with the awareness provided by the indirect cortical route (specifically, processing by the prefrontal cortex), we can override the direct route and take control of our emotional responses (LeDoux, 1996; LeDoux & Phelps, 2008; Öhman, 2008). It is possible that the direct route may be the primary processing pathway for individuals with emotional disorders (L I N K to Chapter Twelve: Psychological Disorders, pp. 440–445) and the indirect, cortical pathway is not able to override the processing initiated by the direct route. This would result in difficulty or inability to control our emotions, or inability to extinguish fears we've already acquired (LeDoux, 1996; LeDoux & Phelps, 2008).

Emotions even work differently depending on which side of the brain is involved. ●

One area of investigation has been the frontal lobes. Researchers have found that positive emotions are associated with the left frontal lobe of the brain, whereas negative feelings such as sadness, anxiety, and depression seem to be a function of the right frontal lobe (R. J. Davidson, 2003; Geschwind & Iacoboni, 2007; Heilman, 2002). In studies where the electrical activity of the brain has been tracked using an electroencephalograph, L I N K to Chapter Two: The Biological Perspective, pp. 62–63, left frontal lobe activation has been associated with pleasant emotions while right frontal lobe activity has been associated with negative emotional states (R. J. Davidson, 2003). Furthermore, increased left frontal lobe activity has been found in individuals trained in meditation, and for the participants in this study, greater left frontal lobe activity was accompanied by a reduction in their anxiety as well as a boost in their immune system (R. J. Davidson et al., 2003).

The ability to interpret the facial expressions of others as a particular emotion also seems to be a function of one side of the brain more than the other. Researchers have found that when people are asked to identify the emotion on another person's face, the right hemisphere is more active than the left, particularly in women (Voyer & Rodgers, 2002). This difference begins weakly in childhood but increases in adulthood, with children being less able to identify negative emotions as well as positive emotions when compared to adults (Barth & Boles, 1999; Lane et al., 1995). This finding is consistent with early research that assigns the recognition of faces to the right hemisphere (Berent, 1977; Ellis, 1983).

Other types of emotional processing involve a variety of other brain areas. Different brain areas take primary roles based on the different ways you use to control your emotions, but there is a degree of overlap across several of the strategies. For

Emotions even work differently depending on which side of the brain is involved.

⊙▸ Simulate recognizing facial expressions of emotion on **MyPsychLab**

example, some common strategies for regulating one's emotions include distraction, reappraisal, and controlling the influence of emotions on decision making. All three of these strategies take advantage of the lateral prefrontal cortex and anterior cingulate cortex and, as you might expect from the earlier discussion, the amygdala also comes into play (J. S. Beer, 2009). However, distraction appears to be supported by activity in the anterior cingulate cortex, and reappraisal is supported by activity in the lateral orbitofrontal cortex; both are accompanied by lower activity in the amygdala (J. S. Beer, 2009). ⊙▸ Simulate on **MyPsychLab**

THE BEHAVIOR OF EMOTION: EMOTIONAL EXPRESSION How do people behave when they are in the grip of an emotion? Facial expressions, body movements, and actions indicate to others how a person feels. Frowns, smiles, and sad expressions combine with hand gestures, the turning of one's body, and spoken words to produce an understanding of emotion. People fight, run, kiss, and yell along with countless other actions stemming from the emotions they feel.

Facial expressions can vary across different cultures, although some aspects of facial expression seem to be universal. (See Figure 8.4 for some examples of universal facial expressions.) Charles Darwin (1898) was one of the first to theorize that emotions were a product of evolution and, therefore, universal: all human beings, no matter what their culture, would show the same facial expression because the facial muscles evolved to communicate specific information to onlookers. For example, an angry face would signal to onlookers that they should act submissively or expect a fight. Darwin's ideas were not in line with the behaviorist movement of the early and middle twentieth century, which promoted environment rather than heredity as the cause of behavior. Nonetheless, other researchers have since found evidence of a

FIGURE 8.4 Facial Expressions of Emotion
Facial expressions appear to be universal. For example, these faces are interpreted as showing (a) anger, (b) fear, (c) disgust, (d) happiness, (e) surprise, and (f) sadness by people of cultures all over the world. Although the situations that cause these emotions may differ from culture to culture, the expression of particular emotions remains strikingly the same.

universal nature in at least seven basic emotions, giving more support to the evolutionary perspective within psychology (Ekman, 1973; Ekman & Friesen, 1969, 1971). **LINK** to Chapter One: The Science of Psychology, p. 15. Even children who are blind from birth can produce the appropriate facial expressions for any given situation without ever having witnessed those expressions on others. This finding strongly supports the idea that emotional expressions have their basis in biology rather than in learning (Charlesworth & Kreutzer, 1973; Fulcher, 1942).

In their research, Ekman and Friesen found that people of many different cultures (Japanese, Europeans, Americans, and even the Fore tribe of New Guinea) can consistently recognize at least seven facial expressions: anger, fear, disgust, happiness, surprise, sadness, and contempt (Ekman & Friesen, 1969, 1971). Although the emotions and the related facial expressions appear to be universal, exactly when, where, and how an emotion is expressed may be determined by the culture. **Display rules** that can vary from culture to culture (Ekman, 1973; Ekman & Friesen, 1969) are learned ways of controlling displays of emotion in social settings. For example, Japanese people have strict social rules about showing emotion in public situations—they simply do not show emotion, remaining cool, calm, and collected, at least on the *outside*. But in a more private situation, such as a parent scolding a child within the home, the adult's facial expression would easily be recognized as "angry" by people of any culture. The emotion is universal, and the way it is expressed on the face is universal; whether it is expressed or displayed, however, depends on the learned cultural rules for displaying emotion.

Display rules are different between cultures that are individualistic (placing the importance of the individual above the social group) and those that are collectivistic (placing the importance of the social group above that of the individual). Whereas the culture of the United States is individualistic, for example, the culture of Japan is collectivistic. At least part of the difference between the two types of display rules may be due to these cultural differences (Edelmann & Iwawaki, 1987; Hofstede, 1980; Hofstede et al., 2002). **LINK** to Chapter Eleven: Theories of Personality and Intelligence, pp. 421–422.

Display rules are also different for males and females. Researchers looking at the display rules of boys and girls found that boys are reluctant to talk about feelings in a social setting, whereas girls are expected and encouraged to do so (Polce-Lynch et al., 1998). With adults, researchers looking at the expression of anger in the workplace found that women are generally less willing than men to express negative emotions, although factors such as status complicate the findings somewhat (Domagalski & Steelman, 2007).

SUBJECTIVE EXPERIENCE: LABELING EMOTION The third element of emotion is interpreting the subjective feeling by giving it a label: anger, fear, disgust, happiness, sadness, shame, interest, and so on. Another way of labeling this element is to call it the "cognitive element" because the labeling process is a matter of retrieving memories of previous similar experiences, perceiving the context of the emotion, and coming up with a solution—a label. ☑●⌐Survey on **MyPsychLab**

The label a person applies to a subjective feeling is at least in part a learned response influenced by that person's language and culture. Such labels may differ among people of different cultural backgrounds. For example, researchers in one study (Tsai et al., 2004) found that Chinese Americans who were still firmly rooted in their original Chinese culture were far more likely to use labels to describe their emotions that referred to bodily sensations (such as "dizzy") or social relationships (such as "friendship") than were more "Americanized" Chinese Americans and European Americans, who tended to use more directly emotional words (such as "liking" or "love").

display rules learned ways of controlling displays of emotion in social settings.

☑●⌐**Survey** Participate in a survey on how you deal with your emotions on **MyPsychLab**

FIGURE 8.5 Common Sense Theory of Emotion

In the common sense theory of emotion, a stimulus (snarling dog) leads to an emotion of fear, which then leads to bodily arousal (in this case, indicated by shaking) through the autonomic nervous system (ANS).

	Stimulus	First response	Second response
Common sense theory "I'm shaking because I'm afraid."	Snarling dog	FEAR Conscious fear	ANS arousal

So which of the three elements is the most important?

In another study, even the subjective feeling of happiness showed cultural differences (Kitayama & Markus, 1994). In this study, Japanese and U.S. students were found to associate a general positive emotional state with entirely different circumstances. In the case of the Japanese students, the positive state was more associated with friendly or socially engaged feelings. The students from the United States associated their positive emotional state more with feelings that were socially disengaged, such as pride. This finding is a further reflection of the differences between collectivistic and individualistic cultures.

● So which of the three elements is the most important?

In the early days of psychology, it was assumed that feeling a particular emotion led first to a physical reaction and then to a behavioral one. Seeing a snarling dog in one's path causes the feeling of fear, which stimulates the body to arousal, followed by the behavioral act of running. People are aroused because they are afraid. (See Figure 8.5.)

8.8 How do the James-Lange and Cannon-Bard theories of emotion differ?

JAMES-LANGE William James (1884, 1890, 1894), who was also the founder of the functionalist perspective in the early history of psychology, ⓛⓘⓝⓚ to Chapter One: The Science of Psychology, pp. 7–8, disagreed with the idea that emotion led to bodily arousal which then led to action. He believed that the order of the components of emotions was quite different. At nearly the same time, a physiologist and psychologist in Denmark, Carl Lange (1885), came up with an explanation of emotion so similar to James's that the two names are used together to refer to the theory—the **James-Lange theory of emotion**. (See Figure 8.6.)

In this theory, a stimulus of some sort (for example, the large snarling dog) produces a physiological reaction. This reaction, which is the arousal of the "fight-or-flight" sympathetic nervous system (wanting to run), produces bodily sensations such as increased heart rate, dry mouth, and rapid breathing. James and Lange believed that the physical arousal led to the labeling of the emotion (*fear*). Simply put, "I am afraid because I am aroused," "I am embarrassed because my face is red," "I am nervous because my stomach is fluttering," and "I am in love because my heart rate increases when I look at her or him."

James-Lange theory of emotion   theory in which a physiological reaction leads to the labeling of an emotion.

FIGURE 8.6 James-Lange Theory of Emotion

In the James-Lange theory of emotion, a stimulus leads to bodily arousal first, which is then interpreted as an emotion.

	Stimulus	First response	Second response
James-Lange theory "I'm afraid because I'm shaking."	Snarling dog	ANS arousal, changes in body	FEAR Conscious fear

FIGURE 8.7 **Cannon-Bard Theory of Emotion**
In the Cannon-Bard theory of emotion, a stimulus leads to activity in the brain, which then sends signals to arouse the body and interpret the emotion at the same time.

What about people who have spinal cord injuries that prevent the sympathetic nervous system from functioning? Although James-Lange would predict that these people should show decreased emotion because the arousal that causes emotion is no longer there, this does not in fact happen. Several studies of people with spinal cord injuries report that these people are capable of experiencing the same emotions after their injury as before, and sometimes even more intensely (Bermond et al., 1991; Chwalisz et al., 1988).

CANNON-BARD Physiologists Walter Cannon (1927) and Philip Bard (1934) theorized that the emotion and the physiological arousal occur more or less at the same time. Cannon, an expert in sympathetic arousal mechanisms, did not feel that the physical changes caused by different emotions were distinct enough to allow them to be perceived as different emotions. Bard expanded on this idea by stating that the sensory information that comes into the brain is sent simultaneously (by the thalamus) to both the cortex and the organs of the sympathetic nervous system. The fear and the bodily reactions are, therefore, experienced at the same time—not one after the other. "I'm afraid and running and aroused!" (See Figure 8.7.)

This theory, known as the **Cannon-Bard theory of emotion**, also had its critics. K. S. Lashley (1938) stated that the thalamus would have to be very sophisticated to make sense of all the possible human emotions and relay them to the proper areas of the cortex and body. It would seem that other areas of the brain must be involved in processing emotional reactions. Studies of people with spinal cord injuries seem to suggest that emotions can be experienced without feedback from the sympathetic organs to the cortex; these studies were cited as a criticism of the James-Lange theory. At first these investigations seem to support the Cannon-Bard version of emotions: People do not need feedback from those organs to experience emotion. However, there is an alternate pathway that does provide feedback from these organs to the cortex; this is the *vagus nerve*, one of the cranial nerves (LeDoux, 1994). The existence of this feedback pathway makes the case for Cannon-Bard a little less convincing.

8.9 What are the key elements in cognitive arousal theory, the facial feedback hypothesis, and the cognitive-mediational theory of emotion?

SCHACHTER-SINGER AND COGNITIVE AROUSAL THEORY The early theories talked about the emotion and the physical reaction, but what about the mental interpretation of those components? In their **cognitive arousal theory**, Schachter and Singer (1962) proposed that two things have to happen before emotion occurs: the physical arousal and a labeling of the arousal based on cues from the surrounding environment. These two events happen at the same time, resulting in the labeling of the emotion. (See Figure 8.8.)

Cannon-Bard theory of emotion theory in which the physiological reaction and the emotion are assumed to occur at the same time.

cognitive arousal theory theory of emotion in which both the physical arousal and the labeling of that arousal based on cues from the environment must occur before the emotion is experienced.

FIGURE 8.8 Schachter-Singer's Cognitive Arousal Theory of Emotion
Schachter-Singer's cognitive arousal theory is similar to the James-Lange theory but adds the element of cognitive labeling of the arousal. In this theory, a stimulus leads to both bodily arousal and the labeling of that arousal (based on the surrounding context), which leads to the experience and labeling of the emotional reaction.

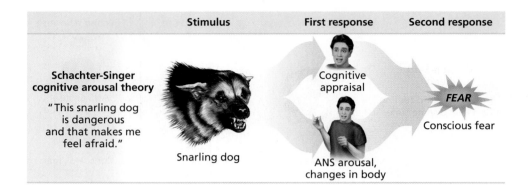

Stimulus	First response	Second response

Schachter-Singer cognitive arousal theory

"This snarling dog is dangerous and that makes me feel afraid."

Snarling dog

Cognitive appraisal

ANS arousal, changes in body

FEAR

Conscious fear

For example, if a person comes across a snarling dog while taking a walk, the physical arousal (heart racing, eyes opening wide) is accompanied by the thought (cognition) that this must be fear. Then and only then will the person experience the fear emotion. In other words, "I am aroused in the presence of a scary dog; therefore, I must be afraid." Evidence for this theory was found in what is now a classic experiment, described in the accompanying Classic Studies in Psychology feature. ✹⃞Explore on **MyPsychLab**

✹⃞Explore the different theories of emotion on **MyPsychLab**

classic studies in psychology
The Angry/Happy Man

In 1962, Stanley Schachter and Jerome Singer designed an experiment to test their theory that emotions are determined by an interaction between the physiological state of arousal and the label, or cognitive interpretation, that a person places on the arousal. Male student volunteers were told that they were going to answer a questionnaire about their reactions to a new vitamin called Suproxin. In reality, they were all injected with a drug called epinephrine, which causes physical arousal in the form of increased heart rate, rapid breathing, and a reddened face—all responses that happen during a strong emotional reaction.

Each student then participated in one of two conditions. In one condition, a confederate* posing as one of the participants started complaining about the experimenter, tearing up his questionnaire and storming out. In the other condition, there was one man who acted more like he was very happy, almost giddy and playing with some of the objects in the room. The "angry" man and the "happy" man in both conditions deliberately behaved in the two different ways as part of the experiment.

After both conditions had played out, participants in each of the two conditions were asked to describe their own emotions. The participants who had been exposed to the "angry" man interpreted their arousal symptoms as anger, whereas those exposed to the "happy" man interpreted their arousal as happiness. In all cases, the actual cause of arousal was the epinephrine, and the physical symptoms of arousal were identical. The only difference between the two groups of participants was their exposure to the two different contexts. Schachter and Singer's theory would have predicted exactly these results: Physiological arousal has to be interpreted cognitively before it is experienced as a specific emotion.

*Confederate: someone who is cooperating with another person on some task.

Although this classic experiment stimulated a lot of research, much of that research has failed to find much support for the cognitive arousal theory of emotion (Reisenzein, 1983, 1994). But this theory did serve to draw attention to the important role that cognition plays in determining emotions. The role of cognition in emotion has been revisited in more modern theories of emotion, as you will see in the following discussions.

QUESTIONS FOR FURTHER DISCUSSION

1. How might observing the emotions of others under more normal circumstances (i.e., not in a drugged state) affect a person's own emotional state?

2. According to Schachter and Singer's theory, for your first date with a person, should you choose a happy movie or a sad one?

3. In this experiment, what was the independent variable manipulated by the experimenters? What was the dependent variable?

4. This experiment used deception, as the participants were not told the true nature of the injection they received. What kind of ethical problems might have arisen from this deception? What problems would the experimenters have had in getting this study approved by an ethics committee today?

THE FACIAL FEEDBACK HYPOTHESIS: SMILE, YOU'LL FEEL BETTER In his (1898) book *The Expression of the Emotions in Man and Animals*, Charles Darwin stated that facial expressions evolved as a way of communicating intentions, such as threat or fear, and that these expressions are universal within a species rather than specific to a culture. He also believed (as in the James-Lange theory) that when such emotions are expressed freely on the face, the emotion itself intensifies—meaning that the more one smiles, the happier one feels.

Modern psychologists have proposed a theory of emotion that is consistent with much of Darwin's original thinking. Called the **facial feedback hypothesis**, this explanation assumes that facial expressions provide feedback to the brain concerning the emotion being expressed, which in turn not only intensifies the emotion but also actually *causes* the emotion (Buck, 1980; Ekman, 1980; Ekman & Friesen, 1978; Keillor et al., 2002). (See Figure 8.9.)

Does that mean that I don't smile because I'm happy—I'm happy because I smile?

As the old song goes, "put on a happy face" and yes, you'll feel happier, according to the facial feedback hypothesis. One fairly recent study does cast some doubt on the validity of this hypothesis, however. If the facial feedback hypothesis is correct, then people who have facial paralysis on both sides of the face should be unable to experience emotions in a normal way. But a case study conducted on just such a

> Does that mean that I don't smile because I'm happy—I'm happy because I smile?

The facial feedback hypothesis assumes that changing your own facial expression can change the way you feel. Smiling makes people feel happy, and frowning makes people feel sad. This effect seems to have an impact on the people around us as well. If this is true, this smiling woman may make the airline steward handing her the food feel good, too. Is it hard for you to stay in a bad mood when the people around you are smiling and laughing?

Stimulus	First response	Second response

Facial feedback theory → ANS arousal in face → Facial expression → Cognitive interpretation of face motions → *FEAR*

FIGURE 8.9 Facial Feedback Theory of Emotion
In the facial feedback theory of emotion, a stimulus such as this snarling dog causes arousal and a facial expression. The facial expression then provides feedback to the brain about the emotion. The brain then interprets the emotion and may also intensify it.

FIGURE 8.10 Lazarus's Theory of Emotion In Lazarus's cognitive-mediational theory of emotion, a stimulus causes an immediate appraisal (e.g., "The dog is snarling and not behind a fence, so this is dangerous"). The cognitive appraisal results in an emotional response, which is then followed by the appropriate bodily response.

	Stimulus	First response	Second response
Lazarus's cognitive-mediational theory		Appraisal of threat · FEAR	Bodily response

cognitive-mediational theory theory of emotion in which a stimulus must be interpreted (appraised) by a person in order to result in a physical response and an emotional reaction.

person revealed that although she was unable to express emotions on her paralyzed face, she could respond emotionally to slides meant to stimulate emotional reactions, just as anyone else would (Keillor et al., 2002). Clearly, the question of how much the actual facial expression determines the emotional experience has yet to be fully answered.

LAZARUS AND THE COGNITIVE-MEDIATIONAL THEORY   As mentioned in the Classic Studies in Psychology feature, Schachter and Singer's (1962) study stressed the importance of cognition, or thinking, in the determination of emotions. One of the more modern versions of cognitive emotion theories is Lazarus's **cognitive-mediational theory** (1991). In this theory, the most important aspect of any emotional experience is how the person interprets, or appraises, the stimulus that causes the emotional reaction. To *mediate* means to "come between," and in this theory, the cognitive appraisal mediates by coming between the stimulus and the emotional response to that stimulus.

For example, remember the person who encountered a snarling dog while walking through the neighborhood? According to Lazarus, the appraisal of the situation would come *before* both the physical arousal and the experience of emotion. If the dog is behind a sturdy fence, the appraisal would be something like "no threat." The most likely emotion would be annoyance, and the physical arousal would be minimal. But if the dog is not confined, the appraisal would more likely be "danger—threatening animal!" and would be followed by an increase in arousal and the emotional experience of fear. In other words, it's the *interpretation* of the arousal that results in the emotion of fear, not the labeling as in the Schachter-Singer model, and the interpretation comes first. (See Figure 8.10.)

Not everyone agrees with this theory, of course. Some researchers believe that emotional reactions to situations are so fast that they are almost instantaneous, which would leave little time for a cognitive appraisal to occur first (Zajonc, 1998). Others (Kilhstrom et al., 2000) have found that the human brain can respond to a physical threat before conscious thought enters the picture. The simple spinal cord reflex of pain withdrawal discussed in Chapter Two is an example of this—the reflex occurs so quickly that the brain itself is not involved, and the experience of pain is consciously felt *after* the injured body part is jerked away from the painful stimulus. Ⓛ Ⓘ Ⓝ Ⓚ to Chapter Two: The Biological Perspective, p. 51.

Which theory is right?   Which theory is right?

Human emotions are so incredibly complex that it might not be out of place to say that all of the theories are correct to at least some degree. In certain situations, the cognitive appraisal might have time to mediate the emotion that is experienced (such as falling in love), whereas in other situations, the need to act first and think and feel later is more important. (See Figure 8.11.)

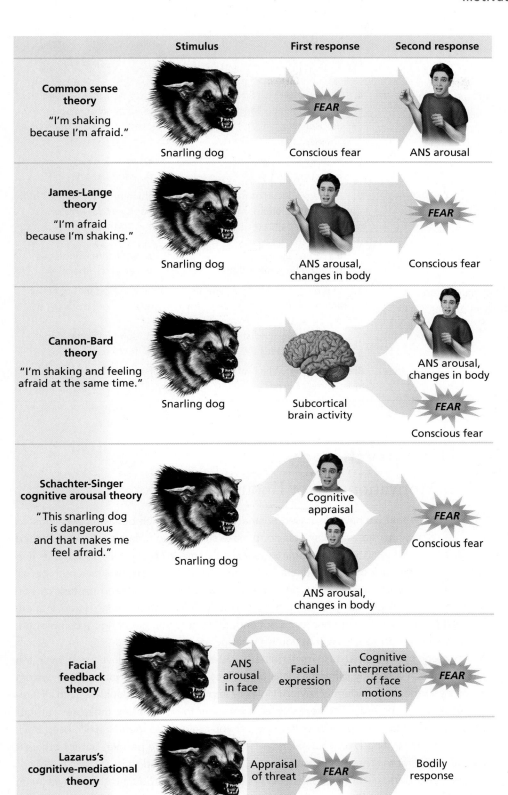

	Stimulus	First response	Second response
Common sense theory "I'm shaking because I'm afraid."	Snarling dog	*FEAR* Conscious fear	ANS arousal
James-Lange theory "I'm afraid because I'm shaking."	Snarling dog	ANS arousal, changes in body	*FEAR* Conscious fear
Cannon-Bard theory "I'm shaking and feeling afraid at the same time."	Snarling dog	Subcortical brain activity	ANS arousal, changes in body *FEAR* Conscious fear
Schachter-Singer cognitive arousal theory "This snarling dog is dangerous and that makes me feel afraid."	Snarling dog	Cognitive appraisal ANS arousal, changes in body	*FEAR* Conscious fear
Facial feedback theory		ANS arousal in face → Facial expression → Cognitive interpretation of face motions	*FEAR*
Lazarus's cognitive-mediational theory		Appraisal of threat → *FEAR*	Bodily response

FIGURE 8.11 Comparison of Theories of Emotion
These figures represent the six different theories of emotion as discussed in the text.

practice quiz How much do you remember?

Pick the best answer.

1. Which of the following is NOT one of the three elements of emotion?
   a. subjective experience
   b. behavior
   c. attention
   d. physical reaction

2. Emotional stimuli travel to the _____ by both a fast subcortical route and a slower cortical route.
   a. thalamus
   b. amygdala
   c. left hemisphere
   d. right hemisphere

3. The theory of emotion that states that the thalamus sends sensory information to the cortex and the sympathetic organs at the same time is the _____ theory.
   a. James-Lange
   b. Cannon-Bard
   c. Schachter-Singer
   d. facial feedback

4. In Schachter and Singer's classic study, participants who were exposed to the "angry" man interpreted their physiological arousal as _____, whereas those who were exposed to the "happy" man interpreted their arousal as _____.
   a. angry; happy.
   b. happy; angry.
   c. happy; happy.
   d. angry; angry.

5. Leslie smiles a lot in the classroom, which in turn prompts his students to smile, making them feel happier too. This effect is best explained by which of the following theories of emotion?
   a. James-Lange
   b. cognitive-mediational
   c. Schachter-Singer
   d. facial feedback

6. In the _____ theory of emotion, the most important aspect of an emotional experience is the interpretation, or appraisal, of the stimulus.
   a. cognitive-mediational
   b. Cannon-Bard
   c. James-Lange
   d. facial feedback

Brainstorming: Which of these theories of emotion do you feel is most correct? Why?

ANSWERS ON PAGE AK–2

applying psychology to everyday life
When Motivation Is Not Enough

 Now that we have discussed a variety of ways in which behavior gets initiated or maintained, what can you do to make sure you complete the tasks you need to finish or address the commitments you've made? Many college students find it difficult to keep track of all of their class assignments and projects, and to remember all of the things they are supposed to do—and when to do them. Keeping on task can be especially challenging when you might not be exactly thrilled about doing some of them in the first place. As such, if motivation is not enough to help you get things accomplished, what else can you do to ensure that you do what needs to be done?

A variety of time- and task-management systems have been developed over the years, each with a slightly different focus on various aspects of motivation. One system suggests you should first identify key principles or important areas in your life (such as family, education, career, etc.). The next step is to sort your to-do list using those key categories, ranking your tasks by priority or in the order you need to do them. Finally, keep track of each item by plotting it on your calendar. This works for some people, but for others it may sound like more steps than you want to do, or feel you need to do.

The book *Getting Things Done: The Art of Stress-Free Productivity* by David Allen and his "Getting Things Done" (or "GTD") methodology can provide a useful structure for a wide range of people who need help, well, in getting things done (Allen, 2001, 2008). Think back to Jennifer, the college student who ran into difficulties after starting college. With a system like GTD, she may have improved her chances of being more successful her first year.

The GTD method consists of five stages of processing your "stuff" into actual outcomes, identifying "next actions" you can actually take to gain and maintain control of your tasks and commitments. The five stages of the GTD method are:

1. Capture anything and everything that has your attention, getting it out of your head and physically collected in one place. This place can be a folder, notebook, computer program, spreadsheet, a set of index cards, or the like.

2. Process and define what you can take action on and identify the next steps. For example, instead of "do my research paper," identify actionable next steps such as "pinpoint topic, collect articles, schedule meeting to discuss ideas with classmates," for example.

3. Organize information and reminders into categories or contexts, based on how and when you need them. For example, if you need to send an e-mail or text message to your group partners, you probably need to have your phone or computer to do so; "phone" or "computer" might be a context that you use.

4. Complete weekly reviews of your projects, next actions, and new items. To get things done, you need to review what you need to do.

5. Do your next actions, in the appropriate context or time frame for doing so.

Adapted from David Allen's (2001) *Getting Things Done: The Art of Stress-Free Productivity* (2001) and *Making It All Work* (2008).

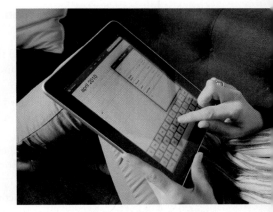

How do you keep track of all of your class assignments, appointments, and deadlines?

· ·

In this discussion we've only highlighted aspects of one specific approach for organizing and keeping on top of all those things you need to get done. A variety of time- and task-management systems and tools are available, many more than we can cover in this textbook. Finding an approach or strategy that works best for you will likely pay off, not only now while you are in school but also in areas of your personal and future professional lives as well. Take some time now and investigate available strategies that will help you get organized and stay on track to meet your obligations in a timely manner. If you do, the next time you find that motivation and emotion are not enough to prompt you to get what you need done taken care of, you'll be glad you did.

chapter summary

((•⬤⎯Listen on **MyPsychLab**   Listen to an audio file of your chapter **www.MyPsychLab**

Approaches to Understanding Motivation

8.1 How do psychologists define motivation, and what are the key elements of the early instinct and drive-reduction approaches to motivation?

- Motivation is the process by which activities are started, directed, and sustained so that physical and psychological needs are fulfilled.
- Instinct approaches proposed that some human actions may be motivated by instincts, which are innate patterns of behavior found in both people and animals.
- Drive-reduction approaches state that when an organism has a need (such as hunger), the need leads to psychological tension that motivates the organism to act, fulfilling the need and reducing the tension.
- Primary drives involve the needs of the body, whereas acquired (secondary) drives are those learned through experience. Homeostasis is the tendency of the body to maintain a steady state.

8.2 What are the characteristics of the three types of needs?

- The need for achievement is a strong desire to succeed in achieving one's goals, both realistic and challenging.
- The self-theory of emotion links the need for achievement to the concept of locus of control. A belief in control over one's life leads to more attempts to achieve, even in the face of failure. Those who believe that they have little control over what happens to them are more likely to develop learned helplessness.

- The need for affiliation is the desire to have friendly social interactions and relationships with others as well as the desire to be held in high regard by others.
- The need for power concerns having control over others, influencing them, and having an impact on them. Status and prestige are important to people high in this need.

8.3 What are the key elements of the arousal and incentive approaches to motivation?

- In arousal theory, a person has to maintain an optimal level of arousal. People who need more arousal than others are called sensation seekers.
- In the incentive approach, an external stimulus may be so rewarding that it motivates a person to act toward that stimulus even in the absence of a drive.

8.4 How do Maslow's humanistic approach and self-determination theory explain motivation?

- Maslow proposed a hierarchy of needs, beginning with basic physiological needs and ending with transcendence needs. The more basic needs must be met before the higher needs can be fulfilled.
- Self-determination theory (SDT) is a model of motivation in which three basic needs are seen as necessary to an individual's successful development: autonomy, competence, and relatedness.
- Intrinsic motivation occurs when people act because the act itself is satisfying or rewarding, whereas extrinsic motivation occurs when people receive an external reward (such as money) for the act.

Psychoactive Drugs and Addiction

8.5 How does drug addiction occur?

- Drugs that are physically addictive cause the user's body to crave the drug. When deprived of the drug, the user will go through physical withdrawal.

- Drug tolerance occurs as the user's body becomes conditioned to the level of the drug. After a time, the user must take more and more of the drug to get the same effect.

- In psychological dependence, the user believes that he or she needs the drug to function well and maintain a sense of well-being. Any drug can produce psychological dependence.

- Stimulants are drugs that increase the activity of the nervous system, particularly the sympathetic division and the central nervous system.

- Depressants are drugs that decrease the activity of the nervous system.

- Narcotics are pain-relieving drugs of the depressant class that are derived from the opium poppy and include opium, morphine, and heroin.

- Hallucinogenics are stimulants that alter the brain's interpretation of sensations, creating hallucinations. Three synthetically created hallucinogens are LSD, PCP, and MDMA.

- Three naturally occurring hallucinogens are mescaline, psilocybin, and marijuana.

- Marijuana is a mild hallucinogen, producing a mild euphoria and feelings of relaxation in its users. Larger doses can lead to hallucinations and paranoia. It contains substances that are carcinogenic and impairs learning and memory.

Sexual Motivation

8.6 What motivates sexual behavior and its variations?

- Alfred Kinsey conducted a series of sexual behavior surveys revealing some highly controversial findings about the kinds of sexual behavior common among people in the United States.

- Janus and Janus published the results of a large-scale survey of sexual behavior in the United States. Their survey results did not differ widely from those of Kinsey but looked at many more types of sexual behavior and factors related to sexual behavior than did Kinsey's surveys.

- Research suggests that there are biological differences between heterosexuals and homosexuals and that there may be genetic influences as well.

issues in psychology: What Is the Evolutionary Purpose of Homosexuality?

- The kin selection hypothesis states that homosexual men may insure the continuation of their genes by nurturing family members such as nieces and nephews.

Emotion

8.7 What are the three elements of emotion?

- Emotion is the "feeling" aspect of consciousness and includes physical, behavioral, and subjective (cognitive) elements.

8.8 How do the James-Lange and Cannon-Bard theories of emotion differ?

- The James-Lange theory states that a stimulus creates a physiological response, which then leads to the labeling of the emotion.

- The Cannon-Bard theory asserts that the physiological reaction and the emotion are simultaneous, as the thalamus sends sensory information to both the cortex of the brain and the organs of the sympathetic nervous system.

8.9 What are the key elements in cognitive arousal theory, the facial feedback hypothesis, and the cognitive-mediational theory of emotion?

- In Schachter and Singer's cognitive arousal theory, both the physiological arousal and the actual interpretation of that arousal must occur before the emotion itself is experienced. This interpretation is based on cues from the environment.

classic studies in psychology: The Angry/Happy Man

- In the facial feedback hypothesis, facial expressions provide feedback to the brain about the emotion being expressed on the face, intensifying the emotion.

- In the cognitive-mediational theory of emotion, the cognitive component of emotion (the interpretation) precedes both the physiological reaction and the emotion itself.

- Those participants who were exposed to the "angry" man interpreted their physical arousal as anger, whereas those who were exposed to the "happy" man interpreted their physical arousal as happiness.

applying psychology to everyday life: When Motivation Is Not Enough

- Motivation and emotion are sometimes not enough to prompt human behavior.

- Time- or task-management systems can help you keep track of commitments and accomplish specific tasks and general goals.

TEST yourself

ANSWERS ON PAGE AK–2

✓●—[Study and **Review** on **MyPsychLab**   Ready for your test? More quizzes and a customized plan. **www.MyPsychLab**

Pick the best answer.

1. The approach to motivation that forced psychologists to consider the hereditary factors in motivation was the _____ approach.
   - **a.** arousal
   - **b.** drive-reduction
   - **c.** instinct
   - **d.** incentive

2. The need for money is an example of a(n) _____ drive.
   - **a.** primary
   - **b.** acquired
   - **c.** innate
   - **d.** instinctive

3. Jocelyn needs to be the one whose ideas are always used and craves prestige among others. She drives an expensive car and wears nothing but the most expensive clothes. Jocelyn is high in the need for _____.
   - **a.** achievement.
   - **b.** affiliation.
   - **c.** power.
   - **d.** attention.

4. People who are always looking for a challenge may be high in the need for _____.
  a. achievement.
  b. affiliation.
  c. power.
  d. attention.

5. Evidence from a study with 2-year-olds who were given an opportunity to explore a black box with a hole in it suggests that sensation seeking may be _____.
  a. learned.
  b. abnormal.
  c. acquired over time.
  d. innate.

6. Gene is trying to choose a snack. There is a bowl of fruit on the table, but there's also a candy bar that he bought yesterday. The fact that Gene feels drawn to choose the candy bar instead of the fruit is an example of the power of _____.
  a. needs.
  b. drives.
  c. incentives.
  d. arousal.

7. According to Maslow, a person who wants to become self-actualized must first satisfy _____.
  a. higher needs before other more basic needs.
  b. more basic needs such as food and safety.
  c. needs for creativity, justice, and the appreciation of beauty.
  d. needs for achievement, affiliation, and power.

8. Shontia works at a day care center. The pay is low and the hours are long, but she loves being around children and has no desire to look for a higher-paying job. Shontia's motivation appears to be _____.
  a. intrinsic.
  b. extrinsic.
  c. selfish.
  d. external.

9. Jackie used Ecstasy while she was in college, but now that she has a government job she has avoided using any recreational drugs. Although she had no problem quitting, she still finds that every now and then she gets a strong craving to use Ecstasy again. Her craving is most likely the result of _____.
  a. psychological dependence.
  b. physical dependency.
  c. withdrawal.
  d. none of the above.

10. Which of the following is NOT a naturally occurring substance?
  a. nicotine
  b. amphetamine
  c. caffeine
  d. cocaine

11. Which of the following is NOT a depressant?
  a. alcohol
  b. valium
  c. PCP
  d. barbiturate

12. "Magic mushrooms" are the source of _____.
  a. marijuana.
  b. psilocybin.
  c. mescaline.
  d. Ecstasy.

13. High doses of marijuana can lead to _____.
  a. death.
  b. hallucinations and delusions.
  c. extreme arousal.
  d. none of the above.

14. The most recent surveys indicate that about _____ percent of men and _____ percent of women are predominantly homosexual.
  a. 22; 17
  b. 15; 10
  c. 5; 9
  d. 9; 5

15. Bisexual people _____.
  a. have multiple relationships with men and women at the same time.
  b. are equally attracted to both sexes.
  c. can be either male or female.
  d. rarely have long-term, monogamous relationships.

16. Your heart is racing, your breathing is rapid, and your mouth is dry. What emotion are you experiencing?
  a. anger
  b. fear
  c. happiness
  d. It is not always possible to distinguish one emotion from another by physiological reactions only.

17. Dora is experiencing positive emotions while Milly is experiencing negative emotions. If researchers are examining EEG recordings of their brains, where are they most likely to see increases in activity?
  a. in Dora's left frontal lobe
  b. in Milly's right frontal lobe
  c. in their thalamic regions
  d. both a and b are correct.

18. The _____ is a brain structure that allows us to quickly and unconsciously respond to potentially dangerous stimuli before we are completely conscious of the threat.
  a. thalamus
  b. hippocampus
  c. prefrontal cortex
  d. amygdala

19. The _____ theory of emotion would predict that people with spinal cord injuries that prevent them from experiencing sympathetic arousal would show decreased emotion.
  a. James-Lange
  b. Cannon-Bard
  c. Schachter-Singer
  d. facial feedback

20. In Schachter and Singer's classic study, participants were physically aroused by _____.
  a. exposure to a "happy" man.
  b. exposure to an "angry" man.
  c. receiving epinephrine.
  d. watching an exciting film.

21. The theory of emotion that owes a lot to Darwin's work is the _____ theory.
  a. James-Lange
  b. Cannon-Bard
  c. Schachter-Singer
  d. facial feedback

8 motivation and emotion

8.1 **8.2** p. 272

- **types**
  - **intrinsic:** actions are rewarding or satisfying in and of themselves
  - **extrinsic:** actions are performed because they lead to some sort of external outcome

Motivation

(process by which activities are started, directed, and continued so that physical or psychological needs or wants are met)

- **instinct**
  - biologically determined/innate patterns of behavior
  - old approach: instincts are mainly descriptions, not explanations; idea that some behavior is hereditary remains an important focus

- **psychological needs**
  - psychological needs have been highlighted in some theories (e.g., McClelland)
  - Dweck suggests that the need for achievement is linked to a person's view of self (fixed or changeable) and locus of control

- **drive reduction**
  - **need:** a requirement of some material that is essential for survival of the organism
  - **primary drives:** those drives that involve needs of the body
  - **acquired (secondary) drives:** those drives that are learned through experience of conditioning

8.3 **8.4** p. 276

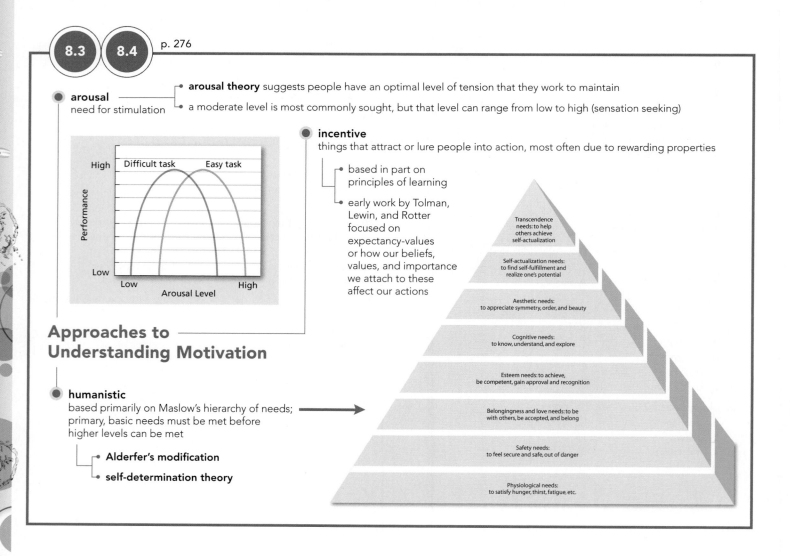

- **arousal**
  need for stimulation
  - **arousal theory** suggests people have an optimal level of tension that they work to maintain
  - a moderate level is most commonly sought, but that level can range from low to high (sensation seeking)

- **incentive**
  things that attract or lure people into action, most often due to rewarding properties
  - based in part on principles of learning
  - early work by Tolman, Lewin, and Rotter focused on expectancy-values or how our beliefs, values, and importance we attach to these affect our actions

Approaches to Understanding Motivation

- **humanistic**
  based primarily on Maslow's hierarchy of needs; primary, basic needs must be met before higher levels can be met
  - **Alderfer's modification**
  - **self-determination theory**

Transcendence needs: to help others achieve self-actualization

Self-actualization needs: to find self-fulfillment and realize one's potential

Aesthetic needs: to appreciate symmetry, order, and beauty

Cognitive needs: to know, understand, and explore

Esteem needs: to achieve, be competent, gain approval and recognition

Belongingness and love needs: to be with others, be accepted, and belong

Safety needs: to feel secure and safe, out of danger

Physiological needs: to satisfy hunger, thirst, fatigue, etc.

8.5 p. 282

What motivates people to use drugs and why do some become addicted to certain drugs?

→ **physical dependence:** user's body needs a drug to function; drug tolerance and withdrawal are warning signs/symptoms

→ **psychological dependence:** user believes drug is needed to function

Psychoactive Drugs and Addiction

(drugs that alter thinking, perception, or memory)

types
- **stimulants:** increase functioning of nervous system
- **depressants:** have sedative effect
- **narcotics:** euphoria-producing and pain-relieving drugs derived from opium
- **hallucinogens:** alter brain's interpretation of sensations

8.6 p. 288

motivation study of sexual behavior (not the sex act) focuses on when/with whom/under what circumstances sexual activity occurs

- Kinsey pioneered the study of different types of sexual behavior; suggested sexual orientation occurred on a continuum, not an either/or basis (see Table 8.3)
- The Janus Report (first large-scale survey since Kinsey) examined both normal and deviant sexual behavior (see Table 8.4)

Sexual Motivation

sexual orientation person's sexual attraction and affection for members of the opposite or same sex

key concepts
- **heterosexual:** attraction to opposite sex; most common and socially acceptable
- **homosexual:** attraction to one's own sex
- **bisexual:** attraction to both sexes

- sexual orientation is likely the product of both biology (i.e. brain structure, genetics) and environment

8.7 8.8 8.9 p. 294

physiological arousal is created by the sympathetic nervous system and is associated with brain activity in specific areas (e.g., the amygdala) and right or left hemisphere activity

emotional expressions can vary across cultures but some expressions seem to be universal; display rules also vary across cultures and according to gender

subjective labeling of emotion is largely a learned response, influenced by both language and culture

Emotion

(is "feeling" aspect of consciousness, characterized by physiological arousal, specific expressive behavior, and inner awareness of feelings)

- Lazarus's **cognitive-mediational theory**
- **facial feedback hypothesis** (based on ideas from Darwin)
- **James-Lange theory**
- **Cannon-Bard theory**
- **cognitive arousal theory** (Schacter-Singer)

Various Theories of Emotion

have been suggested, each with a slightly different focus and interpretation →

9

stress and health

why study health and stress?

How are health and stress related?
Stress is not a rare experience but something
that all people experience in varying degrees
every day. This chapter will explore
the sources of stress in daily life, the factors
that can make the experience of coping
with stress easier or more difficult,
and how stress influences physical and
mental health, as well as ways to cope
with the stresses of everyday life
and extraordinary experiences.

chapter outline

Stress and Stressors

**Physiological Factors:
Stress and Health**

**ISSUES IN PSYCHOLOGY:
Health Psychology and Stress**

Stress, Hunger, and Eating

Stress and Sexual Dysfunction

Coping with Stress

**APPLYING PSYCHOLOGY
TO EVERYDAY LIFE:
Exercising for Mental Health**

Laughter: The Best Medicine?

Secretary to psychologist: "Doctor, there is a patient here who thinks he is invisible."

Psychologist: *"Tell him I can't see him right now."*

I often dream about being carried away by a giant squirrel. Does that make me a nut?

Everyone has a photographic memory. Some just don't have film.

What's the difference between a behaviorist and a magician?

A behaviorist pulls habits out of rats!

They may not be the funniest jokes you've ever heard, but many of you probably chuckled a bit while reading them. Why begin a chapter on stress and health with a series of jokes? For many years now, psychologists and other researchers have known that humor is a great stress reliever (Berk et al., 1989, 2009; Dixon, 1980; Lefcourt et al., 1995; Wooten, 1980). In the last decade, researchers in **psychoneuroimmunology** (the study of the effects of psychological factors such as stress, emotions, thinking, and behavior on the body's disease-fighting system) have found two possible reasons for the stress-reducing benefits of laughter. In one study (Berk et al., 2008), researchers Dr. Lee Berk and Dr. Stanley Tan found that laughing significantly *increases* the level of health-protecting hormones (beta-endorphins, a group of chemicals that help ease depression, and human growth hormone, which helps with immunity to diseases). They also found that just *looking forward* to a positive and humorous laughing experience can significantly *decrease* levels of potentially damaging hormones: cortisol, a major stress hormone, epinephrine (adrenaline), and dopac, a by-product of dopamine metabolism. In another study, these researchers and their colleagues found that laughter has another health benefit: repetitive, joyous laughter causes the body to respond as if receiving moderate exercise, which enhances mood and immune system activity, lowers both bad cholesterol and blood pressure, raises good cholesterol, and decreases stress hormones (Berk et al., 2009).

The moral of the story: Laugh it up!

learning objectives

9.1 How do psychologists define stress?

9.2 What kinds of external events can cause stress?

9.3 What are some psychological factors in stress?

9.4 How does stress affect the physical functioning of the body and its immune system?

9.5 How do cognitive factors and personality differences affect the experience of stress?

9.6 What social factors influence stress reactions?

9.7 What is hunger, and how do social factors influence a person's experience of hunger?

9.8 What are some problems in eating behavior, and how are they affected by biology and culture?

9.9 How can stress lead to sexual problems?

9.10 What are some ways in which people cope with stress reactions?

9.11 How is coping with stress affected by culture and religion?

9.12 What are the psychological benefits of exercise?

psychoneuroimmunology the study of the effects of psychological factors such as stress, emotions, thoughts, and behavior on the immune system.

stress the term used to describe the physical, emotional, cognitive, and behavioral responses to events that are appraised as threatening or challenging.

stressors events that cause a stress reaction.

distress the effect of unpleasant and undesirable stressors.

I feel like that most of the time!

Taking a test is just one of many possible stressors in a college student's life. What aspects of college life have you found to be stressful? Do other students experience the same degree of stress in response to the same stressors?

Stress and Stressors

Every day, each person faces some kind of challenge, big or small. Just deciding what to wear to work or school can be a challenge for some people, whereas others find the drive to the workplace or school the most challenging part of the day. There are decisions to be made and changes that will require adapting plans already made. Sometimes there are actual threats to well-being—an accident, a fight with the boss, a failed exam, or losing a job, to name a few. All of these challenges, threats, and changes require people to respond in some way.

Definition of Stress

9.1 How do psychologists define stress?

Stress is the term used to describe the physical, emotional, cognitive, and behavioral responses to events that are appraised* as threatening or challenging.

Stress can show itself in many ways. Physical problems can include unusual fatigue, sleeping problems, frequent colds, and even chest pains and nausea. People under stress may behave differently, too: pacing, eating too much, crying a lot, smoking and drinking more than usual, or physically striking out at others by hitting or throwing things. Emotionally, people under stress experience anxiety, depression, fear, and irritability, as well as anger and frustration. Mental symptoms of stress include problems in concentration, memory, and decision making, and people under stress often lose their sense of humor.

● I feel like that most of the time!

Most people experience some degree of stress on a daily basis, and college students are even more likely to face situations and events that require them to make changes and adapt their behavior: Assigned readings, papers, studying for tests, juggling jobs, car problems, relationships, and dealing with deadlines are all examples of things that can cause a person to experience stress. Some people feel the effects of stress more than others because what one person might consider a threat might be appraised as an opportunity by another. Stress-causing events are called **stressors**; they can come from within a person or from an external source and range from relatively mild to severe.

What Are Stressors?

Events that can become stressors range from being stuck behind a person in the 10-items-or-less lane of the grocery store who has twice that amount to dealing with the rubble left after a tornado or a hurricane destroys one's home. Stressors can range from the deadly serious (hurricanes, fires, crashes, combat) to the merely irritating and annoying (delays, rude people, losing the car keys). Stressors can even be imaginary, as when a couple puts off doing their income tax return, imagining that they will have to pay a huge tax bill, or when a parent imagines the worst happening to a teenage child who isn't yet home from an evening out.

There are two kinds of stressors: those that cause **distress**, which occurs when people experience unpleasant stressors, and those that cause *eustress*, which results from positive events that require the body to adapt or change (a term first coined by Hans Selye in 1936). Marriage, a job promotion, and having a baby may all be positive events for most people, but they all require a great deal of change in people's habits, duties, and even lifestyle, thereby creating stress.

---

*Appraised: in this sense, evaluated or judged in terms of importance or significance.

Researchers now define **eustress** as the optimal amount of stress that people need to promote health and well-being. The arousal theory presented in Chapter Eight is based on the idea that a certain level of stress, or arousal, is actually necessary for people to feel content (Zuckerman, 1994). ⓛⓘⓝⓚ to Chapter Eight: Motivation and Emotion, pp. 276–278. That arousal can be viewed in terms of eustress. Many students are aware that experiencing a little anxiety or stress is helpful to them because it motivates them to study, for example.

A number of events, great and small, good and bad, can cause us to feel "stressed out." The next section looks at how life's big deals and little hassles contribute to our overall stress experience. ⊙▶ Simulate on **MyPsychLab**

⊙▶ Simulate stress and stressors on **MyPsychLab**

Environmental Stressors: Life's Ups and Downs

9.2 What kinds of external events can cause stress?

CATASTROPHES Losing one's home in a tornado is an example of a stressor called a **catastrophe**, an unpredictable event that happens on a large scale and creates tremendous amounts of stress and feelings of threat. Wars, hurricanes, floods, fires, airplane crashes, and other disasters are all examples of catastrophes. The devastation caused by Hurricane Katrina on August 29, 2005, is a prime example of such an event. A Category 3 hurricane, Katrina laid waste to the north-central coastal area of the Gulf of Mexico. In New Orleans, the damage from Katrina was increased by the levees' failure to hold back floodwaters. Eighty percent of the city and many neighboring areas were flooded for weeks (Swenson & Marshall, 2005). Rates of mental illness, including stress disorders like posttraumatic stress disorder (PTSD) ⓛⓘⓝⓚ to Chapter Twelve: Psychological Disorders, p. 443, nearly doubled from pre-hurricane values (Kessler et al., 2006).

MAJOR LIFE CHANGES Thankfully, most people do not have to face the extreme stress of a catastrophe. But stress is present even in relatively ordinary life experiences and does not have to come from only negative events, such as job loss. Sometimes big, positive events, such as marriage or going to college, also require a person to make adjustments and changes—and adjustments and changes are really at the core of stress, according to early researchers in the field (Holmes & Rahe, 1967).

The Social Readjustment Rating Scale (SRRS) Holmes and Rahe (1967) believed that any life event that required people to change, adapt, or adjust their life-styles would result in stress. Like Selye, they assume that both negative events (such as getting fired) and positive events (such as getting a promotion) demand that a person adjust in some way, and so both kinds of events are associated with stress. Holmes and Rahe devised a way to measure the amount of stress in a person's life by having that person add up the total "life change units" associated with each major event in their **Social Readjustment Rating Scale (SRRS)**. The researchers sampled 394 people, giving them a list of events, such as divorce, pregnancy, or taking a vacation. The people in the sample were told that, on a scale of 0 (no changes required of the person experiencing the event) to 100 (extreme changes required), marriage represented 50 "life change units." This gave those being sampled a "yardstick" of sorts, by which they could assign a number to each event; these numbers became the life change units associated with each event (divorce, marriage, pregnancy, or a change in living conditions, for example) on the SRRS.

Scores of 150 or below were not associated with any significant problems, but scores between 150 and 199 were considered a "mild life crisis" and associated with a 33 percent increase in the risk of that person experiencing an illness or accident in the

eustress   the effect of positive events, or the optimal amount of stress that people need to promote health and well-being.

catastrophe   an unpredictable, large-scale event that creates a tremendous need to adapt and adjust as well as overwhelming feelings of threat.

Social Readjustment Rating Scale (SRRS)   assessment that measures the amount of stress in a person's life over a one-year period resulting from major life events.

near future (when compared to persons not experiencing any crisis). Scores between 200 and 299 were labeled "moderate life crisis" and associated with a 50 percent increase in risk, whereas scores over 300 were considered a "major life crisis" and represented an 80 percent increase in risk (Holmes & Masuda, 1973). Illness includes not only physical conditions such as high blood pressure, ulcers, or migraine headaches but mental illness as well. In one study, researchers found that stressful life events of the kind listed in the SRRS were excellent predictors of the onset of episodes of major depression (Kendler & Prescott, 1999).

The SRRS was later revised (Miller & Rahe, 1997) to reflect changes in the ratings of the events in the 30 intervening years. Miller and Rahe found that overall stress associated with many of the items on the original list had increased by about 45 percent from the original 1967 ratings.

How can stress cause a person to have an accident? Many studies conducted on the relationship between stress and accidents in the workplace have shown that people under a lot of stress tend to be more distracted and less cautious and, therefore, place themselves at a greater risk for having an accident (Hansen, 1988; Sherry et al., 2003).

The SRRS as it was originally designed seems more appropriate for adults who are already established in their careers. A version of the SRRS that uses as life events things more likely to be experienced by college students is the **College Undergraduate Stress Scale (CUSS)**. This scale looks quite different from Holmes and Rahe's original scale because the stressful events listed and rated include those that would be more common or more likely to happen to a college student. For example, the highest events on the CUSS are being raped and finding out you are HIV positive, both earning a rating of 100. The lowest rating of 40 is associated with falling asleep in class.

● How can falling asleep in class be stressful? It's what happens when the professor catches you that's stressful, isn't it?

Ah, but if you fall asleep in class, even if the professor doesn't catch on, you'll miss the lecture notes. You might then have to get the notes from a friend, find enough money to pay for the copy machine, try to read your friend's handwriting, and so on—all stressful situations. Actually, all the events listed on both scales are stressful not just because some of them are emotionally intense but also because so many little details, changes, adjustments, adaptations, frustrations, and delays are caused by the events themselves. The death of a spouse, for example, requires a lot of tasks: planning the funeral, deciding what to do with the spouse's clothes and belongings, getting the notice in the obituaries, answering all of the condolence cards with a thank-you card, dealing with insurance and changing names on policies, and on and on and on. In other words, major life events create a whole host of hassles.

HASSLES Although it's easy to think about big disasters and major changes in life as sources of stress, the bulk of the stress we experience daily comes from little frustrations, delays, irritations, minor disagreements, and similar annoyances. These daily annoyances are called **hassles** (Lazarus, 1993; Lazarus & Folkman, 1984). Experiencing major changes in one's life is like throwing a rock into a pond: There will be a big splash, but the rock itself is gone. What is left behind are all the ripples in the water that came from the impact of the rock. Those "ripples" are the hassles that arise from the big event.

Lazarus and Folkman (1984) developed a "hassles" scale that includes items such as "misplacing or losing things" and "troublesome neighbors." A person taking the test for hassles would rate each item in the scale in terms of how much of a hassle that particular item was for the person. The ratings range between 0 (no hassle or didn't occur) to 3 (extremely severe hassle). Whereas the major life events of Holmes and Rahe's scale (1967) may have a long-term effect on a person's chronic physical and mental health, the day-to-day minor annoyances, delays, and irritations that affect immediate health and well-being are far better predictors of short-term ill-

How can falling asleep in class be stressful? It's what happens when the professor catches you that's stressful, isn't it?

College Undergraduate Stress Scale (CUSS) assessment that measures the amount of stress in a college student's life over a one-year period resulting from major life events.

hassles the daily annoyances of everyday life.

nesses such as headaches, colds, backaches, and similar symptoms (Burks & Martin, 1985; DeLongis et al., 1988; Dunn et al., 2006). In one study, researchers found that among 261 participants who experienced headaches, scores on a scale measuring the number and severity of daily hassles were significantly better predictors of headaches than were scores on a life events scale (Fernandez & Sheffield, 1996). The researchers also found that it was not so much the number of daily hassles that predicted headaches but rather the perceived severity of the hassles.

Another study has indicated that hassles may also come from quite different sources depending on a person's developmental stage (Ellis et al., 2001). In this study, researchers surveyed 270 randomly selected people from ages 3–75. The participants were asked to check off a list of daily hassles and pleasures associated with having "bad days" and "good days," respectively, as well as ranking the hassles in terms of frequency and severity of impact. For children ages 3–5, getting teased was the biggest daily hassle. For children in the 6–10 age-group, the biggest hassle was getting bad grades. Children 11–15 years old reported feeling pressured to use drugs, whereas older adolescents (ages 16–22) cited trouble at school or work. Adults found fighting among family members the greatest source of stress, whereas the elderly people in the study cited a lack of money, and such hassles as going shopping, doctor's appointments, and bad weather. ☑•⌐**Survey** on **MyPsychLab**

☑•⌐**Survey** Participate in a survey on what stresses you out on **MyPsychLab**

practice quiz   How much do you remember?

(9.1) (9.2)

Pick the best answer.

1. The optimal amount of stress that people need to promote their health and sense of well-being is called _____.
   a. intensity.
   b. distress.
   c. eustress.
   d. acute stress.

2. Research has shown that _____ have a long-term effect on physical and mental health, but _____ have a greater impact on short-term health.
   a. hassles; major life events
   b. major life events; hassles
   c. major life events; catastrophes
   d. hassles; castastrophes

3. The College Undergraduate Stress Scale rates being raped as equally stressful when compared with which of the following?
   a. death of a close family member
   b. concerns about being pregnant
   c. being accused of rape
   d. finding out that one is HIV-positive

Brainstorming: When during the school year are you most likely to come down with a cold or experience other symptoms such as headaches? What hassles and stressors are also present at those times? What steps could you take to minimize the effects of these stressors?

ANSWERS ON PAGE AK–2

Psychological Stressors: Stress and the Mind

Although several specific stressors (such as marriage, car problems, etc.) have already been mentioned, the psychological reasons why people find these events stressful fall into several categories.

9.3 What are some psychological factors in stress?

PRESSURE   When there are urgent demands or expectations for a person's behavior coming from an outside source, that person is experiencing **pressure**. Pressure occurs when people feel that they must work harder, faster, or do more, as in meeting a deadline or studying for final exams.

Time pressure is one of the most common forms of pressure. Although some people claim to "work well under pressure," the truth is that pressure can have a negative impact on a person's ability to be creative. Research within actual work settings strongly indicates that when time pressure is applied to workers who are trying to come up with creative, innovative ideas, creativity levels decrease dramatically. This is

pressure   the psychological experience produced by urgent demands or expectations for a person's behavior that come from an outside source.

the case even though the workers may think they have been quite productive because of the effort they have made (Amabile et al., 2002).

UNCONTROLLABILITY Another factor that increases a person's experience of stress is the degree of control that the person has over a particular event or situation. The less control a person has, the greater the degree of stress. Researchers in both clinical interviews and experimental studies have found that lack of control in a situation actually enhances the symptoms of posttraumatic stress disorder (Breier et al., 1987).

In studies carried out in a nursing home with the elderly residents as the participants, researchers Rodin and Langer (Langer & Rodin, 1976; Rodin & Langer, 1977) found that those residents who were given more control over their lives (e.g., being able to choose activities and their timing) were more vigorous, active, and sociable than those in the control group. Similarly, employees at mental health clinics who have more input into and control over policy changes experience less stress than those who believe themselves to have little control (Johnson et al., 2006). A more recent study found that retirees experience more happiness and less stress when retirement is by their choice and not forced upon them, regardless of whether the retirement was rapid or gradual (Calvo et al., 2009).

Residents in retirement homes and nursing homes benefit both physically and psychologically when they can choose for themselves the activities in which they wish to participate, such as this exercise class. What are some other means of control residents might experience?

The increase in stress that comes from lack of control explains the relationship between unpredictability and stress as well. When potentially stressful situations are unpredictable, as in police work, the degree of stress experienced is increased. An unpredictable situation is one that is not controllable, which may at least partially explain the increase in stress. In one study, rats were either given an electric shock after a warning tone or given a shock with no warning. The rats receiving the unpredictable shocks developed severe stomach ulcers (Weiss, 1972).

FRUSTRATION **Frustration** occurs when people are blocked or prevented from achieving a desired goal or fulfilling a perceived need. As a stressor, frustration can be *external*, such as when a car breaks down, a desired job offer doesn't come through after all, or a possession is stolen. Losses, rejections, failures, and delays are all sources of external frustration.

Obviously, some frustrations are minor and others are more serious. The seriousness of a frustration is affected by how important the goal or need actually is. A person who is delayed in traffic while driving to the mall to do some shopping just for fun will be less frustrated than a person who is trying to get to the mall before it closes to get that last-minute forgotten and important anniversary gift.

Internal frustrations, also known as *personal frustrations*, occur when the goal or need cannot be attained because of internal or personal characteristics. For example, someone who wants to be an astronaut might find that severe motion sickness prevents him or her from such a goal. If a man wants to be a professional basketball player but is only 5 feet tall and weighs only 85 pounds, he may find that he cannot achieve that goal because of his physical characteristics. A person who wants to be an engineer but who has no math skills would find it difficult to attain that goal.

People make several typical responses when frustrated. The first is *persistence*, or the continuation of efforts to get around whatever is causing the frustration. Persistence may involve making more intense efforts or changing the style of response. For example, anyone who has ever put coins into a drink machine only to find that the drink does not come out has probably (1) pushed the button again, more forcefully, and (2) pushed several other buttons in an effort to get some kind of response from the machine. If neither of these strategies works, many people may hit or kick the machine itself in an act of aggression.

frustration the psychological experience produced by the blocking of a desired goal or fulfillment of a perceived need.

Aggression, or actions meant to harm or destroy, is unfortunately another typical reaction to frustration. Early psychologists in the field of behaviorism proposed a connection between frustration and aggression, calling it the *frustration–aggression hypothesis* (Dollard et al., 1939; Miller et al., 1941). ⓛⓘⓝⓚ to Chapter Ten: Social Psychology, p. 371. Although they believed that some form of frustration nearly always precedes aggression, that does not mean that frustration *always* leads to aggression. In fact, aggression is a frequent and persistent response to frustration, but it is seldom the first response. In a reformulation of the frustration–aggression hypothesis, Berkowitz (1993) stated that frustration creates an internal "readiness to aggress" but that aggression will not follow unless certain external cues are also present. For example, if the human source of a person's frustration is far larger and stronger in appearance than the frustrated person, aggression is an unlikely outcome!

Okay, so if the person who ticked you off is bigger than you—if aggression isn't possible—what can you do?

One could try to reason with the person who is the source of frustration. Reasoning with someone is a form of persistence. Trying to "get around" the problem is another way in which people can deal with frustration. Another possibility is to take out one's frustrations on less threatening, more available targets in a process called **displaced aggression**. Displaced aggression is a form of **displacement**, one of the psychological defense mechanisms discussed in Chapter Eleven, ⓛⓘⓝⓚ to Chapter Eleven: Theories of Personality and Intelligence, p. 389. Anyone who has ever been frustrated by incidents that occurred at work or school and then later yelled at another person (such as a spouse, parent, child, etc.) has experienced displaced aggression. The person one really wants to strike out at is one's boss, the teacher, or whoever or whatever caused the frustration in the first place. Since that could be dangerous, the aggression is reserved for another less threatening or weaker target. For example, unemployment and financial difficulties are extremely frustrating, because they block a person's ability to maintain a certain standard of living and acquire possessions. In one study, male unemployment and single parenthood were the two factors most highly correlated to rates of child abuse (Gillham et al., 1998). Another study (Campbell & Wolf, 2003) found that unemployment is also one of the factors correlated most highly with the murder of abused women, creating four times the risk of murder for women in abusive relationships. Both studies are examples of displaced aggression toward the weaker targets of children and women. Such targets often become *scapegoats*, or habitual targets of displaced aggression. Scapegoats are often pets, children, spouses, and even minority groups (who are seen as having less power). ⓛⓘⓝⓚ to Chapter Ten: Social Psychology, pp. 364–365.

Another possible reaction to frustration is **escape or withdrawal**. Escape or withdrawal can take the form of leaving, dropping out of school, quitting a job, or ending a relationship. Some people manage a psychological escape or withdrawal into apathy (ceasing to care about or act upon the situation), fantasy (which is only a temporary escape), or the use of drugs. Obviously the last-named reaction can lead to even more problems.

CONFLICT **Conflict** is the psychological distress that occurs when a person has to choose between different and incompatible or opposing goals. These goals can be physical needs, psychological drives, wishes, or even external demands. There are several forms of conflict.

In an **approach–approach conflict**, a person experiences a desire for two goals, each of which is attractive. An example of this conflict might be the need to choose between the chocolate cake or the key lime pie for dessert or from among several good choices for a date to the prom. "Six on one hand, half a dozen on the other" is a phrase that sums up this conflict nicely.

aggression actions meant to harm or destroy.

displaced aggression taking out one's frustrations on some less threatening or more available target, a form of displacement.

displacement psychological defense mechanism in which emotional reactions and behavioral responses are shifted to targets that are more available or less threatening than the original target.

escape or withdrawal leaving the presence of a stressor, either literally or by a psychological withdrawal into fantasy, drug abuse, or apathy.

conflict the psychological distress occurring when a person has to choose between different and incompatible or opposing goals.

approach–approach conflict conflict occurring when a person must choose between two desirable goals.

Okay, so if the person who ticked you off is bigger than you—if aggression isn't possible—what can you do?

These parents are fighting in front of their obviously distressed daughter. In some instances, a child who experiences this kind of frustration might act out aggressively toward a sibling or a pet in a form of displaced aggression.

This couple has just purchased their first house, a rite of passage for many young couples. The decision to become a home owner, with the "pulls" of privacy and earning equity and the "pushes" of mortgage payments and upkeep, is often an approach–avoidance conflict.

avoidance–avoidance conflict   conflict occurring when a person must choose between two undesirable goals.

approach–avoidance conflict   conflict occurring when a person must choose or not choose a goal that has both positive and negative aspects.

Avoidance–avoidance conflicts are much more stressful than approach–approach. In this conflict, the choice is between two or more goals or events that are unpleasant. This type of conflict is so common that numerous phrases can be used to symbolize it, for example, "caught between a rock and a hard place," "between the devil and the deep blue sea," "out of the frying pan into the fire," and "lose-lose situation." Because neither alternative is pleasant, many people avoid making a choice by delaying decisions (Tversky & Shafir, 1992). For example, people who are fearful of dental procedures might face the conflict of suffering the pain of a toothache or going to the dentist.

Approach–avoidance conflicts are a little different in that they only involve one goal or event. That goal or event may have both positive and negative aspects that make the goal appealing and unappealing at the same time. For example, marriage is a big decision to make for anyone and usually has both its attractive features, such as togetherness, sharing good times, and companionship, and also its negative aspects, such as disagreements, money issues, and mortgages. This is perhaps the most stressful of all of the types of conflict, causing many people to vacillate* or be unable to decide for or against the goal or event.

---

*Vacillate: to go back and forth between one decision and another.

practice quiz   How much do you remember?

9.3

Pick the best answer.

1. When people have to work harder, do more work, or work faster, they are experiencing _____.
   a. frustration.
   b. uncontrollability.
   c. pressure.
   d. conflict.

2. The stress-increasing effects of uncontrollability are related to the effects of _____ on stress.
   a. frustration
   b. unpredictability
   c. pressure
   d. conflict

3. Eduardo is on his way to an important job interview when his car breaks down on the highway. Eduardo is likely to experience what kind of frustration?
   a. external
   b. internal
   c. personal
   d. uncontrollable

4. The first response that people typically make to frustration is _____.
   a. persistence.
   b. increasing efforts.
   c. varying efforts.
   d. aggression.

5. Jasmine has just been offered an opportunity to teach at a small college in a rural area of Kansas. On the one hand, she really needs a job and the money it would bring would allow her to pay off some debts. But the college is in a very small town far away from any major cities and has very little to offer in the way of amusements. She would also be far away from her family and friends. Jasmine is facing what type of conflict in deciding whether or not to accept the job?
   a. approach–approach
   b. avoidance–avoidance
   c. approach–avoidance
   d. eustress

Physiological Factors: Stress and Health

9.4 How does stress affect the physical functioning of the body and its immune system?

Chapter Two discussed in detail the function of the *autonomic nervous system* (ANS), the part of the human nervous system that is responsible for automatic, involuntary, and life-sustaining activities. The ANS consists of two divisions, the *parasympathetic* and the *sympathetic*. It is the sympathetic nervous system (the "fight-or-flight" system) that reacts when the human body is subjected to stress: Heart rate increases, digestion slows or shuts down, and energy is sent to the muscles to help deal with whatever action the stressful situation requires. The parasympathetic system returns the body to normal, day-to-day functioning after the stress is ended. If the stress is great enough and lasts long enough, the parasympathetic system may shut the body down, causing a collapse into what some people might call "nervous exhaustion." Both systems figure prominently in a classic theory of the body's physiological reactions to stress, the general adaptation syndrome.

The General Adaptation Syndrome

Psychologist Hans Selye was the founder of the field of research concerning stress and its effects on the human body. He studied the sequence of physiological reactions that the body goes through when adapting to a stressor. This sequence (see Figure 9.1) is called the **general adaptation syndrome (GAS)** and consists of three stages (Selye, 1956):

✳ Explore on **MyPsychLab**

✳ **Explore** Selye's General Adaptation Syndrome on **MyPsychLab**

- **Alarm:** When the body first reacts to a stressor, the sympathetic nervous system is activated. The adrenal glands release hormones that increase heart rate, blood pressure, and the supply of blood sugar, resulting in a burst of energy. Reactions such as fever, nausea, and headache are common.

- **Resistance:** As the stress continues, the body settles into sympathetic division activity, continuing to release the stress hormones that help the body fight off, or resist, the stressor. The early symptoms of alarm lessen, and the person or animal may actually feel better. This stage will continue until the stressor ends or the organism has used up all of its resources. Researchers have found that one of the hormones released under stress, noradrenaline, actually seems to affect the brain's processing of pain, so that when under stress a person may experience a kind of analgesia (insensitivity to pain) if, for example, the person hits an arm or a shin (Delaney et al., 2007).

- **Exhaustion:** When the body's resources are gone, exhaustion occurs. Exhaustion can lead to the formation of stress-related diseases (i.e., high blood pressure or a weakened immune system) or the death of the organism if outside help is unavailable (Stein-Behrens et al., 1994). When the stressor ends, the parasympathetic division activates and the body attempts to replenish its resources.

Alarm and resistance are stages that people experience many times throughout life, allowing people to adapt to life's demands (Selye, 1976). It is the prolonged secretion of the stress hormones during the exhaustion stage that can lead to the most harmful effects of stress. It was this aspect of Selye's work that convinced other researchers of the connection between stress and certain "diseases of adaptation" as Selye termed them. The most common of these diseases are ulcers and high blood pressure.

general adaptation syndrome (GAS) the three stages of the body's physiological reaction to stress, including alarm, resistance, and exhaustion.

FIGURE 9.1 **General Adaptation Syndrome**

The diagram at the top shows some of the physical reactions to stress in each of the three stages of the general adaptation syndrome. The diagram at the bottom shows the relationship of each of the three stages to the individual's ability to resist a stressor. In the alarm stage, resistance drops at first as the sympathetic system quickly activates. But resistance then rapidly increases as the body mobilizes its defense systems. In the resistance stage, the body is working at a much increased level of resistance, using resources until the stress ends or the resources run out. In the exhaustion stage, the body is no longer able to resist as resources have been depleted, and at this point disease and even death are possible.

Immune System and Stress

As Selye first discovered, the **immune system** (the system of cells, organs, and chemicals in the body that responds to attacks on the body from diseases and injuries) is affected by stress. The field of *psychoneuroimmunology* concerns the study of the effects of psychological factors such as stress, emotions, thinking, and behavior on the immune system (Ader; 2003; Cohen & Herbert, 1996; Kiecolt-Glaser, 2009; Kiecolt-Glaser et al., 1995, 1996, 2002). Researchers in this field have found that stress triggers the same response in the immune system that infection triggers (Maier & Watkins, 1998). Certain enzymes and other chemicals (including antibodies) are created by immune cells when the immune cells, or white blood cells, encounter an infection in the body. The white blood cells surround the bacteria or other infectious material and release the chemicals and enzymes into the bloodstream. From there, these chemicals activate receptor sites on the *vagus nerve*, the longest nerve that connects the body to the brain. It is the activation of these receptor sites that signals the brain that the body is sick, causing the brain to respond by further activation of the immune system.

immune system the system of cells, organs, and chemicals of the body that responds to attacks from diseases, infections, and injuries.

Stress activates this same system but starts in the brain rather than in the bloodstream. The same chemical changes that occur in the brain when it has been alerted by the vagus nerve to infection in the body occurred in laboratory animals when they were kept isolated from other animals or given electric shocks (Maier & Watkins, 1998). This has the effect of "priming" the immune system, allowing it to more successfully resist the effects of the stress, as in Selye's resistance stage of the GAS.

Hormones also help the immune system fight the effects of stress. Researchers (Morgan et al., 2009) have found that a hormone called dehydroepiandrosterone (DHEA), known to provide antistress benefits in animals, also aids humans in stress toleration—perhaps by regulating the effects of stress on the hippocampus (part of the limbic system). ⓛⓘⓝⓚ to Chapter Two: The Biological Perspective, pp. 66–67.

So stress actually increases the activity of the immune system? But then how does stress end up causing those diseases, such as high blood pressure?

The positive effects of stress on the immune system only seem to work when the stress is not a continual, chronic condition. As stress continues, the body's resources begin to fail in the exhaustion phase of the general adaptation to stress (Kiecolt-Glaser et al., 1987, 1995, 1996; Prigerson et al., 1997). In one study, college students who were undergoing a stressful series of exams were compared to a group of similar students relaxing during a time of no classes and no exams (Deinzer et al., 2000). The exam group tested significantly lower for immune system chemicals that help fight off disease than did the relaxing control group, even as long as 14 days after the exams were over. The suppression of immune system functioning by stress apparently can continue even after the stress itself is over.

One reason that the early stress reaction is helpful but prolonged stress is not might be that the stress reaction, in evolutionary terms, is meant for only a short-term response, such as running from a predator (Sapolsky, 2004). That level of intense bodily and hormonal activity isn't meant to go on and on, as it does for human beings in the modern, stress-filled life we now know. Humans experience the stress reaction over prolonged periods of times and in situations that are not necessarily life threatening, leading to a breakdown in the immune system. (See Figure 9.2.)

HEART DISEASE Of course, anything that can weaken the immune system can have a negative effect on other bodily systems. For example, stress has been shown to put people at a higher risk for heart attacks and strokes at least in part because the liver does not have a chance to clear the fat and cholesterol from the bloodstream. The result is clogged arteries and eventually the possibility of heart attacks. In one study, middle-aged men were questioned about stress, diet, and lifestyle factors and were examined for biological risk factors for heart disease: obesity, high blood sugar, high triglycerides (a type of fatty acid found in the blood), and low levels of HDL or "good" cholesterol. (See Figure 9.3.) Stress and the production of stress hormones were found to be strongly linked to all four factors: The more stress the workers were exposed to in their work environment and home life, the more likely they were to exhibit these risk factors (Brunner et al., 2002).

Other studies have produced similar findings. One study looked at the heart health of people who suffered acute stress reactions after the 9/11 terrorist attacks and found a 53 percent increase in heart ailments over the three years following the attacks (Holman et al., 2008). Another large-scale study conducted around the same time

> So stress actually increases the activity of the immune system? But then how does stress end up causing those diseases, like high blood pressure?

FIGURE 9.2 Stress Duration and Illness
In this graph, the risk of getting a cold virus increases greatly as the months of exposure to a stressor increase. Although a stress reaction can be useful in its early phase, prolonged stress has a negative impact on the immune system, leaving the body vulnerable to illnesses such as a cold. *Source:* Cohen et al. (1998).

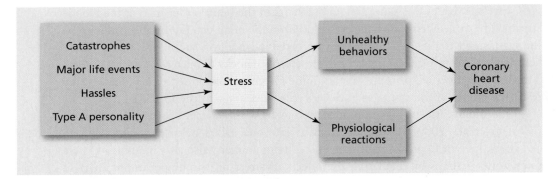

FIGURE 9.3 Stress and Coronary Heart Disease
The box on the left represents various sources of stress (Type A personality refers to someone who is ambitious, always working, and usually hostile). In addition to the physical reactions that accompany the stress reaction, an individual under stress may be more likely to engage in unhealthy behavior such as overeating, drinking alcohol or taking other kinds of drugs, avoiding exercise, and acting out in anger or frustration. This kind of behavior also contributes to an increased risk of coronary heart disease.

found that work stress is highly associated with an increased risk of coronary heart disease due to negative effects of stress on the autonomic nervous system and glandular activity (Chandola et al., 2008). Prolonged stress is simply not good for the heart.

Stress can also lead to certain unhealthy behaviors, such as drinking alcohol; smoking; eating all the wrong, high-fat, high-calorie "comfort" foods; and avoiding exercise—all factors associated with poor health.

DIABETES   Review the last paragraph, and it becomes obvious that weight problems may also become associated with stress. One chronic illness sometimes associated with excessive weight gain is *diabetes*, specifically **Type 2 diabetes** (Type 1 diabetes is associated with failure of the pancreas to secrete enough insulin, necessitating medication, and is usually diagnosed before the age of 40.) Type 2 diabetes is associated with excessive weight gain and occurs when pancreas insulin levels become less efficient as the body size increases. Type 2 diabetes can respond favorably to proper diet, exercise, and weight loss, but may also require medication. Typically, it is associated with older adults, but with the rise in obesity among children, more cases of Type 2 diabetes in children are now occurring.

While controllable, diabetes is a serious disorder that has now been associated with an increased risk of Alzheimer's disease, although memory loss appears to be slower for diabetic Alzheimer patients than for nondiabetic Alzheimer's patients (Sanz et al., 2009). Several ongoing longitudinal studies strongly suggest that Type 2 diabetes not only is associated with mental decline in middle-aged individuals (Nooyens et al., 2010), but also stress can compound the risk of that mental decline (Reynolds et al., 2010).

CANCER   Cancer is not one disease but rather a collection of diseases that can affect any part of the body. Unlike normal cells, which divide and reproduce according to genetic instructions and stop dividing according to those same instructions, cancer cells divide without stopping. The resulting tumors affect the normal functioning of the organs and systems they invade, causing organs to fail and eventually killing the organism. People, animals, and plants can have cancer.

Although stress itself cannot give a person cancer, it can have a suppressing effect on the immune system, making the unchecked growth of cancer more likely. In particular, an immune system cell called a **natural killer cell** has as its main functions the suppression of viruses and the destruction of tumor cells (Herberman & Ortaldo, 1981). Stress has been shown to depress the release of natural killer cells, making it more difficult for the body's systems to fight cancerous growths (Zorilla et al., 2001). The hormone adrenaline is released under stress and has been found to interfere with a protein that normally would suppress the growth of cancer cells (Sastry et al.,

Type 2 diabetes   disease involving failure of the pancreas to secrete enough insulin, necessitating medication, usually diagnosed before the age of 40 and can be associated with obesity.

natural killer cell   immune system cell responsible for suppressing viruses and destroying tumor cells.

2007). In other research, stress has been linked to the accumulation of genetic errors that can lead to the formation of cancer cells and tumors: Stress causes the release of hormones such as adrenaline and noradrenaline that, over time, can cause mistakes in the instructions given by the genes to the cells of the body. (Among these mistakes is damage to the telomeres, structures at the ends of chromosomes that control the number of times a cell can reproduce.) As these mistakes "pile up" over the years, cells can begin to grow out of control, causing the growth of tumors and possibly cancer (Kiecolt-Glaser et al., 2002). One study found that stress increases the risk of cervical cancer in women (Fang et al., 2008).

OTHER HEALTH ISSUES   Heart disease and cancer are not the only diseases affected by stress. Prolonged, chronic stress has been linked to changes in the immune system's ability to fight off inflammation (Miller et al., 2007). Other studies have shown that children in families experiencing ongoing stress are more likely to develop fevers with illness than are other children (Wyman et al., 2007). (Oddly enough, this same study showed that in children stress actually seems to improve the function of their natural killer cells—just the opposite effect that is seen in adults.) A review of research and scientific literature (Cohen et al., 2007) found stress to be a contributing factor in many human diseases, including not only heart disease but also depression and HIV/AIDS.

The physical effects of stress on the body and the immune system are only part of the picture of the influence of stress in daily life. The next section looks at how cognitive factors such as how one interprets a stressful event and psychological factors such as one's personality type can affect the impact of stress. First, let's take a brief look at a field of psychology that has arisen in response to our increased understanding of health and its relationship to psychological and behavioral factors.

issues in psychology
Health Psychology and Stress

In the last three decades, people have become more aware of health issues and their relationship to what we do, what we eat, whom we see, and how we think. A relatively new branch of psychology has begun to explore these relationships.

Health psychology focuses on how our physical activities, psychological traits, and social relationships affect our overall health and rate of illnesses. Psychologists who specialize in this field are typically clinical or counseling psychologists and may work with medical doctors in a hospital or clinic setting, although there are health psychologists who are primarily engaged in teaching and research. Some health psychologists focus on health and wellness issues in the workplace or public health issues such as disease prevention through immunizations or nutrition education. Others are more concerned with health care programs that service all levels of the socioeconomic layers of society (Marks et al., 2005).

Health psychologists seek to understand how behavior (such as use of drugs, optimism, personality, or type of food eaten) can affect a person's ability to fight off illnesses—or increase the likelihood of getting sick. They want to know how to prevent illness and how factors like poverty, wealth, religion, social support, personality, and even one's ethnicity can affect health. In this age of a new focus on health care, health psychology is destined to become a more important force in future research.

QUESTIONS FOR FURTHER DISCUSSION

1. How have some of the factors studied by health psychologists affected you in recent months?

2. What health issues might arise in the college or university setting that could have a positive or negative impact on your psychological and physical well-being?

health psychology   area of psychology focusing on how physical activities, psychological traits, and social relationships affect overall health and rate of illnesses.

primary appraisal the first step in assessing stress, which involves estimating the severity of a stressor and classifying it as either a threat or a challenge.

The Influence of Cognition and Personality on Stress

9.5 How do cognitive factors and personality differences affect the experience of stress?

COGNITIVE FACTORS IN STRESS: LAZARUS'S COGNITIVE APPRAISAL APPROACH
Cognitive psychologist Richard Lazarus developed a cognitive view of stress called the *cognitive-mediational theory* of emotions, in which the way people think about and appraise a stressor is a major factor in how stressful that particular stressor becomes (Lazarus, 1991, 1999; Lazarus & Folkman, 1984). **LINK** to Chapter Eight: Motivation and Emotion, p. 302. According to Lazarus, there is a two-step process in assessing a stressor's degree of threat or harm and how one should react to that stressor. (See Figure 9.4.)

PRIMARY APPRAISAL The first step in appraising a stressor is called **primary appraisal**. It involves estimating the severity of the stressor and classifying it as a threat (something that could be harmful in the future), a challenge (something to be met and defeated), or a harm or loss that has already occurred. For example, a student who has not read the text or taken good notes will certainly appraise an upcoming exam as threatening, but if that student has studied, read, and feels prepared, the upcoming exam is much more likely to be appraised as an opportunity to do well.

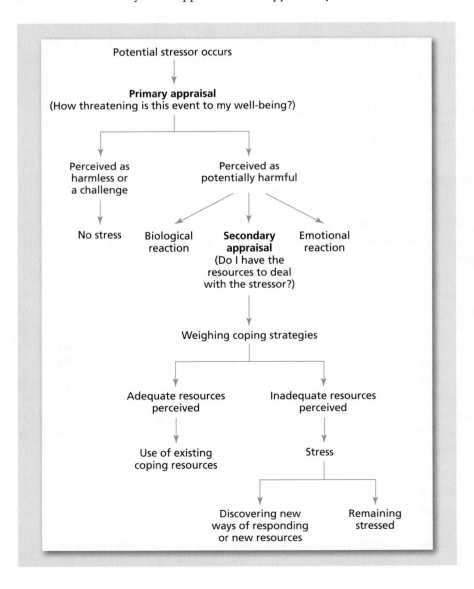

FIGURE 9.4 Responses to a Stressor
Lazarus's Cognitive Appraisal Approach. According to this approach, there are two steps in cognitively determining the degree of stress created by a potential stressor. Primary appraisal involves determining if the potential stressor is a threat. If it is perceived as a threat, secondary appraisal occurs in addition to the bodily and emotional reactions. Secondary appraisal involves determining the resources one has to deal with the stress, such as time, money, and physical ability. Inadequate resources lead to increased feelings of stress and the possibility of developing new resources to deal with the stress.

Perceiving a stressor as a challenge instead of a threat makes coping with the stressor or the harm it may already have caused more likely to be successful, whereas perceiving it as an embarrassment or imagining failure or rejection is more likely to lead to increased stress reactions, negative emotions, and an inability to cope well (Folkman, 1997; Lazarus, 1993). Think positive!

SECONDARY APPRAISAL In **secondary appraisal**, people who have identified a threat or harmful effect must estimate the resources that they have available for coping with the stressor. Resources might include social support, money, time, energy, ability, or any number of potential resources, depending on the threat. If resources are perceived as adequate or abundant, the degree of stress will be considerably less than if resources are missing or lacking.

As an example, let's say that a person's position at a firm has just been downsized. That's a fairly big stressor in most situations, but the degree of stress experienced and the coping abilities of that person will depend on both primary appraisal and secondary appraisal. In most cases, primary appraisal might go something like this: "I've lost my job! I need a job, so this is bad, very bad!" ("This is a threat!") The secondary appraisal might result in the following: "I don't have much money in savings, and the job market for my skills is pretty bad right now. I don't have anyone I can borrow money from or live with while I'm looking for more work. I'm going to lose everything!" ("I don't have the resources to deal with this!") Contrast that person's situation with this person's primary appraisal situation: "I've been let go, but that's not so bad. I wanted to look for a new job anyhow." ("This is a challenge.") The secondary appraisal might be: "I have some money in savings, and I can live with my brother for a while if nothing turns up quickly—I should be fine." ("I have the resources to deal with this.") Which person is going to experience more stress and have more health problems as a consequence?

Personality Factors in Stress

Of course, how one cognitively assesses a stressor has a lot to do with one's personality. People with certain kinds of personality traits—such as aggressiveness or a naturally high level of anxiety, for example—seem to create more stress for themselves than may exist in the actual stressor. Even as long ago as the early 1930s, psychologists had evidence that personality characteristics are a major factor in predicting health. A longitudinal study begun in 1932 (Lehr & Thomae, 1987) found that personality was almost as important to longevity (how long people live) as genetic, physical, and lifestyle factors. Other researchers have found that people who live to be very old—into their nineties and even over 100 years—tend to be relaxed, easygoing, cheerful, and active. People who have opposite personality traits such as aggressiveness, stubbornness, inflexibility, and tenseness typically do not live as long as the average life expectancy (Levy et al., 2002).

Those personality traits are some of the factors associated with two personality types that have been related to how people deal with stress and the influence of certain personality characteristics on coronary heart disease.

TYPE A AND TYPE B In 1974, medical doctors Meyer Friedman and Ray Rosenman published a book titled *Type A Behavior and Your Heart*. The book was the result of studies spanning three decades of research into the influence of certain personality characteristics and coronary heart disease

secondary appraisal the second step in assessing a threat, which involves estimating the resources available to the person for coping with the stressor.

"He always times 60 Minutes."
© The New Yorker Collection 1983 Mischa Richter from cartoonbank.com. All Rights Reserved.

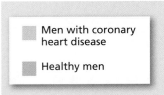

Men with coronary heart disease

Healthy men

FIGURE 9.5 Personality and Coronary Heart Disease
The two bars on the left represent men with Type A personalities. Notice that within the Type A men, there are more than twice as many who suffer from coronary heart disease as those who are healthy. The two bars on the right represent men with Type B personalities. Far more Type B personalities are healthy than Type A personalities, and there are far fewer Type B personalities with coronary heart disease when compared to Type A personalities.
Source: Miller et al. (1991, 1996).

> What about people who don't blow their top but try to keep everything in instead? Wouldn't that be bad for a person's health?

Type A personality   person who is ambitious, time conscious, extremely hardworking, and tends to have high levels of hostility and anger as well as being easily annoyed.

Type B personality   person who is relaxed and laid-back, less driven and less competitive than Type A, and slow to anger.

Type C personality   pleasant but repressed person, who tends to internalize his or her anger and anxiety and who finds expressing emotions difficult.

(Friedman & Kasanin, 1943; Friedman & Rosenman, 1959; Rosenman et al., 1975). Since then, numerous researchers have explored the link between what Friedman called Type A and Type B personalities.

Type A people are workaholics—they are very competitive, ambitious, hate to waste time, and are easily annoyed. They feel a constant sense of pressure, and they have a strong tendency to try to do several things at once. Often successful but frequently unsatisfied, they always seem to want to go faster and do more, and they get easily upset over small things. A typical Type A finds it difficult to relax and do nothing—Type A people take work with them on vacation, a laptop to the beach, and do business over the phone in the car.

In 1961, the *Western Collaborative Group Study* (Rosenman et al., 1975) assessed 3,500 men and followed them for eight years. For example, participants were asked to agree or disagree with statements such as "I can relax without guilt," in which strong agreement indicates a Type B personality. The results were that Type A men were three times more likely to develop heart disease than Type B men. **Type B** people are not that competitive or driven, tend to be easygoing and slow to anger, and seem relaxed and at peace. Type B people are more likely to take a book to the beach to cover up their face than to actually read the book. (See Figure 9.5.)

The *Framingham Heart Study* found that the risk of coronary heart disease for women who work and are also Type A is four times that of Type B working women (Eaker & Castelli, 1988). Other research has narrowed the key factors in Type A personality and heart disease to one characteristic: hostility* (Frederickson et al., 2000; Matthews et al., 2004; Williams, 1999; Williams et al., 1980). Williams and his colleagues used the *Minnesota Multiphasic Personality Inventory*, a personality test that looks for certain characteristics that include the level of hostility. **LINK** to Chapter Eleven: Theories of Personality and Intelligence, p. 408. In this study, 424 patients who had undergone exploratory surgery for coronary heart disease were examined, and the presence of heart disease was related both to being Type A and to being hostile, with hostility being the more significant factor in the hardening of the arteries to the heart (Williams, 2001; Williams et al., 1980). Several studies have consistently linked hostility to an increased risk of coronary heart disease (Brondolo et al., 2003; Chang et al., 2002; Markovitz et al., 1997; Siegler et al., 2003).

Even children may not escape the hostility–heart disease link. A recent study has found that children and adolescents who scored high on assessments of hostility were more likely to show physical changes such as obesity, resistance to insulin, high blood pressure, and elevated levels of triglycerides three years after the initial measurements of hostility had been made (Raikkonen et al., 2003).

● What about people who don't blow their top but try to keep everything in instead? Wouldn't that be bad for a person's health?

TYPE C   A third personality type was identified by researchers Temoshok and Dreher (1992) as being associated with a higher incidence of cancer. **Type C** people tend to be very pleasant and try to keep the peace but find it difficult to express emotions, especially negative ones. They tend to internalize their anger and often experience a sense of despair over the loss of a loved one or a loss of hope. They are often lonely. These personality characteristics are strongly associated with cancer, and people who have cancer and this personality type often have thicker cancerous tumors as well (Eysenck, 1994a, 1994b; Temoshok & Dreher, 1992). Just as the stress of hostility puts the cardiovascular systems of Type A people at greater

---

*Hostility: feelings of conflict, anger, and ill will that are long lasting.

risk, the internalized negative emotions of the Type C personality may increase the levels of harmful stress hormones, weaken the immune system, and slow recovery. The one exception to these findings may be in women at risk for breast cancer: A study of over 9,000 women found no connection between personality traits and increased or decreased risk of breast cancer (Bleiker et al., 2008).

A word of caution here: "personality-type" theories have come under criticism in recent years. Many consider them to be too simplistic—many people would not fall easily into one type or another. Nevertheless, many of the personality traits associated with these types do seem to be associated with stress and longevity. Many of the characteristics of the Type A personality, for example, fit the description of a major personality trait called *neuroticism,* the tendency to worry, be moody, and emotionally intense. ⓁⒾⓃⓀ to Chapter Eleven: Theories of Personality and Intelligence, p. 402. One longitudinal study's findings indicate that these characteristics are associated with an increased risk of an earlier death because people with these traits engage in poor health habits—poor diet, excessive drinking, smoking, and lack of exercise, to name a few (Mroczek et al., 2009).

⬛▶️ Read on MyPsychLab

THE HARDY PERSONALITY Not all Type A people are prone to heart disease. Some people actually seem to thrive on stress instead of letting stress wear them down. These people have what is called the **hardy personality**, a term first coined by psychologist Suzanne Kobasa (1979). Hardy people (call them "Type H") differ from ordinary, hostile Type A people and others who suffer more ill effects due to stress in three ways:

- Hardy people have a deep sense of *commitment* to their values, beliefs, sense of identity, work, and family life.

- Hardy people also feel that they are in *control* of their lives and what happens to them.

- Hardy people tend to interpret events in primary appraisal differently than people who are not hardy. When things go wrong, they do not see a frightening problem to be avoided but instead a *challenge* to be met and answered.

Why would those three characteristics (often known as the three "C's" of hardiness) lessen the negative impact of stress? Commitment makes a person more willing to make sacrifices and deal with hardships than if commitment were lacking. Think about it: Have you ever had a job that you hated? Every little frustration and every snag were very stressful, right? Now think about doing something you love to do. The frustrations and snags that inevitably come with any endeavor just don't seem quite as bad when you are doing something you really want to do, do they?

As for control, uncontrollability is one of the major factors cited as increasing stress, as discussed earlier in this chapter. Seeing events as challenges rather than as problems also changes the level of stress experienced. This difference is similar to that felt when riding a roller coaster: If riding the coaster is your own idea, it's fun; if someone makes you ride it, it's not fun.

The four personality types discussed so far can be summed up this way: If life gives you lemons,

- Type A people get enraged and throw the lemons back, having a minor heart attack while doing so.

TYPE Z BEHAVIOR

⬛▶️ Read and learn more about Type C on **MyPsychLab**

Regular exercise—whether alone or in the company of family and friends—increases the functioning of the immune system and helps give people a sense of control over their health. Having a sense of control decreases feelings of stress, which also helps the immune system to function well.

hardy personality   a person who seems to thrive on stress but lacks the anger and hostility of the Type A personality.

- Type C people don't say anything but fume about the lemons inside where no one can see.
- Type B people gather all the lemons and make lemonade.
- Hardy people (Type H) gather the lemons, make lemonade, sell it, turn it into a franchise business, and make millions. (Remember, laughing is good for you!)

EXPLANATORY STYLE: OPTIMISTS AND PESSIMISTS In addition to personality type, other personal factors have an influence on people's reactions to stressors. One of these factors is the attitude that people have toward the things that happen to them in life.

Optimists are people who always tend to look for positive outcomes. For an optimist, a glass is half full, whereas for a pessimist, the glass is half empty. **Pessimists** seem to expect the worst to happen. Researchers have found that optimism is associated with longer life and increased immune system functioning. Mayo Clinic researchers conducted a longitudinal study of optimists and pessimists (as assessed by a scale) over a period of 30 years (Maruta et al., 2002). The results for pessimists were not good: They had a much higher death rate than did the optimists, and those that were still living in 1994 had more problems with physical and emotional health, more pain, less ability to take part in social activities, and less energy than optimists. The optimists had a 50 percent lower risk of premature death and were calmer, more peaceful, and happier than the pessimists (Maruta et al., 2002). An earlier study linked being optimistic to higher levels of helper T cells (immune system cells that direct and increase the functioning of the immune system) and higher levels of natural killer cells, the body's antivirus, anticancer cells (Segerstrom et al., 1998; Segerstrom & Sephton, 2010).

Martin Seligman is a social learning psychologist who developed the concept of *learned helplessness,* Ⓛ Ⓘ Ⓝ Ⓚ to Chapter Four: Learning, p. 150, and began the positive psychology movement. Seligman (2002) has outlined four ways in which optimism may affect how long a person lives:

1. Optimists are less likely to develop learned helplessness, the tendency to stop trying to achieve a goal that has been blocked in the past.

2. Optimists are more likely than pessimists to take care of their health by preventive measures (such as going to the doctor regularly and eating right) because they believe that their actions make a difference in what happens to them. (Remember, this is a characteristic of hardy people as well.)

3. Optimists are far less likely than pessimists to become depressed, and depression is associated with mortality because of the effect of depression on the immune system.

4. Optimists have more effectively functioning immune systems than pessimists, perhaps because they experience less psychological stress.

Seligman (1998) has also found that optimists are more successful in their life endeavors than pessimists. Optimistic politicians win more elections, optimistic students get better grades, and optimistic athletes win more contests.

Whoa—optimistic students get better grades? How do I become an optimist? Sign me up!

Whoa—optimistic students get better grades? How do I become an optimist? Sign me up!

Optimism is mostly a matter of controlling mood or emotional reactions to situations. Psychiatrist Dr. Susan Vaughan (2000) has some good advice for optimistic people who want to keep a positive outlook:

- **Alternative thinking:** Optimists tend to take bad things that happen less personally, coming up with alternative explanations for why the bad thing happened. For example, optimists tend to attribute poor exam grades to the difficulty of that particular material or to not having enough time to study. They appraise it as a challenge and assume that they will perform more successfully in the future.

optimists people who expect positive outcomes.

pessimists people who expect negative outcomes.

- **Downward social comparison:** Many people make themselves feel better by comparing their performance to that of less competent others, making them feel better and protecting self-esteem. Optimists use *downward social comparison* frequently.

- **Relaxation:** Optimists use relaxation as a way to improve mood, such as exercising, meditating, or reading a good book.

HOW TO BECOME AN OPTIMISTIC THINKER   The way to become an optimist is to monitor one's own thinking. Recognition of negative thoughts is the first step, followed by disputing those same negative thoughts (Seligman, 2002). The problem is that most people don't really think about their thoughts or characterize them as negative or pessimistic, which means that the damaging effects of such thinking are left uncontrolled. Here's a plan to follow to become an optimistic thinker:

1. When a bad mood strikes, stop and think about what just went through your head.

2. When you've recognized the negative statements, treat them as if they came from someone else—someone who is trying to make your life miserable. Think about the damage the statement is doing to you.

3. Argue with those thoughts. Challenge each negative statement and replace it with a more positive statement.

   Example:

1. "I'll never get this term paper finished, it's too hard and there's so much going on that it's impossible!" What words in this statement make it pessimistic? "Never" is a long time. Why is it too hard? Is it really impossible, or just difficult? Is it just one part of the paper that seems so hard, or is it the whole thing?

2. "That statement isn't going to help me at all. It just makes me feel worse and that makes me unmotivated to work on the paper."

3. "I can finish the term paper. I'm just going to have to devote more time to working on it. I can make a timetable for finishing the different parts of the paper and stop spending so much time watching television and escaping into other activities that can wait until the paper is finished. I've been in situations like this before and managed, so I can manage now, too."

Notice that the third way of thinking is much more positive and hopeful. It includes ways to get around what seemed too hard or impossible in the negative statement. Essentially, the last step in becoming a more optimistic thinker is to learn to argue with yourself and correct distorted or faulty thinking.

How can I recognize distorted thinking when it's my own thoughts in the first place?

Recognizing faulty thinking can be difficult at first. The following questions may help people to hone in on negative thinking:

1. In thinking about the thoughts you have had in the last few hours, how many of them were negative thoughts? How could you change those thoughts to be more positive?

2. When thinking about people you know who make a lot of negative self-statements or who are always minimizing their efforts or putting themselves down, how does their behavior make you feel? How do you think their behavior makes them feel?

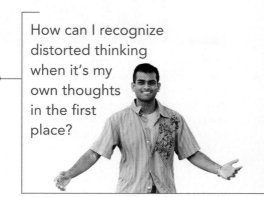

How can I recognize distorted thinking when it's my own thoughts in the first place?

practice quiz How much do you remember?

Pick the best answer.

1. In the _____ stage of the GAS, the person may actually start to feel better.
   a. alarm
   b. resistance
   c. exhaustion
   d. termination

2. The activation of the immune system response by stress differs from the activation of that system by illness in that _____.
   a. illness activates areas in the brain first.
   b. stress increases the release of natural killer cells.
   c. stress activates a different immune response than does illness.
   d. stress activates areas in the brain first.

3. According to Lazarus, secondary appraisal involves _____.
   a. estimating the severity of the stressor.
   b. classifying the stressor as a threat or challenge.
   c. deciding whether the stressor is a problem.
   d. estimating the resources a person has available for coping.

4. Adam is very ambitious and driven to succeed. He is easily angered, always wants to be working, and finds it hard to relax. According to research, Adam _____.

   a. is at a high risk for coronary heart disease.
   b. is a hardy personality.
   c. is a Type B personality.
   d. is a Type C personality.

5. Which of the following is NOT one of the three "C's" of the hardy personality?
   a. commitment
   b. callousness
   c. control
   d. challenge

6. Optimism has been associated with all of the following except _____.
   a. taking care of one's health.
   b. increased rates of learned helplessness.
   c. lower rates of depression.
   d. healthy immune systems.

ANSWERS ON PAGE AK–2

Social Factors in Stress: People Who Need People

9.6 What social factors influence stress reactions?

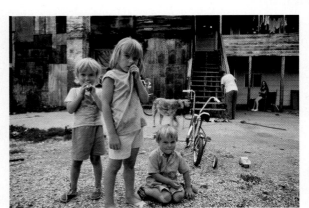

Poverty can lead to many conditions that increase the degree of stress experienced by both adults and children. These children, for example, may face an increased risk of malnutrition, illness, and exposure to violence because of the conditions under which they must live.

👁‍🗨 Watch a video on rude atmospheres in the workplace on **MyPsychLab**

As stated earlier, much of the stress in everyday life comes from having to deal with other people and with the rules of social interaction. Overcrowding, for example, is a common source of stress and may be one reason for the increase in *road rage*, or the tendency for drivers to become excessively enraged by ordinary traffic frustrations, sometimes resulting in serious injuries, assaults, and even death (AAA Foundation for Traffic Safety, 1997). Two prominent social factors in creating stressful living conditions that are both economically based are poverty and job stress.

POVERTY Living in poverty is stressful for many reasons. Lack of sufficient money to provide the basic necessities of life can lead to many stressors for both adults and children: overcrowding, lack of medical care, increased rates of disabilities due to poor prenatal care, noisy environments, increased rates of illness (such as asthma in childhood) and violence, and substance abuse (Aligne et al., 2000; Bracey, 1997; Leroy & Symes, 2001; Park et al., 2002; Renchler, 1993; Rouse, 1998; Schmitz et al., 2001).

JOB STRESS Even if a person has a job and is making an adequate salary, stresses associated with the workplace add to daily stressors. Some of the typical sources of stress in the workplace include the workload, lack of variety or meaningfulness in work, lack of control over decisions, long hours, poor physical work conditions, and lack of job security (Murphy, 1995). 👁‍🗨 Watch on **MyPsychLab**

Stress at work can result in the same symptoms as stress from any other source: headaches, high blood pressure, indigestion, and other physical symptoms; anxiety, irritability, anger, depression, and other psychological symptoms; and behavioral symptoms such as overeating, drug use, poor job performance, or changes in family relationships (Anschuetz, 1999).

There are times when I feel like I've just had it with school and all the work the teachers pile on—is that something like workplace stress?

Burnout One of the more serious effects of workplace stress is a condition called burnout. **Burnout** can be defined as negative changes in thoughts, emotions, and behavior as a result of prolonged stress or frustration (Miller & Smith, 1993). Symptoms of burnout are extreme dissatisfaction, pessimism, lowered job satisfaction, and a desire to quit. Although burnout is most commonly associated with job stress, college students can also suffer from burnout when the stresses of college life—term papers, exams, assignments, and the like—become overwhelming. The emotional exhaustion associated with burnout can be lessened when a person at risk of burnout is a member, within the work environment, of a social group that provides support and also the motivation to continue to perform despite being exhausted (Halbesleben & Bowler, 2007).

HOW CULTURE AFFECTS STRESS When a person from one culture must live in another culture, that person may experience a great deal of stress. *Acculturation* means the process of adapting to a new or different culture, often the dominant culture (Sodowsky et al., 1991). The stress resulting from the need to change and adapt to the dominant or majority culture is called **acculturative stress** (Berry & Kim, 1998; Berry & Sam, 1997).

The method by which a minority person enters into the majority culture can also have an impact on the degree of stress that person will experience (Berry & Kim, 1988). *Integration* involves maintaining one's original cultural identity while still forming positive relationships with dominant culture members. For example, a person may observe cultural traditions in the home but interact with members of the dominant culture according to local customs, dress, and expectations. For people who choose integration, acculturative stress is usually low (Ward & Rana-Deuba, 1999).

In *assimilation*, the minority person gives up the old cultural identity and completely adopts the ways of the majority culture. Assimilation leads to moderate levels of stress, most likely owing to the loss of cultural patterns and rejection by other members of the minority culture who have not chosen assimilation (LaFromboise et al., 1993; Lay & Nguyen, 1998).

Separation is a pattern in which the minority person rejects the majority culture's ways and tries to maintain the original cultural identity. Members of the minority culture refuse to learn the language of the dominant culture, and they live where others from their culture live, socializing only with others from their original culture. Separation results in a fairly high degree of stress, and that stress will be even higher if the separation is forced (by discrimination from the majority group) rather than voluntary (self-imposed withdrawal from the majority culture).

The greatest acculturative stress will most likely be experienced by people who have chosen to be *marginalized*; that is, they neither maintain contact with the original culture nor join the majority culture. They essentially live on the "margins" of both cultures without feeling or becoming part of either culture and without a social support system. Marginalized individuals do not have the security of the familiar culture of origin or the acceptance of the majority culture and may suffer a loss of identity and feel alienated from others (Roysircai-Sodowsky & Maestas, 2000).

I hear the term *social support system* all the time now. Exactly what is it?

burnout negative changes in thoughts, emotions, and behavior as a result of prolonged stress or frustration.

acculturative stress stress resulting from the need to change and adapt a person's ways to the majority culture.

There are times when I feel like I've just had it with school and all the work the teachers pile on—is that something like workplace stress?

This Buddhist group is celebrating Songkran, the New Year, by performing their cultural ritual of pouring water over their elders' palms. Although they are wearing clothing typical of people living in Los Angeles, California, where the ceremony is taking place, they still maintain some of their old cultural traditions.

I hear the term *social support system* all the time now. Exactly what is it?

Coping with illness is always made easier when one has social support. Here, a man recovering in the hospital is visited by a volunteer and her dog. Animals are also a good source of social support, and people who have animals have been shown to recover from illnesses and stressors more quickly (Allen et al., 2002).

THE POSITIVE BENEFITS OF SOCIAL SUPPORT A **social support system** is the network of friends, family members, neighbors, coworkers, and others who can offer help to a person in need. That help can take the form of advice, physical or monetary support, information, emotional support, love and affection, or companionship. Research has consistently shown that having a good social support system is of critical importance in a person's ability to cope with stressors: People with good social support systems tend to live longer and are less likely to die from illnesses or injuries than those without such support (Gardner & Oswald, 2004; Kulik & Mahler, 1989, 1993; Vaillant, 2002). Social support has been found to have a positive effect on the immune system (Holt-Lunstad et al., 2003) and improves the mental health and physical functioning of people who have *lupus*, a chronic inflammatory disease that can affect nearly any part of the body (Sutcliffe et al., 1999; Ward et al., 1999) as well as those with cancer and HIV (Carver & Antoni, 2004; Gonzalez et al., 2004).

Social support can make a stressor seem less threatening because people with such support know that help is available. Having people to talk to about one's problems reduces the physical symptoms of stress—talking about frightening or frustrating events with others can help people think more realistically about the threat, for example, and talking with people who have had similar experiences can help put the event into perspective. **LINK** to Chapter Thirteen: Psychological Therapies, pp. 479–480. How people think about a stressor is also a powerful influence on their ability to cope, as the next section will discuss.

---

practice quiz How much do you remember?

9.6

Pick the best answer.

1. Which of the following is NOT a typical source of stress in the workplace?
   a. heavy workload
   b. lack of variety
   c. lack of shift work
   d. lack of job security

2. Which of the following is NOT a symptom of burnout?
   a. pessimism
   b. dissatisfaction
   c. optimism
   d. desire to quit

3. Larysa moved from Ukraine to the United States. She learned to speak and write English, changed her last name so that it would sound more "American," and no longer maintains any of her old culture's styles of dress or customs. Larysa has used which method of entering the majority culture?

   a. integration
   b. assimilation
   c. separation
   d. marginalization

4. Social support _____.
   a. has a positive benefit on health.
   b. can improve the physical functioning of cancer patients.
   c. can improve the physical functioning of people with HIV.
   d. shows all of the above.

Brainstorming: In general, studies show that people who have social support are better able to deal with the effects of stress, but this does not mean that all social relationships have a positive effect on one's ability to cope. How can the people in your life interfere with your ability to handle stress, and what are some positive ways in which you can reduce that interference?

ANSWERS ON PAGE AK–2

Stress, Hunger, and Eating

The eating habits of people today have become a major concern and a frequent topic of news programs, talk shows, and scientific research. There are countless pills, supplements, and treatments to help people eat less or to eat more. Eating is a basic survival behavior that reduces a primary drive. It is also a form of recreation for many, and the attractive presentations and social environment of many eating experiences are a powerful incentive.

social support system the network of family, friends, neighbors, coworkers, and others who can offer support, comfort, or aid to a person in need.

9.7 What is hunger, and how do social factors influence a person's experience of hunger?

The Physiology of Hunger

The physical hunger drive involves several factors. If the stomach is empty and contracted, hunger usually occurs. Another factor is the insulin response. **Insulin** and **glucagon** are hormones that are secreted by the pancreas to control the levels of fats, proteins, and carbohydrates in the whole body, including glucose (blood sugar). Insulin, normally released in greater amounts after eating has begun, causes a feeling of more hunger because of a drop in blood sugar levels. High blood sugar (which is more likely when one eats sugary foods and white breads, rice, and pasta) leads to more insulin released, which leads to a low blood sugar level, increased appetite, and the tendency to overeat. Also, part of the hypothalamus stops the eating response as blood sugar increases, while another part controls the beginning of eating as insulin levels go up (Neary et al., 2004). (L)(I)(N)(K) to Chapter Two: The Biological Perspective, p. 67.

Social Components of Hunger

The physical controls of hunger are not enough to explain all eating behavior. People often eat when they are not really hungry or just because the food looks so good or smells so good. Social cues also tell people to eat, such as the convention of eating breakfast, lunch, and dinner at certain times. A large part of that "convention" is actually the result of classical conditioning. (L)(I)(N)(K) to Chapter Four: Learning, pp. 123–124. The body becomes conditioned to respond with the hunger reflex at certain times of the day; through association with the act of eating, those times of the day have become conditioned stimuli for hunger. Classical conditioning may cause insulin levels to increase even *before* food is eaten, just as Pavlov's dogs salivated before getting food (Rodin, 1981, 1985).

Cultural factors and gender also play a part in determining hunger and eating habits. In one study, a questionnaire about eating habits was given to both men and women from the United States and Japan. Although no significant differences in what initiates eating existed for men in either culture, women in the United States were found to be much more likely to start eating for emotional reasons, such as depression. Japanese women were more likely to eat because of hunger signals or social demands (Hawks et al., 2003). In this same study, both men and women from the United States were more likely to eat while watching television or movies than were Japanese men and women. Both culture and gender must be taken into account when studying why and under what circumstances people eat.

Maladaptive Eating Problems

9.8 What are some problems in eating behavior, and how are they affected by biology and culture?

Many people weigh far more than they should, whereas others weigh far less. Why do some people get so fat? Is it just overeating?

OBESITY Several factors create *obesity*, a condition in which the body weight of a person is 20 percent or more over the ideal body weight for that person's height. A significant factor in obesity is heredity. There appear to be several sets of genes, some on different chromosomes, which influence a person's likelihood of becoming obese (Barsh et al., 2000). If there is a history of obesity in a particular family, each family member has a risk of becoming obese that is double or triple the risk of people who do not have a family history of obesity (Bouchard, 1997).

glucagon hormone that is secreted by the pancreas to control the levels of fats, proteins, and carbohydrates in the body by increasing the level of glucose in the bloodstream.

insulin a hormone secreted by the pancreas to control the levels of fats, proteins, and carbohydrates in the body by reducing the level of glucose in the bloodstream.

Another factor is certainly overeating. Around the world, as developing countries get stronger economies and their food supplies become stable, the rates of obesity increase dramatically and quickly (Barsh et al., 2000). Foods become more varied and enticing* as well, and an increase in variety is associated with an increase in eating beyond the physiological need to eat (Raynor & Epstein, 2001). In industrialized societies when workers spend more hours in the workplace, there is less time available for preparing meals at home and more incentive to dine out (Chou et al., 2004). When the "dining out" choices include fast food and soft drinks, as is so often the case, obesity rates increase. At about 31 percent, the United States has the highest rate of obesity in the world (Friedman, 2000, 2003; Marik, 2000; Mokdad et al., 2001). Over the last 20 years, rates of obesity in developing countries have tripled. Of children from developing countries such as China, the Middle East, Southeast Asia, and the Pacific Islands, 10 to 25 percent are overweight and another 2 to 10 percent are obese (Hossain et al., 2007).

Two other disorders of eating that cause weight fluctuations in the opposite direction of obesity are anorexia nervosa and bulimia nervosa. Both are classified as clinical (mental) disorders in the *Diagnostic and Statistical Manual of Mental Disorders, Fourth Edition, Text Revision or DSM-IV-TR* (American Psychiatric Association, 2000), which is a listing of disorders and their symptoms used by psychological professionals to make a diagnosis. Both disorders are discussed in a later chapter. (LINK) to Chapter Twelve: Psychological Disorders, pp. 448-450.

Stress and Sexual Dysfunction

9.9 How can stress lead to sexual problems?

What about when people have problems with sex, like impotence? A **sexual dysfunction** is a problem with sexual functioning, or the physical workings of the sex act. Several categories of stressors may lead to potential sexual dysfunction. Problems can occur because of organic factors (i.e., illness or side effects from drugs, chronic illnesses such as diabetes), sociocultural factors (such as negative attitudes toward sexual behavior), or psychological factors stemming from either personality problems, traumatic events, or relationship problems. More commonly, such problems may stem from a combination of these stressors.

Sociocultural influences are often a source of psychological stress leading to sexual dysfunction. In the United States and some other Western cultures, instruction from their parents (both direct and indirect teaching) leads many people to form negative attitudes toward sex and sexual activities, such as masturbation. Certain religious upbringings may also foster a sense of guilt about sex and interest in sex. In one study, a relationship between conservative, religious traditionalism and sexual attitudes was found for married members of Jewish, Protestant, and Catholic faiths (Purcell, 1985). The research showed that the more conservative and traditional the married couples were, the less interest and pleasure they took in sexual activity and the more they experienced guilt, shame, and sexual inhibitions. In non-Western cultures, such as that of India, sex may be seen as not only a duty of married couples but also as a joy to be celebrated within the context of producing children (Gupta, 1994). In particular, women in India may have an entirely different attitude toward sex because a woman's status in Indian culture depends greatly on her ability to bear children.

Psychological stressors also include individual psychological problems, such as low self-esteem, anxiety over performance of the sex act, depression, self-consciousness about one's body image, anxiety disorders, or a history of previous sexual abuse or assault. For

sexual dysfunction a problem in sexual functioning.

---

*Enticing: attractive; desirable.

table 9.1 Organic or Stress-Induced Dysfunctions

Sexual Desire Disorders	Hypoactive Sexual Desire Disorder: Ongoing, abnormally low desire for sexual activity.
	Sexual Aversion Disorder: Fear and disgust of sexual contact.
Sexual Arousal Disorders	Female Sexual Arousal Disorder: Desire for sexual activity is present, but physical discomfort and lack of pleasure are experienced during sexual activity.
	Male Erectile Disorder: A male cannot maintain an erection long enough to complete the sexual act.
Orgasmic Disorders	Male Orgasmic Disorder: A male cannot achieve orgasm through vaginal stimulation, even though fully aroused.
	Female Orgasmic Disorder: A female cannot achieve an orgasm even though fully aroused.
	Premature Ejaculation: Some men experience orgasm shortly after penetration, which can cause feelings of sexual inadequacy because the partner does not have time to achieve orgasm.
Sexual Pain Disorders	Vaginismus: Persistent contractions of the vaginal muscles, causing sexual intercourse to be painful or impossible.
	Dyspareunia: Pain in the genitals that can occur before, during, or after intercourse can be experienced by either sex.

example, women who were sexually molested in childhood are two to four times more likely to suffer pain in the pelvic area on a chronic basis (Reiter & Milburn, 1994).

Another source of psychological stress leading to sexual dysfunctions is the relationship between the two sexual partners. The sexual dysfunction may be only an outward symptom of an underlying problem with the relationship. Examples of such problems might be unresolved arguments, resentment of the partner who feels he or she has less power and influence over the relationship, lack of trust, infidelities, lack of physical attractiveness to the partner, or even lack of sexual skills on the part of one or both partners (Alperstein, 2001).

Organic or stress-induced dysfunctions are types of sexual problems caused by physical disorders, such as nerve damage, or by psychological stress, such as worry and anxiety. (Because body and mind influence each other's functioning, it is difficult to separate these dysfunctions into purely organic and purely stress-induced disorders.) Sexual dysfunctions involve problems in three possible areas of sexual activity: sexual interest, arousal, and response.

Table 9.1 lists some of the more common physical sexual dysfunctions that may be caused by organic factors or psychological stressors such as those discussed at the beginning of this section. For all of the sexual dysfunctions, treatment can include medication, psychotherapy, hormone therapy, stress reduction, and behavioral training. Male erectile disorder is now commonly treated with drug therapy.

organic or stress-induced dysfunction sexual problem caused by physical disorder or psychological stress.

practice quiz How much do you remember?

9.7 9.8 9.9

Pick the best answer.

1. Which of the following is not one of the physiological factors in hunger?
   a. stomach
   b. pancreas
   c. hypothalamus
   d. corpus callosum

2. Which of the following is not a sexual dysfunction stemming from an organic physical disorder?
   a. sexual desire disorder
   b. frotteurism
   c. male erectile disorder
   d. sexual aversion disorder

3. In _____, the person may have the desire for sexual activity but be unable to physically participate.
   a. sexual desire disorder
   b. sexual pain disorder
   c. sexual arousal disorder
   d. orgasmic disorder

ANSWERS ON PAGE AK-2

I have exams and my job and my relationship to worry about, so I feel pretty stressed out—how do people deal with all the stress they face every day?

coping strategies actions that people can take to master, tolerate, reduce, or minimize the effects of stressors.

problem-focused coping coping strategies that try to eliminate the source of a stressor or reduce its impact through direct actions.

emotion-focused coping coping strategies that change the impact of a stressor by changing the emotional reaction to the stressor.

Ignore it? But won't that just make matters worse?

An audience watches what is obviously a funny movie, one of the more popular choices for film-goers. A large part of the success of such comedies can be attributed to the human need to laugh—laughter helps us cope with many of life's stresses.

Coping with Stress

● I have exams and my job and my relationship to worry about, so I feel pretty stressed out—how do people deal with all the stress they face every day?

So far, this chapter has talked about what stress is and the factors that can magnify its effects, as well as the effects of stress on a person's physical health. Part of dealing with stress is in knowing those kinds of things so that changes can be made in the factors that are controllable. **Coping strategies** are actions that people can take to master, tolerate, reduce, or minimize the effects of stressors, and they can include both behavioral strategies and psychological strategies.

9.10 What are some ways in which people cope with stress reactions?

Problem-Focused Coping

One type of coping strategy is to work on eliminating or changing the stressor itself. When people try to eliminate the source of a stress or reduce its impact through their own actions, it is called **problem-focused coping** (Folkman & Lazarus, 1980; Lazarus, 1993). For example, a student might have a problem understanding a particular professor. The professor is knowledgeable but has trouble explaining the concepts of the course in a way that this student can understand. Problem-focused coping might include talking to the professor after class, asking fellow students to clarify the concepts, getting a tutor, or forming a study group with other students who are also having difficulty to pool the group's resources.

Emotion-Focused Coping

Problem-focused coping can work quite well but is not the only method people can use. Most people use both problem-focused coping and **emotion-focused coping** to successfully deal with controllable stressful events (Eschenbeck et al., 2008; Folkman & Lazarus, 1980; Lazarus, 1993; Stowell et al., 2001). Emotion-focused coping is a strategy that involves changing the way a person feels or emotionally reacts to a stressor. This reduces the emotional impact of the stressor and makes it possible to deal with the problem more effectively. For example, the student who is faced with a professor who isn't easy to understand might share his concerns with a friend, talking it through until calm enough to tackle the problem in a more direct manner. Emotion-focused coping also works for stressors that are uncontrollable and for which problem-focused coping is not possible. Someone using emotion-focused coping may decide to view the stressor as a challenge rather than a threat, decide that the problem is a minor one, write down concerns in a journal, or even ignore the problem altogether.

● Ignore it? But won't that just make matters worse?

True, ignoring a problem is not a good strategy when a person can actively do something about solving the problem. But when it is not possible to change or eliminate the stressor, or when worrying about the stressor can be a problem itself, ignoring the problem is not a bad idea. Researchers working with people who had suffered heart attacks found that those people who worried about a future attack were more likely to suffer from symptoms of posttraumatic stress, such as nightmares and poor sleep (both factors that increase the risk of a future heart attack), than were the people who tried to ignore their worries (Ginzburg et al., 2003).

Using humor can also be a form of emotion-focused coping, as the old saying "laughter is the best medicine" suggests. A recent study on the effects of laughter found that laughter actually boosted the action of the immune system by increasing the work of natural killer cells (cells that attack viruses in the body). In this study, participants were shown a humor video for one hour. Blood samples were taken 10 minutes before the viewing, 30 minutes into the viewing, 30 minutes after viewing, and 12 hours after viewing the humor video. There were significant increases in natural killer cell activity and nearly half a dozen other immune system cells and systems, with some effects lasting the full 12 hours after the video ended (Berk et al., 2001).

Meditation as a Coping Mechanism

Meditation is a mental series of exercises meant to refocus attention and achieve a trancelike state of consciousness. ⓁⒾⓃⓀ to Chapter Six: Consciousness and Cognition, p. 199. Meditation can produce a state of relaxation that can aid in coping with the physiological reactions to a stressful situation.

CONCENTRATIVE MEDITATION Have you ever found yourself staring out into space, or at some little spot on the wall or table, only to realize that your mind has been a complete blank for the last several minutes?

The state just described is really nothing more than **concentrative meditation**, the form of meditation best known to the general public. In concentrative meditation, the goal is to focus the mind on some repetitive or unchanging stimulus (such as a spot or the sound of one's own heart beating) so that the mind can forget daily hassles and problems and the body can relax. In fact, Herbert Benson (Benson, 1975; Benson et al., 1974a, 1974b) found that meditation produces a state of relaxation in which blood pressure is lowered, alpha waves (brain waves associated with relaxation) are increased, and the amounts of melatonin secreted at night (the hormone that helps induce sleep) are increased.

Some people say that if you meditate for only 20 minutes a day, you don't have to sleep at night. Unfortunately research has shown this to be untrue (Murphy & Donavan, 1997). Research does show that concentrative meditation is a good way to relax and lower blood pressure in adolescents and adults, men and women, and both whites and African Americans (Barnes et al., 1997; Rainforth et al., 2007; Schneider et al., 1995; Wenneberg et al., 1997). It isn't the only way, as reading a good book or taking a warm bath also produces relaxation. Even simply resting for the same amount of time as one might meditate can be just as relaxing. The advantage of meditation is that people can do it almost anywhere, even in the classroom just before a big test. (It would be a little difficult to take a warm bath then.)

Other research has suggested that concentrative meditation can reduce levels of chronic pain (Kabat-Zinn et al., 1986), moderate symptoms of anxiety, depression, and hostility (Kabat-Zinn et al., 1985), and decrease stress levels in cancer patients (Speca et al., 2000). Reducing stress levels in cancer patients through meditation will increase the likelihood of recovery and reduce the incidence of recurrence.

THE EFFECTS OF MEDITATION Meditation for only 20 minutes can produce lowered blood pressure in people with hypertension (high blood pressure). It can calm anxiety, help people get to sleep, and help people deal with stress (Murphy & Donavan, 1997).

✳ Explore on MyPsychLab

9.11 How is coping with stress affected by culture and religion?

How Culture Affects Coping

Imagine this scene: You are driving out in the country when you come upon an elderly man working on a large wooden box, polishing it with great care. You stop to talk to the man and find out that the box is his own coffin, and he spends his days getting it ready, tending to it with great care. He isn't frightened of dying and doesn't feel strange about polishing his own coffin. How would you react?

If you were from the same rural area of Vietnam as the elderly man, you would probably think nothing strange is going on. For elderly people in the Vietnamese culture, thoughts of death and the things that go along with dying, such as a coffin, are not as

meditation mental series of exercises meant to refocus attention and achieve a trancelike state of consciousness.

concentrative meditation form of meditation in which a person focuses the mind on some repetitive or unchanging stimulus so that the mind can be cleared of disturbing thoughts and the body can experience relaxation.

This man is practicing Zen yoga meditation. Meditation increases relaxation and helps to lower blood pressure and muscle tension.

✳ Explore coping strategies on MyPsychLab

These Peruvian villagers in a cemetery are honoring their loved ones who have passed away. The Day of the Dead is not only a celebration of the lives of those who have passed on but also a celebration for the living, who use this holiday to gain a sense of control over one of life's most uncontrollable events—death itself. What rituals or ceremonies do people of other cultures use to cope with death?

stressful as they are to people from Western cultures. In fact, *stress* isn't all that common a term in Vietnamese society compared to Western societies (Phan & Silove, 1999).

In the case of people living in Vietnam and even Vietnamese immigrants to other countries, mental illness is explained by an imbalance between the male and female elements of a person, or by a loss of soul, evil spirits, or a weakening of the nerves. Coping with stress in Vietnamese culture may include performing rituals, consulting a fortune-teller, or eating certain foods (Phan & Silove, 1999). In many Asian cultures, meditation is a common stress-relief tool, including the art of tai chi, a form of meditational exercise (Yip, 2002).

Obviously, culture is an important factor in the kinds of coping strategies an individual may adopt and even in determining the degree of stress that is experienced. Mental health professionals should make an effort to include an assessment of a person's cultural background as well as immediate circumstances when dealing with adjustment problems due to stress.

How Religion Affects Coping

A belief in a higher power can also be a source of great comfort in times of stress. There are several ways that religious beliefs can affect the degree of stress people experience and the ability to cope with that stress (Hill & Butter, 1995; Pargament, 1997).

First, most people who hold strong religious beliefs belong to a religious organization and attend regular religious functions, such as services at a synagogue, mosque, temple, or church. This membership can be a vital part of a person's social support system (Koenig et al., 1999).

Another way that religion helps people cope involves the rituals and rites that help people feel better about personal weaknesses, failures, or feelings of inadequacy (Koenig et al., 2001). These include rituals such as confession of sins or prayer services during times of stress. Finally, religious beliefs can give meaning to things that otherwise seem to have no meaning or purpose, such as viewing death as a pathway to a paradise, or the destruction of one's home in a natural disaster as a reminder to place less attachment on material things.

Many religions also encourage healthy behavior and eating habits through their prohibitions on such activities as overeating, drinking alcohol, smoking, drug use, and sexual activity outside marriage. Some research even suggests that people with religious commitments live longer than those who have no such beliefs, although this is correlational research and should not be interpreted as concluding that religious belief causes longer life expectancies (Hummer et al., 1999; Koenig et al., 1999; Strawbridge et al., 1997; Thoresen & Harris, 2002). ⊙▶⎯Simulate on **MyPsychLab**

⊙▶⎯**Simulate** factors in stress reduction on **MyPsychLab**

practice quiz   How much do you remember?

9.10   9.11

Pick the best answer.

1. When a person tries to cope by eliminating or changing the stressor directly, it is known as _____.
   a. a defense mechanism.
   c. self-focused coping.
   b. problem-focused coping.
   d. emotion-focused coping.

2. Kareem is relaxing in a chair with his eyes closed. As he sits quietly, he is focusing on the sound of his own breathing and is clearing his mind of other thoughts. Kareem is practicing

   _____.
   a. sensory deprivation.
   b. concentrative meditation.
   c. receptive meditation.
   d. implosive meditation.

3. Which of the following is NOT one of the ways that religion helps people reduce or cope with stress?
   a. Religion can provide a strong social support system.
   b. Religion includes rituals that can help people feel better about their failings.
   c. Most religions promote healthy lifestyles.
   d. Religion isolates people from those who are different.

Brainstorming: Think of some problem that you have faced in the not-too-distant past. What kind of coping did you use? Did you face the problem directly or did you try to deal with your emotional reaction to the problem? Or both?

applying psychology to everyday life
....

Exercising for Mental Health

9.12 What are the psychological benefits of exercise?

You've heard it many times in your life: Exercise is good for you.

Exercise makes the heart healthier, raises the body's metabolic rate to help maintain a healthy weight, raises "good" cholesterol and lowers "bad" cholesterol, strengthens bones, improves sleep quality, reduces tiredness, increases natural killer cell activity to help ward off viruses and cancer, and is a great way to reduce the effects of stress (Courneya et al., 2009; Fiatarone et al., 1993; Manson et al., 2002; Peters et al., 2009). Aerobic exercise has also been found to reduce feelings of tiredness and increase energy in young adults who, because of a sedentary lifestyle, have been diagnosed with persistent fatigue (Puetz et al., 2008).

Now researchers are finding that exercise is good for your mental health as well as your physical health. Exercise has been found to help reduce symptoms in those menopausal women who experience anxiety or depression during the physical and chemical changes of menopause (Nelson et al., 2008). A survey of research on exercise and mental health has shown that exercise can also reduce the more severe symptoms of anxiety and depression disorders. The author of the survey suggests that mental health professionals should more widely prescribe exercise (Ströhle, 2008). Individuals who exercise not only report lower levels of anxiety and depression, but also experience lower levels of stress and anger. One recent study found that regular exercise reduced the anxiety levels of patients suffering from a variety of chronic medical conditions by 20 percent. This benefit was obtained with exercise programs of 30 minutes or less over a period of 3 to 12 weeks—anything longer and patients were less likely to continue (Herring et al., 2010).

It may be difficult to fit an exercise program into one's busy schedule at first, but the benefits to physical and mental health are powerful persuaders to do so. And remember—joyous laughter counts as exercise, too.

Exercising regularly benefits not only physical health but mental health as well—both powerful motivators to get moving!

....

chapter summary ((•⁃[Listen on MyPsychLab Listen to an audio file of your chapter www.MyPsychLab

Stress and Stressors

9.1 How do psychologists define stress?
- Stress is the physical, emotional, and behavioral responses that occur when events are identified as threatening or challenging.
- Stress that has a negative impact is called distress. Eustress is the optimal amount of stress that people need to function well.

9.2 What kinds of external events can cause stress?
- Catastrophes are events such as floods or crashes that can result in high levels of stress, including acute stress disorder and posttraumatic stress disorder.
- Major life changes create stress by requiring adjustments. Major life changes have an impact on chronic health problems and risk of accidents.
- Hassles are the daily frustrations and irritations experienced by people that have an impact on day-to-day health.

9.3 What are some psychological factors in stress?
- Four sources of stress are pressure, uncontrollability, frustration, and conflict.
- Frustration, which can be internal or external, may result in persistence, aggression, displaced aggression, or withdrawal.

Physiological Factwors: Stress and Health
- The autonomic nervous system consists of the sympathetic system, which responds to stressful events, and the parasympathetic system, which restores the body to normal functioning after the stress has ceased.

9.4 How does stress affect the physical functioning of the body and its immune system?
- The general adaptation syndrome is the body's reaction to stress and includes three stages of reaction: alarm, resistance, and exhaustion.

* Stress causes the immune system to react as though an illness or invading organism has been detected, increasing the functioning of the immune system.

* As the stress continues or increases, the immune system can begin to fail.

issues in psychology: Health Psychology and Stress

* The relatively new field of health psychology focuses on the effects of physical activities, psychological traits, and social relationships on overall health and rate of illnesses.

9.5 How do cognitive factors and personality differences affect the experience of stress?

* The cognitive appraisal approach states that how people think about a stressor determines, at least in part, how stressful that stressor will become.

* The first step in appraising a stressor is called primary appraisal, in which the person determines whether an event is threatening, challenging, or of no consequence. Threatening events are more stressful than those seen as challenging.

* The second step is secondary appraisal, in which the person assesses the resources available to deal with the stressor, such as time, money, and social support.

* Type A personalities are ambitious, time conscious, hostile, and angry workaholics who are at increased risk of coronary heart disease, primarily due to their anger and hostility.

* Type B personalities are relaxed and easygoing and have one-third the risk of coronary heart disease as do Type A personalities, if male, and one-fourth the risk if female and working outside the home.

* Type C personalities are pleasant but repressed, internalizing their negative emotions.

* Hardy people are hard workers who lack the anger and hostility of the Type A personality, instead seeming to thrive on stress.

* Optimists look for positive outcomes and experience far less stress than pessimists, who take a more negative view.

9.6 What social factors influence stress reactions?

* Several social factors can be a source of stress or increase the effects of stress: poverty, stresses on the job or in the workplace, and entering a majority culture that is different from one's culture of origin.

* Burnout is a condition that occurs when job stress is so great that the person develops negative thoughts, emotions, and behavior as well as an extreme dissatisfaction with the job and a desire to quit.

* The four methods of acculturation are integration, assimilation, separation, and marginalization.

* Social support systems are important in helping people cope with stress.

Stress, Hunger, and Eating

9.7 What is hunger, and how do social factors influence a person's experience of hunger?

* The physiological components of hunger include signals from the stomach and the hypothalamus and the increased secretion of insulin.

* The social components of hunger include social cues for times meals are to be eaten, cultural customs and food preferences, and the use of food as a comfort device or escape from unpleasantness.

* Some people may be externals who respond to the anticipation of eating by producing an insulin response, increasing the risk of obesity.

9.8 What are some problems in eating behavior, and how are they affected by biology and culture?

* Maladaptive eating problems include obesity, anorexia, and bulimia.

* Bodily processes, genetics, eating habits, and culture all influence what, when, and how we eat during times of stress.

Stress and Sexual Dysfunction

9.9 How can stress lead to sexual problems?

* Sexual dysfunctions are problems with sexual functioning. They may be caused by physical problems, stress, or psychological problems.

* Organic or stress-induced dysfunctions are caused by a physical problem or by stress and can affect sexual interest, arousal, and response.

Coping with Stress

9.10 What are some ways in which people cope with stress reactions?

* Problem-focused coping is used when the problem can be eliminated or changed so that it is no longer stressful or so that the impact of the stressor is reduced.

* Emotion-focused coping is often used with problem-focused coping and involves changing one's emotional reactions to a stressor.

* Meditation can produce a state of relaxation and reduce the physical reactions common to stressful situations.

* Concentrative meditation involves focusing inward on some repetitive stimulus, such as one's breathing.

9.11 How is coping with stress affected by culture and religion?

* Different cultures perceive stressors differently, and coping strategies will also vary from culture to culture.

* People with religious beliefs also have been found to cope better with stressful events.

applying psychology to everyday life: Exercising for Mental Health

9.12 What are the psychological benefits of exercise?

* Exercise not only produces physical benefits such as reduction of heart disease, cancer, and weight, but also reduces anxiety and depression.

TEST yourself

ANSWERS ON PAGE AK–2

✔●─⎸Study and Review on MyPsychLab   Ready for your test? More quizzes and a customized plan. www.MyPsychLab

Pick the best answer.

1. Which of the following is a cognitive symptom of stress?
   a. frequent colds   **c.** overeating
   b. anxiety   **d.** memory problems

2. How do today's researchers differ from Selye in their view of eustress?
   a. They feel that eustress is more harmful than distress.
   b. They have not found evidence of eustress.

   c. They believe that a certain level of eustress is necessary to promote health.
   d. They believe that distress can be helpful instead of harmful.

3. Unpredictable, large-scale events that create a great deal of stress and feelings of threat are called _____.
   a. major life events.   **c.** hassles.
   b. catastrophes.   **d.** major hassles.

4. Lisa's score on the SRRS was 380. According to Holmes and Rahe, Lisa is probably suffering from a _____.
   a. mild life crisis.
   b. moderate life crisis.
   c. major life crisis.
   d. mild stress disorder.

5. Researchers found that the _____ of daily hassles was a far better predictor of headaches than were scores on a life events scale.
   a. number
   b. type
   c. positive quality
   d. perceived severity

6. For which of the following groups of people would going shopping or experiencing bad weather be more stressful than for the other groups, according to Ellis et al. (2001)?
   a. children
   b. adolescents
   c. young adults
   d. elderly people

7. Which of the following is NOT a source of stress as discussed in the text?
   a. pressure
   b. uncontrollability
   c. predictability
   d. frustration

8. Who reformulated the frustration–aggression hypothesis?
   a. Dollard
   b. Berkowitz
   c. Miller
   d. Lazarus

9. Phrases such as "caught between a rock and a hard place" and "out of the frying pan, into the fire" refer to _____ conflicts.
   a. approach–approach
   b. avoidance–avoidance
   c. approach–avoidance
   d. multiple approach–avoidance

10. When a person has to make a choice among several goals and each goal has both its good points and its bad points, the person is experiencing a(n) _____ conflict.
    a. approach–approach
    b. avoidance–avoidance
    c. approach–avoidance
    d. multiple approach–avoidance

11. In which of Selye's stages is death a possible outcome?
    a. alarm
    b. resistance
    c. reaction
    d. exhaustion

12. Appraising a stressor as a challenge results in _____ than if the stressor is appraised as a threat.
    a. more stress
    b. less stress
    c. less successful coping
    d. more negative emotions

13. Joe rarely takes any work home, preferring to leave his work worries at the office. He is not ambitious and likes to have a lot of leisure time when it is possible. He is also easygoing and doesn't lose his temper often, preferring to avoid conflict. Which of the following statements about Joe is most likely true?
    a. Joe is a Type A personality.
    b. Joe is a Type B personality.
    c. Joe is a Type C personality.
    d. Joe's risk of coronary heart disease is high.

14. Tad seems to thrive on stress and feels very much in control of his life. He would probably be labeled a _____ personality.
    a. Type A
    b. Type B
    c. Type C
    d. hardy

15. Which of the following is NOT one of the three methods suggested by Vaughan to promote a positive, optimistic mood?
    a. alternative thinking
    b. relaxation
    c. using a scapegoat
    d. downward social comparison

16. Acculturative stress is lowest for people who choose _____ as their method of entering the majority culture.
    a. integration
    b. assimilation
    c. separation
    d. marginalization

17. When we eat, the pancreas releases _____, which lowers blood sugar and can increase the feeling of hunger.
    a. glucose
    b. insulin
    c. thyroxin
    d. adrenaline

18. According to Rodin, some people may produce insulin in response to anticipating food as a result of _____.
    a. genetic tendencies.
    b. biological sensitivity.
    c. classical conditioning.
    d. operant conditioning.

19. If there is a history of obesity in a family, each family member has _____ of becoming obese compared to people without such a family history.
    a. the same risk
    c. five times the risk
    b. double or triple the risk
    d. less risk

20. Which of the following is not one of the three areas affected by sexual dysfunctions?
    a. sexual reproduction
    b. sexual arousal
    c. sexual interest
    d. sexual response

21. _____ is more a problem of timing than anything else.
    a. Male orgasmic disorder
    c. Dyspareunia
    b. Female orgasmic disorder
    d. Premature ejaculation

22. Shawna is having trouble in algebra. She goes to the school's academic help center for tutoring and spends extra time working algebra problems at home. Shawna's method of coping is _____.
    a. problem focused.
    b. emotion focused.
    c. defensive focused.
    d. internal.

23. Who among the following probably has the least ability to cope effectively with stress?
    a. Marian, a very religious person
    b. Mei Ling, who comes from a culture that emphasizes the family
    c. Jackie, who has few friends and whose family lives far away from her
    d. Lenora, who meditates every day

9 stress and health

9.1 **9.2** p. 312

stress is the physical, emotional, cognitive, and behavioral response to events that are appraised as threatening or challenging; first studied systematically by Hans Selye

Stress and Stressors

stress-causing events are called stressors; can come from external or internal sources; range from mild to severe

- negative events cause distress; positive events cause eustress, the optimal level of stress required to facilitate healthy adaptation and well-being

- external stress-causing events may include catastrophes, major life changes, and daily hassles (differ according to developmental stage)

- can be assessed systematically (e.g., Social Readjustment Rating Scale, College Undergraduate Stress Scale)

9.3 p. 315

pressure
urgent demands or expectations and uncontrollability

frustration
due to external (losses, rejections, failures, delays) or internal (personal characteristics) factors; can result in several typical responses

- **persistence**
- **aggression**
- **escape/withdrawal**
(suicide is a drastic form of escape)

Psychological Stressors
(psychological stressors are often related to external events)

conflict
- **approach–approach conflict**
- **avoidance–avoidance conflict**
- **approach–avoidance conflict**
- **multiple approach–avoidance conflicts**

9.4 p. 319

Physiological Factors

the **autonomic nervous system (ANS)** figures prominently in the body's physiological reactions to stress

Hans Selye identified the **general adaption syndrome (GAS)**, the sequence of physiological reactions the body goes through when adapting to a stressor

- **alarm**
- **resistance**
- **exhaustion**

the field of **psychoneuroimmunology** focuses on the effects of stress on the immune system

9.5 p. 324

Lazarus's cognitive–mediational theory of emotions
suggests an individual's appraisal of a stressor is a major factor in determining how stressful that stressor becomes

- **primary appraisal**
- **secondary appraisal**

personality differences
affect how one assesses a stressor, the coping strategies used, and possible health outcomes

- **Type A**
- **Type B**
- **Type C**
- **"Type H"**

Cognitive and Personality Factors

explanatory style
optimists tend to look for positive outcomes, whereas pessimists seem to expect the worst

- Seligman (originally studied concept of learned helplessness) began the positive psychology movement; has suggested that optimism leads to longer life and greater success in life endeavors

- optimism is associated with controlling mood or emotional reactions; can be a learned skill through alternative thinking, downward social comparison, relaxation, and correcting faulty thinking

9.6 p. 330

Social Factors in Stress

- a great deal of stress can come from dealing with other people and social interactions
- poverty and job stress are prominent, economically based social factors that lead to stressful living conditions
  - poverty results in lack of basic life necessities
  - job stress may be related to workload, lack of control or job security, work schedule, and low job satisfaction
- culturally, stress is affected by status of acculturation (adapting to a new, different, or often dominant culture) and the method chosen to adapt
  - **integration**
  - **assimilation**
  - **separation**
  - **marginalization**
- in general, having a positive social support system that provides various forms of help (e.g., monetary, physical, emotional support) is a good predictor for healthy aging and longevity

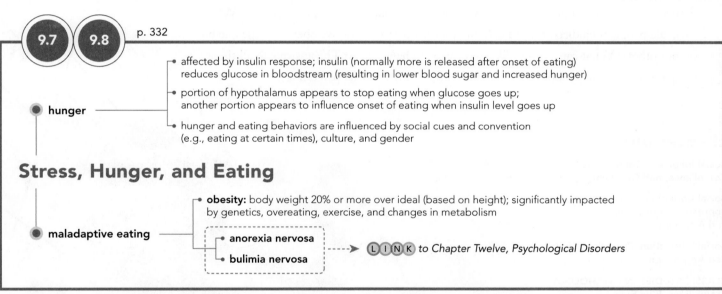

9.7 **9.8** p. 332

Stress, Hunger, and Eating

- **hunger**
  - affected by insulin response; insulin (normally more is released after onset of eating) reduces glucose in bloodstream (resulting in lower blood sugar and increased hunger)
  - portion of hypothalamus appears to stop eating when glucose goes up; another portion appears to influence onset of eating when insulin level goes up
  - hunger and eating behaviors are influenced by social cues and convention (e.g., eating at certain times), culture, and gender
- **maladaptive eating**
  - **obesity:** body weight 20% or more over ideal (based on height); significantly impacted by genetics, overeating, exercise, and changes in metabolism
  - **anorexia nervosa**
  - **bulimia nervosa**

  (L I N K) to Chapter Twelve, Psychological Disorders

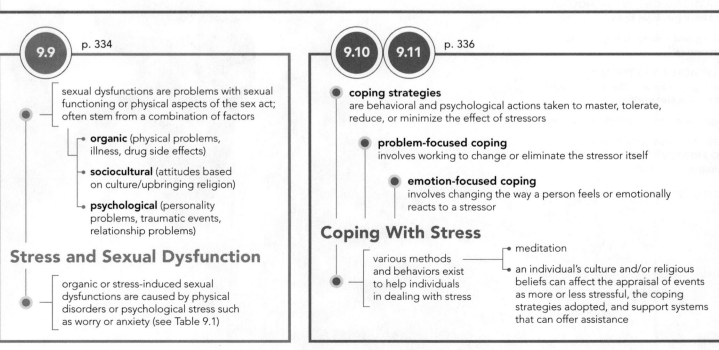

9.9 p. 334

Stress and Sexual Dysfunction

- sexual dysfunctions are problems with sexual functioning or physical aspects of the sex act; often stem from a combination of factors
  - **organic** (physical problems, illness, drug side effects)
  - **sociocultural** (attitudes based on culture/upbringing religion)
  - **psychological** (personality problems, traumatic events, relationship problems)
- organic or stress-induced sexual dysfunctions are caused by physical disorders or psychological stress such as worry or anxiety (see Table 9.1)

9.10 **9.11** p. 336

Coping With Stress

- **coping strategies** are behavioral and psychological actions taken to master, tolerate, reduce, or minimize the effect of stressors
  - **problem-focused coping** involves working to change or eliminate the stressor itself
  - **emotion-focused coping** involves changing the way a person feels or emotionally reacts to a stressor
- various methods and behaviors exist to help individuals in dealing with stress
  - meditation
  - an individual's culture and/or religious beliefs can affect the appraisal of events as more or less stressful, the coping strategies adopted, and support systems that can offer assistance

10

social psychology

why study social psychology?

If people lived in total isolation from other people, there would be no reason to study
the effect that other people have on the behavior of individuals and groups. But human
beings are social creatures—we live with others, work with others, and play with others.
The people who surround us all of our lives have an impact on our beliefs and values,
decisions and assumptions, and the way we think about other people in general. Why are
some people prejudiced toward certain other people? Why do we obey some people but
not others? What causes us to like, to love, or to hate others? The answers to all these
questions and many more can be found in the study of social psychology.

chapter outline

**Social Influence: Conformity,
Compliance, and Obedience**

**Social Cognition: Attitudes,
Impression Formation,
and Attribution**

**Social Interaction: Prejudice, Love,
and Aggression**

**CLASSIC STUDIES IN PSYCHOLOGY:
Brown Eyes, Blue Eyes**

**Liking and Loving: Interpersonal
Attraction**

**PSYCHOLOGY IN THE NEWS:
Facing Facebook—The Social Nature
of Online Networking**

Aggression and Prosocial Behavior

**APPLYING PSYCHOLOGY
TO EVERYDAY LIFE:
Anatomy of a Cult**

The Michelangelo Phenomenon: Sculpting Your Partner

The concept of *self* is one that many psychologists have studied over the years. There is the concept of self as an *intra*personal one—the beliefs that an individual holds about his or her own abilities and characteristics, including the *ideal self*, the abilities and characteristics that an individual aspires to have. (L)(I)(N)(K) to Chapter Eleven: Theories of Personality and Intelligence, p. 399. But researchers are now looking at the *inter*personal self, the way in which an individual's close partners can help or hinder that person in the pursuit of the self's goals (Rusbult et al., 2009a, 2009b, 2009c).

In the *Michelangelo phenomenon* (famed sculptor Michelangelo Buonarroti felt that a sculptor merely releases the ideal figure from a block of stone), an individual's close friends, relatives, romantic partners, or colleagues help that individual "release" the ideal self that lies within by adapting to that person's basic traits and skills, providing opportunities for enhancement, and influencing the person's further personality development of those ideal aspects (Rusbult et al., 2009a). For example, if Latashia would like to become less shy, her boyfriend Antoine might encourage that aspect of her ideal self to develop by providing her with opportunities to tell their friends a funny story she had told to him. Antoine is in a sense "directing" Latashia's development. Over time, Latashia's behavior in these specific situations will become stable components of her sense of self. This effect of the significant other or others on a person's self-concept is particularly effective when it involves affirmation—the positive support of a person's goals for the ideal self (Drigotas et al., 1999; Kumashiro et al., 2009). In a very real sense, then, we look into the "mirror" of our partners' eyes and see ourselves as they see us. This is simply one example of the influence that others can have on the individual, one area of study in the broad field of social psychology.

learning objectives

10.1 What factors influence people to conform to the actions of others?

10.2 How is compliance defined, and what are four common ways to gain the compliance of another?

10.3 What factors make obedience more likely?

10.4 What are the three components of an attitude, how are attitudes formed, and how can attitudes be changed?

10.5 How do people react when attitudes and behavior are not the same?

10.6 What are social categorization and implicit personality theories?

10.7 How do people try to explain the actions of others?

10.8 How are prejudice and discrimination different?

10.9 Why are people prejudiced, and how can prejudice be stopped?

10.10 What factors govern attraction and love, and what are some different kinds of love?

10.11 How is aggressive behavior determined by biology and learning?

10.12 What is altruism, and how is deciding to help someone related to the presence of others?

10.13 Why do people join cults?

social psychology   the scientific study of how a person's thoughts, feelings, and behavior are influenced by the real, imagined, or implied presence of others.

social influence   the process through which the real or implied presence of others can directly or indirectly influence the thoughts, feelings, and behavior of an individual.

conformity   changing one's own behavior to match that of other people.

Sure, I follow the herd—not out of brainless obedience, mind you, but out of a deep and abiding respect for the concept of community."
©The New Yorker Collection 2003 Alex Gregory from cartoonbank.com. All Rights Reserved.

Chapter One defined psychology as the scientific study of behavior and mental processes, including how people think and feel. The field of social psychology also looks at behavior and mental processes but includes as well the social world in which we exist, as we are surrounded by others to whom we are connected and by whom we are influenced in so many ways. It is not the same field as *sociology*, which is the study and classification of human societies. Sociology studies the big picture: how entire groups of people live, work, and play. Although social psychology does look at group behavior, it is more concerned with the individual person within the group and the influence of the group on the individual.

Social psychology is the scientific study of how a person's behavior, thoughts, and feelings are influenced by the real, imagined, or implied presence of others. Although there are several sections in this chapter, there are really only three main areas under discussion: *social influence*, the ways in which a person's behavior can be affected by other people; *social cognition*, the ways in which people think about other people; and *social interaction*, the positive and negative aspects of people relating to others.

Social Influence: Conformity, Compliance, and Obedience

People live in a world filled with other people. An infant is born into a world with adults who have an impact on the infant's actions, personality, and growth. Adults must interact with others on a daily basis. Such interactions provide ample opportunity for the presence of other people to directly or indirectly influence the behavior, feelings, and thoughts of each individual in a process called **social influence**. There are many forms of social influence. People can influence others to follow along with their own actions or thoughts, to agree to do things even when the person might prefer to do otherwise, and to be obedient to authorities. The mere presence of others can even influence the way people perform tasks successfully or unsuccessfully.

Conformity

10.1 **What factors influence people to conform to the actions of others?**

Have you ever noticed someone looking up at something? Did the urge to look up to see what that person was looking at become so strong that you actually found yourself looking up? This common practical joke always works, even when people suspect that it's a joke. It clearly demonstrates the power of **conformity**: changing one's own behavior to more closely match the actions of others.

In 1936, social psychologist Muzafer Sherif conducted a study in which participants were shown into a darkened room and exposed to a single point of light. Under those conditions, a point of light will seem to move because of tiny, involuntary movements of the eye. Ⓛ Ⓘ Ⓝ Ⓚ to Chapter Three: Sensation and Perception, pp. 109–111. The participants were not told of this effect and reported the light moved anywhere from a few inches to several feet. When a confederate (a person chosen by the experimenter to deliberately manipulate the situation) also gave estimates, the original participants began to make estimates of motion that were more and more similar to those of the confederate (Sherif, 1936). This early experiment on conformity has been criticized because the judgments being made were ambiguous* (i.e., the light wasn't really moving, so any estimate within reason would sound good). Would participants be so easily swayed if the judgments were more specifically measurable and certain?

*Ambiguous: having no clear interpretation or able to be interpreted in many ways rather than just one way.

ASCH'S CLASSIC STUDY ON CONFORMITY Solomon Asch (1951) conducted the first of his classic studies on conformity by having seven participants gather in a room. They were told that they were participating in an experiment on visual judgment. They were then shown a white card with only one line on it followed by another white card with three lines of varying lengths. The task was to determine which line on the second card was most similar to the line on the first card (see Figure 10.1).

In reality, only the next-to-the-last person in the group was a real participant. The others were all confederates (people following special directions from the experimenter) who were instructed to pick the same *incorrect* line from the comparison lines. Would the real participant, having heard the others pick what seemed to be the wrong answer, change to conform to the group's opinion? Surprisingly, the participants conformed to the group answer a little over one-third of the time. Asch also found that the number of confederates mattered: Conformity increased with each new confederate until there were four confederates; more than that did not increase the participants' tendency to conform (Asch, 1951). In a later experiment, Asch (1956) found that conformity decreased if there was just one confederate who gave the correct answer—apparently, if participants knew that there was at least one other person whose answer agreed with their own, the evidence of their own eyes won out over the pressure to conform to the group. Subsequent research in the United States has found less conformity among participants, perhaps suggesting that the Asch conformity effect was due to the more conforming nature of people in the era and culture of the United States in the 1950s (Lalancette & Standing, 1990; Nicholson et al., 1985; Perrin & Spencer, 1980, 1981). In other cultures, however, studies have found conformity effects similar to those in Asch's study (Neto, 1995). Still others have found even greater effects of conformity in collectivist cultures such as Hong Kong, Japan, and Zimbabwe (Bond & Smith, 1996; Kim & Markus, 1999). This cultural difference may exist only when face-to-face contact is a part of the task, however. One study found that when the Asch judgment task is presented in an online format (participants were in communi-

Standard line

1 2 3

Comparison lines

FIGURE 10.1 Stimuli Used in Asch's Study
Participants in Asch's famous study on conformity were first shown the standard line. They were then shown the three comparison lines and asked to determine to which of the three was the standard line most similar. Which line would you pick? What if you were one of several people, and everyone who answered ahead of you chose line 3?
How would that affect your answer?
Source: Adapted from Asch (1956).

Watch a video about conformity on **MyPsychLab**

What about gender—are men or women more conforming?

groupthink kind of thinking that occurs when people place more importance on maintaining group cohesiveness than on assessing the facts of the problem with which the group is concerned.

On April 20, 2010, an explosion on the *Deepwater Horizon* oil drilling rig in the Gulf of Mexico. Oil flowed into the Gulf for three months, but the environmental impact will no doubt be felt for years. How might groupthink apply in this situation?

cation but not able to see each other), the cultural difference disappears (Cinnirella & Green, 2007). Watch on **MyPsychLab**

● What about gender—are men or women more conforming?

Research shows that gender differences are practically nonexistent unless the situation involves behavior that is not private. If it is possible to give responses in private, conformity is no greater for women than for men, but if a public response is required, women do tend to show more conformity than men (Eagly, 1987; Eagly et al., 2000; Eagly & Carly, 2007). This effect may be due to the socialization that women receive in being agreeable and supportive; however, the difference in conformity is quite small.

THE HAZARDS OF GROUPTHINK Shortly after the terrorist attack on the World Trade Center in New York, President George W. Bush and his administration made the decision to invade Iraq, find Saddam Hussein, and stop him before he could use his "weapons of mass destruction" that the administration and its advisers believed were hidden in Iraq. This decision to invade a country that had not committed an open act of war against the United States was made and executed *without* building any broad-based support from allies. Although there were advisers who thought the action to be a mistake, no one person was willing to stand up to the rest of the group and challenge the group's decision and assumptions. Many now see this decision (a costly decision in terms of lost lives and casualties, huge amounts of monetary expenditures, and—according to many—the tarnishing of the diplomatic status of the United States in the eyes of the rest of the world) as a prime example of **groupthink**. Groupthink occurs when people within a group feel it is more important to maintain the group's cohesiveness than to consider the facts realistically (Hogg & Hains, 1998; Janis, 1972, 1982; Schafer & Crichlow, 1996). Other examples include the sinking of the *Titanic* in 1912 (the group responsible for designing and building the ship assumed it was unsinkable and did not even bother to include enough lifeboats on board for all the passengers), the *Challenger* disaster of 1986 in which a part on the shuttle was known by a few to be unacceptable (but no one spoke up to delay the launch), and the Bay of Pigs disaster during the Kennedy administration. Table 10.1 summarizes several

table 10.1 Characteristics of Groupthink

CHARACTERISTIC	DESCRIPTION
Invulnerability*	Members feel they cannot fail—the group can do no wrong.
Rationalization	Members explain away warning signs and help each other rationalize their decision.
Lack of introspection	Members do not examine the ethical implications of their decision because they believe that they cannot make immoral choices.
Stereotyping	Members stereotype their enemies as weak, stupid, or unreasonable. Those who oppose the group, therefore, have no worthwhile opinions.
Pressure	Members pressure each other not to question the prevailing opinion and prevent those who disagree from speaking up.
Lack of disagreement	Members do not express opinions that differ from the group consensus in a "don't rock the boat" mentality.
Self-deception	Members share in the illusion that they all agree with the decision.
Insularity	Self-appointed "mind guards" prevent the group (and particularly the leader) from hearing disruptive but potentially useful information from people who are outside the group.

Source: Janis (1972, 1982).

*Invulnerability: quality of being unable to be attacked or harmed.

"symptoms" of groupthink devised by social psychologist and groupthink expert Irving Janis (1972, 1982).

Several things can be done to minimize the possibility of groupthink (Hart, 1998; McCauley, 1998; Moorhead et al., 1998). For example, leaders should remain impartial, and the entire group should seek the opinions of people outside the group. Any voting should be done on secret ballots rather than by a show of hands, and it should be made clear that group members will be held responsible for decisions made by the group.

Compliance

10.2 How is compliance defined, and what are four common ways to gain the compliance of another?

I have a friend who watches infomercials on the shopping channels and buys stuff that isn't worth the money or that doesn't work like it's supposed to work. Why do people fall for pitches like that?

Marketing products is really very much a psychological process. In fact, the whole area of **consumer psychology** is devoted to figuring out how to get people to buy things that someone is selling. (L)(I)(N)(K) to Appendix B: Applied Psychology and Psychology Careers. But infomercials are not the only means by which people try to get others to do what they want them to do. **Compliance** occurs when people change their behavior as a result of another person or group asking or directing them to change. The person or group asking for the change in behavior typically doesn't have any real authority or power to command a change; when that authority does exist and behavior is changed as a result, it is called *obedience*, which is the topic of the next major section of this chapter.

A number of techniques that people use to get the compliance of others clearly show the relationship of compliance to the world of marketing, as they refer to techniques that door-to-door salespersons would commonly use.

FOOT-IN-THE-DOOR TECHNIQUE Let's say that a neighbor asks you to keep an eye on his house while he is on vacation. You agree, thinking that it's a rather small request. Later that day, or perhaps even in the same conversation, the neighbor asks if you would kindly water his plants while he's gone. This is a little bit more involved and requires more of your time and energy—will you do it? If you are like most people, you probably will comply with this second larger request.

When compliance with a smaller request is followed by a larger request, people are quite likely to comply because they have already agreed to the smaller one and they want to behave consistently with their previous response (Cialdini et al., 1995; Dillard, 1990, 1991; Freedman & Fraser, 1966; Meineri & Guéguen, 2008). This is called the **foot-in-the-door technique** because the first small request acts as an opener. (Salespeople once literally stuck a foot in the door to prevent the occupant from shutting it so they could continue their sales pitch, hence, the name.)

DOOR-IN-THE-FACE TECHNIQUE Closely related to the foot-in-the-door technique is its opposite: the **door-in-the-face technique** (Cialdini et al., 1975). In this method, the larger request comes first, which is usually refused. This is followed by a second smaller and more reasonable request that often gets compliance. An example of this would be if the neighbor first asked you to take care of his dog and cat in your home. After you refused to do so, the neighbor might ask if you would at least water his plants, which you would probably do.

LOWBALL TECHNIQUE Another compliance technique, also common in the world of sales, is called the **lowball technique** (Bator & Cialdini, 2006; Burger & Petty, 1981;

I have a friend who watches infomercials on the shopping channels and buys stuff that isn't worth the money or that doesn't work like it's supposed to work. Why do people fall for pitches like that?

consumer psychology branch of psychology that studies the habits of consumers in the marketplace.

compliance changing one's behavior as a result of other people directing or asking for the change.

foot-in-the-door technique asking for a small commitment and, after gaining compliance, asking for a bigger commitment.

door-in-the-face technique asking for a large commitment and being refused and then asking for a smaller commitment.

lowball technique getting a commitment from a person and then raising the cost of that commitment.

that's-not-all technique a sales technique in which the persuader makes an offer and then adds something extra to make the offer look better before the target person can make a decision.

norm of reciprocity assumption that if someone does something for a person, that person should do something for the other in return.

obedience changing one's behavior at the command of an authority figure.

Weyant, 1996). In this technique, once a commitment is made, the cost of that commitment is increased. (In the sense used here, *cost* does not necessarily mean money; *cost* can also mean time, effort, or other kinds of sacrifices.) For example, let's say that a professor agrees to write a textbook for a publishing company. Once committed to that process, the professor discovers that the task involves not only writing but also traveling to meet with editors, working nights and weekends to meet deadlines, and making the commitment to take time off from her teaching job to finish the text on time for publication. (This example is purely hypothetical, of course.)

A more common example will occur to anyone who has ever bought a car. The commitment to buy the car at one low price is quickly followed by the addition of other costs, such as extended warranties, additional options, taxes and fees, and so on, causing the buyer to spend more money than originally intended.

THAT'S-NOT-ALL TECHNIQUE Finally, there is the now familiar technique of the infomercial salesperson: the **that's-not-all technique**. In this compliance tactic, the person doing the persuading makes an offer, but before the target of the offer can make a decision, the persuader throws in something extra to make the deal look even better (Burger, 1986). See if this sounds familiar:

> *"But wait—that's not all! If you act now, we'll send you this 15-piece set of genuine faux carving knives as a bonus!"*

This technique relies on the **norm of reciprocity**, which basically assumes that if someone does something for a person, the person should do something in return (Burger et al., 2009; Fehr & Gächter, 2000; Gouldner, 1960). This is also the principle used by organizations that give out free, unasked-for samples, such as the free address stickers that come with many requests for charitable donations. By offering something that the consumer did not ask for in the first place, the persuader has activated the norm of reciprocity. Now the consumer feels as though the persuader has "given" something and the consumer should respond by giving in to the persuader's request to buy the product.

Cultural differences exist in people's susceptibility to these techniques. For the foot-in-the-door technique in particular, research has shown that people in individualist cultures (such as the United States) are more likely to comply with the second request than are people in collectivist cultures (such as Japan). The research suggests that people in collectivist cultures are not as concerned with being consistent with previous behavior because they are less focused on their inner motivation than are people in individualist cultures, who are more concerned with their inner motives and consistency (Cialdini et al., 1999; Petrova et al., 2007). **LINK** to Chapter Eleven: Theories of Personality and Intelligence, pp. 421–422.

Obedience

10.3 What factors make obedience more likely?

There is a difference between the concepts of compliance, which is agreeing to change one's behavior because someone else asks for the change, and **obedience**, which is changing one's behavior at the direct order of an authority figure. A salesperson who wants a person to buy a car has no real power to force that person to buy, but an authority figure is a person with social power—such as a police officer, a teacher, or a work supervisor—who has the right to demand certain behavior from the people under the authority figure's command or supervision.

How far will people go in obeying the commands of an authority figure? What factors make obedience more or less likely? These are some of the questions that researchers have been investigating for many years. The answers to these questions became very important not only to researchers but also to people everywhere after the atrocities committed by the soldiers in Nazi Germany—soldiers who were "just following orders."

MILGRAM'S SHOCKING RESEARCH Social psychologist Stanley Milgram set out to find answers to these questions. He was aware of Asch's studies of conformity and wondered how much impact social influence could have on a behavior that was more meaningful than judging the length of lines on cards. He designed what has become one of the most famous (even notorious*) experiments in the history of psychology.

Through ads placed in the local newspaper, Milgram recruited people who were told that they would be participating in an experiment to test the effects of punishment on learning behavior (Milgram, 1964a, 1974). The participants believed that they had randomly been assigned to either the "teacher" role or the "learner" role, when in fact the "learner" was an actor already aware of the situation. The "teacher" was given a sample 45-volt shock from the chair in which the "learner" was strapped during the experiment. The task for the learner was a simple memory test for paired words.

The "teacher" was seated in front of a machine through which the shocks would be administered and the level of the shocks changed. (See Figure 10.2.) For each mistake made by the "learner," the "teacher" was instructed to increase the level of shock by 15 volts. The "learner" (who was not actually shocked) followed a carefully arranged script, showing discomfort, asking for the experiment to end, screaming, and even falling silent as if unconscious—or dead. As the "teachers" became reluctant to continue administering the shocks, the experimenter in his white lab coat, which

---

*Notorious: widely and unfavorably known.

FIGURE 10.2 Control Panel in Milgram's Experiment
In Stanley Milgram's classic study on obedience, the participants were presented with a control panel like this one. Each participant ("teacher") was instructed to give electric shocks to another person (the "learner," who only pretended to be shocked). At what point do you think you would have refused to continue the experiment?

signified authority said, for example, "The experiment requires you to continue" or "You must continue," and reminded the "teacher" that the experimenter would take full responsibility for the safety of the "learner."

How many of the participants continued to administer what they believed were real shocks? Milgram surveyed psychiatrists, college students, and other adults prior to the experiments for their opinions on how far the participants would go in administering shocks. Everyone predicted that the participants would all refuse to go on at some point, with most believing that the majority of the participants would start refusing as soon as the "learner" protested—150 volts. None of those he surveyed believed that any participant would go all the way to the highest voltage.

So were they right? Far from it—in the first set of experiments, 65 percent of the "teachers" went all the way through the experiment's final 450-volt shock level, although many were obviously uncomfortable and begged to be allowed to stop. Of those "teachers" who did protest and finally stop, not one of them stopped before reaching 300 volts!

So what happened? Were those people sadists? Why would they keep shocking someone like that?

● So what happened? Were those people sadists? Why would they keep shocking someone like that?

No one was more stunned than Milgram himself. He had not believed that his experiments would show such a huge effect of obedience to authority. These results do not appear to be some random "fluke" resulting from a large population of sadistic people residing in the area. These experiments have been repeated at various times, in the United States and in other countries, and the percentage of participants who went all the way consistently remained between 61 and 66 percent (Blass, 1999).

That's incredible— I just don't believe that I could do something like that to someone else.

● That's incredible—I just don't believe that I could do something like that to someone else.

EVALUATION OF MILGRAM'S RESEARCH Researchers have looked for particular personality traits that might be associated with high levels of obedience but have not found any one trait or group of traits that consistently predicts who will obey and who will not in experiments similar to Milgram's original studies (Blass, 1991). The people who "went all the way" were not necessarily more dependent or susceptible to being controlled by others; they were simply people like most other people, caught in a situation of "obey or disobey" the authority. Although some have suggested that Milgram's results may have been due to the same kind of foot-in-the-door technique of persuasion as discussed earlier, with participants more likely to go on with each next demanding step of the experiment because they had already agreed to the smaller increments of shock, as yet no research supports this idea (Gilbert, 1981).

Milgram's research also raised a serious ethical question: How far should researchers be willing to go to answer a question of interest? Some have argued that the participants in Milgram's studies may have suffered damaged self-esteem and serious psychological stress from the realization that they were willing to administer shocks great enough to kill another person, just on the say-so of an experimenter (Baumrind, 1964). Milgram (1964b) responded to the criticism by citing his follow-up study of the participants, in which he found that 84 percent of the participants were glad to have been a part of the experiment and only 1.3 percent said that they were sorry they had been in the experiment. A follow-up psychiatric exam one year later also found no signs of harm or trauma to the participants. Even so, most psychologists do agree that under the current ethical rules that exist for such research, this study would never be allowed to happen today. **LINK** to Chapter One: The Science of Psychology, pp. 30–31. ◉ Watch on MyPsychLab

Even so, psychologist Jerry Burger (2009) attempted a partial replication of Milgram's classic study. Berger only allowed his participants to continue the experiment

Watch classic video footage of Milgram's obedience study on **MyPsychLab** up to the point at which they heard the learner's first verbal protests (150 volts). He then estimated, based on the percentage of his participants when compared to Milgram's participants who went to the end of the shock range, the obedience rates of his modern participants. He found that his estimated rates of obedience were only slightly lower than those of Milgram's earlier study. It may be that the tendency to obey an authority figure is still almost as strong as it was nearly half a century ago.

practice quiz How much do you remember?

10.1 10.2 10.3

Pick the best answer.

1. A person's conformity in a situation like the Asch line study is most likely to be strongest when _____.
   a. the person is in the room with only one other person.
   b. at least one other person agrees with the person.
   c. that person is from Japan.
   d. that person is from the United States.

2. In groupthink, members of the group _____.
   a. have an illusion of invulnerability.
   b. avoid stereotyping those who hold an opposing viewpoint.
   c. like to "rock the boat" every now and then.
   d. sometimes question the moral "rightness" of the group.

3. When members of a cult are trying to enlist a new recruit, they start by asking the recruit to make a small commitment, such as attending a short meeting or helping out at a social function. Then the commitments get more involved, such as staying for a longer period of time and eventually for major donations of money and moving in with the cult members. This is most like which of the following techniques?

   a. foot-in-the-door technique
   b. door-in-the-face technique
   c. lowball technique
   d. that's-not-all technique

4. Which of the following has been shown to be true concerning the "teachers" in Milgram's experiment?
   a. Most of the "teachers" were sorry to have been a part of the experiment.
   b. They were found to be psychologically weak-minded people.
   c. Only a very small percentage showed any signs of psychological problems after one year.
   d. They were not ordinary people.

Brainstorming: Can you think of a time when you obeyed someone in uniform? What went through your mind when you decided to obey? Was there a time when you changed your mind about something because everyone else disagreed with you? How might Asch's conformity effect come into play when a jury is trying to get a unanimous vote of guilty or not guilty?

ANSWERS ON PAGE AK–2

Social Cognition: Attitudes, Impression Formation, and Attribution

attitude a tendency to respond positively or negatively toward a certain person, object, idea, or situation.

Social cognition focuses on the ways in which people think about other people and how those cognitions influence behavior toward those other people. In this section, we'll concentrate on how we perceive others and form our first impressions of them, as well as how we explain the behavior of others and ourselves.

Attitudes

One area of social cognition concerns the formation and influence of attitudes on the behavior and perceptions of others. An **attitude** can be defined as a tendency to respond positively or negatively to a certain idea, person, object, or situation (Triandis, 1971). This tendency, developed through peoples' experiences as they live and work with others, can affect the way they behave toward those ideas, people, objects, and situations and can include opinions, beliefs, and biases. In fact, attitudes influence the way people view these things *before* they've actually been exposed to them (Petty et al., 2003).

What do you mean—how can an attitude have an effect on something that hasn't happened yet?

What do you mean—how can an attitude have an effect on something that hasn't happened yet?

Attitudes are not something people have when they are born. They are learned through experiences and contact with others and even through direct instruction from parents, teachers, and other important people in a person's life. Because attitudes involve a positive or negative evaluation of things, it's possible to go into a new situation, meet a new person, or be exposed to a new idea with one's "mind already made up" to like or dislike, agree or disagree, and so on (Eagly & Chaiken, 1993; Petty et al., 2003). For example, children are known for making up their minds about certain foods before ever tasting them, simply because the foods are "green." Those children may have tried a green food in the past and disliked it and now are predisposed* to dislike any green food whether they've tasted it or not.

The ABC Model of Attitudes

10.4 What are the three components of an attitude, how are attitudes formed, and how can attitudes be changed?

Attitudes are actually made up of three different parts, or components, as shown in Figure 10.3. These components should not come as a surprise to anyone who has been reading the other chapters in this text because, throughout the text, references have been made to personality and traits being composed of the ways people think, feel, and act. By using certain terms to describe these three things, psychologists have come up with a handy way to describe the three components of attitudes (Eagly & Chaiken, 1993, 1998).

AFFECTIVE COMPONENT The *affective component* of an attitude is the way a person feels toward the object, person, or situation. *Affect* is used in psychology to mean "emotions" or "feelings," so the affective component is the emotional component. For example, some people might feel that country music is fun and uplifting.

BEHAVIOR COMPONENT The *behavior component* of an attitude is the action that a person takes in regard to the person, object, or situation. For example, a person who

---

*Predisposed: referring to a tendency to respond in a particular way based on previous experience.

FIGURE 10.3 Three Components of an Attitude
Attitudes consist of the way a person feels and thinks about something, as well as the way the person chooses to behave. If you like country music, you are also likely to think that country music is good music. You are also more likely to listen to this style of music, buy this type of music, and even go to a performance. Each of the three components influences the other two.

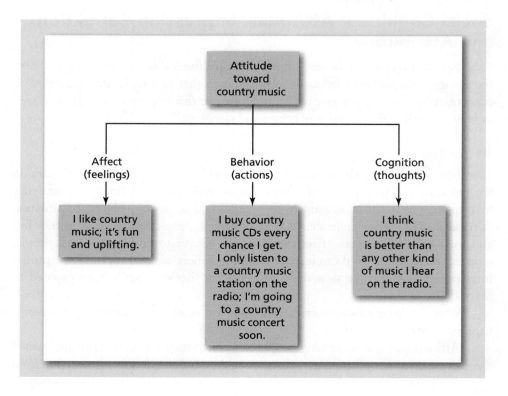

feels that country music is fun is likely to turn to a country music station on the car radio, buy country music CDs, or go to a country music concert.

COGNITIVE COMPONENT   Finally, the *cognitive component* of an attitude is the way a person thinks about the person, object, or situation. These thoughts, or cognitions, include beliefs and ideas about the focus of the attitude. For example, the country music lover might believe that country music is superior to other forms of music.

So if you know what someone thinks or feels about something, you can predict what that person will do, right?

Oddly enough, attitudes turn out to be pretty poor predictors of actual behavior in a number of controlled research studies. One survey of such research conducted in the 1960s found that what people say and what people do are often two very different things (Wicker, 1971). One factor in matching attitudes and behavior concerns how specific the attitude itself is. People may hold a general attitude about something without reflecting that attitude in their actual behavior. For example, doctors generally hold the attitude that people should do everything they can to protect their health and promote wellness, yet many doctors still smoke tobacco, fail to exercise, and often get too little sleep. But a very specific attitude, such as "exercise is important to my immediate health" will more likely be associated with the behavior of exercising (Ajzen, 2001; Ajzen & Fishbein, 2000).

Some attitudes are stronger than others, and strong attitudes are more likely to predict behavior than weak ones. A person who quit smoking because of failing health might have a stronger attitude toward secondhand smoke than someone who quit smoking on a dare, for example. The importance or salience* of a particular attitude in a given situation also has an impact on behavior—the more important the attitude appears, the more likely the behavior will match the attitude. Someone who is anti-smoking might be more likely to confront a smoker breaking the rules in a hospital, for example, than a smoker outside the building (Eagly & Chaiken, 1998).

Attitude Formation

Attitude formation is the result of a number of different influences with only one thing in common: They are all forms of learning.

DIRECT CONTACT   One way in which attitudes are formed is by direct contact with the person, idea, situation, or object that is the focus of the attitude. For example, a child who tries Brussels sprouts for the first time and dislikes them will form a negative attitude about Brussels sprouts. Later that negative attitude may be generalized to other foods that are green or have a similar taste.

DIRECT INSTRUCTION   Another way attitudes are formed is through direct instruction, either by parents or some other individual. Parents may tell their children that smoking cigarettes is dangerous and unhealthy, for example. Some children will form a negative attitude about smoking as a result.

INTERACTION WITH OTHERS   Sometimes attitudes are formed because the person is around other people with that attitude. If a person's friends, for example, all hold the attitude that smoking is cool, that person is more likely to think that smoking is cool as well (Eddy et al., 2000; Hill, 1990). The attitudes and behavior of teachers, parents, and siblings matter as well. Researchers found that a nonsmoking mother, teacher, or brother had a strong influence on both girls and boys (who are less likely to smoke), although the influence of all three on boys seemed to fade over a seven-year follow-up study (Shean et al., 1994).

> So if you know what someone thinks or feels about something, you can predict what that person will do, right?

---

*Salience: importance or having the quality of being obvious or easily seen.

VICARIOUS CONDITIONING (OBSERVATIONAL LEARNING) Many attitudes are learned through the observation of other people's actions and reactions to various objects, people, or situations. Just as a child whose mother shows a fear of dogs may develop a similar fear, a child whose mother or father shows a positive attitude toward classical music may grow into an adult with a similarly positive attitude. The emotional components of an attitude can be learned by observing the emotional reactions of others, and the behavioral components can be observed and imitated.

Attitudes are not only influenced by other people in a person's immediate world but also by the larger world of the educational system (many attitudes may be learned in school or through reading books) and the mass media of magazines, television, and the movies—a fact of which advertisers and marketing experts are well aware (Gresham & Shimp, 1985; MacKenzie et al., 1986).

Attitude Change: The Art of Persuasion

Sometimes people learn attitudes that aren't necessarily good ones, right? So can attitudes change?

> Sometimes people learn attitudes that aren't necessarily good ones, right? So can attitudes change?

Because attitudes are learned, they are also subject to change with new learning. The world is full of people, companies, and other organizations that want to change peoples' attitudes. It's all about the art of **persuasion**, the process by which one person tries to change the belief, opinion, position, or course of action of another person through argument, pleading, or explanation.

Persuasion is not a simple matter. Several factors become important in predicting how successful any persuasive effort at attitude change might be. These factors include the following:

- **Source:** The *communicator* is the person delivering the message. There is a strong tendency to give more weight to people who are perceived as experts, as well as those who seem trustworthy, attractive, and similar to the person receiving the message (Eagly & Chaiken, 1975; Petty & Cacioppo, 1986, 1996; Priester & Petty, 1995).

- **Message:** The actual message should be clear and well organized (Booth-Butterfield, 1996). It is usually more effective to present both sides of an argument to an audience that has not yet committed to one side or the other (Crowley & Hoyer, 1994; Petty & Cacioppo, 1996; Petty et al., 2003). Messages that are directed at producing fear are more effective if they produce only a moderate amount of fear and also provide information about how to avoid the fear-provoking consequences (Kleinot & Rogers, 1982; Meyrick, 2001; Petty, 1995; Rogers & Mewborn, 1976).

- **Target Audience:** The characteristics of the people who are the intended target of the message of persuasion are also important in determining the effectiveness of the message. The age of the audience members can be a factor, for example. Researchers have found that people who are in the young adult stage of the late teens to the mid-twenties are more susceptible to persuasion than are older people (Visser & Krosnick, 1998).

How easily influenced a person is will also be related to the way people tend to process information. In the **elaboration likelihood model** of persuasion (Petty & Cacioppo, 1986), it is assumed that people either elaborate (add details and information) based on what they hear (the facts of the message), or they do not elaborate at all, preferring to pay attention to the surface characteristics of the message (length, who delivers it, how attractive the message deliverer is, etc.). Two types of processing are hypothesized in this model: **central-route processing**, in which people attend to the content of the message, and **peripheral-route processing**, a style of information

persuasion the process by which one person tries to change the belief, opinion, position, or course of action of another person through argument, pleading, or explanation.

elaboration likelihood model model of persuasion stating that people will either elaborate on the persuasive message or fail to elaborate on it and that the future actions of those who do elaborate are more predictable than those who do not.

central-route processing type of information processing that involves attending to the content of the message itself.

peripheral-route processing type of information processing that involves attending to factors not involved in the message, such as the appearance of the source of the message, the length of the message, and other noncontent factors.

processing that relies on peripheral cues (cues outside of the message content itself) such as the expertise of the message source, the length of the message, and other factors that have nothing to do with the message content. This style of processing causes people not to pay attention to the message itself but instead to base their decisions on those peripheral factors (Petty & Cacioppo, 1986; Stiff & Mongeau, 2002). For example, the author once participated on a jury panel in which one woman voted "guilty" because the defendant had "shifty eyes" and not because of any of the evidence presented.

Cognitive Dissonance: When Attitudes and Behavior Clash

10.5 How do people react when attitudes and behavior are not the same?

As stated earlier, sometimes what people say and what they do are very different. I once pointed this out to a friend of mine who was behaving this way, and he got really upset over it. Why did he get so upset?

When people find themselves doing things or saying things that don't match their idea of themselves as smart, nice, or moral, for example, they experience an emotional discomfort (and physiological arousal) known as **cognitive dissonance** (Aronson, 1997; Festinger, 1957; Kelly et al., 1997). When people are confronted with the knowledge that something they have done or said was dumb, immoral, or illogical, they suffer an inconsistency in cognition. For example, they may have a cognition that says "I'm pretty smart" but also the cognition "That was a dumb thing to do," which causes a dissonance. (*Dissonance* is a term referring to an inconsistency or lack of agreement.)

When people experience cognitive dissonance, the resulting tension and arousal are unpleasant, and their motivation is to change something so that the unpleasant feelings and tension are reduced or eliminated. There are three basic things that people can do to reduce cognitive dissonance:

1. Change their conflicting behavior to make it match their attitude.
2. Change their current conflicting cognition to justify their behavior.
3. Form new cognitions to justify their behavior.

Take the example of Larry, who is a college graduate and a cigarette smoker. On one hand, Larry is educated enough to know that cigarette smoking is extremely harmful, causing lung problems, cancer, and eventually death. On the other hand, Larry enjoys smoking, feeling that it calms him and helps him deal with stress—not to mention the fact that he's thoroughly addicted and finds it difficult to quit. His attitude (smoking is bad for you) doesn't match his behavior. Larry is experiencing cognitive dissonance and knows he needs to do something to resolve his dilemma.*

If Larry chooses the first way of dealing with cognitive dissonance, he'll quit smoking, no matter how difficult it is. As long as he is working at changing the conflicting behavior, his dissonance will be reduced. But what if he can't quit? He might decide that smoking isn't as bad as everyone says it is, which changes his original conflicting attitude (Option Two). He might also form a new attitude by deciding that if he smokes "light" cigarettes, he's reducing his risk enough to justify continuing smoking (Option Three).

※─ Explore on **MyPsychLab**

---

*Dilemma: a problem involving a difficult choice.

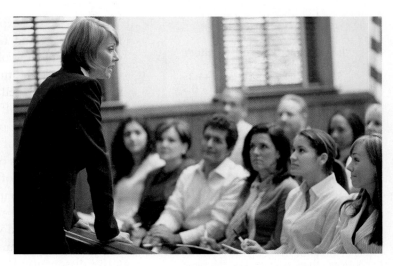

How the jurors in this courtroom interpret and process the information they are given will determine the outcome of the trial. Those who listen carefully to what is said by persons involved in the trial are using central-route processing. There may be some jurors, however, who are more affected by the appearance, dress, attractiveness, or tone of voice of the lawyers, defendant, and witnesses. When people are persuaded by factors other than the message itself, it is called peripheral-route processing.

> As stated earlier, sometimes what people say and what they do are very different. I once pointed this out to a friend of mine who was behaving this way, and he got really upset over it. Why did he get so upset?

cognitive dissonance sense of discomfort or distress that occurs when a person's behavior does not correspond to that person's attitudes.

※─ Explore cognitive dissonance and attitude change on **MyPsychLab**

Inducement	Attitude
$1	+1.35
$20	– 0.5
Control	– .45

*Based on a –5 to +5 scale, where –5 means "extremely boring" and +5 means "extremely interesting"

FIGURE 10.4 Cognitive Dissonance: Attitude Toward a Task

After completing a boring task, some participants were paid $1 and some $20 to convince others waiting to do the same task that the task was interesting and fun. Surprisingly, the participants who were paid only $1 seemed to change their own attitude toward the task, rating it as interesting, whereas those who were paid $20 rated the task no differently than a control group did.

Source: Adapted from Festinger and Carlsmith (1959).

In a classic experiment conducted at Stanford University by psychologist Leo Festinger and colleague James Carlsmith (Festinger & Carlsmith, 1959), each male student volunteer was given an hour-long, very boring task of sorting wooden spools and turning wooden pegs. After the hour, the experimenters asked the participant to tell the female volunteer in the waiting room that the task was enjoyable. While half of the participants were paid only $1 to try to convince the waiting woman, the other participants were paid $20. (In the late 1950s, $20 was a considerable sum of money—the average income was $5,000, the average car cost $3,000, and gas was only 25 cents a gallon.)

At the time of this study, many researchers would have predicted that the more the participants were paid to lie, the more they would come to like the task, because they were getting more reinforcement ($20) for doing so. But what actually happened was that those participants who were paid only $1 for lying actually convinced themselves that the task was interesting and fun. The reason is cognitive dissonance: Participants who were paid only $1 experienced discomfort at thinking that they would lie to someone for only a dollar. Therefore, they must not be lying—the task really was pretty interesting, after all, and fun, too! Those who were paid more experienced no dissonance because they knew exactly why they were lying—for lots of money—and the money was a sufficient amount to explain their behavior to their satisfaction. Although most people don't want to be thought of as liars, back then, getting paid enough money to fill the gas tank of one's car three or four times over was incentive enough to tell what probably seemed to be a harmless fib. Those who were paid only $1 had to change their attitude toward the task so that they would not really be lying and could maintain their self-image of honesty. (See Figure 10.4.)

practice quiz   How much do you remember?

(10.4) (10.5)

Pick the best answer.

1. Which of the following represents the cognitive component of an attitude?
   a. "I just love Italian food!"
   b. "Tonight, we're going to that new Italian restaurant."
   c. "Italian food is the best of the European cuisines."
   d. "I'm going to make lasagna tonight."

2. Lilly's mother always listens to the classic rock station on her car radio, so Lilly has grown up hearing that music and noticing how much her mother enjoys it. Now Lilly says that classic rock is her favorite music, too. Lilly's attitude toward classic rock was most likely acquired through _____.
   a. direct contact.
   b. direct instruction.
   c. interaction with others.
   d. vicarious conditioning.

3. Physical attractiveness is most involved in which of the following aspects of persuasion?
   a. the source
   b. the message
   c. the audience
   d. the media

4. Which of the following is not one of the elements of effective persuasion?
   a. the source or communicator
   b. characteristics of the message
   c. presence of supporters
   d. characteristics of the audience

5. "I didn't like the sermon at all today. It was too long, and that preacher wasn't dressed up enough" would be an example of which type of processing?
   a. central-route processing
   b. peripheral-route processing
   c. cognitive-route processing
   d. visual-route processing

6. In the famous Festinger experiment, participants were paid either $1 or $20 to lie to a woman in the waiting room about how interesting the task really was. The participants who convinced themselves that the task really was fun were the ones who were _____.
   a. paid immediately.
   b. paid after one day.
   c. paid only $1.
   d. paid $20.

Brainstorming: How much money would it take for you to lie to someone you did not know about doing a task similar to the one in Festinger's experiment? What difference would it make if you did know the person somewhat? What if you knew the person well?

At this job fair in Shanghai, China, thousands of applicants wait hopefully in line for an opportunity to get a job interview. Making a good first impression is important in any job interview situation, but when the competition numbers in the thousands, the people who will most likely get interviews are those who are neatly dressed and well-groomed.

Impression Formation and Attribution

When one person meets another for the first time, it is the first opportunity either person will have to make initial evaluations and judgments about the other. That first opportunity is a very important one in **impression formation**, the forming of the first knowledge a person has about another person. Impression formation includes assigning the other person to a number of categories and drawing conclusions about what that person is likely to do—it's really all about prediction. In a sense, when first meeting another person, the observer goes through a process of concept formation similar to that discussed in Chapter Six. Impression formation is another kind of social cognition.

There is a *primacy effect* in impression formation: The first time people meet someone, they form an impression of that person that persists even though they may later have other contradictory information about that person (DeCoster & Claypool, 2004; Luchins, 1957). So the old saying is pretty much on target: First impressions do count.

Impression formation is one of a number of phenomena that are all part of **social cognition**, the mental processes that people use to make sense out of the social world around them.

10.6 What are social categorization and implicit personality theories?

Social Categorization

One of the processes that occur when people meet someone new is the assignment of that person to some kind of category or group. This assignment is usually based on characteristics the new person has in common with other people or groups with whom the perceiver has had prior experience. This **social categorization** is mostly automatic and occurs without conscious awareness of the process (Macrae & Bodenhausen, 2000). Although this is a natural process (human beings are just born categorizers) **LINK** to Chapter Six: Consciousness and Cognition, pp. 209–211, sometimes it can cause problems. When the characteristics used to categorize the person are superficial* ones that have become improperly attached to certain ideas, such as "red hair equals a bad

impression formation the forming of the first knowledge that a person has concerning another person.

social cognition the mental processes that people use to make sense of the social world around them.

social categorization the assignment of a person one has just met to a category based on characteristics the new person has in common with other people with whom one has had experience in the past.

---

*Superficial: on the surface.

temper," social categorization can result in a **stereotype**, a set of characteristics that people believe is shared by all members of a particular social category (Fiske, 1998). Stereotypes (though not always negative) are very limiting, causing people to misjudge what others are like and often to treat them differently as a result. Add the process of stereotyping to the primacy effect and it becomes easy to see how important first impressions really are. That first impression not only has more importance than any other information gathered about a person later on but may include a stereotype that is resistant to change as well (Hilton & von Hipple, 1996; Hugenberg & Bodenhausen, 2003).

It sounds as though we'd be better off if people didn't use social categorization.

● It sounds as though we'd be better off if people didn't use social categorization.

Social categorization does have an important place in the perception of others. It allows people to access a great deal of information that can be useful about others, as well as helping people to remember and organize information about the characteristics of others (Macrae & Bodenhausen, 2000). The way to avoid falling into the trap of negatively stereotyping someone is to be aware of existing stereotypes and apply a little critical thinking: "Okay, so he's a guy with a tattoo on his arm. That doesn't mean that he's overly aggressive—it just means he has a tattoo."

Implicit Personality Theories

The categories into which people place others are based on something called an **implicit personality theory**. Implicit personality theories are sets of assumptions that people have about how different types of people, personality traits, and actions are all related and form in childhood (Dweck et al., 1995; Erdley & Dweck, 1993). For example, many people have an implicit personality theory that includes the idea that happy people are also friendly people and people who are quiet are shy. Although these assumptions or beliefs are not necessarily true, they do serve the function of helping to organize *schemas*, or mental patterns that represent (in this case) what a person believes about certain "types" of people. (The concept of schema here is similar to the complex schemes proposed by Piaget. (LINK) to Chapter Seven: Development Across the Life Span, p. 240.) Of course, schemas formed in this way can easily become stereotypes when people have limited experience with others who are different from themselves, especially in superficial ways such as skin color or other physical characteristics (Levy et al., 1998).

There is evidence to suggest that implicit personality theories may differ from culture to culture as well as from individual to individual. For example, one study found that Americans and Hong Kong Chinese people have different implicit personality theories about how much the personality of an individual is able to change. Whereas Americans assume that personality is relatively fixed and unchanging, Chinese people native to Hong Kong assume that personalities are far more changeable (Chiu et al., 1997).

Attribution

10.7 How do people try to explain the actions of others?

Another aspect of social cognition is the need people seem to have to explain the behavior of other people. Have you ever watched someone who was doing something you didn't understand? Chances are you were going through a number of possible explanations in your head: "Maybe he's sick, or maybe he sees something I can't see," and so on. It seems to be human nature to want to know why people do the things they do so that we know how to behave toward them and decide whom we might want

stereotype a set of characteristics that people believe is shared by all members of a particular social category.

implicit personality theory sets of assumptions about how different types of people, personality traits, and actions are related to each other.

to use as role models. If no obvious answer is available, people tend to come up with their own reasons. People also need an explanation for their own behavior. This need is so great that if an explanation isn't obvious, it causes the distress known as cognitive dissonance. The process of explaining both one's own behavior and the behavior of other people is called **attribution**. ✴ Explore on MyPsychLab

CAUSES OF BEHAVIOR   **Attribution theory** was originally developed by social psychologist Fritz Heider (1958) as a way of explaining not only why things happen but also why people choose the particular explanations of behavior that they do. There are basically two kinds of explanations—those that involve an external cause and those that assume that causes are internal.

When the cause of behavior is assumed to be from external sources, such as the weather, traffic, educational opportunities, and so on, it is said to be a **situational cause**. The observed behavior is assumed to be caused by whatever situation exists for the person at that time. For example, if John is late, his lateness might be explained by heavy traffic or car problems.

On the other hand, if the cause of behavior is assumed to come from within the individual, it is called a **dispositional cause**. In this case, it is the person's internal personality characteristics that are seen as the cause of the observed behavior. Someone attributing John's behavior to a dispositional cause, for example, might assume that John was late because his personality includes being careless of his and other people's time.

These kinds of attributions also have an emotional component. When people are happy in a marriage, for example, researchers have found that when a spouse's behavior has a positive effect, the tendency is to attribute it to an internal cause ("he did it because he wanted me to feel good"). When the effect is negative, the behavior is attributed to an external cause ("she must have had a difficult day"). But if the marriage is an unhappy one, the opposite attributions occur: "He is only being nice because he wants something from me" or "She's being mean because it's her nature to be crabby" (Fincham et al., 2000; Karney & Bradbury, 2000).

Fundamental Attribution Error

But what else determines which type of cause a person will use? For example, what determines how people explain the behavior of someone they don't already know or like?

The most well-known attributional bias is the **fundamental attribution error**, which is the tendency for people to overestimate the influence of another person's internal characteristics on behavior and underestimate the influence of the situation (whereas in explaining our own behavior, the tendency to use situational attributions instead of personal is called the *actor–observer bias*). In other words, people tend to explain the actions of others based on what "kind" of person they are rather than looking for outside causes such as social influences or situations (Blanchard-Fields et al., 2007; Harman, 1999; Jones & Harris, 1967; Leclerc & Hess, 2007; Weiner, 1985). (For example, people hearing about Milgram's "shock" study tend to assume that something is wrong with the "teachers" in the study rather than explaining their behavior within the circumstances of the situation.)

But why do we do that? Why not assume an external cause for everyone?

When people observe themselves, they are very aware of the situational influences on their own behavior. For example, tardy John was actually the one driving to work, and he knows that heavy traffic and a small accident made him late to work—he was *there*, after all. But someone else looking at John's behavior doesn't have the opportunity to see all of the possible situational influences and has only John himself in focus and, thus, assumes that John's tardiness is caused by some internal personality flaw.

---

attribution   the process of explaining one's own behavior and the behavior of others.

attribution theory   the theory of how people make attributions.

situational cause   cause of behavior attributed to external factors, such as delays, the action of others, or some other aspect of the situation.

dispositional cause   cause of behavior attributed to internal factors such as personality or character.

fundamental attribution error   the tendency to overestimate the influence of internal factors in determining behavior while underestimating situational factors.

✴ Explore internal and external attribution on MyPsychLab

But what else determines which type of cause a person will use? For example, what determines how people explain the behavior of someone they don't already know or like?

But why do we do that? Why not assume an external cause for everyone?

Other research has shown that when students are given an opportunity to make attributions about cheating, they make the fundamental attribution error and demonstrate actor-observer bias: If others are cheating, it's because they are not honest people, but if the students themselves are cheating it is because of the situation (Bogle, 2000).

Although the fundamental attribution error has been found in American culture (Jones & Harris, 1967), would the same error occur in a culture that is very different from American culture, such as in Japan? This is the question asked by researchers Masuda and Kitayama (2004), who had both American and Japanese participants ask a target person to read a prewritten attitudinal statement. The participants were then asked to give their opinion on the target's real attitude. American participants made the classic error, assuming that the target's attitude matched the reading. The Japanese participants, however, assumed that the person's attitude might be different from the statement—the person might have been under social obligation to write the piece. Japanese society is a collectivistic culture, and a Japanese person might expect to write a paper to please a teacher or employer, even though the paper's contents do not necessarily express the writer's attitudes. A summary of the research in cross-cultural differences in attribution provides further support for the idea that the fundamental attribution error is not a universal one (Peng et al., 2000). The work of Miller (1984) and many other researchers (Blanchard-Fields et al., 2007; Cha & Nam, 1985; Choi & Nisbett, 1998; Choi et al., 1999; Lee et al., 1996; Morris & Peng, 1994; Morris et al., 1995; Norenzayan et al., 1999) strongly suggests that in more interdependent, collectivist cultures found in China, Hong Kong, Japan, and Korea people tend to assume that external situational factors are more responsible for the behavior of other people than are internal dispositional factors. This finding is exactly the reverse of the fundamental attribution error so common in individualist Western cultures such as the United States.

Even age is a factor in how likely someone is to fall prey to the fundamental attribution error. Several studies (Blanchard-Fields & Horhota, 2005; Follett & Hess, 2002; Leclerc & Hess, 2007) have found that older adults show a stronger bias toward attributing the actions of another to internal causes than do younger people.

practice quiz   How much do you remember?

10.6   10.7

Pick the best answer.

1. Which of the following statements about stereotypes is FALSE?
   a. Stereotypes are forms of social categories.
   b. Stereotypes are sets of characteristics that people believe are true for all members of a particular social category.
   c. Stereotypes are governed by the recency effect.
   d. Stereotypes are very limiting and can cause discrimination.

2. Mental patterns that represent what a person believes about certain types of people are called _____.
   a. schemas.
   c. attributions.
   b. stereotypes.
   d. attitudes.

3. Elizabeth's room is almost always a mess. Her parents attribute this to Elizabeth's laziness. This is an example of a _____ cause.
   a. situational
   c. dispensational
   b. dispositional
   d. superficial

4. John was late to class, and his friend Eddie assumes that John simply doesn't care about being on time. But when Eddie is late the next day, he blames it on heavy traffic. With regard to John being late, Eddie has made the _____.
   a. egocentric error.
   b. fundamental attribution error.
   c. assumption error.
   d. false consensus error.

5. In Asian cultures, people tend to explain the behavior of others as a result of _____.
   a. bad genes.
   b. internal dispositions.
   c. situational factors.
   d. personality traits.

Social Interaction: Prejudice, Love, and Aggression

Social influence and social cognition are two of three main areas included in the field of social psychology. The third major area has to do with social interactions with others, or the relationships between people, both casual and intimate. Social interactions include prejudice and discrimination, liking and loving, and aggression and prosocial behavior.

Prejudice and Discrimination

10.8 How are prejudice and discrimination different?

In the section about attitudes, we discussed the idea that some attitudes—stereotypes—can be formed by using only superficial information about a person or group of people. When a person holds an unsupported and often negative stereotyped attitude about the members of a particular social group, it is called **prejudice**. When prejudicial attitudes cause members of a particular social group to be treated differently than others in situations that call for equal treatment, it is called **discrimination**. Prejudice is the attitude and discrimination is the behavior that can result from that attitude. Although laws can be made to minimize discriminatory behavior, it is not possible to have laws against holding certain attitudes. In other words, discrimination can be controlled and in some cases eliminated, but the prejudicial attitude that is responsible for the discrimination cannot be so easily controlled or eliminated.

Types of Prejudice and Discrimination

There are many kinds of prejudice. There are also many kinds of discrimination that occur as a result of prejudice, notably: ageism, or prejudicial attitudes toward the elderly or teenagers (among others); sexism; racism, or prejudice toward those from different ethnic groups; prejudice toward those from different religions, those from different economic levels, those who are overweight, those who are too thin, and so on. Prejudice can also vary in terms of what type of people or groups make the most likely targets. In any society, there will always be **in-groups** and **out-groups**, or "us" versus "them." The in-group is all the people with whom a particular person identifies, and the out-groups are everyone else (Brewer, 2001; Hewstone et al., 2002; Tajfel & Turner, 1986). The formation of in-groups and out-groups begins in childhood (Ruble et al., 2004) and continues as children become adults.

Once an in-group is established, prejudice toward and discriminatory treatment of the out-group or groups soon follow (Brewer, 2001). Members of the out-groups are usually going to become stereotyped according to some superficial characteristic, such as skin color or hair color, and getting rid of a stereotype once formed is difficult at best (Cameron et al., 2001; Hamilton & Gifford, 1976).

The **realistic conflict theory** of prejudice states that increasing prejudice and discrimination are closely tied to an increasing degree of conflict between the in-group and the out-group when those groups are seeking a common resource, such as land or available jobs (Horowitz, 1985; Taylor & Moghaddam, 1994). Because the examples of this kind of prejudice from history and modern times are so numerous, we will list only a few: the conflict between the early Crusaders and the Muslims, between the Jewish people and the Germans, the hatred between the Irish Catholics and the Irish Protestants, and the conflict between the native population of you-name-the-country and the colonists who want that land. The section that follows is a classic study that illustrates how easily in-groups and out-groups can be formed and how quickly prejudice and discrimination follow.

On September 6, 1957, this high school in Little Rock, Arkansas, became integrated, allowing African American students to attend school with white students. The practice of segregating black and white school children was discrimination, and the desegregation laws were aimed at stopping that discrimination. But the attitudes of prejudice persisted even after the legal discrimination was stopped and to some degree still exist today. The courts can make laws against discrimination, but changing prejudicial attitudes is much more difficult.

"First, can we agree that it's a big backyard?"
©The New Yorker Collection 2002 Charles Barsotti from cartoonbank.com. All Rights Reserved.

prejudice negative attitude held by a person about the members of a particular social group.

discrimination treating people differently because of prejudice toward the social group to which they belong.

in-groups social groups with whom a person identifies; "us."

out-groups social groups with whom a person does not identify; "them."

realistic conflict theory theory stating that prejudice and discrimination will be increased between groups that are in conflict over a limited resource.

classic studies in psychology

Brown Eyes, Blue Eyes

 In a small town in Iowa in 1968, a few days after the assassination of Dr. Martin Luther King, Jr., a second-grade teacher named Jane Elliot tried to teach her students a lesson in prejudice and discrimination. She divided her students into two groups, those with blue eyes and those with brown eyes.

On the first day of the lesson, the blue-eyed children were given special privileges, such as extra time at recess and getting to leave first for lunch. She also told the blue-eyed children that they were superior to the brown-eyed children, telling the brown-eyed children not to bother taking seconds at lunch because it would be wasted. She kept the blue-eyed children and the brown-eyed children apart (Peters, 1971).

When Elliot became critical of the brown-eyed out-group, she soon found that the blue-eyed children also began to criticize, belittle, and viciously attack the brown-eyed children. By the end of the day, the blue-eyed children felt and acted superior, and the brown-eyed children were miserable. The lowered test scores of the brown-eyed children reflected their misery. Two days later, the brown-eyed children became the favored group and the effects from the first two days appeared again but in reverse this time: The blue-eyed children began to feel inferior and their test scores dropped.

The fact that test scores reflected the treatment received by the out-group is a stunning one, raising questions about the effects of prejudice and discrimination on the education of children who are members of stereotyped out-groups. That the children were so willing to discriminate against their own classmates, some of whom were their close friends before the experiment, is also telling. In his book about this classroom experiment, *A Class Divided*, Peters (1971) reported that the students who were part of the original experiment, when reunited 15 years later to talk about the experience, said that they believed that this early experience with prejudice and discrimination helped them to become less prejudiced as young adults.

QUESTIONS FOR FURTHER DISCUSSION

1. Is there anything about this experiment that you find disturbing?
2. How do you think adults might react in a similar experiment?
3. Are there any ethical concerns with what Elliot did in her classroom?
4. What kinds of changes might have occurred in the personalities and performances of the children if the experiment had continued for more than two days with each group?

These Korean demonstrators were protesting the riots that followed the 1992 not guilty verdict of the four police officers who were videotaped beating Rodney King. The riots lasted six days, killing 42 people and damaging 700 buildings in mainly Korean and other Asian American neighborhoods. As the most recent immigrants to the area, the Asian American population of Los Angeles, California, became the scapegoats for aggression.

SCAPEGOATING Conflicts between groups are usually greater when there are other pressures or stresses going on, such as war, economic difficulties, or other misfortunes. When such pressures exist, the need to find a *scapegoat* becomes stronger. A scapegoat is a person or a group, typically a member or members of an out-group, who serves as the target for the frustrations and negative emotions of members of the in-group. (The term comes from the ancient Jewish tradition of sending a goat out into the wilderness with the symbolic sins of all the people on its head.)

Scapegoats are going to be the group of people with the least power, and the newest immigrants to any area are typically those who have the least power at that time. That is why many social psychologists believe that the rioting that took place in Los Angeles, California, in the spring of 1992 occurred in the areas it did. This was the time of the infamous Rodney King beating. Rodney King was an African American man who was dragged out of his car onto the street and severely beaten by four police officers. The beating was caught on tape by a bystander. At the trial, the officers were found not guilty of assault with a deadly weapon. This decision was followed by a series of violent riots (Knight, 1996).

The puzzling thing about these riots is that the greatest amount of rioting and violence did not take place in the neighborhoods of the mostly white police officers or in the African American neighborhoods. The rioting was greatest in the neighborhoods of the Asian Americans and Asians who were the most recent immigrants to the area. When a group has only recently moved into an area, as the Asians had, that group has the least social power and influence in that new area. So the rioters took out their frustrations *not* on the people seen as directly responsible for those frustrations but on the group of people with the least power to resist.

How People Learn Prejudice

10.9 Why are people prejudiced, and how can prejudice be stopped?

As was clearly demonstrated in the brown eyes–blue eyes experiment discussed in the Classic Studies in Psychology feature, even children are, under the right circumstances, prone to developing prejudiced attitudes. Is all prejudice simply a matter of learning, or are there other factors at work? Several theories have been proposed to explain the origins and the persistence of prejudice. In **social cognitive** theory, prejudice is seen as an attitude that is formed as other attitudes are formed, through direct instruction, modeling, and other social influences on learning.

SOCIAL IDENTITY THEORY In **social identity theory**, three processes are responsible for the formation of a person's identity within a particular social group and the attitudes, concepts, and behavior that go along with identification with that group (Tajfel & Turner, 1986). The first process is *social categorization*, as discussed earlier in this chapter. Just as people assign categories to others (such as black, white, student, teacher, and so on) to help organize information about those others, people also assign themselves to social categories to help determine how they should behave. The second element of social identity theory is *identification*, or the formation of one's **social identity**. A social identity is the part of one's self-concept that includes the view of oneself as a member of a particular social group within the social category—typically, the in-group. The third aspect of social identity theory is **social comparison**, Festinger's (1954) concept in which people compare themselves favorably to others to improve their own self-esteem: "Well, at least I'm better off than that person." (Members of the out-group make handy comparisons.)

With respect to prejudice, social identity theory helps to explain why people feel the need to categorize or stereotype others, producing the in-group sense of "us versus them" that people adopt toward out-groups. Prejudice may result, at least in part, from the need to increase one's own self-esteem by looking down on others.

STEREOTYPE VULNERABILITY As discussed previously, stereotypes are the widespread beliefs a person has about members of another group. Not only do stereotypes affect the way people perceive other people, but also stereotypes can affect the way people see themselves and their performance (Snyder et al., 1977). **Stereotype vulnerability** refers to the effect that a person's knowledge of another's stereotyped opinions can have on that person's behavior (Steele, 1992, 1997). Research has shown that when people are aware of stereotypes that are normally applied to their own group by others, they feel anxious about behaving in ways that might support that stereotype. This fear results in anxiety and self-consciousness that have negative effects on their performance in a kind of **self-fulfilling prophecy**, or the effect that expectations can have on outcomes.

Social comparison involves comparing yourself to others so that your self-esteem is protected. What do you think each of these young girls might be thinking?

social cognitive referring to the use of cognitive processes in relation to understanding the social world.

social identity theory theory in which the formation of a person's identity within a particular social group is explained by social categorization, social identity, and social comparison.

social identity the part of the self-concept including one's view of self as a member of a particular social category.

social comparison the comparison of oneself to others in ways that raise one's self-esteem.

stereotype vulnerability the effect that people's awareness of the stereotypes associated with their social group has on their behavior.

self-fulfilling prophecy the tendency of one's expectations to affect one's behavior in such a way as to make the expectations more likely to occur.

Stereotype vulnerability is highly related to *stereotype threat*, in which members of a stereotyped group are made anxious and wary of any situation in which their behavior might confirm a stereotype (Hyde & Kling, 2001; Steele, 1999). In one study, researchers administered a difficult verbal test to both Caucasian and African American participants (Steele & Aronson, 1995). Half of the African American participants were asked to record their race on a demographic* question before the test, making them very aware of their minority status. Those participants showed a significant decrease in scores on the test when compared to the other participants, both African American and Caucasian, who did not answer such a demographic question. They had more incorrect answers, had slower response times, answered fewer questions, and demonstrated more anxiety when compared to the other participants (Steele & Aronson, 1995). Similar effects of stereotype threat on performance also have been found in women (Gonzales et al., 2002; Steele, 1997; Steele et al., 2002) and for athletes in academic settings (Yopyk & Prentice, 2005). ◉▸ Watch on **MyPsychLab**

Overcoming Prejudice

The best weapon against prejudice is education: learning about people who are different from you in many ways. The best way to learn about others is to have direct contact with them and learn to see them as people rather than as outsiders or strangers. *Intergroup contact* is very common in college settings, for example, where students and faculty from many different backgrounds live, work, and study together. Because they go through many of the same experiences (midterms, finals, and so on), people from these diverse** backgrounds find common ground to start building friendships and knowledge of each other's cultural, ethnic, or religious differences.

EQUAL STATUS CONTACT   Contact between social groups can backfire under certain circumstances, however, as seen in a famous study (Sherif et al., 1961) called the "Robber's Cave." In this experiment conducted at a summer camp called Robber's Cave, 22 white, well-adjusted 11- and 12-year-old boys were divided into two groups. The groups each lived in separate housing and were kept apart from each other for daily activities. During the second week, after in-group relationships had formed, the researchers scheduled highly competitive events pitting one group against the other. Intergroup conflict quickly occurred, with name-calling, fights, and hostility emerging between the two groups.

The third week involved making the two groups come together for pleasant, noncompetitive activities, in the hopes that cooperation would be the result. Instead, the groups used the activities of the third week as opportunities for more hostility. It was only after several weeks of being forced to work together to resolve a series of crises (created deliberately by the experimenters) that the boys lost the hostility and formed friendships between the groups. When dealing with the crises, the boys were forced into a situation of **equal status contact**, in which they were all in the same situation with neither group holding power over the other. Equal status contact has been shown to reduce prejudice and discrimination. It appears that personal involvement with people from another group must be cooperative and occur when all groups are equal in terms of power or status to have a positive effect on reducing prejudice (Pettigrew & Tropp, 2000; Robinson & Preston, 1976).

THE "JIGSAW CLASSROOM"   One way to ensure that contact between people from different backgrounds will occur in a cooperative fashion is to make success at a task depend on the cooperation of each person in a group of people of mixed abilities or

◉▸ Watch a video about prejudice on **MyPsychLab**

Intergroup contact is one of the best ways to combat prejudice. When people have an opportunity to work together, as the students in this diverse classroom do, they get to know each other on common ground. Can you think of the first time you had direct contact with someone who was different from you? How did that contact change your viewpoint?

equal status contact   contact between groups in which the groups have equal status with neither group having power over the other.

---

*Demographic: having to do with the statistical characteristics of a population.
**Diverse: different, varied.

statuses. If each member of the group has information that is needed to solve the problem at hand, a situation is created in which people must depend on one another to meet their shared goals (Aronson et al., 1978). Ordinarily, school classrooms are not organized along these lines but are instead more competitive and, therefore, more likely to create conflict between people of different abilities and backgrounds.

In a **"jigsaw classroom,"** students have to work together to reach a specific goal. Each student is given a "piece of the puzzle," or information that is necessary for solving the problem and reaching the goal (Aronson et al., 1978; Clarke, 1994). Students then share their information with other members of the group. Interaction between diverse students is increased, making it more likely that those students will come to see each other as partners and form friendly relationships rather than labeling others as members of an out-group and treating them differently. This technique works at the college level as well as in the lower school grades (Johnson et al., 1991; Lord, 2001).

"jigsaw classroom" educational technique in which each individual is given only part of the information needed to solve a problem, causing the separate individuals to be forced to work together to find the solution.

practice quiz How much do you remember?

⬤ 10.8 ⬤ 10.9

Pick the best answer.

1. The behavioral component of prejudice is _____.
   a. discrimination.
   b. stereotyping.
   c. implicit personality theorizing.
   d. holding a negative attitude toward a person.

2. The most likely predictor of the development of prejudice and discrimination between two groups is the degree of _____ between the groups.
   a. differences
   b. conflict
   c. distance
   d. emotionality

3. In teacher Jane Elliot's classic study, the most startling finding was that the _____.
   a. blue-eyed children were kinder to their brown-eyed peers.
   b. brown-eyed children were less prejudiced.
   c. test scores of each group decreased when it was the out-group.
   d. children were unwilling to discriminate with respect to the others.

4. Which of the following is not an element of social identity theory?
   a. reference group
   b. social identity
   c. social comparison
   d. superordinate goals

5. Which situation would be least likely to result in a decrease of prejudice?
   a. asking people to work on separate projects but in the same room
   b. asking people to work on a common task
   c. giving each person a piece of information to share with the others to solve a problem
   d. people of various backgrounds helping rescue others from a flood

Brainstorming: What was the first time you became aware that you had a prejudiced attitude toward something or someone? How did you confront that knowledge?

ANSWERS ON PAGE AK–2

Liking and Loving: Interpersonal Attraction

Prejudice pretty much explains why people don't like each other. What does psychology say about why people like someone else? There are some "rules" for those whom people like and find attractive. Liking or having the desire for a relationship with someone else is called **interpersonal attraction**, and there's a great deal of research on the subject. (Who wouldn't want to know the rules?)

The Rules of Attraction

10.10 What factors govern attraction and love, and what are some different kinds of love?

Several factors are involved in the attraction of one person to another, including both superficial physical characteristics, such as physical beauty and proximity, as well as elements of personality.

interpersonal attraction liking or having the desire for a relationship with another person.

proximity physical or geographical nearness.

reciprocity of liking tendency of people to like other people who like them in return.

PHYSICAL ATTRACTIVENESS When people think about what attracts them to other people, one of the topics that usually arises is the physical attractiveness of the other person. Some research suggests that physical beauty is one of the main factors that influence people's choices for selecting people they want to know better, although other factors may become more important in the later stages of relationships (Eagly et al., 1991; Feingold, 1992; White, 1980).

PROXIMITY—CLOSE TO YOU The closer together people are physically, such as working in the same office building or living in the same dorm, the more likely they are to form a relationship. **Proximity** refers to being physically near someone else. People choose friends and lovers from the pool of people available to them, and availability depends heavily on proximity.

One theory about why proximity is so important involves the idea of repeated exposure to new stimuli. The more people experience something, whether it is a song, a picture, or a person, the more they tend to like it. The phrase "it grew on me" refers to this reaction. When people are in physical proximity to each other, repeated exposure may increase their attraction to each other.

BIRDS OF A FEATHER—SIMILARITY Proximity does not guarantee attraction, just as physical attractiveness does not guarantee a long-term relationship. People tend to like being around others who are *similar* to them in some way. The more people find they have in common with others—such as attitudes, beliefs, and interests—the more they tend to be attracted to those others (Hartfield & Rapson, 1992; Moreland & Zajonc, 1982; Neimeyer & Mitchell, 1998). Similarity as a factor in relationships makes sense when seen in terms of validation of a person's beliefs and attitudes. When other people hold the same attitudes and beliefs and do the same kinds of actions, it makes a person's own concepts seem more correct or valid.

When Opposites Attract

Isn't there a saying that "opposites attract"? Aren't people sometimes attracted to people who are different instead of similar?

There is often a grain of truth in many old sayings, and "opposites attract" is no exception. Some people find that forming a relationship with another person who has *complementary* qualities (characteristics in the one person that fill a need in the other) can be very rewarding (Carson, 1969; Schmitt, 2002). Research does not support this view of attraction, however. It is similarity, not complementarity, that draws people together and helps them stay together (Berscheid & Reis, 1998; McPherson et al., 2001).

RECIPROCITY OF LIKING Finally, people have a very strong tendency to like people who like them, a simple but powerful concept referred to as **reciprocity of liking**. In one experiment, researchers paired college students with other students (Curtis & Miller, 1986). Neither student in any of the pairs knew the other member. One member of each pair was randomly chosen to receive some information from the experimenters about how the *other* student in the pair felt about the first member. In some cases, target students were led to believe that the other students liked them and, in other cases, that the targets disliked them.

When the pairs of students were allowed to meet and talk with each other again, they were friendlier, disclosed more information about themselves, agreed with the other person more, and behaved in a warmer manner *if they had been told* that the other student liked them. The other students came to like these students better as well, so liking produced more liking.

The only time that liking someone does not seem to make that person like the other in return is if a person suffers from feelings of low self-worth. In that case, finding out that someone likes you when you don't even like yourself makes you question his or her motives. This mistrust can cause you to act unfriendly to that person, which makes the person more likely to become unfriendly to you in a kind of self-fulfilling prophecy (Murray et al., 1998).

psychology in the news

Facing Facebook—The Social Nature of Online Networking

There are some interesting research findings concerning the online networking phenomenon. For example, people using particular sites seem to have certain things in common. The findings of one study suggest that the student's choice of social network sites is related to racial identity, ethnic identity, and the education level of the student's parents (Hargittai, 2007). White students prefer Facebook, and Hispanic students prefer MySpace; and while Asian and Asian American students use Facebook more than MySpace, they use less popular sites like Xanga and Friendster more than any other ethnic group does. The more education the parents have, the more likely the student is to use Facebook and Xanga, and the less likely to use MySpace.

In another study, researchers found that young people who already experience positive social relationships use the online sites to enhance those same relationships, contrary to the stereotyped view that it would be the socially inept who would gravitate toward the anonymous nature of online networking (Mikami et al., 2010). Those who are less well adjusted either did not use social networking sites or used them in more negative ways: using excessive bad language, making hostile remarks, showing aggressive gestures, or posting unflattering or suggestive photographs.

Finally, a recent study's findings suggest that users of social networking sites spend a lot more time on "social searching," which is defined as searching a site for specific information about a certain person, group, or event, than they do on "social browsing," defined as surveying the site without any specific target in mind (Wise et al., 2010). Users were also found to be more emotionally and positively engaged when searching rather than browsing. Again, this runs counter to the complaints of some who feel that such sites encourage time-wasting browsing. Instead, people are actively searching for information they desire.

QUESTIONS FOR FURTHER DISCUSSION

1. Why might certain networking sites be more attractive to one ethnicity over another?
2. How do you find yourself using networking sites, and how does that relate to the findings of these studies?

Love Is a Triangle—Robert Sternberg's Triangular Theory of Love

Dictionary definitions of love refer to a strong affection for another person due to kinship, personal ties, sexual attraction, admiration, or common interests.

But those aren't all the same kind of relationships. I love my family and I love my friends, but in different ways.

Psychologists generally agree that there are different kinds of love. One psychologist, Robert Sternberg, outlined a theory of what he determined were the three main components of love and the different types of love that combinations of these three components can produce (Sternberg, 1986, 1988b, 1997a).

> But those aren't all the same kind of relationships. I love my family and I love my friends, but in different ways.

romantic love type of love consisting of intimacy and passion.

companionate love type of love consisting of intimacy and commitment.

THE THREE COMPONENTS OF LOVE According to Sternberg, love consists of three basic components: intimacy, passion, and commitment.

Intimacy, in Sternberg's view, refers to the feelings of closeness that one has for another person or the sense of having close emotional ties to another. Intimacy in this sense is not physical but psychological. Friends have an intimate relationship because they disclose things to each other that most people might not know, they feel strong emotional ties to each other, and they enjoy the presence of the other person.

Passion is the physical aspect of love. Passion refers to the emotional and sexual arousal a person feels toward the other person. Passion is not simply sex; holding hands, loving looks, and hugs can all be forms of passion.

Commitment involves the decisions one makes about a relationship. A short-term decision might be, "I think I'm in love." An example of a more long-term decision is, "I want to be with this person for the rest of my life." ◉─|Watch on **MyPsychLab**

◉─|Watch a video on Sternberg's triangular theory of love on **MyPsychLab**

THE LOVE TRIANGLES A love relationship between two people can involve one, two, or all three of these components in various combinations. The combinations can produce seven different forms of love, as seen in Figure 10.5.

Two of the more familiar and more heavily researched forms of love from Sternberg's theory are romantic love and companionate love. When intimacy and passion are combined, the result is the more familiar **romantic love**, which is sometimes called passionate love by other researchers (Bartels & Zeki, 2000; Diamond, 2003; Hartfield, 1987). Romantic love is often the basis for a more lasting relationship. In many Western cultures, the ideal relationship begins with liking, then becomes romantic love as passion is added to the mix, and finally becomes a more enduring form of love as a commitment is made.

📖─|Read and learn more about the labeling theory of passionate love on **MyPsychLab**

When intimacy and commitment are the main components of a relationship, it is called **companionate love**. In companionate love, people who like each other, feel emotionally close to each other, and understand one another's motives have made a commitment to live together, usually in a marriage relationship. Companionate love is often the binding tie that holds a marriage together through the years of parenting, paying bills, and lessening physical passion (Gottman & Krokoff, 1989; Steinberg & Silverberg, 1987). In many non-Western cultures, companionate love is seen as more sensible. Choices for a mate on the basis of compatibility are often made by parents or matchmakers rather than the couple themselves (Duben & Behar, 1991; Hortaçsu, 1999; Jones, 1997; Thornton & Hui-Sheng, 1994). 📖─|Read on **MyPsychLab**

Liking
Intimacy

Romantic Love
Passion

Consumate Love
Intimacy + Passion + Commitment

Companionate
Commitment

Infatuation

Fatuous Love

Empty Love

FIGURE 10.5 Sternberg's Triangular Theory of Love
This diagram represents the seven different kinds of love that can result from combining the three components of love: intimacy, passion, and commitment. Notice that three of these types of love sound less desirable or positive than the others. What is the one key element missing from the less positive types of love?
Source: Adapted from Sternberg (1986b).

Finally, when all three components of love are present, the couple has achieved *consummate love*, the ideal form of love that many people see as the ultimate goal. This is also the kind of love that may evolve into companionate love when the passion lessens during the middle years of a relationship's commitment.

practice quiz How much do you remember?

10.10

Pick the best answer.

1. Which of the following is not one of the reasons given by the text for interpersonal attraction?
   a. physical attractiveness
   b. similarity
   c. personality
   d. proximity

2. The more you see someone, the more likely you are to _____ that person.
   a. dislike
   b. like
   c. grow tired of
   d. be annoyed by

3. A person who is very low in self-worth is less likely to be affected by the _____.
   a. halo effect.
   b. mere exposure effect.
   c. need complementarity effect.
   d. reciprocity of liking effect.

4. According to Sternberg, the emotional and physical arousal a person feels for another is the _____ component of love.
   a. intimacy
   b. passion
   c. commitment
   d. psychological

ANSWERS ON PAGE AK–2

Aggression and Prosocial Behavior

Unfortunately, violence toward others is another form of social interaction. When one person hurts or tries to destroy another person deliberately, either with words or with physical behavior, psychologists call it **aggression**. One common cause of aggressive behavior is frustration, which occurs when a person is prevented from reaching some desired goal. The concept of aggression as a reaction to frustration is known as the frustration–aggression hypothesis (Berkowitz, 1993; Miller et al., 1941). Many sources of frustration can lead to aggressive behavior. Pain, for example, produces negative sensations that are often intense and uncontrollable, leading to frustration and often aggressive acts against the nearest available target (Berkowitz, 1993). Loud noises, excessive heat, the irritation of someone else's cigarette smoke, and even awful smells can lead people to act out in an aggressive manner (Anderson, 1987; Rotton & Frey, 1985; Rotton et al., 1979; Zillmann et al., 1981).

Frustration is not the only source of aggressive behavior. Many early researchers, including Sigmund Freud (1930), believed that aggression was a basic human instinct. In Freud's view, aggression was part of the death instinct that drove human beings to destroy both others and themselves, and he believed that if aggression were not released it would cause illness. But if aggression is an instinct present in all humans, it should occur in far more similar patterns across cultures than it does. Instinctual behavior, as often seen in animals, is not modifiable by environmental influences. Modern approaches try to explain aggression as a biological phenomenon or a learned behavior.

Aggression and Biology

10.11 How is aggressive behavior determined by biology and learning?

There is some evidence that human aggression has at least partially a genetic basis. Studies of twins have shown that if one identical twin has a violent temper, the identical sibling will most likely also have a violent temper. This agreement between

aggression behavior intended to hurt or destroy another person.

social role the pattern of behavior that is expected of a person who is in a particular social position.

twins' personalities happens more often with identical twins than with fraternal twins (Miles & Carey, 1997; Rowe et al., 1999). It may be that some gene or complex of genes makes certain people more susceptible to aggressive responses under the right environmental conditions.

As discussed in Chapter Two, certain areas of the brain seem to control aggressive responses. The amygdala and other structures of the limbic system have been shown to trigger aggressive responses when stimulated in both animals and humans (Adams, 1968; Albert & Richmond, 1977; LaBar et al., 1995; Scott et al., 1997). Charles Whitman, the Tower of Texas sniper, who in 1966 killed his mother, his wife, and then shot and killed 12 more people before finally being killed by law enforcement officers, left a note asking for an examination of his brain. An autopsy did reveal a tumor that was pressing into his amygdala (Lavergne, 1997).

There are also chemical influences on aggression. Testosterone, a male sex hormone, has been linked to higher levels of aggression in humans (Archer, 1991). This may help to explain why violent criminals tend to be young, male, and muscular. They typically have high levels of testosterone and low levels of serotonin, another important chemical found in the brain (Alexander et al., 1986; Brown & Linnoila, 1990; Coccaro & Kavoussi, 1996; Dabbs et al., 2001; Robins, 1996).

● **Don't some people get pretty violent after drinking too much? Does alcohol do something to those brain chemicals?**

Alcohol does have an impact on aggressive behavior. Psychologically, alcohol acts to release inhibitions, making people less likely to control their behavior even if they are not yet intoxicated. Biologically, alcohol affects the functioning of many neurotransmitters and in particular is associated with a decrease in serotonin (Virkkunen & Linnoila, 1996). ⓁⒾⓃⓀ to Chapter Two: The Biological Perspective, p. 49. In one study, volunteers were asked to administer electric shocks to an unseen "opponent" in a study reminiscent of Milgram's shock experiment. The actual responses to the shock were simulated by a computer, although the volunteers believed that the responses were coming from a real person. The volunteers were told it was a test of reaction time and learning (Bushman, 1997). Volunteers participated both before consuming alcohol and after consuming alcohol. Participants were much more aggressive in administering stronger shocks after drinking.

The Power of Social Roles

Although frustration, genetics, body chemicals, and even the effects of drugs can be blamed for aggressive behavior to some degree, much of human aggression is also influenced by learning. The social learning theory explanation for aggression states that aggressive behavior is learned (in a process called observational learning) by watching aggressive models get reinforced for their aggressive behavior (Bandura, 1980; Bandura et al., 1961). ⓁⒾⓃⓀ to Chapter Four: Learning, pp. 151–153. Aggressive models can be parents, siblings, friends, or people on television.

There is some evidence to suggest that even taking on a particular *social role*, such as that of a soldier, can lead to an increase in aggressive behavior. A **social role** is the pattern of behavior that is expected of a person who is in a particular social position. For example, "doctor" is a social role that implies wearing a white coat, asking certain types of questions, and writing prescriptions, among other things.

A deeply disturbing experiment was conducted by famed social psychologist Philip Zimbardo at Stanford University in 1971. The experiment was recorded on film from the beginning to a rather abrupt end: About 70 young men, most of whom were college students, volunteered to participate for two weeks. They were told that they would be randomly assigned the social role of either a guard or a prisoner in the

Don't some people get pretty violent after drinking too much? Does alcohol do something to those brain chemicals?

This photograph shows a "guard" searching a "prisoner" in Zimbardo's famous Stanford prison experiment. The students in the experiment became so deeply involved in their assigned roles that Zimbardo had to cancel the experiment after only five days—less than half the time originally scheduled for the study.

experiment. The "guards" were given uniforms and instructions not to use violence but to maintain control of the "prison." The "prisoners" were booked at a real jail, blindfolded, and transported to the campus "prison," actually the basement of one of the campus buildings. On day 2, the prisoners staged a revolt (not planned as part of the experiment), which was quickly crushed by the guards. The guards then became increasingly more aggressive, using humiliation to control and punish the prisoners. For example, prisoners were forced to clean out toilet bowls with their bare hands. The staff observing the experiment had to release five of the prisoners who became so upset that they were physically ill. The entire experiment was canceled on the fifth day, after one of the prisoners reported to Zimbardo that what the experimenters were doing to the young men was terrible (Zimbardo, 1971).

The conclusions of Zimbardo and his colleagues highlighted the influence that a social role, such as that of "guard," can have on perfectly ordinary people. Although history is full of examples of people behaving horribly to others while filling a particular role, one need not travel very far into the past to find an example. ⊙ Watch on MyPsychLab

During the war in Iraq in 2003, an army reserve general was suspended from duty while an investigation into reported prisoner abuses was conducted. Between October and December 2003, investigators found numerous cases of cruel, humiliating, and other startling abuses of the Iraqi prisoners by the army military police stationed at the prison of Abu Ghraib (Hersh, 2004). Among the cruelties reported were pouring cold water on naked detainees, beating them with a broom handle or chair, threatening them with rape, and one case of actually carrying out the threat. How could any normal person have done such things? The "guards" in the Stanford prison study were normal people, but the effect of putting on the uniform and taking on the social role of guard changed their behavior radically. Is it possible that a similar factor was at work at Abu Ghraib? The behavior of the guards at Abu Ghraib was not part of a formal, controlled study, so further research will be needed to determine to what degree the social roles at work in situations like this influence the kind of behavior seen in this real-life example.

Could people such as these guards be aggressive because they were abused as children? No one can deny that abused children are exposed to powerful models of aggression. Their abusing parents get reinforced for their aggressive behavior when they get what they want from the child. No one can deny that there are people who were abused who go on to become abusers. Contrary to popular belief, however, most children who suffer abuse do *not* grow up to become abusers themselves—only one-third of abused children do so (Kaufman & Zigler, 1993; Oliver, 1993). Some abused children receive help and overcome the damage from their childhood, whereas others withdraw, isolating themselves rather than becoming abusive (Dodge et al., 1990). ⊙ Read on MyPsychLab

Violence in the Media and Aggression

I've heard that violent television programs can cause children to become more aggressive. How true is that?

Bandura's early study on the effects of an aggressive model viewed over a movie screen on small children was one of the first attempts to investigate the effect of violence in the media on children's aggressive behavior (Bandura et al., 1963). ⓁⒾⓃⓀ to Chapter Four: Learning, pp. 151–153. Since then, many researchers

A U.S. soldier mistreats an Iraqi prisoner at the Abu Ghraib prison in Iraq. Investigators into alleged abuses at this prison found numerous sadistic and brutal acts committed by U.S. military personnel on the prisoners.

⊙ Watch classic footage of Zimbardo's Stanford prison experiment on MyPsychLab

⊙ Read and learn more about child abuse on MyPsychLab

I've heard that violent television programs can cause children to become more aggressive. How true is that?

have examined the impact of television and other media violence on the aggressive behavior of children of various ages. The earliest conclusions were similar: Children who are exposed to high levels of violent media are more aggressive than children who are not (Baron & Reiss, 1985; Bushman & Huesmann, 2001; Centerwall, 1989; Geen & Thomas, 1986; Huesmann & Miller, 1994; Huesmann et al., 1997; Huesmann et al., 2003; Villani, 2001). More recent research suggests strongly that these earlier studies have been seriously flawed in several ways, and often subject to a bias held by the general population: Violent video games are bad for you.

Why does this bias exist? It's not really new: Television shows from the 1960s were often criticized for being too violent, despite the fact that shows of this era never showed realistic violence—no blood, no wounds, no carnage! Violent video games have come under similar fire in their turn. The tragic shootings at schools all over the United States have, at least in part, been blamed on violent video games that the students seemed to be imitating.

Recent research now strongly suggests that linking video games to school shooters is a mistake. There are many other factors left out or otherwise skipped over when conducting this type of research. One meta-analysis (a careful statistical analysis of a large number of studies on a particular topic, able to more accurately measure the sizes of research effects than any one smaller study can measure) of 26 studies examining the relationship between exposure to media violence and violent aggressive behavior concluded that size effects were too small to provide evidence for a correlational relationship between the two variables (Savage & Yancey, 2008). The authors of the study stress that variables such as socioeconomic status, parent's education level, parental violence, conditions of neglect, and intelligence levels of the participants would need to be methodically controlled in any study of aggression and media effects—all of these factors have been linked to both variables.

Another meta-analysis (Ferguson & Kilburn, 2009) came to similar conclusions. These researchers found evidence of poor measures of aggressive behavior (remember the importance of operational definitions from Chapter One?) as well as a tendency for publication bias: the willingness of journal editors to publish studies with relatively small effect sizes (i.e., small correlations between the variables) as long as the conclusions of the study were in line with the popular consensus of the times. In a later study Ferguson (2010) found that the presence of depression and depressive symptoms was a much more relevant predictor of violent aggression than the playing of violent video games. Remember, many of the school shooters in years past showed or left evidence of depressive symptoms prior to their aggressive acts. Adachi and Willoughby (in press), in an examination of previous correlational studies, point out that many of these studies have two major limitations. First, these earlier studies failed to consider the video games used in the research in terms of their difficulty levels, the pace of the action, and the competitive level—they looked only at violent content, ignoring these other factors. Second, the particular measures of aggression used could also be seen as measuring competitiveness, a major flaw in the operational definition of a key variable. Are those studies measuring aggressive behavior, or are they measuring competitive behavior? Finally, it is important to realize that the bulk of research examining the effects of media violence on aggressive behavior is correlational, not experimental. Remember, correlation does NOT prove causation—no study has yet shown that playing violent video games *causes* increased aggression! Ⓛ Ⓘ Ⓝ Ⓚ to Chapter One: The Science of Psychology, pp. 23–25.

Prosocial Behavior

prosocial behavior socially desirable behavior that benefits others.

Another and far more pleasant form of human social interaction is **prosocial behavior**, or socially desirable behavior that benefits others rather than brings them harm.

10.12 **What is altruism, and how is deciding to help someone related to the presence of others?**

ALTRUISM One form of prosocial behavior that almost always makes people feel good about other people is **altruism**, or helping someone in trouble with no expectation of reward and often without fear for one's own safety. Although no one is surprised by the behavior of a mother who enters a burning house to save her child, some people are often surprised when total strangers step in to help, risking their own lives for people they do not know.

Sociobiologists—scientists who study the evolutionary and genetic bases of social organizations in both animals and humans—see altruistic behavior as a way of preserving one's genetic material, even at the cost of one's own life. This is why the males of certain species of spiders, for example, seem to willingly become "dinner" for the female mates they have just fertilized, ensuring the continuation of their genes through the offspring she will produce (Koh, 1996). It also explains the mother or father who risks life and limb to save a child. But why do people risk their own lives to help total strangers? More importantly, why do people sometimes refuse to help when their own lives are not at risk? ☑•⎯Survey on **MyPsychLab**

Why People Won't Help

On March 13, 1964, at about 3:15 in the morning, a man who didn't even know Catherine "Kitty" Genovese caught her in the parking lot of her apartment complex, stabbed her, left, and then came back nearly half an hour later to rape and stab her to death in the entryway of the complex. A police investigation determined that at least 38 people heard or watched some part of the fatal attack from their apartment windows. Not one of these people—Kitty's neighbors—called the police until after the attack was over (Delfiner, 2001; Gado, 2004; Rosenthal, 1964).

People were outraged by the apparent indifference and lack of sympathy for the poor woman's plight. Why did those people simply stand by and watch or listen? Social psychologists would explain that the lack of response to Kitty Genovese's screams for help was not due to indifference or a lack of sympathy but instead to the presence of other people.

Forty-three years later on June 23, 2007, 27-year-old LaShanda Calloway was stabbed to death during an argument in a convenience store. It took two minutes for someone to call 911. Surveillance video captured the attack, including the five shoppers who stepped over her bleeding form and continued shopping. One customer did stop—to take a picture of Ms. Calloway as she lay dying on the floor (Hegeman, 2007). When other people are present at the scene or are assumed to be present, individuals are affected by two basic principles of social psychology: the bystander effect and diffusion of responsibility.

The **bystander effect** refers to the finding that the likelihood of a bystander (someone observing an event and close enough to offer help) to help someone in trouble decreases as the number of bystanders increases. If only one person is standing by, that person is far more likely to help than if there is another person, and the addition of each new bystander decreases the possibility of helping behavior even more (Darley & Latané, 1968; Eagly & Crowley, 1986; Latané & Darley, 1969). In the case of Kitty Genovese, there were 38 "bystanders" at the windows of the apartment buildings, and none of them helped. Five shoppers stepped over the bleeding body of LaShanda Calloway, and none of them helped.

But why does the number of bystanders matter? ●⎯⎯⎯⎯⎯⎯⎯⎯⎯⎯⎯

Diffusion of responsibility is the phenomenon in which a person fails to take responsibility for either action or inaction because of the presence of other people who are seen to share the responsibility (Figure 10.6) (Leary & Forsyth, 1987). Diffusion of

altruism prosocial behavior that is done with no expectation of reward and may involve the risk of harm to oneself.

bystander effect referring to the effect that the presence of other people has on the decision to help or not help, with help becoming less likely as the number of bystanders increases.

diffusion of responsibility occurring when a person fails to take responsibility for actions or for inaction because of the presence of other people who are seen to share the responsibility.

☑•⎯Survey Participate in a survey: Could you be a hero? on **MyPsychLab**

But why does the number of bystanders matter?

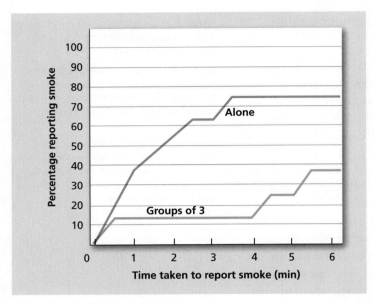

FIGURE 10.6 Elements Involved in Bystander Response

As you can see in the accompanying graph, the time taken to report smoke and the percentage of people reporting smoke both depended on how many people were in the room at the time the smoke was observed. If alone, a person was far more likely to report the smoke and report it more quickly than when there were three people in the room.

Source: Latané and Darley (1969).

responsibility is a form of attribution in which people explain why they acted (or failed to act) as they did because of others. "I was just following orders," "Other people were doing it," and "There were a lot of people there, and I thought one of them would do something" are all examples of statements made in such situations. Kitty Genovese received no help because there were too many potential "helpers," and not one of the people listening to her cries for help took the responsibility to intervene—they thought surely someone else was doing something about it.

FIVE DECISION POINTS IN HELPING BEHAVIOR In all of the experiments reported in the preceding section, there were people who did try to help in every condition. What kind of decision-making process might they have gone through before deciding to help? What are the requirements for deciding when help is needed? Darley and Latané (1968) identified several decision points that a bystander must face before helping someone in trouble. These decision points are outlined in Table 10.2.

Aside from the factors listed in the table, there are other influences on the decision to help. For example, the more ambiguity* there is in a situation, the less likely it becomes that the situation will be defined as an emergency. If there are other people nearby, especially if the situation is ambiguous, bystanders may rely on the actions of the others to help determine whether or not the situation is an emergency. Since all the bystanders are doing this, the situation will very likely be seen as a nonemergency because no one is moving to help.

Another factor is the mood of the bystanders. People in a good mood are generally more likely to help than people in a bad mood, but oddly enough, they are not as likely to help if helping would destroy the good mood. Gender of the victim is also a factor, with women more likely to receive help than men if the bystander is male, but not if the bystander is female. Physically attractive people are more likely to be helped. Victims who look like "they deserve what is happening" are also less likely to be helped. For example, a man lying on the side of the street who is dressed in shabby clothing and appears to be drunk will be passed by, but if he is dressed in a business suit, people are more likely to stop and help. Racial and ethnicity differences between victim and bystander also decrease the probability of helping (Richards & Lowe, 2003; Tukuitonga & Bindman, 2002).

*Ambiguity: having the quality of being difficult to identify specific elements of the situation.

table 10.2 Help or Don't Help: Five Decision Points

DECISION POINT	DESCRIPTION	FACTORS INFLUENCING DECISION
Noticing	Realizing that there is a situation that might be an emergency.	Hearing a loud crash or a cry for help.
Defining an Emergency	Interpreting the cues as signaling an emergency.	Loud crash is associated with a car accident; people are obviously hurt.
Taking Responsibility	Personally assuming the responsibility to act.	A single bystander is much more likely to act than when others are present (Latané & Darley, 1969).
Planning a Course of Action	Deciding how to help and what skills might be needed.	People who feel they have the necessary skills to help are more likely to help.
Taking Action	Actually helping.	Costs of helping (e.g., danger to self) must not outweigh the rewards of helping.

practice quiz How much do you remember?

Pick the best answer.

1. Which of the following has not been studied as a cause of aggressive behavior?
   a. frustration
   b. pain
   c. alcohol
   d. marijuana

2. The area of the brain that is most involved in aggression is the _____.
   a. amygdala.
   b. pineal gland.
   c. cerebellum.
   d. cortex.

3. Which of the following statements is TRUE?
   a. Abused children always grow up to become abusers.
   b. Abused children rarely grow up to become abusers.
   c. Abused children grow up to become abusers about one-third of the time.
   d. Children who were not abused do not grow up to become abusers.

4. According to the bystander effect, Leshan is more likely to get help if there is (are) _____.
   a. no other people standing nearby.
   b. only one other person standing nearby.
   c. several people standing nearby.
   d. a crowd of people standing nearby.

5. Once a situation has been defined as an emergency, the next step in the decision-making process is _____.
   a. noticing.
   b. taking action.
   c. taking responsibility.
   d. planning a course of action.

ANSWERS ON PAGE AK–2

applying psychology to everyday life
Anatomy of a Cult

10.13 Why do people join cults?

The term **cult** literally refers to any group of people with a particular religious or philosophical set of beliefs and identity. In the strictest sense of the word, the Roman Catholic Church and Protestantism are cults within the larger religion of Christianity. But for most people the term *cult* has a negative connotation*: a group of people whose religious or philosophical beliefs and behavior are so different from that of mainstream organizations that they are viewed with suspicion and seen as existing on the fringes of socially acceptable behavior. Although many cults exist without much notice from more mainstream groups, at times members of cults have horrified the public with their actions.

One of the most well-remembered and often cited examples of a cult gone horribly wrong was that of the People's Temple in Jonestown, Guyana, headed by Jim Jones. Originally a Christian offshoot, the People's Temple became a cult under Jones's dictatorial leadership. In 1978, when Jones felt threatened by reporters coming to Guyana, he instructed the entire cult of over 900 people to commit suicide by either drinking cyanide-laced drinks or shooting each other. A total of 914 people died, including 274 children (Chidester, 2003).

While the mainstream Mormon Church, or Church of Jesus Christ of Latter Day Saints, banned polygamy in the early 1900s, Warren Jeffs, the leader and "prophet" of the 10,000-member Fundamentalist Church of Jesus Christ of Latter Day Saints, was arrested in 2006 for arranging "marriages" of his adult male followers to underage girls and is currently serving a minimum 10-year sentence in the Utah State Prison (Winslow, 2007).

In 1978, the Reverend Jim Jones, leader of the People's Temple in Jonestown, Guyana, ordered his followers to drink poisoned drinks or shoot each other. Of the cult members, 640 adults died and 274 children were either killed by their own hands or those of their parents.

Why would any person get so caught up in cult beliefs that polygamy, suicide, and in some cases, murder become desired behaviors? What kind of person joins a cult in the first place? Although there is no particular personality profile associated with cult membership, cult members do appear to have been in some psychological distress at the time of recruitment by the cult. People who are under a lot of stress, dissatisfied with their lives, unassert-

cult any group of people with a particular religious or philosophical set of beliefs and identity.

---
*Connotation: the meaning of a word or concept that is more suggestive than directly stated.

ive, gullible, dependent, feel a desire to belong to a group, and those who are unrealistically idealistic ("we can solve all the world's problems if everyone will just love each other") are the most likely targets of cult recruitment (Langone, 1996). Young people rebelling against parental authority or trying to become independent of families are prime targets.

Cult leaders also have certain techniques of persuasion that are common to most cult organizations. The first step is usually something called "love-bombing" by current cult members, who shower the recruits with affection and attention and claim to understand just how the potential cult members feel. Then efforts are made to isolate the recruits from family and friends who might talk them out of joining. This is accomplished in part by keeping the recruits so busy with rigid rituals, ways of dress, meditations, and other activities that they do not allow the recruits time to think about what is happening. All of these activities also serve to wear down the resistance of the recruits. Cults also teach their members how to stop questioning thoughts or criticisms, which are typically seen as sins or extremely undesirable behavior. Access to people and information outside the cult is either kept to a well-guarded minimum or totally shut off (Singer & Lalich, 1995; Zimbardo & Hartley, 1985).

Commitments to the cult are small at first, such as attending a music concert or some other cult function. Eventually, the cult requests a major step, such as quitting one's job, turning over money or property to the cult, or similar commitments. Leaving a cult is quite difficult, as members of the cult in good standing will often track down a "deserter." Parents, friends, and other family members have been known to hire special "deprogrammers" to help their loved one recover from cult membership, willingly or unwillingly. Sometimes people actually have to "kidnap" their loved one out of the cult environment. Nevertheless, as difficult as it is to leave, 90 percent or more of cult members do eventually get out (Barker, 1983; Galanter, 1983).

Cults have existed all through recorded history and will probably continue to exist in the future. Most cults do not pose a physical threat to their members or others, but the examples of the followers of Jim Jones, David Koresh, and Osama bin Laden clearly demonstrate that cults, like any group of people, can become deadly.

QUESTIONS FOR FURTHER DISCUSSION
1. In what ways are the methods used by cults on new recruits similar to the methods used by the military when training new soldiers?
2. Is it ethical for the family members of an adult to "kidnap" and deprogram a cult member?
3. Which methods of compliance do cults seem to use to recruit new members?

chapter summary ((•─[Listen on **MyPsychLab**   Listen to an audio file of your chapter www.MyPsychLab

- Social psychology is the scientific study of how a person's thoughts, feelings, and behavior are influenced by the real, imagined, or implied presence of other people.

Social Influence: Conformity, Compliance, and Obedience

10.1 What factors influence people to conform to the actions of others?

- Asch used a set of comparison lines and a standard line to experiment with conformity, finding that subjects conformed to group opinion about one-third of the time, and that conformity increased as the number of confederates rose to four, and conformity decreased if just one confederate gave the correct answer.

- Cross-cultural research has found that collectivistic cultures show more conformity than individualistic cultures. Gender differences do not exist in conformity unless the response is not private, in which case women are more conforming than men.

- Groupthink occurs when a decision-making group feels that it is more important to maintain group unanimity and cohesiveness than to consider the facts realistically.

- Minimizing groupthink involves impartial leadership, seeking outside opinions, stating problems in an objective manner, breaking large groups into subgroups, encouraging questions and alternate solutions, using secret ballots, and holding group members responsible for the decisions made by the group.

10.2 How is compliance defined, and what are four common ways to gain the compliance of another?

- Compliance occurs when a person changes behavior as a result of another person asking or directing that person to change.

- Four common ways of getting compliance from others are the foot-in-the-door technique, the door-in-the-face technique, the lowball technique, and the that's-not-all technique.

10.3 What factors make obedience more likely?

- Milgram did experiments in which he found that 65 percent of people obeyed the authority figure of an experimenter even if it meant hurting, injuring, or possibly killing another person with an electric shock.

Social Cognition: Attitudes, Impression Formation, and Attribution

10.4 What are the three components of an attitude, how are attitudes formed, and how can attitudes be changed?

- Attitudes are tendencies to respond positively or negatively to ideas, persons, objects, or situations.

- The three components of an attitude are the affective (emotional) component, the behavioral component, and the cognitive component.

- Attitudes are often poor predictors of behavior unless the attitude is very specific or very strong.

- Direct contact with the person, situation, object, or idea can help form attitudes.

- Attitudes can be formed through direct instruction from parents or others.

- Interacting with other people who hold a certain attitude can help an individual form that attitude.

- Attitudes can also be formed through watching the actions and reactions of others to ideas, people, objects, and situations.

- Persuasion is the process by which one person tries to change the belief, opinion, position, or course of action of another person through argument, pleading, or explanation.

- The key elements in persuasion are the source of the message, the message itself, and the target audience.

- In the elaboration likelihood model, central-route processing involves attending to the content of the message itself, whereas peripheral-route processing involves attending to factors not involved in the message, such as the appearance of the source of the message, the length of the message, and other noncontent factors.

10.5 How do people react when attitudes and behavior are not the same?

- Cognitive dissonance is discomfort or distress that occurs when a person's actions do not match the person's attitudes.

- Cognitive dissonance is lessened by changing the conflicting behavior, changing the conflicting attitude, or forming a new attitude to justify the behavior.

- Impression formation is the forming of the first knowledge a person has about another person.

- The primacy effect in impression formation means that the very first impression one has about a person tends to persist even in the face of evidence to the contrary.

- Impression formation is part of social cognition, or the mental processes that people use to make sense out of the world around them.

10.6 What are social categorization and implicit personality theories?

- Social categorization is a process of social cognition in which a person, upon meeting someone new, assigns that person to a category or group on the basis of characteristics the person has in common with other people or groups with whom the perceiver has prior experience.

- One form of a social category is the stereotype, in which the characteristics used to assign a person to a category are superficial and believed to be true of all members of the category.

- An implicit personality theory is a form of social cognition in which a person has sets of assumptions about different types of people, personality traits, and actions that are assumed to be related to each other.

- Schemas are mental patterns that represent what a person believes about certain types of people. Schemas can become stereotypes.

10.7 How do people try to explain the actions of others?

- Attribution is the process of explaining the behavior of others as well as one's own behavior.

- A situational cause is an explanation of behavior based on factors in the surrounding environment or situation.

- A dispositional cause is an explanation of behavior based on the internal personality characteristics of the person being observed.

- The fundamental attribution error is the tendency to overestimate the influence of internal factors on behavior while underestimating the influence of the situation.

Social Interaction: Prejudice, Love, and Aggression

10.8 How are prejudice and discrimination different?

- Prejudice is a negative attitude that a person holds about the members of a particular social group. Discrimination occurs when members of a social group are treated differently because of prejudice toward that group.

- There are many forms of prejudice, including ageism, sexism, racism, and prejudice toward those who are too fat or too thin.

- In-groups are the people with whom a person identifies, whereas out-groups are everyone else at whom prejudice tends to be directed.

- Conflict between groups increases prejudice and discrimination according to realistic conflict theory.

- Scapegoating refers to the tendency to direct prejudice and discrimination at out-group members who have little social power or influence. New immigrants are often the scapegoats for the frustration and anger of the in-group.

classic studies in psychology: Brown Eyes, Blue Eyes

- A schoolteacher divided her class into brown-eyed children and blue-eyed children to teach them a lesson about prejudice. The children quickly began to discriminate against whichever group was the out-group during a certain time period.

10.9 Why are people prejudiced, and how can prejudice be stopped?

- Social cognitive theory views prejudice as an attitude acquired through direct instruction, modeling, and other social influences.

- Social identity theory sees a person's formation of a social sense of self within a particular group as being due to three things: social categorization (which may involve the use of reference groups), social identity (the person's sense of belonging to a particular social group), and social comparison (in which people compare themselves to others to improve their own self-esteem).

- Stereotype vulnerability refers to the effect that a person's knowledge of the stereotypes that exist against his or her social group can have on that person's behavior.

- People who are aware of stereotypes may unintentionally come to behave in a way that makes the stereotype real in a self-fulfilling prophecy.

- Intergroup contact is more effective in reducing prejudice if the groups have equal status.
- Prejudice and discrimination can also be reduced when a superordinate goal that is large enough to override all other goals needs to be achieved by all groups.
- Prejudice and discrimination are reduced when people must work together to solve a problem because each person has an important key to solving the problem, creating a mutual interdependence. This technique used in education is called the "jigsaw classroom."

Liking and Loving: Interpersonal Attraction

10.10 What factors govern attraction and love, and what are some different kinds of love?

- Interpersonal attraction refers to liking or having the desire for a relationship with another person.
- People tend to form relationships with people who are in physical proximity to them.
- People are attracted to others who are similar to them in some way.
- People may also be attracted to people who are different from themselves, with the differences acting as a complementary support for areas in which each may be lacking.
- People tend to like other people who like them in return, a phenomenon called the reciprocity of liking.
- Love is a strong affection for another person due to kinship, personal ties, sexual attraction, admiration, or common interests.
- Sternberg states that the three components of love are intimacy, passion, and commitment.
- Romantic love is intimacy with passion, companionate love is intimacy with commitment, and consummate love contains all three components.

psychology in the news: Facing Facebook—The Social Nature of Online Networking

Aggression and Prosocial Behavior

10.11 How is aggressive behavior determined by biology and learning?

- Aggression is behavior intended to hurt or destroy another person and may be physical or verbal. Frustration is a major source of aggression.

- Biological influences on aggression may include genetics, the amygdala and limbic system, and testosterone and serotonin levels.
- Social roles are powerful influences on the expression of aggression. Social learning theory states that aggression can be learned through direct reinforcement and through the imitation of successful aggression by a model.
- Studies of the connection between violent media exposure and increased levels of aggression have been methodologically flawed in the past, and more recent research finds little evidence of a connection between the two variables, citing instead variables such as depression and competitiveness.
- Prosocial behavior is behavior that is socially desirable and benefits others.

10.12 What is altruism, and how is deciding to help someone related to the presence of others?

- Altruism is prosocial behavior in which a person helps someone else without expectation of reward or recognition, often without fear for his or her own safety.
- The bystander effect means that people are more likely to get help from others if there are one or only a few people nearby rather than a larger number. The more people nearby, the less likely it is that help will be offered.
- When others are present at a situation in which help could be offered, there is a diffusion of responsibility among all the bystanders, reducing the likelihood that any one person or persons will feel responsibility for helping.
- The five steps in making a decision to help are noticing, defining an emergency, taking responsibility, planning a course of action, and taking action.

applying psychology to everyday life: Anatomy of a Cult

10.13 Why do people join cults?

- People who join cults tend to be under stress, unhappy, unassertive, gullible, dependent, idealistic, and want to belong. Young people are also more likely to join cults than are older people.
- Cults use love-bombing, isolation, rituals, and activities to keep the new recruits from questions and critical thinking. Cults also use the foot-in-the-door technique.

TEST yourself

ANSWERS ON PAGE AK–2.

✓● Study and Review on MyPsychLab   Ready for your test? More quizzes and a customized plan. www.MyPsychLab

Pick the best answer.

1. Studies have found the degree of conformity to be greater in _____ cultures.
   a. collectivistic
   b. individualistic
   c. Western
   d. European

2. To prevent groupthink, members of a group should do all but which of the following?
   a. Have the leader of the group remain impartial.
   b. Seek outside opinions.
   c. Discourage questions and alternate solutions.
   d. Use secret ballots.

3. Maria's fellow professor asked her to teach an honors class in the spring. Maria agreed only to soon find out that teaching such a course also meant that she would have to attend meet-ings of the honors professors, go to honors-oriented conventions, and take on special advising duties. Maria had fallen victim to the _____ technique.
   a. foot-in-the-door
   b. door-in-the-face
   c. lowball
   d. that's-not-all

4. Some researchers believe that Milgram's results were a form of the _____ technique of persuasion.
   a. foot-in-the-door
   b. door-in-the-face
   c. lowball
   d. that's-not-all

5. Jerry goes to a lot of dog races because he enjoys them and loves to see the dogs run. For Jerry, going to the dog races a lot represents the _____ component of an attitude.
   a. psychological
   b. behavioral
   c. cognitive
   d. affective

6. The public service messages that encourage parents to sit down with their children and talk frankly about drugs are promoting which method of attitude formation?
   a. direct contact
   b. direct instruction
   c. vicarious conditioning
   d. observational learning

7. Researchers have found that a _____ degree of fear in a message makes it more effective, particularly when it is combined with _____.
   a. maximum; information about how to prevent the fearful consequences
   b. minimum; threats
   c. moderate; threats
   d. moderate; information about how to prevent the fearful consequences

8. Sandy was a juror in the trial of a man accused of stealing guns from a sporting goods store. The defendant was not very well-spoken and came from a very poor background, but Sandy listened carefully to the evidence presented and made her decision based on that. Sandy was using _____ processing.
   a. central-route
   b. peripheral-route
   c. cognitive-route
   d. visual-route

9. Which of the following is not one of the three things people do to reduce cognitive dissonance?
   a. change their behavior
   b. change their attitude
   c. form a new attitude
   d. ignore the conflict

10. Gerard goes to his job interview dressed in patched blue jeans, a torn t-shirt, and sandals. His hair is uncombed and he hasn't shaved in a few days. Obviously, Gerard knows nothing about _____.
    a. cognitive dissonance.
    b. attitude formation.
    c. impression formation.
    d. groupthink.

11. Sets of assumptions that people have about how different types of people, personality traits, and actions are all related to each other are called _____.
    a. social categorization.
    b. implicit personality theories.
    c. urban legends.
    d. stereotypes.

12. If behavior is assumed to be caused by internal personality characteristics, this is known as _____.
    a. a situational cause.
    b. a dispositional cause.
    c. a fundamental attribution error.
    d. actor–observer bias.

13. The people with whom a person identifies most strongly are called the _____.
    a. referent group.
    b. in-group.
    c. out-group.
    d. "them" group.

14. Prejudice and discrimination are least likely to develop in which of the following situations?
    a. two different groups of immigrants competing for jobs
    b. two different religious groups, in which each believes that its religion is the right one
    c. two different groups, with one group being blamed for the economic difficulties of the other
    d. two different groups dealing with the aftermath of a hurricane

15. The _____ explanation of prejudice assumes that the same processes that help form other attitudes form prejudiced attitudes.
    a. scapegoat
    b. authoritarian
    c. social cognitive
    d. psychodynamic

16. Patrick is very proud of his Irish heritage and thinks of himself as an Irish American. Patrick has a strong _____.
    a. social identity.
    b. reference group.
    c. social category.
    d. stereotype vulnerability.

17. The self-fulfilling prophecy is a negative outcome of _____.
    a. social identity.
    b. reference grouping.
    c. scapegoating.
    d. stereotype vulnerability.

18. The "Robber's Cave" experiment showed the value of _____ in combating prejudice.
    a. "jigsaw classrooms"
    b. equal status contact
    c. subordinate goals
    d. stereotyping vulnerability

19. Sarah found her soulmate, Jon, when she moved to a small town in Florida. According to research in interpersonal attraction, the most likely explanation for them to "find" each other is _____.
    a. karma.
    b. personal attractiveness.
    c. fate.
    d. proximity.

20. According to Sternberg, married (committed) people who also have intimacy and passion are in the form of love called _____ love.
    a. companionate
    b. romantic
    c. affectionate
    d. consummate

21. The concept of aggression as a basic human instinct driving people to destructive acts was part of early _____ theory.
    a. humanistic
    b. behavioral
    c. psychoanalytical
    d. cognitive

22. The hormone that seems most involved in aggression is _____.
    a. testosterone.
    b. serotonin.
    c. dopamine.
    d. estrogen.

23. Which of the following factors have been cited by recent studies as flaws in the early research on violent video games and aggression?
    a. publication bias
    b. poorly constructed measures of aggression
    c. Both a and b have been cited as flaws.
    d. Neither a nor b; there are no flaws in the research.

24. To which two processes do most social psychologists attribute the failure of Kitty Genovese's neighbors to help her?
    a. bystander effect and altruism
    b. aggression and diffusion of responsibility
    c. altruism and diffusion of responsibility
    d. bystander effect and diffusion of responsibility

25. Cries for help, shouting, and loud noises all help with which step in the decision process for helping?
    a. noticing
    b. defining an emergency
    c. taking responsibility
    d. taking action

26. Cults use all of the following except _____ to gain new members.
    a. love-bombing
    b. isolation
    c. "foot-in-the-door" technique
    d. talking with parents of the recruit

10 social psychology

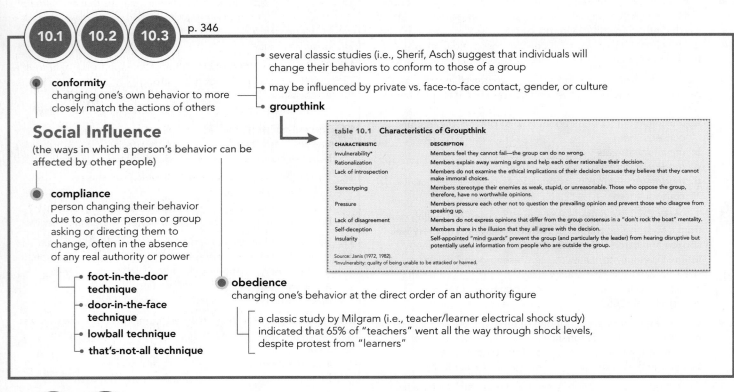

10.1 **10.2** **10.3** p. 346

- **conformity**
  changing one's own behavior to more
  closely match the actions of others

Social Influence

(the ways in which a person's behavior can be
affected by other people)

- **compliance**
  person changing their behavior
  due to another person or group
  asking or directing them to
  change, often in the absence
  of any real authority or power

  - **foot-in-the-door technique**
  - **door-in-the-face technique**
  - **lowball technique**
  - **that's-not-all technique**

- several classic studies (i.e., Sherif, Asch) suggest that individuals will
  change their behaviors to conform to those of a group
- may be influenced by private vs. face-to-face contact, gender, or culture
- **groupthink**

table 10.1 Characteristics of Groupthink

CHARACTERISTIC	DESCRIPTION
Invulnerability*	Members feel they cannot fail—the group can do no wrong.
Rationalization	Members explain away warning signs and help each other rationalize their decision.
Lack of introspection	Members do not examine the ethical implications of their decision because they believe that they cannot make immoral choices.
Stereotyping	Members stereotype their enemies as weak, stupid, or unreasonable. Those who oppose the group, therefore, have no worthwhile opinions.
Pressure	Members pressure each other not to question the prevailing opinion and prevent those who disagree from speaking up.
Lack of disagreement	Members do not express opinions that differ from the group consensus in a "don't rock the boat" mentality.
Self-deception	Members share in the illusion that they all agree with the decision.
Insularity	Self-appointed "mind guards" prevent the group (and particularly the leader) from hearing disruptive but potentially useful information from people who are outside the group.

Source: Janis (1972, 1982).
*Invulnerability: quality of being unable to be attacked or harmed.

- **obedience**
  changing one's behavior at the direct order of an authority figure

  - a classic study by Milgram (i.e., teacher/learner electrical shock study)
    indicated that 65% of "teachers" went all the way through shock levels,
    despite protest from "learners"

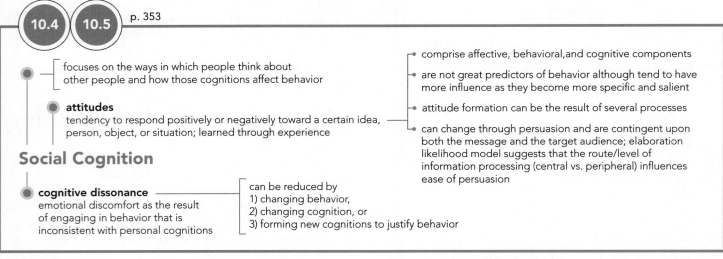

10.4 **10.5** p. 353

- focuses on the ways in which people think about
  other people and how those cognitions affect behavior

- **attitudes**
  tendency to respond positively or negatively toward a certain idea,
  person, object, or situation; learned through experience

Social Cognition

- **cognitive dissonance**
  emotional discomfort as the result
  of engaging in behavior that is
  inconsistent with personal cognitions

  can be reduced by
  1) changing behavior,
  2) changing cognition, or
  3) forming new cognitions to justify behavior

- comprise affective, behavioral, and cognitive components
- are not great predictors of behavior although tend to have
  more influence as they become more specific and salient
- attitude formation can be the result of several processes
- can change through persuasion and are contingent upon
  both the message and the target audience; elaboration
  likelihood model suggests that the route/level of
  information processing (central vs. peripheral) influences
  ease of persuasion

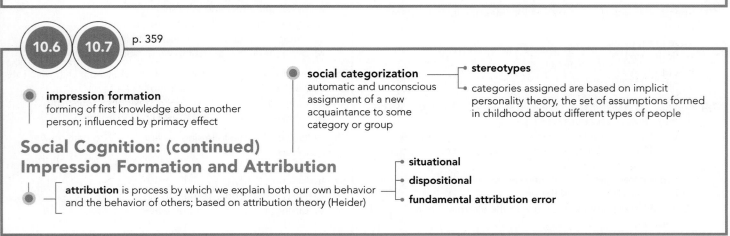

10.6 **10.7** p. 359

- **impression formation**
  forming of first knowledge about another
  person; influenced by primacy effect

- **social categorization**
  automatic and unconscious
  assignment of a new
  acquaintance to some
  category or group

  - **stereotypes**
  - categories assigned are based on implicit
    personality theory, the set of assumptions formed
    in childhood about different types of people

Social Cognition: (continued)
Impression Formation and Attribution

- **attribution** is process by which we explain both our own behavior
  and the behavior of others; based on attribution theory (Heider)

  - **situational**
  - **dispositional**
  - **fundamental attribution error**

10.8 **10.9** p. 363

prejudice
unsupported and negative stereotypes
(e.g., ageism, sexism, racism, etc.)
about members of a particular social group

- **social cognitive theory**
- **social identity theory**
- **stereotype vulnerability**
- **prejudice**

Social Interaction Prejudice and Discrimination

discrimination
occurs when prejudicial attitudes cause members
of a social group to be treated differently than
others in situations calling for equal treament

can vary based on existence of in-groups and out-groups

realistic conflict theory
suggests that when resources are limited, prejudice and discrimination are closely
tied to an increasing degree of conflict between groups that seek common resources

scapegoating

10.10 p. 367

liking or having the desire for a relationship
with someone else; can be influenced by
a variety of factors

- **physical attractiveness**
- **proximity**
- **similarity**
- **complementary qualities**
- **reciprocity of liking**

Liking and Loving: Interpersonal Attraction

love
strong affection for another person due to kinship, personal ties, sexual attraction,
admiration, or common interests

Sternberg's triangular theory suggests different components and types of love

---

10.11 **10.12** p. 371

aggression
occurs when one person verbally
or physically hurts or tries to
destroy another person; often
the result of frustration

- aggression may be partly attributed to genetics and
  can be triggered by variations in brain function
  (i.e., amygdala activation) and internal or external
  chemical influences (e.g., testosterone, alcohol)
- much of aggression is influenced by learning
  but not totally deterministic; social roles can
  also have an influence

Aggression and Prosocial Behavior

prosocial, or socially
desirable, behavior
benefits others

- **altruism:** helping someone with no expectation of reward
  and often at personal risk
- can be influenced by helper's mood and victim's gender,
  attractiveness, or "just rewards"; racial and ethnic differences
  can decrease probability of helping
- refusal to help another can be negatively affected by the
  presence of others (bystander effect/diffusion of responsibility)
  rather than indifference or a lack of sympathy; also influenced
  by individual's appraisal of situation (see Table 10.2)

11

theories of personality and intelligence

why study personality?

Personality is the sum total of who you are—your attitudes and reactions, both physical and emotional. It's what makes each person different from every other person in the world. How can any study of human behavior not include the study of who we are and how we got to be that way?

chapter outline

Theories of Personality and Intelligence

The Man and the Couch: Sigmund Freud and the Psychodynamic Perspective

The Behaviorist and Social Cognitive Views of Personality

The Third Force: Humanism and Personality

Trait Theories: Who Are You?

Assessment of Personality

Intelligence

The Biology of Personality and Intelligence: Behavioral Genetics

CLASSIC STUDIES IN PSYCHOLOGY: Geert Hofstede's Four Dimensions of Cultural Personality

APPLYING PSYCHOLOGY TO EVERYDAY LIFE: The Biological Basis of the Big Five

Not-So-Identical Twins

Many people have heard the story of the "Jim" twins, James Arthur Springer and James Edward Lewis, identical twins separated at the age of 1 month. At age 39 Springer and Lewis were the first set of twins studied by University of Minnesota psychologist Thomas Bouchard, who examined the differences and similarities between identical and fraternal twins raised apart from each other (Bouchard et al., 1990).

The two "Jims" shared interests in mechanical drawing and carpentry, a love of math and a dread of spelling in high school, and smoked and drank the same amount. It is understandable that many researchers attribute these similarities to the shared genetic material of the "Jim" twins. But since Springer and Lewis were both raised in Ohio by parents from relatively similar socioeconomic backgrounds, how much of their similarity to each other might be due to those conditions? And how would genetics explain that they both divorced women named Linda before marrying women named Betty? Are there genes for "divorce Linda, marry Betty?" Obviously not.

Then there's the case of Oskar and Jack. Like the "Jim" twins, they also exhibited a number of similarities in personality and behavior. No one would accuse Oskar and Jack of being raised in similar environments. Born in Trinidad at the time Hitler was rising to power, Jack Yufe was raised by their Jewish father in Trinidad as a Jew, while their mother took Oskar Stohr to occupied Czechoslovakia, where he attended a Nazi-run school and was at one time a Hitler youth. In terms of environment, Oskar and Jack were not-so-identical twins.

If the researchers in the twin study had dug a little deeper, they would also have found countless differences between the twins in the study. To automatically assume that similarities between identical twins are all caused by genetic influences and that differences are caused by environmental influences is bad science. The fact is that any two randomly selected people will find that they have countless things in common, none of which is likely to be caused by hereditary factors.

learning objectives

11.1 What is personality, and how do the various perspectives in psychology view personality?

11.2 How did Freud's historical view of the mind and personality form a basis for psychodynamic theory?

11.3 How did Jung, Adler, Horney, and Erikson modify Freud's theory?

11.4 How does modern psychoanalytic theory differ from that of Freud?

11.5 How do behaviorists and social cognitive theorists explain personality?

11.6 How do humanists such as Carl Rogers explain personality?

11.7 What are the history and current views of the trait perspective?

11.8 What are the advantages and disadvantages of the following measures of personality: interviews, projective tests, behavioral assessment, personality inventories, and online personality tests?

11.9 How do psychologists define intelligence, and how do various theories of intelligence differ?

11.10 How is intelligence measured, and how are intelligence tests constructed?

11.11 What is intellectual disability, and what are its causes?

11.12 What defines giftedness, and does being intellectually gifted guarantee success in life?

11.13 What part do biology, heredity, environment, and culture play in personality and intelligence?

study tip

As you are reading this chapter, remember to use the SQ3R method discussed on pages PIA-6–PIA-8 in *Psychology in Action*. Breaking your reading into small sections will help you get more out of every chapter.

Watch Episode 13: *Personality* and Episode 11: *Intelligence* in the MyPsychLab video series

personality the unique and relatively stable ways in which people think, feel, and behave.

character value judgments of a person's moral and ethical behavior.

temperament the enduring characteristics with which each person is born.

Sigmund Freud (1856–1939) was the founder of the psychodynamic movement in psychology. Many of his patients sat or reclined on the couch above while he sat in a chair, listening to them and developing his psychoanalytic theory of personality.

Theories of Personality and Intelligence

11.1 What is personality, and how do the various perspectives in psychology view personality?

Personality is the unique way in which each individual thinks, acts, and feels throughout life. Personality should not be confused with **character**, which refers to value judgments made about a person's morals or ethical behavior; nor should it be confused with **temperament**, the enduring characteristics with which each person is born, such as irritability or adaptability. Temperament is based in one's biology through genetic influences, prenatal influences, or a combination of those influences, and forms the basis on which one's larger personality is built. Both character and temperament are vital parts of personality, however. Every adult personality is a combination of temperaments and personal history of family, culture, and the time during which they grew up (Kagan, 2010).

Personality is an area of the still relatively young field of psychology in which there are several ways in which the characteristic behavior of human beings can be explained. However, the investigation of personality goes back quite some time. For example, the physiological roots of personality were postulated as early as the fourth century B.C.E. by Empedocles and later by Hippocrates, with Hippocrates' work later influencing Galen in the second century C.E. (Dumont, 2010). Hippocrates and Galen believed that temperament or personality was related to the relative balance of the four physical humors of the body: blood, black bile, yellow bile, and phlegm.

No single explanation of personality exists in part because personality is still difficult to measure precisely and scientifically, and different perspectives of personality have arisen. At present, there are four traditional perspectives, or viewpoints, in personality theory:

- The *psychodynamic perspective* had its beginnings in the work of Sigmund Freud and still exists today. It focuses on the role of the unconscious mind in the development of personality. This perspective is also heavily focused on biological causes of personality differences.

- The *behaviorist perspective* is based on the theories of learning as discussed in Chapter Four. This approach focuses on the effect of the environment on behavior.

- The *humanistic perspective* first arose as a reaction against the psychoanalytic and behaviorist perspectives and focuses on the role of each person's conscious life experiences and choices in personality development.

- The *trait perspective* differs from the other three in its basic goals: The psychoanalytic, behaviorist, and humanistic perspectives all seek to explain the process that causes personality to form into its unique characteristics, whereas trait theorists are more concerned with the end result—the characteristics themselves. Although some trait theorists assume that traits are biologically determined, others make no such assumption.

The Man and the Couch: Sigmund Freud and the Psychodynamic Perspective

11.2 How did Freud's historical view of the mind and personality form a basis for psychodynamic theory?

Freud's Cultural Background

It's hard to understand how Freud developed his ideas about personality without knowledge of the world in which he and his patients lived. Born in the Austro-Hungarian Empire in 1856, Freud's family moved to Vienna when he was only 4 years old. He lived there until 1938, when Germany occupied Austria. Freud, being of Jewish background, moved to England to escape the Nazis. Freud practiced during a period in European history known as the Victorian Age, a time of sexual repression. The prevalent belief was that sex should take place only in the context of marriage and then only to make babies. To enjoy sexual intercourse was considered a sin.

Men were understood to be unable to control their "animal" desires at times, and so a good Victorian husband would father several children with his wife and then turn to a mistress for sexual comfort, leaving his virtuous* wife untouched. Women, especially those of the upper classes, were not supposed to have sexual urges. It is no wonder that many of Freud's patients were wealthy women with problems stemming from unfulfilled sexual desires or sexual repression. Freud's "obsession" with sexual explanations for abnormal behavior seems more understandable in light of his cultural background and that of his patients.

Freud came to believe that there were layers of consciousness in the mind. His belief in the influence of the unconscious mind on conscious behavior, published in *The Psychopathology of Everyday Life* (Freud, 1901), shocked the Victorian world.

The Unconscious Mind

Freud believed that the mind was divided into three parts: the preconscious, conscious, and unconscious minds (Freud, 1900). (See Figure 11.1.) While no one really disagreed with the idea of a conscious mind in which one's current awareness exists, or even the idea of a preconscious mind containing memories, information, and events of which one can easily become aware, the **unconscious mind** (also called "the unconscious") was the real departure for the professionals of Freud's day. Freud theorized that a part of the mind remains hidden at all times, surfacing only in symbolic form in dreams and in some of the behavior people engage in without knowing why they have done so. Even when a person makes a determined effort to bring a memory out of the

---

*Virtuous: morally excellent.

unconscious mind level of the mind in which thoughts, feelings, memories, and other information are kept that are not easily or voluntarily brought into consciousness.

FIGURE 11.1 Freud's Conception of the Personality
This iceberg represents the three levels of the mind. The part of the iceberg visible above the surface is the conscious mind. Just below the surface is the preconscious mind, everything that is not yet part of the conscious mind. Hidden deep below the surface is the unconscious mind, feelings, memories, thoughts, and urges that cannot be easily brought into consciousness. While two of the three parts of the personality (ego and superego) exist at all three levels of awareness, the id is completely in the unconscious mind.

id part of the personality present at birth and completely unconscious.

pleasure principle principle by which the id functions; the immediate satisfaction of needs without regard for the consequences.

ego part of the personality that develops out of a need to deal with reality, mostly conscious, rational, and logical.

reality principle principle by which the ego functions; the satisfaction of the demands of the id only when negative consequences will not result.

unconscious mind, it will not appear directly, according to Freud. Freud believed that the unconscious mind was the most important determining factor in human behavior and personality.

The Divisions of the Personality

Based on observations of his patients, Freud believed that personality itself could be divided into three parts, each existing at one or more levels of conscious awareness (see Figure 11.1). The way these three parts of the personality develop and interact with one another became the heart of his theory (Freud, 1923, 1933, 1940).

ID: IF IT FEELS GOOD, DO IT The first and most primitive part of the personality, present in the infant, is the **id**. *Id* is a Latin word that means "it." The id is a completely unconscious, pleasure-seeking, amoral part of the personality that exists at birth, containing all of the basic biological drives: hunger, thirst, self-preservation, and sex, for example.

● Wait a minute—Freud thought babies have sex drives?

Yes, Freud thought babies have sex drives, which shocked and outraged his colleagues and fellow Victorians. By "sex drive" he really meant "pleasure drive," the need to seek out pleasurable sensations. People do seem to be pleasure-seeking creatures, and even infants seek pleasure from sucking and chewing on anything they can get into their mouths. Thinking about what infants are like when they are just born provides a good picture of the id. Infants are demanding, irrational, illogical, and impulsive. They want their needs satisfied immediately, and they don't care about anyone else's needs or desires. (A word of caution: The fact that infant behavior seems to fit Freud's concept of the id is not proof that the id exists. It simply means that Freud came up with the concept of the id to fit what he already knew about infants.)

Freud called this need for satisfaction the **pleasure principle**, which can be defined as the desire for immediate gratification of needs with no regard for the consequences. The pleasure principle can be summed up simply as "if it feels good, do it."

EGO: THE EXECUTIVE DIRECTOR People normally try to satisfy an infant's needs as quickly as possible. Infants are fed when hungry, changed when wet, and tended to whenever they cry. But as infants begin to grow, adults start denying them their every wish. There will be things they cannot touch or hold, and they must learn to wait for certain things, such as food. Freud would say that reality has reared its ugly head, and the id simply cannot deal with the reality of having to wait or not getting what it wants. Worse still would be the possibility of punishment as a result of the id's unrestrained actions.

According to Freud, to deal with reality, a second part of the personality develops called the **ego**. The ego, from the Latin word for "I," is mostly conscious and is far more rational, logical, and cunning than the id. The ego works on the **reality principle**, which is the need to satisfy the demands of the id only in ways that will not lead to negative consequences. This means that sometimes the ego decides to deny the id its desires because the consequences would be painful or too unpleasant.

For example, while an infant might reach out and take an object despite a parent's protests, a toddler with the developing ego will avoid taking the object when the parent says "No!" to avoid punishment—but may go back for the object when the parent is not looking. A simpler way of stating the reality principle, then, is "if it feels good, do it, but only if you can get away with it."

Superego: The Moral Watchdog

If everyone acted on the pleasure principle, the world would be pretty scary. How does knowing right from wrong come into Freud's theory?

If everyone acted on the pleasure principle, the world would be pretty scary. How does knowing right from wrong come into Freud's theory?

Freud called the third and final part of the personality, the moral center of personality, the **superego**. The superego (also Latin, meaning "over the self") develops as a preschool-aged child learns the rules, customs, and expectations of society. The superego contains the **conscience**—the part of the personality that makes people feel guilt, or *moral anxiety*, when they do the wrong thing. It is not until the conscience develops that children have a sense of right and wrong. (Note that the term *conscience* is a different word from *conscious*. They may look and sound similar, but they represent totally different concepts.) ☀ Explore on MyPsychLab

THE ANGEL, THE DEVIL, AND ME: HOW THE THREE PARTS OF THE PERSONALITY WORK TOGETHER Anyone who has ever watched cartoons while growing up has probably seen these three parts of the personality shown in animated form—the id is usually a little devil, the superego an angel, and the ego is the person or animal caught in the middle, trying to decide what action to take. Images such as these appear often in animated films, with one of the more recent examples in *The Emperor's New Groove* when a character argues with his angel and devil over disposing of the emperor.

So, the id makes demands, the superego puts restrictions on how those demands can be met, and the ego has to come up with a plan that will quiet the id but satisfy the superego. Sometimes the id or the superego does not get its way, resulting in a great deal of anxiety for the ego itself. This constant state of conflict is Freud's view of how personality works; it is only when the anxiety created by this conflict gets out of hand that disordered behavior arises.

The **psychological defense mechanisms** are ways of dealing with stress through unconsciously distorting one's perception of reality. These defense mechanisms were mainly outlined and studied by Freud's daughter, Anna Freud, who was a psychoanalyst (Benjafield, 1996; A. Freud, 1946). In order for the three parts of the personality to function, the constant conflict among them must be managed, and Freud assumed that the defense mechanisms were one of the most important tools for dealing with the anxiety caused by this conflict. A list of the defense mechanisms, their definitions, and examples of each appears in Table 11.1.

superego part of the personality that acts as a moral center.

conscience part of the superego that produces guilt, depending on how acceptable behavior is.

psychological defense mechanisms unconscious distortions of a person's perception of reality that reduce stress and anxiety.

☀ Explore the id, ego, and superego on MyPsychLab

denial psychological defense mechanism in which the person refuses to acknowledge or recognize a threatening situation.

repression psychological defense mechanism in which the person refuses to consciously remember a threatening or unacceptable event, instead pushing those events into the unconscious mind.

rationalization psychological defense mechanism in which a person invents acceptable excuses for unacceptable behavior.

projection psychological defense mechanism in which unacceptable or threatening impulses or feelings are seen as originating with someone else, usually the target of the impulses or feelings.

reaction formation psychological defense mechanism in which a person forms an opposite emotional or behavioral reaction to the way he or she really feels to keep those true feelings hidden from self and others.

displacement redirecting feelings from a threatening target to a less threatening one.

table 11.1 The Psychological Defense Mechanisms

	EXAMPLE
Denial: refusing to recognize or acknowledge a threatening situation.	Ben is an alcoholic who denies being an alcoholic.
Repression: "pushing" threatening or conflicting events or situations out of conscious memory.	Elise, who was sexually abused as a child, cannot remember the abuse at all.
Rationalization: making up acceptable excuses for unacceptable behavior.	"If I don't have breakfast, I can have that piece of cake later on without hurting my diet."
Projection: placing one's own unacceptable thoughts onto others, as if the thoughts belonged to them and not to oneself.	Keisha is attracted to her sister's husband but denies this and believes the husband is attracted to her.
Reaction formation: forming an emotional reaction or attitude that is the opposite of one's threatening or unacceptable actual thoughts.	Matt is unconsciously attracted to Ben but outwardly voices an extreme hatred of homosexuals.
Displacement: expressing feelings that would be threatening if directed at the real target onto a less threatening substitute target.	Sandra gets reprimanded by her boss and goes home to angrily pick a fight with her husband.
Regression: falling back on childlike patterns as a way of coping with stressful situations.	Four-year-old Jeff starts wetting his bed after his parents bring home a new baby.
Identification: trying to become like someone else to deal with one's anxiety.	Marie really admires Suzy, the most popular girl in school, and tries to copy her behavior and dress.
Compensation (substitution): trying to make up for areas in which a lack is perceived by becoming superior in some other area.	Reggie is not good at athletics, so he puts all of his energies into becoming an academic scholar.
Sublimation: turning socially unacceptable urges into socially acceptable behavior.	Alain, who is very aggressive, becomes a professional hockey player.

practice quiz   How much do you remember?

11.1 11.2

Pick the best answer.

1. Although Chien's parents have told him that he attended his grandmother's funeral when he was 9 years old, he has no memory of the funeral. According to Freud, Chien's memory of the funeral may be in the _____ mind.
   a. preconscious
   b. conscious
   c. conscience
   d. unconscious

2. Which of Freud's parts of the personality is most like a director?
   a. id
   b. ego
   c. superego
   d. unconscious

3. According to Freud, which part of the personality makes the person feel guilt when doing the wrong thing?
   a. ego
   b. superego
   c. conscious
   d. conscience

4. In Freud's view of the personality, the part that is present at birth and focused on immediate gratification or pleasure is the

   _____.
   a. conscience.
   b. id.
   c. ego.
   d. superego.

5. Kelly is convinced that a supervisor in her office is very attracted to her, even though he has shown no outward signs of interest in her. She watches the supervisor frequently and makes excuses to be near him or to talk to him. She interprets everything he says as a veiled reference to his desire for her. If Kelly's supervisor actually has no romantic interest in her, we might conclude that Kelly is _____.
   a. rationalizing.
   b. repressing.
   c. projecting.
   d. regressing.

6. Rusty drinks beer all day long, often passing out in a stupor after several hours of steady drinking. Yet he refuses to admit that he has a drinking problem, saying that "it's only beer," and he continues to drink. Rusty is most likely using which defense mechanism?
   a. denial
   b. repression
   c. displacement
   d. reaction formation

ANSWERS ON PAGE AK–2

regression psychological defense mechanism in which a person falls back on childlike patterns of responding in reaction to stressful situations.

identification defense mechanism in which a person tries to become like someone else to deal with anxiety.

compensation (substitution) defense mechanism in which a person makes up for inferiorities in one area by becoming superior in another area.

sublimation channeling socially unacceptable impulses and urges into socially acceptable behavior.

fixation disorder in which the person does not fully resolve the conflict in a particular psychosexual stage, resulting in personality traits and behavior associated with that earlier stage.

psychosexual stages five stages of personality development proposed by Freud and tied to the sexual development of the child.

oral stage first stage occurring in the first year of life in which the mouth is the erogenous zone and weaning is the primary conflict.

So the id exists at birth, but the other two parts of the personality develop later— how much later? When is personality finished?

Stages of Personality Development

So the id exists at birth, but the other two parts of the personality develop later—how much later? When is personality finished?

For Freud, the three parts of the personality develop in a series of stages. Because he focused heavily on the sex drive, he believed that the stages were determined by the developing sexuality of the child. At each stage, a different *erogenous zone*, or area of the body that produces pleasurable feelings, becomes important and can become the source of conflicts. Conflicts that are not fully resolved can result in **fixation**, or getting "stuck" to some degree in a stage of development. The child may grow into an adult but will still carry emotional and psychological "baggage" from that earlier fixated stage.

Because the personality, or *psyche*, develops as a result of sexual development, Freud called these the **psychosexual stages** of personality development.

ORAL STAGE: WEANING AND ORAL FIXATION The first stage is called the **oral stage** because the erogenous zone is the mouth. This stage occurs from the birth of the infant to about 1 or 1½ years and is dominated by the id. The conflict that can arise here, according to Freud, will be over weaning (taking the mother's breast away from the child, who will now drink from a cup). Weaning that occurs too soon or too late can result in too little or too much satisfaction of the child's oral needs, resulting in the activities and personality traits associated with an orally fixated adult personality: overeating, drinking too much, chain smoking, talking too much, nail biting, gum chewing, and a tendency to be either too dependent and optimistic (when the oral needs are overindulged) or too aggressive and pessimistic (when the oral needs are denied).

ANAL STAGE: TOILET TRAINING AND ANAL FIXATION As the child becomes a toddler (1 or 1½ years to 3 years), Freud believed that the erogenous zone moves from the mouth to the anus, because he also believed that children got a great deal of pleasure from both withholding and releasing their feces at will. This stage is, therefore, called the **anal stage**.

Obviously, Freud thought that the main area of conflict here is toilet training, the demand that the child use the toilet at a particular time and in a particular way. This invasion of reality is part of the process that stimulates the development of the ego during this stage. Fixation in the anal stage, from toilet training that is too harsh, can take one of two forms. The child who rebels openly against the demands of the parents and other adults will refuse to go in the toilet, instead defecating where and when he or she feels like doing it. According to Freud, this translates in the adult as a person who sees messiness as a statement of personal control and who is somewhat destructive and hostile. These *anal expulsive personalities* (so called because as children they expelled their feces as children purposefully) are what most people would call "slobs." Some children, however, are terrified of making a mess and rebel passively—refusing to go at all or retaining the feces. No mess, no punishment. As adults, they are stingy, stubborn, and excessively neat. This type is called the *anal retentive personality*.

Freud believed that mothers should breast-feed their infants to satisfy an infant's need for oral gratification in the oral stage of psychosexual development. The age at which an infant was weaned from the breast was a critical factor in psychoanalytic theory.

PHALLIC STAGE As the child grows older (3 to 6 years), the erogenous zone finally shifts to the genitals. Children have discovered the differences between the sexes by now, and most have also engaged in perfectly normal self-stimulation of the genitals, or masturbation. One can only imagine the horror of the Victorian parent who discovered a child engaged in masturbation. People of that era believed that masturbation led to all manner of evils, including mental illness.

This awakening of sexual curiosity and interest in the genitals is the beginning of what Freud termed the **phallic stage**. (The word *phallic* comes from the Greek word *phallos* and means "penis.") Freud believed that when boys realized that the little girl down the street had no penis they developed a fear of losing the penis, a fear he called *castration anxiety,* while girls developed *penis envy* because they were missing a penis. If this seems an odd focus on male anatomy, remember the era—the Western world at that time was very male oriented and male dominated. Fortunately, nearly all psychoanalysts have long since abandoned the concept of penis envy (Horney, 1939, 1973; Slipp, 1993). The conflict in the phallic stage centers on the child's awakening sexual feelings. Freud essentially believed that boys develop both sexual attraction to their mothers and jealousy of their fathers during this stage, a phenomenon called the **Oedipus complex**. (Oedipus was a king in a Greek tragedy who unknowingly killed his father and married his mother.)

The sexual attraction is not that of an adult male for a female but more of a sexual curiosity that becomes mixed up with the boy's feelings of love and affection for his mother. Of course, his jealousy of his father leads to feelings of anxiety and fears that his father, a powerful authority figure, might get angry and do something terrible—remember that castration anxiety? To deal with this anxiety, two things must occur by the time the phallic stage ends. The boy will *repress* his sexual feelings for his mother and *identify* with his father. (*Identification* is one of the defense mechanisms used to combat anxiety.) The boy tries to be just like his father in every way, taking on the father's behavior, mannerisms, values, and moral beliefs as his own, so that Daddy won't be able to get angry with him. Girls go through a similar process called the

anal stage second stage occurring from about 1 to 3 years of age, in which the anus is the erogenous zone and toilet training is the source of conflict.

phallic stage third stage occurring from about 3 to 6 years of age, in which the child discovers sexual feelings.

Oedipus complex/Electra complex situation occurring in the phallic stage in which a child develops a sexual attraction to the opposite-sex parent and jealousy of the same-sex parent.

latency fourth stage occurring during the school years, in which the sexual feelings of the child are repressed while the child develops in other ways.

psychoanalysis Freud's term for both the theory of personality and the therapy based on it.

Electra complex, with their father as the target of their affections and their mother as the rival. The result of identification is the development of the superego, the internalized moral values of the same-sex parent.

What happens when things go wrong? If a child does not have a same-sex parent with whom to identify, or if the opposite-sex parent encourages the sexual attraction, fixation can occur. Fixation in the phallic stage usually involves immature sexual attitudes as an adult. People who are fixated in this stage, according to Freud, will often exhibit promiscuous* sexual behavior and be very vain. The vanity is seen as a cover-up for feelings of low self-worth arising from the failure to resolve the complex, and the lack of moral sexual behavior stems from the failure of identification and the inadequate formation of the superego. In addition, men with this fixation may be "mama's boys" who never quite grow up, and women with this fixation may look for much older father figures to marry.

Now the child is about 6 years old and, if he or she has passed through the first three stages successfully, all three parts of the personality will be in place. What next? The personality may be in place, but the place it is in is only 6 years old. Freud named two more periods, one a kind of "holding pattern" and the other the final coming to terms with one's own sexuality.

LATENCY STAGE: BOYS HAVE COOTIES AND GIRLS ARE YUCKY Remember that by the end of the phallic stage, children have pushed their sexual feelings for the opposite sex into the unconscious in another defensive reaction, repression. From age 6 to the onset of puberty, children will remain in this stage of hidden, or *latent*, sexual feelings; this stage is accordingly called **latency**. In this stage, children grow and develop intellectually, physically, and socially but not sexually. This is the age at which boys play with other boys, girls play only with girls, and each thinks the opposite sex is pretty awful.

GENITAL STAGE When puberty does begin, the sexual feelings that were once repressed can no longer be ignored. Bodies are changing and sexual urges are once more allowed into consciousness, but these urges will no longer have the parents as their targets. When children are 3, their parents are their whole world. When they are 13, their parents have to walk 20 paces behind them in the mall so none of the 13-year-olds' friends will see them. Instead, the focus of sexual curiosity and attraction will become other adolescents or music stars, movie stars, and other objects of adoration. Since Freud tied personality development into sexual development, the genital stage represented the final process in Freud's personality theory as well as the entry into adult social and sexual behavior. Table 11.2 summarizes the stages of the psychosexual theory of personality development.

The Neo-Freudians

11.3 How did Jung, Adler, Horney, and Erikson modify Freud's theory?

At first Freud's ideas were met with resistance and ridicule by the growing community of doctors and psychologists but over time, he was able to amass a sizeable following. Eventually though, a number of early psychoanalysts, objecting to Freud's emphasis on biology and particularly on sexuality, broke away from a strict interpretation of psychoanalytic theory, instead altering the focus of **psychoanalysis** (the term Freud

Carl Jung (1875–1961) was a Swiss psychoanalyst who eventually broke away from Freud's emphasis on the sexual content of the unconscious mind. He formed his own theory of analysis known as analytical psychology.

---

*Promiscuous: having sexual relations with more than one partner.

table 11.2 Freud's Psychosexual Stages

STAGE	AGE	FOCUS OF PLEASURE	FOCUS OF CONFLICTS	DIFFICULTIES AT THIS STAGE AFFECT LATER...
Oral	Birth to 1½ years old	Oral activities (such as sucking, feeding, and making noises with the mouth)	Weaning	• Ability to form interpersonal attachments • Basic feelings about the world • Tendency to use oral forms of aggression, such as sarcasm • Optimism or pessimism • Tendency to take charge or be passive
Anal	1½ to 3 years old	Bowel and bladder control	Toilet training	• Sense of competence and control • Stubbornness or willingness to go along with others • Neatness or messiness • Punctuality or tardiness
Phallic	3 to 6 years old	Genitals	Sexual awareness	• Development of conscience through identification with same-sex parent • Pride or humility
Latency	6 years old to puberty	Social skills (such as the ability to make friends) and intellectual skills; dormant period in terms of psychosexual development	School, play, same-sex friendships	• Ability to get along with others
Genital	Puberty to death	Sexual behavior	Sexual relationship with partner	• Immature love or indiscriminate hate • Uncontrollable working or inability to work

Note: Freud thought that the way a person finds pleasure or is prevented from satisfying urges for pleasure at each stage affects personality. Thus, like Erikson's stage model described in Chapter Seven, Freud's model argues that the way a person deals with particular psychological challenges or potential areas of conflict has long-term effects on personality.

applied to both his explanation of the workings of the unconscious mind and the development of personality and the therapy he based on that theory) to the impact of the social environment. At the same time they retained many of Freud's original concepts such as the id, ego, superego, and the defense mechanisms. These early psychoanalysts became the **neo-Freudians**, or "new" Freudian psychoanalysts. This section briefly covers some of the more famous neo-Freudians.

JUNG Carl Gustav Jung ("YOONG") disagreed with Freud about the nature of the unconscious mind. Jung believed that the unconscious held much more than personal fears, urges, and memories. He believed that there was not only a **personal unconscious**, as described by Freud, but a **collective unconscious** as well (Jung, 1933).

According to Jung, the collective unconscious contains a kind of "species" or "racial" memory, memories of ancient fears and themes that seem to occur in many folktales and cultures. Jung called these collective, universal human memories **archetypes**. There are many archetypes, but two of the more well known are the *anima/animus* (the feminine side of a man/the masculine side of a woman) and the *shadow* (the dark side of personality, called the "devil" in Western cultures). The side of one's personality that is shown to the world is termed the *persona*. ◉ Watch on MyPsychLab

neo-Freudians followers of Freud who developed their own competing psychodynamic theories.

personal unconscious Jung's name for the unconscious mind as described by Freud.

collective unconscious Jung's name for the memories shared by all members of the human species.

archetypes Jung's collective, universal human memories.

◉ Watch classic video footage on the unconscious with Carl Jung on MyPsychLab

Dr. Karen Horney (1885–1952) took issue with Freud's emphasis on sexuality, especially the concept of penis envy. She emphasized the importance of feelings of basic anxiety in personality development during early childhood.

According to Horney, of the three ways children deal with anxiety, which way do you think this child might be using?

It sounds as if all of these theorists became famous by ditching some of Freud's original ideas. Is Freud even worth studying anymore?

basic anxiety anxiety created when a child is born into the bigger and more powerful world of older children and adults.

neurotic personalities personalities typified by maladaptive ways of dealing with relationships in Horney's theory.

ADLER Alfred Adler also disagreed with Freud over the importance of sexuality in personality development. Adler (1954) developed the theory that people, as young and helpless children, all develop feelings of inferiority when they compare themselves to the more powerful, superior adults in their world. For Adler the driving force behind all human endeavors, emotions, and thoughts was not the seeking of pleasure but the seeking of superiority. The defense mechanism of *compensation* (see Table 11.1), in which people try to overcome feelings of inferiority in one area of life by striving to be superior in another area, figured prominently in Adler's theory.

HORNEY Karen Horney ("HORN-EYE") did not study directly with Freud but studied his work and taught psychoanalysis at the Psychoanalytic Institutes of Berlin and later New York (1967, 1973). She left the institute because of disagreements with Freud over the differences between males and females and the concept of penis envy, which she strongly rejected. She countered this concept with that of "womb envy," stating that men felt the need to compensate for their lack of childbearing ability by striving for success in other areas (Burger, 1997).

Rather than focusing on sexuality, Horney emphasized the child's sense of **basic anxiety**, the anxiety created in a child born into a world so much bigger and more powerful than the child. While people whose parents give them love, affection, and security will overcome this anxiety, others with less secure upbringings will develop **neurotic personalities** and maladaptive ways of dealing with relationships. Some children, according to Horney, try to deal with their anxiety by moving toward people, becoming dependent and clingy. Others move against people, becoming aggressive, demanding, and cruel. Finally, a third way of coping identified by Horney is to move away from people by withdrawing from personal relationships.

ERIKSON Erik Erikson (1950, 1959, 1982) was an art teacher who became a psychoanalyst by studying with Anna Freud. He also broke away from Freud's emphasis on sex, preferring instead to stress the social relationships that are important at every stage of life. Erikson's eight psychosocial stages are discussed in detail in Chapter Seven. ⓁⒾⓃⓀ to Chapter Seven: Development Across the Life Span, pp. 250–251.

● It sounds as if all of these theorists became famous by ditching some of Freud's original ideas. Is Freud even worth studying anymore?

Current Thoughts on Freud and the Psychodynamic Perspective

11.4 How does modern psychoanalytic theory differ from that of Freud?

Although Freud's psychoanalytic theory seems less relevant in today's sexually saturated world, many of his concepts have remained useful and still form a basis for many modern personality theories. The idea of the defense mechanisms has had some research support and has remained useful in clinical psychology as a way of describing people's defensive behavior and irrational thinking. The concept of an unconscious mind also has some research support. As strange as the idea of an unconscious mind that guides behavior must have seemed to Freud's contemporaries, modern researchers have had to admit that there are influences on human behavior that exist outside of normal conscious awareness. Although much of this research has taken place in the area of hypnosis and subliminal perception (Borgeat & Goulet, 1983; Bryant &

McConkey, 1989; Kihlstrom, 1987, 1999, 2001), other researchers have looked at the concept of implicit memory and implicit learning (Frensch & Runger, 2003). (L)(I)(N)(K) to Chapter Five: Memory, pp. 172–173.

CRITICISMS OF THE PSYCHODYNAMIC PERSPECTIVE This might be a good time to point out a very important fact about Freud's theory: He did no experiments to arrive at his conclusions about personality. His theory is based on his own observations (case studies) of numerous patients. Basing his suppositions on his patients' detailed memories of their childhoods and life experiences, he interpreted their behavior and reminiscences to develop his theory of psychoanalysis. He felt free to interpret what his patients told him of their childhoods as fantasy or fact, depending on how well those memories fit in with his developing theory. For example, many of Freud's patients told him that they were sexually abused by fathers, brothers, and other close family members. Freud was apparently unable to accept these memories as real and decided that they were fantasies, making them the basis of the Oedipal conflict. He actually revised his original perceptions of his patients' memories of abuse as real in the face of both public and professional criticism from his German colleagues (Masson, 1984).

Freud based much of his diagnoses of patients' problems on the interpretations of dreams and the results of the patient's free association (talking about anything without fear of negative feedback). These "sources" of information are often criticized as being too ambiguous and without scientific support for the validity of his interpretations. The very ambiguity of these sources of information allowed Freud to fit the patient's words and recollections to his own preferred interpretation, as well as increasing the possibility that his own suggestions and interpretations, if conveyed to the patient, might alter the actual memories of the patient, who would no doubt be in a very suggestible state of mind during therapy (Grünbaum, 1984).

Another criticism of Freud's theory concerns the people whose dreams, recollections, and comments form the basis for his theory of psychoanalysis. Freud's clients were almost all wealthy Austrian women living in the Victorian era of sexual repression. Critics state that basing his theory on observations made with such a demographically restricted group of clients promoted his emphasis on sexuality as the root of all problems in personality, as women of that social class and era were often sexually frustrated. Freud rarely had clients who did not fit this description, and so his theory is biased in terms of sexual frustrations (Robinson, 1993).

Although most professionals today view Freud's theory with a great deal of skepticism, his influence on the modern world cannot be ignored. Freudian concepts have had an enormous impact on literature, movies, and even children's cartoons over the last hundred years. People who have never taken a course in psychology are familiar with some of Freud's most basic concepts, such as the defense mechanisms. He was also one of the first theorists to emphasize the importance of childhood experiences on personality development—in spite of the fact he did not work extensively with children. (He did present at least one case study of a 5-year-old boy, "Little Hans," in which Freud gained much of his information from the boy's father, who was providing the actual treatment.)

Only in the last several decades have people had the necessary tools to examine the concepts of the unconscious mind. One can only wonder how Freud might have changed his theory in light of what is known about the workings of the human brain and the changes in society that exist today.

practice quiz   How much do you remember?

11.2 11.3 11.4

Pick the best answer.

1. An area of the body that produces pleasurable sensations is called an _____ zone.
   a. erogenous
   b. fixation
   c. Oedipal
   d. phallic

2. In which psychosexual stage might fixation result in a person who is excessively neat and fussy?
   a. oral
   b. anal
   c. phallic
   d. genital

3. In which psychosexual stage does the defense mechanism of identification figure prominently?
   a. oral
   b. anal
   c. phallic
   d. latency

4. In which psychosexual stage are the sexual feelings repressed?
   a. oral
   b. anal
   c. phallic
   d. latency

5. According to Jung, the part of the mind containing universal human memories is called the _____ unconscious.
   a. personal
   b. cognitive
   c. collective
   d. animistic

6. Which of the neo-Freudians discussed in the text talked about neurotic personalities as moving toward people, moving against people, or moving away from people?
   a. Jung
   b. Adler
   c. Horney
   d. Erikson

Brainstorming: What aspects of psychodynamic theory do you think still have relevance in today's world? Was there one neo-Freudian whose theory appealed to you, and if so, why?

ANSWERS ON PAGE AK–2

---

habits in behaviorism, sets of well-learned responses that have become automatic.

social cognitive learning theorists theorists who emphasize the importance of both the influences of other people's behavior and the influences of a person's own expectancies of learning.

Read and learn more about behaviorists Dollard and Miller's four critical situations on **MyPsychLab**

So how does a pattern of rewarding certain behavior end up becoming part of some kind of personality pattern?

The Behaviorist and Social Cognitive Views of Personality

At the time that Freud's theory was shocking the Western world, another psychological perspective was also making its influence known. In Chapter Four the behavioral theories of classical and operant conditioning were discussed in some detail. *Behaviorists* (researchers who use the principles of conditioning to explain the actions and reactions of both animals and humans) and *social cognitive theorists* (researchers who emphasize the influence of social and cognitive factors on learning) have a very different view of personality.

11.5 How do behaviorists and social cognitive theorists explain personality?

For the behaviorist, personality is nothing more than a set of learned responses or **habits** (DeGrandpre, 2000; Dollard & Miller, 1950). In the strictest traditional view of Watson and Skinner, everything a person or animal does is a response to some environmental stimulus that has been reinforced or strengthened by a reward in some way. Read on **MyPsychLab**

So how does a pattern of rewarding certain behavior end up becoming part of some kind of personality pattern?

Think about how a traditional behaviorist might explain a shy personality. Beginning in childhood, a person might be exposed to a parent with a rather harsh discipline style (stimulus). Avoiding the attention of that parent would result in fewer punishments and scoldings, so that avoidance response is negatively reinforced—the "bad thing" or punishment is avoided by keeping out of sight and quiet. Later, that child might generalize that avoidance response to other authority figures and adults, such as teachers. In this way, a pattern (habit) of shyness would develop.

Of course, many learning theorists today do not use only classical and operant conditioning to explain the development of the behavior patterns referred to as personality. **Social cognitive learning theorists**, who emphasize the importance of both the influences of other people's behavior and of a person's own expectancies on learning, hold that observational learning, modeling, and other cognitive learning techniques can lead to the formation of patterns of personality. LINK to Chapter Four: Learning, p. 147.

One of the more well-researched learning theories that includes the concept of cognitive processes as influences on behavior is the social cognitive theory of Albert Bandura. In the **social cognitive view**, behavior is governed not just by the influence of external stimuli and response patterns but also by cognitive processes such as anticipating, judging, and memory as well as learning through the imitation of models. In fact, you might remember Bandura's work with observation learning and imitation of models from his Bobo doll study. Ⓛ Ⓘ Ⓝ Ⓚ to Chapter Four: Learning, pp. 151–153.

Bandura's Reciprocal Determinism and Self-Efficacy

Bandura (1989) believes that three factors influence one another in determining the patterns of behavior that make up personality: the environment, the behavior itself, and personal or cognitive factors that the person brings into the situation from earlier experiences (see Figure 11.2). These three factors each affect the other two in a reciprocal, or give-and-take, relationship. Bandura calls this relationship **reciprocal determinism**.

As can be seen in Figure 11.2, the environment includes the actual physical surroundings, the other people who may or may not be present, and the potential for reinforcement in those surroundings. The intensity and frequency of the behavior will not only be influenced by the environment but will also have an impact on that environment. The person brings into the situation previously reinforced responses (personality, in other words) and mental processes such as thinking and anticipating.

Here's how this might work: Richard walks into a classroom filled with other students, but no teacher is present at this time. (This is the *environment*.) Part of Richard's *personal* characteristics includes the desire to have attention from other people by talking loudly and telling jokes, which has been very rewarding to him in the past (past reinforcements are part of his cognitive processes, or expectancies of future rewards for his behavior). Also in the past, he has found that he gets more attention when an authority figure is not present. His *behavior* will most likely be to start talking and telling jokes, which will continue if he gets the reaction he expects from his fellow students. If the teacher walks in (the *environment* changes), his behavior will change. If the other students don't laugh, his behavior will change. In the future Richard might be less likely to behave in the same way because his expectations for reward (a cognitive element of his *personal* variables) are different.

One of the more important personal variables that Bandura talks about is **self-efficacy**—a person's expectancy of how effective his or her efforts to accomplish a goal will be in any particular circumstance (Bandura, 1998). (Self-efficacy is not the same concept as *self-esteem*, which is the positive values a person places on his or her sense of worth.)

People's sense of self-efficacy can be high or low, depending on what has happened in similar circumstances in the past (success or failure), what other people tell them about their competence, and their own assessment of their abilities. For example, if Fiona has an opportunity to write an extra-credit paper to improve her grade in psychology, she will be more likely to do so if her self-efficacy is high: She has gotten good grades on such papers in the past, her teachers have told her that she writes well, and she knows she can write a good paper. According to Bandura, people high in self-efficacy are more persistent and expect to succeed, whereas people low in self-efficacy expect to fail and tend to avoid challenges (Bandura, 1998).

Rotter's Social Learning Theory: Expectancies

Julian Rotter (1966, 1978, 1981, 1990) devised a theory based on a basic principle of motivation derived from Thorndike's Law of Effect: People are motivated to seek

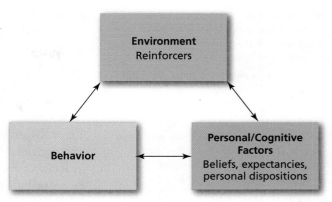

FIGURE 11.2 Reciprocal Determinism
In Bandura's model of reciprocal determinism, three factors influence behavior: the environment, which consists of the physical surroundings and the potential for reinforcement; the person (personal/cognitive characteristics that have been rewarded in the past); and the behavior itself, which may or may not be reinforced at this particular time and place.

social cognitive view learning theory that includes cognitive processes such as anticipating, judging, memory, and imitation of models.

reciprocal determinism Bandura's explanation of how the factors of environment, personal characteristics, and behavior can interact to determine future behavior.

self-efficacy individual's expectancy of how effective his or her efforts to accomplish a goal will be in any particular circumstance.

locus of control the tendency for people to assume that they either have control or do not have control over events and consequences in their lives.

expectancy a person's subjective feeling that a particular behavior will lead to a reinforcing consequence.

humanistic perspective the "third force" in psychology that focuses on those aspects of personality that make people uniquely human, such as subjective feelings and freedom of choice.

According to Rotter, what would be the most likely form of locus of control experienced by this young woman?

It's always 'Sit,' 'Stay,' 'Heel'—never 'Think,' 'Innovate,' 'Be yourself.'"
©The New Yorker Collection 1990 Peter Steiner from cartoonbank.com. All Rights Reserved.

reinforcement and avoid punishment. He viewed personality as a relatively stable set of *potential* responses to various situations. If in the past, a certain way of responding led to a reinforcing or pleasurable consequence, that way of responding would become a pattern of responding, or part of the "personality" as learning theorists see it.

One very important pattern of responding in Rotter's view became his concept of **locus of control**, the tendency for people to assume that they either have control or do not have control over events and consequences in their lives. **LINK** to Chapter Eight: Motivation and Emotion, p. 275. People who assume that their own actions and decisions directly affect the consequences they experience are said to be *internal* in locus of control, whereas people who assume that their lives are more controlled by powerful others, luck, or fate are *external* in locus of control (MacDonald, 1970; Rotter, 1966). Rotter associated people high in internal locus of control with the personality characteristics of high achievement motivation (the will to succeed in any attempted task). Those who give up too quickly or who attribute events in their lives to external causes can fall into patterns of learned helplessness and depression (Abramson et al., 1978, 1980; Gong-Guy & Hammen, 1980).

Like Bandura, Rotter (1978, 1981) also believed that interacting factors would determine the behavioral patterns that become an individual's personality. For Rotter, two key factors influence a person's decision to act in a certain way, given a particular situation: expectancy and reinforcement value. **Expectancy** is fairly similar to Bandura's concept of self-efficacy in that it refers to the person's subjective feeling that a particular behavior will lead to a reinforcing consequence. A high expectancy for success is similar to a high sense of self-efficacy and is also based on past experiences with successes and failures. *Reinforcement value* refers to an individual's preference for a particular reinforcer over all other possible reinforcing consequences. Things or circumstances that are particularly appealing to us have a higher reinforcement value than other possible reinforcers.

Current Thoughts on the Behaviorist and Social Cognitive Views

Behaviorism as an explanation of the formation of personality has its limitations. The classic theory does not take mental processes into account when explaining behavior, nor does it give weight to social influences on learning. The social cognitive view of personality, unlike traditional behaviorism, does include social and mental processes and their influence on behavior. Unlike psychoanalysis, the concepts in this theory can and have been tested under scientific conditions (Backenstrass et al., 2008; Bandura, 1965; Catanzaro et al., 2000; DeGrandpre, 2000; Domjan et al., 2000; Skinner, 1989). Some of this most recent research has investigated how people's expectancies can influence their control of their own negative moods. Some critics think that human personality and behavior are too complex to be explained on the basis of interacting cognitions and external stimuli. Others, however, point out that this viewpoint has enabled the development of therapies based on learning theory that have become effective in changing undesirable behavior. **LINK** to Chapter Thirteen: Psychological Therapies, pp. 473–476.

The Third Force: Humanism and Personality

11.6 How do humanists such as Carl Rogers explain personality?

As first discussed in Chapter One, in the middle of the twentieth century the pessimism of Freudian psychodynamic theory with its emphasis on conflict and animalistic needs, together with the emphasis of behaviorism on external control of behavior, gave rise to a third force in psychology: the **humanistic perspective**. Humanists such as Carl Rogers and Abraham Maslow wanted psychology to focus on the things that make people uniquely human, such as subjective emotions and the freedom to choose one's own destiny. As Maslow's theory was discussed more fully in Chapter Eight, in this chapter the discussion of the humanistic view of personality will focus on Carl Rogers's theory.

Carl Rogers and Self-Concept

Like Maslow, Rogers (1961) believed that human beings are always striving to fulfill their innate capacities and capabilities and to become everything that their genetic potential will allow them to become. This striving for fulfillment is called the **self-actualizing tendency**. An important tool in human self-actualization is the development of an image of oneself, or the **self-concept**. The self-concept is based on what people are told by others and how the sense of **self** is reflected in the words and actions of important people in one's life, such as parents, siblings, coworkers, friends, and teachers.

REAL AND IDEAL SELF Two important components of the self-concept are the **real self** (one's actual perception of characteristics, traits, and abilities that form the basis of the striving for self-actualization) and the **ideal self** (the perception of what one should be or would like to be). The ideal self comes primarily from those important, significant others in a person's life, most often the parents. Rogers believed that when the real self and the ideal self are very close or similar to each other, people feel competent and capable, but when a mismatch occurs between the real self and ideal self, anxiety and neurotic behavior can be the result. (See Figure 11.3.)

The two halves of the self are more likely to match if they aren't that far apart at the start. When a person has a realistic view of the real self, and the ideal self is actually attainable, a problem of a mismatch doesn't usually arise. It is when a person's view of self is distorted or the ideal self is impossible to attain that problems develop. Once again, it is primarily how the important people (who can be either good or bad influences) in a person's life react to the person that determines the degree of agreement between real and ideal selves.

CONDITIONAL AND UNCONDITIONAL POSITIVE REGARD Rogers defined **positive regard** as warmth, affection, love, and respect that come from the significant others (parents, admired adults, friends, and teachers) in people's experience. Positive regard is vital to people's ability to cope with stress and to strive to achieve self-actualization. Rogers believed that **unconditional positive regard**, or love, affection, and respect with no strings attached, is necessary for people to be able to explore fully all that they can achieve and become. Unfortunately, some parents, spouses, and friends give **conditional positive regard**; that is, love, affection, respect, and warmth depend, or seem to depend, on doing what those people want.

Here is an example: As a freshman, Sasha was thinking about becoming a math teacher, a computer programmer, or an elementary school teacher. Karen, also a freshman, already knew that she was going to be a doctor. Whereas Sasha's parents had told her that what she wanted to become was up to her and that they would love her no matter what, Karen's parents had made it very clear to her as a small child that they expected her to become a doctor. She was under the very strong impression that if she tried to choose any other career, she would lose her parents' love and respect. Sasha's parents were giving her unconditional positive regard, but Karen's parents (whether or not they intended to do so) were giving her conditional positive regard. Karen was obviously not as free as Sasha to explore her potential and abilities.

self-actualizing tendency the striving to fulfill one's innate capacities and capabilities.

self-concept the image of oneself that develops from interactions with important, significant people in one's life.

self an individual's awareness of his or her own personal characteristics and level of functioning.

real self one's perception of actual characteristics, traits, and abilities.

ideal self one's perception of whom one should be or would like to be.

positive regard warmth, affection, love, and respect that come from significant others in one's life.

unconditional positive regard positive regard that is given without conditions or strings attached.

conditional positive regard positive regard that is given only when the person is doing what the providers of positive regard wish.

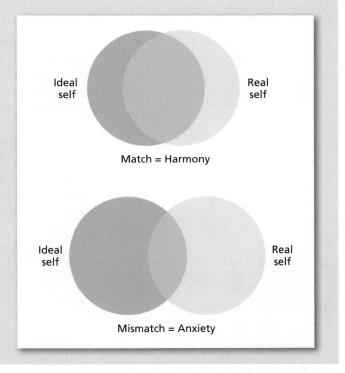

FIGURE 11.3 Real and Ideal Selves According to Rogers, the self-concept includes the real self and the ideal self. The real self is a person's actual perception of traits and abilities, whereas the ideal self is the perception of what a person would like to be or thinks he or she should be. When the ideal self and the real self are very similar (matching), the person experiences harmony and contentment. When there is a mismatch between the two selves, the person experiences anxiety and may engage in neurotic behavior.

fully functioning person a person who is in touch with and trusting of the deepest, innermost urges and feelings.

For Rogers, a person who is in the process of self-actualizing, actively exploring potentials and abilities and experiencing a match between the real self and ideal self, is a **fully functioning person**. Fully functioning people are in touch with their own feelings and abilities and are able to trust their innermost urges and intuitions (Rogers, 1961). To become fully functioning, a person needs unconditional positive regard. In Rogers's view, Karen would not have been a fully functioning person.

● What kind of people are considered to be fully functioning? Is it the same thing as being self-actualized?

> What kind of people are considered to be fully functioning? Is it the same thing as being self-actualized?

Although the two concepts are highly related, there are some subtle differences between them. Self-actualization is a goal that people are always striving to reach, according to Maslow (1987). **LINK** to Chapter Eight: Motivation and Emotion, pp. 279–281. In Rogers's view, only a person who is fully functioning is capable of reaching the goal of self-actualization. To be fully functioning is a necessary step in the process of self-actualization. Maslow (1987) listed several people whom he considered to be self-actualized people, including Albert Einstein, Mahatma Gandhi, and Eleanor Roosevelt. These were people whom Maslow found to have the self-actualized qualities of being creative, autonomous, and unprejudiced. In Rogers's view, these same people would be seen as having trusted their true feelings and innermost needs rather than just going along with the crowd.

Current Thoughts on the Humanistic View of Personality

Humanistic views of personality paint a very rosy picture. Some critics believe that the picture is a little too rosy, ignoring the more negative aspects of human nature. For example, would humanistic theory easily explain the development of sociopathic personalities who have no conscience or moral nature? Or could a humanist explain the motivation behind terrorism?

Humanistic theory is also very difficult to test scientifically. Little research support exists for this viewpoint, which could be considered more of a philosophical than a psychological explanation of human behavior. Its greatest impact has been in the development of therapies designed to promote self-growth and help people reach a better understanding of themselves and others. **LINK** to Chapter Thirteen: Psychological Therapies, pp. 470–472.

practice quiz   How much do you remember?

11.5 **11.6**

Pick the best answer.

1. According to behaviorists, personality is _____.
   a. driven by unconscious forces.
   b. a set of learned responses.
   c. motivated by a striving for success.
   d. a collection of specific traits.

2. Which of the following is not one of Bandura's three factors in reciprocal determinism?
   a. environment
   b. the person
   c. traits
   d. behavior

3. Sandy is playing a trivia game with her friends. When it is her turn, she gets the category of geography. She knows very little about geography and has never done well in this category in the past, so her sense of self-efficacy is likely to be _____.
   a. low.
   b. high.
   c. just right.
   d. unaffected by the game.

4. Stefan knows that he is pretty good at art, but his parents have never encouraged him to develop art as a career because they don't feel that artists have "real" jobs. As a result, Stefan feels that he should concentrate on a more practical career to please his parents. If Stefan is working to be who he should be, according to his parents, he is being influenced by his _____.
   a. self-concept.
   b. real self.
   c. superego.
   d. ideal self.

5. Rogers believed that in order for people to become fully functioning, they must receive _____ from the important people in their lives.
   a. unconditional positive regard
   b. conditional positive regard
   c. positive reinforcement
   d. positive modeling

Trait Theories: Who Are You?

11.7 What are the history and current views of the trait perspective?

As discussed in the introduction to this chapter, **trait theories** are less concerned with explaining personality development and changing personality than they are with describing personality and predicting behavior based on that description. A **trait** is a consistent, enduring way of thinking, feeling, or behaving, and trait theories attempt to describe personality in terms of a person's traits.

Allport

One of the earliest attempts to list and describe the traits that make up personality can be found in the work of Gordon Allport (Allport & Odbert, 1936). Allport and his colleague H. S. Odbert literally scanned the dictionary for words that could be traits, finding about 18,000, then paring that list down to 200 traits after eliminating synonyms. Allport believed (with no scientific evidence, however) that these traits were literally wired into the nervous system to guide one's behavior across many different situations and that each person's "constellation" of traits was unique. (In spite of Allport's lack of evidence, behavioral geneticists have found support for the heritability of personality traits, and these findings are discussed in the next section of this chapter.) 👁️⃣|Watch on MyPsychLab

Cattell and the 16PF

Two hundred traits is still a very large number of descriptors. How might an employer, for example, be able to judge the personality of a potential employee by looking at a list of 200 traits? A more compact way of describing personality was needed. Raymond Cattell (1990) defined two types of traits as surface traits and source traits. **Surface traits** are like those found by Allport, representing the personality characteristics easily seen by other people. **Source traits** are those more basic traits that underlie the surface traits. For example, exhibiting shyness, being quiet, and disliking crowds might all be surface traits related to the more basic source trait of **introversion**, a tendency to withdraw from excessive stimulation.

Using a statistical technique that looks for groupings and commonalities in numerical data called *factor analysis*, Cattell identified 16 source traits (Cattell, 1950, 1966). Although he later determined that there might be another seven source traits to make a total of 23 (Cattell & Kline, 1977), he developed his assessment questionnaire, *The Sixteen Personality Factor (16PF) Questionnaire* (Cattell, 1995), based on just 16 source traits. These 16 source traits are seen as trait dimensions, or continuums, in which there are two opposite traits at each end, with a range of possible degrees for each trait measurable along the dimension. For example, someone scoring near the "reserved" end of the "reserved/outgoing" dimension would be more introverted than someone scoring in the middle or at the opposite end (see Figure 11.4).

The Big Five: OCEAN, or the Five-Factor Model of Personality

Sixteen factors are still quite a lot to discuss when talking about someone's personality. Later researchers attempted to reduce the number of trait dimensions to a more manageable number, with several groups of researchers arriving at more or less the same five trait dimensions (Botwin & Buss, 1989; Jang et al., 1998; McCrae & Costa, 1996). These five dimensions have become known as the **five-factor model** or the **Big Five** and represent the core description of human personality—that is, the only dimensions necessary to understand what makes us tick.

---

trait theories theories that endeavor to describe the characteristics that make up human personality in an effort to predict future behavior.

trait a consistent, enduring way of thinking, feeling, or behaving.

surface traits aspects of personality that can easily be seen by other people in the outward actions of a person.

source traits the more basic traits that underlie the surface traits, forming the core of personality.

introversion dimension of personality in which people tend to withdraw from excessive stimulation.

five-factor model (Big Five) model of personality traits that describes five basic trait dimensions.

👁️—|Watch classic video footage on personality traits with Allport on **MyPsychLab**

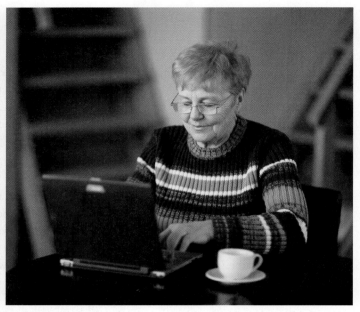

FIGURE 11.4 Cattell's Self-Report Inventory
An example of personality profiles based on Cattell's 16PF self-report inventory. The two groups represented are airline pilots and writers. Airline pilots, when compared to writers, tend to be more conscientious, relaxed, self-assured, and far less sensitive. Writers, on the other hand, were more imaginative and better able to think abstractly.
Source: Cattell (1973).

openness one of the five factors; willingness to try new things and be open to new experiences.

conscientiousness the care a person gives to organization and thoughtfulness of others; dependability.

extraversion dimension of personality referring to one's need to be with other people.

extraverts people who are outgoing and sociable.

introverts people who prefer solitude and dislike being the center of attention.

agreeableness the emotional style of a person that may range from easygoing, friendly, and likeable to grumpy, crabby, and unpleasant.

neuroticism degree of emotional instability or stability.

These five trait dimensions can be remembered by using the acronym OCEAN, in which each of the letters is the first letter of one of the five dimensions of personality.

- **Openness** can best be described as a person's willingness to try new things and be open to new experiences. People who try to maintain the status quo and who don't like to change things would score low on openness. High scorers tend to be more creative, imaginative, and nonconforming.

- **Conscientiousness** refers to a person's organization and motivation, with people who score high in this dimension being those who are careful about being places on time and careful with belongings as well. Someone scoring low on this dimension, for example, might always be late to important social events or borrow belongings and fail to return them or return them in poor condition.

- **Extraversion** is a term first used by Carl Jung (1933), who believed that all people could be divided into two personality types: **extraverts** and **introverts**. Extraverts are outgoing and sociable, whereas introverts are more solitary and dislike being the center of attention.

- **Agreeableness** refers to the basic emotional style of a person, who may be good-natured, easygoing, trusting, and helpful (at the high end of the scale) or grumpy, crabby, and hard to get along with (at the low end).

- **Neuroticism** refers to emotional instability or stability. People who are excessive worriers, overanxious, and moody would score high on this dimension, whereas those who are more even-tempered, calm, and secure would score low.

Costa and McCrae believed that these five traits were not interdependent. In other words, knowing someone's score on extraversion would not give any information about scores on the other four dimensions, allowing for a tremendous amount of variety in personality descriptions. ✳ Explore on MyPsychLab

✳ Explore the five-factor model on MyPsychLab

Current Thoughts on the Trait Perspective

Some theorists have cautioned that personality traits will not always be expressed in the same way across different situations. Walter Mischel, a social cognitive theorist, has emphasized that there is a **trait–situation interaction** in which the particular circumstances of any given situation are assumed to influence the way in which a trait is expressed (Mischel & Shoda, 1995). An outgoing extravert, for example, might laugh, talk to strangers, and tell jokes at a party. That same person, if at a funeral, would still talk and be open, but the jokes and laughter would be less likely to occur. However, the five-factor model provides a dimensional approach to classifying personality structure (as opposed to a categorical approach), which is consistent with proposed changes for the upcoming edition of the *Diagnostic and Statistical Manual of Mental Disorders* (*DSM-5*) and has implications for the diagnosis of personality disorders (Widiger & Trull, 2007).

As mentioned earlier, the five-factor model has been studied and tested by numerous researchers. Cross-cultural studies have found evidence of these five trait dimensions in 11 different cultures, including Japan, the Philippines, Germany, China, and Peru (Digman, 1990; John et al., 1988; McCrae et al., 2000, 2005; McCrae & Terracciano, 2007; Paunonen et al., 1996; Piedmont et al., 2002). This cultural commonality raises the question of the origins of the Big Five trait dimensions: Are child-rearing practices across all those cultures similar enough to result in these five aspects of personality, or could these five dimensions have a genetic component that transcends cultural differences? A later section will discuss the evidence for a genetic basis of the Big Five.

trait–situation interaction the assumption that the particular circumstances of any given situation will influence the way in which a trait is expressed.

practice quiz How much do you remember?

11.7

Pick the best answer.

1. Who believed that traits existed as part of the nervous system?
   a. Costa and McCrae
   b. Allport
   c. Cattell
   d. Rogers

2. According to Cattell, traits that are numerous and can easily be seen by other people are called _____ traits.
   a. central
   b. cardinal
   c. surface
   d. source

3. In the Big Five theory of personality, "C" stands for _____.
   a. conscientiousness.
   b. consciousness.
   c. contrariness.
   d. complexity.

4. Elsie's daughter gave her a microwave oven for her birthday. Elsie has never used a microwave and is scared to use this one. Instead, she lets it sit in her kitchen and refuses to let her daughter teach her how to use it. Elsie would probably score very low on _____.
   a. agreeableness.
   b. neuroticism.
   c. introversion.
   d. openness.

ANSWERS ON PAGE AK-2

Assessment of Personality

11.8 What are the advantages and disadvantages of the following measures of personality: interviews, projective tests, behavioral assessment, personality inventories, and online personality tests?

With all the different theories of personality, how do people find out what kind of personality they have?

With all the different theories of personality, how do people find out what kind of personality they have?

The methods for measuring or assessing personality vary according to the theory of personality used to develop those methods, as one might expect. However, most psychological professionals doing a personality assessment on a client do not necessarily tie themselves down to one theoretical viewpoint only; they prefer to take a more *eclectic* view of personality. The eclectic view is a way of choosing the parts of different theories that seem to best fit a particular situation, rather than using only one theory to explain a phenomenon. Looking at behavior from all four perspectives can often bring insights into a person's behavior that would not easily come from taking only one perspective. Many professionals will not only use several different perspectives but also several of the assessment techniques that follow. Even so, certain methods are more commonly used by certain kinds of theorists, as can be seen in Table 11.3.

Personality assessments may also differ in the purposes for which they are conducted. For example, sometimes a researcher may administer a personality test to participants in a research study so that the participants may be classified according to certain personality traits. There are personality tests available to people who simply want to learn more about their own personalities. Finally, clinical and counseling psychologists, psychiatrists, and other psychological professionals use these personality assessment tools in the diagnosis of disorders of personality. (L)(I)(N)(K) to Chapter Twelve: Psychological Disorders, pp. 455–457.

table 11.3   Who Uses What Method?

TYPE OF ASSESSMENT	MOST LIKELY USED BY...
Interviews	Psychoanalysts, Humanistic Therapists
Projective Tests	Psychoanalysts
Rorschach	
Thematic Apperception Test	
Behavioral Assessments	Behavioral and Social Cognitive Therapists
Direct Observation	
Rating Scales	
Frequency Counts	
Personality Inventories	Trait Theorists
Sixteen Personality Factor Questionnaire (16PF)	
Neuroticism/Extraversion/Openness Personality Inventory (NEO-PI)	
Minnesota Multiphasic Personality Inventory, Version II (MMPI-2)	
Myers-Briggs Type Indicator (MBTI)	
Eysenck Personality Questionnaire (EPQ)	
Keirsey Temperament Sorter II	
California Psychological Inventory (CPI)	

Interviews

Some therapists ask questions and record the answers in a survey process called an **interview**. (LINK) to Chapter One: The Science of Psychology, p. 22. This type of interview, unlike a job interview, is likely to be *unstructured* and to flow naturally from the beginning dialogue between the client and the psychologist.

Problems with Interviews

So an interview is a kind of self-report process? ●

Yes, when psychologists interview clients, clients must report on their innermost feelings, urges, and concerns—all things that only they can directly know. The same problems that exist with self-report data (such as surveys) exist with interviews. Clients can lie, distort the truth, misremember, or give what they think is a socially acceptable answer instead of true information. Interviewers themselves can be biased, interpreting what the client says in light of their own belief systems or prejudices. Freud certainly did this when he refused to believe that his patients had actually been sexually molested as children, preferring to interpret that information as a fantasy instead of reality (Russell, 1986).

Another problem with interviews is something called the **halo effect**, which is a tendency to form a favorable or unfavorable impression of someone at the first meeting, so that all of a person's comments and behavior after that first impression will be interpreted to agree with the impression—positively or negatively. The halo effect can happen in any social situation, including interviews between a psychological professional and a client. First impressions really do count, and people who make a good first impression because of clothing, personal appearance, or some other irrelevant* characteristic will seem to have a "halo" hanging over their heads—they can do no wrong after that (Lance et al., 1994; Thorndike, 1920). (Sometimes the negative impression is called the "horn effect.")

Projective Tests

Psychoanalysts have a goal in dealing with their clients that other personality theorists do not share: The psychoanalyst wishes to uncover the unconscious conflicts, desires, and urges that affect the client's conscious behavior. No other theorist assigns such importance to the unconscious mind, so psychoanalysts use assessment methods that are meant to "get at" those unconscious, hidden emotions and events.

Think about the definition of the defense mechanism of **projection**: placing, or "projecting," one's own unacceptable thoughts onto others, as if the thoughts actually belonged to those others. What if a person could project unacceptable, unconscious thoughts onto some harmless, ambiguous stimulus, like a picture? For example, have you ever tried to see "shapes" in the clouds? You might see a house where another person might see the same cloud as a horse. The cloud isn't really either of those things but can be *interpreted* as one or the other, depending on the person doing the interpretation. That makes a cloud an ambiguous stimulus—one that is capable of being interpreted in more than one way.

In just this way, psychoanalysts (and a few other psychologists) show their clients ambiguous visual stimuli and ask the clients to tell them what they see. The hope is that the client will project those unconscious concerns and fears onto the visual stimulus, revealing them to the analyst. Tests using this method are called **projective tests**. Although such tests can be used to explore a client's personality, they are more commonly used as a diagnostic tool to uncover problems in personality.

So an interview is a kind of self-report process?

interview method of personality assessment in which the professional asks questions of the client and allows the client to answer, either in a structured or unstructured fashion.

halo effect tendency of an interviewer to allow positive characteristics of a client to influence the assessments of the client's behavior and statements.

projection defense mechanism involving placing, or "projecting," one's own unacceptable thoughts onto others, as if the thoughts actually belonged to those others and not to oneself.

projective tests personality assessments that present ambiguous visual stimuli to the client and ask the client to respond with whatever comes to mind.

---

*Irrelevant: not applying to the case or example at hand.

FIGURE 11.5 Rorschach Inkblot Example

A facsimile of a Rorschach inkblot. A person being tested is asked to tell the interviewer what he or she sees in an inkblot similar to the one shown. Answers are neither right nor wrong but may reveal unconscious concerns. What do you see in this inkblot?

THE RORSCHACH INKBLOTS One of the more well-known projective tests is the **Rorschach inkblot test**, developed in 1921 by Swiss psychiatrist Hermann Rorschach (ROR-shok). There are 10 inkblots, five in black ink on a white background and five in colored inks on a white background. (See Figure 11.5 for an image similar to a Rorschach-type inkblot.)

People being tested are asked to look at each inkblot and simply say whatever it might look like to them. Using predetermined categories and responses commonly given by people to each picture (Exner, 1980), psychologists score responses on key factors, such as reference to color, shape, figures seen in the blot, and response to the whole or to details.

Rorschach tested thousands of inkblots until he narrowed them down to the 10 in use today. They are still frequently used to describe personality, diagnose mental disorders, and predict behavior (Watkins et al., 1995; Weiner, 1997).

THE TAT First developed in 1935 by psychologist Henry Murray and his colleagues (Morgan & Murray, 1935), the **Thematic Apperception Test (TAT)** consists of 20 pictures, all black and white, that are shown to a client. The client is asked to tell a story about the person or people in the picture, who are all deliberately drawn in ambiguous situations (see Figure 11.6). Again, the story developed by the client is interpreted by the psychoanalyst, who looks for revealing statements and projection of the client's own problems onto the people in the pictures.

These are only two of the more well-known projective tests. Other types of projective tests include the Sentence Completion test, Draw-A-Person, and House-Tree-Person. In the Sentence Completion test, the client is given a series of sentence beginnings, such as "I wish my mother..." or "Almost every day I feel..." and asked to finish the sentence, whereas in the Draw-A-Person and House-Tree-Person, the client is asked to draw the named items.

But how can anyone know if the interpretation is correct? Isn't there a lot of room for error?

● But how can anyone know if the interpretation is correct? Isn't there a lot of room for error?

PROBLEMS WITH PROJECTIVE TESTS Projective tests are by their nature very **subjective** (valid only within the person's own perception), and interpreting the answers of clients is almost an art. It is certainly not a science and is not known for its accuracy. Problems lie in the areas of reliability and validity. *Reliability* is defined as the tendency of a test to give the same score every time it is administered to the same person

Rorschach inkblot test projective test that uses 10 inkblots as the ambiguous stimuli.

Thematic Apperception Test (TAT) projective test that uses 20 pictures of people in ambiguous situations as the visual stimuli.

subjective referring to concepts and impressions that are only valid within a particular person's perception and may be influenced by biases, prejudice, and personal experiences.

FIGURE 11.6 Thematic Apperception Test Example

A sample from the Thematic Apperception Test (TAT). When you look at this picture, what story does it suggest to you? Who are the people? What is their relationship?

or group of people, and *validity* is defined as the ability of the test to measure what it is intended to measure. Projective tests, with no standard grading scales, have both low reliability and low validity (Gittelman-Klein, 1978; Lilienfeld, 1999; Wood et al., 1996). A person's answers to the Rorschach, for example, might be quite different from one day to the next, depending on the person's mood and what scary movie might have been on television the previous night.

Projective tests may sound somewhat outdated in today's world of MRIs and PET scans, but many practicing clinical psychologists and psychiatrists still use this type of testing (Butcher & Rouse, 1996; Camara et al., 2000). Some psychologists believe that the latest versions of these tests and others like them still have practical use and some validity (Ganellen, 1996; Weiner, 1997), especially when a client's answers on these tests are used as a starting point for digging deeper into the client's recollections, concerns, and anxieties. However, more reliable and objective methods for assessing personality are available, as the next section discusses.

Somehow, I can't see a behaviorist using any of these tests; they're too "mental"—do behaviorists even measure personality?

Behavioral Assessments

Behaviorists do not typically want to "look into the mind." Because behaviorists assume that personality is simply defined as habitually learned responses to stimuli in the environment, the preferred method for a behaviorist would be to watch that behavior unfold in the real world.

In **direct observation**, the psychologist observes the client engaging in ordinary, everyday behavior, preferably in the natural setting of home, school, or workplace, for example. A therapist who goes to the classroom and observes that tantrum behavior occurs only when a child is asked to do something involving fine motor abilities (like drawing or writing) might be able to conclude that the child has difficulty with those skills and throws a tantrum to avoid the task.

Other methods often used by behavioral therapists and other assessors are rating scales and frequency counts. In a **rating scale**, a numerical rating is assigned, either by the assessor or the client, for specific behaviors (Nadeau et al., 2001). In a **frequency count**, the assessor literally counts the frequency of certain behaviors within a specified time limit. Educators make use of both rating scales and frequency counts to diagnose behavioral problems such as attention deficit/hyperactivity disorder (ADHD) and aspects of personality such as social skill level through the various grade levels.

PROBLEMS WITH BEHAVIORAL ASSESSMENTS Problems with these assessments can include the observer effect (when a person's behavior is affected by being watched) and observer bias, which can be controlled by having multiple observers and correlating their observations with one another. **LINK** to Chapter One: The Science of Psychology, pp. 20–21. As with any kind of observational method, there is no control over the external environment. A person observing a client for a particular behavior may not see that behavior occur within the observation time—much as some car problems never seem to show up when the mechanic is examining the car.

Personality Inventories

Trait theorists are typically more interested in personality descriptions. They tend to use an assessment known as a **personality inventory**, a questionnaire that has a standard list of questions and only requires certain specific answers, such as "yes," "no," and "can't decide." The standard nature of the questions (everyone gets the same list) and the lack of open-ended answers make these assessments far more objective and reliable than projective tests (Garb et al., 1998), although they are still a form of self-report. One such personality inventory is Cattell's 16PF, described earlier in this

---

Somehow, I can't see a behaviorist using any of these tests; they're too "mental"—do behaviorists even measure personality?

direct observation assessment in which the professional observes the client engaged in ordinary, day-to-day behavior in either a clinical or natural setting.

rating scale assessment in which a numerical value is assigned to specific behavior that is listed in the scale.

frequency count assessment in which the frequency of a particular behavior is counted.

personality inventory paper and pencil or computerized test that consists of statements that require a specific, standardized response from the person taking the test.

THE PESSIMIST AND THE PARANOID

chapter. Costa and McCrae (2000) have recently revised their original *Neuroticism/ Extraversion/Openness Personality Inventory (NEO-PI)*, which is based on the five-factor model of personality traits (discussed on pages 401–403).

Another inventory in common use is the *Myers-Briggs Type Indicator (MBTI)*. This inventory is based on the ideas of Carl Jung and looks at four personality dimensions. The sensing/intuition (S/I) dimension includes people who prefer to rely on what they can see, hear, and so on through their own physical senses (*sensing*) and, on its opposite end, those who look for patterns and trust their hunches (*intuition*). Sensing people are very detail oriented, preferring to work only with the known facts, whereas intuitive people are more willing to use metaphors and analogies and to look for possibilities. The thinking/feeling (T/F) dimension runs from those who prefer to use logic, analysis, and experiences that can be verified as facts (*thinking*) to those who tend to make decisions based on their personal values and emotional reactions (*feeling*). Introversion/extraversion (I/E) is the same classic dimension that began with Jung and is represented in nearly every personality theory, including the Big Five. Perceiving/judging (P/J) describes those who are willing to adapt and modify decisions, be spontaneous, and who are naturally curious and tend to put off making a final decision so that all possibilities are covered (*perceiving,*) as well as those who are the opposite: the action-oriented, decisive, get-the-task-done-and-don't-look-back type (*judging*). These four dimensions can differ for each individual, resulting in 16 (4 × 4) possible personality types: ISTJ, ISTP, ISFP, ISFJ, and so on (Briggs & Myers, 1998).

The Myers-Briggs is often used to assess personality to help people know the kinds of careers for which they may best be suited. For example, a person who scored high on the extravert, sensing, thinking, and judging dimensions would be an ESTJ. A typical description of this personality type would be a person who needs to analyze information and bring order to the outer world. Such people are organizers, energetic in completing tasks, and practical. They also take their responsibilities seriously and expect others to do so as well. School administrators, for example, are often ESTJs.

Other common personality tests include the Eysenck Personality Questionnaire (Eysenck & Eysenck, 1993), the Keirsey Temperament Sorter II (Keirsey, 1998), the California Psychological Inventory (Gough, 1995), and the Sixteen Personality Factor Questionnaire (Cattell, 1994).

THE MMPI-2 By far the most common personality inventory is the *Minnesota Multiphasic Personality Inventory, Version II*, or *MMPI-2*, which specifically tests for abnormal behavior patterns in personality (Butcher & Rouse, 1996; Butcher et al., 2000, 2001). This questionnaire consists of 567 statements such as "I am often very tense" or "I believe I am being plotted against." The person taking the test must answer "true," "false," or "cannot say." The MMPI has ten clinical scales and eight validity scales in addition to numerous subscales. Each scale tests for a particular kind of behavior. The behavior patterns include relatively mild personality problems, such as excessive worrying and shyness, as well as more serious disorders such as schizophrenia and depression. **(LINK)** to Chapter Twelve: Psychological Disorders, pp. 445, 451.

Read and learn more about clinical scales of the MMPI-2 on **MyPsychLab**

Read on **MyPsychLab**

How can you tell if a person is telling the truth on a personality inventory?

● How can you tell if a person is telling the truth on a personality inventory?

Validity scales, which are built into any well-designed psychological inventory, are intended to indicate whether or not a person taking the inventory is responding honestly. Responses to certain items on the test will indicate if people are trying to make themselves look better or worse than they are, for example, and certain items are repeated throughout the test in a slightly different form, so that anyone trying to "fake" the test will have difficulty responding to those items consistently (Butcher et al., 2001). For example, if one of the statements is "I am always happy" and a person responds "true" to that statement, the suspicion would be that this person is trying to look better than he or she really is. If several of the validity scale questions are answered in this way, the conclusion is that the person is not being honest.

PROBLEMS WITH PERSONALITY INVENTORIES The advantage of personality inventories over projective tests and interviews is that inventories are standardized (i.e., everyone gets exactly the same questions and the answers are scored in exactly the same way). In fact, responses to inventories are often scored on a computer. Observer bias and bias of interpretation are simply not possible because this kind of assessment is objective rather than subjective. The validity and reliability of personality inventories are generally recognized as being greatly superior to those of projective tests (Anastasi & Urbina, 1997).

There are some problems, however. The validity scales, for example, are a good check against cheating, but they are not perfect. Some people are still able to fake their answers and respond in what they feel are the socially appropriate ways (Anastasi & Urbina, 1997; Hicklin & Widiger, 2000). Despite the best intentions of the test creators, individual responses to specific questions may also vary as they may be interpreted in different ways by different individuals and are very likely to be subject to cultural influences (Kagan, 2010). Other problems have to do with human nature itself: Some people may develop a habit of picking a particular answer rather than carefully considering the statement, whereas others may simply grow tired of responding to all those statements and start picking answers at random.

practice quiz How much do you remember?

11.8

Pick the best answer.

1. Which of the following methods would NEVER be used by a behaviorist?
   a. interview
   b. projective test
   c. direct observation
   d. personality inventory

2. Which method of personality assessment offers the most objective measurement?
   a. interview
   b. projective test
   c. direct observation
   d. personality inventory

3. Observer bias would be a problem for any of the following methods except _____.
   a. interview.
   b. projective test.
   c. direct observation.
   d. personality inventory.

Brainstorming: Should employers require prospective employees to take a personality test? Why or why not? Would such a requirement make more sense in certain professions, and what professions might those be?

ANSWERS ON PAGE AK–2

Intelligence

Has someone ever told you that you were "smart"? Have you ever referred to someone else as "smart"? Does being "smart" mean that we are high in intelligence, and what exactly do we mean by the term *intelligence*?

Definition

11.9 How do psychologists define intelligence, and how do various theories of intelligence differ?

Is intelligence merely a score on some test, or is it practical knowledge of how to get along in the world? Is it making good grades or being a financial success or a social success? Ask a dozen people and you will probably get a dozen different answers. Psychologists have come up with a workable definition that combines many of the ideas just mentioned: They define **intelligence** as the ability to learn from one's experiences,

intelligence the ability to learn from one's experiences, acquire knowledge, and use resources effectively in adapting to new situations or solving problems.

g factor the ability to reason and solve problems, or general intelligence.

s factor the ability to excel in certain areas, or specific intelligence.

intelligence quotient (IQ) a number representing a measure of intelligence, resulting from the division of one's mental age by one's chronological age and then multiplying that quotient by 100.

Survey Participate in a survey: What is intelligence? on **MyPsychLab**

Watch classic video footage on mental-age testing with the Stanford-Binet on **MyPsychLab**

acquire knowledge, and use resources effectively in adapting to new situations or solving problems (Sternberg & Kaufman, 1998; Wechsler, 1975). These are the characteristics that individuals need in order to survive in their culture. **Survey** on **MyPsychLab**

Theories of Intelligence

Although we have defined intelligence in a general way, there are differing opinions of the specific knowledge and abilities that make up the concept of intelligence. Charles Spearman (1904) defined intelligence as two primary abilities: the wider ability of *general intelligence*, labeled as **g factor**, and task-specific abilities in certain areas such as music, business, or art, labeled as **s factor** for *specific intelligence*. Some later theorists have suggested that intelligence cannot be defined so simply and have therefore proposed different aspects and abilities. The idea of multiple intelligences was proposed by Howard Gardner (1993b, 1999a), and his theory orginally listed seven different kinds of intelligence but later added an eighth and a ninth (Gardner, 1998, 1999b). Yet another theory suggests that there are three kinds of intelligence. Robert Sternberg's (1988a, 1997b, 2005) triarchic theory of intelligence suggests that intelligence comprises analytical, creative, and practical aspects.

Measuring Intelligence

11.10 How is intelligence measured, and how are intelligence tests constructed?

The history of intelligence testing spans the twentieth century and has at times been marked by controversies and misuse. A full history of how intelligence testing developed would take at least an entire chapter, so this section will discuss only some of the better-known forms of testing and how they came to be.

It doesn't sound like intelligence would be easy to measure on a test—how do IQ tests work, anyway?

The measurement of intelligence by some kind of test is a concept that is less than a century old. It began when educators in France realized that some students needed more help with learning than others did. They thought that if a way could be found to identify these students more in need, they could be given a different kind of education than the more capable students. **Watch** on **MyPsychLab**

BINET'S MENTAL ABILITY TEST In those early days, the French Ministry of Eduction asked a French psychologist named Alfred Binet to design a formal test of intelligence that would help identify children who were unable to learn as quickly or as well as others, so that they could be given remedial education. Eventually, he and colleague Théodore Simon came up with a test that distinguished not only between fast and slow learners but also between children of different age-groups as well (Binet & Simon, 1916). They noticed that the fast learners seemed to give answers to questions that older children might give, whereas the slow learners gave answers that were more typical of a younger child. Binet decided that the key element to be tested was a child's *mental age*, or the average age at which children could successfully answer a particular level of questions.

STANFORD-BINET AND IQ Lewis Terman (1916), a researcher at Stanford University, adopted German psychologist William Stern's method for comparing mental age and *chronological age* (number of years since birth) for use with the translated and revised Binet test. Stern's (1912) formula was to divide the mental age (MA) by the chronological age (CA) and multiply the result by 100 to get rid of any decimal points. The resulting score is called an **intelligence quotient**, or **IQ**. (A quotient is a number that results from dividing one number by another.)

It doesn't sound like intelligence would be easy to measure on a test—how do IQ tests work, anyway?

$$IQ = MA/CA \times 100$$

For example, if a child who is 10 years old were to take the test and score a mental age of 15 (be able to answer the level of questions typical of a 15-year-old), the IQ would look like this:

$$IQ = 15/10 \times 100 = 150$$

The quotient has the advantage of allowing testers to compare the intelligence levels of people of different age-groups. Today, the *Stanford-Binet Intelligence Scales, Fifth Edition (SB5)* (Roid, 2003) uses age-group comparison norms, such as the Wechsler tests (see the next section), and is often used by educators to make decisions about the placement of students into special educational programs, both for those with disabilities and for those with exceptionalities. Many children are given this test in the second grade, or age 7 or 8. The SB5 yields an overall estimate of intelligence, verbal and nonverbal domain scores, all of which are comprised of five primary areas of cognitive ability—fluid reasoning, knowledge, quantitative processing, visual–spatial processing, and working memory (Roid, 2003). See Table 11.4 for descriptions of some items similar to those from the SB5.

THE WECHSLER TESTS Although the original Stanford-Binet test is now in its fifth edition and includes different questions for people of different age-groups, it is not the only IQ test that is popular today. David Wechsler (Wechsler 2002, 2003, 2008) was the first to devise a series of tests designed for specific age groups. Originally dissatisfied with the fact that the Stanford-Binet was designed for children but was being administered to adults, he developed an IQ test specifically for adults. He later designed tests specifically for older school-age children and preschool children, as well as those in the early grades. The Wechsler Adult Intelligence Scale (WAIS-IV), the Wechsler Intelligence Scale for Children (WISC-IV), and the Wechsler Preschool and Primary Scale of Intelligence (WPPSI-III) are the three versions of this test, and in the United States these tests are now used more frequently than the Stanford-Binet. In earlier editions, another way these tests differed from the Stanford-Binet was by having both a verbal and a performance (nonverbal) scale, as well as providing an overall score of intelligence (the original Stanford-Binet was composed predominantly of verbal items). While still using both verbal and non-verbal items, the WISC-IV and WAIS-IV organizes items into four index scales that provide an overall score of intelligence and index scores related to four specific cognitive domains: verbal comprehension, perceptual reasoning, working memory, and processing speed. Table 11.5 has sample items for each of the four index scales from the WAIS-IV.

table 11.4	**Paraphrased Sample Items from the Stanford-Binet Intelligence Test**	
AGE*	**TYPE OF ITEM**	**DESCRIPTION OF ITEM**
2	Board with three differently shaped holes	Child can place correct shape into matching hole on board.
4	Building block bridge	Child can build a simple bridge out of blocks after being shown a model.
7	Similarities	Child can answer such questions as "In what way are a ship and a car alike?"
9	Digit reversal	Child can repeat four digits backwards.
Average adult	Vocabulary	Child can define 20 words from a list.

*Age at which item typically is successfully completed.

Source: Roid (2003).

table 11.5 Simulated Sample Items from the Wechsler Adult Intelligence Scale (WAIS-IV)

SIMULATED SAMPLE TEST ITEMS

Verbal Comprehension Index

Similarities	In what way are a circle and a triangle alike? In what way are a saw and a hammer alike?
Vocabulary	What is a hippopotamus? What does "resemble" mean?
Information	What is steam made of? What is pepper? Who wrote *Tom Sawyer*?

Perceptual Reasoning Index

Block Design	After looking at a pattern or design, try to arrange small cubes in the same pattern.
Matrix Reasoning	After looking at an incomplete matrix pattern or series, select an option that completes the matrix or series.
Visual Puzzles	Look at a completed puzzle and select three components from a set of options that would re-create the puzzle, all within a specified time limit.

Working Memory Index

Digit Span	Recall lists of numbers, some lists forward and some lists in reverse order, and recall a mixed list of numbers in correct ascending order.
Arithmetic	Three women divided 18 golf balls equally among themselves. How many golf balls did each person receive? If two buttons cost $.15, what will be the cost of a dozen buttons?

Processing Speed Index

Symbol Search	Visually scan a group of symbols to identify specific target symbols, within a specified time limit.
Coding	Learn a different symbol for specific numbers and then fill in the blank under the number with the correct symbol. (This test is timed.)

Simulated items and descriptions similar to those in the *Wechsler Adult Intelligence Scale—Fourth Edition* (2008).

TEST CONSTRUCTION: GOOD TEST, BAD TEST? All tests are not equally good tests. Some tests may fail to give the same results on different occasions for the same person when that person has not changed—making the test useless. These tests would be considered unreliable. **Reliability** of a test refers to the test producing consistent results each time it is given to the same individual or group of people. For example, if Nicholas takes a personality test today and then again in a month or so, the results should be very similar if the personality test is reliable. Other tests might be easy to use and even reliable, but if they don't actually measure what they are supposed to measure, they are also useless. These tests are thought of as "invalid" (untrue) tests. **Validity** is the degree to which a test actually measures what it's supposed to measure. Another aspect of validity is the extent to which an obtained score accurately reflects the intended skill or outcome in real-life situations, or *ecological validity*, not just validity for the testing or assessment situation. For example, we hope that someone who passes his test for a driver's license will also be able to safely operate a motor vehicle when he is actually on the road. When evaluating a test, consider what a specific test score means and to what, or to whom, it is compared?

Take the hypothetical example of Professor Stumpwater, who for reasons best known only to him believes that intelligence is related to a person's golf scores. Let's say that he develops an adult intelligence test based on golf scores. What do we need to look at to determine if his test is a good one?

Standardization of Tests First of all, we would want to look at how he tried to standardize his test. *Standardization* refers to the process of giving the test to a large group of people that represents the kind of people for whom the test is designed. Standardization groups are chosen randomly from the population for whom the test is intended and, like all samples, must be representative of that population. Ⓛ Ⓘ Ⓝ Ⓚ to

reliability the tendency of a test to produce the same scores again and again each time it is given to the same people.

validity the degree to which a test actually measures what it's supposed to measure.

Appendix A: Statistics in Psychology. If a test is designed for children, for example, then a large sample of randomly selected children would be given the test. All test subjects would take the test under the same conditions. In the professor's case, this would mean that he would have to allow his sample members to play the same number of rounds of golf on the same course under the same weather conditions, and so on.

Norms The scores from the standardization group would be called the *norms*, the standards against which all others who take the test would be compared. Most tests of intelligence follow a *normal curve*, or a distribution in which the scores are the most frequent around the *mean*, or average, and become less and less frequent the further from the mean they occur (see Figure 11.7). LINK to Appendix A: Statistics in Psychology.

On the Wechsler IQ test, the percentages under each section of the normal curve represent the percentage of scores falling within that section for each *standard deviation (SD)* from the mean on the Wechsler IQ test. The standard deviation is the average variation of scores from the mean. LINK to Appendix A: Statistics in Psychology.

In the case of the professor's golf test, he might find that a certain golf score is the average, which he would interpret as average intelligence. People who scored extremely well on the golf test would be compared to the average, as well as people with unusually poor scores.

The normal curve allows IQ scores to be more accurately estimated. The old IQ scoring method using the simple formula devised by Stern produces raw ratio IQ scores that start to become meaningless as the person's chronological age passes 16 years. (Once a person becomes an adult, the idea of questions geared to a particular age-group loses its power. For example, what kind of differences would there be between questions designed for a 30-year-old versus a 40-year-old?) Test designers replaced the old ratio IQ of the earlier versions of IQ tests with **deviation IQ scores**, which are based on the normal curve distribution (Eysenck, 1994a): IQ is assumed to be normally distributed with a mean IQ of 100 and a typical standard deviation of about 15 (the standard deviation can vary according to the particular test). An IQ of 130, for example, would be two standard deviations above the mean, whereas an IQ of 70 would be two standard deviations below the mean, and in each case the person's score is being compared to the population's average score. **Simulate** on **MyPsychLab**

With respect to validity and reliability, the professor's test fares poorly. If the results of the professor's test were compared with other established intelligence tests, there would probably be no relationship at all. Golf scores have nothing to do with intelligence, so the test is not a valid, or true, measure of intelligence.

On the other hand, his test might work well for some people and poorly for others on the question of reliability. Some people who are good and regular golfers tend to score about the same for each game that they play, so for them, the golf score IQ

deviation IQ scores a type of intelligence measure that assumes that IQ is normally distributed around a mean of 100 with a standard deviation of about 15.

Simulate using the normal curve on **MyPsychLab**

FIGURE 11.7 The Normal Curve
The percentages under each section of the normal curve represent the percentage of scores falling within that section for each standard deviation (SD) from the mean. Scores on intelligence tests are typically represented by the normal curve. The dotted vertical lines each represent one standard deviation from the mean, which is always set at 100. For example, an IQ of 115 on the Wechsler represents one standard deviation above the mean, and the area under the curve indicates that 34.13 percent of the population falls between 100 and 115 on this test. LINK to Appendix A: Statistics in Psychology. Note: The figure shows the mean and standard deviation for the Stanford-Binet Fourth Edition (Stanford-Binet 4). The Stanford-Binet Fifth Edition was published in 2003 and now has a mean of 100 and a standard deviation of 15 for composite scores.

Standard Deviations	-4	-3	-2	-1	0	1	2	3	4
Wechsler IQ	40	55	70	85	100	115	130	145	160
Stanford-Binet 4 IQ	36	52	68	84	100	116	132	148	164
Cumulative %	0.003	0.135	2.275	15.856	50.00	84.134	97.725	99.865	99.997

would be fairly reliable. But others, especially those who do not play golf or play infrequently, would have widely varying scores from game to game. For those people, the test would be very unreliable, and if a test is unreliable for some, it's not a good test.

A test can fail in validity but still be reliable. If for some reason Professor Stumpwater chose to use height as a measure of intelligence, an adult's score on Stumpwater's "test" would always be the same, as height does not change by very much after the late teens. But the opposite is not true. If a test is unreliable, how can it accurately measure what it is supposed to measure? For example, adult intelligence remains fairly constant. If a test meant to measure that intelligence gives different scores at different times, it's obviously not a valid measure of intelligence.

> Just because an IQ test gives the same score every time a person takes it doesn't mean that the score is actually measuring real intelligence, right?

That's right—think about the definition of intelligence for a moment: the ability to learn from one's experiences, acquire knowledge, and use resources effectively in adapting to new situations or solving problems. How can anyone define what "effective use of resources" might be? Does everyone have access to the same resources? Is everyone's "world" necessarily perceived as being the same? Intelligence tests are useful measuring devices but should not necessarily be assumed to be measures of all types of intelligent behavior, or even good measures for all groups of people, as the next section discusses.

IQ TESTS AND CULTURAL BIAS The problem with trying to measure intelligence with a test that is based on an understanding of the world and its resources is that not everyone comes from the same "world." People raised in a different culture, or even a different economic situation, from the one in which the designer of an IQ test is raised are not likely to perform well on such a test—not to mention the difficulties of taking a test that is written in an unfamiliar language or dialect. In the early days of immigration, people from non-English-speaking countries would score very poorly on intelligence tests; in some cases they were denied entry to the United States on the basis of such tests (Allen, 2006).

It is very difficult to design an intelligence test that is completely free of *cultural bias*, a term referring to the tendency of IQ tests to reflect, in language, dialect, and content, the culture of the person or persons who designed the test. A person who comes from the same culture (or even the same socioeconomic background) as the test designer may have an unfair advantage over a person who is from a different cultural or socioeconomic background (Helms, 1992). If people raised in an Asian culture are given a test designed within a traditional Western culture, many items on the test might make no sense to them. For example, one kind of question might be: Which one of the five is least like the other four?

DOG—CAR—CAT—BIRD—FISH

The answer is supposed to be "car," which is the only one of the five that is not alive. But a Japanese child, living in a culture that relies on the sea for so much of its food and culture, might choose "fish," because none of the others are found in the ocean. That child's test score would be lower but not because the child is not intelligent.

Attempts have been made to create intelligence tests that are as free of cultural influences as is humanly possible. Many test designers have come to the conclusion that it may be impossible to create a test that is completely free of cultural bias (Carpenter et al., 1990). Instead, they are striving to create tests that are at least *culturally fair*. These tests use questions that do not create a disadvantage for people whose culture differs from that of the majority. Many items on a "culture fair" test require the use of nonverbal abilities, such as rotating objects, rather than items about verbal knowledge that might be culturally specific.

Just because an IQ test gives the same score every time a person takes it doesn't mean that the score is actually measuring real intelligence, right?

How might these two women, apparently from different cultures, come to an agreement on what best defines intelligence?

If intelligence tests are so flawed, why do people still use them? ●—————

The one thing that IQ tests do well is predict academic success for those who score at the higher and lower ends of the normal curve. (For those who score in the average range of IQ, the predictive value is less clear.) The kinds of tests students are given in school are often similar to intelligence tests, and so people who do well on IQ tests typically do well on other kinds of academically oriented tests as well, such as the Scholastic Assessment Test (SAT), the American College Test (ACT), the Graduate Record Exam (GRE), and actual college examinations. These achievement tests are very similar to IQ tests but are administered to groups of people rather than to individuals. 📖●┤Read on MyPsychLab

> If intelligence tests are so flawed, why do people still use them?

📖●┤Read and learn more about intelligence tests and testing on **MyPsychLab**

practice quiz   How much do you remember?

11.9 **11.10**

Pick the best answer.

1. According to Spearman, a traditional IQ test would most likely measure _____.
   a. practical intelligence.
   b. specific intelligence.
   c. general intelligence.
   d. emotional intelligence.

2. Using the Stanford-Binet IQ formula, what IQ would a person have whose mental age is 10 and whose chronological age is 15?
   a. 150
   b. 1.50
   c. 0.67
   d. 67

3. Lia is 10 years old. The intelligence test that would most likely be used to determine her IQ is the _____.
   a. WAIS-IV.
   b. WISC-IV.
   c. WPPSI-III.
   d. Dove Test.

4. Professor Beckett designed an IQ test. To standardize this test, the professor should be careful to do which of the following?

   a. Use only a small sample to prevent possible cheating on the test.
   b. Select the people in the sample from the population of people for whom the test is designed.
   c. Select only university professors to take the test so that they can critique the questions on the test.
   d. Test each member of the sample under different conditions.

5. _____ would be the problem in a test that provides a consistent score for some people each time it is administered but yields different scores for other people.
   a. Reliability
   b. Validity
   c. Standardization
   d. Normalization

Brainstorming: How do you personally define IQ? Are there various components or aspects? Why or why not?

ANSWERS ON PAGE AK–2.

Individual Differences in Intelligence: Intellectual Disability and Giftedness

Another use of IQ tests is to identify people who differ from those of average intelligence by a great degree. Although one such group is composed of those who are sometimes called "geniuses" (who fall at the extreme high end of the normal curve for intelligence), the other group is made up of people who, for various reasons, are considered intellectually delayed and whose IQ scores fall well below the mean on the normal curve.

INTELLECTUAL DISABILITY

11.11 What is intellectual disability, and what are its causes?

Intellectual disability (formerly *mental retardation*) is defined in several ways. First, the person's IQ score must fall below 70, or two standard deviations below the mean on the normal curve. Second, the person's *adaptive behavior* (skills that allow people to live independently, such as being able to work at a job, the ability to communicate well with others, and grooming skills such as being able to get dressed, eat, and bathe with little or no help) is severely below a level appropriate for the person's age. Finally, these limitations must be present before the age of 18 years. Intellectual disability occurs in about 3 percent of the population (American Psychiatric Association, 2000). Although the older term *mental retardation* is still sometimes used to refer to the condition of intellectual disability, individuals with this condition may more commonly be referred to as *developmentally delayed*, meaning that their behavioral and cognitive

intellectual disability condition in which a person's behavioral and cognitive skills exist at an earlier developmental stage than the skills of others who are the same chronological age; may also be referred to as developmentally delayed. This condition was formerly known as mental retardation.

So how would a professional go about deciding whether or not a child is developmentally delayed? Is the IQ test the primary method?

skills exist at an earlier developmental stage than the skills of others who are the same chronological age (Smith & Mitchell, 2001).

So how would a professional go about deciding whether or not a child has an intellectual disability? Is the IQ test the primary method?

A diagnosis of intellectual disability is based not only on IQ tests scores but also on the strengths and weaknesses of the person in adaptive functioning, and the onset of impairments in intellectual functioning and adaptive behavior is before 18 years of age (American Psychiatric Association, 2000). Recent recommendations from the American Association on Intellectual and Developmental Disabilities (AAIDD) also require deficits in more than one area, that is, not only in intellectual functioning but also in adaptive behavior that may be conceptual, social, or practical in nature (AAIDD, 2009; Schalock et al., 2010).

CLASSIFICATIONS Intellectual disability can range from mild to profound. Even with their flaws, IQ test scores are still used to classify the various levels of disability. In its current form, the *Diagnostic and Statistical Manual of Mental Disorders, Fourth Edition, Text Revision (DSM-IV-TR)* ⓛⓘⓝⓚ to Chapter Twelve: Psychological Disorders p. 437, provides diagnostic and descriptive information across four categories of mental retardation. (Note—the *DSM-IV-TR* was published before the term "intellectual disability" became prevalent and still uses the term "mental retardation"). Individuals with *Mild Mental Retardation* make up the vast majority of those with developmental delay (85%), typically have IQ scores between 55–70, can reach a sixth-grade skill level, and are capable of living independently with sufficient skills training and support. In comparison, *Moderate Mental Retardation* corresponds to IQ scores between 40–55 and 10% of the intellectually disabled population. These individuals can reach a second-grade skill level and may work and live in supervised and sheltered environments (American Psychiatric Association, 2000).

The two greatest levels of intellectual and adaptive impairment are represented in the *DSM-IV-TR* by classifications of Severe and Profound. *Severe Mental Retardation* is diagnosed in about 3–4% of the intellectually disabled population, associated with IQ scores of 25–40, and individuals at this level of impairment may learn basic self-care and communication skills but require constant supervision. The greatest level of impairment has a prevalence rate of 1–2% in those with intellectual disability. Individuals with *Profound Mental Retardation* have IQ scores below 25, have a very limited ability to demonstrate learning but may be able to perform very simple tasks, and most often require constant care, supervision, and someone to provide for their every need (American Psychiatric Association, 2000).

Causes What causes intellectual disability? It's not just environmental factors, like lead or mercury poisoning. These causes, along with the others listed earlier as environmental considerations of the American Association on Intellectual and Developmental Disabilities guidelines, are said to produce *familial retardation* (Schroeder, 2000), a delay related to living in poverty conditions and one that usually produces relatively mild retardation.

The three most common biological causes of intellectual disability are Down syndrome, ⓛⓘⓝⓚ to Chapter Seven: Development Across the Life Span, p. 232, fetal alcohol syndrome, and fragile X syndrome. *Fetal alcohol syndrome* is a condition that results from exposing a developing embryo to alcohol, and intelligence levels can range from below average to levels associated with intellectual disability (Olson & Burgess, 1997). In *fragile X syndrome*, a male has a defect in a gene on the X chromosome of the 23rd pair, leading

Down syndrome is caused by the presence of an extra chromosome in what would normally be only a pair of the number 21 chromosomes. The extra genetic material causes intellectual disability of varying degrees and the distinct facial features seen in these four young adults, all of whom have Down syndrome. Many people with this disorder lead productive and well-adjusted lives, some with supervision and some entirely on their own.

to a deficiency in a protein needed for brain development. Depending on the severity of the damage to this gene, symptoms of fragile X syndrome can range from mild to severe or profound intellectual disability (Dykens et al., 1994; Valverde et al., 2007).

There are many other causes of intellectual disability (Murphy et al., 1998). Lack of oxygen at birth, damage to the fetus in the womb from diseases, infections, or drug use by the mother, and even diseases and accidents during childhood can lead to intellectual disability.

One thing should always be remembered: Intellectual disability affects a person's *intellectual* capabilities and adaptive behaviors. Individuals with intellectual disability are just as responsive to love and affection as anyone else and need to be loved and to have friends just as all people do. Intelligence is only one characteristic; warmth, friendliness, caring, and compassion also count for a great deal and should not be underrated.

gifted the 2 percent of the population falling on the upper end of the normal curve and typically possessing an IQ of 130 or above.

GIFTEDNESS

11.12 **What defines giftedness, and does being intellectually gifted guarantee success in life?**

At the other end of the intelligence scale* are those who fall on the upper end of the normal curve (see Figure 11.7, p. 413) above an IQ of 130 (about 2 percent of the population). The term applied to these individuals is **gifted**, and if their IQ falls above 140 to 145 (less than half of 1 percent of the population), they are often referred to as highly advanced or *genius*.

I've heard that geniuses are sometimes a little "nutty" and odd. Are geniuses, especially the really high IQ ones, "not playing with a full deck," as the saying goes?

People have long held many false beliefs about people who are very, very intelligent. One common phrase around the turn of the twentieth century was "early ripe, early rot," which meant that people expected young geniuses to lose their genius early in life (Shurkin, 1992). Other beliefs were that gifted people are weird and socially awkward, physically weak, and more likely to suffer from mental illnesses. From these beliefs comes the "mad scientist" of the cinema (think "Dr. Evil" of *Austin Powers*) and the "evil geniuses" of literature—Dr. Frankenstein, Dr. Jekyll, and Superman's archenemy,** Lex Luthor, to name a few.

These beliefs were shattered by a groundbreaking study that was initiated in 1921 by Lewis M. Terman, the same individual responsible for the development of the Stanford-Binet (page 410). Terman (1925) selected 1,528 children to participate in a longitudinal study. **LINK** to Chapter Seven: Development Across the Life Span, p. 230. These children, 857 boys and 671 girls, had IQs (as measured by the Stanford-Binet) ranging from 130 to 200. The early findings of this major study (Terman & Oden, 1947) demonstrated that the gifted were socially well adjusted and often skilled leaders. They were also above average in height, weight, and physical attractiveness, putting an end to the myth of the weakling genius. Terman was able to demonstrate not only that his gifted children were *not* more susceptible to mental illness than the general population, but also that they were actually more resistant to mental illnesses than those of average intelligence. Only those with the highest IQs (180 and above) were found to have some social and behavioral adjustment problems *as children* (Janos, 1987).

Terman's "Termites," as they came to be called, were also typically successful as adults. They earned more academic degrees and had higher occupational and financial success than their average peers (at least, the men in the study had occupational

> I've heard that geniuses are sometimes a little "nutty" and odd. Are geniuses, especially the really high IQ ones, "not playing with a full deck," as the saying goes?

Actor Colin Clive portrayed the character of Dr. Frankenstein in one of the earliest film adaptations of Mary Shelley's original novel, *Frankenstein*. In this 1931 version, the prototypical mad scientist and his odd assistant Fritz (played by veteran character actor Dwight Frye) prepare to bring their monster to life. This is only one example of how the myth of the "mad genius" became part of the popular culture.

---

*Scale: a graded series of tests or performances used in rating individual intelligence or achievement.
**Archenemy: a main enemy; the most important enemy.

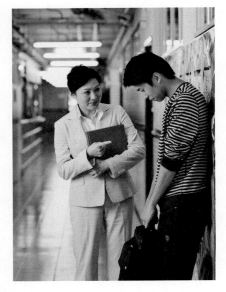

This scene is no doubt played out in many schools, across many cultures. While this young man might need encouragement for his academic life, how he does in school may not be due as much to his scholarly success as to his emotional intelligence—how aware he is and how well he manages his own emotions, motivation, empathy, and social skills. In some theorists' views, academic success alone is not enough—you must also be able to relate well to others in an often demanding social world.

> That all sounds very nice, but how can anything like this be measured?

emotional intelligence the awareness of and ability to manage one's own emotions as well as the ability to be self-motivated, able to feel what others feel, and socially skilled.

success—women at this time did not typically have careers outside the home). Researchers Zuo and Cramond (2001) examined some of Terman's gifted people to see if their identity formation as adolescents was related to later occupational success. ⓁⒾⓃⓀ to Chapter Seven: Development Across the Life Span, pp. 256–257. They found that most of the more successful "Termites" had in fact successfully achieved a consistent sense of self, whereas those who were less successful had not done so.

A book by Joan Freeman called *Gifted Children Grown Up* (Freeman, 2001) describes the results of a similar longitudinal study of 210 gifted and nongifted children in Great Britain. One of the more interesting findings from this study is that gifted children who are "pushed" to achieve at younger and younger ages, sitting for exams long before their peers would do so, often grow up to be disappointed, somewhat unhappy adults. Freeman points to differing life conditions for the gifted as a major factor in their success, adjustment, and well-being: Some lived in poverty and some in wealth, for example. Yet another longitudinal study (Torrance, 1993) found that in both gifted students and gifted adults there is more to success in life than intelligence and high academic achievement. In that study, liking one's work and having a sense of purpose in life, a high energy level, and persistence were also very important factors. If the picture of the genius as mentally unstable is a myth, so, too, is the belief that being gifted will always lead to success, as even Terman found in his original study.

EMOTIONAL INTELLIGENCE What about people who have a lot of "book smarts" but not much common sense? There are some people like that, who never seem to get ahead in life, in spite of having all that so-called intelligence. It is true that not everyone who is intellectually able is going to be a success in life (Mehrabian, 2000). Sometimes the people who are most successful are those who didn't do all that well in the regular academic setting.

One of the early explanations for why some people who do poorly in school succeed in life and why some who do well in school don't do so well in the "real" world was that success relies on a certain degree of **emotional intelligence**, the awareness of and ability to manage one's own emotions as well as the ability to be self-motivated, to feel what others feel, and to be socially skilled (Persaud, 2001).

The concept of emotional intelligence was first introduced by Salovey and Mayer (1990) and later expanded upon by Goleman (1995). Goleman proposed that emotional intelligence is a more powerful influence on success in life than more traditional views of intelligence. One who is emotionally intelligent possesses self-control of emotions such as anger, impulsiveness, and anxiety. Empathy, the ability to understand what others feel, is also a component, as are an awareness of one's own emotions, sensitivity, persistence even in the face of frustrations, and the ability to motivate oneself (Salovey & Mayer, 1990).

● That all sounds very nice, but how can anything like this be measured?

Is there research to support this idea? In one study, researchers asked 321 participants to read passages written by nonparticipants and try to guess what the nonparticipants were feeling while they were writing (Mayer & Geher, 1996). The assumption was that people who were good at connecting thoughts to feelings would also have a high degree of empathy and emotional intelligence. The participants who more correctly judged the writers' emotional experiences (assessed by both how well each participant's emotional judgments agreed with a group consensus and the nonparticipant's actual report of feelings) also scored higher on the empathy measure and lower on the defensiveness measure. These same participants also had higher SAT scores (self-reported), leading Mayer and colleagues to conclude not only that emotional intelligence is a valid and measurable concept but also that general intelligence and emotional intelligence may be related: Those who are high in emotional intelligence are also smarter in the traditional sense (Mayer et al., 2000).

Although his own work and that of his colleagues provide empirical support for the concept of emotional intelligence, Mayer (1999) has criticized the presentation of emotional intelligence in popular magazines and best-selling (but nonscientific) books. In an online article for the American Psychological Association, he states: "the popular literature's implication—that highly emotionally intelligent people possess an unqualified advantage in life—appears overly enthusiastic at present and unsubstantiated by reasonable scientific standards."

behavioral genetics field of study devoted to discovering the genetic bases for personality characteristics.

The Biology of Personality and Intelligence: Behavioral Genetics

What about genetics? How much of our personality and intelligence is inherited?

> What about genetics? How much of our personality and intelligence is inherited?

The field of **behavioral genetics** is devoted to the study of just how much of an individual's personality, intelligence, and other behavioral characteristics is due to inherited traits. Animal breeders have known for a long time that selective breeding of certain animals with specific desirable traits can produce changes not only in size, fur color, and other physical characteristics but also in the temperament of the animals (Isabel, 2003; Trut, 1999). As stated earlier in this chapter, temperament consists of the characteristics with which each person is born and is, therefore, determined by biology to a great degree. If the temperaments of animals can be influenced by manipulating patterns of genetic inheritance, then it is only one small step to assume that at least those personality characteristics related to temperament in human beings may also be influenced by heredity.

Animal breeders have an advantage over those who are studying the influence of genes in human behavior. Those who breed animals can control the mating of certain animals and the conditions under which those animals are raised. Human research cannot ethically or practically develop that degree of control and so must fall back on the accidental "experiments" of nature and opportunity, studies of twins and adopted persons.

11.13 What part do biology, heredity, environment, and culture play in personality and intelligence?

Twin Studies

The difference between monozygotic (identical) and dizygotic (fraternal) twins was discussed in Chapter Seven. L I N K to Chapter Seven: Development Across the Life Span, p. 234. As discussed previously, identical twins share 100 percent of their genetic material, having come from one fertilized egg originally, whereas fraternal twins share only about 50 percent of their genetic material as any other pair of siblings would. By comparing identical twins to fraternal twins, especially when twins can be found who were not raised in the same environment (like Oskar and Jack or the "Jim" twins in the opening story), researchers can begin to find evidence of possible genetic influences on various traits, including personality. (See Figure 11.8.)

The results of the Minnesota twin study have revealed that identical twins are more similar than fraternal twins or unrelated people in intelligence, leadership abilities, the tendency to follow rules, and the tendency to uphold traditional cultural expectations (Bouchard, 1997; Finkel & McGue, 1997); nurturance,* empathy,** and

James Arthur Springer and James Edward Lewis, otherwise known as the "Jim" twins and as referenced in the chapter opener. Although separated shortly after birth and reunited at age 39, they exhibited many similarities in personality and personal habits. Although genetics may explain some of these similarities, what other factors might also be at work?

---

*Nurturance: affectionate care and attention.
**Empathy: the ability to understand the feelings of others.

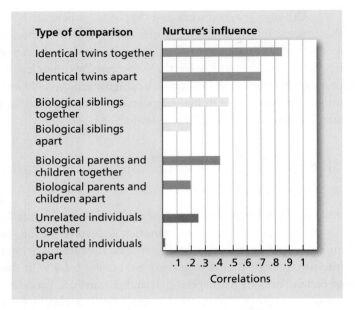

FIGURE 11.8 Correlations Between IQ Scores of Persons with Various Relationships
In the graph on the left, the degree of genetic relatedness seems to determine the agreement (correlation) between IQ scores of the various comparisons. For example, identical twins, who share 100 percent of their genes, are more similar in IQ than fraternal twins, who share only about 50 percent of their genes, even when raised in the same environment. In the graph on the right, identical twins are still more similar to each other in IQ than are other types of comparisons, but being raised in the same environment increases the similarity considerably.

assertiveness (Neale et al., 1986); and aggressiveness (Miles & Carey, 1997). This similarity holds even if the twins are raised in separate environments.

By comparing the IQs of these two types of twins reared together (similar environments) and reared apart (different environments), as well as persons of other degrees of relatedness, researchers can also get a general, if not exact, idea of how much influence heredity has over the trait of intelligence (see Figure 11.8). As can be easily seen from the chart, the greater the degree of genetic relatedness, the stronger the correlation is between the IQ scores of those persons. The fact that genetically identical twins show a correlation of 0.86 means that the environment must play a part in determining some aspects of intelligence as measured by IQ tests. If heredity alone were responsible, the correlation between genetically identical twins should be 1.00. At this time, researchers have determined that the estimated *heritability* (proportion of change in IQ within a population that is caused by hereditary factors) for intelligence is about 0.50 or 50 percent (Plomin & DeFries, 1998; Plomin & Spinath, 2004). Furthermore, the impact of genetic factors increases with increasing age, but the set of genes or genetic factors remains the same. The effects of the same set of genes become larger with increasing age (Posthuma et al., 2009).

● Wait a minute—if identical twins have a correlation of 0.86, wouldn't that mean that intelligence is 86 percent inherited?

Although the correlation between identical twins is higher than the estimated heritability of 0.50, that similarity is not entirely due to the twin's genetic similarity. Twins who are raised in the same household obviously share very similar environments as well. Even twins who are reared apart are usually placed in homes that are similar in socioeconomic and ethnic background—more similar than one might think. So when twins who are genetically similar are raised in similar environments, their IQ scores are also going to be similar. However, similar environmental influences become less important over time (where genetic influences increase over time), accounting for only

> Wait a minute—if identical twins have a correlation of 0.86, wouldn't that mean that intelligence is 86 percent inherited?

about 20 percent of the variance in intelligence by age 11 or 12 (Posthuma et al., 2009). In turn, environmental influences tend not to be a factor by adolescence, and with the increasing impact of genetic factors, it has been suggested that the heritability of intelligence might be as high as .91 or 91 percent by the age of 65 (Posthuma et al., 2009).

One of the things that people need to understand about heritability is that estimates of heritability apply only to changes in IQ within a *group* of people, *not to the individual people themselves*. Each individual is far too different in experiences, education, and other nongenetic factors to predict exactly how a particular set of genes will interact with those factors in that one person. Only differences among people *in general* can be investigated for the influence of genes (Dickens & Flynn, 2001). Genes always interact with environmental factors, and in some cases extreme environments can modify even very heritable traits, as would happen in the case of a severely malnourished child's growth pattern.

classic studies **in psychology**

Geert Hofstede's Four Dimensions of Cultural Personality

In the early 1980s, organizational management specialist Geert Hofstede conducted a massive study into the work-related values of employees of IBM, a multinational corporation (Hofstede, 1980; Hofstede et al., 2002). The study surveyed workers in 64 countries across the world. Hofstede analyzed the data collected from this survey and found four basic dimensions of personality along which cultures differed.

1. **Individualism/collectivism:** *Individualistic cultures* tend to have loose ties between individuals, with people tending to look after themselves and their immediate families only. Members of such cultures have friends based on shared activities and interests and may belong to many different loosely organized social groups. Autonomy,* change, youth, security of the individual, and equality are all highly valued. In contrast, in a *collectivistic culture*, people are from birth deeply tied into very strong in-groups, typically extended families that include grandparents, aunts and uncles, and cousins. Loyalty to the family is highly stressed, and care of the family is placed before care of the individual. Group membership is limited to only a few permanent groups that have tremendous influence over the individual. The values of this kind of culture are duty, order, tradition, respect for the elderly, group security, and respect for the group status and hierarchy.** The United States and Great Britain are examples of individualistic cultures, whereas Japan, China, Korea, Mexico, and Central America are much more collectivistic.

2. **Power distance:** This dimension refers to the degree to which the less powerful members of a culture accept and even expect that the power within the culture is held in the hands of a select few rather than being more evenly distributed. Countries such as the Philippines, Mexico, many Arab countries, and India were found to be high in such expectations, whereas countries such as Austria, Sweden, Australia, Great Britain, and the United States were low in power distance.

3. **Masculinity/femininity:** Referring to how a culture distributes the roles played by men and women within a culture, this dimension varies more for the men within a culture than for the women. "Masculine" cultures are assertive and competitive, although more so for men than for women, and "feminine" cultures are more modest and caring. Both men and women in "feminine" countries have similar, caring values, but in "masculine" countries, the women are not quite as

"I told my parents that if grades were so important they should have paid for a smarter egg donor."

---

*Autonomy: the quality of being self-directed or self-controlled.
**Hierarchy: in this sense, a body of persons in authority over others.

assertive and competitive as the men, leading to a greater difference between the sexes in masculine countries. Japan, Austria, Venezuela, Italy, Switzerland, Mexico, Ireland, Jamaica, the United States, Great Britain, and Germany were found to be masculine countries, whereas Sweden, Norway, the Netherlands, Denmark, Costa Rica, Yugoslavia, Finland, Chile, Portugal, Thailand, and Guatemala were ranked as more feminine.

4. **Uncertainty avoidance:** Some cultures are more tolerant of uncertainty, ambiguity,* and unstructured situations. Cultures that do not tolerate such uncertainty and lack of structure tend to have strict rules and laws with lots of security and safety measures and tend toward a philosophical/religious belief of One Truth (and "we have it!"). Cultures that are more accepting of uncertainty are more tolerant of different opinions and have fewer rules. They tend to allow many different religious beliefs to exist side by side and are less anxious and emotional than people in uncertainty-avoiding countries. Uncertainty-avoiding countries include Greece, Portugal, Guatemala, Uruguay, Belgium, El Salvador, Japan, Yugoslavia, and Peru, whereas those that are more tolerant of uncertainty include Singapore, Jamaica, Denmark, Sweden, Hong Kong, Ireland, Great Britain, Malaysia, India, Philippines, the United States, Canada, and Indonesia.

Note that the Big Five personality dimensions of Costa and McCrae (2000) are not necessarily in competition with Hofstede's dimensions. Hofstede's dimensions are *cultural* personality traits, whereas those of the Big Five refer to individuals.

QUESTIONS FOR FURTHER DISCUSSION

1. Was your own culture listed for any of these dimensions? If so, do you agree with the personality dimension assigned to your culture?

2. If your culture was not listed for a personality dimension, where do you think your culture would fall on that dimension?

---

*Ambiguity: the quality of being uncertain and indistinct.

practice quiz   How much do you remember?

11.11 **11.12** **11.13**

Pick the best answer.

1. Jarod is 35 years old, but his cognitive abilities and adaptive living skills never progressed beyond the level of a second-grade child. Jarod would be classified as _____ intellectually disabled.
   a. mildly
   b. moderately
   c. severely
   d. profoundly

2. A male with developmental delay caused by a protein deficiency stemming from chromosome damage probably suffers from _____.
   a. Down syndrome.
   b. fetal alcohol syndrome.
   c. hydrocephaly.
   d. fragile X syndrome.

3. Elizabeth was tested while in grade school, and was found to have an IQ of 134. Elizabeth's intelligence level can be labeled as _____.
   a. average.
   b. somewhat above normal.
   c. gifted.
   d. genius.

4. Which of the following statements about the successful "Termites" in the Terman and Oden (1959) study is NOT true?
   a. The successful men earned more money.
   b. The successful men were less likely to have consistent senses of identity.
   c. The unsuccessful men were less healthy.
   d. The unsuccessful men held jobs of lower prestige.

5. Twin studies, in which identical twins reared together or reared apart, are compared to each other and to fraternal twins reared under similar conditions are a part of the field of _____.
   a. adoption studies.
   b. neurogenetics.
   c. learning theory.
   d. behavioral genetics.

6. Which of the following countries would be most likely to have an individualistic trait, according to Hofstede?
   a. Japan
   b. Vietnam
   c. England
   d. Brazil

applying psychology to everyday life

The Biological Basis of the Big Five

In 1796, Dr. Franz Joseph Gall, a German physician, developed a theory of personality traits based on the shape of a person's skull. This theory became very popular in the nineteenth century and was known as *phrenology*. Gall believed that certain areas of the brain were responsible for certain aspects of personality, and that the skull itself would bulge out according to which of these traits were dominant (Finger, 1994; Simpson, 2005). As psychology became a scientific area of its own, nonscience-based ideas such as phrenology were soon relegated to the realm of pseudoscience.

How odd, then, that a recent study by Dr. Colin DeYoung and colleagues (DeYoung et al., 2010) seems to suggest that there are indeed certain areas of the brain associated with certain personality traits. Specifically, DeYoung and colleagues believe they have evidence for the biological seat of four of the Big Five: extraversion, neuroticism, agreeableness, and conscientiousness.

In their study, 116 volunteers answered a questionnaire about their Big Five personality traits. The participants were then subjected to a structural magnetic resonance imaging technique for identifying the volume of specific areas of the brain. One participant was found to be near the group average for personality traits; that individual's brain image was used as a reference image to which the other participants' scans were compared.

The trait of *extraversion* was associated with a higher volume in the medial orbitofrontal cortex (underside of frontal lobe, directly above the eyes). This area of the brain is associated with recognizing the value of rewarding information. *Neuroticism* was associated with lower brain volume in several areas responding to threat, punishment, and negative emotions. Reduced volumes were found in the dorsomedial prefrontal cortex (toward the top and middle of the prefrontal cortex) and in the left posterior hippocampus. Neuroticism was also associated with higher brain volume in the middle cingulate cortex (cortical component of limbic system), associated with error detection and response to pain. Areas of the brain associated with the intentions of actions and mental states of others were correlated to *agreeableness*, with the area of the posterior cingulate cortex showing a greater volume in individuals high in that trait and a lesser volume in the left superior temporal sulcus. *Conscientiousness* seemed to be associated with the left lateral prefrontal cortex, an area located on the side of the frontal lobes involved in planning, working memory, and voluntary control of behavior. (The researchers did look at areas that might be associated with the fifth of the Big Five traits, *openness*, but failed to find any significant differences.)

This study, and the others like it that are sure to follow, is part of the growing area of personality neuroscience and an important step in linking personality to the physical structure and functioning of the brain. No skull bulges needed!

QUESTIONS FOR FURTHER DISCUSSION

1. We use personality assessments to make predictions about employment, marriage, and stability among others. What might it mean for the future if a brain scan becomes part of personality assessment?

2. If personality traits are so closely linked with brain structure, what does that say about the plasticity of personality? Are people able to change their traits? Their behavior?

chapter summary

Theories of Personality and Intelligence

11.1 What is personality, and how do the various perspectives in psychology view personality?

- Personality is the unique way individuals think, feel, and act. It is different from character and temperament but includes those aspects.
- The four traditional perspectives in the study of personality are the psychodynamic, behavioristic (including social cognitive theory), humanistic, and trait perspectives.

The Man and the Couch: Sigmund Freud and the Psychodynamic Perspective

11.2 How did Freud's historical view of the mind and personality form a basis for psychodynamic theory?

- The three divisions of the mind are the conscious, preconscious, and unconscious. The unconscious can be revealed in dreams and Freudian slips of the tongue.
- The three parts of the personality are the id, ego, and superego.
- The id works on the pleasure principle while the ego works on the reality principle.
- The superego is the moral center of personality, containing the conscience, and is the source of moral anxiety.
- The conflicts between the demands of the id and the rules and restrictions of the superego lead to anxiety for the ego, which uses defense mechanisms to deal with that anxiety.
- The personality develops in a series of psychosexual stages: oral (id dominates), anal (ego develops), phallic (superego develops), latency (period of sexual repression), and genital (sexual feelings reawaken with appropriate targets).
- The Oedipus and Electra complexes (sexual "crushes" on the opposite-sex parent) create anxiety in the phallic stage, which is resolved through identification with the same-sex parent.
- Fixation occurs when conflicts are not fully resolved during a stage, resulting in adult personality characteristics reflecting childhood inadequacies.

11.3 How did Jung, Adler, Horney, and Erikson modify Freud's theory?

- The neo-Freudians changed the focus of psychoanalysis to fit their own interpretation of the personality, leading to the more modern version known as the psychodynamic perspective.
- Jung developed a theory of a collective unconscious.
- Adler proposed feelings of inferiority as the driving force behind personality.
- Horney developed a theory based on basic anxiety and rejected the concept of penis envy.
- Erikson developed a theory based on social rather than sexual relationships, covering the entire life span.

11.4 How does modern psychoanalytic theory differ from that of Freud?

- Current research has found support for the defense mechanisms and the concept of an unconscious mind that can influence conscious behavior, but other concepts cannot be scientifically researched.

The Behaviorist and Social Cognitive Views of Personality

11.5 How do behaviorists and social cognitive theorists explain personality?

- Behaviorists define personality as a set of learned responses or habits.
- The social cognitive view of personality includes the concept of reciprocal determinism, in which the environment, characteristics of the person, and the behavior itself all interact.
- Self-efficacy is a characteristic in which a person perceives a behavior as more or less effective based on previous experiences, the opinions of others, and perceived personal competencies.
- Locus of control is a determinant of personality in which one either assumes that one's actions directly affect events and reinforcement one experiences or that such events and reinforcements are the result of luck, fate, or powerful others.
- Personality, in the form of potential behavior patterns, is also determined by an interaction between one's expectancies for success and the perceived value of the potential reinforcement.
- Behaviorist personality theory has scientific support but is criticized as being too simplistic.

The Third Force: Humanism and Personality

11.6 How do humanists such as Carl Rogers explain personality?

- Humanism developed as a reaction against the negativity of psychoanalysis and the deterministic nature of behaviorism.
- Carl Rogers proposed that self-actualization depends on proper development of the self-concept.
- The self-concept includes the real self and the ideal self. When these two components do not match or agree, anxiety and disordered behavior result.
- Unconditional positive regard from important others in a person's life helps the formation of the self-concept and the congruity of the real and ideal selves, leading to a fully functioning person.
- Humanistic theory is not scientifically researched but has been effective in therapy situations.

Trait Theories: Who Are You?

11.7 What are the history and current views of the trait perspective?

- Trait theorists describe personality traits in order to predict behavior.
- Allport first developed a list of about 200 traits and believed that these traits were part of the nervous system.
- Cattell reduced the number of traits to between 16 and 23 with a computer method called factor analysis.
- Several researchers have arrived at five trait dimensions that have research support across cultures, called the Big Five or five-factor model. The five factors are openness, conscientiousness, extraversion, agreeableness, and neuroticism.
- Cross-cultural research has found support for the five-factor model of personality traits in a number of different cultures.
- Future research will explore the degree to which child-rearing practices and heredity may influence the five personality factors.
- Behavior genetics is a field of study of the relationship between heredity and personality.

Assessment of Personality

11.8 What are the advantages and disadvantages of the following measures of personality: interviews, projective tests, behavioral assessment, personality inventories, and online personality tests?

- Interviews are used primarily by psychoanalysts and humanists and can include structured or unstructured interviews.

- Disadvantages of interviews can include the halo effect and bias of interpretation on the part of the interviewer.

- Projective tests are based on the defense mechanism of projection and are used by psychoanalysts. Projective tests include the Rorschach inkblot test and the Thematic Apperception Test.

- Projective tests can be useful in finding starting points to open a dialogue between therapist and client but have been criticized for being low in reliability and validity.

- Behavioral assessments are primarily used by behaviorists and include direct observation of behavior, rating scales of specific behavior, and frequency counts of behavior.

- Behavioral assessments have the disadvantage of the observer effect, which causes an observed person's behavior to change, and observer bias on the part of the person doing the assessment.

- Personality inventories are typically developed by trait theorists and provide a detailed description of certain personality traits. They are objective tests rather than subjective.

- The NEO-PI is based on the five-factor model, whereas the Myers-Briggs Type Indicator is based on Jung's theory of personality types.

- The MMPI-2 is designed to detect abnormal personality.

- Personality inventories include validity scales to prevent cheating, but such measures are not perfect and cheating is sometimes possible.

Intelligence

11.9 How do psychologists define intelligence, and how do various theories of intelligence differ?

- Intelligence is the ability to understand the world, think rationally or logically, and use resources effectively when faced with challenges or problems.

- Spearman proposed general intelligence, or g factor, as the ability to reason and solve problems, whereas specific intelligence, or s factor, includes task-specific abilities in certain areas such as music, business, or art.

- Gardner proposed nine different types of intelligence, ranging from verbal, linguistic, and mathematical to interpersonal and intrapersonal intelligence.

- Stemberg proposed three types of intelligence: analytical, creative, and practical.

- Emotional intelligence is viewed as a powerful influence on success in life.

11.10 How is intelligence measured, and how are intelligence tests constructed?

- The Stanford-Binet Intelligence Test yields an IQ score that was once determined by dividing the mental age of the person by the chronological age and multiplying that quotient by 100 but now involves comparing a person's score to a standardized norm.

- The Wechsler Intelligence Tests yield four index scores derived from both verbal and nonverbal subtests and an overall score of intelligence.

- Standardization, validity, and reliability are all important factors in the construction of an intelligence test.

- Deviation IQs are based on the normal curve, defining different levels of intelligence based on the deviation of scores from a common mean.

- IQ tests are often criticized for being culturally biased.

11.11 What is intellectual disability and what are its causes?

- Intellectual disability or developmental delay is a condition in which IQ falls below 70 and adaptive behavior is severely deficient for a person of a particular chronological age.

- The four levels of delay are mild (55–70 IQ), moderate (40–55 IQ), severe (25–40 IQ), and profound (below 25 IQ).

- Causes of intellectual disability include deprived environments as well as chromosome and genetic disorders and dietary deficiencies.

11.12 What defines giftedness, and does being intellectually gifted guarantee success in life?

- Gifted persons are defined as those having IQ scores at the upper end of the normal curve (130 or above).

The Biology of Personality and Intelligence: Behavioral Genetics

11.13 What part do biology, heredity, environment, and culture play in personality and intelligence?

- Studies of twins and adopted children have found support for a genetic influence on many personality traits, including intelligence, leadership abilities, traditionalism, nurturance, empathy, assertiveness, neuroticism, and extraversion.

- Stronger correlations are found between IQ scores as genetic relatedness increases. Heritability of IQ is estimated at 0.50.

classic studies in psychology: Geert Hofstede's Four Dimensions of Cultural Personality

- Hofstede's cross-cultural management study revealed four basic dimensions of personality along which cultures may vary: individualism/collectivism, power distance, masculinity/femininity, and uncertainty avoidance.

applying psychology to everyday life: The Biological Basis of the Big Five

- Personality neuroscience is a growing area of research, and brain structure differences associated with some aspects of the Big Five dimensions of personality have been identified using structural MRI.

TEST yourself

✓•⌐**Study** and **Review** on **MyPsychLab**   Ready for your test? More quizzes and a customized plan. www.MyPsychLab

Pick the best answer.

1. Which of the following is the definition of personality?
   a. the characteristics with which each person is born
   b. the moral and ethical behavior of a person
   c. the unique way an individual thinks, feels, and acts
   d. changes in behavior according to experiences

2. Freud's emphasis on sex and sexual development was mostly due to _____.
   a. his own problems with sexuality.
   b. the culture within which he and his patients existed at the time.
   c. an increase in sexual deviancy across Europe in the nineteenth century.
   d. the influence of his colleagues.

3. Stephen wants a new MP3 player he saw in the local electronics store, but he doesn't have enough money to pay for it. Which structure of Stephen's personality would urge him to take the player while no one in the store was looking?
   a. id   c. superego
   b. ego   d. libido

4. Which structure of the personality, according to Freud, works on the reality principle?
   a. id   c. superego
   b. ego   d. libido

5. The _____ develops in the _____ stage as a result of identification.
   a. ego; oral   c. superego; phallic
   b. id; oral   d. superego; latency

6. Three-year-old Brandon has watched his father, a chef, when he prepares meals for the family. This year, Brandon has asked for a play kitchen for his birthday. Freud would say that Brandon is beginning the process of _____ as a way of resolving his Oedipal conflict.
   a. compensation   c. sublimation
   b. identification   d. denial

7. Tina's boss gives her a bad review, making Tina feel lousy. When she arrives at home, she yells at her husband and children. Tina is likely displaying _____.
   a. escape.
   b. withdrawal.
   c. displacement.
   d. projection.

8. According to Adler, children who compare themselves to older children and adults often tend to be _____.
   a. underachieving.
   b. non-competitive.
   c. more competent.
   d. filled with feelings of inferiority.

9. Research has begun to show some support for which of Freud's concepts?
   a. the existence of an id, ego, and superego
   b. the order of the psychosexual stages
   c. the concept of an unconscious mind
   d. the existence of the Oedipus complex

10. To explain a person's personality, behaviorists would look to _____.
    a. early childhood emotional traumas.
    b. the kind of love, warmth, and affection given to the person by his or her parents.
    c. the early experiences of rewards and punishments for certain behavior.
    d. the constellation of personality traits possessed by the person.

11. For Bandura, one of the most important person variables in determining personality is _____.
    a. self-efficacy.   c. reinforcement value.
    b. expectancy.   d. self-motivation.

12. Unlike the psychodynamic view, the social cognitive view of personality _____.
    a. tries to explain how people become the people they are.
    b. stresses the importance of early childhood in personality development.
    c. is fully able to explain all the complexities of human behavior.
    d. has been scientifically tested.

13. The striving for fulfillment of one's potential is called _____.
    a. self-concept.   c. self-actualization.
    b. self-efficacy.   d. locus of control.

14. According to Rogers, anxiety and neurotic behavior result from _____.
    a. unconscious conflicts and desires.
    b. a mismatch between the real self and ideal self.
    c. receiving too much unconditional positive regard from significant others.
    d. learned habits of behavior.

15. Which of the following viewpoints has different goals from the other three?
    a. psychoanalytic   c. humanism
    b. behaviorism   d. trait theory

16. How many source traits did Cattell use in developing his personality inventory?
    a. 5   c. 16
    b. 10   d. 23

17. The five-factor model of personality traits includes all but which of the following?
    a. openness   c. extraversion
    b. self-sufficiency   d. neuroticism

18. Dr. Jackson is constantly late for her classes and often shows up late for her office hours, leaving students waiting in the hallway outside her door for nearly an hour at times. Using the five-factor model, which dimension would show a very low score for Dr. Jackson?
    a. self-sufficiency   c. agreeableness
    b. openness   d. conscientiousness

19. The study of the inherited portions of personality is called _____.
    a. twin studies.   c. behavioral genetics.
    b. adoptive studies.   d. adoptive genetics.

20. According to Hofstede, cultures that have many strict rules and laws with lots of security and safety measures and that tend to hold only one philosophical or religious belief are high in _____.
    a. individualism.
    b. power distance.
    c. masculinity.
    d. uncertainty avoidance.

21. If a client is having trouble talking about what is bothering him, a psychoanalyst might turn to a(n) _____ to probe the client's unconscious conflicts.
    a. objective test
    b. projective test
    c. personality inventory
    d. observational study

22. The Rorschach test has people _____.
    a. tell stories about a picture with people in it.
    b. answer hundreds of questions about their feelings and thoughts.
    c. perform tasks while an observer watches through a one-way mirror.
    d. look at ambiguous visual stimuli and tell what they think they are.

23. Which type of assessment would have the least problem with reliability?
    a. subjective test
    b. projective test
    c. personality inventory
    d. observational study

24. Which of the following is not a type of behavioral assessment?
    a. direct observation
    b. Thematic Apperception Test
    c. rating scale
    d. frequency count

25. Which of the following is based on the five-factor model?
    a. NEO-PI
    b. MBTI
    c. MMPI-2
    d. 16PF

26. Which of the following is NOT part of the traditional definition of intelligence?
    a. ability to adapt
    b. ability to solve problems
    c. ability to be creative
    d. ability to use resources effectively

27. In Terman's study of gifted children, social and behavioral problems were found only in those _____.
    a. with IQs of 150 or higher.
    b. with IQs of 180 or higher.
    c. with IQs of 180 or higher in adulthood.
    d. with IQs of 180 or higher in childhood.

28. Goleman has proposed that _____ intelligence is a more powerful influence on success in life than other forms of intelligence.
    a. analytical
    b. creative
    c. practical
    d. emotional

29. Keneisha is only 11 years old, but she can answer questions that most 15-year-olds can answer. Fifteen is Keneisha's _____.
    a. chronological age.
    b. mental age.
    c. IQ.
    d. standard age.

30. Which of the following makes the Wechsler tests different from the Stanford-Binet?
    a. The Wechsler tests are administered to individuals.
    b. The Wechsler is designed only for children.
    c. The Stanford-Binet is designed only for adults.
    d. Different Wechsler tests are available for different age groups.

31. A test that gives similar scores for a person each time the person takes it is considered to be a _____ test.
    a. reliable
    b. valid
    c. standardized
    d. creative

32. When a test allows a person from one particular background to have an unfair advantage over persons from other backgrounds, it is called _____.
    a. culturally free.
    b. culturally fair.
    c. culturally biased.
    d. unreliable.

33. Marcos's mother drank heavily while pregnant with him, and he has been diagnosed with mild intellectual disability. Marcos most likely suffers from_____.
    a. Down syndrome.
    b. fetal alcohol syndrome.
    c. fragile X syndrome.
    d. cretinism.

34. The current estimate of heritability of intelligence is _____.
    a. 0.90.
    b. 0.86.
    c. 0.50.
    d. 0.34.

35. Personality neuroscience is an emerging field, offering evidence of a possible relationship between various aspects of personality with _____.
    a. brain structure and function.
    b. the structure and function of individual neurons.
    c. skull shape and size.
    d. neuroticism.

11 theories of personality and intelligence

11.1   p. 386

personality
unique way in which each individual thinks, acts, and feels throughout life

- psychodynamic
- behavioral and social cognitive views
- humanistic
- trait

Theories of Personality

perspectives/theories
different ways of viewing and explaining personality

psychodynamic perspective
basic aspects

- mind made up of different levels of awareness—conscious, preconscious, and unconscious (see Figure 11.1)
- personality stems from interplay and conflict between demands made by the id, restrictions set forth by the superego, and direction by the ego
- disordered behavior is product of constant conflict and anxiety; ego uses unconscious defense mechanisms as ways to manage anxiety/conflict among three parts of personality (see Table 11.1)

11.2   11.3   11.4   p. 386

psychosexual stages of personality development

- id exists at birth; ego and superego develop in childhood
- different erogenous zones are sources of conflict as individual ages; unresolved conflicts result in individuals getting stuck or fixated at that stage

(see Table 11.2)

a group of Freud's students and followers of the psychoanalytic perspective, called the neo-Freudians, modified his theory and altered the focus of psychoanalysis

- Jung
- Adler
- Horney
- Erikson

Psychodynamic Perspective

- modern psychodynamic theory maintains focus on unconscious mind, concept of defense mechanisms is still useful
- despite several criticisms, Freud's theory still important—first to suggest personality develops through stages, that we are not always consciously aware of reasons for behavior, and early life experiences influence who we are later in life

11.5   11.6   p. 396

behavioral and social cognitive

- for behaviorists, personality is set of learned responses and habits, gained through classical and operant conditioning
- in social cognitive view, both learning (individual and through imitation of models) and cognitive processes (such as anticipation, judgment, and memory) are important

Bandura: focused on self-efficacy and idea that personality is result of reciprocal determinism between environment, behavior, and individual's personal or cognitive factors

Rotter: focused on locus of control and how expectancy and reinforcement value influences someone's behavior/personality

Behavioral, Social Cognitive, and Humanistic Perspectives

humanistic
referred to as the third force in psychology (after psychoanalysis and behaviorism); based largely on work of Rogers and Maslow

Rogers: like Maslow, believed that humans have self-actualizing tendency

self-concept: image of oneself

self-actualization: achieving all of one's innate capacities and capabilities

when there is congruence between real and ideal selves, one is considered to be fully functioning and capable of reaching the goal of self-actualization

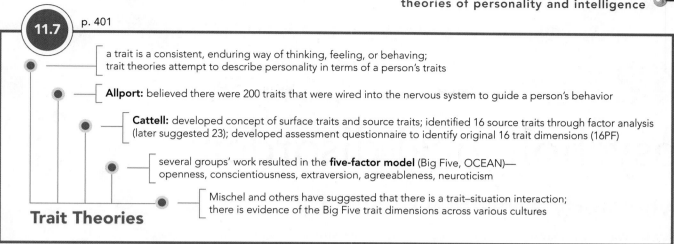

11.7 p. 401

- a trait is a consistent, enduring way of thinking, feeling, or behaving; trait theories attempt to describe personality in terms of a person's traits

- **Allport:** believed there were 200 traits that were wired into the nervous system to guide a person's behavior

- **Cattell:** developed concept of surface traits and source traits; identified 16 source traits through factor analysis (later suggested 23); developed assessment questionnaire to identify original 16 trait dimensions (16PF)

- several groups' work resulted in the **five-factor model** (Big Five, OCEAN)— openness, conscientiousness, extraversion, agreeableness, neuroticism

- Mischel and others have suggested that there is a trait–situation interaction; there is evidence of the Big Five trait dimensions across various cultures

Trait Theories

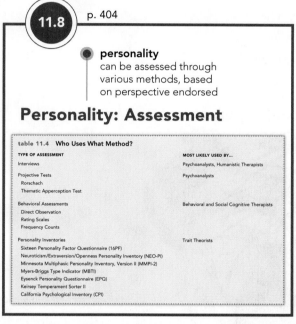

11.8 p. 404

- **personality** can be assessed through various methods, based on perspective endorsed

Personality: Assessment

table 11.4 Who Uses What Method?

TYPE OF ASSESSMENT	MOST LIKELY USED BY...
Interviews	Psychoanalysts, Humanistic Therapists
Projective Tests	Psychoanalysts
Rorschach	
Thematic Apperception Test	
Behavioral Assessments	Behavioral and Social Cognitive Therapists
Direct Observation	
Rating Scales	
Frequency Counts	
Personality Inventories	Trait Theorists
Sixteen Personality Factor Questionnaire (16PF)	
Neuroticism/Extraversion/Openness Personality Inventory (NEO-PI)	
Minnesota Multiphasic Personality Inventory, Version II (MMPI-2)	
Myers-Briggs Type Indicator (MBTI)	
Eysenck Personality Questionnaire (EPQ)	
Keirsey Temperament Sorter II	
California Psychological Inventory (CPI)	

11.9 **11.10** p. 409

- **theories**
  - **Spearman:** intelligence comprised of two primary abilities, general intelligence (g factor) and task-specific intelligence (s factor)
  - **Gardner's multiple intelligences:** overall intelligence comprises nine different types
  - **Sternberg's triarchic theory:** intelligence comprises three different aspects (analytical, creative, practical)

Intelligence
(the ability to learn from one's experiences, acquire knowledge, and use resources effectively

- **measuring intelligence**
  - **tests**
    - **Binet's Mental Ability Test**
    - **Stanford-Binet**
    - **Wechsler Tests**
    - first formal test created by Binet and Simon to help identify students who needed learning assistance
  - **test construction**
    - good tests are valid, reliable, and have standardized administration, scoring, and comparison norms

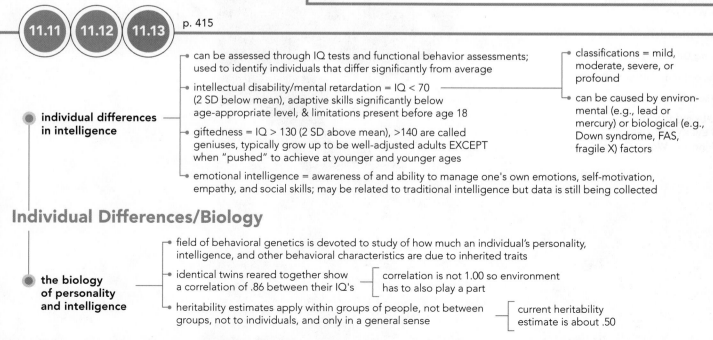

11.11 **11.12** **11.13** p. 415

- **individual differences in intelligence**
  - can be assessed through IQ tests and functional behavior assessments; used to identify individuals that differ significantly from average
  - intellectual disability/mental retardation = IQ < 70 (2 SD below mean), adaptive skills significantly below age-appropriate level, & limitations present before age 18
    - classifications = mild, moderate, severe, or profound
    - can be caused by environmental (e.g., lead or mercury) or biological (e.g., Down syndrome, FAS, fragile X) factors
  - giftedness = IQ > 130 (2 SD above mean), >140 are called geniuses, typically grow up to be well-adjusted adults EXCEPT when "pushed" to achieve at younger and younger ages
  - emotional intelligence = awareness of and ability to manage one's own emotions, self-motivation, empathy, and social skills; may be related to traditional intelligence but data is still being collected

Individual Differences/Biology

- **the biology of personality and intelligence**
  - field of behavioral genetics is devoted to study of how much an individual's personality, intelligence, and other behavioral characteristics are due to inherited traits
  - identical twins reared together show a correlation of .86 between their IQ's
    - correlation is not 1.00 so environment has to also play a part
  - heritability estimates apply within groups of people, not between groups, not to individuals, and only in a general sense
    - current heritability estimate is about .50

12
psychological disorders

why study abnormal behavior?

Because abnormal behavior is all around us, many questions arise:
How should one react? What should be done to help? What kind of person
develops a mental illness? Could this happen to someone close to you? The
key to answering these questions is to develop an understanding of just what
is meant by abnormal behavior and the different ways in which behavior can
depart from the "normal" path.

chapter outline

What Is Abnormality?

ISSUES IN PSYCHOLOGY:
Abnormality Versus Insanity

Models of Abnormality

Diagnostic and Statistical Manual
of Mental Disorders, Fourth Edition,
Text Revision (DSM-IV-TR)

Anxiety Disorders: What,
Me Worry?

Mood Disorders: The Effect of Affect

Eating Disorders

Schizophrenia: Altered Reality

Personality Disorders

APPLYING PSYCHOLOGY
TO EVERYDAY LIFE:
Taking the Worry Out of Exams

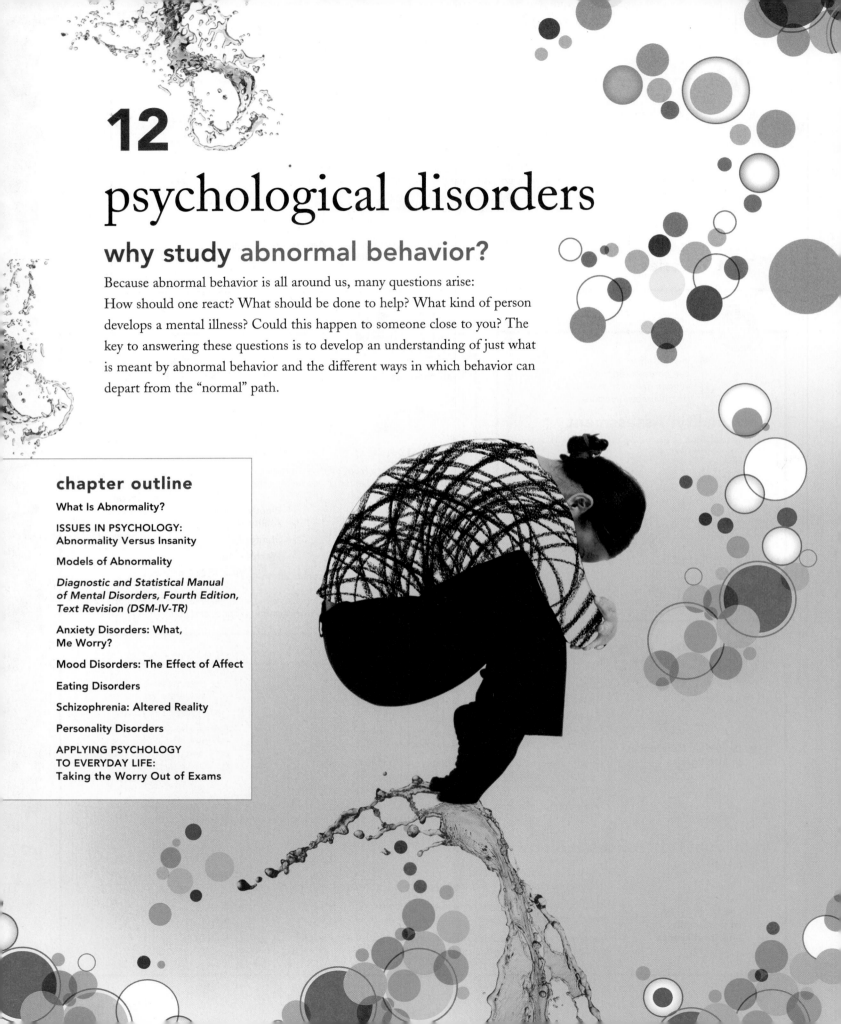

The Psychological Impact of Disasters

When disaster strikes, it leaves in its wake both physical and psychological damage. Hurricane Katrina, a Category 3 hurricane that ripped across the Gulf Coast of the United States in August of 2005, is still causing serious emotional disturbances for many people, especially children and adolescents who experienced the devastation (McLaughlin et al., 2009; McLaughlin et al., 2010).

A little more than a year ago, a new disaster unfolded in the Gulf of Mexico, far more slowly but in many ways, no less devastating. On April 20, 2010, a deep-water oil rig in the Gulf exploded and began to release anywhere from 35,000 to 60,000 barrels of crude oil each day—and possibly more—the equivalent, some say, of more than 15 *Exxon Valdez* spills, the Alaskan disaster of 1989, which is still causing psychological problems of its own today (Macdonald et al., 2010; National Wildlife Federation, 2010).

Dr. Steven Picou, a sociology professor at the University of South Alabama, has been studying the psychological impact of the *Valdez* oil spill for 21 years. He and other researchers found that the unfolding effects of that disaster included escalation of depression, posttraumatic stress disorder, anxiety disorders, and other mental-health problems long after the original spill. An oil-spill-related suicide occurred 4 full years *after* the *Valdez* spill. A charter boat captain in Alabama became severely depressed over the loss of his livelihood and committed suicide just a little over *2 months* after the BP spill (Kam, 2010).

The BP spill is expected to set off a chain reaction of tragedies and mental disorders relating to the stresses of failing fishing industries, decreased tourism, and health issues caused by the oil that is lingering in the Gulf (and beyond) as well as washing up on shore; it is a chain reaction that may be felt for decades. Within 4 months of the spill, an increase in the number of reported deaths was seen in the population of chronically homeless people of the Gulf Coast area. Many of the deaths are believed to have been caused by stress-induced heart attacks, as well as the result of suicide (Kam, 2010). To date, hundreds of claims have been filed against BP for the stress, anxiety, and psychophysiological disorders brought on by the oil spill. The litigation over these claims is a major stressor in and of itself, and decades of unfolding psychological harm may lie ahead.

learning objectives

12.1 How has mental illness been explained in the past, how is abnormal behavior defined today, and what is the impact of cultural differences in defining abnormality?

12.2 How can psychological disorders be explained within the biological and psychological models?

12.3 What are the different types of psychological disorders, and how common are they?

12.4 What are the different types of anxiety disorders, their symptoms, and their causes?

12.5 What are the different types of mood disorders and their causes?

12.6 What are the two primary types of eating disorders, how do they differ, and who are they most likely to affect?

12.7 What are the main symptoms, types, and causes of schizophrenia?

12.8 How do the various personality disorders differ, and what is thought to be the cause of personality disorders?

study tip

As you are reading this chapter, take a look back at pages PIA-9–PIA-12 in *Psychology in Action* for some ways to reduce the stress and anxiety of studying and finishing assignments.

👁—⎤**Watch** Episode 17: *Psychological Disorders and Therapies* in the MyPsychLab video series

> I've heard people call the different things other people do "crazy" or "weird." How do psychologists decide when people are really mentally ill and not just a little odd?

psychopathology the study of abnormal behavior.

What Is Abnormality?

> I've heard people call the different things other people do "crazy" or "weird." How do psychologists decide when people are really mentally ill and not just a little odd?

Exactly what is meant by the term *abnormal behavior*? Abnormal compared to what? Who gets to decide what is normal and what is not? Has the term always meant what it means now? These are just a few questions that come to mind when thinking about the study of abnormal behavior, or **psychopathology**.

A Very Brief History of Psychological Disorders

12.1 How has mental illness been explained in the past, how is abnormal behavior defined today, and what is the impact of cultural differences in defining abnormality?

Dating from as early as 3000 B.C.E., archaeologists have found human skulls bearing the evidence of an ancient surgical technique. The skulls have holes cut into them, and the holes were made while the person was still living. Many of the holes show evidence of healing, meaning that the person survived the process. The process of cutting holes into the skull of a living person is called "trepanning" (also spelled *trephining*). Although trepanning is still done today to relieve pressure of fluids on the brain, in ancient times the reason may have had more to do with releasing the "demons" possessing the poor victim (Gross, 1999). Ancient peoples might well have assumed that some among them who were behaving oddly were possessed by evil spirits.

Hippocrates (460–377 B.C.E.), a Greek physician during the time in which the rest of the world and even many Greeks believed in the demonic possession explanation of mental illness, challenged that belief with his assertion that illnesses of both the body and the mind were the result of imbalances in the body's vital fluids, or *humors*. Although Hippocrates was not correct in his assumptions about the humors of the body (phlegm, black bile, blood, and yellow bile), his was the first recorded attempt to explain abnormal behavior as due to some biological process.

Moving forward in time, people of the Middle Ages believed in spirit possession (a belief influenced by the teachings of the Roman Catholic Church and the remnants of other religious/cultural systems) as one cause of abnormal behavior. The treatment of choice for such maladies was a religious one: *exorcism*, or the formal casting out of the demon through a religious ritual (Lewis, 1995). During the Renaissance, belief in demonic possession (in which the possessed person was seen as a victim) gave way to a belief in witchcraft, and some mentally ill persons were likely called witches and put to death.

These human skulls clearly show the signs of trepanning, a process in which ancient priests or medicine men cut holes into the skulls of a living person, perhaps to release the "demons" that were making the person's behavior odd or disturbed. Some who were treated in this way must have survived, as the holes show some evidence of healing.
Source: American Museum of Natural History.

What Is Abnormal?

Defining abnormal behavior or abnormality is not as simple as it might seem at first. The easy way out is to say that abnormal behavior is behavior that is not normal, but what does that mean? It's complicated, as you'll see by considering different criteria for determining abnormality. ☑•⌐Survey on MyPsychLab

STATISTICAL DEFINITION One way to define *normal* and *abnormal* is to use a statistical definition. Frequently occurring behavior would be considered normal, and behavior that is rare would be abnormal. That kind of definition works fine with a behavior such as talking to others, as the two rarer possibilities would be not talking to anyone at all and talking too much to too many people—both of which would be considered abnormal. But what about a behavior such as happiness? Is a medium level of happiness really the "norm" most people strive to reach? A total lack of happiness would be abnormal, but should a person who is very happy really be labeled abnormal? Statistical definitions of abnormality wouldn't work for intelligence either, as only intellectual disability (the lower end of a distribution of intelligence in a population) would be considered undesirable and abnormal (Troisi & McGuire, 2002). People possessing a higher degree of intelligence than is "normal" are actually highly respected.

SOCIAL NORM DEVIANCE Another way of defining abnormality is to see it as something that goes against the norms or standards of the society in which the individual lives. For example, refusing to wear clothing in a society that does not permit nudity would be seen as abnormal. But deviance (variation) from social norms is not always labeled as negative, abnormal behavior. For instance, a person who decides to become a monk and live in a monastery in the United States would be exhibiting unusual behavior, and certainly not what the society considers a standard behavior, but it wouldn't be a sign of abnormality.

The **situational context** (the social or environmental setting of a person's behavior) can also make a difference in how behavior is labeled. For example, if a man comes to a therapist complaining of people listening in on his phone conversations and spying on all his activities, the therapist's first thought might be that the man is suffering from feelings of persecution. But if the man then explains that he is in a witness protection program, the complaints take on an entirely different and quite understandable tone.

SUBJECTIVE DISCOMFORT One sign of abnormality is when the person experiences a great deal of **subjective discomfort**, or emotional distress while engaging in a particular behavior. A woman who suffers from a fear of going outside her house, for example, would experience a great deal of anxiety when trying to leave home and distress over being unable to leave. However, all behavior that might be considered abnormal does not necessarily create subjective discomfort in the person committing the act—a serial killer, for example, does not experience emotional distress after taking someone's life, and some forms of disordered behavior involve showing no emotions at all.

INABILITY TO FUNCTION NORMALLY Behavior that does not allow a person to fit into society or function normally can also be labeled abnormal. This kind of behavior is termed **maladaptive**, meaning that the person finds it hard to adapt to the demands of day-to-day living. Maladaptive behavior includes behavior that may initially help a person cope but has harmful or damaging effects. For example, a woman who cuts herself to relieve anxiety does experience initial relief but is harmed by the action. Maladaptive behavior is a key element in the definition of abnormality.

By what criterion (or criteria) of abnormality might this person be considered abnormal? Would your perception of him change if he was not in front of a business offering tax services?

☑•⌐Survey Participate in a survey: Are you normal? on **MyPsychLab**

situational context the social or environmental setting of a person's behavior.

subjective discomfort emotional distress or emotional pain.

maladaptive anything that does not allow a person to function within or adapt to the stresses and everyday demands of life.

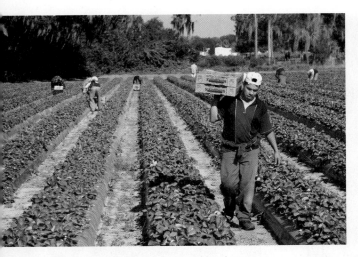

A migrant farming background has been found to be related to increased symptoms of anxiety and depression among college students of Mexican heritage when compared to those without a migrant background.

Read and learn more about culture-bound syndromes on **MyPsychLab**

So how do psychologists decide what is abnormal?

sociocultural perspective perspective in which abnormal behavior (as well as normal behavior) is seen as the product of the learning and shaping of behavior within the context of the family, the social group to which one belongs, and the culture within which the family and social group exist.

cultural relativity the need to consider the unique characteristics of the culture in which behavior takes place.

culture-bound syndromes disorders found only in particular cultures.

THE SOCIOCULTURAL PERSPECTIVE What's normal in one culture may be abnormal in another culture. In the **sociocultural perspective** of abnormality, abnormal behavior (as well as normal behavior) is seen as the product of behavioral shaping within the context of family influences, the social group to which one belongs, and the culture within which the family and social group exist. In particular, cultural differences in abnormal behavior must be addressed when psychological professionals are attempting to assess and treat members of a culture different from that of the professional. **Cultural relativity** is a term that refers to the need to consider the unique characteristics of the culture in which the person with a disorder was nurtured to be able to correctly diagnose and treat the disorder (Castillo, 1997). For example, in most traditional Asian cultures, mental illness is often seen as a shameful thing that brings disgrace to one's family. It may be seen as something inherited and, therefore, as something that would hurt the marriage chances of other family members, or it may be seen as stemming from something the family's ancestors did wrong in the past (Ritts, 1999; Ying, 1990). This leads many Asian people suffering from disorders that would be labeled as depression or even schizophrenia to report bodily symptoms rather than emotional or mental ones because bodily ailments are more socially acceptable (Fedoroff & McFarlane, 1998; Lee, 1995; Ritts, 1999). Furthermore, certain disorders unique to specific cultures, called **culture-bound syndromes**, are only found in particular cultures. For example, anorexia nervosa and bulimia nervosa are most often found in Western societies. **Read** on **MyPsychLab**

It is important to take into account other background and influential factors such as socioeconomic status and education level. Another area of awareness should be primary language and, if applicable, degree of acculturation. Psychosocial functioning has been part of the diagnostic process for some time now, but traditionally, greater attention has been paid to specifically identifying symptoms of pathology rather than focusing on the environmental factors that influence an individual's overall level of functioning (Ro & Clark, 2009). For example, in one recent study, college students of Mexican heritage with migrant farming backgrounds reported more symptoms of anxiety and depression as compared to nonmigrant college students of Mexican heritage (Mejía & McCarthy, 2010). The nature of migrant farming poses different stressors than those faced by nonmigrant families.

A Working Definition of Abnormality

So how do psychologists decide what is abnormal?

To get a clear picture of abnormality, it is often necessary to consider all of the factors discussed in the preceding section. Psychologists and other psychological professionals must consider several different criteria when determining whether or not a behavior is abnormal (at least two of these criteria must be met to form a diagnosis of abnormality):

1. Is the behavior unusual, such as experiencing severe panic when faced with a stranger or being severely depressed in the absence of any stressful life situations?
2. Does the behavior go against social norms? (And keep in mind that social norms change over time—e.g., homosexuality was once considered a psychological disorder rather than a variation in sexual orientation.)
3. Does the behavior cause the person significant subjective discomfort?
4. Is the behavior maladaptive, or does it result in an inability to function?
5. Does the behavior cause the person to be dangerous to self or others, as in the case of someone who tries to commit suicide or who attacks other people without reason?

Abnormal behavior that includes at least two of these five criteria is perhaps best classified by the term **psychological disorder**, which is defined as any pattern of behavior that causes people significant distress, leads them to harm themselves or others, or harms their ability to function in daily life.

Before moving on, it is important to clarify how the term *abnormality* is different from the term *insanity*. ⊙➤ Simulate on **MyPsychLab**

> **psychological disorder** any pattern of behavior that causes people significant distress, causes them to harm others, or harms their ability to function in daily life.

⊙➤ **Simulate** the definition of psychological disorders on **MyPsychLab**

issues in psychology
Abnormality Versus Insanity

Although only psychological professionals can diagnose disorders and determine the best course of treatment for someone who suffers from mental illness, lawyers and judges are charged with determining how the law should address crimes committed under the influence of mental illness. Psychologists and psychiatrists determine whether or not certain behavior is abnormal, but they do not decide whether a certain person is insane. In the United States, *insanity* is not a psychological term; it is a legal term used to argue that a mentally ill person who has committed a crime should not be held responsible for his or her actions because that person was unable to understand the difference between right and wrong at the time of the offense. This argument is called the *insanity defense*.

Many people are diagnosed with psychological disorders either before or after committing crimes. If an individual with schizophrenia burns down a house because he believes God has told him to do it, he has certainly committed a crime—but is he truly guilty? Supporters of the insanity defense might argue that he is not.

It is important to keep in mind that not everyone who has been diagnosed with a psychological disorder is a good candidate to use the insanity defense to plead innocent to a criminal charge. Very few people use the insanity defense in court, and, of those people, only a small percentage are found innocent by reason of insanity.

This photograph shows Keith, Deanna, Joshua, and Luck Laney of New Chapel Hill, Texas, in seemingly happier times. On May 12, 2003, Deanna Laney killed her two young sons by crushing their heads with rocks, believing that God had ordered her to kill her children. On the day of the killings, Deanna suffered a number of visual and auditory hallucinations. She was found innocent by reason of insanity in 2004 and has been committed to a maximum security state hospital, where she is undergoing treatment for paranoid schizophrenia.

QUESTIONS FOR FURTHER DISCUSSION
1. Should the insanity defense be permitted? Why or why not?
2. In what situations should a person exonerated of a crime due to the insanity defense still be required to face some sort of penalty, such as community service or financial restitution?

Models of Abnormality

What causes psychological disorders? ●─────

In Chapter Eleven several different theories of personality were discussed. These theories of personality can be used to describe and explain the formation of not only ordinary behavior and personality but disordered behavior and abnormal personality as well. How one explains disordered behavior, then, depends on which theoretical model is used to explain personality in general.

What causes psychological disorders?

biological model model of explaining behavior as caused by biological changes in the chemical, structural, or genetic systems of the body.

12.2 How can psychological disorders be explained within the biological and psychological models?

The Biological Model: Medical Causes for Psychological Disorders

One model that was not discussed in Chapter Eleven is the **biological model**, which proposes that psychological disorders have a biological or medical cause (Gamwell & Tomes, 1995). This model explains disorders such as anxiety, depression, and schizophrenia as caused by chemical imbalances, genetic problems, brain damage and dysfunction, or some combination of those causes. For example, as you may recall from the discussion of trait theory and the five-factor theory of personality traits ⓛⓘⓝⓚ to Chapter Eleven: Theories of Personality and Intelligence, pp. 401–403, evidence suggests that basic personality traits are as much influenced by genetic inheritance as they are by experience and upbringing, even across cultures (Bouchard, 1994; Herbst et al., 2000; Jang et al., 1996; Loehlin, 1992; Loehlin et al., 1998). One of the Big Five factors was neuroticism, for example, and it is easy to see how someone who scores high in neuroticism would be at greater risk for anxiety-based disorders.

The biological or medical model has had a great deal of influence, especially in the language used to describe disorders: *mental illness*, *symptoms of disorder*, and terms such as *diagnosis*, *mental patient*, *mental hospital*, *therapy*, and *remission* all come from medical terminology. The use of such terms, though still widespread, may tend to bias the assumptions of professionals who are not psychiatrists or medical doctors toward a biological cause for disordered behavior or the idea that disorders might be diseases that can be "cured." Many disorders can effectively be controlled but may not be fully resolved. ⓛⓘⓝⓚ to Chapter Thirteen: Psychological Therapies, p. 491.

The Psychological Models

Although biological explanations of psychological disorders are influential, they are not the only ways or even the first ways in which disorders are explained. Several psychological models, as follows, attempt to explain disordered behavior as the result of various forms of emotional, behavioral, or thought-related malfunctioning.

PSYCHODYNAMIC VIEW: HIDING PROBLEMS The psychodynamic model, based on the work of Freud and his followers, ⓛⓘⓝⓚ to Chapter Eleven: Theories of Personality and Intelligence, pp. 386–395, explains disordered behavior as the result of repressing one's threatening thoughts, memories, and concerns in the unconscious mind (Carducci, 1998). These repressed thoughts and urges try to resurface, and disordered behavior develops as a way of keeping the thoughts repressed. According to this view, a woman who has unacceptable thoughts of sleeping with her brother-in-law might feel "dirty" and be compelled to wash her hands every time those thoughts threaten to become conscious, ridding herself symbolically of the "dirty" thoughts.

BEHAVIORISM: LEARNING PROBLEMS Behaviorists, who define personality as a set of learned responses, have no trouble explaining disordered behavior as being learned just like normal behavior (Skinner, 1971; Watson, 1913). For example, when Emma was a small child, a spider dropped onto her leg, causing her to scream and react with fear. Her mother made a big fuss over her, giving her lots of attention. Each time Emma saw a spider after this, she screamed again, drawing attention to herself. Behaviorists would say that Emma's fear of the spider was classically conditioned and that her screaming reaction was positively reinforced by all the attention.

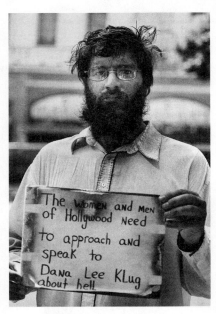

Some homeless people suffer from mental disorders, such as this man, who seems to believe that he has knowledge that others lack—a symptom typical of several serious disorders possibly linked to chemical imbalances or structural defects in the nervous system, according to the biological model.

COGNITIVE PERSPECTIVE: THINKING PROBLEMS **Cognitive psychologists** study the way people think, remember, and mentally organize information; they see abnormal behavior as resulting from illogical thinking patterns (Mora, 1985). A cognitive psychologist might explain Emma's fear of spiders as distorted thinking: "All spiders are vicious and will bite me, and I will die!" Emma's particular thinking patterns put her at a higher risk of depression and anxiety than those of a person who thinks more logically.

> **cognitive psychologists** psychologists who study the way people think, remember, and mentally organize information.
>
> **biopsychosocial model** perspective in which abnormal behavior is seen as the result of the combined and interacting forces of biological, psychological, social, and cultural influences.

Biopsychosocial Perspective: All of the Above

The biological, psychological, and sociocultural influences on abnormality are no longer seen as independent causes of abnormal behavior. Instead, these influences are seen to interact with one another to cause the various forms of disorders. For example, a person may have a genetically inherited tendency for a type of disorder, such as anxiety, but may not develop a full-blown disorder unless the family and social environments produce the right stressors at the right time in development. How accepting of such disorders the particular culture is will also play a part in determining the exact degree and form that anxiety disorder might take. This is known as the **biopsychosocial model** of disorder, which has become a very influential way to view the connection between mind and body.

Diagnostic and Statistical Manual of Mental Disorders, Fourth Edition, Text Revision (DSM-IV-TR)

12.3 **What are the different types of psychological disorders, and how common are they?**

In 1952, the first edition of the *Diagnostic and Statistical Manual of Mental Disorders (DSM)* was published to help psychological professionals diagnose psychological disorders. The current version of the *DSM* is called the *Diagnostic and Statistical Manual of Mental Disorders, Fourth Edition, Text Revision (DSM-IV-TR)* (American Psychiatric Association, 2000).

Categories in the *DSM-IV-TR*

The *DSM-IV-TR* describes about 250 different psychological disorders. Each disorder is discussed in terms of its symptoms, the typical path the disorder takes as it progresses, and a checklist of specific criteria that must be met in order for the diagnosis of that disorder to be made. The manual also divides these disorders and relevant facts about the person being diagnosed along five different categories, or axes. A psychologist or psychiatrist assesses the person on each of these five axes.

Axis I, Clinical Disorders, contains the disorders that bring most people to the attention of a psychological professional. A few of the sixteen categories of disorders that can be diagnosed on Axis I include mood disorders, anxiety disorders, schizophrenia and other psychotic disorders, eating disorders, and disorders usually first diagnosed in infancy, childhood, or adolescence such as ADHD (American Psychiatric Association, 2000). With one exception, all of the psychological disorders are listed on this axis. The exception is the personality disorders, which are listed on Axis II along with mental retardation (now most often called *intellectual disability*). The reason for this is that, unlike most psychological disorders that appear at some later point in a person's life, personality disorders are a part of the individual's personality and are, therefore, relatively stable and enduring. As an integral part of the personality, affecting relationships, careers, and behavior, personality disorders seem more similar to a condition such as mental retardation, which is a developmental disorder affecting many areas of the individual's life.

Axis III includes physical disorders that affect a person's psychological *adjustment*, such as juvenile diabetes, chromosome disorders such as Klinefelter's syndrome, and high blood pressure. (In psychology, the term *adjustment* refers to a person's ability to function normally in everyday life.) Axis IV contains information about problems in the person's life that might affect adjustment, such as the death of a loved one, the loss of a job, or poverty. Finally, Axis V, Global Assessment of Functioning, is an overall judgment made by the psychological professional of the person's mental health and adjustment, literally a rating on a scale of 0 to 100. For example, scores of 91–100 would be interpreted as superior functioning, 71–80 as temporary problems due to stress, and 41–50 as indicative of serious symptoms or impairment in functioning. ✳ Explore on **MyPsychLab**

✳ Explore the axes of the *DSM-IV-TR* on **MyPsychLab**

That sounds like a lot of possible disorders, but most people don't get these problems, right?

How Common Are Psychological Disorders?

That sounds like a lot of possible disorders, but most people don't get these problems, right?

Psychological disorders are more common than most people might think. In any given year, about 26.2 percent of American adults over age 18 suffer from a mental disorder; that comes to about 57.7 million people in the United States. Statistically, mental disorders are the leading cause of disability in the United States and Canada (National Institute of Mental Health, 2010). It is quite common for people to suffer from more than one mental disorder at a time, such as a person with depression who also has a substance-abuse disorder, or a person with an anxiety disorder who also suffers from sleep disorders. Approximately 45 percent of individuals with a mental disorder meet the criteria for two or more disorders (National Institute of Mental Health, 2010). Table 12.1 lists the percentages of selected psy-

table 12.1   Yearly Occurrence of Psychological Disorders in the United States

CATEGORY OF DISORDER	SPECIFIC DISORDER	PERCENTAGE OF U.S. POPULATION AND NUMBER AFFECTED*
Depressive disorders	All types	9.5% or 20.9 million
	Major depressive disorder	6.7% or 14.8 million
	Dysthymic disorder	1.5% or 3.3 million
	Bipolar disorder	2.6% or 5.7 million
Schizophrenia	All types	1.1% or 2.4 million
Anxiety disorders	All types	18.1% or 40 million
	Panic disorder	2.7% or 6 million
	Obsessive-compulsive disorder	1% or 2.2 million
	Posttraumatic stress disorder	3.5% or 7.7 million
	Generalized anxiety disorder	3.1% or 6.8 million
	Social phobia	6.8% or 15 million
	Agoraphobia	0.8% or 1.8 million
	Specific phobia	8.7% or 19.2 million

*Percentage of adults over age 18 affected annually and approximate number within the population based on 2004 United States Census data.

Adapted from National Institute of Mental Health (2010).

chological disorders in the United States. (Note that this table does not include all of the disorders that occur in the 57.7 million adults in the United States mentioned earlier in this paragraph.)

The Pros and Cons of Labels

With its lists of disorders and their corresponding symptoms, the *DSM-IV-TR* helps psychological professionals diagnose patients and provide those patients with labels that explain their conditions. In the world of psychological diagnosis and treatment, labels such as *depression, anxiety*, and *schizophrenia* can be very helpful: They make up a common language in the mental health community, allowing psychological professionals to communicate with each other clearly and efficiently. Labels establish distinct diagnostic categories that all professionals recognize and understand, and they help patients receive effective treatment.

Statistically speaking, about 1 out of every 5 of the people in this crowd probably suffers from some form of psychological disorder.

Labels can also be dangerous, however—or, at the very least, overly prejudicial. In 1972, researcher David Rosenhan asked healthy participants to enter psychiatric hospitals and complain that they were hearing voices. All of the participants, whom Rosenhan called "pseudopatients," were admitted into the hospitals and diagnosed with either schizophrenia or manic depression. Once the pseudopatients were admitted, they stopped pretending to be ill and acted as they normally would, but the hospital staff's interpretation of the pseudopatients' normal behavior was skewed by the label of mental illness. For example, hospital workers described one pseudopatient's relatively normal relationships with family and friends as evidence of a psychological disorder, and another pseudopatient's note-taking habits were considered to be a pathological behavior. The pseudopatients had been diagnosed and labeled, and those labels stuck, even when actual symptoms of mental illness disappeared. Rosenhan concluded that psychological labels are long lasting and powerful, affecting not only how other people see mental patients but how patients see themselves (Rosenhan, 1973).

Labels can be time-saving and even life-saving tools, but they can also bias us, affect our judgment, and give us preconceived notions that may very well turn out to be false. Just to be clear, the diagnostic labels listed in the *DSM-IV-TR* are intended to help both psychologists and patients, and they *do* help. As you read on, remember the power that labels have to shape our perceptions of reality.

Before describing some of the various categories and types of disorders, a word of caution: It's very easy to see oneself in these disorders. Medical students often become convinced that they have every one of the symptoms for some rare, exotic disease they have been studying. Psychology students studying abnormal behavior can also become convinced that they have some mental disorder, a problem that can be called "psychology student's syndrome." The problem is that so many psychological disorders are really ordinary variations in human behavior taken to an extreme. For example, some people are natural-born worriers. They look for things that can go wrong around every corner. That doesn't make them disordered—it makes them pessimistic worriers. Remember, it doesn't become a disorder until the worrying gets out of hand, causing significant distress; leads them to harm themselves or others; or affects their ability to function in everyday life. So if you start "seeing" yourself or even your friends and family in any of the following discussions, don't panic—all of you are *probably* okay.

practice quiz How much do you remember?

Pick the best answer.

1. Who would be most likely to assume that psychological disorders are caused by an imbalance in the fluids of the body?
   a. an ancient Egyptian physician
   b. a modern psychiatrist
   c. an ancient Greek physician
   d. a physician of the Middle Ages

2. Luis has started having feelings of fearfulness about going to school. He has begun to suffer from headaches and stomachaches and has missed several days of school already. Luis's condition is abnormal from the _____ definition.
   a. statistical
   b. situational context
   c. social deviance
   d. subjective discomfort

3. In the United States, insanity is not a _____ term; it is a _____ term.
   a. behavioral; psychoanalytic
   b. legal; medical
   c. legal; psychological
   d. psychological; legal

4. Which model of abnormality explains abnormal behavior as caused by illogical thinking?
   a. psychodynamic
   b. cognitive
   c. behavioral
   d. biopsychosocial

5. Elliot is attracted to his beautiful cousin, Ginny, but knows that she is too closely related to him. He believes he has successfully overcome this forbidden attraction but still finds that every time Ginny is near him he is overwhelmed with feelings of anxiety and feels the need to wash his hands. Which model of abnormality would most likely explain Elliot's behavior?
   a. psychodynamic
   b. cognitive
   c. behavioral
   d. biological

6. Which of the following is NOT a correct match?
   a. Axis V—Global Assessment of Functioning
   b. Axis I—Personality Disorders
   c. Axis III—General Medical Conditions
   d. Axis IV—Psychosocial and Environmental Problems

Brainstorming: What might be the advantages of explaining disorders within the biopsychosocial model rather than using a biological or psychological model only?

ANSWERS ON PAGE AK-2

Anxiety Disorders: What, Me Worry?

12.4 What are the different types of anxiety disorders, their symptoms, and their causes?

The category of **anxiety disorders** includes all disorders in which the most dominant symptom is excessive or unrealistic anxiety. Anxiety can take very specific forms, such as a fear of a specific object, or it can be a very general emotion, such as that experienced by someone who is worried and doesn't know why.

But doesn't everybody have anxiety sometimes? What makes it a disorder?

● But doesn't everybody have anxiety sometimes? What makes it a disorder?

Everyone does have anxiety, and some people have a great deal of anxiety at times. When talking about anxiety disorders, the anxiety is either excessive—greater than it should be given the circumstances—or unrealistic. If final exams are coming up and a student hasn't studied enough, that student's anxiety is understandable and realistic. But a student who has studied, has done well on all the exams, and is very prepared and still worries *excessively* about passing is showing an unrealistic amount of anxiety. (For more about test anxiety, see the Applying Psychology to Everyday Life section in this chapter.) People who are in danger of losing their job might experience quite a bit of anxiety, but its source is obvious and understandable. But someone whose life is going well, and for whom nothing bad is looming in the future, and who still feels extremely anxious may be experiencing an anxiety disorder. **Free-floating anxiety** is the term given to anxiety that seems to be unrelated to any realistic, known factor, and it is often a symptom of an anxiety disorder (Freud & Gay, 1977).

Phobic Disorders: When Fears Get Out of Hand

One of the more specific anxiety disorders is a **phobia**, an irrational, persistent fear of something. The "something" might be an object or a situation or may involve social interactions. For example, many people would feel fear if they suddenly came upon

anxiety disorders disorders in which the main symptom is excessive or unrealistic anxiety and fearfulness.

free-floating anxiety anxiety that is unrelated to any realistic, known source.

phobia an irrational, persistent fear of an object, situation, or social activity.

table 12.2   Common Phobias and Their Scientific Names

FEAR OF	SCIENTIFIC NAME
Washing and bathing	Ablutophobia
Spiders	Arachnophobia
Lightning	Ceraunophobia
Dirt, germs	Mysophobia
Snakes	Ophidiophobia
Darkness	Nyctophobia
Fire	Pyrophobia
Foreigners, strangers	Xenophobia
Animals	Zoophobia

Source: Adapted from Culbertson (2003).

Many people get nervous when they have to speak in front of an audience. Fear of public speaking is a common social phobia. Can you remember a time when you experienced a fear like this?

a live snake as they were walking and would take steps to avoid the snake. Although those same people would not necessarily avoid a *picture* of a snake in a book, a person with a phobia of snakes would. Avoiding a live snake is rational; avoiding a picture of a snake is not.

SOCIAL PHOBIAS (SOCIAL ANXIETY DISORDER) **Social phobias** (also called *social anxiety disorders*) involve a fear of interacting with others or being in a social situation and are some of the most common phobias people experience (World Health Organization International Consortium in Psychiatric Epidemiology, 2000). People with a social phobia are afraid of being evaluated in some negative way by others, so they tend to avoid situations that could lead to something embarrassing or humiliating. They are very self-conscious as a result. Common types of social phobia are stage fright, fear of public speaking, and fear of urinating in a public restroom. Not surprisingly, people with social phobias often have a history of being shy as children (Sternberger et al., 1995).

SPECIFIC PHOBIAS   A **specific phobia** is an irrational fear of some object or specific situation, such as a fear of dogs, or a fear of being in small, enclosed spaces (**claustrophobia**). Other specific phobias include a fear of injections (*trypanophobia*), fear of dental work (*odontophobia*), fear of blood (*hematophobia*), and fear of heights (**acrophobia**). For a listing of common phobias, see Table 12.2.

AGORAPHOBIA   Another type of phobia is **agoraphobia**, a Greek name that literally means "fear of the marketplace." Although that makes it sound like a social phobia, agoraphobia is a little more complicated. It is actually the fear of being in a place or situation (social or not) from which escape is difficult or impossible if something should go wrong (American Psychiatric Association, 2000). So individuals with agoraphobia are often afraid not only of crowds but also of crossing bridges, traveling in a car or plane, eating in restaurants, and sometimes even of leaving the house. To be in any of these situations or to even think about being in such situations can lead to extreme feelings of anxiety and even panic attacks (see the following section about panic attacks).

If a person has agoraphobia, it might be difficult to even go to work or to the store, right?

Exactly. People with specific phobias can usually avoid the object or situation without too much difficulty, and people with social phobias may simply avoid jobs and situations that involve meeting people face to face. But people with agoraphobia cannot avoid their phobia's source because it is simply being outside in the real world.

If a person has agoraphobia, it might be difficult to even go to work or to the store, right?

social phobia   fear of interacting with others or being in social situations that might lead to a negative evaluation.

specific phobia   fear of objects or specific situations or events.

claustrophobia   fear of being in a small, enclosed space.

acrophobia   fear of heights.

agoraphobia   fear of being in a place or situation from which escape is difficult or impossible.

Agoraphobia includes a fear of crossing bridges, although this bridge is enough to test anyone's courage.

panic attack sudden onset of intense panic in which multiple physical symptoms of stress occur, often with feelings that one is dying.

panic disorder disorder in which panic attacks occur frequently enough to cause the person difficulty in adjusting to daily life.

panic disorder with agoraphobia fear of leaving one's familiar surroundings because one might have a panic attack in public.

obsessive-compulsive disorder disorder in which intruding, recurring thoughts or obsessions create anxiety that is relieved by performing a repetitive, ritualistic behavior or mental act (compulsion).

Award-winning actor Tony Shalhoub portrays Adrian Monk, a former policeman turned detective. Monk has a large number of anxiety disorders ranging from phobias (fear of milk, for example) to extreme obsessive-compulsive disordered behavior. His OCDs involve cleaning and touching post-like objects, to name only two.

A severe case of agoraphobia can make a person's home a prison, leaving the person trapped inside unable to go to work, shop, or engage in any kind of activity that requires going out of the home.

Panic Disorder

Fourteen-year-old Dariya was sitting in science class watching a film. All of a sudden, she started feeling really strange. Her ears seemed to be stuffed with cotton and her vision was very dim. She was cold, had broken out in a sweat, and felt extremely afraid for no good reason. Her heart was racing and she immediately became convinced that she was dying. A friend sitting behind her saw how pale she had become and tried to ask her what was wrong, but Dariya couldn't speak. She was in a state of panic and couldn't move.

Dariya's symptoms are the classic symptoms of a **panic attack**, a sudden onset of extreme panic with various physical symptoms: racing heart, rapid breathing, a sensation of being "out of one's body," dulled hearing and vision, sweating, and dry mouth (Kumar & Oakley-Browne, 2002). Many people who have a panic attack think that they are having a heart attack and can experience pain as well as panic, but the symptoms are caused by the panic, not by any actual physical disorder. Psychologically, the person having a panic attack is in a state of terror, thinking that this is it, death is happening, and many people may feel a need to escape. The attack happens without warning and quite suddenly. Although some panic attacks can last as long as half an hour, some last only a few minutes, with most attacks peaking within 10 to 15 minutes.

Having a panic attack is not that unusual, especially for adolescent girls and young adult women (Eaton et al., 1994; Hayward et al., 1989, 2000). Researchers have also found evidence that cigarette smoking greatly increases the risk of panic attacks in adolescents and young adults (Johnson, 2000; Zvolensky et al., 2003). Regardless of the age of onset, it is only when panic attacks become so frequent that they affect a person's ability to function in day-to-day life that they become a **panic disorder**. When a fear of having panic attacks in a public place prevents the person from going out into unfamiliar or exposed places, it is called **panic disorder with agoraphobia**.

Many people try to figure out what triggers a panic attack and then do their best to avoid the situation if possible. If driving a car sets off an attack, they don't drive. If being in a crowd triggers an attack, they don't go where crowds are. It is easy to see how having panic disorder can often lead to agoraphobia. Psychologists and psychiatrists will classify a person as having either a panic disorder with agoraphobia or a panic disorder without agoraphobia.

Obsessive-Compulsive Disorder

Sometimes people get a thought running through their head that just won't go away, such as when a song gets stuck in one's mind. If that particular thought causes a lot of anxiety, it can become the basis for an **obsessive-compulsive disorder** or OCD. OCD is a disorder in which intruding* thoughts that occur again and again (obsessions, such as a fear that germs are on one's hands) are followed by some repetitive, ritualistic behavior or mental acts (compulsions, such as repeated hand washing or counting). The compulsions are meant to lower the anxiety caused by the thought (Soomro, 2001).

---

*Intruding: forcing one's way in; referring to something undesirable that enters awareness.

I knew someone who had just had a baby, and she spent the first few nights home with the baby checking it to see if it was breathing—is that an obsessive-compulsive disorder?

No, almost all new parents check their infant's breathing frequently at first. Remember psychology student's syndrome? Everyone experiences a little obsessive thinking from time to time or has some small ritual that just makes them feel better. The difference is whether or not a person *likes* to perform the ritual (but doesn't *have* to do it) or feels *compelled* to perform the ritual and feels extreme anxiety if unable to complete it. The distress caused by a failure or an inability to successfully complete the compulsive behavior or mental act is a defining feature of OCD.

Acute Stress Disorder (ASD) and Posttraumatic Stress Disorder (PTSD)

Both general and specific stressors were discussed in Chapter Nine, Stress and Health. Two anxiety disorders—*Acute Stress Disorder* and *Posttraumatic Stress Disorder*—are related to exposure to significant and traumatic stressors. The severe stress and anxiety experienced by people after 9/11, Hurricane Katrina, and the April 2010 oil spill in the Gulf of Mexico can lead to **acute stress disorder (ASD)**. The symptoms of ASD occur within 4 weeks of the traumatic event and include anxiety, dissociative symptoms (such as emotional numbness/lack of responsiveness, not being aware of surroundings, dissociative amnesia), recurring nightmares, sleep disturbances, problems in concentration, and moments in which people seem to "relive" the event in dreams and flashbacks for as long as 1 month following the event. One recently published study gathered survey information from Katrina evacuees at a major emergency shelter and found that 62 percent of those sampled met the criteria for having acute stress disorder (Mills et al., 2007).

When the symptoms associated with ASD last more than 1 month, the disorder is then called **posttraumatic stress disorder (PTSD)**. In the same study (Mills et al., 2007), researchers concluded that 38 to 49 percent of all the evacuees sampled were likely at risk of developing PTSD that would still be present 2 years after the disaster. Furthermore, whereas the onset of ASD occurs within 4 weeks of the traumatic event, the symptoms of PTSD may not occur until 6 months or later after the event (American Psychiatric Association, 2000). Treatment of these stress disorders may involve psychotherapy and the use of drugs to control anxiety. LINK to Chapter Thirteen: Psychological Therapies, pp. 487–488.

Researchers have found that women have almost twice the risk of developing PTSD than do men and that the likelihood increases if the traumatic experience took place before the woman was 15 years old (Breslau et al., 1997, 1999). Children may also suffer different effects from stress than do adults. Severe PTSD has been linked to a decrease in the size of the hippocampus in children with the disorder (Carrion et al., 2007). The hippocampus is important in forming new long-term declarative memories (LINK to Chapter Five: Memory, pp. 172–173), and this may have a detrimental effect on learning and the effectiveness of treatments for these children. Some life experiences also lend themselves to people experiencing traumatic events. For example, the rate of PTSD (self-reported) among combat-exposed military personnel has tripled since 2001 (Smith et al., 2008).

acute stress disorder (ASD) a disorder resulting from exposure to a major stressor, with symptoms of anxiety, dissociation, recurring nightmares, sleep disturbances, problems in concentration, and moments in which people seem to "relive" the event in dreams and flashbacks for as long as 1 month following the event.

posttraumatic stress disorder (PTSD) a disorder resulting from exposure to a major stressor, with symptoms of anxiety, dissociation, nightmares, poor sleep, reliving the event, and concentration problems, lasting for more than 1 month.

I knew someone who had just had a baby, and she spent the first few nights home with the baby checking it to see if it was breathing—is that an obsessive-compulsive disorder?

After the BP oil spill in April of 2010, anywhere from 35 to 45 percent of people living around or near the Gulf of Mexico reported suffering symptoms of stress (Abramson et al., 2010).

What about people who are just worriers? Can that become a disorder?

generalized anxiety disorder disorder in which a person has feelings of dread and impending doom along with physical symptoms of stress, which lasts 6 months or more.

magnification the tendency to interpret situations as far more dangerous, harmful, or important than they actually are.

all-or-nothing thinking the tendency to believe that one's performance must be perfect or the result will be a total failure.

overgeneralization the tendency to interpret a single negative event as a never-ending pattern of defeat and failure.

minimization the tendency to give little or no importance to one's successes or positive events and traits.

Anxiety disorders can affect children as well as adults.

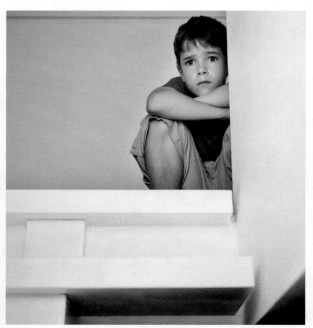

Generalized Anxiety Disorder

● What about people who are just worriers? Can that become a disorder?

Remember free-floating anxiety? That's the kind of anxiety that has no real external source and may be experienced by people with **generalized anxiety disorder**, in which excessive anxiety and worries (apprehensive expectations) occur more days than not for at least 6 months. People with this disorder may also experience anxiety about a number of events or activities (such as work or school performance). These feelings of anxiety persist 6 months or more and have no real source that can be pinpointed, nor can the person control the feelings even if an effort is made to do so.

People with this disorder are just plain worriers (Ruscio et al., 2001). They worry *excessively* about money, their children, their lives, their friends, the dog, as well as things no one else would see as a reason to worry. They feel tense and edgy, get tired easily, and may have trouble concentrating. They have muscle aches, they experience sleeping problems, and are often irritable—all signs of stress. Generalized anxiety disorder is often found occurring with other anxiety disorders and depression.

Causes of Anxiety Disorders

Different perspectives on how personality develops offer different explanations for anxiety disorders. For example, the *psychodynamic model* sees anxiety as a kind of danger signal that repressed urges or conflicts are threatening to surface (Freud & Gay, 1977). A phobia is seen as a kind of displacement, in which the phobic object is actually only a symbol of whatever the person has buried deep in his or her unconscious mind—the true source of the fear. A fear of knives might mean a fear of one's own aggressive tendencies, or a fear of heights may hide a suicidal desire to jump.

Behaviorists believe that anxious behavioral reactions are learned. They see phobias, for example, as nothing more than classically conditioned fear responses, as was the case with "Little Albert" (Rachman, 1990; Watson & Rayner, 1920). Ⓛⓘⓝⓚ to Chapter Four: Learning, p. 128.

Cognitive psychologists see anxiety disorders as the result of illogical, irrational thought processes. One way in which people with anxiety disorders show irrational thinking (Beck, 1976, 1984) is through **magnification**, or the tendency to "make mountains out of molehills" by interpreting situations as being far more harmful, dangerous, or embarrassing than they actually are. In panic disorder, for example, a person might interpret a racing heartbeat as a sign of a heart attack instead of just a momentary arousal.

Another distorted thought process is **all-or-nothing thinking**, in which a person believes that his or her performance must be perfect or the result will be a total failure. **Overgeneralization** (a single negative event interpreted as a never-ending pattern of defeat), jumping to conclusions without facts to support that conclusion, and **minimization** (giving little or no emphasis to one's successes or positive events and traits) are other examples of irrational thinking.

Growing evidence exists that *biological* factors contribute to anxiety disorders. Generalized anxiety disorder, for example, has been linked to an imbalance in several neurotransmitters in the nervous system, including lower levels of both serotonin and GABA (Brawman-Mintzer & Lydiard, 1997; Rynn et al., 2000). Lower levels of these neurotransmitters may reduce the ability to calm reactions to stress. Research has linked panic disorder to a possible defect in the way serotonin binds to its receptors in the nervous system (Neumeister et al., 2004). Recent studies with mice have indicated that an area of the hippocampus known as the ventral hippocampus (vHPC) may help control anxiety by "talking" to the medial prefrontal cortex, the area of the brain important in processing emotional awareness (Adhikari et al., 2010). (L I N K) to Chapter Two: The Biological Perspective, p. 70.

Some evidence suggests that these chemical imbalances may have a genetic component; that is, anxiety disorders such as obsessive-compulsive disorder, phobias, and panic disorder can be passed from parent to child through more than just observational learning (Karayiorgou et al., 1997; Lesch et al., 1996; Logue et al., 2003). Twin studies have provided more evidence of a genetic basis for anxiety disorders, particularly panic disorder and the phobias. Some studies have found that the heritability of panic disorder is about 44 percent, agoraphobia about 39 percent, and anxiety disorder about 30 percent (Hettema et al., 2001; Tsuang et al., 2004; Villafuerte & Burmeister, 2003). Neuroimaging studies using the PET and fMRI scanning techniques, (L I N K) to Chapter Two: The Biological Perspective, p. 63, have revealed that the amygdala, an area of the limbic system, is more active in phobic people responding to pictures of spiders than in nonphobic people (LeDoux, 2003; Rauch et al., 2003).

Anxiety disorders are found around the world, although the particular form the disorder takes might be different in various cultures. For example, in some Latin American cultures anxiety can take the form of *ataque de nervios*, or "attack of nerves," in which the person may have fits of crying, shout uncontrollably, experience sensations of heat, and become very aggressive, either verbally or physically. These attacks usually come after some stressful event such as the death of a loved one (American Psychiatric Association, 2000). Several syndromes that are essentially types of phobias are specific to certain cultures. For example, *koro* (found primarily in China and a few other South Asian and East Asian countries) involves a fear that one's genitals are shrinking (Pfeiffer, 1982), and TKS (found primarily in Japan) involves excessive fear and anxiety, but in this case it is the fear that one will do something in public that is socially inappropriate or embarrassing, such as blushing, staring, or having an offensive body odor (Kirmayer, 1991). Panic disorder is found almost universally at about the same rate all over the world (Weissman et al., 1997). ⊙—[Watch on **MyPsychLab**

affect in psychology, a term indicating "emotion" or "mood."

mood disorders disorders in which mood is severely disturbed.

⊙—[Watch a video about anxiety disorders on **MyPsychLab**

Mood Disorders: The Effect of Affect

12.5 What are the different types of mood disorders and their causes?

In psychological terms, the word **affect** is used to mean "emotion" or "mood." **Mood disorders** are a disturbance in emotion and are also referred to as affective disorders. Although the range of human emotions runs from deep, intense sadness and despair to extreme happiness and elation, under normal circumstances people stay in between those extremes—neither too sad nor too happy, but content (see Figure 12.1). It is when stress or some other factor pushes a person to one extreme or the other that mood disorders can result. Mood disorders can be relatively mild or moderate (straying only a short distance from the "average"), or they can be extreme (existing at either end of the full range). Mild to moderate depression is called *dysthymia*, while moder-

Extreme sadness	Mild sadness	Normal emotions	Mild elation	Extreme elation

FIGURE 12.1 The Range of Emotions Most people experience a range of emotions over the course of a day or several days, such as mild sadness, calm contentment, or mild elation and happiness. A person with a mood disorder experiences emotions that are extreme and, therefore, abnormal.

major depression severe depression that comes on suddenly and seems to have no external cause, or is too severe for current circumstances.

manic having the quality of excessive excitement, energy, and elation or irritability.

bipolar disorder severe mood swings between major depressive episodes and manic episodes.

ate mood swings (from sad to elated) are called *cyclothymia* (Klein et al., 2000). Both forms are chronic* and usually last two years or more.

Major Depression

When a deeply depressed mood comes on fairly suddenly and either seems to be too severe for the circumstances or exists without any external cause for sadness, it is called **major depression**. Major depression would fall at the far extreme of sadness on Figure 12.1. People suffering from major depression are depressed for most of every day, take little or no pleasure in any activities, feel tired, have trouble sleeping or sleep too much, experience changes in appetite and significant weight changes, experience excessive guilt or feelings of worthlessness, have trouble concentrating, and may have thoughts of death or suicide, including suicide attempts. Death by suicide is a real risk faced by people suffering from major depression. Some people with this disorder also suffer from delusional thinking and may experience hallucinations. Most of these symptoms occur on a daily basis, lasting for the better part of the day (American Psychiatric Association, 2000).

Major depression is the most common of the diagnosed mood disorders (see Figure 12.2) and is about twice as common in women as it is in men (American Psychiatric Association, 2000). This is true even across various cultures (Blazer et al., 1994; Weissman et al., 1993). Many possible explanations have been proposed for this gender difference, including the different hormonal structure of the female system (menstruation, hormonal changes during and after pregnancy, menopause, etc.) and different social roles played by women in the culture (Blehar & Oren, 1997). Research has found little support for hormonal influences in general, instead finding that the role of hormones and other biological factors in depression is unclear. Instead, studies have found that the degree of differences between male and female rates of depression is decreasing and is nonexistent in college students and single adults, leading some to conclude that social factors such as marital status, career type, and number of children may have more importance in creating the gender difference than biological differences (McGrath et al., 1992; Nolen-Hoeksema, 1990; Weissman & Klerman, 1977).

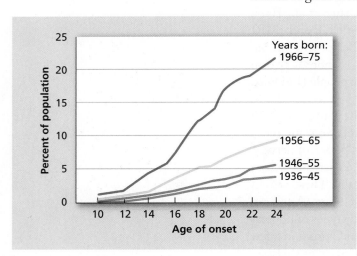

FIGURE 12.2 Prevalence of Major Depressive Disorder

As the most common mood disorder, major depressive disorder has seen an increase in diagnosis with each decade. From 1936 to 1945, the prevalence of major depression in the population was about 3 percent, with the onset of symptoms occurring at around ages 18 to 20. By 1966 to 1975, the prevalence had jumped to about 23 percent of the population, and the age of onset had dropped to the early teens.

Bipolar Disorders

Major depression is sometimes referred to as a *unipolar disorder* because the emotional problem exists at only one end, or "pole," of the emotional range. When a person suffers from severe mood swings that go all the way from severe depression to **manic** episodes (excessive excitement, energy, and elation), that person is said to suffer from a **bipolar disorder**, meaning that emotions cycle between the two poles of possible emotions (American Psychiatric Association, 2000). Unlike mild or moderate mood disorders, there is usually no external cause for the extreme ups and downs of the bipolar person. The depressive phases of a bipolar person are indistinguishable from major depression but give way to manic episodes that may last from a few weeks to a few months. In these manic episodes, the person is extremely happy or euphoric** without any real cause to be so happy. Restlessness, irritability, an inability to sit still or remain

---

*Chronic: long-lasting or occurring frequently over a long period of time.

**Euphoric: having a feeling of vigor, well-being, or high spirits.

inactive, and seemingly unlimited energy are also common. The person may seem silly to others and can become aggressive when not allowed to carry out the grand (and sometimes delusional) plans that are often the hallmark of the manic phase. Speech may be rapid and jump from one topic to another. Oddly, people in the manic state are often very creative until their lack of organization renders their attempts at being creative useless (Blumer, 2002; McDermott, 2001; Rothenberg, 2001).

That sounds almost like a description of an overactive child—can't sit still, can't concentrate—are the two disorders related?

The answer to that question is actually part of an ongoing controversy. There does seem to be a connection between attention-deficit/hyperactivity disorder (ADHD) and the onset of bipolar disorder in adolescence (Carlson et al., 1998), but only a small percentage of children with ADHD go on to develop bipolar disorder. The symptoms of bipolar disorder include irrational thinking and other manic symptoms that are not present in ADHD (Geller et al., 1998). Confusion between the two disorders arises because hyperactivity (excessive movement and an inability to concentrate) is a symptom of both disorders. Researchers compared children diagnosed with both bipolar disorder and ADHD to children diagnosed with ADHD only on measures of academic performance and a series of neurological tests (Henin et al., 2007). They found that the two groups responded in very similar ways, showing the same deficits in information-processing abilities, with only one exception: The children with both disorders performed more poorly on one measure of processing speed when compared to children with only ADHD. The researchers concluded that the neurological deficits often observed in children with bipolar disorder are more likely to be due to the ADHD rather than the bipolar disorder itself. Children with bipolar disorder also seem to suffer from far more severe emotional and behavioral problems than those with ADHD (Ferguson-Noyes, 2005; McDougall, 2009).

Watch on MyPsychLab

That sounds almost like a description of an overactive child— can't sit still, can't concentrate—are the two disorders related?

Watch a video on bipolar disorder on MyPsychLab

Causes of Mood Disorders

Explanations of depression and other mood disorders today come from the perspectives of behavioral, social cognitive, and biological theories as well as genetics.

Behavioral theorists link depression to learned helplessness (Seligman, 1975, 1989), whereas social cognitive theorists point to distortions of thinking such as blowing negative events out of proportion and minimizing positive, good events (Beck, 1976, 1984). In the social cognitive view, depressed people continually have negative, self-defeating thoughts about themselves, which depress them further in a downward spiral of despair. Learned helplessness (discussed in Chapter Four) has been linked to an increase in such self-defeating thinking and depression in studies with people who have experienced uncontrollable, painful events (Abramson et al., 1978, 1980). This link does not necessarily mean that negative thoughts *cause* depression; it may be that depression increases the likelihood of negative thoughts (Gotlib et al., 2001). One study found that when comparing adolescents who were depressed to those who were not, the depressed group faced risk factors specifically associated with the social cognitive environment, such as being female or a member of an ethnic minority, living in poverty, regularly using drugs (including tobacco and alcohol), and engaging in delinquent behavior (Costello et al., 2008). In contrast, those in the nondepressed group of adolescents were more likely to come from two-parent households; had higher self-esteem; and felt connected to parents, peers, and school. Clearly, learned helplessness in the face of discrimination, prejudice, and poverty may be associated with depression in these adolescents. A recent study has also found that when therapists focus

Depression may be caused by conflicts with others, learned reactions, illogical thought patterns, or chemical imbalances—or some combination of all of these factors.

Read and learn more about seasonal affective disorder on **MyPsychLab**

on helping clients to change their way of thinking, depression improves significantly when compared to therapy that focuses only on changing behavior. These results lend support to the cognitive explanation of distorted thinking as the source of depression (Strunk et al., 2010).

Biological explanations of mood disorders focus on the effects of brain chemicals such as serotonin, norepinephrine, and dopamine; drugs used to treat depression and mania typically affect the levels of these three neurotransmitters, either alone or in combination (Cohen, 1997; Cummings & Coffey, 1994; Ruhe et al., 2007).

Some people find that they only get depressed at certain times of the year. In particular, depression seems to set in during the winter months and goes away with the coming of spring and summer. **Seasonal affective disorder (SAD)** is a mood disorder that is caused by the body's reaction to low levels of light present in the winter months (Partonen & Lonnqvist, 1998). Read on **MyPsychLab**

Genes also play a part in mood disorders. The fact that the more severe mood disorders are not a reaction to some outside source of stress or anxiety but rather seem to come from within the person's own body, together with the tendency of mood disorders to appear in genetically related individuals at a higher rate, suggests rather strongly that inheritance may play a significant part in these disorders (Barondes, 1998; Farmer, 1996). Evidence exists for specific genes associated with major depression on chromosome 11 and with bipolar disorder on chromosome 18 (Levinson, 2006; McMahon et al., 2001; Stine et al., 1995). More than 65 percent of people with bipolar disorder have at least one close relative with either bipolar disorder or major depression (Craddock et al., 2005; National Institute of Mental Health Genetics Workgroup, 1998; Sullivan et al., 2000). Twin studies have shown that if one identical twin has either major depression or bipolar disorder, the chances that the other twin will also develop a mood disorder are about 40 to 70 percent (Muller-Oerlinghausen et al., 2002).

Eating Disorders

12.6 What are the two primary types of eating disorders, how do they differ, and who are they most likely to affect?

Anorexia Nervosa

Anorexia nervosa, often called simply **anorexia**, is a condition in which a person (typically young and female) reduces eating to the point that a weight loss of 15 percent below expected body weight or more is the result (Rideout, 2005). At a weight loss of 40 percent below expected body weight, hospitalization is necessary. Hormone secretion becomes abnormal, especially in the thyroid and adrenal glands. The heart muscles become weak, and heart rhythms may alter. Other physical effects of anorexia include diarrhea, loss of muscle tissue, sleeplessness, low blood pressure, and lack of menstruation in females.

Some individuals with anorexia will eat in front of others (whereas individuals with bulimia tend to binge eat as secretly as possible) but then force themselves to throw up or take large doses of laxatives. They are often obsessed with exercising and with food—cooking elaborate meals for others while eating nothing themselves.

seasonal affective disorder (SAD) a mood disorder caused by the body's reaction to low levels of sunlight in the winter months.

anorexia nervosa (anorexia) a condition in which a person reduces eating to the point that a weight loss of 15 percent below the ideal body weight or more occurs.

They have extremely distorted body images, seeing fat where others see only skin and bones.

What causes anorexia is not yet fully understood. Some theories involve biological explanations. Others point to psychological factors such as sexual abuse, perfectionism with a desire to control as many aspects of one's life as possible, and family dysfunction (Abraham & Llewellyn-Jones, 2001; Mitchell, 1985).

What can be done to treat anorexia? If the anorexic weight loss is severe (40 percent or more below expected normal weight), dehydration, severe chemical imbalances, and possibly organ damage may result. Hospitalization should occur before this dangerous point is reached. Psychological counseling will also be part of the hospital treatment, which may last from 2 to 4 months. Those individuals with anorexia who are not so severely malnourished as to be in immediate danger can be treated outside of the hospital setting, typically receiving supportive psychotherapy, behavioral therapy, and perhaps group therapy. Family therapy is nearly always appropriate when the family of the individual with anorexia is contributing in some way to the behavior. ⓁⒾⓃⓀ to Chapter Thirteen: Psychological Therapies, p. 479. The prognosis for full recovery is not as hopeful as it should be; only 40 to 60 percent of all individuals with anorexia who receive treatment will make a recovery. For some individuals with anorexia who do gain weight, the damage already done to the heart and other body systems may still be so great that an early death is a possibility (Neumarker, 1997).

👁 Watch on MyPsychLab

Bulimia Nervosa

Bulimia nervosa, often called **bulimia**, is a condition in which a person develops a cycle of "bingeing" or overeating enormous amounts of food at one sitting, and then using inappropriate methods for avoiding weight gain (American Psychiatric Association, 2000; Rideout, 2005). Most individuals with bulimia engage in "purging" behaviors, such as deliberately vomiting after the binge or misuse of laxatives, but some may not, using other inappropriate methods to avoid weight gain such as fasting the day or two after the binge or engaging in excessive exercise (American Psychiatric Association, 2000). There are some similarities to anorexia: The victims are usually female, are obsessed with their appearance, diet excessively, and believe themselves to be fat even when they are quite obviously not fat. But individuals with bulimia are typically a little older than individuals with anorexia at the onset of the disorder—early 20s rather than early puberty. Individuals with bulimia often maintain a normal weight, making the disorder difficult to detect. The most obvious difference between the two conditions is that the bulimic individual will eat, and eat to excess, bingeing on huge amounts of food—an average of 3,500 calories in a single binge and as much as 50,000 calories in one day (Humphries, 1987; Mitchell et al., 1981; Oster, 1987).

But wait a minute—if individuals with bulimia are so concerned about gaining weight, why do they binge at all?

The binge itself may be prompted by an anxious or a depressed mood, social stressors, feelings about body weight or image, or intense hunger after attempts to diet. The binge continues due to a lack of, or impairment in, self-control once the binge begins. The individual is unable to control when to stop eating or how much to eat. Eating one cookie while trying to control weight can lead to a binge—after all, since the diet is completely blown, why not go all out? This kind of thought process is another example of the cognitive distortion of all-or-nothing thinking.

Like anorexia, bulimia comes with many serious health consequences: severe tooth decay and erosion of the lining of the esophagus from the acidity of the vomiting, enlarged salivary glands, potassium, calcium, and sodium imbalances that can be

This young model is not merely thin; by medical standards she is probably at a weight that would allow her to be labeled as anorexic. The "thin is in" mentality that dominates the field of fashion design models is a major contributor to the Western cultural concept of very thin women as beautiful and desirable. The model pictured here is a far cry from the days of sex symbol Marilyn Monroe, who was rumored to be a size 12.

👁 Watch a video on anorexia on MyPsychLab

But wait a minute— if individuals with bulimia are so concerned about gaining weight, why do they binge at all?

bulimia nervosa (bulimia) a condition in which a person develops a cycle of "bingeing," or overeating enormous amounts of food at one sitting, and then using unhealthy methods to avoid weight gain.

very dangerous, damage to the intestinal tract from overuse of laxatives, heart problems, fatigue, and seizures (Berg, 1999).

Several research studies indicate a genetic component for both bulimia and anorexia (Fumeron et al., 2001; Strober et al., 2000; Vink et al., 2001). Psychological issues of control have also been cited, but biological evidence suggests that brain chemistry, and in particular low levels of the neurotransmitter *serotonin*, is involved in both bulimia and anorexia (Fumeron et al., 2001; Jimerson et al., 1997; Kaye, 2005). Other studies point to the role of leptin, a hormone that has also been implicated in obesity (Ferron et al., 1997; Monteleone et al., 2002). Individuals with anorexia may have too much leptin, whereas individuals with bulimia may have too little (Frederich et al., 2002). Women with bulimia may also be more impulsive in their eating behavior because of the way in which their brains function. Compared to nonbulimic women, the bulimic women in a recent study had lower levels of activity in areas of the brain believed to be responsible for self-control, including the inferior prefrontal cortex and anterior cingulate cortex (Marsh et al., 2009).

Treatment of bulimia can involve many of the same measures taken to treat anorexia: hospitalization, drug therapy to affect serotonin levels, and psychotherapy. The prognosis for recovery from bulimia is somewhat more hopeful than that for anorexia. Cognitive therapy, which involves helping clients understand how illogical and irrational their thought patterns have become, has been successful in treating bulimia (DeAngelis, 2002). Ⓛ Ⓘ Ⓝ Ⓚ to Chapter Thirteen: Psychological Therapies, pp. 476–478.

CULTURE AND EATING DISORDERS Although many researchers have believed eating disorders, especially anorexia, are culture-bound syndromes that only show up in cultures obsessed with being thin (as many Western cultures are), eating disorders are also found in non-Western cultures (Miller & Pumariega, 1999). The difference between Western and non-Western cultures lies in the rate at which such disorders appear. For example, Chinese and Chinese American women are far less likely to suffer from eating disorders than are non-Hispanic white women (Pan, 2000). Why wouldn't Chinese American women be more likely to have eating disorders after being exposed to the Western cultural obsession with thinness? Pan (2000) assumes that whatever Chinese cultural factors "protect" Chinese women from developing eating disorders may also still have a powerful influence on Chinese American women.

One challenge with looking at anorexia and bulimia in other cultures is that the behavior of starving oneself may be seen in other cultures as having an entirely different purpose than in Western cultures. One key component of anorexia, for example, is a fear of being fat, a fear that is missing in many other cultures. Yet women in those cultures have starved themselves for other socially recognized reasons: religious fasting or unusual ideas about nutrition (Castillo, 1997).

Anorexia and bulimia have also been thought to occur only rarely in African American women, but that characterization seems to be changing. Researchers are seeing an increase in anorexia and bulimia among young African American women of all socioeconomic levels (Crago et al., 1996; Mintz & Betz, 1988; Pumariega & Gustavson, 1994). If clinicians and doctors are not aware that these disorders can affect more than the typical white, young, middle-class to upper-middle-class woman, important signs and symptoms of eating disorders in non-white or non-Western people may allow these disorders to go untreated until it is too late.

practice quiz   How much do you remember?

Pick the best answer.

1. An irrational fear of blood would be a _____.
   a. social phobia.
   b. specific phobia.
   c. type of agoraphobia.
   d. type of acrophobia.

2. Nicole worries that someone might come into her house at night while she is sleeping and helpless. She checks the locks on the doors and windows several times before she can relax enough to go to bed. Her constant checking of the locks is most similar to _____.
   a. a compulsion.
   b. an obsession.
   c. a panic disorder.
   d. a phobia.

3. Anxiety, recurring nightmares, sleep disturbances, and concentration problems that occur for more than 1 month after a major stressor are likely symptoms of _____.
   a. acute stress disorder.
   b. posttraumatic stress disorder.
   c. pretraumatic stress disorder.
   d. general stress disorder.

4. Sandy has the tendency to make everything seem so much worse than it usually is. Beck would say that Sandy has a tendency to _____.
   a. overgeneralize.
   b. minimize.
   c. do all-or-nothing thinking.
   d. magnify.

5. Macha woke up one morning in a very sad mood and couldn't think of any reason why she should feel that way. The feeling got worse as the day went on, and although in the days and weeks to follow she occasionally felt normal, she had more sad days than normal. Her feelings were so intense that she couldn't sleep, ate too much, and couldn't take joy in anything. Macha is most likely suffering from _____.
   a. dysthymia.
   b. cyclothymia.
   c. major depression.
   d. bipolar disorder.

6. Trent was always coming up with grand plans for making money, none of which lasted very long before he abandoned them. The latest scheme is to buy a huge tract of land and build an expensive "dude" ranch where people can come to learn how to train their horses, eat at a four-star restaurant, and stay in luxury accommodations—all this in spite of the fact that Trent and his wife don't have the money to buy the land, knowledge of how to run a hotel, or have a four-star chef handy. Trent may have _____.
   a. dysthymia.
   b. cyclothymia.
   c. major depression.
   d. bipolar disorder.

7. One of the main differences between anorexia nervosa and bulimia nervosa is that the individual with anorexia nervosa _____.
   a. is obsessed about body weight.
   b. tends to be female.
   c. weighs 15 percent or more below expected body weight.
   d. can suffer from heart problems.

8. Bulimia nervosa, unlike anorexia nervosa, _____.
   a. produces an obsession with food.
   b. is hard to detect because the person's weight is often normal.
   c. is not physically harmful.
   d. involves starvation.

Brainstorming: How might the proliferation of various media and the Internet affect the development of eating disorders in cultures not previously impacted by them?

ANSWERS ON PAGE AK-2

Schizophrenia: Altered Reality

Once known as *dementia praecox*, a Latin-based term meaning "out of one's mind before one's time," **schizophrenia** was renamed by Eugen Bleuler, a Swiss psychiatrist, to better illustrate the division (*schizo-*) within the brain (*phren*) among thoughts, feelings, and behavior that seems to take place in people with this disorder (Bleuler, 1911; Möller & Hell, 2002). Because the term literally means "split mind," it has often been confused with dissociative identity disorder, which was at one time called "split personality." A more modern definition of schizophrenia describes it as a long-lasting **psychotic** disorder (involving a severe break with reality), in which there is an inability to distinguish what is real from fantasy as well as disturbances in thinking, emotions, behavior, and perception.

12.7 What are the main symptoms, types, and causes of schizophrenia?
Symptoms

Schizophrenia includes several different kinds of symptoms. Disorders in thinking are a common symptom and are called **delusions**. Although delusions are not prominent in all forms of schizophrenia, they are the symptom that most people

schizophrenia   severe disorder in which the person suffers from disordered thinking, bizarre behavior, hallucinations, and inability to distinguish between fantasy and reality.

psychotic   term applied to a person who is no longer able to perceive what is real and what is fantasy.

delusions   false beliefs held by a person who refuses to accept evidence of their falseness.

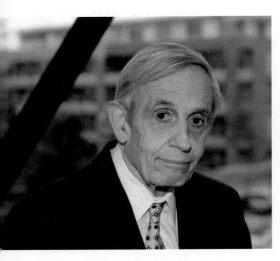

Dr. John Nash is a famous mathematician who won the Nobel Prize for mathematics in 1994. His fame, however, is more due to the fact that Nash once suffered from a form of schizophrenia in which he experienced delusions of persecution. He at one time believed that aliens were trying to contact him through the newspaper (delusions of reference). His life story and remarkable recovery from schizophrenia are portrayed in the 2001 movie *A Beautiful Mind*, which starred Russell Crowe as Nash.

associate with this disorder. Delusions are false beliefs about the world that the person holds and that tend to remain fixed and unshakable even in the face of evidence that disproves the delusions. Common schizophrenic delusions include *delusions of persecution*, in which people believe that others are trying to hurt them in some way; *delusions of reference*, in which people believe that other people, television characters, and even books are specifically talking to them; *delusions of influence*, in which people believe that they are being controlled by external forces, such as the devil, aliens, or cosmic forces; and *delusions of grandeur* in which people are convinced that they are powerful people who can save the world or have a special mission (American Psychiatric Association, 2000).

Delusional thinking alone is not enough to merit a diagnosis of schizophrenia, as there is a separate category of psychotic disorders called **delusional disorders**, in which the primary symptom is some form of delusion. In schizophrenia, other symptoms must be present (American Psychiatric Association, 2000; Black & Andreason, 1999). Speech disturbances are common: People with schizophrenia will make up words, repeat words or sentences persistently, string words together on the basis of sounds (called *clanging*, such as "come into house, louse, mouse, mouse and cheese, please, sneeze"), and experience sudden interruptions in speech or thought. Thoughts are significantly disturbed as well, with individuals with schizophrenia having a hard time linking their thoughts together in a logical fashion.

People with schizophrenia may also have **hallucinations**, in which they hear voices or see things or people that are not really there. Hearing voices is actually more common and one of the key symptoms in making a diagnosis of schizophrenia (Kuhn & Nasar, 2001; Nasar, 1998). Hallucinations involving touch, smell, and taste are less common but also possible.

Emotional disturbances are also a key feature of schizophrenia. **Flat affect** is a condition in which the person shows little or no emotion. Emotions can also be excessive and/or inappropriate—a person might laugh when it would be more appropriate to cry or show sorrow, for example.

The person's behavior may also become disorganized and extremely odd. For example, some forms of schizophrenia are accompanied by periods of complete immobility, whereas others may involve weird facial grimaces and odd gesturing. According to the American Psychiatric Association (2000), at least two or more of the following symptoms must be present frequently for at least 1 month to diagnose schizophrenia: delusions, hallucinations, disturbed speech, disturbed emotions, and disturbed behavior. Symptoms in general must also persist for at least 6 months.

Attention is also a problem for many people with schizophrenia. They seem to have trouble "screening out" information and stimulation that they don't really need, causing them to be unable to focus on information that is relevant (Asarnow et al., 1991; Luck & Gold, 2008).

Categories of Schizophrenia

Although all people with schizophrenia share the symptoms already discussed to a certain degree, the way in which these symptoms show up in behavior can be used to distinguish among several different types of schizophrenia. There are five subtypes of schizophrenia and two categories of symptoms (American Psychiatric Association, 2000). Three of the subtypes will be highlighted along with the two symptom categories that are seen across the different subtypes.

DISORGANIZED People suffering from **disorganized** schizophrenia are very confused in speech, have vivid and frequent hallucinations, and tend to have very inappropriate affect (emotion) or flat affect. They are very socially impaired, unable to engage

delusional disorder a psychotic disorder in which the primary symptom is one or more delusions.

hallucinations false sensory perceptions, such as hearing voices that do not really exist.

flat affect a lack of emotional responsiveness.

disorganized type of schizophrenia in which behavior is bizarre and childish, and thinking, speech, and motor actions are very disordered.

in the normal social rituals of daily life. Giggling, silliness, nonsensical speech, and neglect of cleanliness are common. They may not bathe or change clothing and may urinate or defecate in public, either because of incontinence or a deliberate wish to shock onlookers.

CATATONIC **Catatonic** schizophrenia is less common and involves very disturbed motor behavior. The person doesn't respond to the outside world and either doesn't move at all, maintaining often odd-looking postures for hours on end (a condition known as *catatonia*) or moves about wildly in great agitation. It's as if there are only two "speeds" for the catatonic, totally off or totally on.

PARANOID People diagnosed with **paranoid** schizophrenia suffer from hallucinations and delusions. Auditory* hallucinations are common, and the delusions are typically persecution, grandeur, or extreme jealousy of another or several other persons. Although their thinking is not as scattered as that of someone with disorganized schizophrenia, their delusions tend to be bizarre** but very systematic.

Another way of categorizing schizophrenia is to look at the kind of symptoms that predominate. **Positive symptoms** appear to reflect an excess or distortion of normal functions, such as hallucinations and delusions. **Negative symptoms** appear to reflect a decrease of normal functions, such as poor attention or lack of affect (American Psychiatric Association, 2000).

Positive symptoms are associated with overactivity in the subcortical dopamine areas of the brain. Dopamine-reducing drugs used to treat schizophrenia are usually effective for these symptoms, and the outlook for recovery is generally good (Davis et al., 1991; Penn, 1998).

Negative symptoms include the inability to filter out stimuli to focus attention, flat affect, problems with producing speech, apathy, and withdrawal from others. Negative symptoms, unlike positive symptoms, are associated with *lower* than normal activity in the cortical dopamine systems of the brain and problems in the functioning of the frontal lobe. Studies have found that those with schizophrenia and primarily negative symptoms have decreased blood flow to the frontal lobe areas (Davis et al., 1991; Perlstein et al., 2001) and enlarged ventricles (the fluid-filled spaces within the brain) when compared to people without schizophrenia (Serban et al., 1990). Unfortunately, this also means that the outlook for recovery from schizophrenia with predominantly negative symptoms is not good, as these symptoms do not respond well to medications that are effective with schizophrenia with predominantly positive symptoms.

Causes of Schizophrenia

When trying to explain the cause or causes of schizophrenia, the biopsychological model prevails. Biological explanations of schizophrenia have generated a significant amount of research pointing to genetic origins, inflammation in the brain, chemical influences (dopamine, GABA, glutamate, and other neurotransmitters), and brain structural defects (frontal lobe defects, deterioration of neurons, and reduction in white matter integrity) as the causes of schizophrenia (Gottesman & Shields, 1982; Harrison, 1999; Kety et al., 1994; Nestor et al., 2008; Söderlund et al., 2009). Dopamine was first suspected when amphetamine users began to show schizophrenia-like psychotic symptoms. One of the side effects of amphetamine usage is to increase the

Nathaniel Ayers, a homeless musician, is pictured in 2003 in front of The Midnight Mission shelter in Los Angeles, California. Mr. Ayers's life is the subject of the 2009 movie *The Soloist* starring Jamie Foxx. Mr. Ayers was a Julliard-trained musician who became mentally ill.

catatonic type of schizophrenia in which the person experiences periods of statue-like immobility mixed with occasional bursts of energetic, frantic movement, and talking.

paranoid type of schizophrenia in which the person suffers from delusions of persecution, grandeur, and jealousy, together with hallucinations.

positive symptoms symptoms of schizophrenia that are excesses of behavior or occur in addition to normal behavior; hallucinations, delusions, and distorted thinking.

negative symptoms symptoms of schizophrenia that are less than normal behavior or an absence of normal behavior; poor attention, flat affect, and poor speech production.

---

*Auditory: having to do with hearing.
** Bizarre: extremely unusual or weird.

release of dopamine in the brain. Drugs used to treat schizophrenia decrease the activity of dopamine in areas of the brain responsible for some of the positive symptoms such as overactivity. However, the prefrontal cortex (an area of the brain involved in the planning and organization of information) of people with schizophrenia has been shown to produce lower levels of dopamine than normal (Harrison, 1999), resulting in attention deficits (Luck & Gold, 2008) and poor organization of thought, negative symptoms of the disorder.

Further support for a biological explanation of schizophrenia comes from studies of the incidence of the disorder across different cultures. If schizophrenia were caused mainly by environmental factors, rates of schizophrenia would be expected to vary widely from culture to culture. In fact, about 7 to 8 individuals out of 1,000 will develop schizophrenia in their lifetime, regardless of the culture (Saha et al., 2005; Torrey, 1987).

Family, twin, and adoption studies have provided strong evidence that genes are a major means of transmitting schizophrenia. The highest risk for developing schizophrenia if one has a blood relative with the disorder is faced by monozygotic (identical) twins, who share 100 percent of their genetic material, with a risk factor of about 50 percent (Cardno & Gottesman, 2000; Gottesman & Shields, 1976, 1982; Gottesman et al., 1987). Dizygotic twins, who share about 50 percent of their genetic material, have about a 17 percent risk, the same as a child with one parent with schizophrenia. As genetic relatedness decreases, so does the risk (see Figure 12.3).

Adoption studies also support the genetic basis of schizophrenia. In one study, the biological and adoptive relatives of adoptees with schizophrenia were compared to a control group of adoptees without schizophrenia but from similar backgrounds and conditions (Kety et al., 1994). The adoptees with schizophrenia had relatives with schizophrenia but *only among their biological relatives.* When the prevalence of schizophrenia was compared between the biological relatives of the adoptees with schizophrenia and the biological relatives of the control group, the rate of the disorder in the relatives of the group with schizophrenia was 10 times higher than in the control group (Kety et al., 1994). ⊙▸ Simulate on **MyPsychLab**

● There's something I don't understand. If one identical twin has the gene and the disorder, shouldn't the other one always have it, too? Why is the rate only 50 percent?

If schizophrenia were entirely controlled by genes, identical twins would indeed both have the disorder at a risk of 100 percent, not merely 50 percent.

There's something I don't understand. If one identical twin has the gene and the disorder, shouldn't the other one always have it, too? Why is the rate only 50 percent?

⊙▸ **Simulate** the diagnosis of schizophrenia on **MyPsychLab**

FIGURE 12.3 Genetics and Schizophrenia
This chart shows a definite pattern: The greater the degree of genetic relatedness, the higher the risk of schizophrenia in individuals related to each other. The only individual to carry a risk even close to that of identical twins (who share 100 percent of their genes) is a person who is the child of two parents with schizophrenia.
Source: Gottesman (1991).

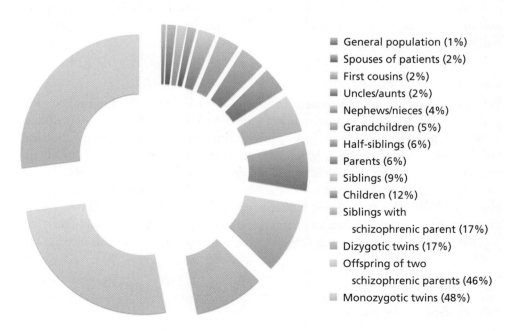

- General population (1%)
- Spouses of patients (2%)
- First cousins (2%)
- Uncles/aunts (2%)
- Nephews/nieces (4%)
- Grandchildren (5%)
- Half-siblings (6%)
- Parents (6%)
- Siblings (9%)
- Children (12%)
- Siblings with schizophrenic parent (17%)
- Dizygotic twins (17%)
- Offspring of two schizophrenic parents (46%)
- Monozygotic twins (48%)

Obviously, environment also has some influence on the development of schizophrenia. One model that has been proposed is the **stress-vulnerability model**, which assumes that persons with the genetic "markers" for schizophrenia have a physical vulnerability to the disorder but will not develop schizophrenia unless they are exposed to environmental or emotional stress at critical times in development, such as puberty (Harrison, 1999; Weinberger, 1987). That would explain why only one twin out of a pair might develop the disorder when both carry the genetic markers for schizophrenia—the life stresses for the affected twin were different from those of the one who remained healthy. The immune system is activated during stress, and one recent study has found that in recent-onset schizophrenia (the early stages of the disorder) the brain's immune system secretes high levels of an inflammation-fighting substance, indicating a possible infection (Söderlund et al., 2009). This leads to the possibility that schizophrenia might one day be treatable with anti-inflammatory medications.

The development of brain-scanning techniques such as magnetic resonance imaging (MRI) and functional MRI (fMRI) has made studies of the structure as well as the functioning of the brains of those with schizophrenia possible. In one study, researchers using *diffusion tensor imaging* (DTI), **LINK** to Chapter Two: The Biological Perspective, p. 62, in addition to other neurological testing found that, when compared to healthy control participants, participants with schizophrenia showed structural differences in two particular areas of the brain (Nestor et al., 2008). Specifically, areas known as the cingulum bundle (CB, consisting of fibers underlying the cingulate gyrus linking parts of the limbic system) and the uncinate fasciculus (UF, neural fibers linking the frontal lobe to the temporal lobe) were found to have significantly less myelin coating on the axons of the neurons within the bundle. This makes these areas of the brain less efficient in sending neural messages to other cells, resulting in decreased memory and decision-making ability. The CB has been implicated in other studies of schizophrenia using DTI and suggest that the less myelin and lower neural efficiency are partly responsible for attention problems in schizophrenia (Kubicki et al., 2009) and that lower white matter integrity in areas of the frontal lobe might be associated with a genetic predisposition to schizophrenia (Camchong et al., 2009). Measuring cortical thickness and tracking changes in the volume of gray matter and white matter is also providing valuable information about the abnormal patterns of brain development in schizophrenia and other disorders (Gogtay et al., 2008; Gogtay & Thompson, 2010; Goldman et al., 2009).

Nestor et al. (2008) used diffusion tensor imaging to investigate schizophrenia. Two of the brain areas examined were the cingulum bundle (CB) and the uncinate fasciculus (UF), two fiber pathways. The cingulum bundle is depicted in the image above. For individuals with schizophrenia, both the CB and UF fiber pathways were found to have neurons with significantly less myelin, making them less efficient in information transfer, and resulting in decreased memory and decision-making ability.
Image courtesy of Dr. Paul Nestor.

Personality Disorders

12.8 How do the various personality disorders differ, and what is thought to be the cause of personality disorders?

Personality disorders are a little different from other psychological disorders in that the disorder does not affect merely one aspect of the person's life, such as a higher than normal level of anxiety or a set of distorted beliefs, but instead affects the entire life adjustment of the person. The disorder is the personality itself, not one aspect of it. In personality disorder, a person has an excessively rigid, maladaptive pattern of behavior and ways of relating to others (American Psychiatric Association, 2000). This rigidity and inability to adapt to social demands and life changes make it very difficult for the individual with a personality disorder to fit in with others or have relatively normal

stress-vulnerability model explanation of disorder that assumes a biological sensitivity, or vulnerability, to a certain disorder will result in the development of that disorder under the right conditions of environmental or emotional stress.

personality disorders disorders in which a person adopts a persistent, rigid, and maladaptive pattern of behavior that interferes with normal social interactions.

social relationships. The *DSM-IV-TR* lists ten types personality disorders across three basic categories (American Psychiatric Association, 2000): those in which the people are seen as odd or eccentric by others (Paranoid, Schizoid, Schizotypal), those in which the behavior of the person is very dramatic, emotional, or erratic (Antisocial, Borderline, Histrionic, Narcissistic), and those in which the main emotion is anxiety or fearfulness (Avoidant, Dependent, Obsessive-Compulsive).

Antisocial Personality Disorder

One of the most well researched of the personality disorders is **antisocial personality disorder**. People with antisocial personality disorder are literally "against society." The antisocial person, sometimes called a *sociopath*, habitually breaks the law, disobeys rules, tells lies, and uses other people without worrying about their rights or feelings. The person with antisocial personality seems to have no real conscience to create guilt feelings when the person does something morally wrong. As a consequence, people with this disorder typically feel no remorse or guilt at lying, cheating, stealing, or even more serious crimes such as murder.

The first thing that usually comes to most people's minds when they hear the term *sociopath* is the *serial killer*, a person who kills others for the excitement and thrill of killing without feeling any guilt. However, most antisocial personalities are not killers. Typically they borrow money or belongings and don't bother to repay the debt or return the items, they are impulsive, they don't keep their commitments either socially or in their jobs, and they tend to be very selfish, self-centered, manipulative, and unable to feel deep emotions.

There is a definite gender difference in antisocial personality disorder, with nearly three times to six times as many males diagnosed with this disorder as females (American Psychiatric Association, 2000; Paris, 2004).

Borderline Personality Disorder

People with **borderline personality disorder** have relationships with other people that are intense and relatively unstable. They are often moody, manipulative, and untrusting of others. Periods of depression are not unusual, and some may engage in excessive spending, drug abuse, or suicidal behavior (suicide attempts may be part of the manipulation the borderline personality uses against others in a relationship). Emotions are often inappropriate and excessive, leading to confusion with *histrionic personality disorder*. What makes the individual with borderline personality different is the confusion over identity issues, in which the person may be unable to focus on consistent life goals, career choices, friendships, and even sexual behavior (American Psychiatric Association, 2000).

This disorder is nearly two to three times more frequent in women than in men (American Psychiatric Association, 2000; Swartz et al., 1990). Numerous causes such as genetic or hormonal influences, childhood experiences with incest or other abuse, and a poor mother–infant relationship during the years in which the identity is forming have all been suggested as a cause of the disorder (Torgersen, 2000; Widiger & Weissman, 1991; Zanarini, 2000).

Causes of Personality Disorders

Cognitive-behavioral theorists talk about how specific behavior can be learned over time through the processes of reinforcement, shaping, and modeling. More cognitive explanations involve the belief systems formed by the personality disordered persons, such as the paranoia, extreme self-importance, and fear of being unable to cope by oneself of the paranoid, narcissistic, and dependent personalities, for example.

There is some evidence of genetic factors in personality disorders (Reichborn-Kjennerud, 2008). Close biological relatives of people with disorders such as antisocial, schizotypal, and borderline are more likely to have these disorders than those who are not related (American Psychiatric Association, 2000; Battaglia et al., 1995; Faraone et al., 1999; Nigg & Goldsmith, 1994). Adoption studies of children whose biological parents had antisocial personality disorder show an increased risk for that disorder in those children, even though they are raised in a different environment by different people (American Psychiatric Association, 2000). A longitudinal study has linked the temperaments of children at age 3 to antisocial tendencies in adulthood, finding that those children with lower fearfulness and inhibitions were more likely to show antisocial personality characteristics in a follow-up study at age 28 (Glenn et al., 2007).

Other causes of personality disorders have been suggested. Antisocial personalities are emotionally unresponsive to stressful or threatening situations when compared to others, which may be one reason they are not afraid of getting caught (Arnett et al., 1997; Blair et al., 1995; Lykken, 1995). This unresponsiveness seems to be linked to lower than normal levels of stress hormones in antisocial persons (Fairchild et al., 2008; Lykken, 1995).

Disturbances in family relationships and communication have also been linked to personality disorders and, in particular, to antisocial personality disorder (Benjamin, 1996; Livesley, 1995). Childhood abuse, neglect, overly strict parenting, overprotective parenting, and parental rejection have all been offered as possible causes, complicating the picture of the development of personality disorders. It is safe to say that many of the same factors (genetics, social relationships, and parenting) that help to create ordinary personalities also create disordered personalities.

practice quiz — How much do you remember?

12.7 12.8

Pick the best answer.

1. Charles believed that a famous song by a popular musical group carried a special, secret message meant only for him. This would be an example of a delusion of _____.
   a. persecution.
   b. reference.
   c. influence.
   d. grandeur.

2. In an old movie, a madman made weird faces and sounds, jumped about wildly in his cell, and laughed and giggled constantly. This bizarre behavior is typical of _____ schizophrenia.
   a. disorganized
   b. catatonic
   c. paranoid
   d. depressed

3. In which type of schizophrenia is an individual most likely to have delusions of grandeur?
   a. disorganized
   b. catatonic
   c. paranoid
   d. depressed

4. Which of the following statements about antisocial personality disorder is TRUE?
   a. Most people with this disorder are vicious killers.
   b. Most people with this disorder are men.
   c. People with this disorder suffer terrible guilt but commit crimes anyway.
   d. People with this disorder feel emotions very deeply and intensely.

Brainstorming: Do you think it is possible for someone with a personality disorder to change his or her maladaptive behavior with the help of psychotherapy? Are there any personality disorders that might be more changeable than others?

ANSWERS ON PAGE AK-2

applying psychology to everyday life

Taking the Worry Out of Exams

Imagine this scenario: You sit down to take your midterm exam, feeling that you are prepared and ready. Once you get the test in front of you, well, maybe you start to feel just a bit more nervous, your hands get sweaty, your stomach may ache; and when you look at the first question—your mind becomes a complete blank!

These are a few of the common symptoms of *test anxiety*, the personal experience of possible negative consequences or poor outcomes on an exam or evaluation, accompanied by a cluster of cognitive, affective, and behavioral symptoms (Zeidner & Matthews, 2005). *Cognitive* symptoms may consist of worrying excessively about an exam, expecting to do poorly no matter how hard you study, or even finding it hard to start studying in the first place. Then, while taking the test, you might find you do not understand certain directions or questions, "go blank" when looking at the items, or feel like you cannot concentrate on the exam in front of you because your mind keeps wandering. *Affective* or emotional symptoms may include body tension and heightened physiological arousal, including sweaty palms, upset stomach, difficulty breathing, and the like, prior to and/or during the exam. *Behavioral* aspects may include procrastination, deficient study skills, or avoiding studying altogether.

While not yet recognized as a clinical disorder in the *DSM-IV-TR*, test anxiety has caused countless students considerable stress and agony over the years. Remember "psychology student's syndrome"? You may not really have any of the psychological disorders we've discussed in this chapter, but chances are good that you *have* experienced test anxiety a time or two. One way to make the development of a true anxiety disorder less likely is to deal realistically with milder forms of anxiety *before* they escalate, and the main intent of this section is to help you achieve that.

So, what can you do if you experience test anxiety and want to get your worrying under control? First, determine why you want to do well on the test in the first place. Do you really want to demonstrate your understanding of the material, or are you hoping just to pass? Try to find an internal motivation to do well on the exam rather than simply relying on extrinsic reasons. Even if you are taking a test in a subject you don't necessarily enjoy, try to identify something **you** want to accomplish, and get your focus off the goal of simply earning a passing grade.

Second, develop some type of strategy for controlling both your cognitive state and behavior, before and during the exam. Review the study tips we presented in the Psychology in Action section of this book. As mentioned there, if you are well prepared, you are less likely to worry. Avoid cramming and take advantage of the additive effects of distributed practice. Refer back to that information and review suggestions that will help you manage your tasks and your time. Schedule regular study sessions and avoid or limit distractions (e-mail, phone, text messages, television, noisy roommates, and the like may seem to provide welcome escapes from studying, but they will only keep you from your intended goal). You've read the chapter on Learning (or at least you should have!), and you now know that spacing out your study and using meaningful, elaborative rehearsal over multiple study periods is going to yield much better results than an all-out cramming marathon the night before an exam. **LINK** to Psychology in Action: Secrets for Surviving College and Improving Your Grades, pp. PIA-9–PIA-12.

The way you approach an exam can have a significant impact on the testing experience and how you manage yourself during that exam (Davis et al., 2008). Instead of focusing on how nervous you are and how sure you are that you aren't going to be able to remember anything, turn that thinking around and recognize how much energy you have going in to the exam (Dundas et al., 2009). Positive self-talk can be very valuable in this kind of situation (and is a good example of cognitive therapy at work). A recent study demonstrated that competence-priming (imagining a person who is successful at a related task) lowered the relationship between test anxiety and test performance (Lang & Lang, 2010). Lastly, instead of focusing on the whole exam, take control and address one question at a time, first answering the questions you know—that will build your confidence and help you progress through the test. Also control your body, try to stay relaxed, and breathe normally. If you get distracted, consciously redirect yourself back to the next question. Before you know it, you will have completed the entire exam—whew!

chapter summary

((•◦⎡**Listen** on **MyPsychLab**   Listen to an audio file of your chapter **www.MyPsychLab**

What Is Abnormality?

- Psychopathology is the study of abnormal behavior.

12.1 How has mental illness been explained in the past, how is abnormal behavior defined today, and what is the impact of cultural differences in defining abnormality?

- In ancient times, holes were cut in an ill person's head to let out evil spirits in a process called trepanning. Hippocrates believed that mental illness came from an imbalance in the body's four humors, whereas demonic possession was offered as an explanation during the Middle Ages. During the Renaissance, some of the mentally ill were likely labeled as witches.

- Abnormal behavior can be defined as behavior that is statistically rare, is deviant from social norms, causes subjective discomfort, does not allow day-to-day functioning, or causes a person to be dangerous to self or others.

- Cultural relativity refers to the need to consider the norms and customs of another culture when diagnosing a person from that culture with a disorder.

issues in psychology: Abnormality Versus Insanity

- In the United States, *insanity* is a legal term, not a psychological term.

Models of Abnormality

12.2 How can psychological disorders be explained within the biological and psychological models?

- In biological models of abnormality, the assumption is that mental illnesses are caused by chemical or structural malfunctions in the nervous system.

- Psychodynamic theorists assume that abnormal behavior stems from repressed conflicts and urges that are fighting to become conscious.

- Behaviorists see abnormal behavior as learned.

- Cognitive theorists see abnormal behavior as coming from irrational beliefs and illogical patterns of thought.

Diagnostic and Statistical Manual of Mental Disorders, Fourth Edition, Text Revision (DSM-IV-TR)

12.3 What are the different types of psychological disorders, and how common are they?

- *Diagnostic and Statistical Manual of Mental Disorders, Fourth Edition, Text Revision (DSM-IV-TR)* is a manual of psychological disorders and their symptoms.

- There are five axes in the *DSM-IV-TR*, which include clinical disorders, personality disorders and mental retardation, general medical conditions, psychosocial and environmental problems, and a global assessment of functioning.

- Over one-fifth of all adults over age 18 suffer from a mental disorder in any given year. Major depression is one of the most common psychological disorders worldwide.

Anxiety Disorders: What, Me Worry?

12.4 What are the different types of anxiety disorders, their symptoms, and their causes?

- Anxiety disorders are all disorders in which the most dominant symptom is excessive and unrealistic anxiety.

- Phobias are irrational, persistent fears. The three types of phobias are social phobias, specific phobias, and agoraphobia.

- Obsessive-compulsive disorder consists of an obsessive, recurring thought that creates anxiety and a compulsive, ritualistic, and repetitive behavior or mental act that reduces that anxiety.

- Panic disorder is the sudden and recurrent onset of intense panic for no reason, with all the physical symptoms that can occur in sympathetic nervous system arousal, and is sometimes accompanied by agoraphobia.

- Significant and traumatic stressors can lead to acute stress disorder or posttraumatic stress disorder. The diagnosis differs according to duration and onset but includes symptoms of anxiety, dissociation, nightmares, and reliving the event.

- Generalized anxiety disorder is a condition of intense and unrealistic anxiety that lasts 6 months or more.
- Psychodynamic explanations point to repressed urges and desires that are trying to come into consciousness, creating anxiety that is controlled by the abnormal behavior.
- Behaviorists state that disordered behavior is learned through both operant conditioning and classical conditioning techniques.
- Cognitive psychologists believe that excessive anxiety comes from illogical, irrational thought processes.
- Biological explanations of anxiety disorders include chemical imbalances in the nervous system, in particular serotonin and GABA systems.
- Genetic transmission may be responsible for anxiety disorders among related persons.

Mood Disorders: The Effect of Affect

12.5 What are the different types of mood disorders and their causes?

- Mood disorders, also called affective disorders, are severe disturbances in emotion.
- Dysthymia is a moderate depression that is typically a reaction to some external stressor, whereas cyclothymia consists of moderate mood swings usually tied to an external stressor.
- Major depression has a sudden onset and is extreme sadness and despair, typically with no obvious external cause. It is the most common of the mood disorders and is twice as common in women as in men.
- Bipolar disorders are severe mood swings from major depressive episodes to manic episodes of extreme elation and energy with no obvious external cause.
- Psychodynamic theories see depression as anger at authority figures from childhood turned inward on the self.
- Learning theories link depression to learned helplessness.
- Cognitive theories see depression as the result of distorted, illogical thinking.
- Biological explanations of mood disorders look at the function of serotonin, norepinephrine, and dopamine systems in the brain.
- Mood disorders are more likely to appear in genetically related people with higher rates of risk for closer genetic relatives.

Eating Disorders

12.6 What are the two primary types of eating disorders, how do they differ, and who are they most likely to affect?

- Maladaptive eating problems include anorexia and bulimia.
- Individuals with anorexia or bulimia are typically female, obsessed with appearance, diet excessively, and have distorted body images; biological, psychological, and cultural factors are likely.
- Genetics, low levels of serotonin, and insensitivity to leptin (a hormone that influences appetite) may play a part in anorexia and bulimia.

Schizophrenia: Altered Reality

- Schizophrenia is a split between thoughts, emotions, and behavior. It is a long-lasting psychotic disorder in which reality and fantasy become confused.

12.7 What are the main symptoms, types, and causes of schizophrenia?

- Symptoms of schizophrenia include delusions (false beliefs about the world), hallucinations, emotional disturbances, attentional difficulties, disturbed speech, and disordered thinking.
- The three types of schizophrenic behavior are disorganized, catatonic, and paranoid.
- Positive symptoms are excesses of behavior associated with increased dopamine activity, whereas negative symptoms are deficits in behavior associated with decreased dopamine activity.
- Biological explanations for schizophrenia prevail and focus on dopamine, structural defects in the brain, and genetic influences. Rates of risk of developing schizophrenia increase drastically as genetic relatedness increases, with the highest risk faced by an identical twin whose twin sibling has schizophrenia.

Personality Disorders

12.8 How do the various personality disorders differ, and what is thought to be the cause of personality disorders?

- Personality disorders are extremely rigid, maladaptive patterns of behavior that prevent a person from normal social interactions and relationships.
- In antisocial personality disorder a person has no conscience and uses people for personal gain. A rare form is the serial killer.
- In borderline personality disorder a person is clingy, moody, unstable in relationships, and suffers from problems with identity.
- Cognitive-learning theorists see personality disorders as a set of learned behavior that has become maladaptive—bad habits learned early on in life. Belief systems of the personality disordered person are seen as illogical.
- Biological relatives of people with personality disorders are more likely to develop similar disorders, supporting a genetic basis for such disorders.
- Biological explanations look at the lower than normal stress hormones in antisocial personality disordered persons as responsible for their low responsiveness to threatening stimuli.
- Other possible causes of personality disorders may include disturbances in family communications and relationships, childhood abuse, neglect, overly strict parenting, overprotective parenting, and parental rejection.

applying psychology to everyday life: Taking the Worry Out of Exams

- Test anxiety is a common and very distressing experience for many students.
- Several things can be done to reduce test anxiety, including preparation and relaxation exercises.

TEST yourself

ANSWERS ON PAGE AK-2.

✓● Study and Review on MyPsychLab   Ready for your test? More quizzes and a customized plan. www.MyPsychLab

Pick the best answer.

1. Survivors of natural disasters like Hurricane Katrina in 2005 and the 2010 BP oil spill in the Gulf of Mexico may experience higher incidences of _____:
   a. depression.
   b. posttraumatic stress disorder.
   c. anxiety disorders.
   d. all of the above.

2. What was the most likely reason that ancient peoples performed trepanning on others?
   a. to relieve fluid pressure on the brain
   b. to look into the brain to see what was wrong
   c. to release evil spirits that were in the person's head
   d. to restore balance to the body's humors

3. Michael decided to give up his job teaching at a small community college in Florida and become a monk. He moved to a nearby town with a monastery, took his vows, and is now living quite happily as a member of that religious order. By what definition might Michael's behavior be considered abnormal?
   a. statistical
   b. subjective discomfort
   c. maladaptive
   d. harmful to self

4. Which model of abnormality talks about rewards, shaping, and imitation as ways of developing abnormal behavior?
   a. psychodynamic
   b. behavioral
   c. cognitive
   d. biological

5. Which axis of the *DSM-IV-TR* would a therapist use to classify the loss of a person's job?
   a. I
   b. II
   c. III
   d. IV

6. When anxiety is unrelated to any known, realistic factor, it is called _____.
   a. free-floating anxiety.
   b. panic.
   c. a phobia.
   d. acute.

7. Alisa hates to go over bridges. This is a mild form of _____.
   a. social phobia.
   b. specific phobia.
   c. agoraphobia.
   d. claustrophobia.

8. Professor Albus always checked the door to his office before leaving for class, lunch, or home. He would pull it closed and then rattle the doorknob three times to make sure that it was locked. He does this because he keeps thinking that he hasn't really locked it well. His thoughts about this are a form of _____.
   a. obsession.
   b. compulsion.
   c. anxiety attack.
   d. door phobia.

9. When a person experiences sudden attacks of intense fear, racing heart, dizziness, and other physical signs of stress, and refuses to go away from home for fear one of these attacks will happen again, it is most properly called _____.
   a. an anxiety attack.
   b. a panic attack.
   c. panic disorder.
   d. panic disorder with agoraphobia.

10. Lori went to great lengths to plan a surprise party for her mother's 70th birthday. "Oh, if she finds out about this, the whole thing will be ruined, it'll be a disaster!" Her sister tried to tell her that even if the party ended up not being a surprise, their mother would be happy and have fun, but Lori was convinced that it would be horrible. According to a cognitive theorist, Lori is engaging in _____.
    a. minimization.
    b. all-or-nothing thinking.
    c. overgeneralization.
    d. magnification.

11. Which term does not belong?
    a. bipolar
    b. hypochondria
    c. dysthymia
    d. major depression

12. Which mood disorder consists of mostly manic episodes with only a few episodes of depression?
    a. bipolar
    b. unipolar
    c. dysthymia
    d. major depression

13. Which mood disorder consists of a consistent, extremely sad mood?
    a. bipolar
    b. cyclothymia
    c. mania
    d. major depression

14. Unlike individuals with anorexia, individuals with bulimia _____.
    a. often purge themselves to stay thin.
    b. are obsessed with being too thin.
    c. can do damage to their health.
    d. may appear to be normal in weight.

15. The role of _____, a neurotransmitter, may provide clues to both bulimia and anorexia.
    a. serotonin
    b. insulin
    c. dopamine
    d. norepinephrine

16. A character in an old movie was a street person who wore aluminum foil on his head to protect his brain from the thought-controlling rays of the government. This is an example of a _____ delusion.
    a. persecution
    b. reference
    c. influence
    d. grandeur

17. Which of the following is not a typical symptom of schizophrenia?
    a. overly rational thinking
    b. inappropriate emotions
    c. delusions
    d. hallucinations

18. In which category of schizophrenia would a person be who remains motionless for long periods of time?
    a. catatonic
    b. disorganized
    c. paranoid
    d. undifferentiated

19. David Koresh, leader of the ill-fated Branch Davidians in Waco, Texas, believed that he was "God's Anointed One," who would bring about the end of the world. This is a _____ delusion.
    a. jealous
    b. grandiose
    c. persecutory
    d. somatic

20. Erik gets really anxious before and during exams. What are two strategies he might focus on?
    a. not sleeping the night before an exam and skipping breakfast
    b. improving his studying/preparation beforehand and learning relaxation techniques
    c. really focusing on how anxious he is and breathing rapidly
    d. waiting until his anxiety is at its worst and then just ignoring it

12 psychological disorders

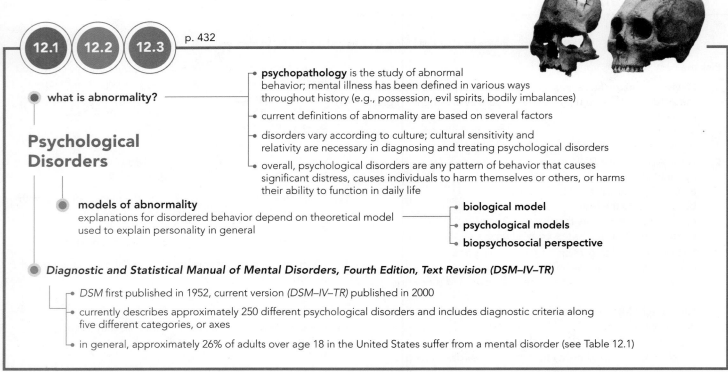

p. 432

12.1 **12.2** **12.3**

Psychological Disorders

what is abnormality?

- **psychopathology** is the study of abnormal behavior; mental illness has been defined in various ways throughout history (e.g., possession, evil spirits, bodily imbalances)
- current definitions of abnormality are based on several factors
- disorders vary according to culture; cultural sensitivity and relativity are necessary in diagnosing and treating psychological disorders
- overall, psychological disorders are any pattern of behavior that causes significant distress, causes individuals to harm themselves or others, or harms their ability to function in daily life

models of abnormality
explanations for disordered behavior depend on theoretical model used to explain personality in general

- **biological model**
- **psychological models**
- **biopsychosocial perspective**

Diagnostic and Statistical Manual of Mental Disorders, Fourth Edition, Text Revision (DSM–IV–TR)

- *DSM* first published in 1952, current version (*DSM–IV–TR*) published in 2000
- currently describes approximately 250 different psychological disorders and includes diagnostic criteria along five different categories, or axes
- in general, approximately 26% of adults over age 18 in the United States suffer from a mental disorder (see Table 12.1)

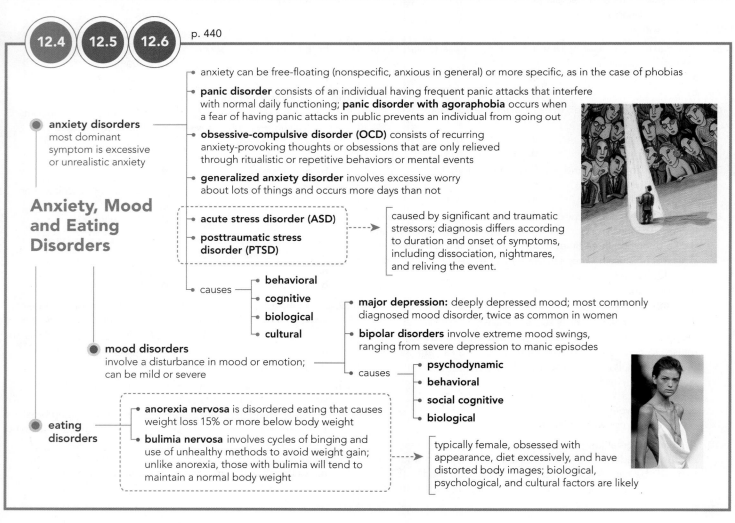

p. 440

12.4 **12.5** **12.6**

Anxiety, Mood and Eating Disorders

anxiety disorders
most dominant symptom is excessive or unrealistic anxiety

- anxiety can be free-floating (nonspecific, anxious in general) or more specific, as in the case of phobias
- **panic disorder** consists of an individual having frequent panic attacks that interfere with normal daily functioning; **panic disorder with agoraphobia** occurs when a fear of having panic attacks in public prevents an individual from going out
- **obsessive-compulsive disorder (OCD)** consists of recurring anxiety-provoking thoughts or obsessions that are only relieved through ritualistic or repetitive behaviors or mental events
- **generalized anxiety disorder** involves excessive worry about lots of things and occurs more days than not

acute stress disorder (ASD)

posttraumatic stress disorder (PTSD)

caused by significant and traumatic stressors; diagnosis differs according to duration and onset of symptoms, including dissociation, nightmares, and reliving the event.

causes
- **behavioral**
- **cognitive**
- **biological**
- **cultural**

mood disorders
involve a disturbance in mood or emotion; can be mild or severe

- **major depression:** deeply depressed mood; most commonly diagnosed mood disorder, twice as common in women
- **bipolar disorders** involve extreme mood swings, ranging from severe depression to manic episodes

causes
- **psychodynamic**
- **behavioral**
- **social cognitive**
- **biological**

eating disorders

- **anorexia nervosa** is disordered eating that causes weight loss 15% or more below body weight
- **bulimia nervosa** involves cycles of binging and use of unhealthy methods to avoid weight gain; unlike anorexia, those with bulimia will tend to maintain a normal body weight

typically female, obsessed with appearance, diet excessively, and have distorted body images; biological, psychological, and cultural factors are likely

p. 451

schizophrenia
psychotic disorder involving a break with reality and disturbances
in thinking, emotions, behavior, and perceptions

primary symptoms
are often classified
as positive (in excess
or in addition to normal
functions) or negative
(absence or decrease
in normal functions)

- **delusions**
- **disturbed or disorganized thoughts**
- **hallucinations**
- **changes in mood**
- **disorganized or odd behavior**

categories
- **disorganized**
- **catatonic**
- **paranoid**

causes

- positive symptoms appear to be associated with overactivity of dopamine areas of brain; negative with lower dopamine activity; related to dopamine hypothesis
- genetics and brain structural defects have been implicated
- biological roots supported by universal lifetime prevalence across cultures of approximately 7–8 people out of 1,000; genetics supported by twin and adoption studies
- **stress-vulnerability model:** suggests people with genetic markers for schizophrenia will not develop the disorder unless they are exposed to environmental or emotional stress at critical times in development

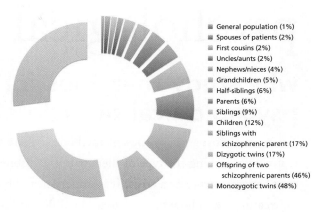

- General population (1%)
- Spouses of patients (2%)
- First cousins (2%)
- Uncles/aunts (2%)
- Nephews/nieces (4%)
- Grandchildren (5%)
- Half-siblings (6%)
- Parents (6%)
- Siblings (9%)
- Children (12%)
- Siblings with schizophrenic parent (17%)
- Dizygotic twins (17%)
- Offspring of two schizophrenic parents (46%)
- Monozygotic twins (48%)

Schizophrenia and Personality Disorders

personality disorders
involve excessively rigid and maladaptive patterns of behavior
and ways of relating to others

- **antisocial personality disorder**
- **borderline personality disorder**
- causes

- **psychodynamic**
- **cognitive-behavioral**
- genetic factors play a role, with many showing increased rates of heritability
- variances in stress tolerance and disturbances in family relationships and communication have also been linked to personality disorders

Odd or Eccentric Types
Paranoid
Schizoid
Schizotypal

Dramatic or Erratic Types
Antisocial
Borderline
Histrionic
Narcissistic

Anxious or Fearful Types
Avoidant
Dependent
Obsessive-Compulsive

13

psychological therapies

why study therapies for psychological disorders?

There are almost as many therapy methods as there are disorders. Correctly matching the type of therapy to the disorder can mean the difference between a cure or a crisis. It is important to know the choices available for treatment and how they relate to the different kinds of disorders so that an informed decision can be made and the best possible outcome can be achieved for mental health and wellness.

chapter outline

Two Kinds of Therapy

The Early Days: Ice-Water Baths and Electric Shocks

Psychotherapy Begins

Humanistic Therapy: To Err Is Human

Behavior Therapies: Learning One's Way to Better Behavior

Cognitive Therapies: Thinking Is Believing

Group Therapies: Not Just for the Shy

PSYCHOLOGY IN THE NEWS: Mental Health on Campus

Does Psychotherapy Really Work?

Biomedical Therapies

APPLYING PSYCHOLOGY TO EVERYDAY LIFE: Virtual Realities

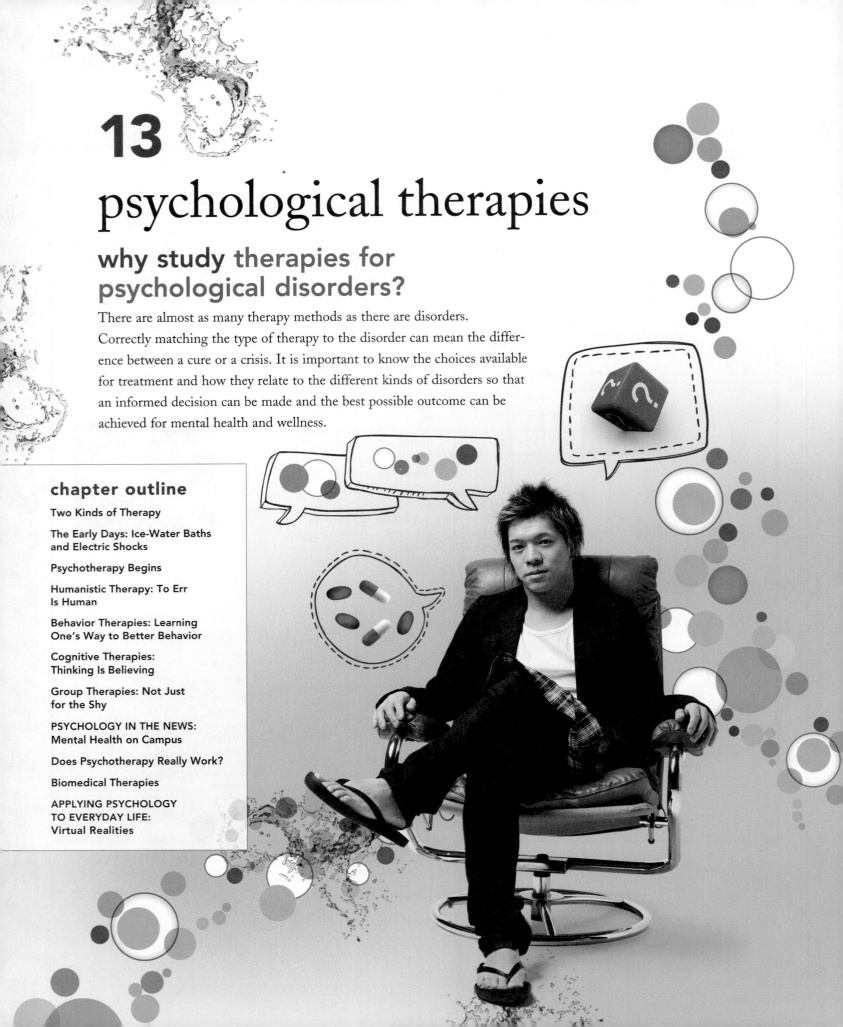

Have you noticed how often television programs, especially medical dramas, take their plots almost directly from newspaper headlines or real situations? A number of years ago, there was an excellent but short-lived medical show called *Chicago Hope*. On one episode, the neurosurgeon worked with a psychiatrist to help a young boy who suffered from obsessive-compulsive disorder (OCD), which caused him to count constantly and left him unable to live a normal life. The neurosurgeon severed some of the neural fibers in an area of the brain called the *cingulate gyrus*, believed to be responsible for the obsessive behavior. In the television program, of course, the surgery is successful.

In real life, this surgery is seen as a treatment of last resort for not only certain OCDs, but also chronic pain. It is called *bilateral anterior cingulotomy* and is discussed near the end of this chapter (Christmas et al., 2004). When this surgery works, its success is attributed to the involvement of this area of the brain in controlling tasks that demand attention (Crottaz-Herbette & Menon, 2006; Davis et al., 2000).

Unfortunately, further research has shown that this procedure does not have as positive a result as the magical world of television might lead you to believe. In a long-term follow-up of 44 patients, each the recipient of a cingulotomy for OCD, only 32 percent of the 44 patients actually responded to the surgery with significant improvement; another 14 percent showed modest signs of improvement, and there were side effects of the surgery: memory problems, apathy, urinary problems, and seizures (Dougherty et al., 2002). The researchers concluded that cingulotomy was perhaps not the best treatment for OCD.

This anecdote illustrates the difficulty of finding the right therapy or combination of therapies to treat disorders. Different disorders require different kinds of therapies, and not all disorders can be completely eliminated. Therapies can take many forms, depending on the particular psychological explanation and approach to the disorder—which will then determine the basis of the therapy. In this chapter, we'll explore many of these forms of therapy and their relative success for various disorders.

learning objectives

13.1 What are the two modern ways in which psychological disorders can be treated, and how have they been treated in the past?

13.2 What were the basic elements of Freud's psychoanalysis, and how does psychoanalysis differ today?

13.3 What are the basic elements of the humanistic therapies known as person-centered therapy and Gestalt therapy?

13.4 How do behavior therapists use classical and operant conditioning to treat disordered behavior?

13.5 What are the goals and basic elements of cognitive therapies such as cognitive–behavioral therapy and rational–emotive behavior therapy?

13.6 What are the various types of group therapies and the advantages and disadvantages of group therapy?

13.7 How effective is psychotherapy, and how is the effectiveness of psychotherapy influenced by cultural, ethnic, and gender differences?

13.8 What are the various types of drugs used to treat psychological disorders?

13.9 How are electroconvulsive therapy and psychosurgery used to treat psychological disorders today?

13.10 How might computers be used in psychotherapy?

study tip

As you are reading this chapter, take a look back at page PIA-6–PIA-8 in *Psychology in Action* for some ways to get more out of this chapter as you read through it.

👁—Watch Episode 17: *Psychological Disorders and Therapies* in the MyPsychLab video series

👁—Watch a video on the history of mental institutions in the United States on **MyPsychLab**

therapy   treatment methods aimed at making people feel better and function more effectively.

psychotherapy   therapy for mental disorders in which a person with a problem talks with a psychological professional.

biomedical therapy   therapy for mental disorders in which a person with a problem is treated with biological or medical methods to relieve symptoms.

insight therapies   therapies in which the main goal is helping people to gain insight with respect to their behavior, thoughts, and feelings.

action therapy   therapy in which the main goal is to change disordered or inappropriate behavior directly.

Two Kinds of Therapy

When talking about treating psychological disorders, there are two main types of **therapy** (treatment methods aimed at making people feel better and function more effectively). In one type of therapy based in psychological techniques, people tell the therapist about their problems, and the therapist listens and tries to help them understand those problems or assists them in changing the behaviors related to the problem. The other type of therapy uses medical interventions to bring the symptoms under control. Although we can separate treatments into these two larger categories, many effective treatments combine facets of both. Just as there as is no one single "cause" of a disorder (Maxmen et al., 2009), different psychological treatments are often used in tandem or combined with biomedical interventions.

13.1 **What are the two modern ways in which psychological disorders can be treated, and how have they been treated in the past?**

The kind of therapy that involves application of psychological principles is called **psychotherapy,** whereas the kind of therapy that uses medical methods is called **biomedical therapy.**

Psychotherapy

The goal of most psychotherapy is to help both mentally healthy and psychologically disordered persons understand themselves better (Goin, 2005; Wolberg, 1977). Because understanding of one's motives and actions is called *insight*, therapies aimed mainly at this goal are called **insight therapies**. A therapy that is directed more at changing behavior than providing insights into the reasons for that behavior is called **action therapy**. Many psychological professionals use a combination of insight and action therapeutic methods.

Biomedical Therapy

The other main type of therapy uses some biological treatment in the form of a medical procedure to bring about changes in the person's disordered behavior. Biomedical therapies include the use of drugs, surgical methods, and electric shock treatments. It is important to understand that biomedical therapy often eliminates or alleviates the symptoms of a disorder while psychotherapy addresses issues associated with the disorder, and when used together, these two types of therapy facilitate each other (Maxmen et al., 2009). For example, when medications are needed, individuals taking the proper medications are going to benefit more from psychotherapy as their symptoms will be better controlled. Furthermore, psychotherapy, not medication, is going to help them better understand what the symptoms of their disorder are and facilitate adjustment, other coping strategies, and proactive ways of addressing the disorder or its related outcomes (Maxmen et al., 2009).

The Early Days: Ice-Water Baths and Electric Shocks

As discussed in Chapter Twelve, although psychological or social causes might have been identified for some disorders, until the late 1700s, people suffering severe mental illnesses were sometimes thought to be possessed by demons or evil spirits, and the "treatments" to rid the person of these spirits were severe and deadly. Even within the last 200 years, a period of supposedly more "enlightened" awareness, the mentally ill did not always receive humane* treatment.👁—Watch on **MyPsychLab**

---

*Humane: marked by compassion, sympathy, or consideration for humans (and animals).

Early Treatment of the Mentally Ill

I've seen movies about mental hospitals, and they didn't look like great places to be in even now—how bad was it back then? What did people do with relatives who were mentally ill?

The first truly organized effort to do something with mentally ill persons began in England in the middle of the sixteenth century. Bethlehem Hospital in London (later known as "Bedlam") was converted into an asylum (a word meaning "place of safety") for the mentally ill. In reality, the first asylums were little more than prisons where the mentally ill were chained to their beds. "Treatments" consisted of blood-letting (which more often than not led to death or the need for lifelong care for the patient), beatings, ice baths in which the person was submerged until passing out or suffering a seizure, and induced vomiting in a kind of spiritual cleansing (Hunt, 1993). This cleansing or purging was meant to rid the body of physical impurities so that the person's mind and soul could function more perfectly.

Pinel's Reforms

It was not until 1793 that efforts were made to treat the mentally ill with kindness and guidance—known as "moral treatment"—rather than beating them or subjecting them to the harsh physical purging that had been commonplace. It was at this time that Philippe Pinel personally unchained the inmates at La Bicêtre Asylum in Paris, France, beginning the movement of humane treatment of the mentally ill (Brigham, 1844; Curtis, 1993).

Psychotherapy Begins

So what exactly happens in psychoanalysis? I've heard lots of stories about it, but what's it really like?

In a sense, Freud took the old method of physical cleansing to a different level. Instead of a physical purge, cleansing for Freud meant removing all the "impurities" of the unconscious mind that he believed were responsible for his patients' psycho-logical and nervous disorders. (Freud was a medical doctor and referred to the people who came to him for help as "patients.") The impurities of the unconscious mind were considered to be disturbing thoughts, socially unacceptable desires, and immoral urges that originated in the id, the part of the personality that is itself unconscious and driven by basic needs for survival and pleasure. ⓁⒾⓃⓀ to Chapter Eleven: Theories of Personality and Intelligence, p. 388.

Psychoanalysis

Freud believed that his patients used these unconscious thoughts to prevent anxiety, and as such, the thoughts would not be easily brought into conscious awareness. Freud designed a therapy technique to help his patients feel more relaxed, open, and able to explore their innermost feelings without fear of embarrassment or rejection. This method was called **psychoanalysis**, and it is an insight therapy that emphasizes revealing the unconscious conflicts, urges, and desires that are assumed to cause disordered emotions and behavior (Freud, 1904b; Mitchell & Black, 1996). This is the original reason for the couch in Freud's version of psychoanalysis; people lying on the couch were more relaxed and would, Freud thought, feel more dependent and childlike, making it easier for them to "get at" those early childhood memories. An additional plus was that he could sit behind the patients at the head of the couch and take notes. Because the patients were unable to see his reactions to what they said, they remained unaffected by his reactions.

I've seen movies about mental hospitals, and they didn't look like great places to be in even now—how bad was it back then? What did people do with relatives who were ill that way?

In this famous painting by French artist Robert Fleury, French psychiatrist Dr. Philippe Pinel orders the chains removed from patients at a Paris asylum for insane women. Pinel was one of the first psychiatrists to recommend humane treatment of the mentally ill.

So what exactly happens in psychoanalysis? I've heard lots of stories about it, but what's it really like?

psychoanalysis an insight therapy based on the theory of Freud, emphasizing the revealing of unconscious conflicts.

"Why do you think you cross the road?"

13.2 What were the basic elements of Freud's psychoanalysis, and how does psychoanalysis differ today?

Freud also made use of two techniques to try to get at the repressed information in his patients' unconscious minds. These techniques were interpreting dreams and allowing patients to talk freely about anything that came to mind.

Dream Interpretation

Dream interpretation, or the analysis of the elements within a patient's reported dream, formed a large part of Freud's psychoanalytic method. Freud believed that repressed material often surfaced in dreams, though in symbolic form. The **manifest content** of the dream was the actual dream and its events, but the **latent content** was the hidden, symbolic meaning of those events that would, if correctly interpreted, reveal the unconscious conflicts that were creating the nervous disorder (Freud, 1900).

Free Association

The other technique for revealing the unconscious mind was a method originally devised by Freud's coworker, Josef Breuer (Breuer & Freud, 1895). Breuer encouraged his patients to freely say whatever came into their minds without fear of being negatively evaluated or condemned. As the patients talked, they began to reveal things that were loosely associated with their flow of ideas, often revealing what Breuer felt were hidden, unconscious concerns. Freud adopted this method of **free association**, believing that repressed impulses and other material were trying to "break free" into consciousness and would eventually surface using this technique.

RESISTANCE AND TRANSFERENCE Other components of Freud's original psychoanalytic method were **resistance** (the point at which the patient becomes unwilling to talk about certain topics due to them being uncomfortably close to repressed material) and **transference** (when the therapist becomes a symbol of a parental authority figure from the past). Therapists can also experience *countertransference*, in which the therapist has a transference reaction to the patient. This reaction might not always be to the patient's benefit. As in all of the therapeutic approaches, peer and professional supervision helps therapists recognize potential issues in providing effective therapy.

Evaluation of Psychoanalysis and Psychodynamic Approaches

Freud's original theory on which he based his interpretations of his patients' revelations has been criticized as having several flaws (see Chapter Eleven). These included the lack of scientific research to support his claims, his unwillingness to believe some of the things revealed by his patients when those revelations did not fit into his view of the world, and his almost obsessive need to assume that sexual problems were at the heart of nearly every nervous disorder.

Although some psychoanalysts today still use Freud's original methods, which could take years to produce results, most modern psychoanalysts have greatly modified the way a psychoanalytic session is conducted. The couch is gone, and the *client* (a term used to support the active role of the person seeking help and to avoid implying "sickness," as might result when using the term *patient*) may sit face-to-face with

manifest content the actual content of one's dream.

latent content the symbolic or hidden meaning of dreams.

free association psychoanalytic technique in which a patient was encouraged to talk about anything that came to mind without fear of negative evaluations.

resistance occurring when a patient becomes reluctant to talk about a certain topic, by either changing the subject or becoming silent.

transference in psychoanalysis, the tendency for a patient or client to project positive or negative feelings for important people from the past onto the therapist.

the therapist. The client may also stand or walk about. Rather than remaining quiet until the client says something revealing, the modern psychoanalyst is far more **directive**, asking questions, suggesting helpful behavior, and giving opinions and interpretations earlier in the relationship, which helps speed up the therapeutic process. Today's psychoanalysts also focus less on the id as the motivator of behavior; instead they look more at the ego or sense of self as the motivating force behind all actions (Prochaska & Norcross, 2003). Some psychoanalysts also focus more on the process of transference than on other typical aspects of traditional psychoanalysis, leading to the more general method called **psychodynamic therapy**. Psychodynamic therapy is typically shorter in duration than traditional psychoanalysis.

Even so, all of the psychodynamic techniques require the client to be fairly intelligent and verbally able to express his or her ideas, feelings, and thoughts effectively. People who are extremely withdrawn or who suffer from the more severe psychotic disorders are not good candidates for this form of psychotherapy. People who have nonpsychotic adjustment disorders, such as anxiety, somatoform, or dissociative disorders, are more likely to benefit from psychodynamic therapy.

directive therapy in which the therapist actively gives interpretations of a client's statements and may suggest certain behavior or actions.

psychodynamic therapy a newer and more general term for therapies based on psychoanalysis, with an emphasis on transference, shorter treatment times, and a more direct therapeutic approach.

interpersonal therapy (IPT) form of therapy for depression which incorporates multiple approaches and focuses on interpersonal problems.

eclectic approach to therapy that results from combining elements of several different approaches or techniques.

Interpersonal Psychotherapy

Interpersonal psychotherapy (IPT) is a psychotherapy developed to address depression. It is an insight therapy that focuses on relationships of the individual with others and the interplay between mood and the events of everyday life (Bleiberg & Markowitcz, 2008). It is based on the interpersonal theories of Adolph Meyer and Harry Stack Sullivan, along with the attachment theory of John Bowlby, and emphasizes interpersonal relationships and functioning (Bleiberg & Markowitcz, 2008). It is one of the few theories derived from psychodynamic thinking that does have some research support for its effectiveness in treating depression, particularly when combined with medication (Mufson et al., 2004; Reynolds et al., 1999). Despite its origins, IPT is not considered to be a psychodynamic therapy because it combines aspects of humanistic and cognitive–behavioral therapies, making it truly **eclectic**.

Psychotherapy often takes place one-on-one, with a client and therapist exploring various issues together to achieve deeper insights or to change undesirable behavior.

practice quiz How much do you remember?

13.1 **13.2**

Pick the best answer.

1. Psychotherapies that attempt to change disordered behavior directly are known as _____ therapies.
   a. insight
   b. action
   c. biomedical
   d. psychoanalytic

2. In the sixteenth century, purging or _____ was sometimes used as a means to rid the body of physical impurities so that the person's mind and soul could improve.
   a. ice bathing
   b. bloodletting
   c. beating
   d. spiritual cleansing

3. In _____, a psychoanalyst encourages the patient to talk about whatever comes to mind.
   a. free association
   b. dream interpretation
   c. resistance
   d. transference

4. The psychoanalyst knows that repressed information is just "below the surface" of the conversation when the patient begins to experience _____.
   a. free association.
   b. dream interpretation.
   c. resistance.
   d. transference.

5. Compared to traditional psychoanalysis, modern psychodynamic therapy is _____.
   a. more directive.
   b. less directive.
   c. more action oriented.
   d. more focused on the id.

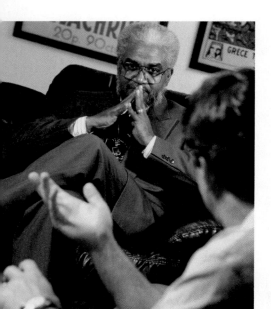

A Rogerian person-centered therapist listens with calm acceptance to anything the client says. A sense of empathy with the client's feelings is also important.

So the key to getting over unhappiness would be to get the real and ideal selves closer together? How does a therapist do that?

Humanistic Therapy: To Err Is Human

Unlike psychodynamic therapists, humanistic theorists do not focus on unconscious, hidden conflicts. Instead, humanists focus on conscious, subjective experiences of emotion and people's sense of self, as well as the more immediate experiences in their daily lives rather than early childhood experiences of the distant past (Cain & Seeman, 2001; Rowan, 2001; Schneider et al., 2001). ⓛⓘⓝⓚ to Chapter One: The Science of Psychology, p. 13. Humanistic therapy emphasizes the importance of the choices made by individuals and the potential to change one's behavior. The two most common therapy styles based on humanistic theory are Carl Rogers's person-centered therapy and Fritz Perls's Gestalt therapy; both are primarily insight therapies.

13.3 What are the basic elements of the humanistic therapies known as person-centered therapy and Gestalt therapy?

Tell Me More: Rogers's Person-Centered Therapy

Chapter Eleven discussed the basic elements of Rogers's theory of personality, which emphasizes the sense of self (Rogers, 1961). To sum it up quickly, Rogers proposed that everyone has a *real self* (how people see their actual traits and abilities) and an *ideal self* (how people think they should be). The closer the real and ideal selves match up, the happier and more well adjusted the person. To have these two self-concepts match, people need to receive *unconditional positive regard*, which is love, warmth, respect, and affection without any conditions attached. If people think that conditions are placed on the love and affection they receive, their ideal selves will be determined by those conditions and become more difficult to achieve, resulting in a mismatch of selves and unhappiness.

● So the key to getting over unhappiness would be to get the real and ideal selves closer together? How does a therapist do that?

Rogers believed that the goal of the therapist should be to provide the unconditional positive regard that has been absent from the troubled person's life and to help the person recognize the discrepancies between the real and ideal selves. He also believed that the person would actually have to do most of the work, talking out problems and concerns in an atmosphere of warmth and acceptance from the therapist. Therefore, he originally called the people in this therapy relationship "clients" instead of "patients," to put the therapeutic* relationship on a more equal footing. As a result, Rogers's therapy is very **nondirective** because the person actually does all the real work, with the therapist merely acting as a sounding board. Later, the term *client* was changed to the even more neutral term *person*. His therapy is now called **person-centered therapy** because the person is truly the center of the process.

FOUR BASIC ELEMENTS Rogers saw four key elements as being necessary in any successful person–therapist relationship: reflection, unconditional positive regard, empathy, and authenticity.

Reflection **Reflection** refers to the technique the therapist must use to allow clients to continue to talk and have insights without the interference of the therapist's interpretations and possible biases. The only way to ensure that a therapist will not control the stream of ideas coming from clients is for the therapist to simply restate what people have already said in slightly different words but with

nondirective therapy style in which the therapist remains relatively neutral and does not interpret or take direct actions with regard to the client, instead remaining a calm, nonjudgmental listener while the client talks.

person-centered therapy a nondirective insight therapy based on the work of Carl Rogers in which the client does all the talking and the therapist listens.

reflection therapy technique in which the therapist restates what the client says rather than interpreting those statements.

---

*Therapeutic: providing or assisting in a cure.

the same exact meaning. Reflection is literally a kind of mirroring of clients' statements. Here's an example from one of Rogers's own therapy sessions with a client (Meador & Rogers, 1984, p. 143):

CLIENT: I just ain't no good to nobody, never was, and never will be.

ROGERS: Feeling that now, hm? That you're just no good to yourself, no good to anybody. Never will be any good to anybody. Just that you're completely worthless, huh?—Those really are lousy feelings. Just feel that you're no good at all, hm?

CLIENT: Yeah.

Unconditional Positive Regard Another key element of person-centered therapy is the warm, accepting, completely uncritical atmosphere that the therapist must create for clients. Having respect for clients and their feelings, values, and goals, even if they are different from those of the therapist, is called **unconditional positive regard**.

Empathy The therapist also has to be able to acknowledge what clients are feeling and experiencing by using a kind of understanding called **empathy**. This involves listening carefully and closely to what clients are saying and trying to feel what they feel. Therapists must also avoid getting their own feelings mixed up with clients' feelings (e.g., countertransference).

Authenticity Finally, the therapist must show **authenticity** in a genuine, open, and honest response to the client. It is easier for some professionals to "hide" behind the role of the therapist, as was often the case in psychoanalysis. In person-centered therapy, the therapist has to be able to tolerate a client's differences without being judgmental.

MOTIVATIONAL INTERVIEWING A variation of client-centered therapy is *motivational interviewing*, or MI (Miller & Rollnick, 2002), which Hal Arkowitz and William R. Miller have described as "client-centered therapy with a twist" (p. 6). In contrast to client-centered, MI has specific goals: to reduce ambivalence about change and to increase intrinsic motivation to bring that change about (Arkowitcz & Miller, 2008). For a therapist, the four principles of MI are express empathy, develop discrepancy between the client's present behaviors and values, roll with resistance, and support the client's self-efficacy (Miller & Rollnick, 2002).

Gestalt Therapy

Another therapy based on humanistic ideas is called **Gestalt therapy**. The founder of this therapeutic method was Fritz Perls, who believed that people's problems often stemmed from hiding important parts of their feelings from themselves. If some part of a person's personality, for example, is in conflict with what society says is acceptable, the person might hide that aspect behind a false "mask" of socially acceptable behavior. As happens in Rogers's theory when the real and ideal selves do not match, in Gestalt theory the person experiences unhappiness and maladjustment when the inner self does not match the mask (Perls, 1951, 1969).

That sounds pretty much like the same thing, only with slightly different words. How is Gestalt therapy different from person-centered therapy?

The two therapy types are similar because they are both based in humanism. But whereas person-centered therapy is nondirective, allowing the client to talk out concerns and eventually come to insights with only minimal guidance from the therapist, Gestalt therapists are very directive, often confronting clients about the statements

unconditional positive regard referring to the warmth, respect, and accepting atmosphere created by the therapist for the client in person-centered therapy.

empathy the ability of the therapist to understand the feelings of the client.

authenticity the genuine, open, and honest response of the therapist to the client.

Gestalt therapy form of directive insight therapy in which the therapist helps clients to accept all parts of their feelings and subjective experiences, using leading questions and planned experiences such as role-playing.

That sounds pretty much like the same thing, only with slightly different words. How is Gestalt therapy different from person-centered therapy?

In Gestalt therapy, it is not unusual to find a client talking to an empty chair. The chair represents some person from the past with whom the client has unresolved issues, and this is the opportunity to deal with those issues.

they have made. This means that a Gestalt therapist does more than simply reflect back clients' statements; instead, a Gestalt therapist actually leads clients through a number of planned experiences, with the goal of helping clients to become more aware of their own feelings and take responsibility for their own choices in life, both now and in the past. These experiences might include a dialogue* that clients have with their own conflicting feelings in which clients actually argue both sides of those feelings. Clients may talk with an empty chair to reveal their true feelings toward the person represented by the chair or take on the role of a parent or other person with whom they have a conflict so that the clients can see things from the other person's point of view. The Gestalt therapist pays attention to body language as well as to the events going on in the client's life at the time of therapy. Unlike psychoanalysis, which focuses on the *hidden past*, Gestalt therapy focuses on the *denied past*. Gestalt therapists do not talk about the unconscious mind. They believe everything is conscious but that it is possible for some people to simply refuse to "own up" to having certain feelings or to deal with past issues. By looking at the body language, feelings both stated and unstated, and the events in the life of the client, the therapist gets a *gestalt*—a whole picture—of the client.

Evaluation of the Humanistic Therapies

Humanistic therapies have been used to treat psychological disorders, help people make career choices, deal with workplace problems, and in marriage counseling. Person-centered therapy in particular can be a very "hands-off" form of therapy because it is so nondirective: Most often, there's nothing that the therapist says that the client has not already said, so the therapist runs a lower risk of misinterpretation. However, omission or not reflecting some things back might be a source of error.

Unfortunately, humanistic therapies have several of the same drawbacks as Freudian psychoanalysis and other forms of modern psychodynamic therapy. There is little experimental research to support the basic ideas on which this type of therapy is founded, but humanists have always preferred to use case studies to build their theories. People must be intelligent, verbal, and able to express their thoughts, feelings, and experiences in a logical manner, which makes humanistic therapies a somewhat less practical choice for treating the more serious mental disorders such as schizophrenia. ✳-[Explore on **MyPsychLab**

✳-[Explore the different schools of therapy on **MyPsychLab**

---

*Dialogue: a conversation or exchange of ideas between two or more persons.

practice quiz   How much do you remember?

13.3

Pick the best answer.

1. Humanistic therapies are different from psychoanalysis because the humanistic therapies are _____.
   a. more directive.
   b. action oriented.
   c. focused only on conscious thoughts and behavior.
   d. insight therapies.

2. Which of the following is not one of the four basic elements of Rogers's person-centered therapy?
   a. conditional positive regard
   b. empathy
   c. reflection
   d. authenticity

3. Which of the following types of therapy makes the greatest use of body language?
   a. psychoanalysis
   b. person-centered therapy
   c. Gestalt therapy
   d. Rogerian therapy

4. Nicole's therapist has her talk to an empty chair and pretend she is talking to her father. Nicole's therapist is most likely a _____ therapist.
   a. psychodynamic
   b. person-centered
   c. Gestalt
   d. Freudian

Brainstorming: Which of the forms of psychotherapy discussed so far would probably work best for a very shy and withdrawn person? Why?

Behavior Therapies: Learning One's Way to Better Behavior

The last chapter talked about how behaviorists have a very different way of looking at abnormality—it's all learned. So do behaviorists do any kind of therapy?

That's right—the basic concept behind behaviorism is that all behavior, whether "normal" or "abnormal," is learned through the same processes of classical and operant conditioning. Unlike the psychodynamic and humanistic therapies, **behavior therapies** are action based rather than insight based. Their aim is to change behavior through the use of the same kinds of learning techniques that people (and animals) use to learn any new responses. The abnormal or undesirable behavior is not seen as a symptom of anything else but rather is the problem itself. Learning created the problem, and new learning can correct it (Onken et al., 1997; Skinner, 1974; Sloan & Mizes, 1999).

13.4 How do behavior therapists use classical and operant conditioning to treat disordered behavior?

Therapies Based on Classical Conditioning

Classical conditioning is the learning of involuntary responses by pairing a stimulus that normally causes a particular response with a new, neutral stimulus. After enough pairings, the new stimulus will also cause the response to occur. ⓛ ⓘ ⓝ ⓚ to Chapter Four: Learning, pp. 122–130. Through classical onditioning, old and undesirable automatic responses can be replaced by desirable ones. Several techniques have been developed using this type of learning to treat disorders such as phobias, obsessive-compulsive disorder, and similar anxiety disorders.

Using learning techniques to change undesirable behavior and increase desirable behavior has a long history (Hughes, 1993; Lovaas, 1987; Lovaas et al., 1966). Originally called **behavior modification**, the more recent adaptation of these techniques is **applied behavior analysis**. The newer term better highlights the need for a functional analysis of the behavior to be modified, which is then followed by the use of conditioning techniques to modify the behavior.

SYSTEMATIC DESENSITIZATION **Systematic desensitization**, in which a therapist guides the client through a series of steps meant to reduce fear and anxiety, is normally used to treat phobic disorders. It consists of a three-step process. First, the client must learn to relax through deep muscle relaxation training. Next, the client and the therapist construct a list, beginning with the object or situation that causes the least fear to the client, eventually working up to the object or situation that produces the greatest degree of fear. Finally, under the guidance of the therapist the client begins at the first item on the list that causes minimal fear and looks at it, thinks about it, or actually confronts it, all while remaining in a relaxed state. By pairing the old conditioned stimulus (the fear object) with a new relaxation response that is incompatible* with the emotions and physical arousal associated with fear, the person's fear is reduced and relieved. The person then proceeds to the next item on the list of fears (called a *hierarchy of fears*) until the phobia is gone. It is even possible to use a computer-generated virtual reality technique for desensitization (Rothbaum et al., 1995).

AVERSION THERAPY Another way to use classical conditioning is to reduce the frequency of undesirable behaviors, such as smoking or overeating, by teaching the

---

*Incompatible: referring to two or more things that cannot exist together or at the same time.

The last chapter talked about how behaviorists have a very different way of looking at abnormality—it's all learned. So do behaviorists do any kind of therapy?

behavior therapies action therapies based on the principles of classical and operant conditioning and aimed at changing disordered behavior without concern for the original causes of such behavior.

behavior modification or **applied behavior analysis** the use of learning techniques to modify or change undesirable behavior and increase desirable behavior.

systematic desensitization behavior technique used to treat phobias, in which a client is asked to make a list of ordered fears and taught to relax while concentrating on those fears.

This device allows the delivery of high levels of nicotine to the smoker in a process known as rapid smoking. Rapid smoking is an aversive technique for helping people to quit smoking and is based on the classical conditioning principle of counterconditioning.

Could you use aversion therapy to help someone with a phobia?

Read and learn more about EMDR on **MyPsychLab**

aversion therapy form of behavioral therapy in which an undesirable behavior is paired with an aversive stimulus to reduce the frequency of the behavior.

exposure therapies behavioral techniques that expose individuals to anxiety- or fear-related stimuli, under carefully controlled conditions, to promote new learning.

flooding technique for treating phobias and other stress disorders in which the person is rapidly and intensely exposed to the fear-provoking situation or object and prevented from making the usual avoidance or escape response.

client to pair an aversive (unpleasant) stimulus with the stimulus that results in the undesirable response in a process called **aversion therapy**. For example, someone who wants to stop smoking might go to a therapist who uses a *rapid-smoking* technique, in which the client is allowed to smoke but must take a puff on the cigarette every 5 or 6 seconds. As nicotine is a poison, such rapid smoking produces nausea and dizziness, both of which are unpleasant effects.

● Could you use aversion therapy to help someone with a phobia?

Because phobias are already very unpleasant, aversive conditioning is not the most useful method of therapy. Although desensitization remains one of the more common therapies for phobias, it does not always bring quick results.

EXPOSURE THERAPIES Behavioral techniques that introduce the client to situations, under carefully controlled conditions, which are related to their anxieties or fears, are called **exposure therapies**. Exposure can be accomplished through a variety of routes and is intended to promote new learning. It can be *in vivo* ("in life"), where the client is exposed to the actual anxiety-related stimulus; *imaginal*, where the client visualizes or imagines the stimulus; and even *virtual*, where virtual reality (VR) technology is used (Najavits, 2007). (For more information on virtual reality in psychology, see the Applying Psychology to Everyday Life feature at the end of this chapter.)

For example, if Chang-sun has social phobia (fairly rare for Korean males at a lifetime prevalence of only about 0.1 percent) (Sadock et al., 2007), for in vivo exposure he might have to attend a social event; for imaginal exposure he might be asked to visualize himself attending a social event; and for virtual exposure, Chang-sun might experience a social event, such as attending a dinner party, through VR technology.

Exposure methods can introduce the feared stimulus gradually, or quite suddenly. A gradual, or *graded* exposure, involves the client and therapist developing a fear hierarchy as in systematic desensitization: Exposure begins at the least feared event and progresses through to the most feared, similar to desensitization. If the exposure is rapid and intense, it begins with the most feared event and is called **flooding** (Gelder, 1976; Olsen, 1975). Flooding is used under very controlled conditions and, like graded exposure, produces extinction of the conditioned fear response by preventing an escape or avoidance response (e.g., Chang-sun would not be allowed to leave the party). For that reason, exposure therapy is sometimes called exposure and response prevention.

Eye-movement desensitization reprocessing, or EMDR, is a type of therapy that uses exposure techniques, most often in the treatment of posttraumatic stress disorder (PTSD). It involves imaginal flooding, cognitive reprocessing and desensitization of the fearful event, and rapid eye movements or other bilateral stimulation (Shapiro, 2001). It is also used with phobias and other anxiety-related disorders, although this therapy is most commonly used for PTSD. Read on **MyPsychLab**

Therapies Based on Operant Conditioning

Operant conditioning techniques include reinforcement, extinction, shaping, and modeling to change the frequency of voluntary behavior. LINK to Chapter Four: Learning, pp. 143–146, 151–153. In the treatment of psychological disorders, the goal is to reduce the frequency of undesirable behavior and increase the frequency of desirable responses.

One advantage of using operant conditioning to treat a problem behavior is that usually results are quickly obtained rather than having to wait through years of more insight-oriented forms of therapy. When the goal is to bring the behavior under control (rather than finding out why it occurs in the first place), operant and other behavioral techniques are very practical. There's an old joke about a man whose fear of things hiding under his bed is cured by a behavioral therapist in one night. The therapist simply cut the legs off the bed.

MODELING **Modeling**, or learning through the observation and imitation of a model, is discussed in Chapter Four. Use of modeling as a therapy is based on the work of Albert Bandura, which states that a person with specific fears or someone who needs to develop social skills can learn to do so by watching someone else (the model) confront those fears or demonstrate the needed social skills (Bandura et al., 1969). In **participant modeling**, a model demonstrates the desired behavior in a step-by-step, gradual process. The therapist encourages the client to imitate the model in the same gradual, step-by-step manner (Bandura, 1986; Bandura et al., 1974). The model can be a person actually present in the same room with the client or someone viewed on video. For example, a model might first approach a dog, then touch the dog, then pet the dog, and finally hug the dog. A child (or adult) who fears dogs would watch this process and then be encouraged to repeat the steps that the model demonstrated.

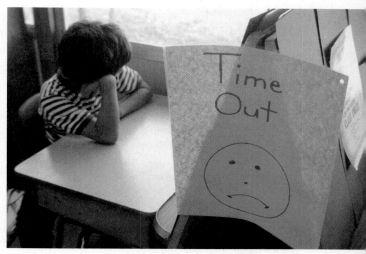

This boy is sitting in the "time-out" corner at his school. By removing the attention that he found rewarding, the teacher is attempting to extinguish the behavior that earned the boy a time-out. Do you see anything in this time-out corner that might make it less effective?

Behavioral therapists can give parents or others advice and demonstrations on how to carry out behavioral techniques. Once a person knows what to do, modeling is a fairly easy technique. Modeling has been effective in helping children with dental fears (Klorman et al., 1980; Ollendick & King, 1998), social withdrawal (O'Connor, 1972), obsessive-compulsive disorder (Roper et al., 1975), and phobias (Hintze, 2002).

USING REINFORCEMENT **Reinforcement** is the strengthening of a response by following it with some pleasurable consequence (positive reinforcement) or the removal of an unpleasant stimulus (negative reinforcement). Reinforcement of both types can form the basis for treatment of people with behavioral problems.

Token Economies In a **token economy**, objects that can be traded for food, candy, treats, or special privileges are called *tokens*. Clients earn tokens for behaving correctly or accomplishing behavioral goals and can later exchange those tokens for things that they want. They may also lose tokens for inappropriate behavior. This trading system is a token economy. (LINK) to Chapter Four: Learning, p. 145. Token economies have also been used successfully in modifying the behavior of relatively disturbed persons in mental institutions, such as people with schizophrenia or depressed persons (Dickerson et al., 1994; Glynn, 1990; McMonagle & Sultana, 2002).

Contingency Contracting Another method based on the use of reinforcement involves making a **contingency contract** with the client (Salend, 1987). This contract is a formal agreement between therapist and client (or teacher and student, or parent and child) in which both parties' responsibilities and goals are clearly stated. Such contracts are useful in treating specific problems such as drug addiction (Talbott & Crosby, 2001), educational problems (Evans & Meyer, 1985; Evans et al., 1989), and eating disorders (Brubaker & Leddy, 2003). Because the stated tasks, penalties, and reinforcements are clearly stated and consistent, both parties are always aware of the consequences of acting or failing to act within the specifications of the contract. This makes this form of behavioral treatment fairly effective. Consistency is one of the most effective tools in using both rewards and punishments to mold behavior. (LINK) to Chapter Four: Learning, pp. 141–142.

USING EXTINCTION **Extinction** involves the removal of a reinforcer to reduce the frequency of a particular response. In modifying behavior, operant extinction often involves removing one's attention from the person when that person is engaging in an

modeling learning through the observation and imitation of others.

participant modeling technique in which a model demonstrates the desired behavior in a step-by-step, gradual process while the client is encouraged to imitate the model.

reinforcement the strengthening of a response by following it with a pleasurable consequence or the removal of an unpleasant stimulus.

token economy the use of objects called tokens to reinforce behavior in which the tokens can be accumulated and exchanged for desired items or privileges.

contingency contract a formal, written agreement between the therapist and client (or teacher and student) in which goals for behavioral change, reinforcements, and penalties are clearly stated.

extinction the removal of a reinforcer to reduce the frequency of a behavior.

time-out an extinction process in which a person is removed from the situation that provides reinforcement for undesirable behavior, usually by being placed in a quiet corner or room away from possible attention and reinforcement opportunities.

cognitive therapy therapy in which the focus is on helping clients recognize distortions in their thinking and replace distorted, unrealistic beliefs with more realistic, helpful thoughts.

arbitrary inference distortion of thinking in which a person draws a conclusion that is not based on any evidence.

selective thinking distortion of thinking in which a person focuses on only one aspect of a situation while ignoring all other relevant aspects.

What are these unrealistic beliefs?

inappropriate or undesirable behavior. With children, this removal of attention may be a form of **time-out**, in which the child is removed from the situation that provides reinforcement (Kazdin, 1980). In adults, a simple refusal by the other persons in the room to acknowledge the behavior is often successful in reducing the frequency of that behavior.

Evaluation of Behavior Therapies

Behavior therapies may be more effective than other forms of therapy in treating specific behavioral problems, such as bed-wetting, overeating, drug addictions, and phobic reactions (Burgio, 1998; Wetherell, 2002). More-serious psychological disorders, such as severe depression or schizophrenia, do not respond as well overall to behavioral treatments, although improvement of specific symptoms can be achieved (Glynn, 1990; McMonagle & Sultana, 2002). Bringing symptoms under control is an important step in allowing a person to function normally in the social world, and behavior therapies are a relatively quick and efficient way to eliminate or greatly reduce such symptoms.

Cognitive Therapies: Thinking Is Believing

13.5 What are the goals and basic elements of cognitive therapies such as cognitive–behavioral therapy and rational–emotive behavior therapy?

Cognitive therapy (Beck, 1979; Freeman et al., 1989) was developed by Aaron T. Beck and is focused on helping people change their ways of thinking. Rather than focusing on the behavior itself, the cognitive therapist focuses on the distorted thinking and unrealistic beliefs that lead to maladaptive behavior (Hollon & Beck, 1994), especially those distortions relating to depression (Abela & D'Allesandro, 2002; McGinn, 2000). The goal is to help clients test, in a more objective, scientific way, the truth of their beliefs and assumptions, as well as their attributions concerning both their own behavior and the behavior of others in their lives. **LINK** to Chapter Ten: Social Psychology, pp. 360–362. Then they can recognize thoughts that are distorted and negative and replace them with more positive, helpful thoughts. Because the focus is on changing thoughts rather than gaining deep insights into their causes, this kind of therapy is primarily an action therapy.

Beck's Cognitive Therapy

What are these unrealistic beliefs?

Cognitive therapy focuses on the distortions of thinking. **LINK** to Chapter Eleven: Theories of Personality and Intelligence, pp. 396–398. Here are some of the more common distortions in thought that can create negative feelings and unrealistic beliefs in people:

- **Arbitrary inference:** This refers to "jumping to conclusions" without any evidence. Arbitrary means to decide something based on nothing more than personal whims. Example: "Suzy canceled our lunch date—I'll bet she's seeing someone else!"

- **Selective thinking:** In selective thinking, the person focuses only on one aspect of a situation, leaving out other relevant facts that might make things seem less negative. Example: Peter's teacher praised his paper but made one comment about needing to check his punctuation. Peter assumes that his paper is lousy and that the teacher really didn't like it, ignoring the other praise and positive comments.

- **Overgeneralization:** Here a person draws a sweeping conclusion from one incident and then assumes that the conclusion applies to areas of life that have nothing to do with the original event. Example: "I insulted my algebra teacher. I'll flunk and I'll never be able to get a decent job—I'll end up on welfare."

- **Magnification and minimization:** Here a person blows bad things out of proportion while not emphasizing good things. Example: A student who has received good grades on every other exam believes that the C she got on the last quiz means she's not going to succeed in college.

- **Personalization:** In personalization, an individual takes responsibility or blame, for events that are not really connected to the individual. Example: When Sandy's husband comes home in a bad mood because of something that happened at work, she immediately assumes that he is angry with her.

A cognitive therapist tries to get clients to look at their beliefs and test them to see how accurate they really are. The first step is to identify an illogical or unrealistic belief, which the therapist and client do in their initial talks. Then the therapist guides the client through a process of asking questions about that belief, such as "When did this belief of mine begin?" or "What is the evidence for this belief?"

Don't those questions sound like critical thinking, which was discussed in Chapter One?

Cognitive therapy really is critical thinking applied to one's own thoughts and beliefs. Just as cognitive psychology grew out of behaviorism, ⓛⓘⓝⓚ to Chapter One: The Science of Psychology, pp. 10–11, 13, therapies using cognitive methods have behavioral elements within them as well, leading to the term **cognitive–behavioral therapy (CBT)**.

Cognitive–behavioral therapy, or CBT, focuses on the present rather than the past (like behaviorism) but also assumes that people interact with the world with more than simple, automatic reactions to external stimuli. People observe the world and the people in the world around them, make assumptions and inferences* based on those observations or cognitions, and then decide how to respond (Rachman & Hodgson, 1980). As a form of cognitive therapy, CBT also assumes that disorders come from illogical, irrational cognitions and that changing the thinking patterns to more rational, logical ones will relieve the symptoms of the disorder, making it an action therapy. Cognitive–behavioral therapists may also use any of the tools that behavioral therapists employ to help clients alter their actions. The three basic goals of any cognitive–behavioral therapy follow.

1. Relieve the symptoms and help clients resolve the problems.

2. Help clients develop strategies that can be used to cope with future problems.

3. Help clients change the way they think from irrational, self-defeating thoughts to more rational, self-helping, positive thoughts.

Ellis and Rational–Emotive Behavior Therapy (REBT)

Albert Ellis proposed a version of CBT called **rational–emotive behavioral therapy (REBT)** in which clients are taught a way to challenge their own irrational beliefs with more rational, helpful statements (Ellis, 1997, 1998). Here are some examples of irrational beliefs:

- Everyone should love and approve of me (if they don't, I am awful and unlovable).

- When things do not go the way I wanted and planned, it is terrible and I am, of course, going to get very disturbed. I can't stand it!

---

*Inferences: conclusions drawn from observations and facts.

Sidebar / margin note:

Don't those questions sound like critical thinking, which was discussed in Chapter One?

overgeneralization distortion of thinking in which a person draws sweeping conclusions based on only one incident or event and applies those conclusions to events that are unrelated to the original.

magnification and minimization distortions of thinking in which a person blows a negative event out of proportion to its importance (magnification) while ignoring relevant positive events (minimization).

personalization distortion of thinking in which a person takes responsibility or blame for events that are unconnected to the person.

cognitive–behavioral therapy (CBT) action therapy in which the goal is to help clients overcome problems by learning to think more rationally and logically.

rational–emotive behavior therapy (REBT) cognitive–behavioral therapy in which clients are directly challenged in their irrational beliefs and helped to restructure their thinking into more rational belief statements.

But I've felt that way at times. Why are these statements so irrational?

● But I've felt that way at times. Why are these statements so irrational?

Notice that these statements have one thing in common: It's either all or nothing. Can a person really expect the love and affection of every single person? Is it realistic to expect things to work as planned every time? Rational–emotive behavioral therapy is about challenging these types of "my way or nothing" statements, helping people to realize that life can be good without being "perfect." In REBT, therapists take a very directive role, challenging the client when the client makes statements like those listed earlier, assigning homework, using behavioral techniques to modify behavior, and arguing with clients about the rationality of their statements.

Evaluation of Cognitive and Cognitive–Behavioral Therapies

Cognitive and cognitive–behavioral therapies are less expensive than the typical insight therapy because they are comparatively short-term therapies. As in behavior therapy, clients do not have to dig too deep for the hidden sources of their problems. Instead, cognitive-based therapies get right to the problems themselves, helping clients deal with their symptoms more directly. In fact, one of the criticisms of these therapies as well as behavior therapies is that they treat the symptom, not the cause. However, it should be noted that in the cognitive viewpoint, the maladaptive thoughts are seen as the cause of the problems, not merely the symptoms. There is also an element of potential bias because of the therapist's opinions as to which thoughts are rational and which are not (Westen, 2005).

Nevertheless, cognitive and cognitive–behavioral therapies have considerable success in treating many types of disorders, including depression, stress disorders, eating disorders, anxiety disorders, personality disorders, and even—in addition to other forms of therapy—some types of schizophrenia (Barlow et al., 2007; Beck, 2007; Clark, Beck, & Brown, 1989; Clark et al., 2009; DeRubeis et al., 1999; Holcomb, 1986; Jay & Elliot, 1990; Kendall, 1983; Kendall et al., 2008; McGinn, 2000; Meichenbaum, 1996; Mueser et al., 2008; Resick et al., 2008; Turk et al., 2008; Young et al., 2008). As an offshoot of behaviorism, the learning principles that are the basis of cognitive–behavioral therapies are considered empirically sound (Barlow et al., 2007; Masters et al., 1987). For a summary of the various types of psychotherapies discussed up to this point, see Table 13.1.

table 13.1 Characteristics of Psychotherapies

TYPE OF THERAPY	GOAL	KEY PEOPLE
Psychodynamic therapy	Insight	Freud
Person-centered therapy	Insight	Rogers
Gestalt therapy	Insight	Perls
Behavior therapy	Action	Watson, Jones, Skinner, Bandura
Cognitive therapy	Action	Beck
CBT	Action	Various professionals
REBT	Action	Ellis

Group Therapies: Not Just for the Shy

An alternative to individual therapy, in which the client and the therapist have a private, one-on-one session, is to gather a group of clients with similar problems together and have the group discuss problems under the guidance of a single therapist (Yalom, 1995).

13.6 What are the various types of group therapies and the advantages and disadvantages of group therapy?

Types of Group Therapies

Group therapy can be accomplished in several ways. The therapist may use either an insight or a cognitive–behavioral style, although person-centered, Gestalt, and behavior therapies seem to work better in group settings than psychodynamic and cognitive–behavioral therapies (Andrews, 1989).

In addition to the variations in the style of therapy, the group structure can also vary. There may be small groups formed of related persons or other groups of unrelated persons that meet without the benefit of a therapist. Their goal is to share their problems and provide social and emotional support for each other.

FAMILY COUNSELING One form of group therapy is **family counseling** or **family therapy**, in which all of the members of a family who are experiencing some type of problem—marital problems, problems in child discipline, or sibling rivalry, for example—are seen by the therapist as a group. The therapist may also meet with one or more family members individually at times, but the real work in opening the lines of communication among family members is accomplished in the group setting (Frankel & Piercy, 1990; Pinsof & Wynne, 1995). The family members may include grandparents, aunts and uncles, and in-laws as well as the core family. This is because family therapy focuses on the family as a whole unit or system of interacting "parts." No one person is seen as "the problem" because all members of the family system are part of the problem: They are experiencing it, rewarding it, or by their actions or inactions causing it to occur in the first place.

The goal in family therapy, then, is to discover the unhealthy ways in which family members interact and communicate with one another and change those ways to healthier, more productive means of interaction. Family therapists work not only with families but also with couples who are in a committed relationship with the goal of improving communication, helping the couple to learn better ways of solving their problems and disagreements, and increasing feelings of intimacy and emotional closeness (Christensen et al., 1995; Heavey et al., 1993).

SELF-HELP GROUPS Therapists are often in short supply, and they also charge a fee for leading group-therapy sessions. In addition, many people may feel that a therapist who has never had, for example, a drug problem would be unable to truly understand their situation. They may also feel that someone who has experienced addiction and beaten it is more capable of providing real help. This, rather than just concerns about the cost of therapy, is the main reason some people choose to meet with others who have problems similar to their own, with no therapist in charge. Called **self-help groups** or **support groups**, these groups are usually formed around a particular problem. Some examples of self-help groups are Alcoholics Anonymous, Overeaters Anonymous, and Narcotics Anonymous, all of which have groups meeting all over the country at almost any time of the day or night. There are countless smaller support groups for nearly every condition imaginable, including anxiety, phobias, having a parent with dementia, having difficult children, depression, and

In family therapy, all family members participate in therapy sessions, with the therapist guiding them through open communication. Although it appears that the young boy in the corner is the focus of this session, all family members are encouraged to see how their own behavior may contribute to the problem behavior.

family counseling (family therapy) a form of group therapy in which family members meet together with a counselor or therapist to resolve problems that affect the entire family.

self-help groups (support groups) a group composed of people who have similar problems and who meet together without a therapist or counselor for the purpose of discussion, problem solving, and social and emotional support.

In self-help groups, the person or persons leading a group are not specialists or therapists but just members of the group. They often have the same problem as all of the other people in the room, which is the strength of this type of program—people may be more likely to trust and open up to someone who has struggled as they have.

dealing with stress—to name just a few. The advantages of self-help groups are that they are free and provide the social and emotional support that any group session can provide (Bussa & Kaufman, 2000). Self-help groups do not have leaders but instead have people who volunteer monthly or weekly to lead individual meetings. So the person who is in charge of organizing the meetings is also a member of the group with the same problem as all the other members. 📖 Read on **MyPsychLab**

📖 Read and learn more about different kinds of self-help groups on **MyPsychLab**

Advantages of Group Therapy

There are several advantages to group therapy:

- Lower cost. Because the therapist can see several clients at one time, this type of therapy is usually less expensive than individual therapy.
- Exposure to the ways in which other people view and handle the same kinds of problems.
- The opportunity for both the therapist and the person to see how that person interacts with others.
- Social and emotional support from people who have problems that are similar or nearly identical to one's own. This advantage is an important one; studies have shown that breast cancer patients who were part of a group-therapy process had much higher survival and recovery rates than those who received only individual therapy or no psychotherapy (Fawzy et al., 1993; Spiegel et al., 1989). Another study found that adolescent girls in Africa, suffering from depression due to the stresses of the war in Uganda, experienced significant reductions in depression when treated with group therapy (Bolton et al., 2007).
- An extremely shy person may initially have great difficulty speaking up in a group setting but cognitive–behavioral group therapy can be effective for social phobia (Heimberg & Becker, 2002; Turk et al., 2008).

In group therapy, several people who share similar problems gather with a therapist to discuss their feelings and concerns. The presence of others who are going through the same kind of emotional difficulties can be comforting as well as provide the opportunity for insights into one's own problems by hearing about the problems of others.

Disadvantages of Group Therapy

Group therapy is not appropriate for all situations, and there can be disadvantages:

- The therapist is no longer the only person to whom secrets and fears are revealed, which may make some people reluctant to speak freely.
- The client must share the therapist's time during the session.
- People with severe psychiatric disorders involving paranoia, such as schizophrenia, may not be able to tolerate group-therapy settings.

A survey and comparison of the effectiveness of both individual and group therapy found that group therapy is only effective if it is long term and that it is more effective when used to promote skilled social interactions rather than as an attempt to decrease the more bizarre symptoms of delusions and hallucinations (Evans et al., 2000).

EVALUATION OF GROUP THERAPY Group therapy can provide help to people who might be unable to afford individual psychotherapy. It can also provide social and emotional support to people who may improve significantly from simply knowing that they are not the only people to suffer from whatever their particular problem may be. People who are not comfortable in social situations or who have trouble speaking in front of others may not find group therapy as helpful as those who are more verbal and social by nature. It is also important to note that group therapy can be used in combination with individual and biomedical therapies.

practice quiz How much do you remember?

Pick the best answer.

1. Cade is trying to stop biting his fingernails. He wears a rubber band around each of his wrists and, whenever he finds himself biting his nails, he snaps the band. Cade is using a form of _____ to modify his nail-biting behavior.
   a. systematic desensitization
   b. aversion therapy
   c. flooding
   d. extinction

2. The reality television shows that deliberately force people to face their "worst fears" are most similar to which therapy technique?
   a. systematic desensitization
   b. aversion therapy
   c. flooding
   d. extinction

3. At Skinner Elementary School, teachers pass out "skinner bucks" to students who turn in papers on time, obey the teacher, and finish their homework. The paper "bucks" can be used at the end of the week to trade for special treats or game-playing time on the classroom computer. This system most resembles a _____.
   a. participant modeling technique.
   b. contingency contract.
   c. group extinction procedure.
   d. token economy.

4. Which of the following would be an unlikely strategy for a rational–emotive behavior therapist to use in treating a client?
   a. arguing with the client's statements
   b. repeating what the client has just said without interpreting it
   c. giving the client homework
   d. pointing out irrational beliefs to the client

5. Maya is upset because her supervisor teased her about turning in her report several hours late. Although her supervisor was quite pleased with the report itself and told Maya that her work was excellent, Maya remains unhappy. Beck would say that Maya is guilty of _____.
   a. arbitrary inference.
   b. selective thinking.
   c. personalization.
   d. defective thinking.

6. Which person might benefit the least from a group-therapy environment?
   a. Azul, who has a phobia of cats
   b. Richard, who has a drinking problem
   c. Jasmine, who is experiencing auditory hallucinations
   d. Elena, who suffers from depression

7. Six members of Nicole's statistics class would meet every Saturday to go over their notes and try to figure out what the teacher had told them during his rambling lectures. If part of every Saturday's session is spent sharing feelings about the teacher and venting their anger and resentment, Nicole's study group could be said to serve as _____.
   a. a support group.
   b. family therapy.
   c. an awareness training group.
   d. a guided-discovery group.

Brainstorming: What might be some benefits to participating in group counseling on a college campus? What kind of challenges might be present?

ANSWERS ON PAGE AK–2

psychology in the news
Mental Health on Campus

The college experience is supposed to be one of intellectual and social development, but for many people it is also a time of strife and stress. From exams to living conditions (commuting, new roommates, living in a dorm), relationship issues (immediate family, significant others), and adjustment in general (balancing school/work/family), college life can be quite stressful. The shootings and other campus crises over the past few years are just one indicator of the level of psychological dysfunction that can occur in extreme circumstances.

These circumstances can make preexisting conditions worse or prompt the development of new psychological disorders. According to the American College Counseling Association's 2009 National Survey of Counseling Center Directors, of the 2.6 million students represented in the survey, approximately 270,000 sought counseling (Gallagher, 2009). Of those students receiving services in college counseling centers, 16 percent are referred for psychiatric evaluation and 25 percent are on psychiatric medication. The majority of counseling center directors believe there is an increase in the number of students coming to campus already on psychiatric medication, and there is a trend toward a greater number of students on campus recognized with severe psychological problems. Increases are being noted in medication management, crisis intervention, learning disabilities, self-injury (e.g., self-cutting), illicit drug use, alcohol abuse, eating disorders, and sexual assault concerns or problems related to earlier sexual abuse (Gallagher, 2009).

As revealed by the 2009–2010 Community College Counselors Survey, these increases are especially troublesome given the added stress of the ongoing economic situation in the United States. Consequences of economic stressors include increases in enrollment, more signs of anxiety and depression in both students and college employees, and an increased need for mental-health services (American College Counseling Association's Community College Task Force, 2010). The top four presenting problems were stress, depression, anxiety disorders, and academic problems.

So what can you do with this information? First, if you are not familiar with your college's counseling resources, learn more about what is offered. Even if you do not have a serious psychological disorder, counselors can assist you in identifying and developing effective coping strategies. Second, take care of yourself, get enough sleep, eat healthy (not just instant noodles or fast food), exercise, and make time to relax. Finally, know that you are not alone if you do experience difficulties and that a variety of resources are likely available to help you along the path to your college degree. ☑•⌐Survey on **MyPsychLab**

☑•⌐**Survey** Participate in a survey: How do you take care of your mental health? on **MyPsychLab**

QUESTIONS FOR FURTHER DISCUSSION

1. Do you know any of your fellow students who have used your college's counseling center? If so, what was their experience like?

2. What do you believe to be the greatest stressor in college life today?

Does Psychotherapy Really Work?

> There sure are a lot of psychotherapies, but do any of them really work?

There sure are a lot of psychotherapies, but do any of them really work?

In the 1950s, Hans Eysenck published one of the earliest studies on the effectiveness of therapy. His conclusion—that the people receiving psychotherapy did not recover at any higher rate than those who had no psychotherapy and that the passage of time alone could account for all recovery.

Studies of Effectiveness

13.7 How effective is psychotherapy, and how is the effectiveness of psychotherapy influenced by cultural, ethnic, and gender differences?

Eysenck's classic survey created a major controversy within the world of clinical and counseling psychology. Other researchers began their own studies to find evidence that would contradict Eysenck's findings. One such effort reviewed studies that the researchers considered to be well controlled and concluded that the psychotherapies did not differ from one another in effectiveness (Luborsky et al., 1975). Of course, that can mean either that the psychotherapies were all equally effective or that they were all equally ineffective. (Note—many psychological professionals take an eclectic approach, using more than one psychotherapy technique.)

Studying the effectiveness of psychotherapy presents numerous problems. Controlled studies can be done using an experimental group of people who receive a particular psychotherapy and a control group of people who are put on a waiting list, but this is less than ideal. The control group is not getting the attention from the therapist, for one thing, and so there would be no placebo-effect expectations about getting better because of therapy (Shapiro & Shapiro, 1997). Also, not all therapies take the same amount of time to be effective. For example, psychoanalysis, even in its short form, takes longer than a behavioral therapy. In a short-term study, behavioral therapy would obviously look more effective. Action therapies such as behavior therapy measure the success of the therapy differently

THE SEVEN DWARFS AFTER THERAPY

than do insight therapies; in a behavioral therapy the reduction of the undesired behavior is easy to measure objectively, but gaining insights and feelings of control, self-worth, self-esteem, and so on are not as easily evaluated (Shadish et al., 2002).

Studies that do not use empirical* procedures but instead try to determine if the clients who have been helped by the therapy in general are plagued by problems such as experimenter bias (the therapist expects the therapy to work and is also the one assessing the progress of the client), the inaccuracies of self-report information, and the same placebo-effect expectations cited by Shapiro and Shapiro (Seligman, 1995; Wampold, 1997).

Nevertheless, more recent surveys have shown that people who have received psychotherapy believe that they have been helped more often than not (*Consumer Reports*, 1995; Kotkin et al., 1996). The *Consumer Reports* research was a survey of the magazine's readers in which those who had been or were currently clients in psychotherapy rated the effectiveness of the therapy they received. Here are the findings from a summary of this and several other similar surveys (Lambert & Ogles, 2004; Seligman, 1995; Thase, 1999):

- An estimated 75–90 percent of people feel that psychotherapy has helped them.
- The longer a person stays in therapy, the greater the improvement.

Other studies have found that some psychotherapies are more effective for certain types of disorders (Clarkin et al., 2007; Hollon et al., 2002) but that no one psychotherapy is the most effective or works for every type of problem.

Characteristics of Effective Therapy

So how does a person with a problem know what kind of therapist to go to? How do you pick a good one?

As discussed before, many psychological professionals today take an eclectic view of psychotherapy, using a combination of methods or switching methods to fit the particular client's needs or specific problems.

The *common factors approach* in psychotherapy is a modern approach to eclecticism and focuses on those factors common to successful outcomes from different forms of therapy (Norcross, 2005). These factors are seen as the source of the success rather than specific differences among therapies. The most important common factor of a successful psychotherapy may be the relationship between the client and the therapist, known as the **therapeutic alliance**. This relationship should be caring, warm, and accepting, and be characterized by empathy, mutual respect, and understanding. Therapy should also offer clients a *protected setting* in which to release emotions and reveal private thoughts and concerns and should help clients understand why they feel the way they do and provide them with ways to feel better. Other common factors in therapy effectiveness are *opportunity for catharsis* (relieving pent-up emotions), *learning and practice of new behaviors*, and *positive experiences* for the client (Norcross, 2005).

An ongoing area of research in psychology is related to identifying those treatments and other aspects of treatment that work best for specific disorders. Especially in today's modern age of managed health care and tight budgets, clients benefit through evidence-based practice, or empirically validated treatment. Evidence-based practice includes systematic reviews of relevant

therapeutic alliance the relationship between therapist and client that develops as a warm, caring, accepting relationship characterized by empathy, mutual respect, and understanding.

So how does a person with a problem know what kind of therapist to go to? How do you pick a good one?

"I like to think that each generation will need a little less therapy than the generation before."

---

*Empirical: capable of being verified or disproved by observation or experiment.

and valid information that ranges from assessment to intervention (American Psychological Association, 2005; Hunsley & Mash, 2008; Nathan & Gorman, 2007). Some examples of evidence-based, or empirically validated, treatments are exposure therapies, cognitive–behavioral, and cognitive processing for PTSD (Ehlers et al., 2010; Najavits, 2007; Resick et al., 2008), cognitive–behavioral treatment for panic disorder with agoraphobia (Barlow et al., 2007; Craske & Barlow, 2008), cognitive–behavioral group therapy for social anxiety disorder (Turk et al., 2008), cognitive therapy for depression (Young et al., 2008), antipsychotic drugs for schizophrenia (Sharif et al., 2007), and interpersonal psychotherapy for depression (Bleiberg & Markowitcz, 2008).

Cultural, Ethnic, and Gender Concerns in Psychotherapy

Consider the following situation (adapted from Wedding, 2004).

> *K. is a 24-year-old Korean American. She lived with her parents, who were both born and reared in Korea before moving to the United States as adults. She came to a therapist because she was depressed and unhappy with her lack of independence. Her father was angry about her plans to marry a non-Korean. Her therapist immediately began assertiveness training and role-playing to prepare K. to deal with her father. The therapist was disappointed when K. failed to keep her second appointment.*

This example of an actual case demonstrates a problem that exists in the therapist–client relationship for many clients when the ethnicity or culture of the client is different from that of the therapist. This cultural difference makes it difficult for therapists to understand the exact nature of their clients' problems and for clients to benefit from therapies that do not match their needs (Matsumoto, 1994; Moffic; 2003; Wedding, 2004). The values of different cultures and ethnic groups are not universally the same. How, for example, could a female therapist who is white, from a upper-middle-class family, and well educated understand the problems of a Hispanic adolescent boy from a poor family living in substandard housing if she did not acknowledge the differences between them? In this case, gender, ethnicity, and economic background of client and therapist are all vastly different.

In the case of K., for example, the therapist mistakenly assumed that the key to improving K.'s situation was to make her more assertive and independent from her family, particularly her father. This Western idea runs counter to Korean cultural values. Korean culture stresses interdependence, not independence. The family comes first, obedience to one's elders is highly valued, and "doing one's own thing" is not acceptable. K.'s real problem may have been her feelings of guilt about her situation and her father's anger. She may have wanted help in dealing with her family situation and her feelings about that situation, not help in becoming more independent.

For therapy to be effective, the client must continue in treatment until a successful outcome is reached. K. never came back after the first session. One of the problems that can occur when the culture or ethnic backgrounds of the client and therapist are mismatched, as in K.'s case, is that the therapist may project his or her values onto the client, failing to achieve true empathy with the client's feelings or even to realize what the client's true feelings are, thus causing the client to drop out of therapy. Studies of such situations have found that members of minority racial or ethnic groups drop out of therapy at a significantly higher rate than the majority group clients (Brown et al., 2003; Cooper et al., 2003; Flaherty & Adams, 1998; Sue, 1977, 1992; Sue et al., 1994; Vail, 1976; Vernon & Roberts, 1982).

Traditional forms of psychotherapy, developed mainly in Western, individualistic cultures, may need to be modified to fit the more collectivistic, interdependent cultures. For example, Japanese psychologist Dr. Shigeru Iwakabe has pointed out that the typical "talking cure" practiced by many psychotherapists—including psychodynamic and humanistic therapists—may have to be altered to a nontalking cure and the use of nonverbal tasks (like drawing) due to the reluctance of many traditional Japanese people to talk openly about private concerns (Iwakabe, 2008).

Are differences in gender that important? For example, do women prefer female therapists, but men would rather talk to another man?

Research on gender and therapist–client relationships varies. When talking about white, middle-class clients, it seems that both men and women prefer a female therapist (Jones et al., 1987). But African American clients were more likely to drop out of therapy if the therapist was the *same* sex as the client (Vail, 1976); male Asian clients seemed to prefer a male therapist; and female Asian clients stayed in therapy equally long with either male or female therapists (Flaherty & Adams, 1998; Flaskerud, 1991). (Although several of the references cited are older ones, they represent the most recent studies for these specific findings.)

Four barriers to effective psychotherapy exist when the culture or ethnic backgrounds of client and therapist are different (Sue & Sue, 2008):

1. **Culture-bound values.** Including individual centered versus other (or others) centered, verbal/emotional/behavioral expressiveness, communication patterns from client to counselor, nuclear family, and so forth (Sue & Sue, 2008). Differing cultural values can cause therapists to fail at forming an empathetic relationship (Sattler, 1977; Wedding, 2004).

2. **Class-bound values.** Adherence to time schedules, ambiguous approach to problems, looking for long-range goals (Sue & Sue, 2008). Clients from impoverished backgrounds may have values and experiences that the therapist cannot understand (Wedding, 2004).

3. **Language.** Use of Standard English, emphasis on verbal communication (Sue & Sue, 2008). Speaking different languages becomes a problem in understanding what both client and therapist are saying and in psychological testing (Betancourt & Jacobs, 2000; Lewis, 1996).

4. **Nonverbal communication.** Body language, or nonverbal communication, can also differ between cultures and ethnicities. The physical distance between the client and therapist, the use of gestures, and eye contact, for example, can cause misunderstandings during the session and in interpretation of the client's moods and intentions (Galanti, 1997; Like et al., 1996). People in some cultures are content with long periods of silence, whereas others are not; direct eye contact is desirable in some cultures and offensive in others; and even facial expressions of emotion vary from very expressive (as with Hispanic people) to nonexpressive (as with many Asian people).

The American Psychiatric Association (2000a) has included a guide for therapists concerning cultural issues and culture-bound syndromes such as *koro*. (L)(I)(N)(K) to Chapter Twelve: Psychological Disorders, p. 445. All therapists need to make an effort to become aware of cultural differences, culture-bound syndromes, and possible gender issues. Sociopolitical issues should also be examined (Sue & Sue, 2008).

Cybertherapy: Therapy in the Computer Age

Although psychotherapy is usually accomplished by the client or clients speaking face-to-face with the therapist, a new type of therapy is now available to people in

cybertherapy psychotherapy that is offered on the Internet. Also called online, Internet, or Web therapy or counseling.

biomedical therapies therapies that directly affect the biological functioning of the body and brain.

psychopharmacology the use of drugs to control or relieve the symptoms of psychological disorders.

antipsychotic drugs drugs used to treat psychotic symptoms such as delusions, hallucinations, and other bizarre behavior.

need who own a computer. **Cybertherapy** refers to psychotherapy that is offered on the Internet, and the people who practice it are called *cybertherapists*. Although this method of delivery may have the advantages of lower or no cost, availability of therapy opportunities for those unable to get to a therapist easily (such as people living in a remote or rural area), access to support groups online, and relative anonymity, there are dangers. There is no guarantee that the cybertherapist has any credentials or training in psychotherapy. Although some therapists use voice or video conferencing, some only use text-based chat. When there is no face-to-face or voice-to-voice contact, the therapist has no access to body language or vocal tones in trying to assess a client's emotional and psychological state. For further information on this subject, an excellent list of the various forms that cybertherapy can take and the strengths and weaknesses of each has been developed by Dr. Azy Barak, a psychologist at the University of Haifa in Israel and an expert in Internet psychotherapy (Barak, 1999; Barak & Hen, 2008; Barak & Suler, 2008). (For more on the application of computers in psychology, see the Applying Psychology to Everyday Life feature.)

A group of researchers in Germany found that people who were treated as inpatients and then allowed to "meet" with a group therapist in an Internet chat room showed a significantly lower risk of negative changes in their mental status than a control group (Golkaramnay et al., 2007). The dropout rate from the Internet group was very low, and most patients "attended" the chat room sessions, which suggests that the ease of using a computer to connect to a group-therapy session may be a viable option for some people needing continued therapy opportunities.

Biomedical Therapies

Just as a therapist trained in psychoanalysis is more likely to use that technique, a therapist whose perspective on personality and behavior is biological will most likely turn to medical techniques to manage disordered behavior. Even psychotherapists who are not primarily biological in orientation may combine psychotherapy with medical treatments that are supervised by a medical doctor working with the psychologist. As medical doctors, psychiatrists are almost inevitably biological in perspective and, thus, use **biomedical therapies** (directly affecting the biological functioning of the body and brain) in addition to any psychotherapy technique they may favor. The biomedical therapies fall into three categories: drug therapy, shock therapy, and surgical treatments.

Psychopharmacology

13.8 What are the various types of drugs used to treat psychological disorders?

The use of drugs to control or relieve the symptoms of a psychological disorder is called **psychopharmacology**. Although these drugs are sometimes used alone, they are more often combined with some form of psychotherapy and are more effective as a result (Kearney & Silverman, 1998; Keller et al., 2000). There are four basic categories of drugs used to treat psychotic disorders, anxiety disorders, the manic phase of mood disorders, and depression. ✴-[Explore on **MyPsychLab**

ANTIPSYCHOTIC DRUGS Drugs used to treat psychotic symptoms, such as hallucinations, delusions, and bizarre behavior, are called **antipsychotic drugs**. The three categories of antipsychotic drugs are *typical neuroleptics, atypical neuroleptics,* and *partial dopamine agonists.* The first of the typical neuroleptics to be developed was *chlorpromazine* (Jones & Pilowsky, 2002). The term *neuroleptic* comes from the French word *neuroleptique,* which means "to have an effect on neurons." Table 13.2 lists several of these antipsychotic drugs and their side effects.

✴-[Explore drugs commonly used to treat psychiatric disorders on **MyPsychLab**

table 13.2 Types of Drugs Used in Psychopharmacology

CLASSIFICATION	TREATMENT AREAS	SIDE EFFECTS	EXAMPLES
Antipsychotic: Typical Neuroleptic	Positive (excessive) symptoms such as delusions or hallucinations	Motor problems, tardive dyskinesia	chlorpromazine, droperidol, haloperidol
Antipsychotic: Atypical Neuroleptic	Positive and some negative symptoms of psychoses	Fewer than typical neuroleptics; clozapine may cause serious blood disorder	risperidone, clozapine, aripiprazole
Antianxiety: Minor Tranquilizers	Symptoms of anxiety and phobic reactions	Slight sedative effect; potential for physical dependence	xanax, ativan, valium
Antimanic	Manic behavior	Potential for toxic buildup	lithium, anticonvulsant drugs
Antidepressants: MAOIs	Depression	Weight gain, constipation, dry mouth, dizziness, headache, drowsiness, insomnia, some sexual arousal disorders	iproniazid, isocarboxazid, phenelzine sulfite, tranylcypromine sulfate
Antidepressants: Tricyclics	Depression	Skin rashes, blurred vision, lowered blood pressure, weight loss	imipramine, desipramine, amitriptyline, doxepin
Antidepressants: SSRIs	Depression	Nausea, nervousness, insomnia, diarrhea, rash, agitation, some sexual arousal problems	fluoxetine, sertraline, paroxetine

These drugs work by blocking certain dopamine receptors in the brain, thereby reducing the effect of dopamine in synaptic transmission (Csernansky et al., 2002). However, because they block more pathways in the dopamine system than are involved in psychosis, with prolonged use they tend to cause problems such as *tardive dyskinesia*, a syndrome causing the person to make repetitive, involuntary jerks and movements of the face, lips, legs, and body (Jones & Pilowsky, 2002).

The atypical neuroleptics also suppress dopamine but to a much greater degree in the one dopamine pathway that seems to cause psychotic problems. These drugs also block or partially block certain serotonin receptors, resulting in fewer negative side effects and occasionally some improvement in the more negative symptoms of schizophrenia such as withdrawal, apathy, and reduced communication (Jones & Pilowsky, 2002).

Clozapine, an atypical neuroleptic, can cause a potentially fatal reduction in the white blood cells of the body's immune system in a very small percentage of people. For this reason, the blood of patients on clozapine is closely monitored (Jones & Pilowsky, 2002).

How long do people generally have to take these antipsychotic medications?

In some cases, a person might have a psychotic episode that lasts only a few months or a few years and may need drug treatment only for that time. But in most cases, especially in schizophrenia that starts in adolescence or young adulthood, the medication must be taken for the rest of the person's life.

Long-term use of neuroleptics, particularly the older typical drugs, has been associated with a decrease in cognitive functioning (Terry et al., 2002, 2003). A newer class of atypical neuroleptics called partial dopamine agonists affects the release of dopamine rather than blocking its receptors in the brain (Tamminga, 2002). (An *agonist* is any chemical substance that can stimulate a reaction within the synapse.) ⓛⓘⓝⓚ to Chapter Two: The Biological Perspective, p. 50. By 2005 the only one of these drugs that had been approved by the Food and Drug Administration for use in the treatment of schizophrenia was aripiprazole (Abilify). The hope is that these newer drugs will not only produce fewer negative side effects but also have less impact

How long do people generally have to take these antipsychotic medications?

antianxiety drugs drugs used to treat and calm anxiety reactions, typically minor tranquilizers.

antidepressant drugs drugs used to treat depression and anxiety.

on the thought processes of those persons taking these drugs. In one recent study, the atypical neuroleptics were also found to lower the risk of violent behavior in patients with schizophrenia who are receiving their medication through community-based treatment centers (Swanson et al., 2004).

ANTIANXIETY DRUGS There are currently two kinds of drugs used to treat anxiety disorders, from mild anxiety to the more serious anxiety of social phobias, simple phobias, and panic disorder. The traditional **antianxiety drugs** are the minor tranquilizers or *benzodiazepines* such as Xanax, Ativan, and Valium. All of these drugs have a sedative effect and in the right dose can relieve symptoms of anxiety within half an hour of taking the drug (Uretsky, 2002). Although many side effects are possible, the main concern in using these drugs is their potential for addiction as well as abuse in the form of taking larger doses to "escape" (National Institute on Drug Abuse [NIDA], 2002).

In the last several years use of the benzodiazepines to treat anxiety has declined, and physicians and therapists have begun to prescribe **antidepressant drugs** to treat anxiety disorders such as panic disorder, obsessive-compulsive disorder, and posttraumatic stress disorder. Although the antidepressants take from 3 to 5 weeks to show any effect, they are not as subject to abuse as the minor tranquilizers and have fewer of the same side effects.

ANTIMANIC DRUGS For many years, the treatment of choice for bipolar disorder and episodes of mania has been *lithium*, a metallic chemical element that in its salt form (lithium carbonate) evens out both the highs and the lows of bipolar disorder. It is generally recommended that treatment with lithium continue at maintenance levels in people with recurring bipolar disorder. Lithium affects the way sodium ions in neuron and muscle cells are transported, although it is not clear exactly how this affects mood. Side effects typically disappear quickly, although the use of lithium has been associated with weight gain. Diet needs to be controlled when taking lithium because lowered levels of sodium in the diet can cause lithium to build up to toxic levels, as can any substance that removes water from the body such as the caffeine in sodas, tea, and coffee.

Anticonvulsant drugs, normally used to treat seizure disorders, have also been used to treat mania. Examples are carbamazepine, valproic acid (Depakote), and lamotrigine. These drugs can be as effective in controlling mood swings as lithium and can also be used in combination with lithium treatments (Bowden et al., 2000; Thase & Sachs, 2000). When bouts of mania include psychotic symptoms (as in affective psychosis), patients are often treated with antipsychotic drugs in addition to a combination of anticonvulsants or antidepressants (Tohen et al., 2003).

ANTIDEPRESSANT DRUGS As is so often the case in scientific discoveries, the first types of drugs used in the treatment of depression were originally developed to treat other disorders. Iproniazid, for example, was used to treat tuberculosis symptoms in the early 1950s and was found to have a positive effect on mood, becoming the first modern *antidepressant* (Trujillo & Chinn, 1996). This drug became the first of the *monoamine oxidase inhibitors (MAOIs)*, a class of antidepressants that blocks the activity of an enzyme called monoamine oxidase. Monoamine oxidase is the brain's "cleanup worker" because its primary function is to break down the neurotransmitters norepinephrine, serotonin, and dopamine—the three neurotransmitters most involved in control of mood. Under normal circumstances, the excess neurotransmitters are broken down *after* they have done their "job" in mood control. In depression, these neurotransmitters need more time to do their job, and the MAOIs allow them that time by inhibiting the enzyme's action.

Some common MAOIs in use today are isocarboxazid (Marplan), phenelzine sufate (Nardil), and tranylcypromine sulfate (Parnate). These drugs can produce some unwanted side effects, although in most cases the side effects decrease or disappear with continued treatment: weight gain, constipation, dry mouth, dizziness, headache, drowsiness or insomnia, and sexual arousal disorders are possible. People taking MAOIs should also be careful about eating certain smoked, fermented, or pickled foods, drinking certain beverages, or taking some other medications due to a risk of severe high blood pressure in combination with these substances (Geddes & Butler, 2002).

The second category of antidepressant drug to be developed is called the *tricyclic antidepressants*. These drugs were discovered in the course of developing treatments for schizophrenia (Trujillo & Chinn, 1996). Tricyclics, so called because of their molecular structure consisting of three rings (cycles), increase the activity of serotonin and norepinephrine in the nervous system by inhibiting their reuptake into the synaptic vesicles of the neurons. ⓛⓘⓝⓚ to Chapter Two: The Biological Perspective, pp. 49–50. Some common tricyclics are imipramine (Tofranil), desipramine (Norpramin, Pertofrane), amitriptyline (Elavil), and doxepin (Sinequan, Adapin). Side effects of these drugs, which may also decrease over the course of treatment, are very similar to those of the MAOIs but can also include skin rashes, blurred vision, lowered blood pressure, and weight loss (American Psychiatric Association, 2000b; Geddes & Butler, 2002).

The effect of the MAOIs and the tricyclics on the action of the three critical neurotransmitters led researchers to try to develop drugs that would more specifically target the critical neural activity involved in depression with fewer negative side effects. This led to the development of the *selective serotonin reuptake inhibitors (SSRIs)*, drugs that inhibit the reuptake process of only serotonin. This causes fewer side effects while still providing effective antidepressant action, making these drugs relatively safe when compared to the older antidepressants. But like the other two classes of antidepressants, the SSRIs may take from 2 to 6 weeks to produce effects. Some of the better-known SSRIs are fluoxetine (Prozac), sertraline (Zoloft), and paroxetine (Paxil).

electroconvulsive therapy (ECT) form of biomedical therapy to treat severe depression in which electrodes are placed on either one or both sides of a person's head and an electric current is passed through the electrodes that is strong enough to cause a seizure or convulsion.

13.9 How are electroconvulsive therapy and psychosurgery used to treat psychological disorders today?

Electroconvulsive Therapy

Many people are—well—*shocked* to discover that **electroconvulsive therapy (ECT)** is still in use to treat cases of severe depression. ECT involves the delivery of an electric shock to either one side or both sides of a person's head, resulting in a seizure or convulsion of the body and the release of a flood of neurotransmitters in the brain (American Psychiatric Association [APA] Committee on Electroconvulsive Therapy, 2001). The result is an almost immediate improvement in mood. ECT is used not only in severe cases of depression that have not responded to drug treatments or psychotherapy, or where the side effects of medication are not acceptable, but also in the treatment of several other severe disorders, such as schizophrenia and severe mania, that are not responding to alternate treatments (APA Committee on Electroconvulsive Therapy, 2001).

In the 1930s, doctors actually were researching the possible uses of inducing seizures in treating schizophrenia, although the seizures were induced through means of a drug (camphor) in those early experiments. It was Italian researchers Cerletti and Bini who first used electricity to induce a seizure in a man with schizophrenia,

Electroconvulsive therapy consists of applying an electric shock to one or both sides of the head. The result is rapid improvement in mood. It has been shown to be most effective in treating severe depression that has not responded to medication or where medication side effects cannot be tolerated.

psychosurgery surgery performed on brain tissue to relieve or control severe psychological disorders.

prefrontal lobotomy psychosurgery in which the connections of the prefrontal cortex to other areas of the brain are severed.

What are some of the side effects? Wasn't there something from an earlier chapter about this therapy affecting memory?

But I thought lobotomies left most people worse off than before—didn't it take away their emotions or something?

The woman on the left is Rosemary Kennedy, sister of President John F. Kennedy. The man on the right is her father, U.S. Ambassador to Great Britain Joseph Kennedy. About 6 years after this photograph was taken, Rosemary, who had mild intellectual disability and whose behavior had become difficult to control, was subjected to a transorbital lobotomy. The results were disastrous, and she remained institutionalized until her death on January 7, 2005.

who fully recovered after only 11 such treatments (Endler, 1988; Fink, 1984; Shorter, 1997). Soon doctors were using ECT on every kind of severe mental disorder. In those early days, no anesthesia was used because the shock was severe enough to result in a loss of consciousness (most of the time). Broken bones, bitten tongues, and fractured teeth were not untypical "side effects."

Today's ECT is far more controlled and humane. It is only used to treat severe disorders and written and informed consent is required in most states. ECT has been found to be most useful for severe depression that has not responded to medications or psychotherapy and in cases where suicide is a real possibility or has already been attempted. ECT works more quickly than antidepressant medications, so it can play an important role in helping to prevent suicide attempts (APA Committee on Electroconvulsive Therapy, 2001). However, ECT should not be considered a "cure." It is a way to get a person suffering from severe depression into a state of mind that is more receptive to other forms of therapy or psychotherapy.

● What are some of the side effects? Wasn't there something from an earlier chapter about this therapy affecting memory?

ECT does have several negative side effects, some of which last longer than others. Memory is definitely affected, as ECT disrupts the consolidation process and prevents the formation of long-term memories. ⓁⒾⓃⓀ to Chapter Five: Memory, pp. 188–189. This causes both retrograde amnesia, the loss of memories for events that happen close to the time of the treatment, and anterograde amnesia, the rapid forgetting of new material (APA Committee on Electroconvulsive Therapy, 2001; Lisanby et al., 2000; Weiner, 2000). The retrograde effects can extend to several months before and a few weeks after treatment and the older memories may return with time, whereas the anterograde amnesia is more temporary, clearing up in a few weeks after treatment. Only a very few patients suffer more severe and long-lasting cognitive difficulties, and it is not easy to determine whether these difficulties originate with the treatment or the disorder the person exhibits (Smith, 2001). When ECT is used today, an effort is made to reduce as many side effects as possible. The modern patient is given muscle relaxants to reduce the effects of the convulsion as well as a very short-term anesthetic.

Psychosurgery

Just as surgery involves cutting into the body, **psychosurgery** involves cutting into the brain to remove or destroy brain tissue for the purpose of relieving symptoms of mental disorders. One of the earliest and best-known psychosurgical techniques is the **prefrontal lobotomy**, in which the connections of the prefrontal cortex to other areas of the brain are severed. The lobotomy was developed in 1935 by Portuguese neurologist Dr. Antonio Egas Moniz, who was awarded the Nobel Prize in medicine for his contribution to psychosurgery (Cosgrove & Rauch, 1995; Freeman & Watts, 1937). Walter Freeman and James W. Watts modified Moniz's technique and developed a procedure called the *transorbital lobotomy*, during which an instrument resembling an ice pick, called a leucotome, was inserted through the back of the eye socket and into the brain to sever the brain fibers. It was this technique that became widely used, and unfortunately sometimes overused, in the pursuit of relief for so many people suffering from mental illness.

● But I thought lobotomies left most people worse off than before—didn't it take away their emotions or something?

Although it is true that some of the early lobotomy patients did seem less agitated, anxious, and delusional, it is also true that some early patients did not survive the surgery (about 6 percent died, in fact) and others were left with negative changes in personality: apathy, lack of emotional response, intellectual dullness, and childishness, to name a few. Fortunately, the development of antipsychotic drugs, beginning with chlorpromazine, together with the results of long-term studies that highlighted serious side effects of lobotomies, led to the discontinuation of lobotomies as a psychosurgical technique (Cosgrove & Rauch, 1995; Swayze, 1995). Some famous recipients of the last decades of lobotomies (and the disorders for which the procedure was performed) were Rosemary Kennedy, sister of John F. Kennedy (mild intellectual disability), and Rose Williams, sister of playwright Tennessee Williams (schizophrenia). 📖 Read on MyPsychLab

Are there any psychosurgical techniques in use today since the lobotomy is no longer used?

The lobotomy is gone, but there is a different, and more modern technique that was mentioned in the chapter opener called **bilateral anterior cingulotomy**. In this technique magnetic resonance imaging, Ⓛ Ⓘ Ⓝ Ⓚ to Chapter Two: The Biological Perspective, pp. 61–62, is used to guide an electrode to a specific area of the brain called the cingulate gyrus. This area connects the frontal lobes to the limbic system, which controls emotional reactions. By running a current through the electrode, a very small and specific area of brain cells can be destroyed. This process is called *deep lesioning*. Ⓛ Ⓘ Ⓝ Ⓚ to Chapter Two: The Biological Perspective, p. 60. Cingulotomies have been shown to be effective in about one-third to one-half of cases of major depression, bipolar disorder, and certain forms of obsessive-compulsive disorder that have not responded to any other therapy techniques (Dougherty et al., 2002; Kuhn et al., 2010; Spangler et al., 1996). Because this is deliberate brain damage and quite permanent, all other possible treatments must be exhausted before a bilateral cingulotomy will be performed, and, unlike the early days of lobotomies, it can be performed only with the patient's full and informed consent (Rodgers, 1992; Spangler et al., 1996). Because of the ethical, social, and legal implications of psychosurgery in general, today only a very small number of such surgeries are carried out in a few medical centers across the world (Cosgrove & Rauch, 1995).

EMERGING TECHNIQUES Some new noninvasive techniques for effecting changes in the brain were discussed in Ⓛ Ⓘ Ⓝ Ⓚ Chapter Two, including *repetitive transcranial magnetic stimulation* (rTMS), where magnetic pulses are applied to the cortex and *transcranial direct current stimulation* (tDCS), which uses scalp electrodes to pass very low amplitude direct currents to the brain. These new and exciting strategies are being evaluated as possible treatment options for a variety of psychological disorders including PTSD and depression (Boggio et al., 2009; Nitsche et al., 2009). Another technique highlighted in Ⓛ Ⓘ Ⓝ Ⓚ Chapter Two was *deep brain stimulation*; it is being evaluated as a treatment modality for both depression and OCD (Harvard Mental Health Letter, 2010; Huff et al., 2010).

Many psychological professionals today believe that combining psychotherapy with medical therapies—particularly drug therapy—is a more effective approach to treating many disorders. A person dealing with depression may be given an antidepressant drug to alleviate symptoms but may also still need to talk about what it's like to deal with depression and with needing the medication. Cognitive–behavioral therapy in combination with drug therapy has been shown to be particularly effective in treating depression (Dew et al., 2007; Frank et al., 2007; Rohde et al., 2008). Another study has found that women with recurrent depression benefit from a combination of treatment with antidepressants and monthly maintenance psychotherapy (Frank et al., 2007).

bilateral anterior cingulotomy psychosurgical technique in which an electrode wire is inserted into the anterior cingulate gyrus, with guidance from magnetic resonance imaging, to destroy a very small portion of that brain area with electric current.

Are there any psychosurgical techniques in use today since the lobotomy is no longer used?

📖 Read and learn more about the history of lobotomy on MyPsychLab

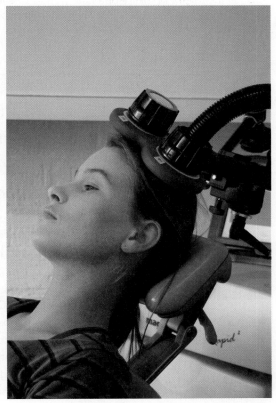

Repetitive transcranial magnetic stimulation (rTMS) uses a pulsating magnetic field to activate specific parts of the brain's surface. As seen above, by placing an electromagnet on the scalp, TMS can be used to stimulate small areas of the cortex and is being evaluated as a way to control some psychological symptoms, such as those related to depression and PTSD. Photo courtesy of Martijn Arns, http://www.brainclinics.com

practice quiz How much do you remember?

Pick the best answer.

1. Which of the following statements about the effectiveness of psychotherapy is FALSE?
   a. In surveys, 75 to 90 percent of people reported that therapy has helped them.
   b. The longer a person stays in therapy, the less effective it is.
   c. Psychotherapy without drugs seems to work as well as psychotherapy with drugs.
   d. No one psychotherapy is effective for all disorders.

2. For psychotherapy to be effective, _____.
   a. the therapist must provide a protected setting for clients to reveal their feelings.
   b. the therapist should maintain emotional distance from the client.
   c. clients and therapists should avoid warmth in their relationship.
   d. therapists should choose one style of therapy for all of their clients.

3. Of the following, all are potential barriers to effective therapy listed by Sue and Sue (2008) when the culture or ethnic backgrounds of therapist and client are different except _____.
   a. language.
   b. cultural values.
   c. social class.
   d. age.

4. The newest drugs being developed to treat psychotic symptoms are the _____.
   a. typical neuroleptics.
   b. atypical neuroleptics.
   c. anticonvulsants.
   d. partial dopamine agonists.

5. For which disorders have antidepressants NOT been used?
   a. panic disorder
   b. dissociative amnesia
   c. obsessive-compulsive disorder
   d. posttraumatic stress disorder

6. Electroconvulsive shock therapy is useful in preventing suicide attempts because it _____.
   a. is more effective than drug therapies.
   b. has few negative side effects.
   c. works more quickly than antidepressants.
   d. makes people happy.

7. The risk of permanent brain damage is greatest with _____.
   a. cybertherapy.
   b. ECT.
   c. psychosurgery.
   d. bilateral ECT.

Brainstorming: What are some of the possible drawbacks of using medication to treat disordered behavior, beyond any side effects of the medications themselves?

ANSWERS ON PAGE AK-2

applying psychology to everyday life
Virtual Realities

13.10 How might computers be used in psychotherapy?

Virtual reality is a software-generated, three-dimensional simulated environment. Imagine yourself playing a video game, but instead of viewing your character on the screen in front of you, you are immersed in the visual and auditory world created by the game designers, seeing and hearing through the eyes and ears of your character. While playing a video game in this manner might be a lot of fun, there are some very practical uses of virtual reality (VR) for treating psychological disorders.

One of the main uses of VR as a therapy incorporates exposure therapy of some form. Exposure therapy involves preventing a person with a phobia, for example, from avoiding the presentation of the phobic object—preventing the typical avoidance response and eventually resulting in extinction of the conditioned fear. Using VR ensures that the person being treated cannot avoid exposure as the sight and sound of the animal, open spaces, or whatever the phobia involves are always right in front of him or her. A study that is being conducted at the University of Manchester, England, and led by Professor Nick Tarrier is focused on helping people with phobias about driving cars by having them wear sophisticated goggles that allow them to experience a virtual driving environment (University of Manchester, 2009). Special sensors on chest and fingers measure anxiety levels. The real advantage of VR psychotherapy here is that there is no physical risk to the phobic driver, therapist, or other drivers on a real road.

Posttraumatic stress disorder (PTSD) is another mental-health issue benefiting from the use of VR psychotherapy. Cases of this disorder are rising (and with the BP oil spill disaster discussed in Chapter Twelve and other such stressors, psychologists expect the number of PTSD cases to continue to rise), and traditional treatments are not always effective. Virtual reality psychotherapy allows the safe use of exposure therapy, already thought to be a highly

Some behavioral therapists now use virtual reality to expose patients to phobic objects and situations—like the cabin of an airplane. As part of systematic desensitization, this patient receives exposure to anxiety-provoking visual displays through a virtual reality headset. Credit: Charles Undermost, Delft University of Technology.

promising treatment for PTSD (Mary Ann Liebert, Inc./Genetic Engineering News, 2010). Another advantage is the more vivid and realistic imagery possible with VR, especially for patients who may not be highly skilled in visualization and are asked to "imagine" the scenarios that disturb them. Think also of the portability of VR: there are currently handheld VR devices that eventually could be used to deliver therapy for PTSD, for example, to survivors of earthquakes, tsunamis, hurricanes, and other massive disasters around the world.

QUESTIONS FOR FURTHER DISCUSSION

1. What other disorders can you think of that might benefit from virtual reality psychotherapy?

2. Can you think of any disadvantages to this method of therapy?

chapter summary ((•─Listen on MyPsychLab   Listen to an audio file of your chapter www.MyPsychLab

Two Kinds of Therapy

13.1 What are the two modern ways in which psychological disorders can be treated, and how have they been treated in the past?

- Psychotherapy involves a person talking to a psychological professional about the person's problems.
- Psychotherapy for the purpose of gaining understanding into one's motives and actions is called insight therapy, whereas psychotherapy aimed at changing disordered behavior directly is called action therapy.
- Biomedical therapy uses a medical procedure to bring about changes in behavior.

The Early Days: Ice-Water Baths and Electric Shocks

- Mentally ill people began to be confined to institutions called asylums in the mid-1500s. Treatments were harsh and often damaging.
- Philippe Pinel became famous for demanding that the mentally ill be treated with kindness, personally unlocking the chains of inmates at Bicêtre Asylum in Paris, France.

Psychotherapy Begins

- Sigmund Freud developed a treatment called psychoanalysis that focused on releasing a person's hidden, repressed urges and concerns from the unconscious mind.

13.2 What were the basic elements of Freud's psychoanalysis, and how does psychoanalysis differ today?

- Psychoanalysis uses interpretation of dreams, free association, positive and negative transference, and resistance to help patients reveal their unconscious concerns.
- Freud's original therapy technique is criticized for its lack of scientific research and his own personal biases that caused him to misinterpret much of what his patients revealed.
- Modern psychodynamic therapists have modified the technique so that it takes less time and is much more direct, and they do not focus on the id and sexuality as Freud did.

Humanistic Therapy: To Err Is Human

13.3 What are the basic elements of the humanistic therapies known as person-centered therapy and Gestalt therapy?

- Humanistic therapies focus on the conscious mind and subjective experiences to help clients gain insights.
- Person-centered therapy is very nondirective, allowing the client to talk through problems and concerns while the therapist provides a supportive background.
- The four basic elements of person-centered therapy are reflection of the client's statements by the therapist, unconditional positive regard

given to the client by the therapist, empathy of the therapist for the client, and authenticity of the therapist in the client's perception.

- Gestalt therapy is more directive, helping clients to become aware of their feelings and to take responsibility for their choices in life.
- Gestalt therapists try to help clients deal with things in their past that they have denied and will use body language and other nonverbal cues to understand what clients are really saying.
- Humanistic therapies are also not based in experimental research and work best with intelligent, highly verbal persons.

Behavior Therapies: Learning One's Way to Better Behavior

- Behavior therapies are action therapies that do not look at thought processes but instead focus on changing the abnormal or disordered behavior itself through classical or operant conditioning.

13.4 How do behavior therapists use classical and operant conditioning to treat disordered behavior?

- Classical conditioning techniques for changing behavior include systematic desensitization, aversion therapy, and flooding.
- Therapies based on operant conditioning include modeling, reinforcement and the use of token economies, and extinction.
- Behavior therapies can be effective in treating specific problems, such as bed-wetting, drug addictions, and phobias, and can help improve some of the more troubling behavioral symptoms associated with more severe disorders.

Cognitive Therapies: Thinking Is Believing

13.5 What are the goals and basic elements of cognitive therapies such as cognitive–behavioral therapy and rational–emotive behavior therapy?

- Cognitive therapy is oriented toward teaching clients how their thinking may be distorted and helping clients to see how inaccurate some of their beliefs may be.
- Some of the cognitive distortions in thinking include arbitrary inference, selective thinking, overgeneralization, magnification and minimization, and personalization.
- Cognitive–behavioral therapies are action therapies that work at changing a person's illogical or distorted thinking.
- The three goals of cognitive–behavioral therapies are to relieve the symptoms and solve the problems, to develop strategies for solving future problems, and to help change irrational, distorted thinking.
- Rational–emotive behavior therapy is a directive therapy in which the therapist challenges clients' irrational beliefs, often arguing with clients and even assigning them homework.

- Although CBT has seemed successful in treating depression, stress disorders, and anxiety, it is criticized for focusing on the symptoms and not the causes of disordered behavior.

Group Therapies: Not Just for the Shy

13.6 What are the various types of group therapies and the advantages and disadvantages of group therapy?

- Group therapy has the advantages of low cost, exposure to other people with similar problems, social interaction with others, and social and emotional support from people with similar disorders or problems. It has also been demonstrated to be very effective for people with social anxiety.
- Disadvantages of group therapy can include the need to share the therapist's time with others in the group, the lack of a private setting in which to reveal concerns, and the inability of people with severe disorders to tolerate being in a group.
- Group therapy can be accomplished using many styles of psychotherapy and may involve treating people who are all part of the same family, as in family counseling.
- Group therapy can also be accomplished without the aid of a trained therapist in the form of self-help or support groups composed of other people who have the same or similar problems.
- Group therapy is most useful to persons who cannot afford individual therapy and who may obtain a great deal of social and emotional support from other group members.

psychology in the news: Mental Health on Campus

- Campus life is often very stressful, and many students arrive on campus already in therapy for a diagnosed disorder.
- Students should make use of the available resources on college campuses, such as counseling centers.

Does Psychotherapy Really Work?

- Eysenck's early survey of client improvement seemed to suggest that clients would improve as time passed, with or without therapy.

13.7 How effective is psychotherapy, and how is the effectiveness of psychotherapy influenced by cultural, ethnic, and gender differences?

- Surveys of people who have received therapy suggest that psychotherapy is more effective than no treatment at all.
- Surveys reveal that from 75 to 90 percent of people who receive therapy improve, the longer a person stays in therapy the better the improvement, and psychotherapy works as well alone as with drugs.
- Some types of psychotherapy are more effective for certain types of problems, and no one psychotherapy method is effective for all problems.
- Effective therapy should be matched to the particular client and the particular problem, there should exist a therapeutic alliance between therapist and client, and a protected setting in which clients can release emotions and reveal private thoughts is essential.
- When the culture, ethnic group, or gender of the therapist and the client differs, misunderstandings and misinterpretations can occur due to differences in cultural/ethnic values, socioeconomic differences, gender roles, and beliefs.
- The four barriers to effective psychotherapy that exist when the backgrounds of client and therapist differ are language, cultural values, social class, and nonverbal communication.
- Cybertherapy is therapy that is offered on the Internet. Cybertherapists may or may not be trained in psychotherapy, but cybertherapy offers the advantages of anonymity and therapy for people who cannot otherwise get to a therapist.

Biomedical Therapies

- Biomedical therapies include the use of drugs, induced convulsions, and surgery to relieve or control the symptoms of mental disorders.

13.8 What are the various types of drugs used to treat psychological disorders?

- Antipsychotic drugs are used to control delusions, hallucinations, and bizarre behavior and include the typical neuroleptics, atypical neuroleptics, and partial dopamine agonists.
- Antianxiety drugs are used to treat anxiety disorders and include the benzodiazepines and certain antidepressant drugs.
- Antimanic drugs are used to treat bipolar disorder and include lithium and certain anticonvulsant drugs.
- Antidepressant drugs are used in the treatment of depression and include monoamine oxidase inhibitors (MOAIs), tricyclic antidepressants, and selective serotonin reuptake inhibitors (SSRIs).

13.9 How are electroconvulsive therapy and psychosurgery used to treat psychological disorders today?

- Electroconvulsive therapy, or ECT, is used to treat severe depression, bipolar disorder, and schizophrenia and involves the use of a muscle relaxant, a short-term anesthetic, and induction of a seizure under controlled conditions.
- One of the earliest psychosurgeries was the prefrontal lobotomy, in which the front part of the frontal lobe was cut away from the back part of the brain, producing effects ranging from a disappearance of symptoms to a lack of emotional response and dulling of mental functions.
- Modern psychosurgery includes the bilateral cingulotomy, used to treat major depression, bipolar disorders, and certain forms of obsessive-compulsive disorder that have not responded to other forms of treatment.
- Emerging technologies for treatment of psychological disorders include repetitive transcranial magnetic stimulation (rTMS), transcranial direct current stimulation (tDCS), and deep brain stimulation.

applying psychology to everyday life: Virtual Realities

13.10 How might computers be used in psychotherapy?

- Virtual reality therapy is a computer-based simulation of environments that can be used to treat disorders such as phobias and PTSD with less risk than that of actual exposure to anxiety-provoking stimuli.
- VRT is particularly useful as a delivery system for exposure therapy.

TEST yourself

ANSWERS ON PAGE AK-2

✓ [Study and Review on MyPsychLab](www.MyPsychLab) Ready for your test? More quizzes and a customized plan. www.MyPsychLab

Pick the best answer.

1. Larisa is going to a therapist to gain a better understanding of what makes her do the things she does. This type of therapy is known as _____ therapy.
   a. insight
   b. action
   c. behavioral
   d. biomedical

2. It was _____ who is most credited with the "moral treatment" movement for using kindness and guidance with the mentally ill.
   a. Sigmund Freud
   b. Josef Breuer
   c. Jean Martin Charcot
   d. Philippe Pinel

3. The actual content of a dream is the _____ content, according to Freud.
- **a.** repressed
- **b.** latent
- **c.** manifest
- **d.** sexual

4. A psychoanalyst may rely on the technique of _____, which allows the patient to talk about anything that comes to mind.
- **a.** positive transference
- **b.** negative transference
- **c.** free association
- **d.** dream analysis

5. In _____, a person-centered therapist must show an honest and open response to the client and not hide behind the professional role of therapist.
- **a.** reflection
- **b.** unconditional positive regard
- **c.** empathy
- **d.** authenticity

6. Gestalt therapy differs from person-centered therapy because _____.
- **a.** it is based in humanistic theory.
- **b.** it focuses on the unconscious mind.
- **c.** it is directive rather than nondirective.
- **d.** it is an insight therapy.

7. What kind of person would probably get the least benefit from a humanistic therapy?
- **a.** one who is bright but confused about self-image
- **b.** one who is very talkative and open in discussing feelings
- **c.** one who enjoys exploring the inner workings of the mind
- **d.** one who has a hard time putting things into words in a logical manner

8. Lashonna was afraid of dogs. She wanted to get over this fear, so she began by thinking about seeing a dog but staying calm. Then she walked past her neighbor's dog in its fenced yard until she no longer felt afraid. Next, she visited a pet store and petted a dog while the salesperson held it. Finally, she bought herself a puppy and was no longer afraid. Lashonna's method is most like _____.
- **a.** systematic desensitization.
- **b.** aversion therapy.
- **c.** flooding.
- **d.** extinction.

9. When the exposure to a feared object is rapid and intense rather than slow and gradual, it is called _____.
- **a.** systematic desensitization.
- **b.** aversion therapy.
- **c.** flooding.
- **d.** extinction.

10. Yvonne sat down with her daughter, Camille, and together they wrote out a list of things that Camille was expected to do each day and the rewards she would get if she accomplished them, as well as the penalties she would face if she did not do them. This is most like which technique?
- **a.** token economy
- **b.** time-out
- **c.** extinction
- **d.** contingency contracting

11. Which therapy style can be compared to a drill sergeant–private style of therapeutic relationship?
- **a.** person-centered
- **b.** Gestalt
- **c.** rational–emotive behavioral
- **d.** cognitive

12. Which of the following is not one of the three goals of cognitive–behavioral therapy?
- **a.** helping the client gain insight
- **b.** relieving the symptoms and resolving the problems
- **c.** helping the client develop strategies for future problem solving
- **d.** helping the client to think in a more rational, self-helping way

13. Stephan sees a text message from a phone number he does not recognize on his girlfriend's phone. He immediately assumes his girlfriend is seeing someone else and the phone number belongs to that person. Beck would say that Stephan has engaged in what type of distorted thinking?
- **a.** arbitrary inference
- **b.** selective thinking
- **c.** overgeneralization
- **d.** personalization

14. Which of the following is a disadvantage of group therapy?
- **a.** Clients share the therapist's time.
- **b.** Clients see how other people have handled the problem.
- **c.** Clients get social support from others.
- **d.** Clients interact with others socially.

15. When Carson began acting out, her parents took her to a therapist who suggested that her parents may have caused the problem by using the wrong kind of discipline. The kind of therapy that might best help Carson would probably be _____.
- **a.** a support group of other disturbed children.
- **b.** an insight therapy.
- **c.** a cognitive therapy.
- **d.** family therapy.

16. Which of the following is not one of the problems in studying the effectiveness of psychotherapy?
- **a.** All therapies take the same amount of time to be effective.
- **b.** Control groups have no expectations about getting better.
- **c.** Some therapies measure success differently and are not easily evaluated.
- **d.** There may be experimenter bias.

17. Cindy is a white, upper-middle-class graduate student in clinical psychology doing her first internship in juvenile court. Her first client is an angry 15-year-old African American boy. Which of the following might be barriers to effective therapy in this situation?
- **a.** social class
- **b.** nonverbal communication
- **c.** cultural values
- **d.** All of these might be barriers.

18. When a person on an antipsychotic drug develops repetitive, involuntary jerks and movements of the face, lips, legs, and body, this is called _____.
- **a.** the "Thorazine" shuffle.
- **b.** neuroleptic syndrome.
- **c.** tardive dyskinesia.
- **d.** psychotic syndrome.

19. The use of antianxiety drugs to treat anxiety disorders is gradually being phased out in favor of treatment with _____ drugs.
- **a.** antidepressant
- **b.** antimanic
- **c.** antipsychotic
- **d.** sedative

20. Which neurotransmitter is not one of the three that seems to be involved in depression and the drugs that treat depression?
- **a.** norepinephrine
- **b.** serotonin
- **c.** dopamine
- **d.** epinephrine

21. Before the use of electricity, seizures were induced in psychotic patients by means of _____.
- **a.** ice-cold water.
- **b.** bloodletting.
- **c.** camphor.
- **d.** opium.

22. In bilateral anterior cingulotomy _____.
- **a.** the front of the brain is cut away from the back.
- **b.** a thin wire electrode is used to destroy a small area of brain tissue.
- **c.** an electric shock is used to stimulate certain areas of the brain.
- **d.** a drug is injected into the brain to destroy a small area of brain tissue.

23. Virtual reality (VR) techniques have been useful in the treatment of which of the following disorders?
- **a.** phobias
- **b.** mania
- **c.** posttraumatic stress disorder
- **d.** both a and c

13 psychological therapies

13.1 **13.2** p. 466

modern treatments
- psychotherapy
- biomedical therapy

early interventions
- historically, psychological or social causes identified for some disorders; for others, individuals with mental illness were believed to be possessed by demons or evil spirits
- organized treatment began in England around the middle 1500s
- Pinel started the "moral treatment" movement in France

Psychological Therapies

Freud's psychoanalysis and related techniques
- Freud developed the technique of **psychoanalysis**, an insight therapy aimed at revealing unconscious conflicts, urges, and desires
- **dream interpretation**
- **free association**
- **modern psychodynamic approach**

interpersonal therapy (IPT)
- eclectic therapy with some theoretical roots in the psychodynamic approach but combines aspects from humanistic and cognitive–behavioral therapies

"Why do you think you cross the road?"

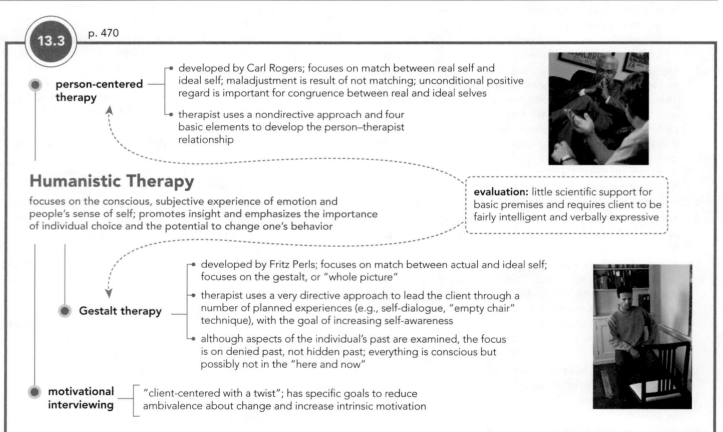

13.3 p. 470

person-centered therapy
- developed by Carl Rogers; focuses on match between real self and ideal self; maladjustment is result of not matching; unconditional positive regard is important for congruence between real and ideal selves
- therapist uses a nondirective approach and four basic elements to develop the person–therapist relationship

Humanistic Therapy

focuses on the conscious, subjective experience of emotion and people's sense of self; promotes insight and emphasizes the importance of individual choice and the potential to change one's behavior

evaluation: little scientific support for basic premises and requires client to be fairly intelligent and verbally expressive

Gestalt therapy
- developed by Fritz Perls; focuses on match between actual and ideal self; focuses on the gestalt, or "whole picture"
- therapist uses a very directive approach to lead the client through a number of planned experiences (e.g., self-dialogue, "empty chair" technique), with the goal of increasing self-awareness
- although aspects of the individual's past are examined, the focus is on denied past, not hidden past; everything is conscious but possibly not in the "here and now"

motivational interviewing
- "client-centered with a twist"; has specific goals to reduce ambivalence about change and increase intrinsic motivation

13.4 **13.5** **13.6** p. 473

- **behavior therapies**
  action-based therapies operating on the premise that all behaviors, both normal and abnormal, are learned; applied behavior analysis involves functional analysis and learning techniques to increase desirable behaviors and decrease undesirable behaviors

  - techniques based on classical conditioning—pairing of stimuli
  - techniques based on operant conditioning—reinforcement, extinction, shaping, and modeling
  - **evaluation:** more effective than others for specific behavioral problems (e.g., bed-wetting, overeating, drug addictions, phobic reactions)

Action Therapies

- **cognitive therapies**
  action-based therapies that focus on helping people change their ways of thinking; emphasis on identifying distorted and unrealistic beliefs that lead to maladaptive behavior and problem emotions and then replacing them with more positive, helpful thoughts

  - **Beck's cognitive therapy** identifies several common cognitive distortions (e.g., arbitrary inference, selective thinking, etc.)
  - **cognitive–behavioral therapy (CBT)** uses cognitive methods that have behavioral elements within them as well
  - **rational–emotive behavior therapy (REBT)** developed by Ellis; teaches clients to challenge their irrational beliefs
  - **evaluation:** typically shorter and less expensive than insight therapies; treating the symptom, not the cause, is both a feature and a criticism; especially effective for many disorders, including depression, anxiety disorders, and personality disorders

- alternative to individual therapy; group of clients meet together to discuss similar problems with a single therapist or pair of therapists
  - may use a variety of styles, but person-centered, Gestalt, and behavioral seem to work best; may also take several different forms

- **self-help groups** may also be effective; do not have a therapist directly involved
- **family counseling:** all members of family are seen by therapist as a group

- **evaluation:** advantages include lower cost, exposure to ways other people view and handle similar problems, social and emotional support; disadvantages include greater exposure, less one-on-one contact with therapist, and some problems hard to treat in a group setting

Group Therapies

13.7 **13.8** **13.9** p. 482

- effectiveness is not easy to study due to different theories, techniques, time frames for success, etc.; tendency of some therapists to be eclectic (using variety of techniques) is also a challenge
  - where effective, greater success is often tied to the relationship between the therapist and client (therapeutic alliance), a sense of safety, and longer time in therapy

- cultural, ethnic, and gender concerns should also be examined; these factors can affect not only the therapeutic alliance but also identification of actual problem(s) and treatment options

Does Psychotherapy Work?

- **psychopharmacology**
  the use of drugs to control or relieve the symptoms of a psychological disorder; may be used alone or in combination with other therapies (see Table 13.2)

- **electroconvulsive therapy**
  - still used to treat severe depression and a few other disorders that have not responded to other forms of treatment
  - involves the application of an electric shock and resulting seizure that appears to normalize the balance of neurotransmitters within the brain
  - traditional side effects (extreme memory loss, broken bones) have been minimized by lower levels of current and the use of both muscle relaxers and anesthesia

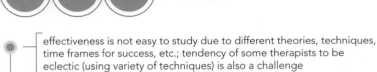

Biomedical Therapies — **psychosurgery**
  - used as a last resort, involves cutting into the brain to remove or destroy brain tissues associated with symptoms of a mental disorder
  - prefrontal lobotomies were widely used in the mid-1900s up until the development of antipsychotic drugs
  - at present, bilateral anterior cingulotomy (involves selective areas of cingulate gyrus) is used, primarily for obsessive-compulsive disorder; has also been used with depression and bipolar disorder

- **emerging technologies**
  - repetitive transcranial magnetic stimulation (rTMS)
  - transcranial direct current stimulation (tDCS)
    - being evaluated as treatment options for PTSD and depression, and other disorders
  - deep brain stimulation for depression and OCD

appendix A
statistics in psychology

A.1 Why do psychologists use statistics?

why study statistics?

Psychology is a science, and scientists must have ways of describing, summarizing, and analyzing the numerical data gathered through systematic observation and experimentation. Statistics allow researchers to do all of these things in a meaningful, logical fashion.

Many students in psychology wonder why the field uses such seemingly complicated mathematics. The answer is easy. Psychologists base their field on research findings. Data are collected, and they have to be analyzed. *Statistics* is the field that gives us the tools to do that.

Psychologists have to be able to do two things with the data they collect. The first is to summarize the information from a study or experiment. This is the role of **descriptive statistics**. The second is to make judgments and decisions about the data. We are interested if groups differ from each other. We are also interested in how one group of variables is related to another. This second emphasis is known as **inferential statistics**.

Statistical analysis is a way of trying to account for the error that exists in almost any body of data. A **statistic** is typically a number that represents some measure of central tendency or variability. These are described later in this appendix. Statistics are calculated from a **sample**. The same number calculated from a population is called a **parameter**. If you asked what the average height of teenage males was, and you calculated the average from just your high school, that average would be a statistic. If you tested every teenage male on earth, the average would be a parameter. As you can see, parameters are very rarely calculated. Thus, **statistics** is the branch of mathematics that is concerned with the collection and interpretation of data from samples (Agresti & Finlay, 1997; Aron et al., 2005). Psychology is only one of many fields that use the following types of statistics.

Descriptive Statistics

Descriptive statistics are a way of organizing numbers and summarizing them so that they can be understood. There are two main types of descriptive statistics:

- **Measures of Central Tendency.** Measures of central tendency are used to summarize the data and give you one score that seems typical of your sample.
- **Measures of Variability.** Measures of variability are used to indicate how spread out the data are. Are they tightly packed or are they widely dispersed?

The actual descriptive statistics are best understood after we explain the concept of a frequency distribution.

 A.1 Why do psychologists use statistics?

Descriptive Statistics

 A.2 What types of tables and graphs represent patterns in data?

 A.3 What types of statistics examine central tendencies in data?

 A.4 What types of statistics examine variations in data?

Inferential Statistics

 A.5 How can statistics be used to determine if differences in sets of data are large enough to be due to something other than chance variation?

 A.6 How are statistics used to predict one score from another?

 A.7 Why are skills in statistics important to psychology majors?

descriptive statistics   a way of organizing numbers and summarizing them so that patterns can be determined.

inferential statistics   statistical analysis of two or more sets of numerical data to reduce the possibility of error in measurement and to determine if the differences between the data sets are greater than chance variation would predict.

statistic   a measure of central tendency or variability computed from a sample.

sample   group of subjects selected from a larger population of subjects, usually selected randomly.

parameter   a number representing some measure of central tendency or variability within a population.

statistics   branch of mathematics concerned with the collection and interpretation of numerical data.

A-1

frequency distribution   a table or graph that shows how often different numbers or scores appear in a particular set of scores.

histogram   a bar graph showing a frequency distribution.

polygon   line graph showing a frequency distribution.

normal curve   a special frequency polygon in which the scores are symmetrically distributed around the mean, and the mean, median, and mode are all located on the same point on the curve, with scores decreasing as the curve extends from the mean.

bell curve   alternate name for the normal curve, which is said to be shaped like a bell.

table A.1   A Frequency Distribution

NUMBER OF GLASSES PER DAY	NUMBER OF PEOPLE OUT OF 30 (FREQUENCY)
1	0
2	1
3	2
4	4
5	5
6	6
7	5
8	4
9	2
10	1

A.2 What types of tables and graphs represent patterns in data?

One way psychologists get started in a research project is to look at their data, but just looking at a list of numbers wouldn't do much good. So we make a graph or chart. Then we can look for patterns.

Frequency Distributions

A **frequency distribution** is a table or graph that shows how often different numbers, or scores, appear in a particular set of scores. For example, let's say that you have a sample of 30 people, the size of some psychology classes. You ask them how many glasses of water they drink each day. You could represent the answers as shown in Table A.1. Just by looking at this table, it is clear that typical people drink between 4 and 8 glasses of water a day.

Tables can be useful, especially when dealing with small sets of data. Sometimes a more visual presentation gives a better "picture" of the patterns in a data set, and that is when researchers use graphs to plot the data from a frequency distribution. One common graph is a **histogram**, or a bar graph. Figure A.1 shows how the same data from Table A.1 would look in a bar graph.

Another type of graph used in frequency distributions is the **polygon**, a line graph. Figure A.2 shows the same data in a polygon graph.

The Normal Curve

Frequency polygons allow researchers to see the shape of a set of data easily. For example, the number of people drinking glasses of water in Figure A.2 is easily seen to be centered about 6 glasses (central tendency) but drops off below 4 glasses and above 8 glasses a day (variability). Our frequency polygon has a high point, and the frequency decreases on both sides.

A common frequency distribution of this type is called the **normal curve**. It has a very specific shape and is sometimes called the **bell curve**. Look at Figure A.3. This curve is almost a perfect normal curve, and many things in life are not that perfect. The normal curve is used as a model for many things that are measured, such as intelligence, height, or weight, but even those measures only come close to

FIGURE A.1 A Histogram
Histograms, or bar graphs, provide a visual way to look at data from frequency distributions. In this graph, for example, the height of the bars indicates that most people drink between 4 and 8 glasses of water (represented by the five highest bars in the middle of the graph).

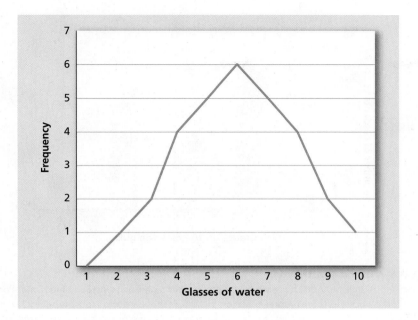

FIGURE A.2 A Polygon
A polygon is a line graph that can represent the data in a frequency distribution in much the same way as a bar graph but allows the shape of the data set to be easily viewed.

a perfect distribution (provided large numbers of people are measured). One of the reasons that the normal curve is so useful is that it has very specific relationships to measures of central tendency and a measurement of variability, known as the standard deviation.

OTHER DISTRIBUTION TYPES Distributions aren't always normal in shape. Some distributions are described as *skewed*. This occurs when the distribution is not even on both sides of a central score with the highest frequency (as in our example). Instead, the scores are concentrated toward one side of the distribution. For example, what if a study of people's water-drinking habits in a different class revealed that most people drank around 7 to 8 glasses of water daily, with no one drinking more than 8? The frequency polygon shown in Figure A.4 reflects this very different distribution.

FIGURE A.3 The Normal Curve
The normal curve, also known as the bell curve because of its unique shape, is often the way in which certain characteristics such as intelligence or weight are represented in the population. The highest point on the curve typically represents the average score in any distribution.

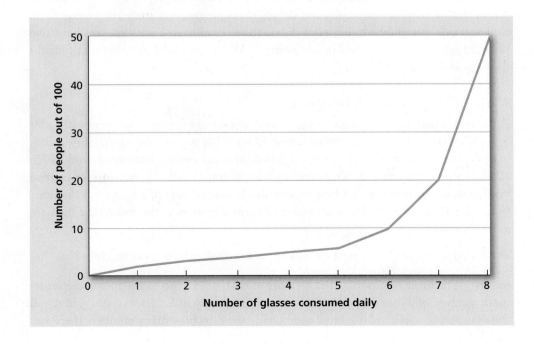

FIGURE A.4 A Frequency Polygon
Skewed distributions are those in which the most frequent scores occur at one end or the other of the distribution, as represented by this frequency polygon in which most people are seen to drink at least 7 to 8 glasses of water each day.

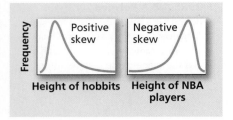

FIGURE A.5 Skewed Distribution
These frequency polygons show how distributions can be skewed in two different directions. The graph on the left represents the frequency of heights among hobbits (the little people from the fantasy *The Lord of the Rings*) and is positively skewed because the long "tail" goes to the right, or positive direction. The graph on the right shows the frequency of heights among NBA basketball players and is negatively skewed—the tail points to the left.

FIGURE A.6 A Bimodal Distribution
When a distribution is bimodal, it means that there are two high points instead of just one. For example, in the pop-quiz scores represented on this graph there are two "most frequent" scores—6 and 8. This most likely represents two groups of students, with one group being less successful than the other.

In this case, scores are piled up in the high end with most people drinking 7 or 8 glasses of water a day. The graphs in Figure A.5 show a **skewed distribution**. Skewed distributions are called positively or negatively skewed, depending on where the scores are concentrated. A concentration in the high end would be called **negatively skewed**. A concentration in the low end would be called **positively skewed**. The direction of the extended tail determines whether it is positively (tail to right) or negatively (tail to left) skewed. Here's an example. What do you think about the distribution of heights of hobbits (the little guys from *The Lord of the Rings*) and NBA basketball players (who are usually tall)? Might not these frequency distributions of height in Figure A.5 be appropriate?

Some frequency polygons show two high points rather than just one (see Figure A.6) and are called **bimodal distributions**. In this example, we have a distribution of scores from a 10-point pop quiz, and we see that one group of students seemed to do well and one group didn't. Bimodal distributions usually indicate that you have two separate groups being graphed in one polygon. What would the distribution of height for men and women look like?

Measures of Central Tendency

A frequency distribution is a good way to look at a set of numbers, but there's still a lot to look at—isn't there some way to sum it all up? One way to sum up numerical data is to find out what a "typical" score might be, or some central number around which all the others seem to fall. This kind of summation is called a **measure of central tendency**, or the number that best represents the central part of a frequency distribution. There are three different measures of central tendency: the mean, the median, and the mode.

A.3 What types of statistics examine central tendencies in data?

MEAN The most commonly used measure of central tendency is the **mean**, the arithmetic average of a distribution of numbers. That simply indicates that you add up all the numbers in a particular set and then divide them by how many numbers there are.

skewed distribution frequency distribution in which most of the scores fall to one side or the other of the distribution.

negatively skewed a distribution of scores in which scores are concentrated in the high end of the distribution.

positively skewed a distribution of scores in which scores are concentrated in the low end of the distribution.

bimodal distribution frequency distribution in which there are two high points rather than one.

measure of central tendency numbers that best represent the most typical score of a frequency distribution.

mean the arithmetic average of a distribution of numbers.

This is usually the way teachers get the grade point average for a particular student, for example. If Rochelle's grades on the tests she has taken so far are 86, 92, 87, and 90, then the teacher would add 86 + 92 + 87 + 90 = 335, and then divide 355 by four (the number of scores) to get the mean, or grade point average, of 88.75. Here is the formula for the mean:

$$\text{Mean} = \Sigma X/N$$

What does this mean?

- Σ is a symbol called sigma. It is a Greek letter, and it is also called the summation sign.
- X represents a score. Rochelle's grades are represented by X.
- ΣX means add up or sum all the X scores, or
  $\Sigma X = 86 + 92 + 87 + 90 = 355$.
- N means the number of scores. In this case, there are four grades.

  We then divide the sum of the scores (ΣX) by N to get the mean or

$$\text{Mean} = \Sigma X/N = \frac{355}{4} = 88.75$$

The mean is a good way to find a central tendency if the set of scores clusters around the mean with no extremely different scores that are either far higher or far lower than the mean.

MEDIAN

I remember that sometimes my teacher would "curve" the grades for a test, and it was always bad when just one person did really well and everyone else did lousy—is that what you mean about extremely different scores?

Yes, the mean doesn't work as well when there are extreme scores, as you would have if only two students out of an entire class had a perfect score of 100 and everyone else scored in the 70s or lower. If you want a truer measure of central tendency in such a case, you need one that isn't affected by extreme scores. The **median** is just such a measure. A median is the score that falls in the middle of an *ordered* distribution of scores. Half of the scores will fall above the median, and half of the scores will fall below it. If the distribution contains an odd number of scores, it's just the middle number, but if the number of scores is even, it's the average of the two middle scores. The median is also the 50th percentile. Look at Table A.2 for an example of the median.

The mean IQ of this group would be 114.6, but the median would be 101 (the average between Evan with 102 and Fethia with 100, the average of the two middle numbers). This may not look like much of a difference, but it's really a change of about 13.6 IQ points—a big difference. Also, think about measures of income in a particular area. If most people earn around $35,000 per year in a particular area, but there are just a few extremely wealthy people in the same area who earn $1,000,000 a year, a mean of all the annual incomes would no doubt make the area look like it was doing much better than it really is economically. The median would be a more accurate measure of the central tendency of such data.

I remember that sometimes my teacher would "curve" the grades for a test, and it was always bad when just one person did really well and everyone else did lousy—is that what you mean about extremely different scores?

median the middle score in an ordered distribution of scores, or the mean of the two middle numbers; the 50th percentile.

table A.2	**Intelligence Test Scores for 10 People**								
NAME	Allison	Ben	Carol	Denise	Evan	Fethia	George	Hal	Inga	Jay
IQ	160	150	139	102	102	100	100	100	98	95

mode   the most frequent score in a distribution of scores.

bimodal   condition in which a distribution has two modes.

measures of variability   measurement of the degree of differences within a distribution or how the scores are spread out.

range   the difference between the highest and lowest scores in a distribution.

MODE   The **mode** is another measure of central tendency in which the most frequent score is taken as the central measure. In the numbers given in the previous example, the mode would be 100 because that number appears more times in the distribution than any other. Three people have that score. This is the simplest measure of central tendency and is also more useful than the mean in some cases, especially when there are two sets of frequently appearing scores. For example, suppose a teacher notices that on the last exam the scores fall into two groups, with about 15 students making a 95 and another 14 students making a 67. The mean *and* the median would probably give a number somewhere between those two scores—such as 80. That number tells the teacher a lot less about the distribution of scores than the mode would because, in this case, the distribution is **bimodal**—there are two very different yet very frequent scores. (See Figure A.6 for another example.)

Measures of Central Tendency and the Shape of the Distribution

When the distribution is normal or close to it, the mean, median, and mode are the same or very similar. There is no problem. When the distribution is not normal, then the situation requires a little more explanation.

SKEWED DISTRIBUTIONS   If the distribution is skewed, then the mean is pulled in the direction of the tail of the distribution. The mode is still the highest point, and the median is between the two. Let's look at an example. In Figure A.7 we have a distribution of salaries at a company. A few people make a low wage, most make a midlevel wage, and the bosses make a lot of money. This gives us a positively skewed distribution with the measures of central tendency placed as in the figure. As mentioned earlier, with such a distribution, the median would be the best measure of central tendency to report. If the distribution were negatively skewed (tail to the left), the order of the measures of central tendency would be reversed.

BIMODAL DISTRIBUTIONS   If you have a bimodal distribution, then none of the measures of central tendency will do you much good. You need to discover why you have seemingly two groups in your one distribution.

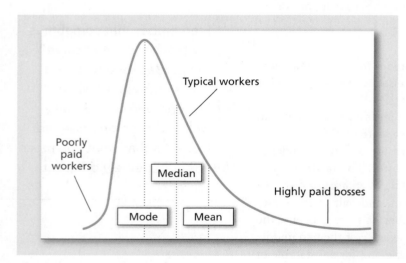

FIGURE A.7 Positively Skewed Distribution

In a skewed distribution, the high scores on one end will cause the mean to be pulled toward the tail of the distribution, making it a poor measure of central tendency for this kind of distribution. For example, in this graph many workers make very little money (represented by the mode), while only a few workers make a lot of money (the tail). The mean in this case would be much higher than the mode because of those few high scores distorting the average. In this case, the median is a much better measure of central tendency because it tends to be unaffected by extremely high or extremely low scores such as those in this distribution.

Measures of Variability

A.4 What types of statistics examine variations in data?

Descriptive statistics can also determine how much the scores in a distribution differ, or vary, from the central tendency of the data. These **measures of variability** are used to discover how "spread out" the scores are from each other. The more the scores cluster around the central scores, the smaller the measure of variability will be, and the more widely the scores differ from the central scores, the larger this measurement will be.

There are two ways that variability is measured. The simpler method is by calculating the **range** of the set of scores, or the difference between the highest score and the lowest score in the set of scores. The range is somewhat limited as a measure of variability when there are extreme scores in the distribution. For example, if you look at Table A.2, the range of those IQ scores would be 160–95, or 65. But if you just look at the numbers, you can see that there really isn't that much variation except for the three highest scores of 139, 150, and 160.

The other measure of variability that is commonly used is the one that is related to the normal curve, the **standard deviation**. This measurement is simply the square root of the average squared difference, or deviation, of the scores from the mean of the distribution. The mathematical formula for finding the standard deviation looks complicated, but it is really nothing more than taking each individual score, subtracting the mean from it, squaring that number (because some numbers will be negative and squaring them gets rid of the negative value), and adding up all of those squares. Then this total is divided by the number of scores and the square root of that number is the standard deviation. In the IQ example, it would go like this:

standard deviation the square root of the average squared deviation from the mean of scores in a distribution; a measure of variability.

$$\text{Standard Deviation Formula } SD = \sqrt{[\Sigma(X - M)^2/N]}$$

The mean (M) of the 10 IQ scores is 114.6. To calculate the standard deviation we

1. Subtract each score from the mean to get a deviation score $\rightarrow (X - M)$.

2. We square each deviation score $\rightarrow (X - M)^2$.

3. We add them up. Remember that's what the sigma (Σ) indicates $\rightarrow \Sigma(X - M)^2$.

4. We divide the sum of the squared deviation by N (the number of scores) $\rightarrow \Sigma(X - M)^2/N$

5. We take the square root ($\sqrt{\ }$) of the sum for our final step.

$$\sqrt{[\Sigma(X - M)^2/N]}$$

The process is laid out in Table A.3.

The standard deviation is equal to 23.5. What that tells you is that this particular group of data deviates, or varies, from the central tendencies quite a bit—there are

table A.3   Finding the Standard Deviation

SCORE	DEVIATION FROM THE MEAN ($X \pm M$)	SQUARED DEVIATION
160.00	45.40	2,061.16
	(ex. 160 − 114.60 = 45.40)	($45.40^2 = 2,061.16$)
150.00	35.40	1,253.16
139.00	24.40	595.36
102.00	−12.60	158.76
102.00	−12.60	158.76
100.00	−14.60	213.16
100.00	−14.60	213.16
100.00	−14.60	213.16
98.00	−16.60	275.56
95.00	−19.60	384.16
Sum of Scores		
(ΣX) = 1,146.00	($\Sigma X - M$) = 0.00	($\Sigma X - M)^2$ = 5,526.40
Mean = ($\Sigma X)/N$		Standard Deviation
= 1,146/10 = 114.60		= $\sqrt{[\Sigma(X - M)^2/N]}$
		= $\sqrt{5,526.40/10}$ = 23.5

z score a statistical measure that indicates how far away from the mean a particular score is in terms of the number of standard deviations that exist between the mean and that score.

some very different scores in the data set, or in this particular instance, three noticeably different scores.

This procedure may look very complicated. Let us assure you that computers and inexpensive calculators can figure out the standard deviation simply by entering the numbers and pressing a button. No one does a standard deviation by hand anymore.

How does the standard deviation relate to the normal curve? Let's look at the classic distribution of IQ scores. It has a mean of 100 and a standard deviation of 15 as set up by the test designers. It is a bell curve. With a true normal curve, researchers know exactly what percent of the population lies under the curve between each standard deviation from the mean. For example, notice that in the percentages in Figure A.8, one standard deviation above the mean has 34.13 percent of the population represented by the graph under that section. These are the scores between the IQs of 100 and 115. One standard deviation below the mean (–1) has exactly the same percent, 34.13, under that section—the scores between 85 and 100. This means that 68.26 percent of the population falls within one standard deviation from the mean, or one average "spread" from the center of the distribution. For example, "giftedness" is normally defined as having an IQ score that is two standard deviations *above* the mean. On the Wechsler Intelligence Scales, this means having an IQ of 130 or greater because the Wechsler's standard deviation is 15. But if the test a person took to determine giftedness was the Stanford-Binet Fourth Edition (the previous version of the test), the IQ score must have been 132 or greater because the standard deviation of that test was 16, not 15. The current version, the Stanford-Binet Fifth Edition, was published in 2003 and it now has a mean of 100 and a standard deviation of 15 for composite scores.

Although the "tails" of this normal curve seem to touch the bottom of the graph, in theory they go on indefinitely, never touching the base of the graph. In reality, though, any statistical measurement that forms a normal curve will have 99.72 percent of the population it measures falling within three standard deviations either above or below the mean. Because this relationship between the standard deviation and the normal curve does not change, it is always possible to compare different test scores or sets of data that come close to a normal curve distribution. This is done by computing a **z score**, which indicates how many standard deviations you are away from the mean. It is calculated by subtracting the mean from your score and dividing by the standard deviation. For example, if you had an IQ of 115, your z score would be 1.0. If you had an IQ of 70, your z score would −2.0. So on any exam, if you had a positive z score,

FIGURE A.8 IQ Normal Curve
Scores on intelligence tests are typically represented by the normal curve. The dotted vertical lines each represent one standard deviation from the mean, which is always set at 100. For example, an IQ of 116 on the Stanford-Binet Fourth Edition (Stanford-Binet 4) represents one standard deviation above the mean, and the area under the curve indicates that 34.13 percent of the population falls between 100 and 116 on that test. The Stanford-Binet Fifth Edition was published in 2003 and it now has a mean of 100 and a standard deviation of 15 for composite scores.

Standard Deviations	-4	-3	-2	-1	0	1	2	3	4
Wechsler IQ	40	55	70	85	100	115	130	145	160
Stanford-Binet 4 IQ	36	52	68	84	100	116	132	148	164
Cumulative %	0.003	0.135	2.275	15.856	50.00	84.134	97.725	99.865	99.997

you did relatively well. A negative z score means you didn't do as well. The formula for a z score is:

$$Z = (X - M)/SD$$

Inferential Statistics

A.5 How can statistics be used to determine if differences in sets of data are large enough to be due to something other than chance variation?

Descriptive methods of statistics are not useful when it comes to comparing sets of numbers or scores to see if there are differences between them that are great enough to be caused by something other than chance variation. Inferential statistics consist of statistical techniques that allow researchers to determine the difference between results of a study that are meaningful and those that are merely due to chance variations. Inferential statistics also allow researchers to draw conclusions, or make *inferences*, about the results of research and about whether those results are only true for the specific group of animals or people involved in the study, or whether the results can be applied to, or *generalized* to, the larger population from which the study participants were selected.

For example, in the Cheryan (Cheryan et al., 2009) study described in Chapter One, there were a lot of variables that simply could not be controlled completely, even with random assignment of participants to the two conditions. (L)(I)(N)(K) to Chapter One: The Science of Psychology, pp. 4–5. For example, there was no guarantee that random assignment would account for the interfering effects of female participants who might have really liked the science fiction toys, posters, and pizza they saw in one of the test conditions. Maybe any difference found between the males and females was due to pure luck or chance and not to the variables under study.

In any analysis that compares two or more sets of data, there's always the possibility of error in the data that comes from either within the group (all participants in one group, for example, will not be exactly like each other) or differences between groups (the experimental group and the control group are formed with different people, so there are differences between the two groups that have nothing to do with the manipulations of the experimenter). When researchers want to know if the differences they find in the data that come from studies like the Cheryan experiment are large enough to be caused by the experimental manipulation and *not* just by the chance differences that exist within and between groups, they have to use a kind of statistical technique that can take those chance variations into account. These kinds of statistical analysis use inferential statistics.

Inferential statistical analysis also allows researchers to determine how much confidence they should have in the results of a particular experiment. As you might remember, results from other kinds of studies that look for relationships—observations, surveys, and case studies—are often analyzed with descriptive statistics, especially correlations. But experiments look for *causes* of relationships, and researchers want to have some evidence that the results of their experiments really mean what they think they mean.

There are many different kinds of inferential statistical methods. The method that is used depends on the design of the experiment, such as the number of independent and dependent variables or the number of experimental groups. All inferential statistics have one thing in common—they look for differences in group measurements that are **statistically significant**. Statistical significance is a way to test differences to

statistically significant referring to differences in data sets that are larger than chance variation would predict.

see how likely those differences are to be real and not just caused by the random variations in behavior that exist in everything animals and people do.

For example, in a classic study investigating the effects of intrinsic versus extrinsic motivation on children's creativity, Dr. Teresa Amabile's 1982 study showed that the collages of the children who were promised prizes (an extrinsic reward) were judged to be less creative than those of the children who created collages just for fun. But was that difference between the creativity scores of the two groups a real difference, or was it merely due to chance variations in the children's artistic creations? Dr. Amabile used an inferential test on her results that told her that the difference was too big to be just chance variations, which means her results were *significant*—they were most likely to be real differences. How likely? Tests of significance give researchers the probability that the results of their experiment were caused by chance and not by their experimental manipulation. For example, in one test called a ***t*-test**, the scores of the children's artwork would have been placed into a formula that would result in a single number (t) that evaluates the probability that the difference between the two group means is due to pure chance or luck. That number would be compared to a value that exists in a table of possible t values, which tells researchers the probability of the result is due to chance or luck. If the number obtained by the calculation is bigger than the value in the table, there will be a probability associated with that number in the table. The probability, symbolized by the letter p, will tell researchers the probability of the difference was due to chance. In Dr. Amabile's case, the probability was $p < .05$ which means the probability that the results were due to chance alone was less than 5 out of 100. Another way of stating the same result is that Dr. Amabile could be 95 percent certain that her results were real and not due to chance. Dr. Amabile would thus report that the study found a **significant difference**, which means a difference thought not to be due to chance.

There are several statistic techniques to test if groups are different from each other. Here are some common ones you might encounter if you read journal articles.

- *t*-test—determines if two means are different from each other.
- *F*-test or analysis of variance—determines if three or more means are different from each other. Can also evaluate more than one independent variable at a time.
- chi-square—compares frequencies of proportions between groups to see if they are different. For example, the proportion of women hired at a company is too low and might indicate discrimination. *Chi* is pronounced like the beginning of the word kite. Don't say "chee." It will be ugly.

If you do take a statistics course, you will find out that most analyses are done by computers and you don't have to manually go through the long formulas.

A.6 How are statistics used to predict one score from another?

We've already talked about the correlation coefficient. Let's see how psychologists can predict one variable from another by using it. (L I N K) to Chapter One: The Science of Psychology, pp. 23–25.

The Correlation Coefficient

A *correlation* is a measure of the relationship between two or more variables. For example, if you wanted to know if scores on the SAT are related to grade point average, you could get SAT scores and GPAs from a group of people and enter those numbers into a mathematical formula, which will produce a number called the **correlation coefficient**. The correlation coefficient represents the direction of the relationship and

t-test type of inferential statistical analysis typically used when two means are compared to see if they are significantly different.

significant difference a difference between groups of numerical data that is considered large enough to be due to factors other than chance variation.

correlation coefficient a number that represents the strength and direction of a relationship existing between two variables.

its strength. Chapter One (pages 23–25) discusses correlation in more detail and also emphasizes that correlation does not allow the assumption that one variable causes the other.

Is the formula for the correlation coefficient really complicated? ●

Is the formula for the correlation coefficient really complicated?

Actually, the definitional formula for finding a correlation coefficient is not very complicated. Here it is:

$$r = \frac{\Sigma Z_x Z_y}{n}$$

The r is the *correlation coefficient*, the number representing the strength and direction of the relationship between the two variables. Z_x and Z_y are the z scores for each score. If you remember, the z score tells you how many standard deviations a score is away from the mean. You would calculate the Z_x and Z_y for each subject, multiply, and add them up. Then divide by the number of subjects. There is a very complicated-looking formula based on the raw scores.

$$r = \frac{\Sigma XY - \frac{\Sigma X \Sigma Y}{N}}{\sqrt{\left(\Sigma X^2 - \frac{(\Sigma X)^2}{N}\right)\left(\Sigma Y^2 - \frac{(\Sigma Y)^2}{N}\right)}}$$

Don't worry. You can do all this work on inexpensive calculators or on computers using common statistical programs or spreadsheets. Let's take the following example of two sets of scores, one on a test of drawing ability with scores from 1 (poor) to 5 (excellent) and the other on a test of writing ability using the same scale.

	Drawing (X)	Writing (Y)
Student 1	3	5
Student 2	1	2
Student 3	2	3
Student 4	4	4
Student 5	1	3
Student 6	4	6
Student 7	2	3
Student 8	3	4
Student 9	5	5
Student 10	1	2

If we plugged our data set into our calculator or spreadsheet, we would find that r (the correlation coefficient) equals 0.86. That would indicate a fairly strong correlation. If you continue studies in statistics, you will find out how to see if the correlation coefficient we calculated is statistically significant or, if you recall, not due to just dumb luck when we picked our subjects. In our case, the r is very significant and would happen by chance only 1 in 100 times!

Remember that the correlation coefficient has values that range between +1.0 and −1.0. The closer the r is to these values, the stronger the relationship. A positive r means a positive relationship, whereas a negative r means a negative relationship.

Our example had us trying to see if two scores were related. It is also possible to see if three or more scores are related with various techniques. The most common one is called multiple regression.

A.7. Why are skills in statistics important to psychology majors?

We have taken a look at describing data—seeing if groups differ from each other and seeing if two variables are related to each other. Those are the basic ideas of psychological statistics. The more advanced techniques are just bigger and better versions of these ideas. Many psych students sometimes panic at the thought of taking statistics. However, it is crucial to the field and not really that hard if you put your mind to it and don't freeze yourself up. Here's a practical hint. Students with good research and statistical skills are much more employable and make more money than those who don't try to master research skills. It's nice to care about people, but you need all the skills you can get in today's world. Statistics and research design is one really profitable set of skills.

chapter summary   ((•–[Listen on **MyPsychLab**   Listen to an audio file of your chapter **www.MyPsychLab**

A.1 Why do psychologists use statistics?
- Statistics is a branch of mathematics that involves the collection, description, and interpretation of numerical data.

Descriptive Statistics
- Descriptive statistics are ways of organizing numbers and summarizing them so that they can be understood.
- Inferential statistics are ways of determining if groups are different and if two or more variables are related.

A.2 What types of tables and graphs represent patterns in data?
- Frequency distributions are tables or graphs that show the patterns in a set of scores and can be a table, a bar graph or histogram, or a line graph or polygon.

A.3 What types of statistics examine central tendencies in data?
- Measures of central tendency are ways of finding numbers that best represent the center of a distribution of numbers and include the mean, median, and mode.
- The normal curve is a special frequency polygon that is symmetrical and has the mean, median, and mode as the highest point on the curve.

A.4 What types of statistics examine variations in data?
- Measures of variability provide information about the differences within a set of numbers and include the range and the standard deviation.

Inferential Statistics

A.5 How can statistics be used to determine if differences in sets of data are large enough to be due to something other than chance variation?
- Inferential statistics involves statistical analysis of two or more sets of numerical data to reduce the possibility of error in measurement and determine statistical significance of the results of research.

A.6 How are statistics used to predict one score from another?
- The correlation coefficient is a number that represents the strength and direction of a relationship existing between two variables.

A.7 Why are skills in statistics important to psychology majors?
- Students who understand the process of research and the statistical methods used in research are more desirable to many university and business institutions than those who lack such skills.

TEST yourself   ANSWERS ON PAGE AK-2

✓•–[Study and Review on **MyPsychLab**   Ready for your test? More quizzes and a customized plan. **www.MyPsychLab**

Pick the best answer.

1. The correlation coefficient provides all of the following types of information EXCEPT _____.
   a. whether or not there is a relationship between the variables.
   b. the strength of the relationship between the variables.
   c. the cause of the relationship between the variables.
   d. the direction of the relationship between the variables.

2. Another name for a bar graph is a _____.
   a. polygon.
   b. histogram.
   c. normal curve.
   d. line graph.

3. A table that shows how often different scores appear in a set of scores is called a frequency _____.
   a. polygon.
   b. histogram.
   c. normal curve.
   d. distribution.

4. In the set of numbers 2, 2, 2, 3, 5, 5, 6, 8, 15, the median would be _____.
   a. 5.75.
   b. 5.33.
   c. 5.
   d. 2.

5. In the same set of numbers in Question 4, the mode would be _____.
   a. 5.75.
   b. 5.33.
   c. 5.
   d. 2.

6. In a skewed distribution, the scores _____.
   a. have two high points instead of one.
   b. fall to one side of the distribution.
   c. are evenly distributed around the mean.
   d. fall on both sides of the mean.

7. The normal curve is a special kind of _____.
   a. frequency distribution.
   b. scattergram.
   c. measure of central tendency.
   d. pie chart.

8. The normal curve has a special relationship with the _____.
   a. range.   c. standard deviation.
   b. median.   d. mode.

9. In the normal curve, _____.
   a. the mean, median, and mode are all on the highest point of the curve.
   b. the mean is on the highest point, while the median and mode are on either side of the mean.
   c. the median is on the highest point, while the mean and mode are on either side of the median.
   d. the standard deviation is located at the highest point of the curve.

10. What approximate percent of the population is said to fall between one standard deviation above and one standard deviation below the mean on a normal curve?
    a. 50 percent   c. 100 percent
    b. 34 percent   d. 68 percent

11. Errors in data _____.
    a. come only from within a group.
    b. come only from between different groups.
    c. come from both between and within groups.
    d. can be completely eliminated by random assignment.

12. When the goal is to compare sets of numbers or scores to see if the differences between them are greater than chance variations, researchers use _____.
    a. descriptive statistics.   c. analytical statistics.
    b. inferential statistics.   d. their intuition.

13. Inferential statistics are used when researchers want to know about _____.
    a. the range of the highest to lowest scores.
    b. causes of differences in data.
    c. central tendencies in data.
    d. variability in data.

14. Dr. Asimov finds that the results of his t-test are significant at $p < .01$. That means that he can be _____.
    a. totally certain that the results are not due to chance.
    b. totally certain that the results are due to chance.
    c. 1 percent certain that the results are not due to chance.
    d. 99 percent certain that the results are not due to chance.

appendix B

applied psychology and psychology careers

why study applied psychology?

Many different kinds of psychologists study or work in many different fields. Whereas early psychologists were still discovering the processes that govern the human mind, today's psychologists are more often applying information and principles gained from research to people in the real world. Why study careers in psychology? With so many different areas of focus, a career in psychology can be varied and exciting. There is much more to psychology than helping people who have mental health problems.

Professor John Gambon of Ozarks Technical Community College in Springfield, Missouri, is an industrial/organizational psychologist who has been studying violence in the workplace and gathering data for presentation to his classes. Recently, Gambon has found himself moving into another area of applied psychology: forensic psychology. He has had the opportunity to be an expert witness for the defense in two different trials, testifying about the accuracy and problems with eyewitness testimony as outlined by psychologist Elizabeth Loftus. **LINK** to Chapter Five: Memory, pp. 179–180. In one trial, the defendant was accused of an armed robbery that had taken place at night. In the other trial, the defendant was accused of a double homicide. The kinds of things Gambon spoke about on the witness stand included the length of time between the incidents and the questioning of the eyewitnesses, the concept of "weapons focus" and its tendency to wipe out memories of the face of the perpetrator, the lighting at the scene of the crime, and so on. He also showed an instructional video he had made in which people rush into Gambon's classroom and hit him with water balloons, yelling, "That was for last fried eggs!" Later, when answering a survey about the incident, the students witnessing this incident in the video all reported in writing that the statement yelled at the end was "That was for last Friday!" Clearly, this is one example of the flaws inherent in eyewitness testimony. Forensic psychology is just one of many areas in which psychological principles can be applied to the issues and concerns of everyday life. This appendix will look at several areas of applied psychology, as well as the types of careers that are open to someone who studies psychology today. We will also return to the issue of workplace violence later in this appendix.

What Is Applied Psychology?

B.1 What is the definition of applied psychology?

Psychology as a Career

B.2 What are the different types of psychological professionals?

B.3 What kinds of careers are available to someone with a master's degree in psychology?

B.4 What kinds of careers are available to someone with a bachelor's degree in psychology?

B.5 What are the areas of specialization in psychology?

Psychology Beyond the Classroom

B.6 How does psychology interact with other career fields?

Psychology and Work

B.7 What are industrial/organizational psychology and human factors psychology?

APPLYING PSYCHOLOGY TO EVERYDAY LIFE: Techniques Used by Sports Psychologists

B.8 What are some techniques used in sports psychology?

What Is Applied Psychology?

B.1 What is the definition of applied psychology?

The term **applied psychology** refers to using findings from psychological research to solve real-world problems. The psychological professional, who might be a psychiatrist, psychologist, or even a psychiatric social worker (as described later in this appendix), may do testing or use some other type of assessment and then describe a plan of action intended to solve whatever problem is of concern. As is evident in the opening comments about John Gambon, you can see that his training in psychology and his specialized knowledge enabled him to testify in court as an expert witness. This is a practical application of psychological tools to a real problem—the professional literally "applies" psychology.

> It seems to me that psychology could be useful in a lot of different areas, not just education. In fact, wasn't that what all those "Applying Psychology" sections at the end of each chapter were about?

● It seems to me that psychology could be useful in a lot of different areas, not just education. In fact, wasn't that what all those "Applying Psychology" sections at the end of each chapter were about?

Every chapter in this text (and even this appendix) does end with some application of psychology to the real world. The field of applied psychology isn't just one field but rather a lot of different areas that all share the common goal of using psychology in a practical way. A large number of areas can be considered applied psychology, including one of the broadest areas of psychology: clinical and counseling psychology. For example, health psychologists examine the effects of stress on physical as well as mental health; educational and school psychologists look for ways to improve student learning and apply the findings to the classroom; sports psychologists help athletes prepare themselves mentally for competition; human factors psychologists deal with the way people and machines interact; forensic psychologists deal with psychological issues within the legal system; and industrial/organizational (I/O) psychologists deal with the work environment. In addition, environmental psychologists examine the interaction of people with their surroundings at work, in social settings, and in schools, homes, and other buildings. Those surroundings include not just the physical structures but also the particular population of people who live, work, and play in those surroundings. Other psychologists look at the factors that influence people to buy certain products, analyze the best ways to market a product, and examine the buying habits of the typical consumer.

This appendix includes information on the different roles of psychological professionals and the type of education required for many professions, along with a brief overview of many of the specialized areas in psychology. The remainder of this appendix briefly explores how psychology can be used in practical ways in several different areas of life: the environment, law, education, the military, sports, and the world of work.

Psychology as a Career

When most people think of psychology as a potential career, they assume certain things about the profession: For example, to help people with their problems one has to be a psychologist, all psychologists are doctors, and all psychologists counsel mentally ill people. None of these assumptions is completely true.

Types of Psychological Professionals

B.2 What are the different types of psychological professionals?

Several types of professionals work in psychology. These professionals have different training with different focuses and may have different goals.

applied psychology the use of psychological concepts in solving real-world problems.

PSYCHIATRISTS A **psychiatrist** has a medical doctorate (M.D.) degree and is a medical doctor who has specialized in the diagnosis and treatment of psychological disorders. Like any other medical doctor who may specialize in emergency medicine, treating the diseases of the elderly, treating infants and children, or any other special area of medicine, psychiatrists are able to write prescriptions and perform medical procedures on their patients. They simply have special training in the diagnosis and treatment of disorders that are considered to be mental disorders, such as schizophrenia, depression, or extreme anxiety. Because they are medical doctors, they tend to have a biopsychological perspective on the causes and treatments for such disorders.

PSYCHIATRIC SOCIAL WORKERS A **psychiatric social worker** is trained in the area of social work and usually possesses a master of social work (MSW) degree and may be licensed in the state in which he or she works as a licensed clinical social worker (LCSW). These professionals focus more on the social conditions that can have an impact on mental disorders, such as poverty, overcrowding, stress, and drug abuse. They may administer psychotherapy (talking with clients about their problems), and they often work in a clinical setting where other types of psychological professionals are available.

PSYCHOLOGISTS A **psychologist** doesn't have medical training but instead undergoes intense academic training, learning about many different areas of psychology before choosing an area in which to specialize. Psychologists may have either a doctor of philosophy (Ph.D.) or doctor of psychology (Psy.D.) degree. (People who hold a master of science or M.S. degree are not usually called psychologists except in a few states. They can be called therapists or counselors, or they may be teachers or researchers.)

What's the difference between a Ph.D. and a Psy.D.?

The Ph.D. is a type of degree that usually indicates the highest degree of learning available in almost any subject area—psychology, the study of languages, education, philosophy, the sciences, and many others. It is typically very research oriented, and earning the degree usually requires a previous master's degree in addition to course work for the doctorate itself, as well as a dissertation—a scholarly work of research in the area of focus that is as long as a book and may even be published as a book.

The Psy.D. is a type of degree developed in the late 1970s that is focused less on research and more on the practical application of psychological principles (Peterson, 1976, 1982). In addition to academic course work such as that required for the Ph.D., this degree may require a major paper instead of a dissertation, with the difference being that the paper is not a report of research designed and conducted by the student but is rather a large-scale term paper. Each year of a Psy.D. program will also require the student to participate in a *practicum*—an actual experience with observing and eventually conducting therapy and treatments under supervision.

Unlike psychiatrists, psychologists typically cannot prescribe medicines or perform medical procedures. Some states are seeking legislative changes to allow psychologists to prescribe psychotropic medications if they receive special education in the use of prescription drugs. Such privileges were first pursued by the U.S. military. The reasoning behind this move, for which the American Psychological Association has been lobbying since 1984, involves both cost and the delay in receiving mental health services. If a person sees a psychologist and then

psychiatrist a medical doctor who specializes in the diagnosis and treatment of psychological disorders.

psychiatric social worker a social worker with some training in therapy methods who focuses on the environmental conditions that can have an impact on mental disorders, such as poverty, overcrowding, stress, and drug abuse.

psychologist a professional with an academic degree and specialized training in one or more areas of psychology.

What's the difference between a Ph.D. and a Psy.D.?

Psychologists specialize in many different areas and work in many different settings. This child psychologist is evaluating the young boy by using puppets and dolls to encourage the boy to talk about his feelings.

has to go to a psychiatrist for medical prescriptions, the cost can be prohibitive. There are also fewer psychiatrists in some states than in others, causing long waits for mental health services from those doctors—delays that can sometimes lead to an increase in suicide rates for patients who are not getting the help they need. As of November 2011, only two states (New Mexico and Louisiana) have successfully afforded prescription privileges to psychologists.

Some psychologists provide counseling or therapy and use a variety of techniques and approaches. ⓁⒾⓃⓀ to Chapter Thirteen: Psychological Therapies, pp. 466–480. However, many psychologists do no counseling at all. There are psychologists who only engage in assessment, those who teach at colleges or universities, those who do only research in those same institutions or for industries, and those who do a combination of teaching and research (and some that do a combination of teaching, research, and counseling or clinical practice). Other psychologists are involved in designing equipment and workplaces, developing educational methods, or working as consultants to businesses and the court system.

Although becoming a psychologist requires a doctorate degree of some kind, many career fields can benefit from a 4-year college degree in psychology as the basis of that career or going on to obtain a master's degree in psychology.

Careers with a Master's Degree in Psychology

B.3 What kinds of careers are available to someone with a master's degree in psychology?

While individuals earning a master's degree in psychology are not typically able to engage in the level of independent research or practice of psychology as someone with a doctoral degree, they can still work in a variety of areas, both within and beyond the field of psychology. They may work directly under the supervision of a doctoral psychologist if they are engaged in clinical, counseling, school psychology, or in assessment. Others work outside of the field in jobs requiring research or analysis skills and work in health, industry, or government areas.

For those who are interested in counseling or in providing therapy, many states allow individuals with master's degrees and prerequisite training and supervision experiences to become licensed to provide unsupervised counseling and therapy. Titles may vary by state, but some of the areas and titles associated with licensed master's level work include licensed marriage and family therapist (LMFT), licensed professional counselor (LPC), licensed mental health counselor (LMHC), or licensed clinical social worker (LCSW). These individuals may work in a larger organization or work independently in private practice. Beyond these areas, some individuals with a master's degree in psychology become certified or licensed to serve as school counselors at various levels and may work in an elementary school, middle school, or high school.

Careers with a Bachelor's Degree in Psychology

B.4 What kinds of careers are available to someone with a bachelor's degree in psychology?

Although people earning only the baccalaureate (bachelor's) degree in psychology cannot be called psychologists or provide therapy in a private practice, there are many career fields open to such a person. More than 1 million bachelor's degrees in psychology have been awarded since 1970, and since 2000 the number has increased each year (Landrum, 2009; Snyder & Dillow, 2010). A bachelor's degree in psychology

Constance Newman (left) is a Peace Corps volunteer. Using skills she developed while obtaining a bachelor's degree in psychology, Constance is trying to help this Mbankono woman understand the importance of having her child immunized against diseases such as measles.

can be highly flexible and adaptable to many different kinds of careers (Landrum, 2009; Landrum & Davis, 2007; Schwartz, 2000). While surveys, both by the American Psychological Association and others, reveal many may work in health-related or social fields, individuals with a bachelor's degree in psychology may be employed in research development or research management, administration, business, education and teaching, professional services, sales, or management (Grocer & Kohout, 1997; Landrum, 2009),

Other possible careers include marketing researcher, social worker, and communications specialist (Landrum & Davis, 2007; Schwartz, 2000). With its emphasis on critical thinking and empirical observation, psychology trains people for a variety of potential workplace environments and requirements. Psychology is an excellent major even if you intend to do graduate work in some other career: Business, law, childcare, teaching, and management are only a few of the areas that relate to psychology.

Many people with a bachelor's degree in psychology work in health-related fields, such as this woman who is lecturing about depression at a medical clinic.

Areas of Specialization

You said that some psychologists teach or do research. What kind of research do they do? ●

Psychologists may focus their energies in many different areas. They conduct experiments, surveys, observations, and so on to gather more information for their particular field of interest, to find support for current theories, or to develop new ones. Let's look at some of the areas in which psychologists may specialize.

> You said that some psychologists teach or do research. What kind of research do they do?

B.5 What are the areas of specialization in psychology?

CLINICAL PSYCHOLOGY   Even though not all psychologists do counseling or therapy, many psychologists do. **Clinical psychology** is the most similar of the areas to psychiatry in that professionals with this focus traditionally work with individuals who have more serious forms of mental illness. It is also the area of specialization with the largest number of psychologists. Clinical psychologists, like psychiatrists, diagnose and treat psychological disorders in people. However, the clinical psychologist cannot prescribe drugs or medical therapies (with the exceptions discussed earlier, of course) but instead relies on listening or observing the client's problems, possibly administering psychological tests, and then providing explanations for the client's behavior and feelings or directing them in specific actions to make positive changes in his or her life.

COUNSELING PSYCHOLOGY **Counseling psychology** is similar to clinical psychology in that this type of psychologist diagnoses and treats problems. The difference is that a counseling psychologist usually works with relatively healthy people who have less severe forms of mental illness or problems, such as adjustment to college, marriage, family life, and work problems. As of 2008, nearly 73 percent of surveyed psychologists currently providing health services identified themselves as clinical psychologists or counseling psychologists (Michalski et al., 2010). (LINK) to Chapter One: The Science of Psychology, p. 16.

DEVELOPMENTAL PSYCHOLOGY **Developmental psychology** focuses on the study of change, or development. Developmental psychologists are interested in changes in the way people think, in how people relate to others, and in the ways people feel over the entire span of life. These psychologists work in academic settings such as colleges and universities and may do research in various areas of development. They do not provide therapy. (LINK) to Chapter Seven: Development Across the Life Span, pp. 230–231.

clinical psychology   area of psychology in which the psychologists diagnose and treat people with psychological disorders that may range from mild to severe.

counseling psychology   area of psychology in which the psychologists help people with problems of adjustment.

developmental psychology   area of psychology in which the psychologists study the changes in the way people think, relate to others, and feel as they age.

EXPERIMENTAL PSYCHOLOGY   **Experimental psychology** encompasses several different areas such as learning, memory, thinking, perception, motivation, and language. The focus of these psychologists, however, is on doing research and conducting studies and experiments with both people and animals in these various areas. They tend to work in academic settings, especially in large universities. ⓁⒾⓃⓀ to Chapter One: The Science of Psychology, p. 16.

SOCIAL PSYCHOLOGY   **Social psychology** focuses on how human behavior is affected by the presence of other people. For example, social psychologists explore areas such as prejudice, attitude change, aggressive behavior, and interpersonal attraction. Although most social psychologists work in academic settings teaching and doing research, some work in federal agencies and big business doing practical (applied) research. Many social psychologists are experimental psychologists who perform their experiments in real-world settings rather than the laboratory to preserve the natural reactions of people. When people are in an artificial setting, they often behave in self-conscious ways, which is not the behavior the researcher wishes to study. ⓁⒾⓃⓀ to Chapter Ten: Social Psychology, p. 346.

PERSONALITY PSYCHOLOGY   **Personality psychology** focuses on the differences in personality among people. These psychologists may look at the influence of heredity on personality. They study the ways in which people are both alike and different. They study the development of personality and do personality assessment. They may be involved in forming new theories of how personality works or develops. Personality psychologists work in academic settings, doing research and teaching. ⓁⒾⓃⓀ to Chapter Eleven: Theories of Personality and Intelligence, p. 386.

PHYSIOLOGICAL PSYCHOLOGY   **Physiological psychology** focuses on the study of the biological bases of behavior. Many professionals now refer to this area as *behavioral neuroscience* or *biopsychology*. Physiological psychologists study the brain, nervous system, and the influence of the body's chemicals, such as hormones and the chemicals in the brain, on human behavior. They also study the effects of drug use and possible genetic influences on some kinds of abnormal and normal human behavior, such as schizophrenia or aspects of intelligence. Most physiological psychologists, like experimental psychologists, work in an academic setting. ⓁⒾⓃⓀ to Chapter Two: The Biological Perspective, p. 42.

NEUROPSYCHOLOGY   **Neuropsychology** is an area within the field of psychology in which professionals explore the relationships between the brain systems and behavior. Neuropsychologists may be engaged in research or be more focused on the assessment, diagnosis, treatment, and/or rehabilitation of individuals with various neurological, medical, neurodevelopmental, or psychiatric conditions (National Academy of Neuropsychology, 2001). ⓁⒾⓃⓀ to Chapter Two: The Biological Perspective, p. 42.

COMPARATIVE PSYCHOLOGY   **Comparative psychology** focuses exclusively on animals and animal behavior. By comparing and contrasting animal behavior with what is already known about human behavior, comparative psychologists can contribute to the understanding of human behavior by studying animals. Research in animal behavior also helps people to learn how to treat animals more humanely and to coexist with the animals in a common environment. Comparative psychologists might work in animal laboratories in a university or may do observation and studies of animals in the animals' natural habitats.

---

experimental psychology   area of psychology in which the psychologists primarily do research and experiments in the areas of learning, memory, thinking, perception, motivation, and language.

social psychology   area of psychology in which the psychologists focus on how human behavior is affected by the presence of other people.

personality psychology   area of psychology in which the psychologists study the differences in personality among people.

physiological psychology   area of psychology in which the psychologists study the biological bases of behavior.

neuropsychology   area of psychology in which the psychologists specialize in the research or clinical implications of brain–behavior relationships.

comparative psychology   area of psychology in which the psychologists study animals and their behavior for the purpose of comparing and contrasting it to human behavior.

Psychologists in these areas may do research that is directed at discovering basic principles of human behavior (basic research), or they may engage in research designed to find solutions to practical problems of the here and now (applied research). There are many other areas in which psychologists may specialize that focus almost exclusively on applied research. These areas are those most often associated with applied psychology.

Psychology Beyond the Classroom

B.6 How does psychology interact with other career fields?

Psychology and Health

Health psychology focuses on the relationship of human behavior patterns and stress reactions to physical health, with the goal of improving and helping to maintain good health while preventing and treating illness. For example, a health psychologist might design a program to help people lose weight or stop smoking. Stress management techniques are also a major focus of this area. Health psychologists may work in hospitals, clinics, medical schools, health agencies, academic settings, or private practice.

In a recent study (Kerwin et al., 2010), researchers found an association between obesity in older women and a decline in memory functioning in those women. This finding was particularly true for women carrying the excess weight around their hips (pear shapes) and less so for women carrying the excess weight around their waists (apple shapes). The study controlled for other health variables, such as diabetes, heart disease, and stroke. This is a good example of the kind of research that health psychologists conduct. Other areas they study include the influence of optimistic attitudes on the progress of disease, the link between mental distress and health, and the promotion of wellness and hope in an effort to prevent illness. **L·I·N·K** to Chapter Nine: Stress and Health, p. 323.

Psychology and Education

Educational psychology is concerned with the study of human learning. As educational psychologists come to understand some of the basic aspects of learning, they develop methods and materials for aiding the process of learning. For example, educational psychologists helped to design the phonics method of teaching children to read. This type of psychologist may have a doctorate of education (Ed.D.) rather than a Ph.D. and typically works in academic settings.

What types of research might an educational psychologist conduct? The August 2011 issue of *Journal of Educational Psychology* included articles on the role that bilingualism plays in elementary students' performance on math word problems; the influences of mood on text comprehension; and an investigation of potential sources and influences of Bandura's ideas of self-efficacy on academics and self-regulation in French third-graders, **L·I·N·K** to Chapter Eleven: Theories of Personality and Intelligence, p. 397—just to name a few.

School psychology is related to, but not at all the same as, educational psychology. Whereas educational psychologists may do research and develop new learning techniques, school psychologists may take the results of that research or those methods and apply them in the actual school system. School psychologists work directly with children in the school setting. They do testing and other forms of assessment to place

health psychology area of psychology in which the psychologists focus on the relationship of human behavior patterns and stress reaction to physical health.

educational psychology area of psychology in which the psychologists are concerned with the study of human learning and development of new learning techniques.

school psychology area of psychology in which the psychologists work directly in the schools, doing assessments, educational placement, and diagnosing educational problems.

This woman is a health psychologist. She is helping this girl to control her fear of receiving an injection by letting her act out giving an injection to a special doll.

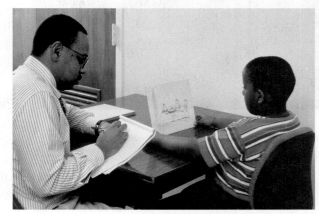

School psychologists often administer tests to assess a child's intelligence or psychological well-being. The young boy's description of the drawing he is holding will help this psychologist determine the boy's emotional state.

sports psychology area of psychology in which the psychologists help athletes and others to prepare themselves mentally for participation in sports activities.

children in special programs or to diagnose educational problems such as dyslexia or attention-deficit/hyperactivity disorder. They may act as consultants to teachers, parents, and educational administrators. Counseling students is actually a relatively small part of the school psychologist's job, although counseling takes a much bigger role when tragedies strike a school. When traumatic events such as the unexpected and tragic death of a classmate or even larger-scale tragedies such as the numerous school shootings of the past decade take place, school psychologists are often called on to offer help and counseling to students.

Psychology and Sports

Sports psychology is a relatively new and fast-growing field in which the main focus is on helping athletes and others involved in sports activities prepare mentally, rather than just physically, for participation in sports. The idea behind this field is that a superior physical performance is not enough to guarantee success. Rather, the mind must be prepared for the activity by setting clear, short-term goals, holding positive thoughts, using visualization of the goal, stopping negative thoughts, and other techniques based primarily in the cognitive perspective. For example, a sports psychologist might have a golfer, who has been having trouble with the accuracy of her drives, perform visualization exercises, mentally seeing herself hit the ball down the fairway again and again. Sports psychologists work in athletic organizations and may have a private practice or do consulting work. (For more on the techniques used in sports psychology, see the Applying Psychology to Everyday Life feature at the end of this appendix.)

A Fort Lewis Army psychologist demonstrates a headset from the "Virtual Reality Iraq" therapy program on April 18, 2007, in Spanaway, Washington. The virtual-reality program, which simulates the sights, sounds, and smells of combat, will be used in working with soldiers suffering from posttraumatic stress disorder.

Psychology and the Military

Within the military, psychologists work in a variety of areas ranging from assessment to teaching, management, research, and the provision of mental health services. The variety of psychologists in this field may include clinical, counseling, experimental, I/O, or human factors and may reflect any specialty area in the field of psychology. In short, these psychologists apply psychological skills to human issues in military environments, working with both military personnel and their families (American Psychological Association, Division 19, 2010). One poignant example: The rise of suicides in the armed forces associated with the conflicts in Iraq and Afghanistan has placed unprecedented demands on both the military and military families (Berman et al., 2010).

Psychology and the Law

Psychologists have often been involved in the world of legal matters in various ways. Social psychologists often do research in the areas of criminal behavior and may consult with attorneys or other agents of the court system on such topics as witness credibility, jury selection, and the kind of influences that exist for decision-making processes. Developmental psychologists may become involved in determining the accuracy of and influences on the testimony of children and adolescents, as well as the needs of children caught up in a custody battle between divorced or divorcing parents. Cognitive psychologists may become expert witnesses on the accuracy of memory and eyewitness testimony or ways to determine the truth or falsehood of statements made by witnesses or defendants. Clinical psychologists may deliver their services directly to incarcerated prisoners or may conduct assessments of intelligence and/or mental status to determine whether or not a person charged with a crime should stand trial.

All of the forms of psychological involvement in legal matters mentioned here can be considered as part of the growing field of **forensic psychology**. Forensic psychology is the practice of psychology related to the legal system, and it involves examining criminal evidence and aiding law enforcement investigations into criminal activities. Some forensic psychologists provide information and advice to officials in the legal system, such as lawyers or judges; some act as expert witnesses (as did Professor John Gambon in the opening story); some actually diagnose and treat criminals within the prison system; and others may administer psychological tests to criminal defendants. Forensic psychologists may aid either the prosecution or the defense in a trial by helping to determine which potential jurors would be the best or worst choices. This type of professional may do consulting work in addition to maintaining a regular private practice in clinical or counseling psychology, or may work entirely within the justice system as a police psychologist, or a full-time jury expert, for example.

forensic psychology area of psychology concerned with people in the legal system, including psychological assessment of criminals, jury selection, and expert witnessing.

environmental psychology area of psychology in which the focus is on how people interact with and are affected by their physical environments.

Psychology and the Environment

Another broad area in which psychological principles can be applied to solve practical problems is the area of managing the environment. **Environmental psychology** is an area that focuses on the relationship between human behavior and the environment in which the behavior takes place, such as an office, store, school, dormitory, or hospital. Because researchers in this field deal directly with behavior in a particular setting, their research is always conducted in that setting rather than in a laboratory. Environmental psychologists may work with other professionals such as urban or city planners, economists, engineers, and architects, helping those professionals to plan the most efficient buildings, parks, housing developments, or plants.

practice quiz How much do you remember?

Pick the best answer.

1. Which of the following professionals in psychology focuses more on the social conditions that affect mental disorders?
   a. psychiatrist
   b. therapist
   c. psychiatric social worker
   d. psychologist

2. Which of the following specialties in psychology is most similar to the medical field of psychiatry?
   a. clinical
   b. counseling
   c. personality
   d. experimental

3. Chevene is interested in becoming a psychologist. He is most interested in how people become attracted to other people. He would most likely specialize in _____ psychology.
   a. comparative
   b. developmental
   c. sports
   d. social

4. The study of the effects of psychological stress on the growth rate of cancer cells would most likely be the work of _____ psychologists.
   a. environmental
   b. forensic
   c. health
   d. military

5. Which type of psychologist would be more likely to administer an IQ test to a child to determine the child's eligibility for a gifted program?
   a. educational
   b. school
   c. developmental
   d. personality

ANSWERS ON PAGE AK-2

Psychology and Work

B.7 What are industrial/organizational psychology and human factors psychology?

Work is a very important part of most people's lives. People often spend more time at work than they do with their families or in social activities. One of the largest branches of applied psychology focuses on how psychology can help people in management, productivity, morale, and many other areas of the world of work.

Industrial/organizational (I/O) psychology is concerned with the relationships between people and their work environments. I/O psychologists may help in personnel selection, administer job performance assessments, design work schedules that help workers adjust to new time periods of work hours with less difficulty, or design new work areas to increase morale and productivity. Psychologists in this field may study the behavior of entire organizations. They are often hired by corporations and businesses to deal with the hiring and assessment of employees. They may research and develop ways for workers to be more efficient and productive. They may work in business, government agencies, and academic settings.

A specific kind of I/O specialist, called a *human factors engineer*, focuses on designing machines, furniture, and other devices that people have to use so that those devices are the most practical, comfortable, and logical for human use. **Human factors psychology** consists of these researchers and designers who study the way humans and machines interact with each other. They may work directly in the companies involved in the design of appliances, airplane controls, and the operation of computers or other mechanical devices.

Human factors psychologists design machines that are more practical and comfortable for people to use. For example, this keyboard is designed to reduce the risk of pain in the wrists and increase accuracy in typing.

Psychologists working in I/O settings apply psychological principles and theories to the workplace. For example, Maslow's humanistic theory and hierarchy of needs has had a powerful influence on the field of management (Heil et al., 1998). Douglas McGregor, in his explanations of two different styles of management (McGregor, 1960), relates the older and less productive "Theory X" (workers are unmotivated and need to be managed and directed) to Maslow's lower needs and the newer, more productive style of management called "Theory Y" (workers want to work and want that work to be meaningful) to the higher needs.

Industrial/organizational psychology got its start near the beginning of the twentieth century with the work of Walter D. Scott, a former student of famed physiologist and founder of the first psychological laboratory, Wilhelm Wundt. Scott applied psychological principles to hiring, management, and advertising techniques (Schultz & Schultz, 2004). He also wrote one of the first books about the application of psychology to industry and advertising, called *The Theory and Practice of Advertising* (Scott, 1908). Another early figure in the newly developing field of industrial/organizational psychology was Hugo Münsterberg, a psychologist also trained by Wundt, who conducted research on such varied topics as the power of prayer and eyewitness testimony (Hothersall, 1995). Münsterberg wrote a book about eyewitness testimony called *On the Witness Stand* (1907) and later wrote *Psychology and Industrial Efficiency* (1913).

The I/O field became important during World War I when the army needed a way to test the intelligence of potential recruits. Psychologist Robert Yerkes, who would later become known for his groundbreaking research in comparative psychology while working with the great apes, developed the Army Alpha and Army Beta tests. The Army Alpha test was used with applicants who were able to read, whereas the

industrial/organizational (I/O) psychology area of psychology concerned with the relationships between people and their work environment.

human factors psychology area of industrial/organizational psychology concerned with the study of the way humans and machines interact with each other.

Army Beta test was administered to applicants who were illiterate (McGuire, 1994; Yerkes, 1921).

In the mid-1920s a series of studies conducted by Elton Mayo for the Western Electric Company (Franke & Kaul, 1978; Parsons, 1992; Roethlisberger & Dickson, 1939) broadened the field. These were the first studies to view the workplace as a social system rather than as just a production line. Instead of treating workers as simply other pieces of equipment, these studies suggested that allowing workers some input into the decision-making process not only improved worker morale* but also reduced workers' resistance to changes in the workplace. These studies led the way for others to examine how management of employees and production could be improved. Management theories and strategies may also be applied to other kinds of settings such as schools, colleges, and universities. The following section takes a closer look at the development of these theories.

---

*Morale: a sense of common purpose, enthusiasm, confidence, and loyalty.

issues in psychology
Workplace Violence

Acts of violence in the workplace have increased dramatically in the past few decades—nearly tripling in the 1980s alone (Baron, 1993). Psychologists are devoting time and energy to studying the reasons for this violence and are looking for ways to recognize and prevent future incidents. Some highlights from research in workplace violence show that people in some types of jobs face a higher probability of becoming a victim of a crime because of the characteristics of the job. For example, three of the most likely such occupations are police officers, corrections officers, and taxi drivers (Centers for Disease Control and Prevention, 2009). For taxi drivers (along with convenience-store clerks), it is the availability of cash and the solitary nature of the job that entices many criminals to attempt robbery. In the case of police and correctional officers, violence is part of the very nature of their job. Consider the following statistics:

The aftermath of workplace violence: A somber crowd gathers at a candlelight vigil Sunday, August 8, 2010, in honor of the victims of a workplace shooting at a Connecticut beer distribution company. Only one week prior to this vigil, Omar Thornton killed eight coworkers and wounded two others before killing himself at the Hartford Distributors building.

- Between 1992 and 2006, there were 11,613 workplace homicide victims reported. Of those homicides, 11.6 police officers out of every 100,000 were killed on the job compared to 4.0 out of every 100,000—the national average for all occupations.
- From 2004 to 2008 there was an average of 564 work-related homicides each year—10 percent of all fatal work injuries.
- Four out of every 5 homicide victims in 2008 were male.
- Men were more likely to be killed by an assailant, while women were more likely to be killed by a relative or personal acquaintance.
- In 2008, there were 30 multiple-fatality workplace homicide incidents, with an average of 2 people dying in each incident. Most were shot, and in 12 percent of the shootings the assailants were coworkers or former coworkers (Bureau of Labor Statistics, 2010).

Industrial/organizational psychologists have developed a term for the employee who becomes highly violent and commits violent crimes resulting in serious injury or death to other employees: the *berserker*. What are the characteristics of persons who "go berserk" in the workplace? Typically, they have at least a high school diploma or some college. Their self-esteem, or sense of worth as a person, is intimately tied to their job. They tend to like watching violent television or movies. There is a small correlation between berserkers and those with delusional disorders: People who become violent in the workplace are also somewhat likely to suffer from a delusional disorder, such as paranoia. ⓁⒾⓃ Ⓚ to Chapter Twelve: Psychological Disorders, pp. 451–453.

Prevention of violence in the workplace can include some simple, commonsense steps as well as more complicated training and preparation (Arbury, 2005; Harvey & Keashly, 2003; Security Director's Report, 2008; Vandenbos & Bulatao, 1996):

- entrances and exits that are well lighted
- presence of video cameras or security guards, especially at night
- criminal background checks performed on all potential new employees
- training managers and supervisors to identify signs of potential workplace violence, including such things as employees (1) who have a tendency to use verbal threats or who use low-grade acts of violence, such as pushing or shoving; (2) who are fascinated with and have access to firearms; or (3) who appear desensitized to television and movie violence and show a preference for watching such media.

Other Areas in Industrial/Organizational Psychology

There are many other areas of research and study in the field of industrial/organization psychology. Table B.1 briefly lists some of these areas of specialization.

table B.1   Areas in I/O Psychology

AREAS IN INDUSTRY	AREAS IN ORGANIZATIONS
Job analysis	Social behavior of work teams
Job evaluation and compensation	Job satisfaction
Characteristics critical to effective management	Personality characteristics critical to job performance
Personnel recruiting, selection, and placement	Relationships between management and workers
Occupational training	Leadership characteristics and training
Examination of working conditions	Consumer psychology
Interviewing and testing	Motivational concerns
Performance appraisal and feedback	Conflict management

practice quiz   How much do you remember?

Pick the best answer.

1. Alejandro works in a factory and is responsible for making sure that the office equipment made in the factory is practical and easy to use. He sometimes suggests changes in the design of certain equipment to accomplish this goal. Alejandro is most likely what type of psychologist?
   a. forensic
   b. human factors
   c. industrial/organizational
   d. management/design

2. One of the early figures in I/O psychology who examined the behavior of eyewitnesses in the courtroom was _____.
   a. Wilhelm Wundt.
   b. Walter D. Scott.
   c. Hugo Münsterberg.
   d. Robert Yerkes.

3. Violence in the workplace can come from which of the following sources?
   a. a fellow employee
   b. a disgruntled lover or spouse
   c. an outside person, such as a robber
   d. all of the above

ANSWERS ON PAGE AK-2

applying psychology to everyday life

Techniques Used by Sports Psychologists

B.8   What are some techniques used in sports psychology?

Many athletes become frustrated when their performance seems to be less than it could be or when they reach some "roadblock" on their way to achieving new goals. The techniques that follow are designed to help athletes get around the roadblocks and get the most out of their performance. The same techniques are also helpful in the careers of acting, musical performance, professional speaking, teaching, or any career in which there is an element of a public performance.

1. *Visualization.* In this technique, athletes try to "see" their performance in their minds as if watching from the sidelines before actually doing it.

2. *Imagery/mental rehearsal.* Similar to visualization, imagery can be used to mentally rehearse the desired performance. Instead of visualizing oneself as if from the sidelines, however, imagery/mental rehearsal involves actually "seeing" and "feeling" the performance in one's mind from one's own viewpoint. This helps prepare the muscles that will be used for action.

3. *Distraction desensitization.* Athletes can be trained to ignore distractions, such as the shouts of spectators.

4. *Thought stopping.* People often have negative thoughts about things that might happen: "I'm going to miss it, I just know it!" is a good example of a negative, self-defeating thought. Sports psychologists train athletes to stop such thoughts in the making, replacing them with more positive thoughts: "I can do this. I've done it before and it was easy."

5. *Confidence training.* Another thing that sports psychologists do is try to build confidence and self-esteem in the athletes who come to them for help. Lack of confidence in one's own abilities is a major roadblock.

6. *Focus training.* Athletes can also be trained to focus attention, often through the use of hypnosis, concentrative meditation, or similar psychological techniques.

7. *Relaxation training.* Athletes can be trained to use special breathing methods, tension and relaxation of muscles, and other strategies for relaxation to reduce anxiety and tension before a performance.

8. *Autogenic training.* Autogenic essentially means "from within the self." In the sense used here, autogenic training involves helping athletes learn about their physiological responses to stress. Once learned, athletes can gain control over these responses, such as learning to slow one's heart rate or to lower anxiety.

9. *Fostering realistic goals and expectations.* Sports psychologists try to teach athletes that although setting goals is important, setting unrealistic goals can lead to burnout, frustration, and feelings of failure. Sports psychologists try to help athletes modify their expectations and goals to be more realistic.

10. *Fostering team unity.* Sports psychologists may also work with entire teams of athletes, helping them to become a unit that works as one single "organism" while still providing support for each individual athlete.

Relaxation training is becoming a very important part of any athlete's training. Here the Wisconsin Badgers college football team participates in a relaxation exercise before the big game. What other career areas might be improved by relaxation training?

chapter summary

((•–[Listen on **MyPsychLab**   Listen to an audio file of your chapter www.MyPsychLab

What Is Applied Psychology?

B.1 What is the definition of applied psychology?

• Applied psychology refers to using psychological principles and research to solve problems in the real world.

Psychology as a Career

B.2 What are the different types of psychological professionals?

• Different types of psychological professionals vary by level of education and training. Examples include psychiatrists, psychiatric social workers, and psychologists.

• Psychologists hold either a Ph.D. or Psy.D. degree.

B.3 What kinds of careers are available to someone with a master's degree in psychology?

• Individuals with a master's degree may work under the supervision of a doctoral-level psychology professional, practice independently if licensed, or operate in private or educational settings.

B.4 What kinds of careers are available to someone with a bachelor's degree in psychology?

• Education, statistical consulting, administration and other business occupations, as well as health services are examples of careers that a person with a bachelor's degree in psychology might enter.

B.5 What are the areas of specialization in psychology?

• Areas of specialization include clinical and counseling psychology, developmental, experimental, social, personality, physiological, neuropsychology, and comparative psychology.

Psychology Beyond the Classroom

B.6 How does psychology interact with other career fields?

• Health psychology is an area in which the goal is to discover relationships between human behavior, including stress factors, and physical health with the intention of preventing and treating ill health.

• Educational psychologists study the processes of human learning to develop new techniques and methods, whereas school psychologists apply those methods in the school, administer assessments, recommend placement, and provide counseling and diagnosis of educational problems.

• Sports psychologists help athletes prepare themselves mentally for participation in sports.

• Psychologists working in the military represent almost all subfields of psychology and work with both military personnel and their families in military environments.

• Psychologists may act as expert witnesses for legal matters, help in jury selection, provide clinical services to defendants or prisoners, or perform psychological assessment of criminals in the field of forensic psychology.

• Environmental psychology looks at the relationship between human behavior and the physical environment in which that behavior takes place.

Psychology and Work

B.7 What are industrial/organizational psychology and human factors psychology?

• Industrial/organizational psychology is concerned with how people function in and are affected by their work environments.

• Human factors is a type of I/O psychology in which the focus is on the way humans and machines interact with each other, designing or helping to design the machines people use in various science and industrial settings.

applying psychology to everyday life: Techniques Used by Sports Psychologists

B.8 What are some techniques used in sports psychology?

• Sports psychologists use many techniques to help athletes better their performances, including visualization, imagery, thought stopping, confidence training, relaxation training, and fostering team unity.

TEST yourself

ANSWERS ON PAGE AK-2

✓• Study and Review on MyPsychLab   Ready for your test? More quizzes and a customized plan. www.MyPsychLab

Pick the best answer.

1. Carrie would like to work as a psychological professional, but she is not interested in teaching, scientific research, or in becoming a medical doctor. She would like to be able to call herself a psychologist and provide therapy for her clients. What type of degree would be best for Carrie to pursue?
 a. a master's degree in psychology
 b. a Ph.D.
 c. a Psy.D.
 d. a master's degree in social work

2. What type of professional would help people with adjustments to stress, work problems, or marital difficulties?
 a. clinical psychologist   **c.** developmental psychologist
 b. personality psychologist   **d.** counseling psychologist

3. Dr. Branco is studying the changes that occur in people's working memory ability as they age from youth to late adulthood. Dr. Branco's area of specialization is most likely in _____ psychology.
 a. social   **c.** comparative
 b. personality   **d.** developmental

4. _____ psychologists do research and conduct experiments with people and animals in the areas of learning, memory, thought processes, perception, and language.
 a. Experimental   **c.** Developmental
 b. Comparative   **d.** Social

5. The view that panic attacks occur because of a malfunction in a small area of the brain normally responsible for alerting the person to real danger is most compatible with which area of specialization in psychology?
 a. developmental   **c.** physiological
 b. health   **d.** human factors

6. What type of psychologist would be most likely to provide a psychological assessment of an individual applying for early release from a penitentiary?
 a. industrial/organizational   **c.** forensic
 b. clinical   **d.** environmental

7. City planners who want the new public library to be accessible to all and logically organized into different areas, each with a different function, might consult what type of psychologist?
 a. developmental   **c.** social
 b. physiological   **d.** environmental

8. Which type of psychologist is most concerned with increasing the productivity of workers by increasing morale and manipulating work shifts?
 a. industrial/organizational   **c.** forensic
 b. clinical   **d.** environmental

9. Alexis is about to compete on the balance beam and begins to have second thoughts about her ability. She realizes that such negative thoughts will not help and tells herself that this is something she has done perfectly in practice and that she can do it perfectly now. Alexis's ability to replace her negative thinking with more helpful, positive thinking is a form of _____.
 a. visualization.
 b. thought stopping.
 c. distraction desensitization.
 d. autogenic training.

10. The psychologist tells Michaela that she needs to "be the ball," or try to see herself actually hitting the ball over the net. The psychologist is using _____.
 a. distraction desensitization.
 b. thought stopping.
 c. imagery/mental rehearsal.
 d. focus training.

answer key

Chapter 1

Practice Quiz page 12
1.c 2.d 3.b 4.b 5.d 6.a 7.b
Practice Quiz page 17
1.b 2.d 3.d 4.b 5.c 6.c
Practice Quiz page 23
1.b 2.c 3.a 4.c 5.d
Practice Quiz page 32
1.a 2.b 3.b 4.d 5.c 6.c 7.b 8.d
Test Yourself pages 36–37
1.a 2.b 3.c 4.b 5.d 6.d 7.a 8.a 9.d 10.a 11.c 12.d
13.d 14.a 15.d 16.a 17.d 18.c 19.b 20.a 21.b 22.a
23.d 24.d 25.b 26.c 27.c 28.b 29.c 30.c

Chapter 2

Practice Quiz page 51
1.b 2.d 3.a 4.d 5.c 6.c
Practice Quiz page 59
1.a 2.c 3.d 4.b 5.a 6.b 7.a 8.a
Practice Quiz page 67
1.d 2.b 3.a 4.c 5.a
Practice Quiz page 73
1.b 2.a 3.a 4.c 5.c
Test Yourself pages 76–77
1.a 2.b 3.d 4.b 5.c 6.d 7.c 8.a 9.a 10.b 11.a
12.d 13.d 14.c 15.a 16.b 17.c 18.d 19.b
20.c 21.d 22.a 23.c 24.b 25.b

Chapter 3

Practice Quiz page 84
1.b 2.d 3.a 4.d
Practice Quiz page 91
1.b 2.c 3.d 4.b 5.a
Practice Quiz page 96
1.a 2.c 3.a 4.d
Practice Quiz page 102
1.c 2.a 3.b 4.b 5.a 6.c
Practice Quiz page 112
1.b 2.c 3.a 4.c 5.a 6.b
Test Yourself pages 116–117
1.b 2.c 3.a 4.d 5.c 6.b 7.b 8.b 9.b 10.c 11.d 12.c 13.b
14.a 15.a 16.d 17.c 18.a 19.a 20.c 21.b 22.d 23.a 24.c

Chapter 4

Practice Quiz pages 127
1.a 2.b 3.b 4.d 5.a 6.b
Practice Quiz page 130
1.b 2.c 3.c 4.a 5.d
Practice Quiz page 134
1.d 2.a 3.c 4.d
Practice Quiz pages 147
1.a 2.c 3.d 4.c 5.d 6.c 7.a
Practice Quiz page 153
1.c 2.b 3.d 4.b 5.a 6.b
Test Yourself pages 158–159
1.c 2.b 3.a 4.d 5.c 6.b 7.a 8.b 9.a 10.c 11.d 12.d 13.c 14.a
15.a 16.c 17.b 18.c 19.d 20.a 21.b 22.a 23.c 24.d 25.c

Chapter 5

Practice Quiz page 166
1.c 2.a
Practice Quiz page 175
1.a 2.b 3.d 4.b 5.d 6.a 7.b 8.c
Practice Quiz page 181
1.a 2.b 3.d 4.d 5.c
Practice Quiz page 184
1.b 2.d 3.b 4.a
Practice Quiz page 190
1.a 2.c 3.b 4.c 5.d 6.d 7.a 8.a
Test Yourself pages 193
1.c 2.b 3.b 4.c 5.b 6.a 7.a 8.c 9.d 10.d 11.c 12.c
13.c 14.d 15.d 16.a 17.d 18.b 19.c 20.a 21.a 22.d

Chapter 6

Practice Quiz page 207
1.b 2.c 3.a 4.c 5.c 6.d 7.d 8.b
Practice Quiz page 214
1.b 2.c 3.a 4.b 5.d
Practice Quiz page 217
1.a 2.b 3.c 4.b
Practice Quiz page 222
1.c 2.a 3.b 4.d 5.c
Test Yourself pages 225
1.b 2.c 3.a 4.c 5.b 6.d 7.a 8.c 9.d 10.a 11.c 12.a
13.b 14.b 15.d 16.a 17.b 18.a 19.c 20.b 21.a 22.d

Chapter 7

Practice Quiz page 233
1.b 2.c 3.b 4.d
Practice Quiz page 237
1.a 2.c 3.d 4.b 5.b 6.d
Practice Quiz page 246
1.d 2.b 3.a 4.c 5.a
Practice Quiz page 251
1.b 2.a 3.d 4.c
Practice Quiz page 253
1.b 2.c 3.b 4.a 5.d
Practice Quiz page 257
1.c 2.c 3.b 4.a 5.b
Practice Quiz page 262
1.b 2.d 3.c 4.a 5.c 6.b 7.c
Practice Quiz page 263
1.d 2.b 3.c
Test Yourself pages 266–267
1.c 2.b 3.d 4.c 5.d 6.b 7.c 8.c 9.d 10.b 11.c 12.d
13.a 14.b 15.a 16.c 17.c 18.d 19.a 20.c 21.a 22.a
23.a 24.b 25.d 26.b 27.a 28.c 29.c 30.a

Chapter 8

Practice Quiz page 276
1.c 2.d 3.b 4.a
Practice Quiz page 282
1.b 2.c 3.d 4.b
Practice Quiz page 288
1.c 2.b 3.c 4.a

Practice Quiz page 294
1.d 2.b 3.a 4.c 5.b
Practice Quiz page 304
1.c 2.b 3.b 4.a 5.d 6.a
Test Yourself pages 306–307
1.c 2.b 3.c 4.a 5.d 6.c 7.b 8.a 9.a 10.b 11.c 12.b
13.b 14.d 15.c 16.d 17.d 18.d 19.a 20.c 21.d

Chapter 9

Practice Quiz page 315
1.c 2.b 3.d
Practice Quiz page 318
1.c 2.b 3.a 4.a 5.c
Practice Quiz page 330
1.b 2.d 3.d 4.a 5.b 6.b
Practice Quiz page 332
1.c 2.c 3.b 4.d

Practice Quiz page 335
1.d 2.b 3.c
Practice Quiz page 338
1.b 2.b 3.d
Test Yourself pages 340–341
1.d 2.c 3.b 4.c 5.d 6.d 7.c 8.b 9.b 10.d 11.d 12.b 13.b
14.d 15.c 16.a 17.b 18.c 19.b 20.a 21.d 22.a 23.c

Chapter 10

Practice Quiz page 353
1.c 2.a 3.a 4.c
Practice Quiz page 358
1.c 2.c 3.a 4.c 5.b 6.c
Practice Quiz page 362
1.c 2.a 3.b 4.b 5.c
Practice Quiz page 367
1.a 2.b 3.c 4.d 5.a
Practice Quiz page 371
1.c 2.b 3.d 4.b
Practice Quiz page 377
1.d 2.a 3.c 4.b 5.c
Test Yourself pages 380–381
1.a 2.c 3.c 4.a 5.b 6.b 7.d 8.a 9.d 10.c 11.b 12.b 13.b 14.d
15.c 16.a 17.d 18.b 19.d 20.d 21.c 22.a 23.c 24.d 25.a 26.d

Chapter 11

Practice Quiz page 390
1.d 2.b 3.d 4.b 5.c 6.a
Practice Quiz page 396
1.a 2.b 3.c 4.d 5.c 6.c
Practice Quiz page 400
1.b 2.c 3.a 4.d 5.a

Practice Quiz page 403
1.b 2.c 3.a 4.d
Practice Quiz page 409
1.b 2.d 3.d
Practice Quiz page 415
1.c 2.d 3.b 4.b 5.a
Practice Quiz page 422
1.b 2.d 3.c 4.b 5.d 6.c
Test Yourself pages 426–427
1.c 2.b 3.a 4.b 5.c 6.b 7.c 8.d 9.c 10.c 11.a 12.d
13.c 14.b 15.d 16.c 17.b 18.d 19.c 20.d 21.b 22.d
23.c 24.b 25.a 26.c 27.d 28.d 29.b 30.d 31.a 32.c 33.b 34.c 35.a

Chapter 12

Practice Quiz page 440
1.c 2.d 3.d 4.b 5.a 6.b
Practice Quiz page 451
1.b 2.a 3.b 4.d 5.c 6.d 7.c 8.b
Practice Quiz pages 457
1.b 2.a 3.c 4.b
Test Yourself pages 461
1.b 2.c 3.a 4.b 5.d 6.a 7.c 8.a 9.d 10.b 11.b
12.a 13.d 14.d 15.a 16.c 17.a 18.a 19.b 20.b

Chapter 13

Practice Quiz page 469
1.b 2.b 3.a 4.c 5.a
Practice Quiz page 472
1.c 2.a 3.c 4.c
Practice Quiz page 481
1.b 2.c 3.d 4.b 5.b 6.c 7.a
Practice Quiz page 492
1.b 2.a 3.d 4.d 5.b 6.c 7.c
Test Yourself pages 494–495
1.a 2.d 3.c 4.c 5.d 6.c 7.d 8.a 9.c 10.d 11.c 12.a
13.a 14.a 15.d 16.a 17.d 18.c 19.a 20.d 21.c 22.b 23.d

Appendix A

Test Yourself pages A-12–A-13
1.a 2.b 3.d 4.c 5.c 6.b 7.a 8.c 9.a 10.d 11.c 12.b 13.b 14.d

Appendix B

Practice Quiz page B-9
1.c 2.a 3.d 4.c 5.b
Practice Quiz page B-12
1.b 2.c 3.d
Test Yourself pages B-14
1.c 2.d 3.d 4.a 5.c 6.c 7.d 8.a 9.b 10.c

absolute threshold: the lowest level of stimulation that a person can consciously detect 50 percent of the time the stimulation is present 82.

accommodation: as a monocular cue, the brain's use of information about the changing thickness of the lens of the eye in response to looking at objects that are close or far away 106.

acculturative stress: stress resulting from the need to change and adapt a person's ways to the majority culture 331.

acquired (secondary) drives: those drives that are learned through experience or conditioning, such as the need for money or social approval 273.

acrophobia: fear of heights 441.

action potential: the release of the neural impulse consisting of a reversal of the electrical charge within the axon 45.

action therapy: therapy in which the main goal is to change disordered or inappropriate behavior directly 466.

activity theory: theory of adjustment to aging that assumes older people are happier if they remain active in some way, such as volunteering or developing a hobby 262.

acute stress disorder (ASD): a disorder resulting from exposure to a major stressor, with symptoms of anxiety, dissociation, recurring nightmares, sleep disturbances, problems in concentration, and moments in which people seem to "relive" the event in dreams and flashbacks for as long as 1 month following the event 443.

adolescence: the period of life from about age 13 to the early twenties, during which a young person is no longer physically a child but is not yet an independent, self-supporting adult 253.

adrenal glands: endocrine glands located on top of each kidney that secrete over 30 different hormones to deal with stress, regulate salt intake, and provide a secondary source of sex hormones affecting the sexual changes that occur during adolescence 59.

aerial (atmospheric) perspective: the haziness that surrounds objects that are farther away from the viewer, causing the distance to be perceived as greater 106.

affect: in psychology, a term indicating "emotion" or "mood" 445.

afferent (sensory) neuron: a neuron that carries information from the senses to the central nervous system 52.

afterimages: images that occur when a visual sensation persists for a brief time even after the original stimulus is removed 89.

aggression: actions meant to harm or destroy; behavior intended to hurt or destroy another person 317, 371.

agonists: chemical substances that mimic or enhance the effects of a neurotransmitter on the receptor sites of the next cell, increasing or decreasing the activity of that cell 48.

agoraphobia: fear of being in a place or situation from which escape is difficult or impossible 441.

agreeableness: the emotional style of a person that may range from easygoing, friendly, and likeable to grumpy, crabby, and unpleasant 402.

alcohol: the chemical resulting from fermentation or distillation of various kinds of vegetable matter 285.

algorithms: very specific, step-by-step procedures for solving certain types of problems 212.

all-or-none: referring to the fact that a neuron either fires completely or does not fire at all 45.

all-or-nothing thinking: the tendency to believe that one's performance must be perfect or the result will be a total failure 444.

alpha waves: brain waves that indicate a state of relaxation or light sleep 200.

altered state of consciousness: state in which there is a shift in the quality or pattern of mental activity as compared to waking consciousness 198.

altruism: prosocial behavior that is done with no expectation of reward and may involve the risk of harm to oneself 375.

amphetamines: stimulants that are synthesized (made) in laboratories rather than being found in nature 283.

amygdala: brain structure located near the hippocampus, responsible for fear responses and memory of fear 67.

anal stage: second stage occurring from about 1 to 3 years of age, in which the anus is the erogenous zone and toilet training is the source of conflict 391.

andropause: gradual changes in the sexual hormones and reproductive system of middle-aged males 259.

anorexia nervosa (anorexia): a condition in which a person reduces eating to the point that a weight loss of 15 percent below the ideal body weight or more occurs 448.

antagonists: chemical substances that block or reduce a cell's response to the action of other chemicals or neurotransmitters 48.

anterograde amnesia: loss of memory from the point of injury or trauma forward, or the inability to form new long-term memories 172.

antianxiety drugs: drugs used to treat and calm anxiety reactions, typically minor tranquilizers 488.

antidepressant drugs: drugs used to treat depression and anxiety 488.

antipsychotic drugs: drugs used to treat psychotic symptoms such as delusions, hallucinations, and other bizarre behavior 486.

antisocial personality disorder: disorder in which a person has no morals or conscience and often behaves in an impulsive manner without regard for the consequences of that behavior 456.

anxiety disorders: disorders in which the main symptom is excessive or unrealistic anxiety and fearfulness 440.

applied behavior analysis (ABA): modern term for a form of functional analysis and behavior modification that uses a variety of behavioral techniques to mold a desired behavior or response 146.

applied psychology: the use of psychological concepts in solving real-world problems B-2.

approach–approach conflict: conflict occurring when a person must choose between two desirable goals 317.

approach–avoidance conflict: conflict occurring when a person must choose or not choose a goal that has both positive and negative aspects 318.

arbitrary inference: distortion of thinking in which a person draws a conclusion that is not based on any evidence 476.

archetypes: Jung's collective, universal human memories 393.

arousal theory: theory of motivation in which people are said to have an optimal (best or ideal) level of tension that they seek to maintain by increasing or decreasing stimulation 276.

association areas: areas within each lobe of the cortex responsible for the coordination and interpretation of information, as well as higher mental processing 70.

attachment: the emotional bond between an infant and the primary caregiver 247.

attitude: a tendency to respond positively or negatively toward a certain person, object, idea, or situation 353.

attribution: the process of explaining one's own behavior and the behavior of others 361.

attribution theory: the theory of how people make attributions 361.

auditory canal: short tunnel that runs from the pinna to the eardrum 93.

auditory nerve: bundle of axons from the hair cells in the inner ear 94.

authenticity: the genuine, open, and honest response of the therapist to the client 471.

authoritarian parenting: style of parenting in which parent is rigid and overly strict, showing little warmth to the child 260.

authoritative parenting: style of parenting in which parents combine warmth and affection with firm limits on a child's behavior 261.

automatic encoding: tendency of certain kinds of information to enter long-term memory with little or no effortful encoding 180.

autonomic nervous system (ANS): division of the PNS consisting of nerves that control all of the involuntary muscles, organs, and glands 54.

availability heuristic: estimating the frequency or likelihood of an event based on how easy it is to recall relevant information from memory or how easy it is for us to think of related examples 213.

aversion therapy: form of behavioral therapy in which an undesirable behavior is paired with an aversive stimulus to reduce the frequency of the behavior 474.

avoidance–avoidance conflict: conflict occurring when a person must choose between two undesirable goals 318.

axon: tubelike structure that carries the neural message to other cells 43.

axon terminals: branches at the end of the axon 47.

barbiturates: depressant drugs that have a sedative effect 284.

basic anxiety: anxiety created when a child is born into the bigger and more powerful world of older children and adults 394.

basic-level type: an example of a type of concept around which other similar concepts are organized, such as "dog," "cat," or "pear" 210.

behavior modification: the use of operant conditioning techniques to bring about desired changes in behavior; the use of learning techniques to modify or change undesirable behavior and increase desirable behavior (may also be referred to as applied behavior analysis) 145, 473.

behavior therapies: action therapies based on the principles of classical and operant conditioning and aimed at changing disordered behavior without concern for the original causes of such behavior 473.

behavioral genetics: field of study devoted to discovering the genetic bases for personality characteristics 419.

behaviorism: the science of behavior that focuses on observable behavior only 11.

bell curve: alternate name for the normal curve, which is said to be shaped like a bell A-2.

benzodiazepines: drugs that lower anxiety and reduce stress 284.

bilateral anterior cingulotomy: psychosurgical technique in which an electrode wire is inserted into the anterior cingulate gyrus, with guidance from magnetic resonance imaging, to destroy a very small portion of that brain area with electric current 491.

bimodal: condition in which a distribution has two modes A-6.

bimodal distributions: frequency distribution in which there are two high points rather than one A-4.

binocular cues: cues for perceiving depth based on both eyes 105.

binocular disparity: the difference in images between the two eyes, which is greater for objects that are close and smaller for distant objects 107.

biofeedback: use of feedback about biological conditions to bring involuntary responses, such as blood pressure and relaxation, under voluntary control 146.

biological model: model of explaining behavior as caused by biological changes in the chemical, structural, or genetic systems of the body 436.

biological preparedness: referring to the tendency of animals to learn certain associations, such as taste and nausea, with only one or a few pairings due to the survival value of the learning 129.

biological psychology or behavioral neuroscience: branch of neuroscience that focuses on the biological bases of psychological processes, behavior, and learning 42.

biomedical therapy: therapy for mental disorders in which a person with a problem is treated with biological or medical methods to relieve symptoms 466.

biomedical therapies: therapies that directly affect the biological functioning of the body and brain 486.

biopsychological perspective: perspective that attributes human and animal behavior to biological events occurring in the body, such as genetic influences, hormones, and the activity of the nervous system 14.

biopsychosocial model: perspective in which abnormal behavior is seen as the result of the combined and interacting forces of biological, psychological, social, and cultural influences 437.

bipolar disorder: severe mood swings between major depressive episodes and manic episodes 446.

bisexual: person attracted to both men and women 291.

blind spot: area in the retina where the axons of the three layers of retinal cells exit the eye to form the optic nerve, insensitive to light 87.

borderline personality disorder: maladaptive personality pattern in which the person is moody, unstable, lacks a clear sense of identity, and often clings to others 456.

bottom-up processing: the analysis of the smaller features to build up to a complete perception 111.

brightness constancy: the tendency to perceive the apparent brightness of an object as the same even when the light conditions change 103.

Broca's aphasia: condition resulting from damage to Broca's area, causing the affected person to be unable to speak fluently, to mispronounce words, and to speak haltingly 71.

bulimia nervosa (bulimia): a condition in which a person develops a cycle of "bingeing," or overeating enormous amounts of food at one sitting, and then using unhealthy methods to avoid weight gain 449.

burnout: negative changes in thoughts, emotions, and behavior as a result of prolonged stress or frustration 331.

bystander effect: referring to the effect that the presence of other people has on the decision to help or not help, with help becoming less likely as the number of bystanders increases 375.

caffeine: a mild stimulant found in coffee, tea, and several other plant-based substances 284.

Cannon-Bard theory of emotion: theory in which the physiological reaction and the emotion are assumed to occur at the same time 299.

case study: study of one individual in great detail 21.

catastrophe: an unpredictable, large-scale event that creates a tremendous need to adapt and adjust as well as overwhelming feelings of threat 313.

catatonic: type of schizophrenia in which the person experiences periods of statue-like immobility mixed with occasional bursts of energetic, frantic movement, and talking 453.

central nervous system (CNS): part of the nervous system consisting of the brain and spinal cord 50.

central-route processing: type of information processing that involves attending to the content of the message itself 356.

centration: in Piaget's theory, the tendency of a young child to focus only on one feature of an object while ignoring other relevant features 242.

cerebellum: part of the lower brain located behind the pons that controls and coordinates involuntary, rapid, fine motor movement 65.

cerebral hemispheres: the two sections of the cortex on the left and right sides of the brain 68.

cerebrum: the upper part of the brain consisting of the two hemispheres and the structures that connect them 71.

character: value judgments of a person's moral and ethical behavior 386.

circadian rhythm: a cycle of bodily rhythm that occurs over a 24-hour period 199.

classical conditioning: learning to make an involuntary (reflex) response to a stimulus other than the original, natural stimulus that normally produces the reflex 123.

claustrophobia: fear of being in a small, enclosed space 441.

clinical psychology: area of psychology in which the psychologists diagnose and treat people with psychological disorders that may range from mild to severe B-5.

closure: the tendency to complete figures that are incomplete (Gestalt principle of perception) 104.

cocaine: a natural drug derived from the leaves of the coca plant 284.

cochlea: snail-shaped structure of the inner ear that is filled with fluid 94.

cognitive arousal theory: theory of emotion in which both the physical arousal and the labeling of that arousal based on cues from the environment must occur before the emotion is experienced 299.

cognitive development: the development of thinking, problem solving, and memory 240.

cognitive dissonance: sense of discomfort or distress that occurs when a person's behavior does not correspond to that person's attitudes 357.

cognitive neuroscience: study of the physical changes in the brain and nervous system during thinking 13.

cognitive perspective: modern perspective that focuses on memory, intelligence, perception, problem solving, and learning 13.

cognitive perspective: modern theory in which classical conditioning is seen to occur because the conditioned stimulus provides information or an expectancy about the coming of the unconditioned stimulus 130.

cognitive psychologists: psychologists who study the way people think, remember, and mentally organize information 437.

cognitive therapy: therapy in which the focus is on helping clients recognize distortions in their thinking and replace distorted, unrealistic beliefs with more realistic, helpful thoughts 476.

cognitive universalism: theory that concepts are universal and influence the development of language 220.

cognitive–behavioral therapy (CBT): action therapy in which the goal is to help clients overcome problems by learning to think more rationally and logically 477.

cognitive-mediational theory: theory of emotion in which a stimulus must be interpreted (appraised) by a person in order to result in a physical response and an emotional reaction 302.

collective unconscious: Jung's name for the memories shared by all members of the human species 393.

College Undergraduate Stress Scale (CUSS): assessment that measures the amount of stress in a college student's life over a one-year period resulting from major life events 314.

companionate love: type of love consisting of intimacy and commitment 370.

comparative psychology: area of psychology in which the psychologists study animals and their behavior for the purpose of comparing and contrasting it to human behavior B-6.

compensation (substitution): defense mechanism in which a person makes up for inferiorities in one area by becoming superior in another area 390.

compliance: changing one's behavior as a result of other people directing or asking for the change 349.

computed tomography (CT): brain-imaging method using computer-controlled X-rays of the brain 61.

concentrative meditation: form of meditation in which a person focuses the mind on some repetitive or unchanging stimulus so that the mind can be cleared of disturbing thoughts and the body can experience relaxation 337.

concepts: ideas that represent a class or category of objects, events, or activities 209.

concepts maps: an organized visual representation of knowledge consisting of concepts and their relationships to other concepts PIA-11.

concrete operations stage: Piaget's third stage of cognitive development in which the school-age child becomes capable of logical thought processes but is not yet capable of abstract thinking 243.

conditional positive regard: positive regard that is given only when the person is doing what the providers of positive regard wish 399.

conditioned emotional response (CER): emotional response that has become classically conditioned to occur to learned stimuli, such as a fear of dogs or the emotional reaction that occurs when seeing an attractive person 128.

conditioned response (CR): learned reflex response to a conditioned stimulus 123.

conditioned stimulus (CS): stimulus that becomes able to produce a learned reflex response by being paired with the original unconditioned stimulus 123.

conditioned taste aversion: development of a nausea or aversive response to a particular taste because that taste was followed by a nausea reaction, occurring after only one association 129.

cones: visual sensory receptors found at the back of the retina, responsible for color vision and sharpness of vision 86.

confirmation bias: the tendency to search for evidence that fits one's beliefs while ignoring any evidence that does not fit those beliefs 215.

conflict: the psychological distress occurring when a person has to choose between different and incompatible or opposing goals 317.

conformity: changing one's own behavior to match that of other people 346.

conscience: part of the superego that produces guilt, depending on how acceptable behavior is 389.

conscientiousness: the care a person gives to organization and thoughtfulness of others; dependability 402.

consciousness: a person's awareness of everything that is going on around him or her at any given moment, which is used to organize behavior 198.

conservation: in Piaget's theory, the ability to understand that simply changing the appearance of an object does not change the object's nature 242.

consolidation: the changes that take place in the structure and functioning of neurons when a memory is formed 188.

constructive processing: referring to the retrieval of memories in which those memories are altered, revised, or influenced by newer information 182.

consumer psychology: branch of psychology that studies the habits of consumers in the marketplace 349.

contiguity: the tendency to perceive two things that happen close together in time as being related (Gestalt principle of perception) 105.

contingency contract: a formal, written agreement between the therapist and client (or teacher and student) in which goals for behavioral change, reinforcements, and penalties are clearly stated 475.

continuity: the tendency to perceive things as simply as possible with a continuous pattern rather than with a complex, broken-up pattern (Gestalt principle of perception) 104.

continuous reinforcement: the reinforcement of each and every correct response 135.

control group: subjects in an experiment who are not subjected to the independent variable and who may receive a placebo treatment 27.

convergence: the rotation of the two eyes in their sockets to focus on a single object, resulting in greater convergence for closer objects and lesser convergence if objects are distant 107.

convergent thinking: type of thinking in which a problem is seen as having only one answer, and all lines of thinking will eventually lead to that single answer, using previous knowledge and logic 216.

coping strategies: actions that people can take to master, tolerate, reduce, or minimize the effects of stressors 336.

corpus callosum: thick band of neurons that connects the right and left cerebral hemispheres 68.

correlation: a measure of the relationship between two variables 23.

correlation coefficient: a number derived from the formula for measuring a correlation and indicating the strength and direction of a correlation 23, A-10.

cortex: outermost covering of the brain consisting of densely packed neurons, responsible for higher thought processes and interpretation of sensory input 67.

counseling psychology: area of psychology in which the psychologists help people with problems of adjustment B-5.

creativity: the process of solving problems by combining ideas or behavior in new ways 216.

critical periods: times during which certain environmental influences can have an impact on the development of the infant 236.

critical thinking: making reasoned judgments about claims 33.

cross-sectional design: research design in which several different age-groups of participants are studied at one particular point in time 230.

cross-sequential design: research design in which participants are first studied by means of a cross-sectional design but are also followed and assessed for a period of no more than six years 230.

cult: any group of people with a particular religious or philosophical set of beliefs and identity 377.

cultural relativity: the need to consider the unique characteristics of the culture in which behavior takes place 434.

culture-bound syndromes: disorders found only in particular cultures 434.

curve of forgetting: a graph showing a distinct pattern in which forgetting is very fast within the first hour after learning a list and then tapers off gradually 185.

cybertherapy: psychotherapy that is offered on the Internet. Also called online, Internet, or Web therapy or counseling 486.

dark adaptation: the recovery of the eye's sensitivity to visual stimuli in darkness after exposure to bright lights 88.

decay: loss of memory due to the passage of time, during which the memory trace is not used 186.

declarative memory: type of long-term memory containing information that is conscious and known 173.

deep lesioning: insertion of a thin, insulated wire into the brain through which an electrical current is sent that destroys the brain cells at the tip of the wire 60.

delta waves: long, slow waves that indicate the deepest stage of sleep 200.

delusional disorder: a psychotic disorder in which the primary symptom is one or more delusions 452.

delusions: false beliefs held by a person who refuses to accept evidence of their falseness 451.

dendrites: branchlike structures that receive messages from other neurons 43.

denial: psychological defense mechanism in which the person refuses to acknowledge or recognize a threatening situation 389.

dependent variable: variable in an experiment that represents the measurable response or behavior of the subjects in the experiment 26.

depressants: drugs that decrease the functioning of the nervous system 283.

depth perception: the ability to perceive the world in three dimensions 105.

descriptive statistics: a way of organizing numbers and summarizing them so that patterns can be determined A-1.

developmental psychology: area of psychology in which the psychologists study the changes in the way people think, relate to others, and feel as they age B-5.

deviation IQ scores: a type of intelligence measure that assumes that IQ is normally distributed around a mean of 100 with a standard deviation of about 15 413.

diffusion: process of molecules moving from areas of high concentration to areas of low concentration 44.

diffusion of responsibility: occurring when a person fails to take responsibility for actions or for inaction because of the presence of other people who are seen to share the responsibility 375.

direct observation: assessment in which the professional observes the client engaged in ordinary, day-to-day behavior in either a clinical or natural setting 407.

directive: therapy in which the therapist actively gives interpretations of a client's statements and may suggest certain behavior or actions 469.

discrimination: treating people differently because of prejudice toward the social group to which they belong 363.

discriminative stimulus: any stimulus, such as a stop sign or a doorknob, that provides the organism with a cue for making a certain response in order to obtain reinforcement 143.

disorganized: type of schizophrenia in which behavior is bizarre and childish, and thinking, speech, and motor actions are very disordered 452.

displaced aggression: taking out one's frustrations on some less threatening or more available target, a form of displacement 317.

displacement: psychological defense mechanism in which emotional reactions and behavioral responses are shifted to targets that are more available or less threatening than the original target; redirecting feelings from a threatening target to a less threatening one 317, 389.

display rules: learned ways of controlling displays of emotion in social settings 297.

dispositional cause: cause of behavior attributed to internal factors such as personality or character 361.

distress: the effect of unpleasant and undesirable stressors 312.

distributed practice: spacing the study of material to be remembered by including breaks between study periods 185.

disuse: another name for decay, assuming that memories that are not used will eventually decay and disappear 186.

divergent thinking: type of thinking in which a person starts from one point and comes up with many different ideas or possibilities based on that point 216.

dizygotic twins: often called fraternal twins, occurring when two eggs each get fertilized by two different sperm, resulting in two zygotes in the uterus at the same time 234.

dominant: referring to a gene that actively controls the expression of a trait 232.

door-in-the-face technique: asking for a large commitment and being refused and then asking for a smaller commitment 349.

double-blind study: study in which neither the experimenter nor the subjects know if the subjects are in the experimental or control group 28.

drive: a psychological tension and physical arousal arising when there is a need that motivates the organism to act in order to fulfill the need and reduce the tension 273.

drive-reduction theory: approach to motivation that assumes behavior arises from physiological needs that cause internal drives to push the organism to satisfy the need and reduce tension and arousal 273.

echoic memory: the brief memory of something a person has just heard 166.

eclectic: approach to therapy that results from combining elements of several different approaches or techniques 469.

educational psychology: area of psychology in which the psychologists are concerned with the study of human learning and development of new learning techniques B-7.

efferent (motor) neuron: a neuron that carries messages from the central nervous system to the muscles of the body 52.

ego: part of the personality that develops out of a need to deal with reality, mostly conscious, rational, and logical 388.

egocentrism: the inability to see the world through anyone else's eyes 242.

eidetic imagery: the ability to access a visual memory for 30 seconds or more 166.

elaboration likelihood model: model of persuasion stating that people will either elaborate on the persuasive message or fail to elaborate on it and that the future actions of those who do elaborate are more predictable than those who do not 356.

elaborative rehearsal: a method of transferring information from STM into LTM by making that information meaningful in some way 171.

electroconvulsive therapy (ECT): form of biomedical therapy to treat severe depression in which electrodes are placed on either one or both sides of a person's head and an electric current is passed through the electrodes that is strong enough to cause a seizure or convulsion 489.

electroencephalogram (EEG): a recording of the electrical activity of large groups of cortical neurons just below the skull, most often using scalp electrodes 62.

electroencephalograph: machine designed to record the electroencephalogram 62.

embryo: name for the developing organism from two weeks to eight weeks after fertilization 236.

embryonic period: the period from two to eight weeks after fertilization, during which the major organs and structures of the organism develop 236.

emotion: the "feeling" aspect of consciousness, characterized by a certain physical arousal, a certain behavior that reveals the emotion to the outside world, and an inner awareness of feelings 294.

emotional intelligence: the awareness of and ability to manage one's own emotions as well as the ability to be self-motivated, able to feel what others feel, and socially skilled 418.

emotion-focused coping: coping strategies that change the impact of a stressor by changing the emotional reaction to the stressor 336.

empathy: the ability of the therapist to understand the feelings of the client 471.

encoding: the set of mental operations that people perform on sensory information to convert that information into a form that is usable in the brain's storage systems 164.

encoding failure: failure to process information into memory 186.

encoding specificity: the tendency for memory of information to be improved if related information (such as surroundings or physiological state) available when the memory is first formed is also available when the memory is being retrieved 176.

endocrine glands: glands that secrete chemicals called hormones directly into the bloodstream 57.

environmental psychology: area of psychology in which the focus is on how people interact with and are affected by their physical environments B-9.

enzymatic degradation: process by which structure of neurotransmitter is altered so it can no longer act on a receptor 50.

episodic memory: type of declarative memory containing personal information not readily available to others, such as daily activities and events 173.

equal status contact: contact between groups in which the groups have equal status with neither group having power over the other 366.

escape or withdrawal: leaving the presence of a stressor, either literally or by a psychological withdrawal into fantasy, drug abuse, or apathy 317.

eustress: the effect of positive events, or the optimal amount of stress that people need to promote health and well-being 313.

evolution perspective: perspective that focuses on the biological bases of universal mental characteristics that all humans share 15.

excitatory synapse: synapse at which a neurotransmitter causes the receiving cell to fire 48.

expectancy: a person's subjective feeling that a particular behavior will lead to a reinforcing consequence 398.

expectancy-value theories: incentive theories that assume the actions of humans cannot be predicted or fully understood without understanding the beliefs, values, and the importance that a person attaches to those beliefs and values at any given moment in time 279.

experiment: a deliberate manipulation of a variable to see if corresponding changes in behavior result, allowing the determination of cause-and-effect relationships 25.

experimental group: subjects in an experiment who are subjected to the independent variable 27.

experimental psychology: area of psychology in which the psychologists primarily do research and experiments in the areas of learning, memory, thinking, perception, motivation, and language B-6.

experimenter effect: tendency of the experimenter's expectations for a study to unintentionally influence the results of the study 28.

explicit memory: memory that is consciously known, such as declarative memory 173.

exposure therapies: behavioral techniques that expose individuals to anxiety- or fear-related stimuli, under carefully controlled conditions, to promote new learning 474.

extinction: the disappearance or weakening of a learned response following the removal or absence of the unconditioned stimulus (in classical conditioning) or the removal of a reinforcer (in operant conditioning); the removal of a reinforcer to reduce the frequency of a behavior 125, 475.

extraversion: dimension of personality referring to one's need to be with other people 402.

extraverts: people who are outgoing and sociable 402.

extrinsic motivation: type of motivation in which a person performs an action because it leads to an outcome that is separate from or external to the person 272.

facial feedback hypothesis: theory of emotion that assumes that facial expressions provide feedback to the brain concerning the emotion being expressed, which in turn causes and intensifies the emotion 301.

false positive: error of recognition in which people think that they recognize some stimulus that is not actually in memory 179.

family counseling (family therapy): a form of group therapy in which family members meet together with a counselor or therapist to resolve problems that affect the entire family 479.

fertilization: the union of the ovum and sperm 234.

fetal period: the time from about eight weeks after conception until the birth of the child 236.

fetus: name for the developing organism from eight weeks after fertilization to the birth of the baby 236.

figure–ground: the tendency to perceive objects, or figures, as existing on a background 103.

five-factor model (Big Five): model of personality traits that describes five basic trait dimensions 401.

fixation: disorder in which the person does not fully resolve the conflict in a particular psychosexual stage, resulting in personality traits and behavior associated with that earlier stage 390.

fixed interval schedule of reinforcement: schedule of reinforcement in which the interval of time that must pass before reinforcement becomes possible is always the same 135.

fixed ratio schedule of reinforcement: schedule of reinforcement in which the number of responses required for reinforcement is always the same 137.

flashbulb memories: type of automatic encoding that occurs because an unexpected event has strong emotional associations for the person remembering it 180.

flat affect: a lack of emotional responsiveness 452.

flooding: technique for treating phobias and other stress disorders in which the person is rapidly and intensely exposed to the fear-provoking situation or object and prevented from making the usual avoidance or escape response 474.

foot-in-the-door technique: asking for a small commitment and, after gaining compliance, asking for a bigger commitment 349.

forensic psychology: area of psychology concerned with people in the legal system, including psychological assessment of criminals, jury selection, and expert witnessing B-9.

formal concepts: concepts that are defined by specific rules or features 210.

formal operations stage: Piaget's last stage of cognitive development, in which the adolescent becomes capable of abstract thinking 243.

free association: psychoanalytic technique in which a patient was encouraged to talk about anything that came to mind without fear of negative evaluations 468.

free-floating anxiety: anxiety that is unrelated to any realistic, known source 440.

frequency count: assessment in which the frequency of a particular behavior is counted 407.

frequency distribution: a table or graph that shows how often different numbers or scores appear in a particular set of scores A-2.

frequency theory: theory of pitch that states that pitch is related to the speed of vibrations in the basilar membrane 94.

frontal lobes: areas of the brain located in the front and top, responsible for higher mental processes and decision making as well as the production of fluent speech 69.

frustration: the psychological experience produced by the blocking of a desired goal or fulfillment of a perceived need 316.

fully functioning person: a person who is in touch with and trusting of the deepest, innermost urges and feelings 400.

functional fixedness: a block to problem solving that comes from thinking about objects in terms of only their typical functions 215.

functional magnetic resonance imaging (fMRI): MRI-based brain-imaging method that allows for functional examination of brain areas through changes in brain oxygenation 63.

functionalism: early perspective in psychology associated with William James, in which the focus of study is how the mind allows people to adapt, live, work, and play 7.

fundamental attribution error: the tendency to overestimate the influence of internal factors in determining behavior while underestimating situational factors 361.

g factor: the ability to reason and solve problems, or general intelligence 410.

gender: the behavior associated with being male or female 251.

gender identity: the individual's sense of being male or female 251.

gender roles: the culture's expectations for masculine or feminine behavior, including attitudes, actions, and personality traits associated with being male or female in that culture 252.

gender schema theory: theory of gender identity acquisition in which a child develops a mental pattern, or schema, for being male or female and then organizes observed and learned behavior around that schema 253.

general adaptation syndrome (GAS): the three stages of the body's physiological reaction to stress, including alarm, resistance, and exhaustion 319.

generalized anxiety disorder: disorder in which a person has feelings of dread and impending doom along with physical symptoms of stress, which lasts 6 months or more 444.

generativity: providing guidance to one's children or the next generation, or contributing to the well-being of the next generation through career or volunteer work 260.

germinal period: first two weeks after fertilization, during which the zygote moves down to the uterus and begins to implant in the lining 235.

Gestalt psychology: early perspective in psychology focusing on perception and sensation, particularly the perception of patterns and whole figures 9.

Gestalt therapy: form of directive insight therapy in which the therapist helps clients to accept all parts of their feelings and subjective experiences, using leading questions and planned experiences such as role-playing 473.

gifted: the 2 percent of the population falling on the upper end of the normal curve and typically possessing an IQ of 130 or above 417.

glial cells: cells that provide support for the neurons to grow on and around, deliver nutrients to neurons, produce myelin to coat axons, clean up waste products and dead neurons, influence information processing, and, during prenatal development, influence the generation of new neurons 43.

glucagon: hormone that is secreted by the pancreas to control the levels of fats, proteins, and carbohydrates in the body by increasing the level of glucose in the bloodstream 333.

gonads: sex glands; secrete hormones that regulate sexual development and behavior as well as reproduction 59.

grammar: the system of rules governing the structure and use of a language 218.

groupthink: kind of thinking that occurs when people place more importance on maintaining group cohesiveness than on assessing the facts of the problem with which the group is concerned 348.

gustation: the sensation of a taste 96.

habits: in behaviorism, sets of well-learned responses that have become automatic 396.

habituation: tendency of the brain to stop attending to constant, unchanging information 83.

hallucinations: false sensory perceptions, such as hearing voices that do not really exist 452.

hallucinogenics: drugs including hallucinogens and marijuana that produce hallucinations or increased feelings of relaxation and intoxication 283.

hallucinogens: drugs that cause false sensory messages, altering the perception of reality 286.

halo effect: tendency of an interviewer to allow positive characteristics of a client to influence the assessments of the client's behavior and statements 405.

hardy personality: a person who seems to thrive on stress but lacks the anger and hostility of the Type A personality 327.

hassles: the daily annoyances of everyday life 314.

health psychology: area of psychology focusing on how physical activities, psychological traits, and social relationships affect overall health and rate of illnesses; area of psychology in which the psychologists focus on the relationship of human behavior patterns and stress reactions to physical health 323, B-7.

heroin: narcotic drug derived from opium that is extremely addictive 285.

hertz (Hz): cycles or waves per second, a measurement of frequency 93.

heterosexual: person attracted to the opposite sex 291.

heuristic: an educated guess based on prior experiences that helps narrow down the possible solutions for a problem. Also known as a "rule of thumb" 212.

higher-order conditioning: occurs when a strong conditioned stimulus is paired with a neutral stimulus, causing the neutral stimulus to become a second conditioned stimulus 126.

hindsight bias: the tendency to falsely believe, through revision of older memories to include newer information, that one could have correctly predicted the outcome of an event 182.

hippocampus: curved structure located within each temporal lobe, responsible for the formation of long-term memories and the storage of memory for location of objects 66.

histogram: a bar graph showing a frequency distribution A-2.

homeostasis: the tendency of the body to maintain a steady state 273.

homosexual: person attracted to the same sex 291.

hormones: chemicals released into the bloodstream by endocrine glands 58.

human development: the scientific study of the changes that occur in people as they age from conception until death 230.

human factors psychology: area of industrial/organizational psychology concerned with the study of the way humans and machines interact with each other B-10.

humanistic perspective: the "third force" in psychology that focuses on those aspects of personality that make people uniquely human, such as subjective feelings and freedom of choice 398.

hypothalamus: small structure in the brain located below the thalamus and directly above the pituitary gland, responsible for motivational behavior such as sleep, hunger, thirst, and sex 66.

hypothesis: tentative explanation of a phenomenon based on observations 18.

iconic memory: visual sensory memory, lasting only a fraction of a second 166.

id: part of the personality present at birth and completely unconscious 388.

ideal self: one's perception of whom one should be or would like to be 399.

identification: defense mechanism in which a person tries to become like someone else to deal with anxiety 390.

identity versus role confusion: fifth stage of personality development in which the adolescent must find a consistent sense of self 257.

imaginary audience: type of thought common to adolescents in which young people believe that other people are just as concerned about the adolescent's thoughts and characteristics as they themselves are 255.

immune system: the system of cells, organs, and chemicals of the body that responds to attacks from diseases, infections, and injuries 320.

implicit memory: memory that is not easily brought into conscious awareness, such as procedural memory 172.

implicit personality theory: sets of assumptions about how different types of people, personality traits, and actions are related to each other 360.

impression formation: the forming of the first knowledge that a person has concerning another person 359.

incentive approaches: theories of motivation in which behavior is explained as a response to the external stimulus and its rewarding properties 279.

incentives: things that attract or lure people into action 279.

independent variable: variable in an experiment that is manipulated by the experimenter 26.

industrial/organizational (I/O) psychology: area of psychology concerned with the relationships between people and their work environment B-10.

inferential statistics: statistical analysis of two or more sets of numerical data to reduce the possibility of error in measurement and to determine if the differences between the data sets are greater than chance variation would predict A-1.

information-processing model: model of memory that assumes the processing of information for memory storage is similar to the way a computer processes memory in a series of three stages 164.

in-groups: social groups with whom a person identifies; "us" 363.

inhibitory synapse: synapse at which a neurotransmitter causes the receiving cell to stop firing 48.

insight: the sudden perception of relationships among various parts of a problem, allowing the solution to the problem to come quickly 149.

insight therapies: therapies in which the main goal is helping people to gain insight with respect to their behavior, thoughts, and feelings 466.

insomnia: the inability to get to sleep, stay asleep, or get a good quality of sleep 205.

instinct approach: approach to motivation that assumes people are governed by instincts similar to those of animals 272.

instinctive drift: tendency for an animal's behavior to revert to genetically controlled patterns 145.

instincts: the biologically determined and innate patterns of behavior that exist in both people and animals 272.

insulin: a hormone secreted by the pancreas to control the levels of fats, proteins, and carbohydrates in the body by reducing the level of glucose in the bloodstream 333.

integrity: sense of wholeness that comes from having lived a full life and the ability to let go of regrets; the final completion of the ego 261.

intellectual disability: condition in which a person's behavioral and cognitive skills exist at an earlier developmental stage than the skills of others who are the same chronological age; may also be referred to as developmentally delayed. This condition was formerly known as mental retardation 415.

intelligence quotient (IQ): a number representing a measure of intelligence, resulting from the division of one's mental age by one's chronological age and then multiplying that quotient by 100 410.

intelligence: the ability to learn from one's experiences, acquire knowledge, and use resources effectively in adapting to new situations or solving problems 409.

interneuron: a neuron found in the center of the spinal cord that receives information from the afferent neurons and sends commands to the muscles through the efferent neurons. Interneurons also make up the bulk of the neurons in the brain 52.

interpersonal attraction: liking or having the desire for a relationship with another person 367.

interpersonal therapy (IPT): form of therapy for depression which incorporates multiple approaches and focuses on interpersonal problems 469.

interview: method of personality assessment in which the professional asks questions of the client and allows the client to answer, either in a structured or unstructured fashion 405.

intimacy: an emotional and psychological closeness that is based on the ability to trust, share, and care, while still maintaining a sense of self 260.

intrinsic motivation: type of motivation in which a person performs an action because the act itself is rewarding or satisfying in some internal manner 272.

introversion: dimension of personality in which people tend to withdraw from excessive stimulation 401.

introverts: people who prefer solitude and dislike being the center of attention 402.

irreversibility: in Piaget's theory, the inability of the young child to mentally reverse an action 243.

James-Lange theory of emotion: theory in which a physiological reaction leads to the labeling of an emotion 298.

"jigsaw classroom": educational technique in which each individual is given only part of the information needed to solve a problem, causing the separate individuals to be forced to work together to find the solution 367.

just noticeable difference (jnd or the difference threshold): the smallest difference between two stimuli that is detectable 50 percent of the time 82.

kinesthetic sense: sense of the location of body parts in relation to the ground and each other 99.

language: a system for combining symbols (such as words) so that an unlimited number of meaningful statements can be made for the purpose of communicating with others 218.

latency: fourth stage occurring during the school years, in which the sexual feelings of the child are repressed while the child develops in other ways 392.

latent content: the symbolic or hidden meaning of dreams 468.

latent learning: learning that remains hidden until its application becomes useful 148.

law of effect: law stating that if an action is followed by a pleasurable consequence, it will tend to be repeated, and if followed by an unpleasant consequence, it will tend not to be repeated 131.

learned helplessness: the tendency to fail to act to escape from a situation because of a history of repeated failures in the past 151.

learning/performance distinction: referring to the observation that learning can take place without actual performance of the learned behavior 151.

levels-of-processing model: model of memory that assumes information that is more "deeply processed," or processed according to its meaning rather than just the sound or physical characteristics of the word or words, will be remembered more efficiently and for a longer period of time 165.

light adaptation: the recovery of the eye's sensitivity to visual stimuli in light after exposure to darkness 88.

limbic system: a group of several brain structures located primarily under the cortex and involved in learning, emotion, memory, and motivation 65.

linear perspective: the tendency for parallel lines to appear to converge on each other 105.

linguistic relativity hypothesis: the theory that thought processes and concepts are controlled by language 220.

locus of control: the tendency for people to assume that they either have control or do not have control over events and consequences in their lives 398.

longitudinal design: research design in which one participant or group of participants is studied over a long period of time 230.

long-term memory (LTM): the system of memory into which all the information is placed to be kept more or less permanently 170.

lowball technique: getting a commitment from a person and then raising the cost of that commitment 349.

LSD (lysergic acid diethylamide): powerful synthetic hallucinogen 286.

magnetic resonance imaging (MRI): brain-imaging method using radio waves and magnetic fields of the body to produce detailed images of the brain 61.

magnification: the tendency to interpret situations as far more dangerous, harmful, or important than they actually are 444.

magnification and minimization: distortions of thinking in which a person blows a negative event out of proportion to its importance (magnification) while ignoring relevant positive events (minimization) 477.

maintenance rehearsal: practice of saying information to be remembered over and over in one's head in order to maintain it in short-term memory 170.

major depression: severe depression that comes on suddenly and seems to have no external cause, or is too severe for current circumstances 446.

maladaptive: anything that does not allow a person to function within or adapt to the stresses and everyday demands of life 433.

manic: having the quality of excessive excitement, energy, and elation or irritability 446.

manifest content: the actual content of one's dream 468.

marijuana: mild hallucinogen (also known as *pot or weed*) derived from the leaves and flowers of a particular type of hemp plant 287.

MDMA (Ecstasy or X): designer drug that can have both stimulant and hallucinatory effects 286.

mean: the arithmetic average of a distribution of numbers A-4.

means–end analysis: heuristic in which the difference between the starting situation and the goal is determined and then steps are taken to reduce that difference 213.

measure of central tendency: numbers that best represent the most typical score of a frequency distribution A-4.

measures of variability: measurement of the degree of differences within a distribution or how the scores are spread out A-6.

median: the middle score in an ordered distribution of scores, or the mean of the two middle numbers; the 50th percentile A-5.

meditation: mental series of exercises meant to refocus attention and achieve a trancelike state of consciousness 337.

medulla: the first large swelling at the top of the spinal cord, forming the lowest part of the brain, which is responsible for life-sustaining functions such as breathing, swallowing, and heart rate 64.

memory: an active system that receives information from the senses, puts that information into a usable form, organizes it as it stores it away, and then retrieves the information from storage 164.

memory trace: physical change in the brain that occurs when a memory is formed 186.

menopause: the cessation of ovulation and menstrual cycles and the end of a woman's reproductive capability 258.

mental images: mental representations that stand for objects or events and have a picture-like quality 208.

mental set: the tendency for people to persist in using problem-solving patterns that have worked for them in the past 215.

mescaline: natural hallucinogen derived from the peyote cactus buttons 286.

minimization: the tendency to give little or no importance to one's successes or positive events and traits 444.

mirror neurons: neurons that fire when an animal or person performs an action and also when an animal or person observes that same action being performed by another 70.

misinformation effect: the tendency of misleading information presented after an event to alter the memories of the event itself 182.

mode: the most frequent score in a distribution of scores A-6.

modeling: learning through the observation and imitation of others 475.

monocular cues (pictorial depth cues): cues for perceiving depth based on one eye only 105.

monozygotic twins: identical twins formed when one zygote splits into two separate masses of cells, each of which develops into a separate embryo 234.

mood disorders: disorders in which mood is severely disturbed 445.

morphemes: the smallest units of meaning within a language 218.

morphine: narcotic drug derived from opium, used to treat severe pain 285.

motion parallax: the perception of motion of objects in which close objects appear to move more quickly than objects that are farther away 106.

motivation: the process by which activities are started, directed, and continued so that physical or psychological needs or wants are met 272.

motor cortex: ear section of the frontal lobe, responsible for sending motor commands to the muscles of the somatic nervous system 70.

motor pathway: nerves coming from the CNS to the voluntary muscles, consisting of efferent neurons 54.

Müller-Lyer illusion: illusion of line length that is distorted by inward-turning or outward-turning corners on the ends of the lines, causing lines of equal length to appear to be different 109.

myelin: fatty substances produced by certain glial cells that coat the axons of neurons to insulate, protect, and speed up the neural impulse 44.

narcolepsy: sleep disorder in which a person falls immediately into REM sleep during the day without warning 206.

narcotics: a class of opium-related drugs that suppress the sensation of pain by binding to and stimulating the nervous system's natural receptor sites for endorphins 283.

natural concepts: concepts people form as a result of their experiences in the real world 210.

natural killer cell: immune system cell responsible for suppressing viruses and destroying tumor cells 322.

nature: the influence of our inherited characteristics on our personality, physical growth, intellectual growth, and social interactions 230.

need: a requirement of some material (such as food or water) that is essential for survival of the organism 273.

need for achievement (nAch): a need that involves a strong desire to succeed in attaining goals, not only realistic ones but also challenging ones 274.

need for affiliation (nAff): the need for friendly social interactions and relationships with others 274.

need for power (nPow): the need to have control or influence over others 275.

negative reinforcement: the reinforcement of a response by the removal, escape from, or avoidance of an unpleasant stimulus 134.

negative symptoms: symptoms of schizophrenia that are less than normal behavior or an absence of normal behavior; poor attention, flat affect, and poor speech production 453.

negatively skewed: a distribution of scores in which scores are concentrated in the high end of the distribution A-4.

neo-Freudians: followers of Freud who developed their own competing psychodynamic theories 393.

nerves: bundles of axons coated in myelin that travel together through the body 44.

nervous system: an extensive network of specialized cells that carries information to and from all parts of the body 42.

neurofeedback: form of biofeedback using brain-scanning devices to provide feedback about brain activity in an effort to modify behavior 146.

neuron: the basic cell that makes up the nervous system and that receives and sends messages within that system 43.

neuroplasticity: the ability within the brain to constantly change both the structure and function of many cells in response to experience or trauma 53.

neuropsychology: area of psychology in which the psychologists specialize in the research or clinical implications of brain–behavior relationships B-6.

neuroscience: a branch of the life sciences that deals with the structure and function of neurons, nerves, and nervous tissue 42.

neurotic personalities: personalities typified by maladaptive ways of dealing with relationships in Horney's theory 394.

neuroticism: degree of emotional instability or stability 402.

neurotransmitter: chemical found in the synaptic vesicles that, when released, has an effect on the next cell 47.

neutral stimulus (NS): stimulus that has no effect on the desired response 123.

nicotine: the active ingredient in tobacco 284.

night terrors: relatively rare disorder in which the person experiences extreme fear and screams or runs around during deep sleep without waking fully 204.

nightmares: bad dreams occurring during REM sleep 204.

nondirective: therapy style in which the therapist remains relatively neutral and does not interpret or take direct actions with regard to the client, instead remaining a calm, nonjudgmental listener while the client talks 470.

non-REM (NREM) sleep: any of the stages of sleep that do not include REM 200.

norm of reciprocity: assumption that if someone does something for a person, that person should do something for the other in return 350.

normal curve: a special frequency polygon in which the scores are symmetrically distributed around the mean, and the mean, median, and mode are all located on the same point on the curve, with scores decreasing as the curve extends from the mean A-2.

nurture: the influence of the environment on personality, physical growth, intellectual growth, and social interactions 230.

obedience: changing one's behavior at the command of an authority figure 350.

object permanence: the knowledge that an object exists even when it is not in sight 241.

objective introspection: the process of examining and measuring one's own thoughts and mental activities 6.

observational learning: learning new behavior by watching a model perform that behavior 151.

observer bias: tendency of observers to see what they expect to see 20.

observer effect: tendency of people or animals to behave differently from normal when they know they are being observed 20.

obsessive-compulsive disorder: disorder in which intruding, recurring thoughts or obsessions create anxiety that is relieved by performing a repetitive, ritualistic behavior or mental act (compulsion) 442.

occipital lobe: section of the brain located at the rear and bottom of each cerebral hemisphere containing the visual centers of the brain 68.

Oedipus complex/Electra complex: situation occurring in the phallic stage in which a child develops a sexual attraction to the opposite-sex parent and jealousy of the same-sex parent 391.

olfaction (olfactory sense): the sensation of smell 98.

olfactory bulbs: two projections just under the front of the brain that receive information from the receptors in the nose located just below; areas of the brain located just above the sinus cavity and just below the frontal lobes that receive information from the olfactory receptor cells 66, 99.

openness: one of the five factors; willingness to try new things and be open to new experiences 402.

operant: any behavior that is voluntary 132.

operant conditioning: the learning of voluntary behavior through the effects of pleasant and unpleasant consequences to responses 131.

operational definition: definition of a variable of interest that allows it to be directly measured 26.

opium: substance derived from the opium poppy from which all narcotic drugs are derived 285.

opponent-process theory: theory of color vision that proposes visual neurons (or groups of neurons) are stimulated by light of one color and inhibited by light of another color 90.

optimists: people who expect positive outcomes 328.

oral stage: first stage occurring in the first year of life in which the mouth is the erogenous zone and weaning is the primary conflict 390.

organic or stress-induced dysfunction: sexual problem caused by physical disorder or psychological stress 335.

out-groups: social groups with whom a person does not identify; "them" 363.

ovaries: the female gonads 59.

overgeneralization: the tendency to interpret a single negative event as a never-ending pattern of defeat and failure; distortion of thinking in which a person draws sweeping conclusions based on only one incident or event and applies those conclusions to events that are unrelated to the original 444, 477.

overlap (interposition): the assumption that an object that appears to be blocking part of another object is in front of the second object and closer to the viewer 105.

ovum: the female sex cell, or egg 234.

pancreas: endocrine gland; controls the levels of sugar in the blood 58.

panic attack: sudden onset of intense panic in which multiple physical symptoms of stress occur, often with feelings that one is dying 442.

panic disorder: disorder in which panic attacks occur frequently enough to cause the person difficulty in adjusting to daily life 442.

panic disorder with agoraphobia: fear of leaving one's familiar surroundings because one might have a panic attack in public 442.

parallel distributed processing (PDP) model: a model of memory in which memory processes are proposed to take place at the same time over a large network of neural connections 165.

parameter: a number representing some measure of central tendency or variability within a population A-1.

paranoid: type of schizophrenia in which the person suffers from delusions of persecution, grandeur, and jealousy, together with hallucinations 453.

parasympathetic division: part of the ANS that restores the body to normal functioning after arousal and is responsible for the day-to-day functioning of the organs and glands 55.

parietal lobes: sections of the brain located at the top and back of each cerebral hemisphere containing the centers for touch, taste, and temperature sensations 69.

partial reinforcement effect: the tendency for a response that is reinforced after some, but not all, correct responses to be very resistant to extinction 135.

participant modeling: technique in which a model demonstrates the desired behavior in a step-by-step, gradual process while the client is encouraged to imitate the model 475.

participant observation: a naturalistic observation in which the observer becomes a participant in the group being observed 20.

PCP: synthesized drug now used as an animal tranquilizer that can cause stimulant, depressant, narcotic, or hallucinogenic effects 286.

peak experiences: according to Maslow, times in a person's life during which self-actualization is temporarily achieved 280.

perception: the method by which the sensations experienced at any given moment are interpreted and organized in some meaningful fashion 102.

perceptual set (perceptual expectancy): the tendency to perceive things a certain way because previous experiences or expectations influence those perceptions 111.

peripheral nervous system (PNS): all nerves and neurons that are not contained in the brain and spinal cord but that run through the body itself 54.

peripheral-route processing: type of information processing that involves attending to factors not involved in the message, such as the appearance of the source of the message, the length of the message, and other noncontent factors 356.

permissive indulgent: permissive parenting in which parents are so involved that children are allowed to behave without set limits 261.

permissive neglectful: permissive parenting in which parents are uninvolved with a child or child's behavior 261.

permissive parenting: style of parenting in which parent makes few, if any, demands on a child's behavior 261.

personal fable: type of thought common to adolescents in which young people believe themselves to be unique and protected from harm 255.

personal unconscious: Jung's name for the unconscious mind as described by Freud 393.

personality: the unique and relatively stable ways in which people think, feel, and behave 386.

personality disorders: disorders in which a person adopts a persistent, rigid, and maladaptive pattern of behavior that interferes with normal social interactions 455.

personality inventory: paper and pencil or computerized test that consists of statements that require a specific, standardized response from the person taking the test 407.

personality psychology: area of psychology in which the psychologists study the differences in personality among people B-6.

personalization: distortion of thinking in which a person takes responsibility or blame for events that are unconnected to the person 477.

person-centered therapy: a nondirective insight therapy based on the work of Carl Rogers in which the client does all the talking and the therapist listens 470.

persuasion: the process by which one person tries to change the belief, opinion, position, or course of action of another person through argument, pleading, or explanation 356.

pessimists: people who expect negative outcomes 328.

phallic stage: third stage occurring from about 3 to 6 years of age, in which the child discovers sexual feelings 391.

phobia: an irrational, persistent fear of an object, situation, or social activity 440.

phonemes: the basic units of sound in language 218.

physical dependence: condition occurring when a person's body becomes unable to function normally without a particular drug 282.

physiological psychology: area of psychology in which the psychologists study the biological bases of behavior B-6.

pineal gland: endocrine gland located near the base of the cerebrum; secretes melatonin 58.

pinna: the visible part of the ear 93.

pitch: psychological experience of sound that corresponds to the frequency of the sound waves; higher frequencies are perceived as higher pitches 94.

pituitary gland: gland located in the brain that secretes human growth hormone and influences all other hormone-secreting glands (also known as the master gland) 58.

place theory: theory of pitch that states that different pitches are experienced by the stimulation of hair cells in different locations on the organ of Corti 94.

placebo effect: the phenomenon in which the expectations of the participants in a study can influence their behavior 28.

plagiarism: the copying of someone else's exact words (or a close imitation ofthe words) and presenting them as yourown PIA-13.

pleasure principle: principle by which the id functions; the immediate satisfaction of needs without regard for the consequences 388.

polygon: line graph showing a frequency distribution A-2.

pons: the larger swelling above the medulla that connects the top of the brain to the bottom and that plays a part in sleep, dreaming, left–right body coordination, and arousal 64.

population: the entire group of people or animals in which the researcher is interested 22.

positive regard: warmth, affection, love, and respect that come from significant others in one's life 399.

positive reinforcement: the reinforcement of a response by the addition or experience of a pleasurable stimulus 133.

positive symptoms: symptoms of schizophrenia that are excesses of behavior or occur in addition to normal behavior; hallucinations, delusions, and distorted thinking 453.

positively skewed: a distribution of scores in which scores are concentrated in the low end of the distribution A-4.

positron emission tomography (PET): brain-imaging method in which a radioactive sugar is injected into a person and a computer compiles a color-coded image of the activity of the brain 63.

posttraumatic stress disorder (PTSD): a disorder resulting from exposure to a major stressor, with symptoms of anxiety, dissociation, nightmares, poor sleep, reliving the event, and concentration problems, lasting for more than 1 month 443.

pragmatics: aspects of language involving the practical ways of communicating with others, or the social "niceties" of language 219.

prefrontal lobotomy: psychosurgery in which the connections of the prefrontal cortex to other areas of the brain are severed 490.

prejudice: negative attitude held by a person about the members of a particular social group 363.

preoperational stage: Piaget's second stage of cognitive development in which the preschool child learns to use language as a means of exploring the world 241.

pressure: the psychological experience produced by urgent demands or expectations for a person's behavior that come from an outside source 315.

primacy effect: tendency to remember information at the beginning of a body of information better than the information that follows 178.

primary appraisal: the first step in assessing stress, which involves estimating the severity of a stressor and classifying it as either a threat or a challenge 324.

primary drives: those drives that involve needs of the body such as hunger and thirst 273.

primary reinforcer: any reinforcer that is naturally reinforcing by meeting a basic biological need, such as hunger, thirst, or touch 133.

proactive interference: memory problem that occurs when older information prevents or interferes with the learning or retrieval of newer information 187.

problem solving: process of cognition that occurs when a goal must be reached by thinking and behaving in certain ways 212.

problem-focused coping: coping strategies that try to eliminate the source of a stressor or reduce its impact through direct actions 336.

procedural (nondeclarative) memory: type of long-term memory including memory for skills, procedures, habits, and conditioned responses. These memories are not conscious but are implied to exist because they affect conscious behavior 172.

projection: psychological defense mechanism in which unacceptable or threatening impulses or feelings are seen as originating with someone else, usually the target of the impulses or feelings; defense mechanism involving placing, or "projecting," one's own unacceptable thoughts onto others, as if the thoughts actually belonged to those others and not to oneself 389, 405.

projective tests: personality assessments that present ambiguous visual stimuli to the client and ask the client to respond with whatever comes to mind 405.

prosocial behavior: socially desirable behavior that benefits others 374.

prototype: an example of a concept that closely matches the defining characteristics of a concept 210.

proximity: physical or geographical nearness 368.

proximity: the tendency to perceive objects that are close to each other as part of the same grouping (Gestalt principle of perception) 104.

psilocybin: natural hallucinogen found in certain mushrooms 286.

psychiatric social worker: a social worker with some training in therapy methods who focuses on the environmental conditions that can have an impact on mental disorders, such as poverty, overcrowding, stress, and drug abuse 16, B-3.

psychiatrist: a medical doctor who has specialized in the diagnosis and treatment of psychological disorders 16, B-3.

psychoactive drugs: drugs that alter thinking, perception, and memory 282.

psychoanalysis: Freud's term for both the theory of personality and the therapy based on it; an insight therapy based on the theory of Freud, emphasizing the revealing of unconscious conflicts 10, 392, 467.

psychodynamic perspective: modern version of psychoanalysis that is more focused on the development of a sense of self and the discovery of other motivations behind a person's behavior than sexual motivations 12.

psychodynamic therapy: a newer and more general term for therapies based on psychoanalysis, with an emphasis on transference, shorter treatment times, and a more direct therapeutic approach 469.

psychological defense mechanisms: unconscious distortions of a person's perception of reality that reduce stress and anxiety 389.

psychological dependence: the feeling that a drug is needed to continue a feeling of emotional or psychological well-being 283.

psychological disorder: any pattern of behavior that causes people significant distress, causes them to harm others, or harms their ability to function in daily life 435.

psychologist: a professional with an academic degree and specialized training in one or more areas of psychology 16, B-3.

psychology: the scientific study of behavior and mental processes 4.

psychoneuroimmunology: the study of the effects of psychological factors such as stress, emotions, thoughts, and behavior on the immune system 311.

psychopathology: the study of abnormal behavior 432.

psychopharmacology: the use of drugs to control or relieve the symptoms of psychological disorders 486.

psychosexual stages: five stages of personality development proposed by Freud and tied to the sexual development of the child 390.

psychosurgery: surgery performed on brain tissue to relieve or control severe psychological disorders 490.

psychotherapy: therapy for mental disorders in which a person with a problem talks with a psychological professional 466.

psychotic: term applied to a person who is no longer able to perceive what is real and what is fantasy 451.

puberty: the physical changes that occur in the body as sexual development reaches its peak 254.

punishment: any event or object that, when following a response, makes that response less likely to happen again 139.

punishment by application: the punishment of a response by the addition or experience of an unpleasant stimulus 139.

punishment by removal: the punishment of a response by the removal of a pleasurable stimulus 139.

random assignment: process of assigning subjects to the experimental or control group randomly, so that each subject has an equal chance of being in either group 27.

range: the difference between the highest and lowest scores in a distribution A-6.

rapid eye movement (REM): stage of sleep in which the eyes move rapidly under the eyelids and the person is typically experiencing a dream 200.

rating scale: assessment in which a numerical value is assigned to specific behavior that is listed in the scale 407.

rational–emotive behavior therapy (REBT): cognitive–behavioral therapy in which clients are directly challenged in their irrational beliefs and helped to restructure their thinking into more rational belief statements 477.

rationalization: psychological defense mechanism in which a person invents acceptable excuses for unacceptable behavior 389.

reaction formation: psychological defense mechanism in which a person forms an opposite emotional or behavioral reaction to the way he or she really feels to keep those true feelings hidden from self and others 389.

real self: one's perception of actual characteristics, traits, and abilities 399.

realistic conflict theory: theory stating that prejudice and discrimination will be increased between groups that are in conflict over a limited resource 363.

reality principle: principle by which the ego functions; the satisfaction of the demands of the id only when negative consequences will not result 388.

recall: type of memory retrieval in which the information to be retrieved must be "pulled" from memory with very few external cues 177.

recency effect: tendency to remember information at the end of a body of information better than the information at the beginning of it 178.

receptor sites: three-dimensional proteins on the surface of the dendrites or certain cells of the muscles and glands, which are shaped to fit only certain neurotransmitters 47.

recessive: referring to a gene that influences the expression of a trait only when paired with an identical gene 232.

reciprocal determinism: Bandura's explanation of how the factors of environment, personal characteristics, and behavior can interact to determine future behavior 397.

reciprocity of liking: tendency of people to like other people who like them in return 368.

recognition: the ability to match a piece of information or a stimulus to a stored image or fact 177.

reflection: therapy technique in which the therapist restates what the client says rather than interpreting those statements 470.

reflex arc: the connection of the afferent neurons to the interneurons to the efferent neurons, resulting in a reflex action 52.

regression: psychological defense mechanism in which a person falls back on childlike patterns of responding in reaction to stressful situations 390.

reinforcement: any event or stimulus that, when following a response, increases the probability that the response will occur again; the strengthening of a response by following it with a pleasurable consequence or the removal of an unpleasant stimulus 132, 475.

reinforcers: any events or objects that, when following a response, increase the likelihood of that response occurring again 133.

relative size: perception that occurs when objects that a person expects to be of a certain size appear to be small and are, therefore, assumed to be much farther away 105.

reliability: the tendency of a test to produce the same scores again and again each time it is given to the same people 412.

REM behavior disorder: a rare disorder in which the mechanism that blocks the movement of the voluntary muscles fails, allowing the person to thrash around and even get up and act out nightmares 203.

REM paralysis: the inability of the voluntary muscles to move during REM sleep 203.

REM rebound: increased amounts of REM sleep after being deprived of REM sleep on earlier nights 203.

replication in research: repetition of a study or experiment to see if the same results will be obtained in an effort to demonstrate reliability of results 19.

representative heuristic: assumption that any object (or person) sharing characteristics with the members of a particular category is also a member of that category 212.

representative sample: randomly selected sample of subjects from a larger population of subjects 22.

repression: psychological defense mechanism in which the person refuses to consciously remember a threatening or unacceptable event, instead pushing those events into the unconscious mind 389.

resistance: occurring when a patient becomes reluctant to talk about a certain topic, by either changing the subject or becoming silent 468.

resting potential: the state of the neuron when not firing a neural impulse 45.

reticular formation (RF): an area of neurons running through the middle of the medulla and the pons and slightly beyond that is responsible for general attention, alertness, and arousal 64.

retrieval cue: a stimulus for remembering 176.

retrieval: getting information that is in storage into a form that can be used 164.

retroactive interference: memory retrieval problem that occurs when newer information prevents or interferes with the retrieval of older information 187.

retrograde amnesia: loss of memory from the point of some injury or trauma backwards, or loss of memory for the past 189.

reuptake: process by which neurotransmitters are taken back into the synaptic vesicles 49.

reversible figures: visual illusions in which the figure and ground can be reversed 103.

rods: visual sensory receptors found at the back of the retina, responsible for noncolor sensitivity to low levels of light 86.

romantic love: type of love consisting of intimacy and passion 370.

Rorschach inkblot test: projective test that uses 10 inkblots as the ambiguous stimuli 406.

s factor: the ability to excel in certain areas, or specific intelligence 410.

sample: group of subjects selected from a larger population of subjects, usually selected randomly A-1.

scaffolding: process in which a more skilled learner gives help to a less skilled learner, reducing the amount of help as the less skilled learner becomes more capable 244.

scheme: in this case, a mental concept formed through experiences with objects and events 240.

schizophrenia: severe disorder in which the person suffers from disordered thinking, bizarre behavior, hallucinations, and inability to distinguish between fantasy and reality 451.

school psychology: area of psychology in which the psychologists work directly in the schools, doing assessments, educational placement, and diagnosing educational problems B-7.

scientific method: system of gathering data so that bias and error in measurement are reduced 18.

seasonal affective disorder (SAD): a mood disorder caused by the body's reaction to low levels of sunlight in the winter months 448.

secondary appraisal: the second step in assessing a threat, which involves estimating the resources available to the person for coping with the stressor 325.

secondary reinforcer: any reinforcer that becomes reinforcing after being paired with a primary reinforcer, such as praise, tokens, or gold stars 133.

selective attention: the ability to focus on only one stimulus from among all sensory input 169.

selective thinking: distortion of thinking in which a person focuses on only one aspect of a situation while ignoring all other relevant aspects 476.

self: an individual's awareness of his or her own personal characteristics and level of functioning 399.

self-actualization: according to Maslow, the point that is seldom reached at which people have sufficiently satisfied the lower needs and achieved their full human potential 279.

self-actualizing tendency: the striving to fulfill one's innate capacities and capabilities 399.

self-concept: the image of oneself that develops from interactions with important, significant people in one's life 399.

self-determination theory (SDT): theory of human motivation in which the social context of an action has an effect on the type of motivation existing for the action 281.

self-efficacy: individual's expectancy of how effective his or her efforts to accomplish a goal will be in any particular circumstance 397.

self-fulfilling prophecy: the tendency of one's expectations to affect one's behavior in such a way as to make the expectations more likely to occur 365.

self-help groups (support groups): a group composed of people who have similar problems and who meet together without a therapist or counselor for the purpose of discussion, problem solving, and social and emotional support 479.

semantic memory: type of declarative memory containing general knowledge, such as knowledge of language and information learned in formal education 173.

semantic network model: model of memory organization that assumes information is stored in the brain in a connected fashion, with concepts that are related stored physically closer to each other than concepts that are not highly related 174.

semantics: the rules for determining the meaning of words and sentences 218.

sensation seeker: someone who needs more arousal than the average person 277.

sensation: the process that occurs when special receptors in the sense organs are activated, allowing various forms of outside stimuli to become neural signals in the brain 82.

sensorimotor stage: Piaget's first stage of cognitive development in which the infant uses its senses and motor abilities to interact with objects in the environment 241.

sensory adaptation: tendency of sensory receptor cells to become less responsive to a stimulus that is unchanging 83.

sensory conflict theory: an explanation of motion sickness in which the information from the eyes conflicts with the information from the vestibular senses, resulting in dizziness, nausea, and other physical discomfort 102.

sensory memory: the very first stage of memory; the point at which information enters the nervous system through the sensory systems 166.

sensory pathway: nerves coming from the sensory organs to the CNS consisting of afferent neurons 54.

serial position effect: tendency of information at the beginning and end of a body of information to be remembered more accurately than information in the middle of the body of information 177.

sexual deviance: behavior that is unacceptable according to societal norms and expectations 290.

sexual dysfunction: a problem in sexual functioning 334.

sexual orientation: a person's sexual attraction and affection for members of either the opposite or the same sex 290.

shape constancy: the tendency to interpret the shape of an object as being constant, even when its shape changes on the retina 103.

shaping: the reinforcement of simple steps in behavior that lead to a desired, more complex behavior 143.

short-term memory (STM): the memory system in which information is held for brief periods of time while being used 169.

significant difference: a difference between groups of numerical data that is considered large enough to be due to factors other than chance variation A-10.

similarity: the tendency to perceive things that look similar to each other as being part of the same group (Gestalt principle of perception) 104.

single photon emission computed tomography (SPECT): neuroimaging method that is similar to PET but uses a different radioactive tracer and can be used to examine brain blood flow 63.

single-blind study: study in which the subjects do not know if they are in the experimental or the control group 28.

situational cause: cause of behavior attributed to external factors, such as delays, the action of others, or some other aspect of the situation 361.

situational context: the social or environmental setting of a person's behavior 433.

size constancy: the tendency to interpret an object as always being the same actual size, regardless of its distance 103.

skewed distribution: frequency distribution in which most of the scores fall to one side or the other of the distribution A-4.

skin senses: the sensations of touch, pressure, temperature, and pain 99.

sleep apnea: disorder in which the person stops breathing for nearly half a minute or more 206.

sleepwalking (somnambulism): occurring during deep sleep, an episode of moving around or walking around in one's sleep 204.

social categorization: the assignment of a person one has just met to a category based on characteristics the new person has in common with other people with whom one has had experience in the past 359.

social cognition: the mental processes that people use to make sense of the social world around them 359.

social cognitive: referring to the use of cognitive processes in relation to understanding the social world 365.

social cognitive learning theorists: theorists who emphasize the importance of both the influences of other people's behavior and the influences of a person's own expectancies of learning 396.

social cognitive view: learning theory that includes cognitive processes such as anticipating, judging, memory, and imitation of models 397.

social comparison: the comparison of oneself to others in ways that raise one's self-esteem 365.

social identity: the part of the self-concept including one's view of self as a member of a particular social category 365.

social identity theory: theory in which the formation of a person's identity within a particular social group is explained by social categorization, social identity, and social comparison 365.

social influence: the process through which the real or implied presence of others can directly or indirectly influence the thoughts, feelings, and behavior of an individual 346.

social phobia: fear of interacting with others or being in social situations that might lead to a negative evaluation 441.

social psychology: area of psychology in which the psychologists focus on how human behavior is affected by the presence of other people B-6.

social psychology: the scientific study of how a person's thoughts, feelings, and behavior are influenced by the real, imagined, or implied presence of others 346.

Social Readjustment Rating Scale (SRRS): assessment that measures the amount of stress in a person's life over a one-year period resulting from major life events 313.

social role: the pattern of behavior that is expected of a person who is in a particular social position 372.

social support system: the network of family, friends, neighbors, coworkers, and others who can offer support, comfort, or aid to a person in need 332.

sociocultural perspective: perspective that focuses on the relationship between social behavior and culture; perspective in which abnormal behavior (as well as normal behavior) is seen as the product of the learning and shaping of behavior within the context of the family, the social group to which one belongs, and the culture within which the family and social group exist 13, 434.

soma: the cell body of the neuron responsible for maintaining the life of the cell 43.

somatic nervous system: division of the PNS consisting of nerves that carry information from the senses to the CNS and from the CNS to the voluntary muscles of the body 54.

somatosensory cortex: area of neurons running down the front of the parietal lobes responsible for processing information from the skin and internal body receptors for touch, temperature, body position, and possibly taste 69.

somesthetic senses: the body senses consisting of the skin senses, the kinesthetic sense, and the vestibular senses 99.

source traits: the more basic traits that underlie the surface traits, forming the core of personality 401.

specific phobia: fear of objects or specific situations or events 441.

spinal cord: a long bundle of neurons that carries messages between the body and the brain and is responsible for very fast, lifesaving reflexes 51.

spontaneous recovery: the reappearance of a learned response after extinction has occurred 126.

sports psychology: area of psychology in which the psychologists help athletes and others to prepare themselves mentally for participation in sports activities B-8.

standard deviation: the square root of the average squared deviations from the mean of scores in a distribution; a measure of variability A-7.

statistic: a measure of central tendency or variability computed from a sample A-1.

statistically significant: referring to differences in data sets that are larger than chance variation would predict A-9.

statistics: branch of mathematics concerned with the collection and interpretation of numerical data A-1.

stem cells: special cells found in tissues of the body that are capable of manufacturing other cell types when those cells need to be replaced due to damage or wear and tear 54.

stereotype: a set of characteristics that people believe is shared by all members of a particular social category 360.

stereotype vulnerability: the effect that people's awareness of the stereotypes associated with their social group has on their behavior 365.

stimulants: drugs that increase the functioning of the nervous system 283.

stimulatory hallucinogenics: drugs that produce a mixture of psychomotor stimulant and hallucinogenic effects 286.

stimulus discrimination: the tendency to stop making a generalized response to a stimulus that is similar to the original conditioned stimulus because the similar stimulus is never paired with the unconditioned stimulus 125.

stimulus generalization: the tendency to respond to a stimulus that is only similar to the original conditioned stimulus with the conditioned response 125.

stimulus motive: a motive that appears to be unlearned but causes an increase in stimulation, such as curiosity 276.

stimulus substitution: original theory in which Pavlov stated that classical conditioning occurred because the conditioned stimulus became a substitute for the unconditioned stimulus by being paired closely together 130.

storage: holding onto information for some period of time 164.

stress: the term used to describe the physical, emotional, cognitive, and behavioral responses to events that are appraised as threatening or challenging 312.

stressors: events that cause a stress reaction 312.

stress-vulnerability model: explanation of disorder that assumes a biological sensitivity, or vulnerability, to a certain disorder will result in the development of that disorder under the right conditions of environmental or emotional stress 455.

structuralism: early perspective in psychology associated with Wilhelm Wundt and Edward Titchener, in which the focus of study is the structure or basic elements of the mind 6.

subjective: referring to concepts and impressions that are only valid within a particular person's perception and may be influenced by biases, prejudice, and personal experiences 406.

subjective discomfort: emotional distress or emotional pain 433.

sublimation: channeling socially unacceptable impulses and urges into socially acceptable behavior 390.

subordinate concept: the most specific category of a concept, such as one's pet dog or a pear in one's hand 210.

successive approximations: small steps in behavior, one after the other, that lead to a particular goal behavior 143.

superego: part of the personality that acts as a moral center 389.

superordinate concept: the most general form of a type of concept, such as "animal" or "fruit" 209.

surface traits: aspects of personality that can easily be seen by other people in the outward actions of a person 401.

sympathetic division (fight-or-flight system): part of the ANS that is responsible for reacting to stressful events and bodily arousal 55.

synapse (synaptic gap): microscopic fluid-filled space between the synaptic knob of one cell and the dendrites or surface of the next cell 47.

synaptic knob: rounded areas on the end of the axon terminals 47.

synaptic vesicles: saclike structures found inside the synaptic knob containing chemicals 47.

synesthesia: disorder in which the signals from the various sensory organs are processed in the wrong cortical areas, resulting in the sense information being interpreted as more than one sensation 81.

syntax: the system of rules for combining words and phrases to form grammatically correct sentences 218.

systematic desensitization: behavior technique used to treat phobias, in which a client is asked to make a list of ordered fears and taught to relax while concentrating on those fears 473.

***t*-test:** type of inferential statistical analysis typically used when two means are compared to see if they are significantly different A-10.

temperament: the behavioral characteristics that are fairly well established at birth, such as easy, difficult, and slow to warm up; the enduring characteristics with which each person is born 246, 386.

temporal lobes: areas of the brain located along the side, starting just behind the temples, containing the neurons responsible for the sense of hearing and meaningful speech 69.

teratogen: any factor that can cause a birth defect 236.

testes: the male gonads 59.

texture gradient: the tendency for textured surfaces to appear to become smaller and finer as distance from the viewer increases 106.

thalamus: part of the limbic system located in the center of the brain, this structure relays sensory information from the lower part of the brain to the proper areas of the cortex and processes some sensory information before sending it to its proper area 66.

that's-not-all technique: a sales technique in which the persuader makes an offer and then adds something extra to make the offer look better before the target person can make a decision 350.

Thematic Apperception Test (TAT): projective test that uses 20 pictures of people in ambiguous situations as the visual stimuli 406.

therapeutic alliance: the relationship between therapist and client that develops as a warm, caring, accepting relationship characterized by empathy, mutual respect, and understanding 483.

therapy: treatment methods aimed at making people feel better and function more effectively 466.

theta waves: brain waves indicating the early stages of sleep 200.

thinking (cognition): mental activity that goes on in the brain when a person is organizing and attempting to understand information and communicating information to others 207.

thyroid gland: endocrine gland found in the neck; regulates metabolism 58.

time-out: an extinction process in which a person is removed from the situation that provides reinforcement for undesirable behavior, usually by being placed in a quiet corner or room away from possible attention and reinforcement opportunities 476.

token economy: type of behavior modification in which desired behavior is rewarded with tokens; the use of objects called tokens to reinforce behavior in which the tokens can be accumulated and exchanged for desired items or privileges 145, 475.

top-down processing: the use of preexisting knowledge to organize individual features into a unified whole 111.

trait: a consistent, enduring way of thinking, feeling, or behaving 401.

trait theories: theories that endeavor to describe the characteristics that make up human personality in an effort to predict future behavior 401.

trait–situation interaction: the assumption that the particular circumstances of any given situation will influence the way in which a trait is expressed 403.

transduction: the process of converting outside stimuli, such as light, into neural activity 82.

transference: in psychoanalysis, the tendency for a patient or client to project positive or negative feelings for important people from the past onto the therapist 468.

trial and error (mechanical solution): problem-solving method in which one possible solution after another is tried until a successful one is found 212.

trichromatic theory: theory of color vision that proposes three types of cones: red, blue, and green 88.

Type 2 diabetes: disease involving failure of the pancreas to secrete enough insulin, necessitating medication, usually diagnosed before the age of 40 and can be associated with obesity 322.

Type A personality: person who is ambitious, time conscious, extremely hardworking, and tends to have high levels of hostility and anger as well as being easily annoyed 326.

Type B personality: person who is relaxed and laid-back, less driven and less competitive than Type A, and slow to anger 326.

Type C personality: pleasant but repressed person, who tends to internalize his or her anger and anxiety and who finds expressing emotions difficult 326.

unconditional positive regard: positive regard that is given without conditions or strings attached; referring to the warmth, respect, and accepting atmosphere created by the therapist for the client in person-centered therapy 399, 471.

unconditioned response (UCR): an involuntary (reflex) response to a naturally occurring or unconditioned stimulus 123.

unconditioned stimulus (UCS): a naturally occurring stimulus that leads to an involuntary (reflex) response 123.

unconscious mind: level of the mind in which thoughts, feelings, memories, and other information are kept that are not easily or voluntarily brought into consciousness 387.

unilateral spatial neglect: condition produced most often by damage to the parietal lobe association areas of the right hemisphere resulting in an inability to recognize objects or body parts in the left visual field 71.

validity: the degree to which a test actually measures what it's supposed to measure 412.

variable interval schedule of reinforcement: schedule of reinforcement in which the interval of time that must pass before reinforcement becomes possible is different for each trial or event 137.

variable ratio schedule of reinforcement: schedule of reinforcement in which the number of responses required for reinforcement is different for each trial or event 137.

vestibular senses: the sensations of movement, balance, and body position 99.

vicarious conditioning: classical conditioning of a reflex response or emotion by watching the reaction of another person 128.

visual accommodation: the change in the thickness of the lens as the eye focuses on objects that are far away or close 86.

volley principle: theory of pitch that states that frequencies from about 400 Hz to 4000 Hz cause the hair cells (auditory neurons) to fire in a volley pattern, or take turns in firing 95.

waking consciousness: state in which thoughts, feelings, and sensations are clear and organized, and the person feels alert 198.

Wernicke's aphasia: condition resulting from damage to Wernicke's area, causing the affected person to be unable to understand or produce meaningful language 71.

withdrawal: physical symptoms that can include nausea, pain, tremors, crankiness, and high blood pressure, resulting from a lack of an addictive drug in the body systems 282.

working memory: an active system that processes the information in short-term memory 169.

Yerkes-Dodson law: law stating performance is related to arousal; moderate levels of arousal lead to better performance than do levels of arousal that are too low or too high. This effect varies with the difficulty of the task: Easy tasks require a high-moderate level, whereas more difficult tasks require a low-moderate level 277.

z score: a statistical measure that indicates how far away from the mean a particular score is in terms of the number of standard deviations that exist between the mean and that score A-8.

zone of proximal development (ZPD): Vygotsky's concept of the difference between what a child can do alone versus what that child can do with the help of a teacher 244.

zygote: cell resulting from the uniting of the ovum and sperm 234.

references

AAA Foundation for Traffic Safety. (1997). *Aggressive driving: Three studies*. Washington, DC: Louis Mizell.

Abadinsky, H. (1989). *Drug abuse: An introduction*. Chicago: Nelson-Hall Series in Law, Crime, and Justice.

Abbott, L., Nadler, J., & Rude, R. K. (1994). Magnesium deficiency in alcoholism: Possible contribution to osteoporosis and cardiovascular disease in alcoholics. *Alcoholism, Clinical & Experimental Research, 18*(5), 1076–1082.

Abe, K., Amatomi, M., & Oda, N. (1984). Sleepwalking and recurrent sleep talking in children of childhood sleepwalkers. *American Journal of Psychiatry, 141*, 800–801.

Abel, G. G., & Osborn, C. A. (1992). The paraphilias: The extent and nature of sexually deviant and criminal behavior. In J. M. W. Bradford (Ed.), *Psychiatric Clinics of North America, 15*(3), (pp. 675–687). Philadelphia: W. B. Saunders.

Abela, J. R. Z., & D'Allesandro, D. U. (2002). Beck's cognitive theory of depression: The diathesis-stress and causal mediation components. *British Journal of Clinical Psychology, 41*, 111–128.

Åberg, M. A., Pedersen, N. L., Torén, K., Svartengren, M., Bäckstrand, B., Johnsson, T., Cooper-Kuhn, C. M., Åberg, N. D., Nilsson, M., & Kuhn, H. G. (2009). Cardiovascular fitness is associated with cognition in young adulthood. *Proceedings of the National Academy of Sciences, 106*(49), 20906–20911.

Abraham, S., & Llewellyn-Jones, D. (2001). *Eating disorders, the facts* (5th ed). London: Oxford University Press.

Abraham, W. C., & Williams, J. M. (2003). Properties and mechanisms of LTP maintenance. *The Neuroscientist, 9*(6), 463–474.

Abramson, L. Y., Garber, J., & Seligman, M. E. P. (1980). Learned helplessness in humans: An attributional analysis. In J. Garber & M. E. P. Seligman (Eds.), *Human Helplessness* (pp. 3–34). New York: Academic Press.

Abramson, L. Y., Seligman, M. E. P., & Teasdale, J. D. (1978). Learned helplessness in humans: Critique and reformulation. *Journal of Abnormal Psychology, 87*, 49–74.

Acheson, D. J., MacDonald, M. C., & Postle, B. R. (2010). The interaction of concreteness and phonological similarity in verbal working memory. *Journal of Experimental Psychology: Learning, Memory and Cognition, 36*(1), 17–36.

Adachi, P. J. C. & Willoughby, T. (in press). The effect of violent video games on aggression: Is it more than just the violence?, *Aggression and Violent Behavior* [doi: 10.1016/j.avb.2010.12.002].

Adams, D. B. (1968). The activity of single cells in the midbrain and hypothalamus of the cat during affective defense behavior. *Archives Italiennes de Biologie, 106*, 243–269.

Adams, R. J. (1987). An evaluation of colour preferences in early infancy. *Infant Behaviour and Development, 10*, 143–150.

Addis, D. R., Leclerc, C. M., Muscatell, K., & Kensinger, E. A. (2010). There are age-related changes in neural connectivity during the encoding of positive, but not negative, information. *Cortex, 46*, 9.

Ader R. (2003). Conditioned immunomodulation: Research needs and directions. *Brain, Behavior, and Immunity, 17*(1), 51–57.

Adhikari, A., Topiwala, M. A., & Gordon, J. A. (2010). Synchronized activity between the ventral hippocampus and the medial prefrontal cortex during anxiety. *Neuron, 65*(2), 257–269.

Adler, A. (1954). *Understanding human nature*. New York: Greenburg Publisher.

Adler, S. R., Fosket, J. R., Kagawa-Singer, M., McGraw, S. A., Wong-Kim, E., Gold, E., & Sternfeld, B. (2000) Conceptualizing menopause and midlife: Chinese American and Chinese women in the U.S. *Maturitas 35*(1), 11–23.

Adolphs, R., & Tranel, D. (2003). Amygdala damage impairs emotion recognition from scenes only when they contain facial expressions. *Neuropsychologia, 41*, 1281–1289.

Adolphs, R., Gosselin, F., Buchanan, T. W., Tranel, D., Schyns, P., & Damasio, A. R. (2005). A mechanism for impaired fear recognition after amygdala damage. *Nature, 433*, 68–72.

Aghajanian, G. K., & Marek, G. J. (1999). Serotonin and hallucinogens. *Neuropsychopharmacology, 21*, 16S–23S.

Agnati, L. F., Bjelke, B., & Fuxe, K. (1992). Volume transmission in the brain. *American Scientist, 80*, 362–373.

Agresti, A., & Finlay, B. (1997). *Statistical Methods for the Social Sciences*. Upper Saddle River, NJ: Prentice Hall.

Aguiar, A., & Baillargeon, R. (2003). Perseverative responding in a violation-of-expectation task in 6.5-month-old infants. *Cognition, 88*(3), 277–316.

Ahlskog, J. E. (2003). Slowing Parkinson's disease progression: Recent dopamine agonist trials. *Neurology, 60*(3), 381–389.

Ahn, W. (1998). Why are different features central for natural kinds and artifacts? The role of causal status in determining feature centrality. *Cognition, 69*, 135–178.

Ainsworth, M. D. S. (1985). Attachments across the life span. *Bulletin of the New York Academy of Medicine, 61*, 792–812.

Ainsworth, M. D. S., Blehar, M. C., Waters, E., & Wall, S. (1978). *Patterns of attachment: A study of the strange situation*. Hillsdale, NJ: Erlbaum.

Aitchison, J. (1992). Good birds, better birds, and amazing birds: The development of prototypes. In P. J. Arnaud & H. Béjoint (Eds.), *Vocabulary and applied linguistics* (pp. 71–84). London: Macmillan.

Ajzen, I. (2001). Nature and operation of attitudes. *Annual Review of Psychology, 52*, 27–58.

Ajzen, I., & Fishbein, M. (2000). Attitudes and the attitude–behavior relation: Reasoned and automatic processes. In W. Stroebe & M. Hewstone (Eds.), *European review of social psychology* (pp. 1–33). New York: Wiley.

Alarcón, R. D., Becker, A. E., Lewis-Fernández, R., Like, R. C., Desai, P., Foulks, E., Gonzales, J., Hansen, H., Kopelowicz, A., Lu, F. G., Oquendo, M. A., & Primm, A. (2009). Issues for DSM-V: The role of culture in psychiatric diagnosis. *The Journal of Nervous and Mental Disease, 197*(8), 559–660.

Albert, D. J., & Richmond, S. E. (1977). Reactivity and aggression in the rat: Induction by alpha–adrenergic blocking agents injected ventral to anterior septum but not into lateral septum. *Journal of Comparative and Physiological Psychology, 91*, 886–896 [DBA] *Physiology and Behavior, 20*, 755–761.

Alderfer, C. P. (1972). *Existence, relatedness and growth: Human needs in organisational settings*. New York: Free Press.

Alexander, G., DeLong, M. R., & Strick, P. L. (1986). Parallel organization of functionally segregated circuits linking basal ganglia and cortex. *Annual Review of Neuroscience, 9*, 357–381.

Aligne, C. A., Auinger, P., Byrd, R. S., & Weitzman, M. (2000). Risk factors for pediatric asthma contributions of poverty, race, and urban residence. *American Journal of Respiratory Critical Care Medicine, 162*(3), 873–877.

Alkon, D. (1989). Memory storage and neural systems. *Scientific American, 261*(1), 42–50.

Allen, D. (2001). *Getting things done: the art of stress-free productivity*. New York: Viking Adult.

Allen, D. (2008). *Making it all work*. New York: Viking Adult.

Allen, F. (1994). *Secret formula*. New York: HarperCollins.

Allen, G. E. (2006). *Intelligence tests and immigration to the United States, 1900–1940*. Hoboken, NJ: Wiley.

Allen, G., & Parisi, P. (1990). Trends in monozygotic and dizygotic twinning rates by maternal age and parity. Further analysis of Italian data, 1949–1985, and rediscussion of U.S. data, 1964–1985. *Acta Genetic Medicine and Gemellology, 39*, 317–328.

Allen, K., Blascovich, J., & W. Mendes. (2002). Cardiovascular reactivity and the presence of pets, friends, and spouses: The truth about cats and dogs. *Psychosomatic Medicine, 64*, 727–739.

Alloy, L. B., & Clements, C. M. (1998). Hopelessness theory of depression: Tests of the symptom component. *Cognitive Therapy and Research, 22*, 303–335.

Allport, G. W., & Odbert, H. S. (1936). Trait names: A psycho-lexical study. *Psychological Monographs, 47*(211).

Alm, H., & Nilsson, L. (1995). The effects of a mobile telephone conversation on driver behaviour in a car following situation. *Accident Analysis and Prevention, 27*(5), 707–715.

Alperstein, L. (2001, May). *For two: Some basic perspectives and skills for couples therapy*. Paper presented at the XXXIII Annual Conference of the American Association of Sex Educators, Counselors, and Therapists, San Francisco.

Alzheimer's Association. (2010). Alzheimer's disease facts and figures. *Alzheimer's and Dementia, 6*, 4–54.

Amabile, T., Hadley, C. N., & Kramer, S. J. (2002).Creativity under the gun. *Harvard Business Review, 80*(8), 52–60.

Amabile, T. M., DeJong, W., & Lepper, M. R. (1976). Effects of externally imposed deadlines on subsequent intrinsic motivation. *Journal of Personality and Social Psychology, 34*, 92–98.

Amat, J., Baratta, M. V., Paul, E., Bland, S. T., Watkins, L. R., & Maier, S. F. (2005). Medial prefrontal cortex determines how stressor controllability affects behavior and dorsal raphe nucleus. *Nature Neuroscience, 8*(3), 365–371.

American Academy of Pediatrics. (1995). Health supervision for children with Turner syndrome. *Pediatrics, 96*(6), 1166–1173.

American Association on Intellectual and Developmental Disabilities [AAIDD]. (2009). FAQ on intellectual disability. Retrieved June 8, 2010, from www.aamr.org/content_104.cfm

American College Counseling Association's (ACCA) Community College Task Force (2010). *2009–2010 Community college counselors survey*. Retrieved August 12, 2010, from www.collegecounseling.org/pdf/2009-2010_Community_College_Counselors_Survey_Results.pdf

American College Counseling Association's Community College Task Force (2010). 2009-2010 Community College Counselors Survey. *The American College Counseling Association (ACCA),*. Retrieved from http://www.collegecounseling.org/pdf/2009-2010_Community_College_Counselors_Survey_Results.pdf

American Psychiatric Association. (2000). *DSM-IV-TR: Diagnostic and statistical manual of mental disorders* (4th ed., Text Revision). Washington, DC: American Psychicatric Association.

American Psychiatric Association. (2000a). Appendix I: Outline for cultural formulation and glossary of culture-bound syndromes. In *DSM-IV-TR: Diagnostic and statistical manual of mental disorders* (4th ed., Text Revision). Washington, DC: American Psychicatric Association.

American Psychiatric Association. (2000b). Practice guidelines for the treatment of patients with major depressive disorder (revision). *American Journal of Psychiatry, 157* (Suppl. 4), 1–45.

American Psychiatric Association. (2009). Report of the DSM-V Neurodevelopmental Disorders Work Group [Electronic Version] from "http://www.psych.org/Main-Menu/Research/DSMIV/DSMV/DSMRevisionActivities/DSM-V-Work-Group-Reports/Neurodevelopmental-Disorders-Work-Group-Report.aspx"

American Psychiatric Association (2009). Report of the DSM-V Personality and Personality Disorders Work Group. Retrieved from http://www.dsm5.org/ProgressReports/Pages/0904ReportoftheDSM-VPersonalityandPersonalityDisordersWorkGroup.aspx.

American Psychiatric Association (2010). APA modifies DSM naming convention to reflect publication changes. Retrieved from American Psychiatric Association website http://www.dsm5.org/Newsroom/Documents/DSM-Name-Change.pdf

American Psychiatric Association Committee on Electroconvulsive Therapy. (2001). *The practice of electroconvulsive therapy: Recommendations for treatment, training, and privileging,* (2nd ed.). Washington, DC: American Psychiatric Association.

American Psychological Association. (2002). Ethical principles of psychologists and code of conduct. American Psychologist, 57, 1060–1073.

American Psychological Association (2005). Policy Statement on Evidence-Based Practice in Psychology. Retrieved from http://www.apa.org/practice/guidelines/evidence-based.pdf

American Psychological Association Division 19 (2010). Society for Military Psychology. Retrieved from http://www.apadivision19.org/about.htm

American Psychological Association. (2002). Ethical principles of psychologists and code of conduct. *American Psychologist, 57,* 1060–1073.

Anastasi, A., & Urbina, S. (1997). *Psychological testing* (7th ed.). Upper Saddle River, NJ: Prentice-Hall.

Anderson, C. A. (1987). Temperature and aggression: Effects on quarterly, yearly, and city rates of violent and nonviolent crime. *Journal of Personality and Social Psychology, 52*(6), 1161–1173.

Anderson, C. A., Berkowitz, L., Donnerstein, E., Huesmann, L. R., Johnson, J. D., Linz, D., Malamuth, N. M., & Wartella, E. (2003). The influence of media violence on youth. *Psychological Science in the Public Interest, 4*(3), 81–110.

Anderson, L. W., Krathwohl, D. R., Airasian, P. W., Cruikshank, K. A., Mayer, R. E., Pintrich, P. R., Raths, J., & Wittrock, M. C. (Eds.). (2001). *A taxonomy for learning, teaching, and assessing—A revision of Bloom's Taxonomy of Educational Objectives.* New York: Addison Wesley Longman.

Anderson, M. C., & Neely, J. H. (1995). Interference and inhibition in memory retrieval. In E. L. Bjork & R. A. Bjork (Eds.). *Handbook of perception and cognition, Vol. 10. Memory.* San Diego, CA: Academic Press.

Andrews, J. D. W. (1989). Integrating visions of reality: Interpersonal diagnosis and the existential vision. *American Psychologist, 44,* 803–817.

Anschuetz, B. L. (1999). The high cost of caring: Coping with workplace stress. *The Journal, the Newsletter of the Ontario Association of Children's Aid Societies, 43*(3), 1–63.

Antuono, P. G., Jones, J. L., Wang, Y., & Li, S. (2001). Decreased glutamate [plus] glutamine in Alzheimer's disease detected in vivo with (1)H-MRS at 0.5 T. *Neurology, 56*(6), 737–742.

Arbury, S. (2005). Workplace Violence: Training Young Workers in Preventative Strategies. *NFIB Business Toolbox, March 4.*

Archer, J. (1991). The influence of testosterone on human aggression. *British Journal of Psychology, 82,* 1–28.

Arkowitz, H., & Miller, W. R. (2008). Learning, applying, and extending motivational interviewing. In H. Arkowitz, H. A. Westra, W. R. Miller, & S. Rollnick (Eds.). *Motivational interviewing in the treatment of psychological disorders* (pp. 1–25). New York: Guilford Press.

Armstrong, R. (1997). When drugs are used for rape. *Journal of Emergency Nursing, 23*(4), 378–381.

Arnett, P. A., Smith, S. S., & Newman, J. P. (1997). Approach and avoidance motivation in psychopathic criminal offenders during passive avoidance. *Journal of Personality and Social Psychology, 72*(6), 1413–1428.

Aron, A., Aron, E., & Coups, E. (2005). *Statistics for the behavioral and social sciences: Brief course.* (4th edition). Upper Saddle River, NJ: Prentice-Hall.

Aronson, E. (1997). Back to the future. Retrospective review of Leon Festinger's—A theory of cognitive dissonance. *American Journal of Psychology, 110,* 127–137.

Aronson, E., Blaney, N., Stephan, C., Sikes, J., & Snapp, M. (1978). *The jigsaw classroom.* Beverly Hills, CA: Sage.

Asarnow, R. F., Granholm, E., & Sherman, T. (1991). Span of apprehension in schizophrenia. In H. A. Nasrallah (Ed.), *Handbook of Schizophrenia, Vol. 5.* In S. R. Steinhauer, J. H. Gruzelie, & J. Zubin (Eds.), *Neuropsychology, psychophysiology and information processing* (pp. 335–370). Amsterdam: Elsevier.

Asch, S. E. (1951). Effects of group pressure upon the modification and distortion of judgement. In H. Guetzkow (Ed.), *Groups, leadership and men.* Pittsburgh: Carnegie Press.

Asch, S. E. (1956). Studies of independence and conformity: A minority of one against a unanimous majority. *Psychological Monographs, 70,* (Whole no. 416).

Aserinsky, E., & Kleitman, N. (1953). Regularly occurring periods of eye motility, and concomitant phenomena, during sleep. *Science, 118,* 273–274.

Ash, M. G. (1998). *Gestalt psychology in German culture, 1890–1967: Holism and the quest for objectivity.* Cambridge: Cambridge University Press.

Assaf, Y., & Pasternak, O. (2008). Diffusion tensor imaging (DTI)-based white matter mapping in brain research: A review. *Journal of Molecular Neuroscience, 34*(1), 51–61.

Atkinson, R. C., & Shiffrin, R. M. (1968). Human memory: A proposed system and its control processes. In K. W. Spence & J. T. Spence (Eds.). *The psychology of learning and motivation* (Vol. 2, pp. 89–105). New York: Academic Press.

Atladóttir, H. O., Pedersen, M. G., Thorsen, C., Mortensen, P. B., Deleuran, B., Eaton, W. W., & Parner, E. T. (2009). Association of family history of autoimmune diseases and autism spectrum disorders. *Pediatrics, 124*(2), 687–694.

Babiloni, C., Vecchio, F., Buffo, P., Buttiglione, M., Cibelli, G., & Rossini, P. M. (2010). Cortical responses to consciousness of schematic emotional facial expressions: A high-resolution EEG study. *Human Brain Mapping, 8,* 8.

Backenstraß, M., Pfeiffer, N., Schwarz, T., Catanzaro, S. J., & Mearns, J. (2008). Reliability and validity of the German version of the Generalized Expectancies for Negative Mood Regulation (NMR) Scale. *Diagnostica, 54,* 43–51.

Backer, B., Hannon, R., & Russell, N. (1994). *Death and dying: Understanding and care* (2nd ed.). Albany, NY: Delmar.

Baddeley, A. (1988). Cognitive psychology and human memory. *Trends in Neurosciences, 11,* 176–181.

Baddeley, A. D. (1986). *Working memory.* London Oxford University Press.

Baddeley, A. D. (1996). Exploring the central executive. *Quarterly Journal of Experimental Psychology, 49A,* 5–28.

Baddeley, A. D. (2003). Working memory: Looking back and looking visual forward. *Nature Reviews Neuroscience, 4*(10), 829–839.

Baddeley, A. D., & Hitch, G. (1974). Working memory. In G. A. Bower (Ed.), *The psychology of learning and motivation, 8* (pp. 47–89). New York: Academic Press.

Baddeley, A. D., & Larson, J. D. (2007). The phonological loop unmasked? A comment on the evidence for a "perceptual-gestural" alternative. *Quarterly Journal of Experimental Psychology, 60*(4), 497–504.

Baehr, E. K., Revelle, W., & Eastman, C. I. (2000). Individual difference in the phase amplitude of the human circadian temperature rhythm: With an emphasis on morningness-eveningness. *Journal of Sleep Research, 9,* 117–127.

Baer, D. M., Wolf, M. M., & Risley, T. R. (1968). Some current dimensions of applied behavior analysis. *Journal of Applied Behavior Analysis, 1,* 91–97.

Bahrick, H. (1984). Fifty years of second language attrition: Implications for programmatic research. *Modern Language Journal, 68,* 105–118.

Bailey, J., Dunne, M. P., & Martin, N. G. (2000). Genetic and environmental influences on sexual orientation and its correlates in an Australian twin sample. *Journal of Personality and Social Psychology, 78*(3), 524–536.

Bailey, J. M., & Pillard, R. C. (1991). A genetic study of male sexual orientation. *Archives of General Psychiatry, 48,* 1089–1096.

Bailey, J. M., & Zucker, K. J. (1995). Childhood sex-typed behavior and sexual orientation: A conceptual analysis and quantitative review. *Developmental Psychology, 31,* 43–55.

Bailey, J. M., Pillard, R. C., Neale, M. C., & Agyei, Y. (1993). Heritable factors influence sexual orientation in women. *Archives of General Psychiatry, 50,* 217–223.

Bailey, J., Dunne, M. P., & Martin, N. G. (2000). Genetic and environmental influences on sexual orientation and its correlates in an Australian twin sample. *Journal of Personality and Social Psychology, 78*(3), 524–536.

Baillargeon, R. (1986). Representing the existence and the location of hidden objects: Object permanence in 6- and 8-month-old infants. *Cognition, 23,* 21–41.

Baker, L. D., Frank, L. L., Foster-Schubert, K., Green, P. S., Wilkinson, C. W., McTiernan, A., et al. (2010). Effects of aerobic exercise on mild cognitive impairment: A controlled trial. *Archives of Neurology, 67*(1), 71–79.

Ball, K., Berch, D. B., Helmers, K. F., Jobe, J. B., Leveck, M. D., Marsiske, M., Morris, J. N., Rebok, G. W., Smith, D. M., Tennstedt, S. L., Unverzagt, F. W., & Willis, S. L. (2002). Advanced Cognitive Training for Independent and Vital Elderly Study Group. Effects of cognitive training interventions with older adults: A randomized controlled trial. *Journal of the American Medical Association, 288,* 2271–2281.

Baltes, P. B., Reese, H. W., & Nesselroade, J. R. (1988). *Introduction to research methods, life-span developmental psychology.* Hillsdale, NJ: Erlbaum.

Bandura, A. (1965). Influence of models' reinforcement contingencies on the acquisition of imitative responses. *Journal of Social Psychology, 1,* 589–595.

Bandura, A. (1980). The social learning theory of aggression. In R. A. Falk & S. S. Kim (Eds.), *The war system: An interdisciplinary approach* (p. 146). Boulder, CO: Westview Press.

Bandura, A. (1986). *Social foundations of thought and action: A social cognitive theory.* Englewood Cliffs, NJ: Prentice Hall.

Bandura, A. (1998). Exploration of fortuitous determinants of life paths. *Psychological Inquiry, 9*, 95–99.

Bandura, A., & Rosenthal, T. L. (1966). Vicarious classical conditioning as a functioning of arousal level. *Journal of Personality and Social Psychology, 3*, 54–62.

Bandura, A., Blanchard, E. B., & Ritter, B. (1969). Relative efficacy of desensitization and modeling approaches for inducing behavioral, affective, and attitudinal changes. *Journal of Personality and Social Psychology, 13*, 173–199.

Bandura, A., Jeffrey, R. W., & Wright, C. L. (1974). Efficacy of participant modeling as a function of response induction aids. *Journal of Abnormal Psychology, 83*, 56–64.

Bandura, A., Ross, D., & Ross, S. A. (1961). Transmission of aggression through imitation of aggressive models. *Journal of Abnormal and Social Psychology, 63*, 575–582.

Bandura, A., Ross, D., & Ross, S. A. (1963). Imitation of film-mediated aggressive models. *Journal of Abnormal and Social Psychology, 66*, 3–11.

Barak, A. (1999). Psychological applications on the Internet: A discipline on the threshold of a new millennium. *Applied and Preventive Psychology, 8*, 231–246.

Barak, A., & Hen, L. (2008). Exposure in cyberspace as means of enhancing psychological assessment. In A. Barak (Ed.), *Psychological aspects of cyberspace: Theory, research, applications* (pp. 129–162). Cambridge, UK: Cambridge University Press.

Barak, A., & Suler, J. (2008). Reflections on the psychology and social science of cyberspace. In A. Barak (Ed.), *Psychological aspects of cyberspace: Theory, research, applications* (pp. 1–12). Cambridge, UK: Cambridge University Press.

Bard, P. (1934). On emotional expression after decortication with some remark on certain theoretical views. *Psychological Review, 41*, 309–329, 424–449.

Bargh, J. A., Chen, M., & Burrows, C. (1996). Automaticity of social behavior: Direct effects of trait construct and stereotype activation on action. *Journal of Personality and Social Psychology, 71*(2), 230–244.

Barker, E. (1983). The ones who got away: People who attend Unification Church workshops and do not become Moonies. In E. Barker (Ed.), *Of gods and men: New religious movements in the West*. Macon, GA: Mercer University Press.

Barkley, R. A., Murphy, K. R., & Fischer, M. (2008). *ADHD in adults: What the science says*. New York: Guilford Press.

Barlow, D. H., Allen, L. B., & Basden, S. L. (2007). Psychological treatments for panic disorders, phobias, and generalized anxiety disorder. In P. E. Nathan & J. M. Gorman (Eds.), *A guide to treatments that work* (3rd ed., pp. 351-394). New York, NY: Oxford University Press.

Barnes, A. M., & Carey, J. C. (2002, January). Common problems of babies with trisomy 18 or 13. Rochester, NY, *Support Organization for Trisomy 18, 13, and Related Disorders*, January 11, New York: Soft Publications.

Barnes, V., Schneider, R., Alexander, C., & Staggers, F. (1997). Stress, stress reduction, and hypertension in African Americans: An updated review. *Journal of the National Medical Association, 89*(7), 464–476.

Barnyard, P., & Grayson, A. (1996). *Introducing psychological research*. London: Macmillan Press.

Baron, J. N., & Reiss, P. C. (1985). Same time, next year: Aggregate analyses of the mass media and violent behavior. *American Sociological Review, 50*, 347–363.

Baron, S. A. (1993). *Violence in the workplace*. Ventura, CA: Pathfinder Publishing of California.

Barondes, S. H. (1998). *Mood genes: Hunting for origins of mania and depression*. New York: W. H. Freeman.

Barone, J. J., & Roberts, H. R. (1996). Caffeine consumption. *Food Chemistry and Toxicology, 34*, 119–129.

Barsalou, L. W. (1992). *Cognitive psychology: An overview for cognitive scientists*. Hillsdale, NJ: Lawrence Erlbaum.

Barsch, J. (1996). *Barsch learning style inventory* (rev. ed.). Novato, CA: Academic Therapy Publications.

Barsh, G. S., Farooqi, I. S., & O'Rahilly, S. (2000). Genetics of body-weight regulation. *Nature, 404*, 644–651.

Barstow, A. L. (1995). *Witchcraze: A new history of the European witch hunts*. London: Pandora.

Bartels, A., & Zeki, S. (2000). The neural basis of romantic love. *NeuroReport, 11*, 3829–3834.

Barth, J. M., & Boles, D. B. (1999, September,). *Positive relations between emotion recognition skills and right hemisphere processing*. Paper presented at the 11th Annual Convention of the American Psychological Society, Denver, CO.

Bartholomew, K. (1990). Avoidance of intimacy: An attachment perspective. *Journal of Social and Personal Relationships, 7*, 147–178.

Bartlett, F. C. (1932). *Remembering: A study in experimental ad social psychology*. Cambridge, UK: Cambridge University Press.

Bartlett, N. R. (1965). Dark and light adaptation. In C. H. Graham (Ed.), *Vision and visual perception*. New York: Wiley.

Barton, M. E., & Komatsu, L. K. (1989). Defining features of natural kinds and artifacts. *Journal of Psycholinguistic Research, 18*, 433–447.

Bartoshuk, L. M. (1993). The biological basis for food perception and acceptance. *Food Quality and Preference, 4*(1/2), 21–32.

Bartoshuk, L. M., Duffy, V. B., Hayes, J. E., Moskowitz, H. R., & Snyder, D. J. (2006). Psychophysics of sweet and fat perception in obesity: Problems, solutions and new perspectives. *Philosophical Transactions of the Royal Society of London. Series B, Biological Sciences, 361*(1471), 1137–1148.

Bartoshuk, L. M., Fast, K., & Snyder, D. J. (2005). Differences in our sensory worlds. *Current Directions in Psychological Science, 14*(3), 122–125.

Basadur, M., Pringle, P., & Kirkland, D. (2002). Crossing cultures: Training effects on the divergent thinking attitudes of Spanish-speaking South American managers. *Creativity Research Journal, 14*(3, 4), 395–408.

Bastien, C. H., Morin, C. M., Ouellet, M., Blais, F. C., Bouchard, S. (2004). Cognitive-behavioral therapy for insomnia: Comparison of individual therapy, group therapy, and telephone consultations. *Journal of Consulting and Clinical Psychology, 72*(4), 653–659.

Bates, J. E. (1989). Applications of temperament concepts. In G. A. Kohnstamm, J. E. Bates, & M. K Rothbart (Eds.), *Temperament in childhood* (pp. 323–355). New York: Wiley.

Bator, R. J., & Cialdini, R. B. (2006). "The nature of consistency motivation: Consistency, aconsistency, and anticonsistency in a dissonance paradigm." *Social Influence, 1*, 208–233.

Battaglia, M., Bernardeschi, L., Franchini, L., Bellodi, L., & Smeraldi, E. (1995). A family study of schizotypal disorder. *Schizophrenia Bulletin, 2*(1)1, 133–146.

Baumrind, D. (1964). Some thoughts on ethics of research: After reading Milgram's "Behavioral Study of Obedience." *American Psychologist, 19*, 421–423.

Baumrind, D. (1967). Child care practices anteceding three patterns of preschool behavior. *Genetic Psychology Monograph, 75*, 43–88.

Baumrind, D. (1991). The influence of parenting style on adolescent competence and substance abuse. *Journal of Early Adolescence, 11*(1), 56–95.

Baumrind, D. (1997). Necessary distinctions. *Psychological Inquiry, 8*, 176–182.

Baumrind, D. (2005). Patterns of parental authority and adolescent autonomy. In J. Smetana (Ed.), *New directions for child development: Changes in parental authority during adolescence* (pp. 61–69). San Francisco: Jossey-Bass.

Bayliss, D. M., Baddeley, J. C., & Gunn, D. M. (2005). The relationship between short-term memory and working memory: Complex span made simple? *Memory, 13*(3–4), 414–421.

Bechtel, W. & Abrahamsen, A. (2002). *Connectionism and the mind: Parallel processing, dynamics, and evolution in networks* (2nd ed.). Oxford, UK: Basil Blackwell.

Beck, A. T. (1976). *Cognitive therapy and the emotional disorders*. New York: International Universities Press.

Beck, A. T. (1979). *Cognitive therapy and the emotional disorders*. New York: Penguin Books.

Beck, A. T. (1984). Cognitive approaches to stress. In C. Lehrer & R. L. Woolfolk (Eds.), *Clinical guide to stress management*. New York: Guilford Press.

Beck, J. S. (2007). Cognitive therapy for personality disorders. Retrieved November 17, 2010, from http://www.academyofct.org/Library/InfoManage/Guide.asp?FolderID=196.

Beckman, M. & Pierrehumbert, J. (1986). Intonational structure in English and Japanese. *Phonology Year Book III*, 15–70.

Beer, J. S. (2009). The neural basis of emotion regulation: Making emotion work for you and not against you. In M. S. Gazzaniga (Ed.), *The Cognitive Neurosciences* (pp. 961–972). Cambridge, MA: MIT Press.

Behne, T., Carpenter, M., & Tomasello, M. (2005). One-year-olds comprehend the communicative intentions behind gestures in a hiding game. *Developmental Science, 8*, 492–499.

Békésy, G. V. (1960). *Experiments in Hearing* (E. G. Wever, Trans.). New York: McGraw-Hill.

Belsky, J. (2005). Differential susceptibility to rearing influence: An evolutionary hypothesis and some evidence. In B. Ellis & D. Bjorklund (Eds.), *Origins of the social mind: Evolutionary psychology and child development* (pp. 139–163). New York: Guilford Pres.

Belsky, J., & Johnson, C. D. (2005). Developmental outcome of children in day care. In J. Murph, S. D. Palmer, & D. Glassy (Eds.), *Health in child care: A manual for health professionals* (4th ed., pp. 81–95). Elks Grove Village, IL: American Academy of Pediatrics.

Belsky, J., Vandell, D., Burchinal, M., Clarke-Stewart, K. A., McCartney, K., Owen, M., & NICHD Early Child Care Research Network. (2007). Are there long-term effects of early child care? *Child Development, 78*, 681–701.

Bem, S. L. (1981). Gender schema theory: A cognitive account of sex typing. *Psychological Review, 88*, 354–364.

Bem, S. L. (1987). Gender schema theory and the romantic tradition. In P. Shaver & C. Hendrick (Eds.), *Review of personality and social psychology* (Vol. 7, pp. 251-271). Newbury Park, CA: Sage.

Bem, S. L. (1993). Is there a place in psychology for a feminist analysis of the social context? *Feminism and Psychology, 3*, 247–251.

Benjafield, J. J. G. (1996). *A history of psychology*. Boston: Allyn & Bacon.

Benjamin, S. L. (1996). An interpersonal theory of personality disorders. In J. F. Clarkin & M. F. Lenzenweger (Eds.), *Major theories of personality disorder*. New York: Guilford Press.

Ben-Shakhar, G., Bar-Hillel, M., Bliu, Y., Ben-Abba, E., & Flug, A. (1986). Can graphology predict occupational success? Two empirical studies and some methodological ruminations. *Journal of Applied Psychology, 71*, 645–653.

Benson, H. (1975). *The relaxation response*. New York: Morrow.

Benson, H., Beary, J., & Carol, M. (1974a). The relaxation response. *Psychiatry, 37*, 37–46.

Benson, H., Rosner, B. A., Marzetta, B. R., & Klemchuk, H. M. (1974b). Decreased blood pressure in pharmacologically treated hypertensive patients who regularly elicited the relaxation response. *Lancet, 1*(7852), 289–291.

Benton, D., & Parker, P. Y. (1998). Breakfast, blood glucose, and cognition. *American Journal of Clinical Nutrition, 67*(S), 772S–778S.

Berent, S. (1977). Functional asymmetry of the human brain in the recognition of faces. *Neuropsychologia, 15*, 829–831.

Berg, F. (1999). Health risks associated with weight loss and obesity treatment programs. *Journal of Social Issues, 55*(2), 277–297.

Berk L., Tan, S. A., & Berk, D. (2008, April). *Cortisol and catecholamine stress hormone decrease is associated with the behavior of perceptual anticipation of mirthful laughter.* Presented at the 121st Annual Meeting of the American Physiological Society, San Diego, California.

Berk, L. E. (1992). Children's private speech: An overview of theory and the status of research. In R. M. Diaz & L. E. Berk (Eds.), *Private speech: From social interaction to self-regulation* (pp. 17–53). Hillsdale, NJ: Erlbaum.

Berk, L. E., & Spuhl, S. T. (1995). Maternal interaction, private speech, and task performance in preschool children. *Early Childhood Research Quarterly, 10*, 145–169.

Berk, L. S., Felten, D. L., Tan, S. A., Bittman, B. B., & Westengard, J. (2001). Modulation of neuroimmune parameters during the eustress of humor-associated mirthful laughter. *Alternative Therapy Health Medicines, 7*(2), 62–72, 74–76.

Berk, L. S., Tan, S. A., Fry, W. F., Napier, B., J., Lee, J. W., Hubbard, R. W., Lewis, J. E., & Eby, W. C. (1989). Neuroendrocrine and stress hormone changes during mirthful laughter. *American Journal of the Medical Sciences. 298*(6), 390–396.

Berk, L., Prowse, M., Petrofsky, J. S., Batt, J., Laymon, M., Bains, G., Daher, N., Tan, S., & Berk, D. (2009, May). *Laughercise: Health benefits similar of exercise lowers cholesterol and systolic blood pressure.* Presented at the Association for Psychological Science 21st Annual Convention, San Francisco, California.

Berkowitz, L. (1993). *Aggression: Its causes, consequences and control.* New York: McGraw-Hill.

Berman, A., Bradley, J. C., Carroll, B., Certain, R. D., Gabrelcik, J. C., Green, R., et al. (2010). *The challenge and the promise: Strengthening the force, preventing suicide and saving lives. Final report of the Department of Defense task force on the prevention of suicide by members of the armed forces.* Washington, DC.

Bermond, B., Nieuwenhuyse, B., Fasotti, L., & Schuerman, J. (1991). Spinal cord lesions, peripheral feedback, and intensities of emotional feelings. *Cognition and Emotion, 5*, 201–220.

Bernat, E., Shevrin, H., & Snodgrass, M. (2001). Subliminal visual oddball stimuli evoke a P300 component. *Clinical Neurophysiology, 112*, 159–171.

Berry, J. W., & Kim, U. (1998). Acculturation and mental health. In P. R. Dasen, J. W. Berry, & N. Sartorius (Eds.), *Health and cross-cultural psychology: Toward applications* (pp. 207–236). Newbury Park, CA: Sage.

Berry, J. W., & Sam, D. L. (1997). Acculturation and adaptation. In J. W. Berry, M. H. Segall, & C. Kagitcibasi (Eds.), *Handbook of cross-cultural psychology, Vol. 3: Social behaviour and applications* (2nd ed., pp. 291–326). Boston: Allyn & Bacon.

Berscheid, E., & Reis, H. T. (1998). Attraction and close relationships. In D. T. Gilbert & S. T. Fiske et al. (Eds.), *The handbook of social psychology, Vol. 2* (4th ed., pp. 193–281), New York: McGraw-Hill.

Berteretche, M. V., Dalix, A. M., Cesar d'Ornano, A. M., Bellisle, F., Khayat, D., & Faurion, A. (2004). Decreased taste sensitivity in cancer patients under chemotherapy. *Supportive Care in Cancer, 12*(8), 571–576.

Bertram, L., & Tanzi, R. E. (2005). The genetic epidemiology of neurodegenerative disease. *The Journal of Clinical Investigation, 115*(6), 1449–1457.

Best, D. L., & Williams, J. E. (2001). Gender and culture. In D. Matsumoto (Ed.), *The handbook of culture and psychology* (pp. 195–212). New York: Oxford University Press.

Betancourt, J. R., & Jacobs, E. A. (2000). Language barriers to informed consent and confidentiality: The impact on women's health. *Journal of American Medical Women's Association, 55*, 294–295.

Beyer, B. K. (1995). *Critical thinking.* Bloomington, IN: Phi Delta Kappa Educational Foundation.

Beyreuther, K., Biesalski, H. K., Fernstrom, J. D., Grimm, P., Hammes, W. P., Heinemann, U., Kempski, O., Stehle, P., Steinhart, H., & Walker, R. (2007). Consensus meeting: Monosodium glutamate, an update. *European Journal of Clinical Nutrition, 61*, 304–313.

Bigler, E. D., Johnson, S. C., Anderson, C. V., Blatter, D. D., Gale, S. D., Russo, A. A., Ryser, D. K., Macnamara, S. E., Bailey, B. R., & Hopkins, R. O. (1996). Traumatic brain injury and memory: The role of hippocampal atrophy. *Neuropsychology, 10*, 333–342.

Binet, A., & Simon, T. (1916). *The development of intelligence in children.* Baltimore: Williams & Wilkins.

Bivens, J. A., & Berk, L. E. (1990). A longitudinal study of the development of elementary school children's private speech. *Merill-Palmer Quarterly, 36*, 443–463.

Bjork, R. A., & Bjork, E. L. (1992). A new theory of disuse and an old theory of stimulus fluctuation. In A. Healy, S. Kosslyn, & R. Shiffrin (Eds.), *From learning processes to cognitive processes: Essays in honor of William K. Estes* (Vol. 2, pp. 35–67). Hillsdale, NJ: Erlbaum.

Bjork, R. A., & Whitten, W. B. (1974). Recency-sensitive retrieval processes in long-term free recall. *Cognitive Psychology, 6*, 173–189.

Black, D. W., & Andreasen, N. C. (1999). Schizophrenia, schizophreniform disorder, and delusional (paranoid) disorders. In R. E. Hales et al. (Eds.), *Textbook of psychiatry* (3rd ed., pp. 425–477). Washington, DC: American Psychiatric Press.

Blackmon, L. R., Batton, D. G., Bell, E. F., Engle, W. A., Kanto, W. P., Martin, G. I., Rosenfeld, W. N., Stark, A. R., & Lemons, J. A. (Committee on Fetus and Newborn). (2003). Apnea, sudden infant death syndrome, and home monitoring. *Pediatrics, 111*(4), 914–917.

Blair, R. J. R., Sellars, C., Strickland, I., Clark, F., Williams, A. O., Smith, M., & Jones, L. (1995). Emotion attributions in the psychopath. *Personality and Individual Differences, 19*(4), 431–437.

Blanchard, M., & Main, M. (1979). Avoidance of the attachment figure and social-emotional adjustment in day-care infants. *Developmental Psychology, 15*, 445–446.

Blanchard, R. (2001). Fraternal birth order and the maternal immune hypothesis of male homosexuality. *Hormones and Behavior, 40*(2), 105–114.

Blanchard-Fields, F., & Horhota, M. (2005). Age differences in the correspondence bias: When a plausible explanation matters. *Journals of Gerontology Series B: Psychological Sciences and Social Sciences, 60*(5), 259–267.

Blanchard-Fields, F., Chen, Y., Horhota, M., & Wang, M. (2007). Cultural differences in the relationship between aging and the correspondence bias. *Journals of Gerontology Series B: Psychological Sciences and Social Sciences, 62*(6), 362–365.

Blass, T. (1991). Understanding behavior in the Milgram obedience experiment: The role of personality, situations, and their interactions. *Journal of Personality and Social Psychology, 60*, 398–413.

Blass, T. (1999). The Milgram paradigm after 35 years: Some things we now know about obedience to authority. *Journal of Applied Social Psychology, 25*, 955–978.

Blazer, D. G., Kessler, R. C., McGonagle, K. A., & Swartz, M. S. (1994). The prevalence and distribution of major depression in a national community sample: The National Comorbidity Survey. *American Journal of Psychiatry, 151*, 979–986.

Bledsoe, C. H., & Cohen, B. (1993). *Social dynamics of adolescent fertility in sub-Saharan Africa.* Washington DC: National Academy Press.

Blehar, M. C., & Oren, D. A. (1997). Gender differences in depression. *Medscape General Medicine, 1*(2). Retrieved June 27, 2004, from http://www.medscape.com/viewarticle/719236

Bleiberg, K. L., & Markowitcz, J. C. (2008). Interpersonal psychotherapy for depression. In D. H. Barlow (Ed.), *Clinical handbook of psychological disorders* (pp. 306-327). New York, NY: The Guilford Press.

Bleuler, E. (1911, reissued 1950). *Dementia praecox or the group of schizophrenias.* New York: International Universities Press.

Blits, B., & Bunge, M. B. (2006). Direct gene therapy for repair of the spinal cord. *Journal of Neurotrauma, 23*(3–4), 508–520.

Block, N. (2005). Two neural correlates of consciousness. *Trends in Cognitive Sciences, 9*, 41–89.

Bloom, B. S. (Ed.). (1956) *Taxonomy of educational objectives, the classification of educational goals—Handbook I: Cognitive domain.* New York: McKay.

Bloom, L. (1974). Talking, understanding and thinking. In R. Schiefelbusch & L. L. Lloyd (Eds.), *Language perspectives: Acquisition, retardation and intervention.* New York: Macmillan.

Bloom, P. (2000). *How children learn the meaning of words.* Cambridge, MA: MIT Press.

Blumer, D. (2002). The illness of Vincent van Gogh. *American Journal of Psychiatry, 159*(4), 519–526.

Bock, R. (1993, August). *Understanding Klinefelter syndrome: A guide for XXY males and their families.* NIH Publication No. 93-3202. National Institutes of Health, Office of Research Reporting. Washington, DC: Retrieved August 10, 2010, from http://www.nichd.nih.gov/publications/pubs/klinefelter.cfm

Bodrova, E., & Leong, D. J. (1996). *Tools of the mind: The Vygotskian approach to early childhood education.* Englewood Cliffs, NJ: Prentice Hall.

Boggio, P. S., Campanha, C., Valasek, C. A., Fecteau, S., Pascual-Leone, A., & Fregni, F. (2010). Modulation of decision-making in a gambling task in older adults with transcranial direct current stimulation. *The European Journal of Neuroscience, 31*(3), 593–597.

Boggio, P. S., Fregni, F., Valasek, C., Ellwood, S., Chi, R., Gallate, J., et al. (2009). Temporal lobe cortical electrical stimulation during the encoding and retrieval phase reduces false memories. *PLoS One, 4*(3), e4959.

Boggio, P. S., Rocha, M., Oliveira, M. O., Fecteau, S., Cohen, R. B., Campanha, C., et al. (2009). Noninvasive brain stimulation with high-frequency and low-intensity repetitive transcranial magnetic stimulation treatment for posttraumatic stress disorder. *The Journal of Clinical Psychiatry, 29*, 29.

Bogle, K. D. (2000). Effect of perspective, type of student, and gender on the attribution of cheating. *Proceedings of the Oklahoma Academy of Science, 80*, 91–97.

Bolton, P., Bass, J., Betancourt, T., Speelman, L., Onyango, G., Clougherty, K. F., et. al. (2007). Interventions for depression symptoms among adolescent survivors of war and displacement in northern Uganda. *Journal of Medical Association, 298*, 519–527.

Bond, R. A., & Smith, P. B. (1996). Culture and conformity: A meta-analysis of studies using Asch's (1952, 1956) line judgment task. *Psychological Bulletin, 119*, 111–137.

Bondarenko, L. A. (2004). Role of methionine in nocturnal melatonin peak in the pineal gland. *Bulletin of Experimental Biological Medicine, 137*(5), 431–432.

Bonnelykke, B. (1990). Maternal age and parity as predictors of human twinning. *Acta Genetic Medicine and Gemellology, 39*, 329–334.

Booth-Butterfield, S. (1996). Message characteristics. *Steve's primer of practical persuasion and influence.* Retrieved August 2, 2004, from http://www.austincc.edu/colangelo/1311/persuasivecharacteristics.htm

Borgeat, F., & Goulet, J. (1983, June). Psychophysiological changes following auditory subliminal suggestions for activation and deactivation. *Perceptual and Motor Skills, 56*(3), 759–766.

Borges, M. A., Stepnowsky, M. A., & Holt, L. H. (1977). Recall and recognition of words and pictures by adults and children. *Bulletin of the Psychonomic Society, 9*, 113–114.

Boroditsky, L. (2001). Does language shape thought? Mandarin and English speakers' conceptions of time. *Cognitive Psychology, 43*(1), 1–22.

Boroditsky, L. (2009). How does our language shape the way we think? In M. Brockman (Ed.). *What's next? Dispatches on the future of science* (pp. 116–129). New York: Vintage.

Bosworth, H. B., & Schaie, K. W. (1997). The relationship of social environment, social networks, and health outcomes in the Seattle Longitudinal Study: Two analytical approaches. *Journals of Gerontology Series B: Psychological Sciences and Social Sciences, 52*(5), 197–205.

Botwin, M. D., & Buss, D. M. (1989). The structure of act data: Is the Five-Factor Model of personality recaptured? *Journal of Personality and Social Psychology, 56*, 988–1001.

Bouchard, C., Tremblay, A., Nadeau, A., Dussault, J., Despres, J. P., Theriault, G., Lupien, P. J., Serresse, O., Boulay, M. R., & Fournier, G. (1990). Long-term exercise training with constant energy intake. 1: Effect on body composition and selected metabolic variables. *International Journal on Obesity, 14*(1), 57–73.

Bouchard, T. (1994). Genes, environment, and personality. *Science, 264*, 1700–1701.

Bouchard, T. J., & Segal, N. L. (1985). Environment and IQ. In B. B. Wolman (Ed.), *Handbook of intelligence: Theories, measurements, and applications* (pp. 391–464). New York: Wiley.

Bouchard, T. J., Jr. (1997). Whenever the twain shall meet. *The Science, 37*(5), 52–57.

Bowden, C. L., Calabrese, J. R., McElroy, S. L., Gyulai, L., Wassef, A., Petty, F., Pope, H. G., Jr., Chou, J. C., Keck, P. E., Jr., Rhodes, L. J., Swann, A. C., Hirschfeld, R. M., & Wozniak, P. J. (2000). For the Divalproex Maintenance Study Group. A randomized, placebo-controlled 12-month trial of divalproex and lithium in treatment of outpatients with bipolar I disorder. *Archives of General Psychiatry, 57*(5), 481–489.

Bowman, E. S. (1996). Delayed memories of child abuse: Part II: An overview of research findings relevant to understanding their reliability and suggestibility. *Dissociation: Progress in the Dissociative Disorders, 9*, 232–243.

Boyd, C. H., & Peeler, C. M. (May, 2004). *Highlighting vs note taking: A comparison of students' performance on tests.* Poster presented at 16th Annual Convention of the American Psychological Society, Chicago.

Boyd, L. A., & Winstein, C. J. (2004). Cerebellar stroke impairs temporal but not spatial accuracy during implicit motor learning. *Neurorehabilitation and Neural Repair, 18*(3), 134–143.

Boyson-Bardies, B., deHalle, P., Sagart, L., & Durand, C. (1989). A cross-linguistic investigation of vowel formats in babbling. *Journal of Child Language, 16*, 1–17.

Bracey, G. (1997). A few facts about poverty. *Phi Delta Kappan, 79*, 163–164.

Braio, A., Dunn, R., Beasley, T. M., Quinn, P., & Buchanan, K. (1997). Incremental implementation of learning style strategies among urban low achievers. *Journal of Educational Research, 91*, 15–25.

Braun, S. R. (1996). *Buzz: the science and lore of alcohol and caffeine,* pp. 137-169. New York: Oxford University Press.

Brawman-Mintzer, O., & Lydiard, R. B. (1997). Biological basis of generalized anxiety disorder. *Journal of Clinical Psychiatry, 58*(3), 16–25.

Brazelton, T. B. (1992). *Touchpoints: Your child's emotional and behavioral development.* Reading, MA: Addison-Wesley.

Brecher, M., Wang, B. W., Wong, H., & Morgan, J. P. (1988). Phencyclidine and violence: Clinical and legal issues. *Journal of Clinical Psychopharmacology, 8*, 397–401.

Breier, A., Albus, M., Pickar, D., Zahn, T. P., Wolkowitz, O. M., & Paul, S. M. (1987). Controllable and uncontrollable stress in humans: Alterations in mood, neuroendocrine and psychophysiological function. *American Journal of Psychiatry, 144*, 1419–1425.

Breland, K., & Breland, M. (1961). The misbehavior of organisms. *American Psychologist. 16*, 681–684.

Bremmer, J. D. (2005). *Brain imaging handbook.* New York: W. W. Norton.

Brennan, J. F. (2002). *History and systems of psychology* (6th ed.). Upper Saddle River, NJ: Prentice Hall.

Breslau, N., Chilcoat, H. D., Kessler, R. C., Peterson, E. L., & Lucia, V. C. (1999). Vulnerability to assaultive violence: Further specification of the sex difference in post-traumatic stress disorder. *Psychological Medicine, 29*, 813–821.

Breslau, N., Davis, G. C., Andreski, P., & Peterson, E. L. (1997). Sex differences in post-traumatic stress disorder. *Archives of General Psychiatry, 54*(11), 1044–1048.

Breuer, J., & Freud, S. (1895). *Studies on hysteria (cathartic method). Special Edition, 2*, 1–309.

Brewer, M. B. (2001). Ingroup identification and intergroup conflict: When does in-group love become outgroup hate? In R. D. Ashmore, L. Jussim, & D. Wilder (Eds.), *Social identity, intergroup conflict, and conflict reduction.* New York: Oxford University Press.

Briem, V., & Hedman, L. R. (1995). Behavioural effects of mobile telephone use during simulated driving. *Ergonomics, 38*, 2536–2562.

Briggs, K. C., & Myers, I. B. (1998). *The Myers-Briggs Type Indicator-Form M.* Palo Alto, CA: Consulting Psychologists Press.

Brigham, A. (1844). Asylums exclusively for the incurably insane. Classic article in *The American Journal of Psychiatry, 151*, 50–70.

Broadbent, D. (1958). *Perception and communication.* Elmsford, NY: Pergamon.

Brondolo, E., Rieppi, R., Erickson, S. A., Bagiella, E., Shapiro, P. A., McKinley, P., & Sloan, R. P. (2003). Hostility, interpersonal interactions, and ambulatory blood pressure. *Psychosomatic Medicine, 65*, 1003–1011.

Bronkhorst, A. W. (2000). The cocktail party phenomenon: A review on speech intelligibility in multiple-talker conditions. *Acta Acustica united with Acustica 86*, 117–128.

PDF available from http://eaa-fenestra.org/products/acta-acustica/most-cited/acta_86_2000_Bronkhorst.pdf

Brooks, J. G., & Brooks, M. G. (1993). *In search of understanding: The case for constructivist classrooms.* Alexandria, VA: The Association for Supervision and Curriculum Development.

Brown, C., Taylor, J., Green, A., Lee, B. E., Thomas, S. B., & Ford, A. (2003). *Managing depression in African Americans: Consumer and provider perspectives.* (Final Report to Funders). Pittsburgh: Mental Health Association of Allegheny County.

Brown, G. L., & Linnoila, M. I. (1990). CSF serotonin metabolite (5–HIAA) studies in depression, impulsivity, and violence. *Journal of Clinical Psychiatry, 51*(4), 31–43.

Brown, J. (1958). Some tests of the decay theory of immediate memory. *Quarterly Journal of Experimental Psychology, 10*, 12–21.

Brown, K. M., Li, X. Y., Descalzi, G., Kim, S. S., Chen, T., Shang, Y. Z., Zhuo, M., Houslay, M. D., & Abel, T. (2009). Sleep deprivation impairs cAMP signaling in the hippocampus. *Nature, 461* (7267): 1122-1125.

Brown, P. K., & Wald, G. (1964). Visual pigments in single rods and cones of the human retina. *Science, 144*, 45.

Brown, R. (1973). *A first language: The early stages.* Cambridge, MA: Harvard University Press.

Brown, R., & McNeill, D. (1966). The "tip of the tongue" phenomenon. *Journal of Verbal Learning and Verbal Behavior, 5*(4), 325–337.

Brown, W. M., Finn, C. J., Cooke, B. M., & Breedlove, S. M. (2002). Differences in finger length ratios between self-identified "butch" and "femme" lesbians. *Archives of Sexual Behavior, 31*(1), 123–127.

Browne, D. (2004). Do dolphins know their own minds? *Biology and Philosophy, 19*, 633–653.

Browne, M. N., & Keeley, S. M. (2009). *Asking the right questions: A guide to critical thinking* (9th ed., pp. 37–129). Upper Saddle River, NJ: Pearson Prentice-Hall.

Broyles, S. (2006). Subliminal advertising and the perpetual popularity of playing to people's paranoia. *Journal of Consumer Affairs, 40*(2), 392–406.

Brubaker, D. A., & Leddy, J. J. (2003). Behavioral contracting in the treatment of eating disorders. *The Physician and Sportsmedicine, 31*(9).

Brunner, E. J., Hemingway, H., Walker, B., Page, M., Clarke, P., Juneja, M., Shipley, M. J., Kumari, M., Andrew, R., Seckl, J. R., Papadopoulos, A., Checkley, S., Rumley, A., Lowe, G. D., Stansfeld, S. A., & Marmot, M. G. (2002). Adrenocortical, autonomic and inflammatory causes of the metabolic syndrome: Nested case-control study. *Circulation, 106*, 2659–2665.

Bryan, E. B., & Hallett, F. (2001). *Guidelines for professionals. Twins and triplets: The first five years and beyond.* London: Multiple Births Foundation.

Bryan, J., & Freed, F. (1982). Corporal punishment: Normative data and sociological and psychological correlates in a community college population. *Journal of Youth and Adolescence, 11*(2), 77–87.

Bryant, R. A., & McConkey, K. M. (1989). Hypnotic blindness: A behavioral and experimental analysis. *Journal of Abnormal Psychology, 98*, 71–77.

Brzustowicz, L. M., Simone, J., Mohseni, P., Hayter, J. E., Hodgkinson, K. A., Chow, E. W., & Bassett, A. S. (2004). Linkage disequilibrium mapping of schizophrenia susceptibility to the CAPON region of chromosome 1q22. *American Journal of Human Genetics, 74*(5), 1057–1063.

Buccino, G., Binkofski, F., & Riggio, L. (2004). The mirror neuron system and action recognition. *Brain and Language, 89*(2), 370–376.

Buccino, G., Binkofski, F., Fink, G. R., Fadiga, L., Fogassi, L., Gallese, V., et al. (2001). Action observation activates premotor and parietal areas in a somatotopic manner: An fMRI study. *European Journal of Neuroscience, 13*(2), 400–404.

Bucher, B. D., & Lovaas, O. I. (1967). Use of aversive stimulation in behavior modification. In M. R. Jones (Ed.), *Miami Symposium on the Prediction of Behavior 1967: Aversive Stimulation*, 77–145. Coral Gables: University of Miami Press.

Buck, R. (1980). Nonverbal behavior and the theory of emotion: The facial feedback hypothesis. *Journal of Personality and Social Psychology, 38*, 811–824.

Bullock, T. H., Bennett, M. V., Johnston, D., Josephson, R., Marder, E., & Fields, R. D. (2005). Neuroscience. The neuron doctrine, redux. *Science, 310*(5749), 791–793.

Bunge, M. (1984). What is pseudoscience? *The Skeptical Inquirer, 9*(1), 36–46.

Bunge, M. B., & Pearse, D. D. (2003). Transplantation strategies to promote repair of the injured spinal cord. *Journal of Rehabilitative Research and Development, 40*(4), 55–62.

Bureau of Labor Statistics. (2010). *Census of fatal occupational injuries.* Retrieved August 9, 2010, from http://www.bls.gov/iif/oshcfoi1.htm

Burger, J. J. M. (1997). The psychoanalytic approach: Neo-Freudian theory, application, and assessment. *Personality* (4th ed.). Pacific Grove, CA: Brooks/Cole.

Burger, J. M. (2009). Replicating Milgram: Would people still obey today? *American Psychologist, 64*, 1–11.

Burger, J. M., & Petty, R. E. (1981). The low-ball compliance technique: Task or person commitment? *Journal of Personality and Social Psychology, 40*, 492–500.

Burger, J. M., Sanchez, J. Imberi, J. E., & Grande, L. R. (2009). The norm of reciprocity as an internalized social norm: Returning favors even when no one finds out. *Social Influence, 4*(1), 11–17.

Burgio, K. L. (1998). Behavioral vs. drug treatment for urge urinary incontinence in older women: A randomized controlled trial. *Journal of the American Medical Association, 280*, 1995–2000.

Burke, D. M., MacKay, D. G., Worthley, J. S., & Wade, E. (1991). On the tip of the tongue: What causes word finding failures in young and older adults. *Journal of Memory and Language, 30*, 542–579.

Burks, N., & Martin, B. (1985). Everyday problems and life change events: Ongoing versus acute sources of stress. *Journal of Human Stress, 11,* 27–35.

Burns, J. F. (May 24, 2010). British medical council bars doctor who linked vaccine with autism. *New York Times.*

Bush, G., Frazier, J. A., Rauch, S. L., Seidman, L. J., Whalen, P. J., Jenike, M. A., et al. (1999). Anterior cingulate cortex dysfunction in Attention-Deficit/Hyperactivity Disorder revealed by fMRI and the Counting Stroop. *Biological Psychiatry, 45*(12), 1542–1552.

Bush, G., Spencer, T. J., Holmes, J., Shin, L. M., Valera, E. M., Seidman, L. J., et al. (2008). Functional magnetic resonance imaging of methylphenidate and placebo in Attention-Deficit/Hyperactivity Disorder during the Multi-Source Interference Task. *Archives of General Psychiatry, 65*(1), 102–114.

Bushman, B. J. (1997). Effects of alcohol on human aggression: Validity of proposed explanations. In M. Galanter (Ed.), Recent developments in alcoholism. Vol. 1: Alcohol and violence—Epidemiology, neurobiology, psychology, family issues (pp. 227–243). New York: Plenum Press.

Bushman, B. J., & Huesmann, L. R. (2001). Effects of televised violence on aggression. In D. G. Singer & J. L. Singer (Eds.), *Handbook of children and the media* (Ch. 11, pp. 223–254). Thousand Oaks, CA: Sage.

Buss, D. M., Larsen, R. J., Westen, D., & Semmelroth, J. (1992). Sex differences in jealousy: Evolution, physiology, and psychology. *Psychological Science, 3,* 251–255.

Bussa, B., & Kaufman, C. (2000). What can self-help do? *The Journal of the California Alliance of the Mentally Ill, 2*(2), 34–45.

Butcher, J. N., & Rouse, S. V. (1996). Personality: Individual differences and clinical assessment. *Annual Review of Psychology, 47,* 87–111.

Butcher, J. N., Graham, J. R., Ben-Poarth, Y. S., Tellegen, A., Dahlstrom, W. G., & Kaemmer, B. (2001). *Minnesota Multiphasic Personality Inventory-2. Manual for administration, scoring, and interpretation* (Rev. ed.). Minneapolis: University of Minnesota Press.

Butcher, J. N., Rouse, S. V., & Perry, J. N. (2000). Empirical description of psychopathology in therapy clients: Correlates of MMPI-2 scales. In J. N. Butcher (Ed.), *Basic sources on the MMPI-2* (pp. 487–500). Minneapolis: University of Minnesota Press.

Cabeza, R., & Nyberg, L. (2000). Imaging cognition II: An empirical review of 275 PET and fMRI studies. *Journal of Cognitive Neuroscience, 12*(1), 1–47.

Cabeza, R., Anderson, N. D., Locantore, J. K. & McIntosh, A. R. (2002). Aging gracefully: Compensatory brain activity in high-performing older adults. *NeuroImage, 17*(3), 1394–1402.

Cain, D., & Seeman, J. (Eds.). (2001). *Humanistic psychotherapies: Handbook of research and practice.* Washington, DC: APA Publications.

Cajal, S. Ramón y (1995). Histology of the nervous system of man and vertebrates (translated from the French by Neely Swanson and Larry W. Swanson). New York, NY: Oxford University Press.

Calon, F., Julien, C., Tremblay, C., Phivilay, A., Berthiaume, L., & Julien, P. (2008). Evidencing dietary risk factors of Alzheimer's disease in 3XTg-AD mice: The role of trans and omega-3 fatty acids. *Alzheimer's and Dementia, 4*(4), T158–T159.

Calvo, E. Haverstick, K. & Sass, S. A. (2009). Gradual retirement, sense of control, and retirees' happiness. *Research on Aging, 31,* 112–135.

Camara, W. J., Nathan, J. S., & Puente, A. E. (2000). Psychological test usage: Implications in professional psychology. *Professional Psychology: Research and Practice, 31*(2), 141–154.

Camchong, J., Lim, K. O., Sponheim, S. R., & Macdonald, A. W. (2009). Frontal white matter integrity as an endophenotype for schizophrenia: Diffusion tensor imaging in monozygotic twins and patients' nonpsychotic relatives. *Frontiers in Human Neuroscience, 3,* 35.

Cameron, J., Banko, K. M., & Pierce, W. D. (2001). Pervasive negative effects of rewards on intrinsic motivation: The myth continues. *The Behavior Analyst, 24,* 1–44.

Cameron, J. R., Hansen, R., & Rosen, D. (1989). Preventing behavioral problems in infancy through temperament assessment and parental support programs. In W. B. Carey & S. C. McDevitt (Eds.), *Clinical and educational applications of temperament research* (pp. 155–165). Amsterdam: Swets & Zeitlinger.

Cami, J., Farre, M., Mas, M., Roset, P. N., Poudevida, S., Mas, A., San, L., & de la Torre, R. (2000). Human pharmacology of 3,4-methylenedioxymethamphetamine ("ecstasy"): Psychomotor performance and subjective effects. *Journal of Clinical Psychopharmacology, 20,* 455–466.

Campbell, J. C., & Wolf, A. D. (2003). Risk factors for femicide in abusive relationships: Results from a multisite case control study. *American Journal of Public Health, 93*(7).

Cannon, W. B. (1927). The James-Lange theory of emotion: A critical examination and an alternative theory. *American Journal of Psychology, 39,* 10–124.

Cannon, W. B., & Washburn, A. L. (1912). An explanation of hunger. *American Journal of Physiology, 29,* 444–454.

Cardno, A. G., & Gottesman, II. (2000). Twin studies of schizophrenia: From bow-and-arrow concordances to star wars Mx and functional genomics. *American Journal of Medical Genetics, 97*(1), 12–17.

Carducci, B. (1998). *The psychology of personality.* Pacific Grove, CA: Brooks/Cole Publishing Co.

Carey, B. (2009, December 21). Building a search engine of the brain, slice by slice. *New York Times.* Retrieved June 10, 2010, from http://www.nytimes.com/2009/12/22/health/22brain.html?ref=henry_gustav_molaison

Carlson, G. A., Jensen, P. S., & Nottelmann, E. D. (Eds.). (1998). Current issues in childhood bipolarity [Special issue]. *Journal of Affective Disorders, 51.*

Carnot, M. J., Dunn, B., Cañas, A. J., Gram, P., & Mudloon, J. (2001). Concept maps vs. Web pages for information searching and browsing. Retrieved from the Internet on May 28, 2008, at http://www.ihmc.us/users/acanas/publications/CMapsVSWebPagesExp1/CMapsVSWebPagesExp1.htm

Carpenter, P. A., Just, M. A., & Shell, P. (1990). What one intelligence test measures: A theoretical account of the processing in the Raven Progressive Matrices test. *Psychological Review, 97*(3), 404–431.

Carr, E. G., & Lovaas, O. I. (1983). Contingent electric shock as a treatment for severe behavior problems. In S. Axelrod & J. Apsche (Eds.), *The effects of punishment on human behavior* (pp. 221–245). New York: Academic Press.

Carrion, V. G., Weems, C. F., & Reiss, A. L. (2007). Stress predicts brain changes in children: A pilot longitudinal study on youth stress, posttraumatic stress disorder, and the hippocampus. *Pediatrics, 119*(3), 509–516.

Carruthers, M. (2001). A multifactorial approach to understanding andropause. *Journal of Sexual and Reproductive Medicine, 1,* 69–74.

Carskadon, M. A., & Dement, W. C. (2005). Normal human sleep overview. In M. H. Kryger, T. Roth, & W. C. Dement (Eds.), *Principles and practice of sleep medicine* (4th ed., pp. 13–23). Philadelphia: Elsevier/Saunders.

Carson, R. C. (1969). *Interaction concepts of personality.* Chicago: Aldine.

Carter, C., Bishop, J., & Kravits, S. L. (2006). Keys to success: Building successful intelligence for college, career, and life (5th ed.). Englewood Cliffs, NJ: Prentice Hall.

Carter, C., Bishop, J., Kravits, S. L., & D'Agostino, J. V. (Ed. consultant). (2002). *Keys to college studying: Becoming a lifelong learner.* Upper Saddle River, NJ: Prentice Hall.

Carver, C. S., & Antoni, M. H. (2004). Finding benefit in breast cancer during the year after diagnosis predicts better adjustment 5 to 8 years after diagnosis. *Health Psychology, 26,* 595–598.

Cassidy, A., Bingham, S., & Setchell, K. D. R. (1994). Biological effects of a diet of soy protein rich in isoflavones on the menstrual cycle of premenopausal women. *American Journal of Clinical Nutrition, 60,* 333–340.

Castillo, R. J. (1997). Eating disorders. In R. J. Castillo (Ed.), *Culture and mental illness: A client-centered approach* (p. 152). Pacific Grove, CA: Brooks/Cole.

Catanzaro, S. J., Wasch, H. H., Kirsch, I., & Mearns, J. (2000). Coping-related expectancies and dispositions as prospective predictors of coping responses and symptoms: Distinguishing mood regulation expectancies, dispositional coping, and optimism. *Journal of Personality, 68,* 757–788.

Cattell, R. B. (1950). *Personality: A systematic, theoretical, and factual study.* New York: McGraw-Hill.

Cattell, R. B. (Ed.). (1966). *Handbook of multivariate experimental psychology.* Chicago: Rand McNally.

Cattell, R. B. (1973). *Personality and mood by questionnaire.* San Francisco: Jossey-Bass.

Cattell, R. B. (1990). Advances in Cattellian personality theory. In L. A. Pervin (Ed.), *Handbook of personality: Theory and research* (pp. 101–110). New York: Guilford Press.

Cattell, R. B. (1994). *Sixteen Personality Factor Questionnaire* (5th ed.). Champaign, IL: Institute for Personality and Ability Testing.

Cattell, R. B. (1995). Personality structure and the new fifth edition of the 16PF. *Educational and Psychological Measurement, 55*(6), 926–937.

Cattell, R. B., & Kline, P. (1977). *The scientific analysis of personality and motivation.* New York: Academic Press.

Cave, K. R., & Kim, M. (1999). Top-down and bottom-up attentional control: On the nature of interference from a salient distractor. *Perception and Psychophysics, 61,* 1009–1023.

Centers for Disease Control and Prevention (CDC). (2008). Annual smoking-attributable mortality, years of potential life lost, and economic costs—United States, 2000–2004. *Morbidity and Mortality Weekly Report, 57*(45), 1226–1228.

Centers for Disease Control and Prevention. (2008, October 3). Morbidity and Mortality Weekly Report. HIV Prevalence Estimates—United States, 2006 Centers for Disease Control and Prevention. Atlanta, GA: U.S. Centers for Disease Control and Prevention.

Centers for Disease Control and Prevention. (2009a). HIV/AIDS Surveillance Report 2007 (Vol. 19). National Center for Chronic Disease Prevention and Health Promotion. Atlanta, Georgia.

Centerwall, B. S. (1989). Exposure to television as a risk factor for violence. *American Journal of Epidemiology, 129,* 643–652.

Cepeda, N. J., Pashler, H., Vul, E., Wixted, J. T., & Rohrer, D. (2006). Distributed practice in verbal recall tasks: A review and quantitative synthesis. *Psychological Bulletin, 132,* 354–380.

Cermak, L., & Craik, F. (1979). *Levels of processing in human memory.* Hillsdale, NJ: Erlbaum.

Cha, J. H., & Nam, K. D. (1985). A test of Kelley's cube theory of attribution: A cross-cultural replication of McArthur's study. *Korean Social Science Journal, 12,* 151–180.

Chaddock, L., Hillman, C. H., Buck, S. M., & Cohen, N. J. (in press). Aerobic fitness and executive control of relational memory in preadolescent children. *Medicine and Science in Sports and Exercise.*

Chandola, T., Britton, A., Brunner, E., Hemingway, H., Malik, M., Kumari, M., Badrick, E., Kivimaki, M., & Marmot, M. (2008). Work stress and coronary heart disease: What are the mechanisms? *European Heart Journal.,* doi:10.1093/eurheartj/ehm584

Chang, P. P., Ford, D. E., Meoni, L. A., Wang, N., & Klag, M. J. (2002). Anger in young men and subsequent premature cardiovascular disease: The precursors study. *Archives of Internal Medicine, 162,* 901–906.

Charlesworth, W. R., & Kreutzer, M. A. (1973). Facial expression of infants and children. In P. Ekman (Ed.), *Darwin and facial expression: A century of research in review.* New York: Academic.

Chen, J. Y. (2007). Do Chinese and English speakers think about time differently? Failure of replicating Boroditsky (2001). *Cognition, 104*(2), 427–436.

Chen, L. Y., Rex, C. S., Sanaiha, Y., Lynch, G., & Gall, C. M. (2010). Learning induces neurotrophin signaling at hippocampal synapses. *Proceedings of the National Academy of Sciences, USA 107*(15), 7030–7035.

Chen, R., & Ende, N. (2000). The potential for the use of mononuclear cells from human umbilical cord blood in the treatment of amyotrophic lateral sclerosis in SOD1 mice. *Journal of Medicine, 31,* 21–31.

Cheng, H., Cao, Y., & Olson, L. (1996). Spinal cord repair in adult paraplegic rats: Partial restoration of hind limb function. *Science, 273,* 510–513.

Cherry, E. C. (1953). Some experiments on the recognition of speech, with one and with two ears. *Journal of the Acoustical Society of America, 25*(5), 975–979.

Cheryan, S., Plaut, V., Davis, P., & Steele, C. (2009). Ambient belonging: How stereotypical cues impact gender participation in computer science. *Journal of Personality and Social Psychology, 97*(6), 1045–1060.

Chess, S., & Thomas, A. (1986). *Temperament in clinical practice.* New York: Guilford Press.

Chesterton, L. S., Barlas, P., Foster, N. E., Baxter, G. D., & Wright, C. C. (2003). Gender differences in pressure pain threshold in healthy humans. *Pain, 101,* 259–266.

Chidester, D. (2003). *Salvation and suicide: Jim Jones, the Peoples Temple, and Jonestown* (Rev. ed., pp. 1–51). Bloomington: Indiana University Press.

Chinn, A.B. & Trujillo, K.A. (1996). Drugs and the brain: A World Wide Web tutorial in neuropsychopharmacology. *Society for Neuroscience Abstracts, 22,* 246.

Chiu, C., Hong, Y., & Dweck, C. S. (1997). Lay dispositionism and implicit theories of personality. *Journal of Personality and Social Psychology, 73,* 19–30.

Choi, I., & Nisbett, R. E. (1998). Situational salience and cultural differences in the correspondence bias and in the actor–observer bias. *Personality and Social Psychology Bulletin, 24,* 949–960.

Choi, I., Nisbett, R. E., & Norenzayan, A. (1999). Causal attribution across cultures: Variation and universality. *Psychological Bulletin, 125,* 47–63.

Chomsky, N. (1957). *Syntactic structures.* The Hague: Mouton.

Chomsky, N. (1964). *Current issues in linguistic theory.* The Hague: Mouton.

Chomsky, N. (1981). Principles and parameters in syntactic theory. In N. Hornstein & D. Lightfoot (Eds.), *Explanation in linguistics: The logical problem of language acquisition.* London: Longman.

Chomsky, N. (1986). *Knowledge of language: Its nature, origin and use.* New York: Praeger.

Chomsky, N. (2006). *Language and mind* (3rd ed.). New York: Cambridge University Press.

Chomsky, N., Belletti, A., & Rizzi, L. (2002). *On nature and language.* New York: Cambridge University Press.

Chou, S. Y., Grossman, M., & Saffer, H. (2004). An economic analysis of adult obesity: Results from the behavioral risk factor surveillance system. *Journal of Health Economics, 23,* 565–587.

Christensen, A., Jacobson, N. S., & Babcock, J. C. (1995). Integrative behavioral couple therapy. In N. S. Jacobson & A. S. Gurman (Eds.), *Clinical handbook of couple therapy* (pp. 31–64). New York: Norton.

Christmas, D., Morrison, C., Eljamel, M. S., & Matthews, K. (2004). Neurosurgery for mental disorders. *Advances in Psychiatric Treatment,10,* 189-199.

Chwalisz, K., Diener, E., & Gallagher, D. (1988). Autonomic arousal feedback and emotional experience: Evidence from the spinal cord injured. *Journal of Personality and Social Psychology, 54,* 820–828.

Cialdini, R., Vincent, J., Lewis, S., Catalan, J., Wheeler, D., & Darby, B. (1975). Reciprocal concessions procedure for inducing compliance: The door–in–the–face technique. *Journal of Personality and Social Psychology, 31,* 206–215.

Cialdini, R., Wosinska, W., Barrett, D., Butner, J., & Gornik–Durose, M. (1999). Compliance with a request in two cultures: The differential influence of social proof and commitment/consistency on collectivists and individualists. *Personality and Social Psychology Bulletin, 25,* 1242–1253.

Cialdini, R. B., Trost, M. R., & Newsom, J. T. (1995). Preference for consistency: The development of a valid measure and the discovery of surprising behavioral implications. *Journal of Personality and Social Psychology, 69,* 318–328.

Ciardiello, A. V. (1998). Did you ask a good question today? Alternative cognitive and metacognitive strategies. *Journal of Adolescent and Adult Literacy, 42,* 210–219.

Cinnirella, M., & Green, B. (2007). Does "cyber-conformity" vary cross-culturally? Exploring the effect of culture and communication medium on social conformity. *Computers in Human Behavior, 23*(4), 2011–2025.

Clancy, S. A., McNally, R. J., Schacter, D. L., Lenzenweger, M. F., & Pitman, R. K. (2002). Memory distortion in people reporting abduction by aliens. *Journal of Abnormal Psychology, 111*(3), 455–461.

Clark, A. (1991). *Microcognition: Philosophy, cognitive science, and parallel distributed processing.* Cambridge, MA: MIT Press, reprint edition (1989).

Clark, D. A., Beck, A. T., & Brown, G. (1989). Cognitive mediation in general psychiatric outpatients: A test of the content-specificity hypothesis. *Journal of Personality and Social Psychology, 56,* 958–964.

Clark, D. A., Hollifield, M., Leahy, R. L., & Beck, J. S. (2009). Theory of cognitive therapy. In G. Gabbard, J. S. Beck, and J. Wright (Eds.), *Textbook of psycho-*

therapeutic treatments in psychiatry, pp. 165-200. Washington, DC: American Psychiatric Press.

Clarke, A. R., Barry, R. J., McCarthy, R., Selikowitz, M., Johnstone, S. J., Hsu, C. I., et al. (2007). Coherence in children with Attention-Deficit/Hyperactivity Disorder and excess beta activity in their EEG. *Clinical Neurophysiology, 118*(7), 1472–1479.

Clarke, J. (1994). Pieces of the puzzle: The jigsaw method. In S. Sharan (Ed.), *Handbook of cooperative learning methods* (pp. 34–50). Westport, CT: Greenwood Press.

Clarkin, J. F., Levy, K. N., Lenzenweger, M. F., & Kernberg, O. F. (2007). Evaluating three treatments for borderline personality disorder: A multiwave study. *American Journal of Psychiatry, 164*(6), 922–928.

Coates, J. (1986). *Women, men, and language.* New York: Longman.

Coccaro, E. F., & Kavoussi, R. J. (1996). Neurotransmitter correlates of impulsive aggression. In D. M. Stoff & R. B. Cairns (Eds.), *Aggression and violence* (pp. 67–86). Mahwah, NJ: Erlbaum.

Coffield, F., Moseley, D., Hall, E., & Ecclestone, K. (2004). Should we be using learning styles? What research has to say about practice. *Learning and Skills Research Centre.* www.WSRD.ac.uk

Coffield, F., Moseley, D., Hall, E., Ecclestone, K. (2004). *Learning styles and pedagogy in post-16 learning. A systematic and critical review.* London: Learning and Skills Research Centre.

Cohen, L. J. (1997). Rational drug use in the treatment of depression. *Pharmacotherapy, 17,* 45–61.

Cohen, N. J., Eichenbaum, R., Decedo, J. C., & Corkin, S. (1985). Preserved learning capacity in amnesia: Evidence for multiple memory systems. In L. S. Squire & N. Butters (Eds.), *Neuropsychology of memory.* New York: Guilford Press.

Cohen, S., & Herbert, T. B. (1996). Health psychology: Psychological factors and physical disease from the perspective of human psychoneuroimmunology. *Annual Review of Psychology, 47,* 113–142.

Cohen, S., Frank, E., Doyle, B. J., Skoner, D. P., Rabin, B. S., & Gwaltney, J. M. (1998). Types of stressors that increase susceptibility to the common cold. *Health Psychology, 17,* 214–223.

Cohen, S., Janicki-Deverts, D., & Miller, G. E. (2007). Psychological stress and disease. *Journal of the American Medical Association, 298*(14), 1685–1687.

Coker, T., Austin, S., & Schuster, M. (2009). The health and health care of lesbian, gay, and bisexual adolescents. *Annual Review of Public Health, 31,* 457–477.

Colcombe, S. J., Erickson, K. I., Raz, N., Webb, A. G., Cohen, N. J., McAuley, E., & Kramer, A. F. (2003). Aerobic fitness reduces brain tissue loss in aging humans. *Journal of Gerontology Series A: Biological Sciences and Medical Sciences, 58,* 176–180.

Colligan, J. (1983). Musical creativity and social rules in four cultures. *Creative Child and Adult Quarterly, 8,* 39–44.

Collins, A. M., & Loftus, E. F. (1975). A spreading activation theory of semantic processing. *Psychological Review, 82,* 407–428.

Collins, A. M., & Quillian, M. R. (1969). Retrieval time from semantic memory. *Journal of Verbal Learning and Verbal Behaviour, 8,* 240–247.

Collins, C. J., Hanges, P. J., & Locke, E. A. (2004). The relationship of achievement motivation to entrepreneurial behavior: A meta-analysis. *Human Performance, 17*(1), 95–117.

Colom, R., Shih, P. C., Flores-Mendoza, C., & Quiroga, M. A. (2006). The real relationship between short-term memory and working memory. *Memory, 14*(7), 804–813.

Committee on Animal Research and Ethics. (2004). *Research with animals in psychology.* Retrieved October 12, 2004, from www.apa.org/science/animal2.html

Conrad, R., & Hull, A. J. (1964). Information, acoustic confusion, and memory span. *British Journal of Psychology, 55,* 429–432.

Consumer Reports. (1995, November). Mental health: Does psychotherapy help? 734–739.

Conway, M. A., Cohen, G., & Stanhope, N. (1992). Very long-term memory for knowledge acquired at school and university. *Applied Cognitive Psychology, 6,* 467–482.

Coolidge, F. L. (2006). *Dream interpretation as a psychotherapeutic technique.* London: Radcliffe.

Cooper, L. A., Gonzales, J. J., Gallo, J. J., Rost, K. M., Meredith, L. S., Rubenstein, L. V., Wang, N. Y., & Ford, D. E. (2003). The acceptability of treatment for depression among African-American, Hispanic, and White primary care patients. *Medical Care, 41*(4), 479–489.

Corbetta, M., Kincade, M. J., Lewis, C., Snyder, A. Z., & Sapir, A. (2005). Neural basis and recovery of spatial attention deficits in spatial neglect. *Nature Neuroscience, 8,* 1603–1610.

Cosgrove, G. R., & Rauch, S. L. (1995). Psychosurgery. *Neurosurgery Clinics of North America, 6,* 167–176.

Cosgrove, K. P., Mazure, C. M., & Staley, J. K. (2007). Evolving knowledge of sex differences in brain structure, function, and chemistry. *Biological Psychiatry, 62*(8), 847–855.

Costa, P. T., Jr., & McCrae, R. R. (2000). The Revised NEO Personality Inventory (NEO PI-R). In J. Cheek & E. M. Donahue (Eds.), *Handbook of personality inventories.* New York: Plenum.

Costello, D. M., Swendsen, J., Rose, J. S., & Dierker, L. C. (2008). Risk and protective factors associated with trajectories of depressed mood from adolescence to early adulthood. *Journal of Consulting and Clinical Psychology, 76*(2), 173–183.

Courage, M. L., & Howe, M. L. (2002). From infant to child: The dynamics of cognitive change in the second year of life. *Psychological Bulletin, 128,* 250–277.

Courneya, K. S., Sellar, C. M., Stevinson, C., McNeely, M. L., Peddle, C. J., Friedenreich, C. M., Tankey, K., Basi, S., Chua, N., Mazurek, A., & Reiman, T. (2009). Randomized controlled trial of the effects of aerobic exercise on physical functioning and quality of life in lymphoma patients. *Journal of Clinical Oncology, 27*(27), 4605–4612.

Cowan, N. (1988). Evolving conceptions of memory storage, selective attention, and their mutual constraints within the human information processing system. *Psychological Bulletin, 104*, 163–191.

Cowan, N. (1995) *Attention and memory: An integrated framework.* Oxford Psychology Series, No. 26. Oxford University Press.

Cowan, N. (2001). The magical number 4 in short-term memory: A reconsideration of mental storage capacity. *Behavioral and Brain Sciences, 24*, 97–185.

Cowan, N., Elliott, E. M., Saults, J. S., Morey, C. C., Mattox, S., Hismjatullina, A., & Conway, A. R. A. (2005). On the capacity of attention: Its estimation and its role in working memory and cognitive aptitudes. *Cognitive Psychology, 51*(1), 42–100.

Craddock, N., O'Donovan, M. C., & Owen, M. J. (2005). The genetics of schizophrenia and bipolar disorder: Dissecting psychosis. *Journal of Medical Genetics, 42*, 288–299.

Crago, M. B., Shisslak, C. M., & Estes, L. S. (1996). Eating disturbances among American minority groups: A review. *International Journal of Eating Disorders, 19*, 239–248.

Craik, F. I. M. (1970). The fate of primary memory items in free recall. *Journal of Verbal Learning and Verbal Behavior, 9*, 143–148.

Craik, F. I. M. (1994). Memory changes in normal aging. *Current Directions in Psychological Science, 3*(5), 155–158.

Craik, F. I. M., & Lockhart, R. S. (1972). Levels of processing. A framework for memory research. *Journal of Verbal Learning and Verbal Behaviour, 11*, 671–684.

Craik, F. I. M., & Tulving, E. (1975). Depth of processing and the retention of words in episodic memory. *Journal of Experimental Psychology: General, 104*, 268–294.

Craske, M. G., & Barlow, D. H. (2008). Panic disorder and agoraphobia. In D. H. Barlow (Ed.), *Clinical handbook of psychological disorders* (pp. 1-64). New York, NY: The Guilford Press.

Crawford, M., & Unger, R. (2004). *Women and gender: A feminist psychology* (4th ed.). Boston: McGraw-Hill.

Crick, F. & Koch, C. (2003). A framework for consciousness. *Nature Neuroscience, 6*, 119–127.

Crick, F., & Koch, C. (1990). Towards a neurobiological theory of consciousness. *Seminars in the Neurosciences, 2*, 263–275.

Critchfield, T. S., Haley, R., Sabo, B., Colbert, J., & Macropoulis, G. (2003). A half century of scalloping in the work habits of the United States Congress. *Journal of Applied Behavior Analysis, 36*(4), 465–486.

Crottaz-Herbette S., & Menon V. (2006). Where and when the anterior cingulate cortex modulates attentional response: combined fMRI and ERP evidence. *Journal of Cognitive Neuroscience, 18*(5), 766-780.

Crowley, A. E., & Hoyer, W. D. (1994). An integrative framework for understanding two-sided persuasion. *Journal of Consumer Research, 20*, 561–574.

Csernansky, J. G., Mahmoud, R., & Brenner, R. (2002). A comparison of reperidone and haloperidol for the prevention of relapse in patients with schizophrenia. *New England Journal of Medicine, 346*, 16–22.

Csikszentmihalyi, M. (1996). *Creativity: Flow and the psychology of discovery and invention.* New York: Harper Perennial.

Csikszentmihalyi, M. (1997). *Finding flow: The psychology of engagement with everyday life.* New York: Basic Books.

Culbertson, F. (2003). *The phobia list.* Retrieved June 22, 2004, from www.phobialist.com

Cummings, J. L., & Coffey C. E. (1994). Neurobiological basis of behavior. In C. E. Coffey & J. L. Cummings (Eds.), *Textbook of geriatric neuropsychiatry* (pp. 72–96). Washington, DC: American Psychiatric Press.

Cummings, S. R., & Melton, L. J., III. (2002). Epidemiology and outcomes of osteoporotic fractures. *Lancet, 359*(9319), 1761–1767.

Curtis, R. C., & Miller, K. (1986). Believing another likes or dislikes you: Behaviors making the beliefs come true. *Journal of Personality and Social Psychology, 51*, 284–290.

Curtis, R. H. (1993). *Great lives: Medicine.* New York: Charles Scribner's Sons Books for Young Readers.

Cytowic, R. E. (1989). Synesthesia and mapping of subjective sensory dimensions. *Neurology, 39*, 849–850.

Dabbs, J. M., Jr., Bernieri, F. J., Strong, R. K., Campo, R., & Milun, R. (2001). Going on stage: Testosterone in greetings and meetings. *Journal of Research in Personality, 35*, 27–40.

Dalenberg, C. J. (1996). Accuracy, timing and circumstances of disclosure in therapy of recovered and continuous memories of abuse. *The Journal of Psychiatry and Law, 24*(2), 229–275.

Daly, M., Wilson, M., & Weghorst, S. J. (1982). Male sexual jealousy. *Ethology and Sociobiology, 3*, 11–27.

Damasio, H., Grabowski, T., Frank, R., Galaburda, A. M., & Damasion, A. R. (1994). The return of Phineas Gage: Clues about the brain from the skull of a famous patient. *Science, 264*, 1102–1105.

Dani, J., Burrill, C., & Demmig-Adams, B. (2005). The remarkable role of nutrition in learning and behavior. *Nutrition and Food Science, 35*(4), 258–263.

Darley, J. M., & Latané, B. (1968). Bystander intervention in emergencies: Diffusion of responsibility. *Journal of Personality and Social Psychology, 8*, 377–383.

Darwin, C. (1859). *The origin of species by means of natural selection.* London: John Murray.

Darwin, C. (1898). *The expression of the emotions in man and animals.* New York: D. Appleton.

Daum, I., & Schugens, M. M. (1996). On the cerebellum and classical conditioning. *Current Directions in Psychological Science, 5*, 58–61.

Davidson, R. J. (2003). Affective neuroscience and psychophysiology: Toward a synthesis. *Psychophysiology, 40*(5), 655–665.

Davidson, R. J., Putman, K. M., & Larson, C. L. (2000). Dysfunction in the neural circuitry of emotion regulation—A possible prelude to violence. *Science, 289*, 591–594.

Davies, I. R. L., Laws, G., Corbett, G. G., & Jerrett, D. J. (1998a). Cross-cultural differences in colour vision: Acquired "colour blindness" in Africa. *Personality and Individual Differences, 25*, 1153–1162.

Davies, I. R. L., Sowden, P., Jerrett, D. T., Jerrett, T., & Corbett, G. G. (1998b). A cross-cultural study of English and Setswana speakers on a colour triads task: A test of the Sapir-Whorf hypothesis. *British Journal of Psychology, 89*, 1–15.

Davis, C. J., Harding, J. W., & Wright, J. W. (2003). REM sleep deprivation induced deficits in the latency-to-peak induction and maintenance of longterm potentiation within the CA1 region of hippocampus. *Brain Research, 973*, 293–297.

Davis, H. A., DiStefano, C., & Schutz, P. A. (2008). Identifying patterns of appraising tests in first-year college students: Implications for anxiety and emotion regulation during test taking. [doi: 10.1037/a0013096]. *Journal of Educational Psychology, 100*(4), 942–960.

Davis, K. D., Hutchison, W. D., Lozano, A. M., Tasker, R. R., & Dostrovsky, J. O. (2000). Human anterior cingulate cortex neurons modulated by attention-demanding tasks. *Journal of Neurophysiology, 83*(6), 2575–2577.

Davis, K. F., Parker, K. P., & Montgomery, G. (2004). Sleep in infants and young children: Part 1: Normal sleep. *Journal of Pediatric Healthcare, 18*(2), 65–71.

Davis, K. L., Kahn, R. S., Ko, G., & Davidson, M. (1991). Dopamine in schizophrenia: A review and reconceptualization. *American Journal of Psychiatry, 148*, 1474–1486.

Davis, M., & Whalen, P. J. (2001). The amygdala: Vigilance and emotion. *Molecular Psychiatry, 6*, 13–34.

Dawood, K., Pillard, R. C., Horvath, C., Revelle, W., & Bailey, J. M. (2000). Familial aspects of male homosexuality. *Archives of Sexual Behavior, 29*(2).

De Valois, R. L., & De Valois, K. K. (1993). A multi-stage color model. *Vision Research, 33*(8), 1053–1065.

De Valois, R. L., & Jacobs, G. H. (1968). Primate color vision, *Science, 162*, 553–540.

Dębiec, J., Díaz-Mataix, L., Bush, D. E. A., Doyère, V., & LeDoux, J. E. (2010). The amygdala encodes specific sensory features of an aversive reinforcer. *Nature Neuroscience, 13*, 536–537.

Dean, G., & Kelly, I. W. (2000). Does astrology work? Astrology and skepticism 1975–2000. In P. Kurtz (Ed.), *Skepticism: A 25 Year Retrospective* (pp. 191–207). Amherst, NY: Prometheus Books.

DeAngelis, T. (2002). Promising treatments for anorexia and bulimia: Research boosts support for tough-to-treat eating disorders. *APA Monitor on Psychology, 33*(3), 38–43.

DeCasper, A. J., & Fifer, W. P. (1980). Of human bonding: Newborns prefer their mothers' voices. *Science, 208*, 1174–1176.

DeCasper, A. J., & Spence, M. J. (1986). Prenatal maternal speech influence on newborns' perception of sounds. *Infant Behaviour and Development, 9*, 133–150.

deCharms, R. (1968). *Personal causation.* New York: Academic Press.

Deci, E. L., & Ryan, R. M. (1985). *Intrinsic motivation and self-determination in human behavior.* New York: Plenum.

Deci, E. L., Eghrari, H., Patrick, B. C., & Leone, D. R. (1994). Facilitating internalization: The self-determination theory perspective. *Journal of Personality, 62*, 119–142.

Deci, E. L., Koestner, R., & Ryan, R. M. (1999). A meta-analytic review of experiments examining the effects of extrinsic rewards on intrinsic motivation. *Psychological Bulletin, 125*, 627–668.

DeCoster, J., & Claypool, H. M. (2004). A meta-analysis of priming effects on impression formation supporting a general model of informational biases. *Personality and Social Psychology Review, 8*(1), 2–27.

DeGrandpre, R. J. (2000). A science of meaning: Can behaviorism bring meaning to psychological science? *American Psychologist, 55*, 721–739.

Deinzer, R., Kleineidam, C. H., Winkler, R., Idel, H., & Bachg, D. (2000). Prolonged reduction of salivary immunoglobulin A (slgA) after a major academic exam. *International Journal of Psychophysiology, 37*, 219–232.

Delagrange, P., & Guardiola-Lemaitre, B. (1997). Melatonin, its receptors, and relationships with biological rhythm disorders. *Clinincal Neuropharmacology, 20*, 482–510.

Delaney, A. J., Crane, J. W., & Sah, P. (2007). Noradrenaline modulates transmission at a central synapse by a presynaptic mechanism. *Neuron, 56*(6), 880–892.

Delfiner, R. (2001, November 16). "Kitty Left at Death's Door." *New York Post.*

DeLongis, A., Lazarus, R. S., & Folkman, S. (1988). The impact of daily stress on health and mood: Psychological and social resources as mediators. *Journal of Personality and Social Psychology, 54*(3), 486–495.

Dement, W. C. (1960). The effect of dream deprivation. *Science, 131*, 1705–1707.

Dement, W. C. (1974). *Some must watch while some must sleep.* New York: W. H. Freeman.

Dement, W. C., Henry, P., Cohen, H., & Ferguson, J. (1969). Studies on the effect of REM deprivation in humans and animals. In K. H. Pribram (Ed.), *Mood, states, and mind.* Baltimore: Penguin.

Demers, R. A. (1988). Linguistics and animal communication. In F. J. Newmeyer (Ed.), *Language form and language function* (pp. 314–335). Cambridge, MA: MIT Press.

Dempster, F. N., & Farris, R. (1990). The spacing effect: Research and practice. *Journal of Research and Development in Education 23*(2), 97–101.

Dennett, D. C. (1991). *Consciousness explained.* New York: Little, Brown.

Denno, D. W. (2002). Crime and consciousness: Science and involuntary acts. *Minnesota Law Review, 87,* 269–399.

Department of Health. (2007). Total deaths and leading cause of death by age group. *2007 Data Book.* Retrieved from the Internet on December 3, 2008 at http://www.ofm.wa.gov/databook/human/st10.asp

Deregowski, J. B. (1969). Perception of the two-pronged trident by two- and three-dimensional perceivers. *Journal of Experimental Psychology, 82,* 9–13.

DeRubeis, R. J., Gelfand, L. A., Tang, T. Z., & Simons, A. D. (1999). Medications versus cognitive behavior therapy for severely depressed outpatients: Mega-analysis of four randomized comparisons. *American Journal of Psychiatry, 156*(7), 1007–1013.

Dew, M. A., Whyte, E. M., Lenze, E. J., Houck, P. R., Mulsant, B. H., Pollock, B. G., Stack, J. A., Bensasi, S., & Reynolds, C. F. (2007). Recovery from major depression in older adults receiving augmentation of antidepressant pharmacotherapy. *American Journal of Psychiatry, 164*(6), 892–899.

DeYoung, C. G., Hirsh, J. B., Shane, M. S., Papademetris, X., Rajeevan, N., & Gray, J. R. (2010). Testing predictions from personality neuroscience: Brain structure and the Big Five. *Psychological Science, 21*(6), 820–828.

Diamond, L. M. (2003). What does sexual orientation orient? A biobehavioral model distinguishing romantic love and sexual desire. *Psychological Review, 110,* 173–192.

Diamond, M. (1995). Biological aspects of sexual orientation and identity. In L. Diamant & R. McAnulty (Eds.), *The psychology of sexual orientation, behavior, and identity: A handbook* (pp. 45–80). Westport, CT: Greenwood Press.

Diamond, M., & Sigmundson, H. K. (1997). Sex reassignment at birth. Long-term review and clinical implications. *Archives of Pediatric Adolescent Medicine, 151*(3), 298–304.

Dickens, W. T., & Flynn, J. R. (2001 April). Heritability estimates vs. large environmental effects: The IQ paradox resolved. *Psychological Review, 108*(2), 346–369.

Dickerson, F., Ringel, N., Parente, F., & Boronow, J. (1994). Seclusion and restraint, assaultiveness, and patient performance in a token economy. *Hospital and Community Psychiatry, 45,* 168–170.

Digman, J. M. (1990). Personality structure: Emergence of the five-factor model. *Annual Review of Psychology, 41,* 417–440.

Dillard, J. (1990). Self-inference and the foot-in-the-door technique: Quantity of behavior and attitudinal mediation. *Human Communication Research, 16,* 422–447.

Dillard, J. (1991). The current status of research on sequential–request compliance techniques. *Personality and Social Psychology Bulletin, 17,* 282–288.

Dinges, D. F. (1995). An overview of sleepiness and accidents. *Journal of Sleep Research, 4*(2), 4–14.

Dixon, N. F. (1980). Humor: A cognitive alternative to stress? In I. Sarason and C. D. Spielberger (Eds.), *Stress and Anxiety* (Vol. 7, pp. 281–289). Washington, DC: Hemisphere.

Dodge, K. A., Bates, J. E., & Pettit, G. S. (1990). Mechanisms in the cycle of violence. *Science, 250,* 1678–1683.

Dolcos, F., LaBar, K. S., Cabeza, R. & Purves, D. (2005). Remembering one year later: Role of the amygdala and the medial temporal lobe memory system in retrieving emotional memories. *Proceedings of the National Academy of Sciences, USA.* doi: 10.1073/pnas.0409848102

Dollard, J., & Miller, N. F. (1950). *Personality and psychotherapy.* New York: McGraw-Hill.

Dollard, J., Doob, L. W., Miller, N. E., Mowrer, O. H., & Sears, R. R. (1939). *Frustration and aggression.* New Haven, CT: Yale University Press.

Domagalski, T. A., & Steelman, L. A. (2007). The impact of gender and organizational status on workplace anger expression. *Management Communication Quarterly, 20*(3), 297–315.

Dominey, P. F., & Dodane, C. (2004). Indeterminacy in language acquisition: The role of child-directed speech and joint attention. *Journal of Neurolinguistics, 17*(2–3), 121–145.

Donovan, J. J., & Radosevich, D. R. (1999). A meta-analytic review of the distribution of practice effect: Now you see it, now you don't. *Journal of Applied Psychology, 84,* 795–805.

Dougherty, D. D., Baer, L., Cosgrove, G. R., Cassem, E. H., Price, B. H., Nierenberg, A. A., Jenike, M. A., & Rauch, S. L. (2002). Prospective long-term follow-up of 44 patients who received cingulotomy for treatment-refractory obsessive-compulsive disorder. *The American Journal of Psychiatry, 159*(2), 269–275.

Drenth, P. J., Thierry, H., Willems, P. J., & de Wolff, C. J. (1984). *Handbook of work and organizational psychology.* Chichester, UK: Wiley.

Drever, B. D., Anderson, W. G. L., Johnson, H., O'Callaghan, M., Seo, S., Choi, D-Y., Riedel, G., & Platt, B. (2008). Memantine acts as a cholinergic stimulant in the mouse hippocampus. *The Journal of Alzheimer's Disease, 12*(4), 319-333.

Drigotas, S. M., Rusbult, C. E., Wieselquist, J., & Whitton, S. (1999). Close partner as sculptor of the ideal self: Behavioral affirmation and the Michelangelo phenomenon. *Journal of Personality and Social Psychology, 77,* 293–323.

Drysdale, M. T., Ross, J. L., & Schulz, R. A. (2001). Cognitive learning styles and academic performance in 19 first-year university courses: Successful students versus students at risk. *Journal of Education for Students Placed at Risk, 6,* 271–289.

Duben, A., & Behar, C. (1991). *Istanbul households: Marriage, family and fertility 1880–1940.* Cambridge, NY: Cambridge University Press.

Dubowitz, H., & Bennett, S. (2007). Physical abuse and neglect of children. *Lancet, 369*(9576), 1891–1899.

Dudai, Y. (2004). The neurobiology of consolidations, or, how stable is the engram? *Annual Review of Psychology, 55,* 51–86.

Duker, P. C. & Seys, D. M. (1996). Long-term use of electrical aversion treatment with self-injurious behaviors. *Research in Developmental Disabilities, 17,* 293–301.

Dumont, F. (2010). *A history of personality psychology.* New York, NY: Cambridge University Press.

Duncan, R. M. (1995). Piaget and Vygotsky revisited: Dialogue or assimilation? *Developmental Review, 15,* 458–472.

Dundas, I., Wormnes, B. R., & Hauge, H. (2009). Making exams a manageable task. *Nordic Psychology, 61*(1), 26–41.

Dunn, J. C., Whelton, W. J., & Sharpe, D. (2006). Maladaptive perfectionism, hassles, coping, and psychological distress in university professors. *Journal of Counseling Psychology, 53*(4), 511–523.

Dunn, R., Beaudry, J. S., & Klavas, A. (1989). Survey of research on learning styles. *Educational Leadership, 46*(6), 50–57.

Dunn, R., Della Valle, J., Dunn, K., Geisert, G., Sinatra, R., & Zenhausern, R. (1986). The effects of matching and mismatching students' mobility preferences on recognition and memory tasks. *Journal of Educational Research, 79,* 267–272.

Dunn, R., Denig, S., & Lovelace, M. K. (2001, February 1). Multiple intelligences and learning styles: Two sides of the same coin or different strokes for different folks? *Teacher Librarian.* 28, pp. 9–15.

Dunn, R., Griggs, S. A., Olson, J., Gorman, B., & Beasley, M. (1995). A meta-analytic validation of the Dunn and Dunn model of learning-style preferences. *Journal of Educational Research, 88,* 353–361.

Durrant, M. (Ed.). (1993). *Aristotle's De anima in focus.* London: Routledge.

Durso, F., Rea, C., & Dayton, T. (1994). Graph-theoretic confirmation of restructuring during insight. *Psychological Science, 5,* 94–98.

Dweck, C. (1986). Motivational processes affecting learning. *American Psychologist, 41*(10), 1040–1048.

Dweck, C. S. (1999). *Self-theories: Their role in motivation, personality and development.* Philadelphia: Psychology Press.

Dweck, C. S., & Leggett, E. L. (1988). A social-cognitive approach to motivation and personality. *Psychological Review, 95,* 256–273.

Dweck, C. S., & Molden, D. C. (2008). Self-theories: The construction of free will. In J. Baer, J. C. Kaufman, & R. F. Baumeister (Eds.), *Are we free? Psychology and free will* (pp. 44–64). New York: Oxford University Press.

Dweck, C. S., Chiu, C., & Hong, Y. (1995). Implicit theories and their role in judgments and reactions: A world from two perspectives. *Psychological Inquiry, 6,* 267–285.

Dweck, C., & Elliott, E. (1983). Achievement motivation. In P. Mussen (Ed.), *Handbook of child psychology: Vol. 4. Socialization, personality, and social development* (pp. 643–691). New York: Wiley.

Dykens, E. M., Hodapp, R. M., & Leckman, J. F. (1994). *Behavior and development in fragile X syndrome.* Thousand Oaks, CA: Sage.

Eagleman, D. M. (2001). Visual illusions and neurobiology. *Nature reviews: Neuroscience, 2*(12), 920–926.

Eagly, A., & Crowley, M. (1986). Gender and helping behavior: A meta-analytic review of the social psychological literature. *Psychological Bulletin, 100,* 283–308.

Eagly, A. H. (1987). *Sex difference in social behavior: A social-role interpretation.* Hillsdale, NJ: Erlbaum.

Eagly, A. H., & Carli, L. L. (2007). *Through the labyrinth: The truth about how women become leaders,* pp. 119–136. Boston: Harvard Business School Press.

Eagly, A. H., & Chaiken, S. (1993). *The psychology of attitudes.* Fort Worth, TX: Harcourt Brace.

Eagly, A. H., & Chaiken, S. (1998). Attitude structure and function. In D. T. Gilbert, S. T. Fiske, & G. Lindzey (Eds.), *The handbook of social psychology* (4th ed., pp. 269–322). New York: McGraw-Hill.

Eagly, A. H., Ashmore, R. D., Makhijani, M. G., & Longo, L. C. (1991). What is beautiful is good, but . . . : A meta-analytic review of the physical attractiveness stereotype. *Psychological Bulletin, 110,* 109–128.

Eagly, A. H., Wood, W., & Diekman, A. B. (2000). Social role theory of sex differences and similarities: A current appraisal. In T. Eckes & H. M. Trautner (Eds.), *The developmental social psychology of gender* (pp. 123–174). Mahwah, NJ: Erlbaum.

Eaker, E. D., & Castelli, W. P. (1988). Type A behavior and mortality from coronary disease in the Framingham Study. *New England Journal of Medicine, 319,* 1480–1481.

Eastern Virginia Medical School (2009, May 5). Texting while driving can be deadly, study shows. *ScienceDaily.* Retrieved May 5, 2010, from http://www.sciencedaily.com/releases/2009/05/090504094434.htm

Eaton, W. W., Kessler, R. C., Wittchen, H. U., & Magee, W. J. (1994). Panic and panic disorder in the United States. *American Journal of Psychiatry 151*(3), 413–420.

Ebbinghaus, H. (1885). *Memory: A contribution to experimental psychology.* New York: Dover Publications.

Ebbinghaus, H. (1913). *Memory: A contribution to experimental psychology.* New York: Teachers College Press. (Translated from the 1885 German original.)

Eddy, J., Fitzhugh, E., & Wang, M. (2000). Smoking acquisition: Peer influence and self-selection. *Psychological Reports, 86,* 1241–1246.

Edelmann, R. J., & Iwawaki, S. (1987). Self-reported expression of embarrassment in five European cultures. *Psychologia: An International Journal of Psychology, 30,* 205–216.

Edlund, J. E., Heider, J. D., Scherer, C. R., Farc, M.-M., & Sagarin, B. J. (2006). Sex differences in jealousy in response to actual infidelity. *Evolutionary Psychology, 4,* 462–470.

Ehlers, A., Bisson, J., Clark, D. M., Creamer, M., Pilling, S., Richards, D., Schnurr, P. P., Turner, S., & Yule, W. (2010). Do all psychological treatments really work the same in posttraumatic stress disorder? *Clinical Psychology Review, 30*(2), 269-276.

Eich, E., & Metcalfe, J. (1989). Mood dependent memory for internal vs. external events. *Journal of Experimental Psychology: Learning, Memory and Cognition, 15,* 443–455.

Ekman, P. (1973). Darwin and cross-cultural studies of facial expression. In P. Ekman (Ed.), *Darwin and facial expression: A century of research in review.* New York: Academic Press.

Ekman, P. (1980). Asymmetry in facial expression. *Science, 209,* 833–834.

Ekman, P., & Friesen, W. (1969). The repertoire of nonverbal behavior: Categories, origins, usage, and coding. *Semiotica, 1,* 49–98.

Ekman, P., & Friesen, W. (1971). Constants across cultures in the face and emotion. *Journal of Personality and Social Psychology, 17*(2), 124–129.

Ekman, P., & Friesen, W. V. (1978). *The facial action coding system.* Palo Alto, CA: Consulting Psychologists Press.

Ekman, P., Sorensen, E. R., & Friesen, W. V. (1969). Pan-cultural elements in facial displays of emotion. *Science, 164,* 86–88.

Elkind, D. (1985). Egocentrism redux. *Developmental Review, 5,* 218–226.

Elliott, E., & Dweck, C. (1988). Goals: An approach to motivation and achievement. *Journal of Personality and Social Psychology, 54,* 5–12.

Elliott, L., & Brantley, C. (1997). *Sex on campus: The naked truth about the real sex lives of college students.* New York: Random House.

Ellis, A. (1997). *The practice of rational emotive behavior therapy.* New York: Springer.

Ellis, A. (1998). *The Albert Ellis reader: A guide to well-being using rational emotive behavior therapy.* Secaucus, NJ: Carol Publishing Group.

Ellis, B. J., McFayden-Ketchum, S. A., Dodge, K. A., Pettit, G. S., & Bates, J. E. (1999). Quality of early family relationships and individual differences in the timing of pubertal maturation in girls: A longitudinal test on an evolutionary model. *Journal of Personality and Social Psychology, 77,* 387–401.

Ellis, H. D. (1983). The role of the right hemisphere in face perception. In A. W. Young (Ed.), *Functions of the right cerebral hemisphere* (pp. 33–64). London: Academic Press.

Ellis, L., Ames, M. A., Peckham, W., & Burke, D. (1988). Sexual orientation of human offspring may be altered by severe maternal stress during pregnancy. *The Journal of Sex Research, 25,* 152–157.

Ellis, L. K., Gay, P. E., & Paige, E. (2001). Daily pleasures and hassles across the lifespan. Poster presented at the September annual meeting of the American Psychological Association, San Francisco.

Endler, N. S. (1988). The origins of electroconvulsive therapy (ECT). *Convulsive Therapy, 4,* 5–23.

Engelhardt, C. R., Bartholow, B. D., Kerr, G. T., & Bushman, B. J. (in press). This is your brain on violent video games: Neural desensitization to violence predicts increased aggression following violent video game exposure. *Journal of Experimental Social Psychology.*

Engle, R. W., & Kane, M. J. (2004). Executive attention, working memory capacity, and a two-factor theory of cognitive control. *The Psychology of Learning and Motivation, 44,* 145–199.

Enns, J. T., & Coren, S. (1995). The box alignment illusion: An orientation illusion induced by pictorial depth. *Perception and Psychophysics, 57,* 1163–1174.

Ephraim, P. L., Wegener, S. T., MacKenzie, E. J., Dillingham, T. R., & Pezzin, L. E. (2005). Phantom pain, residual limb pain and back pain in persons with limb loss: Results of a national survey. *Archives of Physical Medicine and Rehabilitation, 86,* 1910–1919.

Epping-Jordan, M., Waltkins, S. S., Koob, G. F., & Markou, A. (1998). Dramatic decreases in brain reward function during nicotine withdrawal. *Nature, 393,* 76–79.

Erdley, C. A., & Dweck, C. S. (1993). Children's implicit personality theories as predictors of their social judgments. *Child Development, 64,* 863–878.

Erickson, K. I., Prakash, R. S., Voss, M. W., Chaddock, L., Hu, L., Morris, K. S., et al. (2009). Aerobic fitness is associated with hippocampal volume in elderly humans. *Hippocampus, 19*(10), 1030–1039.

Erikson, E. (1980). Elements of a psychoanalytic theory of psychosocial development. In S. Greenspan & G. Pollock (Eds.), *The Course of Life, Vol. 1* (pp. 11–61). Washington, DC: U.S. Department of Health and Human Services.

Erikson, E. H. (1950). *Childhood and society.* New York: Norton.

Erikson, E. H. (1959). Growth and crises of the healthy personality. *Psychological Issues, 1,* 50–100.

Erikson, E. H. (1982). *The life cycle completed.* New York: Norton.

Erikson, E. H., & Erikson, J. M. (1997). *The life cycle completed.* New York: Norton.

Escandon, A., Al-Hammadi, N., Galvin, J. E. (2010). Effect of cognitive fluctuation on neuropsychological performance in aging and dementia. *Neurology, 74,* 210–217.

Eschenbeck, H., Kohlmann, C. W., & Lohaus, A. (2008). Gender differences in coping strategies in children and adolescents. *Journal of Individual Differences, 28*(1), 18–26.

Espiard, M. L., Lecardeur, L., Abadie, P., Halbecq, I., & Dollfus, S. (2005). HPPD after psilocybin consumption: A case study. *European Psychiatry, 20*(5–6), 458–460.

Evans, D., Hodgkinson, B., O'Donnell, A., Nicholson, J., & Walsh, K. (2000). The effectiveness of individual therapy and group therapy in the treatment of schizophrenia. In *Best Practice, 5*(3), 1–54.

Evans, I. M., & Meyer, L. H. (1985). *An educative approach to behavior problems: A practical decision model for interventions with severely handicapped learners.* Baltimore: Paul H. Brookes.

Evans, W. H., Evans, S. S., & Schmid, R. E. (1989). *Behavior and instructional management: An ecological approach.* Boston: Allyn & Bacon.

Everson, S. (1995). Psychology. In J. Barnes (Ed.), *The Cambridge companion to Aristotle* (pp. 168–194). Cambridge, UK: Cambridge University Press.

Exner, J. E. (1980). But it's only an inkblot. *Journal of Personality Assessment, 44,* 562–577.

Eysenck, H. (1994a). *Test your IQ.* Toronto: Penguin Books.

Eysenck, H. J. (1957). The effects of psychotherapy: An evaluation. *Journal of Consulting Psychology, 16,* 319–324.

Eysenck, H. J. (1994b). Synergistic interaction between psychosocial and physical factors in the causation of lung cancer. In C. Lewis, C. O'Sullivan, & J. Barraclough (Eds.), *The psychoimmunology of human cancer* (pp. 163–178). London: Oxford University Press.

Eysenck, H. J., & Eysenck, S. B. G. (1993). *Eysenck Personality Questionnaire* [Revised]. London: Hodder & Stoughton Educational.

Fagot, B. I., & Hagan, R. (1991). Observations of parent reactions to sex-stereotyped behaviours: Age and sex effects. *Child Development, 62,* 617–628.

Fairchild, G., Van Goozen, S. H., Stollery, S. J., & Goodyer, I. M. (2008). Fear conditioning and affective modulation of the startle reflex in male adolescents with early-onset or adolescence-onset conduct disorder and healthy control subjects. *Biological Psychiatry 63*(3), 279–285.

Fanselow, M. S., & Gale, G. D. (2003). The amygdala, fear, and memory. *Annals of the New York Academy of Sciences, 985,* 125–134.

Fantz, R. L. (1961). The origin of form perception. *Scientific American, 204,* 66–72.

Fantz, R. L. (1964). Visual experience in infants: Decreased attention to familiar patterns relative to novel ones. *Science, 146,* 668–670.

Faraone, S. V., Tsuang, M. T., & Tsuang, D. W. (1999). *Genetics of mental disorders: A guide for students, clinicians, and researchers.* New York: Guilford Press.

Farmer, A. E. (1996). The genetics of depressive disorders. *International Review of Psychiatry, 8*(4).

Farthing, W. (1992). *The psychology of consciousness.* Upper Saddle River, NJ: Prentice-Hall.

Faucett, J., Gordon, N., & Levine, J. (1994). Differences in postoperative pain severity among four ethnic groups. *Journal of Pain Symptom Management, 9,* 383–389.

Fawzy, F. I., Fawzy, N. W., Hyun, C. S., Elashoff, R., Guthrie, D., Fahey, J. L., & Morton, D. L. (1993). Malignant melanoma effects of an early structured psychiatric intervention, coping, and affective state on recurrence and survival 6 years later. *Archives of General Psychiatry, 50*(9), 681–689.

Fazel-Rezai, R., & Peters, J. F. (2005). P300 wave feature extraction: Preliminary results, in *Proceedings of the 18th Annual Canadian Conference on Electrical and Computer Engineering (CCECE '05,* pp. 390–393). Saskatoon, Saskatchewan, Canada.

Fechner, G. T. (1860). *Elemente der Psykophysik.* Leipzig: Breitkopf und Härtel.

Fedoroff, I. C., & McFarlane, T. (1998). Cultural aspects of eating disorders. In S. S. Kazarian & D. R. Evans (Eds.), *Cultural clinical psychology: Theory, research and practice* (pp. 152–176). New York: Oxford University Press.

Fehr, E., & Gächter, S. (Summer 2000). Fairness and retaliation: The economics of reciprocity. *Journal of Economic Perspectives 14*(3), 159–181.

Feingold, A. (1992). Good-looking people are not what we think. *Psychological Bulletin, 111,* 304–341.

Felder, R. (1993). Reaching the second tier: Learning and teaching styles in college science education. *Journal of College Science Teaching, 23*(5), 286–290.

Felder, R. (1996). Matters of style. *ASEE Prism, 6*(4), 18–23.

Felder, R. M. (2010). Are learning styles invalid? (Hint: No!). *On-Course Newsletter, 18*(1), 2-7.

Felder, R. M. & Brent, R. (2005). Understanding student differences. *Journal of Engineering Education, 94*(1), 57-72.

Felder, R., & Soloman, B. R. M.(2004). Index of Learning Styles (ILS). Retrieved from the Internet on January 7, 2010 at http://www.engr.ncsu.edu/learningstyles/ilsweb.html.

Felder, R. M., & Spurlin, J. E. (2005). Applications, reliability and validity of the index of learning styles. *International Journal of Engineering Education, 21*(1), 103–112.

Feldman, D. H. (2003). Cognitive development in childhood. In R. M. Lerner, M. A. Easterbrooks et al. (Eds.), *Handbook of psychology: Developmental psychology: Vol. 6* (pp. 195–201). New York: Wiley.

Ferguson, C. J. (2010). Blazing angels or resident evil? Can violent video games be a force for good? *Review of General Psychology, 14*(2), 68–81.

Ferguson, C. J. (2010). Video games and youth violence: A prospective analysis in adolescents. *Journal of Youth and Adolescence,* [DOI: 10.1007/s10964-010-9610-x].

Ferguson, C. J. (2011). Video games and youth violence: A prospective analysis in Adolescents. *Journal of Youth Adolescence, 40*(4), 377–391.

Ferguson, C. J., & Kilburn, J. (2009). The Public health risks of media violence: A meta-analytic review. *Journal of Pediatrics, 154,* 759–763.

Ferguson-Noyes, N. (2005). Bipolar disorder in children. *Advanced Nurse Practitioner, 13,* 35.

Fernald, A. (1984). The perceptual and affective salience of mothers' speech to infants. In L. Feagans, C. Garvey, & R. Golinkoff (Eds.), *The origins and growth of communication.* Norwood, NJ: Ablex.

Fernald, A. (1992) Human maternal vocalizations to infants as biologically relevant signals: An evolutionary perspective. In J. H. Barkow, L. Cosmides, & J. Tooby (Eds.), *The adapted mind: Evolutionary psychology and the generation of culture.* New York: Oxford University Press.

Fernandez, E., & Sheffield, J. (1996). Relative contributions of life events versus daily hassles to the frequency and intensity of headaches. *Headache, 36*(10), 595–602.

Feroah, T. R., Sleeper, T., Brozoski, D., Forder, J., Rice, T. B., & Forster, H. V. (2004). *Circadian slow wave sleep and movement behavior are under genetic control in inbred strains of rat.* Paper presented at the American Physiological Society Annual Conference, April 17–21, 2004, Washington, DC.

Ferron, F., Considine, R. V., Peino, R., Lado, I. G., Dieguez, C., & Casanueva, F. F. (1997). Serum leptin concentrations in patients with anorexia nervosa, bulimia nervosa and non-specific eating disorders correlate with the body mass index but are independent of the respective disease. *Clinical Endocrinology (Oxford), 46,* 289–293.

Festinger, L. (1954). A theory of social comparison processes. *Human Relations, 7,* 117–140.

Festinger, L. (1957). *A theory of cognitive dissonance.* Stanford, CA: Stanford University Press.

Festinger, L., & Carlsmith, J. (1959). $1/$20 experiment: Cognitive consequences of forced compliance. *Journal of Abnormal and Social Psychology, 58*(2), 203–210.

Fiatarone, M. (1996). Physical activity and functional independence in aging. *Research Quarterly for Exercise and Sport, 67,* 70–75.

Fiatarone, M. A., O'Neill, E. F., Doyle, N., Clements, K. M., Roberts, S. B., Kehayias, J. J., Lipsitz, L. A., & Evans, W. J. (1993). The Boston FICSIT study: The effects of resistance training and nutritional supplementation on physical frailty in the oldest old. *Journal of American Geriatrics, 41,* 333–337.

Fincham, F. D., Harold, G. T., & Gano-Phillips, S. (2000). The longitudinal association between attributions and marital satisfaction: Direction of effects and role of efficacy expectations. *Journal of Family Psychology, 14,* 267–285.

Finger, S. (1994). *Origins of neuroscience: A history of explorations into brain function.* New York, NY: Oxford University Press.

Fink, M. (1984). Meduna and the origins of convulsive therapy. *American Journal of Psychiatry, 141,* 1034–1041.

Finke, R. (1995). Creative realism. In S. Smith, T. Ward & R. Finke (Eds.), *The creative cognition approach* (pp. 301–326). Cambridge, MA.: Cambridge University Press.

Finkel, D., & McGue, M. (1997). Sex differences and nonadditivity in heritability of the Multidimensional Personality Questionnaire scales. *Journal of Personality and Social Psychology, 72,* 929–938.

Fischl, B., Liu, A., & Dale, A. M. (2001). Automated manifold surgery: Constructing geometrically accurate and topologically correct models of the human cerebral cortex. *IEEE Transactions on Medical Imaging, 20,* 70–80.

Fisher, M., Holland, C., Merzenich, M. M., & Vinogradov, S. (2009). Using neuroplasticity-based auditory training to improve verbal memory in schizophrenia. *The American Journal of Psychiatry, 166*(7), 805–811.

Fisher, R., Salanova, V., Witt, T., Worth, R., Henry, T., Gross, R., et al. (2010). Electrical stimulation of the anterior nucleus of thalamus for treatment of refractory epilepsy. *Epilepsia, 17,* 17.

Fiske, S. T. (1998). Stereotyping, prejudice, and discrimination. In D. T. Gilbert & S. T. Fiske (Eds.), *The handbook of social psychology* (4th ed., Vol. 2, pp. 357–411). New York: McGraw-Hill.

Fitzpatrick, M. (2004). *MMR and autism* (pp. 133–149). New York: Routledge.

Fivush, R., Haden, C., & Reese, E. (1996). Remembering, recounting, and reminiscing: The development of autobiographical memory in social context. In D. C. Rubin (Ed.), *Remembering our past: Studies in autobiographical memory* (pp. 341–359). New York: Cambridge University Press.

Fivush, R., & Nelson, K. (2004). Culture and language in the emergence of autobiographical memory. *Psychological Science, 15*(9), 573.

Flaherty, J. A., & Adams, S. A. (1998). Therapist–patient race and sex matching: Predictors of treatment duration. *Psychiatric Times, 15*(1).

Flaskerud, J. H. (1991). Effects of an Asian client–therapist language, ethnicity and gender match on utilization and outcome of therapy. *Community Mental Health Journal, 27,* 31–42.

Flavell, J. H. (1999). Cognitive development: Children's knowledge about the mind. *Annual Review of Psychology, 50,* 21–45.

Fleming, M. F., & Barry, K. L. (1992). Clinical overview of alcohol and drug disorders. In M. F. Fleming & K. L. Barry (Eds.), *Addictive disorders.* St. Louis: Mosby Year Book.

Flemons, W. W. (2002). Obstructive sleep apnea. *New England Journal of Medicine, 347,* 498–504.

Folkard, S., Arendt, J., & Clark, M. (1993). Can melatonin improve shift workers' tolerance of the night shift? Some preliminary findings. *Chronobiology International: The Journal of Biological and Medical Rhythm Research, 10*(5), 315–320.

Folkman, S. (1997). Positive psychological states and coping with severe stress. *Social Science and Medicine, 45,* 1207–1221.

Folkman, S., & Chesney, M. A. (1995). Coping with HIV infection. In M. Stein & A. Baum (Eds.), *Perspectives in behavioral medicine* (pp. 115–133). Hillsdale, NJ: Erlbaum.

Folkman, S., & Lazarus, R. S. (1980). An analysis of coping in a middle-aged community sample. *Journal of Health and Social Behavior, 21*(3), 219–239.

Follett, K. J., & Hess, T. M. (2002). Aging, cognitive complexity, and the fundamental attribution error. *Journals of Gerontology Series B: Psychological Sciences and Social Sciences, 57,* 312–323.

Forbes, G., Zhang, X., Doroszewicz, K., & Haas, K. (2009). Relationships between individualism-collectivism, gender, and direct or indirect aggression: a study in China, Poland, and the U.S. *Aggressive Behavior, 35*(1), 24–30.

Ford, N., & Chen, S. Y. (2001). Matching/mismatching revisited: An empirical study of learning and teaching styles. *British Journal of Educational Technology, 32*(1), 5–22.

Fornito, A., Yucel, M., & Pantelis, C. (2009). Reconciling neuroimaging and neuropathological findings in schizophrenia and bipolar disorder. *Current Opinion in Psychiatry, 22*(3), 312–319.

Foulkes, D., & Schmidt, M. (1983). Temporal sequence and unit comparison composition in dream reports from different stages of sleep. *Sleep, 6,* 265–280.

Frank, E., Kupfer, D. J., Buysse, D. J., Swartz, H. A., Pilkonis, P. A., Houck, P. R., Rucci, P., Novick, D. M., Grochocinski, V. J., & Stapf, D. M. (2007). Randomized trial of weekly, twice-monthly, and monthly interpersonal psychotherapy as maintenance treatment for women with recurrent depression. *American Journal of Psychiatry, 164*(5), 761–767.

Franke, R. H., & Kaul, J. D. (1978). The Hawthorne experiments: First statistical interpretation. *American Sociological Review, 43,* 623–643.

Frankel, B. R., & Piercy, F. P. (1990). The relationship among selected supervisor, therapist, and client behaviors. *Journal of Marital and Family Therapy, 16,* 407–421.

Frederich, R., Hu, S., Raymond, N., & Pomeroy, C. (2002). Leptin in anorexia nervosa and bulimia nervosa: Importance of assay technique and method of interpretation. *Journal of Laboratory and Clinical Medicine, 139*(2), 72–79.

Freedman, J., & Fraser, S. (1966). Compliance without pressure: The foot-in-the-door technique. *Journal of Personality and Social Psychology, 4,* 195–202.

Freeman, J. (2001). *Gifted children grown up.* London: David Fulton.

Freeman, W., & Watts, J. W. (1937). Prefrontal lobotomy in the treatment of mental disorders. *Southern Medical Journal, 30,* 23–31.

Frensch, P. A., & Runger, D. (2003). Implicit learning. *Current Directions in Psychological Science, 12,* 13–18.

Fresquet, N., Angst, M., & Sandner, G. (2004, August). Insular cortex lesions alter conditioned taste avoidance in rats differentially when using two methods of sucrose delivery. *Behavioral Brain Research, 153*(2), 357–365.

Freud, S. (1900). The interpretation of dreams. *S. E., 4–5.* (cf. J. Crick, Trans., 1999). London: Oxford University Press.

Freud, S. (1901). The psychopathology of everyday life. *S. E., 6,* 1–290.

Freud, S. (1904a). *Psychopathology of everyday life.* New York: Macmillan; London: Fisher Unwin.

Freud, S. (1923). The ego and the id. *S. E., 19,* 12–66.

Freud, S. (1930). *Civilization and its discontents.* New York: Jonathon Cape and Co.

Freud, S. (1931) Female sexuality. *Pelican Freud Library, 7,* 367.

Freud, S. (1933). *New introductory lectures on psycho-analysis.* London: Hogarth Press.

Freud, S. (1940). Splitting of the ego in the process of defence. *International Journal of Psychoanalysis, 22,* 65 [1938], S. E., 23, 275–278.

Freud, S., & Gay, P. (1977). *Inhibitions, symptoms and anxiety. Standard edition of the complete works of Sigmund Freud.* New York: Norton.

Friedman, J. M. (2000). Obesity in the new millennium. *Nature, 404,* 632–634.

Friedman, J. M. (2003). A war on obesity, not the obese. *Science, 299*(5608), 856–858.

Friedman, J. M., & Halaas, J. L. (1998). Leptin and the regulation of body weight in mammals. *Nature, 395,* 763.

Friedman, M., & Kasanin, J. D. (1943). Hypertension in only one of identical twins. *Archives of Internal Medicine, 72,* 767–774.

Friedman, M., & Rosenman, R. H. (1959). Association of specific behavior pattern with blood and cardiovascular findings. *Journal of the American Medical Association, 169,* 1286–1296.

Frontera, W. R., Hughes, V. A., Lutz, K. J., & Evans, W. J. (1991). A cross-sectional study of muscle strength and mass in 45- to 78-year-old men and women. *Journal of Applied Physiology, 71,* 644–650.

Fulcher, J. S. (1942). "Voluntary" facial expression in blind and seeing children. *Archives of Psychology, 38,* 1–49.

Fumeron, F., Betoulle, D., Aubert, R., Herbeth, B., Siest, G., & Rigaud, D. (2001). Association of a functional 5–HT transporter gene polymorphism with anorexia nervosa and food intake. *Molecular Psychiatry, 6,* 9–10.

Furumoto, L. (1979). Mary Whiton Calkins (1863–1930): Fourteenth president of the American Psychological Association. *Journal of the History of Behavioral Sciences, 15,* 346–356.

Furumoto, L. (1991). Portraits of pioneers in psychology. In G. A. Kimble, M. Wertheimer, & C. White (Eds.), *From "Paired associates" to a psychology of self: The intellectual odyssey of Mary Whiton Calkins* (pp. 57–72). Washington, DC: American Psychological Association.

Gable, R. S. (2004). Acute toxic effects of club drugs. *Journal of Psychoactive Drugs. 36*(1), 303–313.

Gado, M. (2004). A cry in the night: The Kitty Genovese murder. *Court TV's Crime Library: Criminal Minds and Methods.* Retrieved August 2, 2004, from www.crimelibrary.com/serial_killers/predators/kitty_genovese/1.html?sect=2.

Galanter, M. (1983). Unification Church ("Moonie") dropouts: Psychological readjustment after leaving a charismatic religious group. *American Journal of Psychiatry, 140*(8), 984–989.

Gallagher, R. P. (2009). National Survey of Counseling Center Directors, 2009. *The American College Counseling Association (ACCA)*. Retrieved from http://www.iacsinc.org/2009%20National%20Survey.pdf

Gamwell, L., & Tomes, N. (1995). *Madness in America: Cultural and medical perspectives of mental illness before 1914*. Ithaca, NY: Cornell University Press.

Ganchrow, J. R., Steiner, J. E., & Munif, D. (1983). Neonatal facial expressions in response to different qualities and intensities of gustatory stimuli. *Infant Behavior Development, 6*, 473–478.

Ganellen, R. J. (1996). *Integrating the Rorschach and the MMPI-2 in personality assessment*. Mahwah, NJ: Erlbaum.

Ganis, G., Thompson, W. L., & Kosslyn, S. M. (2004). Brain areas underlying visual mental imagery and visual perception: An fMRI study. *Brain research. Cognitive Brain Research, 20*(2), 226–241.

Garb, H. N., Florio, C. M., & Grove, W. M. (1998). The validity of the Rorschach and the Minnesota Multiphasic Personality Inventory: Results from metaanalyses. *Psychological Science, 9*, 402–404.

Garcia, J., & Koelling, R. A. (1966). Relation of cue to consequence in avoidance learning. *Psychonomic Science, 4*, 123.

Garcia, J., Brett, L. P., & Rusiniak, K. W. (1989). Limits of Darwinian conditioning. In S. B. Klein & R. R. Mowrer (Eds.), *Contemporary learning theories: Instrumental conditioning theory and the impact of biological constraints on learning* (pp. 237–275). Hillsdale, NJ: Erlbaum.

Gardner, H. (1993a). *Creating minds: An anatomy of creativity seen through the lives of Freud, Einstein, Picasso, Stravinsky, Eliot, Graham, and Ghandi*. New York: Basic Books.

Gardner, H. (1993b). *Multiple intelligences: The theory in practice*. New York: Basic Books.

Gardner, H. (1998). Are there additional intelligences? The case for naturalist, spiritual, and existential intelligences. In J. Kane (Ed.), *Education, information, and transformation* (pp. 111–131). Upper Saddle River, NJ: Merrill-Prentice Hall.

Gardner, H. (1999a). *Intelligence reframed: Multiple intelligences for the 21st century*. New York: Basic Books.

Gardner, H. (1999b, February). Who owns intelligence? *Atlantic Monthly*, 67–76.

Gardner, H., Kornhaber, M. L., & Wake, W. K. (1996). *Intelligence: Multiple perspectives*. Orlando, FL: Harcourt Brace.

Gardner, J., & Oswald, A. J. (2004). How is mortality affected by money, marriage, and stress? *Journal of Health Economics, 23*(6), 1181–1207.

Garland, E. J., & Smith, D. H. (1991). Simultaneous prepubertal onset of panic disorder, night terrors, and somnambulism. *Journal of American Academic Child and Adolescent Psychiatry, 30*(4), 553–555.

Gazzaniga, M. S. (2006). *The ethical brain: The science of our moral dilemmas*. New York: HarperCollins.

Gazzaniga, M. S. (2009). *Human: The science behind what makes us unique*. New York: Harper Perennial.

Geake, J. (2008). Neuromythologies in education. *Educational Research, 50,* 123–133.

Geary, D. C. (2000). Evolution and proximate expression of human paternal investment. *Psychological Bulletin, 126*, 55–77.

Geary, D. C. (2012). Sex differences. In V. S. Ramachandran (Editor-in-chief), *Encyclopedia of human behavior* (2nd ed.). *San Diego*, CA: Elsevier.

Gebhard, P. H., & Johnson, A. B. (1979/1998). *The Kinsey data: Marginal tabulations of 1938–1963 interviews conducted by the Institute for Sex Research*. Philadelphia: W. B. Saunders.

Geddes, D. P. (Ed.) (1954). *An analysis of the Kinsey reports*. New York: New American Library.

Geddes, J., & Butler, R. (2002). Depressive disorders. *Clinical Evidence, 7*, 867–882.

Geen, R. G., & Thomas, S. L. (1986). The immediate effects of media violence on behavior. *Journal of Social Issues, 42*, 7–27.

Geier, J., Bernáth, L., Hudák, M., & Sára, L. (2008). Straightness as the main factor of the Hermann grid illusion. *Perception, 37*(5), 651–665.

Gelder, M. (1976). Flooding. In T. Thompson & W. Dockens (Eds.), *Applications of behavior modification* (pp. 250–298). New York: Academic Press.

Geliebter, A. (1988). Gastric distension and gastric capacity in relation to food intake in humans. *Physiological Behavior, 44*, 665–668.

Geller, B., Williams, M., Zimerman, B., Frazier, J., Beringer, L., & Warner, K. L. (1998). Prepubertal and early adolescent bipolarity differentiate from ADHD by manic symptoms, grandiose delusions, ultra-rapid or ultradian cycling. *Journal of Affective Disorders, 51*(2), 81–91.

Gelman, S. A. (1988). The development of induction within natural kind and artifact categories. *Cognitive Psychology, 20*, 65–95.

Gelman, S. A., & Markman, E. M. (1986). Categories and induction in young children. *Cognition, 23*, 183–209.

Gershoff, E. T. (2000). The short- and long-term effects of corporal punishment on children: A meta-analytical review. In D. Elliman & M. A. Lynch, *The physical punishment of children* (pp. 196–198).

Gershoff, E. T. (2002). Corporal punishment by parents: Effects on children and links to physical abuse. *Child Law Practice, 21* (10), 154-157.

Geschwind, D. H., & Iacoboni, M. (2007). Structural and functional asymmetries of the frontal lobes. In B. L. Miller & J. K. Cummings (Eds.), *The human frontal lobes* (2nd ed., pp. 68–91). New York: Guilford Press.

Gibbons, J. L., Stiles, D. A., & Shkodriani, G. M. (1991). Adolescents' attitudes toward family and gender roles: An international comparison. *Sex Roles, 25*, 625–643.

Giedd, J. N., Blumenthal, J., Jeffries, N. O., Castellanos, F. X., Liui, H., Zijdenbos, A., Paus, T., Evans, A. C., & Rapoport, J. L. (1999). Brain development during childhood and adolescence: A longitudinal MRI study. *Nature Neuroscience, 2*(10), 861–863.

Gilberg, C., & Coleman, M. (2000). *The biology of the autistic syndromes* (3rd ed.). London: MacKeith Press.

Gilbert, S. J. (1981). Another look at the Milgram obedience studies: The role of the graduated series of shocks. *Personality and Social Psychology Bulletin, 7*(4), 690–695.

Gill, S. T. (1991). Carrying the war into the never-never land of psi. *Skeptical Inquirer, 15*(1), 269–273.

Gillespie, M. A., Kim, B. H., Manheim, L. J., Yoo, T., Oswald, F. L., & Schmitt, N. (June, 2002). The development and validation of biographical data and situational judgment tests in the prediction of college student success. Presented in A. M. Ryan (Chair), *Beyond g: Expanding thinking on predictors of college success*. Symposium conducted at the 14th Annual Convention of the American Psychological Society, New Orleans, LA.

Gillham, B., Tanner, G., Cheyne, B., Freeman, I., Rooney, M., & Lambie, A. (1998). Unemployment rates, single parent density, and indices of child poverty: Their relationship to different categories of child abuse and neglect. *Child Abuse and Neglect, 22*(2), 79–90.

Gilligan, C. (1982). *In a different voice: Psychological theory and women's development*. Cambridge, MA: Harvard University Press.

Gillund, G., & Shiffrin, R. M. (1984). A retrieval model for both recognition and recall. *Psychological Review, 91*, 1–67.

Ginzburg, K., Solomon, Z., Koifman, B., Keren, G., Roth, A., Kriwisky, M., Kutz, I., David, D., & Bleich, A. (2003). Trajectories of post-traumatic stress disorder following myocardial infarction: A prospective study. *Journal of Clinical Psychiatry, 64*(10), 1217–1223.

Gittelman-Klein, R. (1978). Validity in projective tests for psychodiagnosis in children. In R. L. Spitzer & D. F. Klein (Eds.), *Critical issues in psychiatric diagnosis* (pp. 141–166). New York: Raven Press.

Glenn, A. L., Raine, A., Mednick, S. A., & Venables, P. (2007). Early temperamental and psychophysiological precursors of adult psychopathic personality. *Journal of Abnormal Psychology, 116*(3), 508–518.

Glenn, D. (2009). Matching teaching style to learning style may not help students. *The Chronicle of Higher Education, December 15th, 2009*. Retrieved January, 6, 2010, from http://chronicle.com/article/Matching-Teaching-Style-to/49497/

Glynn, S. M. (1990). Token economy approaches for psychiatric patients: Progress and pitfalls over 25 years. *Behavior Modification, 14*, 383–407.

Godden, D. R., & Baddeley, A. D. (1975). Context-dependent memory in two natural environments: On land and underwater. *British Journal of Psychology, 66*, 325–331.

Goel, V., & Grafman, J. (1995). Are the frontal lobes implicated in "planning" functions? Interpreting data from the Tower of Hanoi. *Neuropsychologia, 33*(5), 623–642.

Gogtay, N., & Thompson, P. M. (2010). Mapping gray matter development: Implications for typical development and vulnerability to psychopathology. *Brain and Cognition, 72*(1), 6–15.

Gogtay, N., Lu, A., Leow, A. D., Klunder, A. D., Lee, A. D., Chavez, A., Greenstein, D., Giedd, J. N., Toga, A. W., Rapoport, J. L., & Thompson, P. M. (2008). Three-dimensional brain growth abnormalities in childhood-onset schizophrenia visualized by using tensor-based morphometry. *Proceedings of the National Academy of Sciences of the United States of America, 105*(41), 15979–15984.

Goin, M. K. (2005). Practical psychotherapy: A current perspective on the psychotherapies. *Psychiatric Services, 56*(3), 255–257.

Goldman, A. L., Pezawas, L., Mattay, V. S., Fischl, B., Verchinski, B. A., Chen, Q., Weinberger, D. R., & Meyer-Lindenberg, A. (2009). Widespread reductions of cortical thickness in schizophrenia and spectrum disorders and evidence of heritability. *Archives of General Psychiatry, 66*(5), 467–477.

Goldman-Rakic, P. S. (1998). The prefrontal landscape: Implications of functional architecture for understanding human mentation and the central executive. In A. C. Roberts, T. W. Robbins, & L. Weiskrantz (Eds.), *The prefrontal cortex: Executive and cognitive functions* (pp. 87–102). Oxford, UK: Oxford University Press.

Goldsmith, H. H., & Campos, J. (1982). Toward a theory of infant temperament. In R. Emde & R. Harmon (Eds.), *The development of attachment and affiliative systems: Psychobiological aspects* (pp. 161–193). New York: Plenum Press.

Goleman, D. (1982). Staying up: The rebellion against sleep's gentle tyranny. *Psychology Today, 3*, 24–35.

Goleman, D. (1995). *Emotional intelligence: Why it can matter more than IQ*. New York: Bantam Books.

Golkaramnay, V., Bauer, S., Haug, S., Wolf, M., & Kordy, H. (2007). The exploration of the effectiveness of group therapy through an Internet chat as aftercare: A controlled naturalistic study. *Pychotherapy and Psychosomatics, 76*, 219–225.

Gonsalves, B., Reber, P. J., Gitelman, D. R., Parrish, T. B., Mesulam, M. M., & Paller, K. A. (2004). Neural evidence that vivid imagining can lead to false remembering. *Psychological Science, 15*, 655–660.

Gonzales, P. M., Blanton, H., & Williams, K. J. (2002). The effects of stereotype threat and double–minority status on the test performance of Latino women. *Personality and Social Psychology Bulletin, 28*(5), 659–670.

Gonzalez, J. S., Penedo, F. J., Antoni, M. H., Durán, R. E., Fernandez, M. I., McPherson-Baker, S., Ironson, G., Klimas, N. G., Fletcher, M. A., & Schneiderman, N. (2004).

Social support, positive states of mind, and HIV treatment adherence in men and women living with HIV/AIDS. *Health Psychology, 23*(4), 413–418.

Goodglass, H., Kaplan, E., & Barresi, B. (2001). *The assessment of aphasia and related disorders* (3rd ed.). Baltimore: Lippincott, Williams & Wilkins.

Goodman, E. S. (1980). Margaret Floy Washburn (1871–1939) first woman Ph.D. in psychology. *Psychology of Women Quarterly, 5*, 69–80.

Gotlib, I. H., Sivers, H., Canli, T., Kasch, K. L., & Gabrieli, J. D. E. (November, 2001). Neural activation in depression in response to emotional stimuli. In I. H. Gotlib (Chair), *New directions in the neurobiology of affective disorders*. Symposium conducted at the annual meeting of the Society for Research in Psychopathology, Madison, WI.

Gottesman, I. I. (1991). *Schizophrenia genesis: The origins of madness.* New York: W. H. Freeman.

Gottesman, I. I., McGuffin P. & Farmer, A. E. (1987). Clinical genetics as clues to the "Real" genetics of schizophrenia (A decade of modest gains while playing for time). *Schizophrenia Bulletin, 13*, 23-47.

Gottesman, I. I., & Shields, J. (1976). A critical review of recent adoption, twin and family studies of schizophrenia: Behavioural genetics perspectives. *Schizophrenia Bulletin, 2*, 360–401.

Gottesman, I., & Shields, J. (1982). *Schizophrenia: The epigenetic puzzle.* New York: Cambridge University Press.

Gottman, J. M., & Krokoff, L. J. (1989). Marital interaction and satisfaction: A longitudinal view. *Journal of Consulting and Clinical Psychology, 57*, 47–52.

Gough, H. G. (1995). *California Psychological Inventory* (3rd ed.). Palo Alto, CA: Consulting Psychologist-Press.

Gould, J. L., & Gould, C. G. (1994). *The animal mind.* New York: Scientific American Library.

Gould, S. J. (1996). *The mismeasure of man.* New York: Norton.

Gouldner, A. W. (1960). The norm of reciprocity: A preliminary statement. *American Sociological Review, 25*, 161–178.

Graber, J. A., Brooks-Gunn, J., & Warren, M. P. (1995). The antecedents of menarcheal age: Heredity, family environment, and stressful life events. *Child Development, 66*, 346–359.

Gregory, R. L. (1990). *Eye and brain, the psychology of seeing.* Princeton, NJ: Princeton University Press.

Gresham, L. G., & Shimp, T. A. (1985). Attitude toward the advertisement and brand attitudes: A classical conditioning prospective. *Journal of Advertising, 14*(1), 10–17, 49.

Gribbons, B., & Herman, J. (1997) *True and quasi-experimental designs.* Washington, DC: ERIC Clearinghouse on Assessment and Evaluation.

Griffiths, R. R., Richards, W. A., McCann, U., & Jesse, R. (2006). Psilocybin can occasion mystical-type experiences having substantial and sustained personal meaning and spiritual significance. *Psychopharmacology, 187*(3), 1432–2072.

Grocer, S., & Kohout, J. (1997). The 1995 APA survey of 1992 baccalaureate recipients. Washington, DC: American Psychological Association.

Gross, C. G. (1999). A hole in the head. *The Neuroscientist, 5*, 263–269.

Grumbach, M. M., & Kaplan, S. L. (1990). The neuroendocrinology of human puberty: An ontogenetic perspective. In M. M. Grumbach, P. C. Sizonenko, & M. L. Aubert (Eds.), *Control of the onset of puberty* (pp. 1–6). Baltimore: Williams & Wilkins.

Grumbach, M. M., & Styne, D. M. (1998). Puberty: Ontogeny, neuroendocrinology, physiology, and disorders. In J. D. Wilson, D. W. Foster, H. M. Kronenberg, & P. R. Larsen (Eds.), *Williams textbook of endocrinology* (9th ed. pp. 1509–1625). Philadelphia: W. B. Saunders.

Grünbaum, A. (1984). *The foundations of psychoanalysis: A philosophical critique.* Berkeley: University of California Press.

Guilford, J. P. (1967). *The nature of human intelligence.* New York: McGraw-Hill.

Gummerman, K., Gray, C. R., and Wilson, J. M. (1972). An attempt to assess eidetic imagery objectively. *Bulletin of the Psychonomic Society 28*, 115–118.

Gupta, M. (1994). Sexuality in the Indian sub-continent. *Sex and Marital Therapy, 9*, 57–69.

Guthrie, R. V. (2004). *Even the rat was white: A historical view of psychology.* Boston: Allyn & Bacon.

Halbesleben, J. R. B., & Bowler, W. M. (2007). Emotional exhaustion and job performance: The mediating role of motivation. *Journal of Applied Psychology, 91*, 93–106.

Hall, W., & Degenhardt, L. (2009). Adverse health effects of non-medical cannabis use. *Lancet, 374*, 1383–1391.

Hamer, D. H., Hu, S., Magnuson, V. L., Hu, N., & Pattatucci, A. M. L. (1993). A linkage between DNA markers on the X chromosome and male sexual orientation. *Science, 261*, 321–327.

Hamilton, D. L., & Gifford, R. K. (1976). Illusory correlation in interpersonal perception: A cognitive basis of stereotypic judgments. *Journal of Experimental Social Psychology, 12*, 392–407.

Hampton, J. A. (1998). Similarity-based categorization and fuzziness of natural categories. *Cognition, 65*, 137–165.

Handel, S. (1989). *Listening: An introduction to the perception of auditory events.* Cambridge, MA: MIT Press.

Hansen, C. P. (1988). Personality characteristics of the accident involved employee. *Journal of Business and Psychology, 2*(4), 346–365.

Hargittai, E. (2007). Whose space? Differences among users and non-users of social network sites. *Journal of Computer-Mediated Communication, 13*(1), article 14. Retrieved from http://jcmc.indiana.edu/vol13/issue1/hargittai.html

Harlow, H. F. (1958). The nature of love. *American Psychologist, 13*, 573–685.

Harman, G. (1999). Moral philosophy meets social psychology: Virtue ethics and the fundamental attribution error. *Proceedings of the Aristotelian Society, 1998–99, 99*, 315–331.

Harris, J. L., & Qualls, C. D. (2000). The association of elaborative or maintenance rehearsal with age, reading comprehension, and verbal working memory performance. *Aphasiology, 14*(5–6), 515–526.

Harrison, P. J. (1999). The neuropathology of schizophrenia: A critical review of the data and their interpretation. *Brain, 122*, 593–624.

Hart, P. (1998). Preventing groupthink revisited: Evaluating and reforming groups in government. *Organizational Behavior and Human Decision Processes, 73*(2–3), 306–326.

Hartfield, E. (1987). Passionate and companionate love. In R. J. Sternberg & M. L. Barnes (Eds.), *The psychology of love* (pp. 191–217). New Haven, CT: Yale University Press.

Hartfield, E., & Rapson, R. L. (1992). Similarity and attraction in intimate relationships. *Communication Monographs, 59*, 209–212.

Harvard Mental Health Letter (2010). Experts urge caution in using deep brain stimulation. *Harvard Mental Health Letter, 26*(8), 6–7.

Harvey, S. & Keashly, L. (2003). Predicting the risk for aggression in the workplace: Risk factors, self-esteem and time at work. *Social Behaviour and Personality: An International Journal, 31*(8), 807–814.

Hashioka, S., Miklossy, J., Schwab, C., Klegeris, A., & McGeer, P. L. (2008). Adhesion of exogenous human microglia and THP-1 cells to amyloid plaques of postmortem Alzheimer's disease brain. *Journal of Alzheimer's Disease, 14*(3), 345–352.

Hauck, S. J., & Bartke, A. (2001). Free radical defenses in the liver and kidney of human growth hormone transgenic mice. *Journal of Gerontology and Biological Science, 56*, 153–162.

Havighurst R. J., Neugarten B. L., & Tobin S. N. S. (1968). Disengagement and patterns of aging. In B. L. Neugarten (Ed.), *Middle age and aging: A reader in social psychology* (pp. 161–172). Chicago: University of Chicago Press.

Hawks, S. R., Madanat, H. N., Merrill, R. M., Goudy, M. B., & Miyagawa, T. (2003). A cross-cultural analysis of "motivation for eating" as a potential factor in the emergence of global obesity: Japan and the United States. *Health Promotion International, 18*(2), 153–162.

Hayflick, L. (1977). The cellular basis for biological aging. In C. E. Finch & L. Hayflick (Eds.), *Handbook of biology of aging* (p. 159). New York: Van Nostrand Reinhold.

Hayward, C., Killen, J. D., Kraemer, H. C., & Taylor, C. B. (2000). Predictors of panic attacks in adolescents. *Journal of the American Academy of Child and Adolescent Psychiatry, 39*(2), 207–214.

Hayward, C., Killen, J., & Taylor, C. B. (1989). Panic attacks in young adolescents. *American Journal of Psychiatry, 146*(8), 1061–1062.

Hazan, C., & Shaver, P. (1987). Romantic love conceptualized as an attachment process. *Journal of Personality and Social Psychology, 52*, 511–524.

Heavey, C. L., Layne, C., & Christensen, A. (1993). Gender and conflict structure in marital interaction: A replication and extension. *Journal of Consulting and Clinical Psychology, 61*, 16–27.

Hebb, D. O. (1955). Drives and the CNS (Conceptual Nervous System). *Psychological Review, 62*, 243–254.

Hegeman, R. (2007). "Police: Shoppers stepped over victim." Associated Press, July 4. http://abcnews.go.com/US/wireStory?id=3342724.

Heider, F. (1958). *The psychology of interpersonal relations.* New York: Wiley.

Heil, G., Maslow, A., & Stephens, D. (1998). *Maslow on management.* New York: Wiley.

Heilman, K. M. (2002). *Matter of mind: A neurologist's view of brain-behavior relationships.* New York: Oxford University Press.

Heilman, K., Watson, R., & Valenstein, E. (1993). Neglect and related disorders. In K. Heilman and E. Valenstein (Eds.), *Clinical neuropsychology.* New York: Oxford University Press.

Heimberg, R. G., & Becker, R. E. (2002). *Cognitive-behavioral group therapy for social phobia: Basic mechanisms and clinical strategies.* New York: Guilford Press.

Heinicke, C. M., Goorsky, M., Moscov, S., Dudley, K., Gordon, J., Schneider, C., & Guthrie, D. (2000). Relationship-based intervention with at-risk mothers: Factors affecting variations in outcome. *Infant Mental Health Journal, 21*, 133–155.

Heinrich, B. (2000). Testing insight in ravens. In C. Heyes & L. Huber (Eds.), *The evolution of cognition.* Cambridge, MA: MIT Press.

Helms, J. E. (1992). Why is there no study of cultural equivalence in standardized cognitive ability testing? *American Psychologist, 47*(9), 1083–1101.

Henin, A., Mick, E., Biederman, J., Fried, R., Wozniak, J., Faraone, S. V., Harrington, K., Davis, S., & Doyle, A. E. (2007). Can bipolar disorder-specific neuropsychological impairments in children be identified? *Journal of Consulting and Clinical Psychology, 75*(2), 210–220.

Henningfield, J. E., Clayton, R., & Pollin, W. (1990). Involvement of tobacco in alcoholism and illicit drug use. *British Journal of Addition, 85*, 279–292.

Henningfield, J. E., Cohen, C., Slade, J. D. (1991). Is nicotine more addictive than cocaine? *British Journal of Addiction, 86*, 565–569.

Henry, J. (2007, July 30). Professor pans "learning style" teaching method. [London] *Telegraph.* Retrieved March 24, 2010, from http://www.telegraph.co.uk/news/uknews/1558822/Professor-pans-learning-style-teaching-method.html

Herberman, R. B., & Ortaldo, J. R. (1981). Natural killer cells: Their role in defenses against disease. *Science, 214*, 24–30.

Herbst, J. H., Zonderman, A. B., McCrae, R. R., & Costa, P. T., Jr. (2000). Do the dimensions of the Temperament and Character Inventory map a simple genetic architecture? Evidence from molecular genetics and factor analysis. *American Journal of Psychiatry, 157*, 1285–1290.

Herman, L. M., Pack, A. A., & Morrell-Samuels, P. (1993). Representational and conceptual skills of dolphins. In H. L. Roitblatt, L. M. Herman, & P. E. Nachtigall (Eds.), *Language and communication: Comparative perspectives*. Hillsdale, NJ: Erlbaum.

Hernandez, D., & Fisher, E. M. (1996). Down syndrome genetics: Unravelling a multifactorial disorder. *Human Molecular Genetics, 5*, 1411–1416.

Heron, M. P., Hoyert, D. L., Jiaquan Xu, Scott, C., & Tejada-Vera, B. (2008). Deaths: Preliminary Data for 2006. National Vital Statistics Reports, *56*(16), 1–52.

Herring, M. P., O'Connor, P. J., & Dishman, R. K. (2010). The effect of exercise training on anxiety symptoms among patients: A systematic review. *Archives of Internal Medicine, 170*(4), 321–331.

Herrnstein, R. J., & Murray, C. (1994). *The bell curve: The reshaping of American life by differences in intelligence*. New York: Free Press.

Hersh, S. M. (2004, May 10). Annals of national security: Torture at Abu Ghraib. *The New Yorker*.

Herxheimer, A., & Petrie, K. J. (2001). Melatonin for preventing and treating jet lag. *Cocharane Database of Systematic Reviews* (1), CD 001520.

Hettema, J. M., Neale, M. C., & Kendler, K. S. (2001). A review and meta-analysis of the genetic epidemiology of anxiety disorders. *American Journal of Psychiatry, 158*, 1568–1578.

Hewstone, M., Rubin, M., & Willis, H. (2002). Intergroup bias. *Annual Review of Psychology, 53*, 575–604.

Heyes, C. M. (1998). Theory of mind in nonhuman primates. *Behavior and Brain Science, 21*, 101–148.

Hicklin, J., & Widiger, T. A. (2000). Convergent validity of alternative MMPI-2 personality disorder scales. *Journal of Personality Assessment, 75*(3), 502–518.

Hilgard E. R. (1965). *Hypnotic susceptibility*. New York: Harcourt, Brace & World.

Hilgard, E. R. (1991). *A neodissociation interpretation of hypnosis*. In S. J. Lynn & J. W. Rhue (Eds.), *Theories of hypnosis* (pp. 83–104). New York: Guilford Press.

Hilgard, E. R., & Hilgard, J. R. (1994). *Hypnosis in the relief of pain* (Rev. ed.). New York: Brunner/Mazel.

Hill, D. (1990). Causes of smoking in children. In B. Durston & K. Jamrozik, *Smoking and health 1990—The global war. Proceedings of the 7th World Conference on Smoking and Health*, 1–5 April. Perth: Health Department of Western Australia, 205–209.

Hill, J. A. (1998). Miscarriage risk factors and causes: What we know now. *OBG Management, 10*, 58–68.

Hill, P. C., & Butter E. M. (1995). The role of religion in promoting physical health. *Journal of Psychology and Christianity, 14*(2), 141–155.

Hillman, C. H., Pontifex, M. B., Raine, L. B., Castelli, D. M., Hall, E. E., & Kramer, A. F. (2009). The effect of acute treadmill walking on cognitive control and academic achievement in preadolescent children. *Neuroscience, 159*(3), 1044–1054.

Hilton, J. L., & von Hipple, W. (1996). Stereotypes. *Annual Review of Psychology, 47*, 237–271.

Hines, T. (2003). *Pseudoscience and the paranormal: A critical examination of the evidence*. Amherst, NY: Prometheus Books.

Hintze, J. M. (2002). Interventions for fears and anxiety problems. In M. R. Shinn, H. R. Walker, & G. Stoner (Eds.), *Interventions for academic and behavior problems II: Preventive and remedial approaches* (pp. 939–954). Bethesda, MD: National Association of School Psychologists.

Hochman, J. (1994). Buried memories challenge the law. *National Law Journal, 1*, 17–18.

Hodges, J. R. (1994). Retrograde amnesia. In A. Baddeley, B. A. Wilson, & F. Watts (Eds.), *Handbook of memory disorders* (pp. 81–107). New York: Wiley.

Hodgson, B. (2001). *In the arms of Morpheus: The tragic history of laudanum, morphine, and patent medicines*. New York: Firefly Books.

Hodson, D. S., & Skeen, P. (1994). Sexuality and aging: The hammerlock of myths. *The Journal of Applied Gerontology, 13*, 219–235.

Hoffmann, R. & McGuire, S. Y. (2010), Learning and Teaching Strategies. *American Scientist, 98*(5) (September-October): 378–382.

Hoffrage, U., Hertwig, R., & Gigerenzer, G. (2000). Hindsight bias: A by-product of knowledge updating? *Journal of Experimental Psychology: Learning, Memory, and Cognition, 26*, 566–581.

Hofstede, G. H. (1980). *Culture's consequences, international differences in work-related values*. Beverly Hills, CA: Sage.

Hofstede, G. J., Pedersen, P. B., & Hofstede, G. H. (2002). *Exploring culture: Exercises, stories, and synthetic cultures*. Yarmouth, ME: Intercultural Press.

Hogg, M. A., & Hains, S. C. (1998). Friendship and group identification: A new look at the role of cohesiveness in groupthink. *European Journal of Social Psychology, 28*(1), 323–341.

Holcomb, W. R. (1986). Stress inoculation therapy with anxiety and stress disorders of acute psychiatric patients. *Journal of Clinical Psychology, 42*, 864–872.

Holden, C., & Vogel, G. (2002). Plasticity: Time for a reappraisal? *Science, 296*, 2126–2129.

Hollon, S., These, M., & Markowitz, J. (2002). Treatment and prevention of depression. *Psychological Science in the Public Interest, 3*, 39–77.

Hollon, S. D., & Beck, A. T. (1994). Cognitive and cognitive-behavioral therapies. In A. E. Bergin & and S. L. Garfield (Eds.), *Handbook of psychotherapy and behavior change* (4th ed., p. 428). Chichester, UK: Wiley.

Holman, E. A., Silver, R. C., Poulin, M., Andersen, J., Gil-Rivas, V., & McIntosh, D. N. (2008). Terrorism, acute stress, and cardiovascular health: A 3-year national study following the September 11th attacks. *Archives of General Psychiatry, 65*, 73–80.

Holmes, T. H., & Masuda, M. (1973). Psychosomatic syndrome: When mothers-in-law or other disasters visit, a person can develop a bad, bad cold. *Psychology Today, 5*(11), 71–72, 106.

Holmes, T. H., & Rahe, R. H. (1967). The Social Readjustment Rating Scale. *Journal of Psychosomatic Research II*, 213–218.

Holt-Lunstad, J., Uchino, B. N., Smith, T. W., Cerny, C. B., & Nealey-Moore, J. B. (2003). Social relationships and ambulatory blood pressure: Structural and qualitative predictors of cardiovascular function during everyday social interactions. *Health Psychology, 22*, 388–397.

Hood, D. C. (1998). Lower-level visual processing and models of light adaptation. *Annual Review of Psychology, 49*, 503–535.

Hopfinger, J. B., Buonocore, M. H., & Mangun, G. R. (2000). The neural mechanisms of top-down attentional control. *Nature Neuroscience, 3*, 284–291.

Horne, J. A., & Staff, C. H. (1983). Exercise and sleep: Body heating effects. *Sleep, 6*, 36–46.

Horney, K. (1939). *New ways in psychoanalysis*, New York: Norton.

Horney, K. (1967/1973). *Feminine psychology*. New York: Norton.

Horowitz, D. L. (1985). *Ethnic groups in conflict*. Berkeley: University of California Press.

Hortaçsu, N. (1999). The first year of family and couple initiated marriages of a Turkish sample: A longitudinal investigation. *International Journal of Psychology, 34*(1), 29–41.

Hossain, P., Kawar, B., & El Nahas, M. (2007). Obesity and diabetes in the developing world—A growing challenge. *New England Journal of Medicine, 356*(9), 973.

Hothersall, D. (1995). *History of psychology* (pp. 162–165). New York: McGraw-Hill.

Hovland, C. I. (1937). The generalization of conditioned responses. I. The sensory generalization of conditioned responses with varying frequencies of tone. *Journal of General Psychology, 17*, 1251–48.

Hu, P., & Meng, Z. (August, 1996). *An examination of infant–mother attachment in China*. Poster session presented at the meeting of the International Society for the Study of Behavioral Development, Quebec City, Quebec, Canada.

Hu, S., Pattatucci, A. M. L., Patterson, C., Li, L., Fulker, D. W., Cherny, S. S., Kruglyak, L., & Hamer, D. H. (1994). Linkage between sexual orientation and chromosome Xq28 in males but not in females. *Nature Genetics, 11*, 248–256.

Hubel, D. H., & Wiesel, T. N. (1959). Receptive fields of single neurons in the cat's striate cortex. *The Journal of Physiology, 148*, 574–591.

Huesmann, L. R., & Eron, L. (1986). *Television and the aggressive child: A cross-national comparison*. Hillsdale, NJ: Erlbaum.

Huesmann, L. R., & Miller, L. S. (1994). Long-term effects of repeated exposure to media violence in childhood. In L. R. Huesmann (Ed.), *Aggressive behavior: Current perspectives* (pp. 153–183). New York: Plenum Press.

Huesmann, L. R., Moise, J. F., & Podolski, C. L. (1997). The effects of media violence on the development of antisocial behavior. In D. M. Stoff, J. Breiling, & J. D. Maser (Eds.), *Handbook of antisocial behavior* (pp. 181–193). New York: Wiley.

Huesmann, L. R., Moise-Titus, J., Podolski, C. L., & Eron, L. D. (2003). Longitudinal relations between children's exposure to TV violence and their aggressive and violent behavior in young adulthood: 1977–1992. *Developmental Psychology, 39*(2), 201–221.

Huff, W., Lenartz, D., Schormann, M., Lee, S. H., Kuhn, J., Koulousakis, A., Mai, J., Daumann, J., Maarouf, M., Klosterkotter, J., & Sturm, V. (2010). Unilateral deep brain stimulation of the nucleus accumbens in patients with treatment-resistant obsessive-compulsive disorder: Outcomes after one year. *Clinical Neurology and Neurosurgery, 112*(2), 137–143.

Hugenberg, K., & Bodenhausen, G. V. (2003). Facing prejudice: Implicit prejudice and the perception of facial threat. *Psychological Science, 14*, 640–643.

Hughes, J. (1993). Behavior therapy. In T. R. Kratochwill & R. J. Morris (Eds.), *Handbook of psychotherapy with children and adolescents* (pp. 185–220). Boston: Allyn & Bacon.

Hughes, S. M., Harrison, M. A., & Gallup, G. G., Jr. (2007). Sex differences in romantic kissing among college students: An evolutionary perspective. *Evolutionary Psychology 5*(3), 612–631.

Huitt, W., & Hummel, J. (2003). Piaget's theory of cognitive development. *Educational Psychology Interactive*. Valdosta, GA: Valdosta State University. Retrieved 6/14/04 from http://www.edpsycinteractive.org/topics/cognition/piaget.html

Hull, C. L. (1943). *Principles of behavior*. New York: Appleton-Century.

Hummer, R. A., Rogers, R. G., Nam, C. B., & Ellison, C. G. (1999). Religious involvement and U.S. adult mortality. *Demography, 36*(2), 273–285.

Humphries, L. L. (1987). Bulimia: Diagnosis and treatment. *Comprehensive Therapy, 13*, 12–15.

Hunsley, J., & Mash, E. J. (2008). Developing criteria for evidence-based assessment: An introduction to assessments that work. In J. Hunsley & E. J. Mash (Eds.), *A guide to assessments that work* (3rd ed.). New York, NY: The Guilford Press.

Hurley, D. (1989). The search for cocaine's methadone. *Psychology Today, 23*(7/8), 54.

Hurley, S., & Nudds, M. (Eds.). (2006). *Rational animals?* Oxford, UK: Oxford University Press.

Hurvich, L. M., & Jameson, D. (1957). An opponent-process theory of color vision. *Psychological Review, 64*, 384–404.

Hvas, L. (2001). Positive aspects of menopause: A qualitative study. *Maturitas 39*(1), 11–17.

Hyde, J. S., & Kling, K. C. (2001). Women, motivation, and achievement. *Psychology of Women Quarterly, 25*, 264–378.

Hygge, S. A., & Öhman, A. (1976). The relation of vicarious to direct instigation and conditioning of electrodermal responses. *Scandanavian Journal of Psychology, 17*(1), 217–222.

Hyman, I. E., Gilstrap, L. L., Decker, K., & Wilkinson, C. (1998). Manipulating remember and know judgements of autobiographical memories. *Applied Cognitive Psychology, 12*, 371–386.

Hyman, I. E., Jr. (1993). Imagery, reconstructive memory, and discovery. In B. Roskos-Ewoldsen, M. J. Intons-Peterson, & R. E. Anderson (Eds.), *Imagery, creativity, and discovery: A cognitive perspective* (pp. 99–121). The Netherlands: Elsevier Science.

Hyman, I. E., Jr., & Loftus, E. F. (1998). Errors in autobiographical memories. *Clinical Psychology Review, 18*, 933–947.

Hyman, I. E., Jr., & Loftus, E. F. (2002). False childhood memories and eyewitness memory errors. In M. L. Eisen, J. A. Quas, & G. S. Goodman (Eds.), *Memory and suggestibility in the forensic interview* (pp. 63–84). Mahwah, NJ: Erlbaum.

Iacoboni, M., Woods, R. P., Brass, M., Bekkering, H., Mazziotta, J. C., & Rizzolatti, G. (1999). Cortical mechanisms of human imitation. *Science, 286*, 2526–2528.

Iber, C., Ancoli-Israel, S., Chesson Jr., A. L., & Quan, S. F. (2007). *The AASM Manual for the scoring of sleep and associated events: Rules, terminology and technical specifications.* Westchester, IL: American Academy of Sleep Medicine.

Iemmola, F., & Camperio Ciani, A. (2008). New evidence of genetic factors influencing sexual orientation in men: Female fecundity increase in the maternal line. *Archives of Sexual Behavior, 38*(3), 393–399.

Imaizumi, Y. (1998). A comparative study of twinning and triplet rates in 17 countries, 1972–1996. *Acta Genetic Medicine and Gemellology, 47*, 101–114.

Insel, T. R., & Wang, P. S. (2010). Rethinking mental illness. *The Journal of the American Medical Association, 303*(19). 1970–1971.

Irwin, M., Cole, J., & Nicassio, P. (2006). Comparative meta-analysis of behavioral intervention for insomnia and their efficacy in middle aged adults and in older adults 55+ years of age. *Health Psychology, 25*, 3–14.

Isabel, J. (2003). *Genetics: An introduction for dog breeders.* Loveland, CO: Alpine.

Isenberg, D. J. 1986. Group Polarization: A Critical Review and Meta-Analysis. *Journal of Personality and Social Psychology, 50*(6), 1141–1151.

Iwakabe, S. (2008). Psychotherapy integration in Japan. *Journal of Psychotherapy Integration, 18*(1), 103–125.

Iwamoto, E. T., & Martin, W. (1988). A critique of drug self-administration as a method for predicting abuse potential of drugs. *National Institute on Drug Abuse Research Monograph, 1046*, 81457–81465.

Izard, C. (1988). Emotion-cognition relationships and human development. In C. Izard, J. Kagan, & R. Zajonc (Eds.), *Emotions, cognition, and behavior.* New York: Cambridge University Press.

Jackson, R. (2001). *Plato: A beginner's guide.* London: Hoder & Stroughton.

Jackson, T., Iezzi, T., Gunderson, J., Fritch, A., & Nagasaka, T. (2002). Gender differences in pain perception: The mediating role of self-efficacy beliefs. *Sex Roles, 47*, 561–568.

Jaeggi, S. M., Buschkuehl, M., Jonides, J., & Perrig, W. J. (2008). Improving fluid intelligence with training on working memory. *Proceedings of the National Academy of Sciences, USA, 105*(19), 6829–6833.

James, W. (1884). What is an emotion? *Mind, 9*, 188–205.

James, W. (1890). *Principles of psychology.* New York: Henry Holt.

James, W. (1890, 2002). *The principles of psychology (Vols. 1 and 2).* Cambridge, MA: Harvard University Press.

James, W. (1894). The physical basis of emotion. *Psychological Review, 1*, 516–529.

Jameson, M., Diehl, R., & Danso, H. (2007). Stereotype threat impacts college athletes' academic performance. *Current Research in Social Psychology, 12*(5), 68–79.

Jang, K. L., Livesley, W. J., & Vernon, P. A. (1996). Heritability of the Big Five personality dimensions and their facets: A twin study. *Journal of Personality, 64*, 577–591.

Jang, K. L., McCrae, R. R., Angleitner, A., Riemann, R., & Livesley, W. J. (1998). Heritability of facet-level traits in a cross-cultural twin sample: Support for a hierarchical model of personality. *Journal of Personality and Social Psychology, 74*, 1556–1565.

Janis, I. (1972). *Victims of groupthink.* Boston: Houghton-Mifflin.

Janis, I. (1982). *Groupthink* (2nd ed.). Boston: Houghton-Mifflin.

Janos, P. M. (1987). A fifty-year follow-up of Terman's youngest college students and IQ-matched agemates. *Gifted Child Quarterly, 31*, 55–58.

January, D., & Kako, E. (2007). Re-evaluating evidence for linguistic relativity: Reply to Boroditsky (2001). *Cognition, 104*(2), 417–426.

Janus, S. S., & Janus, C. L. (1993). *The Janus report on sexual behavior.* New York: Wiley.

Jay, S. M., & Elliot, C. H. (1990). A stress inoculation program for parents whose children are undergoing medical procedures. *Journal of Consulting and Clinical Psychology, 58*, 799–804.

Jehn, K., Northcraft, G., & Neale, M. (1999). Why differences make a difference: A field study of diversity, conflict, and performance in workgroups. *Administrative Science Quarterly, 44*, 741–763.

Jensen, A. R. (1969). How much can we boost IQ and scholastic achievement? *Harvard Educational Review, 39*, 1–123.

Jester, C. (2000). Introduction to the DVC Learning Style Survey for College. Adapted for the Web by Suzanne Miller, Instructor, Math and Multimedia © Copyright 2000. Retrieved from the Internet on September 7th, 2004, at www.metamath.com/lsweb/dvclearn.htm.

Jimerson, D. C., Wolfe, B. E., Metzger, E. D., Finkelstein, D. M., Cooper, T. B., & Levine, J. M. (1997). Decreased serotonin function in bulimia nervosa. *Archives of General Psychiatry, 54*, 529–534.

John, O. P., Angleitner, A., & Ostendorf, F. (1988). The lexical approach to personality: A historical review of trait taxonomic research. *European Journal of Personality, 2*, 171–203.

Johnson, C. P., Myers, S. M. (Council on Children with Disabilities). (2007). Identification and evaluation of children with autism spectrum disorders. *Pediatrics, 120*(5), 1183–1215.

Johnson, D., Johnson, R., & Smith, K. (1991). *Active learning: Cooperation in the college classroom.* Edna, MN: Interaction Book Company.

Johnson, G. (1995, June 6). Chimp talk debate: Is it really language? *New York Times.*

Johnson, J., Cohen, P., Pine, D. S., Klein, D. F., Kasen, S., & Brook, J. S. (2000). Association between cigarette smoking and anxiety disorders during adolescence and early adulthood. *Journal of the American Medical Association, 284*(18), 2348–2351.

Johnson, M. E., Brems, C., Mills, M. E., Neal, D. B., & Houlihan, J. L. (2006). Moderating effects of control on the relationship between stress and change. *Administration and Policy in Mental Health and Mental Health Services Research, 33*(4), 499–503.

Johnston, L. D., O'Malley, P. M., Bachman, J. G., Schulenberg, J. E. (2007). *Monitoring the Future national survey results on drug use, 1975–2006: Vol. 1. Secondary school students 2006.* Bethesda, MD: National Institute on Drug Abuse; September 2007.

Jones, E. E., & Harris, V. A. (1967). The attribution of attitudes. *Journal of Experimental Social Psychology, 3*, 1–24.

Jones, E. J., Krupnick, J. L., & Kerig, P. K. (1987). Some gender effects in a brief psychotherapy. *Psychotherapy, 24*, 336–352.

Jones, E., Fear, N. T., & Wessely, S. (2007). Shell shock and mild traumatic brain injury: A historical review. *The American Journal of Psychiatry, 164*(11), 1641–1645.

Jones, G. W. (1997). Modernization and divorce: Contrasting trends in Islamic Southeast Asia and the West. *Population and Development Review, 23*(1), 95–113.

Jones, H. M., & Pilowsky, L. S. (2002). Dopamine and antipsychotic drug action revisited. *British Journal of Psychiatry, 181*, 271–275.

Jones, M. K., & Menzies, R. G. (1995). The etiology of fear of spiders. *Anxiety, Stress and Coping, 8*, 227–234.

Judelsohn, R. G. (2007). Vaccine Safety: Vaccines are one of public health's great accomplishments. *Skeptical Inquirer, 31.*6 (November/December), Retrieved June 13, 2010, from http://www.csicop.org/si/show/vaccine_safety_vaccines_are_one_of_public_healthrsquos_great_accomplishment/

Juffer, F., & Rosenboom, L. G. (1997). Infant–mother attachment of internationally adopted children in the Netherlands. *International Journal of Behavioral Development, 20*(1), 93–107.

Julien, R. M., Advokat, C. D., & Comaty, J. E. (2008). *A primer of drug action: A comprehensive guide to the actions, uses, and side effects of psychoactive drugs* (11th ed.). New York: Worth Publishers.

Jung, C. (1933). *Modern man in search of a soul.* New York: Harcourt Brace.

Kabat-Zinn, J., Lipworth, L., & Burney, R. (1985). The clinical use of mindfulness meditation for the self-regulation of chronic pain. *Journal of Behavioral Medicine, 8*, 163–190.

Kabat-Zinn, J., Lipworth, L., Burney, R., & Sellers, W. (1986). Four year follow-up of a meditation-based program for the self regulation of chronic pain: Treatment outcomes and compliance. *Clinical Journal of Pain, 2*, 159–173.

Kable, J. A., Coles, C. D., Lynch, M. E., & Platzman, K. (2008). Physiological responses to social and cognitive challenges in 8-year olds with a history of prenatal cocaine exposure. *Developmental Psychobiology, 50*(3), 251–265.

Kagan, J. (1998). *Galen's prophecy: Temperament in human nature.* (pp. 237–260, 270–274). New York: Basic Books.

Kagan, J. (2010). *The temperamental thread.* New York: Dana Press.

Kagan, J., Snidman, N., Kahn, V., & Towsley, S. (2007). The preservation of two infant temperaments into adolescence. *SRCD Monographs, 72*(2), 76-80.

Kahan, M., & Sutton, N. (1998). Overview: Methadone treatment for the opioid-dependent patient. In B. Brands & J. Brands (Eds.), *Methadone maintenance: A physician's guide to treatment* (pp. 1–15). Toronto, ON: Addiction Research Foundation.

Kahneman, D., & Tversky, A. (1973). On the psychology of prediction. *Psychological Review, 80*, 237–251.

Kahneman, D., Slovic, P., & Tversky, A. (1982). *Judgment under uncertainty: Heuristics and biases.* New York: Cambridge University Press.

Kail, R. & Hall, L. K. (2001). Distinguishing short-term memory from working memory. *Memory and Cognition, 29*(1), 1–9.

Kakko, J., Svanborg, K. D., Kreek, M. J., & Heilig, M. (2003). 1-year retention and social function after buprenorphine-associated relapse prevention treatment for heroin dependence in Sweden: A randomised, placebo-controlled trial. *Lancet, 361*, 662–668.

Kales, A., Soldatos, C., Bixler, E., Ladda, R. L., Charney, D. S., Weber, G., & Schweitzer, P. K. (1980). Hereditary factors in sleepwalking and night terrors. *British Journal of Psychiatry, 137*, 111–118.

Kam, D. (June 29, 2010). Valdez expert: Psychological impact of Gulf oil spill won't fully emerge for years. *The Palm Beach Post,* June 29th, 2010 . Retrieved from the Internet on August 3, 2011 at http://www.palmbeachpost.com/news/valdez-expert-psychological-impact-of-gulf-oil-spill-776588.html

Kamin, L. J. (1995, February). Behind the curve. *Scientific American,* 99–103.

Kandel, E. R., & Schwartz, J. H. (1982). Molecular biology of learning: Modulation of transmitter release. *Science, 218,* 433–443.

Kanne, S. M., Balota, D. A., Storandt, M., McKeel, D. W., Jr., & Morris, J. C. (1998). Relating anatomy to function in Alzheimer's disease: Neuropsychological profiles predict regional neuropathology 5 years later. *Neurology, 50*(4), 979–985.

Karayiorgou, M., Altemus, M., Galke, B., Goldman, D., Murphy, D., Ott, J., & Gogos, J. (1997). Genotype determining low catechol-O-methyltransferase activity as a risk factor for obsessive-compulsive disorder. *Proceedings of the National Academy of Sciences, USA, 94,* 4572–4575.

Karney, B. R., & Bradbury, T. N. (2000). Attributions in marriage: State or trait? A growth curve analysis. *Journal of Personality and Social Psychology, 78,* 295–309.

Karpicke, J. D., & Blunt, J. R. (2011). Retrieval practice produces more learning than elaborative studying with concept mapping. *Science,* DOI: 10.1126scoemce/1199327

Kastenbaum, R., & Costa, P. T., Jr. (1977). Psychological perspective on death. *Annual Review of Psychology, 28,* 225–249.

Katz, V. L. (2007). Spontaneous and recurrent abortion: Etiology, diagnosis, treatment. In V. L. Katz, G. M. Lentz, R. A. Lobo, & D. M. Gershenson (Eds.), *Comprehensive Gynecology* (5th ed). Philadelphia: Mosby Elsevier.

Kaufman, J., & Zigler, E. (1993). The intergenerational transmission of abuse is overstated. In R. J. Gelles & D. R. Loseke (Eds.), *Current controversies on family violence.* Newbury Park, CA: Sage.

Kaveny, M. C. (2001). The case of conjoined twins: Embodiment, individuality, and dependence. *Theological Studies, 62.*

Kaye, W. H., Frank, G. K., Bailer, U. F., Henry, S. E., Meltzer, C. C., Price, J. C., Mathis, C. A., & Wagner, A. (2005). Serotonin alterations in anorexia and bulimia nervosa: New insights from imaging studies. *Physiology & Behavior, 85,* 73–81.

Kaye, W.H., Frank, G.K., Bailer, U.F., Henry, S.E., Meltzer, C.C., Price, J.C., Mathis, C.A., & Wagner, A. (2005). Serotonin alterations in anorexia and bulimia nervosa: new insights from imaging studies. *Physiology & Behavior, 85,* 73–81.

Kazdin, A. E. (1980). Acceptability of time out from reinforcement procedures for disruptive behavior. *Behavior Therapy, 11*(3), 329–344.

Kearney, C. A., & Silverman, W. K. (1998). A critical review of pharmacotherapy for youth with anxiety disorders: Things are not as they seem. *Journal of Anxiety Disorders, 12,* 83–102.

Keillor, J., Barrett, A., Crucian, G., Kortenkamp, S., & Heilman, K. (2002). Emotional experience and perception in the absence of facial feedback. *Journal of the International Neuropsychological Society, 8*(1), 130–135.

Keirsey, D.(1998). *Please understand me ii: Temperament character intelligence.* Del Mar, CA: Prometheus Nemesis Book Company.

Keller, M. B., McCullough, J. P., Klein, D. N., Arnow, B., Dunner, D., Gelenberg, A., Markowitz, J. C., Nemeroff, C. B., Russell, J. M., Thase, M. E., Trivedi, M. H., & Zajecka, J. (2000). A comparison of nefazodone, the cognitive behavioral-analysis system of psychotherapy, and their combination for the treatment of chronic depression. *New England Journal of Medicine, 342*(20), 1462–1470.

Kelly, I. (1980). The scientific case against astrology. *Mercury, 10*(13), 135.

Kelly, J. A., McAuliffe, T. L., Sikkema, K. J., Murphy, D. A., Somlai, A. M., Mulry, G., Miller, J. G., Stevenson, L. Y., & Fernandez, M. I. (1997). Reduction in risk behavior among adults with severe mental illness who learned to advocate for HIV prevention. *Psychiatric Services, 48*(10), 1283–1288.

Kempf, L., & Weinberger, D. R. (2009). Molecular genetics and bioinformatics: An outline for neuropsychological genetics. In T. E. Goldberg & D. R. Weinberger (Eds.), *The genetics of cognitive neuroscience* (pp. 3–26). Cambridge, MA: MIT Press.

Kendall, P. (1983). Stressful medical procedures: Cognitive-behavioral strategies for stress management and prevention. In D. Meichenbaum & M. Jaremko (Eds.), *Stress reduction and prevention.* (pp. 159–190). New York: Plenum Press.

Kendall, P. C., Hudson, J. L., Gosch, E., Flannery-Schroeder, E., & Suveg, C. (2008). Cognitive-behavioral therapy for anxiety disordered youth: A randomized clinical trial evaluating child and family modalities. *Journal of Consulting and Clinical Psychology, 76*(2), 282–297.

Kendler, K. S. (1985). Diagnostic approaches to schizotypal personality disorders: A historical perspective. *Schizophrenia Bulletin, 11,* 538–553.

Kendler, K. S., & Prescott, C. A. (1999). A population-based twin study of lifetime major depression in men and women. *Archives of General Psychiatry, 56*(1), 39–44.

Kenny, A. (1968). Mind and body, In *Descartes: A study of his philosophy* (p. 279). New York: Random House.

Kenny, A. (1994). Descartes to Kant. In A. Kenny (Ed.), *The Oxford history of western philosophy* (pp. 107–192). Oxford, UK: Oxford University Press.

Kenrick, D. T., Griskevicius, V., Neuberg, S. L., & Schaller, M. (2010). Renovating the pyramid of needs: Contemporary extensions built upon ancient foundations. *Perspectives on Psychological Science, 5*(3), 292–314.

Keromoian, R., & Leiderman, P. H. (1986). Infant attachment to mother and child caretaker in an East African community. *International Journal of Behavioral Development, 9,* 455–469.

Kerwin, D. R., Zhang, Y., Kotchen, J. M., Espeland, M. A., Van Horn, L., McTigue, K. M., Robinson, J. G., Powell, L., Kooperberg, C., Coker, L. H., & Hoffmann, R. (2010). The cross-sectional relationship between body mass index, waist–hip ratio, and cognitive performance in postmenopausal women enrolled in the women's health initiative. *Journal of the American Geriatric Society, 58,* 1427–1432. [Article first published online July 14, 2010]. doi: 10.1111/j.1532-5415.2010.02969.x

Kesebir, S., Graham, J., & Oishi, S. (2010). A theory of human needs should be human-centered, not animal-centered. *Perspectives on Psychological Science, 5*(3), 315–319.

Kety, S. S., Wender, P. H., Jacobsen, B., Ingaham, L. J., Jansson, L., Faber, B., & Kinney, D. K. (1994). Mental illness in the biological and adoptive relatives of schizophrenic adoptees. *Archives of General Psychiatry, 51,* 442–455.

Kiecolt-Glaser, J. K., Fisher, L. D., Ogrocki, P., Stout, J. C., Speicher, C. E., & Glaser, R. (1987). Marital quality, marital disruption, and immune function. *Psychosomatic Medicine, 49,* 13–34.

Kiecolt-Glaser, J. K., Glaser, R., Gravenstein, S., Malarkey, W. B., & Sheridan, J. (1996). Chronic stress alters the immune response to influenza virus vaccine in older adults. *Proceedings of the National Academy of Sciences, USA, 93*(7), 3043–3047.

Kiecolt-Glaser, J. K., Marucha, P. T., Malarkey, W. B., & Marcado, A. M. (1995). Slowing of wound healing by psychological stress. *Lancet, 346,* 1194–1196.

Kiecolt-Glaser, J. K., McGuire, L., Robles, T., & Glaser, R. (2002). Psychoneuroimmunology: Psychological influences on immune function and health. *Journal of Consulting and Clinical Psychology, 70,* 537–547.

Kihlstrom, J.,Mulvaney, S.,Tobias,B., & Tobis, I.(2000).The emotional unconscious. In E.Eich, J.Kihlstrom, G.Bower, J.Forgas, & P.Niedenthal (Eds.), *Cognition and emotion,* (pp.30–86). New York:Oxford University Press.

Kihlstrom, J. F. (1987). The cognitive unconscious. *Science, 237,* 1445–1452.

Kihlstrom, J. F. (1999). Conscious and unconscious cognition. In R. J. Sternberg (Ed.), *The nature of cognition* (pp. 173–203). Cambridge, MA: MIT Press.

Kihlstrom, J. F. (2001). Hypnosis and the psychological unconscious. In Howard S. Friedman (Ed.), *Assessment and therapy: Specialty articles from the encyclopedia of mental health* (pp. 215–226). San Diego, CA: Academic Press.

Kihlstrom, J. F. (2002). Memory, autobiography, history. *Proteus: A Journal of Ideas, 19*(2), 1–6.

Kihlstrom, J., Mulvaney, S., Tobias, B., & Tobis, I. (2000). The emotional unconscious. In E. Eich, J. Kihlstrom, G. Bower, J. Forgas, & P. Niedenthal (Eds.), *Cognition and emotion* (pp. 30–86). New York: Oxford University Press.

Kim, H., & Markus, H. R. (1999). Deviance or uniqueness, harmony or conformity? A cultural analysis. *Journal of Personality and Social Psychology, 77,* 785–800.

Kinsey, A. C., Pomeroy, W. B., & Martin, C. E. (1948). *Sexual behavior in the human male.* Philadelphia: W. B. Saunders.

Kinsey, A. C., Pomeroy, W. B., Martin, C. E., & Gebhard, P. H. (1953). *Sexual behavior in the human female.* New York: W. B. Saunders.

Kirby, J. S., Chu, J. A., & Dill, D. L. (1993). Correlates of dissociative symptomatology in patients with physical and sexual abuse histories. *Comprehensive Psychiatry 34,* 250–263.

Kirmayer, L. J. (1991). The place of culture in psychiatric nosology: *Taijin kyofusho* and the *DSM-III-TR. Journal of Nervous and Mental Disease, 179,* 19–28.

Kitamura, T., Saitoh, Y., Takashima, N., Murayama, A., Niibori, Y., Ageta, H., Sekiguchi, M., Sugiyama, H., & Inokuchi, K. (2009). Adult neurogenesis modulates the hippocampus-dependent period of associative fear memory. *Cell, 139*(4), 814–827.

Kitayama, S., & Markus, H. R. (1994). Introduction to cultural psychology and emotion research. In S. Kitayama & H. R. Markus (Eds.), *Emotion and culture: Empirical studies of mutual influence* (pp. 1–22). Washington, DC: American Psychological Association.

Klein, D. N. (2010). Chronic depression: Diagnosis and classification. *Current Directions in Psychological Science, 19*(2), 96–100.

Klein, D., Schwartz, J., Rose, S., & Leader, J. (2000). Five-year course and outcome of dysthymic disorder: A prospective, naturalistic follow-up study. *American Journal of Psychiatry, 157*(6), 931–939.

Klein, S. B., & Mowrer, R. R. (1989). *Contemporary learning theories: Pavlovian conditioning and the status of traditional learning theory.* Hillsdale, NJ: Erlbaum.

Kleinot, M. C., & Rogers, R. W. (1982). Identifying effective components of alcohol misuse prevention programs. *Journal of Studies on Alcohol, 43,* 802–811.

Klorman, R., Hilpert, P. L., Michael, R., LaGana, C., & Sveen, O. B. (1980). Effects of coping and mastery modeling on experienced and inexperienced pedodontic patients' disruptiveness. *Behavior Therapy, 11,* 156–168.

Klüver, H., & Bucy, P. C. (1939). Preliminary analysis of functions of the temporal lobes in monkeys. *Archives of Neurological Psychiatry, 42,* 979–1000.

Knight, A. (1996). *The life of the law: The people and cases that have shaped our society, from King Alfred to Rodney King.* New York: Crown Publishing Group.

Knight, J. A. (1998). Free radicals: Their history and current status in aging and disease. *Annals of Clinical and Laboratory Science, 28,* 331–346.

Kobasa, S. (1979). Stressful life events, personality, and health: An inquiry into hardiness. *Journal of Personality and Social Psychology, 37*(1), 1–11.

Koch C. & Mormann F. (2010). The neurobiology of consciousness. In G. Mashour (Ed.), *Consciousness, awareness, and anesthesia* (pp. 24–46). New York: Cambridge University Press.

Koenig, H. G., Hays, J. C., Larson, D. B., George, L. K., Cohen, H. J., McCullough, M. E., Meador, K. G., & Blazer, D. G. (1999). Does religious attendance prolong survival? A six-year follow-up study of 3,968 older adults. *Journal of Gerontology, 54A,* M370–M377.

Koenig, H. G., McCullough, M. E., & Larson, D. B. (2001). *Handbook of religion and health.* Oxford, UK: Oxford University Press.

Koh, J. K. (1996). A guide to common Singapore spiders. *BP Guide to Nature* series. Singapore: Singapore Science Center.

Kohlberg, L. (1969). Stage and sequence: the cognitive-developmental approach to socialization. In D. A. Goslin (Ed.), *Handbook of socialization: Theory in research* (pp. 347–480). Boston: Houghton-Mifflin.

Kohlberg, L. (1973). Continuities in childhood and adult moral development revisited. In P. Baltes & K. W. Schaie (Eds.), *Life-span development psychology: Personality and socialization*. San Diego, CA: Academic Press.

Köhler, W. (1925, 1992). *Gestalt psychology: An introduction to new concepts in modern psychology (reissue)*. New York: Liveright.

Korn, S. (1984). Continuities and discontinuities in difficult/easy temperament: Infancy to young adulthood. *Merrill Palmer Quarterly, 30*, 189–199.

Kosslyn, S. M. (1983). Mental imagery. In Z. Rubin (Ed.), *The psychology of being human*. New York: Harper & Row.

Kosslyn, S. M., Alpert, N. M., Thompson, W. L., Maljkovic, V., Weise, S. B., Chabris, C. F., Hamilton, S. E. and Buonano, F. S. (1993). Visual mental imagery activates topographically organized visual cortex: PET investigations. *Journal of Cognitive Neuroscience 5*, 263–287.

Kosslyn, S. M., Ball, T. M., & Reiser, B. J. (1978). Visual images preserve metric spatial information: Evidence from studies of image scanning. *Journal of Experimental Psychology: Human Perception and Performance, 4*, 47–60.

Kosslyn, S. M., Ganis, G., & Thompson, W. L. (2001). Neural foundations of imagery. *Nature Reviews Neuroscience 2*, 635–642.

Kosslyn, S. M., Pascual-Leone, A., Felician, O., Camposano, S., Keenan, J. P., Thompson, W. L., Ganis, G., Sukel, K. E., & Alpert, N. M. (1999). The role of area 17 in visual imagery: Convergent evidence from PET and rTMS. *Science 284*, 167–170.

Kosslyn, S. M., Thompson, W. L., Wraga, M. J., & Alpert, N. M. (2001). Imagining rotation by endogenous and exogenous forces: Distinct neural mechanisms for different strategies. *Neuroreport*, 12, 2519–2525.

Kotkin, M., Daviet, C., & Gurin, J. (1996). The *Consumer Reports* mental health survey. *American Psychologist, 51*(10), 1080–1082.

Kouri, E. M., Pope, H. G., & Lukas, S. E. (1999). Changes in aggressive behavior during withdrawal from long-term marijuana use. *Psychopharmacology, 143*, 302–308.

Kratofil, P. H., Baberg, H. T., & Dimsdale, J. E. (1996). Self-mutilation and severe self-injurious behavior associated with amphetamine psychosis. *General Hospital Psychiatry, 18*, 117–120.

Kriegstein, A., & Alvarez-Buylla, A. (2009). The glial nature of embryonic and adult neural stem cells. *Annual Review of Neuroscience, 32*(1), 149–184.

Kristensen, P., & Bjerkedal, T. (2007). Explaining the relation between birth order and intelligence. *Science, 316*(5832), 1717.

Kryger, M., Lavie, P., & Rosen, R. (1999). Recognition and diagnosis of insomnia. *Sleep, 22*, S421–S426.

Kubicki, M., Niznikiewicz, M., Connor, E., Nestor, P., Bouix, S., Dreusicke, M., Kikinis, R., McCarley, R., & Shenton, M. (2009). Relationship between white matter integrity, attention, and memory in schizophrenia: A diffusion tensor imaging study. *Brain Imaging and Behavior, 3*(2), 191–201.

Kübler-Ross, E. (1997). *The wheel of life: A memoir of living and dying*. New York: Touchstone.

Küntay, A., & Slobin, D. I. (2002). Putting interaction back into child language: Examples from Turkish. *Psychology of Language and Communication*, 6, 5–14.

Kuhn, H. W., & Nasar, S. (Eds.). (2001). *The essential John Nash*. Princeton, NJ: Princeton University Press.

Kuhn, J., Gründler, T. O. J., Lenartz, D., Sturm, V., Klosterkötter, J., & Huff, W. (2010). Deep brain stimulation for psychiatric disorders. *Deutsches Ärzteblatt International, 107* (7), 105–113.

Kulik, J. A., & Mahler, H. I. M. (1989). Social support and recovery from surgery. *Health Psychology, 8*, 221–238.

Kulik, J. A., & Mahler, H. I. M. (1993). Emotional support as a moderator of adjustment and compliance after coronary bypass surgery: A longitudinal study. *Journal of Behavioral Medicine, 16*, 45–63.

Kumar, R. (1994). Postnatal mental illness: A transcultural perspective. *Social Psychiatry and Psychiatric Epidemiology, 29*(6), 250–264.

Kumashiro, M., Rusbult, C. E., Coolsen, M. K., Wolf, S. T., van den Bosch, M., & van der Lee, R. (2009). Partner affirmation, verification, and enhancement as determinants of attraction to potential dates: Experimental evidence of the unique effect of affirmation. Unpublished manuscript, Goldsmiths, University of London.

Kupfer, D. J., & Reger, D. A. (2009). Current activities: Report of the DSM-5 task force. Retrieved from http://www.dsm5.org/ProgressReports/Pages/CurrentActivities ReportoftheDSM-VTaskForce%28March2009%29.aspx

Kupfer, D. J., & Reynolds, C. F., III. (1997). Management of insomnia. *New England Journal of Medicine, 336*(5), 341–346.

Kuriki, I., Ashida, H., Murakami, I., & Kitaoka, A. (2008). Functional brain imaging of the Rotating Snakes illusion by fMRI. *Journal of Vision, 8*(10), 16 11–10.

Kvavilashvili, L., Mirani, J., Schlagman, S., Foley, K., & Dornbrot, D. E. (2009). Consistency of flashbulb memories of September 11 over long delays: Implications for consolidation and wrong time slice hypotheses. *Journal of Memory and Language, 61*(4), 556–572.

LaBar, K. S., LeDoux, J. E., Spencer, D. D., & Phelps, E. A. (1995). Impaired fear conditioning following unilateral temporal lobectomy to humans. *Journal of Neuroscience, 15*, 6846–6855.

LaBerge, D. (1980). Unitization and automaticity in perception. In J. H. Flowers (Ed.), *Nebraska Symposium on Motivation* (pp. 53–71). Lincoln: University of Nebraska Press.

Lacayo, A. (1995). Neurologic and psychiatric complications of cocaine abuse. *Neuropsychiatry, Neuropsychology, and Behavioral Neurology, 8*(1), 53–60.

LaFromboise, T., Coleman, H. L. K., & Gerton J. (1993). Psychological impact of biculturalism: Evidence and theory. *Psychological Bulletin, 114*, 395–412.

Lal, S. (2002). Giving children security: Mamie Phipps Clark and the radicalization of child psychology. *American Psychologist, 57*(1), 20–28.

Lalancette, M.-F., & Standing, L. G. (1990). Asch fails again. *Social Behavior and Personality, 18*(1), 7–12.

Lance, C. J., LaPointe, J. A., & Fisicaro, S. (1994). Tests of three causal models of halo rater error. *Organizational Behavior and Human Decision Performance, 57*, 83–96.

Landrum, R. E. (2009). Finding jobs with a psychology bachelor's degree. Washington, DC: American Psychological Association.

Landrum, R. E., & Davis, S. F. (2007). *The psychology major: Career options and strategies for success*, 3rd ed. Upper Saddle River, NJ: Prentice Hall.

Lane, R. D., Kivley, L. S., DuBois, M. A. Shamasundara, P., & Schwartz, G. E. (1995). Levels of emotional awareness and the degree of right hemisphere dominance in the perception of facial emotion. *Neuropsychologia, 33*, 525–538.

Lang, J. W. B., & Lang, J. (2010). Priming competence diminishes the link between cognitive test anxiety and test performance. *Psychological Science, 21*(6), 811–819.

Lange, C. (1885. The emotions. Reprinted in C. G. Lange & W. James (Eds.), *The emotions*. New York: Harner.

Langer, E. J., & Rodin, J. (1976). The effects of enhanced personal responsibility for the aged: A field experiment in an institutional setting. *Journal of Personality and Social Psychology, 34*, 191–198.

Langone, M. C. (1996). Clinical update on cults. *Psychiatric Times, 13*(7), 1–3.

Lapsley, D. K., Milstead, M., Quintana, S. M., Flannery, D., & Buss, R. R. (1986). Adolescent egocentrism and formal operations: Tests of a theoretical assumption. *Developmental Psychology, 22*, 800–807.

Larsen, J. T., Berntson, G. G., Poehlmann, K. M., Ito, T. A., & Cacioppo, J. T. (2008). The psychophysiology of emotion. In M. Lewis, J. M. Haviland-Jones, & L. F. Barrett (Eds.), *Handbook of Emotions* (3rd ed., pp. 180–195). New York: Guilford Press.

Larzelere, R. (1986). Moderate spanking: Model or deterrent of children's aggression in the family? *Journal of Family Violence, 1*(1), 27–36.

Lashley, K. S. (1938). The thalamus and emotion. *The Psychological Review, 45*, 21–61.

Latané, B., & Darley, J. M. (1969). Bystander "apathy." *American Scientist, 57*(2), 244–268.

Laumann, E. O., Paik, A., & Rosen, R. C. (1999). Sexual dysfunction in the United States: Prevalence and predictors. *Journal of the American Medical Association, 281*(6), 537–544.

Launer, L., Masaki, K., Petrovitch, H., Foley, D., & Havlik, R. (1995). The association between midlife blood pressure levels and late-life cognitive function. *Journal of the American Medical Association, 272*(23), 1846–1851.

Laungani, P. (1997). Death in a Hindu Family. In C. M. Parkes, P. Laungani & B. Young (Eds.), *Death and Bereavement Across Cultures* (pp. 52–72). London: Routledge.

Lavergne, G. M. (1997). *A sniper in the tower: The true story of the Texas Tower massacre*. New York: Bantam.

Laws, G., Davies, I., & Andrews, C. (1995). Linguistic structure and nonlinguistic cognition: English and Russian blues compared. *Language and Cognitive Processes, 10*, 59–94.

Lay, C., & Nguyen, T. T. I. (1998). The role of acculturation-related and acculturation non-specific daily hassles: Vietnamese-Canadian students and psychological distress. *Canadian Journal of Behavioural Science, 30*(3), 172–181.

Lazarus, R. S. (1991). *Emotion and adaptation*. New York: Oxford University Press.

Lazarus, R. S. (1993). From psychological stress to the emotions: A history of changing outlooks. *Annual Review of Psychology, 44*, 1–22.

Lazarus, R. S. (1999). *Stress and emotion: A new synthesis*. New York: Springer.

Lazarus, R. S., & Folkman, S. (1984). *Stress, appraisal and coping*. New York: Springer.

Leary, M. R., & Forsyth, D. R. (1987). Attributions of responsibility for collective endeavors. *Review of Personality and Social Psychology, 8*, 167–188.

Leclerc, C. M., & Hess, T. M. (2007). Age differences in the bases for social judgments: Tests of a social expertise perspective. *Experimental Aging Research, 33*(1), 95–120.

LeDoux, J. (2003). The emotional brain, fear, and the amygdala. *Cellular and Molecular Neurobiology, 23*(4–5), 727–738.

LeDoux, J. E. (1996). *The emotional brain: The mysterious underpinnings of emotional life*. New York: Simon & Schuster.

LeDoux, J. E. (2007). The amygdala. *Current Biology, 17*(20), R868–R874.

LeDoux, J. E., & Phelps, E. A. (2008). Emotional networks in the brain. In M. Lewis, J. M. Haviland-Jones, & L. F. Barrett (Eds.), *Handbook of emotions* (3rd ed., pp. 159–179). New York: Guilford Press.

Lee, F., Hallahan, M., & Herzog, T. (1996). Explaining real life events: How culture and domain shape attributions. *Personality and Social Psychology Bulletin, 22*, 732–741.

Lee, M., & Shlain, B. (1986). *Acid dreams: The complete social history of LSD: The CIA, the sixties, and beyond*. New York: Grove Press.

Lee, P. A. (1995). Physiology of puberty. In K. L. Becker (Ed.), *Principles and practice of endocrinology and metabolism* (pp. 822–830). Philadelphia: J. B. Lippincott.

Lee, S. H., Kim, E. Y., Kim, S., & Bae, S. M. (2010). Event-related potential patterns and gender effects underlying facial affect processing in schizophrenia patients. *Neuroscience Research, 7*, 7.

Lefcourt, H. M., Davidson, K., Shepherd, R., & Phillips, M. (1995). Perspective-taking humor: Accounting for stress moderation. *Journal of Social and Clinical Psychology 14*(4), 373–391.

Lehnert, B. (2007). Joint wave-particle properties of the individual photon. *Progress in Physics, 4*(10), 104–108.

Lehr, U., & Thomae, H. (1987). Patterns of psychological aging. *Results from the Bonne Aging Longitudinal Study (BOLSA)*. Stuttgart, Germany: Enke.

Leon, P., Chedraui, P., Hidalgo, L., & Ortiz, F. (2007). Perceptions and attitudes toward the menopause among middle-aged women from Guayaquil, Ecuador. *Maturitas, 57*(3), 233–238.

Leonard, L. (1997). *Children with specific language impairment.* Cambridge, MA: MIT Press.

Leroy, C., & Symes, B. (2001). Teachers' perspectives on the family backgrounds of children at risk. *McGill Journal of Education, 36*(1), 45–60.

Lesch, K. P., Bengel, D., Heils, A., Sabol, S. Z., Greenberg, B. D., Petri, S., Benjamin, J., Muller, C. R., Hamer, D. H., & Murphy, D. L. (1996). Association of anxiety-related traits with a polymorphism in the serotonin transporter gene regulatory region. *Science, 274*(5292), 1527–1531.

Levenson, R. W. (1992). Autonomic nervous system differences among emotions. *Psychological Sciences, 3*, 23–27.

Levenson, R. W., Ekman, P., Heider, K., & Friesen, W. V. (1992). Emotion and autonomic nervous system activity in the Minangkabau of West Sumatra. *Journal of Personality and Social Psychology, 62*, 972–988.

Levinson, D. F. (2006). The genetics of depression: A review. *Biological Psychiatry, 60*(2), 84–92.

Levy, B. R., Slade, M. D., Kunkel, S. R., & Kasl, S. V. (2002). Longevity increased by positive self-perceptions of aging. *Journal of Personality and Social Psychology, 83*, 261–269.

Levy, S. R., Stroessner, S. J., & Dweck, C. S. (1998). Stereotype formation and endorsement: The role of implicit theories. *Journal of Personality and Social Psychology, 74*, 1421–1436.

Lewin, K. (1936). *Principles of topological psychology.* New York: McGraw-Hill.

Lewis, J. R. (1995) *Encyclopedia of afterlife beliefs and phenomenon.* Detroit, MI: Visible Ink Press.

Lilienfeld, S. O. (1999). Projective measures of personality and psychopathology: How well do they work? *Skeptical Inquirer, 23*(5), 32–39.

Lin, C. S., Lyons, J. L., and Berkowitz, F. (2007). Somatotopic identification of language-SMA in language processing via fMRI. *Journal of Scientific and Practical Computing 1*(2), 3–8.

Lin, P. J., & Schwanenflugel, P. J. (1995). Cultural familiarity and language factors in the structure of category knowledge. *Journal of Cross-Cultural Psychology, 26*, 153–168.

Lin, P. J., Schwanenflugel, P. J. & Wisenbaker, J. M. (1990). Category typicality, cultural familiarity, and the development of category knowledge. *Developmental Psychology, 26*, 805–813.

Lindau, S. T., Schumm, P., Laumann, E. O., Levinson, W., O'Muircheartaigh, C. A., & Waite, L. J. (2007). A study of sexuality and health among older adults in the United States. *New England Journal of Medicine, 357*(8), 762–764.

Lindemann, B. (1996). Taste reception. *Physiological Review, 76*, 719–766.

Lisanby, S. H., Maddox, J. H., Prudic, J., Devanand, D. P., & Sackeim, H. A. (2000). The effects of electroconvulsive therapy on memory of autobiographical and public events. *Archives of General Psychiatry, 57*, 581–590.

Livesley, J. W. (Ed.). (1995). *The DSM-IV Personality disorders.* New York: Guilford Press.

Lizskowski, U., Carpenter, M., Striano, T., & Tomasello, M. (2006). 12- and 18-month-olds point to provide information for others. *Journal of Cognition and Development, 7*, 173–187.

Lock, M. (1994). Menopause in cultural context. *Experimental Gerontology, 29*(3–4), 307–317.

Loehlin, J. C. (1992). *Genes and environment in personality development.* Newbury Park, CA: Sage.

Loehlin, J. C., McCrae, R. R., Costa, P. T., Jr., & John, O. P. (1998). Heritabilities of common and measure-specific components of the Big Five personality factors. *Journal of Research in Personality, 32*, 431–453.

Loftus, E. (1975). Leading questions and the eyewitness report. *Cognitive Psychology, 7*, 560–572.

Loftus, J. (2001). America's liberalization in attitudes toward homosexuality, 1973 to 1998. *American Sociological Review, 66*(5), 762–782.

Logue, M. W., Vieland, V. J., Goedken, R. J., & Crowe, R. R. (2003). Bayesian analysis of a previously published genome screen for panic disorder reveals new and compelling evidence for linkage to chromosome 7. *American Journal of Medical Genetics, 121B*, 95–99.

Loo, S. K., Hale, T. S., Macion, J., Hanada, G., McGough, J. J., McCracken, J. T., et al. (2009). Cortical activity patterns in ADHD during arousal, activation and sustained attention. *Neuropsychologia, 47*(10), 2114–2119.

Lord, T. R. (2001). 101 reasons for using cooperative learning in biology teaching. *The American Biology Teacher, 63*(1), 30–38.

Lovaas, O. I. (1964). Cue properties of words: The control of operant responding by rate and content of verbal operants. *Child Development, 35*, 245–256.

Lovaas, O. I. (1987). Behavioral treatment and normal educational and intellectual functioning in young autistic children. *Journal of Consulting and Clinical Psychology, 55*, 3–9.

Lovaas, O. I., Berberich, J. P., Perloff, B. F., & Schaffer, B. (1966). Acquisition of imitative speech by schizophrenic children. *Science, 151*, 705–707.

Lu, S., & Ende, N. (1997). Potential for clinical use of viable pluripotent progenitor cells in blood bank stored human umbilical cord blood. *Life Sciences, 61*, 1113–1123.

Luborsky, L., Singer, B., & Luborsky, L. (1975). Comparative studies of psychotherapies: Is it true that "everyone has won and all must have prizes"? *Archives of General Psychiatry, 32*, 995–1008.

Luby, J. L. (2010). Preschool depression: The importance of identification of depression early in development. *Current Directions in Psychological Science, 19*(2), 91-95.

Luchins, A. S. (1957). Primacy-recency in impression formation. In C. Hovland (Ed.), *The order of presentation in persuasion* (pp. 33–40, 55–61). New Haven, CT: Yale University Press.

Luck, S. J., & Gold, J. M. (2008). The construct of attention in schizophrenia. *Biological Psychiatry, 64*(1), 34–39.

Lucy, J. A., & Shweder, R. A. (1979). Whorf and his critics: Linguistic and nonlinguistic influences on color memory. *American Anthropologist, 81*, 581–615.

Luria, A. R. (1968). *The mind of a mnemonist* (pp. 24, 25). New York: Basic Books.

Lutkenhaus, P., Grossmann, K. E., & Grossman, K. (1985). Infant–mother attachment at twelve months and style of interaction with a stranger at the age of three years. *Child Development, 56*, 1538–1542.

Lydiard, R. B. (2003). The role of GABA in anxiety disorders. *The Journal of Clinical Psychiatry, 64*(Suppl. 3), 21–27.

Lykken, D. T. (1995). *The antisocial personalities.* Hillsdale, NJ: Erlbaum.

Lykken, D. T., & Tellegen, A. (1996). Happiness is a stochastic phenomenon. *Psychological Science, 7*, 186–189.

Lynch, E. B., Coley, J. D., & Medin, D. L. (2000). Tall is typical: Central tendency, ideal dimensions, and graded category structure among tree experts and novices. *Memory & Cognition, 28*(1), 41–50.

Lytton, H., & Romney, D. M. (1991). Parents' sex-differentiated socialization of boys and girls: A meta-analysis. *Psychological Bulletin, 109*, 267–296.

Lyvers, M. (2003). The neurochemistry of psychedelic experiences. *Science and Consciousness Review, 1*, 1–5.

MacDonald, A. P. (1970). Internal-external locus of control and the practice of birth control. *Psychological Reports, 27*, 206.

MacDonald, D., Kabani, N., Avis, D., & Evens, A. C. (2000). Automated 3D extraction of inner and outer surfaces of cerebral cortex from MRI. *NeuroImage, 12*, 340–356.

Macdonald, Ian; Amos, John; Crone, Timothy; Wereley, Steve (2010-05-21). "The Measure of an Oil Disaster". *The New York Times* (The New York Times Company). Retrieved from the Internet on August 3, 2011 at http://www.nytimes.com/2010/05/22/opinion/22macdonald.html.

Mack, J. E. (1994). *Abduction.* New York: Scribner.

MacKenzie, S. B., Lutz, R. J., & Belch, G. E. (1986, May). The role of attitude toward the ad as a mediator of advertising effectiveness: A test of competing explanations. *Journal of Marketing Research, 23*, 130–143.

Macknik, S. L., King, M., Randi, J., Robbins, A., Teller, Thompson, J., & Martinez-Conde, S. (2008). Attention and awareness in stage magic: Turning tricks into research. *Nature Reviews: Neuroscience, 9*(11), 871–879.

Macknik, S. L., & Martinez-Conde, S. (2009). Real magic: Future studies of magic should be grounded in neuroscience. *Nature reviews: Neuroscience, 10*(3), 241–241.

Macquet, P., & Franck, G. (1996). Functional neuroanatomy of human rapid eye movement sleep and dreaming. *Nature, 383*, 163–166.

Macrae, C. N., & Bodenhausen, G. V. (2000). Social cognition: Thinking categorically about others. *Annual Review of Psychology, 51*, 93–120.

Madsen, K. M., Hviid, A., Vestergaard, M., Schendel, D., Wohlfahrt, J., Thorsen, P., Olsen, J., & Melbye, M. (2002). A population-based study of measles, mumps, rubella vaccine and autism. *New England Journal of Medicine, 347*, 1477–1482.

Mahowald, M. W., & Schenck, C. H. (1996). NREM sleep parasomnias. *Neurologic Clinics, 14*, 675–696.

Mai, J. K., Triepel, J., & Metz, J. (1987). Neurotensin in the human brain. *Neuroscience, 22*, 499–524.

Maier, S. F., Amat, J., Baratta, M. V., Paul, E., & Watkins, L. R. (2006). Behavioral control, the medial prefrontal cortex, and resilience. *Dialogues in Clinical Neuroscience, 8*(4), 397–406.

Maier, S. F., & Watkins, L. R. (1998). Cytokines for psychologists: Implications of bidirectional immune-to-brain communication for understanding behavior, mood, and cognition. *Psychological Review, 105*, 83–107.

Maier, S. F., & Watkins, L. R. (2005). Stressor controllability and learned helplessness: The roles of the dorsal raphe nucleus, serotonin, and corticotropin-releasing factor. *Neuroscience and Biobehavioral Reviews, 29*(4–5), 829–841.

Main, M., & Cassidy, J. (1988). Categories of response to reunion with the parent at age 6: Predictable from infant attachment classifications and stable over a 1 month period. *Developmental Psychology, 24*, 415–426.

Main, M., & Hesse, E. (1990). Parents' unresolved traumatic experiences are related to infant disorganized attachment status; Is frightened and/or frightening parental behaviour the linking mechanism? In M. T. Greenberg, D. Cicchetti, & E. M.

Cummings (Eds.), *Attachment in the preschool years: Theory, research and intervention* (pp. 161–182). Chicago: University of Chicago Press.

Main, M., & Solomon, J. (1990). Procedures for identifying infants as disorganized/disoriented during the Ainsworth Strange Situation. In M. T. Greenberg, D. Cicchetti, & E. M. Cummings (Eds.), *Attachment in the preschool years: Theory, research and intervention* (pp. 121–160). Chicago: University of Chicago Press.

Maletic, V., Robinson, M., Oakes, T., Iyengar, S., Ball, S. G., & Russell, J. (2007). Neurobiology of depression: An integrated view of key findings. *The International Journal of Clinical Practice, 61*(12), 2030–2040.

Mander, B. A., Santhanam, S., Saletin, J. M., & Walker, M. P. (2011). Wake deterioration and sleep restoration of human learning. *Current Biology, 21*(5): R183 DOI: 10.1016/j.cub.2011.01.019.

Mandler, G. (1967). Organization and memory. In K. W. Spence & J. T. Spence (Eds.), *The psychology of learning and motivation, Vol. 1* (pp. 327–372). New York: Academic Press.

Mandler, J. M. (2000). Perceptual and conceptual processes. *Journal of Cognition and Development, 1*, 3–36.

Mandler, J. M. (2003). Conceptual categorization. In D. H. Rakison & L. M. Oakes (Eds.), *Early category and concept development: Making sense of the blooming, buzzing confusion* (pp. 103–131). Oxford, UK: Oxford University Press.

Manson, J., Greenland, P., LaCroix, A. Z., Stefanick, M. L., Mouton, C. P., Oberman, A., Perri, M. G., Sheps, D. S., Pettinger, M. B., & Siscovick, D. S. (2002). Walking compared with vigorous exercise for the prevention of cardiovascular events in women. *The New England Journal of Medicine, 347*(10), 716–725.

Manusov, V., & Patterson, M. L. (Eds.). (2006). *The Sage handbook of nonverbal communication* (p. 289). Thousand Oaks, CA: Sage.

Marcus, G. F. (2001). *The algebraic mind: Integrating connectionism and cognitive science (learning, development, and conceptual change).* Cambridge, MA: MIT Press.

Maren, S., & Fanselow, M. S. (1996). The amygdala and fear conditioning: Has the nut been cracked? *Neuron, 16*, 237–240.

Margolin, S., & Kubic, L. S. (1944). An apparatus for the use of breath sounds as a hypnogogic stimulus. *American Journal of Psychiatry, 100*, 610.

Marik, P. E. (2000). Leptin, obesity, and obstructive sleep apnea. *Chest, 118*, 569–571.

Markovitz, J. H., Lewis, C. E., Sanders, P. W., Tucker, D., & Warnock, D. G. (1997). Relationship of diastolic blood pressure with cyclic GMP excretion among young adults (the CARDIA study): Influence of a family history of hypertension. *Journal of Hypertension, 15*(9), 955–962.

Marks, D. F., Murray, M., Evans, B., Willig, C., Sykes, C. M., & Woodall, C. (2005). *Health Psychology: Theory, research and practice* (pp. 3–25). London: Sage.

Marks, K. (2010). Round-the-world teenage sailor Jessica Watson gets hero's welcome in Australia. *The Christian Science Monitor*, May 16, 2010. Retrieved June 27, 2010, from http://www.csmonitor.com/World/Asia-Pacific/2010/0516/Round-the-world-teenage-sailor-Jessica-Watson-gets-hero-s-welcome-in-Australia

Mars, A. E., Mauk, J. E., & Dowrick, P. (1998). Symptoms of pervasive developmental disorders as observed in prediagnostic home videos of infants and toddlers. *Journal of Pediatrics, 132*, 500–504.

Marsh, R., Steinglass, J. E., Gerber, A. J., Graziano O'Leary, K., Wang, Z., Murphy, D., et al. (2009). Deficient activity in the neural systems that mediate self-regulatory control in bulimia nervosa. *Archives of General Psychiatry, 66*(1), 51–63.

Martin, C. L. (2000). Cognitive theories of gender development. In T. Eckes & H. M. Trautner (Eds.), *The developmental social psychology of gender* (pp. 91–121). Mahwah, NJ: Lawrence Erlbaum.

Martin, J. A., & Buckwalter, J. J. (2001). Telomere erosion and senescence in human articular cartilage chondrocytes. *Journal of Gerontology and Biological Science, 56*(4), 172–179.

Martin, L. (2004). Can sleepwalking be a murder defense? Retrieved October 19, 2004, from http://www.lakesidepress.com/pulmonary/Sleep/sleep-murder.htm

Maruta, T., Colligan, R. C., Malinchoc, M., & Offord, K. P. (2002, August). Optimism-pessimism assessed in the 1960s and self-reported health status 30 years later. *Mayo Clinic Proceedings*. 77, 748–753.

Maslow, A. (1943). A theory of human motivation. *Psychological Review, 50*, 370–396.

Maslow, A. (1971). *The farther reaches of human nature.* New York: Viking Press.

Maslow, A. (1987). *Motivation and personality* (3rd ed.). New York: Harper & Row.

Maslow, A., & Lowery, R. (Ed.). (1998). *Toward a psychology of being* (3rd ed.). New York: Wiley.

Masson, J. M. (1984). *The assault on truth: Freud's suppression of the seduction theory.* New York: Farrar, Straus & Giroux.

Masters, J. C., Burish, T. G., Holton, S. D., & Rimm, D. C. (1987). *Behavior therapy: Techniques and empirical finding.* San Diego, CA: Harcourt Brace Jovanovich.

Masters, W., & Johnson, V. (1966). *Human sexual response.* Boston: Little, Brown.

Masters, W. H., & Johnson, V. E. (1970). *Human sexual inadequacy.* Boston: Little, Brown.

Masuda, T., & Kitayama, S. (2004). Perceiver-induced constraint and attitude attribution in Japan and the U.S.: A case for the cultural dependence of the correspondence bias. *Journal of Experimental Social Psychology, 40*, 409–416.

Matsumoto, D. (1994). *People: Psychology from a cultural perspective* (pp. 144–147). Pacific Grove, CA: Brooks-Cole.

Matthew, N. & Dallery, J. (2007). Mercury rising: Exploring the vaccine–autism myth. *Skeptic, 13*(3), Retrieved May 3, 2010, from http://www.skeptic.com/eskeptic/07-06-20/#feature

Matthews, K. A., Gump, B. B., Harris, K. F., Haney, T. L., & Barefoot, J. C. (2004). Hostile behaviors predict cardiovascular mortality among men enrolled in the Multiple Risk Factor Intervention trial. *Circulation, 109*, 66–70.

Maurer, D., & Young, R. (1983). Newborns' following of natural and distorted arrangements of facial features. *Infant Behaviour and Development, 6*, 127–131.

Mavromatis, A. (1987). *Hypnagogia: The unique state of consciousness between wakefulness and sleep.* London: Routledge & Kegan Paul.

Mavromatis, A., & Richardson, J. T. E. (1984). Hypnagogic imagery. *International Review of Mental Imagery, 1*, 159–189.

Maxmen, J. S., Ward, N. G., & Kilgus, M. D. (2009). *Essential psychopathology and its treatment.* New York, NY: W. W. Norton & Company.

Mayer, J. D. (1999). Emotional Intelligence: Popular or scientific psychology? *APA Monitor, 30*(8), 50.

Mayer, J. D., & Geher, G. (1996). Emotional intelligence and the identification of emotion. *Intelligence, 22*, 89–113.

Mayer, J. D., Salovey, P., & Caruso, D. R. (2000). Models of emotional intelligence. In R. J. Sternberg (Ed.), *Handbook of human intelligence* (2nd ed., pp. 396–420). New York: Cambridge University Press.

Maziade, M., Bissonnette, L., Rouillard, E., Martinez, M., Turgeon, M., Charron, L., Pouliot, V., Boutin, P., Cliché, D., Dion, C., Fournier, J. P., Garneau, Y., Lavallee, J. C., Montgrain, N., Nicole, L., Pires, A., Ponton, A. M., Potvin, A., Wallot, H., Roy, M. A., & Merette, C. (Le Groupe IREP). (1997). 6p24–22 region and major psychoses in the Eastern Quebec population. *American Journal of Medical Genetics, 74*, 311–318.

Mazzoni, G. A. L., Loftus, E. F., & Kirsch, I. (2001). Changing beliefs about implausible autobiographical events: A little plausibility goes a long way. *Journal of Experimental Psychology: Applied, 7*(1), 51–59.

McCann, S. J. H., & Stewin, L. L. (1988). Worry, anxiety, and preferred length of sleep. *Journal of Genetic Psychology, 149*, 413–418.

McCauley, C. (1998). Group dynamics in Janis's theory of groupthink: Backward and forward. *Organizational Behavior and Human Decision Processes, 73*(2–3), 142–162.

McClelland, D. C. (1961). *The achieving society.* Princeton, NJ: Van Nostrand.

McClelland, D. C. (1987). *Human motivation.* Cambridge, MA: Cambridge University Press.

McClelland, J. L., & Rumelhart, D. E. (1988). Explorations in parallel distributed processing. Cambridge, MA: MIT Press.

McConaghy, N., Hadzi-Pavlovic, D., Stevens, C., Manicavasagar, V., Buhrich, N., & Vollmer-Conna, U. (2006). Fraternal birth order and ratio of heterosexual/homosexual feelings in women and men. *Journal of Homosexuality, 51*(4), 161–174.

McCrae, R. R., & Costa, P. T. (1990). *Personality in adulthood.* New York: Guilford Press.

McCrae, R. R., & Costa, P. T., Jr. (1996). Toward a new generation of personality theories: Theoretical contexts for the five-factor model. In J. S. Wiggins (Ed.), *The five-factor model of personality: Theoretical perspectives* (pp. 51–87). New York: Guilford.

McCrae, R. R., Costa, P. T., Jr., Ostendorf, F., Angleitner, A., Hrebickova, M., Avia, M. D., Sanz, J., Sanchez-Bernardos, M. L., Kusdil, M. E., Woodfield, R., Saunders, P. R, & Smith, P. B. et al. (2000). Nature over nurture: Temperament, personality, and life span development. *Journal of Personality and Social Psychology, 78*, 173–186.

McCrae R. R., Terracciano A., & 78 Members of the Personality Profiles of Cultures Project (2005). Universal features of personality traits from the observer's perspective: Data from 50 cultures. *Journal of Personality and Social Psychology, 88*, 547–561.

McCrae, R. R., & Terracciano, A. (2007). The Five-Factor model and its correlates in individuals and cultures. In F. J. R. van de Vijver, D. A. van Hemert, & Y. Poortinga (Eds.), *Individuals and cultures in multi-level analysis* (pp. 247–281). Mahwah, NJ: Erlbaum.

McDaniel, M. A., Howard, D. C., & Einstein, G. O. (2009). The read-recite-review study strategy: Effective and portable. *Psychological Science, 20*(4), 516–522.

McDermott, J. F. (2001). Emily Dickinson revisited: A study of periodicity in her work. *American Journal of Psychiatry, 158*(5), 686–690.

McDougall, T. (2009) Nursing children and adolescents with bipolar disorder. *Journal of Child and Adolescent Psychiatric Nursing, 22*: 33–39.

McDougall, W. (1908). *An introduction to social psychology.* London: Methuen & Co.

McEwen, B. S. (2000). The neurobiology of stress: From serendipity to clinical relevance. *Brain Research, 886*, 172–189.

McGaugh, J. L. (2004). The amygdala modulates the consolidation of memories of emotionally arousing experiences, *Annual Review Neuroscience, 27*, 1–28.

McGinn, L. K. (2000). Cognitive behavioral therapy of depression: Theory, treatment, and empirical status. *American Journal of Psychotherapy, 54*, 254–260.

McGinnis, J. M., & Foege, W. H. (1993). Actual causes of death in the United States. *Journal of the American Medical Association, 270*(18), 2207–2212.

McGrath, E., Keita, G. P., Strickland, B. R., & Russo, N. F. (1992). *Women and depression: Risk factors and treatment issues.* Washington, DC: American Psychological Association.

McGregor, D. (1960). *The human side of enterprise.* New York: McGraw-Hill.

McGuire, F. (1994). Army alpha and beta tests of intelligence. In R. J. Sternberg (Ed.), *Encyclopedia of intelligence* (Vol. 1, pp. 125–129.) New York: Macmillan.

McLaughlin, K. A., Fairbank, J. A., Gruber, M. J., Jones, R. T., Lakoma, M. D., Pfefferbaum, B., Sampson, N. A., & Kessler, R. C. (2009). Serious emotional disturbance among youths exposed to Hurricane Katrina 2 years postdisaster. *Journal of the American Academy of Child and Adolescent Psychiatry, 48*(11), 1069–1078.

McLaughlin, K. A., Fairbank, J. A., Gruber, M. J., Jones, R. T., Osofsky, J. D., Pfefferbaum, B., Sampson, N. A., Kessler, R. C. (2010). Trends in serious emotional disturbance among youths exposed to Hurricane Katrina. *Journal of the American Academy of Child Adolescent Psychiatry, 49*(10), 990-1000.

McLaughlin, S. K. & Margolskee, R. F. (1994). Vertebrate taste transduction. *American Scientist, 82,* 538–545.

McMahon, F. J., Simpson, S. G., McInnis, M. G., Badner, J. A., MacKinnon, D. F., & DePaulo, J. R. (2001). Linkage of bipolar disorder to chromosome 18q and the validity of bipolar II disorder. *Archives of General Psychiatry, 58,* 1025–1031.

McMonagle, T., & Sultana, A. (2002). Token economy for schizophrenia (Cochrane Review). In *The Cochrane Library, Issue 2.* Oxford: Update Software.

McPherson, J. M., Smith-Lovin, L., Cook, J. M., (2001). Birds of a feather: Homophily in social networks. *Annual Review of Sociology* 27, 415–444.

Meador, B. D., & Rogers, C. R. (1984). Person-centered therapy. In R. J. Corsini (Ed.), *Current psychotherapies* (3rd ed., pp. 142–195). Itasca, IL: Peacock.

Medical Economics Staff. (1994). *PDR family guide to women's health & prescription drugs.* Montvale, NJ: Medical Economics Company.

Mehrabian, A. (2000). Beyond IQ: Broad-based measurement of individual success potential or "emotional intelligence." *Genetic, Social, and General Psychology Monographs, 126,* 133–239.

Meineri, S. & Guéguen N. (2008). An Application of the Foot-in-the-Door Strategy in the Environmental Field. *European Journal of Social Sciences, 7,* 71–74.

Mejía, O. L., & McCarthy, C. J. (2010). Acculturative stress, depression, and anxiety in migrant farmwork college students of Mexican heritage. *International Journal of Stress Management, 17*(1), 1–20.

Melzack, R., & Wall, P. D. (1965). Pain mechanisms: A new theory. *Science, 150,* 971–979.

Melzack, R., & Wall, P. D. (1996). *The challenge of pain.* London: Penguin Books.

Merikle, M. P. (2000). Subliminal perception. In A. E. Kazdin (Ed.), *Encyclopedia of Psychology* (Vol. 7, pp. 497–499). New York: Oxford University Press.

Merriam-Webster. (2003). *Merriam-Webster's collegiate dictionary* (11th ed.). Springfield, MA: Merriam-Webster.

Mervis, C. B., & Rosch, E. (1981). Categorization of natural objects. *Annual Review of Psychology, 32,* 89–115.

Meyrick, J. (2001). Forget the blood and gore: An alternative message strategy to help adolescents avoid cigarette smoking. *Health Education, 101*(3), 99–107.

Michalski, D., Mulvey, T., & Kohoout, J. (2010). *2008 American Psychological Association survey of psychology health service providers.* Retrieved April 5, 2010, from http://www.apa.org/workforce/publications/08-hsp/report.pdf

Mikami, A. Y., Szwedo, D. E., Allen, J. P., Evans, M. A., & Hare, A. L. (2010). Adolescent peer relationships and behavior problems predict young adults' communication on social networking websites. *Developmental Psychology, 46,* 46–56.

Miles, D. R., & Carey, G. (1997). Genetic and environmental architecture of human aggression. *Journal of Personality and Social Psychology, 72,* 207–217.

Milgram, S. (1964a). Behavioral study of obedience. *Journal of Abnormal and Social Psychology, 67,* 371–378.

Milgram, S. (1964b). Issues in the study of obedience: A reply to Baumrind. *American Psychologist, 19,* 848–852.

Milgram, S. (1974). *Obedience to authority: An experimental view.* New York: Harper & Row.

Miller, G. A. (1956). The magical number seven, plus or minus two: Some limits on our capacity for processing information. *Psychological Review, 63,* 81–97.

Miller, J. G. (1984). Culture and the development of everyday social explanation. *Journal of Personality and Social Psychology, 46,* 961–978.

Miller, K., & Doman, J. M. R. (1996, April). Together forever. *Life Magazine,* 46–56.

Miller, K. E., & Graves, J. C. (2000). Update on the prevention and treatment of sexually transmitted diseases. *American Family Physician, 61,* 379–386.

Miller, L. H., & Smith, A. D. (1993). *The stress solution.* New York: Pocket Books.

Miller, M., & Rahe, R. H. (1997). Life changes scaling for the 1990s. *Journal of Psychosomatic Research, 43*(3), 279–292.

Miller, M. N., & Pumariega, A. (1999). Culture and eating disorders. *Psychiatric Times, 16*(2), 1–4.

Miller, M.N., & Pumariega, A.(1999). *Culture and eating disorders. PsychiatricTimes, 16*(2), 1–4.

Miller, N. E., Sears, S. R., Mowrer, O. H., Doob, L. W., & Dollard, J. (1941). The frustration-aggression hypothesis. *Psychological Review, 48,* 337–342.

Miller, T. Q., Smith, T. W., Turner, C. W., Guijarro, M. L., & Hallet, A. J. (1996). A meta-analytic review of research on hostility and physical health. *Psychological Bulletin, 119,* 322–348.

Miller, T. Q., Turner, C. W., Tindale, R. S., Posavac, E. J., & Dugoni, B. L. (1991). Reasons for the trend toward null findings in research on Type A behavior. *Psychological Bulletin, 110,* 469–485.

Miller, W. R., & Rollnick, S. (2002). *Motivational interviewing: Preparing people for change* (2nd ed.). New York, NY: The Guilford Press.

Mills, M. A., Edmondson, D., & Park, C. L. (2007). Trauma and stress response among Hurricane Katrina evacuees. *American Journal of Public Health, 97*(1), 116–123.

Milner, B., Corkin, S., & Teuber, H. L. (1968). Further analysis of the hippocampal syndrome: 14-year follow-up study of H. M. *Neuropsychologia, 6,* 215–234.

Mintz, L. B., & Betz, N. E. (1988). Prevalence and correlates of eating disordered behaviors among undergraduate women. *Journal of Counseling Psychology, 35,* 463–471.

Mischel, W. (1966). A social learning view of sex differences in behaviour. In E. E. Maccoby (Ed.), *The development of sex differences* (pp. 56–81). Stanford, CA: Stanford University Press.

Mischel, W., & Shoda, Y. (1995). A cognitive-affective system theory of personality: Reconceptualizing situations, dispositions, dynamics, and invariances in personality structure. *Psychological Review, 102,* 246–268.

Mishell, D. R. (2001). Menopause. In M. A. Stenchever et al. (Eds.), *Comprehensive gynecology* (4th ed., pp. 1217–1258). St. Louis, MO: Mosby.

Mitchell, J. E. (1985). *Anorexia nervosa & bulimia, diagnosis and treatment.* Minneapolis: University of Minnesota Press.

Mitchell, J. E., Pyle, R. L., Eckert, E. D. (1981). Frequency and duration of binge-eating episodes in patients with bulimia. *American Journal of Psychiatry, 138,* 835–836.

Mitchell, S. A., & Black, M. J. (1996). *Freud and beyond: A history of modern psychoanalytic thought* [Reprint ed.]. New York: HarperCollins.

Miyatake, A., Morimoto Y., Oishi, T., Hanasaki, N., Sugita, Y., Iijima, S., Teshima. Y., Hishikawa, Y., & Yamamura, Y. (1980). Circadian rhythm of serum testosterone and its relation to sleep: Comparison with the variation in serum luteinizing hormone, prolactin, and cortisol in normal men. *Journal of Clinical Endocrinology and Metabolism, 51*(6), 1365–1371.

Moffic, H. S. (2003). Seven ways to improve "cultural competence." *Current Psychiatry, 2*(5), 78.

Mogil, J. S. (1999). The genetic mediation of individual differences in sensitivity to pain and its inhibition. *Proceedings of the National Academy of Sciences, USA, 96*(14), 7744–7751.

Mokdad, A. H., Bowman, B. A., Ford, E. S., Dietz, W. H., Vinicor, F., Bales, V. S., & Marks, J. S. (2001). Prevalence of obesity, diabetes, and obesity related health risk factors. *Journal of the American Medical Association, 289,* 76–79.

Moll, H., & Tomasello, M. (2007). How 14- and 18-month-olds know what others have experienced. *Developmental Psychology, 43,* 309–317.

Möller, A., & Hell, D. (2002). Eugen Bleuler and forensic psychiatry. *International Journal of Law and Psychiatry, 25,* 351–360.

Money, J. (1994). *Sex errors of the body and related syndromes.* Baltimore: Paul H. Brookes.

Monteleone, P., Martiadis, V., Colurcio, B., & Maj, M. (2002). Leptin secretion is related to chronicity and severity of the illness in bulimia nervosa. *Psychosomatic Medicine, 64,* 874–879.

Moody, R., & Perry, P. (1993). *Reunions: Visionary encounters with departed loved ones.* London: Little, Brown.

Moore, T. E. (1988). The case against subliminal manipulation. *Psychology and Marketing, 5,* 297–316.

Moore, T. H., Zammit, S., Lingford-Hughes, A., Barnes, T. R., Jones, P. B., Burke, M., & Lewis, G. (2007). Cannabis use and risk of psychotic or affective mental health outcomes: A systematic review. *Lancet, 370,* 293–294, 319–328.

Moore-Ede, M. C., Sulzman, F. M., & Fuller, C. A. (1982). *The clocks that time us.* Cambridge, MA: Harvard University Press.

Moorhead, G., Neck, C. P., & West, M. S. (1998). The tendency toward defective decision making within self-managing teams: The relevance of groupthink for the 21st century. *Organizational Behavior and Human Decision Processes, 73*(2–3), 327–351.

Mora, G. (1985). History of psychiatry. In H. I. Kaplan & B. J. Sadock (Eds.), *Comprehensive textbook of psychiatry* (pp. 2034–2054). Baltimore: Williams & Wilkins.

Moreland, R. L., & Zajonc, R. B. (1982). Exposure effects in person perceptions: Familiarity, similarity, and attraction. *Journal of Experimental Social Psychology, 18*(5), 395–415.

Moreno-Manzano V., Rodriguez-Jimenez F. J., Acena-Bonilla J. L., Fustero-Lardies S., Erceg S., Dopazo J., Montaner D., Stojkovic M., Sanchez-Puelles J. M. (2009). FM19G11, a new HIF modulator, affects stem cell differentiation status. *J. Biol Chem 285*(2), 1333–1342

Morgan, C. A., Rasmusson, A., Pietrzak, R. H., Coric, V., Southwick, S. M. (2009). Relationships among plasma dehydroepiandrosterone and dehydroepiandrosterone sulfate, cortisol, symptoms of dissociation, and objective performance in humans exposed to underwater navigation stress. *Biological Psychiatry, 66*(4), 334–340.

Morgan, C. D., & Murray, H. A. (1935). A method for investigating fantasies: The Thematic Apperception Test. *Archives of Neurology and Psychiatry, 34,* 298–306.

Morin, C. M., Bootzin, R. R., Buysse, D. J., Edinger, J. D., Espie, C. A., & Lichstein, K. L. (2006). Psychological and behavioral treatment of insomnia: Update of the recent evidence (1998–2004). *Sleep, 29*(11), 1398–1414.

Morris, M., Nisbett, R. E., & Peng, K. (1995). Causal understanding across domains and cultures. In D. Sperber, D. Premack, & A. J. Premack (Eds.), *Causal cognition: A multidisciplinary debate* (pp. 577–612). Oxford, UK: Oxford University Press.

Morris, M. W., & Peng, K. (1994). Culture and cause: American and Chinese attributions social and physical events. *Journal of Personality and Social Psychology, 67,* 949–971.

Morris, S. (2009, November 20). Devoted husband who strangled wife in his sleep walks free from court. Retrieved June 5, 2011, from http://www.guardian.co.uk/uk/2009/nov/20/brian-thomas-dream-strangler-tragedy

Mortimer, J. A., Snowdon, D. A., & Markesbery, W. R. (2008). Small head circumference is associated with less education in persons at risk for Alzheimer disease in later life. *Alzheimer Disease & Associated Disorders. 22*(3), 249–254.

Moruzzi, G., & Magoun, H. W. (1949). Brainstem reticular formation and activation of the EEG. *Electroencephalographs in Clinical Neurophysiology, 1,* 455–473.

Mowat, F. (1988). *Woman in the mists: The story of Dian Fossey and the mountain gorillas of Africa.* New York: Warner Books.

Mroczek, D. K., Spiro, A., & Turiano, N. A. (2009). Do health behaviors explain the effect of neuroticism on mortality? Longitudinal findings from the VA Normative Aging Study. *Journal of Research in Personality, 43*(4), 653.

Mufson, L. H., Dorta, K. P., Olfson, M., Weissman, M. M., & Hoagwood, K. (2004). Effectiveness research: Transporting interpersonal psychotherapy for depressed adolescents (IPT-A) from the lab to school-based health clinics. *Clinical Child and Family Psychology Review, 7*(4), 251–261.

Mukamel, R., Ekstrom, A. D., Kaplan, J., Iacoboni, M., & Fried, I. (2010). Single-neuron responses in humans during execution and observation of actions. *Current Biology, 20,* 750–756.

Muller-Oerlinghausen, B., Berghofer, A., & Bauer, M. (2002). Bipolar disorder. *Lancet, 359,* 241–247.

Munoz, Daniel (15 May 2010). Australian teenager finishes round-world solo sail. *Reuters.* Retrieved May 15, 2010, from http://www.reuters.com/article/idUS-TRE64E0D920100515.

Münsterberg, H. (1908). *On the witness stand.* New York: Clark, Boardman.

Münsterberg, H. (1913). *Psychology and industrial efficiency.* Boston: Houghton Mifflin

Murdock, B. B., Jr. (1962). The serial position effect in free recall. *Journal of Experimental Psychology, 64,* 482–488.

Murphy, C. C., Boyle, C., Schendel, D., Decouflé, P., & Yeargin-Allsopp, M. (1998). Epidemiology of mental retardation in children. *Mental Retardation and Developmental Disabilities Research Reviews, 4,* 6–13.

Murphy, L. R. (1995). Managing job stress: An employee assistance/human resource management partnership. *Personnel Review, 24*(1), 41–50.

Murphy, M., & Donavan, S. (1997). *The physical and psychological effects of meditation: A review of contemporary research with a comprehensive bibliography.* Petaluma, CA: Institute of Noetic Sciences.

Murray, S. L., Holmes, J. G., MacDonald, G., & Ellsworth, P. C. (1998). Through the looking glass darkly? When self-doubts turn into relationship insecurities. *Journal of Personality and Social Psychology, 75,* 1459–1480.

Muter, P. (1978). Recognition failure of recallable words in semantic memory. *Memory and Cognition, 6*(1), 9–12.

Nadeau, K. G., Quinn, P., & Littman, E. (2001). *AD/HD self-rating scale for girls.* Springfield, MD: Advantage Books.

Naitoh, P., Kelly, T. L., & Englund, C. E. (1989). *Health effects of sleep deprivation* (Naval Health Research Centre, Rep. No. 89-46), San Diego, CA: NHRC.

Najavits, L. M. (2007). Psychosocial treatments for postraumatic stress disorder. In P. E. Nathan & J. M. Gorman (Eds.), *A guide to treatments that work* (3rd ed., pp. 513–530). New York, NY: Oxford University Press.

Naqvi, N., Tranel, D., & Bechara, A. (2006). Visceral and decision-making functions of the ventromedial prefontal cortex. In D. H. Zald & S. L. Rauch (Eds.), *The orbitofrontal cortex* (pp. 325–353). New York: Oxford University Press.

Nasar, S. (1998). *A beautiful mind: A biography of John Forbes Nash, Jr., winner of the Nobel Prize in economics 1994.* New York: Simon & Schuster.

Nathan, P. E., & Gorman, J. M. (2007). *Psychosocial treatments for postraumatic stress disorder* (3rd ed.). New York, NY: Oxford University Press.

National Academy of Neuropsychology. (May, 2001). NAN definition of a clinical neuropsychologist [Electronic version]. Retrieved April 13, 2010, from http://www.nanonline.org/NAN/Files/PAIC/PDFs/NANPositionDefNeuro.pdf

National Center for Health Statistics (NCHS) (2007). Alcohol use. Retrieved July 25, 2007, from http://www.cdc.gov/nchs/fastats/alcohol.htm

National Collegiate Athletic Association (2002). 2002 NCAA graduation rates report. Retrieved September 21, 2007, from NCAA—The National Collegiate Athletic Association: The online resource for the National Collegiate Athletic Association Web site: http://web1.ncaa.org/web_files/grad_rates/2002/index.html.

National Institutes of Health. (2007). *Stem cell basics.* Retrieved February 6, 2008, from http://stemcells.nih.gov/info/basics/

National Institute of Mental Health (NIMH) (2010). The numbers count: Mental disorders in America. Retrieved from http://www.nimh.nih.gov/health/publications/the-numbers-count-mental-disorders-in-america/index.shtml

National Institute of Mental Health (NIMH) Genetics Workgroup. (1998). *Genetics and mental disorders* (NIH Publication No. 98-4268). Rockville, MD: National Institute of Mental Health.

National Institute on Alcoholism and Alcohol Abuse (NIAAA) (2007). Data/Statistical Tables. Retrieved July 25, 2007, from http://www.niaaa.nih.gov/Resources/DatabaseResources/QuickFacts/default.htm

National Institute on Drug Abuse (NIDA). (2002). Research report series—Prescription drugs: Abuse and addiction. National Institutes of Health (NIH). Retrieved July 19, 2008, from http://www.drugabuse.gov/ResearchReports/Prescription/prescription5.html

National Institute on Drug Abuse. (2006, May). NIDA InfoFacts: MDMA (Ecstasy). Retrieved May 5, 2010, from http://www.nida.nih.gov/Infofacts/ecstasy.html

National Safety Council. (2010). National safety council estimates that at least 1.6 million crashes are caused each year by drivers using cell phones and texting. Retrieved June 5, 2011, from http://www.nsc.org/Pages/NSCestimates16millioncrashescausedbydriversusingcellphonesandtexting.aspx

National Sleep Foundation (2009). Can't sleep? What to know about insomnia. Retrieved June 5, 2011, from http://www.sleepfoundation.org/article/sleep-related-problems/insomnia-and-sleep

National Wildlife Federation. (2010). Compare the Exxon Valdez and BP Oil Spills. Retrieved from http://www.nwf.org/Oil-Spill/Effects-on-Wildlife/Compare-Exxon-Valdez-and-BP-Oil-Spills.aspx

Neale, M. C., Rushton, J. P., & Fulker, D. W. (1986). The heritability of items from the Eysenck Personality Questionnaire. *Personality and Individual Differences, 7,* 771–779.

Neary, N. M., Goldstone, A. P., & Bloom, S. R. (2004). Appetite regulations: From the gut to the hypothalamus. *Clinical Endocrinology, 60*(2), 153–160.

Neimark, J. (1996). The diva of disclosure, memory researcher Elizabeth Loftus. *Psychology Today, 29*(1), 48–80.

Neimeyer, R. A., & Mitchell, K. A. (1998). Similarity and attraction: A longitudinal study. *Journal of Social and Personality Relationships, 5,* 131–148.

Neisser, U. (1982). Snapshots or benchmarks? In U. Neisser (Ed.), *Memory observed: Remembering in natural contexts* (pp. 43–48). San Francisco: W. H. Freeman.

Neisser, U., & Harsch, N. (1992). Phantom flashbulbs: False recollections of hearing the news about *Challenger.* In E. Winograd & U. Neisser (Eds.), *Affect and accuracy in recall: Studies of "flashbulb memories"* (pp. 9–31). New York: Cambridge University Press.

Nelson, D. B., Sammel, M. D., Freeman, E. W., Lin, H., Gracia, C. R., & Schmitz, K. H. (2008). Effect of physical activity on menopausal symptoms among urban women. *Medicine and Science in Sports & Exercise, 40*(1), 50–58.

Nestor, P. G., Kubicki, M., Niznikiewicz, M., Gurrera, R. J., McCarley, R. W., & Shenton, M. E. (2008). Neuropsychological disturbance in schizophrenia: A diffusion tensor imaging study. *Neuropsychology, 22*(2), 246–254.

Neto, F. (1995). Conformity and independence revisited. *Social Behavior and Personality, 23*(3), 217–222.

Neumarker, K. (1997). Mortality and sudden death in anorexia nervosa. *International Journal of Eating Disorders, 21,* 205–212.

Neumeister, A., Bain, E., Nugent, A. C., Carson, R. E., Bonne, O., Luckenbaugh, D. A., Eckelman, W., Herscovitch, P., Charney, D. S., & Drevets, W. C. (2004). Reduced serotonin Type 1a receptor binding in panic disorder. *The Journal of Neuroscience, 24*(3), 589–591.

Neville, H. J., & Bavelier, D. (2000). Specificity and plasticity in neurocognitive development in humans. In M. S. Gazzaniga (Ed.), *The New Cognitive Neurosciences* (2nd ed., pp. 83–99). Cambridge, MA: MIT Press.

Nicholson, N., Cole, S., & Rocklin, T. (1985). Conformity in the Asch situation: A comparison between contemporary British and U.S. students. *British Journal of Social Psychology, 24,* 59–63.

Nickell, J. 1995. Crop circle mania wanes: An investigative update. *Skeptical Inquirer 19*(3), 41–43.

Nickerson, R. S., & Adams, J. J. (1979). Long-term memory for a common object. *Cognitive Psychology, 11,* 287–307.

Niedermeyer, E. (2005). Historical aspects. In E. Niedermeyer & F. Lopes da Silva (Eds.), *Electroencephalography: Basic principles, clinical applications, and related fields* (5th ed., pp. 1–15). Philadelphia: Lippincott, Williams & Wilkins.

Nieto, F., Young, T. B., Lind, B. K., Shahar, E., Samet, J. M., Redline, S., D'Agostino, R. B., Newman, A. B., Lebowitz, M. D., & Pickering, T. G. (2000). Association of sleep-disordered breathing, sleep apnea, and hypertension in a large, community-based study. *Journal of the American Medical Association, 283*(14), 1829–1836.

Nigg, J. T. (2006). *What causes ADHD? Understanding what goes wrong and why.* New York, NY: The Guilford Press.

Nigg, J. T. (2010). Attention-Deficit/Hyperactivity Disorder: Endophenotypes, structure, and etiological pathways. *Current Directions in Psychological Science, 19*(1), 24–29.

Nigg, J. T., & Goldsmith, H. H. (1994). Genetics of personality disorders: Perspectives from personality and psychopathology research. *Psychological Bulletin, 115,* 346–380.

Nikolajsen, L., & Jensen, T. S. (2001). Phantom limb pain. *British Journal of Anaesthesia, 87,* 107–116.

Nitsche, M. A., Boggio, P. S., Fregni, F., & Pascual-Leone, A. (2009). Treatment of depression with transcranial direct current stimulation (tDCS): A review. *Experimental Neurology, 219*(1), 14–19.

Nolen-Hoeksema, S. (1990). *Sex differences in depression.* Palo Alto, CA: Stanford University Press.

Nooyens, A. C. J., Baan, C. A., Spijkerman, A. M. W., & Verschuren, W. M. M. (2010). *Type 2 diabetes mellitus and cognitive decline in middle-aged men and women—The Doetinchem Cohort Study.* American Diabetes Association: Diabetes Care.

Norcross, J. C. (2005). A primer on psychotherapy integration. In J. C. Norcross & M. R. Goldfried (Eds.), *Handbook of psychotherapy integration* (2nd ed., pp. 3–23). New York, NY: Oxford University Press.

Norenzayan, A., Choi, I., & Nisbett, R. E. (1999). Eastern and Western perceptions of causality for social behavior: Lay theories about personalities and situations. In D. A. Prentice & D. T. Miller (Eds.), *Cultural divides* (pp. 239–272). New York: Russell Sage Foundation.

Norrbrink Budh, C., Lund, I., Hultling, C., Levi, R., Werhagen, L., Ertzgaard, P., & Lundeberg, T. (2003). Gender-related differences in pain in spinal cord injured individuals. *Spinal Cord, 41,* 122–128.

Nosich, G. M. (2008). *Learning to think things through: A guide to critical thinking across the curriculum* (3rd ed., pp. 2–16). Upper Saddle River, NJ: Prentice-Hall.

Novak, J. D. (1995). Concept mapping: A strategy for organizing knowledge. In S. M. Glynn & R. Duit (Eds.) *Learning science in the schools: Research reforming practice* (pp. 229–245). Mahwah, N. J.: Lawrence Erlbaum Associates.

Novella, S. (2007, November/December). The Anti-Vaccination Movement. *Skeptical Inquirer*. Retrieved May 21, 2010, from http://www.csicop.org/si/show/anti-vaccination_movement/www.guardian.co.uk/science/2007/feb/24/badscience.uknews

Nyberg, L., & Tulving, E. (1996). Classifying human long-term memory: Evidence from converging dissociations. *European Journal of Cognitive Psychology, 8*(2), 163–183.

Oberman, L. M., & Ramachandran, V. S. (2007). The simulating social mind: The role of simulation in the social and communicative deficits of autism spectrum disorders, *Psychological Bulletin, 133*, 310–327.

Ocholla-Ayayo, A. B. C., Wekesa, J. M., & Ottieno, J. A. M. (1993). *Adolescent pregnancy and its implications among ethnic groups in Kenya.* In International Population Conference, Montreal, Canada: International Union for the Scientific Study of Population, *1*, 381–395.

Ochsner, K., & Kosslyn, S. M. (1994). Mental imagery. In V. S. Ramaschandran (Ed.), *Encyclopedia of human behavior.* New York: Academic Press.

O'Connor, R. D. (1972). Relative efficacy of modeling, shaping, and the combined procedures for modification of social withdrawal. *Journal of Abnormal Psychology, 79*, 327–334.

Öhman, A. (2008). Fear and anxiety. In M. Lewis, J. M. Haviland-Jones & L. F. Barrett (Eds.), *Handbook of emotion* (3rd ed., pp. 709–729). New York: Guilford Press.

Ollendick, T. H., & King, N. J. (1998). Empirically supported treatments for children with phobic and anxiety disorders: Current status. *Journal of Clinical Child Psychology, 27*(2), 156–167.

Olsen, P. (1975). *Emotional flooding.* Baltimore: Penguin Books.

Olson, H. C., & Burgess, D. M. (1997). Early intervention for children prenatally exposed to alcohol and other drugs. In M. J. Guralnick (Ed.), *The effectiveness of early intervention* (pp. 109–146). Baltimore: Brookes.

Oman, C. M. (1990). Motion sickness: A synthesis and evaluation of the sensory conflict theory. *Canadian Journal of Physiological Pharmacology, 68*, 294–303.

Onken, L. S., Blaine, J. D., & Battjes, R. J. (1997). Behavioral therapy research: A conceptualization of a process. In S. W. Henggeler & A. B. Santos (Eds.), *Innovative approaches for difficult-to-treat populations* (pp. 477–485). Washington, DC: American Psychiatric Press.

Oster, J. R. (1987). The binge-purge syndrome: A common albeit unappreciated cause of acid-base and fluid-electrolyte disturbances. *Southern Medical Journal, 80*, 58–67.

Oswald, I. (1959). Sudden bodily jerks on falling asleep. *Brain, 82*, 92–103.

Overeem, S., Mignot, E., Gert van Dijk, J., & Lammers, G. J. (2001). Narcolepsy: Clinical features, new pathophysiological insights, and future perspectives. *Journal of Clinical Neurophysiology, 18*(2), 78–105.

Overmier, J. B., & Seligman, M. E. P. (1967). Effects of inescapable shock on subsequent escape and avoidance behavior. *Journal of Comparative Physiology and Psychology, 63*, 23–33.

Owen, A. M., Hampshire, A., Grahn, J. A., Stenton, R., Dajani, S., Burns, A. S. (2010). Putting brain training to the test. *Nature, 465*(7299), 775–778.

Owen, M. T., Easterbrooks, M. A., Chase-Lansdale, L., & Goldberg, W. A. (1984). The relation between maternal employment status and the stability of attachments to mother and to father. *Child Development, 55*, 1894–1901.

Paivio, A. (1971). *Imagery and verbal processes.* New York: Holt, Rinehart & Winston.

Paivio, A. (1986). *Mental representations: A dual coding approach.* New York: Oxford University Press.

Pajonk, F. G., Wobrock, T., Gruber, O., Scherk, H., Berner, D., Kaizl, I., Kierer, A., Muller, S., Oest, M., Meyer, T., Backens, M., Schneider-Axmann, T., Thornton, A. E., Honer, W. G., & Falkai, P. (2010). Hippocampal plasticity in response to exercise in schizophrenia. *Archives of General Psychiatry, 67*(2), 133–143.

Palmer, S. E. (1992). Common region: A new principle of perceptual grouping. *Cognitive Psychology, 24*(3), 436–447.

Palva, J. M., Monto, S., Kulashekhar, S., & Palva, S. (2010). Neuronal synchrony reveals working memory networks and predicts individual memory capacity. *Proceedings of the National Academy of Sciences, USA, 107*(16), 7580–7585.

Pan, A. S. (2000). Body image, eating attitudes, and eating behaviors among Chinese, Chinese-American and non-Hispanic White women. *Dissertation Abstracts International, Section B: The Sciences and Engineering, 61*(1-B), 544.

Pargament, K. I. (1997). *The psychology of religion and coping: Theory, research, and practice.* New York: Guilford Press.

Paris, J. (2004). Gender differences in personality traits and disorders. *Current Psychiatry Reports, 6*, 71–74.

Park, J., Turnbull, A. P., & Turnbull, H. R. (2002). Impacts of poverty on quality of life in families of children with disabilities. *Exceptional Children, 68*, 151–170.

Parsons, H. M. (1992). Hawthorne: An early OBM experiment. *Journal of Organizational Behavior Management, 12*(1), 27–43.

Partonen, T., & Lonnqvist, J. (1998). Seasonal affective disorder. *Lancet, 352*(9137), 1369–1374.

Pashler, H., McDaniel, M., Rohrer, D., & Bjork, R. (2009). Learning styles: concepts and evidence. *Psychological Science in the Public Interest, 9*(3), 106–119.

Paul, B. M., ElvevÅg, B., Bokat, C. E., Weinberger, D. R., & Goldberg, T. E. (2005). Levels of processing effects on recognition memory in patients with schizophrenia. *Schizophrenia Research, 74*(1), 101–110.

Paunonen, S. V., Keinonen, M., Trzbinski, J., Forsterling, F., Grishenko-Roze, N., Kouznetsova, L., & Chan, D. W., et al. (1996). The structure of personality in six cultures. *Journal of Cross Cultural Psychology, 27*, 339–353.

Pavlov, I. (1926). *Conditioned reflexes.* London: Oxford University Press.

Pavlov, I. P. (1906). The scientific investigation of the psychical faculties or processes in the higher animals. *Science, 24*, 613–619.

Pavlov, I. P. (1927). *Conditioned Reflexes: An Investigation of the Physiological Activity of the Cerebral Cortex. Translated and Edited by G. V. Anrep.* London: Oxford University Press.

Peng, K., Ames, D. R., & Knowles, E. D. (2000). Culture and human inference: Perspectives from three traditions. In D. Matsumoto (Ed.) (2001). *The handbook of culture and psychology* (pp. 245–264). New York: Oxford University Press.

Peplau, L. A., & Taylor, S. E. (1997). *Sociocultural perspectives in social psychology: Current readings.* Upper Saddle River, NJ: Prentice-Hall.

Pepperberg, I. M. (1998). Talking with Alex: Logic and speech in parrots. *Scientific American Presents: Exploring Intelligence, 9*(4), 60–65.

Pepperberg, I. M. (2006). Grey Parrot *(Psittacus erithacus)* numerical abilities: Addition and further experiments on a zero-like concept. *Journal of Comparative Psychology, 120*(1), 1–11.

Pepperberg, I. M. (2007). Grey parrots do not always "parrot": The roles of imitation and phonological awareness in the creation of new labels from existing vocalizations. *Language Sciences, 29*(1), 1–13.

Perls, F. (1951). *Gestalt therapy.* New York: Julian Press.

Perls, F. (1969). *Gestalt therapy verbatim.* Moab, UT: Real People Press.

Perlstein, W. M., Carter, C. S., Noll, D. C., & Cohen, J. D. (2001). Relation of prefrontal cortex dysfunction to working memory and symptoms in schizophrenia. *American Journal of Psychiatry, 156*, 1105–1113.

Perrin, S., & Spencer, C. (1980). The Asch effect—A child of its time. *Bulletin of the British Psychological Society, 33*, 405–406.

Perrin, S., Spencer, C. P. (1981). Independence or conformity in the Asch experiment as a reflection of cultural and situational factors. *British Journal of Social Psychology, 20*(3), 205–209.

Persaud, R. (2001). *Staying sane: How to make your mind work for you.* New York: Bantam.

Peters, T. M., Moore, S. C., Gierach, G. L., Wareham, N. J., Ekelund, U., Hollenbeck, A. R., Schatzkin, A., & Leitzmann, M. F. (2009). Intensity and timing of physical activity in relation to postmenopausal breast cancer risk: The prospective NIH=AARP Diet and Health Study. *BMC Cancer, 9*, 349.

Peters, W. A. (1971). *A class divided.* Garden City, NY: Doubleday.

Peterson, C., & Park, N. (2010). What happened to self-actualization? *Perspectives on Psychological Science, 5*(3), 320–322.

Peterson, D. R. (1976). Need for the Doctor of Psychology degree in professional psychology. *American Psychologist, 31*, 792–798.

Peterson, D. R. (1982). Origins and development of the Doctor of Psychology concept. In G. R. Caddy, D. C. Rimm, N. Watson, & J. H. Johnson (Eds.), *Educating professional psychologists* (pp. 19-38). New Brunswick, NJ: Transaction Books.

Peterson, L. R., & Peterson, M. J. (1959). Short-term retention of individual items. *Journal of Experimental Psychology, 58*, 193–198.

Petitto, L. A., & Marentette, P. F. (1991). Babbling in the manual mode: Evidence for the ontogeny of language. *Science, 251*, 1493–1496.

Petitto, L. A., Holowka, S., Sergio, L. E., & Ostry, D. (2001). Language rhythms in baby hand movements. *Nature, 413*, 35.

Petri, H. (1996). *Motivation: Theory, research and application* (4th ed.). Belmont, CA: Wadsworth.

Petrova, P. K., Cialdini, R. B., & Sills S., J. (2007). Compliance, consistency, and culture: Personal consistency and compliance across cultures. *Journal of Experimental Social Psychology 43*: 104–111.

Pettigrew, T. F., & Tropp, L. R. (2000). Does intergroup contact reduce prejudice? Recent meta-analytic findings. In S. Oskamp (Ed.), *Reducing prejudice and discrimination: Social psychological perspectives* (pp. 93–114). Mahwah, NJ: Erlbaum.

Petty, R., & Cacioppo, J. (1986). *Communication and persuasion: Central and peripheral routes to attitude change.* New York: Springer-Verlag.

Petty, R., & Cacioppo, J. (1996). *Attitudes and persuasion: Classic and contemporary approaches* (reprint). Boulder, CO: Westview Press.

Petty, R. E. (1995). Attitude change. In A. Tesser (Ed.), *Advances in social psychology* (pp. 194–255). New York: McGraw-Hill.

Petty, R. E., Wheeler, S. C., & Tormala, Z. L. (2003). Persuasion and attitude change. In T. Millon & M. J. Lerner (Eds.), *Handbook of psychology: Volume 5: Personality and social psychology* (pp. 353–382). Hoboken, NJ: Wiley.

Pezdek, K., & Hodge, D. (1999). Planting false childhood memories in children: The role of event plausibility. *Child Development, 70*, 887–895.

Pezdek, K., Finger, K., & Hodge, D. (1997). Planting false childhood memories: The role of event plausibility. *Psychological Science, 8*, 437–441

Pfeiffer, W. M. (1982). Culture-bound syndromes. In I. Al-Issa (Ed.), *Culture and psychopathology* (pp. 201–218). Baltimore: University Park Press.

Pfurtscheller, G., Allison, B. Z., Bauernfeind, G., Brunner, C., Solis Escalante, T., Scherer, R., Zander, T. O., Mueller-Putz, G., Neuper, C., & Birbaumer, N. (2010). The hybrid BCI. *Frontiers in Neuroprosthetics, 4.*

Phan, T., & Silove, D. (1999). An overview of indigenous descriptions of mental phenomena and the range of traditional healing practices amongst the Vietnamese. *Transcultural Psychiatry, 36*, 79–94.

Piaget, J. (1926). *The language and thought of the child.* New York: Harcourt Brace.

Piaget, J. (1952). *The origins of intelligence in children.* New York: Norton.

Piaget, J. (1962). *Play, dreams and imitation in childhood.* New York: Norton.

Piaget, J. (1983). Piaget's theory. In W. Kessen (Ed.), *Handbook of child psychology: Volume 1. Theoretical models of human development* (pp. 103–128). New York: Wiley.

Piedmont, R. L., Bain, E., McCrae, R. R., & Costa, P. T., Jr. (2002). The applicability of the Five-Factor Model in a sub-Saharan culture: The NEO-PI-R in Shona. In R. R. McCrae & J. Allik (Eds.), *The Five-Factor Model across cultures* (pp. 105–126). New York: Kluwer Academic/Plenum Publishers.

Pinker, S. (1995). Language acquisition. In Gleitman et al. (Eds.), *An invitation to cognitive science* (2nd ed., pp. 135–182). Cambridge: MIT Press.

Pinker, S., & Bloom, P. (1990). Natural language and natural selection. *Behavioral and Brain Sciences, 13*(4), 707–784.

Pinsof, W. M., & Wynne, L. C. (1995). The efficacy of marital and family therapy: An empirical overview, conclusions, and recommendations. *Journal of Marital and Family Therapy, 21*, 585–613.

Plaut, D. C., & McClelland, J. L. (2010). Locating object knowledge in the brain: A critique of Bowers' (2009) attempt to revive the grandmother cell hypothesis. *Psychological Review, 117*, 284–288.

Plomin, R., & DeFries, J. C. (1998, May). Genetics of cognitive abilities and disabilities. *Scientific American*, 62–69.

Plomin, R., & Spinath, F. M. (2004). Intelligence: Genetics, genes, and genomics. *Journal of Personality and Social Psychology, 86*(1), 112–129.

Plomin, R., Owen, M. J., & McGuffin, P. (1994). The genetic basis of complex human behaviors. *Science, 264*(5166), 1733–1739.

Plug, C., & Ross, H. E. (1994). The natural moon illusion: A multi-factor angular account. *Perception, 23*, 321–333.

Plum, F., & Posner, J. B. (1985). *The diagnosis of stupor and coma.* Philadelphia: F. A. Davis.

Pogue-Geile, M. F., & Yokley, J. L. (2010). HYPERLINK "http://cdp.sagepub.com/content/19/4/214.abstract." Current Research on the Genetic Contributors to Schizophrenia. *Current Directions in Psychological Science, 19*, 214–219. doi: 10.1177/0963721410378490.

Polce-Lynch, M., Myers, B. J., Kilmartin, C. T., Forssmann-Falck, R., & Kliewer, W. (1998) Gender and age patterns in emotional expression, body image, and self-esteem: A qualitative analysis. *Sex Roles, 38*, 1025–1050.

Polewan, R. J., Vigorito, C. M., Nason, C. D., Block, R. A., & Moore, J. W. (2006). A cartesian reflex assessment of face processing. *Behavioral and Cognitive Neuroscience Reviews, 3*(5), 3–23.

Pollitt, E., & Matthews, R. (1998). Breakfast and cognition: An integrative summary. *American Journal of Clinical Nutrition, 67*(S), 804S–813S.

Pormerleau, C. S., & Pormerleau, O. F. (1994). Euphoriant effects of nicotine. *Tobacco Control, 3*, 374.

Posthuma, D., de Geus, E. J. C., & Deary, I. J. (2009). The genetics of intelligence. In T. E. Goldberg & D. R. Weinberger (Eds.), *The Genetics of Cognitive Neuroscience.* Cambridge, MA: The MIT Press.

Postman, L. (1975). Tests of the generality of the principle of encoding specificity. *Memory and Cognition, 3*, 663–672.

Powers, M. H. (1984). A computer-assisted problem-solving method for beginning chemistry students. *The Journal of Computers in Mathematics and Science Teaching, 4*(1), 13–19.

Pratkanis, A. R. (1992). The cargo-cult science of subliminal persuasion. *Skeptical Inquirer, 16*, 260–272.

Pratkanis, A. R., & Greenwald, A. G. (1988). Recent perspectives on unconscious processing: Still no marketing applications. *Psychology and Marketing, 5*, 337–353.

Pratt, J. A. (1991). Psychotropic drug tolerance and dependence: Common underlying mechanisms? In E. Pratt (Ed.), *The biological bases of drug tolerance and dependence* (pp. 2–28). London: Academic Press/Harcourt Brace Jovanovich.

Preston, J. D., O'Neal, J. H., & Talaga, M. C. (2008). *Handbook of clinical psychopharmacology for therapists* (5th ed.). Oakland, CA: New Harbinger Publications.

Priester, J. M., & Petty, R. E. (1995). Source attributions and persuasion: Perceived honesty as a determinant of message scrutiny. *Personality and Social Psychology Bulletin, 21*, 637–654.

Prigerson, H. G., Bierhals, A. J., Kasi, S. V., Reynolds, C. F., Shear, M. K., Day, N., Beery, L. C., Newsome, J. T., & Jacobs, S. (1997). Traumatic grief as a risk factor for mental and physical morbidity. *American Journal of Psychiatry, 154I*, 616–623.

Prochaska, J. O., & Norcross, J. C. (2003). *Systems of psychotherapy* (5th ed.). Belmont, CA: Wadsworth.

Puetz, T. W., Flowers, S. S., & O'Connor, P. J. (2008). A randomized controlled trial of the effect of aerobic exercise training on feelings of energy and fatigue in sedentary young adults with persistent fatigue. *Psychotherapy and Psychosomatics, 77*(3), 167–174.

Pumariega, A. J., & Gustavson, C. R. (1994). Eating attitudes in African-American women: The essence. *Eating Disorders: Journal of Treatment and Prevention, 2*, 5–16.

Purcell, S. (1985, August). *Relation between religious orthodoxy and marital sexual functioning.* Paper presented at the meeting of the American Psychological Association, Los Angeles.

Purdy, D., Eitzen, D., & Hufnagel, R. (1982). Are athletes also students? The educational attainment of college athletes. *Social Problems, 29*, 439–448.

Putnam, S. P., & Stifter, C. A. (2002). Development of approach and inhibition in the first year: Parallel findings for motor behavior, temperament ratings and directional cardiac response. *Developmental Science, 5*, 441–451.

Puts, D. A., Jordan, C. L., & Breedlove, S. M. (2006). O brother, where art thou? The fraternal birth-order effect on male sexual orientation. *Proceedings of the National Academy of Sciences, USA, 103*(28), 10531–10532.

Quintero, J. E., Kuhlman, S. J., & McMahon, D. G. (2003). The biological clock nucleus: A multiphasic oscillator network regulated by light. *Journal of Neuroscience, 23*, 8070–8076.

Raaijmakers, J. G. W., & Shiffrin, R. M. (1992). Models for recall and recognition. *Annual Review of Psychology, 43*, 205–234.

Rabins, P., Appleby, B. S., Brandt, J., DeLong, M. R., Dunn, L. B., Gabriels, L., et al. (2009). Scientific and ethical issues related to deep brain stimulation for disorders of mood, behavior, and thought. *Archives of General Psychiatry, 66*(9), 931–937.

Rachman, S. (1990). The determinants and treatments of simple phobias. *Advances in Behavioral Research and Therapy, 12*(1), 1–30.

Rachman, S. J., & Hodgson, R. J. (1980). *Obsessions and compulsions.* Englewood Cliffs, NJ: Prentice Hall.

Rahman, Q., & Hull, M. S. (2005). An empirical test of the kin selection hypothesis for male homosexuality. *Archives of Sexual Behavior, 34*, 461–467.

Raikkonen, K., Matthews, K. A., & Salomon, K. (2003). Hostility predicts metabolic syndrome risk factors in children and adolescents. *Health Psychology, 22*, 279–286.

Rainforth, M. V., Schneider, R. H., Nidich, S. I., Gaylord-King, C., Salerno, J. W., & Anderson, J. W. (2007). Stress reduction programs in patients with elevated blood pressure: A systematic review and meta-analysis. *Current Hypertension Reports, 9*, 520–528.

Ramachandran, V. S., & Blakeslee, S. (1998). *Phantoms in the brain.* New York: Quill William Morrow.

Ramachandran, V. S., & Hubbard, E. M. (2003). Hearing colors, tasting shapes. *Scientific American, 5*, 52–59.

Ranke, M. B., & Saenger, P. (2001, July 28). Turner's syndrome. *Lancet, 358*(9278), 309–314.

Rao, S. C., Rainer, G., & Miller, E. K. (1997) Integration of what and where in the primate prefrontal cortex. *Science, 276*, 821–824.

Ratey, J. J., & Hagerman, E. (2008). *Spark: The revolutionary new science of exercise and the brain.* New York, NY: Little, Brown and Company.

Rauch, S. L., Shin, L. M., & Wright, C. I. (2003). Neuroimaging studies of amygdala function in anxiety disorders. *Annals of the New York Academy of Sciences, 985*, 389–410.

Raynor, H. A., & Epstein, L. H. (2001). Dietary variety, energy regulation and obesity. *Psychological Bulletin, 127*(3), 325–341.

Reason, J. T., & Brand, J. (1975). *Motion sickness.* London: Academic Press.

Reder, L. M., Anderson, J. R., & Bjork, R. A. (1974). A semantic interpretation of encoding specificity. *Journal of Experimental Psychology, 102*, 648–656.

Reichborn-Kjennerud, T. (2008). Genetics of personality disorders. *Psychiatric Clinics of North America, 31*, 421.

Reiner, W. G. (1999). Assignment of sex in neonates with ambiguous genitalia. *Current Opinions in Pediatrics, 11*(4), 363–365.

Reiner, W. G. (September 29, 2000). *The genesis of gender identity in the male: Prenatal androgen effects on gender identity and gender role.* Oral presentation at New York University Child Study Center, Grand Rounds Summary.

Reiter, R., & Milburn, A. (1994). Exploring effective treatment for chronic pelvic pain. *Comtemporary Ob/Gyn, 3*, 84–103.

Renchler, R. (1993). Poverty and learning. *ERIC Digest No. 83*, Eugene, OR: ERIC Clearinghouse on Educational Management. (ERIC Document Reproduction Service No. ED 357 433).

Renner, M. J., & Mackin, R. S. (1998). A life stress instrument for classroom use. *Teaching of Psychology, 25*, 47.

Rescorla, R. (1988). Pavlovian conditioning—It's not what you think. *American Psychologist, 43*, 151–160.

Rescorla, R. A. (1968). Probability of shock in the presence and absence of CS in fear conditioning. *Journal of Comparative and Physiological Psychology, 66*, 1–5.

Rescorla, R. A., & Wagner, A. R. (1972). A theory of Pavlovian conditioning: Variations in the effectiveness of reinforcement and nonreinforcement. In A.H. Black & W.F. Prokasy (Eds.), *Classical conditioning II: Current theory and research* (pp. 64–99). New York: Appleton-Century-Crofts.

Resick, P. A., Monson, C. M., & Rizvi, S. (2008). Posttraumatic stress disorder. In D. H. Barlow (Ed.), *Clinical handbook of psychological disorders* (pp. 65-122). New York, NY: The Guilford Press.

Reynold, C. F., Frank, E., Perel, J. M., Imber, S. D., Cornes, C., Miller, M. D., Mazumdar, S., Houck, P. R., Dew, M. A., Stack, J. A., Pollock, B. G., & Kuper, D. J. (1999). Nortriptyline and Interpersonal Psychotherapy as maintenance therapies for recurrent depression: A randomized controlled trial in patients older than 59 years. *Journal of the American Medical Association 281*(1): 39–45.

Reynolds, J. (2002). *Succeeding in college: Study skills and strategies.* Upper Saddle River, NJ: Prentice-Hall.

Reynolds, R. M., Strachan, M Frier, B. M., Fowkes, F. G., Mitchell, R., Seckl, J. R., Deary, I. J., Walker, B. R., & Prices, J. F. (2010). Morning cortisol levels and cognitive abilities in people with Type 2 diabetes. *American Diabetes Association: Diabetes Care, 33*(4), 714–720.

Rezvani, A. H., & Levin, E. D. (2001). Cognitive effects of nicotine. *Biological Psychiatry, 49*, 258–267.

Richards, C. F., & Lowe, R. A. (2003). Researching racial and ethnic disparities in emergency medicine. *Academic Emergency Medicine, 10*(11), 1169–1175.

Richardson, J., & Morgan, R. (1997). *Reading to learn in the content areas.* Belmont, CA: Wadsworth Publishing Company.

Rideout, T. M. (2005). Eating disorders: Anorexia and bulimia. Eating Disorders Infocenter, Holistic online.com. Retrieved March 30, 2005, from www.holistic-online.com/Remedies/EatingD/EatD_anorexia-bulimia.htm

Rideout, V. J., Foehr, U. G., & Roberts, D. F. (2010). *Generation M2: Media in the lives of 8- to 18-year-olds*: Menlo Park, CA: Henry J. Kaiser Family Foundation.

Ridley, H. (2002). Crop Circle Confession. *Scientific American.* Retrieved February 17, 2010, from http://www.sciam.com/article.cfm?chanID=sa006&articleID=00038B16-ED5F-1D29-97CA809EC588EEDF

Ridley, M. (1999). *Genome: The autobiography of a species in 23 chapters.* London: Fourth Estate.

Rieber, R. W., & Robinson, D. K. (2001). *Wilhelm Wundt in history: The making of a scientific psychology.* New York: Kluwer Academic.

Ritts, V. (1999). Infusing culture into psychopathology: A supplement for psychology instructors. Retrieved from the Internet on June 19, 2004, at www.stlcc.cc.mo.us/mc/users/vritts/psypath.htm.

Rizzolatti, G., Fabbri-Destro, M., & Cattaneo, L. (2009). Mirror neurons and their clinical relevance. *Nature Clinical Practice Neurology, 5*(1), 24–34.

Ro, E., & Clark, L. A. (2009). Psychosocial functioning in the context of diagnosis: Assessment and theoretical issues. *Psychological Assessment, 21*(3), 313–324.

Robins, L. N. (1996). *Deviant children grown up.* Baltimore: Williams & Wilkins.

Robinson, F. P. (1970). *Effective study,* 4th ed. New York: Harper & Row, New York.

Robinson, J. W., & Preston, J. D. (1976). Equal status contact and modification of racial prejudice: A reexamination of the contact hypothesis. *Social Forces, 54*, 911–924.

Robinson, P. (1993). *Freud and his critics.* Berkeley: University of California Press.

Rodgers, J. E. (1992). *Psychosurgery: Damaging the brain to save the mind.* New York: HarperCollins.

Rodin, J. (1981). Current status of the internal-external hypothesis for obesity. *American Psychologist, 36*, 361–372.

Rodin, J. (1985). Insulin levels, hunger, and food intake: An example of feedback loops in body weight regulation. *Health Psychology, 4*, 1–24.

Rodin, J., & Langer, E. J. (1977). Long-term effects of a control-relevant intervention among the institutionalized aged. *Journal of Personality and Social Psychology, 35*, 275–282.

Roediger, H. L. (1990). Implicit memory: Retention without remembering. *American Psychologist, 45*, 1043–1056.

Roediger, H. L., III (2000). Why retrieval is the key process to understanding human memory. In E. Tulving (Ed.), *Memory, consciousness and the brain: The Tallinn Conference* (pp. 52–75). Philadelphia: Psychology Press.

Roediger, H. L., III, & Guynn, M. J. (1996). Retrieval processes. In E. L. Bjork & R. A. Bjork (Eds.), *Memory* (pp. 197–236). New York: Academic Press.

Roethlisberger, F. J., & Dickson, W. J. (1939) *Management and the Worker.* Cambridge, MA: Harvard University Press.

Roffman, R. A., Stephens, R. S., Simpson, E. E., & Whitaker, D. L. (1988). Treatment of marijuana dependence: Preliminary results. *Journal of Psychoactive Drugs, 20*(1), 129–137.

Roffwarg, H. P., Muzio, J. N., & Dement, W. C. (1966). Ontogenetic development of the human sleep-dream cycle. *Science, 152*(3722), 604–619. Rogers, C. (1961). *On becoming a person: A therapist's view of psychotherapy.* Boston: Houghton/Mifflin.

Rogers, R. W., & Mewborn, C. R. (1976). Fear appeals and attitude change: Effects of a threat's noxiousness, probability of occurrence, and the efficacy of the coping responses. *Journal of Personality and Social Psychology, 34*, 54–61.

Rogoff, B. (1994). Developing understanding of the idea of communities of learners. *Mind, Culture, and Activity, 1*(4), 209–229.

Rohde, P., Silva, S. G., Tonev, S. T., Kennard, B. D., Vitiello, B., Kratochvil, C. J., Reinecke, M. A., Curry, J. F., Simons, A. D., March, J. S. (2008). Achievement and maintenance of sustained improvement during TADS continuation and maintenance therapy. *Archives of General Psychiatry, 65*(4), 447–455.

Roid, G. H. (2003). *Stanford-Binet intelligence scales* (5th ed.). Itasca, IL: Riverside.

Rosch, E. (1973). On the internal structure of perceptual and semantic categories. In T. E. Moore (Ed.), *Cognitive development and the acquisition of language* (pp. 111–144). New York: Academic Press.

Rosch, E. (1977). Human categorization. In N. Warren (Ed.), *Advances in cross-cultural psychology, 1*(pp. 1–72). London: Academic Press.

Rosch, E., & Mervis, C. (1975). Family resemblances: Studies in the internal structures of categories. *Cognitive Psychology, 7*, 573–605.

Rosch, E., Mervis, C. B., Gray, W. D., Johnson, D. M., & Boyes-Braem, P. (1976). Basic objects in natural categories. *Cognitive Psychology, 8*, 382–439.

Rosch-Heider, E. (1972). Universals in color naming and memory. *Journal of Experimental Psychology, 93*, 10–20.

Rosch-Heider, E., & Olivier, D. C. (1972). The structure of the color space in naming and memory for two languages. *Cognitive Psychology, 3*, 337–354.

Rose, S., Kamin, L. J., & Lewontin, R. C. (1984). *Not in our genes: Biology, ideology and human nature.* Harmondsworth, UK: Penguin.

Rosenfeld, J. P., Labkovsky, E., Winograd, M., Lui, M. A., Vandenboom, C., & Chedid, E. (2008). The Complex Trial Protocol (CTP): A new, countermeasure-resistant, accurate, P300-based method for detection of concealed information. *Psychophysiology, 45*(6), 906–919.

Rosenhan, D. L. (1973), On being sane in insane places, *Science, 179*, 250–258.

Rosenman, R. H., Brand, R. I., Jenkins, C. D., Friedman, M., Straus, R., & Wurm, M. (1975). Coronary heart disease in the Western Collaborative Group Study, final follow-up experience of 2 years. *Journal of the American Medical Association, 233*, 812–817.

Rosenthal, A. M. (1964). *Thirty-eight witnesses: The Kitty Genovese case.* New York: McGraw-Hill.

Rosenthal, R., & Jacobson, L. (1968). *Pygmalion in the classroom.* New York: Holt, Rinehart & Winston.

Ross, H. E., & Ross, G. M. (1976). Did Ptolemy understand the moon illusion? *Perception, 5*, 377–385.

Rossini, P. M., Altamura, C., Ferreri, F., Melgari, J. M., Tecchio, F., Tombini, M., Pasqualetti, P., & Vernieri, F. (2007). Neuroimaging experimental studies on brain plasticity in recovery from stroke. *Eura Medicophys, 43*(2), 241–254.

Rothbaum, B. O., Hodges, L. F., Kooper, R., Opdyke, D., Williford, J. S., & North, M. (1995). Effectiveness of computer-generated (virtual reality) graded exposure in the treatment of acrophobia. *American Journal of Psychiatry, 152*, 626–628.

Rothbaum, R., Weisz, J., Pott, M., Miyake, K., & Morelli, G. (2000). Attachment and culture: Security in Japan and the U.S. *American Psychologist, 55*, 1093–1104.

Rothenberg, A. (2001). Bipolar illness, creativity, and treatment. *Psychiatric Quarterly, 72*(2), 131–147.

Rotter, J. B. (1954). *Social learning and clinical psychology.* New York: Prentice Hall.

Rotter, J. B. (1966). Generalized expectancies for internal versus external control of reinforcements. *Psychological Monographs, 80* [Whole no. 609].

Rotter, J. B. (1978). Generalized expectancies for problem solving and psychotherapy. *Cognitive Therapy and Research, 2*, 1–10.

Rotter, J. B. (1981). The psychological situation in social learning theory. In D. Magnusson (Ed.), *Toward a psychology of situations: An interactional perspective.* Hillsdale, NJ: Erlbaum.

Rotter, J. B. (1990). Internal versus external control of reinforcement: A case history of a variable. *American Psychologist, 45*, 489–493.

Rotton, J., & Frey, J. (1985). Air pollution, weather, and violent crime: Concomitant time-series analysis of archival data. *Journal of Personality and Social Psychology, 49*, 1207–1220.

Rotton, J., Frey, J., Barry, T., Milligan, M., & Fitzpatrick, M. (1979). The air pollution experience and physical aggression. *Journal of Applied Social Psychology, 9*, 397–412.

Rouse, B. A. (1998). *Substance and mental health statistics source book.* Rockville, MD: Department of Health and Human Services, Substance Abuse and Mental Health Services Administration (SAMHSA).

Rouw, R., & Scholte, H. S. (2007, May 21). Increased structural connectivity in grapheme-color synesthesia. *Nature Neuroscience 10*, 792–797.

Rovet, J. (1993). The psychoeducational characteristics of children with Turner's syndrome. *Journal of Learning Disabilities, 26*, 333–341.

Rowan, J. (2001). *Ordinary ecstasy.* Hove, UK: Brunner-Routledge.

Rowe, D. C., Almeida, D. A., & Jacobson, K. C. (1999). School context and genetic influences on aggression in adolescence. *Psychological Science, 10*, 277–280.

Roysircai-Sodowsky, G. R., & Maestas, M. V. (2000). Acculturation, ethnic identity, and acculturative stress: Evidence and measurement. In R. H. Dana (Ed.), *Handbook of cross-cultural and multicultural assessment* (pp. 131–172). Mahwah, NJ: Erlbaum.

Ruble, D., Alvarez, J., Bachman, M., Cameron, J., Fuligni, A., Garcia Coll, C., & Rhee, E. (2004). The development of a sense of "we": The emergence and implications of children's collective identity. In M. Bennett & F. Sani (Eds.), *The development of the social self.* New York: Psychology Press.

Rudd, P., & Osterberg, L. G. (2002). Hypertension: Context, pathophysiology, and management. In E. J. Topol (Ed.), *Textbook of cardiovascular medicine* (pp. 91–122). Philadelphia: Lippincott, Williams & Wilkins.

Ruhe, H. G., Mason, N. S., & Schene, A. H. (2007). Mood is indirectly related to serotonin, norepinephrine and dopamine levels in humans: A meta-analysis of monoamine depletion studies. *Molecular Psychiatry, 12*(4), 331–359.

Rumelhart, D. E., Hinton, G. E., & McClelland, J. L. (1986). A general framework for parallel distributed processing. In D. E. Rumelhart, J. L. McClelland, & the PDP Research Group (Eds.), *Parallel distributed processing: Explorations in the microstructure of cognition: Vol. 1. Foundations* (pp. 45–76). Cambridge, MA: MIT Press.

Rundus, D. (1971). An analysis of rehearsal processes in free recall. *Journal of Experimental Psychology, 89*, 63–77.

Rusbult, C. E., Finkey, E. J., & Kumashiro, M. (2009a). The Michelangelo phenomenon. *Current Directions in Psychological Science, 18*(1), 305–309.

Rusbult, C. E., Kumashiro, M., Finkel, E., Kirchner, J., Coolsen, M., Stocker, S., & Clarke, J. (2009b). *A longitudinal study of the Michelangelo phenomenon in marital relationships.* Unpublished manuscript, Vrije Universiteit Amsterdam, The Netherlands.

Rusbult, C. E., Kumashiro, M., Kubacka, K. E., & Finkel, E. J. (2009c). "The part of me that you bring out": Ideal similarity and the Michelangelo phenomenon. *Journal of Personality and Social Psychology, 96*, 61–82.

Ruscio, A. M., Borkovec, T. D., & Ruscio, J. (2001). A taxometric investigation of the latent structure of worry. *Journal of Abnormal Psychology, 110*, 413–422.

Russell, D. E. (1986). *The secret trauma: Incest in the lives of girls and women*. New York: Basic Books.

Rutherford, A. (2000). Mary Cover Jones (1896–1987). *The Feminist Psychologist, 27*(3), 25.

Ryan, R. M., & Deci, E. L. (2000). Intrinsic and extrinsic motivations: Classic definitions and new directions. *Contemporary Educational Psychology, 25*, 54–67.

Rynn, M., Scherrer, J., & True, W. R. (2000, November). Generalized anxiety disorder. *Best Practice of Medicine*.

Sabatini, E., Della Penna, S., Franciotti, R., Ferretti, A., Zoccolotti, P., Rossini, P. M., Romani, G. L., & Gainotti, G. (2009). Brain structures activated by overt and covert emotional visual stimuli. *Brain Research Bulletin, 79*(5), 258–264.

Sacks, D. P., Bushman, B. J., & Anderson, C. A. (2011). Do violent video games harm children? Comparing the scientific amicus curiae "experts" in *Brown v Entertainment Merchants Association*. *Northwestern University Law Review Colloquy, 106*, 1–12.

Sacks, O. (1990). *The man who mistook his wife for a hat and other clinical tales*. New York: HarperPerennial.

Sadock, B. J., Kaplan, H. I., & Sadock, V. A. (2007). *Kaplan & Sadock's synopsis of psychiatry: Behavioral sciences/clinical psychiatry* (10th ed.). Philadelphia, PA: Lippincott Williams & Wilkins.

Sagan, C. (1977). *The dragons of Eden: Speculations on the evolution of human intelligence*. New York: Random House.

Saha, S., Chant, D., Welham, J., & McGrath, J. (2005). A systematic review of the prevalence of schizophrenia. *PLoS Medicine, 2*(5), e141.

Salend, S. J. (1987). Contingency management systems. *Academic Therapy, 22*, 245–253.

Salovey, P., & Mayer, J. D. (1990). Emotional intelligence. *Imagination, cognition, and personality, 9*, 185–211.

Salthouse, T. A. (1984). The skill of typing. *Scientific American, 250*(2), 128–135.

Sanders, L. D., Weber-Fox, C. M., & Neville, H. J. (2008). Varying degrees of plasticity in different subsystems within language. In J. R. Pomerantz (Ed.), *Topics in integrative neuroscience: From cells to cognition* (pp. 125–153). New York: Cambridge University Press.

Sands, L. P., & Meredith, W. (1992). Intellectual functioning in late midlife. *Journal of Gerontological and Psychological Science, 47*, 81–84.

Saper, C. B., Chou, T. C., & Scammell, T. E. (2001). The sleep switch: Hypothalamic control of sleep and wakefulness. *Trends in Neurosciences, 24*, 726–731.

Sapir, E. S. (1921). *Language: An introduction to the study of speech*. New York: Harcourt, Brace.

Sapolsky, R. M. (2004). *Why zebras don't get ulcers* (3rd ed., pp. 1, 144–145). New York: Owl Books.

Sastry, K. S., Karpova, Y., Prokopovich, S., Smith, A. J., Essau, B., Gersappe, A., Carson, J. P., Weber, M. J., Register, T. C., Chen, Y. Q., Penn, R. B., & Kulik, G. (2007). Epinephrine protects cancer cells from apoptosis via activation of cAMP-dependent protein kinase and BAD phosphorylation. *Journal of Biological Chemistry, 282*(19), 14094–14100.

Satterly, D. (1987). Piaget and education. In R. L. Gregory (Ed.), *The Oxford companion to the mind* (pp. 110–143). Oxford: Oxford University Press.

Sattler, J. M. (1977). The effects of therapist–client racial similarity. In A. S. Gurman & A. M. Razin (Eds.), *Effective psychotherapy: A handbook of research* (pp. 252–290). Elmsford, NY: Pergamon.

Saunders, B., & Goddard, C. R. (1998). Why do we condone the "physical punishment" of children? *Children Australia, 23*, 23–28.

Savage, J., & Yancey, C. (2008). The effects of media violence exposure on criminal aggression: A meta-analysis. *Criminal Justice and Behavior, 35*(6), 772–791. [DOI: 10.1177/0093854808316487].

Savage-Rumbaugh, S., & Lewin, R. (1994). *Kanzi*. New York: Wiley.

Savage-Rumbaugh, S., Shanker, S., & Taylor, T. J. (1998). *Apes, language and the human mind*. Oxford, UK: Oxford University Press.

Savic, I. & Lindstrom, P. (2008). PET and MRI show differences in cerebral asymmetry and functional connectivity between homo- and heterosexual subjects. *Proceedings of the National Academy of Sciences, USA, 105*(27), 9403–9408.

Savic, I., Berglund, H., & Lindstrom, P. (2005). Brain response to putative pheromones in homosexual men. *Proceedings of the National Academy of Sciences, USA, 102*(20), 7356–7361.

Scarpa, A., Raine, A., Venables, P. H., & Mednick, S. A. (1995). The stability of inhibited/uninhibited temperament from ages 3 to 11 years in Mauritian children. *Journal of Abnormal Child Psychology, 23*, 607–618.

Schachter, S., & Singer, J. E. (1962). Cognitive, social and physiological determinants of emotional states. *Psychological Review, 69*, 379–399.

Schafer, M., & Crichlow S. (1996). Antecedents of groupthink: A quantitative study. *Journal of Conflict Resolution, 40*, 415–435.

Schaie, K. W., & Willis, S. L. (2010). *Handbook of the Psychology of Aging*, 7th ed, pp. 27–29. Maryland Heights, Montana: Academic Press.

Schalock, R. L., Borthwick-Duffy, S. A., Buntinx, W. H. E., Coultier, D. L., & Craig, E. M. P. (2010). *Intellectual disability: Definition, classification, and systems of supports* (11th ed.): American Association on Intellectual and Developmental Disabilities.

Schapiro, A. C. & McClelland, J. L. (2009). A connectionist model of a continuous developmental transition in the balance scale task. *Cognition, 110*(1), 395–411.

Schiller, P. H., & Carvey, C. E. (2005). The Hermann grid illusion revisited. *Perception, 34*(11), 1375–1397.

Schmitt, D. P. (2002). Personality, attachment and sexuality related to dating relationship outcomes: Contrasting three perspectives on personal attribute interaction. *British Journal of Social Psychology, 41*(4), 589–610.

Schmitz, C., Wagner, J., & Menke, E. (2001). The interconnection of childhood poverty and homelessness: Negative impact/points of access. *Families in Society, 82*(1), 69–77.

Schnabel, J. (1994). *Round in circles* (pp. 267–277). London: Hamish Hamilton.

Schneider, K. J., Bugental, J. F. T., & Fraser, J. F. (Eds.). (2001). *Handbook of humanistic psychology*. Thousand Oaks, CA: Sage.

Schneider, R. H., Staggers, F., Alexander, C. N., Sheppard, W., Rainforth, M., Kondwani, K., Smith, S., & King, C. G. (1995). A randomized controlled trial of stress reduction for hypertension in older African Americans. *Hypertension, 26*(5), 820–827.

Schneider, W., Dumais, S., & Shriffrin, R. (1984). *Automatic and control processing and attention*. London: Academic Press.

Schneidman, E. (1983). *Death of man*. New York: Jason Aronson.

Schneidman, E. (1994). *Death: Current perspectives*. New York: McGraw-Hill.

Schols, L., Haan, J., Riess, O., Amoiridis, G., & Przuntek, H. (1998). Sleep disturbance in spinocerebellar ataxias: Is the SCA3 mutation a cause of restless legs syndrome? *Neurology, 51*, 1603–1607

Schroeder, S. R. (2000). Mental retardation and developmental disabilities influenced by environmental neurotoxic insults. *Environmental Health Perspectives 108*(Suppl. 3), 395–399.

Schroth, M. L., & McCormack, W. A. (2000). Sensation seeking and need for achievement among study-abroad students. *The Journal of Social Psychology, 140*, 533–535.

Schultz, D. P., & Schultz, S. E. (2004). *A history of modern psychology*, pp. 239–242. Belmont, CA: Wadsworth.

Schwanenflugel, P., & Rey, M. (1986). Interlingual semantic facilitation: Evidence from common representational system in the bilingual lexicon. *Journal of Memory and Language, 25*, 605–618.

Schwartz, S. K. (2000). *Working your degree*. Retrieved March 6, 2010, from http://cnnfn.cnn.com/2000/12/08/career/q_degreepsychology/

Schweickert, R. (1993). A multinomial processing tree model for degradation and redintegration in immediate recall. *Memory and Cognition, 21*, 168–175.

Schwitzgebel, E. (1999). Representation and desire: A philosophical error with consequences for theory-of-mind research. *Philosophical Psychology, 12*, 157–180.

Scott, S. K., Young, A. W., Calder, A. J., Hellawell, D. J., Aggleton, J. P., & Johnson, M. (1997). Impaired auditory recognition of fear and anger following bilateral amygdala lesions. *Nature, 385*(6613), 254–257.

Scott, W. D. (1908). *The theory and practice of advertising*. Boston, MA: Small, Maynard, & Company.

Security Director's Report (2008). Experts identify four trends in workplace violence. *Institute of Management and Administration, Inc., 8*(6), 1–15.

Segall, M. H., Campbell, D. T., & Herskovits, M. J. (1966). *The influence of culture on perception*. Indianapolis, IN: Bobbs-Merrill.

Segerstrom, S. C., Taylor, S. E., Kemeny, M. E., & Fahey, J. L. (1998). Optimism is associated with mood, coping, and immune change in response to stress. *Journal of Personality and Social Psychology, 74*(6), 1646–1655.

Segerstrom, S.C., & Sephton, S.E. (2010). Optimistic expectancies and cell-mediated immunity: The role of positive affect. *Psychological Science, 21*(3), 448–455.

Seligman, M. (1970). On the generality of the laws of learning. *Psychological Review, 77*, 406–418.

Seligman, M. (1975). *Helplessness: Depression, development and death*. New York: W. H. Freeman.

Seligman, M. (1989). *Helplessness*. New York: W. H. Freeman.

Seligman, M. (1995). The effectiveness of psychotherapy: The *Consumer Reports* study. *American Psychologist, 50*, 965–975.

Seligman, M. (1998). *Learned optimism: How to change your mind and your life* (2nd ed.). New York: Pocket Books.

Seligman, M. (2002). *Authentic happiness*. New York: Free Press.

Seligman, M., & Maier, S. F. (1967). Failure to escape traumatic shock. *Journal of Experimental Psychology, 74*, 1–9.

Selye, H. (1956). *The stress of life*. New York: McGraw-Hill.

Selye, H. (1976). *The stress of life* (Rev. ed.). New York: McGraw-Hill.

Selye, H. A. (1936). Syndrome produced by diverse nocuous agents. *Nature, 138*, 32.

Serban, G., George, A., Siegel, S., DeLeon, M., & Gaffney, M. (1990). Computed tomography scans and negative symptoms in schizophrenia: Chronic schizophrenics with negative symptoms and nonenlarged lateral ventricles. *Acta Psychiatrica Scandinavica, 81*(5), 441–447.

Shackelford, T. K., Buss, D. M., & Bennett, K. (2002). Forgiveness or breakup: Sex differences in responses to a partner's infidelity. *Cognition and Emotion, 16*(2), 299–307.

Shadish, R., Cook, T. D., & Campbell, D. T. (2002). *Experimental and quasi-experimental designs for generalized causal inferences*. New York: Houghton Mifflin.

Shafto, P., & Coley, J. D. (2003). Development of categorization and reasoning in the natural world: Novices to experts, naïve similarity to ecological knowledge. *Journal of Experimental Psychology: Learning, Memory and Cognition, 29*, 641–649.

Shafton, A. (1995). *Dream reader: Contemporary approaches to the understanding of dreams (SUNY series in dream studies)* (pp. 40–46). New York: State University of New York Press.

Shapiro, A. K., & Shapiro, E. (1997). *The powerful placebo*. Baltimore: Johns Hopkins University Press.

Shapiro, F. (2001). *Eye movement desensitization and reprocessing: Basic principles, protocols, and procedures*. New York: Guilford Press.

Shapiro, K. L., Jacobs, W. J., & LoLordo, V. M. (1980). Stimulus relevance in Pavlovian conditioning in pigeons. *Animal Learning and Behavior, 8*, 586–594.

Sharif, Z., Bradford, D., Stroup, S., & Lieberman, J. (2007). Pharmacological treatment of schizophrenia. In P. E. Nathan & J. M. Gorman (Eds.), *A guide to treatments that work* (3rd ed., pp. 203–241). New York, NY: Oxford University Press.

Sharot, T., Delgado, M. R. & Phelps, E. A. (2004). How emotion enhances the feeling of remembering, *Nature Neuroscience, 7*(12), 1376–1380.

Shean, R. E., de Klerk, N. H., Armstrong, B. K., & Walker, N. R. (1994). Seven-year follow-up of a smoking-prevention program for children. *Australian Journal of Public Health, 18*, 205–208.

Sheeber, L. B., & Johnson, J. H. (1992). Child temperament, maternal adjustment, and changes in family life style. *American Journal of Orthopsychiatry, 62*(2), 178–185.

Shekelle, P. G., Hardy, M. L., Morton, S. C., Maglione, M., Mojica, W. A., Suttorp, M. J., Rhodes, S. L., Jungvig, L., & Gagné, J. (2003). Efficacy and safety of ephedra and ephedrine for weight loss and athletic performance: A metaanalysis. *Journal of the American Medical Association, 289*(12), 1537–1545.

Sheldon, S. H. (2002). Sleep in infants and children. In T. L. Lee-Chiong, M. J. Sateia, & M. A. Carskadon (Eds.), *Sleep medicine* (pp. 99–103). Philadelphia: Hanley & Belfus.

Shepard, R. N., & Metzler, J. (1971). Mental rotation of three-dimensional objects. *Science, 171*, 701–703.

Shepard, T. H. (2001). *Catalog of teratogenic agents* (10th ed.). Baltimore: Johns Hopkins University Press.

Sherif, M. (1936). *The psychology of social norms*. New York: Harper & Row.

Sherif, M., Harvey, O. J., White, B. J., Hood, W. R., & Sherif, C. W. (1961). *Intergroup conflict and cooperation: The Robber's Cave experiment*. Norman: University of Oklahoma Book Exchange.

Sherry, P., Gaa, A., Thurlow-Harrison, S., Graber, K., Clemmons, J., & Bobulinski, M. (2003). *Traffic accidents, job stress, and supervisor support in the trucking industry*. Paper presented at the International Institute for Intermodal Transportation, University of Denver, CO.

Shomrat T, Zarrella I., Fiorito G., Hochner B. (2008). The Octopus Vertical Lobe Modulates Short-Term Learning Rate and Uses LTP to Acquire Long-Term Memory. *Current Biology, 18*, 337–342.

Shore, L. A. (1990). Skepticism in light of scientific literacy. *Skeptical Inquirer, 15*(1), 3–4.

Shorey, G. (2001). Bystander non-intervention and the Somalia incident. *Canadian Military Journal*, 19–27.

Shorter E. (1997). *A history of psychiatry: From the era of the asylum to the age of Prozac*. New York: Wiley.

Showalter, E. (1997). *Hystories: Hysterical epidemics and modern culture*. New York: Columbia University Press.

Shuglin, A. (1986). The background chemistry of MDMA. *Journal of Psychoactive Drugs, 18*(4), 291–304.

Shurkin, J. N. (1992). *Terman's kids; The groundbreaking study of how the gifted grow up*. Boston: Little, Brown.

Siegler, I. C., Costa, P. T., Brummett, B. H., Helms, M. J., Barefoot, J. C., Williams, R. B., Dahlstrom, G., Kaplan, B. H., Vitaliano, P. P., Nichaman, M. Z., Day, S., & Rimer, B. K. (2003). Patterns of change in hostility from college to midlife in the UNC alumni heart study predict high-risk status. *Psychosomatic Medicine, 65*, 738–745.

Siegler, R. S. (1996). *Emerging minds: The process of change in children's thinking*. New York: Oxford University Press.

Simon, D. A., & Bjork, R. A. (2001). Metacognition in motor learning. *Journal of Experimental Psychology: Learning, memory, and cognition, 27*(4), 907–912.

Simpson, D. (2005). Phrenology and the neurosciences: Contributions of F. J. Gall and J. G. Spurzheim. *ANZ Journal of Surgery, 75*(6), 475–482.

Singer, M. T., & Lalich, J. (1995). *Cults in our midst*. San Francisco: Jossey-Bass.

Singh-Manoux, A., Richards, M., & Marmot, M. (2003). Leisure activities and cognitive function in middle age: Evidence from the Whitehall II study. *Journal of Epidemiology and Community Health, 57*, 907–913.

Skinner, B. F. (1938). *The behavior of organisms: An experimental analysis*. New York: Appleton-Century-Crofts.

Skinner, B. F. (1971). *Beyond freedom and dignity*. New York: Knopf.

Skinner, B. F. (1974). *About behaviorism*. New York: Knopf.

Skinner, B. F. (1989) The origins of cognitive thought. *Recent Issues in the Analysis of Behavior*, Princeton, NC: Merrill Publishing Company.

Skolnick, A. (1986). Early attachment and personal relationships across the life course. In P. B. Baltes, D. L. Featherman, & R. M. Lerner (Eds.), *Life-span development and behavior* (vol. 7). Hillsdale, NJ: Erlbaum.

Slater, A. (2000). Visual perception in the young infant: Early organisation and rapid learning. In D. Muir & A. Slater (Eds.), *Infant development: The essential readings*. Oxford, UK: Blackwell.

Slipp, S. (1993). *The Freudian mystique: Freud, women and feminism*. New York: New York University Press.

Sloan, D. M., & Mizes, J. S. (1999). Foundations of behavior therapy in the contemporary healthcare context. *Clinical Psychology Review, 19*, 255–274.

Smith, D. (2001). Shock and disbelief. *Atlantic Monthly, 2*, 79–90.

Smith, J. D., & Mitchell, A. (2001). "Me? I'm not a drooler. I'm the assistant": Is it time to abandon mental retardation as a classification? *Mental Retardation, 39*(2), 144–146.

Smith, T. C., Ryan, M. A. K., Wingard, D. L., Sallis, J. F., & Kritz-Silverstein, D. (2008). New onset and persistent symptoms of post-traumatic stress disorder self-reported after deployment and combat exposures: Prospective population based U.S. military cohort study. *British Medical Journal, 336*(7640), 366–371.

Snyder, D. J., & Bartoshuk, L. M. (2009). Epidemiological studies of taste function: Discussion and perspectives. *Annals of the New York Academy of Sciences, 1170*, 574–580.

Snyder, M., Tanke, E. D., & Berscheid, E. (1977). Social perception and interpersonal behavior: On the self-fulfilling nature of social stereotypes. *Journal of Personality and Social Psychology, 35*, 656–666.

Snyder, S. H. (2002), Forty years of neurotransmitters. *Archives of General Psychiatry, 59*, 983–994.

Snyder, T. D., & Dillow, S. A. (2010). *Digest of education statistics 2009* (NCES Publication No. NCES 2010-013). Washington, DC: National Center for Education Statistics, Institute of Education Sciences, U.S. Department of Education.

Söderlund, J., Schröder, J., Nordin, C., Samuelsson, M., Walther-Jallow, L., Karlsson, H., Erhardt, S., & Engberg, G. (2009). Activation of brain interleukin-1β in schizophrenia. *Molecular Psychiatry, 14*(12), 1069.

Sodowsky, G. R., Lai, E. W., & Plake, B. S. (1991). Moderating effects of socio-cultural variables on acculturation attitudes of Hispanics and Asian Americans. *Journal of Counseling & Development, 70*, 194–204.

Soomro, G. M. (2001). Obsessive-compulsive disorder. *Clinical Evidence, 6*, 754–762.

Sowell, E. R., Thompson, P. M., Holmes, C. J., Jernigan, T. L., & Toga, A. W. (1999). In vivo evidence for post-adolescent brain maturation in frontal and striatal regions. *Nature Neuroscience, 2*(10), 859–861.

Spangler, W. D. (1992). Validity of questionnaire and TAT measures of need for achievement: Two meta-analyses. *Psychological Bulletin, 112*, 140–154.

Spangler, W. J., Cosgrove, G. R., Ballantine, H. T., Jr., Cassem, E. H., Rauch, S. L., Nierenberg, A., & Price, B. H. (1996). Magnetic resonance image-guided stereotactic cingulotomy for intractable psychiatric disease. *Neurosurgery, 38*, 1071–1076.

Sparing, R., Mottaghy, F., Ganis, G., Thompson, W. L., Toepper, R., Kosslyn, S. M., & Pascual-Leone, A. (2002). Visual cortex excitability increases during visual mental imagery—A TMS study in healthy human subjects. *Brain Research, 938*, 92–97.

Spearman, C. (1904). "General intelligence" objectively determined and measured. *American Journal of Psychology, 15*, 201–293.

Speca, M., Carlson, L. E., Goodey, E., & Angen, E. (2000). A randomized wait-list controlled clinical trial: The effects of a mindfulness meditation-based stress reduction program on mood and symptoms of stress in cancer outpatients. *Psychosomatic Medicine, 6*, 2613–2622.

Speroff, L., Glass, R. H., & Kase, N. G. (1999). Recurrent early pregnancy loss. In *Clinical Gynecologic endocrinology and infertility* (pp. 1042–1055). Philadelphia: Lippincott, Williams & Wilkins.

Sperry, R. W. (1968). Mental unity following surgical disconnection of the cerebral hemispheres. *The Harvey Lectures*. Series 62, 293–323. New York: Academic Press.

Spiegel, D., Bloom, J. R., & Gottheil, E. (1989). Effects of psychosocial treatment on survival of patients with metastatic breast cancer. *Lancet, 2*, 888–891.

Springer, S. P., & Deutsch, G. (1998). *Left brain, right brain: Perspectives from cognitive neuroscience* (5th ed.). New York: W. H. Freeman.

Squire, L. R., & Slater, P. C. (1978). Anterograde and retrograde memory impairment in chronic amnesia. *Neuropsychologia, 16*, 313–322.

Squire, L. R., Knowlton, B., & Musen, G. (1993). The structure and organization of memory. *Annual Review of Psychology, 44*, 453–495.

Squire, L. R., Slater, P. C., & Chace, P. M. (1975). Retrograde amnesia: Temporal gradient in very long-term memory following electroconvulsive therapy. *Science, 187*, 77–79.

Squire, L., & Kandel, E. (1999). *Memory: From mind to molecule*. New York: Scientific American Library.

Standing, L., Conezio, J., & Haber, R. N. (1970). Perception and memory for pictures: Single-trial learning of 2500 visual stimuli. *Psychonomic Science, 19*, 73–74.

Steele, C. M. (1992). Race and the schooling of Black Americans. *The Atlantic Monthly, 269*(4), 68–78.

Steele, C. M. (1997). A threat in the air: How stereotypes shape intellectual identity and performance. *American Psychologist, 52*, 613–629.

Steele, C. M. (1999, August). Thin ice: "stereotype threat" and Black college students. *The Atlantic Monthly, 284*, 44–54.

Steele, C. M., & Aronson J. (1995). Stereotype threat and the intellectual test performance of African Americans. *Journal of Personality and Social Psychology, 69*, 797–811.

Steele, J., James, J. B., & Barnett, R. C. (2002). Learning in a man's world: Examining the perceptions of undergraduate women in male-dominated academic areas. *Psychology of Women Quarterly, 26*, 46–50.

Stein-Behrens, B., Mattson, M. P., Chang, I., Yeh, M., & Sapolsky, R. (1994). Stress exacerbates neuron loss and cytoskeletal pathology in the hippocampus. *Journal of Neuroscience, 14*, 5373–5380.

Steinberg, L., & Silverberg, S. B. (1987). Influences on marital satisfaction during the middle stages of the family life cycle. *Journal of Marriage and the Family, 49*, 751–760.

Steriade, M., & McCarley, R. W. (1990). *Brainstem control of wakefulness and sleep*. New York: Plenum.

Stern, W. (1912). *The psychological methods of testing intelligence* (G. M. Whipple, Trans.) (Educational Psychology Monograph No. 13). Baltimore, Warwick & York, Inc.

Sternberg, R. J. (1986). A triangular theory of love. *Psychological Review, 93*, 119–135.

Sternberg, R. J. (1988a). *The triarchic mind: A new theory of human intelligence*. New York: Viking-Penguin.

Sternberg, R. J. (1988b). Triangulating love. In R. Sternberg & M. Barnes (Eds.), *The psychology of love* (pp. 119–138). New Haven, CT: Yale University Press.

Sternberg, R. J. (1996). *Successful intelligence: How practical and creative intelligence determine success in life*. New York: Simon & Schuster.

Sternberg, R. J. (1997a). Construct validation of a triangular love scale. *European Journal of Social Psychology, 27,* 313–335.

Sternberg, R. J. (2005). The triarchic theory of successful intelligence. In *Contemporary Intellectual Assessment: Theories, Tests, and Issues*. New York: Guilford Press.

Sternberg, R. J., & Grigorenko, E. L. (2006). Cultural intelligence and successful intelligence. *Group Organization Management, 31,* 27–39.

Sternberg, R. J., & Kaufman, J. C. (1998). Human abilities. *Annual Review of Psychology, 49,* 479–502.

Sternberger, R. R., et al. (1995). Social phobia: An analysis of possible developmental factors. *Journal of Abnormal Psychology, 194,* 526–531.

Stevenson, M. B., Roach, M. A., Leavitt, L. A., Miller, J. F., & Chapman, R. S. (1988). Early receptive and productive language skills in preterm and full-term 8-month-old infants. *Journal of Psycholinguistic Research, 17*(2), 169–183.

Stickgold, R., Hobson, J. A., Fosse, R., & Fosse, M. (2001). Sleep, learning and dreams: Off-line memory reprocessing. *Science, 294,* 1052–1057.

Stiff, J. B., & Mongeau, P. A. (2002). *Persuasive communication* (2nd ed.). New York: Guilford Press.

Stine, C., Xu, J., Koskela, R., McMahon, F. J., Gschwend, M., Friddle, C., Clark, C. D., McInnis, M. G., Simpson, S. G., Breschel, T. S., Vishio, E., Riskin, K., Feilotter, H., Chen, E., Shen, S., Folstein, S., Meyers, D. A., Botstein, D., Marr, T. G., & DePaulo, J. R. (1995). Evidence for linkage of bipolar disorder to chromosome 18 with a parent-of-origin effect. *American Journal of Human Genetics, 57*(6), 1384–1394.

Stowell, J. R., Kiecolt-Glaser, J. K., & Glaser, R. (2001). Perceived stress and cellular immunity: When coping counts. *Journal of Behavioral Medicine, 24*(4), 323–339.

Stratton, K., Gable, A., & McCormick, M. C. (Eds.). (2001a). *Immunization safety review: Thimerosal-containing vaccines and neurodevelopmental disorders*. Washington, DC: National Academies Press.

Stratton, K., Wilson, C. B., & McCormick, M. C. (Eds.). (2001b). *Immunization safety review: Measles-mumps-rubella vaccine and autism*. Washington, DC: National Academies Press.

Straus, M. A. (2000). Corporal punishment of children and adult depression and suicidal ideation. *Beating the devil out of them: Corporal punishment in American families and its effects on children* (pp. 60–77). New York: Lexington Books.

Straus, M. A., & Stewart, J. H. (1999). Corporal punishment by American parents: National data on prevalence, chronicity, severity, and duration, in relation to child, and family characteristics. *Clinical Child and Family Psychology Review, 2,* 55–70.

Straus, M. A., & Yodanis, C. L. (1994). Physical abuse. In M. A. Straus (Ed.), *Beating the devil out of them: Corporal punishment in American families* (pp. 81–98). San Francisco: New Lexington Press.

Strauss, A. S. (2004). The meaning of death in Northern Cheyenne culture. In A. C. G. M. Robben (Ed.), *Death, mourning, and burial: A cross-cultural reader* (pp. 71–76). Malden, MA: Blackwell.

Strawbridge, W. J., Cohen, R. D., Shema, S. J., & Kaplan, G. A. (1997). Frequent attendance at religious services and mortality over 28 years. *American Journal of Public Health, 87,* 957–961.

Strayer, D. L., & Drews, F. A. (2007). Cell-phone-induced driver distraction. *Current Directions in Psychological Science, 16,* 128–131.

Strayer, D. L., & Johnston, W. A. (2001). Driven to distraction: Dual-task studies of simulated driving and conversing on a cellular phone. *Psychological Science, 12,* 462–466.

Strayer, D. L., Drews, F. A., & Crouch, D. J. (2006). A comparison of the cell phone driver and the drunk driver. *Human Factors, 48,* 381–391.

Strober, M., Freeman, R., Lampert, C., Diamond, J., & Kaye, W. (2000). Controlled family study of anorexia nervosa and bulimia nervosa: Evidence of shared liability and transmission of partial syndromes. *American Journal of Psychiatry, 157,* 393–401.

Ströhle, A. (2008). Physical activity, exercise, depression and anxiety disorders. *Journal of Neural Transmission, 116*(6), 777–784.

Stroth, S., Hille, K., Spitzer, M., & Reinhardt, R. (2009). Aerobic endurance exercise benefits memory and affect in young adults. *Neuropsychological Rehabilitation, 19*(2), 223–243.

Strunk, D. R., Brotman, M. A., & DeRubeis, R. J. (2010). The process of change in cognitive therapy for depression: Predictors of early inter-session symptom gains. *Behaviour Research and Therapy, 48*(7), 599–606.

Stubbs, R. J., van Wyk, M. C. W., Johnstone, A. M., & Harbron, C. G. (1996). Breakfasts high in protein, fat or carbohydrate: Effect on within-day appetite and energy balance. *European Journal of Clinical Nutrition, 50,* 409–417.

Stuss, D. T., Binns, M. A., Murphy, K. J., & Alexander, M. P. (2002). Dissociations within the anterior attentional system: Effects of task complexity and irrelevant information on reaction time speed and accuracy. *Neuropsychology, 16,* 500–513.

Sue, D. W., & Sue, D. (2008). *Counseling the culturally diverse*. Hoboken, New Jersey: John Wiley & Sons, Inc.

Sue, S. (1977). Community mental health services to minority groups: Some optimism, some pessimism. *American Psychologist, 32,* 616–624.

Sue, S. (1992). Ethnicity and mental health: Research and policy issues. *Journal of Social Issues, 48*(2), 187–205.

Sue, S., Zane, N., & Young, K. (1994). Research on psychotherapy in culturally diverse populations. In A. Bergin & S. Garfield (Eds.), *Handbook of psychotherapy and behavior change* (pp. 783–817). New York: Wiley.

Sullivan, P. F., Neale, M. C., & Kendler, K. S. (2000). Genetic epidemiology of major depression: Review and meta-analysis, *American Journal of Psychiatry, 157,* 1552–1562.

Sutcliffe, N., Clarke, A. E., Levinton, C., Frost, C., Gordon, C., & Isenberg, D. A. (1999). Associates of health status in patients with systemic lupus erythematosus. *Journal of Rheumatology, 26,* 2352–2356.

Sutherland, P. (1992). *Cognitive development today: Piaget and his critics*. London: Paul Chapman.

Swayze, V. W., II. (1995). Frontal leukotomy and related psychosurgical procedures in the era before antipsychotics (1935–1954): A historical overview. *American Journal of Psychiatry, 152*(4), 505–515.

Swenson, D. D., & Marshall, B. (2005, May 14). Flash flood: Hurricane Katrina's inundation of New Orleans, August 29, 2005. *Times-Picayune,* p. 3.

Taglialatela, J. P., Savage-Rumbaugh, E. S., & Baker, L. A. (2003). Vocal production by a language-competent bonobo (*Pan paniscus*). *International Journal of Comparative Psychology, 24,* 1–17.

Tajfel, H., & Turner, J. C. (1986). The social identity theory of intergroup behaviour. In S. Worchel & W. G. Austin (Eds.), *The psychology of intergroup relations* (Vol. 2, pp. 7–24). New York: Nelson Hall.

Takeuchi, T., Ogilvie, R. D., Murphy, T. I., & Ferrelli, A. V. (2003). EEG activities during elicited sleep onset. REM and NREM periods reflect difference mechanisms of dream generation. *Clinical Neurophysiology, 114*(2), 210–220.

Talbott, G. D. & Crosby, L. R. (2001). Recovery contracts: Seven key elements. In R. H. Coombs (Ed.), *Addiction recovery tools* (pp. 127–144). Thousand Oaks, CA: Sage.

Tamminga, C. A. (2002). Partial dopamine agonists in the treatment of psychosis. *Journal of Neural Transmission, 109,* 411–420.

Taylor, B., Miller, E., Farrington, C. P., Petropoulos, M. C., Favot-Mayaud, I., Li, J., & Waight, P. A. (1999). Autism and measles, mumps, and rubella vaccine: No epidemiological evidence for a causal association. *Lancet, 353,* 2026–2029.

Taylor, C., Manganello, J. A., Lee, S. J., & Rice, J. C. (2010). Mothers' spanking of 3-year-old children and subsequent risk of children's aggressive behavior. *Pediatrics, 125,* 1057–1065.

Taylor, D. M., & Moghaddam, F. M. (1994). *Theories of intergroup relations: International social psychological perspectives* (2nd ed.). Westport, CT: Praeger.

Teigen, K. (1994). Yerkes–Dodson: A law for all seasons. *Theory and Psychology, 4,* 525–547.

Temoshok, L., & Dreher, H. (1992). *The Type C connection: The behavioral links to cancer and your health*. New York: Random House.

Terman, L. M. (1916). *The measurement of intelligence*. Boston: Houghton Mifflin.

Terman, L. M. (1925). *Mental and physical traits of a thousand gifted children (I)*. Stanford, CA: Stanford University Press.

Terman, L. M., & Oden, M. H. (1947). *The gifted child grows up: 25 years' follow-up of a superior group: Genetic studies of genius (Vol. 4)*. Stanford, CA: Stanford University Press.

Terman, L. M., & Oden, M. H. (1959). *The gifted group at mid-life, thirty-five years follow-up of the superior child: Genetic studies of genius (Vol. 3)*. Stanford, CA: Stanford University Press.

Terry, A. V., Jr., Hill, W. D., Parikh, V., Waller, J. L., Evans, D. R., & Mahadik, S. P. (2003). Differential effects of haloperidol, risperidone, and clozapine exposure on cholinergic markers and spatial learning performance in rats. *Neuropsychopharmacology, 28*(2), 300–309.

Thase, M. E. (1999). When are psychotherapy and pharmacotherapy combinations the treatment of choice for major depressive disorders? *Psychiatric Quarterly, 70*(4), 333–346.

Thase, M. E., & Sachs, G. S. (2000). Bipolar depression: Pharmacotherapy and related therapeutic strategies. *Biological Psychiatry, 48*(6), 558–572.

Thiedke, C. C. (2001). Sleep disorders and sleep problems in childhood. *American Family Physician, 63,* 277–284.

Thigpen, C. H., & Cleckley, H. M. (1992, Rev.). *The three faces of Eve*. London: Secker & Warburg.

Thomas, A., & Chess, S. (1977). *Temperament and development*. New York: Brunner/Mazel.

Thomas, N. J. T. (2001). Mental imagery. In E. N. Zalta (Ed.), *The Stanford encyclopedia of philosophy* (Winter 2001). Retrieved January 20, 2008, from http://plato.stanford.edu/entries/mental-imagery/

Thompson, W. W., Price, C., Goodson, B., Shay, D. K., Benson, P., Hinrichsen, V. L., Lewis, E., Eriksen, E., Ray, P., Marcy, S. M., Dunn, J., Jackson, L. A., Lieu, T. A., Black, S., Stewart, G., Weintraub, E. S., Davis, R. L., & DeStefano, F. (2007). Early thimerosal exposure and neuropsychological outcomes at 7 to 10 years. *The New England Journal of Medicine, 357*(13), 1281–1292.

Thoresen, C. E., & Harris, H. S. (2002). Spirituality and health: What's the evidence and what's needed? *Annals of Behavioral Medicine, 24,* 3–13.

Thorndike, E. L. (1911). *Animal Intelligence: Experimental studies*. New York: Macmillan.

Thorndike, E. L. (1920). A constant error on psychological rating. *Journal of Applied Psychology, 5,* 25–29.

Thornton, A., & Hui-Sheng, L. (1994). Continuity and change. In A. Thornton & Hui-Sheng (Eds.), *Social change and the family in Taiwan* (pp. 396–410). Chicago: University of Chicago Press.

Tobach, E. (2001). Development of sex and gender. In J. Worell (Ed.), *Encyclopedia of women and gender* (pp. 315–332). San Diego, CA: Academic Press.

Toga, A. W., & Thompson, P. M. (2003). Mapping brain asymmetry. *Nature Reviews Neuroscience, 4*, 37–48.

Tohen, M., Vieta, E., Calabrese, J., Ketter, T. A., Sachs, G., Bowden, C., Mitchell, P. B., Centorrino, F., Risser, R., Baker, R. W., Evans, A. R., Beymer, K., Dube, S., Tollefson, G. D., & Breier, A. (2003). Efficacy of olanzapine and olanzapinefluoxetine combination in the treatment of bipolar I depression. *Archives of General Psychiatry, 60*(11), 1079–1088.

Tolman, E. C. (1932). *Purposive behavior in animals and man.* New York: Century.

Tolman, E. C., & Honzik, C. H. (1930). Introduction and removal of reward and maze learning in rats. *University of California Publications in Psychology, 4*, 257–275.

Tomasello, M., Carpenter, M., & Lizskowski, U. (2007). A new look at infant pointing. *Child Development, 78*, 705–722.

Torgersen, S. (2000). Genetics of patients with borderline personality disorder. *Psychiatric Clinics of North America, 23*, 1–9.

Torrance, E. P. (1993). The Beyonders in a thirty-year longitudinal study of creative achievement. *Roeper Review, 15*(3), 131–135.

Torrey, E. F. (1987). Prevalence studies in schizophrenia. *British Journal of Psychiatry, 150*, 598–608.

Tran, M.-T. (2010, June 27). Teenage sailor Abby Sunderland one step closer to home. *Los Angeles Times.* Retrieved June 27, 2010, from http://articles.latimes.com/2010/jun/26/local/la-me-0626-abby-sunderland-arrives-20100626

Trappey, C. (1996). A meta-analysis of consumer choice and subliminal advertising. *Psychology and Marketing, 13*, 517–530.

Treisman A. [M.] (2006). How the deployment of attention determines what we see. *Visual Cognition, 14*, 411–443.

Treisman, A. M., & Gelade, G. (1980). A feature integration theory of attention. *Cognitive Psychology, 12*, 97–136.

Treisman, M. (1977). Motion sickness: An evolutionary hypothesis. *Science, 197*, 493.

Tremblay, A., Doucet, E., & Imbeault, P. (1999). Physical activity and weight maintenance. *International Journal of Obesity, 23*(3), S50–S54.

Tresniowski, A. (1999, July 12). Troubled sleep. *People Weekly*, 56–59.

Triandis, H. (1971). *Attitude and attitude change.* New York: Wiley.

Trocmé, N., MacLaurin, B., Fallon, B., Daciuk, J., Billingsley, D., Tourigny, M., Mayer, M., Wright, J., Barter, K., Furford, G., Hornick, J., Sullivan, R., & McKenzie, B. (2001). *Canadian incidence study of reported child abuse and neglect: Final report* (pp. 30–31). Ottawa, ON: Minister of Public Works and Government Services Canada.

Troisi, A., & McGuire, M. (2002). Darwinian psychiatry and the concept of mental disorder. *Human Ethology and Evolutionary Psychology, 23*(4), 31–38.

Troncoso, X. G., Macknik, S. L., Otero-Millan, J., & Martinez-Conde, S. (2008). Microsaccades drive illusory motion in the enigma illusion. *Proceedings of the National Academy of Sciences, USA, 105*(41), 16033–16038.

Trujillo, K. A., & Chinn, A. B. (1996). Antidepressants. *Drugs and the Brain*: California State University. Retrieved from the Internet on July 20, 2004, at www.csusm.edu/DandB/AD.html#history.

Trut, L. M. (1999). Early canid domestication: The Farm-Fox experiment. *Science, 283*.

Tsai, J. L., Simeonova, D. I., & Watanabe, J. T. (2004). Somatic and social: Chinese Americans talk about emotion. *Personality and Social Psychology Bulletin, 30*(9), 1226–1238.

Tsuang, M., Domschke, K., Jerskey, B. A., & Lyons, M. J. (2004). Agoraphobic behavior and panic attack: A study of male twins. *Journal of Anxiety Disorders, 18*(6), 799–807.

Tucker, E. W., & Potocky-Tripodi, M. (2006). Changing heterosexuals' attitudes toward homosexuals: A systematic review of the empirical literature. *Research on Social Work Practice, 16*(2), 176–190.

Tukuitonga, C. F., & Bindman, A. B. (2002). Ethnic and gender differences in the use of coronary artery revascularisation procedures in New Zealand. *New Zealand Medical Journal, 115*, 179–182.

Tulving, E., & Thomson, D. M. (1973). Encoding specificity and retrieval processes in episodic memory. *Psychological Review, 80*, 352–373.

Turk, C. L., Heimberg, R. G., & Magee, L. (2008). Social anxiety disorder. In D. H. Barlow (Ed.), *Clinical handbook of psychological disorders* (pp. 123–163). New York, NY: The Guilford Press.

Turner, W. J. (1995). Homosexuality, Type 1: An Xq28 phenomenon. *Archives of Sexual Behavior, 24*(2), 109–134.

Tusel, D. J., Piotrowski, N. A., Sees, K., Reilly, P. M., Banys, P., Meek, P., & Hall, S. M. (1994). Contingency contracting for illicit drug use with opioid addicts in methadone treatment. In L. S., Harris (Ed.), *Problems of drug dependence: Proceedings of the 56th Annual Scientific Meeting.* (National Institute on Drug Abuse Research Monograph No. 153, pp. 155–160). Washington, DC: U.S. Goverment Printing Office.

Tversky, A., & Kahneman, D. (1973). Availability: A heuristic for judging frequency and probability. *Cognitive Psychology, 5*(2), 207–232.

Tversky, A., & Shafir, E. (1992). The disjunction effect in choice under uncertainty. *Psychological Science, 3*(5), 305–309.

Ulmer, J. L., Parsons, L., Moseley, M., & Gabrieli, J. (Eds.). (2006). White matter in cognitive neuroscience: Advances in diffusion tensor imaging and its applications. *Annals of the New York Academy of Sciences* (Vol. 1064). New York, NY: The New York Academy of Sciences.

Unger, R. (1979). Toward a redefinition of sex and gender. *American Psychologist, 34*, 1085–1094.

Upthegrove, T., Roscigno, V., & Charles, C. (1999). Big money collegiate sports: Racial concentration, contradictory pressures, and academic performance. *Social Science Quarterly, 80*, 718–737.

Uretsky, S. D. (2002). Antianxiety drugs. *Gale Encyclopedia of Medicine.* Gale Group. Retrieved July 19, 2010, from http://www.healthline.com/galecontent/antianxiety-drugs

Vaidya, C. J., Zhao, M., Desmond, J. E., & Gabrieli, J. D. E. (2002). Evidence for cortical encoding specificity in episodic memory: Memory-induced re-activation of picture processing areas. *Neuropsychologia, 40*(12), 2136–2143.

Vail, A. (1976). Factors influencing lower class, black patients' remaining in treatment. *Clinical Psychology, 29*, 12–14.

Vaillant, G. E. (2002). Adaptive mental mechanisms: Their role in a positive psychology. *American Psychologist, 55*, 89–98.

Valverde, R., Pozdnyakova, I., Kajander, T., Venkatraman, J., & Regan, L. (2007). Fragile X mental retardation syndrome: Structure of the KH1-KH2 domains of fragile X mental retardation protein. *Structure, 9*, 1090–1098.

Van de Castle, R. (1994). *Our dreaming mind.* New York: Ballantine Books.

van der Merwe, A., & Garuccio, A. (Eds.). (1994). *Waves and particles in light and matter.* New York: Plenum Press.

van der Stelt, Odin, van der Molen, M., Boudewijn Gunning, W., & Kok, A. (2010). Neuroelectrical signs of selective attention to color in boys with Attention-Deficit/Hyperactivity disorder. *Cognitive Brain Research, 12*(2), 245–264.

VandenBos, G. R., & Bulatao, E. Q. (Eds.). (1996). *Violence on the job: Identifying risks and developing solutions.* Washington DC: American Psychological Association.

Vartanian, L. R. (2000). Revisiting the imaginary audience and personal fable constructs of adolescent egocentricism: A conceptual review. *Adolescence, 35*(140), 639–661.

Vasey, P. L. & VanderLaan, D. P. (2010). An adaptive cognitive dissociation between willingness to help kin and nonkin in Samoan *Fa'afafine. Psychological Science, 21*(2), 292–297.

Vaughan, S. (2000). *Half empty, half full: The psychological roots of optimism.* New York: Harcourt.

Vecsey, C. G., Baillie, G. S., Jaganath, D., Havekes, R., Daniels, A., Wimmer, M., Huang, T., Brown, K. M., Li, X. Y., Descalzi, G., Kim, S. S., Chen, T., Shang, Y. Z., Zhuo, M., Houslay, M. D., & Abel, T. (2009). Sleep deprivation impairs cAMP signaling in the hippocampus. *Nature, 461*(7267), 1122–1125.

Vernon, S. W., & Roberts, R. E. (1982). Use of RDC in a tri-ethnic community survey. *Archives of General Psychiatry, 39*, 47.

Villafuerte, S., & Burmeister, M. (2003). Untangling genetic networks of panic, phobia, fear and anxiety. *Genome Biology, 4*(8), 224.

Villani, S. (2001). Impact of media on children and adolescents: A 10-year review of the research. *Journal of the American Academy on Child and Adolescent Psychiatry, 40*(4), 392–401.

Vink, T., Hinney, A., Van Elburg, A. A., Van Goozen, S. H., Sandkuijl, L. A., Sinke, R. J., Herpertz-Dahlman, B. M., Henebrand, J., Remschmidt, H., Van Engeland, H., & Adan, R. A. (2001). Association between an agouti-related protein gene polymorphism and anorexia nervosa. *Molecular Psychiatry, 6*(3), 325–328.

Virkkunen, M., & Linnoila, M. (1996). Serotonin and glucose metabolism in impulsively violent alcoholic offenders. In D. M. Stoff, & R. B. Cairns (Eds.), *Aggression and violence* (pp. 87–100). Mahwah, NJ: Erlbaum.

Visser, P. S., & Krosnick, J. A. (1998). Development of attitude strength over the life cycle: Surge and decline. *Journal of Personality and Social Psychology, 75*(6), 1389–1410.

Vogel, G. W. (1975). A review of REM sleep deprivation. *Archives of General Psychiatry, 32*, 749–761.

Vogel, G. W. (1993). Selective deprivation, REM sleep. In M. A. Carskadon (Ed.), *The encyclopedia of sleep and dreaming.* New York: Macmillan.

Voineskos, A. N., Lobaugh, N. J., Bouix, S., Rajji, T. K., Miranda, D., Kennedy, J. L., et al. (2010). Diffusion tensor tractography findings in schizophrenia across the adult lifespan. *Brain: A Journal of Neurology, 17*, 17.

Vokey, J. R., & Read J. D. (1985). Subliminal messages: Between the devil and the media. *American Psychologist, 40*, 1231–1239.

Volkow, N. D., Wang, G.-J., Newcorn, J., Telang, F., Solanto, M. V., Fowler, J. S., et al. (2007). Depressed dopamine activity in caudate and preliminary evidence of limbic involvement in adults with Attention-Deficit/Hyperactivity Disorder. *Archives of General Psychiatry, 64*(8), 932–940.

von Helmholtz, H. (1852). On the theory of compound colours. *Philosophical Magazine, 4*, 519–535.

von Helmholtz, H. L. F. (1863). *Die Lehre von den Tonempfindungen als physiologische Grundlage fur die Theorie der Musik* (1954, XX, trans. by Alexander J. Ellis). *On the sensations of tone as a physiological basis for the theory of music.* New York: Dover.

Voss, M. W., Erickson, K. I., Prakash, R. S., Chaddock, L., Malkowski, E., Alves, H., Kim, J. S., Morris, K. S., White, S. M., Wojcicki, T. R., Hu, L., Szabo, A., Klamm, E., McAuley, E., & Kramer, A. F. (2010). Functional connectivity: A source of variance in the association between cardiorespiratory fitness and cognition? *Neuropsychologia, 48*(5), 1394–1406.

Voyer, D., & Rodgers, M. (2002). Reliability of laterality effects in a dichotic listening task with nonverbal material. *Brain and Cognition, 48*, 602–606.

Vygotsky, L. S. (1934/1962). *Thought and language.* Cambridge, MA: MIT Press.

Vygotsky, L. S. (1978). *Mind in society: The development of higher psychological processes.* Cambridge, MA: Harvard University Press.

Vygotsky, L. S. (1987). Thought and word. In R. W. Riebe & A. S. Carton (Eds.), *The collected works of L. S. Vygotsky: Vol. 1. Problems of general psychology* (pp. 243–288). New York: Plenum.

Wahlsten, D. (1997). The malleability of intelligence is not constrained by heritability. In B. Devlin, S. E. Fienberg, & K. Roeder, *Intelligence, genes, and success: Scientists respond to the bell curve* (pp. 71–87). New York: Springer.

Wakefield, A. J., Murch, S. H., Anthony, A., Linnell, J., Casson, D. M., Malik, M., Berelowitz, M., Dhillon, A. P., Thomson, M. A., Harvey, P., Valentine, A., Davies, S. E., & Walker-Smith J., A. (1998). Ileal-lymphoid-nodular hyperplasia, non-specific colitis, and pervasive developmental disorder in children. *The Lancet, 351*, 9103.

Walker, L. J. (1991). Sex differences in moral reasoning. In W. M. Kurtines & J. L. Gewirtz (Eds.), *Handbook of moral behavior and development: Vol. 2. Research* (pp. 333–364). Hillsdale, NJ: Erlbaum.

Walter, C. (2008). Affairs of the lips. *Scientific American Mind, 19*(6), 24.

Wampold, B. E. (1997). Methodological problems in identifying efficacious psychotherapies. *Psychotherapy Research, 7*, 21–43.

Ward, A. S., Li, D. H., Luedtke, R. R., & Emmett-Oglesby, M. W. (1996). Variations in cocaine self-administration by inbred rat strains under a progressive-ratio schedule. *Psychopharmacology, 127*(3), 204–212.

Ward, C., & Rana-Deuba, A. (1999). Acculturation and adaptation revisited. *Journal of Cross-Cultural Psychology, 30*, 422–442.

Ward, J., Mattic, K. R. P., & Hall, W. (1999). *Methadone maintenance treatment and other opioid replacement therapies.* Sydney, Australia: Harwood Academic.

Wartner, U. G., Grossmann, K., Fremmer-Bombik, E., & Suess, G. (1994). Attachment patterns at age six in south Germany: Predictability from infancy and implications for preschool behavior. *Child Development, 65*, 1014–1027.

Washburn, M. F. (1908). *The animal mind: A text-book of comparative psychology.* New York: Macmillan.

Wasserman, E. A., & Miller, R. R. (1997). What's elementary about associative learning? *Annual Review of Psychology, 48*, 573–607.

Watson, J. B. (1913). Psychology as the behaviorist views it. *Psychological Review, 20*, 158–177.

Watson, J. B. (1924). *Behaviorism.* New York: Norton.

Watson, J. B., & Rayner, R. (1920). Conditioned emotional responses. *Journal of Experimental Psychology, 3*, 1–14.

Watson, J. M., & Strayer, D. L. (2010). Supertaskers: Profiles in extraordinary multitasking ability. *Psychonomic Bulletin and Review, 17*(4), 479–485.

Weaver, F. M., Follett, K., Stern, M., Hur, K., Harris, C., Marks, W. J., Jr., et al. (2009). Bilateral deep brain stimulation vs. best medical therapy for patients with advanced Parkinson disease: A randomized controlled trial. *Journal of the American Medical Association, 301*(1), 63–73.

Webb, W. B. (1992). *Sleep: The gentle tyrant* (2nd ed.). Bolton, MA: Ander.

Wechsler, D. (1975). *The collected papers of David Wechsler.* New York: Academic Press.

Wechsler, D. (2002). *WPPSI-III (Wechsler Preschool and Primary Scale of Intelligence—Third Edition) Administration and scoring manual.* San Antonio, TX: Pearson.

Wechsler, D. (2003). *WISC-IV (Wechsler Intelligence Scale for Children—Fourth Edition) Administration and scoring manual.* San Antonio, TX: Pearson.

Wechsler, D. (2008). *WAIS-IV (Wechsler Adult Intelligence Scale—Fourth Edition) Administration and scoring manual.* San Antonio, TX: Pearson.

Wedding, D. (2004). Cross-cultural counseling and psychotherapy. In R. J. Corsini & D. Wedding (Eds.), *Current psychotherapies* (7th ed., p. 485). Itasca, IL: Peacock.

Weinberger, D. R. (1987). Implications of normal brain development for the pathogenesis of schizophrenia. *Archives of General Psychiatry, 44*, 660–668.

Weiner, B. (1985). An attributional theory of achievement motivation. *Psychological Review, 92*, 548–573.

Weiner, I. B. (1997). Current status of the Rorschach Inkblot Method. *Journal of Personality Assessment, 68*, 5–19.

Weiner, R. D. (2000). Retrogade amnesia with electroconvulsive therapy: Characteristics and implications. *Archives of General Psychiatry, 57*, 591–592.

Weis, S., Klaver, P., Reul, J., Elger, C. E., & Fernandez, G. (2004). Temporal and cerebellar brain regions that support both declarative memory formation and retrieval. *Cerebral Cortex, 14*, 256–267.

Weisman, A. (1972). *On dying and denying.* New York: Behavioral Publications.

Weiss, J. M. (1972). Psychological factors in stress and disease. *Scientific American, 26*, 104–113.

Weisse, C. S. (1992). Depression and immunocompetence: A review of the literature. *Psychological Bulletin, 111*, 475–489.

Weissman, M. M., & Klerman, G. L. (1977). Sex differences and the epidemiology of depression. *Archives of General Psychiatry, 34*, 98–111.

Weissman, M. M., Bland, R. C., Canino, G. J., Faravelli, C., Greenwald, S., Hwu, H. G., Joyce, P. R., Karam, E. G., Lee, C. K., Lellouch, J., Lepine, J. P., Newman, S. C., Oakley-Browne, M. A., Rubio-Stipec, M., Wells, J. E., Wickramaratne, P. J., Wittchen, H. U., & Yeh, E. K. (1997). The cross-national epidemiology of panic disorder. *Archives of General Psychiatry, 54*, 305–309.

Weissman, M. M., Bland, R., Joyce, P. R., Newman, S., Wells, J. E., & Wittchen, H. U. (1993). Sex differences in rates of depression: Cross-national perspectives. *Journal of Affective Disorders, 29*, 77–84.

Wender, P. H., Wolf, L. E., & Wasserstein, J. (2001). Adults with ADHD. An overview. *Annals of the New York Academy of Sciences, 931*, 1–16.

Wenneberg, S. R., Schneider, R. H., Walton, K. G., Maclean, C. R., Levitsky, D. K., Mandarino, J. V., Waziri, R., & Wallace, R. K. (1997). Anger expression correlates with platelet aggregation. *Behavioral Medicine, 22*(4), 174–177.

Werker, J. F., & Lalonde, C. E. (1988). Cross-language speech perceptions: Initial capabilities and developmental change. *Developmental Psychology, 24*, 672–683.

Wertheimer, M. (1982). *Productive thinking.* Chicago: University of Chicago Press.

Westen, D. (2005). Cognitive neuroscience and psychotherapy: Implications for psychotherapy's second century. In G. Gabbard, J. Beck, & J. Holmes (Eds.), *Oxford textbook of psychotherapy.* Oxford, UK: Oxford University Press.

Wetherell, J. L. (2002). Behavior therapy for anxious older adults. *Behavior Therapist, 25*, 16–17.

Wever, E. G. (1949). *Theory of Hearing.* New York: John Wiley & Sons.

Wever, E. G., & Bray, C. W. (1930). The nature of acoustic response: The relation between sound frequency and frequency of impulses in the auditory nerve. *Journal of Experimental Psychology, 13*(5), 373–387.

Weyant, J. M. (1996). Application of compliance techniques to direct-mail requests for charitable donations. *Psychology and Marketing, 13*, 157–170

White, G. L. (1980). Physical attractiveness and courtship progress. *Journal of Personality and Social Psychology, 39*, 660–668.

Whorf, B. L. (1956). *Language, thought and reality.* New York: Wiley.

Wicker, A. W. (1971). An examination of the "other variables" explanation of attitude–behavior inconsistency. *Journal of Personality and Social Psychology, 19*, 18–30.

Widiger, T. A., & Trull, T. J. (2007). Plate tectonics in the classification of personality disorder: Shifting to a dimensional model. [doi:10.1037/0003-066X.62.2.71]. *American Psychologist, 62*(2), 71–83.

Widiger, T. A., & Weissman, M. M. (1991). Epidemiology of borderline personality disorder. *Hospital and Community Psychiatry, 42*, 1015–1021.

Wierenga, C. E., Stricker, N. H., McCauley, A., Simmons, A., Jak, A. J., Chang, Y. L., et al. (2010). Increased functional brain response during word retrieval in cognitively intact older adults at genetic risk for Alzheimer's disease. *Neuroimage, 15*, 15.

Williams, J. A., Pascual-Leone, A., & Fregni, F. (2010). Interhemispheric modulation induced by cortical stimulation and motor training. *Physical Therapy, 90*(3), 398–410.

Williams, M. E. (1995). *The American Geriatrics Society's complete guide to aging and mental health.* New York: Random House.

Williams, R. B. (1999). A 69-year-old man with anger and angina. *Journal of the American Medical Association, 282*, 763–770.

Williams, R. B. (2001). Hostility: Effects on health and the potential for successful behavioral approaches to prevention and treatment. In A. Baum, T. A. Revenson, & J. E. Singer (Eds.), *Handbook of Health Psychology.* Mahwah, NJ: Erlbaum.

Williams, R. B., Haney, T. L., Lee, K. L., Kong, Y. H., Blumenthal, J. A., & Whalen, R. E. (1980). Type A behavior, hostility, and coronary atherosclerosis. *Psychosomatic Medicine, 42*(6), 539–549.

Winningham, R. G., Hyman, I. E., Jr., & Dinnel, D. L. (2000). Flashbulb memories? The effects of when the initial memory report was obtained. *Memory, 8*, 209–216.

Winslow, B. (2007). "37,000 'Fundamentalists' counted in and near Utah." *Deseret Morning News.* August 1, 2007. http://www.reckross.com/reference/polygamy/poyltgamy684.html. Accessed on February 19, 2010.

Winton, W. M. (1987). Do introductory textbooks present the Yerkes-Dodson law correctly? *American Psychologist, 42*(2), 202–203.

Wise, K., Alhabash, S., & Park, H. (2010). Emotional responses during social information seeking on Facebook. *Cyberpsychology, Behavior, and Social Networking, 13*(5), 555–562.

Wiseman, R. (2007). *Quirkology: How we discover the big truths in small things* (pp. 7–8, 28–32). New York: Basic Books.

Wolberg, L. R. (1977). *The technique of psychotherapy.* New York: Grune & Stratton.

Wood, J. M., Nezworski, M. T., & Stejskal, W. J. (1996). The comprehensive system for the Rorschach: A critical examination. *Psychological Science, 7*(1), 3–10, 14–17.

Woodhouse, A. (2005). Phantom limb sensation. *Clinical and Experimental Pharmacology and Physiology, 32*(1–2), 132–134.

Wooten, P. (1980). Humor: an antidote for stress. *Holistic Nursing Practice. 10*(2), 49–56.

World Health Organization (WHO) International Consortium in Psychiatric Epidemiology. (2000). Cross-national comparisons of the prevalences and correlates of mental disorders. *Bulletin of the World Health Organization, 78*(4), 413–426.

Wu, C-C., Lee, G. C., & Lai, H-K. (2004). Using concept maps to aid analysis of concept presentation in high school computer textbooks. *Education and Information Technologies, 9*(20), 185–197.

Wyman, P. A., Moynihan, J., Eberly, S., Cox, C., Cross, W., Jin, X., & Caserta, M. T. (2007). Association of family stress with natural killer cell activity and the frequency of illnesses in children. *Archives of Pediatric and Adolescent Medicine, 161*, 228–234.

Wynne, C. (1999). Do animals think? The case against the animal mind. *Psychology Today, 32*(6), 50–53.

Yaffe, K., Vittinghoff, E., Lindquist, K., Barnes, D., Covinsky K. E., Neylan, T., Kluse, M., & Marmar, C. (2010). Posttraumatic stress disorder and risk of dementia among U.S. veterans. *Archives of General Psychiatry, 67*(6), 608–613.

Yalom, I. (1995). *The theory and practice of group psychotherapy* (4th ed.). New York: Basic Books.

Yamaguchi, S., Isejima, H., Matsuo, T., Okura, R., Yagita, K., Kobayashi, M., & Okamura, H. (2003). Synchronization of cellular clocks in the suprachiasmatic nucleus. *Science, 302*, 1408–1412.

Yerkes, R. M. (Ed.). (1921). Psychological examining in the United States Army. *Memoirs of the National Academy of Sciences, 15,* 1–890.

Yerkes, R. M., & Dodson, J. D. (1908). The relation of strength of stimulus to rapidity of habit formation. *Journal of Comparative Neurology and Psychology, 18,* 459–482.

Ying, Y. W. (1990). Explanatory models of major depression and implications for help-seeking among immigrant Chinese-American women. *Culture, Medicine, and Psychiatry, 14,* 393–408.

Yip, Y. L. (2002, Autumn). Pivot–Qi. *The Journal of Traditional Eastern Health and Fitness, 12*(3).

Yopyk, D., & Prentice, D. A. (2005). Am I an athlete or a student? Identify salience and stereotype threat in student-athletes. *Basic and Applied Social Psychology, 27* (4), 29–336.

Young, J. E., Rygh, J. L., Weinberger, A. D., & Beck, A. T. (2008). Cognitive therapy for depression. In D. H. Barlow (Ed.), *Clinical handbook of psychological disorders* (pp. 250–305). New York, NY: The Guilford Press.

Young, S. N. (Ed.) (1996). Melatonin, sleep, aging, and the health protection branch. *Journal of Psychiatry Neuroscience, 21*(3), 161–164.

Yule, G. (1996). *Pragmatics.* Oxford, UK: Oxford University Press.

Zajonc, R. B. (1965). Social facilitation. *Science, 149,* 269–274.

Zajonc, R. B. (1980). Feeling and thinking: Preferences need no inferences. *American Psychologist, 35,* 151–175.

Zajonc, R. B. (1984). On the primacy of affect. *American Psychologist, 39,* 117–123.

Zajonc, R. B. (1998). Emotions. In D. T. Gilbert & S. T. Fiske (Eds.), *Handbook of social psychology* (4th ed., Vol. 1, pp. 591–632). New York: McGraw-Hill.

Zanarini, M. C. (2000). Childhood experiences associated with the development of borderline personality disorder. *Psychiatric Clinics of North America, 23*(1), 89–101.

Zedler, Beatrice (1995). "Mary Whiton Calkins." In M. E. Waithe (Ed.), *A history of women philosophers: Vol. 4* (pp. 103–123). Netherlands: Kluwer Academic Publishers.

Zeidner, M., & Matthews, G. (2005). Evaluative anxiety. In A. Elliott & C. Dweck (Eds.), *Handbook of competence and motivation* (pp. 141–146). New York: Guilford Press.

Zeki, S. (2001). Localization and globalization in conscious vision. *Annual Review of Neuroscience, 24,* 57–86.

Zentall, T. R. (2000). Animal intelligence. In R. J. Sternberg (Ed.), *Handbook of intelligence.* Cambridge, MA: Cambridge University Press.

Zhang, L. (2006). Does student-teacher thinking style match/mismatch matter in students' achievement? *Educational Psychology, 26,* 395–409.

Zilles, K. (1990). Cortex. In G. Paxinos (Ed.), *The human nervous system* (pp. 757–802). San Diego, CA: Academic.

Zillmann, D., Baron, R., & Tamborini, R. (1981). Social costs of smoking: Effects of tobacco smoke on hostile behavior. *Psychology Journal of Applied Social, 11,* 548–561.

Zimbardo, P. (1971). The pathology of imprisonment. *Society, 9*(4–8), 4.

Zimbardo, P. G., & Hartley, C. F. (1985). Cults go to high school: A theoretical and empirical analysis of the initial stage in the recruitment process. *Cultic Studies Journal, 2,* 91–148.

Zisapel, N. (2001). Circadian rhythm sleep disorders: Pathophysiology and potential approaches to management. *CNS Drugs, 15*(4), 311–328.

Zorilla, E. P., Luborsky, L., McKay, J. R., Rosenthal, R., Houldin, A., Tax, A., McCorkle, R., Seligman, D. A., & Schmidt, K. (2001). The relationship of depression and stressors to immunological assays: A meta-analytic review. *Brain, Behavior, and Immunity, 15,* 199–226.

Zuckerman, M. (1979). *Sensation seeking: Beyond the optimal level of arousal.* Hillsdale, NJ: Erlbaum.

Zuckerman, M. (1994). *Behavioral expression and biosocial bases of sensation seeking.* New York: Cambridge University Press.

Zuckerman, M. (2002). Zuckerman-Kuhlman Personality Questionnaire (ZKPQ): An alternative five-factorial model. In B. De Raad & M. Perugini (Eds.), *Big Five assessment* (pp. 377–396). Seattle, WA: Hogrefe & Huber.

Zuo, L., & Cramond, B. (2001). An examination of Terman's gifted children from the theory of identity. *Gifted Child Quarterly, 45*(4), 251–259.

Zvolensky, M. J., Schmidt, M. B., & Stewart, S. H. (2003). Panic disorder and smoking. *Clinical Psychology: Science and Practice, 10,* 29–51.

credits

PHOTO CREDITS

TEXT CREDITS

name index

A

AAA Foundation for Traffic Safety, 330
Abadinsky, H., 282
Abe, K., 204
Abel, G. G., 183
Abela, J. R. Z., 476
Åberg, M. A., 223
Abraham, S., 449
Abraham, W. C., 54
Abrahamsen, A., 165
Abramson, L. Y., 398, 447
Acheson, D. J., 169
Adachi, P. J. C., 374
Adams, D. B., 372
Adams, J. J., 186
Adams, R. J., 239
Adams, S. A., 484, 485
Addis, D. R., 259
Ader, R., 320
Adhikari, A., 445
Adler, A., 394
Adler, S. R., 259
Adolphs, R., 67, 295
Aghajanian, G. K., 286
Agnati, L. F., 49
Agresti, A., A–1
Aguiar, A., 243
Ahn, W., 210
Ainsworth, M. D. S., 247, 248
Aitchison, J., 210
Ajzen, I., 355
Al-Hammadi, N., 15
Albert, D. J., 372
Alderfer, C. P., 280
Alexander, G., 372
Aligne, C. A., 330
Alkon, D., 188
Allen, D., 304, 305
Allen, G., 234
Allen, G. E., 414
Allen, K., 332
Alloy, L. B., 151
Allport, G. W., 401
Alm, H., 199
Alperstein, L., 335
Alvarez-Buylla, A., 44
Alzheimer's Association, 190, 191
Amabile, T., 316
Amabile, T. M., 272, A–10
Amat, J., 150
American Academy of Pediatrics, 232
American Association on Intellectual and Developmental Disabilities [AAIDD], 416

American College Counseling Association's (ACCA) Community College Task Force, 482
American Psychiatric Association, 74, 334, 415, 416, 437, 441, 445, 446, 449, 452, 453, 455, 456, 457, 485, 490
American Psychiatric Association Committee on Electro-convulsive Therapy, 489
American Psychological Association, 31, 484
American Psychological Association Division 19, B–8
Anastasi, A., 409
Anderson, C. A., 152, 371
Anderson, M. C., 187
Andreasen, N. C., 452
Andrews, J. D. W., 479
Anschuetz, B. L., 331
Antoni, M. H., 332
Antuono, P. G., 190
Arbury, S., B–12
Archer, J., 372
Arkowitcz, H., 471
Armstrong, R., 284
Arnett, P. A., 457
Aron, A., A–1
Aronson, E., 357, 367
Aronson, J., 366
Asarnow, R. F., 452
Asch, S. E., 347
Aserinsky, E., 200
Ash, M. G., 9
Assaf, Y., 62
Atkinson, R. C., 166, 170
Atladóttir, H. O., 245

B

Babiloni, C., 83
Backenstrass, M., 398
Backer, B., 263
Baddeley, A., 176, 177, 181
Baddeley, A. D., 164, 169
Bae, S. M., 63
Baehr, E. K., 199
Baer, D. M., 146
Bahrick, H., 170, 182
Bailey, J., 292
Bailey, J. M., 292, 293
Baillargeon, R., 243
Baker, L. D., 223
Ball, K., 259
Baltes, P. B., 230

Bandura, A., 128, 151, 152, 372, 373, 397, 398, 475
Barak, A., 486
Bard, P., 299
Bargh, J. A., 83
Barker, E., 378
Barkley, R. A., 74
Barlow, D. H., 478, 484
Barnes, A. M., 232
Barnes, V., 337
Barnyard, P., 170
Baron, J. N., 374
Baron, S. A., B–11
Barondes, S. H., 448
Barry, K. L., 282
Barsalou, L. W., 122
Barsh, G. S., 333, 334
Bartels, A., 370
Barth, J. M., 295
Bartholomew, K., 248
Bartke, A., 262
Bartlett, F. C., 181
Bartlett, N. R., 88
Barton, M. E., 210
Bartoshuk, L. M., 96, 97
Basadur, M., 217
Bastien, C. H., 206
Bates, J. E., 247
Bator, R. J., 349
Battaglia, M., 457
Baumrind, D., 141, 260, 352
Bavelier, D., 53
Bayliss, D. M., 169
Bechtel, W., 165
Beck, A. T., 444, 447, 476, 478
Beck, J. S., 478
Becker, R. E., 480
Beckman, M., 219
Beer, J. S., 296
Behar, C., 370
Behne, T., 245
Békésy, G. V., 94
Belsky, J., 248
Bem, S. L., 253
Ben-Shakhar, G., 33
Benjafield, J. J. G., 389
Benjamin, S. L., 457
Bennett, S., 139, 140, 141
Benson, H., 337
Berent, S., 295
Berg, F., 450
Berk, L., 311
Berk, L. E., 220
Berk, L. S., 311, 337
Berkowitz, L., 371
Berman, A., B–8
Bermond, B., 299

Bernat, E., 83
Berry, J. W., 331
Berscheid, E., 368
Berteretche, M. V., 129
Bertram, L., 191
Best, D. L., 252
Betancourt, J. R., 485
Betz, N. E., 450
Beyer, B. K., 33
Beyreuther, K., 97
Bigler, E. D., 66
Bindman, A. B., 376
Binet, A., 410
Bivens, J. A., 220
Bjerkedal, T., 231
Bjork, E. L., 186
Bjork, R. A., 178, 185, 186
Black, D. W., 452
Black, M. J., 467
Blackmon, L. R., 206
Blair, R. J. R., 457
Blakeslee, S., 71
Blanchard, M., 248
Blanchard, R., 292
Blanchard-Fields, F., 361, 362
Blass, T., 352
Blatt, S. D., 284
Blazer, D. G., 446
Bledsoe, C. H., 258
Blehar, M. C., 446
Bleiberg, K. L., 469, 484
Bleiker, E. M. A., 327
Bleuler, E., 451
Blits, B., 54
Block, N., 198
Block, R. I., 287
Bloom, L., 244
Bloom, P., 220, 244
Blumer, D., 447
Bock, R., 232
Bodenhausen, G. V., 359, 360
Bodrova, E., 244
Boggio, P. S., 61
Bogle, K. D., 362
Boles, D. B., 295
Bolton, P., 480
Bond, R. A., 347
Bondarenko, L. A., 200
Bonnelykke, B., 234
Booth-Butterfield, S., 356
Borgeat, F., 394
Borges, M. A., 177, 178
Boroditsky, L., 220
Bosworth, H. B., 259
Botwin, M. D., 401
Bouchard, C., 385
Bouchard, T., 436

Bouchard, T. J., 231
Bouchard, T. J., Jr., 333, 419
Bowden, C. L., 488
Bowler, W. M., 331
Bowman, E. S., 183
Boyd, C. H., 188
Boyson-Bardies, B., 219
Bracey, G., 330
Bradbury, T. N., 361
Brand, J. J., 102
Brantley, C., 292
Braun, S. R., 284
Brawman-Mintzer, O., 444
Bray, C. W., 95
Brazelton, T. B., 251
Brecher, M., 286
Breedlove, S. M., 14
Breier, A., 316
Breland, K., 144, 145
Breland, M., 144, 145
Bremmer, J. D., 62
Brennan, J. F., 6, 7
Breslau, N., 443
Breur, J., 468
Brewer, M. B., 363
Briem, V., 199
Briggs, K. C., 408
Brigham, A., 467
Broadbent, D., 168
Brondolo, E., 326
Bronkhorst, A., 168
Brooks, J. G., 243
Brooks, M. G., 243
Brown, C., 484
Brown, G., 478
Brown, G. L., 372
Brown, J., 170, 186
Brown, P. K., 89
Brown, R., 177, 245
Brown, W. B., 14
Browne, D., 198
Browne, M. N., 33
Broyles, S., 83
Brubaker, D. A., 475
Brunner, E. J., 321
Bryan, E. B., 234
Bryan, J., 141
Bryant, R. A., 394–395
Brzustowicz, L. M., 14
Buccino, G., 70
Bucher, B. D., 140
Buck, R., 301
Buckwalter, J. J., 262
Bucy, P. C., 67
Budney, A. J., 287
Bulatao, E. Q., B–12
Bullock, T. H., 44
Bunge, M., 33
Bunge, M. B., 54
Bureau of Labor Statistics, B–11
Burger, J. J. M., 394
Burger, J. M., 349, 350, 352
Burgess, D. M., 416
Burgio, K. L., 476
Burke, D. M., 177

Burks, N., 315
Burmeister, M., 445
Burns, J. F., 246
Bush, G., 67, 74
Bushman, B. J., 152, 372, 374
Buss, D. M., 15, 401
Bussa, B., 480
Butcher, J. N., 407, 408
Butler, R., 489
Butter, E. M., 338

C
Cabeza, R., 67, 259
Cacioppo, J., 356, 357
Cain, D., 470
Cajal, S., 42
Calon, F., 191
Calvo, E., 316
Camara, W. J., 407
Camchong, J., 455
Cameron, J., 281, 363
Cameron, J. R., 247
Cami, J., 286
Campbell, J. C., 317
Camperio Ciani, A., 293
Campos, J., 247, 248
Cannon, W. B., 299
Cardno, A. G., 454
Carducci, B., 436
Carey, B., 188
Carey, G., 372, 420
Carey, J. C., 232
Carli, L. L., 348
Carlsmith, J., 358
Carlson, G. A., 447
Carpenter, P. A., 414
Carr, E. G., 140
Carrion, V. G., 443
Carruthers, M., 259
Carskadon, M. A., 203
Carson, R. C., 368
Carver, C. S., 332
Carvey, C. E., 108
Caselli, W. P., 326
Cassidy, A., 258
Cassidy, J., 248
Castillo, R. J., 434, 450
Catanzaro, S. J., 398
Cattell, R. B., 401, 402, 408
Cave, K. R., 111
Centers for Disease Control and
    Prevention (CDC), 25,
    232, 284, B–11
Centerwall, B. S., 374
Cepeda, N. J., 185
Cermak, L., 165
Cha, J. H., 362
Chaddock, L., 223
Chaiken, S., 354, 355, 356
Chandola, T., 322
Chang, P. P., 326
Charlesworth, W. R., 297
Chen, J. Y., 220
Chen, L. Y., 191
Chen, R., 236

Cheng, H., 53
Cherry, E. C., 168
Cheryan, S., 5, A–9
Chess, S., 246, 247
Chesterton, L. S., 101
Chidester, D., 377
Chinn, A. B., 488, 489
Chiu, C., 360
Choi, I., 362
Chomsky, N., 218, 244
Chou, S. Y., 334
Christensen, A., 479
Christmas, D., 465
Chwalisz, K., 299
Cialdini, R., 349, 350
Cialdini, R. B., 349
Ciardiello, A., 216
Cinnirella, M., 348
Clancy, S. A., 184
Clark, A., 165
Clark, D. A., 478
Clark, L. A., 434
Clarke, A. R., 74
Clarke, J., 367
Clarkin, J. F., 483
Claypool, H. M., 359
Clements, C. M., 151
Coccaro, E. F., 372
Coffey, C. E., 448
Cohen, B., 258
Cohen, L. J., 448
Cohen, N. J., 172
Cohen, S., 320, 321, 323
Colcombe, S. J., 259
Coleman, M., 246
Coley, J. D., 210
Colligan, J., 217
Collins, A. M., 174
Collins, C. J., 274
Colom, R., 169
Committee on Animal Research
    and Ethics, 32
Conrad, R., 169
Consumer Reports, 483
Conway, M. A., 185
Coolidge, F. L., 202
Cooper, L. A., 484
Corbetta, M., 71
Coren, S., 109
Cosgrove, G. R., 490, 491
Costa, P. T., Jr., 263, 401, 408, 422
Costello, D. M., 447
Courage, M. L., 243
Courneya, K. S., 339
Cowan, N., 167, 170, 171
Craddock, N., 448
Crago, M. B., 450
Craik, F., 165
Craik, F. I. M., 165, 171, 178, 259
Cramond, B., 418
Craske, M. G., 484
Crichlow, S., 348
Crick, F., 198
Critchfield, T. S., 136
Crosby, L. R., 475

Crottaz-Herbette, S., 465
Crowley, A. E., 356
Crowley, M., 375
Csernansky, J. G., 487
Csikszentmihalyi, M., 216, 217
Culbertson, F., 441
Cummings, J. L., 448
Cummings, S. R., 258
Curtis, R. C., 368
Curtis, R. H., 467
Cytowic, R. E., 81

D
D'Allesandro, D. U., 476
Dabbs, J. M., Jr., 372
Dalenberg, C. J., 183
Dallery, J., 245
Daly, M., 15
Damasio, H., 21
Darley, J. M., 14, 375, 376
Darwin, C., 15, 296, 301
Daum, I., 188
Davidson, R. J., 295
Davies, I. R. L., 220
Davis, H. A., 458
Davis, K. D., 465
Davis, K. F., 203
Davis, K. L., 453
Davis, M., 295
Davis, S. F., B–5
Dawood, K., 292
De Valois, K. K., 90
De Valois, R. L., 90
Dean, G., 33
DeAngelis, T., 450
Debiec, J., 172, 188
DeCasper, A. J., 239
deCharms, R., 281
Deci, E. L., 272, 281
DeCoster, J., 359
DeFries, J. C., 420
Degenhardt, L., 287
DeGrandpre, R. J., 396, 398
Deinzer, R., 321
Delagrange, P., 200
Delaney, A. J., 319
Delfiner, R., 375
DeLongis, A., 315
Dement, W. C., 202, 203
Demers, R. A., 221
Dempster, F. N., 185
Dennett, D. C., 198
Deregowski, J. B., 112
DeRubeis, R. J., 478
Deutsch, G., 71, 72
Dew, M. A., 491
DeYoung, C. G., 423
Diamond, L. M., 370
Diamond, M., 252, 291
Dickens, W. T., 421
Dickerson, F., 475
Dickson, W. J., B–11
Digman, J. M., 403
Dillard, J., 349
Dillow, S. A., B–4

Dixon, N. F., 311
Dodane, C., 245
Dodge, K. A., 373
Dodson, J. D., 277
Dolcos, F., 180
Dollard, J., 317, 396
Domagalski, T. A., 297
Doman, J. M. R., 235
Dominey, P. F., 245
Domjan, M., 398
Donovan, J. J., 185
Donovan, S., 337
Dougherty, D. D., 465, 491
Dreher, H., 326
Drenth, P., 280
Drews, F. A., 199
Drigotas, S. M., 345
Duben, A., 370
Dubowitz, H., 139, 140, 141
Dudai, Y., 188
Duker, P. C., 140
Dumont, F., 386
Duncan, R. M., 219
Dundas, I., 459
Dunn, R., 315
Durrant, M., 5
Durso, F., 214
Dweck, C., 275
Dweck, C. S., 275, 276, 360
Dykens, E. M., 417

E

Eagleman, D. M., 108
Eagly, A.., 375
Eagly, A. H., 348, 354, 355, 356, 368
Eaker, E. D., 326
Eastern Virginia Medical School, 199
Eaton, W. W., 442
Ebbinghaus, H., 185
Eddy, J., 355
Edelmann, R. J., 297
Edlund, J. E., 15
Ehlers, A., 484
Eich, E., 177
Ekman, P., 294, 297, 301
Elkind, D., 255
Elliot, C. H., 478
Elliott, E., 275
Elliott, L., 292
Ellis, A., 477
Ellis, B. J., 254
Ellis, H. D., 295
Ellis, L., 292
Ellis, L. K., 315
Ende, N., 236
Endler, N. S., 490
Engelhardt, C. R., 152
Engle, R. W., 169
Enns, J. T., 109
Ephraim, P. L., 100
Epping-Jordan, M., 284
Epstein, L. H., 334
Erdley, C. A., 360

Erickson, K. I., 223
Erikson, E., 261
Erikson, E. H., 251, 261, 281, 394
Erikson, J. M., 251
Eron, L., 152
Escandon, A., 15
Eschenbeck, H., 336
Espiard, M. L., 287
Evans, D., 480
Evans, I. M., 475
Evans, W. H., 475
Everson, S., 5
Exner, J. E., 406
Eysenck, H., 326
Eysenck, H. J., 408
Eysenck, S. B. G., 408

F

Fagot, B. I., 253
Fairchild, G., 457
Fang, C. Y., 323
Fanselow, M. S., 67, 295
Fantz, R. L., 239
Faraone, S. V., 457
Farmer, A. E., 448
Farris, R., 185
Farthing, W., 198
Fast, K., 97
Faucett, J., 101
Fawzy, F. I., 480
Fazel-Rezai, R., 83
Fechner, G. T., 82
Fedoroff, I. C., 434
Fehr, E., 350
Feingold, A., 368
Feldman, D. H., 243, 255, 257
Ferguson, C. J., 152, 374
Ferguson-Noyes, N., 447
Fernald, A., 245
Fernandez, E., 315
Feroah, T. R., 200
Ferron, F., 450
Festinger, L., 357, 358, 365
Fiatarone, M., 259
Fiatarone, M. A., 339
Fifer, W. P., 239
Fincham, F. D., 361
Finger, S., 90, 423
Fink, M., 490
Finke, R., 216
Finkel, D., 419
Finlay, B., A–1
Fischer, M., 74
Fischl, B., 67
Fishbein, M., 355
Fisher, E. M., 232
Fisher, M., 222, 223
Fisher, R., 60
Fiske, S. T., 360
Fitzpatrick, M., 245
Fivush, R., 244
Flaherty, J. A., 484, 485
Flaskerud, J. H., 485
Flavell, J. H., 243
Fleming, M. F., 282

Flemons, W. W., 206
Flynn, J. R., 421
Foege, W. H., 259
Folkard, S., 199
Folkman, S., 314, 324, 325, 336
Follett, K. J., 362
Forbes, G., 252
Fornito, A., 67
Forsyth, D. R., 375
Foulkes, D., 203
Frank, E., 284, 491
Franke, R., B–11
Frankel, B. R., 479
Fraser, S., 349
Frederich, R., 450
Fredrickson, B. L., 326
Freed, F., 141
Freedman, J., 349
Freeman, J., 418
Freeman, W., 490
Fregni, F., 61
Frensch, P. A., 395
Fresquet, N., 69
Freud, A., 389
Freud, S., 10, 371, 387, 388, 440, 444, 467, 468
Frey, J., 371
Friedman, J. M., 334
Friedman, M., 326
Friesen, W., 294, 297, 301
Frontera, W. R., 258
Fulcher, J. S., 297
Fumeron, F., 450
Furumoto, L., 7

G

Gable, R. S., 284
Gabrieli, J., 62
Gächter, S., 350
Gado, M., 375
Galanter, M., 378
Galanti, G. A., 485
Gale, G. D., 295
Gallagher, R. P., 481
Galvin, J. E., 15
Gamwell, L., 436
Ganchrow, J. R., 238
Ganellen, R. J., 407
Ganis, G., 209
Garb, H. N., 407
Garcia, J., 129
Gardner, H., 216, 231, 410
Gardner, J., 332
Garland, E. J., 204
Garuccio, A., 84
Gay, P., 440, 444
Gazzaniga, M. S., 72
Geary, D. C., 15
Gebhard, P. H., 289
Geddes, D. P., 289
Geddes, J., 489
Geen, R. G., 374
Geher, G., 418
Geier, J., 108
Gelade, G., 168

Gelder, M., 474
Geller, B., 447
Gelman, S. A., 210, 220
Gershoff, E. T., 140, 141
Geschwind, D. H., 295
Ghoneim, M. M., 287
Gibbons, J. L., 252
Giedd, J. N., 255
Gifford, R. K., 363
Gilberg, C., 246
Gilbert, S. J., 352
Gill, S. T., 33
Gillespie, M. A., 274
Gillham, B., 317
Gilligan, C., 256
Gillund, G., 177, 178
Ginzberg, K., 336
Gittelman-Klein, R., 407
Glenn, A. L., 457
Glynn, S. M., 475, 476
Goddard, C. R., 139
Godden, D. R., 176, 177
Goel, V., 70
Gogtay, N., 455
Goin, M. K., 466
Gold, J. M., 452, 454
Goldman, A. L., 455
Goldman-Rakic, P. S., 188
Goldsmith, H. H., 247, 248, 457
Goleman, D., 216, 418
Golkaramnay, V., 486
Gong-Guy, E., 398
Gonsalves, B., 183
Gonzales, P. M., 366
Gonzalez, J. S., 332
Goodglass, H., 71
Goodman, E. S., 6
Gorman, J. M., 484
Gotlib, I. H., 447
Gottesman, H., 454
Gottesman, I., 453
Gottesman, I. I., 454
Gottman, J. M., 370
Gough, H. G., 408
Gould, C. G., 221
Gould, J. L., 221
Gould, S. J., 231
Gouldner, A. W., 350
Goulet, J., 394
Graber, J. A., 254
Grafman, J., 70
Grayson, A., 170
Green, B., 348
Greenwald, A. G., 83
Gregory, R. L., 109
Gresham, L. G., 356
Griffiths, R. R., 286
Grigorenko, E. L., 231
Grocer, S., B–5
Gross, C. G., 432
Grumbach, M. M., 254
Grünbaum, A., 395
Guardiola-Lemaitre, B., 200
Guéguen, N., 349
Guilford, J. P., 216

Gummerman, K., 167
Gupta, M., 334
Gustavson, C. R., 129, 450
Guthrie, R. V., 6, 7, 8
Guynn, M. J., 176

H

Haber, R. N., 167
Hagan, R., 253
Hagerman, E., 23, 223
Hains, S. C., 348
Halbesleben, J. R. B., 331
Hall, L. K., 169
Hall, W., 287
Hallett, F., 234
Hamer, D. H., 292
Hamilton, D. L., 363
Hammen, C., 398
Hampton, J. A., 210
Handel, S., 168
Hansen, C. P., 314
Hargittai, E., 369
Harlow, H. F., 249
Harman, G., 361
Harris, H. S., 338
Harris, J. L., 171
Harris, V. A., 361, 362
Harrison, P. J., 453, 454, 455
Harsch, N., 180
Hart, P., 349
Hartfield, E., 368, 370
Hartley, C. F., 378
Harvard Mental Health Letter, 491
Harvey, S., B–12
Hauck, S. J., 262
Havighurst, R. J., 262
Hawks, S. R., 333
Hayflick, L., 262
Hayward, C., 442
Hazan, C., 248
Heavey, C. L., 479
Hebb, D. O., 277
Hedman, L. R., 199
Hegeman, R., 375
Heider, F., 361
Heil, G., 280, B–10
Heilman, K., 71
Heilman, K. M., 295
Heimberg, R. G., 480
Heinicke, C. M., 251
Heinrich, B., 149
Hell, D., 451
Helms, J. E., 414
Hen, L., 486
Henin, A., 447
Henningfield, J. E., 284
Herberman, R. B., 322
Herbert, T. B., 320
Herbst, J. H., 436
Herman, L. M., 221
Hernandez, D., 232
Herring, M. P., 339
Herrnstein, R. J., 231
Hersh, S. M., 373

Herxheimer, A., 199
Hess, T. M., 361, 362
Hesse, E., 248
Hettema, J. M., 445
Hewstone, M., 363
Heyes, C. M., 149
Hicklin, J., 409
Hill, D., 355
Hill, J. A., 237
Hill, P. C., 338
Hillman, C. H., 223
Hilton, J. L., 360
Hines, T., 33
Hintze, J. M., 475
Hitch, G., 169
Hochman, J., 183
Hodge, D., 183
Hodges, J. R., 189
Hodgson, B., 285
Hodgson, R. J., 477
Hodson, D. S., 258
Hoffrage, U., 182
Hofstede, G. H., 280, 297, 421
Hofstede, G. J., 280, 297, 421
Hogg, M. A., 348
Holcomb, W. R., 478
Holden, C., 236
Hollon, S., 483
Hollon, S. D., 476
Holman, E. A., 321
Holmes, T. H., 313, 314
Holt-Lunstad, J., 332
Honzik, C. H., 148, 149
Hood, D. C., 88
Hopfinger, J. B., 168
Horhota, M., 362
Horne, J. A., 203
Horney, K., 391, 394
Horowitz, D. L., 363
Hortacsu, N., 370
Hossain, P., 334
Hothersall, D., B–10
Howe, M. L., 243
Hoyer, W. D., 356
Hu, P., 249
Hu, S., 293
Hubbard, E. M., 81
Hubel, D. H., 108
Huesmann, L. R., 152, 374
Huff, W., 491
Hugenberg, K., 360
Hughes, J., 473
Hughes, S. M., 15
Hui-Sheng, L., 370
Huitt, W., 243
Hull, A. J., 169
Hull, C. L., 273
Hull, M. S., 293
Hummel, J., 243
Hummer, R. A., 338
Humphries, L. L., 449
Hunsley, J., 484
Hunt, M., 467
Hurley, S., 198

Hurvich, L. M., 90
Hvas, L., 259
Hyde, J. S., 366
Hygge, S. A., 128
Hyman, I. E., 182, 183
Hyman, I. E., Jr., 182

I

Iacoboni, M., 70, 295
Iber, C., 201
Iemmola, F., 293
Imaizumi, Y., 234
Insel, T. R., 231
Irwin, M., 206
Isabel, J., 419
Iwakabe, S., 485
Iwawaki, S., 297
Izard, C., 58

J

Jackson, R., 6
Jackson, T., 101
Jacobs, E. A., 485
Jacobson, L., 28
Jaeggi, S. M., 223
James, W., 7, 198, 272, 298
Jameson, M., 29, 90
Jang, K. L., 401, 436
Janis, I., 348, 349
Janos, P. M., 417
January, D., 220
Janus, C. L., 290, 291
Janus, S. S., 290, 291
Jay, S. M., 478
Jehn, K., 7
Jensen, A. R., 231
Jensen, T. S., 100
Jimerson, D. C., 450
John, O. P., 403
Johnson, A. B., 289
Johnson, C. D., 248
Johnson, C. P., 245, 246
Johnson, D., 367
Johnson, G., 221
Johnson, J., 442
Johnson, J. H., 247
Johnson, M. E., 316
Johnson, V., 290
Johnston, L. D., 286
Johnston, W. A., 199
Jones, E. E., 361, 362
Jones, E. J., 485
Jones, G. W., 370
Jones, H. M., 486, 487
Jones, M. K., 128
Jordan, C. L., 14
Judelsohn, R. G., 245
Juffer, F., 249
Julien, R. M., 50
Jung, C., 393, 402

K

Kabat-Zinn, J., 337
Kagan, J., 247, 386, 409

Kahan, M., 285
Kahneman, D., 213
Kail, R., 169
Kakko, J., 286
Kako, E., 220
Kales, A., 204
Kam, D., 431
Kandel, E., 188
Kandel, E. R., 188
Kane, M. J., 169
Kanne, S. M., 172
Kaplan, S. L., 254
Karayiorgou, M., 445
Karney, B. R., 361
Kasanin, J. D., 326
Kastenbaum, R., 263
Katz, V. L., 237
Kaufman, C., 480
Kaufman, J., 373
Kaufman, J. C., 410
Kaul, J. D., B–11
Kaveny, M. C., 235
Kavoussi, R. J., 372
Kaye, W. H., 450
Kazdin, A. E., 476
Kearney, C. A., 486
Keashly, L., B–12
Keeley, S. M., 33
Keillor, J., 301, 302
Keirsey, D., 408
Keller, M. B., 486
Kelly, I., 33
Kelly, I. W., 33
Kelly, J. A., 357
Kempf, L., 273
Kendall, P., 478
Kendall, P. C., 478
Kendler, K. S., 147, 314
Kenny, A., 6
Kenrick, D. T., 281
Keromoian, R., 249
Kerwin, D. R., B–7
Kesebir, S., 281
Kety, S. S., 453, 454
Kiecolt-Glaser, J. K., 320, 321, 323
Kihlstrom, J. F., 182, 395
Kilburn, J., 374
Kilhstrom, J., 302
Kim, E. Y., 63
Kim, H., 347
Kim, M., 111
Kim, S., 63
Kim, U., 331
King, N. J., 475
Kinsey, A. C., 288, 290
Kirmayer, L. J., 445
Kitamura, T., 170
Kitayama, S., 298, 362
Klein, D., 446
Klein, S. B., 11
Kleinot, M. C., 356
Kleitman, N., 200
Klerman, G. L., 446
Kline, P., 401

Kling, K. C., 366
Klorman, R., 475
Klüver, H., 67
Knight, A., 365
Knight, J. A., 262
Kobasa, S., 327
Koch, C., 198
Koelling, R. A., 129
Koenig, H. G., 338
Koh, J. K., 375
Kohlberg, L., 255
Köhler, W., 9, 149, 214
Kohout, J., B-5
Komatsu, L. K., 210
Korn, S., 247
Kosslyn, S. M., 208, 209
Kotkin, M., 483
Kouri, E. M., 287
Kratofil, P. H., 283
Kreutzer, M. A., 297
Kriegstein, A., 44
Kristensen, P., 231
Krokoff, L. J., 370
Krosnick, J. A., 356
Kryger, M., 205
Kubic, L. S., 146
Kubicki, M., 455
Kübler-Ross, E., 263
Kuhn, H. W., 452, 491
Kulik, J. A., 332
Kumar, R., 442
Kumashiro, M., 345
Küntay, A., 245
Kupfer, D. J., 205
Kutiki, I., 110
Kvavilashvili, L., 180

L

LaBar, K. S., 295, 372
LaBerge, D., 169
Lacayo, A., 284
LaFromboise, T., 331
Lal, S., 8
Lalancette, M-F., 347
Lalich, J., 378
Lalonde, C. E, 219
Lambert, M. J., 483
Lance, C. J., 405
Landrum, R. E., B-4, B-5
Lane, R. D., 295
Lang, J., 459
Lang, J. W. B., 459
Lange, C., 298
Langer, E. J., 316
Langone, M. C., 378
Lapsley, D. K., 255
Larsen, J. D., 169
Larsen, J. T., 295
Larzelere, R., 141
Lashley, K. S., 299
Latané, B., 14, 375, 376
Launer, L., 259
Laungani, P., 264
Lavergne, G. M., 372

Lavie, P., 205
Laws, G., 220
Lay, C., 331
Lazarus, R. S., 302, 314, 324, 325, 336
Leary, M. R., 375
Leask, J., 167
Leclerc, C. M., 361, 362
Leddy, J. J., 475
LeDoux, J., 445
LeDoux, J. E., 83, 295
Lee, F., 362
Lee, M., 286
Lee, P. A., 434
Lee, S. H., 63
Lefcourt, H. M., 311
Leggett, E. L., 275
Lehnert, B., 84
Lehr, U., 325
Leiderman, P. H., 249
Leon, P., 259
Leonard, L., 70
Leong, D. J., 244
Leroy, C., 330
Lesch, K. P., 445
Levenson, R. W., 295
Levin, E. D., 284
Levinson, D. F., 448
Levy, B. R., 325
Levy, S. R., 360
Lewin, K., 278
Lewin, R., 221
Lewis, J. R., 432, 485
Like, R., 485
Lilienfeld, S. O., 407
Lin, C. S., 63
Lin, P. J., 211
Lindau, S. T., 290
Lindemann, B., 97
Lindström, P., 292
Linnoila, M., 372
Linnoila, M. I., 372
Lisanby, S. H., 490
Livesley, J. W., 457
Lizskowski, U., 245
Llewellyn-Jones, D., 449
Lock, M., 258
Lockhart, R. S., 165, 171
Loehlin, J. C., 436
Loftus, E., 179
Loftus, E. F., 174, 182
Loftus, J., 291
Logue, M. W., 445
Lonnqvist, J., 448
Loo, S. K., 74
Lord, T. R., 367
Lovaas, O. I., 140, 146, 473
Lowe, R. A., 376
Lowery, R., 279
Lu, S., 236
Luborsky, L., 482
Luchins, A. S., 359
Luck, S. J., 452, 454
Lucy, J. A., 220

Luria, A. R., 185
Lutkenhaus, P., 248
Lydiard, R. B., 444
Lykken, D. T., 457
Lynch, E. B., 210, 211
Lytton, H., 252
Lyvers, M., 286, 287

M

MacDonald, A. P., 275, 398
MacDonald, D., 67
Macdonald, I., 431
Mack, J. E., 183
MacKenzie, S. B., 356
Macknik, S. L., 108, 113
Macrae, C. N., 359, 360
Madsen, K. M., 246
Maestas, M. V., 331
Magoun, H. W., 65
Mahler, H. I. M., 332
Mahowald, M. W., 202
Mai, J. K., 58
Maier, S. F., 150, 320, 321
Main, M., 248
Maletic, V., 67
Mandler, G., 180
Mandler, J. M., 210
Manson, J., 339
Manusov, V., 7
March of Dimes Organization, 237
Marcus, G. F., 165
Marek, G. J., 286
Maren, S., 67
Marentette, P. F., 245
Margolin, S., 146
Margolskee, R. F., 96
Marik, P. E., 334
Markman, E. M., 220
Markovitz, J. H., 326
Markowitcz, J. C., 469, 484
Marks, D. F., 323
Marks, K., 229
Markus, H. R., 298, 347
Mars, A. E., 246
Marsh, R., 450
Marshall, B., 313
Martin, B., 315
Martin, C. L., 253
Martin, J. A., 262
Martin, L., 205
Martinez-Conde, S., 113
Maruta, T., 328
Mash, E. J., 484
Maslow, A., 279, 280, 400
Masson, J. M., 395
Masters, J. C., 478
Masters, W., 290
Masuda, M., 314
Masuda, T., 362
Matsumoto, D., 484
Matthew, N., 245
Matthews, G., 458
Matthews, K. A., 326
Maurer, D., 239

Mavromatis, A., 202
Maxmen, J. S., 466
Mayer, J. D., 418, 419
Maziade, M., 14
Mazzoni, G. A., 183-184
McCann, S. J. H., 200
McCarley, R. W., 65
McCarthy, C. J., 434
McCauley, C., 349
McClelland, D. C., 274
McClelland, J. L., 165
McConaghy, N., 292
McConkey, K. M., 394-395
McCormack, W. A., 277
McCrae, R. R., 401, 403, 408, 422
McDermott, J. F., 447
McDonald, J., 431
McDougall, T., 447
McDougall, W., 272
McEwen, B. S., 180
McFarlane, T., 434
McGaugh, J. L., 180
McGinn, L. K., 476, 478
McGinnis, J. M., 259
McGrath, E., 446
McGregor, D., B-10
McGue, M., 419
McGuire, F., B-11
McGuire, M., 433
McLaughlin, K. A., 431
McLaughlin, S. K., 96
McMahon, F. J., 448
McMonagle, T., 475, 476
McNeil, D., 177
McPherson, M., 368
Meador, B. D., 471
Medical Economics Staff, 237
Mehrabian, A., 418
Meichenbaum, D., 478
Meineri, S., 349
Mejia, O. L., 434
Melton, L. J., III, 258
Melzack, R., 100
Meng, Z., 249
Menon, V., 465
Menzies, R. G., 128
Meredith, W., 259
Merikle, M. P., 83
Mervis, C., 211
Mervis, C. B., 210
Merriam-Webster, 278
Metcalfe, J., 177
Metzler, J., 208
Meyer, L. H., 475
Meyrick, J., 356
Michalski, D., B-5
Mikami, A. Y., 369
Milburn, A., 335
Miles, D. R., 372, 420
Milgram, S., 351, 352
Miller, G. A., 169
Miller, J. G., 362
Miller, K., 235, 368

Miller, L. H., 331
Miller, L. S., 374
Miller, M., 314
Miller, M. N., 450
Miller, N. E., 317, 371
Miller, N. F., 396
Miller, R. R., 125
Miller, T. Q., 326
Miller, W. R., 471
Mills, M. A., 443
Milner, B., 141, 188
Mintz, L. B., 450
Mischel, W., 253, 403
Mishell, D. R., 258
Mitchell, A., 416
Mitchell, J. E., 449
Mitchell, K. A., 368
Mitchell, S. A., 467
Miyatake, A., 203
Mizes, J. S., 473
Moffic, H. S., 484
Moghaddam, F. M., 363
Mogil, J. S., 100
Mokdad, A. H., 334
Molden, D. C., 276
Moll, H., 245
Möller, A., 451
Money, J., 252
Mongeau, P. A., 357
Monteleone, P., 450
Moody, R., 202
Moore, T. E., 83
Moore, T. H., 287
Moore-Ede, M. C., 199
Moorhead, G., 349
Mora, G., 437
Moreland, R. L., 368
Moreno-Manzanoa, V., 236
Morgan, C. A., 321
Morgan, C. D., 406
Morin, C., 206
Mormann, F., 198
Morris, M., 362
Morris, M. W., 362
Morris, S., 205
Mortimer, J. A., 190
Moruzzi, G., 65
Moseley, M., 62
Mowat, F., 21
Mowrer, R. R., 11
Mroczek, D. K., 237
Mueser, K. T., 478
Mufson, L. H., 469
Mukamel, R., 70
Muller-Oerlinghausen, B., 448
Munoz, D., 229
Münsterberg, H., B–10
Murdock, B. B., Jr., 177, 178
Murphy, C. C., 417
Murphy, K. R., 74
Murphy, L. R., 330
Murphy, M., 337
Murray, C., 231
Murray, H. A., 406
Murray, S. L., 369

Muter, P., 179
Myers, I. B., 408
Myers, S. M., 245, 246

N
Nadeau, K. G., 407
Najavits, L. M., 474, 484
Nam, K. D., 362
Naqvi, N., 50
Nasar, S., 452
Nathan, P. E., 484
National Academy of
    Neuropsychology, B–6
National Center for Health
    Statistics [NCHS], 285
National Collegiate Athletic
    Association, 29
National Institute of Mental
    Health (NIMH), 438
National Institute of Mental
    Health (NIMH) Genetics
    Workgroup, 448
National Institute on Alcoholism
    and Alcohol Abuse
    [NIAAA], 285
National Institute on Drug Abuse
    [NIDA], 286, 488
National Institutes of Health, 54
National Safety Council, 216
National Sleep Foundation, 205
National Wildlife Federation, 431
Neale, M. C., 420
Neary, N. M., 333
Neely, J. H., 187
Neimark, J., 179
Neimeyer, R. A., 368
Neisser, U., 180
Nelson, D. B., 244, 339
Nelson, K., 244
Nestor, P. G., 453, 455
Neto, F., 347
Neumarker, K., 449
Neumeister, A., 444
Neville, H. J., 53
Newborn, C. R., 356
Nguyen, T. T. I., 331
Nicholson, N., 347
Nickell, J., 34
Nickerson, R. S., 186
Niedermeyer, E., 62
Nieto, F., 259
Nigg, J. T., 74, 457
Nikolajsen, L., 100
Nilsson, L., 199
Nisbett, R. E., 362
Nitsche, M. A., 61, 491
Nolen-Hoeksema, S., 446
Nooyens, A. C., 322
Norcross, J. C., 469, 483
Norenzayan, A., 362
Norrbrink Budh, C., 101
Nosich, G. M., 33
Novella, S., 245
Nudds, M., 198
Nyberg, L., 67, 173

O
O'Connor, R. D., 475
Oakley-Browne, M., 442
Oberman, L. M., 70
Ochoffa-Ayayo, A. B. C., 258
Ochsner, K., 208
Odbert, H. S., 401
Oden, M. H., 417
Ogles, B. M., 483
Öhman, A., 83, 128, 295
Olin, B. R., 284, 286, 287
Oliver, J. F., 373
Olivier, D. C., 220
Ollendick, T. H., 475
Olsen, P., 474
Olson, H. C., 416
Oman, C. M., 102
Onken, L. S., 473
Oren, D. A., 446
Organization of Teratology
    Information Specialists, 237
Ortaldo, J. R., 322
Osborn, C. A., 183
Oserberg, L. G., 259
Oster, J. R., 449
Oswald, A. J., 332
Oswald, I., 202
Overeem, S., 206
Overmier, J. B., 150
Owen, A. M., 222
Owen, M. T., 248

P
Paivio, A., 208
Pajonk, F. G., 223
Palmer, S. E., 105
Palva, J. M., 170
Pan, A. S., 450
Pargament, K. I., 338
Paris, J., 456
Parisi, P., 234
Park, J., 330
Park, N., 281
Parker, P. Y., 163
Parsons, H. M., B–11
Parsons, L., 62
Partonen, T., 448
Pascual-Leone, A., 61
Pasternak, O., 62
Patterson, M. L., 7
Paul, B. M., 165
Paunonen, S. V., 403
Pavlov, I., 122, 124, 125
Pearse, D. D., 54
Peng, K., 362
Penn, D. L., 453
Peplau, L. A., 14
Pepperberg, I. M., 221
Perls, F., 471
Perlstein, W. M., 453
Perrin, S., 347
Perry, P., 202
Persaud, R., 418
Peters, J. F., 83
Peters, T. M., 339

Peters, W. A., 364
Peterson, C., 281
Peterson, D. R., B–3
Peterson, L. R., 170, 186
Peterson, M. J., 170, 186
Petitto, L. A., 245
Petri, H., 272
Petrie, K. J., 199
Petrova, P. K., 350
Pettigrew, T. F., 366
Petty, R., 356, 357
Petty, R. E., 349, 353, 354, 356
Pezdek, K., 183
Pfeiffer, W. M., 445
Pfurtsceller, G., 41
Phan, T., 338
Phelps, E. A., 83, 295
Piaget, J., 219, 240
Piedmont, R. L., 403
Piercy, F. P., 479
Pierrehumbert, J., 219
Pillard, R. C., 292
Pilowsky, L. S., 486, 487
Pinker, S., 220, 221
Pinsof, W. M., 479
Plaut, D. C., 165
Plomin, R., 273, 420
Plug, C., 109
Plum, F., 65
Pogue-Geile, M. F., 14
Polce-Lynch, M., 297
Polewan, R. J., 125
Pope, H. G., 287
Pormerleau, C. S., 284
Pormerleau, O. F., 284
Posner, J. B., 65
Posthuma, D., 420, 421
Postman, L., 171
Potocky-Tripodi, M., 291
Powers, M. H., 243
Pratkanis, A. R., 83
Pratt, J. A., 282
Prentice, D. A., 366
Prescott, C. A., 314
Preston, J. D., 50, 366
Priester, J. M., 356
Prigerson, H. G., 321
Prochaska, J. O., 469
Puetz, T. W., 339
Pumariega, A., 450
Pumariega, A. J., 450
Purcell, S., 334
Purdy, D., 29
Putnam, S. P., 277
Puts, D. A., 14

Q
Qualls, C. D., 171
Quillian, M. R., 174
Quintero, J. E., 200

R
Raaijmakers, J. G. W., 177, 178
Rabins, P., 60
Rachman, S., 444

Rachman, S. J., 477
Radosevich, D. R., 185
Rahe, R. H., 313, 314
Rahman, Q., 293
Raikkonen, K., 326
Rainforth, M. V., 337
Ramachandran, V. S., 70, 71, 81
Rana-Deuba, A., 331
Ranke, M. B., 232
Rao, S. C., 188
Rapson, R. L., 368
Ratey, J. J., 23, 223
Rauch, S. L., 445, 490, 491
Rayner, R., 11, 128, 444
Raynor, H. A., 334
Read, J. D., 83
Reason, J. T., 102
Reder, L. M., 176
Reichborn-Kjennerud, T., 457
Reiner, W. G., 252
Reis, H. T., 368
Reisenzein, R., 301
Reiss, P. C., 374
Reiter, R., 335
Renchler, R., 330
Rescorla, R., 125, 130
Rescorla, R. A., 130
Resick, P. A., 478, 484
Rey, M., 211
Reynolds, C. F., 469
Reynolds, C. F., III, 205
Reynolds, R. M., 322
Rezvani, A. H., 284
Richards, C. F., 376
Richardson, J. T. E., 202
Richmond, S. E., 372
Rideout, T. M., 448, 449
Rideout, V. J., 152
Ridley, H., 34
Ridley, M., 231
Rieber, R. W., 6
Ritts, V., 434
Rizzolatti, G., 70
Ro, E., 434
Roberts, R. E., 484
Robins, L .N., 372
Robinson, D. K., 6
Robinson, J. W., 366
Robinson, P., 395
Rocha, M., 61
Rodgers, J. E., 491
Rodgers, M., 295
Rodin, J., 316, 333
Roediger, H. L., 173
Roediger, H. L. III, 176
Roethlisberger, F. J., B–11
Roffman, R. A., 283
Roffwarg, H. P., 200
Rogers, B., 399, 400, 470
Rogers, C. R., 471
Rogers, R. W., 356
Rogoff, B., 244
Rohde, P., 491
Roid, G. H., 411
Rollnick, S., 471

Romney, D. M., 252
Roper, G., 475
Rosch, E., 210, 211
Rosch-Heider, E., 220
Rose, S., 231
Rosen, R., 205
Rosenboom, L. G., 249
Rosenfeld, J. P., 63
Rosenhan, D. L., 439
Rosenman, R. H., 326
Rosenthal, A. M., 375
Rosenthal, R., 28
Rosenthal, T. L., 128
Ross, G. M., 109
Ross, H. E., 109
Rossini, P. M., 53
Rothbaum, B. O., 473
Rothbaum, R., 249
Rothenberg, A., 447
Rotter, J. B., 275, 278, 397, 398
Rotton, J., 371
Rouse, B. A., 330
Rouse, S. V., 407, 408
Rouw, R., 81
Rovet, J., 232
Rowan, J., 470
Rowe, D. C., 372
Roysircai-Sodowsky, G. R., 331
Ruble, D., 363
Rudd, P., 259
Ruhe, H. G., 448
Rumelhart, D. E., 165, 174
Rundus, D., 170
Runger, D., 395
Rusbult, C. E., 345
Ruscio, A. M., 444
Russell, D. E., 405
Rutherford, A., 11
Ryan, R. M., 272, 281
Rynn, M., 444

S
Sabatini, E., 83
Sachs, G. S., 488
Sacks, D. P., 152
Sacks, O., 69
Sadock, B. J., 474
Saenger, P., 232
Sagan, C., 202
Saha, S., 454
Salend, S. J., 475
Salovey, P., 418
Salthouse, T. A., 259
Sam, D. L., 331
Sanders, L. D., 53
Sands, L. P., 259
Sapir, E. S., 220
Sapolsky, R. M., 321
Sastry, K. S., 323
Satterly, D., 255
Sattler, J. M., 485
Saunders, B., 139
Savage, J., 374
Savage-Rumbaugh, S., 221
Savic, I., 292

Scarpa, A., 247
Schachter, S., 299, 302
Schafer, M., 348
Schaie, K. W., 230, 259
Schalock, R. L., 416
Schapiro, A. C., 165
Schenck, C. H., 202
Schiller, P. H., 108
Schmidt, M., 203
Schmitt, D. P., 368
Schmitz, C., 330
Schnabel, J., 34
Schneider, K. J., 470
Schneider, R. H., 337
Schneider, W., 180
Schneidman, E., 263
Schöls, L., 65
Scholte, H. S., 81
Schroeder, S. R., 416
Schroth, M. L., 277
Schugens, M. M., 188
Schultz, D. P., B–10
Schultz, S. E., B–10
Schwanenflugel, P., 211
Schwanenflugel, P. J., 211
Schwartz, J. H., 188
Schwartz, S. K., B–5
Schweickert, R., 168
Schwitzgebel, E., 243
Scott, S. K., 372
Scott, W. D., B–10
Security Director's Report, B–12
Seeman, J., 470
Segal, N. L., 231
Segall, M. H., 109
Segerstrom, S. C., 328
Seligman, M., 129, 149, 150, 328,
    329, 447, 483
Seligman, M. E. P., 150
Selye, H., 319
Selye, H. A., 312
Sephton, S. E., 328
Serban, G., 453
Seys, D. M., 140
Shackelford, T. K., 15
Shadish, R., 483
Shafir, E., 318
Shafto, P., 210
Shafton, A., 203
Shapiro, A. K., 482
Shapiro, E., 482
Shapiro, F., 474
Shapiro, K. L., 129
Sharif, Z., 484
Sharot, T., 180
Shaver, P., 248
Shean, R. E., 355
Sheeber, L. B., 247
Sheffield, J., 315
Shekelle, P. G., 282
Sheldon, S. H., 203
Shepard, T. H., 237
Shepherd, R. N., 208
Sherif, M., 346, 366
Sherry, P., 314

Shields, J., 453, 454
Shiffrin, R. M., 166, 170, 177, 178
Shimp, T. A., 356
Shlain, B., 286
Shoda, Y., 403
Shomrat, T., 188
Shore, L. A., 33
Shorey, G., 14
Shorter, E., 490
Shuglin, A., 286
Shurkin, J. N., 417
Shweder, R. A., 220
Siegel, S., 125
Siegler, I. C., 326
Siegler, R. S., 243, 255
Sigmundson, H. K., 252
Silove, D., 338
Silverberg, S. B., 370
Silverman, W. K., 486
Simon, D. A., 185
Simon, T., 410
Simpson, D., 423
Singer, J. E., 299, 302
Singer, M. T., 378
Singh-Manoux, A., 259
Skeen, P., 258
Skinner, B. F., 13, 132, 135, 398,
    436, 473
Skolnick, A., 247, 248
Slater, A., 239
Slater, P. C., 189
Slipp, S., 391
Sloan, D. M., 473
Slobin, D. I., 245
Smith, A. D., 331
Smith, D., 490
Smith, D. H., 204
Smith, J. D., 416
Smith, P. B., 347
Smith, T. C., 443
Snyder, D. J., 97
Snyder, M., 365
Snyder, S. H., 48
Snyder, T. D., B–4
Söderlund, J., 453, 455
Sodowsky, G. R., 331
Solomon, J., 248
Soomro, G. M., 442
Sowell, E. R., 255
Spangler, W. D., 274
Spangler, W. J., 491
Sparing, R., 209
Spearman, C., 410
Speca, M., 337
Spence, M. J., 239
Spencer, C., 347
Sperling, G., 166
Speroff, L., 237
Sperry, R. W., 72
Spiegel, D., 480
Spinath, F. M., 273, 420
Springer, S. P., 71, 72
Spuhl, S. T., 220
Squire, L., 188
Squire, L. R., 172, 189

Staff, C. H., 203
Standing, L., 178
Standing, L. G., 347
Steele, C. M., 365, 366
Steele, J., 366
Steelman, L. A., 297
Steen, C., 81
Stein-Behrens, B., 319
Steinberg, L., 370
Steriade, M., 65
Stern, W., 410
Sternberg, R. J., 231, 369, 370, 410
Sternberger, R. R., 441
Stevenson, M. B., 245
Stewart, J. H., 139
Stewin, L. L., 200
Stiff, J. B., 357
Stifter, C. A., 277
Stine, C., 448
Stowell, J. R., 336
Stratton, K., 245
Straus, M. A., 139
Strauss, A. S., 264
Strawbridge, W. J., 338
Strayer, D. L., 199, 216
Strober, M., 450
Ströhle, A., 339
Stroth, S., 223
Strunk, D. R., 448
Stuss, D. T., 168
Styne, D. M., 254
Sue, D., 485
Sue, D. W., 485
Sue, S., 484
Suler, J., 486
Sullivan, P. F., 448
Sultana, A., 475, 476
Sutchliffe, N., 332
Sutherland, P., 243
Sutton, N., 285
Swanson, J. W., 488
Swartz, M., 456
Swayze, V. W., II, 491
Swenson, D. D., 313
Symes, B., 330

T

Tagliatatela, J. P., 221
Tajfel, H., 363, 365
Takeuchi, T., 203
Talbott, G. D., 475
Tamminga, C. A., 487
Tanzi, R. E., 191
Taylor, B., 246
Taylor, C., 142
Taylor, D. M., 363
Taylor, S. E., 14
Teigen, K., 277
Temoshok, L., 326
Terman, L. M., 410, 417
Terracciano, A., 403
Terry, A. V., Jr., 487
Thase, M. E., 483, 488

Thiedke, C. C., 203
Thomae, H., 325
Thomas, A., 246, 247
Thomas, N. J. T., 208
Thomas, S. L., 374
Thompson, P. M., 71, 455
Thompson, W. L., 209
Thompson, W. W., 246
Thomson, D. M., 176
Thoresen, C. E., 338
Thorndike, E. L., 131, 405
Thornton, A., 370
Tobach, E., 252
Toga, A. W., 71
Tohen, M., 488
Tolman, E. C., 148, 149, 278
Tomasello, M., 245
Tomes, N., 436
Torgersen, S., 456
Torrance, E. P., 418
Torrey, E. F., 454
Tran, M.-T., 229
Tranel, D., 295
Trappey, C., 83
Treisman, A. M., 168
Treisman, M., 102, 168
Tresniowski, A., 205
Triandis, H., 353
Trocmé, N., 139, 140
Troisi, A., 433
Troncosco, X. G., 110, 111
Tropp, L. R., 366
Trujillo, K. A., 488, 489
Trull, T. J., 403
Trut, L. M., 419
Tsai, J. L., 297
Tsuang, M., 445
Tucker, E. W., 203, 291
Tukuitonga, C. F., 376
Tulving, E., 165, 171, 173, 176
Turk, C. L., 478, 480, 484
Turner, J. C., 363, 365
Turner, W. J., 293
Tversky, A., 213, 318

U

Ulmer, J. L., 62
Unger, R., 252
University of Manchester, 492
Upthegrove, T., 29
Urbina, S., 409
Uretsky, S. D., 488

V

Vaidya, C. J., 176
Vail, A., 484, 485
Vaillant, G. E., 332
Valverde, R., 417
van der Merwe, A., 84
van der Stelt, O., 74
Vandenbos, G. R., B-12
VanderLaan, D. P., 293
Vartanian, L. R., 255

Vasey, P. L., 293
Vaughan, S., 328
Vernon, S. W., 484
Villafuerte, S., 445
Villani, S., 374
Vink, T., 450
Visser, P. S., 356
Vogel, G., 236
Vogel, G. W., 203
Voineskos, A. N., 62
Vokey, J. R., 83
Volkow, N. D., 74
von Helmholtz, H., 6
von Hipple, W., 360
Voss, M., 223
Voyer, D., 295
Vygotsky, L. S., 14, 219, 244

W

Wagner, A. R., 130
Wahlsten, D., 231
Wakefield, A. J., 245
Wald, G., 89
Walker, L. J., 256
Wall, P. D., 100
Walter, C., 15
Wampold, B. E., 483
Wang, P. S., 231
Ward, C., 331
Ward, J., 286, 332
Wartner, U. G., 248
Washburn, M. F., 7
Wasserman, E. A., 125
Watkins, L. R., 150
Watkins, L. R., 320, 321
Watson, J. B., 11, 128, 436, 444
Watson, J. M., 216
Watts, J. W., 490
Weaver, F. M., 60
Webb, W. B., 199
Wechsler, D., 410, 411
Wedding, D., 484, 485
Weinberger, D. R., 273, 455
Weiner, B., 361
Weiner, I. B., 406, 407
Weiner, R. D., 490
Weis, S., 188
Weisman, A., 263
Weiss, J. M., 316
Weissman, M. M., 445, 446, 456
Wenneberg, S. R., 337
Werker, J. F., 219
Wertheimer, M., 9
Westen, D., 478
Wetherell, J. L., 476
Wever, E. G., 95
Weyant, J. M., 350
Whalen, P. J., 295
White, G. L., 368
Whitten, W. B., 178
Whorf, B. L., 220
Wicker, A. W., 355

Widiger, T. A., 403, 409, 456
Wierenga, C. E., 63
Wiesel, T. N., 108
Williams, J. A., 61
Williams, J. E., 252
Williams, J. M., 54
Williams, M. E., 258
Williams, R. B., 326
Willis, S. L., 230
Willoughby, T., 374
Winningham, R. G., 180
Winslow, B., 377
Winstein, C. J., 188
Winton, W. M., 277
Wise, K., 369
Wiseman, R., 33
Wolberg, L. R., 466
Wolf, A. D., 317
Wood, J. M., 407
Woodhouse, A., 100
Wooten, P., 311
World Health Organization Inter-
   national Consortium in Psy-
   chiatric Epidemiology, 441
Wu, C-C., 287
Wyman, P. A., 323
Wynne, C., 149
Wynne, L. C., 479

Y

Yalom, I., 479
Yamaguchi, S., 200
Yancey, C., 374
Yerkes, R. M., 277, B-11
Ying, Y. W., 434
Yip, Y. L., 338
Yodanis, C. L., 139
Yokley, J. L., 14
Yopyk, D., 366
Young, J. E., 478, 484
Young, R., 239
Young, S. N., 199
Yule, G., 219

Z

Zajonc, R. B., 58, 302, 368
Zanarini, M. C., 456
Zedler, B., 7
Zeidner, M., 458
Zeki, S., 103, 370
Zentall, T. R., 149
Zigler, E., 373
Zilles, K., 67
Zillmann, D., 371
Zimbardo, P., 372, 373
Zimbardo, P. G., 378
Zisapel, N., 200
Zorilla, E. P., 322
Zucker, K. J., 293
Zuckerman, M., 313
Zuckerman, M. 1, 277
Zuo, L., 418
Zvolensky, M. J., 442

subject index

Bolded numbers indicate figures or images

A

Abilify (aripiprazole), 487
Abnormality, 459
  behaviorism, 436
  biological model, 436, 459, 462
  biopsychosocial model, 437
  cognitive model, 437
  defined, 432–435, 459, 462
  maladaptive behavior, 433, 459
  models of, 435–437, 459, 462
  psychodynamic model, 436, 459
  psychological models, 436–437, 459, 462
  psychopathology, 432
  social norm deviance, 433, 459
  sociocultural perspective of, 434
  statistical definition, 433, 459
  subjective discomfort, 433, 459
  in various cultures, 434
  working definition, 434–435
Abortion, spontaneous, 237
Absolute thresholds, 82, 114
  examples of, 82
Abstract concepts, 243
Abu Ghraib, prisoner abuse at, 373, **373**
Acceptance stage, of death/dying, 263
Accommodation, 106–107, 240
Acculturative stress, 331, 340, 343
Acetylcholine, 48, **48**, 49, 66–67, 75, 191
  and Alzheimer's disease, 48
Acquired (secondary) drives, 273, 308
Acquisition in classical conditioning, 124
Acrophobia, 441
Action potential, 45, **46**, 75
Action therapy, 466, 493
Activity theory, 262–263, 266
Actor-observer bias, 361–362, 379, 425
Acute stress disorder (ASD), 443, **443**, 459, 462
Adapin (doxepin), 489
Adaptive behavior, 15, 415
ADHD. *See* Attention-deficit hyperactivity disorder (ADHD)
Adjustment, 439
Adler, Alfred, 10, 394, 424
Adolescence, 253–257, 266, 269
  cognitive development, 254–256
  formal operations, 254–255
  identity *vs.* role confusion, 257
  imaginary audience, 255, 266
  moral development, 255–256, 266, 269

parent/teen conflict, 257
personal fable, 255, 266
physical development, 254
psychosocial development, 256–257
puberty, 254, 266
Adoption studies
  and personality disorders, 457, 460
  and schizophrenia, 454
Adrenal cortex, 59, 76
Adrenal glands, 56, 59, 75, 254
Adrenal medulla, 59, 75
Adrenaline, and stress, 322
Adulthood, 258–263, 266, 269
  activity theory, 262–263, 266
  aging, effects on health, 259
  andropause, 259
  brain, keeping young, 259, **259**
  cognitive development, 259
  death and dying, stages of, 263, 266, 269
  forming relationships, 260
  intimacy, 260, 266
  life review, 261
  memory, changes in, 259
  menopause, 258–259, 266
  morality, dealing with, 261
  parenting, 260–261
  parenting styles, 260–261, 266
  physical and psychological aging, theories of, 262–263
  physical development, 258–259, 266
  psychosocial development, 260–262, 266, 269
Aerial (atmospheric) perspective, 106
Aerobic exercise, and wellness, 339
Aesthetic needs, 279
Affect, 354, 445
Affective component of attitude, 354, 379
Afferent (sensory) neurons, 52
African American psychology, 8–9
After-discharge, 113
Afterimages, 89, **89**
Aggression, 371–376, 380
  and biology, 371–372, 380
  defined, 371, 380
  displaced, 317, **317**, 339
  and frustration, 317, 339, 342
  linked with spanking, 142
  social roles, power of, **372**, 372–373, **373**, 380
  and violence in the media, 151, 373–374, 380

Aging, 252
  activity theory, 262–263
  cellular clock theory, 262, 266, 269
  effects on health, 259
  free radical theory, 262, 266, 269
  wear-and-tear theory, 262
Agonists, 48, 50, 487
Agoraphobia, 441–442, **442**, 459
  panic disorder with, 442
Agreeableness, 402, 423
Ainsworth, Mary, 247
Al-Hazan, 109
Alarm stage, general adaptation syndrome (GAS), 319, 339, 342
Alcohol, 285, **285**, 287
  abuse, signs of, 285
  and aggression, 372
  blood alcohol level, 285
  defined, 285
Alcoholics Anonymous, 479
Alderfer, Clayton, 280
Alex the African gray parrot, **221**
Algorithms, 212, 227
All-or-none firing, 45–46
All-or-nothing thinking, 444
Allen, David, 304
Allport, Gordon, 401, 424
Alpha waves, 62, 200, 202
Altered states of consciousness, 198–199, **199**, 224, 226
  hypnosis, 183
  hypothalamus, 199, 200
  psychoactive drugs, 282–287, 306, 309
  sleep, 199–206
Alternative thinking, and optimists, 328
Altruism, 375, 380
Alzheimer's disease, 15, 27, 28, 54, 63, 67, 172, 189–191, 192
  and acetylcholine, 48
  current research in, 190–191, 192
Amabile, Teresa, 272, A-10
Ambivalent attachment style, **247**, 248, 265
American Academy of Sleep Medicine, 206
American Association on Intellectual and Developmental Disabilities (AAIDD) guidelines, 416
American College Test (ACT), 415

American Psychological Association (APA), 53
Ames room illusion, **111**
Amines, **232**
Amitriptyline (Elavil), 489
Amnesia
  anterograde, 189–190, 192
  infantile, 195
  organic, 189, 195
  retrograde, 189, 192
Amphetamine psychosis, 283
Amphetamines, 283, 287
Amygdala, 67, 76, 99, 295, 372
Anal explusive personality, 391
Anal retentive personality, 391
Anal stage of personality development, 390–391, 424
Analytical psychology, **392**
Andropause, 259, 266
Anger stage, of death/dying, 263
Angry/Happy Man study, 300, 306, 309
Anhidrosis, 100
Anima/animus, 393
Animal Mind, The (Washburn), 7
Animal research, ethical considerations in, 31–32
Animals as social support, **332**
Animism, 241
Anorexia nervosa, 334, 343, 448–449, **449**, 460, 463
Antagonists, 48
Antecedent stimuli, 132
Anterograde amnesia, 172, 189–190, 192
Antianxiety drugs, 488, 494
Anticonvulsant drugs, 488
Antidepressant drugs, 488–489, 494
Antidepressants
  MAOIs, 488–489, 494
  SSRIs (selective serotonin reuptake inhibitors), 50, 488–489, 494, 497
  tricyclics, 489, 494
Antimanic drugs, 488, 494
Antipsychotic drugs, 486–488, 494
Antisocial personality disorder, 456, 460, 463
Anvil, 94
Anxiety, basic, 394, 424
Anxiety disorders, **444**
  causes of, 444–445
  free-floating anxiety, 440
  generalized anxiety disorder, 444, 462

Anxiety disorders (*cont.*)
 obsessive-compulsive disorder
  (OCD), **442,** 442–443,
  459, 462
 panic disorder, 442, 459, 462
 phobic disorders, 440–441
Aphasia, 71
Apparent distance hypothesis, 109
Applied behavior analysis (ABA),
  146, 157, 473, 496
Applied psychology, B-13
 defined, B-2
 reasons for studying, B-1
Approach-approach conflict,
  317, 342
Approach-avoidance conflict, 318,
  318, 342
Aqueous humor, 86
Arbitrary inference, 476
Archetypes, 393
Aripiprazole (Abilify), 487
Aristotle, 5
Arkowitz, Hal, 471
Army Alpha test, B-10
Army Beta test, B-11
Arousal and performance, **277**
Arousal theory, 276–278, 305,
  306, 308
Artificial intelligence (AI), 165
Asch, Solomon, 347–348, 378
 classic study on conformity,
  stimuli used in, **347**
Asian Americans
 and prejudice against, **364,**
  364–365
Assimilation, 240, 331, 340, 343
Association areas, 70–71, 76
Association cortex, 70
Association for Psychological
  Science (APS), 53
Asthma, 330
Astrology, as pseudopsychology, 33
Asylums, 467, 493
Ataque de nervios, 445
Ativan, 284, 488
Attachment, 247–249, 265, 269
Attention as element of
  observational learning, 152
Attention Deficit Disorder
  (ADD), 73
Attention-deficit hyperactivity
  disorder (ADHD), 73–74,
  76, 407
 link with bipolar disorders, 447
Attitudes, 353–357, 379, 392
 affective component, 354, 379
 behavior component, 354–355,
  379
 change in, 356–357, 379
 cognitive component, 355, 379
 components of, **353, 354,** 379
 defined, 353
 formation of, 355–356, 379
Attraction. *See* Interpersonal
  attraction
Attribution
 causes of behavior, 361, 379
 defined, 361

fundamental attribution error,
  361–362, 379
 and impression formation,
  359, 379
Attribution theory, 361, 379
Atypical neuroleptics, 486
Auditory association area, 69
Auditory canal, 93
Auditory hallucinations, 452
Auditory nerve, 94
Authenticity, 471
Authoritarian parenting, 260, 266
Authoritative parenting, 261, 266
Autism, 52, 70, 146
Autism spectrum disorder, 245–246
Autobiographical memory, 163
Autogenic training, B-13
Autokinetic effect, 109
Automatic encoding, 180, 192
Autonomic nervous system (ANS),
  55–57, 75, 319, 339, 342
 parasympathetic division, 56–57,
  75, 319, 339
 sympathetic division, 55–56, 75,
  319, 339
Autonomy, 281
Availability heuristic, 213
Aversion therapy, 473–474, **474**
Avoidance-avoidance conflict,
  318, 342
Avoidant attachment style, 247–248,
  265
Axon terminals, 47
Axons, **43,** 44, 47, 75, 87, 455
 defined, 43

B
Babbling, 245
Bailey, J. Michael, 293
Bandura, Albert, 151–152, 157,
  397, 475
Barak, Azy, 486
Barbiturates/major tranquilizers,
  284, 287
Bard, Philip, 299
Bargaining stage, of death/dying, 263
Bartlett, Frederic, 181
Basic anxiety, 394, 424
Basic-level type, 210
Basilar membrane, 94
Baumrind, Diana, 260, 266
Bay of Pigs disaster, 348
Beautiful Mind, A (movie), **452**
Bechler, Steve, 282
Beck, Aaron T., 476
Beckham, Albert Sidney, 8, 9
Beck's cognitive therapy, 476–477,
  497
Behavior, 4, 355, 357
 modification of, and control,
  10–11
 observable, **4,** 11
Behavior component of attitudes,
  354–355, 379
Behavior modification, 138, 146–147,
  157, 161, 473
 defined, 146

Behavior therapies, 473–476,
  493, 496
 aversion therapy, 473–474, **474**
 classical conditioning, therapies
  based on, 473–474, 493, 496
 evaluation of, 476, 496
 exposure therapies, 474
 flooding, 474
 operant conditioning, 474–476,
  493, 496
 systematic desensitization, 473
Behavioral assessment, 407–409, 425
Behavioral genetics, 231, 265,
  419, 425
Behavioral neuroscience, 42, B-6
Behavioral perspective, 12–13, 35
Behaviorism, 11, 34, 132,
  436, 459
 defined, 11
Behaviorist perspective, 386
Behaviorists, 396, 424
 and dissociative disorders, 451
 and personality disorders, 444, 460
Bell curve, A-2
Belongingness needs, 279, 280, 308
Belsky, Jay, 248
Benson, Herbert, 337
Benzedrine, 283
Benzodiazepines, 50, 284, 488
Berger, Hans, 62
Berk, Lee, 311
Beta-endorphins, 311
Beta waves, 62, 200
Bethlehem Hospital (London,
  England), 467
Bias
 actor-observer, 361–362, 379
 confirmation, 18, 215–216, 224
 courtesy, 22
 cultural, and IQ tests, 414–415
 hindsight, 182, **182,** 192
 observer, 20, 28
Bicêtre Asylum, 467, **467**
Big Five (five-factor model), 401–
  402, 403, 408, 423, 425
Big grain of salt, use of term, 22
Bilateral anterior cingulotomy,
  465, 491
Bilateral cingulotomy, 491
Bilateral ECT, 490
Bimodal distributions, A-4,
  A-4, A-6
bin Laden, Osama, 378
Binet, Alfred, 410
Binet's mental ability test, 410
Binge drinking, **285**
Binge eating, 449
Binocular cues, 107, 115
 to depth perception, **107**
Binocular disparity, 107
Biofeedback, 146, 157
Biological perspective, 40–79
 and anxiety disorders, 444
 learning objectives, 41
Biological preparedness, 129, 156
Biological psychology, 42
Biological rhythms, 199

Biomedical therapies, 466, 486–491,
  493, 494, 496, 497
 defined, 486
 electroconvulsive therapy (ECT),
  489–490, 494, 497
 psychopharmacology, 486–489
 psychosurgery, 490–491, 494, 497
Biopsychological perspective,
  14–15, 35
Biopsychology, 14, B-6
Biopsychosocial model, 437
Bipolar cells, 86
Bipolar disorders, 446–447, 460, 462
Birth order influence on sexual
  orientation, 292
Bisexual orientation, 291, 309
Bleuler, Eugen, 452
Blind observers, 20–21, **21**
Blind spot, 86–87, **87**
Bloodletting, 467
Bobo doll, **151,** 151–152
Body temperature, and sleep,
  202–203
Borderline personality disorder,
  456, 460, 463
Bottom-up processing, 111, 115
Bouchard, Thomas, 385
Bower, David, 34
Bowlby, John, 469
BP oil spill disaster, **348,** 431,
  443, **443**
Brain, 51, 53–54, 58, 75, 79. *See
  also* Hindbrain
 activity during sleep, **201**
 and aggression, 372
 cerebral hemispheres, 68, 71–73,
  73, 79
 clinical studies, 60–61
 and cognitive health, 223
 cortex, 65–71, 76
 CT scans, 61, 75
 electrical stimulation of the brain
  (ESB), 60, 75
 electroencephalography (EEG),
  62, 62–63, 75, 79, 147, 295
 and emotions, 295–296, 309
 functional magnetic resonance
  imaging (fMRI), 13, 63, 76,
  445, 455
 hindbrain, 64–65
 keeping young, 259, **259**
 lesioning studies, 60
 lobes of, **68,** 68–70
 mapping function, 62–63
 and memory, 188–190, 192, 195
 MRI scans, 13, **61,** 61–62,
  75, 455
 PET scans (positron emission
  tomography), 13, 63, 76,
  407, 445, 455
 stimulation, 60–61
 structures of, 63–64, **64,** 76, 79
 studying, **60**
Brain-computer interfaces (BCI), 41
Brain-derived neurotrophic factors
  (BDNF), 191
Brainstorming, 217, 227

Bray, Charles, 95
Breastfeeding, **391**
Breland, Kellar, 144
Breland, Marian, 144
Breuer, Josef, 468
Brightness, 84, 114
Brightness constancy, 103, 114, 115
Broca, Paul, 70
Broca's aphasia, 71, 76
Broca's area, 70–71, 76
Brown-eyed/blue-eyed children
        (experiment), 364, 379
Buddhists, **331**
Bulimia, 334, 343, 449–450
Bundy, Ted, 179, 231
Buonarroti, Michelangelo, 345
Buprenorphine, 285
Burnout, 331, 340
Bush, George W., 348
Bystander effect, 14, 375, 380
        elements involved in, **376**

C
Caffeine, 284, 287
Cajal, Santiago Ramón y, 42
California Psychological Inventory
        (CPI), 408
Calkins, Mary Whiton, 7, **7**
Calloway, LaShanda, 375
Cancer, and stress, 322–323
Cannabinoids, 287
Cannabis sativa, 287
Cannon, Walter, 299
Cannon-Bard theory of emotion,
        299, **299**, 306, 309
        cognitive arousal theory
                (Schachter/Singer), 299–301,
                300, 306, 309
        defined, 299
        facial feedback theory, 301
Carbamazepine, 488
Carbohydrates, 333
Carcinogens, 287
Carlsmith, James, 358
Case studies, 21–22, 35
Castaway (movie), **280**
Castration anxiety, 391
Cataplexy, 206
Catastrophes, 313, 339, 342
Catatonic schizophrenia, 453,
        460, 463
Cattell, Raymond, 401, 403, **424**
        self-report inventory, **402**
Causation, 25
Cellular clock theory, 262,
        266, 269
Central nervous system (CNS),
        51–54, 75, 78
        brain, 51
        damage to, 53
        defined, 51
        spinal cord, 51–52
        stem cells, 54, **54**
Central-route processing, 356, 379
Centration, 242
Cerebellum, 65, **65**, 76, 172, 188
Cerebral cortex, 65

Cerebral hemispheres, 68, 71–73, 79
        specialization of, 72
        split-brain research, 72–73, 76
Cerebrum, 71
Chabert, Lacey, **257**
Challenger space shuttle disaster,
        180, 348
Channels, 44
Character, defined, 386
Chemical senses, 96–99, 114
        olfaction, 98–99, 114, 119
        taste, 96–98, 114
Cheyenne, 264, 266
Chi-square tests, A-10
Chicago Hope (television show), 465
Child-directed speech, 245
Chlorpromazine, 486
Chomsky, Noam, 13, 218, 221, 245
Chorley, Doug, 34
Chromosome problems, 232–233,
        265, 268
Chromosomes, 232, 265
Chronological age, 410
Chunking, 170
Cilia, 98
Cingulate cortex, 67
Cingulate gyrus, 465
Cingulotomies, 491
Cingulum bundle (CB), 455
Circadian rhythm, 199
Circadian rhythm disorders, 207, 226
Clanging, 452
Clark, Kenneth, 8
Clark, Mamie, 8
Class-bound values, 485
Class Divided, A (Peters), 364
Classical conditioning, 121,
        122–127, **124**, 156, 160,
        205, 295, 333, 473–476,
        493, 496
        acquisition, 124
        biological preparedness, 129, 156
        compared to operant
                conditioning, 133
        conditioned emotional response
                (CER), 128, 156
        conditioned response (CR),
                123–125, 156
        conditioned stimulus (CS),
                123–125, 130, 156
        conditioned taste aversion, 129,
                129, 156
        elements of, 123
        extinction, 125–126, **126**
        higher-order conditioning,
                126–127, **127**
        neutral stimulus (NS), 123–124
        Pavlov and the salivating dogs,
                122–124, **123**, **124**, 156
        reinforcers, 126
        spontaneous recovery, 125–126,
                126
        stimulus discrimination, 125, 156
        stimulus generalization, 125, **125**
        stimulus substitution, 130
        unconditioned response (UCR),
                123–125

unconditioned stimulus (UCS),
        123–125, 156
        vicarious conditioning, 128
        why it works, 129–130
Claustrophobia, 441
Climacteric changes, 258, 266
Clinical psychology, B-5
Clinical studies, 52–53
Clive, Colin, **417**
Closure, 104
Clozapine, 487
Cocaine, 49, 283–284, 287
Cochlea, 94
Cochlear implant, 95, **95**
"Cocktail party effect," 168, **168**
Cognition, 147, 207–217, 224, 354
        concepts, 209–211, 224
        creativity, 216–217, 224
        intelligence, 215
        language, 218–221, 265
        learning objectives, 197
        mental exercises for better
                cognitive health, 222–223
        mental imagery, 208–209, 224
        problem solving and decision
                making, 211–216, 224
        schemas, 211, 360
        scripts, 211
Cognitive appraisal approach,
        324, 340
Cognitive arousal theory (Schachter/
        Singer), 299–301, **300**, 306,
        309
Cognitive-behavioral therapy
        (CBT), 477, 491, 493, 497
        evaluation of, 478
Cognitive component of attitudes,
        355, 379
Cognitive development
        adolescence, 254–256
        adulthood, 259
        infancy and childhood
                development, 240–246
        Piaget's theory, 240–243, **241**
Cognitive differences in
        gender, 252
Cognitive dissonance, 357–358,
        358, 379
Cognitive learning theory, 147–151,
        157, 161
        insight learning, 149, 157, 224
        Köhler's smart chimp, 148–149,
                149, 157
        latent learning, 148, **149**, 157
        learned helplessness, 149–151
        Seligman's depressed dogs,
                149–150, **150**, 157
        Tolman's maze-running rats,
                148, **149**, 157
Cognitive map, 148
Cognitive mediational theory of
        emotion, 302, **302**, 306,
        309, 324
Cognitive needs, 279, 308
Cognitive neuroscience, 13
Cognitive perspective, 13,
        35, 130

Cognitive psychologists, 324, 437,
        444, 476
        and personality disorders, 444, 460
Cognitive psychology, 9, 11, 13, 35
        anxiety, view of, 444
Cognitive therapies, 476–478,
        493–494, 497
        Beck's, 476–477, 497
        cognitive-behavioral therapy
                (CBT), 477, 493, 497
        defined, 476
        distortions in thoughts, 477
        evaluation of, 478
        rational-emotive behavioral
                therapy (REBT), 477–478,
                493, 497
Cognitive universalism, 220, 224
Collective unconscious, 393
Collectivism, 421
College athletes and stereotypes, 29
College students and psychological
        disorders, 481–482
College test performances and
        stereotypes, 29
College Undergraduate Stress Scale
        (CUSS), 314, 342
Color, 85
        afterimage, 89, **89**
        color vision, theories of, 88–89
        opponent-process theory, 90
        perception of, 88–89
        trichromatic theory, 88–89, **89**
Color blindness, 90–91, **91**, 114
Color-deficient vision, 90
Columbia space shuttle disaster, 180
Comfort dog, **332**
Commitment, 370, 380
Common factors approach, 483
Common region, 105
Common sense theory of emotion,
        298
Communicator, and persuasion,
        356
Community College Counselors
        Survey, 482
Companionate love, 370, 380
Comparative psychology, B-6
Compensation, 394
Competence, 281
Competence-priming, 459
Complementary, 368
Compliance, 349–350, 379, 381
        defined, 349
        door-in-the-face technique,
                349, 379
        froot-in-the-door technique,
                349, 379
        lowball technique, 349–350, 379
        susceptibility to techniques,
                cultural differences in, 350
        that's-not-all technique, 350, 379
Computed tomography (CT), 61,
        61, 75
Concentrative meditation, 337, 340
Concept
        intelligence, 216
Conception, 234

Concepts, 209–211, 224
  abstract, 243
  basic-level type, 210
  concrete, 243
  formal, 210
  natural, 210
  prototypes, 210–211, **211**, 224
  subordinate, 210
  superordinate, 209–210
Concrete concepts, 243
Concrete operations stage, 243,
  243, 265, 268
Concussions, 189, **189**
Conditional positive regard, 399
Conditioned emotional response
  (CER), 128, 156
Conditioned response (CR),
  123–125, 156
Conditioned stimulus (CS), 123–125,
  130, 156
Conditioned taste aversion, 129,
  129, 156
Conditioning, 11
Conduction hearing impairment,
  95, 114
Cones, 86, **87**, 89, 114
Confidence training, B-13
Confirmation bias, 18, 215–216, 224
Conflict, 317–318, 339, 342
  approach-approach, 317, 342
  approach-avoidance conflict, 318,
    318, 342
  avoidance-avoidance conflict,
    318, 342
  as stressor, 317, 342
Conformity, 346–349, 378, 381
  Asch's classic study on, **347**,
    347–348, 378
  and gender, 348
Confounding variables, 26–27
Congenital analgesia, 100
Congenital insensitivity to pain
  with anhidrosis (CIPA),
  100, **100**
Conjoined twins, 234–235, **235**, 265
Connectionism, 165
Conscience, 389
Conscientiousness, 402, 423
Consciousness, 6, 7, 196–227
  altered states of, 198–199,
    199, 224
  in animals, 198
  defined, 198, 226
  effect of drugs on, **287**
  and hypnosis, 183
  learning objectives, 197
  waking, 198
Conservation, 242–243
Conservation experiment, **242**
Consolidation, 188, 192
Constructive processing of
  memories, 181–182
Constructive processing view of
  memory retrieval, 182
Consumer psychology, 349
Consummate love, 371
Contact comfort, 249, **249**, 265

Contiguity, 104–105
Contingency contract, 475
Continuity, 104
Continuous positive airway pressure
  (CPAP) device, 206
Continuous reinforcement, 135, 157
Contradiction, 18
Control, 5
Control group, 27
Conventional morality, 256, 266
Convergence, 107
Convergent thinking, 216
Cooing, 245
Coping
  and culture, 337–338, 340, 343
  emotion-focused coping, 336–337,
    340, 343
  problem-focused, 336, 340, 343
  and religion, 338, 340, 343
Cornea, 86
Coronary heart disease
  and personality, **326**
  and stress, **322**
Corpus callosum, 68, 76
Correlation, 23–25, **24**, A-10
Correlation coefficient, 23, 24,
  A-10–A-12
Cortex, 65–71, 74, 76
  adrenal, 59, 76
  association, 70
  association areas of, 70–71, 76
  lobes, **68**, 68–70
  motor, 70
  primary auditory, 69
  primary visual, 68
  somatosensory, 69
  structures under, 65–67
  visual association, 68
  wrinkling of, 67–68, 76
Corticalization, 68, **68**, 76
Corticoids, 59, 75
Cortisol, 59
Counseling psychology, B-5
Counterconditioning, 11, **474**
Countertransference, 468
Courtesy bias, 22
Creativity, 216–217, 224
  convergent thinking, 216
  defined, 216
  divergent thinking, 216–217, 224
Critical period for development, 105
Critical periods, 236
Critical thinking, 32–34, 36
  defined, 33
  open mind necessary for, 34
Crop circles, 33, **33**
Cross-cultural research, 14
Cross-sectional design, 230, **231**,
  265, 268
Cross-sequential design, 230, **231**,
  265, 268
Crowe, Russell, **452**
Crystal, Billy, 264
CT scans, 61, 75
Cult
  anatomy of, 377–378

  commitments to, 378
  defined, 377, 380
Cultural bias, and IQ tests,
  414–415, 425
Cultural personality, Hofstede's
  four dimensions of,
  421–422, 425
Cultural psychology, 13
Cultural relativity, 434, 459
Cultural values, as barriers to
  effective psychotherapy,
  484–485
Culturally fair tests, 414
Culture
  and anxiety disorders, 445
  and attachment style, 249
  and compliance, 350
  and conformity, 347
  and coping, 334, 337–338, 340
  and display of emotion, 297
  and eating disorders, 334, 450
  and gender, 252, 266, 269
  and hierarchy of needs, 280
  and hunger, 333
  and IQ tests, 414–415
  and mood disorders, 446
  and personality, 360, 403
  and prototypes, 211
  and stress, 331–332, 340, 343
  views on death, 264, 266
Culture-bound syndromes,
  434, 459
Culture-bound values, 485
Curare, 48, 75
Curve of forgetting, 185, **185**, 192
Cybertherapists, 486
Cybertherapy, 485–486
Cyclothymia, 446, 460
Cystic fibrosis, 232, 265

D
Damon, Johnny, **189**
Dani tribe, 220
Daniel, Robert Prentiss, 8
Danso, Henry, 29
Dark adaptation, 88
Darwin, Charles, 7, 296, 301
Day of the Dead, **338**
Daycare, 248
Death and dying
  cross-cultural views on,
    264, 266
  stages of, 263, 266, 269
Debriefing, 31
Decay theory, 186
Decibels, **92**
Decision making
  creativity, 216–217
  and problem solving, 211–212,
    227
Decision points in helping behavior,
  376, **376**, 380
Declarative memory, 66, 173, **174**,
  192, 194
  episodic, 173, **174**
  semantic, 173, **174**

Deep brain stimulation (DBS),
  60, 491
Deep lesioning, 60, 491
Deep sleep, 202, 203
Deepwater Horizon oil drilling rig
  disaster, **348**, 421
Defense mechanisms, 389, **389**,
  391, 394, 405
Dehydroepiandrosterone
  (DHEA), 321
Delta waves, 63, 200, 202–203
Delusional disorders, 452
Delusions, 451–452, 460, 463
Delusions of grandeur, 452
Delusions of influence, 452
Delusions of persecution, 452
Delusions of reference, 452
Dementia praecox, 451
Dendrites, 43
Denial stage, of death/dying, 263
Denied past, 472
Dennett, Daniel, 198
Depakote (valproic acid), 488
Dependent variables, 26, 35
Depressants, 284, 287, 306, 309
  alcohol, 285, 287
  barbiturates/major tranquilizers,
    284, 287
  benzodiazepines/minor
    tranquilizers, 284
Depression, 150–151. *See also*
  Major depression
  and stress, 314
Depression stage, of death/dying, 263
Depth perception, 105–107, 115
  binocular cues to, 107
  monocular cues to, 105–106
Descartes, René, 5
Description, 4
Descriptive data, 20–21, 23, 34
  case studies, 21–22
  laboratory observation, 21, **21**
  naturalistic observation, **20**,
    20–21, 28, 35
  surveys, 22, **22**
Descriptive statistics, A-1–A-9,
  A-12
Desipramine (Norpramin), 489
Despair, 261
Determinism, reciprocal, 397,
  397, 424
Deuteranopia, 90
Development
  embryonic period, 236, **236**
Development delay, 415–416
  classifications of, **416**
Developmental psychology,
  B-5–B-6
Developmental research designs, 230
  comparison of, **231**
Deviation IQ scores, 413, 425
"Devil's trident," 112, **112**
Dexedrine, 283
Diabetes, 58, **59**
  and stress, 322

Diagnostic and Statistical Manual of Mental Disorders Fourth Edition, Text Revision (DSM-IV-TR), 334, 403, 437–439, 459, 462
axes of, 437–438
Axis I disorders, 438
Axis II disorders, 438–439
Axis III disorders, 439
Axis IV disorders, 439
Axis V disorders, 439
Diary of a Student Revolution, 179
Diazepam (Valium®), 50
Dichromatic vision, 90
Diehl, Robert, 29
Difference threshold, 82, **82**
Difficult babies, 247
Diffusion of responsibility, 14, 375–376
Diffusion tensor imaging (DTI), 62, 455, **455**
Digit-span test, 169, **169**
Direct contact, and attitude formation, 355, 379
Direct instruction, and attitude formation, 355, 379
Direct observation, 407
Direction of the relationship, 24–25
Directive, use of term, 469
Discrimination, **363**, 363–364, 379
defined, 363
types of, 363
Discriminative stimuli, 125, 143–144, 157
Diseases of adaptation, 319
Disorganized-disoriented attachment style, 248, 265
Disorganized schizophrenia, 452–453, 460, 463
Displaced aggression, 317, **317**, 342
Displacement, 317
Display rules, 297
Dispositional attribution, 361, 379
Dispositional cause, 361, 379
Dissociative identity disorder (DID), 21, 451
Dissonance, 357, 379
Distraction, 296
Distraction desensitization, B-13
Distress, 312, 339, 342
Distributed practice, 185, 195
Disuse, 186
Divergent thinking, 216–217, 224
stimulating, **217**
Dizygotic twins, 234, **234**, 265
DNA (deoxyribonucleic acid), 232
molecule, **223**, 268
Dolphins, and language, 221
Dominant genes, 232, **233**, 265
Door-in-the-face technique, 349, 379
Dopamine, 49, **49**, 487
and schizophrenia, 453–454, 463
Dot problem, solution to, **218**
Double-bind studies, 28–29
Double take, 166

Down syndrome, 232, **232**, 265, 416, **416**
Downward social comparison, and optimists, 329
Doxepin (Sinequan), 489
Draw-A-Person, 406
Dream interpretation, 468
Dreams. *See also* Dream interpretation
latent content, 468
manifest content, 468
Drive, 273
Drive-reduction theory, 273–274, **274**, 305, 308
Drug interaction, 284
Drug tolerance, 282, 306
DTI, 62
Dual-task condition, 216, **216**
Dweck, Carol, 275–276, 308
Dysthymia, 446, 460

E
Ear, structure of, **93**, 93–95, 118
Ear canal, 93
Eardrum, 93
Easy babies, 246
Eating disorders, 333–334, 340, 343, 448–450, 460, 472
anorexia nervosa, 334, 343, 448–449, 460, 463
bulimia nervosa, 334, 343, 449–450
culture and, 334, 450
obesity, 333–334, 340, 343
Ebbinghaus, Hermann, 185
Echoic memory, 191, 194
Echoic sensory memory, 167–168, **168**
Eclectic therapies, 469
Ecstasy (X), 286, **286**, 287
Educational psychology, 8, B-7, **B-7**, B-14
Efferent (motor) neurons, 52
Ego, 261–262, 388, 424
Ego integrity, 261
Ego movement, 10
Egocentric speech, 219
Egocentrism, 242, 255
Eidetic imagery, 167
Einstein, Albert, 84, 400
Elaboration likelihood model of persuasion, 356, 379
Elaborative rehearsal, 171
Elavil (amitriptyline), 489
Electra complex, 392, 424
Electrical potential, 44
Electrical stimulation of the brain (ESB), 60, 75
Electroconvulsive therapy (ECT), 61, 189, 192, **489**, 489–490, 494, 497
Electroencephalograph (EEG), **62**, 62–63, 75, 79, 147, 200, **201**
alpha waves, 62, 200, **201**
beta waves, 62, 200, **201**
delta waves, 63, 200, **201**

event-related potential (ERP), 63, 75, 83
theta waves, 62–63, 200, **201**
Elliot, Jane, 364
Ellis, Robert, 477
Embryo, 236
Embryonic period, 236, **236**, 265, 268
Emotion-focused coping, 336–337, 340, 343
Emotional crisis, 251
Emotional intelligence, **418**, 418–419
Emotion(s), 294–309
behavior of, 296–297
Cannon-Bard theory of, 299, **299**, 306, 309
cognitive arousal theory (Schachter/Singer), 299–301, **300**, 306, 309
cognitive-mediational theory, 302, **302**, 306, 309, 324
common sense theory of, **298**
comparison of theories of, **303**, 309
defined, 294, 309
display rules, 297
elements of, 294–298, 306, 309
emotional expressions, 296–297, 309
facial expressions, 295–297, **296**, 309
facial feedback hypothesis, **301**, 301–302, 306, 309
James-Lange theory of, 298, **298**, 306, 308
labeling, 297–298
learning objectives, 271
physiology of, 294–296
range of, **445**
Empathy, 418, 471
Empedocles, 386
Emperor's New Groove, The, 389
Encoding, 164
automatic, 180, 192
Encoding failure, 186, 195
Encoding specificity, 176, 195
End-stopped neurons, 113
Endocrine glands, 57–59, 75, 79
Endogenous, use of term, 49
Endogenous morphine, 49
Endorphins, 49, 75, 101, 285
Enigma (Levant), **110**, 110–111
Enuresis, 207, 226
Environmental psychology, B-9, B-14
Environmental stressors, 313–315, 339, 342
acute stress disorder (ASD), 443, **443**, 459, 462
catastrophes, 313, 339, 342
hassles, 314–315, 339, 342
major life changes, 313, 339, 342
post-traumatic stress disorder (PTSD), 443, 459, 462

Social Readjustment Rating Scale (SRRS), 313–314, 342
Enzymatic degradation, 50
Enzymes, 49–50
Ephedra, 282
Epilepsy, 72
Epinephrine, 49, 59, 75, 300
Episodic long-term memory, 173
Episodic memory, 173, **174**, 192, 194
Equal status contact, 366
Ergot, 286
Erikson, Erik, 10, 250, 251, 257, 280, 394, 424
ego integrity *vs.* despair, 261, 266
generativity *vs.* stagnation, 260, 266
identity *vs.* role confusion, 257
intimacy *vs.* isolation, 260, 266
psychosocial adolescent and adult stages, **250**, 250–251, 266
psychosocial stages of development, **250**, 250–251, 265, 269
Erogenous zone, 390
Escape, and frustration, 317, 342
Esteem needs, 279, 308
Ethics
in animal research, 31–32
of psychological research, 30–32, 35
Eustress, 312–313, 339, 342
Evaluation
of behavior therapies, 476, 496
of cognitive therapies, 478
of group therapy, 480
of humanistic therapy, 472, 496
of psychoanalysis, 468–469, 493
Even the Rat Was White (Guthrie), 8
Event-related potentials (ERPs), 63, 75, 83
Evidence, 33
Evil, Dr., 417
Evolutionary psychologists, 15
Evolutionary perspective, 15, **15**, 34
Excitatory effect, 48
Excitatory neurotransmitters, 48
Excitatory synapses, 48
Exercise, 223, **327**
Exhaustion stage, general adaptation syndrome, 319, 339, 342
Existence needs, 280
Exorcism, 432
Expectancies, 397–398
Expectancy, 130
Expectancy-value theories, 278, 308
Experimental group, 27
Experimental psychologists, 5
Experimental psychology, B-6
Experimenter effect, 28, 33
Experiments, 25–29, 33
Explanation, 4
Explanatory style, 328–329, 342
Explicit memory, 173, **174**
Exposure and response prevention, 474

Exposure therapy, 474, 492
Expression of the Emotions in Man and Animals, The (Darwin), 301
External frustration, 316, 342
Extinction, 143, 157
  in classical conditioning, 125–126, **126**
  in operant conditioning, 475–476
Extraneous variables, 27
Extrasensory perception (ESP), thinking critically about, 215
Extraversion, 402, 423
Extravert, 402
Extrinsic motivation, 271, 308
Extrinsic reward, 281, **281**, 305
Exxon Valdez oil spill, 431
Eye, 347
  how it works, 87–88
  REM (rapid eye movement), 200, **203**
  structure of, **85**, 85–87
Eye-movement desensitization reprocessing (EMDR), 474
Eysenck, Hans, 482
Eysenck Personality Questionnaire, 408

F

F-test, A-10
fa'afafine, 293
Facebook, 369
Facial expressions, 295–297, **296**, 309
Facial feedback hypothesis, **301**, 301–302, 306, 309
Factor analysis, 401, 424
Falater, Scott, 204
False memory syndrome, 182–184, 192
False positives, 179
Familial retardation, 416
Family counseling therapy, 479, **479**, 494
Family studies, and schizophrenia, 454–455
Fear response, 67, 76
Fechner, Gustav, 82
Female sex organs, **57**, 59
Femininity, 421–422
Fertilization, 234
Festinger, Leo, 358
Fetal alcohol syndrome, 416
Fetal period, 236, **236**, 265, 268
Fetus, defined, 236
Fight-or-flight system, 56
Figure-ground illusion, **104**
Figure-ground relationships, 103–104
Five-factor model (Big Five), 401–402, 403, 408, 424
Five-factor test, 401
Fixation, 390, 424
  in the phallic stage, 392

Fixed interval schedule of reinforcement, 135–136, **136**, 157
Fixed ratio schedule of reinforcement, 137
Flashbulb memories, 180, 192
Flat affect, 452
Fleury, Robert, **467**
Flooding, 474
Fluid intelligence, 223
Fluoxetine (Prozac), 489
Focus training, B-13
Foot-in-the-door technqiue, 349, 379
Forensic psychology, B-1, B-9
Forgetting, 184–187, 192, 195
  distributed practice, 185, 195
  encoding failure, 186, 195
  interference theory, 186–187
  memory trace decay, 186, 192, 195
  reasons for, 184–185, **188**
Forgetting curve, 185, **185**, 192
Formal concepts, 210
Formal operations stage, 243, 254–255, 265, 268
Fossey, Diane, 21
Fovea, 88
Fragile X syndrome, 416–417
Framingham Heart Study, 326
Frankenstein, Dr., 417, **417**
Fraternal twins, 420, **420**
  personalities of, 371–372
Free association, 468
Free-floating anxiety, 440
Free nerve endings, 99
Free radical theory, 262, 266, 269
Free radicals, defined, 262
Free will, 13
Freeman, Joan, 418
Freeman, Walter, 490
Freewriting, 217, 227
Frequency, 407
Frequency count, 407, 425
Frequency distribution, A-2, **A-2**, A-12
Frequency polygon, **A-3**
Frequency theory, 94, 114
Freud, Anna, 10, **10**, 389, 394
Freud, Sigmund, 9–10, **10**, 11, 21, 31, 371, **386**, 392, 394–395, 405, 424, 467–468, 493, 496
  conception of the personality, **387**
  cultural background, 386–387
  on dreams, 395
  and psychodynamic perspective, 394–395, 424
  psychosexual stages, 390, **393**, 424
  unconscious mind, **387**, 387–388, 424
Freudian psychoanalysis, 10
Freudian theory, 12
Friedman, Meyer, 325
Friendster, 369
Frontal lobes, 69–70, 76, 295
Frustration
  and aggression, 317, 371
  as stressor, 316, 339, 342

Frustration-aggression hypothesis, 317, 371
Fully functional person, 400
Functional fixedness, 215, 224
Functional magnetic resonance imaging (fMRI), 13, **62**, 63, 76, 83, 209, 407, 445, 455
Functionalism, 7–8
  defined, 7
Fundamental attribution error (actor-observer bias), 361–362, 379, 425
Fundamentalist Church of Jesus Christ of Latter Day Saints, 377

G

g factor (generalized intelligence), 410, 425
GABA (γ-aminobutyric acid/gamma-aminobutyric acid), 49, 75, 444, 453
Gage, Phineas, 21, **21**, 70
Galen, 386
Gall, Franz Joseph, 423
Gambon, John, B-1
Gandhi, Mahatma, 400
Ganglion cells, 86
Gate-control theory, 100–101, 114
Gates in nerves, 44
Gender, 251, 266, 269
  biological influences, 252, 266
  and conformity, 348
  culture and, 266, 269
  defined, 251
  environmental influences, 252, 266, 269
Gender differences
  antisocial personality disorder, 456
  cognitive, 485
  social/personality, 456
Gender identity, 251, 252, 266, 269
Gender role development, 252–253, 266, 269
  gender schema theory, 253, 266, 269
  social learning theory, 252–253
  theories of, 252
Gender roles, 252, 266, 269
Gender schema theory, 253, 266, 269
Gender typing, 252
General adaptation syndrome (GAS), 319, **320**, 339, 342
Generalization, in operant conditioning, 144
Generalized anxiety disorder, 444, 459, 462
Generalized intelligence, 410, 425
Generalized response, strength of, **125**
Generativity, 260, 266
Genes, 232–233, 265, 268
  dominant, 232, **233**
  genetic and chromosome problems, 232–233
  and mood disorders, 448

recessive, 232, **233**
  and sexual orientation, 292–293
Genetics, 232, 419
Genius, 417
Genovese, Catherine "Kitty," 375, 376
Germinal period, 235–236, **236**, 265, 268
Gestalt, defined, 9
Gestalt principles, 115
  of grouping, **104**
  of perception, 103–105
Gestalt psychology, 9, **9**, 34
Gestalt therapy, 9, 471–472, **472**, 493, 496
Getting Things Done: The Art of Stress-Free Productivity (Allen), 304
Getting Things Done (GTD) methodology, 304–305
Gifted, defined, 418
Gifted Children Grown Up (Freeman), 418
Giftedness, 417–418, 425
Glands, 59, 75
Glial cells, 52, 74, 75
  defined, 43
Glucagons, 58, 75, 333
Glutamate, 49, 97
Goal into subgoals, 213, **213**
Gonads, 59, 75
Graded exposure, 474
Graduate Record Exam (GRE), 415
Grammar, 218, 224, 227
Grasping reflex, **239**
Gray matter, 62
Group therapy, **478**, 479–480, 494, 497
  advantages of, 480
  disadvantages of, 480
  evaluation of, 480
  family counseling therapy, 479, **479**, 494
  self-help groups (support groups), **479**, 479–480, 494, 497
  types of, 479–480
Groups, 26–27
Groupthink, 348–349, 378, 381
  characteristics, **348**
  hazards of, 348–349
Growth hormones, 58, 202
Growth needs, 280
Growth spurt, 254
Gustation, 96–98, 114
  defined, 96
Guthrie, Robert V., 8

H

Habits, 396
Habituation, 83, 114
Hair cells, 94
Halcion, 284
Hallucinations, 202, 286, 452
Hallucinogen-persisting perception disorder (HPPD), 287
Hallucinogens, 286–287, 306, 309
  hashish, 287

LSD (lysergic acid diethylamide), 286, 287, 306
marijuana (pot/weed), 287, 306
MDMA (Ecstasy), 286, **286**, 287
mescaline, 286, 306
PCP, 286, 306
psilocybin, 286–287, 306
stimulatory, 286
Halo effect, 405, 425
Hammer, 94
Handedness, 72–73
Hanks, Tom, **280**
Happiness, achieving, 298, 306
Hardy personality, 327–328, 340, 342
Harlow, Harry, 249, 265
Hashish, 287
Hassles, 314–315, 339, 342
Hazards, experimental, 27–28
Health
  aging effects on, 259
  stress and, 319–323, 339, 342
Health psychology, 323, 340, B-7, **B-7**, B-14
Hearing, 91–95, 114, 118, 238
  frequency theory, 93, 94
  inner ear, 94, 114
  middle ear, 94, 114
  outer ear, 93
  pitch, 92
  place theory, 94
  sound, perception of, 92–93
  structure of the ear, **93**, 93–95
  timbre, 92
  volley principle, 95
Hearing impairments, 95
Heart disease, and stress, 321–322, **322**
Heider, Fritz, 361
Hematophobia, 441
Henning, Hans, 97
Hensel, Abby and Brittany, 234–235, **235**, 265
Hering, Edward, 90
Heritability
  defined, 420
  and human behavior, 420
Hermann grid, 108, **108**
Heroin, 285, 306
Hertz (Hz), 93
Heterosexual orientation, 291, 306, 309
Heuristics, 212–214, 224, 227
  availability, 213
  means-end analysis, 213–214
  representative, 212–213
Hierarchy, defined, 279
Hierarchy of fears, 473
Hierarchy of needs, Maslow's, **279**, 279–281, 305, 308
High blood sugar, 319
Higher-order conditioning, 126–127, **127**
Hindbrain, 64–65
  cerebellum, 65, 76
  medulla, 64, 75

pons, 64, 76
reticular formation, 64–65, 76
Hindsight bias, 182, **182**, 192
Hindu, 264, 266
Hippocampus, 48, 66–67, 76, 188, 192, 195, 321, 443
Hippocrates, 386, 432
Histogram, **A-2**
Histronic personality disorder, 456
Hitler, Adolf, 231
Hofstede, Geert, 421
Hofstede's four dimensions of cultural personality, 421–422, 425
Holophrases, 245
Homeless, **436**
Homeostasis, 273, **273**, 305
Homosexual orientation, 291, **292**, 306, 309
  evolutionary purpose of, 293, 306
Hormone therapy, 335
Hormones, 56, 58, 75, 257
  growth, 58, 75
  and stress, 321
Horn effect, 405
Horney, Karen, 394, **394**, 424
Hostility and stress, 326
Hot flashes, 258
House-Tree-Person, 406
Howard, Ruth, 9
Hoyt, Dick, 41
Hoyt, Rick, 41
Human development. *See also* Adolescence; Adulthood; Infancy and childhood development
  building blocks of, 231–233, 265
  defined, 230
  issues in, 230–231, 265, 268
  prenatal, 234–237
Human factors engineer, B-10, **B-10**
Human factors psychology, **B-10**, B-10–B11, B-14
Human growth hormone, 311
Humanism, 13, 35
Humanistic approaches, 279–281, 305, 308
Humanistic perspective, 13, 386, 398–399, 424
  current thoughts on, 400
  self-concept, 399, 424
Humanistic therapy, 470–472, 493, 496
  evaluation of, 472, 496
  Gestalt therapy, 471–472, **472**, 493, 496
  person-centered therapy (Rogers), **470**, 470–471, 493, 496
Humors, 386, 432
Hunger, 340, 343
  cultural factors/gender, 333
  maladaptive eating problems, 333–334, 340, 343
  physiology of, 333, 340, 343

social components of, 333, 340, 343
Huntington's disease, 232
Hurricane Katrina, 313, 431, 443
Hussein, Saddam, 348
Hypersomnia, 207, 226
Hyperthymesia, 163
Hypnic jerk, 202
Hypnogogic images, 202
Hypnosis, 183
Hypoglycemia, 58
Hypothalamus, 58, 66, 76, 199
  and hunger, 333
Hypothesis
  defined, 18
  drawing conclusions, 19
  forming, 18
  testing, 18–19

I

Ice baths, 467, 493
Iconic memory, 166–167, 191, 194
  capacity of, 167
  duration, 167
  function of, 167
  test, **167**
Id, 388, 424
Ideal self, 345, 399, **399**, 424, 470
Identical twins, **419**, 419–420, 454
Identification, 365, 391
Identity *vs.* role confusion, 257, 266, 269
Ikeda, Kikunae, 97
Illness and stress, 321, **321**
Illusions, 115
  defined, 108
Imagery/mental rehearsal, B-13
Imaginal exposure, 474
Imaginary audience, 255, 266
Imipramine (Tofranil), 489
Imitation, as element of observational learning, 153
Immune system
  defined, 310
  and stress, 320–321, 340, 342
Immunizations, **245**, 245–246, 265
Implicit memory, 172, 194
Implicit personality theories, 360, 379
Impression formation, 359, 379
In-groups, 363, 379
In vivo exposure, 474
Incentive approaches, 278, 305, 308
Incentives, defined, 278
Independent variables, 26
Individualism, 421
Industrial/organizational (I/O) psychology, 8, B-10–B-11, B-14
  areas in, B-10–B-11, **B-12**
  defined, B-10
Infancy and childhood development, 238–251, 265, 268
  accommodation, 240
  assimilation, 240

attachment, 247–249, 265, 269
cognitive development, 240–246, 265, 268
concrete operations stage, 243, **243**
Erikson's psychosocial stages of development, **250**, 250–251, 265, 269
formal operations stage, 243
gender development, 251–253, 266, 269
Infancy and childhood development (*cont.*)
  immunizations, **245**, 245–246
  language development, 244–245, 265, 268
  motor development, 239–240, **240**, 265
  physical development, 238–240
  Piaget's stages, 240–243, **241**, 265, 268
  preoperational stage, 241–243
  psychosocial development, 246–251
  reflexes, 238, **239**, 265
  sensorimotor stage, 241
  sensory development, 238–239, 265, 268
  temperament, 246–247, 265, 268
  zone of proximal development (ZPD), 244, 265, 268
Infantile amnesia, 195
Inferential statistics, A-9–A-12
Information-processing model, 164, 191–192, 194
Informed consent, 30–31
Inhibitory effect, 48
Inhibitory neurotransmitters, 48
Inhibitory synapses, 48
Innate behavior, 238
Inner ear, 94, 114
Insanity, 435
Insanity defense, 435
Insight, 214, 224, 227
  defined, 214
Insight learning, 149, 157, 224
Insight therapies, 466, 493
Insomnia, **205**, 205–206, 224, 226
Instant replay, 181
Instinct, 272–273, 305, 308, 371
Instinctive drift, 144–145, 157
Institutional review boards, 30
Insulin, 58, **59**, 75, 333, 340
Integration, 331, 340, 343
Integrity, 261, 266
Intellectual disability, 415–417, 425, 438
  causes of, 416–417, 425
  classifications of, 416, 425
  defined, 415
  Down syndrome, 232, **232**, 265, 416, **416**
  familial retardation, 416
  fragile X syndrome, 416–417
Intelligence, 275, 409–423, 425
  artificial, 165

Intelligence (*cont.*)
  Binet's mental ability test, 410
  chronological age, 410
  defined, 409–410, 425
  deviation IQ scores, 413, 425
  emotional, **418**, 418–419
  Gardner's multiple intelligences, 410
  genetic influences, 419–421, 425
  giftedness, 417–418, 425
  Hofstede's four dimensions of cultural personality, 421–422, 425
  individual differences in, 415–419
  IQ scores correlation with various relationships, **420**
  IQ tests and cultural bias, 414–415, 425
  learning objectives, 385
  measuring, 410–415
  mental age, 410
  mental retardation (developmental delay), 416–417, 425
  normal curve, **413, A-8**
  Spearman's g factor, 410, 425
  standardization of tests, 412–413
  Stanford-Binet and IQ, 410–411, 425
  Sternberg's triarchic theory, 410, 425
  test construction, 412–414
  theories of, 410
  twin studies, 419–421, 425
  Weschler's tests, 411, 425
Intelligence quotient (IQ), 410
  normal curve, **413**
Intelligence tests, **A-5**
Interaction with others, and attitude formation, 355, 379
Interference theory, 186–187, 195
  proactive interference, 187, **187**, 195
  retroactive interference, 187, **187**, 195
Intergroup contact, and prejudice, 366, **366**, 380
Internal frustration, 316, 342
Interneurons, 52
Interpersonal attraction, 367–371, 379
  companionate love, 370
  consummate love, 372
  intimacy, 370
  love, components of, 370
  love triangles, 370
  "opposites attract," 368
  physical attractiveness, 368
  proximity, 368, 379
  reciprocity of liking, 368–369, 379
  romantic love, 370
  rules of, 367–368
  similarity, 368, 379

triangular theory of love, 370, **370**, 380
Interpersonal psychotherapy, 469, **469**, 496
Interposition, 105
Interstimulus interval (ISI), 125
Interval schedule, 135
Interviews, 405, 425
Intimacy, 260, 266, 370, 380
Intonation, 219
Intrinsic motivation, 272, 281, **281**, 308
Introversion, 401
Introvert, 402
Inverse, use of term, 24
Involuntary muscles, 55
Ions, 44, 75
Iris, 86
Irreversibility, 243
Ishihara color test, **91**
Isocarboxazid (Marplan), 488
Isolation, 260
Iwakabe, Shigeru, 485

J
Jackson, Damian, **189**
Jackson, Michael, **180**
Jacobson, Lenore, 28
James, William, 7, 198, 298
James-Lange theory of emotion, 298, **298**, 306, 309
Jameson, Matthew, 29
Janus, Cynthia L., 290, 306
Janus, Samuel S., 290, 306
Janus Report on Sexual Behavior, The, 290, 306
  findings from, **290**, 306, 309
Jeffs, Warren, 377
Jekyll, Dr., 417
Jet lag, 207
"Jigsaw classroom," 366–367, 380
Job stress, 330–331, 340, 343
Johnson, Virginia, 290
Jones, Harold, 11
Jones, Jim, 377, 378
Jones, Mary Cover, 11, **11**
Journaling, 217, 227
Jung, Carl, 10, **392**, 393–394, 402, 408, 424
Just noticeable difference (jnd), 82, **82**, 114

K
Kanzi (bonobo chimpanzee), 221
Keirsey Temperament Sorter II, 408
Kennedy, John F., 180
Kennedy, Rosemary, **490**, 491
Kihlstrom, John, 181
Kin selection hypothesis, 293, 306
Kinesthesia, 101
Kinesthetic sense, 101, 114
  defined, 99
King, Rodney, 364
Kinsey, Alfred, 288–289, **289**, 306, 309

Kitaoka, Abiyoshi, 110
Klinefelter's syndrome, 232, 265
Klüver-Bucy syndrome, 67
Kohlberg, Lawrence, 255, 256, 266, 269
  three levels of morality, **256**
Köhler, Wolfgang, 147, 148–149, 157, 161
Koresh, David, 378
koro, 445, 485
Kosslyn's fictional island, **208**
Kübler-Ross, Elisabeth, 263

L
Labels of psychological disorders, 439
Laboratory observation, 21, **21**, 35
Lamotrigine, 488
Laney, Deanna, 435
Lange, Carl, 298
Language, 69, 218–221, 224, 227, **245**, 265, 268, 485
  animal studies in, 221, 224
  as barrier to effective psychotherapy, 485
  defined, 218, 224
  grammar, 218, 224
  linguistic relativity hypothesis, 220–221
  morphemes, 218
  morphology, 224
  phonemes, 218–219
  pragmatics, 219, 224
  relationship between thought and, 219–221, 224
  semantics, 218
  syntax, 218, 221, 224
  and thinking, 219–221, 227
Language acquisition device (LAD), 218, 245, 265
Language development, stages of, 244–245
Laser-assisted in situ keratomileusis (LASIK), 86
Latency stage in personality development, 392, 424
Latent content of dreams, 468
Latent learning, 148, **149**, 157
Lateral geniculate nucleus (LGN), 90
Laudanum, 285
Laughter, 336, **336**
Law of Effect, 131, 156, 397
Law psychology, B8–B9
Lazarus, Richard, 302, 324
  theory of emotion, **302**, **324**, 342
Learned helplessness, 149–151, **150**, 157, 275, 328, 447
Learning, 120–161
  classical conditioning, 121, 122–127, **124**, 156
  cognitive learning theory, 147–151, 157
  defined, 122, 156, 160
  latent, 148, **149**, 157

learning objectives, 121
observational, 151–153, 157
operant conditioning, 131–147, 156–157
rote, 171, 212, 224
state-dependent, 176, 192
Learning and practice of new behaviors, 483
Learning curve, **149**
Learning/performance distinction, 151
Left hemisphere, 68, 75
Lens, 86–87, **87**, 114
Leptin, 450
Leucotome, 490
Levels-of-processing model, 165, 191, 194
Lewin, Kurt, 278
Lewis, James Edward, 385, 419, **419**
Librium, 284
Life review, 261
Light, 84, 88, 114, 118
Light adaptation, 88
Light sleep, 202
Limbic system, 65–67, 76
Linear perspective, 105
Linguistic relativity hypothesis, 220–221
Lithium, 488
"Little Albert," 11, 30, 128, 444
  conditioning of, **128**
"Little Hans," 395
"Little Peter," 11
Locus of control, 275, 398
Loftus, Elizabeth, 179, **179**, 182, 183–184, 192, B-1
Lohan, Lindsay, **257**
Long, Howard Hale, 9
Long, Karawynn, 154, 157
Long-term memory (LTM), 170–175, 192, 193, 194
  automatic encoding, 180, 192
  constructive processing of memories, 181–182, 195
  declarative memory, 173
  defined, 170
  elaborative rehearsal, 171–172
  encoding, 171
  flashbulb memories, 180, 192
  nondeclarative, 172
  organization of, 174–175
  primacy effect, 178
  procedural LTM, **172**, 172–173
  recall, 177, 192
  recency effect, 178
  recognition, 177, 178, 192
  reconstructive nature of, 177–179, 181–184, 192, 195
  retrieval, 176–179, 195
  retrieval problems, 177–179, 182–184, 192
  types of, 172–175, **174**
Long-term potentiation, 188
Longitudinal design, 230, **231**, 265, 268

Lord of the Rings, The (film), A-4
Love
    companionate, 370, 380
    components of, 370
    consummate, 371
    defined, 369
    love triangles, 370
    passionate, 370
    romantic, 370, 380
    triangular theory of, 369–370, **370**, 380
"love-bombing," 378
Love needs, 279, 281, 308
Lowball technique, 349–350, 379
LSD (lysergic acid diethylamide), 286, 287, 306
Lupus, 332
Luria, A.R., 185
Luthor, Lex, 417

M
Magic, neuroscience of, 112–113, 115
Magical number seven, 169–170
Magnetic resonance imaging (MRI), 13, **61**, 61–62, 75, **209**, 407, 455
Magnification, 444
Magnification and minimization, 477
Maier, Steven F., 150
Maintenance rehearsal, 170
Major depression, 446, **446, 448,** 460, 462
Major life changes, 313, 339, 342
Major tranquilizers, 284
Maladaptive behavior, 433, 459
Maladaptive eating problems. *See* Eating disorders
Male sex organs, **57,** 59
Mamillary body, **66**
Mania, 446
Manic episodes, 446
Manifest content of dreams, 468
Marfan's syndrome, 232
Marginalization, 331, 340, 343
Marijuana, 287, 306
Marplan (isocarboxazid), 488
Marriage, as form of social support, 370
Masculinity, 421
Masking, 167
Maslow, Abraham, 13, 279–281, 305, 308, 398
Maslow's hierarchy of needs, **279,** 279–281, 305, 308
Massed practice, 185
Master gland, pituitary gland as, 58, 75
Masters, William, 290
Masturbation, 290, 391
Maturation, 122
Mayo, Elton, B-11
Maze, 148, **148,** 157
McAdams, Rachel, **257**
McClelland, David C., 274
McDougall, William, 272

McGregor, Douglas, B-10
McVeigh, Timothy, 231
MDMA (Ecstasy), 286, **286,** 287
Mean, 413
Mean (statistics), A-4–A-5
Mean Girls (movie), **257**
Means-end analysis, 213–214
Measures of central tendency, A-4–A-6, A-12
    bimodal distributions, A-6
    mean, A-4–A-5
    median, A-5
    mode, A-6
    and the shape of the distribution, A-6
    skewed distributions, A-6
Measures of variability, A-6–A-9, A-12
    IQ normal curve, **A-8**
    range, A-6
    standard deviation, **A-7,** A-7–A-9
Mechanical solutions, 212, 224
Media, violence in, 151, 373–374, 380
Median, A-5
Meditation, **337,** 337–338, 340, 343
    concentrative, 337, 340
    effects of, 337
Medulla, 64, 76
Melatonin, 58, 199–200
Memory, 13, 65, 162–195, **164**
    autobiographical, 163
    and the brain, 188–190, 192, 195
    changes in, 259
    consolidation, 188, 192
    declarative, 173, 192
    defined, 164, 191
    echoic, 167–168
    effect of ECT on, 189, 192
    as element of observational learning, 152–153
    encoding, 164
    episodic, 173, 192
    flashbulb memories, 180
    forgetting, 184–187, 192, 195
    and hippocampus, 188, 192
    iconic, 166–167, 191
    implicit, 172, 192
    information-processing model, 164, 191–192, 194
    learning objectives, 163
    levels-of-processing model, 165, 191, 194
    long-term, 170–175, 191, 192
    masters of, 163
    models of, 191, 194
    neural activity and structure in formation of, 188
    nondeclarative, 172
    parallel distributed processing (PDP) model, 165, 174, 191, 194
    physical aspects of, 188–190, 192
    procedural, 172–173, 192
    retrieval, 164, 192
    semantic, 173, 192

sensory, 166–168, 191
short-term (STM), 168–170, 191
stages of, 191
storage, 164
three-stage process of, **165,** 166–175, 191
working, 168–170, 191
Memory retrieval problems, 182–184, 192
Memory trace decay, 186, 192, 195
Menopause, 258–259, 266
Mental age, 410
Mental exercises for better cognitive health, 222–223, 224
Mental illness, history of, 432
Mental imagery, 208–209, 224, 227
Mental map, 208
Mental processes, 4
Mental retardation (development delay). *See also* Intellectual disability
    use of term, 415–417, 425
Mental sets, 215
Mescaline, 286, 306
Message, and persuasion, 356–357, 379
Methadone, 285
Methamphetamines, 287
Methedrine, 283
Meyer, Adolph, 469
Michelangelo Buonarroti, 345
Michelangelo phenomenon, 345
Microsaccades, 84, 110–111
Middle ear, 94, 114
Migrant farming, 434, **434**
Mild mental retardation, 416
Milgram, Stanley, **351,** 351–353, 379
    shock experiment, **351,** 351–353, 379
Military psychology, B-8, **B-8,** B-14
Miller, William R., 471
Mind mapping, 217, 227
Minimization, 444
Minnesota Multiphasic Personality Inventory, Version II (MMPI-2), 326, 408, 425
Minor tranquilizers, 284
Minorities in early psychology, 8–9
Mirror neurons, 70, **70**
Miscarriage, 237
Mischel, Walter, 403
Misinformation effect, 182, 192
Mitosis, 234
MMR (measles, mumps, and rubella) vaccine, 245–246
Mnemonic strategies, 178
Mnemonics, 185
Mode, A-6
Modeling, 475
Moderate mental retardation, 416
Modern psychoanalysis, 394–395
Modern psychological perspectives
    behavioral perspective, 12–13, 35
    biopsychological perspective, 14–15, 35

cognitive perspective, 13, 35
    evolutionary perspective, 15, 35
    humanistic perspective, 13, 35
    psychodynamic perspective, 12, 35
    sociocultural perspective, 13–14, 35
Molaison, Henry Gustav, 188, **188**
Moniz, Antonio Egas, 490
Monoamine oxidase, 488
Monoamine oxidase inhibitors (MAOIs), 488, 494
Monochrome color blindness, 90
Monocular cues, 105–106, 115
Monosodium glutamate (MSG), 97
Monozygotic twins, 234, **234,** 265
Monroe, Marilyn, **449**
Mood disorders, 445–448, 460, 462
    biological explanations of, 448, 460
    bipolar disorders, 446–447, 460, 462
    causes of, 447–448, 460, 462
    cyclothymia, 446
    defined, 445
    dysthymia, 446
    and genes, 448
    major depression, 446, **446,** 460, 462
Moon illusion, 109, **109**
Moral anxiety, 389, 424
Moral development, 255–256, 266, 269
Moral dilemma, example of, **256**
Mormon Church, 377
Moro reflex, **239**
Morphemes, 218, 224, 227
Morphine, 285, 306
    endogenous, 49
Morphology, of language, 224
Motion parallax, 106
Motion sickness, 102, 114
Motivation, 271–309
    arousal approaches, 276–278, 305, 308
    defined, 272, 305, 309
    drive-reduction approaches, 273–274, **274,** 305, 308
    Dweck's self-theory of motivation, 275–276
    as element of observational learning, 153
    extrinsic, 271, 272, 281, 308
    humanistic approaches, 279–281, 305, 308
    incentive approaches, 278, 305, 308
    instinct approaches, 272–273, 305, 308
    intrinsic, 281, **281,** 305
    learning objectives, 271
    self-determination theory (SDT), 281, 305, 308
    sexual, 288–294
Motivational interviewing, 471, 496
Motive, 278

Motor cortex, **69**, 70, 76
  and somatosensory cortex, **69**
Motor development, 239–240,
  240, 265
Motor milestones, **240**
Motor neurons, 52
Motor pathway, 54–55
Müller-Lyer illusion, 108–109, **109**
Multiple approach-avoidance
  conflicts, 342
Multiple intelligences, 410
Multiple personalities. *See*
  Dissociative identity
  disorder (DID)
Multiple sclerosis, 44
Münsterberg, Hugo, B-10
"Murder while sleepwalking,"
  204–205
Murray, Henry, 406
Myelin, 44–45, 75
Myers-Briggs Type Indicator
  (MBTI), 408, 425
MySpace, 369

N

Naltrexone, 286
Narcolepsy, 206, 224, 226
Narcotics, 285–286, 287, 306, 309
  heroin, 285, 306
  methadone, 285
  morphine, 285, 306
  opium, 285, 287
Narcotics Anonymous, 479
Nardil (phenelzine sufate), 488
Nasal retinas, 87
Nash, John, **452**
National Institute on Alcoholism
  and Alcohol Abuse, 285
National Survey of Counseling
  Center Directors, 481
Natural concepts, 210, **210**
Natural killer cell, 322
Natural selection, 7
Naturalistic observation, 20, **20**, 35
Nature
  defined, 230
Nature *vs.* nurture, 230–231, 265,
  268, **419**
Necker, Louis Albert, 103
Necker cube, 103, **103**
Need, 273
Need for achievement (nAch), 274,
  276, 305
  and personality, 275–276
Need for affiliation (nAff), 274, 305
Need for power (nPow), 274,
  275, 305
Negative emotions, 295, 297
Negative reinforcement, 133–134,
  139, 156, 283
  punishment by removal, 139–140
Negative symptoms, schizophrenia,
  453, 460, 463
Negatively skewed distributions, A-4
Nembutal, 287
Neo-Freudianism, 35

Neo-Freudians, 392–393, 424
Nerve crossovers, 64
Nerve fibers, implantation of, 53
Nerve hearing impairment, 95
Nerves, 44, 75, 78
Nervous system, 42, 51, 74. *See
  also* Central nervous system
  (CNS); Peripheral nervous
  system (PNS)
  defined, 42
  neural impulse, 44–46, **46**
  neurons, 42–48
  neurotransmitters, **47**, 47–50
  reuptake and enzymes, 49–50
  synapse, **47**, 47–48
Neural impulse, 44–46, **46**
Neural peptides, 49
Neural regulators, 49
Neurilemma, 75
Neurofeedback, 146, 157
Neuroleptics, 486
Neurons, 42–48, 74–75, 78
  mirror, 70, **70**
  structure of, **43**, 43–44
  types of, 52
Neuroplasticity, 53
Neuropsychology, B-6
Neuroscience, defined, 14, 42
Neurotic personalities, 394
Neuroticism, 327, 402, 423, 436
Neuroticism/Extraversion/
  Openness Personality
  Inventory (NEO-PI),
  408, 425
Neurotransmitters, **47**, 47–50,
  75, 444
Neutral stimulus (NS), 123–124, 156
Newman, Constance, **B-4**
News sources, validity of, 52–53
Nicotine, 284, **284**, 287
Night terrors, 204, 207, 224, 226
Nightmares, 204, **204**, 224
Nocturnal leg cramps, 207, 226
Nodes, 44
Non-REM sleep, 200
Non-REM Stage 1, 202, 224, 226
Non-REM Stage 2, 202, 224, 226
Non-REM Stages 3 and 4, 202–203,
  224, 226
Nondeclarative memory, 172
Nondirective therapy, 470
Nonverbal communication,
  as barrier to
  psychotherapy, 485
Noradrenaline, and stress, 319
Norepinephrine, 49, 59, 75, 488
Norm of reciprocity, 350
Normal curve, 413, **413**, A-2–A-3,
  A-3, A-12
Norms, 413–414
Norpramin (desipramine), 489
Nurture
  defined, 230

O

Oakland Growth Study, 11

Obama, Barack, 180
Obedience, 349
  defined, 350
  Milgram's shock experiment,
    351, 351–352, 379
Obesity, 333–334, 340, 343
Object permanence, 241
Objective introspection, 6
  defined, 6
Objectivity, defined, 6
Observable behavior, 4, 11
Observational learning, 151–153,
  157, 161, 355, 379
  attention, 152
  Bandura and the Bobo doll, **151**,
    151–152, 157
  elements of, 152–153
  imitation, 153
  learning/performance
    distinction, 151
  memory, 152–153
  motivation, 153
Observer bias, 20, 28
Observer effect, 20, 425
Obsessive-compulsive disorder
  (OCD), **442**, 442–443, 459,
  462, 465
Occipital lobes, 68–69, 76
OCEAN (acronym), 401–402, 424
Odbert, H.S., 401
Odontophobia, 441
Oedipus complex, 391, 424
Olfaction (olfactory sense), 98–99,
  114, 119, 238
Olfactory bulbs, 66, 99
Olfactory receptor cells, **98**, 98–99
Oligodendrocytes, 44
On the Witness Stand
  (Münsterberg), B-10
One-word speech, 245
Online networking, 369
Openness, 402
Operant conditioning, 13, 131–147,
  156, 160, 161
  antecedent stimuli, 132
  and behavior modification, 138,
    145–146, 157
  biological constraints,
    144–145, 157
  compared to classical
    conditioning, 133
  effect of consequences on
    behavior, 142–143
  extinction, 143, 475–476
  instinctive drift, 144–145, 157
  Law of Effect, 131, 156
  modeling, 473
  punishment, 138–139
  reinforcement, 132–138, 156, 475
  shaping, 143
  stimulus control, 142–143
  therapies based on, 474–476,
    493, 496
  Thorndike's puzzle box, 131, **131**
Operant conditioning chamber, **132**
Operational definition, 26, **26**, 35

Opiates, 285, 287
Opium, 285
Opponent-process theory, 90, 114
Opportunity for catharsis, 483
"Opposites attract," 368
Optic nerve, 88
  crossing of, **88**
Optimists
  and alternative thinking, 328
  developing optimism, 329
  and downward social
    comparison, 329
  and relaxation, 329
  and stress, 328–329, 340, 342
Oral stage in personality
  development, 390, 424
Orbitofrontal cortex, 99
Organ of Corti, 94, 114
Organic amnesia, 189, 195
Orgasm, **335**
Otolith organs, 101
Out-groups, 363, 379
Outer ear, 93
Oval window, 94
Ovaries, 59
Overeaters Anonymous, 479
Overgeneralization, 444, 477
Overlap, 105
Ovum, 234

P

Pacinian corpuscles, 99, 114
Pagano, Father Bernard, 179
Pain, 100–101, 114
  gate-control theory, 100–101
  somatic, 100
  visceral, 100
Painting reflecting light, 88
Pancreas, 58, 75, 333
Panic attack, 442
Panic disorder, 442, 459, 462
  with agoraphobia, 442
Papillae, 96
Parallel distributed processing
  (PDP) model, 165, 174,
  191, 194
Parameter, A-1
Paranoid schizophrenia, 453, 460,
  463
Parasympathetic division, **55, 56,**
  56–57, 75, 319, 339
  defined, 55
Paregoric, 285
Parent/teen conflict, 257, 266
Parenting, 260–261, 266
  authoritarian, 260
  authoritative, 261
  permissive, 261, 266
Parenting styles, 260–261, 266
Parietal lobes, 69, **69**, 76
Parkinson's disease, 54, 75
Parnate (tranylcypromine
  sulfate), 488
Paroxetine (Paxil), 489
Partial dopamine agonists, 486
Partial reinforcement effect,
  134–135, 157

Partial report method, 167
Participant modeling, 475
Participant observation, 20
Participants, 22
Passion, 370, 380
Passionate love, 370, 380
Pavlov, Ivan, **10**, 10–11, 122–123, **123**, 125–126, 129, 156, 160
Paxil (paroxetine), 489
PCP, 286, 306
Peak experiences, 280
Peer pressure, **257**
Penis envy, 391, 394
Penn & Teller, 112, **113**
People's Temple (Jonestown, Guyana), 377, **377**
Pepperberg, Irene, **221**
Perceiving the question, 18
Perception, 102–103, 115, 119
  binocular cues, **105**, 105–106
  brightness constancy, 103
  closure, 104
  common region, 105
  contiguity, 104–195
  continuity, 104
  defined, 102–103
  depth, 105–107
  development of, 105
  factors influencing, 111–112
  figure-ground relationships, 103–104
  Gestalt principles, 103–105
  monocular cues, 105–107
  motion, illusions of, 106
  perceptual illusions, 108–111
  proximity, 104
  shape constancy, 103, **103**
  similarity, 104
  size constancy, 103
Perceptual expectancy, 111, 115
Perceptual illusions, 108–111
  Hermann grid, 108, **108**
  moon illusion, 109, **109**
  Müller-Lyer illusion, 108–109, **109**
Perceptual set, 111, **111**, 115
Perham, Michael, 229
Perimenopause, 258
Peripheral nervous system (PNS), **54**, 54–57, 75, 78
  autonomic nervous system (ANS), 55–57
  somatic nervous system, 54–55, **55**
Peripheral-route processing, 356, **357**, 379
Perls, Fritz, 471
Permissive indulgent parents, 261
Permissive neglectful parents, 261
Permissive parenting, 261, 266
Persistence, and frustration, 316, 342
Persistence of vision, 113
Person-centered therapy (Rogers), **470**, 470–472, 493, 496
  authenticity, 471
  empathy, 471

reflection, 470–471
  unconditional positive regard, 471, 493
Persona, 393
Personal fable, 255, 266
Personal frustration, 316
Personal unconscious, 393
Personality, 384–424
  anal stage, 390–391, 424
  assessment of, **403**, 403–409, 425
  behaviorist and social cognitive view of, 396–398, 424
  behaviorist perspective, 386
  biological roots and summary, 459
  biology of, 419–421
  and coronary heart disease, **326**
  defined, 384, 386, 424
  development stages, 390–392, 424
  divisions of, 388–389
  ego, 388, 424
  genital stage, 392, 424
  humanistic perspective, 386, 398–399, 424
  id, 388, 424
  latency stage, 392, 424
  learning objectives, 385
  and need for achievement, 275–276
  neo-Freudians, 392–393, 424
  oral stage, 390, 424
  phallic stage, 391–392, 424
  psychodynamic perspective, 386, 394–395, 424
  psychological defense mechanisms, 389, **389**, 424
  reciprocal determination, 397, **397**, 424
  self-efficacy, 397, 424
  stress and, 325–329, 340, 342
  superego, 388–389, 424
  theories of, 386–423
  trait perspective, 386, 401–403
  trait theories, 401–403, 424
  unconscious mind, **387**, 387–388, 424
Personality assessments, 404–409, 425
  behavioral assessments, 407, 425
  interviews, 405, 425
  personality inventories, 407–409, 425
  projective tests, 405–407, **406**, 425
  types of, **404**
Personality differences, 324–328, 340
Personality disorders, 455–457, 460, 463
  antisocial personality disorder, 456, 460, 463
  borderline personality disorder, 456, 460, 463
  causes of, 456–457
  defined, 455
  genetic factors, 456
  types of, 455–456
Personality inventories, 407–409, 425
  defined, 407

Eysenck Personality Questionnaire, 408
Minnesota Multiphasic Personality Inventory, Version II (MMPI-2), 326, 408, 425
Myers-Briggs Type Indicator (MBTI), 408, 425
Neuroticism/Extraversion/ Openness Personality Inventory (NEO-PI), 408, 425
  problems with, 409
Personality psychology, B-6
Personalization, 477
Persuasion, 356–357, 379
Pertofrane (desipramine), 489
Pessimists, and stress, 328–329, 340, 342
PET scans (positron emission tomography), 13, 74, 76, 86, 407, 445, 455
Pezdek, Kathy, 183
Phallic stage of personality development, 391–392, 424
Phantom limb pain, 100
Phantoms in the Brain (Ramachandran & Blakeslee), 71
Phencyclidine, 286
Phenelzine sufate (Nardil), 488
Phenylketonuria (PKU), 232, **233**
Phi phenomenon, 110
Philosophers, 5–6
Phobias, 11, 128, 155, 440, **441**, 459
  agoraphobia, 441–442, **442**, 459
  flooding, 474
  scientific names, **441**
  specific, 441
Phobic disorders, 440–441, 459, 462
  social phobias (social anxiety disorders), 441, 459, 462
Phonemes, 218–219, 224, 227
Photons, 84
Photoreactive keratectomy (PRK), 86
Photoreceptors, 86
Phrenology, 423
Physical attractiveness, 368
Physical dependence, 282–283, 306, 309
Physical development
  adolescence, 254, 266, 269
  adulthood, 258–259, 266, 269
  infancy and childhood development, 238–240
Physical exercise for better cognitive health, 222–223
Physiological psychology, B-6
Physiologist, 5
Piaget, Jean, 13, 219, 220, 240, 244, 254, 265
Piaget's theory of cognitive development, 240–243, **241**, 265, 268

concrete operations stage, 243, **243**
formal operations stage, 243, 254–255
preoperational stage, 241–243
sensorimotor stage, 241
Picasso, Pablo, **167**
Picou, Steven, 431
Pictorial depth cues, 105
  examples of, **106**
Pineal gland, 58, 75, 200
Pinel, Philippe
  and humane treatment of the mentally ill, 467, **467**, 493, 496
Pinna, 93
Piriform cortex, 99
Pitch, 92, 94–95
Pituitary gland, 58, 66, 75, 254
PKU, 232, **233**, 265
Place theory, 94, 114
Placebo, defined, 28
Placebo effect, 27–28, 33
Placenta, 235
Plato, 5
Pleasure principle, 388, 424
Polygenic inheritance, 265
Polygon, A-2, **A-3**
Pons, 64, 76
Population, defined, 22
Positive emotions, 295
Positive experiences, 483
Positive psychology, 149
Positive psychology movement, 328
Positive regard, 399
Positive reinforcement, 133–134, 139, 156, 283
Positive symptoms, schizophrenia, 453, 460, 463
Positively skewed distributions, A-4, **A-6**
Positron emission tomography (PET), 13, **62**, 63, 74, 86, 407, 445, 455
Post-traumatic stress disorder (PTSD), 443, 459, 462, 474, 492
Postconventional morality, 256, 266
Poverty, and stress, 330, **330**, 340, 343
Power distance, 421
Practicum, B-3
Pragmatics, 219, **219**, 224, 227
  of language, 219
Preconscious mind, 387
Preconventional morality, 256, 266
Prediction, 5, 19
Prefrontal cortex, 188, 454
Prefrontal lobotomy, 490, 494, 497
Pregnancy, 235–236, **236**
Prejudice, **363**, 379
  defined, 363, 379
  equal status contact, 366
  in-groups, 363, 379
  and intergroup contact, 366, **366**, 380

Prejudice (cont.)
    "jigsaw classroom," 366–367, 380
    learning, 365–366, 379
    out-groups, 363, 379
    overcoming, 366–367, 380
    realistic conflict theory of,
        363, 379
    social identity theory, 365, 379
    stereotype vulnerability,
        365–366, 379
    types of, 363
Prenatal development, 234–237,
        265, 267
    chromosomes, 232, 234
    conception, 234
    DNA (deoxyribonucleic acid),
        232, 234
    genes, 232–233, 265
    genetic and chromosome
        problems, 232–233
    germinal period, 225–226, **226,**
        265, 268
    twinning, 232–233
    zygote, 232, 265
Prenatal hazards, 236
Preoperational stage of cognitive
        development, 241–243,
        265, 268
Presbyopia, 86
Pressure, 315–316, 339, 342
Presynaptic membrane, 47
Preterm, defined, 237
Primacy effect, 178, 192, 359, 379
Primary appraisal, 324–325,
        340, 342
Primary auditory cortex, 69
Primary drives, 273, 305, 308
Primary reinforcers, 132–133, 156
Primary sex characteristics, 254
Primary visual cortex, 68
Princess Bride, The (movie), 264
Principles of Psychology (James), 7
Private speech, 219–220
Proactive interference, 187,
        187, 195
Problem-focused coping, 336,
        340, 343
Problem solving, 211–214, 224, 227
    algorithms, 212, 224
    confirmation bias, 215–216, 224
    creativity, 216–217, 224
    and decision making, 211–212
    defined, 212
    difficulties in, 215–216
    functional fixedness, 215, 224
    heuristics, 212–214, 224
    insight, 214, 224
    mental sets, 215
    problems with, 215–216
    trial and error (mechanical
        solutions), 212, **212,** 224
Procedural (nondeclarative)
        memory, **172,** 172–173,
        174, 192, 194
Profound mental retardation, 416
Projection, defined, 405

Projective tests, 405–407, **406,** 425
Proprioceptors, 101
Prosocial behavior, 371,
        374–376, 380
    altruism, 375, 380
    bystander effect, 375, 380
    decision points in helping
        behavior, 376, **376,** 380
    diffusion of responsibility,
        376–377, 380
Prosser, Inez Beverly, 8
Protanopia, 90
Prototypes, 210–211, **211,** 224
Proximity, 104, 368, 379
Prozac (fluoxetine), 489
Pseudopatients, 439
Psilocybin, 286–287, 306
Psychiatric social worker, 16, **17,**
        B-3
Psychiatrist, 16, 35, B-3
Psychoactive drugs, 282–287, 306,
        309
    alcohol, 285, 287
    defined, 282
    depressants, 284, 287, 306, 309
    hallucinogens, 286–287, 306, 309
    marijuana, 287, 306
    narcotics, 285–286, 287, 306
    physical dependence, 282–283,
        306, 309
    psychological dependence,
        283–287, 306, 309
    stimulants, 283–284, 287, 306,
        309
Psychoanalysis, 9–10, 35, 392,
        467–468, 493, 496
    defined, 10, 467
    dream interpretation, 468,
        493, 496
    evaluation of, 468–469, 493
    free association, 468
    Freud's theory of, 10, 392,
        424, 493
    modern, 395, 467
    resistance, 468
    transference, 468
Psychoanalyst, 10
Psychodynamic perspective, 12, 386,
        394–395, 424, 436, 459
    anxiety, 444, 460
    criticisms of, 395
Psychodynamic theory, 12,
        386, 424
Psychodynamic therapy, 469
Psychological defense mechanisms,
        389, **389,** 424
Psychological dependence,
        283–287, 306, 309
Psychological disorders, 430–463
    abnormality, defined, 432–435,
        459, 462
    anxiety disorders, 440–445,
        450, 462
    brief history of, 432, 459
    in college students, 481–482
    common, 438–439
    labels, 439

learning objectives, 431
    mood disorders, 445–448,
        460, 462
    occurrence in U.S., **438**
    personality disorders, 455–457
    psychoanalysis, 467–468
    psychotherapy, 482–486
    schizophrenia, 451–455, **452,**
        460, 463
    therapy, 464–496
Psychological needs, 263, 265,
        273, 279
Psychological professionals
    specializations of, 16–17
    types of, 16–17, 35
Psychological research, ethics of,
        30–32, 35
Psychological stressors, 315–318,
        339, 342
    conflict, 317–318, 339, 342
    frustration, 316, 339, 342
    pressure, 315–316, 339, 342
    uncontrollability, 316, 339, 342
Psychological therapies, 464–497
    behavior therapies, 473–476,
        493, 496
    characteristics of, **478**
    cognitive therapies, 476–478,
        493–494, 497
    early days of, 466–467, 496
    humanistic therapy, 470–472,
        493, 496
    learning objectives, 465
    psychoanalysis, 467–468
Psychologist, 4, 16, 17, 35, **B-3,**
        B-3–B-4
Psychology
    African American, 8–9
    applied, B-2, B-13
    areas of specialization, 16–17,
        35, B-14
    behavioral perspective, 12–13
    beyond the classroom, B-7–B-9
    biological, 42
    biopsychological perspective,
        14–15
    as a career, B-2–B-4, B-13
    careers with a bachelor's degree
        in, B-4–B-5, **B-5**
    careers with a master's degree
        in, B-4
    clinical, B-5
    cognitive, 9, 11
    cognitive perspective, 13
    comparative, B-6
    consumer, 349
    counseling, B-5
    cultural, 13
    defined, 4, 34
    descriptive methods, 20–21
    developmental, B-5–B-6
    educational, 8, B-7, **B-7,** B-14
    environmental, B-9, B-14
    evolutionary perspective, 15
    experimental, 5, B-6
    forensic, B-1, B-9
    goals of, 4–5
    health, B-7, **B-7,** B-14

history of, 5–8, 34
    human factors, **B-10,**
        B-10–B-11, B-14
    humanistic perspective, 13
    industrial/organizational (I/O),
        8, B-10–B-11, B-14
    issues in, 8–9
    and the law, B-8–B-9
    learning objectives, 3
    and the military, B-8, **B-8,** B-14
    neuropsychology, B-6
    personality, B-6
    physiological, B-6
    positive, 149
    psychiatric social worker, 16,
        17, B-3
    psychiatrists, 16, B-3
    psychodynamic perspective, 12
    psychologists, 4, **B-3,** B-3–B-4
    school, **B-7,** B-7–B-8
    science of, 2–38
    scientific method,
        18, 18–20, 35
    social, 13, 344–380, B-6
    sociocultural perspective,
        13–14, 39
    sports, B-8, B-12–B-13, B-14
    statistics in, A-1–A-13
    and work, **16**
    work settings/subfields of, **16**
Psychology and Industrial Efficiency
        (Münsterberg), B-10
Psychology of Everyday Life, The
        (Freud), 387
Psychology student's syndrome, 439
Psychoneuroimmunology, 311,
        320, 342
Psychopathology, 432, 462
Psychopharmacology, 486–489,
        487, 494, 497
    antianxiety drugs, 488, 494
    antidepressant drugs,
        488–489, 494
    antimanic drugs, 488, 494
    antipsychotic drugs,
        486–488, 494
    types of drugs used in, **487,** 494
Psychosexual stages of personality
        development, 390–392,
        393, 424
Psychosocial development, 260–262
    adolescence, 256–257
    infancy and childhood
        development, 246–251
    stages of, **250**
Psychosurgery, 490–491, 494, 497
Psychotherapies, 10, 466, 493, 496
    interpersonal, 469, **469,** 496
Psychotherapy, 482–486, 494, 497
    characteristics of, **478**
    cultural, ethnic, and gender
        concerns in, 484–485, 494
    effective therapy, characteristics
        of, 483–484
    effectiveness, studies of, 482–483
    virtual reality, 492–493

Psychotic disorder, 452
Ptolemy, 109
Puberty, 254, 266
Punishment, 138–142, **139,** 157, 161
   by application, 139
   consistent, 141–142
   making more effective, 141–142
   problems with, 140–141
   by removal, **139,** 139–140, 157
Pupil, 86
Purity of sound, 92
Pygmalion in the Classroom
     (Rosenthal & Jacobson), 28

Q

Question (scientific method), 18

R

Ramachandan, V.S., 71
Random assignment, 27
Randomization, 27
Range (statistics), A-6
Rapid eye movement, 200. *See also*
     REM behavior disorder;
     REM rebound; REM sleep
Rapid-smoking technique, 474, **474**
Rating scale, 407, 425
Ratio schedule, 135
Rational-emotive behavior therapy
     (REBT), 477–478, 493, 497
Rayner, Rosalie, 11
Real self, 470
Realistic conflict theory of
     prejudice, 363, 379
Realistic goals and expectations,
     fostering, B-13
Reality principle, 388, 424
Recall, 177, 192
   recency effect, 178, 192
   retrieval failure, 177, 192
   serial position effect, 177–178, 192
Recency effect, 178, 192
Receptive-productive lag, 245
Receptor sites, 47
Recessive genes, 232, **233,** 265
Recessive traits, 91
Reciprocal determinism, 397,
     397, 424
Reciprocity of liking, 368–369, 379
Recognition, 177, 178, 192
Red-green color blindness, 90
Reflection, 470–471
Reflex, defined, 123
Reflex arc, **51,** 52, 75
Reflexes, 10, 238, **239,** 265
   grasping, **239**
   rooting, **239**
   startle, **239**
   stepping, **239**
   sucking, **239**
Refraction, 86, **86**
Reinforcement, 13, 132–138, **136,**
     156, 160, 398, 475. *See also*
     Schedules of reinforcement
   negative, 133–134, 157
   pairing punishment with, 138
   partial, 134–135, 157

positive, 133–134, 157
   primary/secondary reinforcers,
     132–133
   schedules of, 134–137
Reinforcers, 126, 133
Relatedness, 281
Relatedness needs, 280
Relationships, mathematical, 22–25
Relative size, 105
Relaxation, and optimists, 329
Relaxation training, B-13
Reliability, of a test, 406, 412, 425
Religion, and coping, 338, 340, 343
REM (rapid eye movement),
     200, **203**
REM behavior disorder, 203, 224
REM myth, 203
REM paralysis, 203, 224
REM rebound, 203
REM sleep, 200, 203, **203,**
     224, 226
   need for, 203–204
Repetitive transcranial magnetic
     stimulation (rTMS), **60,**
     60–61, 75, 491, **491,** 494,
     497
Replicate, use of term, 19
Representative heuristic, 212–213
Representative sample, 22
Repression, 10
Rescorla, Robert, 130
Research guidelines, 30–32
Resistance, 468
Resistance stage, general adaptation
     syndrome, 319, 339, 342
Response, defined, 123
Resting potential, 45
Restless leg syndrome, 207, 226
Results, reporting, 19
Reticular activating system
     (RAS), 65
Reticular formation, 64–65, 76
Retina, 86, 87, **87**
   parts of, 86, **87**
Retrieval, 164, 176–181
   constructive processing view of,
     181–182
Retrieval cues, 176–177, 192
Retrieval failure, 177, 192
Retrieval problems, 182–184
Retroactive interference, 187,
     187, 195
Retrograde amnesia, 189, 192
Reuptake, 49–50, 75
Reversible figures, 103
Right- and left-handedness, 72–73
Right hemisphere, 72–73, 76
Road rage, 330
Robber's cave study, 366
Rods, 86, **87,** 88, 114
Rogers, Carl, 13, 398, 424, 470
   person-centered therapy
     (Rogers), **470,** 470–472,
     493, 496
Rohypnol, 284
Romantic love, 370, 380

Roosevelt, Eleanor, 400
Rooting reflex, **239**
Rorschach, Hermann, 406
Rorschach inkblot test, 406, **406,** 425
Rosenman, Ray, 325
Rosenthal, Robert, 28
Rotating Snakes illusion, 110
Rote learning, 171, 212, 224
Rotter, Julian, 397–398
Rubik's Cube®, 212
Rule of thumb. *See* Heuristics
Rutherford, Ernest, 94

S

s factor (specific intelligence),
     410, 425
Saccades, 167
Saccadic movements, 84
Sacks, Oliver, 68–69
Safety needs, 279, 280
Sample, A-1
Sanchez, Jorge, 8
Sapir, Edward, 220, 224
Sapir-Whorf hypothesis, 220
Saturation, 85, 114
Scaffolding, 244, 265, 268
Scalloping effect, 135, **136**
Scapegoating, **364,** 364–365, 379
Scapegoats, 317
Schachter, Stanley, 300
Schachter-Singer model of
     emotion, 299–301, **300,**
     306, 309
Schedules of reinforcement,
     134–137, **136,** 157, 161
   continuous reinforcement,
     135, 157
   fixed interval schedule,
     135–136, **136**
   fixed ratio schedule, 137
   partial reinforcement effect,
     134–135
   timing of reinforcement,
     134–137, **136**
   variable interval schedule, 136,
     136, 157
   variable ratio schedule, 137,
     137, 157
Schemas, 211, 240, 360, 379
Schizophrenia, 14, **14,** 451–455,
     452, 455, 460, 463
   catatonic, 453, 460, 463
   categories of, 452–453, 460, 463
   causes of, 453–455, 460, 463
   defined, 451
   delusions, 451–452
   disorganized, 452–453, 460, 463
   and genetics, **454**
   mental exercise for better
     cognitive health, 222
   negative symptoms, 453, 460, 463
   paranoid, 453, 460, 463
   positive symptoms, 453, 460, 463
   stress-vulnerability model,
     455, 463
   symptoms, 451–452

Scholastic Assessment Test
     (SAT), 415
School psychology, **B-7,** B-7–B-8
Schwann cells, 44
Scientific method, **18,** 18–20, 35
Scott, Walter D., B-10
Scripts, 211
Seasonal affective disorder
     (SAD), 448
Secondary appraisal, 325, 340, 342
Secondary drives, 273, **274,** 305
Secondary reinforcers, 132–133
Secondary sex characteristics,
     254, 266
Secure attachment style, 247, 265
Seeing. *See also* Sight
   defined, 86, 114
Selective attention, 168
Selective serotonin reuptake
     inhibitors (SSRIs), 50, 489,
     494, 497
Selective thinking, 476
Self, 275, 345, 399, **399,** 424
   ideal, 345
Self-actualization, 13, 279, 400
Self-actualization needs, 279–281
Self-actualizing tendency, 399
Self-concept, 399, 424
   conditional and unconditional
     positive regard, 399–400
   real and ideal self, 399, **399**
Self-determination theory (SDT),
     281, 305, 308
Self-efficacy, 397, 424
Self-esteem, 397
Self-fulfilling prophecy, 365, 379
Self-help groups (support groups),
     479, 479–480, 494, 497
Self-report inventory (Cattell), **402**
Seligman, Martin, 147, 149–150,
     157, 161, 328
Selye, Hans, 312, 313, 319
Semantic memory, 173, 192, 194
Semantic network model, 174–175,
     175, 194
Semantics, 218
Semicircular canals, 101–102
Semipermeable, defined, 44
Senile dementia, 189
Sensation, **99,** 114, 118
   absolute threshold, 82
   chemical senses, 96–99, 114
   defined, 82
   difference threshold, 82
   habituation, 83–84
   hearing, 91–95
   just noticeable difference (jnd), 82
   learning objectives, 81
   olfaction, 98–99, 114, 119
   sensory adaptation, 83, **83**
   sight, 83–91, 114
   somesthetic senses, 99–102, 114
   subliminal perception, 83
   synesthesia, 81
   taste, 96–98, 114
   transduction, 82

Sensation seeker, 277, **278**, 305, 308
Sensorimotor stage, 241, 265, 268
Sensory adaptation, 83, **83**, 114
Sensory conflict theory, 102
Sensory development
    infancy and childhood
        development, 238–239
Sensory memory, 166–168,
        191, 194
    echoic, 167–168, 191
    iconic, 166–167, 191
Sensory neurons, 52
Sensory pathway, 54–55
Sensory receptors, defined, 82
Sensory thresholds, 82–83
Sentence Completion test, 406
Separation, 331, 340, 343
Serial killer, 456
Serial position effect, 177–178,
        178, 192
Serotonin, 49, 50, 75, 372, 450, 463
Serotonin receptors, 487
Sertraline (Zoloft), 489
Severe depression, 189
Severe mental retardation, 416
Sex chromosomes, 232
Sex glands, 254
Sex-linked inheritance, 91
Sex organs, **57**, 59
Sexism, 363
Sexual arousal disorders, 335
Sexual behavior, types of, 288–290,
        306, 309
Sexual behavior surveys (Kinsey),
        key findings from, **289**
Sexual desire orders, 335
Sexual deviance, 290
Sexual dysfunction/problems,
        334–335, 340, 343
    stress-induced (organic)
        dysfunctions, 334–335,
        340, 343
Sexual motivation, 288–294, 306, 309
Sexual orientation, 290–294,
        292, 309
    bisexual, 291, 309
    development of, 14–15, 291–293
    evolutionary purpose, 293
    heterosexual, 291, 306, 309
    homosexual, 291, **292**, 306, 309
Sexual pain disorders, 335
Seyfried, Amanda, **257**
Shadow, 393
Shalhoub, Tony, **442**
Shallow lesioning, 60
Shape constancy, 103, **103**, 115
Shaping, 143, 154, 156
Sherif, Muzafer, 346
Short-term memory (STM),
        168–170, **169**, 191, 194
    capacity, 169–170
    chunking, 170
    defined, 168
    encoding, 168
    interference in, 170, **170**
    maintenance rehearsal, 170
    selective attention, 168

Sickle-cell anemia, 232, 265
Sight, 84–91, 114
    brightness, 84
    color, 85
    dark adaptation, 88
    how the eye works, 87–88
    light, perceptual properties of,
        84–85
    light adaptation, 88
    saturation, 85
    structure of the eye, 85–87
    visible spectrum, 85, **85**
Significant difference, A-10
Similarity, 104, 368, 379
Simon, Théodore, 410
Simple reflex arc, 75
Sinequan (doxepin), 489
Singer, Jerome, 300
Single-blind studies, 28
Single photon emission computed
        tomography (SPECT), 63
Sissy, 252
Situational cause, 361, 379
Situational context, 433
Sixteen Personality Factor
        Questionnaire (16PF), 401,
        402, 407, 408
Size constancy, 103, 115
Skewed distributions, **A-3,**
        A-3–A-4, **A-4,** A-6
Skin
    pain, 100–101
    receptors, **100**
    types of sensory receptors in,
        99–100
Skin senses, defined, 99
Skinner, B.F., 12–13, **13**, 132,
        156, 160
Skinner box, **132**
Sleep, 199–206, 224, 226. *See also*
        Dreams
    alpha waves, 200, 202
    beta waves, 200
    and body temperature, 203
    brain activity during, **201**
    circadian rhythm, 199
    deep, 202, 203
    delta waves, 200, 202–203
    disorders, **204,** 204–207, **205**
    lack of, 203–204
    light, 202
    necessity of, 199–200
    non-REM, 200
    REM sleep, 200, **203,** 203–204
    requirements, 200, 224
    sleep patterns of infants and
        adults, **200**
    sleep spindles, 202
    sleep-wake cycles, 199–200, 224
    stages of, 200–204, 224
    theta waves, 200
    typical night's sleep, **202**
Sleep apnea, 206, 224, 226
Sleep clinics/experts, 206
Sleep deprivation, 203

Sleep disorders, **204, 205,** 224, 226
    circadian rhythm disorders, 207
    enuresis, 207
    hypersomnia, 207
    insomnia, **205,** 205–206, 224
    narcolepsy, 206, 224
    night terrors, 204, 207, 224
    nightmares, 204, **204,** 224
    nocturnal leg cramps, 207
    REM behavior disorder, 204
    restless leg syndrome, 207
    sleep apnea, 206, 224
    sleep spindles, 224
    sleepwalking, 204–205, 224
    somnambulism, 204, 207
Sleep spindles, 202, 224
Sleep-wake cycles, 199–200, 224
Sleeping pills, **283**
Sleeptalking, 224
Sleepwalking, 204–205, 224
Slow to warm up babies, 247
Smell. *See* Olfaction (olfactory sense)
Social browsing, 369
Social categorization, 359–360,
        365, 379
Social cognition, 353–362, 379,
        397, 424
    attitudes, 353–357, 379
    attribution, 360–362, 379
    defined, 353
    implicit personality theories,
        360, 379
    impression formation, 359, 379
    social categorization, 359–360,
        379
Social-cognitive learning theorists,
        396, 424
Social-cognitive perspective, 396
Social-cognitive theory, 365
Social comparison, 365, **365,** 379
Social identity, defined, 365
Social identity theory, 365, 379
Social influence, 346–353, 378, 379
    compliance, 349–350, 379
    conformity, 346–348, 379
    groupthink, 348–349, 379
    obedience, 350–353, 359
Social interaction, 363–367, 379
    prejudice and discrimination,
        363–364, 379
    scapegoating, **364,** 364–365, 379
Social learning theory, 252–253,
        266, 269, 397–398
Social network sites, 369
Social norm deviance, 349, 433
Social phobias (social anxiety
        disorder), 441, 459, 462
Social psychology, 13, 344–380,
        B-6
    defined, 346
    learning objectives, 345
Social Readjustment Rating Scale
        (SRRS), 313–314, 342
Social roles, power of in aggression,
        372, 372–373, **373,** 380

Social searching, 369
Social support system, 332, 340,
        342
Society for Neuroscience (SfN), 53
Sociobiologists, 375
Sociocultural perspective, 13–14,
        434–435
Sociopath, 456
Soma, 54
    defined, 43
Somatic nervous system, 54–55, **55,**
        75, 79
Somatic pain, 100
Somatosensory cortex, 69, **69**
Somesthetic senses, 99–102, 114,
        119
Somnambulism, 204, 207, 226
songkran, **331**
Sonograms, **237**
Sound, 114
    perception of, 92–93
Sound waves, **92,** 92–93
Source, and persuasion, 356–357,
        379
Source traits, 401
Spanking
    linked with aggression, 142
Spatial neglect, 71, 76
Specialization, areas of, 16–17
Specific intelligence, 410, 425
Specific phobias, 441, 459
Sperling, George, 166
Sperry, George, 72
Spinal cord, 51–52, 75, 78
    reflex arc, **51,** 52, 75
Spinocerebellar degeneration, 65
Split-brain experiment, **72**
Split-brain research, 72–73, 76
Spontaneous abortion, 237
Spontaneous recovery, 125–126,
        126
    in operant conditioning, 144
Sports psychology, B-14
    techniques used in, B-12–B-13,
        B-14
Springer, James Arthur, 385, 419,
        419
SSRIs (selective serotonin reuptake
        inhibitors), 50, 488–489,
        494, 497
Stagnation, 260
Standard deviation (SD), 413,
        A-7–A-9
    finding, **A-7**
Standardization of tests, 412–413,
        425
Stanford-Binet Intelligence Scales,
        Fifth edition (SB5), 410
Stanford-Binet intelligence test,
        410–411, 425
    and IQ, 410–411
    paraphrased items from, **411**
Stanford prison experiment
        (Zimbardo), **372,** 372–373
Startle reflex, **239**
State-dependent learning, 176, **176,**
        192

Statistic, defined, A-1
Statistical analysis, A-1
Statistics
    bell curve, A-2
    bimodal distributions, A-4, **A-4**
    chi-square tests, A-10
    correlation coefficient,
        A-10–A-12
    defined, A-1
    descriptive, A-1–A-9
    F-test, A-10
    frequency distribution, A-2, **A-2**
    frequency polygon, **A-3**
    histogram, **A-2**
    inferential, A-9–A12
    measures of central tendency,
        A-4–A-6, A-12
    measures of variability, A-6–A-9,
        A-12
    negatively skewed distributions,
        A-4
    normal curve, A-2–A-3, **A-3,**
        A-12
    parameter, A-1
    polygon, A-2, **A-3**
    positively skewed distributions,
        A-4, **A-6**
    in psychology, A-1–A-13
    sample, A-1
    significant difference, A-10
    skewed distributions, **A-3,**
        A-3–A-4, **A-4**
    statistically significant, use of
        term, A-9
    t test, A-10
    z score, A-8
Steen, Carol, 81
Stem cells, 54, **54,** 235–236
Stepping reflex, **239**
Stereotype threat, 366
Stereotype vulnerability, 365, 379
Stereotypes, 213, 360, 365, 379
    and college athletes, 29
    defined, 360
Stern, William, 410
Sternberg, Robert, 369–370
    triangular theory of love,
        369–370, **370,** 380
    triarchic theory of intelligence,
        410, 425
Steroids, 59
Stimulants, 283–284, 287,
        306, 309
    amphetamines, 283, 287
    caffeine, 284, 287
    cocaine, 283–284, 287
    nicotine, 284, **284,** 287
Stimulatory hallucinogenics, 286
Stimulus, 11
    defined, 123
Stimulus control, 142–143
Stimulus discrimination, 125, 143,
        156
Stimulus generalization, 125, **125**
Stimulus motive, 276
Stimulus substitution, 130

Stirrup, 94, 114
Stohr, Oskar, 385
Storage, 164
Strange Situation, 247–248
Stream of consciousness, 198
Stress, 310–343
    acculturative, 331, 340, 343
    burnout, 331, 340
    cancer and, 322–323
    cognitive factors in, 324–325,
        340, 342
    coping with, 336–338, 340, 343
    coronary heart disease and,
        321–322, **322**
    defined, 312, 339, 342
    diabetes and, 322
    distress, 312
    duration of, and illness, 321, **321**
    emotion-focused coping, 336–
        337, 340, 343
    general adaptation syndrome
        (GAS), 319, **320,** 339, 342
    health and, 319–323, 339, 342
    health disease and, 321–322, **322**
    hunger, and eating, 332–334,
        340, 343
    and immune system, 320–321,
        340, 342
    influence of cognition and
        personality on, 324–329
    job, 330–331, 340, 342
    and Lazarus' cognitive appraisal
        approach, **324,** 342
    learning objectives, 311
    meditation, as coping
        mechanism, 337, **337**
    mental symptoms of, 312
    and optimists, 328–329, 340, 342
    personality factors in, 325–329,
        340, 342
    and pessimists, 328–329, 340,
        342
    and poverty, 330, **330,** 340, 343
    primary appraisal, 324–325, 340,
        342
    problem-focused coping, 336,
        340, 343
    psychological defense
        mechanisms, 389
    secondary appraisal, 325, 340,
        342
    sexual dysfunction and, 334–335,
        340, 343
    social factors in, 330–332, 340,
        343
    social support system, 332, 340,
        343
Stress hormones, 56, 319
Stress-vulnerability model, 455, 463
Stressors, 312–313, 339, 342
    environmental, 313–315
    psychological, 42, 315–318, 339
    responses to, **324**
Stroboscopic motion, 109
Stroke, 53
Structuralism, **6,** 6–7, 35
    defined, 6

Stuttering, 71
Subjective, use of term, 406
Subjective discomfort, 433, 459
Subliminal perception, 83
Subliminal stimuli, 83, 114
Subordinate concept, 210
Substance P, 101
Successive approximation, 143
Sucking reflex, **239**
Sudden infant death syndrome
        (SIDS), 206
Sullivan, Harry Stack, 469
Sultan the chimpanzee, and
        problem solving, 149, **149**
Sumner, Francis Cecil, 7–8, **8**
Sunderland, Abby, 229
Superego, 388–389, 424
Superordinate concept, 209–210
Suprachiasmatic nucleus, 200
Supraliminal, 83
Suproxin, 300
Surface traits, 401
Surveys, 22, **22**
Survival instincts, 273
Sweetness, 97
Symbolic thought, 241
Sympathetic division, **55,** 55–56,
        56, 75, 319, 339
    defined, 55
Synapse (synaptic gap), **47,** 47–48,
        75
Synaptic knob, 47
Synaptic vesicles, 47
Synesthesia, 81, 286
Synesthete, 81
Syntax, 218, 221, 224, 227
Systematic desensitization, 473

T
t-test, A-10
Tabula rasa, 145
Taijin-kyofu-sho (TKS), 445
Tan, Stanley, 311
Tardive dyskinesia, 487
Target audience, and persuasion,
        356–357, 379
Taste, 98–99, 114, 119, 238
Taste aversion conditioning, 129,
        129, 156
Taste buds, 96, **97**
Tay-Sachs disorder, 232, 265
Team unity, fostering, B-13
Telegraphic speech, 245
Television, violence in, 11, **18,** 374
Telomeres, 262
Temperament, 246–247, 265, 268
    defined, 386
Temporal lobes, 67, 69, 76, 188
Temporal retinas, 87
Teratogens, 236, **237**
Terman, Lewis M., 417
Terman's "Termites," 417
Terminal button, 47
Test anxiety, 458–459, 460, 463
Test construction, 412–414

Testes, 59
Testosterone, 203, 372
Tetrahydrocannabinol (THC), 287
Texture gradient, 106
Thalamus, 65–66, 76, 299
That's-not-all technique, 350, 379
Thematic apperception test (TAT),
        406, 425
    example of, **406**
Theory, 4
*Theory and Practice of Advertising,
    The* (Scott), B-10
Theory X/Theory Y, 292, B-10
Therapeutic alliance, 483
Therapist, 5
Therapy
    biomedical therapies, 486–491,
        494, 497
    bloodletting, 467
    cybertherapy, 485–486
    defined, 466
    early days of, 466–467, 496
    electroconvulsive therapy (ECT),
        61, 189, 192, **489,** 489–490,
        494, 497
    ice baths, 467, 493
    mentally ill, early treatment of, 467
    Pinel's reforms, 467, **467**
Theta waves, 62–63, 200
Thinking. *See also* Cognition
    convergent, 216
    critical, 32–34, 36
    defined, 207, 224
    divergent, 216–217, 224
    and language, 219–221, 224, 227
Thomas, Brian, 205
Thompson, Charles Henry, 8
Thorndike, Edward L., 131, 156, 160
    puzzle box, 131, **131**
Thornton, Omar, **B-11**
Thought stopping, B-13
Thyroid gland, 58, 75, 254
Thyroxin, 58, 75
Timbre, 92
Time management, 304–305
Time-out, 146, **475,** 476
Timing of reinforcement, 134–137,
        136. *See also* Schedules of
        reinforcement
Tinnitus, 95
Tip of the tongue phenomena, 177
Titanic, 348
Titchener, Edward, 6
Tofranil (imipramine), 489
Toilet training, 390–391
Toilet training a cat (application),
        154, 154–156, **155,** 157
Token economy, 145–146, 157, 475
Tokens, 146, 475
Tolman, Edward, 147, 157, 161
Tomboy, 252
Tongue, **97**
Top-down processing, 111, 115
Touch, **99,** 238
Tower of Hanoi, 172, **172**
Trait, defined, 401

Trait perspective, 386, 401–403, 424
    current thoughts on, 403
Trait-situation interaction, 403
Transcendence needs, 280
Transcranial direct current
        stimulation (tDCS), 491,
        494, 497
Transduction, 82, 164
Transference, 468
Transorbital lobotomy, 490
Tranylcypromine sulfate
        (Parnate), 488
Trepanning (trephining), 432,
        432, 459
Triage, defined, 65–66
Trial and error (mechanical
        solutions), 212, **212**,
        224, 227
Triangular theory of love, 369–370,
        370, 380
Triarchic theory of intelligence,
        410, 425
Trichromatic theory, 88–89, **89**, 114
Tricyclic antidepressants, 489, 494
Tritanopia, 90
Trump, Donald, **275**
Trypanophobia, 441
Turner's syndrome, 232, 265
Twin studies, 385
    of aggression and biology, 371–372
    of genetic basis for anxiety
            disorders, 445
    and mood disorders, 448
    in personality and intelligence,
            419–421, 425
    and schizophrenia, 454–455
    of sexual orientation, 292–293
Twins, 234–235
    conjoined, 234–235, **235**
    dizygotic, 234, **234**
    monozygotic, 234, **234**
Tympanic membrane, 93
Type 2 diabetes, 322
Type A Behavior and Your Heart
        (Friedman/Rosenman), 325
Type A personality, 325–326,
        340, 342
Type B personality, 325–326,
        340, 342
Type C personality, 326–327,
        340, 342
Type H personality, 327–328,
        340, 342
Typical neuroleptics, 486

U
Umami, 97
Umbilical cord, 235
Uncertainty avoidance, 422
Uncinate fasciculus, 455
Unconditional positive regard, 399,
        424, 470, 471, 493
Unconditioned response (UCR),
        123–125
Unconditioned stimulus (UCS),
        123–125, 156
Unconscious mind, 10
    defined, **387**, 387–388, 424
Uncontrollability, 316, 339, 342
Understanding, 4
Unforgettable (movie), 163
Unilateral spatial neglect, 71, 76
Unipolar disease. *See* Major
        depression
Unpredictability, 137
Unresponsive bystander, 375
Uterus, 235
Uvula, 206

V
Vagus nerve, 299, 320
Validity, of a test, 406, 412, 425
Validity scales, 408
Valium, 50, 284, 488
Valproic acid (Depakote), 488
VanderLaan, Doug, 293
Variable interval schedule of
        reinforcement, 136, **136**, 157
Variable ratio schedule of
        reinforcement, 137, **137**, 157
Variables, 23, 26–27
    confounding, 26–27
    dependent, 26
    extraneous, 27
    independent, 26
Vasey, Paul, 293
Vaughan, Susan, 328
Ventriloquist, defined, 105
Ventromedial prefrontal cortex
        (vmPFC), 150
Vestibular senses, **101**, 101–102,
        114, 119
    defined, 99
    otolith organs, 101
    semicircular canals, 101–102
Vicarious conditioning, 128
    and attitude formation, 356,
        379 (*See also* Observational
        learning)
Vicary, James, 83

Video games, violence in, 374
Vietnam, coping with stress in,
        337–338
Violence
    in the media, 373–374, 380
    and television, 151
Violent cartoons, 26
Virtual exposure, 474
Virtual reality, 492–493, 494, 497
Virtual Reality Iraq therapy
        program, **B-8**
Visceral pain, 100
Visible spectrum, 85, **85**
Vision, 238, 265
Visual accommodation, 86
Visual association cortex, 68
Visual cortex, 68, **68**, 76
Visual illusions, 115
Visualization, B-13
Vitreous humor, 86
Volley principle, 95, 114
Volume, 92
Voluntary muscles, 55, **55**
von Békésy, Georg, 94
von Helmholtz, Hermann, 6, 88, 94
Vygotsky, Lev, 14, 219, 220, 244,
        265, 268
    scaffolding, 244, 265, 268
Vygotsky's theory of cognitive
        development, 244, **244**

W
Wakefield, Andrew, 245, 246, 265
Waking consciousness, 198
Washburn, Margaret F., 6
Watson, Jessica, 229
Watson, John B., 11, **11**, 12, 128
    and Little Albert, 30, 128
Watts, James W., 490
Wavelength, 85
Weaning, 390
Weapons focus, B-1
Wear-and-tear theory of aging, 262
Weber, Ernst, 82
Weber's law of just noticeable
        difference (jnd), 82
Wechsler, David, 411
Wechsler Adult Intelligence Scale
        (WAIS-IV), 411
    paraphrased items from, **411**
Wechsler Intelligence Scale for
        Children (WISC-IV), 411
Wechsler Preschool and Primary
        Scale of Intelligence
        (WPPSI-III), 411

Wechsler tests, 411, 425
Wechsler's Intelligence
        Scales, A-8
Wernicke, Carl, 71
Wernicke's aphasia, 71, 76
Wernicke's area, 71, 76
Wertheimer, Max, 9
Western Collaborative Group Study
        (Rosenman et al), 326
Western Electric Company, B-11
Wever, Ernest, 95
White matter, 62
Whitman, Charles, 372
Whole-sentence speech, 245
Whorf, Benjamin Lee,
        220, 224
Williams, Brad, 163
Williams, Rose, 491
"Wilson," **280**
Withdrawal, 282–283
    and frustration, 317, 342
Womb envy, 394
Women in early psychology, 7, 11
Work settings, **16**
Working memory, 168–170, 191,
        194, 223
Workplace violence, **B-11**,
        B-11–B-12
World Trade Center terrorist
        attack, 348
Worry, and loss of sleep, 205
Wundt, Wilhelm, 6, **6**, B-10

X
Xanax, 284, 488
Xanga, 369

Y
Yerkes, Robert, B-10
Yerkes-Dodson law, 277
Young, Thomas, 88
Yufe, Jack, 385

Z
z score, A-8
Zimbardo, Philip, 372–373
Zoloft (sertraline), 489
Zone of proximal development
        (ZPD), 244, 265, 268
Zucker, Ken, 293
Zuckerman-Kuhlman Personality
        Questionnaire, sample items
        from, **277**
Zygote, 265